MOVE YOUR ASSETS

To Beat Inflation

Ferd Nauheim

New York Institute of Finance • New York, New York 10005

Library of Congress Cataloging in Publication Data

Nauheim, Ferd.
Move Your Assets to Beat Inflation.

Includes index.
1. Finance, Personal. I. Title.
HG179.N373 332.024'01 79-2626819 01

ISBN: 0-13-604611-8

70 Pine Street
New York, New York 10005

Printed in the United States of America

10 9 8 7 6 5 4 3 2 1

To my son,

Steve,

for so generously sharing
his invaluable tax law
knowledge and skills,
whenever asked.

Contents

Introduction

Fighting back

You are being inflated, taxed, interest-rated, engineered, and legislated into spending more and more money. Fighting back—just trying to hold your ground—is a tough, frustrating job. But if you do not fight back successfully, your potential loss is frightening to contemplate. You can lose the ability to maintain the way of life you want for your family and for yourself. That can be a bitter, painful loss.

When inflation, taxation, and interest rates are abnormally high, we *all* get clobbered. Some are hurt more than others, such as the retired couple on a modest fixed pension. But no one fully escapes harm when dollars buy less, when credit costs more, and when the IRS digs into your pockets with greater vigor. Everyone is aware of and concerned about inflation. A recent Roper Poll revealed that 88 percent of those questioned listed inflation as the subject demanding the government's greatest attention. But inflation is only part of the picture. In your effort to fight increasing living costs, whatever you manage to add to your income is taxed at your highest tax bracket: the more income you add, the more you are likely to increase the percentage payable to the IRS. Also, soaring interest rates don't seem to touch you if you are not borrowing, but those rates are one of the reasons why everything you buy costs more.

Rising prices, taxes, and interest rates are not your only

dollar drain. Because of this country's dynamic inventiveness, its marketing muscle, and the directions taken by many legislative thrusts, you are constantly exposed to new things to buy—more reasons to spend. Not so many years ago television was regarded as a luxury. Today it is in the necessity class. Recent engineering developments now make it possible for you to capture on tape any program you wish to see, even if you are away from home—a luxury right now but a family "must" tomorrow. On the legislative side, the Congress requires automobile manufacturers to build into your car new safety features, new energy saving devices, new controls to protect the atmosphere. They all cost money. And those extra costs are added to the already inflated price you pay when you buy your new car.

Don't give up the ship

In any battle it helps to know the strength of the enemy and the capabilities of your own armaments. You can use one yardstick that tells you what is needed in your effort just to keep pace with inflation. Take your own top tax bracket: Let's say it is 43 percent. In other words, the IRS takes 43 percent of your top taxed dollars; you keep 57 percent. Then take the current inflation rate: For this example, we'll use 8 percent. To know what your money must earn for you, if you are to keep up with living costs, divide the 8 percent inflation figure by the 57 percent you keep (8% ÷ 57% = 14%), and you have the answer. If your invested dollars are not earning at least 14 percent, *you are losing ground!*

Earning 14 percent is not impossible if you take into account what the stock brokers call "total return." Total return is the combination of whatever income a stock pays plus any growth in value. If a stock pays a 5 percent dividend and has increased in market value by 9 percent during the year, the total return adds up to 14 percent. Unfortunately, there is no way of providing yourself with a fixed, dependable return of 14 percent—or any other specific percentage. *Maybe* you will realize such a return. You might get more, and you might get less. And in the process of trying, you *might* succumb to the temptation to take excessive risks and end up with a damaging loss.

You have many choices

You must take the necessary risks. You mustn't stand still. You have to battle inflation—*and* escalating taxes, climbing interest rates, and the inescapable spending pressures.

This book gives you some tactics—answers to the question, "What should I do?" Today's economic chaos permits no easy answers. If you are determined to stay ahead of the game and recognize the urgent need to take action, you must examine and weigh a variety of ideas. That is exactly what this structured exploration of ideas helps you do. At the end of each chapter is a simple checklist, entitled "Candidates for Action." This checklist permits you to pinpoint those strategies in closest harmony with you, your thinking, your needs, and your circumstances. The "candidate" ideas you check off will eventually be the seriously considered candidates for the comprehensive personal program you will adopt to increase and protect your income and capital.

Here, then, in conversational, nontechnical language, are many well established strategies. Some minimize risk. Others avoid, reduce, or postpone taxes. Others will give you more money to spend now or in the future, allow your capital to grow, protect your family against needless estate shrinkage, or build strong safeguards around your assets.

Here is your chance to maintain the way of life that you want for your family and for yourself.

FERD NAUHEIM

MOVE YOUR ASSETS

To Beat Inflation

1

Tired Traditions, Blind Faith, and Other Financial Disasters

Just the facts

You are about to read some bitter, shocking facts about the financial condition of the *majority* of U.S. citizens 65 years of age and older. They will shake you up. And that is good. The aim of this opening chapter is to shake you up, to disturb you, to give you an urgent desire to take a hard look at a number of long accepted, habitual ways of thinking about money—to ask yourself if your attitudes are anchored down by traditions that have lost all meaning in today's economic world. The things you heard, read, thought and were taught in the past have a sticky way of living with you. It does not matter how obsolete they may have become; they cling to you, shaping your thoughts and actions consciously or subconsciously. Worst of all, *they can destroy you financially.* There is an urgent need to bring them out into the open, examine them, and—if you recognize any to be obsolete roadblocks or current threats to your financial health—*throw them out*!

For those 65 or over

Not only are most senior members of the population in financial hot water, there is abundant evidence that most people still earning a living in this, the wealthiest of all nations, are making the same errors that led their elders down the path to dollar disaster. The great majority of the American people are smart and hard working. They cherish the good life. And yet in 1976 *U.S. citizens who were 65 years of age or older* were faced with these chilling facts about themselves:*

- *Of all elderly married couples 73 percent had incomes of less than $10,000 a year.*
- *The median income for married couples was $6,640—$128 a week.*
- *Men living alone or with a relative averaged $68 a week.*
- *Women living alone or with a relative averaged $54 a week.*
- *Of all people in this age group, 15.7 percent were classified as "poor," and 33 percent of that category were women.*
- *Barely three-fifths had any income from personal savings and investments, and those who did generally had very small amounts.*
- *One woman out of seven depended on public assistance.*
- *Ninety percent were receiving Social Security benefits, and* that income is included *in the figures you just read.*
- *Many individuals either living in institutions or housed with others, where combined incomes escaped the "poor" label, are not included in these facts.*

When told about the plight of the men and women 65 and older, some recoil and say, "I can't believe it. I know plenty of people that age and older. I don't see that kind of poverty." That is true. Most of us do not see the evidence. To go through life living fairly well, earning a decent income, and then suddenly facing a severe economic drop that gets more terrible with each passing, inflation-packed year is a grim experience. It does more than mutilate people's lifestyles, it devastates their pride. Somehow these people must eat, have shelter, provide themselves with clothing. They are hurt, bewildered, perhaps ashamed. They can hardly be expected to tell everyone they meet, "I get by because I asked my children to help out" or "We manage because we have some good friends who realized the trouble we were in" or "We are on welfare." No. Much suffering of this type remains mercifully hidden.

*Facts quoted are from the Office of Research and Statistics, Social Security Administration, presented in an address at the 103rd Forum of the National Conference on Social Welfare, June 16, 1976.

How did it happen?

As unpleasant as the picture is, however, it must be held up and inspected. As you can see, something is terribly wrong. This nation *is* the wealthiest in the world. Yet the depressingly great number of people who find themselves in such agonizing situations in what have been called "the golden years" did not get there without reason. Most of them did fine during their productive years. In all probability the majority of them were bright, well-informed men and women. *What went wrong?* Unless those who follow uncover, understand, and avoid the pitfalls, they will commit the same mistakes again and again. Probe we must.

What do you think of when I say "money"?

On average, people commit a great error in the way in which they *think* about money. Their handling of money entails a great deal of prejudice, misunderstanding, and fear. Deeply rooted misconceptions give rise to an astonishing amount of indifference. And numerous emotional blocks obstruct the businesslike construction and pursuit of sensible financial plans.

You must therefore try to read on without any prior notions. Throughout this book you are going to read about a broad variety of constructive things to do with dollars. Some will be appropriate to your needs, hopes, and circumstances. But these ideas will be meaningless if they are not translated into action. You must approach them with an appreciation of present-day truths about saving, investing, and conservation. You must also come to these subjects free of deeply imbedded concepts that once were true but that are no longer. You must develop a keen awareness of the current yardsticks to be used when evaluating risks and potential rewards. And you must give the needs of your future years at least as much thoughtful attention as your needs of today.

Financial fears

There is a widespread inclination to fear almost everything to do with financial matters. Everyone enjoys day-to-day spending, but making plans for the financial future is something else. Making such plans entails considering many factors. You have to know what your goals are and put price tags on them. You have to decide how much time you have to get where you want to be. You must review your resources to find out how much you can earmark for your plan, where the money is coming from, how dependably you can adhere to your plan, how it harmonizes with what you have working for you—and more. And then you must learn about the choices you have in pursuing your objective. You will have to narrow those choices down until you make a final selection of the methods you will adopt, and then you must exercise your judgment in picking the providers of the vehicles you have decided to use.

All that scares the hell out of people.

Such feelings, although often irrational, are common and understandable. Everyone fears and shuns the unknown, the unfamiliar. If you are not accustomed to dealing with figures and theories, they can be confusing. If you meet and work with a financial planner, an investment dealer, an insurance agent whom you have not known and worked with before, there is also the question of faith and trust. Lots of people will not even walk into a brokerage office. They are self-conscious about their lack of knowledge. They fear that the amount of capital they may want to put to work will seem too petty—that they will be ignored and embarrassed. If a lack of familiarity is not enough, still other reasons compel too many people to fail themselves financially: confusion, not wanting to make mistakes, a concern that their lack of sophistication and perhaps the size of their purse will embarrass them. These are all very human, totally understandable reasons why countless men and women, sensing an urgent need to put their financial lives on a businesslike basis, suppress their urge and do nothing.

You can't kick the tires

You face another real challenge: you can't kick the tires. A financial plan has little or nothing to see, feel, smell,or taste. It is an intangible object, and the intangible is hard to pin down—difficult to grasp. People tend to walk away from subjects that, on first inspection, elude their understanding. What you are not up on, you are down on. Many dollar-wise ideas are bypassed for a lack of the patient understanding required. But—*and this is a promise*—since technical and intangible ideas are recognized roadblocks to well planned actions, I have made every effort to present the ideas in the following pages in as crystal-clear, as nontechnical, and as tangible terms as possible.

You can't see tomorrow (maybe that's good!)

One of the many other things that bar so many intelligent people from implementing sensible financial plans is inflation. Every time you go into a supermarket, a clothing store, or a restaurant, you get a refresher course on its presence. It hurts. It is the popular topic of conversation. It is featured in your newspapers and magazines. *Inflation is here. It is now. It is today's problem.* You worry, quite properly, about ways to increase your income and to decrease your spending. And, somehow, you manage.

In the battle to keep pace with living costs—to compensate—demands for higher wages are met, wives join their husbands as wage earners, business and professional people increase their charges, a lot of people take on second jobs. Where medium family income in 1978 was $16,000, it rose to $22,000, as both husbands and wives brought home paychecks. Inflation is bringing married women into the work force in unprecedented numbers. At the end of 1978 working wives numbered 40 million. The current prediction is that by 1990 55 percent of all married women will be wage earners. All these measures help to some degree. At least they seem to.

Extra earned income brings with it a comfortable sense of financial well-being. But part of it is false. The hidden troublemaker is the way you are taxed. Federal income tax rates are progressive. As you earn more, a greater *percentage* of your income goes to the IRS. For example, if a husband and wife earn $29,000 in a year and file a joint return, their federal income tax would amount to $5,913. (To avoid needless complexity, we are skipping the normal deductions.) Then for the next five years, inflation stays at a level 8 percent, and they are given 8 percent cost-of-living increases each year. Their wages climb to $42,609. Beautiful! Beautiful, except that they now pay $11,348 in taxes. Their top bracket leaped from 32 to 43 percent. At the same time, the compound effect of five years of inflation at 8 percent means that their *dollars dropped 47 percent in value.* They are worse off, despite their exciting hike in income. But a handsome salary increase *looks* like progress. It makes you feel better. It camouflages the full impact of the one-two punch of compounding inflation and progressive taxation.

The great trouble is that your day-after-day preoccupation with soaring living costs and your constant battle to overcome them rob you of the thought and concentration that your future deserves. Today, like a high fence, blocks your vision of tomorrow, while inflation and taxes only distort it. There seems to be no time to lift your eyes for a look at tomorrow. You are spending more and saving less. You are not in any serious trouble, but you know that you cannot afford to stand still. You must keep running in the effort to hold on to your chosen lifestyle.

The economy is you

We read and hear about how politicians and economists are taking steps to curb inflation, as if it were an animal that had to be domesticated. Maybe these measures will work. Maybe they will not. The more realistic alternative, however, is that *things may very well get worse.* If they do, we can't just sit back and blame "Inflation." If we do, we are blaming ourselves because we are, to some degree, inflation. We are the economy.

Yet we are subjected daily to powerful forces that compel us to spend, spend, spend. Every time the government takes measures to make your life safer, the air purer, the rivers cleaner, the food and the drugs you buy healthier, somebody must pay for the extra costs involved: *you.* Safety-belts, no-lead gas, filters on cigarettes are just a few examples. And every time good old American ingenuity comes out with a new time-or labor-saving gadget for an established product, or every time it adds comfort, beauty, and convenience to the things you use in your daily life, the already inflated price tags grow bigger. Every time something new comes on the market—a household item, a personal or business service, or a leisure time activity—the potent persuaders use the air and the printing presses to tempt you to buy. And they succeed. Items or services that start out as interesting new luxuries quickly become "must-have" necessities. That's been the history of color televisions, power steering, automatic transmissions, air conditioning—all out-of-reach, super-luxury additions when first introduced. Finally, no little part of the surging temptation to spend is the undreamed-of ease of plastic credit. The collection of credit cards in your wallet disguises spending and makes it pain-free.

There is just about no chance at all that living costs are going to go down in the years ahead. The last time they did was in 1954. Living costs, in that year, fell by one-half of 1 percent. And compounding inflationary power is an ever-present force as well. Our example showed that five years of 8-percent inflation does not mean a loss of 40 percent in buying power (5 years times 8 percent); it means that your dollar buys *47 percent* less. Just as interest on money in a savings account enjoys an increased yield through compounding, inflation flourishes in exactly the same way.

Optimism, our national drawback

Knowing that the cost of living is just about sure to keep growing is a valuable forewarning, provided that you take steps to counteract the attack on your dollars, on the way you live, and on the way you hope to live throughout life. Call it realism or pessimism, expect the worst. Such an attitude, however, is almost un-American. One of the reasons why the statistics about senior citizens make such a horror story is that we are a nation of optimists. We believe, sometimes smugly, that tomorrow will take care of itself. The average American worker has an abiding faith in Social Security, the company pension, and the nest egg in the bank. Any two of the three should be all that is needed for a comfortable, worry-free retirement.

Unless the nest egg is big enough to uproot a tree, *it just won't be enough.*

Social Security or Social Insecurity?

Although a good many individuals think of Social Security as the dependable replacement for earnings, it was never intended to fill that role. At best, it was and is properly regarded as a *supplement* to retirement income and nothing more.

Partially because of this mistaken notion, perhaps, there is a great deal of concern about the future of the system—and for mighty good reason. The foundation of the system started rotting away almost as soon as it was born. In 1936 the machinery designed to make the system work was based on the fact that for each potential recipient of benefits there were thirty workers. Those thirty and their employers would pay in for each person taking money out. Twenty years later things had changed radically. Instead of 30-to-1, the ratio was 6-to-1. Another twenty years went by, and it was 3-to-1. By 1990 the ratio is expected to go to 1-to-1. You can see the size of the problem.

Can you hope to collect from Social Security when you reach the required age? The outcome remains to be seen. Plenty of brilliant minds are working on the problem. You cannot fully dismiss the possibility that it *could* be dropped altogether. However, because Social Security is a very, very hot political potato, the chances are that the system will survive. But "survival" does not mean that it will give you as much as you hope for.

Pensions from heaven

Pensions and profit-sharing plans can be the source of generous retirement income. They also can be the source of great disappointment. While you may have the impression that your company's contributions to your plan are yours no matter what occurs, this hope may prove to be an empty one. Most plans contain many "ifs" and "buts." When the *Employee's Retirement Income Security Act (ERISA)* came into being in 1974, the original and widespread belief was that the interests of employees were strongly reinforced. While they were, the Act also had some strongly negative side effects. It is one of the most complex federal laws in the nation's history. The rules and regulations are so rigid and potentially so costly—particularly for small to medium-sized businesses—that tens of thousands of employers have said, *"Too much expense. Too much red tape. Too much government in my business. Too many demands on my time. Too much responsibility on my shoulders. To hell with it."* They cancelled their plans.

Even in the plans that survived ERISA's demands—and there are a good many of them—generally you have no benefits you can call your own until you have been employed by your company for at least ten years. If you change jobs, you may have to start another ten-year waiting period, assuming that your new employer even has a retirement plan.

The leaky nest egg

The so-called "nest egg"—money in a savings account, government savings bonds, commercial bonds, or some similar place—is another potential cause of disillusionment. A person working and earning \$25,000 or \$30,000 a year, for example, may accumulate the equivalent of two or three years worth of gross pay (\$50,000 to \$100,000) and feel that all is well with the world, that the future is provided for. A look at today's life expectancy table can change that feeling of content. We are living longer lives. Medical and nutritional advances have added years to our lives. In the early part of 1979 HEW published a report stating that better than 25 years have been added to the lives of U.S. citizens since the turn of the century.

That's great. But to live longer, you must continue paying for food, shelter, clothing, medical care, and all the rest. To live 15 or 20 years after the customary retirement age of 65 is not uncommon. You can look around and see a good number of people who have gone well beyond their eighties in good health and vigor. Divide the \$50,000 or \$100,000 nest egg by 20 years, and it begins to look less attractive. *And don't forget about inflation.* The probability is that inflation will be as alive and vigorous as you are throughout your retirement years.

The moral is: A nest egg must not be eaten; it must be allowed to hatch and produce. The only nest egg you can feel secure about is one that is big enough to "hatch" the *income* you expect to need when your earnings stop—a "flexible" egg. If it is not earning enough as your retirement years roll on, *you must have control.* Your capital cannot be glued to the nest. You must be able, with the proper counsel and guidance, to make changes, transferring your capital to one or more places with the required muscle.

Reading this book, you will learn how to determine the size of the capital base you should plan for—one big enough to provide you with the income you will need. And although the figure you will arrive at may frighten you—or seem beyond reach—you will very likely come away from what you read with the comforting feeling that there are ways to attain such goals.

"Safe" havens—another comforting myth

One of the more serious misconceptions, which a vast number of people support, is that the wise and conservative thing to do with money is to put it where it is guaranteed. Avoid risk. Take no chances. Adopt the "safe havens" that have been traditional since grandfather's time.

Though a deeply injurious misconception, a staggering percentage of the public share this mistaken belief. The evidence of the widespread acceptance of this time-honored conviction is the amount of money sitting in "safe havens." In 1972, United States government records showed that deposits in commercial banks, mutual savings banks, savings and loan institutions, credit unions, and E and H government savings bonds totaled $914,742,394,000—almost $915 billion. Just five years later, that figure had swelled to $1,527,503,000,000—*more than a trillion and a half dollars!* Clearly, high living costs, high taxes, high interest rates, and huge clouds of uncertainty had combined to create widespread economic fear. Fear goads people to turn to the places where they feel most comfortable, the traditional "safe havens."

How safe are the "safe havens"? To answer that question, we must sharply define not only the full meaning of the word "guaranteed," but also what the haven guarantees.

Another day, another dollar

Today's dollars, which you use to provide yourself with all your needs, are just printed pieces of paper. But they were not always just paper. In the past, U.S. paper currency was so much larger than the familiar bills we now use that they were referred to as "horse blankets." In those days, for example, a $20 bill was printed green on one side and orange-gold on the other. They were called "goldbacks." Underneath Andrew Jackson's picture there was a statement that $20 in gold had been deposited in the Treasury of the United States, payable on demand. Then the government went off the gold standard. The bills were made smaller, and there were no more goldbacks. On the new bill, the legend read that $20 in silver had been deposited in the Treasury of the United States, payable on demand. Have you read any $20 bills lately? The ones you carry now say "Twenty Dollars." That's all. Of course, you may still exchange them. You will be given two tens, four fives, even twenty singles.

In other words, the money you deal with each day of your life is *worth only what it will buy. Nothing else matters.* Buying power is the yardstick. It is the only yardstick. When you put dollars into a "safe haven," the guarantee is that you will get back a certain *number* of dollars (the sum of principal plus interest). You also have the unexpressed guarantee that, regardless of what happens to the buying power of the dollar, you will not be given a single *extra* dollar. The guarantee in no way relates to the dollar's real worth in buying power. The guarantee is unfortunately double-edged.

How safe the "safe havens" are depends largely on the economic storm. Commercial banks, mutual savings banks, savings and loans, credit unions, E and H bonds are all essential to our economy. They render great services to you and to your community. In a variety of ways they enable you to shape

Everything looks so good! (Till the tide comes in.)

your financial life efficiently and effectively, and in a later chapter you will see ways in which they can serve you. But to use these institutions and methods as the places to *entrust all your funds for the things you want for yourself in the years ahead is economic suicide.* You must weigh their value to you against the nature of the economic circumstances: If inflation is bad and getting worse, then the "safe havens" are anything but safe. The massive blindness to this single fact probably accounts for the serious financial plight of most of the over-65 people of this nation.

To evaluate the value of these investments—in your own situation—ask yourself these questions:

1. *How much do your "safe haven" guaranteed dollars earn?*
2. *What remains after you subtract the taxes you pay to IRS on those earnings?*

3. *What is today's inflation rate?*
4. *Does the difference between your answers to entries 2 and 3 represent a profit or loss?*
5. *Other than what they earn,* is there any way *that your guaranteed dollars may increase in number while they remain in the guaranteed-dollar "safe haven"?*

Your answers to those five questions should convince you that what you have is a *guaranteed loss.* If all or a major portion of your dollars are in such places, your buying power is getting smaller and smaller. As you have seen, five years of 8 percent inflation shrinks buying power by 47 percent. *The only value your dollars have is cut almost in half in just five years.*

If your income is not guaranteed, then you might think, rather naturally, that you must take risks to increase your buying power. Yet the popular notion is that risk is something to avoid. In reality, *there is no way of avoiding risk.* As you have just seen, there is an absolute risk of loss when you put money where it cannot grow, where the after-tax return is less than the prevailing rate of inflation. And because inflation constantly hacks away at the buying power of money, dollars in a safe deposit box or buried in the basement face the obvious risk of being worth less when you bring them back into circulation. There is no escape. But if understood, analyzed, and measured, risk can be managed. First, you must discard the mistaken idea that risk can be and must be avoided. It is another harmful misconception.

There can be no profit without risk. Guarantees applied to a quantity of dollars are unyielding and inflexible anchors. When the tide of inflation rolls in, the anchor ensures loss. Guaranteed dollars, while capable of earning more dollars within certain limits, have no chance of growing in real value. Substitute risk for guarantees, and you open the doors to growth opportunity. You give yourself a means of catching up with or even running ahead of inflation.

Are you ready to take a chance?

The degree of risk you can and should accept in any effort to permit your dollars to grow in value is a special and interesting subject. It brings into play a variety of considerations, one of which is your emotional makeup. Some people, recognizing the true character of investment risk and appreciating the rewards that risk can offer, just cannot tolerate anything more than the most modest degree of risk. They are worriers. They lose sleep over their investments. Should they take a deep breath and agree to a carefully planned investment program, they are likely to drop it long before it has had time to accomplish anything for them. Others go to the other extreme. They enjoy high risk and seek it out. They accept unreasonable risks, believing that they will make overnight fortunes. As you read the next chapter, you will see how to evaluate your own degree of risk acceptance and how to adjust to it (if any adjustment is required). The all-important point is that risk is not only unavoidable, it is an element to be recognized, understood, and *put to work for your benefit.*

The capital invaders

Still another flawed financial belief is the moss-covered saying, "Never invade capital." Decades ago the adage was probably sound. The pace of living was far slower. The lures to spend were not the roaring flames they are today. The avenues of communication and their accompanying invitation to mimic the luxuries enjoyed by the super-rich did not exist. The massive availability of instant credit was not present. Even though yields were far more modest than those we know today, invading capital was regarded as a "capital offense." Even as you repeat the warning to yourself, *"Never invade capital,"* you are likely to conjure up a mental image of a snow-haired attorney, pontificating from behind a massive desk.

But times have changed. Today the invasion of capital is not always a bad thing to do. There are some broad exceptions to the old rule. In the financial climate of today, rarely will you find a will, written by the most conservative of lawyers, that does not provide the right for a widow or for the guardians of children to invade capital in order to supplement interest or dividend income if the pressures of inflation so require. When a financial planner tackles the question of providing cash flow for an unknown time period, capital should be treated as the producer of income and not as a sum to be devoured. Flexibility and judicious provisions for intelligent exceptions, however, must give way to a rigid adherence to an ancient, tired precept.

The comfort of procrastination

One of the costliest wastes in the lives of many is the attitude that, "I have no time." Its nearest competitor is the attitude that, "I have plenty of time." Both beliefs are sincere. Today's problems can be overwhelming, crowding out thinking time for anything but immediate emergencies. The feeling that you have plenty of time (expressed most frequently, of course, by those under 40) is even more understandable. A young couple with their first child has difficulty picturing their child wearing the world's most expensive head covering—the cap that goes with the gown at college commencement. That piece of millinery can cost as much as $35,000, but it can be worth a half-million dollars in lifetime income. That is how much more a college educated person may earn compared with those who lack the advantage. By the time the baby, now sucking its toe in the playpen,is ready to doff that cap, the cost might be as high as $75,000.

And retirement? That's for old people—30 or 40 years away. It may never come. ("Dad loved his work, and he *never* retired.") Retirement, however, comes in several forms. There is voluntary retirement, company policy retirement, disability retirement, and (who knows?), if unemployment becomes the increasing problem some predict, retirement by law could become a fact.

No matter how it may come, it is still something way off in the future.

Or is it? Most financial plans that are intended to create a source of capital for spending—for college costs, for retirement, or for other purposes—rely on the systematic accumulation of money. Monthly payments to those accumulation accounts are most common. A 35-year-old says, "No hurry. I have thirty long years ahead of me before I'm likely to retire. Today I can use my money for other things." Perhaps that person has thirty years, perhaps less. With the trend toward earlier

30 YEARS
20 YEARS
10 YEARS
! ?

retirement, it is entirely possible that you might think of retirement as a time of life when you put aside the money-earning career and graduate to a new career, devoting your time and energies to the fulfillment of a dream, whether it pays or not. It could be a career in art, writing, travelling, coaching little league baseball teams, charity, politics—almost anything. If a second career is your dream, the ideal time to make the break is when you are still young enough, healthy enough, and vigorous enough to pursue it with unimpeded enthusiasm. So maybe you don't have thirty years.

And there can be less happy reasons why your retirement might start at an earlier age.

But assume that the full thirty years is the accurate measure. For a monthly program you have 360 opportunities (30 years × 12 months per year) to accumulate the money you desire. Start now, and the amount you have to send forward to the 65-year-old you will be some day is relatively small. Wait ten years, and you have wasted 120 opportunities to help that you-of-the-future. At age 45 you will be compelled to budget a considerably larger amount each month. That could hurt. Wait until you are 55, with only 120 opportunities remaining, and the shadow of the approaching need is getting easier to see. A monthly program of a realistic size might be too heavy a load. It probably will be.

In any accumulation program you have two tools with which to build: time and money. They have equal importance but one big difference. Throughout your working and earning years it is possible to replace wasted money. Wasted time cannot be replaced. It is gone forever.

CANDIDATES FOR ACTION

At the end of each chapter, you have the opportunity to note those things that seemed particularly important and appropriate to you.

Eventually you will assemble all your own notes on the form at the end of the book. The chapter notes will help you to keep track of everything that *hit home* in a convenient, time-saving manner.

Consolidating all your candidates for action will permit you to review, discard, and select the elements you can use to develop your own financial plan—one that is in harmony with your circumstances, needs, hopes, and personal convictions.

Since this opening chapter concentrates on attitudes and mental adjustments in preparation for more specific ideas to follow, there are not many notes to be made. You may want to make your notations on either or both of these points, however:

( ) Transfer of assets in "loss positions."

( ) Use all the time available to me by starting now to accumulate for:

2

Give Yourself Control

The financial pendulum

Not too many years ago, the term "financial balance" had a clear, precise meaning and merited a considerable amount of respect. It was based on the idea that the economy acted like a pendulum. Sometimes we had *in*flation, and sometimes we had *de*flation, periods when a dollar was worth more and bought more. The theorists did not expect that the pendulum effect would be in any way uniform, with equal periods at either end of its swings. They looked to the past and recognized that there were occasional periods when the cost of living dropped and the dollar gained in purchasing power. Advocates of financial balance claimed that the thoughtful, conservative manager of money must have a financial mix. Some capital must be in *flexible* dollars—dollars that were free to grow in value during periods of inflation. And some capital must be in *fixed* dollars—guaranteed dollars that would grow in buying power during periods of deflation.

The period from 1929 through 1973 seemed to justify this even-balance viewpoint. Assume a person bought a fixed annuity paying a guaranteed $100 a month on January 1, 1929. At the same time he or she invested in the Standard & Poor's 500 Industrial Stock Index an amount of money sufficient to provide income of $100 a month at that time. On the day the two investments were made, their combined buying power was $200 a month. From then on, the actual returns have to be adjusted to the actual cost of living, in order to measure the true buying power of the total income received. In most of those forty-four years, realistic buying power stayed amazingly close to the original $200 because of the balance. Some of the years showed rather dramatic results. For example, in 1933 investment income—the income from the Standard & Poor's Index that had started at $100—was down to $47. The annuity income, of course, was at its guaranteed $100, but because living costs were down, the total income of $147 gave the investor buying power of $195. On the other end of the swing in living costs, the impact of inflation was vividly displayed in the final year, 1973. In that year the investment income amounted to $477. That and the $100 from the annuity amounted to $577, which produced actual buying power of $221.

The reason why this concept has disappeared is easy to see. From 1929 through 1942, a dollar was worth more than 100 cents in the grocery store. But 1942 was the last year that witnessed so much strength in our dollar's trading value. Assuming that you got *a dollar's worth for a dollar spent* in 1929, in 1973, the dollar brought home only 38 cents worth of anything. And you know the pounding it has taken since 1973! Depending on when you are reading this paragraph, the chances are that the value is closer to 20 cents.

In 1954 the cost of living went down by one-half of one percent. Since then we have lived through a variety of economic upheavals, and living costs have continued to increase, year after year, regardless of all other factors.

Thinking in reverse

Normal expectations are no longer normal. During periods of recession, living costs are *supposed* to go down, but since 1954 that simply has not happened. There have been serious recessions and mini recessions marked by bad business and grave unemployment problems. Through it all the Consumer Price Index, the government's measure of the cost of living, stubbornly continued to climb uphill.

Nor was this the only departure from normal expectations. Over many decades securities values have been the reliable, tough victor over rising prices. Rule of thumb was that living costs and securities values travelled as a team. When the prices in the supermarket rose, so did values in the securities markets. As a matter of record, securities values generally outpaced rising price tags by a considerable margin, more than compensating for inflation. The related actions were not always instantaneous, but stock prices could be counted on to move up with relative promptness as a reaction to increases in the Consumer Price Index. During the past decade, however, their reaction time has been distressingly slow or totally absent. In a number of those years stock values took sharp drops when tradition called for a strong move in the opposite direction. The stock market just has not been a reliable mirror of living costs. The old adage was, "Securities values will successfully combat inflation if given enough time." The key, of course, is to be found in the last four words . . . *if given enough time.*

No serious student of the market doubts that stock prices can and will resume their historic role, *eventually.* A bargain is a bargain, is a bargain. And if stocks—participation in the ownership of this country's corporate giants—remain static or if they slump while the corporations are continuing to make sound profits and are paying good dividends, catch-up time is inevitable. After all, who but the corporations are collecting the inflated prices?

No evidence leads us to believe that securities values will not move from low levels to new, historic highs. On the contrary, abundant evidence shows that this is precisely what will happen, *in time.* Possibly it has already happened by the time you read this. But at this writing there are far too many undervalued issues, far too many companies at price levels that result in unrealistically high yields, for these distortions, these buying opportunities, to be ignored indefinitely. The distortions *will* be corrected, just as water seeks its own level.

As far as stock values are concerned, the defiance of logic and tradition we have witnessed in recent years is not entirely without precedent. During World War I we had 16-percent inflation and a 50-percent drop in securities values. This was followed by a rocket-like move in stock prices in the early twenties. The aftermath of World War II ushered in a similar performance. Living costs were rising at an annual rate of 9.7 percent while securities values plunged downward; it took nine years for those values to recover.

None of this is at all mysterious. Periods of strong inflation frighten people. They fear their ability to cope with the future. They are uncertain as to what lies ahead. They do not know where to put their money, and they therefore turn to the time-honored, traditional "safe havens": the guaranteed savings account in a bank or savings and loan institution, government bonds, high-grade commercial bonds—all time-honored "safe havens." In times of uncertainty and fear, money flows out of the securities markets into the so-called safe harbors.

There is no escaping the fact that when money is taken *out* of the stock market, stock values move down. When dollars move *into* the stock market, prices go up. The stock market, as is true of any other market, reacts to the laws of supply and demand. But it reacts even more so, for dealings in the stock market are influenced so powerfully by emotions. When securities values are drifting downward, the emotion of fear accelerates the movement. When values are on the rise, the greed emotion takes over, propelling the upward movement. Low prices, which presumably would lure people to the market, actually scare them away. The *emotional* aspect of how individuals handle their money is highlighted by the tendency to turn to the "safe havens" during periods of serious inflation. The *reasoned* response to inflationary pressure is to attack it by putting dollars where they have a chance to increase in number. The purely emotional reaction—fear—motivates people to run to guaranteed vehicles. Putting your money where it *cannot* grow during periods when living costs *are* growing defies common sense. But a departure from common sense is not unusual when decisions spring from emotional impulses.

Summarizing, four points taken as a whole, give us a new look at financial balance:

1. *Securities values have matched or exceeded increasing living costs in the past and will again*—given enough time.
2. *What is enough time cannot be predicted. It can be a fairly long time, or it can be tomorrow.*

3. *Inflation appears to be a permanent guest in our lives, and deflation has become a stranger.*
4. *Emotions create great distortions in the securities markets, but extremes correct themselves*—given enough time.

The response of mutual funds

The new look takes on greater clarity when you study what the mutual fund industry has been doing in recent years. In the entire investment community no segment has been more innovative and more responsive to shifting economic factors and to investor demand than the mutual funds.

In 1969, as a direct reaction to the severe drop in stock market values, mutual funds with portfolios confined to government securities began to appear. They offered the antidote for those who had been hurt with high-potential, high-risk growth funds. Government securities represent exceptional safety and generous yield, the two attributes wanted by investors so recently savaged by their pursuit of growth.

In December, 1974, the Dow-Jones Industrial Average sank to 577.60, and what remained of the public's desire to pursue the quest for capital gains dropped several more notches. High income was king, and minimum risk shared the throne. In response to the homage paid to the royal couple, several dozen money-market funds surfaced. (You will meet money market funds in the next chapter.)

The *Tax Reform Act of 1976* made possible the formation of municipal bond funds, permitted to pass the tax-free privilege along to their shareholders (Chapter 5). The new tax-free mutual funds came to the market and gave the public a triple advantage: good income, freedom from federal taxation, and relative safety.

Then in 1977, as yields in general began to soften, the industry again found an answer by introducing option-income funds. You will see how options operate in Chapter 4. An option-income fund invests in dividend-paying common stocks and then attempts to increase overall income by selling options on the stocks it owns. The concept is that, in the hands of professional investment managers who are skilled at dealing in options, the combination of normal dividend income and the premiums realized from the sale of covered call options gives the investors unusually high income distributions.

The development of these new types of funds gives investors choices tailored to their desires or true needs: good income linked to the great conservatism represented by government securities, money-market instruments capable of producing still greater income, the municipals for those in higher tax brackets who see the need to solve income and tax problems at the same time, or option-income for those willing to accept greater risk for greater return. But the traditional types of mutual funds have not been discarded. Fund families have increased, taking on new members.

All this brings to the surface something more significant than a demonstration of the nimbleness of the mutual fund community. The fund sponsors are, in effect, saying to you, "Here is a complete financial menu. What appeals to your palate today? Do you desire a growth fund, a balanced fund, or a specialty fund? Or, if you prefer, we have some money-market funds, government securities funds, municipal bond funds, tax-deferred funds, and more. And if you like what we serve today and your tastes change tomorrow, just tell the waiter. Our chef is completely versatile." *They are offering you control.*

"Control" has become king

Financial balance has become a deposed monarch. Control has replaced it.

While there once was a time when a degree of financial balance was achieved by putting portions of your assets on one side of the scale and the remainder on the other, that degree of simplicity no longer works. The economy has become turbulent, the impact of national and international events and other portents have become too serious, taxation and legislative facts and possibilities have become too weighty. Most of all, economic uncertainty has become too worrisome a factor.

Control: it is a familiar word with which you can feel at

home. Its meaning is apparent. But that simple term, applied to so complex a subject, calls for some depth of understanding. Try a fuller definition of financial balance:

The ability to control your financial defenses so that you have a reasonable chance to live the way you want to live, no matter what happens to the economy.

Control, taken in that sense, wipes away any visualization of a *tight grip.* It speaks, instead, of flexibility, of freedom to move, of freedom to change.

The first thing it calls for, therefore, is an examination of all the places where your capital is right now. Is any of it fully or relatively inflexible? In the "inflexible" category are such items as certificates of desposit. Long-term ones that you have held for just a short time are quite inflexible; they can be liquidated at any time, but the cost is high. Short-term or long-held ones pose less of a problem, but they do tie your hands to a degree. Holding property such as diamonds, valuable jewelry, old coins, stamps, antiques, and works of art all require your finding a buyer willing to pay what you consider to be a fair price. This can be a time-consuming process, *if* it can be concluded to your satisfaction. Certain real estate investments require thoughtful consideration as to the degree of freedom you have or do not have, should you see the need to sell. There are stocks that the holder is not free to sell until a certain number of years have passed, or until the prohibition has been removed by regulatory authorities. These are known as *letter* or *restricted securities.* Control over your assets is particularly questionable if you are either the sole owner of a business or a partner or stockholder in a closely held corporation. Not only is your freedom of movement a key factor, but also the problems your family may face after you are gone may demand particularly serious study. The types of securities that you own or that you may consider in the future also enter the picture. Stocks that move rather sensationally, either up or down, may be a roadblock if you face the need to sell them when they are depressed. On the other side of the coin, some securities and other investments have given you big paper profits. When you sell them, you will be faced with heavy tax liabilities. (There are answers to the capital gains handicap; you will read about them in Chapter 10.)

Few things in life are flawless. That is abundantly true in this area. But if you buy the idea that it is important to give yourself as much control as you can command, you will avoid obvious traps. You will make a conscious, ongoing effort to minimize capital investments that reduce freedom of movement.

The mutual fund exchange privilege

Returning to the mutual fund example, today you have families of funds offered by the various fund sponsors and distributors. The sizes of the families have grown, as you have seen. Your investment in any fund within the family gives you access to all the cousins, the sisters, and the aunts. As often as you please, you may shift from a growth fund to an income fund, to a balanced fund, to a money-market fund, and so on. The exchange privilege either is free or requires a nominal charge, usually no more than $5 regardless of the size of the holdings. You are not frozen to an investment that matched your views and your needs at inception. When you have reason to believe that the economy's tendencies or your own needs have changed and that your investment direction should be brought into harmony with the altered situation, you may make that change without cost, delay, or red tape. A letter does it for you.

Some investment dealers or individual brokers, particularly those who are financial planners, take it as their personal responsibility to watch the general economy and the performance of the funds they have sold to their clients. When they see strong movements and have sound reason to believe that the time is right for a change in investment objectives, they advise you to take advantage of the exchange privilege and of any other moves that seem advisable.

The use of the mutual fund exchange privilege has reached the point where there are now several commercial services created to help brokers and investors take maximum advantage of this method of control. These organizations are given a record of client's fund holdings. Maintaining a day-to-day record of the fluctuating values of the various funds, each company developed methods of monitoring fund performances and shifts in the general economy, so that certain signals indicate when a shift from one type of investment portfolio to another seems advisable. The brokers or the individual investors are immediately alerted to the suggested action. They are free to act on or to ignore the suggestions. This type of investment technique is called *market timing*. It is evident that the ability to shift from one type of investment portfolio to another with speed, with ease, and without cost gives the investor considerable control.

Do not forget, however, that, except for transfers within a variable annuity, the IRS regards each exchange as a sale and a new purchase. Full consideration must be given to gains and losses.

Control starts with knowing where you are and where you are going.

The conduct of your personal financial management is almost certain to be the most serious business enterprise of your life. It is astonishing how few people operate that business—the business of making it possible to live their lives in styles they want for themselves and for their families—in a *businesslike manner.*

The first thing anyone does when opening a shop, office, or any other type of commercial or professional endeavor, is to establish written records, to set up books. No intelligently run business functions without financial statements. There is an absolute need to be able to examine figures showing how much is coming in, how much is going out, what is owed, what is owing, what assets and liabilities there are, and how these various accounts balance off. Bookkeeping is the indispensable means an owner or partner has of knowing whether progress is being made, if some seemingly minor problem is growing into a major threat, if expenses are getting out of hand, if some assets are proving to be a handicap instead of a help, and so much more. The ability to look at the full picture is no less vital in your day-to-day living. As evidenced by the grim facts revealed at the start of this book, mighty few people give themselves that advantage. It takes a little effort, but it is not complicated or difficult. It is one of the most rewarding steps you can take to organize and improve your financial life. There is an excellent chance that you will find immediate rewards. It is the surest way of giving yourself *control.*

Does the prospect of finding out where you stand intimidate you? Don't let it. The form below deals only with you, what you have, and where it is; and it is for your eyes only. Starting with **Section A, "Monthly Income,"** most of it is clear and simple. The best figure to use for "Earned Income" is actual take-home pay. Using that figure, you don't have to determine what withholdings are or what goes to Social Security. You can leave the Social Security entry, number 7, blank if you enter take-home pay earnings.

As of ________, this is where I stand:
(date)

A. Monthly Income

1. Earnings	$______	7. Social Security	$______
2. Spouse's earnings	______	8. Pension	______
3. Dividends	______	9. Annuity	______
4. Interest	______	10. Other	______
5. Rents	______		
6. Royalties	______	Total	$______

B. Monthly Expenses

1. Household	$______	11. Medical	$______
2. Clothing	______	12. Savings/Investment	______
3. Utilities	______	13. Personal care	______
4. Rent or mortgage	______	14. Personal meals	______
5. Taxes	______	15. Recreation/Education	______
6. Insurance	______	16. Vacation	______
7. Transportation	______	17. Gifts and charity	______
8. Time payments	______	18. Other	______
9. Average charge accounts	______		
10. Maintenance	______	Total	$______

C. Current Assets

		Annual Income Produced	Free	Semi	Frozen
1. Checking account (average)	$______	$______			
2. Savings accounts	______	______			
3. Certificates of deposit	______	______			
4. Home (less mortgage)	______	______			
5. Other real estate, net	______	______			
6. Bonds	______	______			
7. Securities	______	______			
8. Mutual funds	______	______			
9. Annuities	______	______			
10. Life insurance, cash values	______	______			
11. Precious metals	______	______			
12. Business interests	______	______			
13. Other	______	______			
Total	$______				

D. Obligations

1. Loans.................. $______
2. Home mortgage........ ______
3. Other mortgages....... ______
4. Time payments.......... $______
5. Other.................... ______

Total $______

E. Future Sources of Income or Capital

☐ Social Security ☐ Keogh ☐ IRA ☐ Co. Pension ☐ Profit sharing

Anticipations—(This can include inheritances, insurance or legal claim due you, proceeds from sale of business or property, etc.) $______

Total of face value of Life Insurance $______

Monthly income replacement from Disability Insurance $______

F. Future Capital Drains

(This can include any substantial claims you anticipate not included under D, above.) $______

Section B, "Monthly Expenses," may look like a budget. It isn't. It is a record of what really happens and not a structured plan for spending. "Household" includes food, cleaning supplies, and such. For the tax item, if you have earnings and adopted the suggestion that you use take-home pay, all you should fill in for B-5 is whatever additional taxes you pay. When you filed your last federal and state income tax

TO-THE-DOLLAR FIGURES ARE NOT NECESSARY

Round numbers are all you need throughout your financial inventory. Come as close as you can. If, as you go about filling in the figures, a specific entry (such as total dividend income) is out of reach, skip it. Fill in everything you can. There may be three or four items you will not complete because you need information not immediately at hand. The important thing is to keep going and not let the few hard-to-find figures bring everything to a standstill. When you reach the point where you know what the gaps are, you have a clear picture of where to go in order to finish the job. You may have to call on an investment dealer, your insurance agent, your accountant, or your financial planner. No problem. They are there to help you. There is no reason to hesitate. You are unusual if you do not need assistance with the current values of securities, real estate, total dividend income, and cash values of your insurance policies.

reports, did you have to make payments because withholding had been insufficient? Do you pay personal property taxes? Real estate taxes? Sales taxes should not be included. They are included in your normal living expenses. All else in this section may take a little head-scratching, but this record is simply a mirror of what you do, what you spend, day-to-day.

Section C, "Current Assets," asks for a little additional information. Keep in mind that one of the real purposes of this form is to enable you to control your financial life. The four columns, beyond the cash values of your assets, are quite revealing. The first of them, "Annual Income Produced," explains itself. The "Free-Semi-Frozen" entry calls for some judgment. Put a check mark under "Free" if, for example, it is the money in your checking account. That money can be moved at any time you see reason to move it. A certificate of deposit, on the other hand, may be either "semi-free" or "frozen." It is "semi" if it has only a brief time to go. It is "frozen" if the termination is several years away. Annuities are "free" if they are either deferred or in the accumulation process. They are "frozen" if the pay-out period has begun. And so on down the list.

Section D, "Obligations," should show the total sums owed, in contrast with the payments those debts require. The payments have been accounted for under B, "Monthly Expenses." Sections E and F round out the picture. Some of the possibilities covered may not be easily translated to actual dollars and cents. If they can, good; otherwise, just let it go.

Look for immediate benefits

When the form is completed, start looking for immediate benefits. One of the benefits you had in mind when you approached the business of writing your financial statement was to find ways to give yourself maximum control of your financial life. You are also looking for ways to provide yourself with increased current income or a bigger base for the creation of future income. All three goals can be translated to looking for ways to do something about inflation.

Start with "C. Current Assets." The first thing to examine are bare spots under "Annual Income Produced." Not every asset you own is capable of producing income. The equity in your home certainly cannot. But pay particular attention to 1, 5, and 10. Do you have too much money in your checking account earning nothing at all? How much money is really needed there? At the foot of "B. Monthly Expenses," you have a total. Is the amount of money in your checking account a lot more than that total? If so, you have discovered a new source of income. You could put the overflow into a money-market fund paying very high income and still giving you check-writing privileges (see page 50, Chapter 3). The no-cost checks you may write retain your total control, and the shift from no income to high income is an obvious step forward. There are, of course, other ways you can put the excess amount to work as well.

Item 5, "Real Estate," may call attention to an investment in raw land. Raw land produces no income and, in most cases, involves at least an annual tax expense. If the property has been getting more and more valuable, or if there is solid reason to believe that it will sharply increase in value in the relatively near future, all well and good. If not, then it is time for a change. Analyze the circumstances carefully. A piece of raw land bought ten years ago for $50,000 may have doubled in value, which looks good enough until you stop to consider that money invested at 8 percent doubles in nine years. You must consider other things: the taxes you pay on income as opposed to the capital gains tax on the real estate sale, or the annual costs of taxes on the raw land. The point is that investments in non-income-producing real estate require study.

For item 7, "Securities," you must check out each security. The considerations are not too different from those that came into play with raw land. Some securities may pay little or no income but are growth stocks. The question is how much growth have they given? How much growth may they deliver in the months ahead? And how much risk do they entail?

If item 10, "Life Insurance Cash Values," amount to an appreciable sum of money, are they serving you in the best possible manner sitting where they are? You will read about cash values and what you may do with them in the chapter on insurance. You will know your options. You can use them to earn more income, to invest for growth, or to increase your total insurance protection. You have control. Are you exercising it?

You have put checkmarks in the next three columns. At a glance you now know which of your assets can be moved without delay or heavy cost, if you see advantages in moving them. And you see assets that may be moved about with some delay, red tape, or expense. In the final column you see assets that presently are close to immovable. The first of these three columns gives you no cause for concern; you have all the control you could want. The next column, "semi," calls for some study. Unless there is some pressing need or a major advantage to moving one of the assets in that column right now, your main thoughts should be whether you should plan to make some changes when time frees them. If there is a serious reason to transfer one or more assets in this group now, then you have to weigh the costs against the potential gain and reach a conclusion. The "frozen" items might include your biggest assets and your biggest problems.

Your are going to see answers to some of the problems as you go through the coming chapters on gifts, trusts, and ways to ease the tax bite on highly appreciated investments. You may have good reason to consult with specialists about ways of unfreezing some of those assets: your investment dealer, financial planner, insurance broker, lawyer, or accountant.

Now that you have taken a fresh look at what you have and at what it is doing or not doing for you, "Obligations" (part

D) calls for inspection. You may have seen that certain assets are not earning their keep. Just possibly, using them to reduce or eliminate some obligations could be a sound exercise of control. If you do so, you are probably improving "B. Monthly Expenses." And, if you can cut down on B, you are going to be in a position to make some better uses of "A. Monthly Income." There's a good chance that the freed-up income can be put to work earning additional income.

Control can be beautiful.

After you have read future chapters, come back to E and F. Whatever you have checked off (or not checked off), along with the figures you may have entered in sections E and F, will have more meaning for you.

When you compare the totals of sections A and B ("Monthly Income and Monthly Expenses"), you don't have to look hard to see if something is wrong. If what you are spending is more than what is coming in, perhaps you already anticipated this part of the financial statement. You "knew" there was a problem. The review of assets may also point the way to an effective answer. If not, or if the answer is not sufficient to give you proper control of your day-to-day finances, other answers are needed.

Self-control

One answer may be *emotional control.* The temptation to spend can be powerful, aided so substantially today by easy credit. One of the most damaging traps that has given lots of people bad cases of the financial feebles is the uncomplicated way in which installment credit and credit cards make buying so painless. Credit, in itself, is not an evil. Installment buying, used with control, can be a desirable form of enforced saving. Prior to the broad use of "convenient payments," people would save for a long time if they wanted to buy anything as substantial, for example, as an automobile. Today they buy it and then "save" by making regularly scheduled payments.

There are two distinct advantages to the second approach. First, you need not postpone the utility, convenience, and pleasure that car ownership entails. Second and more importantly, the systematic payments bring with it enforced

discipline. If you quit, you are a big loser. Those who decide to save first and fly later can wander away from the saving practice with no injury other than the forsaken goal. Nobody reminds or prods them. They are on their own, and many people simply do not have that kind of stick-to-it character.

The mutual fund industry's historic experience has illustrated the degree to which the threat of loss effectively enforces systematic savings habits. Contractual accumulation plans and voluntary accumulation plans have been offered for many years. The contractual plan calls for prepayment of a substantial portion of the sales charge covering the entire program. The voluntary plan asks for no prepayment. If a person quits a contractual plan in the early years, the prepaid sales charges are not returned. The investor loses that money:

He or she *knows* about that threat of loss. The voluntary planholder makes no prepayment and faces no threat of loss. During the period that practically all contractual plans required payment of half the entire sales charge in the first year, better than 90 percent of all investors completed their plans of ten years or more. During the same period, 80 percent of all voluntary planholders drifted away from their plans by the end of the third year.

Installment purchasing, because it permits the immediate possession of major items, is credited with being one of the reasons for the high living standards of the average American family. Its growth has been dramatic. In 1950, according to a Federal Reserve bulletin, installment credit amounted to a little more than $4.5 billion. In 1976, that figure was close to $185 billion. And then there are credit cards. Credit card buying jumped from $76 million in 1950 to well over $2 billion in 1976. The uncomplicated use of a credit card is a delightful convenience. It avoids the need to carry large sums of cash, which is particularly welcome in these days of high crime. It makes it unnecessary to wait for pay-day to make purchases. It has been so universally accepted that relatively few things cannot be purchased with a credit card. A trip around the world, clothing, furniture, meals—all are yours with credit cards. More gasoline, for example, is bought with credit cards than with cash.

Installment buying, with many months to handle the payments, and credit cards, granting immediate access to a limitless number of items and services, have done much to lubricate the wheels of business and to permit people to enjoy more of the material comforts of life. They are fine. But anything can be overdone.

Budgeting for self-control

Just as no intelligently run business is operated without a financial balance sheet, no business is run without control over money paid out. Cash needs are put on paper, and every effort is made to stick to budgeted expenditures. A *personal expense control,* more commonly called a *budget,* tells where your money is *going to go* instead of telling you, after the fact, where it went. By no means does everyone need a budget.

Quite a few individuals and families have never budgeted their expenses, but they handle living expenses without problems. That is particularly true, of course, if income is so ample that there is little danger of overspending. For others the discipline of planned and controlled spending is almost essential. There is no point in plotting a budget unless everyone involved is determined to be faithful to it. A realistic family budget, therefore, should not be so rigid that living with it proves to be a burden and a cause of conflict. A good budget is like a good bathrobe: It should be broad enough to cover all the essentials and loose enough to be comfortable.

Model budgets do not mean very much. They can be more confusing than helpful. People's ideas, lifestyles, habits, needs, occupations, family makeup, and localities differ far too much. On page 37 of this chapter, there is a list of those things to be included in your budget if you decide that you want to prepare your personal family budget. You may want to list some additional items. The framework provided for you is no more than an organized reminder of essentials to be covered by most family budgets without any suggestions as to percentages. Percentages are up to you.

In putting down a figure for income, include everything. Don't overlook any of the income items on your financial inventory. Do include customary Christmas bonuses or cash gifts you *know* you can rely on for your birthday, anniversary, or other occasions. Add it all up and divide by twelve. Use that figure as the basis for what is available to spend each month.

You have a lot more control over what goes out than over what comes in. You will notice that the checklist divides outgo into three categories. First is for you. To control your financial life in the most satisfactory manner, you have to set aside money for those things most important to you. And there is simply no reason to consider payments you make to strangers before taking care of yourself. Number two category is for those expenses you have little or no way of influencing. You are stuck with them, although, if you have completed and reviewed your personal "This is where I stand" statement, you may have found ways to reduce come of the payments in the "fixed" category. Finally, in the "flexible" portion of the budget

ITEMS TO BE INCLUDED IN YOUR EXPENSE CONTROL

Income

All certain income for year		$______
Providing monthly income of		$______

Outgo

1. Yourself:	Savings and investments (for both emergency fund and major goals)	$______
2. Fixed:	Taxes (other than income tax withholding and Social Security)	$______
	Rent (or house payment)	$______
	Utilities	$______
	Installment payments (including debt repayments)	$______
	Current bills	$______
	Insurance premiums	$______
3. Flexible:	Food	$______
	Clothing	$______
	Home maintenance	$______
	Medical	$______
	Education	$______
	Recreation/vacation	$______
	Gifts and contributions	$______
	Transportation	$______
	Her monthly expenses	$______
	His monthly expenses	$______
	Children's allowances	$______

are those things that you can readily control—some to a minor extent, most to a major extent.

Control involves many things. Tradition and so many things we read and hear serve to firmly implant in our minds that 65 is retirement age. Most people, therefore, base an important part of their financial plans on being ready to supplement retirement income when earnings stop at, or about, age 65.

Independence at age 50

Here is an idea for you: Do some hard thinking about trying to have a replacement for earned income waiting for you at an earlier age. Take age 50. At that time of life it can be nothing less than glorious to be financially free. To have full control of your financial life at 50 suggests a variety of enticing possibilities. At that age it is not unusual for people to become tiptoe careful about their employment. They put aside strong desires to say what they think if what they think could conceivably isolate them from the higher-ups. They are less likely to sound off if they think they are being treated unfairly. They shy away from making radical suggestions, no matter how much they may believe that the idea might prove to be a zinger. They hesitate to accept increased responsibilities, even if it means a healthy increase in pay. They have become smug and comfortable doing what they do and fear that the new challenges could mean even a slight chance of failure. The fact is that the idea of looking for a new job when you are 50 or older is frightening.

And there are other possibilities at that age. By that time of life you have attained a record, a reputation, a depth of knowledge, skill, and experience. You are marketable. When you have those irreplaceable advantages, you are liable to be approached by others to join with them to start a new venture. At such a time you may think you should start a business of your own. The yes or no decisions you make are almost bound to depend on your degree of financial freedom. Either you have the money to join others or go on your own with a promising new venture, or you do not. You have the money to back you up if you say what you want to say, act as you want to act, promote the ideas you believe in—or you do not.

Earning money at age 50 is not the entire picture either. If you have provided yourself with financial freedom, you are in a position to see dreams come to life. You can devote yourself fully to travel, to a cause, to a charity or institution, a low-paying faculty assignment, to politics, to pursuing a new career as a writer, artist, musician, prestidigitator. At 50 you are going to have the health, the vigor, the enthusiasm, and the time to do the things you want to do, without compromise or handicaps—*if you are financially in control.*

Control includes protection

For myriad reasons may may want your control to outlive you. Control of that type can protect people you love; it can build defenses against anticipated avarice, jealousies, and plots. It can provide supervision and ironclad provisions for the benefit of family members who may need such disciplines. It can preserve those things you want preserved.

Total control of all aspects of your financial life encompasses life and disability insurance as well as investments and savings. Insurance provides an unmatched means of filling capital vacuums. Potential capital vacuums can be anticipated, making the adoption of appropriate insurance programs imperative. The appropriateness of an insurance program has no permanency. It changes as surely as the general economy changes and as surely as an individual's earnings, age, family composition, and many other aspects of life change. Control, therefore, calls for review at fairly frequent intervals—review and adjustment.

You should investigate other points beyond what may be needed to counterbalance the drying up of earnings if you should have the misfortune to suffer a long-term disability or die before your time. One of the key considerations lies in the source of your earned income. If you are a sole proprietor, a partner in a business venture, or a major stockholder in a closely held corporation, some problems can be foreseen. Such problems include the following:

- *Some day you may want to retire, or an accident or bad health may force you to retire. If and when this happens, what are the prospects of being able to sell the business, or your interest in it, for a reasonable price?*

- *If you die while still active in the business, what happens with your interest? Is the value lost? Can it be sold? Is there a logical buyer? Will the logical buyer have the funds needed to pay a fair price?*
- *If a partner or a fellow major stockholder dies, what happens? Will an undesirable stranger, an untrained widow or some other unwelcome buyer move in and, perhaps, take charge? If you want to be the buyer, will the necessary purchase price be available to you?*

These and companion problems can be of towering importance. But, since they can be anticipated, you can take control before any of these events occurs. Through insurance a pool of capital can be made available if early retirement becomes a fact. And this particular capital account can be tax-sheltered through the adoption of a suitable retirement plan.

Buy-sell agreements are important tools. With the use of such agreements, understandings can be reached as to the establishment of the fair value of a business. Through life insurance on one another's lives, each partner or stockholder knows that when death takes out any party to the arrangement, cash will be on hand to buy out the deceased member's interest, or to pay the estate for his or her own interest. In the case of a sole proprietorship, a special life insurance policy on your life can enable your estate, a son, a nephew, or a long-term loyal employee to pay a predetermined price for the business. The degree and the importance of this type of control is obvious.

If you have a business in corporate form, there may be a fairly substantial cash surplus. The investment of part of that surplus in a mutual fund withdrawal plan that will pay the premiums on the insurance portion of a buy-sell agreement can be very attractive. The premiums are paid without the need for annual reductions of cash flow. Taxation on the dividends at corporate rates make the taxes delightfully low. The value of the shares are continuously exposed to growth possibilities. The investment remains on the corporation's books as a capital asset. It is an idea worth investigating.

Along with your annual checkup . . .

An annual review of every part of your financial life is an essential ingredient of businesslike control. Those reviews should be shared by your financial planner, investment dealer, insurance agent, lawyer, accountant, real estate broker—if each has played a part in the placement of your working capital and of your arrangements for the future.

CANDIDATES FOR ACTION

- ☐ Availing myself of the exchange privilege through mutual fund investment where a "family of funds" offers varying objectives and investment policies.
- ☐ Completing the "*This is where I stand*" form to put my financial life on a businesslike basis.
- ☐ Study of all assets with objective of increasing my control of my financial life.
- ☐ Analysis of assets as to amount of income and/or growth prospects they offer.
- ☐ Consideration of reducing or eliminating debt and related payments.
- ☐ Preparing a budget.
- ☐ Making financial independence by age 50 my goal.
- ☐ Control of income vacuum possibilities via appropriate life and disability insurance.
- ☐ Buy-sell agreements to control purchase or disposition of business interests.
- ☐ Annual reviews with assistance of:
  - ☐ Investment dealer
  - ☐ Insurance agent
  - ☐ Real estate broker
  - ☐ Lawyer
  - ☐ Accountant
  - ☐ Financial planner

3

Ready Cash

How much cash is enough?

Emergencies

Although everyone needs a cash reserve for emergencies, no one can say how much of a reserve is enough. With no other source of support to help you deal with various types of emergencies, you could settle for a relatively precise formula. Economists claim that employed people need anything from the equivalent of three month's to a year's earned income. For people living on retirement income, two month's of normal living costs has been suggested. Before settling on the amount of your emergency reserve, you should ask yourself several questions. Do you have:

- Hospitalization? *Does it cover all family members in the household? Is there a waiting period? How long is it? Do payments cover surgery, anesthesia, and medical care, in addition to the hospital?*
- Medicare and Medicaid?
- Medical reimbursement policy? *Does it cover the family?*
- *An* employer *who can be counted on to handle all costs of an accident, serious illness, or other unexpected need for cash?*
- *Any* medical problem *that might cause emergencies fairly often?*
- Parents or other close relatives *who, without question, would instantly take over in an emergency?*
- Parents or other close relatives *whose serious illness or injury might require immediate cash assistance?*

The answers to these and to similar questions all bear on your decision as to the size of your particular emergency fund. In general, however, most people have various forms of accident and health protection, so the realistic out-of-pocket cash requirements occasioned by unexpected, emergency situations are rather limited. With average insurance protection, a realistic sum to be regarded as a back-stop for the unexpected is approximately $2,000.

As in other phases of the ready (or guaranteed) cash question, your mental attitude affects how much you feel "safe" with. One part of the answer to the emergency fund question must therefore depend on what is in your mind when you see the phrase "emergency fund." Some people think of such a fund as one capable of handling unexpected car and home repairs, the sudden need for new clothing, an unanticipated gift, and so on. Others regard it as money to cover childbirth, a wedding, and similar family happenings. These attitudes are not to be debated. If Mrs. Blowe is three months pregnant, and the parents-to-be feel that all the costs connected with the impending arrival of a baby constitute an emergency, that's fine. They should base their emergency reserve on that premise. It is not an uncommon practice for a family to have a savings account which they maintain with a firm resolve that, under no circumstances—other than a genuine "must-be-handled-instantly" emergency—will they permit the account to fall below a fixed number of dollars. That sacred base is for emergency use only. Any amount above it is available for specific purchases, for car and home repair, gifts, vacations, what have you. Such an approach succeeds with sufficient self-discipline. If self-control is an acknowledged weakness in your household, you will be better off if the fund for genuine emergency use is a separate entity—a special account, never used for any other purpose and never mingled with any other funds. The key element is that ways to pay for foreseeable and possible future needs must be given full consideration. How you label your reserve for such preparedness is of no importance.

Ready cash for other reasons

Although emergencies are obvious reasons for keeping cash available, they are not the only ones. Seven categories cover most of the reasons why some people insist on having sizable sums of money in a readily available, guaranteed-cash status.

1. *Near-term* certain *need.* *Within a relatively short span of time, you may firmly intend to make a major purchase, pay a loan, make a loan, or lay out cash in some form or another.*
2. *Near-term* maybe *need. There is a* chance *that you may need a large amount of money because a big trip, big purchase, or big cash settlement (such as losing a damage suit) could come up.*
3. Holding pattern. *The family has just come into a sizable sum of money—through the sale of a home, farm or business, through an inheritance, by collecting damages from a lawsuit, or by hitting the state lottery—and wants to take a lot of time deciding what to do with that money on a long-term basis.*
4. Distrust of a currently flagging securities market.
5. A general lack of confidence in securities and real estate investments at all times.
6. Infatuation with dollar guarantees.
7. A personal need for availability. *Perhaps, you are just not happy unless all, or nearly all, capital is within instant reach.*

You can see that, going from entries 1 to 7, more and more emotion asserts itself. Items 1 and 2 are objectively sound reasons for wanting to keep cash readily available. "Holding pattern" individuals probably have some reasons for their attitude, but they must take *some* action to put the money where it can earn income. Number 4, distrust of the current securities market, seems sound on the surface. But it may or may not be valid since, as parts of this book reveal, there are many ways of taking benefits from investments or securities. The door to the securities market must be kept open. The rest of the reasons (5, 6, and 7) stem from pure emotionalism or a lack of knowledge.

Cash-rich but income-poor

These last three attitudes are likely to lead to serious financial problems. Why? The most obvious fact is that inflation is an established fixture in our economy and in the world's economy. Ingoring it does not solve the grave problems it imposes. Having a lot of cash on hand will not necessarily give you the income you need to live. You might be "cash-rich but income-poor."

Ask yourself, "If money is put to work at interest, can the interest earned be enough *after taxes* to compensate for the average increase in living costs?" For example, if we could count on an average annual rate of inflation of 6 percent, then money earning 6 percent *before taxes* has to create a loss. The average income earner would have to find a source of 8-percent to 9-percent interest just to stand still. Yet how many people can have true peace of mind if they base their financial health on simply standing still? Any increase in inflation, any loss of income or capital, any unplanned increase in spending results in a certain loss.

The real question revolves around a single word ... "risk." When people say that they will not invest because investing involves risk, they are accurate—because investment *does* entail risk—but mistaken. They are mistaken because the avoidance of investment risk creates another kind of risk, namely, the risk of losing the ability to keep pace with inflation. Without that ability, you are assured a loss. Bypassing investment because of the risk factor puts you in the position of facing the risks associated with standing still or falling behind; your only hope of even a small profit is based on the chance that living costs will go down. Do you expect that to happen? Investing therefore involves the risk of loss, but it also creates the possibility of reward—profit.

Why "risk" your cash?

Time has proven that investing cash in securities offers a reasonable chance for reward; as such, it is one of the soundest ways of fighting inflation. Look at the records: inflation's impact on the cost of living is measured by the government's Consumer Price Index; one of the most frequently used measurements of securities' performance is the Standard & Poor's 500 Stock Index. From 1945 through 1979, the Consumer Price Index increased by 209.3 percent, while the S&P 500 rose by 507.9 percent. During the same thirty-year period, dividends earned by securities grew 387.4 percent.

Growth, therefore, is the name of the inflation-fighting game. If you have to save a particular number of dollars, you may put them aside in an account, where those dollars are guaranteed. But you have seen that you cannot guarantee the future *buying power* of savings. Before anyone makes the decision to protect a given *number* of dollars—thus accepting buying power risk and refusing all investment risk—the purpose of savings must be explicit.

EXAMPLE: Mr. and Mrs. Kiddee decide that they want their 3-year-old son to attend an important, prestigious college some day. They agree that since college costs are high, it is wise to launch a systematic savings program at once. They learn that, today, four years at the type of college they have in mind costs about $14,000. That means that they must put aside enough money every year, at interest, to reach their goal. By doing a bit of digging, they find that if they save $600 per year at 5½ percent compounded quarterly, they will have what they want.

But they won't. They will *have $14,000, but there is mighty little chance that they will come even close to having what it will take to pay for four years of college. College costs have not kept in step with inflation. They have run ahead of it! The cost of attending a top-ranking private college has been increasing from 7 to 16 percent a year since 1970. If future increases fall someplace between these two figures, the $14,000 that Mr. and Mrs. Kiddee managed to save* would not be enough to pay for even one year of college. *By the time that the Kiddee kid would be ready for college, the cost could be well over $50,000.*

The Kiddees have several options. They may, of course, choose to believe that inflation will go away—that they can ignore it. But if they think that history is not about to reverse itself—that the cost of higher education will keep growing—they must triple the amount of money they will set aside. If they cannot put that much aside, they can put their money where it is freed of the fetters of guarantees and has a chance to grow.

The reasonable approach

Carry that example one step further. If putting one child through college can present such a big, inflation-embroiled problem, just think about the immensely greater problem of retirement. How great a pool of capital must be amassed to adequately supplement retirement income from Social Security and a company pension?

Deciding on how big your cash reserve should be is a question to be answered by means of the fundamental elements of logic—not approached emotionally, not ignored, not avoided. Yet emotions are sometimes so deeply embedded that they cannot be dispatched with logic. And sometimes, as you have seen, there are perfectly sensible reasons for holding impressive sums of money in cash equivalents. If you expect to need a fixed amount of money in the near future, no fluctuating investment makes good sense. When the moment of need arises, liquidating the investment may be difficult, even impossible, because it may be a particularly bad time to sell. Although the security or property may be used as collateral for a loan (interest is usually deductible), negotiations for an acceptable loan can take time, and borrowing costs money. Your needs may be too urgent to wait for a loan. There are, therefore, situations where securities investments are just not suitable. However much you decide to set aside as a reserve and however much you choose to invest represent amounts that only you can judge. The key point is that you make your judgments with reason, not with emotion.

How "ready" should your cash be? banks, bonds, bulls, and bears

Before you make a firm decision that a certain sum of money or a certain percentage of your assets are to be in readily available cash, you must do some thinking about what you really mean by "readily available." Does it mean *today? Within two or three days? Within a week or ten days?* Once you have made that decision, you may more easily decide what price you are willing to pay for the availability you want.

Banks and savings and loan institution

When looking for a safe place to put money, have it earn interest, and always have it quickly available, most people

think of a bank savings account or a savings and loan deposit. Savings and loan institutions are permitted to pay a slightly higher rate than banks. But your money earns money in both types of account. Banks pay *interest,* while the savings and loans pay *dividends.* The IRS, however, regards the savings and loan payments as interest. So even though the paying organization *labels* the earnings as dividends, those payments do not qualify for the $100 dividend exclusion from income on federal tax returns. That exclusion applies only to dividends paid by general securites and mutual funds. With rare exceptions, deposits of up to $40,000 in either type of account are insured by agencies of the United States government. With different ownership registrations, several times the $40,000 is insurable. Both types of banks customarily permit withdrawals on demand from their standard passbook accounts. And both, particularly the savings and loan institutions, are likely to be geographically handy and can be dealt with easily, without formalities or complications. Either type offers an ideal answer for the small emergency account.

Incidentally, the same benefits, with the probable exception of geographic convenience, are available from mutual savings banks and credit unions. Like banks and S&L institutions, they give you a choice of passbook accounts (credit union members make their deposits through the purchase of *shares*) or certificates of deposit. Certificates pay more generous income, but, unless they are held to predetermined maturities, they entail penalties for withdrawals. They do not really qualify as sources of "ready" cash, therefore, if you consider instant availability important.

Savings banks, savings and loan institutions, and credit unions may play important roles for you in keeping cash ready. The great ease of putting your money into and taking it out of these accounts must not be discounted. Very competitive, they make a great effort to offer the most generous return permitted by law. For people in very low tax brackets, they are particularly desirable.

For one thing, the dollars in any of these accounts are safe to the *n*th degree. The $40,000 insured protection is provided by one of three agencies. The Federal Deposit Insurance Corporation (FDIC) insures banks. The Federal Savings and Loan Insurance Corporation covers the thrift institutions, and credit union members are protected by the National Credit Union Administration. All three are agencies of the United States government. The first two have been operating for more than forty years, and no saver has ever lost one penny covered by the insurance. You pay nothing for that protection.

Even within the $40,000 limit, you can easily protect a great deal more.

EXAMPLE: Tom Saver has $40,000 in the Beautiful Money Savings & Loan. His wife, Sally Saver, has an equally large account in the same institution. Both accounts are fully insured. But Tom and Sally can go beyond that limit. In addition to their separate accounts, they are allowed to have a joint account and, assuming that it is valid (with the customary signatures on file, along with the rights of withdrawal), this account may also carry $40,000 worth of insurance. In that way, one couple may have up to $120,000 of free insurance in a single institution.

You want more? You can have more. Nothing in the regulations bars you from opening $40,000 accounts in as many *different* banks, savings and loans, or credit unions as you please—and every one of your accounts will qualify for the maximum insurance.

Quite a few savings and loan institutions also have a little known service that can have particular appeal to people who are elderly or infirm. Operating under different names, it may be called an *interest-income account* in one place and *check-a-month service* in another.

EXAMPLE: Bob and Barbara Olds are no longer as spry as they were in the past. Wed to tradition, they are comfortable only with their money where it has a solid **number** *of dollars guarantee behind it. They have $120,000 in capital from the sale of their home (they now rent an apartment), so they turn to the thrift institutions. They find one with check-a-month service. Bob opens an account with a third of their capital, while Barbara opens her own account with another third. The final third goes into a joint account. Every dime is insured, and they earn 5¾ percent. The savings and loan is instructed to use the interest from the joint account to send a monthly rent check for $175 to their landlord. Out of Bob's interest the savings and loan mails a check for $200 directly to him. Barbara gets a $100 check from her account each month, and another $90 is sent to her brother who is in a nursing home. The Olds never have to go out of their apartment to collect their money for living. They don't have to write checks—or remember to do so—for their rent or for her brother. The convenience is great, and the income will flow forever, because their capital is not being reduced.*

Money-market funds

The problem with such a neat arrangement (as in the Olds' account) is that the yield may not keep pace with rising living costs—higher rents, greater nursing home fees, or the increased price per pound for beef. A higher yield would naturally make such an arrangement more desirable. For many years, savings accounts were almost the only places to put dollars to keep them readily available. Until recently, the average citizen had only one other resort: highly rated corporate bonds, which keep dollars relatively safe, earn a good return, and are quickly and easily convertible to cash. What was not available to those of average means were the safest and highest yielding repositories of money—United States Treasury bills, United States obligations, the obligations of various federal agencies, and certain debt obligations of major banks and corporations. Treasury bills and obligations call for minimums ranging from a low of $10,000 to $100,000 or more. The obligations of federal agencies demand $5,000 to $10,000 minimums, and attractive commercial paper, from $25,000 to $1 million. These minimums barred nearly all individuals from using any of these otherwise inviting, safe, high-yielding, liquid investments. Most people did not have enough cash to buy them.

Then the innovative people in the mutual fund industry created accesses to these very solid producers of top income. Today, many mutual funds have opened the locked doors. Popularly called *money-market funds,* they take the dollars of thousands of individuals and invest in short-term, high-yield government bills and obligations, in top-paying commercial paper, and in other types of investments offering exceptionally generous income. Yields of 10 percent and better are not uncommon. Nothing like common stocks, the investments made by the money-market funds just about eliminates the risk of loss. Rarely do the values change, and their short-term nature permits them to be fully liquid at all times.

For most of these novel mutual funds, you must make a minimum initial investment, which range from $1,000 to $5,000. After that you may invest as little as $100 at a time whenever money comes to hand. Nearly all money-market funds are offered free of sales charge. There are no time restrictions, and there is no charge or penalty for withdrawing money, no matter when. Some funds make a flat monthly service charge—a few dollars a month regardless of the size of your account. Most also impose an annual fee of less than 1 percent of the average balance of your account. In either case, the charges are deducted from the income payments.

Most of these attractive mutual funds now make it possible for you to have part or all of your money the day you want it. You can, for example, put your money into a money-market fund that provides you with free checks. When the need for money comes up, you write a check and cash it the same day. Generally you are required to write checks for no less than $500. That should give you no problems. If you need $200, you can write a check for $500, cash it, and immediately reinvest the $300 dollars in the same money-market account—or put it in your regular checking account. Using the free checks is not the only way of access to your money on a same-day basis. Normally you may arrange to transfer money from the fund to your own bank by telephone or telegram.

These funds compare favorably with savings and loan institutions. In 1979, for example, their yield was 10 percent versus 5½ percent from S&L accounts. The degree of safety is about the same, and the cash is just as available. To a couple like the Olds, the difference rests with the peace of mind they enjoy; they prefer to forego the additional return for the convenience and familiarity of the savings and loan.

Mutual funds

A variety of mutual funds also concentrate on giving you high income. Some invest in nothing but commercial bonds, while others make their investments in high-yielding common stocks and bonds. These funds do not offer the same-day cash facilities available from the money-market funds, but, in most cases, your written request for full or partial withdrawal brings you a check within a week.

(A great many individual securities offer good income combined with the chance of growth or profits; these are discussed in the following chapter.)

Emotionally acceptable financial decisions

Sound logic and human emotions are not necessarily compatible. Your emotions play a powerful part in the things you do—or don't do—about your personal financial planning. Nothing in this or in any other publication has much chance of changing your emotional makeup. Nonetheless, many statements in this book are calculated to influence how you *think* about money, risks, and rewards. For example, in the opening chapter you saw that a number of misconceptions, prejudices, and habits demand reexamination to bring your thinking into balance with the realities of today's economy. These exercises are all matters of logic. Now you must consider where to put

your precious capital—and it is precious. You are engaged in an exploration of the contrasts between traditional safe havens and places that may be less familiar and more intimidating . . . *may* be.

At this stage, a long, deep, inward look becomes critically important for you. You have to weigh your emotions and give grave consideration before you make any substantial dollar decisions. The essence of good financial planning is to arrive at *emotionally acceptable* decisions, which at the same time can provide you with a well-rounded plan to maintain your way of life and your family's way of life . . . while you live and after you are gone.

The key words are *emotionally acceptable.* The soundest of your decisions can lead to frustration and failure if they conflict with your emotional nature. You may accept the rationale of a carefully structured program with sincere enthusiasm, but if long-term adherence to the plan or to key parts of it is not emotionally acceptable to you, it will not endure. For example, highly conservative persons may decide to accept a "reasonable" amount of risk in a systematic long-term monthly investment concept, only to find that they are so concerned about the risks that they become nervous and irritable everytime the market declines a little. Their sleep is disturbed, and the worry interferes with their work. Under such conditions, the program will collapse before many months go by. At the other end of the scale, people with strong speculative inclinations, though initially convinced that they must conserve, will sooner or later become equally ill at ease. They will probably not persevere in their planned programs either, tormented by the "great opportunities for profit" they are losing.

Discontinuing a thoughtfully drawn financial program in its early stages is, in itself, harmful. What is more harmful is the serious possibility that you will make no effort to substitute a plan that is emotionally acceptable. No program at all is the end result, and *that* can be ruinous.

As important as adherence to the plan may be, not everyone is able to look inward, measuring his or her genuine emotional reactions to the kinds of decisions they can live with over long periods of time. The following checklist may help you in that attempt. It is a simple yardstick of your personal reactions to several situations. Answer the questions with absolute frankness. Do not analyze your instinctive mental reactions as you check off your responses. Then score yourself. You may have a clearer picture of what is emotionally acceptable to you, and what is not.

What is emotionally acceptable to you?

1. *Your employer gives you a choice. You may have 7 percent added to your paycheck, starting at once; after taxes you would get to keep about 4½ percent. Or you may take no wage increase now but have the same sum of money go to a deferred compensation plan; the money in the plan will not be taxed until you retire. Your employer's contribution to your plan are paid into a bank trust account, and only you or your heirs may ever touch it, but not until you retire or die.*

   ☐ *A. You take the salary increase.* ☐ *B. You take the plan.*

2. *A savings and loan institution a block from where you live offers a long-term certificate of deposit account paying 8 percent interest. Another savings and loan, which offers 10.1 percent interest, is 6 miles away and in a rather rough neighborhood. You could set up an account by phone and mail. Both are FDIC insured.*

   ☐ *A. You go for the higher return.* ☐ *B. You deal in your area.*

3. *In today's mail you get the exciting news that your name was*

chosen in a contest you had entered. You are the winner of a two-week all-expense trip for two. You have a choice of a trip to Florida or Arizona, or you may go to London, Paris, and Rome. The domestic trip may be taken in the next 60 days. The European trip will not be available for a full year.

☐ *A. You choose the European holiday.*

☐ *B. You opt for the domestic trip.*

4. *You are about to go on a 2,000-mile journey. You have the literature on two airlines: One is a major scheduled airline offering round-trip coach fare of $280; the other is a $190 round-trip fare on a nonscheduled but federally regulated airline, featuring in their literature their fine safety record and the fact that they employ only experienced, senior pilots.*

   ☐ *A. The non-scheduled reduced fare.* ☐ *B. The major airline.*

5. *Your cousin, whom you don't see very often, asks to borrow $1,500 to handle an unexpected expense. He promises to repay you plus any interest you feel is reasonable. You like your cousin, have had no occasion to measure his trustworthiness before, but have no reason to distrust him. You can spare the money but would feel the loss it it were not repaid.*

   ☐ *A. You make the loan.* ☐ *B. You do not.*

6. *You have been interested in an exceptionally attractive group of homes being built about thirty miles from your present residence. You need the extra living space the new homes represent, but the prices have been too high for your means. Now, because of a rumor that a nuclear power plant may be built within five miles of the new homes, the prices have been drastically reduced and you can afford the purchase.*

   ☐ *A. You buy.* ☐ *B. You hold off.*

7. *You have an interesting job as chief of personnel for your company. You are 52 years old. You are comfortable with your work, your associates, and your salary.*

   The company president calls you in. He tells you that a new department is to be formed, dedicated to the improvement of production by developing new ways to train and to motivate employees. Headquarters for the new department are to be in another building several miles away, and it is to be staffed by all new people. You are offered the opportunity to head the new department with a substantial increase in pay.

   ☐ *A. You accept.* ☐ *B. You refuse.*

Before scoring your answers, how do you rate yourself? Perhaps you know your emotional capacities extremely well.

Some people do, and others do not. By rating yourself first and then comparing your evaluation with what the scoring reveals, you might come away with encouraging support for your self-appraisal. If you find a sharp contrast, it will motivate you to indulge in some deeper self-examination. Your conclusion well may be that you are right and the test is wrong, or just the opposite. In either event you probably will get to know yourself just a little bit better. And that is the purpose of the whole exercise.

To evaluate yourself, first think about your emotional reactions to quick decisions, to taking chances, to the need to wait for rewards, to the desire for winning big, and to similar considerations. Now take a pen and mark that point in the following line where you think you belong.

ULTRA |————————————|————————————| CONFIRMED
CONSERVATIVE SPECULATOR

Are you at one of the extremes? In the middle? Some place between the middle and either extreme?

To score yourself on the seven questions, give yourself the following points for every "A" checked. Score no points for any "B."

1A. 1

2A. 3,

3A. 2,

4A. 3,

5A. 2,

6A. 2,

7A. 3.

Now add up your score:

0–4, ultra to very conservative;

5–7, quite careful;

8–12, can abide a fair amount of risk;

13–16, accepts reasoned risk without fear.

Now you know.

CANDIDATES FOR ACTION

To satisfy my desire for immediately available cash, I am particularly interested in:

- ☐ A special savings account for genuine emergencies, one that I will not touch for anything else under any circumstances.
- ☐ Investment in one or more money-market mutual funds offering the use of free checks and/or same-day transfers of cash to my regular bank checking account by telephone or telegram.
- ☐ The use of one or more savings and loan accounts in ways that permit me to have insurance on as much capital as I put into them regardless of the $40,000 limits.
- ☐ The ease and convenience of a check-a-month type plan in a savings and loan institution.

4

Taking Stock of Securities

Chasin' inflation

To thoroughly appreciate inflation's overwhelming impact on your lifestyle, you must consider it from a variety of viewpoints. Throughout this book it will be brought up a number of times. The inflationary force is such a presence in your life that it cannot be mentioned once or twice and forgotten, due to its relative permanence. The Department of Labor's *Consumer Price Index*, which measures the cost of living, reveals that only twice in the past thirty years have prices declined. The cost of living was reduced by 1.8 percent in 1949 and by 0.5 percent in 1954. Just compare these modest declines with the 13 percent inflation rate we saw as recently as 1979. Compare that rate with the 6-percent figure many consider to be "acceptable." Inflation, despite immense and continuous efforts to hold it down, is a vigorous and persistent guest in your financial household.

If we could depend on the inflation rate settling down to a dependable, consistent 6 percent a year, it might seem, at first glance, that we could all relax. Paying 6 percent more for everything we buy sounds relatively easy to handle, but the great destructive force behind inflation is its compounding power. At 6 percent a year, the cost of living doubles in less than twelve years: An "economical" car will cost $10,000, and you will see steaks on sale for $5 a pound. Beyond any question, it is essential that you put some of your money where it is free to fight inflation, to counteract the decreasing value of the dollar, to at least keep pace with rising living costs and progressive taxation.

The best bet

A common expression at the race tracks is, "Let's see where the smart money goes." As reported by *U.S. News & World Report* in July, 1976, the National Bureau of Economic Research, Federal Reserve Board, U.S. Treasury released these figures to show where millionaires put their money:

Corporate stocks	47.9%
Mortgages, life insurance, and other assets	20.2
Real estate	12.3
Bonds	6.1
Tax exempts	4.9
Cash	4.3
Unincorporated business	4.3
	100.0%

Over the years the "smart money" has gone into common stocks, because they have given the public a highly effective weapon in the battle against inflation. There have been and there will be times when the cost of living goes up while stock values go down. For the long pull, however, the reverse has been true. Not only have stock values outrun living costs, but the dividends collected by investors have increased at a pace that outdistanced inflation by a healthy margin. Common stocks, in the long run, seem to be a reasonably good bet.

How much should you invest?

The question as to how much money should be invested in securities calls for a variety of considerations: your age, your health, whether you have ample income, how long current income will continue, what new income can be counted on to replace any income you expect to lose, your emotional acceptance of risks and rewards, others you are responsible for financially, dependable increases of capital on the horizon, the anticipation of major expenditures, and the anticipation of any major threats to your capital. Looming largest are two elements: timing and your emotions. Timing is critical because younger investors can give their money more growth opportunities than older investors. As to the emotional element, you have seen how any thoughtful planning may be sidetracked and hurt if you ignore your fundamental reactions to risks and rewards. You can build with greater solidity and dependability if you give your emotions proper consideration.

Even if you are an ultra-conservative (a fact you probably knew without taking the test), you need not rule out any and all types of investing. There are securities you can live with comfortably. The rest of this chapter deals with the various types of securities open to you, with a brief description of each. No attempt is made to provide detailed coverage of these securities, since this is not intended to be a technical course on the subject. A wealth of literature is available if you want to study each type of security in depth,particularly Victor L. Harper's *Handbook of Investment Products and Services* (The New York Institute of Finance). The aim of the book now in your hands is quite different. These descriptions offer just enough information about the many different ways to have your money working for you to let you select the ways that are *right for you.* Exhaustive facts would only cloud your perspective and blunt your ability to take the actions that appear to be most logical. Here, then, are your investment choices.

If you invest for long-term growth . . .

Common stocks

Don't select just any common stocks; go with those of companies with solid histories of growth. One characteristic of a *growth stock* is a company that consistently plows a large percentage of its profits into research and development, in order to have a flow of new and improved products coming to the marketplace. An equally acceptable sign is a company that makes a practice of putting big parts of its earnings into new plants and equipment, into expansion via the opening of more branches, into increased budgets for advertising and promotion. These organizations generally demonstrate sales growth that outpaces the economy as a whole. They are strong, well-financed, and competitive. Growth companies usually do not pay good dividends. Some pay none at all. Dividends come from profits, and, if profits are channeled to activities leading to further growth, the investors' rewards come from increasing value.

If you invest for current income . . .

Common stocks

In this instance, look for a solid, long-term history of generous dividends. Logically you would expect that where you find a stock of a big, well-managed company that pays high dividends, the investing public would be attracted to it and the law of supply and demand would force the price of the stock up, thus making it a good growth situation. But logic and the stock market do not always keep steady company. If they did, all intelligent investors would be multi-millionaires. Various influences may keep a good dividend payer from becoming a good growth stock. Not the least of them involves the mechanics of paying a dividend. If a stock customarily offers a good yield and is forced up in price, then the yield gets smaller. A stock, for example, selling at $50 a share and paying an annual dividend of $3.50 has a lot of appeal for the income-minded investor. A 7 percent return is good. If the price of the stock moves up to $70 and the dividend stays at $3.50, the percentage of return falls to 5 percent. That return is not very exciting. The result is that the great numbers of income-seeking investors who had come on board for income take the opportunity to bail out with a handsome profit. They take their increased capital to some other investment paying 7 percent or better. The big sell-off pulls the price of the stock down.

Institutional investors play a large role in this financial

"That one has a pretty border."

mechanism—mutual funds, pension funds, life insurance companies, and the like. If a mutual fund, for example, has an announced goal of high income, it cannot afford to continue buying shares of a stock with a decreasing yield. When the institutional investors move into or out of a stock, the move is likely to be massive and the impact on the stock's price substantial.

Preferred stocks

A preferred stock has a fixed dividend rate, and quite a few preferred stocks pay excellent dividends. In addition, there is a strong safety factor. A corporation's bonds normally have slightly higher yields but preferred stockholders, as the term suggests, get preferential treatment. They get paid before holders of the company's common stock, and, should the company fail, they go to the head of the line when the remaining assets are distributed.

Options

In recent years selling options on stock you own has become a fairly popular means of increasing income. Options on certain stocks are bought and sold on option exchanges, just as stocks are bought and sold on exchanges of their own, such as the Daddy of them all, the New York Stock Exchange. An exchange acts as a clearing house, permitting the smooth exchange of buy and sell orders. For example, if you owned 100 shares of XYZ Corp. and it is listed on one or more of the option exchanges, you can tell your stockbroker that you want to *write an option* on that stock. Writing an option is another way of saying that you are selling an option, and it represents a fairly conservative way to markedly increase your investment income. Your broker handles the details. Writing an option on stock that you own is considered "covered," or a *covered option.* Like most things that sound simple, option buying and selling can get rather involved. What follows is a stripped-down explanation of how a covered option works.

EXAMPLE: You have bought 100 shares of XYZ at $50 a share, and that is the current value. The stock pays a fairly good dividend, but you would like to increase your income. Your broker arranges to sell an option for somebody else, Mr. Speculator, to buy your XYZ shares at $50 per share six months from now. The buyer pays a premium of $6 a share, or a total of $600 for that privilege. (For a six-month option on an active stock the premium is usually about 8 or 10 percent of the stock's price.) Some of that goes to commissions and costs, but, keeping to basics, presume that you get it all.

If the price of XYZ goes to $60 before the time runs out, the option buyer calls on you to complete the deal. You have to sell your stock at $50 a share. If you had not sold the option, you would have had $1,000 real or paper profit. You end up with $400 less, but you aren't hurt.

If, instead of the stock going to $60, it drops to $40, the option is never exercised. The buyer is $600 poorer, and you are $600 richer. If you had reasons to sell your stock at $40, your loss would be $400, rather than $1,000. If you do not sell, you are free to pocket your winnings and sell another option.

Why does the option buyer buy? The chances are he likes XYZ and thinks it has a good chance of going to $60 or better. The buyer has the choice of buying 100 shares at $50—a $5,000 investment—but decides to risk less capital by spending $600 on the option. If he exercised his right to buy the stock from you at $50 when the price goes up to $60, he pays you $5,000 but enjoys a $400 profit on a risk of only $600. If he loses his chance to buy—that is, the stock does not go above $56 a share (to make it worth his while to buy)—he loses his $600.

There are other ways to play this game. You may write and sell an option on stock you don't even own. You would have to be at the high speculation end of the risk-acceptance scale to be interested, for the risks are substantial. The technique is called *naked* option writing, and the following example shows you how risky it can be.

EXAMPLE: You do not own any XYZ stock, but you write an option giving a buyer the right to purchase the stock from you at $50 a share. If the price goes to $60 and the option is exercised, you must take a deep breath, buy 100 shares at $60, and sell it at $50. You thus spend $6,000 and collect $5,600, for a net loss of $400. On the other hand, if the stock goes down to $40, you are simply $600 ahead of the game with no investment whatsoever. The big risk is what you may lose if XYZ goes well above $60 a share. Who knows? It could happen.

Those are the ground rules. Other steps can be taken. If you deal with a broker who knows options thoroughly, he or she can introduce you to more sophisticated areas. Some of them can help to reduce risk to something approaching zero.

Corporate bonds

Long-time favorites of conservative investors seeking income are the bonds of financially strong corporations, many of which pay high rates of interest. A bond is evidence of money borrowed. It is quite unlike common stock, which entitles you to share in any distributed profits of a company. At any given time, the stock is worth whatever someone else is willing to pay you for it. A corporate bond represents money owed to you—a debt of the issuing company. It is frequently backed by specific assets. Although bond prices rise and fall, bonds are not inflation-fighting tools; rather, they offer a reasonably safe way of providing yourself with good income. The various types of corporate bonds are industrial, utility, finance, and railroad. If investments in bonds fit you and your needs, it will pay you to become acquainted with what each type represents and what each offers.

U.S. Treasury bills, notes, bonds, and obligations of government agencies

Treasury bills call for minimums that range from $10,000 to $100,000 or more. The obligations of federal agencies usually have $5,000 and $10,000 minimums. The other types usually have $1,000 minimums. Treasury bills mature within one year, notes and bonds mature in no less than twenty-four years, although some with shorter lives are available. What these different government issues pay varies. Treasury bills, for example, have paid from 4¼ percent to 9 percent in recent years. The others pay less. All government issues are considered to be the safest of investments. Those of some government agencies are somewhat less safe, but are extremely conservative investments.

Certificates of deposit (CDs), commercial paper, and bankers' acceptances

Again, these items are strictly for income. They have no attraction from the growth standpoint. Each calls for minimum investments of $100,000, sometimes more, on a short-term basis. The pay is generous, and they are backed by major banks and well-known corporate borrowers. Certificates of deposits of this type are banking instruments, very different from the well-known certificates of deposit that banks and thrift institutions sell to the public. The yields on these CDs are higher, and so are the minimums required.

With such requirements, they are therefore out of reach for most individual investors. Their appealing yields can be realized, however, through investments in money-market mutual funds, for these are what you will find in their portfolios.

If you want a combination of income and inflation-fighting growth . . .

Convertible preferred stocks and bonds

Yes, there is a way of reaching for the best of two worlds. You do give up some yield, but everything in the world of investments exacts a price.

EXAMPLE: You invest in a convertible bond of the Blue Sky Star Co., which is paying a 6 percent dividend. At the time you make the investment, the common stock of Blue Sky is $20 a share. The convertible feature of your investment is the guarantee that you may exchange your bonds for a certain number of shares of Blue Sky common stock at a specified price per share. At the time you buy your bonds, the chances of deriving any benefit from the exchange are remote, unless you pay a stiff premium for the bonds. At a later date, however, the price of the common may rise to the exchange value and well beyond, making your privilege most interesting.

When that price rise occurs, the price of your bond will also rise, and it could even outpace the market price of the common stock for two reasons:

1. *Very likely, the bond pays a bigger dividend than the common stock.*
2. *The price of the common stock may fall back from its high levels, and, if it does, the bond price probably will not drop as much. The bond pays a better dividend, which dividend is fixed. The common stock's dividend is not, and the stock does have the backing that is part and parcel of a corporate debt instrument.*

Here, then, is one way of investing that offers you good income plus a way of dealing with inflation.

Convertible preferred issues are put together in the same way and offer identical advantages. The difference is that, unlike bonds, the preferred stock is not backed up by certain assets.

If you want to accumulate capital for future use . . .

See the "Mutual Fund" portion of this chapter on page 73.

If you want tax avoidance or deferral . . .

Municipal bonds and tax shelters

The facts about municipal bonds are covered in Chapter 5, and Chapter 9 is devoted entirely to tax shelters.

If you want to speculate . . .

Common stocks

Successful speculation is a fine art. There are a number of ways to search for a common stock that may produce spectacular profits for you. One is to join the professional and nonprofessional investors constantly on the lookout for companies that are likely candidates for being taken over by other companies. The financial news, from time to time, carries stories about some corporation announcing its readiness to pay, just for example, $45 a share for the stock of another company presently listed at $25 a share. That kind of news is exciting and wonderful—if you are one of the lucky ones *already owning* some of those shares. Of course, the rush to buy them, once the news is made public, drives the price up to and sometimes beyond the takeover offer.

Being a takeover candidate places a stock in one kind of *special situation.* But a myriad of special situations, ranging from the hiring of a new chief executive to news about a dramatic discovery or invention, may affect the price of the company's stock. For example, research may uncover the fact that a certain pharmaceutical company is on the threshold of a revolutionary breakthrough—a drug calculated to control the common cold. *If* the news is borne out and *if* the Food and Drug Administration approves the sale of the new drug within a reasonable period of time and *if* the competitors are unable to duplicate the discovery, the chances are that the stock of the pharmaceutical firm will, in time, reflect the great profits to be realized—and you have a big winner.

And so it goes.

The astronomical profits people tell stories about most often are made through stock ownership in small, unknown, underfinanced companies with new products that just catch on and, with dizzying speed, become household names. Xerox and Polaroid are two of the Cinderellas that were able to wear the fabled glass slipper. The problem, of course, is that investments in such issues have a splendid chance of being wiped out 100 percent. Speculations of that type should be considered only if you have surplus capital you are willing to lose and can afford to lose without being hurt.

Options

You just read about them.

Commodity futures

Commodity futures contracts may be bought in eggs, sugar, wheat, soybeans, cattle, pork bellies, coffee, orange juice, silver, gold, platinum, wood, and foreign currencies . . . just to name a few. Trading in commodities, you agree to buy a specified quantity of an agricultural product, metal, or currency for delivery at a certain future time at a fixed price. If the price rises before delivery, you sell your contract (not the commodity) at a profit. If the price drops, you have a loss. Prices change to a far greater degree than those of common stocks. This is a very fast moving field.

In fact, speculative risks in commodity futures are so high that there is general agreement that the public loses seven times out of ten. Professionals do a little better. The speculative nature of commodities trading is enhanced by its margin requirements. When you buy a future contract on margin, you put up only 5 to 10 percent of the total involved, whereas the lowest margin allowed when you buy stocks is 50 percent. As a result of the low margin requirement, you make big profits or suffer big losses.

EXAMPLE: You buy a $50,000 futures contract in orange juice, putting up 10 percent ($5,000). Before the expiration of the contract (the delivery date), the price has driven the value of your contract up to $60,000, a 20 percent increase, and you sell. You have done a lot better than make 20 percent on your money. You ***doubled*** *your $5,000. On the other hand, if the value went down only 10 percent, your margin would be gone. You either put up more money or take a $5,000 loss.*

Various commodity exchanges handle the buy and sell orders for commodity futures. Because this area of speculation is so highly charged, sensitive, and involved, most investors put their trading in the hands of specialists. Various investment firms offer several types of accounts, including either discretionary accounts where all decisions are made for you or accounts where you are advised as to what steps to take but the decisions are up to you. Due to the intensive activity surrounding commodity futures, commissions and management fees are relatively high. Funds are also available. Somewhat like mutual funds, these commodity futures funds differ in that they are not as fully liquid. You may take your money out at the end of a month or a quarter but not at your whim, as is true of the more conventional mutual funds. The fund account is the safest for two reasons: First, investors are not subject to margin calls; second, instead of relying on one contract, your investment is spread over various contracts.

A number of areas of fraud have been connected with commodity futures, to the extent that the Commodity Futures Trading Commission (CFTC) has established a "hot line." If you are about to engage in speculations of this nature, you can phone 800-424-9838 to find out if the firm you are planning to deal with has been guilty of violations or if complaints have been lodged against it.

Gold

Throughout most of history gold has been the traditional anchor for people who want their assets in tangible form. For at least three hundred years, given enough time, the price of gold has risen in buying power wherever and whenever inflation increased the cost of living.

From the time when the United States went off the gold standard until January 1, 1975, it was illegal for U.S. citizens to hold or to sell gold. From 1934 until 1971 the U.S. froze the official value of gold at $35 a *troy ounce,* which is the universally accepted weight measurement for gold. The freezing of the price was wholly artificial, and when it was finally allowed to seek its own level, it quickly responded to international inflation pressures and a general uneasiness about unsupported paper currencies. Gold moved from $35 an ounce in 1975 to over $400 an ounce just four years later. Ardent believers in gold as the only safe asset you can own—commonly dubbed the "gold bugs"—contend that the price will go to $700 and better. And there are those who disagree.

One of the leading arguments against putting everything into gold is that owning gold produces no income whatsoever. In fact, since it has an obvious value in itself, as opposed to certificates attesting to your ownership of this, that, or the other thing, gold creates the expense of protecting it from theft. You must insure it or pay for it to be stored—or do both. You must also question how genuine it is, how pure. Answering this question incurs the expense of having it assayed by experts.

Of course, the objections may be overcome to a degree. There are at least six ways to invest in gold:

1. *You can buy* gold deposit certificates. *You put up a minimum amount of money ($2,500 or more is normal), and you are given a certificate as evidence of the fact that a certain amount of gold bullion is being held on deposit in your name. ("Bullion" is a term used to refer to a mass of metal, the value of which is that of the metal itself, unrelated to whatever form it happens to be in.) The actual gold may be in vaults in Switzerland, somewhere in the United States, or elsewhere. You will be told where. You have to pay purchase commission, which is deducted from your investment, and you also pay an annual fee for storage and insurance. Presumably, you would deal only with a well-established company that you can trust. The trust element affects not only your assurance as to the quality of the gold but also your certainty that it is, in fact, stored safely in the amount represented. Your investment is based on your belief that gold will grow in value and that the dollar will fall in value.*
2. *You can buy* gold coins, *such as the South African Krugerrand, the Austrian 100 Crown, or the Mexican 50 Peso. These coins, being minted today, have a known gold content. Investors buy them strictly for their gold content and not for any other value. They are readily available from a variety of sources. Coin dealers, for example, sell them for approximately 5 percent above the actual value of the gold content at the time of purchase. Krugerrands are particularly popular, readily recognized, and seldom counterfeited. They are easy to store and easy to sell. But they too pay no income and require the expense of safekeeping.*

3. Gold bars *can be bought through a dealer whose reputation you know. However, you must be ready to accept the costs and be certain that the dealer will buy them back from you, if and when you want to unload. Selling gold bars on your own would not be easy.*
4. Old gold coins and jewelry *are regarded by a number of dealers as investments. In these areas you have to be particularly careful. One reason for caution is that only experts are capable of evaluating the worth of rare gold coins or fine gold jewelry. The numismatic value of rare coins can be far greater than the value of the gold content. This is even more true of jewelry, whose gold content is of a nature different from bullion or coins. The pure gold in gold bars and bullion is 24 carat, which is too soft for most jewelry; the great bulk of gold jewelry is 14 or 18 carat. Another reason to be careful is that in addition to the lack of income and the safekeeping problems, you must know where you will find your market in the future. The dealer earns a living by buying low and selling high. You must therefore see the value of your purchases increase in market value enough to counterbalance that difference.*
5. Gold futures *involve the same forces as those at work in other commodity speculations. Since buying a futures contract in gold is not done with any thought of ever taking delivery, you are at least relieved of the cost of assaying, storage, and insurance.*
6. Gold mining stocks. *If you are convinced that gold is the inflation hedge you want, this constitutes the one way of investing in it that gives you income and that avoids the costs of storage, protection, and appraisal. You can buy the stocks of gold mining companies that operate in the United States, in Canada, and in South Africa. The yields are appealing. The South African mining stocks, which represent the biggest sources of gold, have paid 15 percent and better. There are dangers, however, whenever your money is invested in a company in a foreign land. You have no way of knowing what might happen, should there be any serious political upheavals.*

Silver

Silver investments present pretty much the same plus and minus aspects you find in gold. The value of silver is inclined to follow that of gold, although there are times when it moves in its own directions because silver is considerably influenced by the law of supply and demand. Silver is used for countless industrial purposes. Every roll of photographic film, for example, uses silver for nothing equals silver's reflective quality. The demand is consistently heavy and the supply relatively limited. On the other side of the coin (a silver coin, of course), silver is remelted and reused to a great extent.

Diamonds

Promoted aggressively, diamonds comprise a reasonable inflation-fighting investment. Propelled by inflation and by the widespread effort to find places to put money where it may maintain buying power, thousands have put their faith in the history of the increasing value of these sparkling stones. A significant part of this interest is generated by those who are extremely busy promoting diamonds as investments. In the early seventies a single U.S. firm offered diamonds for investment purposes. By the end of the decade, more than a hundred were in the business. Primarily they use the mails, the telephone, and display ads.

Indeed, some good things may be said for diamonds as an investment. Since the flow of diamonds to the market is controlled, so too is their price. The control is primarily in the hands of DeBeers Consolidated Mines, Ltd., a London based, publicly traded company. DeBeers, its affiliated companies, and other major factors in the diamond world have successfully managed supply and demand. As a result, the value of diamonds has gone up with little deviation. Another favorable characteristic about diamonds is that they are indestructible: They may be stolen, but they cannot be destroyed. Besides, they make nice jewelry!

Once more, however, if an investment in diamonds appeals to you, you should be aware of the negatives: no income, along with the costs of appraisal, storage, and insurance. Add the possibility of being defrauded; dealing in diamonds demands great expertise. Just one example: It might seem evident that the best assurance of increasing value is derived by buying only "flawless" stones. Authorities on diamonds tell us, however, that it is extremely difficult for experts to be able to certify a stone as absolutely flawless and that the discovery of even a tiny flaw decreases your value by a considerable percentage. Surprisingly, diamonds graded as having slight or very slight flaws generally appreciate in value a good deal more than flawless gems.

Perhaps the biggest concern for potential investors is the question of liquidating their investment. The chief executive of a large, reputable retail jewelry concern expressed such doubts about diamonds for investment purposes. "The only way I would buy diamonds from the public would be if I could buy for a lot less than I can from my normal resources. I have recourse when I buy through normal channels. I lack that when I buy from the public and that important safeguard must be compensated for by an appreciably lower price." He also pointed out that most reputable jewelers are members of the American Gem Society. The Society, in its Code of Ethics, discourages members from telling their customers that one reason for buying diamond jewelry is that it is a good investment. He observed, "I know of very few jewelers who speculate in diamonds."

Stamps, antiques, and works of art

These items all make their claims as suitable objects for investment because of their increasing values. Undeniably such claims have substance, but all the warnings pertaining to precious metals and diamonds hold true with equal force.

If you want to invest but are concerned over your lack of knowledge and experience . . .

Mutual funds

Mutual funds constitute a *method* of investing. This method is capable of serving the needs and wants of those who do wish to invest but who do not have the training, the skills, or the time to do so in a sound, businesslike manner. Hundreds of mutual funds reflect such broad investment aims and policies that you should have no problem finding one or more to match you, your emotional acceptances, your desires. These are the types of funds you may choose from:

- *common stock funds dedicated to long-term growth in a very conservative manner,*
- *common stock funds with a more aggressive approach to long-term growth, open to more profit and exposed to more risk,*
- *common stock funds that are relatively speculative and that are for those willing to accept high risk in the hope of high profits,*
- *common stock funds seeking a combination of growth and income,*
- *common stock funds with income as the chief objective,*
- *bond funds for income,*
- *combinations of common stocks and bonds—balanced funds—offering growth and income in a highly conservative manner,*
- *special situation funds for growth,*
- *common stock funds concentrating on one industry,*
- *common stock funds investing only in securities of nations other than the United States,*
- *option funds,*
- *government securities funds,*
- *money market funds,*
- *tax-free municipal bond funds,*
- *tax-deferred funds.*

Each fund is managed by a group of investment professionals who have extensive sources of information available to them. Their information is drawn from a number of various sources: in-depth examinations of the industries and of individual companies whose securities are of interest; research into the domestic and worldwide economy; constant surveillance of what is happening in the various securities markets; and alertness to all types of legislation, government agency actions, court decisions and allied matters that are or may have impact on securities values. Any fund you invest in has established an investment in anywhere from twenty to more than one hundred different securities. This portfolio of securities is supervised constantly, and possible candidates for future investment are evaluated. The fund's managers buy and sell securities if and when they consider doing so beneficial, and in response to the flow of money in or out of the fund as people invest or liquidate their shares.

Mutual funds are also known as *open-end investment companies.* The term "open-end" stems from the fact that the public may invest in a fund at any time, and, when they do, new shares are created. On the other end, investors may withdraw from the fund whenever they please, for the fund will redeem their shares on demand. You, as a shareholder, become part owner of everything in the fund's portfolio. You and the other shareholders receive all dividends, interest payments, and profits realized from the sale of some of the fund's investments. The fund's fees and expenses are deducted from dividends before distributions are made.

You should be aware of the difference between "load" and "no-load" funds. Traditionally, mutual funds are sold through investment dealer firms, and those sales include a sales charge. The charge (or *load,* as it is sometimes called) enables the firm and its account executives to spend time with investors giving guidance, counsel, and continuing service. In recent years an increasing number of funds have sold directly to the public by advertising in various publications and through the mails. Shares of these funds are sold without sales charge, for there are no salesmen involved; hence they are called *no-load funds.* As is true of so many things in life, you get what you pay for. If you need the help of a knowledgeable securities expert when selecting the appropriate fund, when deciding on which way to invest, or when choosing which of a fund's features and services to adopt, funds with sales charges make sense. The sales charge is a one-time fee, usually ranging from about 4 to 8½ percent of the sum you invest, which is a reasonable amount to pay for the time and continuing attention of a good financial planner or broker. If you feel that you are capable of assembling the prospectuses of various *no-load* mutual funds, digesting their printed materials, and making your own decisions, then you might as well save the sales charge. There is no basis for feeling that one type of fund is superior to the other type of fund because of the method of distribution.

Just as there are many different kinds of mutual funds, there are also many ways of investing in them.

Lump sum. This investment approach is just what it sounds like. If you have a sum of money not doing what it might for you, you make a single investment in a fund. The 8½ percent sales charge (incidentally the maximum charge) may be reduced for lump-sum investments, depending on how big the "lump" is. Funds offer reductions on a sliding scale, going as far down as 1 percent for investments of a million dollars or more.

Handling of dividend and capital gains distributions. When you make lump-sum investments, you make out instructions as to how you want your distributions treated. You may ask to have everything paid to you by check as soon as distributions are made. Or you may have dividends reinvested for you and capital gains paid in cash, or vice-versa. You may change your instructions whenever you please.

Systematic accumulation plans. These plans are also almost self-explanatory. If you are interested in accumulating capital, the funds provide a practical mechanism you can use. You open an account with the mutual fund's minimum initial investment (anything from zero to $5,000), and then you program yourself to make systematic investments of a fixed number of dollars (anything from $25 to $100), monthly, every other month, or on whatever schedule you prefer. The fund uses all distributions you earn, such as dividends, interest, or capital gains, to buy additional shares for you, even fractions of shares so that every penny is at work. The additions to your account from distributions are usually handled without sales charges or transaction fees.

Contractual plans. These systematic plans with a twist are for you, if you have a difficult time being religious about any systematic investment or savings plan. When you adopt a contractual plan, you have to decide to pursue it for a specific period of time, say ten or fifteen years. In the first year you prepay a big part of the sales charge for the full period. Perhaps only half of your first year's investments get invested; the balance is all sales charge. In the years that follow, the sales charge is therefore very low. In effect, you now have something to lose if you quit, which is not true in the voluntary systematic plan. The "something lost-if-you quit" element is why people rarely quit making mortgage payments, car payments, or life insurance payments. If you need that type of discipline, the contractual plan makes sense.

BUY MORE—PAY LESS

The *voluntary systematic plan* or the *contractual plan* brings into play a time-honored investment technique called *dollar-cost-averaging.* It works like magic. It does not matter what you are buying: eggs, gasoline, or shares of General Motors. If the price constantly changes and if you are buying at regular intervals, you can apply this technique and come out ahead.

You and Cousin Louie agree that the Dandy Dollar Fund is a good one for regular monthly investments. You tell Louie that you plan to invest $75 each month. Louie, however, prefers to buy 10 shares each month. Dandy Dollar Fund, during the first year of your separate investments, bounces up and down in value to quite an extent. Here is what would have resulted.

	Price Per Share	*Number of shares you would buy for your $75 a month*	*Cost of Louie's 10 shares each month*
January	$ 8	9.38	$ 80
February	9	8.33	90
March	12	6.25	120
April	11	6.82	110
May	8	9.38	80
June	7	10.71	70
July	7	10.71	70
August	6	12.50	60
September	4	18.75	40
October	5	15.00	50
November	6	12.50	60
December	7	10.71	70

Result: You spent $900.
You own 131.04 shares.
Average price 7.50
Average cost 6.87

Louie spent $900.
Louie owns 120 shares.
Average price 7.50
Average *cost* 7.50

If you enjoy working with figures, try this out with any price variations you want. Start high and end low, or start low and end high—it does not matter. Buying *anything* with changing prices by using an *unchanging number of dollars* always gives you more of what you are buying. And your cost will always be lower than the average price.

Magic? Not really. The answer lies in the fact that the use of this technique automatically slams the brakes on your buying when prices are high—and automatically steps on the gas when prices are low. It takes advantage of price changes in both directions.

Contractual plans have other good points. With a definite term of years involved, you may use low-cost group term life insurance to assure the completion of your plan no matter what happens to you. This point is particularly appealing if, for example, you enter the plan in order to pile up the cash to pay for the college educations of your children. Contractual plans also provide the means of taking out some of your money, if a sudden need arises, and of replacing it later without charge. You can draw up to 90 percent of the assets in your account in that way. In this respect, the term "contractual" is deceptive. You are not tied to a contract. You may drop the plan and take out all your money at any time. The fund, however, must live up to its obligations throughout the full term if you do not drop out.

Letter of intent. Almost all mutual funds that apply a sales charge offer this means of reducing the charge.

EXAMPLE: You have $5,000 to invest in Common Growth Fund, and the prospectus shows that there is a reduction in the sales charge if your investment is as much as $10,000. You know that before a year goes by, you will have $10,000 or more to put into Common Growth. You therefore make the $5,000 investment now and sign a letter of intent, which reflects your intention to invest a total of $10,000 or better within thirteen months. You are then privileged to make your $5,000 investment at the $10,000 sales charge. If, for any reason, you eventually find that you cannot or do not want to put the balance of the money in, you are simply charged for the difference.

Rights of accumulation. Not all funds offer this other approach to reduce sales charges, but a number do. You invest in the fund, and, either on a regular or on a time-to-time basis, you add to your investment. When your total investment reaches an amount, such as $10,000, where there is a sales charge reduction, you automatically become eligible for the lower sales charge on all *future* investments. And so it goes . . . As you attain each plateau accompanied by an additional sales charge reduction, you are entitled to the advantage.

Exchange privilege. You may decide to invest in a mutual fund sponsored by an organization with a number of different mutual funds under its management. If so, you have the right, which you may exercise whenever you please, to order that the shares of your fund be exchanged for shares of equal value of another fund under the same management. You thereby avoid a second sales charge. This feature can be quite advantageous. If, for example, you have shares in a growth fund and are about to retire, you may transfer to a fund stressing generous income. Keep in mind, however, that the IRS considers such exchanges to constitute a sale and new purchase. If you had a profit in the growth fund, it should be reported when you file your tax return.

Withdrawal plans. This service, described in detail in the following chapter, can provide you with a flow of income checks *in whatever amounts you name.*

CANDIDATES FOR ACTION

My main objective when investing in securities is:

- ☐ long-term growth of capital
- ☐ current income
- ☐ accumulation of capital for future use
- ☐ combination of growth and current income
- ☐ tax reduction or avoidance
- ☐ speculation

I am particularly interested in:

- ☐ common stocks
- ☐ preferred stocks
- ☐ convertible securities
- ☐ options
- ☐ commodity futures
- ☐ gold deposit certificates
- ☐ gold bars
- ☐ gold coins
- ☐ old gold coins and/or jewelry
- ☐ gold mining stocks
- ☐ silver
- ☐ diamonds
- ☐ stamps, antiques, works of art

☐ I am interested in mutual funds in line with my objectives

- ☐ lump sum
- ☐ voluntary accumulation plan
- ☐ contractual accumulation plan
- ☐ through investment dealer
- ☐ no-load

5

Beautiful Income

Nearsighted investing

One of the questions asked in a survey of investors conducted by the New York Stock Exchange was why they were investing. Better than 85 percent of those who replied said that they had long-term objectives. Parents of youngsters wanted to be prepared to meet college costs one day. People in their early or middle years wanted to develop a source of supplementary income for the retirement years. Young couples looked forward to the day when they could buy or build a home. These were typical reasons.

All but 15 percent of the people holding securities were long-term investors. Now pick up today's *Wall Street Journal*, the financial section of your local newspaper, or any newspaper or magazine dealing with investment and finance. Look for articles that might have real impact on long-term investment considerations. On a typical day you will look in vain. If you should find one, it would be unusual.

The things you do see in the financial pages are current stories about local, national and international happenings that can have or already have had instant impact on the market . . . laws and wars, things occurring in banking and in politics. You see a variety of statistical yardsticks the nation uses to measure the ups and downs of employment, industrial growth, housing starts, automobile sales, interest rates, consumer debt, and more. Business news embraces quarterly profits and losses, proxy fights, tender offers, new issues, civil suits, antitrust cases, strikes, strike settlements, threats of new strikes, what the market did today, and what the pundits think it will do tomorrow. It's all short-term news, every bit of it.

Short-term news is what you see and hear. And 85 percent of the people who are investing for the long term are making investment decisions based on just about the only financial news they are exposed to. Decisions concerning long-term objectives are based on short-term news. Sometimes you may hear neighbors or friends saying that they are staying out of the market because the Dow Jones or the Standard & Poor's stock averages are low and they have no confidence in the market. This is the equivalent of saying, "The grocery store is having a sale today. Prices have been slashed and are lower than they have been for a long time. I won't buy. Those low prices destroy my confidence." The constant dominance of short-term financial news causes people with long-term financial needs to lose perspective. The end result is that they exercise incredibly bad judgment. Even investment dealers, poisoned by the same exposure to incessant short-term financial news, aid and abet these mistaken actions. They see and hear the same words and music. They sing in harmony with their misguided customers.

The father of a 3-year-old picks up his paper and reads that the stock market lost ground that day. Then he checks a mutual fund he invested in to help pay the costs of his son's college education some day. The value of his shares, reflecting the general market, are down. He decides that the investment was a mistake; he is going to bail out and put the money where it is guaranteed and can earn generous interest. That may, or may not, be a good decision. Later, when you read about short-term trusts and gifts, you may see a way of acting on such a decision in a dollar-wise, tax-wise manner. But simply taking the money out of the mutual fund and putting it into a certificate of deposit is not likely to work out the way you want. You will have taxes to pay on the income, and you will have to worry about the probable cost of that desired college education fourteen or fifteen years from now. The father's decision to change his method of creating an educational fund is based on just one thing: the status of the stock market at one isolated period out of a fifteen-year span.

Were you the parent in this situation, the logical thing to do, when disturbed by some current news, would be to review the entire picture. Originally you started the investment program on the basis of several convictions. To start with, you decided that—no two ways about it—your son was going to have the lifelong advantages of a college education. Next, you looked at present college costs and realized that, high as they are, they are likely to seem like "good-old-days" bargains by the time you will be called on to pay the bills. With that in mind, you then determined that if the costs were going to grow over the next fifteen years, it made good sense to put your set-aside dollars someplace where they, too, might grow. You probably looked at a number of different mutual funds featuring long-term growth as their goals. You settled on one with a good, long-term record. You knew, when you adopted that method and that specific means of investing, that stock values do not stand still. They rise, and they fall. You also knew that you had the unmatched advantage of time on your side—fifteen long years. You knew, or you may have been shown at that time that, for as long as records have been kept, each drop in stock market values has, in time, been followed by an historic, new high.

Recalling those decisions, convictions and knowledge, you finally would ask yourself if it was realistic to discard them because, during a brief portion of the fifteen-year program your mutual fund investment results have been negative? On mature consideration, the chances are that you would not make the error of running for cover and abandoning your long-term plan on the basis of a short-term situation.

Nothing is wrong with putting money where it earns current income *provided* that the reasons are right—*provided* that, if you have a long-term objective, a departure from an investment with a growth potential has been taken with knowledge. Those who know the rules of any contest may, occasionally, temporarily bend them with good effect.

Investing for income

Many people want and should be concentrating on current income. Primarily, these are people in retirement, widows, trustees responsible for investments supporting minor

Many people want current income.

children, students, and handicapped individuals. There are, of course, others, but those named make up the great bulk of the 15 percent who invest for the purpose of meeting living costs now.

The rich feel of money

In addition, quite a few people simply enjoy getting checks and invest for current income, even though their own earned income or that of their spouses is more than adequate and their tax brackets cry out against the quest for extra income now. As is true of so many other aspects of dealing with financial matters, this is a highly emotional area. Logic does not always prevail.

There are, of course, various ways of investing for current income. You have seen detail on some of them in the earlier chapters on savings and investments. The investment chapter called your attention to a number of different investment approaches: common stocks, preferred stocks, corporate bonds, U.S. government securities, money-market instruments, options, convertible stocks and bonds, and annuities. They are all sources of current income. Most of them offer more than income alone. Stocks, whether invested in outright or through convertibles and mutual funds, represent income *and* growth possibilities. Annuities can provide lifetime income, and variable annuities give you a chance to have income that can combat rising living costs.

You, and the people you may consult with, must make the decisions as to which means of providing yourself with current income makes sense for you. Your tax bracket, your age, your personal viewpoint, and your emotional makeup all enter into the decision-making process. No package on anyone's shelf, labeled "Current Income," can be picked up and carried home with satisfaction guaranteed. Putting your money to work is a highly individual, thoughtful process.

Investing in tax-free municipal bonds

The availability of income that need not be reported to IRS has been a fact of life since 1871. In that year the Supreme Court handed down a decision stating that the states cannot tax federal securities and that the federal government cannot tax state securities. Over the years there have been several efforts to induce the Supreme Court to reverse itself, but none succeeded. Because of that decision and a corresponding tax law adopted in 1913, states and municipalities can and do issue bonds that are exempt from federal taxation. Usually they are also exempt from taxation within the state issuing them. If you live in Pennsylvania and buy a municipal bond issued within the state, you pay no taxes to the IRS or to Pennsylvania. Buy one in Maryland, however, and you probably will have to include the income when you file your Pennsylvania income tax report.

Only in recent years have tax-free offerings been of interest to most people. Because of their tax-free status and because municipal bonds are traditionally regarded as having the highest degree of safety next to U.S. government bonds, the yield was quite modest until the mid-sixties. Despite the poor return, the combination of low risk and no tax appealed to banks, trust companies, and insurance companies. They, by law, are required to confine themselves to the most cautious types of investments. The only individual investors attracted by the tax-free lure were those in the uppermost tax brackets. But times have changed: inflation and taxes again.

In the early part of the 1960s the average yield of municipal bonds hovered around 3 percent—not very exciting. At this writing even the most highly rated bonds offer investors yields in the area of 7 to 8 percent. And if you want to drop to those rated less than A, AA or AAA, still higher are available.

How well they may fit you and your needs depends on two basic considerations. Your top tax bracket is the chief element, and your financial goals come a close second. Since this chapter is devoted to the pursuit of *current income,* the goal factor has been resolved. To see the extent to which a tax-free municipal bond investment may help you to increase

Table 1
Amount of taxable income needed to equal 7% tax-free

If you file a joint return: and your taxable income is—	your top tax is—	To equal the *tax-free* 7% yield, you need a *taxable* return of—
$20,000–$24,600	28%	9.72%
24,600–29,900	32	10.59
29,900–35,200	37	11.11
35,200–45,800	43	12.28
45,800–60,000	49	13.73
60,000–85,600	54	15.22
85,600–109,400	59	17.07

your current income, Table 1 tells the story. For the table, a 7 percent tax-free yield has been used. If you make an investment in tax-free issues and your yield is higher, you are that much better off. Incomes and the sliding scale of taxes, of course, go higher. The maximum tax is 70 percent. The taxable yield needed to match a 7 percent tax-free return, in that case, would be 23.33 percent. If you file as an unmarried individual, the tax rates for the same incomes are higher, and *taxable* returns would also have to be higher to equal tax-free income.

The selection problems

If you decide that some part of your capital should be earning tax-free income, the next question is how to select the issues to buy. More problems.

Maturity. Before investing in any municipal issues, decide how long you want your money to be invested. The duration of the investment is important. Municipal bonds amount to promissory notes. You lend money to a municipality, and they promise to refund your money on a specific date and will, until that time, pay you a fixed rate of interest. The redemption date is called the bond's *maturity.* Maturities run from five to thirty years, and some run longer. As a rule, longer maturities are associated with higher yields. On the other hand, since economic conditions are always changing, there is the possibility that new issues coming on the market may offer even more generous yields and that would drive the *value* of long-term bonds down. Short-term issues, therefore, although paying less, have less fluctuation. Hold any of them—long- or short-term—to the end of the line, which is the maturity date, and you get back 100 cents on the dollar.

Quality. Quality is safety. While it is true that municipal bond investments are regarded as second only to U. S. government securities for safety, there are degrees of safety: the more safety you have, the softer the pillow. Standard & Poor's and

Moody's, two highly respected and well-known organizations, rate municipal bonds. Bonds rated A and better are considered to be extremely conservative. There are different types of municipal bonds as well. Most are *general obligation bonds,* backed by the full faith, credit and taxing power of the issuer. *Revenue bonds,* in contrast, derive their ability to pay from revenues earned from toll roads, bridges and like sources. Some revenue bonds are general obligations if secured by a pledge of the issuer's full faith, credit and taxing power.

Diversity. The matter of selection, therefore, seems to be fairly easy, but there are a few exceptions. The first is that there are unbelievable quantities of tax-free issues to choose from. About 33,000 common stocks are traded on the various exchanges and the over-the-counter (OTC) market, but there are more than 150,000 municipal bonds from which you may make your selections! A second exception is another safety consideration. One of the best accepted methods of smart investing is to avoid putting all your eggs into one basket. Professionals agree that it is wise to spread a municipal bond investment over at least twenty different issues. But, on the average, municipal bonds sell for $5,000 each.

Trusts and funds

There are ways of dealing with the selection problem and sidestepping the danger of putting all your eggs into a single basket. Instead of buying individual issues, you may buy shares in a tax-free municipal bond unit investment trust or in a tax-free municipal bond mutual fund.

Unit investment trusts. The trust provides unchanging tax-free income. A professional organization invests in a list of different municipal issues, divides the total value into small units ($100 per unit, for example), and the units are sold to the public. You are required to buy a minumum number of units, such as 50, or $5,000 worth. All the tax-free income earned by the issues represented by your units goes to you. In most cases there is a sales charge of about 4½ percent (the commission paid to the brokerage firm you buy from), but there is no fee for managing the trust. That is because no buying and selling takes place once the original group of issues has been bought.

The sponsoring company's charges for administration, which are usually quite modest, are taken from the income. If the units are offered at a 7 percent yield, you get the 7 percent *after* the deduction of the costs. You are free to cash in whenever you please. If you hold the investment, eventually the issues held by the trust mature. As each one does, the trust receives the full face value and forwards your portion of it to you. The maturity dates in a tax-free unit investment trust frequently are carefully checked to see if they harmonize with an investor's needs.

EXAMPLE: Dr. Joe has decided to join some fellow physicians in the erection of a medical building. For various reasons the project will not start for five years. Dr. Joe finds a tax-free unit investment trust with short-term issues, most of them maturing in five to six years. This gives him a way of earning tax-free income until the time his capital is needed and the secure knowledge that during the period of need, he will get back every penny he invested. He can be unconcerned about any fluctuation in the market values of his units. He won't be selling them, and various municipalities will be redeeming their bonds.

Municipal bond mutual funds. The fund is different in several respects from the trust. It is just like other types of mutual funds in that new shares are created as the public invests, the new money is used to make additional investments for the fund, and shareholders may have their shares redeemed on request. One of the most important differences between the fund and the trust is that the fund is actively managed. This is not an unchanging group of investments with an unchanging yield. The managers buy and sell municipal bond issues whenever they think it advisable to do so, or whenever they have to do so to meet the demands of redeeming shareholders, or when large sums of money come to hand because of new investments. Their aim is to try to increase the yield. Most of the municipal bond funds have no sales charge, but they do have management fees. Due to the constant activity of investors coming in and out, the administrative costs are relatively high. Since the fees and expenses are deducted from income before payments are made to investors, the income tends to be lower than that provided by the trusts.

Automatic reinvestment. The funds have one important advantage if you desire future, but not current income. The fund arranges to take your income distributions, as they become payable to you, and use them to buy additional shares—even fractions of shares in order to use every penny, thus compounding your share ownership. This is done without charge. One combination used by some is to invest in the unit investment trust and arrange to have its income distributions flow into a fund in an effort to get the best of two worlds.

The one other significant difference between the two is that the unit investment trust, once organized, offers the public a fixed number of units. When all the units have been sold, which seldom takes more than a few weeks, no more are available. After that, units are bought and sold in what is referred to as a *secondary market,* just like common stocks. But since the sponsor of the trust makes its specific inventory of units available just once, you cannot use a unit investment trust for a systematic accumulation program. The municipal bond funds, because their shares are offered on a continuing basis, make systematic investing possible. Despite the absence of a continuous offering of trust units, you can always invest in this way. Not only is there the secondary market, but, when the units of a trust are gone, another comes on the market.

Risk. There is some risk of loss in municipal bond investments, as dramatized by the financial problems of New York City and Cleveland. There can be no certainty that other major cities and some states will not find themselves in similar trouble from time to time. Problems of that kind have a tendency to erupt with surprising speed, and holders of bonds backed by the financial strength of the affected municipalities may find that the income they counted on is not forthcoming.

One strong answer to this negative aspect of investing in municipal bonds involves the three extremely important pluses the trusts and funds give you. One is diversification. The second is continuing management, alert to changing conditions and poised to make changes in the portfolio. Even the unmanaged unit investment trusts carefully watch the bonds they hold. If they see signs of impending trouble, they act and do so quickly. The third advantage is that you have the privilege of liquidating your shares whenever it seems wise to do so. An additional answer to the risk factor is the presence of insured municipal bond trusts. An insurance company guarantees the investment against loss.

Do tax-free bonds fit your needs?

By all means tax-free municipal bonds or municipal bond funds, should be given serious consideration. But the tax advantage and all the safety factors provide no protection against the loss of purchasing power when the inflation rate exceeds these tax-free yields. They are ideal in many situations, but unless you have abundant reason to shrug off the impact of inflation municipal bonds should represent only a portion of your holdings. How great that portion should be is a matter calling for your study and guidance.

Which unit investment trust or municipal bond fund should you select? The answer boils down to the yields offered relative to the quality, the ratings of the bonds in the portfolio, the maturity consideration, and the history and reputation of the sponsor.

So much for taxes—what about inflation?

You, as is true of a good many people, may have reason to want generous current income with built-in inflation-fighting capabilities. One dynamic solution is to invest your money where it is capable of growing, producing profits, and skimming some of those profits off the top. A well-lubricated mechanism for this exists in the *mutual fund withdrawal plan.* Here is a fictional case history to demonstrate how it works. For the sake of simplicity, no taxes are given consideration.

EXAMPLE: Mr. Former is 76, and Mrs. Former is two years younger. He retired seven years ago.

Mr. Former's peak earnings just before retirement were $30,000 a year, $2,500 a month. The Formers have just sold the home they lived in for many years. Even though it was fully paid for, the costs of repairs and a recent big jump in real estate taxes dictated the decision to sell. (In the chapter on gifts, you will see a fascinating *action the Formers might have taken instead of selling their home.) After the deduction of real estate commission they netted $90,000. What to do with that money? If they put it to work at 6 percent, along with the $44,000 they have in a savings and loan, here is what they will have:*

Social Security	$ 4,668.
Pension	7,200.
$44,000 savings @ 6 %	2,640.
$90,000 @ 6%	5,400.
Stock dividends	450.
Monthly income	$20,358.

At the time he retired, Former had been earning $2,500 a month. Now he has about $800 less. He has rent to pay, and if his monthly income prior to retirement were to be adjusted for today's actual purchasing power, it would amount to $3,750. Their living expenses have been reduced since he stopped working, but the gap between their previous and present buying power demands a severe curtailment of their lifestyle, and each succeeding year is going to mean still greater sacrifices.

They see the urgency of finding some way to increase income as much as possible, preferably in a way that includes some chance of helping them to keep in step with inflated living costs. They recognize the fact that they cannot afford to start using up their capital, for once it starts shrinking so does their income. It would become a vicious downhill cycle.

They discuss their problem with a financial planner. At his suggestion they look into what a mutual fund withdrawal plan *might do for them. They learn that almost all mutual funds offer a service that permits people investing enough money ($5,000 to $10,000 are the usual minimum investments required to open a withdrawal plan) to state the sizes of the checks they want to receive each month. The withdrawals are unrelated to the fund's performance. If you want x number of dollars, that's what you ask for. If you want more later on, you issue new instructions; or you may decide to take less for a while. You will see the things you must weigh before you decide how much to request.*

The Formers' financial planner calls their attention to the fact that the company stock they had acquired through Mr. Former's years of employment is not helping them at all. With a present value of $30,000, its dividends amount to a petty 1½ percent a year, and there seems to be no reason to look for any improvement. The stock *should be sold. The stock proceeds, the $90,000 from the home sale, and the $44,000 in the savings and loan would then total $164,000. With the planner's help, they pick a suitable mutual fund, sign an application for its withdrawal plan, and invest the $164,000. Their instructions to the fund are: "Send us a check every month for an amount based on an annual withdrawal of 7½ percent. At the end of the first year and of each succeeding year, adjust the monthly sums you will send to reflect 7½ percent of the actual value of the account at that time."*

What does that mean? First, it means that during the first year the Formers will get $1,025 a month. Add in the monthly income from Social Security and the pension, and their total monthly income comes to $2,014, $320 more than they had before. Second, while they are taking money out of the withdrawal account each month, any dividends and realized profits earned by the mutual fund are going into *the account, and any realized profits are adding to the value of their investment. At the end of the first twelve months, assuming that inflation continues and that the investments of the fund reflect that increase, it is entirely possible that their account will have a greater value than it did at the start. If that is the case, their withdrawal for the second year—7½ percent of the new value—will be higher. And so on, year after year.*

When they first learned the degree of control they had over the size of the checks they could request, Mr. and Mrs. Former said, "Let's take 10 percent." But their financial planner said: "That may be a mistake. One thing we want to guard against is any chance of either of you outliving your capital. If you ask for an unreasonable monthly payment, eventually you will run the account out of money and bring it to an end. Nothing will be left in the account and there will be no more checks coming to you. I have found that the best way to decide on the percentage of withdrawal, if you are to go beyond 6 percent, is to base it on your ages. That is why I suggested 7½ percent. If you were in your nineties, I'd say a 9 percent withdrawal would be a good idea for there would be little or no danger of your outliving your capital even with a bad market. I am satisfied that a 7½ percent withdrawal will not only safeguard against your running out of capital, it will permit the value of the account to grow so that you will get automatic cost-of-living increases as the years go by."

The choice of the type of fund to be used for this means of providing income surprised the Formers. Wanting income, they expected the planner to concentrate on funds having income as their major objective. Instead, he favored a fund dedicated to growth of capital. "Two reasons," he said: "Over many years, each of the funds we will consider has shown good growth, averaging better than 9 percent a year. Some years less and some years more, but that has been the average. Income has been very modest, and that's the second reason. Even though your tax bracket is low, there is no reason to pay IRS any more than you must. The withdrawals you will get from a growth fund will represent some return of your own capital, which is free of tax, plus capital gains, only 40 percent of which gets taxed, and a very small amount of dividend income, which is fully taxed. Were you to be in an income fund, there would be little or no capital gains and a fairly large proportion of your income would be fully taxed. While a growth fund involves market risk, funds producing very good income today also represent risk since there is no certainty that the income will continue to be that good."

There is no magic about the withdrawal plan. Should securities values, across the board, go through a bad decline, the chances are that the value of almost any mutual fund's shares will drop in value, too. In that case, when the account is valued at the end of the year and the new amount of the monthly checks is determined, the Formers would get less income than the year before. Part of your decision, when pondering the advisability of using this method of providing yourself with monthly spending money, must be based on your judgment of the future of the economy. If you think that business will be good and that there will be prosperity, you can then feel confident that you are going to have a cash flow that will grow generously. If you are pessimistic, then perhaps this is not for you. Or if you are to use the withdrawal plan method, you might do well to avoid mutual funds seeking growth in value and select instead a hard-working income fund. Pick an income fund with most of its investments in bonds or U. S. government securities.

Freedom of choice. If the fund chosen is part of a family of funds with different objectives, you have the right to shift from one fund to another whenever you please, with little or no cost. That advantage can be most useful. Just suppose, for example, you wanted to use the withdrawal idea now but do not like the present outlook for the stock market. You can launch your plan with an income fund and then, when you see the clouds breaking and expect a new wave of prosperity, you can transfer your account to a growth fund. You are free to move back and forth; generally the greatest cost of doing so is a flat $5 for each change.

You can also take some money out of the fund if you wish. If, while taking your monthly checks, you decide you need $1,000 or so for a trip, it is yours for the asking. Some of the mutual funds make no charge for the withdrawal plan services; others have modest service fees.

Annuities

Do not confuse withdrawal plans and annuities just because each makes monthly payments. They seem to be lookalikes, but there are extreme differences. Annuities normally guarantee that you get payments as long as you live, even if you break all longevity records. You have no such guarantee from a withdrawal plan. As you have seen, if you go overboard on the amount you draw, or even if there is a prolonged and severe period of falling securities values, you could use up all the capital in the account. That would be the end: no more account and no more checks. The second big difference is that, generally, when an annuitant dies, *nothing* goes to his estate. With a withdrawal plan, *everything* remaining goes to the estate. Under no circumstances does any part of the assets left in your account at your death belong to the mutual fund.

You can buy annuity contracts in any of three basic ways. For current income you simply write a check and buy the contract. Your second choice is to buy a *deferred annuity,* also a single purchase, but with the stipulation that you are to receive no payments till some future time. The third approach is to buy a future annuity by making systematic payments over a period of time.

Annuities are very interesting income producers. They come in several shapes and styles. You may buy a *fixed annuity,* a *variable annuity,* or a contract giving you the freedom to move back and forth between the two types at will. To reduce confusion, you should first acquaint yourself with the differences between a *fixed annuity* and a *variable annuity.*

Fixed annuities

The names, in themselves, give you a good part of the answer. A *fixed annuity* guarantees a lifetime payout of monthly checks for fixed sums of money. Year after year, you will receive monthly checks for an unchanging amount. When offering a *fixed* annuity contract, the insurance company says, "In consideration of the amount of money you have turned over to us and the payout option you have specified, we guarantee to pay you *x* number of dollars each month for as long as you live. We are taking the gamble on what happens to our own investments, which is the source of the regular sums you will get."

Variable annuities

A *variable annuity* guarantees a lifetime payout of monthly checks of a varying sum of money. When offering a *variable* annuity contract, the insurance company says, "In consideration of the amount of money you have turned over to us and the payout option you have specified, we guarantee to pay you the *value* of a fixed number of *investment units* for as long as you live. How long you may live is our risk, but the investment risk is yours." The investment influencing the size of your monthly checks is just like a mutual fund. A number of variable annuity contracts use mutual funds as the investment. Each month, on the day your check is to be prepared, your units are multiplied by that day's unit value, and, of course, that value constantly fluctuates.

Wrap-around annuities

This newest type of annuity contract brings together two sponsoring companies, a life insurance company, and an investment management company with a group, or family, of mutual funds. The combination gave birth to the descriptive name, *wrap-around annuity,* for it is an annuity contract wrapped around the investment portion of the package, one or more of the mutual funds.

As with all annuities there are two parts—the period before annuity payouts begin and the payout period itself—the annuity portion. During the initial period you make your own investment decision. You specify which member of the mutual fund family you want. And then you are free to shift your investment, whenever you please, to any of the other funds in the group. You are permitted to move back and forth, in whatever manner and at whatever intervals you choose. You pay no fee for those transfers. The attractiveness of this feature, of course, is that you have the opportunity to put yourself in a fund dedicated to high yields when yields are more desirable than the pursuit of growth of capital. And then, when you have reason to believe that stock values are going to rise you order that your money be moved to the growth side. After the annuity payout period has started you still are permitted to transfer from one fund to another once each year.

It is critically important to you to have the money you invest earning and growing as much as possible, without undue risk, before the annuity payments start. The more money in your account on the day your account is annuitized the bigger the monthly checks will be. The wrap-around concept gives you a good deal of control throughout that building effort.

Options

The options on payout vary a good deal, but the major ones offered by most companies are:

1. guaranteed income for life,
2. guaranteed income for husband and/or wife, *the income continuing for as long as either one of them lives, and*
3. ten years certain, *which means that income is guaranteed for life, and if you should die before ten years of the annuity payout period have gone by, a beneficiary you name receives the monthly checks until the ten-year period is up.*

How much will you be paid?

When you buy an immediate fixed annuity you will be told, to the penny, how much you will be paid each month. If you take an immediate variable annuity you will be told the exact amount of the *first payment*. After that the payments will vary, and no one can state what the payments will amount to. They may be more and may be less than the initial one. You will see why in a moment. Should you elect a deferred annuity, or buy your annuity on a systematic accumulation basis, there is no way you can be told what the eventual payments will be since there is no way of knowing how much of the money you put into the account will earn, or change in value before the payouts begin.

How much you will be paid is arrived at by means of a formula the insurance companies use. The formula is made up of various elements including:

1. *the payout option you elect,*
2. *your age and sex if it is a single life contract, or the ages and sexes of both parties if it is a two life contract,*
3. *the current market value of your investment in the contract,*
4. *the insurance company's risk factor and the costs of marketing and administering the contract.*

The insurance companies all use a standard life expectancy table when arriving at the sums to be paid out.

As you know, the fixed annuity payout just keeps rolling along with absolutely no change for as long as you, or you and another party, may live.

The very first payment for a variable annuity is determined in the same way. Once the company has that figure they then relate it to the share value of whatever mutual fund is the investment medium, or to the unit value (identical to a per share value) of the company's own pooled investment account.

EXAMPLE: You write a check for $90,000 and buy an immediate variable annuity contract. The company, applying its formula, tells you that your first check will amount to $600. (The figures used in this example are pulled out of the air, and are not intended to indicate actual payouts.) At that time the company's pooled account has a value of $12 per unit. Your initial payout of $600 is divided by the $12 unit cost ($600 ÷ $12 = 50). Your check amounts to the value of 50 units at that time. Now you are married to 50 units. The number of units applied to you never will change, but the unit value will constantly change since the value is based on the day-to-day fluctuations of the several dozens of securities that make up the pooled *account. If the company used a mutual fund for the investment it would operate in exactly the same way, but we would speak of share value instead of unit value.*

Now it is time for your second check to go in the mail and at that time, 30 days later, the unit value is $12.44. That month your check will be $622. If the unit value is $11.92 you will be paid $596. And so it goes from month to month for as long as you live. The big hope and expectation, of course, is that the investments will succeed in increasing the unit value in pace with, or going beyond, inflation. That is the hope, but, unlike the fixed annuity, it is not guaranteed.

Tax deferral

Although this chapter is devoted to current income, several other benefits of both deferred, single premium and systematic-payment annuities have so many benefits to offer that this is an appropriate time to discuss them. Until the annuity payout period arrives, the money in the account earns money, and you are not required to pay taxes on those earnings. Taxes are deferred until the payout period. Not only does this lighten your tax load for a period of time, but the chances are that when you do have to pay, your tax bracket will be lower. That is because you probably will have retired by the time annuity payments begin.

Single-premium (or single-pay) deferred annuities provide high yields throughout the deferred period; in 1979, 8-percent to 9-percent yields were not uncommon. When combined with the tax deferral, this becomes most attractive. The untaxed yield, remaining in the account, has a compounding effect, and it does not take very many years for your original pay-in to have doubled or better, depending on the number of years involved. Until the annuity payout period starts—and only until then—the money in the deferred account is yours if you should need it. You can withdraw part or all of it with little or no penalty. The terms offered by various insurance companies differ. With some there is no penalty for early withdrawal, while others make some charges if the money is taken out after only three years, or six years, and so on. And the tax situation on any withdrawals you may take prior to the annuity payout period is interesting. Your money has been in there earning money, and, at some time, you have to pay the postponed taxes. But IRS says that if you do not draw out more money than you put in originally, you can continue to put off the tax liability. Once you go past your original investment, then taxes become payable.

Here is an additional way to use the deferred, single-pay annuity to good advantage. The only type of property that can pass from you to your family entirely free of income tax is life insurance. Anything you can do to increase your life insurance within your means and in keeping with your circumstances merits your consideration. If, for example, you are paying tax on $47,200 of income, you are in the 50-percent tax bracket; to buy additional life insurance you would have to earn twice as much money as you would pay out in premiums. If, however, you had a deferred annuity growing on an untaxed basis, you could make annual withdrawals—tax-free—to pay your premiums. The cost of your insurance would be cut in half.

Still another possibility adds to the flexibility of the deferred, single-pay annuity. Assume that the contract is with a company with the requirement that the deferral must end by a certain age, say age 70. When you reach that age, you automatically lose the valuable privilege of sheltering the income. It also brings to an end the right to take any withdrawals other than the annuity payments to be made in keeping with the chosen option. However, there is a way of extending the deferral period. While remaining the owner of the contract, you may designate some young member of your immediate family—your son, perhaps—as the annuitant. There is the possibility that some gift tax liability may come into play if this is done, but you can appreciate the benefit.

If you buy an annuity for someone else and that other person is designated as annuitant and contract owner, it is a gift and subject to the federal gift tax. This can be avoided, though, if you make yourself the contract owner and name the other person as the annuitant. In this way, since you are the owner, you are in control of the contract. You are free to name someone else as the annuitant at any time prior to the start of the annuity payout date. Handle it that way, and there will be no gift until your son starts receiving the annuity payments. Taxes on earnings are payable by the donor and any appreciation in the value of the account increases the donor's taxable estate.

What about inflation? The very favorable tax deferral helps to keep the yield in a strong position as an opponent of inflation. Furthermore, if the contract is for a variable annuity, the opportunities to challenge inflation effectively are multiplied. The fact that it is a *variable* annuity in no way changes the tax advantages. The privileges and options also remain the same.

Annuities represent just one aspect of what insurance companies have to offer, an area covered more fully in the next chapter.

CANDIDATES FOR ACTION

To satisfy my desire for as generous a flow of income as I can manage, without taking needless risks, I am particularly interested in:

- ☐ Municipal bonds individually selected
- ☐ Municipal bond unit investment trusts
- ☐ Municipal bond managed funds
- ☐ A combination of the trust and the fund
- ☐ A mutual fund withdrawal plan
- ☐ A fixed annuity
- ☐ A variable annuity
- ☐ A wrap-around annuity
- ☐ A single-pay deferred annuity

6

Insuring to be Sure

A vital part of your financial plan

This chapter on insurance is, by no means, a detailed course on this very involved subject. A meaningful course would require not a chapter, but a number of books. Insurance—particularly life insurance, annuities, and disability income replacement—is integral to sound financial planning. What is presented is an overview of the functions of insurance, the types of insurance you may use as building blocks when constructing your financial plan, and the tax and income considerations that should be weighed.

Life insurance encompasses a great variety of benefits, possibilities, and solutions. Of all the many types of insured protection, life insurance is the most fruitful for most people. With a signature and the payment of a modest sum of money, a person with negligible assets suddenly establishes an appreciable estate . . . through life insurance. The lives of widows and children are cushioned against the economic shock of the sudden removal of the breadwinner . . . through life insurance. The need either to break up a lucrative family business or to sell investments at a time when prices are unfavorable is avoided because of the cash made available . . . through life insurance. A mortgaged home passes on to its inheritors, free and clear . . . through life insurance. And while these benefits of life insurance are among the most important, there are many others, including those that do not depend on the death of the person insured.

How much is enough?

The biggest question concerning life insurance is, "How much is enough?" Although there is no precise answer to that question, obviously it is seldom asked. Most people buy or are sold life insurance protection on a random, bits-and-pieces, uncoordinated basis.

As a result, life insurance proceeds seldom amount to enough to keep survivors out of severe financial trouble. The

average life insurance policy per insured family in this, the wealthiest nation in the history of the world, is less than $30,000.* Invested at 6 percent, that produces $34.60 a week (before taxes), a sum that could not be expected to do much for a widow—certainly not a widow with one or more children. Add Social Security, and the survivors of the breadwinner are still in an impossible economic fix. In 1970 the Life Insurance Agency Management Association conducted a survey of widows whose husbands had died before age 65. They found that half of them had received not more than $5,000 in insurance, that only 8 percent of them had received more than $25,000, and that 25 percent of them were forced to spend all they received immediately. A more recent research project in this area, conducted by the Anchor Corporation, provided these additional grim facts:

1. *Over 50 percent of all widows had used up all death benefits within six months;*
2. *25 percent had exhausted all insurance proceeds within 60 days;*
3. *the average of all death benefits—from insurance, Social Security, Veterans Administration, pensions, and so on—combined, was just about $12,000; and*
4. *the average sum of death costs (hospital, doctors, funeral) came to $4,000.*

It is abundantly clear that most people do not take the time to try to estimate what insurance protection they need to protect the family against economic disaster. A prospect proudly told a seasoned life insurance agent that his family was well protected because he had $25,000 in life insurance. The agent unsmilingly commented, "You don't expect to stay dead very long, do you?"

If you plan to remain dead . . .

How much is enough?

Over the years countless people—economists, financial

*The American Council of Life Insurance reported that in 1976 the average American family carried $29,800 in life insurance protection.

planners, insurance experts, tax and legal counselors, investment advisors, and others—have suggested a variety of yardsticks. The frustrating fact, however, is that so many factors have to be weighed that no simple set of rules can do the job. "How much is enough" can be answered only after you have taken into account your age, marital status, support obligations and/or desires, earned income, other income, capital, tax situation, survivor's ability to be self-supporting, availability of after-death income that can be counted on, and more.

This much is clear: "how much is enough?" is a question that gives rise to constantly changing answers as you go through life. A graphic demonstration of this appeared in an article in the magazine *Money* in 1974. Under the caption "The changing need for protection," the author presented these figures:

Age 25 —Income: $15,000
No House
Net Worth: Negligible
No children
INSURANCE: $25,000

Age 35 —Income: $20,000
Mortgage: $15,000
Net Worth: $10,000
Three young children
INSURANCE: $150,000

Age 45 —Income: $30,000
Mortgage: $5,000
Net Worth: $45,000
Children approaching college
INSURANCE: $200,000

Age 55 —Income: $35,000
Mortgage paid off
Net Worth: $75,000
Children grown
INSURANCE: $165,000

Age 65 —Pension: $9,000
Social Security: $5,400
Net Worth: $150,000
INSURANCE: $25,000

It becomes apparent that one of the most meaningful approaches to the question "How much is enough?" is to ask several other questions.

Ready money. Do you now support other people? How much would *they* need if you are not here? Do you have any notion of what your estate taxes and probate costs might amount to? Your lawyer can help you with the answer to that question. When you have the answer, the next point to be considered—and a critical one—is how much ready money will become available, within a reasonable period of time after your death, to handle estate taxes and probate costs without requiring the forced sale of securities, real estate, or business interests? What makes this particular question so important is the realization that, if a sale is necessary, the timing could be painfully undesirable.

Money for final expenses. The amount of cash needed for final expenses is another item to be added to the list. Final expenses include all hospital and doctor bills stemming from a terminal illness—an unpalatable subject for you to think about, but one that must not be ignored. Final expenses can run from $5,000 to astronomical sums. Medical costs, including nursing care, simply know no limits. Medical costs have been increasing in a frightening manner. Major medical insurance, if you have it, may seem to be the answer, removing the need for concern. But do not count on it. Nursing care, for example, frequently is not covered, and the costs for around-the-clock nurses required for any prolonged period can be ruinous.

Cost of living. How much will the family's living costs be reduced? If your present income and living standards are on the high side, the percentage saved will be negligible. At the lower end of the income scale, family expenses could be reduced by as much as 25 percent to 35 percent.

Capital or income? Should your family live on capital or income? The answer to this one has to be based on the age or ages of those who may survive you and on the anticipated, after-tax amount of capital. Will your family's established life-style by sustainable by combining income and a gradual erosion of capital? Or must it be fully supportable by income with capital remaining relatively intact?

The need figure

Once all these measurements are taken and a *need* figure established, subtract Social Security and all other income that will continue for certain, and you will know how much life insurance is needed ideally. Once all the decisions have been made and acted on, you must review the need figure at relatively frequent intervals. Many believe that a review of their insurance is as important and should be as consistent as annual physical and dental checkups.

The many kinds of life insurance

Insurance serves a variety of purposes and comes in a variety of forms. It is made available by a great number of companies, which fall into either of two categories. *Stock companies* are owned by shareholders. *Mutual companies* are owned by the insured. There are two types of mutual companies: *Participating* mutual companies generally charge more and pay dividends to their insured, the dividends representing the difference between the premium you pay for a specific type of insurance policy and the company's costs; *nonparticipating* mutual companies offer their insurance at lower premiums. The dividends paid by the participating companies are not taxable but are not guaranteed. If they are not paid-up, the premiums are higher than you would pay to a nonparticipating company.

Term insurance

The foundation of all life insurance is protection. *Term* insurance offers pure protection, nothing else. As the title implies, the insurance is made available for a specific term of time. It is the lowest cost type of life insurance that can be bought because it has no value beyond protection. If you outlive the term, you pay premiums and get nothing back. *You have to die to win.* But, beyond any question, you get the most protection for your family for what you pay.

Buying term insurance. There are different ways of buying term insurance.

Level term is bought for a certain number of years: 1, 5, 10, 15, or 20 years, for example. Normally, term insurance premiums increase as you grow older. "Level term" actually means "level premium." The premium is uniform for the life of the policy. It provides an answer to the problem of very high cost per thousand dollars of normal term coverage at older ages.

Renewable term costs more, but it guarantees that the policy may be renewed without a medical examination at each renewal period until you are 65 years old.

Convertible term permits you, at any time prior to reaching age 65, to convert to ordinary (sometimes called "straight" or "whole") life insurance without a medical examination. Since term insurance becomes more costly each year, it is quite expensive after age 65.

Reducing term starts with a certain amount of insured protection, which is reduced year after year. It is frequently used to give you the certainty that something you are paying off in installments over a period of years will be paid for in full no matter how soon you die. Reducing-term insurance is therefore commonly linked to mortgage payments. For example, you have a $100,000 mortgage on your home and a $100,000 reducing-term policy tied to your mortgage obligation. You start out with $100,000 coverage, and that amount of protection keeps getting smaller in step with the decreasing principal in your mortgage payments, over and above interest and taxes. By the time the mortgage is paid off, your insured protection is reduced to zero. This type of insurance is also used to cover accumulations for college education—for just about anything involving long-term payments on your part. It is one way of relieving your survivors of debt.

Reducing term is used in other ways as well. A lot depends, once again, on your attitude and your emotional approach to your financial life. A young couple, charged up with ambition and abundant confidence, may decide that the early years of married life—while their children need total protection and a mother at home to care for their upbringing—is the period of greatest life insurance need. It may be their conviction that the husband will, without doubt, climb to great heights in his career. They are confident that, by the time the children have grown up, his income and his acquisition of assets will become substantial enough to diminish the importance of life insurance protection. For them, therefore, reducing term is an ideal answer: They will have maximum protection during the early years, and the protection will diminish as income increases—one balancing the other.

Then there is the philosophy, somewhat akin to the confident young couple's, that a sound program is to use a portion of income for protection and another portion—perhaps an equal amount—for investment. In another see-saw effect, this approach amounts to a term policy that reduces as the investment accumulation grows. It could be dubbed an *"I want-x-amount-dead-or-alive" approach*. It can be a meaningful answer to the question as to whether a fixed amount of insurance protection is as realistic as you might wish it to be in this inflationary economy. The investment portion can be the means of fighting the inflation battle.

Ordinary (whole or straight) life

Ordinary life insurance combines protection and savings. One essential difference between ordinary and term is that ordinary offers protection *until* you die while term protects you against the *possibility* of dying before the term expires. Another way of putting it is that term is protection against the *risk* of death, while ordinary protects against the *certainty* of death, whether it occurs tomorrow or off in the far distant future.

Cash value versus face value. Ordinary insurance is sometimes referred to as *cash value* insurance, because it is really a combination of reducing term and savings. The *cash value* represents the savings portion. As a rule, there is no cash value, or savings, until the end of the second year that the policy has been in force. The cash value increases year by year, since part of each premium paid is for protection and part for savings. As savings increase, the amount of protection decreases. In the average case, if a person dies at age 65, the

BORROWING THE CASH VALUES IN YOUR ORDINARY LIFE POLICY

As your ordinary life policy gets older, it gets better. The interest you pay when you borrow cash values is specified in your policy, and your insurance policy is stuck with it. Some old policies have rates as low as 3 percent, and a great number have rates that do not go beyond 6 percent. Even recently issued policies may enable you to borrow your cash values for as little as 8 percent. *Compare those rates with current bank rates.* The bargain is obvious and immense. If you compare the rate with what you pay for some installment purchases, the difference is still more dramatic.

You are permitted to borrow all or part of the accumulated cash values in your policy. And it is not like a bank loan. There is no date on which the money must be repaid. You may never pay it back if you choose not to. You are not even required to pay the interest. What you borrow and the interest you owe are subtracted from the amount paid to your estate when you die. If, however, the sum borrowed and the buildup of interest reach the point where they exceed the total cash value, the policy may be cancelled and you will lose that much of your insured protection. If the money you borrow is invested, your family may be ahead despite the reduced amount of insurance because the investment will be part of your estate.

Good strategy is to borrow when bank rates are high and repay when they are low. Also, if inflation stays with us (particularly if it is at a high level), you will repay your loan with cheaper dollars than you take out. Another factor to consider when weighing the pros and cons of repaying the loan is what the borrowed money is producing for you.

If you do want to borrow some or all of your cash values, just phone your agent or send a written request to the insurance company. If you worry about the reduced value of your policy due to unpaid borrowings and unpaid interest, you can counterbalance them with an equal amount of low cost term insurance.

payment to the beneficiary is half from cash value and half from the insurance company's reserves. If you live to a very old age, the cash values cover the full face amount of the policy. Upon payment of the death benefit (the *face value* of the policy), no cash values remain. If you surrender your policy, you will be paid whatever the cash value amounts to at that time. As long as the company retains the cash values, interest accumulates, and you pay no taxes on those earnings. If you cannot make the premium payments, you have three choices:

1. *Cash values may be used to pay the premiums until they have been exhausted.*
2. *The cash values may be applied to the purchase of* a paid-up *policy in whatever amount the available cash can buy.*
3. *You can apply the cash values to the purchase of extended term insurance.*

Types of ordinary life insurance. Level-pay life entails the payment of unchanging premiums until you die.

Limited-pay life amounts to a prepayment on a whole life policy. The payments may extend for 10, 20, or 30 years, or they can be "by age 65." When the payments for the agreed period have been completed, the policy is fully paid and remains in force as long as you live.

Single-pay life (also called single-premium life) is a means of discounting the costs of ordinary life insurance. The entire premium is paid at one time in a lump sum at the start of the policy. Because the insurance company has the extra money for so much longer, it reduces the overall premium cost. The policy can be discounted at any time and the cash values withdrawn, and are not taxed until they equal the original premium.

Endowment, to a specific age or for a period of years, puts the greatest emphasis on the saving portion, for it guarantees to pay no less than the face amount of the policy, whether you live or die. In other words, since it is a life insurance policy, should you die before the term of the endowment ends your beneficiaries get paid. If you do not die, the insurance company sends you a check at the end of the term. The check is at least equal to the face amount and, because of the accrued interest, might contain enough of a surplus to pay for the protection you enjoyed while covered. Endowments are used for various purposes where there is a long-term, high-cost goal. Some people use this method to prepare for college costs; whether they live or die, the money will be there. Its great weaknesses are its inability to react to inflation and its usually low yield.

ORDINARY LIFE VERSUS TERM

There is a constant debate regarding the relative merits of ordinary life and term insurance. The defenders of ordinary insurance contend that:

- *It is the only permanent protection you can buy and that permanence is vital. Term does, indeed, expire at the end of a specific period of time, and no protection remains.*
- *History shows, indisputably, that term policies are allowed to lapse much more often than ordinary—another point for the permanence issue.*
- *Ordinary, tied as it is to enforced savings, does something for you beyond pure protection.*
- *Term insurance disappears at the very time that you are approaching the end of your lifespan. At that time, when you may be retired and your earnings have ceased, when insurance dollars may be particularly important to those you leave behind, the chances are that you will be both uninsured and uninsurable. There are ways of buying* term to age 100, *but the costs are high, and, usually, the amount of protection you may buy is severely limited.*

Those who champion term insurance make a big point of the fact that when you want protection against the possibility of premature death, you should give your family as much protection as your premium dollars can buy. Because of the savings feature, ordinary greatly dilutes the amount of protection for the dollar. In the place of maximum protection, you are given a costly way of saving money. They say that you can handle your own saving program in considerably better ways. They also point to the fact that the longer you *save* in your ordinary life program, the more you are simply shifting the risk factor from the shoulders of the insurance company onto your own. Your cash values will be what your estate will be paid, with little or no money coming out of the insurance company's pockets.

There is logic on both sides of the debate. The pluses and minuses for each type of life insurance constitute one reason why many individuals use a combination of the two. When you take the time to determine what your own insured protection should be, the chances are that you will be looking at a huge sum of money. It may not be practical for you even to consider buying that much ordinary life. Your answer may be to buy as much ordinary life as you can afford comfortably and to cover the balance of your protection needs with term.

To some extent you may have done so already. It is not unusual for employed people to have some ordinary life insurance they have bought on their own, supplemented by company-provided group insurance. In most situations company-provided insurance is term. The reducing-term linked to a home mortgage is to be considered, too. That form of protection reduces the overall amount needed since, one way or another, those who survive you will have no mortgage payments to make. Your home, if you have one, will be fully paid for.

A family plan is a combination of ordinary and decreasing term policies, and it is used, under many different titles, in many different ways. Basically, the concept is that permanent life insurance is provided for the breadwinner, along with reducing-term insurance. Thus it creates *greater* protection during the years when children and earnings are small and *diminishing* protection as your own earnings and savings grow. Sometimes the lives of a spouse and children are covered by a term portion until they reach certain ages.

Split-dollar or *split-life* is a sophisticated concept used more often in business planning than in individual plans. In essence, two parties pay the premiums on a single policy on one person's life. As an example, a father may agree to pay that part of an ordinary life premium *equal to the increase in the cash value each year.* The son pays only for the pure protection portion. The son's payments are much less than they would be were he to buy the same amount of protection in term insurance. Since the cash value increases each year and the protection decreases accordingly, what the son actually has is a very low-cost decreasing-term policy. Were the son to die, the father would receive the cash value portion, and the son's estate would receive the balance. In this case, one way for the son to keep the protection at the original level is to have an increasing-term rider tacked onto the policy. *Increasing term,* as the title suggests, operates on the same principal as decreasing term, but in reverse. Each year its face value grows bigger.

Where split-dollar is used in business as a fringe benefit or as part of other business planning, the IRS takes the position that the difference between the employee's cost of protection and the cost for a decreasing-term policy with the same face value, constitutes "extra compensation" and must be reported as such. It is assumed, therefore, that when split-dollar is used within the family, IRS would regard the transaction in the same light, considering the difference in cost as a gift. It is most improbable, however, that the amount of the gift will exceed the annual exclusion, particularly if husband and wife combine their exclusion privileges. These are subjects you will read about in Chapter 7.

The use of split-life as a fringe benefit in business is attractive. If you are in business yourself and you want to do something for some special employees, this is one way you can handle the problem. Many employee fringe benefits have to be free of discrimination. If you give it to one, you are compelled to give it to everyone. Not so with split-life. Also, it costs you little or nothing. The part of the premium you pay each year is an amount equal to that year's cash value. Eventually the cash values you are paying out come back to you or to your company. Your hand-picked employee or employees are getting additional life insurance at a bargain price. If an employee is 45 years old, for example, his or her share of the annual premium will be about $3 per thousand. To buy term insurance on their own, the cost would be closer to $25 a thousand. That is a whopping difference.

Even if you are not an owner or major stockholder of the firm you work for, you might be able to benefit from split-life. Perhaps you know or believe—hope?—that the executives of your firm would welcome a "low-to-no"-cost way of doing something for you and maybe for some others. Bring the idea to them. It might be wise, under such circumstances, to line up an insurance agent or financial planner who understands the subject and is ready to visit with your top brass to answer their questions and to close the sale.

Insurance and inflation

Along with everyone else, the life insurance industry has been thoroughly aware of inflation-created problems. They have recognized the fact that insurance that might have been adequate at its inception can become hopelessly inadequate years later. You might decide that, all factors considered, your family will need $150,000 if you are out of the picture right now. But ten, fifteen, or twenty years from now, your $150,000 policy might have lost so much of its down-to-earth purchasing power that your intentions have been severely blunted. You may, of course, buy more and more insurance as the years go by, but that idea is not very appealing. The expense of the additions would be compounded by ever higher rates because of your increasing age. And then there is the likelihood that you would not want the burden of evaluating and making the add-on decisions over the years. In response to this general concern, the life insurance people have come forth with some new products.

Variable life insurance

The first product on the scene, variable life insurance, is not very far away from the concept of variable annuities (Chapter 5). Part of the premium dollars you send to a company selling variable life insurance goes into a special investment account. The investment account is similar to that of the variable annuity or of a mutual fund. The dollars of thousands of individuals are in the one account, which is managed by a team of investment professionals for the benefit of all. They invest in the shares of companies which, in their judgment, are most likely to provide growth in value sufficient to stay in step with or stride ahead of the cost of living.

The life insurance contract, which you buy with a stipulated face value, includes a guarantee that, when you die, your family will get *no less* than that value. Your family could get a good deal more if the investment pool has performed well. The hope is that the value of your insurance will stay pretty much in line with the purchasing power of the dollar. Thus, if the value of the dollar is cut in half twenty years after you take out a $150,000 policy, it is possible that your family could be paid $300,000 or more, should you decide to die at that stage of the game. In the early years a significant portion of your premium dollar goes to cover the normal risk, administrative, and distribution costs, which are part and parcel of all life insurance. In the long run, the portion channeled to the investment grows, and so do your opportunities to see the face value grow.

Variable life insurance, in all other respects, is ordinary life and has cash values, but there is no guarantee as to the number of dollars your cash values will amount to at any given point. The cash values rise and fall with the value of the investment portfolio. The cost of variable life is greater than for normal ordinary life insurance. The guarantee of the minimum payment and the cost of maintaining the special investment account are reflected in the premiums you pay.

Increasing variable life

This type of contract takes one step more. You take a $150,000 policy, and the face amount automatically increases by 3 percent a year without any change in premium. In addition, as with variable life, part of your premium dollar is in a managed investment account. There is the possibility that the eventual payout may be a good deal more than the total of the face amount *and* the annual 3-percent increases. The cost of this policy, for obvious reasons, is higher than you would pay for variable life.

Adjustable life

A more recent newcomer, this type of insurance contract has two new features of interest.

Automatic increase of face value. The first is an automatic change in the face value of your policy at predetermined intervals, based on the Consumers' Price Index or some other yardstick. The bad news is that, as the face value climbs upwards, so do your premiums; the good news is that until you reach your fifty-second birthday, you are permitted to have your insurance increased regardless of your insurability. For instance, at age 35 you may buy an adjustable life contract with $150,000 face value. Three years later, due to increases in living costs, the company moves the value up to $170,000 and your premiums increase accordingly. You do not have to say yes to the increases in protection and premium. It is up to you. You may decide to keep everything where it was. But suppose, before the next cycle has passed, that you suffer a heart attack from which you recover. There is now a good chance that you would not be okayed for a new or increased insurance contract if you had to respond to a health questionnaire or take a physical. Despite your illness, if the face value of your policy goes up to $200,000 in your forty-first year, the company may not deny you if you are willing to pay the new premium.

"Mixable" life insurance. The second element of importance is that adjustable life contracts are comprised of a flexible mix of life insurance products. In effect, you may tell the insurance company what kind of protection you want and what you are able to pay. The company will structure a contract for you, tailored to your specifications. And you may change your specifications. That can be a help through inflationary periods. Let's say that you have been paying your premiums regularly until a time when, because of rising living costs or any other reason, they become too expensive for you. You want to lower your costs, but you do not want to lower your family's protection. In that case you advise your agent or the company that you want to pay less but maintain the same benefits. They make the alteration possible by reducing your premium to the amount you have specified and arranging a new product mix for you. There are, of course, limits to the company's ability to make such changes, but it is another way of dealing with inflation.

Taxation of insurance proceeds

Life insurance proceeds are *not* taxed as income by the federal government. Your heirs pay no taxes on them. They are, however, included in your estate when you die. Once included, they become subject to federal estate taxation. Since life insurance proceeds constitute a big portion of many an estate, you can reduce your estate taxes considerably by keeping your life insurance proceeds out of your estate. Depending on your circumstances you might want to give away your policies, retaining only the protection they provide.

Giving your policies away

New and exisitng life insurance policies can be given away. For example, a husband can transfer ownership of one or all of his policies to his wife, to his children—to anyone. This privilege extends to group life policies as well, but you must surrender all rights of ownership. This means that you may not retain the right to change beneficiaries, the right to borrow, pledge, or assign the policy, or the right to alter or elect any of the settlement options; nor may you surrender the policy. The gift has to be absolute. The new owner acquires all those rights, including the right to pay premiums if you do not.

Giving away your life insurance policies can be a difficult decision to make. That is especially true if you have large cash values in the policies and do not want to relinquish the privilege of borrowing those values at the relatively low rates they entail. A compromise may prove to be more acceptable. You can convert your high cash value policy or policies to paid-up life contracts. You then apply the annual premiums you have been in the custom of paying to the purchase of a new policy to be owned by your spouse or children.

Giving a policy with substantial cash values could create gift tax problems. The cash value, at the time the transfer of ownership takes place, would definitely constitute a gift. If it amounts to $3,000 or less, there is no problem. If it goes beyond that, however, the excess is taxable. Should the recipient be your wife, you can of course take advantage of the marital gift exclusion: the first $100,000 is tax-free, but half of whatever the gift amounts to is deducted from the marital deduction when the estate tax is to be paid. The marital deduction refers to that part of your estate which may be passed on to your spouse free of federal tax. The deduction may be $250,000 or half of your assets, whichever amounts to more. There are some side effects to be considered, but this subject is discussed in detail in Chapter 7.

Life insurance trusts

Normally, the realistic expectation is that a wife outlives her husband. So let's look at the estate tax problems from the husband's point of view for the sake of making a simple point.

The transfer of insurance policies from husband to wife removes those big assets from one estate and throws them into the other. If she passes away after her husband, her taxable estate is not reduced by the marital deduction and the tax on those insurance proceeds can be quite large. If she has children, this is a real problem.

A very effective solution to the problem is to create an *insurance trust.* Briefly stated, you transfer all rights to your life insurance policies to the trust. This transfer must be irrevocable. You cannot change your mind ever. The trust becomes the owner of your insurance, and your wife is named as trustee. As trustee she will pay the premiums, which, if you choose, can be provided by you as annual gifts. For the average policy the gifts are likely to fall within the $3,000 annual exclusion. The terms of the trust are that she is to enjoy all the income produced by the insurance proceeds as long as she shall live. Upon her death the assets in the trust are to be turned over to your children, and at that point the trust expires. This approach removes the insurance proceeds from both your estate and your wife's.

And there are other benefits. At the time of your death, the amount of cash needed to pay final expenses, taxes, and probate costs might require some undesirable sales of the estate's assets. For example, the only sizable asset might be a family-owned business, and its sale or the sale of an important percentage of it might be totally unwelcome. The trust, however, could buy the business, using the cash from the insurance benefits, thus keeping the business in the family.

Life insurance settlement options

From a financial planning viewpoint, you must give serious attention to the settlement options you choose: (1) who your beneficiary or beneficiaries are to be and (2) how the payments are to be made. You may pass up the second privilege if you feel that it is up to those you leave behind to make their own decisions. However, this type of reasoning could be nothing more than an emotional desire not to participate in plans concerning your own death which, while understandable, is not good planning. So if you recognize the fact that the recipients of your insurance proceeds may not be trained in the handling of large sums of money, it is clearly prudent to make decisions regarding appropriate settlement methods while you are alive and in full possession of your mental faculties. By taking action on the settlement choices, you can protect your heirs from well-intended or not so well-intended friends, relatives, and outsiders, as well as from creditors. You can not only reduce probate expense, but you can also fortify against the immense problems sometimes resulting from a common disaster that takes your life and your spouse's at the same time. It is a good idea to coordinate the settlement options with your will and with the provisions of whatever other life insurance policies you own.

The commonplace settlement options include the payment of the death claim in:

1. *all cash,*
2. *income only,*
3. *income for a certain period,*
4. *income until a certain sum is paid out, or*
5. *income for life.*

Review your existing policies

Study your existing life policies. Most of us are inclined to overlook the terms of life insurance contracts bought years ago. Old policies should be reviewed to ascertain whether births, deaths, and marriages that may have occurred since the policy was written require changes as to prime and contingent beneficiaries. Have the proceeds been protected from creditors and judgments? Are all the considerations and safeguards built into current policies present in older contracts, such as automatic loans to assure against lapse? Are premiums being paid in the most economical way? Are the settlement options in harmony with newer policies?

Insurance and your will

A thoughtful approach to the terms of your will (discussed in Chapter 12) is likely to include one or more steps that may serve to assure the carrying-out of your wishes. For example, a man planning his will may come to the conclusion that a trust would produce enough income for his wife and that the assets should go to his children after she is gone. At the same time he might recognize the need to provide his wife with a cash flow that goes beyond the income likely to be produced. The trustee is therefore permitted to invade capital systematically. This may solve the problem for the wife, but it could leave the children with little or nothing. The trustee is further authorized, under those circumstances, to buy an appropriate amount of life insurance on the wife's life; the children, of course, would be the beneficiaries.

In the same vein, if your will calls for specific sums to be paid out to one or more recipients at regular intervals, the trustee may be empowered to sell some assets and to use the proceeds to buy an annuity or a mutual fund withdrawal account for such purposes. Great care must be taken to avoid *directing* the trustee to take such action; such a directive could disqualify the important marital deduction. The trustee may be given the *suggestion* and the *right* to make such a decision—but he or she should not be directed to do so.

A sound idea, where the need is seen, might be to contract for a separate life insurance policy with instructions in your will that the eventual proceeds from that policy are to be used to pay estate taxes and/or all other final expenses. This policy could help to avoid the need either to sell all or part of a family business, or to liquidate securities or real estate holdings while they are in the doldrums. It also clarifies what is often a cloudy question: What part of the estate is to pay those final expenses?

The will expresses your wishes as to who should get what and in what manner. Life insurance settlement options, to a great extent, do the same. That is why you should exercise care that your will and any previously chosen life insurance settlement options are coordinated—that each is in harmony with the other.

If there is any chance that your wife may be widowed while your children are still minors, give attention to what happens with Social Security. As long as the children are under age 18 or, if they continue to be students, under 22, Social Security benefits remain at a relatively high level. As soon as the children have passed those limits, however, the payments are drastically reduced until your wife reaches her sixty-second birthday. It may be important to prepare for supplemental income to bridge that period through life insurance and the adoption of the "period certain" option.

Disability insurance

If earned income is a sizeable factor in a family's financial life—as it most surely is in most cases—the need to guard against a long-term disability is undeniable. Statistically, one out of three people die prematurely, and *the chance of a long-term disability is even greater.*

How much income replacement protection is needed? To start with, most regular expenses would continue, regardless of the fact that the wage earner may be confined to bed. Figure out which expenses would be suspended or reduced. Daily transportation and lunches are clearly items you can eliminate, as are taxes on the wage earner's salary (which is now nonexistent). What else comes to mind? Jot them down. Beyond the day-to-day costs of living, what is going to happen to other parts of your family financial plan? Insurance premiums must be paid unless your policy contains a provision that in the event of disability premiums will be waived, and programmed investments, savings, and other elements of the basic financial structure could collapse or be seriously disrupted.

How long would earned income continue to flow despite the disability? If you are a business owner, income might continue indefinitely. But if yours is a proprietary shop or if you are a professional or a commissioned salesperson, an immediate stoppage of income is all too likely. As a corporate executive, on the other hand, you may know that your salary will flow for an extended period of time. The variances are great.

Before you decide on how much income replacement protection you need, weigh the Social Security factor. For example, if you are not yet 65 and fully insured under Social Security, and if you have a medically determinable physical or mental impairment that can be expected to result in death or that can be expected to last for a continuous period of not less than twelve months, you are entitled to the same monthly payments you would receive had you reached age 65 and retired. There is a waiting period of five successive months, but the benefits are retroactive to the first month of disability. There are also additional cash benefits if you have a wife age 62 or over, or a wife of any age if caring for a child 18 or younger. Reduced benefits are available if not fully insured and there are other technical details involved, but the point is that Social Security may be the source of some meaningful benefits. They must be considered before any precise action on disability protection is taken.

The remaining areas of income protection embrace the broad fields of casualty, accident, health, and hospitalization. These are involved subjects. You should discuss them with insurance agents who are specialists in those fields.

CANDIDATES FOR ACTION

- ☐ Term insurance
- ☐ Level term
- ☐ Renewable term
- ☐ Convertible term
- ☐ Reducing term

- ☐ Ordinary life
- ☐ Borrowing cash values from existing ordinary policies
- ☐ Level-pay life
- ☐ Limited-pay life
- ☐ Single-pay life
- ☐ Endowment
- ☐ Family plan
- ☐ Split-dollar
  - ☐ Family ☐ Business
- ☐ Variable life
- ☐ Increasing variable life
- ☐ Adjustable life
- ☐ Gifts of life insurance
- ☐ Life insurance trust
- ☐ Review of existing policies
- ☐ Check settlement options and will
- ☐ Disability insurance

7

Gifts That Gladden the Giver

For a number of reasons you may find gift-giving appealing. The emotional reasons are obvious. Making gifts to members of your immediate family, while you are still around to be thanked and appreciated, is rewarding in itself. When a gift also serves to reduce current income or estate taxes, the reward is sweeter. It is also gratifying to know that your family will be better off with estate taxes reduced as the result of gift-giving. Gifts to charity or to favorite institutions such as your old school can be particularly gratifying. In some cases attendant publicity can be an important plus for your business or profession. Giving, properly handled, can help to ease the problem of disposing of assets that represent large capital gains tax liabilities.

Taxes and gift-giving

The *Tax Reform Act of 1976* severely reduced some of the popular tax advantages of gift-giving. But it did not take away *all* the advantages. Because the benefits have been rather sharply reduced, it is all the more important to know all you can about the remaining benefits to the giver as well as to the receiver.

Annual Exclusions

Until the *Tax Reform Act of 1976* was enacted, you had two types of giving that went untaxed. One was the *lifetime exemption,* which is now a thing of the past. Once in your lifetime you were permitted to give away a total of $30,000 free of gift tax. You didn't have to give it away in a single gift or to a single individual. All in all you could give away that much tax-free, or a married couple could give away $60,000. Too bad, but it is no more.

The other tax-free giving permitted was–and remains–*the annual exclusion.* As big as the lifetime exemption may have seemed, the annual exclusion is, or can be, a lot bigger. You are entitled to give as much as $3,000 a year, each year, to each of as many people as you please. You and your spouse, if in agreement, may give away $6,000 each year to each of as many people as you please. If you have ten children and your children each have ten children, you and your mate could give $6,000 to each child and to each grandchild on an annual basis, year after year. And you would have no gift tax liability.

And that isn't all. As you will soon see, gift-giving has become a bit involved. In a lot of cases, what you save in taxes on one end you lose at the other end, but not with the annual exclusion. The "other end" is what must be paid in taxes when your *taxable estate* has been determined. The full value of some of your gifts get added back to the taxable estate value, but not those gifts permitted under the annual exclusion. They are not classified as *taxable gifts,* which is extremely important.

If you have a relatively to substantially large estate and if you are more eager to have it pass to those you love instead of going to nameless, faceless tax collectors, pay a lot of attention to the annual exclusion. It is one of the best escape hatches you have. You can adopt annual gift programs for the benefit of family members—even for faithful, valued employees—with very happy results.

Gift and estate taxes

One of the sharpest bites made by TRA '76 (*Tax Reform Act of 1976*) was the elimination of the difference in the tax on gifts made while living, and on assets in your taxable estate after death. Until then there was a whopping 25 percent difference. Every lawyer, accountant, tax advisor, or financial planner would counsel affluent clients to make substantial gifts and pay the gift taxes, in order to reduce the oppressive estate tax. The saving meant a lot to survivors.

TRA '76 made gift and estate taxes identical. Furthermore, the Act said that all taxable gifts made after January 1, 1977 had to be added back to the taxable estate and taxed. Any *taxes* already paid for the gifts may be deducted, but every penny of the taxable gifts is added to the value of your taxable estate. The fact that the money or property went out of your hands and control long ago makes no difference.

There is more. As is true of your federal income taxes, gift taxes are on a sliding scale, but IRS plays "catch-up" with you. The scale runs from a low of 18 percent to a high of 70 percent. You might start making some modest taxable gifts this year, paying at the low end of the scale. But if, for example, you later make a six-figure gift, the tax is based on adding up all the taxable gifts you have given, plus the new one, and the total determines the tax you pay. Sure, you get credit for whatever taxes you paid previously on the included gifts, but you cannot escape the arithmetic that pegs the point on the scale for the size of the tax. It is cumulative.

Unified tax credits

It is easy to misunderstand many things about the tax laws. When the 1976 *Tax Reform Act* killed the $30,000 annual exemption, it also killed a $60,000 exemption every estate had been entitled to until that time. In its place it created *unified tax credits.* The credit started at $30,000 in 1977, climbed gradually to a maximum of $47,000 in 1981. At first glance this change struck a number of people as a costly come-down. But just the opposite, it is a more generous measure than the $60,000 exemption. The key to understanding the former exemption is that $60,000 of the *assets* of an estate would not be taxed; but the unified tax credit reduces the *tax* to be paid, not the *amount* to be taxed. To fully appreciate this point, look at Table 2. As you can see, an estate big enough to claim the top tax credit of $47,000, in 1981 and thereafter, is immensely better off than if the old $60,000 exemption had remained on the books—$115,625 better off.

Table 2. The unified tax credit

Unified Tax Credit		Equal to dollar amount that is free of tax
1977	$30,000	$120,667
1978	34,000	134,000
1979	38,000	147,333
1980	42,500	161,563
1981	47,000	175,625

The unified tax credits apply to gifts and to estate taxes, but not twice. If you give away, in taxable gifts, $175,625 worth of assets in your lifetime, you pay no gift taxes thanks to the $47,000 credit. However, not a penny of that credit remains to be applied to your taxable estate. If you take advantage of half of the credit, your estate has half the remaining credit available, but no more.

TRA '76 further obstructed your giving gifts with the hope of leaving more money for the family after death. While past taxes that were paid on taxable gifts may be subtracted from the net estate tax, there is one exception. If any taxable gifts are made within three years prior to death, *both* the value of the gifts *and* the taxes that were paid are added back to the gross value of the estate. The old law also regarded gifts made within that three-year period as gifts made in contemplation of death, but there were allowable exceptions. No longer. The three-year rule is flat and noncontestable.

For people of wealth, therefore, many of the estate tax reduction techniques of the past are gone. On the other hand, people of more moderate circumstances had their situations improved.

Marital deductions

Earlier tax laws provided a marital deduction; in essence, it said that half of all the property a married couple owned could be passed to the other without tax. The new law says that the marital deduction may be as much as $250,000 or half the assets, whichever is *greater*. "Greater" is a splendid word. Combine the increased marital deduction and the new unified tax credit, and many families have no estate tax problems at all. You can die with a taxable estate (what is left after taxes and final debts have been subtracted) of $400,000. If you had elected to take the maximum marital deduction of $250,000, the remainder would be $150,000. Your estate tax would amount to $38,800. A unified tax credit of $47,000 means the estate pays no tax at all. This figuring assumes, of course, that you did not use up the tax credit on taxable gifts while living.

It is not always good to take advantage of the $250,000 maximum marital deduction. It is vital that you look ahead. Take the classic case of the successful husband.

EXAMPLE: At his death everything, except the man himself, looks fine. Of the couple's property, $250,000 goes to his widow tax-free. The remaining $150,000 also escapes tax, probably passed along in a trust that provides income to her as long as she lives and then becomes the property of the children. (You will read about this popular type of trust in detail when you come to Chapter 8). Everything seems to be in the best possible order.

But what happens when she dies?

For the sake of simplicity let's say that she still has the $250,000 and that the $150,000 in the trust has remained intact. When she goes, there is no marital deduction. The entire $250,000 is now subject to tax. The net tax amounts to $23,800: $70,800 less the $47,000 unified tax credit.

Now the question is, what would have happened if our man had not used the maximum deduction but had left half of his estate ($200,000) to his wife with the balance going into the trust? Under those circumstances there would have been a $7,800 tax on his estate since he left an extra $50,000 that did not get the marital deduction tax protection and that occasioned a tax exceeding the credit. Her estate, too, would have been taxed an identical sum. The combined estate taxes would have amounted to $15,600, instead of $23,800. The children would have had an extra $8,200.

As a rule of thumb, you will generally find that you get the lowest combined estate taxes if you divide the estate into equal amounts. Any property the wife owns, added to her inheritance, may put her taxable estate at a level that could make it wise to make no use of the marital deduction.

And, speaking of marital deductions, there is also a *marital gift tax deduction*. A man or wife may make a tax-free gift to the other of as much as $100,000. The next $100,000 is fully taxed, and all thereafter is subject to *half* the regular rates. Again, what you make on the apples you lose on the oranges. Any part of the marital gift tax deduction used comes off the estate tax marital deduction.

Life insurance as a gift

In Chapter 5, "Insurance," you saw that existing or new life insurance policies, even group policies, may be given away to beneficiaries or to a life insurance trust. Handled properly, this transfer removes the life insurance proceeds from your estate. Because life insurance proceeds can be such a significant part of your estate, it pays to examine four major reasons why it can pay to give your life insurance policies away.

1. *Although many life insurance gifts do not have values exceeding the $3,000 annual exclusion and thus are not free from gift tax, others create a gift tax liability. The value on which the gift tax is based is not the amount of coverage involved. The gift value is the cost of the policy, and, if it is an existing policy, whatever cash values have accumulated. The gift value, therefore, is generally so much smaller than the face value of the policy, the gift tax becomes a relatively minor consideration.* Just about any other gift of substance would incur a tax based on its full value.
2. *When you give away a life insurance policy, as opposed to many other properties of value, you are not sacrificing income or potential gains.*
3. *Were you to give away real estate or securities, the recipient's cost base would be your cost plus any gift tax you paid. If the recipient eventually sells the property at a loss, however, the cost base becomes the property's fair market value as of the time the gift was made. Not so with life insurance. The cost base is the replacement cost of the policy at the time of the gift, and the recipient-beneficiary receives the insurance proceeds free of income tax.*
4. *Unlike most other items of value that you might give, the recipients are not likely to cash in any insurance policy and dissipate the proceeds.*

Giving without hurting (too much)

The gift of a policy that you have held for a long time and that has large cash values presents two serious problems. First of all, the cash values may be large enough to make the gift tax a considerable problem. The second factor is that you may be reluctant to make the gift because you cut yourself off from the opportunity to borrow those cash values. The interest rates are usually appetizingly low. There is no way that permits you to have any control over the cash value if the gift is to produce the desired tax benefits. You must rid yourself of all incidents of ownership. Control over the cash values is a vital incident of ownership.

This two-fold problem can be dealt with in any of three ways.

1. *You can take your cash values, cancel the policy, and make a gift of a new one with the same face value.*
2. *You can borrow the cash values, give away the policy, and then make annual gifts to the recipient to cover the cost of the premiums and the interest on the loan. If the cash value is sufficient, you may also use it to reduce the loan on a progressive basis.*
3. *You can borrow the cash values and turn the cash over to the recipient in the form of a noninterest-bearing demand loan,* with the suggestion that the money be invested in a portfolio of income-producing securities. The dividend could be used for premiums, interest payments, and the reduction of the cash value loan.*

Cutting the strings

One element of life insurance gifts has to be watched with care. The annual exclusion is a privilege that applies only to gifts of *present interest.* An outright gift with no strings attached creates no problems. If, on the other hand, a stipulation restricts the recipient's right to cash in the policy or to borrow against the cash values, the gift then becomes a gift of *future interest.* The annual exclusion does not apply, and the gift becomes taxable.

*The tax court in the case of *IRS vs. Lester Crown* [67 TC No. 88, 1977] ruled that intra-family noninterest loans do not give rise to gift tax liability. This decision may be challenged and overthrown, but it has not been at the time of this writing.

Giving your child an insurance policy

Minors may be the recipients of life insurance policies if handled under the *Uniform Gifts to Minors Act.* Be certain that you do not have yourself named as trustee or custodian. Were you to die while serving as trustee or custodian, the insurance proceeds end up in your estate, which is what you wish to avoid.

The gift of an insurance policy to a minor constitutes a gift of future interest, unless (1) the trustee or custodian is given explicit rights to use any cash values or the interest produced by cash values for the benefit of the minor until the child reaches age 21; and (2), at that age, any unspent sums become available to him or her.

Giving a minor child ownership of an ordinary life insurance policy on your life can be unusually interesting. Insofar as an ordinary life policy accumulates cash values over the years, the proceeds eventually go to your child who, by that time, will probably be an adult. The cash values, under those circumstances, are not included in your taxable estate, nor does your child have any tax liability.

The combination gift. When the insurance is first given, the new policy has no value and no gift tax problem. It could incur a gift tax, however, if you paid the premiums over the years. Your child can become the premium payer if you make a combination gift. At the time the insurance is given, you could also make a gift of mutual fund shares sufficient to produce the amount of income necessary to meet the premium payments. If the income is insufficient, the custodian has the right to liquidate shares as needed. One of the easier ways to plan this combination gift is to make the fund gift a withdrawal plan, with the fund instructed to send the exact amount of the premiums directly to the insurance company on the due dates.

Short-term trusts: A gift of income

One of the most useful tools available to you, for a variety of purposes, is the *short-term trust.* Although it is sometimes called the reversionary trust or the Clifford trust, a more colorful title for it might be "borrow my money-making machine." It is capable of doing two important jobs. First of all, it is a means of shifting tax liabilities from you, if you are in a fairly high tax bracket, to the trust itself or to someone in a relatively low tax bracket. In many cases the trust, or the individual you make the trust for, is not required to pay any tax at all. The second of this trust's important functions is that when you put it to work (in ways you will read about shortly), it enables you to give away income to someone you have been helping, or want to help, at greatly reduced cost.

Very briefly, this is what is involved. You have an asset that produces little or no income, or income you can afford to do without for at least ten years and a day. If you do not have such an asset, if you do not have the cash to make a suitable

I'll lend you my money-making machine.

investment, or if you want only to create a trust to accumulate income for future use, you can manage to put aside an appropriate sum of money each year for ten years. In one way or another, you must be in a position to provide the basic ingredient that makes the short-term trust work—an income-producing asset or a "money-making machine." If the asset you put into the trust produces little or no income but if you wish to give the beneficiary either a flow of income now or accumulated income later, then the trustee may have to sell the asset and use the proceeds to buy a suitable, income-producing investment. The ten-year factor is another must. The Internal Revenue says that a short-term trust must last for more than ten years or for the life of the beneficiary. Ten years and a day is frequently designated in these trusts.

A lawyer prepares the trust document, providing that the recipient is to receive the income produced by your asset for the full term of the trust. This payment can be on a monthly, quarterly, semi-annual, or annual basis. In an *accumulation trust,* the beneficiary does not receive the income as it becomes available. Instead, the income accumulates for later use. In either case, when the trust comes to an end after the specified number of years, or when the beneficiary dies, all the assets in the trust come back to you. That is why this arrangement is sometimes called a *reversionary trust.*

Who should and who should not make use of this type of trust? You may not use it if its only purpose is to save taxes; the IRS would reject it. You make it serve a sound economic purpose, such as aiding someone in the family, supporting the costs of higher education, and so on. The income may not be used to pay normal support costs of a minor child, for example, if you are the parent and legally required to provide such support. The short-term trust is most useful to you if you are enjoying good earned income. It is also useful if your investments are producing interest or dividend income that you do not need now to maintain your lifestyle. You reason, however, that when you eventually retire you will require that additional income to supplement Social Security, a pension plan, or whatever else you may have. This sort of trust is *not* for you if you think that, because of your age or health, you might need this income from your savings or investments in less than ten years. The trust is irrevocable. You cannot start it today and change your mind next week, next month, or next year. If must run its full course before the asset comes back to you for your own use. If its irrevocability constitutes a problem, avoid it.

As the maker of the trust, you may give yourself a good deal of control by appointing yourself as the trustee, or you and your spouse may serve as co-trustees. As trustee you may manage the investment as you see fit. You may sell or reinvest the assets, as well as collect rents, interest, or dividends. However, you are legally responsible to act in the best interests of the beneficiary. For instance, since the purpose of the trust is to provide income for the beneficiary, you may not sell an income-producing asset and replace it with a new investment that holds forth great promise of profit but pays little or no income. That sort of control is self-serving and contrary to the interests of the beneficiary. You could be successfully sued. As trustee you may not change the beneficiary or any of the beneficiary's rights. You are barred from borrowing against the assets in the trust unless you put up adequate security and pay realistic interest.

Taxes and the trust

The law recognizes a trust as a person. So, since the trust may receive and accumulate income, it is treated as a tax-payer. The trust is allowed an annual deduction of $100 instead of a personal exemption, and it is further allowed a $100 exclusion for dividends received from domestic corporations.

The short-term trust does not save estate taxes, since you are not permanently removing any property from your estate. Yet it often incurs a gift tax, which is based not on the actual value of the property but on the "income value." The *income value* is arrived at by consulting the Internal Revenue Service gift valuation table (Table 3). This table specifies what percentage of the funding asset's value is to be considered a gift. The percentages are based on the number of years involved. A ten-year trust, for instance, is valued at 44.1605 percent of the value of the asset. Therefore, if a couple wants to fund a trust in a manner that would not exceed the $6,000-a-year limit of their combined annual exclusion, they may put as much as $13,500 of assets into the trust without a gift tax (44.1605% of $13,500 = $5,962).

Table 3. IRS Gift Valuations:
Short-term trusts for 10 to 20 years

Number of Years in Trust	Value of Gift (%)
10	44.1605
11	47.3212
12	50.3031
13	53.1161
14	55.7699
15	58.2735
16	60.6354
17	62.8636
18	64.9656
19	66.9487
20	68.8195

One final observation. Depending on the nature of the asset you put into a trust, you *might* receive some realized capital gains during the trust's life. These can be handled in either of two ways: (1) You have to report and pay taxes on those gains in the year or years received; or (2), if the trust is written accordingly, the gains may be treated as income payable to the beneficiary.

Some typical cases

To put some flesh and bones on this technique, here are some typical applications of short-term trusts at work.

Helping Mother. *John Taylor is 45 years old, has a good job, and has managed to put some money aside for the future. His wife's mother is an 82-year-old widow living on a very limited income. She gets $160 a month from Social Security and $145 a month from the proceeds of a life insurance policy on her late husband. She lives in a fully paid small house. Mary and John have been helping her by* *sending a check each month for $200. John is in the 39-percent tax bracket.*

In order to write those checks, amounting to $2,400 a year, John must earn almost $3,500 before taxes. So John has a lawyer prepare a short-term trust. Into it he puts a $40,000 asset earning 6-percent income. The trust pays Mary's mother $200 a month, and she becomes the taxpayer. But, since she was receiving the $200 check each month before he adopted the trust, her minimal tax obligations remain the same while Mary and John save $1,560 a year—a total savings of $15,600 for the life of the trust. In this case, as in any short-term trust that is to operate as long as the income beneficiary lives, the manner of determining the income value is handled differently. Instead of the value being based on the specific number of years the trust is to exist, it is based on the beneficiary's life expectancy. Here is a brief sample of the IRS life expectancy table your lawyer or accountant will use to see what the value amounts to:

Age	Gift Value
70	41.294%
75	34.194
80	27.098
85	21.070
90	15.922

In the case of the trust for the Taylor's mother, therefore, the income value of the asset in the trust amounts to approximately $11,000 ($40,000 × 27.098% = $10,839.20).

A Boost for a Young Couple. *Jerry, son of Paul and Paula Perceptive, is just about to start his career as a physician. He has finished his internship at the hospital and opened his own office. Jerry married Peggy while still in medical school, and in a few months they are going to have their first child.*

Paul and Paula both feel that the young couple need far more life insurance than they can afford. At the same time, Dad prefers not to obligate himself to the routine of making regular premium payments over a period of years. Being in a 50-percent tax bracket, whatever he spends costs him double. So a short-term trust is used. As step one, Paul buys a $100,000 term policy on his son's life and names Peggy, the expecting mother, as owner and beneficiary. As step two, Paul, with his lawyer's help, creates a short-term trust. To *fund the trust, Paul invests $13,500 in an income-oriented mutual fund. At the time of the investment it has a 6-percent yield. The trust is instructed to pay the annual premiums on the insurance policy.*

Add up the advantages. Paul accomplishes what he wants by giving the young people the added protection he knows they should have. He pays out $700 for the first year's premium and buys $13,500 worth of fund shares to go into the trust, knowing he'll get them back. He makes a gift of the income which, after taxes, would have netted him only 3 percent a year if he used it for his own benefit. Dr. Jerry, the recipient of these benefits, has only the income tax to pay. At his low income level, the tax is probably less than $200 a year. Dad's ten-year tax saving is about $2,000. By the time the trust terminates, everyone anticipates that young Dr. Jerry will be able to pay his own premiums. And, by the way, the property that funds the trust does not have sufficient income value to involve any gift tax, so it qualifies for the annual exclusion.

If Paul does not choose to spend the $700 for the first-year insurance premium, he can create the trust and wait one year until the trust has the income needed to initiate the policy.

Our Boy's Going to College. *Hank and Hilda Mason have been married six years. They have a 3-year-old son, Tommy, and they are determined that their boy is going to go to the best college money will buy. They take time out to inquire as to how much money it takes to buy four years of higher education these days. The answer, they learn, is about $25,000 covering tuition, room, and food alone. They could put aside about $1,000 a year for the next 15 years, for interest or dividends could make up the difference. On the other hand, they will have to pay taxes on whatever their set-aside dollars earn; and, since college costs have been rising faster than most other costs, who can guess what four years of college may cost fifteen years ahead? No one can say for sure, but most people are willing to guess that the costs will probably be frighteningly higher than today's frighteningly high costs. The answer seems to be to put aside at least $1,000 a year, and where it may earn growing income and where whatever it may earn has its growth accelerated by compounding. Finally, the Masons should take steps to shield the income from being diluted by needless taxation. As the years go by, Hank's income will probably be going up, and so will his tax rate.*

The answer, of course, is a short-term accumulation trust. Hank and Hilda could, as one way of funding this trust, make annual investments in one or more stocks or a mutual fund. Of particular appeal to the Masons is the knowledge that the mutual fund shares accumulated will revert to them when the trust expires. In time, those shares will be used as a source of extra income when Hank retires.

This trust is the taxpayer, but, with the annual deduction and exemption, it pays no income taxes for a long time. If and when it does reach that point, the taxes are minimal. At the time the trust starts paying out money to cover college costs, Tommy becomes the taxpayer. The IRS has a formula for determining what taxes he will pay, giving full credit to those already paid by the trust. If the boy has no other income, he will of course be at the low end of the tax bracket totem pole.

The Masons, in their determination to give their boy the advantages of higher education, could also guard against the possibility of Hank's dying before completing the investment program. The investment could be made in a mutual fund contractual plan that includes low-cost group life insurance. The insurance feature, which is optional, guarantees that if Hank dies before the planned investments have been completed, the dollars needed to carry on with the program will be provided. The goal of having a sum of money that will help pay the cost of Tommy's college is protected.

One precaution: Since the costs of college educations are not considered child support items, all the income accumulated in the trust and paid to the college **may become taxable to Dad** *if he doesn't handle the bills properly. If Dad signs any form that says he will be responsible for tuition and/or other payments, or even if he merely accepts bills from the college and forwards those bills to the trustee—or even pays them as trustee—he is in tax trouble. He should return the bills, state in writing that he is not responsible for the payments, and tell the college how the bills should be addressed.*

Other uses

Of the innumerable uses for the short-term trust, these three examples indicate the various directions they may take. In all instances the services of an attorney are needed to write the trust instrument.

Give your child future wealth. Have a short-term trust created for your youngster: the younger the child, the better; the more time involved, the better. You put into the trust an asset capable of earning $1,000 a year. Unless the child has other income, this income is all tax-tree. Each year you, as trustee, turn the income over to your sister Helen whom you appoint as custodian. Helen uses the annual income to buy, in your child's name under the *Uniform Gifts to Minors Act,* an annual premium-deferred annuity. At the end of the short-term trust, your assets come back to you. The deferred annuity, which might have been paying 8 percent or better tax-deferred earnings, is now worth $16,000 or better, and it keeps compounding tax-sheltered income until your son or daughter needs or wants the payouts to start. Left until age 50 or better, this source of future income for your child can be well over $100,000. What did it cost you? You gave up $1,000 in income each year for ten years, a total of $10,000. Subtract from that total whatever your top tax bracket would have required you to pay out in federal and state taxes. The remainder is what it cost you to give your young one a handsome base for future income: For $5,000 or $6,000, you made a six-figure gift.

If a trust is not appropriate. You just read how Hank and Hilda Mason adopted a short-term trust to accumulate money for a college education. They adopted it because it not only offered a solution to their problem, but it also provided a base for future retirement income for themselves. In other cases, however, such a trust might not be advisable. Maybe you have no need for an extra source of future income. Perhaps you prefer to accumulate for future college costs in a way that will not depend on the income that can be produced but that will make planned use of the asset itself. Also, some people—parents, grandparents, uncles, or aunts—might be able to put aside enough assets to produce income for financing college and then to have the assets turn over to your child or children as a financial base for their careers. In such cases a reversionary trust would be inappropriate.

The simple way to handle either of these situations is to make a single investment or a single series of investments registered in the name of the child under the *Uniform Gifts to Minors Act,* with an adult serving as custodian. A custodianship is very much like a trust, but it is much simpler. No trust agreement or any other type of document is used. You simply register any shares purchased as, *"Hank Mason, as Custodian for Tom Mason, a minor under the Uniform Gifts to Minors Act."* That is all. No report or accounting is required. But this type of custodianship is totally inflexible. It cannot be revoked.

When your child becomes an adult, which may be at age 18 or 21, depending on state law, the property must be turned over to him or her. The variance in state laws is still another reason why it is vital that you consult with your attorney or CPA.

As custodian you have very broad powers. You can manage the assets in the account, making whatever changes you deem appropriate, provided that you act in the best interests of the minor. Interest and dividend payments may be put into a savings account, stocks or bonds, reinvested, or spent for the support of the child. It is a parent's obligation to support a child, however, so it is generally safe not to use any cash flow from the investment to pay for things that come under the heading of support (paying for a college education, as mentioned earlier, is not considered a "support" item). In any event, if you use the assets for support, you have to include that part of the income in your own tax return.

Although any competent adult may serve as custodian, it is safer if you, as the donor of the assets, do not list yourself. If you die before the custodianship ends, the assets are included in your estate. You can name your spouse or any other adult, and it is a good precaution to write a simple, witnessed letter naming a successor custodian just in case the original custodian dies or is otherwise unable to function. Without such a letter, the state appoints a successor—a procedure that can be complicated and time-consuming.

Giving Appreciated Securities. The *Uniform Gifts to Minors Act* can be used to dispose of appreciated securities in a way that eliminates or sharply reduces the capital gains tax liability.

EXAMPLE: The Masons own some securities that have grown in *value from $2,000 to $6,000. Were they to sell, the Masons would have to pay a capital gains tax, as follows: 60 percent of the gain ($2,400) is excluded, leaving $1,600, which is included with their ordinary income. Hank's top bracket is 43% (as a married individual, filing a joint return on income exceeding $35,200 but less than $45,800), so the tax amounts to $688. Instead of selling, Hank and Hilda give the stock to Tommy under the Act, naming Tommy's uncle, Josephus, as custodian. Josephus, acting in the interests of his nephew, sells the security, which appears to have a dim future. He invests the proceeds in shares of a mutual fund. Now Tommy is the taxpayer, and his cost base is the same as his Dad's. He has a $4,000 profit. He* *too, of course, may exclude 60 percent of the gain and is subject to tax, at his ordinary income rate, on the remaining $1,600. But Tommy has the same $1,000 exemption everyone else is entitled to, and that exemption reduces the $1,600 of income to the taxable sum of $600 at the minimum tax rate of 14%—$224 compared with Hank's $688.*

For this illustration a $6,000 gift was used because it comes within the Masons' annual exclusion and eliminates any gift tax. If the Masons happened to have considerably more than $6,000 in highly appreciated stock, real estate, or anything else, and if they liked this way of transferring it on a tax-free basis, they could make such gifts to their boy annually. The gift would lose its force only at the time when Tommy has a good deal of other income.

Such gifts should be made under the *Uniform Gifts to Minors Act* with your spouse named as custodian. All states permit the gift of securities to be made under the Act. Almost all states accept the fact that gifts of life insurance may be made in the same way.

Charitable gifts

Of all tax favored forms of giving, none offers as many pluses as properly handled gifts to charity. What makes them so desirable is the manner in which they offer solutions to two major problems: how to permanently remove or greatly reduce assets from your final estate, and how to deal with highly appreciated assets. The second problem can be monumental if you need more income and if your appreciated asset produces little or no income. If you sell it, you give up a substantial part of your gain in taxes. If you do not sell it, you not only have unsatisfactory yield, but you are also in the dangerous position of having an important percentage of your capital linked to the future welfare of one company or of one piece of real estate. Amazingly the answer, in many cases, may be simply to give the asset away. A gift to a charity, college, university, hospital, religious institution, an organization engaged in medical or scientific research, and so on, furnishes tax benefits (under Section 170 (C) of the Internal Revenue Code), provided that the institution chosen is recognized by

IRS. The government subsidizes such organizations by treating contributions to them in a tax-favored manner. Just to demonstrate the breadth of the possibilities, here is a rather dramatic illustration.

EXAMPLE: Our couple is Ben and Bertha Needer. Ben has been in poor health and has just retired at age 50.

The Needers never managed to save money. Their only income is $290 a month disability from Social Security. They live in a barn of a house, which they have owned for more than forty years. And you probably are wondering how people in such circumstances could possibly be interested in taxes, for surely they will have none to pay. You are right. But just follow what the favorable tax treatment made available by a charitable remainder trust can do for them.

When the Needers bought their home almost three decades ago, they paid $11,000 for it. The old place had gotten a bit the worse for wear. The neighborhood, fortunately, had not; it is a good neighborhood. Current value of the home, sitting on a third of an acre of good residential real estate, is an amazing $85,000.

As the scene opens, a real estate man is at the house urging Ben and Bertha to sell. If they do sell, they will have a capital gain of $74,000: 60 percent of the gain is excluded, leaving $29,600 on which they will be required to pay income tax. As a married couple filing jointly, they must pay $5,457. The net amount they will realize from the sale is $79,543. If they put that money to work at 6 percent interest, they will have income of $4,773 a year; $398 a month. That is a long step forward, even though they will probably have to spend about $2,000 a year on apartment rental.

jointly, they must pay $5,457. The net amount they will realize from the sale is $79,543. If they put that money to work at 6 percent interest, they will have income of $4,773 a year; $398 a month. That is a long step forward, even though they will probably have to spend about $2,000 a year on apartment rental.

jointly, they must pay $5,457. The net amount they will realize from the sale is $79,543. If they put that money to work at 6 percent interest, they will have income of $4,773 a year; $398 a month. That is a long step forward, even though they will probably have to spend about $2,000 a year on apartment rental.

They are in a very high tax bracket. They decide to give their highly appreciated home to charity. They too will enjoy inflation fighting income for as long as either of them lives, and they will have still another substantial benefit.

The IRS permits the Gottits to deduct up to 30 percent of all their other taxable income if the gift is big enough to equal that amount. If the amount they are allowed to deduct is greater than 30 percent of their other income, they may take like deductions each year, for as many as five additional years, until the full *remainder interest* of the gift has been deducted. Remainder interest, a term used by the IRS, is arrived at through the application of a formula that takes into consideration the dollar value of the income the beneficiaries are likely to receive, based on their ages and sexes. This is subtracted from the current market value of the gift and the balance constitutes the total tax deduction that may be taken.

The examples of the Needers and the Gottits dealt with gifts of their homes, but your charitable gift may be any asset. You may donate stocks, investment real estate, jewelry, an art collection—anything of genuine value. If you donate cash, and you certainly may, the deduction can be as much as 50 percent of your taxable income because no capital gains are involved.

It is clear that this type of giving can be of great value to you if you have highly appreciated assets which you hesitate to sell because of the capital gains tax liability. It is an exciting, economical way of taking an appreciated asset now earning little or no income and moving it to a position where it will earn generous income you cannot outlive.

The charitable remainder trust

The ways of giving to yourself when giving to charity described above are made possible by your employing a *charitable remainder trust.* At the heart of the trust is a gift to a charity recognized by IRS as qualifying under Section 170(c) of the Internal Revenue Code. Most big charities, universities, and hospitals—and countless small ones—are on that approved list.

The gift must be irrevocable. You surrender all rights to

the asset with two exceptions. First, you retain the right to receive income for the rest of your life, or for the duration of the lives of as many people as you choose, provided that each income beneficiary is alive at the time the trust becomes effective. The second right you keep is that you are privileged to change the designation of the charity that is to be the ultimate owner of the asset, provided that the substitute charity also qualifies under 170(c).

Here is what happens

You have a stock you bought for $20,000 with a current value of $200,000. You, or your lawyer or financial planner, advise the Help Your Brother or Sister Charity Foundation that you intend to donate the stock to them through a charitable remainder trust. A representative of the HYBOSCF meets with you and your advisor, and you all agree on the terms of the trust. You are given the choice of electing the form of charitable remainder trust you want: an *annuity trust* or a *unitrust.* The big difference is that the annuity trust will give you monthly payments of a *fixed sum of money,* and the unitrust will make *varying monthly payments.*

The stock you donate will be sold. You don't sell it. The charity sells it, and, because it is a bona fide 170(c) organization, it is not taxed on the capital gain. Because of the absence of any tax resulting from the sale, your income is based on the full current value of the stock. The charity invests the money. If you choose an annuity trust your monthly checks will be for an unchanging percentage of the value of the stock you donated on the day you completed the donation. If you selected the unitrust, your monthly checks will be for an unchanging percentage of the *changing value* of the investment made with the proceeds realized from the sale of the donated stock. On a specific date each year, or at pre-agreed more frequent intervals, the investment will be evaluated and your fixed percentage of income will be adjusted accordingly. For example, your first payment will be 8 percent of $200,000 (8 percent is just used for example, it could be more or less), which amounts to $16,000 a year, or $1,333.33 a month. The next evaluation might find the value at $190.000. In that case the monthly checks will be $1,266.66. The investment's value might then go to $220,000, and that would give you monthly checks of $1,466.66.

Your next choice concerns who is to receive the income. You can be the sole recipient, or it can be you and your spouse, or you may specify that your children and any grandchildren presently alive are to be subsequent income beneficiaries after you and your spouse are deceased. You may specify that the income is to be paid out for no less than 20 years even if none of the named income recipients are still alive, with the further provision that at the end of the 20-year term the income payments will continue to go to a named beneficiary, or beneficiaries, for as long as they live.

Understandably, the more lives involved the lower the monthly payments. One of the fundamental factors used when determining what the monthly payouts will be is the expectation of how long the youngest beneficiary may live. The 20-year provision is also going to reduce the amount paid out. Top monthly benefits go to a single life recipient and the older he or she is the bigger the payout.

A trustee is appointed to see to it that the terms of the trust are carried out properly. You may make *suggestions* regarding the investment of the money realized from the sale of the asset you donated, but the trustee is boss. Your suggestions may or may not be followed, for the interests of the charity have to be considered. After all, the charity is the ultimate owner of your donation. In most cases, however, your choices are likely to be honored. For example, you elected a unitrust because you want the chance to offset inflation with increasing income. At one time you may be convinced that an investment in a group of securities selected for high income will be best for you. At a later date you may conclude that the time has come to shift to common stocks with strong growth potential, so you suggest to the trustee that it might be a good idea to make the transfer. Your income is based on a fixed percentage of the ever-changing value of the total investment. The greater the growth, via high income that is reinvested, or via increasing values, the better for you and the better for the charity.

Unitrust. The income paid to you by a unitrust is based on a fixed percentage of whatever the changing market of the trust property happens to be on a specific date, or dates, each year. IRS requires that the percentage must be at least 5 percent. You may specify 7 or 8 percent, for example. The IRS has approved 11 percent in a few cases. If you ask for an unrealistic amount, the charity probably will reject your gift. The changing value of the property in the unitrust makes it a source of varying income and an appropriate method if you want the triple advantage of:

1. *a tax deduction in the year the gift is made, and for as many as 5 more years if justified by the size of the donation,*
2. *a reduction of estate taxes, and*
3. *a flow of checks that have the possibility of providing automatic cost-of-living increases.*

Annuity trust. If you choose to have unchanging income, then the annuity trust is the proper choice. The dollar amount of the income it pays never changes. This type of trust may be the right choice if: the income is intended to handle a series of unchanging payments, if you expect securities values to fall over a long period, or if you are emotionally better suited to dependably fixed income rather than to unpredictable income.

Giving appreciated property to a charity. *Mr. Otto Giver was an executive of a big corporation. After 41 years of service, he retired at age 66. Over the years he was in a stock accumulation plan, and he also received some company stock as bonuses from time to time. Today his stock is worth $180,000. His cost was $72,000, and the stock pays a 2-percent dividend ($3,600). The common stock is the only sizeable asset they own.*

Otto and his wife, Olga, have no children. Before retiring, Otto's salary was $45,000 a year. Today, they find they cannot live up to the standards they once enjoyed and have become accustomed to. From all sources, including Social Security, they have $2,330 a month. This amount does not constitute poverty, but it is a big drop from the $3,750 a month they had been getting, particularly in light of inflation.

With his lawyer's help, Otto creates a unitrust. He makes an irrevocable gift in trust of all his stock. The recipient is his old school, a nonprofit college. The trust contains these provisions:

1. *The trust is to sell the stock.*
2. *The proceeds of the sale, after normal brokerage commissions*

are deducted, are to be invested in shares of PDQ Mutual Fund Withdrawal Plan.

3. *The trust is to order that the plan send monthly checks to Otto as long as he lives and to Olga, if she outlives him, for as long as she lives.*
4. *Monthly payments for the first year are to be based on a withdrawal of 8 percent of the original investment.*
5. *At the end of each twelve-month period, the payments for the twelve months ahead are to be determined by recalculating an 8 percent withdrawal of the value of the shares at that date.*
6. *After both die, the trust is to end, and the property is to go to the college.*

The year the gift is made, Otto's taxable income is about $20,000. But, having made a gift of appreciated property with a current value of $180,000, he earns an additional deduction amounting to 30 percent of his taxable income.

The discounted value of the remainder interest in his donation is far in excess of 30 percent of his taxable income. As a result, he is taxed on $14,000 instead of $20,000, and it gives him the further great economy of putting him in a lower tax bracket.

The size of Otto's gift is so much greater than his income that he is also allowed to carry forward his charitable deduction privilege five more years. Altogether, therefore, he has substantial tax savings for a total of six years.

Otto and Olga now have $1,000 extra coming to them each month and fewer tax dollars going out. The threat contained in having their financial future hanging on the welfare of a single company is gone. Also gone is the worry about the big capital gain tax that had barred them from needed action. A significant part of the $180,000 was removed from Otto's taxable estate, reducing future estate taxes.

There are other tax-favored ways of giving to charity, but the charitable remainder trust offers the most substantial benefits.

Pooled income trusts

Another popular way to handle charitable contributions, a pooled income trust, is not too far apart from the charitable remainder trust in what it does for you and how it operates. As with the unitrust and the annuity trust, your charitable gift deduction for cash or unappreciated assets may be equal to 50 percent of your normal income tax or, for appreciated assets, 30 percent of your income tax. You also have the same right to take deductions for as much as five additional years, should the size of the donation justify the extension. But it has several major differences.

First, unlike the charitable remainder trust, the *pooled income trust* has a fund made up of the donations of thousands of individuals. The fund is managed by the charity or by a professional investment organization retained by the charity. You, as a donor, receive your prorated share of the income earned. You have a life income interest in the fund, or you and your spouse have life interests. Some charitable institutions limit the number of beneficiaries to two, while others permit you to name successor beneficiaries who continue to get income for as long as they live. Any beneficiaries named must be alive at the time you make the gift.

The pooled income fund differs also in how it is taxed. The income that you and other beneficiaries earn is taxed as ordinary income, whereas in a unitrust and an annuity trust your taxes may be part ordinary income, part capital gains, and part return of capital. (In charitable remainder trusts, you have a certain amount of leeway in specifying the percentage of income to be paid to you. If the actual interest or dividend income earned is insufficient to provide those payments, the balance is made up with realized profits or with some return of capital.) But with pooled income all your income is subject to ordinary income tax.

The third major difference is that, unless you favor a particular charity or nonprofit institution, you may shop around to find one with a pooled income fund investing its money in a way that fits your needs and ideas. Older people, for example, might prefer to draw their income from an investment in high-yielding bonds, caring more about steady generous income than they care about long-term growth of income.

Charitable gift annuity

This type of annuity offers you still another way of making a donation to an institution of your choice in a manner that provides lifelong income for one or two lives. Consisting of a contract between you and the institution, the annuity provides that, for a certain payment made by you, the institution promises to pay the annuity income for as long as you, or for as long as you or your spouse, shall live.

There are some sharp differences between this arrangement and the previous ones. To start with, this is a genuine annuity, and the amount you are paid is based to a great extent on your age or on the two ages. Age is irrelevant in a pooled income trust and it is only a minor consideration in the charitable remainder trusts. Second, while there may be some nontaxable return of capital in the charitable remainder trust and none at all in the pooled income trust, there is always a nontaxable return of capital portion in the charitable gift annuity. Third, the institution itself makes a guarantee, backed by all its assets and resources, that the income will continue for as long as you shall live. Although the risks are minor, the two other annuities offer no such guarantee. Although it is conceivable that, through bad management, the capital producing the income for donors to the charitable remainder trust and to the pooled income trust could be exhausted, if the capital did actually give out, then that would be that. The institution would have no obligation to use its other resources to take over. The final difference is that this annuity is the only one of the three where you might use appreciated property as your donation and be required to pay capital gains taxes. If the asset you donate is sold, you have the tax to pay, but it is spread out over your life expectancy, greatly reducing its impact.

You may also, using this approach, contract for a deferred annuity with a starting date of your own choosing. The income you eventually get will be based, in part, on the value of your original donation plus the tax-sheltered, compounded interest that accumulates before the annuity period starts. Not only does this interest increase your income materially, but it also gives you greater tax benefits.

Incidentally, the IRS regards the charitable gift annuity as part donation and part annuity purchase. The deductibility, therefore, is reduced.

Pause before giving a cash donation to a favorite institution

Your favorite hospital, where you had your appendix removed so painlessly some years ago, has a capital fund-raising drive to erect a new building. You decide to give $1,000. Before writing the check, it may pay to review any securities you are holding. You might find one with a current value of $1,000. You might have paid only $250 for that stock, and you may still have a lot of faith in the company. Give the stock to the hospital. You will get a tax deduction for a $1,000 donation. Then take the $1,000 of cash you were going to donate and replace the stock at the current price. You now have the same number of shares in the same company from which you expect great things. You also have a new cost base which, if you are right about the stock's future, will call for a much lighter capital gains tax when you sell.

Where to go?

These descriptions of the charitable remainder trusts, the pooled income trust, and the charitable gift annuity have sufficient depth to enable you to appreciate the potential benefits they offer and to evaluate their suitability (or lack of suitability) in your personal circumstances. While reading about these methods of helping a favorite charity, school, religious, medical, or educational facility, your own pet project may have come to mind.

But the paperwork involved in tailoring these methods to your needs and wants calls for a fair amount of technical knowledge. So not every charitable and nonprofit organization is prepared to handle donations of this type. The charitable remainder trust may or may not be a well-known device to the organization of your choice, but it is a form of charitable giving that can be applied to almost any recipient with the help of a knowledgeable lawyer. Certainly the pooled income trust is not to be found in any but very large institutions, and the charitable gift annuity is probably rarer still.

If you do not have a particular charity in mind but if you

still want to investigate or activate one of these ideas, you should approach an institution such as The Salvation Army. This and other sizeable organizations have well-staffed Living Gifts Branches with personnel steeped in the required know-how. Their professionalism in tailoring donations to the wishes of donors can be extremely helpful to you. The same is true of a number of big universities and hospitals. Any of them will be happy to work with you to your mutual advantage.

CANDIDATES FOR ACTION

- ☐ Annual exclusion gifts
- ☐ Gifts of life insurance
- ☐ Gifts of life insurance to minors
- ☐ Short-term trusts to:
  - ☐ take over help for a family member
  - ☐ give a boost to a young couple or son or daughter launching a career
  - ☐ prepare for future college costs
  - ☐ other thoughts
- ☐ Two-part program for child—short-term accumulation trust and annuity
- ☐ Gift of appreciated asset to minor child
  - ☐ Once
  - ☐ Annual program
- ☐ Combination gift to child—life insurance on self, linked to mutual fund withdrawal plan as premium payer
- ☐ Charitable remainder trust
- ☐ Pooled income fund
- ☐ Charitable gift annuity
- ☐ Donating appreciated stock instead of cash and replacing stock

8

Putting Your Trust in Trusts

Trusts are for the nonwealthy too

Earlier chapters of this book acquainted you, to some extent, with trusts. You know about the short-term (or reversionary) trust and about the charitable remainder trust. A more thorough examination of just what a trust is, where it came from, what it can and cannot do, can be rewarding. Few financial devices are more useful, so the better you know trusts the more you will be able to appreciate what one or more might be able to accomplish for you. All in all, trusts provide one of the strongest, most dependable, and most rigidly enforced means of dealing with property.

Despite the important advantages and safeguards trusts embrace, however, there are certain words that make a good many people uncomfortable. "Trusts" is one of them. When you speak to some people about using a trust, they draw back. For them the term creates visions of batteries of high-powered lawyers, bankers, courts, and big fees. A certain amount of tradition, in the minds of many, has put "trusts" and "estates" (another trigger word) in the exclusive province of multimillionaires. At one time, you seldom heard of anyone—other than people of great wealth—using a trust of any kind. That impression was widespread many years ago. It was not factual and most certainly is not the case today.

The origin of trusts

The interesting thing is that trusts originally came into being to solve a problem for people who had less wealth than anyone else. They go all the way back to the thirteenth century. At least there is no recorded history of any type of trust prior to that time. In the thirteenth century the very strict Order of Franciscan Friars in England forbade any individual or any group of individuals to own anything whatsoever. As you can appreciate, this requirement caused severe problems. The Friars were not salaried, but in the normal course of events numbers of them inherited property or were in possession of a certain amount of wealth at the time they joined the Order. The rules were so restrictive, however, that under no circumstances were they permitted to keep any possessions of any kind, nor could they exercise any control over any assets. The solution they arrived at was essentially a trust arrangement: a Friar who was to receive property put it into the hands of an outside party he trusted. That individual was given written instructions stating what was to be done with the asset and how, eventually, it was to be distributed.

The idea was simple and serviceable. It was fully accepted by the English courts and adopted by the legal profession as a method that could serve various purposes for many people other than the Friars. The written instructions became known as "trusts." The people given the responsibility to carry out the trust's instructions were called "trustees."

In those days sailing captains were away on voyages that frequently took many months, even years. The trust idea fitted one of their most serious needs. They were able to have a trust drawn instructing a trustee as to how they wanted their properties handled while they were away and in the event that they failed to return. It became a practice to pay fees to trustees charged with duties of that nature, and in time special trust companies were formed for that express purpose. Today, as you know, there are many trust companies, and many banks have trust departments. These are professional trustees. You may or may not have need for professionals for the type of trusts you may decide to use. More likely you and your spouse will serve as trustees for one another, and another family member or good friend may share that role with you. In such cases there are generally no fees.

PROBATE

When property is inherited by means of a will, or through a trust that is incorporated in a will—*a testamentary trust*—normal Probate Court procedure can bring about severe burdens in terms of dollars, time, and unwelcome publicity. The Court, in order to determine that the terms of the will are legal and that the provisions can and will be carried out properly, requires an inventory and a full appraisal of all property conveyed by the will and/or the testamentary trust. Lawyers, accountants, and appraisers must be paid. Those costs can eat up from 7 to 10 percent of the gross value of the property—even more. In some complicated estates the time element may constitute a serious handicap for the beneficiaries. A term of years can pass before the property becomes available to them. Finally, whatever passes through Probate Court is a matter of public record, open to the eyes of individuals and to the press.

The negative elements of probate make it evident that you may accomplish some important good for yourself and for your beneficiaries if you take steps to keep all or major portions of your estate out of probate.

Probate is not all bad. A great deal can be gained by having the terms of a will and the interests of beneficiaries subjected to independent judicial review, and by having the assets in the probate estate properly inventoried and evaluated.

The basics

The fundamentals of a trust are quite simple.

EXAMPLE: Joe Blue is finishing his breakfast coffee when wife, Mary, comes to him and hands him a $20 bill and a note she has just written. She says, "Joe, I know that you are busy and have a lot on your mind, so I have written out something I want you to do for me while you are downtown today." The note says that he is to use the $20 she has handed to him to buy a fruit basket and to take it to Mary's sister, Pinkie, who is convalescing from an operation. Pinkie is a patient at the City Hospital. The note goes on to say that maybe Pinkie has been discharged and went home. Mary will call the hospital and inquire. If Pinkie has gone home, she will phone him at his office to tell him to forget the whole deal and return the $20 when he comes home.

You have just read about a trust. The letter of instruction amounts to the *trust instrument*. Mary is the trust's *creator*.

Joe is the *trustee*, charged with carrying out the terms of the trust. Pinkie is the *beneficiary*. Mary has given herself the right to cancel the trust and get her twenty dollars back. The trust, therefore, is *revocable*. Mary may have said, "If I find that Pinkie has been discharged, I'll let you know. In any event you are to buy the fruit basket and send it to Pinkie wherever she is." Had those been her instructions the trust would have been *irrevocable*. The $20 handed to Joe provides the *funding of the trust*.

Why would you need a trust?

Trusts are used for a variety of purposes. The elimination or the reduction of tax liabilities is a major use. The avoidance of probate costs, delays, and publicity is another important objective. Trusts are frequently created, however, for other reasons. A trust may serve a very useful purpose without saving anything in taxes or probate. Trusts are used:

- *to protect family members from their own inexperience and lack of training in the handling of capital,*
- *to put safeguards around children and incompetents.*
- *to ensure that your ideas are carried out exactly as you wish,*
- *to curb spendthrifts,*
- *to avoid undesirable and wasteful uses of capital stemming from greed, gullibility, jealousy, family feuds, and other emotional elements.*

The ideal situation, of course, is when a trust serves a number of purposes—saving taxes, avoiding probate and providing protection and control.

What a trustee does

Trustees have specifically defined legal duties, backed by the penalties to which they expose themselves if they fail to live up to their obligation or to behave in keeping with the high standards prescribed for trustees.

THE LANGUAGE OF TRUSTS

A few of the special terms that occur in the world of trusts:

Settlor—The person who has a trust written for his or her use is the *settlor, creator, grantor,* or *donor.*

Trustee—The person named in the trust instrument as responsible for the management of the trust's handling of assets and carrying out the trust's instructions for the sole benefit of the beneficiary or beneficiaries.

Trust instrument—The terms, conditions, and instructions of the trust, in writing.

Testamentary trust—A trust that is part of a will and does not come into existence until the settlor dies.

Inter vivos trust—Also called a *living trust,* it is created while the settlor is alive. The trust is in being once created.

Pour-over trust—An inter vivos trust that inherits assets via the settlor's will or other instrument. Also referred to as *spill-over trust.*

Sprinkle and spray—Instructions in a trust instrument giving the trustee broad discretionary power as to the distribution of income to the beneficiaries.

Funding of trust—A trust must have some money or property so that it can create income or capital growth for the beneficiaries. Whatever the settlor provides for that purpose constitutes the *funding of the trust.*

Probate estate—That portion of a person's estate subject to review by the probate court, not necessarily the same as the *gross estate* or the *taxable estate.*

Trustees are required to obey the instructions contained in the trust instrument. Generally they may not part from those instructions without the permission of a court or the creator of the trust. The universal yardstick for the diligence with which trustees must carry out their duties is that ". . . he is under a duty to exercise such care and skill in the administration of the trust as a man of ordinary prudence would exercise in dealing with his own property. Moreover, if the trustee has greater skill he is under duty to exercise that greater skill."

If trustees are found to have done less than is expected of them, or if they have failed to use their skills solely for the best interests of the beneficiaries, they face various penalties. They may be called upon to reach into their own pockets to make good losses, if it can be shown that they lacked prudence. In some situations they may even be fined or imprisoned.

Permanence and *uniformity of administration* are expected of trusts. Trustees, therefore, may not walk away from their responsibilities. To be relieved of them, they must apply to the proper court or, depending on the instructions of the trust instrument, win the consent of all the people who are benefiting from or who will benefit from the trust.

The kinds of trusts

Fundamentally, there are two types of trusts: testamentary trusts and inter vivos trusts. A *testamentary trust* is created by provisions written into your will, and it does not come into being until you die. An *inter vivos trust* is created and can actually start functioning while you are still alive; it is also called a *living trust.* Living trusts have become increasingly popular. As an example, close to 85,000 living trusts were reported to the IRS in 1964. Today there are more than 200,000.

Trusts, as you have seen, may be of short duration with the remaining assets returned to you at the end of a specific time period spelled out in the trust instrument. Trusts may also last for very long periods, up to but not more than twenty-one years beyond the life of a person specified in the trust and alive at the time the trust was created.

Living trusts and testamentary trusts have these advantages in common:

- *Tax-saving opportunities are available.*
- *The interests of beneficiaries can be protected.*
- *Distribution of capital and income can be channeled in various ways in keeping with your wishes.*
- *Continuing management can be assured as to investment and the uses of income and capital for various beneficiaries.*
- *The special problems of providing for minors can be handled without the need to deal with guardianship problems.*

Trusts you leave behind

Testamentary trusts, compared with outright bequests granted in your will, may seem almost identical, but there are some critical differences. Take the case of the wealthy Mrs. Brown. She and her lawyer discuss her wishes. Her idea is to leave everything to her son and daughter-in-law, confident that, after they are gone, their children will inherit her considerable estate. Mrs. Brown's lawyer, however, cautions against that.

Instead, he points out the advantages of using a testamentary trust. The trust would provide that the property left by Mrs. Brown would be left to the grandchildren with all income going to the son and daughter-in-law as long as they shall live. After they both are gone, the property goes to their children. This arrangement, the lawyer explains, accomplishes three important things. First, it eliminates all taxes on the property when it passes from her son and his wife to the grandchildren, since it was the grandchildren's property right along. Second, since Mrs. Brown's son never has had any experience in handling money and investments, the trust is written to make certain that the property's management is in competent hands. Finally, it eliminates all doubts that the grandchildren will, absolutely, be the eventual inheritors.

Trusts you can live with

A *living trust* has these advantages, in addition to those it shares with testamentary trusts:

- *You avoid probate. Unlike the testamentary trust, the living trust exists prior to the creator's death. If the creator dies during the term of the trust, the property in the trust is ordinarily not subject to probate. This feature can represent substantial savings. It also permits the assets, or the income from the assets, to become available to your beneficiaries without the delays that probate can involve. And, while whatever passes through probate court is a matter of public record and open to publicity, the facts about a living trust are not available to public scrutiny.*
- *Since a testamentary trust comes into being through the terms of a will, there is a risk that it may never come into being at all. Wills must be examined by the probate court. If a will is found to be legally unsound or if the will is successfully challenged by a private party, it is entirely possible that there will be no trust. In contrast, the probate court has no jurisdiction over living trusts,*

and, although they can be contested, wills are generally easier to overturn.

- *A living trust may permit the lawyer drafting the trust a broader choice of the most favorable state laws. If, for example, the laws of the state where you reside are less desirable than those of the state either where a beneficiary or trustee lives or where the property is located, you can usually designate that the terms of the trust shall comply with the laws of the selected state. That degree of flexibility is not present in a testamentary trust.*
- *Living trusts give you the opportunity to see the trust in operation so that changes and adjustments may be made should the need become evident.*
- *Where a living trust exists, your will may specify that certain assets, such as pension plan proceeds, shall be left to the trust. This privilege is known as the "pour-over" provision, more fully discussed below.*

The living trust simplified

Setting up a living trust, particularly if you are not going to fund it with any substantial amount of cash or property, may call for disproportionate legal expense. Also, if you go to most trust companies or to the trust departments of most banks, you might find that they will not accept a trust account funded for less than $250,000. The solution is to deal with a bank trust department that offers a *standard living trust.* Some banks have established simplified trust instruments that anyone may use. But you have to be willing to accept the trust terms the bank provides and be satisfied that the bank will do a good job of managing the money you put into the trust. Bank trust departments offering standard trusts accept only cash for the funding, and they charge a fee in the area of 1 percent a year. It is a streamlined way of having your own living trust, and the cost is low.

A living trust may be revocable or irrevocable.

Revocable living trusts

You may place property in the trust and name yourself as trustee. You may also name a professional trustee or an investment manager to act as a co-trustee. You can, as a matter

of fact, name any competent person as trustee or co-trustee. As creator of the trust, you retain the right to cancel it at any time.

When you reserve the right to revoke, you should be aware of the consequences. All income produced by the property in the trust is taxable to you, and you do not avoid or reduce federal estate taxes. Probate is avoided, however, for the property in the trust does not become part of your probate estate. Since you retain full control over the property in the trust, there is no gift at the time the trust is created. Since a gift is not completed, you have no gift tax liability at that time. The revocability also permits you to change your mind. You may take back any and all assets in the trust whenever you choose. The free hand you have also permits you to appoint a money manager as trustee, for example, and to oversee his or her operation of the trust so that you can form your own judgment as to the manager's capabilities. You have total freedom to substitute another trustee or simply to end the trust.

Irrevocable living trusts

In contrast with the revocable trust, when a trust is irrevocable, taxes may be saved. To gain these advantages, you must give up certain rights. No strings may be attached to the provisions of the trust. You may not reserve the right to revoke or significantly alter the trust. Generally you may not receive any of the income earned by the investment of the property in the trust. Your rights to invade the property in the trust, to change the beneficiaries, or to alter the rights of the beneficiaries are all severely limited. Since the surrender of all rights to the assets you place in the trust takes place at the time the trust is created, the establishment of the trust constitutes an outright gift and may be subject to gift taxation in that year. The amount of that tax depends on the value of the gift. Any advantage of having assets in the trust removed from your taxable estate is subject to the "contemplation of death" provision. Should you die within three years of the time that the trust is activated, the gift is considered to have been made in contemplation of death, and the assets remain in your taxable estate.

The pour-over provision

You may establish a living trust and fund it with any amount of capital or property you choose, with the thought that, through your will, the funding will become more substantial. This capability gives you an exceptional degree of control and some first-rate benefits, because the trust exists and is operating while you are able to keep an eye on it.

EXAMPLE: Oscar Observe has his lawyer create a living trust for him, and he puts $20,000 in cash into it. He names himself as trustee, and he names a professional investment advisory firm as co-trustee. The advisor is charged with the responsibility of handling the investment of the money in a manner that produces little or no income but that attempts to produce growth of capital. Oscar now sits back and watches. Over a period of time he will have a basis for *judgment as to the co-trustee's abilities. If he is unhappy with what the advisor does, he may discharge him and bring in another. In this way he gives himself the satisfaction that, before he goes, the investment of the funds in the trust will be in competent hands . . . Mrs. Observe will be well-served.*

Increasing your children's inheritance

Oscar has several large life insurance policies, a valuable rare coin collection, and a substantial interest in the profit sharing plan his employer provides. Oscar makes his living trust the beneficiary of his life insurance policies. The will specifies that his coin collection should be sold to a reputable coin dealer whom he names and that the proceeds are to go to the living trust. He further states that his interest in the profit sharing plan shall be paid to the living trust. When Oscar dies, therefore, the trust swells in value. The trust instrument instructs Oscar's successor trustee and the co-trustee to switch from investments aimed at growth of capital to investments calculated to give the trust beneficiary, Mrs. Observe, generous income.

The insurance proceeds, the money realized from the sale of the coins, and the cash coming from the profit sharing plan have been "poured over" into the trust. The advantages are most desirable.

1. *Oscar has tested and is satisfied with how the assets in the trust will be handled.*
2. *The assets he poured over to the trust from his life insurance escape the costs of probate.*
3. *While he lived, Oscar enjoyed all the control he could possibly want as to which assets would go to the trust. All he had to do was to change his will whenever he pleased.*
4. *While he lived, Oscar was in charge; he was free to adjust and to amend the management of the trust as he saw fit. He could even change the terms of the trust itself, if the state in which he lived permitted him to do so. He could name his successor trustee, which could be his widow, any of his children, his lawyer, or anyone else he cared to name.*
5. *His original funding of the trust did not have to be in an amount as great as the $20,000 used in our example. It could have been as modest as a minimum investment in a mutual fund.*

An important tax-reducing trust

As discussed in the gifts chapter, the *1976 Tax Reform Act* makes it quite difficult to remove assets from your taxable estate because gift and estate taxes are now uniform. One of the remaining advantages, however, is that the gift tax itself is not charged back to the estate, unless the gift was made within three years of the date of death. In some instances this can represent worthwhile savings.

A major way of taking a big bite out of estate taxes is available via the trust route. You also read about the marital deduction and saw that the knowledgeable use of trusts can be linked to that deduction to reduce or eliminate estate taxes. Here is an examination of the steps to be taken and the reasons why the trust approach might be important to you if you are married.

Without a trust. *Peter Trend dies, and his will leaves all he has to his wife, Geraldine. After all expenses have been paid, his adjusted gross estate amounts to $400,000. Here is what happens:*

Peter's adjusted gross estate	$400,000
Less marital deduction	– 250,000
Taxable amount	$150,000
Tax before tax credit	$ 38,000[1]
Less tax credit	– 47,000[2]
Actual tax to be paid	$ -0-

1. Tax based on Unified Rate Schedule is $38,800.
2. Maximum credit, as of 1981 and thereafter ($47,000), exceeds Peter's taxes, therefore nothing is owed.

No taxes on a $400,000 estate is good news. But the Trends had two children. So let's see what happens when Geraldine passes away. She has inherited all of Peter's $400,000 estate, so let's assume that her adjusted gross estate also amounts to $400,000 when she dies. Now taxes become a big issue. Almost one-fifth of all the money the Trends had worked to accumulate will go to the tax collector and not to their children. Let's see.

Geraldine's adjusted gross estate	$400,000
Taxes before tax credit	$121,800[1]
Less tax credit	– 47,000
Actual tax to be paid	$ 74,800

1. On $400,000 the tax is $70,800 on the first $250,000 plus 34% of the excess $150,000 which is $51,000 (.34 × $150,000). The tax is $121,800 ($70,800 + $51,000).

Remember, too, that this example does not include two big items: the extra drains on the estate from probate costs and state death taxes in excess of the credit allowed against the federal estate tax.

The use of a trust could have given the children an extra $51,000.

With a trust. *When Peter dies, his will instructs that $250,000 is to go to Geraldine under the marital estate deduction and that the re-*mainder *is to go into a trust. As long as Geraldine lives, she is to receive all the income the property in the trust produced, but the property belongs to the children. In addition, the trust may permit her to have some of the principal if the trustees have reason to think she needs extra money.*

Now, when Geraldine dies, she has only $250,000 in her estate. The $150,000 in the trust does not belong to her. All that is hers is the income it produces while she lives. At her death, the $250,000 goes straight to the children with no tax. The children get that, and they get Geraldine's money—a total of $400,000, less the taxes on Geraldine's $250,000. Here's how the money from Geraldine is taxed.

Geraldine's money	$250,000
Tax before tax credit	$ 70,800
Less tax credit	− 47,000
Actual taxes to be paid	$ 23,800

Quite a different from $74,800 where there was no trust! With the trust, the children receive the extra $51,000, not Uncle Sam.

But the children could have had $8,200 more.

When Peter died, $250,000, the biggest marital deduction allowed, was taken. That was why Geraldine came into full possession of $250,000 and the trust received $150,000. Suppose Peter's $400,000 had been evenly divided between Geraldine and the trust? (The regulations say that the marital deduction may be the greater of $250,000 or half of the gross estate. This does not mean that you are required *to take the greater of the two.) If it had been, half the estate would have passed to Geraldine, and the other half, after taxes, would go into a trust. Peter's estate, after subtracting the marital deduction of $200,000, and Geraldine's estate of $200,000 at her death were each taxed $7,800—a total tax on both estates of only $15,600. (If Geraldine died within ten years of Peter's death, it would be less. Uncle Sam would have allowed some credit for the tax paid on Peter's estate.)*

The decision to take one-half of the adjusted gross estate as the *marital deduction, instead of the $250,000 allowable, would have given the children that extra $8,200.*

You may be considerably more concerned about providing for your spouse, as opposed to saving assets for your children. It is not at all unusual for people to conclude that their children have demonstrated their ability to provide for themselves and that there is no need, therefore, to put their financial interest ahead of that of a surviving partner. This factor must be weighed when you instruct your attorney regarding the marital deduction election.

The decision about the marital deduction—whether to take the $250,000 or half the adjusted gross estate—is important only if your estate amounts to $500,000 or less. In such borderline cases, the decision calls for serious study so that all possible advantages and pitfalls in this area of planning can be considered, although the usual decision is to take half. On considerably larger estates, there is little question about the desirability of making the marital deduction half of your adjusted gross estate: the larger the estate, the greater the tax savings when you use this type of trust. On the other hand, in modest estates, whatever can be saved can be extremely important: the less people have, the more each dollar counts.

The many kinds of trusts

Charitable remainder trusts were explored at some length in the gift chapter, and the fundamentals of the life insurance trust were related in the chapter on insurance. But these two by no means represent the only trusts available to you.

Marital deduction trusts

Sometimes that part of a couple's property coming under the tax-free marital deduction must be considered carefully. Either husband or wife, or both, might be untrained and inefficient at handling money. Or a serious illness or accident could put either or both of them in a position where businesslike investing, watching, and supervising of an important sum of money are out of the question.

An accepted way of avoiding such problems is through the use of the marital deduction trust. Mr. Reem, for example, might be keenly aware of his wife's particular weakness with money. She is a completely reckless spender. A protective wall must be put around the part of his estate that will go straight to her. Her marital deduction portion does not have that protection. To provide the needed safeguard, the portion of the estate qualifying for the marital deduction might be put into a trust. The idea behind the marital deduction is to permit roughly half of the estate to be taxed on Mr. Reem's death and the other half on his wife's death. (Since tax rates increase as total assets in the estate increase, splitting assets evenly between husband and wife keeps tax rates at the lowest possible level.) The assumption is that the portion of the estate escaping tax on his death is taxable because she owns it outright.

The tax law permits the use of a trust without disturbing the marital deduction privilege *if the wife's rights in the trust are the equivalent of outright ownership.* Obviously, if the wife is given the right to draw out all or any part of the assets in the trust as she sees fit, she has the equivalent of outright ownership. But the tax law is not that severe; it does not require that degree of equivalent ownership. Instead, the tax law accepts a minimum degree of outright ownership as enough, and, if the trust provides for at least that much or more, the marital deduction is still available. The minimum degree of equivalent ownership requires that all the income from the trust must be payable for life to the wife, annually or more frequently, and that the wife has the power to name who gets the remainder of the property after she dies. The power to name this recipient can be restricted to individuals she names in her will. The husband can even provide that, if the wife fails to name those who are to receive the remainder in *her* will, the remainder shall be distributed according to the directions he has provided in his own will.

From the husband's viewpoint and as a further protection of any children, the marital deduction trust has another advantage. If Mrs. Reem remarries, her new husband cannot touch the money in the marital trust, nor will he get any should he outlive her, unless she puts instructions to that effect in her will.

What Mr. Reem can do, then, is to create two trusts: trust A and trust B. Both trusts call for trustees to serve along with Mrs. Reem, as another means of protecting her from impulsive and unwise uses of her property. Trust A, the marital deduction trust, pays all income to Mrs. Reem, and she has at least the minimum equivalent of outright ownership in it. Whatever she leaves when she dies will be used as she directs in her will. Because she has that power estate taxes are not saved. The entire value of the trust will be part of her estate. The property in trust B is what is left in Mr. Reem's estate after the estate tax is paid. Trust B is to pay Mrs. Reem income for life, and then the property goes to the children.

The assumption in this example is that Mr. Reem's estate is larger than his wife's. This is the usual case, but not always. Also, it is assumed that he is the first to die—again the usual situation. The marital deduction, however, as structured in the law, does not discriminate between the sexes. A wife's estate is eligible for the marital deduction, where the property has been left to the husband, according to the same rules as applied to Mr. Reem in our example. If the wife's estate is larger than the husband's, using the marital deduction in her estate makes sense. Where the estates are relatively equal, it may be a good idea to avoid the marital deduction altogether.

Short-term trust

This type of trust, primarily used to produce income or to accumulate income for others and to transfer the tax liability from the donor to the recipient, has been covered in some detail in the last chapter on gifts. Here are two further examples of the great versatility of short-term trusts.

1. *Income you don't need.* You are having no problem meeting your living expenses, and you are doing whatever you enjoy doing. A new source of income opens up for you. Either you become the income beneficiary of a trust, you win a contest providing income for a period of years, a book you wrote becomes a producer of generous royalties, or what-have-you. At any rate, you are happy about the income, but you really do not need it now, particularly in your present tax bracket. You have a son or daughter, niece, nephew, aged parents, aunt or uncle, who are having financial problems and

who are in tax brackets well under your own. You can have your lawyer make an irrevocable assignment of income through the use of a short-term trust. In other words, you give up all rights to that income for at least ten years or for the life of the person who is to get the income. The income recipient becomes the taxpayer, and, when the trust period ends, the property and the income of course are yours. Your lawyer should be certain that the laws of your state permit the assignment of income. The IRS definitely does permit it, provided that you observe all of the normal requirements of a short-term trust.

2. *Combining a short-term trust and interest-free loans.* When you read about *short-term trusts* in the chapter on gifts, you saw that a gift tax may be involved, a tax based on the IRS Gift Valuation table.

One possible way of establishing an income-producing, short-term trust that is free of gift tax is to use an *interest-free loan.* Interest-free loans came into prominence several years ago when the tax court heard a case that the IRS brought against a taxpayer by the name of Crown. Crown had loaned money to a member of the family and charged no interest. The IRS said, "Okay, you can do what you like about waiving interest, but in our view the interest which would normally be paid constitutes a gift. You must pay a gift tax." The tax court, however, sided with the Crown family saying that individuals should be free to do as they please with their money and that no law requires people to charge a member of the family interest if they choose not to do so. No tax had to be paid. The IRS has maintained its attitude, but, to date, the tax court decision has held up. It may, or may not continue to have validity. Check carefully before you adopt this approach.

Here is what you can do: You create a short-term trust for the benefit of a family member you want to help. The chances are that the individual being helped is in a tax bracket lower than your own. You fund the trust with a very small amount of money or with some other property. Once the trust has been established, you then make an interest-free loan to the trust. You may choose to lend cash, stock, or income-producing real estate. Whatever you lend to the trust produces income, which is paid to the beneficiary. The income is not taxable to you. Since the loan is not part of the funding of the trust, it is not bound to the "more-than-ten-year" provision, which is required of the funding of short-term trusts. You can withdraw the loaned property whenever you please. Under those circumstances there is no occasion to determine the IRS Gift Valuation table, which is based on the number of years the property is in the trust.

Family gift and leaseback trusts

If you are engaged in a profession or business, if you own the building you occupy in your occupation, or if you own valuable equipment required by your work, you have the opportunity to save taxes and to produce income for your children or others. You can create a trust by putting your building or equipment in the trust and then by leasing the property or equipment from the trustee, who distributes the rental you pay to your children. Your business may deduct whatever rent you pay as a legitimate business expense, thus reducing its taxes. Your children are the taxpayers on the rental income, at their tax bracket.

Several precautions must be taken if you are to avoid a successful IRS challenge. First of all, you must surrender all control over the property you put into the trust. To do so, you or your spouse may not be trustee. The trustee should be a totally independent person or a company acting strictly for the benefit of your children. Second, a valid lease should be written, and the rent you pay for use of either the building or the equipment must be realistic—what you would expect to pay were you dealing with a stranger. Finally, you must rent the space or the equipment for a genuine business reason. You should be able to prove that you have an unquestioned business need for the space or equipment.

The Internal Revenue Service has attacked *family gift and leaseback trusts*, but, when they are properly structured, the tax courts have ruled against IRS. As is true with all trusts but particularly with those the IRS has been fighting, the assistance of a capable lawyer is essential.

Appointing the trustee

The choice of the trustee when you create a trust requires a good deal of thoughtful care. Are the assets in the trust substantial? Are the terms of the trust complex? Are or will children and grandchildren be beneficiaries of the trust? Are the laws of the state at cross purposes with your wishes? All these elements must be taken into account.

In a vast number of instances the creator and spouse serve as co-trustees, an arrangement that can work out very well. In other cases, a friend or member of the family may be considered as sole trustee or as a co-trustee. The question then arises as to whether this individual is capable of handling all the details—if the person has the time, the willingness, and the good health essential to carrying out the duties. In many instances, it may be the wiser course to use a professional, such as a trust company or the trust department of a bank. Many people object to the use of professional trustees, however, because of the impersonal nature with which their duties are generally performed.

Successor trustees

Particularly in situations where children and grandchildren are involved successor trustees have to be considered. If the trust is likely to outlive you and your spouse, or even your children, you might be better off thinking of a trust company or trust department. In any event, the naming of family members as successors logically should take into account the need to deal with descending ages.

The laws of some states do not permit trustees to delegate their investment duties to anyone else. In some jurisdictions this restriction would bar a trustee from making investments in a mutual fund or from turning the investment problems over to an investment advisory firm. Your trust instrument, however, may authorize such investments. In that case the trustee is free to follow the instructions of the trust.

The sprinkle and spray provision

The selection of the trustee and of successor trustees becomes particularly sensitive when the trust document includes instructions to "sprinkle and spray." To *sprinkle and spray* means that the trust income is to be used, at the discretion of the trustee, where, how, and when needed. This type of use is in contrast to the idea of paying out the income in a methodical, uniform manner. Under the sprinkle and spray concept, the trustee may conclude that it is wise to withhold income for some periods and to be generous with it at other times. He or she may also, for example, have the right to decide that, under the given circumstances, one beneficiary should receive more income than others. Clearly, decisions of that nature must be in extremely trustworthy hands.

The sprinkle and spray idea can be important. To illustrate, assume that a couple has two adult children at the time they and their lawyer prepares A and B trusts for them. The elder son, Charlie, at 38, has a good executive job and is moving right up the corporate ladder in his firm. Robert, their 36-year-old son, has had a disabling illness since childhood. As a result he never has been able to take anything but temporary employment and goes through long periods where he cannot work or even find a job. The trusts, in this case, provide that after both parents are gone, all income goes to the two boys with the property in the trusts eventually going to grandchildren living at the time the trusts were adopted. A sprinkle and spray provision in the trust instructions specifies that when the trusts start distributing income to the two sons, the trustee is to exercise his or her best judgment as to where the income is needed most and to handle the distributions accordingly.

CANDIDATES FOR ACTION

- ☐ Testamentary trust
- ☐ Living trust
  - ☐ Revocable ☐ Irrevocable
- ☐ Pour-over provision
- ☐ Standardized living trust
- ☐ Marital trust
- ☐ A and B trusts
- ☐ Irrevocable assignment of income short-term trust
- ☐ Short-term trust combined with interest-free loans
- ☐ Sprinkle-and-spray provision

9

Bask in the Shade of Tax Shelters

For the welfare of the nation

A lot of the things said and written about tax shelters give the impression that they are illegal, unethical, and immoral. The fact is that tax shelters exist because they have been created by the Congress of the United States. They were created to encourage people to put their money into investments that, under other circumstances, would be extremely unattractive because of the high risks involved.

But these investments are vital to the good and welfare of the nation. For example, it is clearly desirable for us to find more oil and gas within our own borders. In order to find it there must be money to pay for exploration. Drilling in unproven ground, however—wildcatting—represents immense risks. Only one exploration in ten finds any oil, and only one in forty is commercially rewarding. But the effort to find new sources of oil and gas must go on. That is why Uncle Sam permits those who provide the needed capital to deduct 100 percent of their investments for the costs of drilling dry holes. The tax shelter is justified and logical. You need not blush and try to hide the fact that you invested in a tax shelter. You are helping yourself and your country at the same time.

Avoiding, reducing, postponing—but not evading

In part, the misunderstanding about tax shelters—tax loopholes—comes about because of some confusion caused by two similar words: "avoidance" and "evasion." *Tax avoidance* is entirely legal and ethical; it helps you pay for your food and shelter. *Tax evasion* provides you with free food and shelter at a federal institution. Tax avoidance is but one of three ways in which shelters can help you to ease your tax burden. Shelters can *avoid, reduce,* or *postpone* taxes. "Postponement" may sound like the least of the three, but it is by no means a weak sister. Tax postponement—*tax deferral*—amounts to an interest-free loan, and it can be a most advantageous portion of your financial plans. So the publicized efforts of Congress to "plug up loopholes" is not as much related to efforts to eliminate government-sponsored shelters as they are intended to correct certain so-called distortions and abuses. These "loopholes" were the targets of the *Tax Reform Act of 1976.*

Nonrecourse loans

One of that Act's major thrusts was to curtail tax writeoffs based to a great extent on nonrecourse loans. A *nonrecourse loan* is a device that made a great number of tax-sheltered offerings immensely attractive. A partnership would be formed, and individuals would advance a small percentage of the capital required—as little as ten percent in many cases, with the remaining 90 percent provided via a loan. The general partners accepted full responsibility, and the limited partners had no liability for repayment of the loan. But even though they owed no part of the borrowed capital, the limited partners were permitted to take tax deductions based on the grand total of the money in the venture. TRA '76 put a stop to this practice by stating that most limited partner deductions had to be based on the money that the individuals actually invested—*the money at risk*—and no more. One major exception was certain real estate projects. This exception was made for the simple reason that the government wants to encourage investment in housing, particularly subsidized housing for the elderly and the poor. Clearly, without special inducements, it would be difficult to attract capital for such poor investment risks as housing projects for the elderly and the poor. It is equally clear that there is a critical need for such housing.

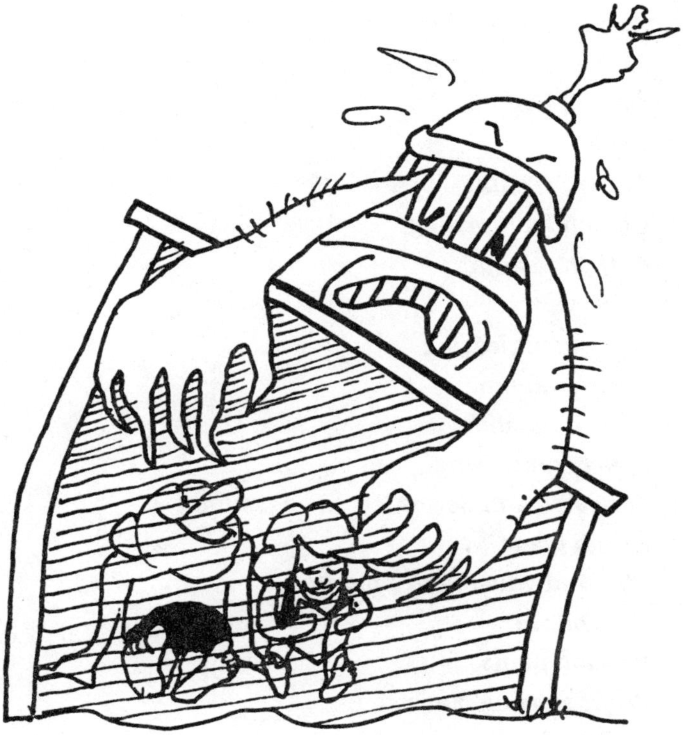

What's left?

Despite the shrinkage of shelters with highly attractive writeoffs, the tax shelter field is far from dead. As one observer expressed it, "For every government lawyer trying to bar the imaginative expansion of the easement of tax liabilities, there are ten lawyers in private practice burning the midnight oil to dream up new ways to stretch and circumvent the rules and regulations." Not all means of avoiding, reducing, or deferring taxes are sophisticated, technically involved, or subject to attack by the government. But many still fit that description. Currently available shelters include:

Municipal bonds
Municipal bond funds
Annuities, fixed

Annuities, variable
Real estate limited partnerships
Oil and gas
Coal
Cattle breeding
Chinchilla breeding
Catfish farming
Timber
Equipment leasing
Record albums
Book publishing
Sport franchising
Series EE and Series HH savings bonds
Keogh plans
IRA—Indvidual Retirement Accounts
IRA rollovers
Pension plans
Profit sharing plans
Deferred compensation
Salary reduction plans

Who needs tax shelters?

When you go beyond some of the simpler items on the list, such as the Series EE bonds and the various retirement plans, tax shelters are not for everyone. It is generally agreed that the more involved tax-sheltered investments should be adopted only by people with these qualifications:

1. *in the 50-percent tax bracket or higher, and having at least $50,000 of net worth exclusive of ownership of home and car;*
2. *$200,000 of net worth regardless of income tax bracket;*
3. *the 35-percent tax bracket or better for real estate investments;*
4. *an unusual capital gain situation or an uncharacteristic bulge in income, as in the case of the sale of a business or piece of property.*

People with substantial unearned income—income from dividends, interest, rent, royalties, and similar sources, are subject to a maximum tax of 70 percent as opposed to the 50 percent ceiling on income earned from personal services. If you are in the 70-percent bracket, therefore, you do need favorable tax treatment.

Keep in mind that what might appear to be a fine tax shelter could actually hurt you financially. For instance, the investment or the return on it might give you "tax preference income" resulting in your moving up from a top 50-percent bracket to the 70-percent bracket.

Other considerations

The excesses practiced prior to TRA '76 gave many people a distorted viewpoint about tax shelters. The rules have changed, but the old motivations prevail to a great extent. All too many individuals look solely at the tax aspects and ignore normal investment considerations. The only proper way to evaluate a tax shelter is to start with the question, *"Does it make good sense without the tax benefit?"* Regardless of tax advantages, a bad investment is a bad investment. The risks that may be present can wipe out the entire investment. On top of that, the IRS is on solid ground should it disallow the favorable tax treatment if it can establish the fact that the investment was made for the *sole purpose* of tax avoidance. And rules may be changed. In some cases the fabric of a tax shelter suggests the likelihood of an eventual attack. Should the attack occur and the IRS wins in the tax court, you could be damaged. And the damage can be deep. A number of investors go into some tax shelters only on an annual basis. A few years ago the IRS suddenly declared a long-established silver straddles shelter illegal, and it disallowed tax deductions retroactively, going back three years!

Timing is another ingredient. As the end of the year approaches, people become particularly concerned about taxes and look about for steps they may take before December 31. As a result a lot of tax-shelter activity starts up in the closing months of each year. The closing months, however, do not constitute the best time to become involved in tax shelters. Early in the year you have better choices from a greater number of possibilities.

Types of shelters

There is no need to discuss all the tax-sheltered investments itemized on pages 175, 176, since some of them are covered in other chapters of this book—fixed and variable annuities, municipal bond funds, and others.

Limited partnerships

The typical limited partnership is organized by individuals who serve as general partners. They create the company, run it, and sell participation to others. The investors are the limited partners, who share in any profits but whose losses are usually limited to the money they invest.

Limited partnerships are a particularly popular form of tax shelter, because of certain advantages they enjoy over corporations. Any tax deductions generated by a corporation are strictly for the benefit of the corporation itself. There is no way that those tax deductions are permitted to flow through to the shareholders. But a limited partnership is permitted to pass its tax deductions along to the partners. In addition, the limited partners enjoy the freedom from liability that a corporation provides for its shareholders. Finally, a partnership is free of direct taxation. The tax advantage is that the limited partners may take their proper share of a variety of expenses and losses experienced by the business as their own deductions and apply them against their gross income from all sources. Even though they have no responsibility for the repayment of money borrowed by the business, they take as a legitimate deduction the interest paid on loans. They also have deductions for depreciation on real estate, development and drilling costs in oil and gas ventures, leasing of equipment, and more.

While they offer attractive advantages, don't leap before taking a long, hard look. A limited partnership must be studied with care. They sometimes are loaded very heavily in favor of the organizers. Take care regarding any conflicts of interest. You should ask questions like: Are the general partners giving out contracts to unrelated companies that they own or have interests in, at inflated prices? Are there excessive developer, promoter, or legal fees? Who is the first in line for distributions? Five measures can help you evaluate the soundness of a limited partnership:

1. *80 percent of the anticipated proceeds should be earmarked to finance the project with no more than 20 percent going to the general partners as fees.*
2. *Tax deductions should be supportable, not unduly subject to challenge from IRS.*
3. *There must be a reasonable chance of economic success.*
4. *The venture should be structured so that the investment can ultimately earn enough to pay off deferred taxes.*
5. *The general partners should have a good history of experience, skill, stability, and financial strength.*

Keogh plans

It may surprise you to see Keogh Plans and individual retirement accounts discussed as tax shelters. But that is what they are. They are two of the better tax shelters available, and neither one of them is subject to attack by IRS.

Keogh, in its present form, has a lot to offer. Since October 10, 1962, when HR-10, better known as the *Keogh Act,* was passed by the Congress, its liberality has been increasing. When the law was first enacted, the most you were allowed to put toward your retirement under its tax umbrella was $2,500 a year. Now it is $7,500 or even more, as you will see. Until Keogh was brought into being, employees of corporations were just about the only people earning money who could put aside some of their earnings in a tax-favored manner in order to prepare for the retirement years.

Eligibility. If you are self-employed, you may have a Keogh Plan. Even this measure of eligibility has broadened. Originally, the self-employment yardstick meant that you had to have an unincorporated business of your own, or as a partner you had to be operating as a professional, earning your living as a freelance writer, artist, architect, or what-have-you. Now you are permitted to have a full-time job with a corporation, be a participant in that company's pension or profit sharing plan, and still have a Keogh Plan if you do some moonlighting in an unincorporated enterprise of your own.

Benefits. Assuming that you are eligible, you are permitted to contribute the lesser of $7,500 or 15 percent of your gross earned income to your plan each year. (*Earned income* is the money you make from your personal services, as opposed to interest, dividends, or profits made from investments.) The big tax shelter is this: Whatever part of your earned income you pay into your plan you need not report to the IRS as income that year. That is a very important privilege. If your top tax bracket is, say, 40 percent, then Uncle Sam is lending you $400 for each $1,000 going into your Keogh Plan—and *it is interest-free.* If you are all the way up to the 70-percent bracket, you are in effect borrowing money without cost at the rate of $700 for each $1,000 you put into your plan each year. You pay taxes eventually, but even that is a soft landing.

Not only do you get these great tax postponements on your contributions, you get the same break on whatever your Keogh account money earns year after year. Under normal circumstances, the money you put into your Keogh Plan must remain in it until you reach 59½, at which time, if you desire, you can take it out. By the time you are 70½, you are required to start withdrawing the money. There are two exceptions to the 59½ rule: (1) If you become permanently disabled, you may draw your money; (2) should you die, the money in the account goes to your beneficiaries.

If all of that sounds too good to be true, you are right. The rules also state that if you have one or more full-time employees who have been with you for three years or more, you must establish Keogh Plans for each of them and you must contribute the same percentage of their wages as you contribute for yourself. Here is how that works.

EXAMPLE: You earn $50,000 a year and contribute the full 15 percent of your earnings ($7,500) to your account. That is the legal limit. Sally Thayer, your administrative assistant, earns $12,000 a year. You must contribute 15 percent of her earnings to her plan ($1,800 a year). However, since the rule says that you are limited to 15 percent or $7,500, whichever is less, *if you earn $75,000, you may not put more than 10 percent of your earnings in your own plan ($7,500), and you are permitted to contribute the same* percentage *for Sally—only $1,200 instead of $1,800. Even if you earn $50,000 or less, you do not have to put a full 15 percent in for yourself. If you have a dozen qualified employees, you may decide that you are ahead of the game if you hold your own contribution to something less—10 percent, 8 percent, whatever you want.*

There are some good things about contributing to employee accounts. For one thing, it is a deductible expense. The government shares the costs with you. Second, it is an attractive fringe benefit that can help to hold good workers and that makes the job more inviting when you are trying to recruit new ones. A third factor is that your accountant will show you how you may reduce your employee contributions by whatever you pay to the Social Security taxes of included employees.

Voluntary contributions. A big plus comes under the heading of "voluntary contributions." If you have even one covered employee, you and the employee are both permitted to make additional contributions to your own account. Your voluntary contributions may amount to as much as $2,500 or 10 percent of earned income, whichever is less. One big difference between regular and voluntary contributions is that voluntary contributions are not tax-deferred. You may not deduct those sums when you report your income to the IRS. However, whatever that extra money in your account earns remains untaxed until you withdraw, which is a valuable privilege. The one remaining distinction between regular and voluntary contributions is that voluntary contributions may be withdrawn, without penalty, whenever you want.

When income is $15,000 or less. There is a special exemption to the rule limiting contributions to *15 percent of gross earned income or $7,500, whichever is less.* If your gross annual income from all sources—and that includes dividends, interest, salary, and self-employment earnings—is less than $15,000, you are permitted to put as much as $750 a year into your Keogh Plan. It does not matter what percentage of your income that $750 happens to be. This exemption can be of particular importance to families with more than one wage earner.

EXAMPLE: Moe and Molly Kelly are married. Moe earns better than $35,000 a year. Molly embroiders place mats, and she has a few shops that buy them from her. She is therefore self-employed. Her earnings amount to $1,500 a year on average. What Moe earns does not matter. Her gross income is what does matter. All her income adds up to a good deal less than $15,000, so she is entitled to have *her own Keogh Plan and may put $750 a year into it, even though that amounts to 50 percent of her earnings.*

When the tax collector cometh. Eventually you will take the money out of your Keogh account, and the tax collector will be waiting for you.

If you withdraw the money in the form of monthly income, you are taxed at whatever your tax rate is at that time. The withdrawals are treated as earned income, as opposed to investment income, and the likelihood is that you won't be withdrawing until you have retired. If that is the case, you will probably be in a reduced tax bracket.

If, instead of withdrawing the money on a regular basis, you take it out all at once, the tax treatment becomes somewhat involved. It works this way:

EXAMPLE: If the lump-sum distribution amounts to $20,000 or less, half of it is exempt—free of any tax. Next, you deal with anything over $20,000, up to $70,000

You take 20 percent of the amount over $20,000 (but under $70,000), and subtract that amount from the $10,000 exemption. The result is your total deduction. You pay ordinary tax on the remainder.

You get a lump-sum distribution of $50,000.

Tax exemption on first $20,000	$10,000
Less 20% of the remaining $30,000	−6,000
Total exemption	$ 4,000
Total taxable amount	$46,000

If the account amounts to more than $70,000, you get very special treatment.

IRS permits you to use the *ten-year-averaging rule.* The ten-year-averaging is a bonus. The taxes you will pay over a ten-year period are based on a complicated IRS formula. The big advantage is that you avoid the need to pay a big tax in a single year, throwing you into an abnormally high tax bracket which would apply to the lump-sum payout and to all your other income as well.

You can do even better if you take advantage of the *rollover* provision, which is described later in this chapter.

The regulations also permit you to direct your payout to:

- *trusts,*
- *annuities,*
- *custodian accounts using mutual funds,*
- *insurance,*
- *endowments or annuity policies (just about all mutual funds and insurance companies have custodian accounts established for Keogh accounts),*
- *face amount certificates,*
- *savings and loan accounts,*
- *banks,*
- *credit unions, or*
- *some special government bonds.*

You are also allowed to split the contribution. For example, you may split it between mutual funds and life insurance. If you do so, the life insurance portion must be less than 50 percent of the investment, 25 percent if term insurance is used.

Defined benefit Keogh

The newest expansion of Keogh benefits lets you go beyond the annual tax-sheltered $7,500 contribution. Under the *defined benefit plan,* available only to employees of corporations, you may now decide, within certain limits, what you want your retirement income to be and make contributions calculated to provide that income. How much you may contribute is based on two elements: your age and your annual earned income. How much the Act says you may contribute is displayed in Table 4. The percentages apply to top yearly compensation, but the ceiling is $50,000. The amount you may contribute is based on what it would take to fund a straight life annuity starting at age 65. The percentage of your compensation to be contributed, since it is based on your age when you enter this plan, remains constant. The maximum amount you are allowed to contribute to a defined benefit Keogh plan is about $11,000 a year on a tax-deferred basis. That amount is interestingly more than the former $7,500 limit.

Table 4.
The defined benefit Keogh plan scale

Age	% of Earned Income
30 or under	6.5
35	5.4
40	4.4
45	3.6
50	3.0
55	2.5
60 or over	2.0

One aspect of the defined benefit Keogh and the normal Keogh Plan is the impact of investment results. If you use the defined plan and if the money in the account builds up too much due to good investment results, you must cut back on the amounts contributed. You may not exceed the defined benefit. This is not true of the standard Keogh Plan. Investment results have no bearing on what you contribute. It does not matter how much the earnings make the account grow; you are not required to reduce contributions, nor are you called on to increase contributions being made for your employees should investment results cause the fund to drop in value.

Individual retirement accounts

After the *Keogh Act* was passed, just about everybody who worked for a corporation or who was self-employed had a tax-saving way of building up a retirement nest egg. But people who did not work for corporations were empty-handed. Then in 1975 Congress opened the doors for that group of some fifty million wage earners. And this tax shelter, the Individual Retirement Account (IRA), keeps getting more generous, as has Keogh.

You will find many more savings and loan institutions, banks, mutual funds, and insurance companies that promote IRAs than those that talk up Keogh Plans, because IRAs are so simple and Keogh Plans are more or less technical and involved. An IRA, as its name implies, is just an account, but Keogh is a *plan*. Because it is a plan, much care must be taken to be sure that it is legally proper at its inception and throughout its life. IRA originally required annual reporting, but even that requirement was eliminated by the *Revenue Act of 1978*. Today no annual returns are called for unless a penalty has been imposed.

Eligibility. You may have your own IRA if you are not already participating in a tax-qualified retirement plan, such as a corporate pension plan, a profit sharing plan, a qualified bond purchase plan, or a Keogh Plan. Be careful. If you *were* in a qualified plan for as much as a single day, you are disqualified from the use of an IRA for the entire calendar year. Next year is okay, but not this year. If you have pension rights or are receiving pension payments from a previous job, however, there is no problem. These do not bar you from having an IRA.

Contributions. Assuming that you are eligible, you may contribute the lesser of $1,500 or 15 percent of your earned income to your account on an annual basis. As with Keogh, you pay no current tax on the money you put in, nor do you pay taxes on whatever the money in your account earns until you start withdrawing. The withdrawal portion is the same as with Keogh. Nothing comes out until age 59½, unless you become permanently disabled or die; and you must start drawing your money by the time you are 70½. In actual practice, if you simply must have the money in your account due to a real emergency you may take it out. You pay the deferred tax at that time and a 10-percent penalty.

If you are an employer, IRA is not like Keogh. You may contribute to employee IRAs, *but you do not have to*. You may even pick and choose, making IRA contributions to one person without doing it for others. Say, for instance, that you have a particularly valuable employee you want to favor: He or she sets up an IRA, and you make annual contributions. Your contributions are counted as salary and are, therefore, deductible as a business expense. Your employee can deduct your contributions from current income, deferring any taxes on it until the end of the line. One of the particularly attractive rulings in this connection is that, although your employee is limited to the lesser of $1,500 or 15 percent of his or her own contributions to an IRA, you, as a contributing employer, may contribute to the plan as much as $7,500 a year or 15 percent of his or her earned income, whichever is the lower figure.

Taxation. At any time after age 59½, you may take all of the money out of the account, or you may elect to have monthly payments coming to you. Take all of it at once, and you will pay ordinary income tax on the money, but you are allowed to use five-year-averaging to reduce the tax bite. On page 182, you saw how ten-year-averaging is a big benefit. The principal is somewhat the same. It is not as good a deal as ten-year averaging, but it is a lot better than no break at all.

If you are employed and your spouse is not, each of you may have an individual IRA. The total deductible under those circumstances is $1,750 a year, $875 into each plan. If both of you are wage earners and neither is participating in any qualified plan, each may have an IRA and each may contribute the lesser of $1,500 or 15 percent of your earnings.

The roll-over privilege—a possible bonanza. Whenever a qualified plan in which you have been a participant is terminated, the lump-sum payout becomes taxable *unless* it is "rolled over" into an IRA. Although this is a particularly valuable tax shelter, the roll-over privilege has not attracted as much attention as it deserves. The probable reason is the general impression—a mistaken one—that the opportunities to take advantage of the privilege are rare. Actually, there are at least seven circumstances where the IRA roll-over can be utilized:

1. *at normal retirement,*
2. *when taking early retirement,*
3. *when quitting your job,*
4. *when you are fired,*
5. *when your employing company fails,*
6. *when your company is sold and the plan is dropped, and*
7. *when your employer discontinues a plan.*

The essence of the privilege is that it becomes available whenever a qualified plan is *terminated.* That is the key word.

Regardless of the reason, the dollars coming to you may be rolled over into an IRA, and immediate tax liabilities are avoided. The earnings continue to be tax-sheltered. The sum rolled over can be in six, even seven figures. There is no limit.

Vesting. Vesting relates to the number of years you have been in a plan and to the percentage of the money that has been contributed on your behalf and that truly belongs to you. Nearly all pension and profit sharing plans have a vesting provision. You might be in a plan with a regulation that says until you have been a participant for no less than three years, no part of the money on the books in your name is yours. In another plan—and this is a commonplace provision—each year another 10 percent of the money contributed to your account is unquestionably yours. At the end of ten years, all of it belongs to you. This does not mean that you may take that money whenever you want, but it does mean that when you retire you are *fully vested* and that you will get all the money in your account as either a lump sum or in regular payments. It all depends on the terms of your plan and what options are open to you.

Yet even if you were not fully vested, you get everything in your account if the company terminates the plan. Vesting is no part of the consideration if the company you work for terminates a plan because it fails. (The company's failure, by the way, does not put your qualified plan money in jeopardy. The company is compelled to keep that money in an escrow account where it may not be used for any other purpose, nor may it be attached by creditors.) Even if the company sells out or decides to discontinue the plan for any other reason, you and all other covered employees automatically become fully vested. You *do not* become fully vested just because you retire, take early retirement, quit, or get fired. In other words, if the *plan* terminates, you are fully vested. If *you* terminate, you are not, unless you have been a participant for the required number of years to have reached that happy state.

These are the requirements if you are going to roll over a lump-sum payout from a qualified plan to an IRA:

- *All the money coming out of the old plan must be paid out to you within a single tax year before you reach age 70½.*

- *The portion of the payout you are to roll over must go into the special IRA you create for this purpose within sixty days of the time you receive it. At one time you were required to roll over all your payout, but current regulations allow you to hold any part you want. The part you do hold out becomes taxable at your ordinary rate in the year the money comes to you.*
- *If you made any voluntary contributions to the old plan, that money may not be included in the transfer to the IRA. Any money already earned by voluntary contributions, however, may remain as part of the assets rolled over.*
- *If the payout from the old plan is in the form of anything other than money—stocks or bonds, for example—you must either put exactly what you received (less voluntary contributions) into the IRA or make arrangements with the trustees of the old plan to convert such property to cash before the payout.*
- *You may roll over assets from one IRA to another IRA, or from an Individual Retirement Annuity, as often as once each year. Roll-overs from other types of qualified plans to IRAs may be made as often as the proper conditions permit.*
- *The assets in an IRA roll-over may not be used as loan collateral.*
- *The roll-over should not be made into an existing IRA. It is better to keep an existing IRA and establish a new one to accept the roll-over. No additions may be made to the IRA roll-over account other than its earnings.*
- *Withdrawal restrictions are the same as for other IRAs.*
- *When you roll over to an IRA and do not later roll over to another qualified plan, you sacrifice the right to any capital gain treatment and to the special ten-year averaging permitted when there is a lump-sum distribution from a qualified plan.*
- *Withdrawals from the IRA are treated as ordinary income.*

The loss of the capital gain and averaging opportunities, which sometimes may be applied if no roll-over is made, should be weighed to see which course is better.

A typical case. *At age 50, John Wagner received $80,000 as a lump-sum payout from a terminated pension plan. He banks it and works for another fifteen years. John is in a 32-percent tax bracket. Since he was not age 59½ and was therefore not eligible for the special tax treatment given a lump-sum payout from a qualified plan, John paid $25,600 in taxes on the payout. The remaining $54,400 was invested and earned 5 percent less taxes. By age 65, when he retired, he had $113,093 (not counting taxes paid on the 5 percent interest).*

If John had rolled over the $80,000 into an IRA and the account had earned 5 percent, which would have been tax-deferred, at age 65 he would have had $166,314—$55,000 more. At that point, when he started withdrawing, he would have to pay ordinary income taxes on the withdrawals, but, having retired, his tax bracket would probably be lower.

Because the sums going into IRA roll-overs out of pension and profit sharing plans can be quite large, the IRS in a private letter ruling has given the green light to breaking a roll-over up into two or more IRAs. In that way it becomes a simple matter to put the money into more than one investment vehicle, making your financial planning more flexible. One part, for example, might go into a deferred annuity, another into a growth mutual fund, and still another into a high-yielding commercial bond fund.

U. S. Savings Bonds

Series E and Series H Savings Bonds have been long-term favorites of many savers wanting a tax shelter. Backed by the full faith and credit of the United States, they offer the ultimate in safety. The interest payments are exempt from all state and local taxes. Federal taxes on the income they earn is deferred until maturity. If lost, stolen, or destroyed, the bonds can be replaced. Their immense popularity has been helped, to a great extent, by the facts that they may be bought in very small denominations and that a vast number of employed individuals have had the ease and convenience of buying them on a programmed basis by means of payroll deductions. They are available at banks, savings and loan institutions, and some post offices. They may be bought by mail from the Bureau of Public Debt, Securities Transactions Department, Washington, D.C., 20226, or you can ask your bank to order them for you. The HH Series must be bought from a Federal Reserve bank or by mail from the Bureau.

On January 10, 1979, far-reaching changes were made in these familiar saving vehicles. It was decreed that, as of January 2, 1980, E bonds would be replaced by EE bonds and H bonds would step aside for HH bonds. But the doubling up of the alphabetical designations does not mean that the benefits doubled. Interest earned by the old E bonds was tax-deferred until cashed, nor were any limits put on the length of time they could earn tax-postponed interest for you. The new EE bonds have a lifespan of eleven years, and that is the end of the line—no guaranteed extensions. They may be exchanged for HH bonds, however, thus continuing the deferral on federal taxation of the interest earned.

EE bonds. No longer are $25 bonds available. The smallest denomination of EE bonds is $50, and the biggest is $10,000. Sorry, no more $100,000 bonds. One big change is that now you buy EE bonds for half of their face value. The old E bonds, with a life span of five years, sold for 75 percent of face value. The yield on EE bonds is a straight 6½ percent if held for five or more years. They are not redeemable for six months after you buy them, and you pay a price if you redeem them before five years. The price you pay is that you get less interest—4 percent after two months, 4½ percent in the first year, and the interest gradually increases until the fifth year when it reaches the full 6½ percent. You may not buy more than $15,000 worth, at the issue price, in any year.

HH bonds. These bonds, available in $500, $1,000, $5,000, and $10,000 denominations, sell for face value. The yield is a straight 6½ percent, unless you redeem them before maturity. Interest is paid by check mailed to you twice a year. Maturity is ten years with no extensions. If you acquire HH bonds by exchanging series E and EE bonds, there is no penalty if you redeem prior to maturity.

As is true of EE bonds, you pay no state or local taxes on the interest your HH bonds earn. Federal taxes on HH bond interest is payable when received. The annual limit on purchases is $20,000.

Use EE bonds to handle college costs on a tax-free basis. While it is fine to defer federal taxes on EE bond income, the time comes when those taxes must be paid—*unless.* The "unless" can be handled in this way. You have a young child, and in time you want that child to have a college education. You start putting money aside to cover future college costs by purchasing EE bonds on a consistant basis over a long period of years. Instead of registering the EE bonds in your own name, put them in the name of your child, not as co-owner but as *sole owner.* You can name yourself or anyone else as beneficiary.

Instead of allowing the annual build-up of interest to be deferred, have your child declare the interest each year. If he or she has no other income or at least not enough to require a tax payment, there will be no tax to pay. The very first year of this program, have a Form 1040 filed in your child's name, reporting the EE bond income. Now your offspring is on record as having made the choice to report the EE bond interest income as it accrues. As long as the child's income stays under the taxable level, no further 1040s need be filed. Keep a copy of the first report in your safe deposit box as proof of the original choice. Eventually, when college time comes, your child may redeem the EE bonds and owe nothing to the IRS.

And, speaking of beneficiaries, the new EE bonds, in contrast with the old E bonds, permit you to change beneficiaries whenever you please.

If you have E or H bonds. Any that were issued from 1941 through 1952 will stop paying interest after forty years—in 1981 to 1992. If you cash them in, Uncle Sam will be at your elbow waiting to collect the deferred taxes. You can continue the tax shelter when they mature by trading them in for HH bonds. In that case you will start receiving income in cash twice a year, enjoy the tax deferral, and, of course, you still are free of state and local taxation.

H bonds bought prior to July 1959 will mature and stop earning any interest for you sometime (depending on the date or dates they were first issued) between February 1982 and May 1989. These will have to be cashed as the maturity dates arrive. You are not permitted to exchange them for HH bonds.

Real estate tax shelters

Real estate investments have a fundamental attraction for almost everyone. The solidity and permanance of real estate, as well as its history of increasing value, have broad appeal in themselves. Now that TRA '76 has stripped so many other tax shelters of their brightest attractions, leaving real estate practically untouched, the desirability of some real estate limited partnerships and other real estate investments has been greatly heightened. Not the least of their charms is that many real estate investment programs eliminate one of the greatest detractions of the past—relatively modest sums can be invested.

A real estate tax-sheltered investment can bring together cash flow, tax deductions over a period of years, leverage, a means of fighting inflation, and the possibility of a capital gain at the end of the line. There can be no question about the need for excellent management in the hands of reliable, experienced people. Real estate projects are just as open to bad judgment, error, and dishonesty as any other type of business.

Leverage in a real estate shelter is available because you can take tax deductions based on the full cost of a building even though a major part of the cost represents borrowed money. As a limited partner you have no liability for the borrowings. No other shelter can offer that. Even in a conservative program it is possible for you to enjoy dollar-for-dollar tax writeoffs at the start and then, while enjoying tax-sheltered cash flow over the next eight years or so, you may have deductions amounting to an additional 40 to 50 percent. Deductions can amount to as much as 350 percent in some programs. More often than not, you have a full return of invested dollars in approximately five years while your interest in the program continues.

Drawbacks. Although TRA '76 left real estate king of the tax-shelter hill, it did curb the goodies to some extent. Until 1988 deductions for construction costs must be spread over the useful life of the asset—20 percent for residential construction and 14½ percent for nonresidential. After 1988 the deductions for construction costs may be applied over a 10-year period. Prior to that time the 10-year rule applies only to construction cost interest and taxes.

Where the program embraces subsidized housing for the elderly and the poor, accelerated depreciation may be used. This, plus the high leverage made possible by government-guaranteed loans and rent subsidies, improve the tax loss attraction. The negative factor, however, is the ultimate value of such properties when depreciation has run out and the time for disposing of them arrives. Chapter 11 covers, in some detail, a variety of real estate investment techniques.

Oil and gas drilling funds

Drilling has been, and still is, the most heavily adopted tax shelter for people looking for significant tax relief along with attractive income and capital gain possibilities. This country's dependence on imported oil and gas, increasing domestic usage, and the shrinkage of oil and gas supplies all create a constant demand for capital to finance exploration. And, as stated in the opening paragraph of this chapter, the government does what it can to encourage people to put money into the efforts to find new sources by providing strong tax incentives.

There are, basically, two types of limited partnerships available: (1) publicly offered drilling funds, registered with the SEC, and (2) private placements. While each private placement is smaller than the SEC-registered partnerships, it is estimated that they account for twice as many investment dollars as the public offerings. The big oil companies do a considerable amount of drilling on an exploration basis, but 90 percent of all wildcat drilling is done by independents, accounting for three-quarters of all major new fields. Wildcatting is the term used when an exploration is carried out in an area where no successful wells exist.

Diversification versus wildcatting. One of the principal attractions of the typical offering is that the risk element is reduced by two types of diversification.

For one thing, it is not unusual for fifty to one hundred explorations to be packaged into a single program. You are not exposed to the extreme risk of putting all your investment into a single exploratory well—win or lose. Spreading your invested dollars over so many probes almost eliminates the possibility of coming up with nothing but dry holes. On the other hand, it also reduces the amount of profit from the winners. If you are involved in a program with sixty explorations and the outcome is twenty dry holes, twenty marginal producers, and twenty good producers, the one-third at the top of the scale is considerably watered down by the losers and the mediocre successes. But you have not been wiped out. If the geologists who put the program together are good and their luck is good, you might have enough gushers to make you a big winner despite the negatives.

The second element of diversification—and a most important one—is that the sixty exploratory wells in our hypothetical example are divided over three types of fields. The first category is that of *producing wells.* Some drillings are sited next to a producing well. Oil may be coming out of the ground at Charlie's Gulch, and the geologists have determined that the well is capturing oil from an underground chamber of certain fairly well-defined proportions. They have decided that it probably will pay to sink another well to penetrate the same source. Or the specialists decide that a far deeper penetration of a producing area is needed to get maximum production. Second, some of the exploratory drilling is done in *proven fields.* A proven field is somewhat removed from a producing well, but not too far. Within a limited area there may be one or more producing wells, and it appears immensely logical that the drilling of a new well at the center of a triangle of producers should be productive. There is no absolute certainty that this will be the result, but all studies and sound thinking indicate the advisability of making the attempt. These and similar situations, where proximity to winners is involved, are the proven field drillings. Finally, wildcatting is the long-shot—the big win if you win at all. It is also the big chance that you will end up with nothing.

The reason wildcatting pays off so well is that the exploration companies pay proportionately for the right to drill in each of these three types of geography. Sinking a new well in conjunction with a producing well, as you may expect, gives the person or people with the rights to that piece of real estate a strong bargaining position. If you want to move in on Tex Smith's territory, he might agree provided you make it very much worth his while. You will probably foot the bill for all or most of the costs and pay a handsome price for the drilling privilege. You also will have to agree that a sizable percentage of whatever oil comes out of your well will belong to Tex Smith. To a reduced degree this rationale applies to the rights to explore proven ground. But wildcatting is another story. Not only will it cost far less to get the rights to do your exploration, but also the chances are you will be able to do it without sharing anything you find. Very few wells result from wildcatting. The odds against winning are huge. For that reason

WHEN 100% IS LESS THAN 100%

It is far from uncommon to misunderstand the statements about potential tax savings. A tax shelter's offering statement may say that you will get "*an immediate 100-percent deduction when you invest.*" What could be nicer? You visualize yourself writing a check for $5,000 for the investment and deducting $5,000 from the taxes you pay to IRS.

But that is not the way it works.

Say that your top tax bracket is 40 percent. You invest $5,000 in the Tax-Shelter-of-the-Week on the strength of the fact that you are to get that immediate 100-percent deduction. But what this means is that when you file your federal income tax report this year, you are permitted to pay no tax on $5,000 of your normally taxable income. If you had not made the investment, you would have paid $2,000 to IRS as your tax on that $5,000 (40% of $5,000 = $2,000). You hold on to the $2,000, instead of sending it to the government, *but you still are $3,000 out of pocket.*

Not only that. The chances are that the deduction was allowed because the tax on your $5,000 investment was *deferred.* You have postponed the time when the tax must be paid. This is quite helpful to you, but it is a far cry from paying no tax at all—ever.

the wildcatting portion of the typical exploration package is generally extremely small.

The advantages. These two conservative elements of diversification, therefore, are importantly helpful to you if you invest in an exploration program. They protect you from the risks of extreme speculation. The tax shelter, added to that, makes the package extremely attractive if your tax bracket is high enough. Many experts say that it should be 50 percent or more. You can recover more than you invest because you get tax deductions as you go into the program, and part of whatever income comes out of the program is tax-free. An investor in the 70 percent bracket, for example, can make a $10,000 investment with only $3,000 actually at risk, because if he had not made the investment the remaining $7,000 would have been paid out in taxes. The deductions stemming from intangible drilling costs, such as wages, fuel, repairs, equipment rental, drilling rigs, chemicals, site preparation, and the like, are subject to 15-percent tax-preference minimum tax. This applies only to the productive wells.

Of the money spent for the drilling of unsuccessful explorations—the dry holes—100 percent is deductible. From 60 to 80 percent is deductible for the successful wells, and up to 22 percent of gross income is tax-free thanks to statutory depletion allowances. Income from the producing wells continues as long as the well continues to produce—eight to fifteen years or longer in most instances.

As is true with any type of limited partnership, great care should be taken to study the terms of the partnership agreement, the knowledge, experience, and integrity of the general partners and all other details. With the consent of the general partners, you, as a limited partner, may sell your interest at any time, and, if the successful wells are still producing, you may have a capital gain.

Due to the great popularity of oil and gas investments, some people, other than potential investors, have been attracted. A fair number of questionable people and practices have been unable and unwilling to resist the abundance of public interest. The Securities and Exchange Commission, concerned, as they should be, about some of the illegal and borderline activities, have issued warnings to the public. Here are some of the examples they have used to show how far some promoters go to lure your investment:

- *Prospective investors were told that the common stock being offered would yield a 10 percent return and double in price within the first year, and that the investor would be able to send his or her children to college on a $500 investment in that stock.*
- *Prospective limited partners were told that "scientific equipment" designed and built by the promoter would improve the risk-reward ratio 400 percent in wildcat prospecting for oil and gas. No such equipment existed. The promoter, whose most relevant prior experience was working as a service station attendant, was represented to the potential investor as having engineering and business degrees as well as extensive oil and gas field experience.*
- *Investors were not told that a "psychic" was paid $100,000 to select sites for drilling.*
- *Investors' funds were used to pay for the European and Bahamian vacations of the promoter, leaving no money to pay for drilling wells.*

- *"Producing wells" indicated on the map shown to investors for the purpose of inducing them to invest had not been drilled.*
- *Prospective investors were told that the purchase of a fractional undivided interest was a "safe investment" without disclosing the high degree of risk.*

SEC suggests that you check the following before going into any oil exploration investment:

1. *Is the offering filed with SEC? If so, you should have been given a copy of the prospectus or offering circular.*
2. *Has the offering been filed with the State Securities Commission of your state or of the state in which the promoters are located? Do not hesitate to contact those agencies for any information you feel you should have.*
3. *Ask for a copy of any geological report that may have been prepared, especially if the offering is a private offering. Such reports are not assurances of the presence of oil, gas, or coal. They often contain references to "provide reserves" or "probable reserves," which are only estimates and do not assure that total production will be substantial or that production will be at a profitable rate.*
4. *Review the geological report with a geologist, petroleum engineer, or other person who is knowledgeable and unaffiliated with the company and who can evaluate this type of investment.*
5. *If you find that you need assistance, contact the SEC's Office of Consumer Affairs or one of the SEC's regional or branch offices.*

And the other tax shelters

The additional tax shelters listed at the start of this chapter bring into play a broad variety of factors and technicalities. The laws and regulations, the changing interpretation of those rules and regulations, "tax reform" legislation forever being written, the question as to which of those shelters will endure—all combine to suggest that there is little reason to devote your time to a study of how each of them operate. They should not be overlooked and ignored. Those that survive the decisions of Congress, IRS challenges, and tax court decisions may merit your investigation.

CANDIDATES FOR ACTION

- ☐ Keogh plan
- ☐ Keogh defined benefit
- ☐ IRA
- ☐ IRA roll-over
- ☐ Series EE bonds
- ☐ Series HH bonds
- ☐ College accumulation with Series EE
- ☐ Redeeming Series E and H bonds
- ☐ Real estate limited partnerships
- ☐ Subsidized housing real estate limited partnerships
- ☐ Oil and gas limited partnerships
- ☐ Other tax shelters

10

Locked-In Gains and Forms of Registration

Locked-in gains

It is not unusual for people to have securities or real estate that have enjoyed considerable appreciation since the original investments are made. While it is delightful to see sizable profits in any investment, the profit can bring with it some serious problems. Two of the more commonplace problems are these:

EXAMPLE 1. Mr. Kent has a piece of real estate that has grown in value in a spectacular manner. He bought it in 1962 for $18,000. Today, because of developments in adjacent areas, it is worth $150,000. The land is undeveloped, producing no income. Kent not only has no income from his investment, he pays taxes on it each year and the taxes have been mounting with reassesments as the value has increased. Furthermore, he is now 65, has retired, and could use the income the land value could produce if he sold the property. If he sells, however, he has $132,000 of taxable profits. While he is required to pay a tax on only 40 percent of the profit, his gross taxable income for the year goes sky high, increasing his top bracket. The net result, in this example, is that Mr. Kent would end up with a lot less than the current market value of his property.

EXAMPLE 2. For more than forty years Mr. Goodson worked for a big corporation, rising from a junior executive position to a place near the top. Over that period of time he acquired a large holding of the company shares. Some he bought, some were contributed as a matching encouragement to invest in the company, some were *bonuses, and some were bought at prices well under the market via stock options. Mr. Goodson is about to retire. He has over $350,000 worth of the stock paying a 5-percent dividend. His cost base is extremely low. The company stock represents better than 85 percent of all his assets. He is uneasy about a new management group that has moved in. He fears for the welfare of the company and for the future value of the stock. If he sells and reinvests his money, his income after taxes is likely to be sharply reduced. If he holds and the stock acts as he fears it might, his retirement years look grim.*

The challenge is to find ways to side-step the capital gains tax problems or to modify them sufficiently to release locked-in holdings.

Effective side-stepping

One of the most effective steps, if appropriate, is the charitable remainder trust, which is covered in some detail in the chapter on gifts. The charitable remainder trust significantly minimizes the capital gain tax, provides you (or you and your spouse) generous life-long income, permits immediate tax deductions for the gift, and can give you the gratification of doing something substantial for a worthy cause. This type of trust is not at all appropriate, however, if you want to pass your assets along to other family members. It should be considered only if you have no children, or if your children are extremely well-established financially and do not have any need for your assets. It may also be suitable if the property in question is only a minor part of your estate. It is vital to recognize the fact that the charitable remainder trust involves an irrevocable gift to the institution you choose. It becomes the property of that institution when you and any other income recipients die.

Two other approaches to the locked-in problem are frequently used when there are heirs to consider. Neither of them eliminates the capital gain, but each reduces it—softens the blow—materially.

Installment sales

Mr. Kent, who is concerned with his highly appreciated undeveloped real estate, has a son, Kenneth Kent. At the advice of his financial planner, Mr. Kent decides to make an installment sale of his property to Kenneth. IRS Code 453 sanctions the installment sale and the tax benefits involved. It is a technique that the IRS watches with care. The installment sale contract should be prepared by your lawyer, but it can be important for you to be familiar with the fundamental details. Here are the provisions:

1. *In most cases the installment sale, when used to move out of a high capital gain position, is a family transaction. When the sale is made by Mr. Kent to his son, it is with the thought that Kenneth will sell the property, reinvesting the proceeds in a manner that will help him to meet his installment obligations to his father. Since this must be a legitimate business transaction, Kenneth*

must therefore purchase the property at current market value. Thus, when Kenneth sells the property he is likely to realize approximately the same amount he agreed to pay. He will have no capital gain or loss unless the value has changed after he makes the purchase from his father.

2. *The IRS always has insisted that there must be no prearrangement for the second sale—Kenneth's sale of the property. If the installment sale is to be accepted as a legitimate business arrangement, efforts to find a buyer must not start until after the installment sale agreement is in force. The tax court has not gone along with the IRS position on this, but since IRS has continued to insist on its belief, many lawyers insist that there should be no appearance or reason for suspicion that the second sale was set up in advance. For that reason Kenneth is advised to do nothing about selling the property during the first year.*
3. *The installment agreement must provide that the interest Kenneth pays be no less than 6 percent. If the sales contract does not provide for that much interest, the IRS will require that the rate be 7 percent. If the terms, involving 6 percent or more interest and curtailment of the principal sum, prove to be too burdensome, Mr. Kent can ease the problem for his son. He can give him annual cash gifts of $3,000—or $6,000 with Mrs. Kent's cooperation—as tax-free annual exclusion gifts.*
4. *With the exception of real estate transactions, the sale price may be no less than $1,000.*
5. *The buyer must not be involved in the business of dealing in whatever kind of property is involved. If Kenneth were a real estate agent, he would be barred from the installment purchase of his father's real estate.*
6. *The installments must consist of no less than two payments. Each must be in a different tax year of the seller.*
7. *The payments made in the first year must not exceed 30 percent of the selling price.*
8. *The buyer must be a competent adult. If Kenneth had been 12 years old, the sale could not have been made to him directly. In that case an irrevocable trust would have to be created. Since the law regards a trust as a competent adult, Mr. Kent would sell the property to the trust. The trustee would deal with Mr. Kent and handle all transactions. Kenneth would be the beneficiary of the trust, and Mr. Kent would have no interest in or control over the trust.*

These are the advantages to be realized by Mr. Kent:

1. *The income Mr. Kent receives would be based on the full market value of the property as opposed to the income earned by what would have been left after taxes had he made a normal sale.*
2. *The payments Kenneth makes to his father would be comprised of three elements: Some would be tax-free return of capital, another portion would be interest, and the third part would be capital gain. Since the capital gain would be spread over a long period of years, the annual capital gain that Mr. Kent would have to report and include as part of his ordinary income (40 percent of the gain) will be substantially less than would have been the case had he made an outright sale. The impact on his total income and the resulting top bracket, therefore, will greatly reduce his total tax cost.*

When Kenneth sells the real estate he will have to find a place to invest the money in a manner that will help him meet the agreed payments to his father. How much of a problem this may be will depend, to a great extent, on the terms of the purchase agreement. In most installment sale transactions between parent and child, it is assumed that when the parent dies the child will inherit that portion of the property remaining unpaid. Whatever portion does remain unpaid, however, will be included in Mr. Kent's taxable estate.

A mutual fund withdrawal plan frequently is used to fund an installment sale, with uniform payments of the agreed sums going directly to the seller.

Private annuities

Commercial annuities are available from insurance companies and are sold only for cash. Private annuities may be provided by individuals who are not in the business of offering, creating, or selling annuities; these may be bought by transferring property of value.

Private annuities are capable of giving the buyer—the person who transfers an asset in exchange for annuity payments—any of three advantages. In some cases, a combination of two or all of those benefits can be realized. As is true of the installment sale, it (1) allows the spread of capital gains over a period of years, thus softening the tax liability, (2) it is a means of moving assets paying no, or little income, in a manner that provides good income and excellent cash flow, and (3) it is a means of removing some of the asset from one's taxable estate. The provider of the annuity also may enjoy some worthwhile advantages.

To illustrate how the private annuity works we will stay with Mr. Kent, his son, Kenneth, and Mr. Kent's unimproved real estate with a current value of $150,000 and a cost base of $18,000. Since Mr. Kent is eager to get rid of his nonincome-paying property and does not want to sacrifice a substantial part of his gain via the taxes that would result from an outright sale, he transfers the property to his son Kenneth. In consideration Kenneth promises to make monthly annuity payments to him for as long as he and/or Mrs. Kent may live. The amount Kenneth will pay each month is arrived at by using an IRS formula and IRS tables. The formula is based on Mr. and Mrs. Kent's life expectancies, on the original cost and current value of the property, and on a 6-percent interest factor.

The private annuity formula departs from commercial annuity determinations in some interesting ways. The result is that the senior Kents will get a bigger check each month than any insurance company would provide. The first item of difference is that there is no need to consider a sales commission, overhead, reserves, or profits. The second is that insurance companies and IRS use different life expectancy tables. The insurance company figures that, on average, their annuitants who start receiving payments at Mr. Kent's age—65—will live another fifteen years. The money they expect to pay out to those annuitants, therefore, is to be spread over that period of time. The IRS, looking at its Standard Mortality Table, bases its payout estimate on a shorter period, thirteen years.

This reasoning may sound arbitrary, but there is some sound reasoning behind the difference. Normally, a person who buys an annuity from an insurance company, knows that when he is gone, or when he and his wife are gone, the company keeps whatever is left. For that reason people who are not in good health or who are in hazardous occupations are less interested in annuities than those who expect to live long lives. They expect to beat the insurance company. In contrast, those who enter into private annuity contracts *want* the buyer—usually one of their own children—to have whatever is left. This is not a matter of theory. Long-term records show that people who have commercial annuity contracts actually live longer.

The third difference between private and commercial annuities is that where the IRS requires that the interest factor in a private annuity contract be 6 percent, insurance companies use lower rates. To more fully appreciate the difference, in our example Kenneth would have to pay his father about $18,500 a year, whereas a commercial annuity would pay only $14,250. As a matter of fact, Mr. Kent would get a good deal less than $14,250 from the commercial contract since, in order to buy it, he would first have to sell his land and pay the capital gains tax. (Commercial annuities are sold only for cash; only a private annuity can be bought with appreciated property.) The commercial monthly annuity payments, therefore, would amount to about half as much, for Mr. Kent would have had so much less money with which to buy the contract.

At the heart of the private annuity tax advantage is the fact that when property is exchanged for a private annuity, no capital gain tax is due at that time. The gain is spread over the years of payout. The advantage is the same as in the case of the installment sale. The circumstances are identical. There is one important provision that must be observed. If Kenneth's promise to make the payments is *secured* in any way, the capital gain becomes fully taxable in the year the exchange takes place. The tax advantage is lost. In other words, the annuity contract must not provide that there is to be any lien on the real estate or on any other property, as a guarantee of the annuity payments.

Looking at the private annuity sale from Kenneth's viewpoint, you must consider several elements. As was true in the installment sale, Kenneth will sell the real estate and put the proceeds where it is likely to help him make the required payments. He has no capital gain, having bought and sold at current market value, and in this case there is no need to delay his sale of the asset. A mutual fund withdrawal plan again may prove to be his best choice for the investment. And, again, annual tax-free gifts of $3,000 to $6,000 from Mr. and Mrs. Kent may be used as a means of helping him keep up with the payment schedule.

Keep in mind, in weighing the private annuity, that an annuity sale with a single buyer such as Mr. Kent, cannot be looked upon as a sound business proposition by itself, Actually, it is a means of accomplishing certain tax advantages. It is a poor business proposition because, unlike the annuities sold by insurance companies, the end result is based on a single life. It is not spread over thousands of lives allowing for the long-term experience on which actuarial tables are based, protecting the interests of the seller. If Mr. and Mrs. Kent live abnormally long lives, Kenneth could be in trouble. If they die prematurely Kenneth has a windfall profit, on which he must pay taxes. Regardless of how long or short the Kents' lives may be, a sharp increase or a sharp decrease in the value of the investment can also make big differences. Should Mr. Kent predecease his wife, the value of the annuity to be paid to Mrs. Kent would be part of his estate.

Parents, when aware of the fact that the required annuity payments can create problems, sometimes make the transaction part sale and part gift. Under those circumstances it can be arranged that the annuity payments be held to a level where the investment of the property and the gift, combined, produce ample income to eliminate any hardship. There probably would be a gift tax involved. This possibility must be put on the scale when considering the plan.

If Kenneth was married, the possibility that he could predecease his father must be thought about. He would not want this wife to be saddled with this responsibility of continuing the annuity payments. Decreasing term life insurance on Kenneth's life, with his own wife as beneficiary, would be a sound precaution.

The capital gains if you sell your home

There is a good chance that the biggest capital gain you will have in your life will be the result of appreciation in value of the home you live in. Real estate values have risen astronomically in most areas across the nation. To live in a home you bought for $50,000 with a current market value of $150,000 (which is not unusual) may be very gratifying until you try to figure how you can take advantage of that great growth in value. If you sell, you may face a staggering tax liability, and, at the same time, you must find a new place to live and will be forced to pay a greatly inflated price for that dwelling.

Happily, the framers of our tax structure appreciated those problems and have given you certain privileges. The tax breaks related to the sale of a home are restricted to the sale of your *principal residence.* They do not apply to a house you may have bought as an investment. They do not apply to that place at the beach or the lodge in the mountains you bought for your vacations. Your principal residence can be a house, a condominium or coop apartment, your boat, camper, mobile home, or any other place of dwelling that you customarily use as your living quarters—your home and not your "home away from home." The interpretations of *principal residence,* however, have been quite generous. You are not called on to prove that you have used the place for any specific length of time. You do not even have to be living in it at the time you sell it.

When you sell your principal residence and realize a profit, you may postpone the payment of any tax on the profit. You may even postpone it forever. You will be allowed to defer any capital gains tax on your profit provided that:

1. *What you pay for the new dwelling is as much as or more than the adjusted sales price you received for your old home. (The* adjusted sales price *is the gross amount of the sale minus your sales costs, which may include commissions, legal fees, and anything you spend within the ten days prior to the sale, to make the house more attractive and in good repair, provided that you paid those bills within thirty days after the sale was made.)*
2. *You purchase the new residence eighteen months before and no later than eighteen months after selling your former home.*
3. *You occupy the new home within that same period of time, establishing it as your new principal residence.*
4. *If you build a new principal residence for yourself, construction must be started before the end of eighteen months after your home is sold and you must occupy the new home within two years of the sale. (The IRS has interpreted "start of construction" to mean that you have bought a lot, have a loan commitment for*

construction, and have obtained a building permit for the home you are going to construct, even though you have not broken ground. The two-year deadline applies only when you, or a contractor, are erecting a new home expressly for you. The time limit is eighteen months if you rebuild an existing building, or if you buy and complete a partially constructed house, or if you agree to buy a condominium unit still being constructed. "Occupying" means actually living in the new home. Moving furniture in does not satisfy the definition.)

You do not have to pay the deferred taxes unless you eventually sell the new home and do not, at that time, follow the same course (that is, buying still another residence paying as much or more than you received).

Long enough may be forever. Even then you may not have to pay taxes, because *if you are 55 years of age, or older,* you may sell your home, pocket up to $100,000 profit, and pay no tax on that amount of capital gain. This is a once-only special privilege. In this case it is required that, during three of the five years immediately preceding the date you exchange or sell your home, you use the home as your principal residence. The three years do not have to be successive; three years in aggregate will suffice. Or, if you are 65 or older at the time you sell or exchange the property, proof that you made the home your principal residence in any five out of the past eight years is adequate.

Should the profit you realize amount to more than $100,000, then 40 percent of the excess has to be reported as ordinary income in the year the sale is made. Nor is that all. Let's say you have sold your residence and have realized $150,000 profit. The $100,000 is tax-free, and you owe a capital gain tax on the remaining $50,000 of profit—*unless* you buy still another home. This time, however, you do not have to pay as much or more than you received because your one-time $100,000 exclusion may be subtracted from what you pay, and you are still free of tax liability for the other $50,000 of profit. You get two tax savings for the price of one.

Forms of registration

Many things that people do with their assets stem from tradition or limited understanding. Traditionally, a couple register their bank accounts in joint name, and this tradition frequently carries over to the ownership of other assets. Many married people have the notion that registration in joint ownership eliminates the need for writing a will. Everything, they figure, is beautifully simple. Husband and wife have their bank accounts, stocks, and the house in joint name. If either one dies, the other automatically becomes sole owner. Why pay a lawyer to write a complicated will? They are wrong. Joint ownership makes good sense in many cases, but not in all of them. And there are various joint diseases in joint ownership.

Joint ownership

There are three commonly used types of joint ownership in a property:

1. *joint tenancy,*
2. *tenancy by the entirety, and*
3. *tenancy in common.*

1. *Joint tenancy* is a form wherein two or more people have ownership in a property. The interests are equal. While living, any of the joint owners may do what they want with their portions. They may sell them or give them away even if the disposition of their interests is opposed by the other or others. When they die, however, their interests go to the remaining owner or owners.

2. *Tenancy by the entirety* is a form used exclusively by a husband and wife. Neither may do anything with his or her share unless there is mutual agreement. When either dies, the entire property belongs to the other. The tenancy by entirety automatically ceases to exist if the couple is divorced. (A *joint tenancy by the entirety with right of severance* provides an unusual degree of freedom. One of the joint tenants, without consent of the other, may sell or give his or her share to a third party, making the third party a tenant in common with the remaining original tenant. Generally this is not possible with a tenant by the entirety).

3. *Tenancy in common* involves no rights of survivorship. Each tenant owns an unidivided interest in the property,

which means that each tenant owns no specifically identified portion, but rather an unchanging percentage of the whole. Tenants involved in this type of ownership may sell or give away their interest. They may also dispose of it through wills. This last provision is not true of any other form of joint ownership.

Jointly registered safe deposit boxes. There is a fairly widespread belief that if a man and wife have a bank safe deposit box registered in both names, then all the contents of the box are automatically jointly owned. There is no basis in law for such a belief. The ownership of stocks and deeds in a jointly held safe deposit box depends on how each is actually registered and not where it is stored.

It also depends on whether the couple are living in a state with community property laws. Although these laws vary from one state to the next, one concept is common to all: Anything and everything a married couple acquires or earns throughout their married lives belongs to them jointly. When either partner dies, the remaining mate becomes full owner of it. There are eight community property states: Arizona, California, Idaho, Louisiana, Nevada, New Mexico, Texas, and Washington. Community property states—and some others as well—do not sanction tenancy by the entirety. Several of the states that do recognize this form of ownership permit it to apply only to real estate.

The good, the bad, and the dubious. Joint ownership, in its various forms, has its good points and its bad points. Here are the positive factors . . .

1. *From a psychological standpoint many married couples want joint ownership. It provides a strong bond, a feeling of togetherness, a sense of mutual trust, a common financial base.*
2. *In the event of an emergency, either a husband or wife can get to the assets in a jointly registered bank account instantly.*
3. *Some state laws protect jointly held property from creditors making claims against the first to die. This usually applies only to husband and wife joint ownerships.*
4. *It is possible that some or all of the assets held jointly may escape being included in the taxable estate of the first of a married couple to die.*

5. *Any property passing to a surviving spouse through joint ownership is out of the probate estate and thus normal probate costs are saved. This does not, however, mean that there are no costs involved in the transfer of ownership.*
6. *Because probate is bypassed, there is presumably no delay in the passing of the assets to the survivor, nor is there any publicity.*
7. *There may be some income tax savings. Savings can be realized if the filing of separate returns results in lower tax brackets, or if it permits increased exemptions, credits, and deductions. Many states do not allow these tax savings in regard to savings accounts, savings bonds, or where one of the joint owners provided all the funds that purchased the jointly held property. The chances are that there is no benefit regarding Federal taxes since the law permits income splitting on joint returns no matter how the property is registered. Some states do not have a similar provision, and in those cases the separate returns could provide an advantage.*
8. *Where securities are held in joint ownership and the dividends are paid to a co-owner who does not otherwise use the $100 dividend exclusion, there is a clear advantage.*

The fractional share rule deals with the possibility that the full value of the property might be included in the estate of the first spouse to die. The fractional share rule in TRA '76 provides that only *half* the value is considered part of the estate of the first to die if four requirements are met:

1. *The joint interest must be created by one or both of the spouses for property acquired after 1976.*
2. *In relation to personal property, the creation of the joint interest must have been a taxable gift and reported for gift tax purposes.*
3. *When the property involved is real estate, an election to treat the creation of the joint interest as a taxable gift must have been made and reported at the time.*
4. *Only a husband and wife may be the joint owners.*

The fractional share rule applies only to husband and wife joint ownerships created after December 31, 1976. Joint ownerships that were created prior to that date may be dissolved and recreated under the new rule. As to joint ownerships that were created before December 31, 1976, the survivor has the burden of proving that part of all of the jointly held property was originally purchased with his or her own funds, or that the property was received as an inheritance or a gift.

The negatives of joint ownership are:

1. *Spouses with jointly owned assets sacrifice full control. Ordinarily neither one has the sole right to use, manage, invest, borrow against, sell, and what not. Arguments, separation, or divorce can create severe problems.*
2. *If husband and wife have property in joint ownership and they die simultaneously, there can be great problems concerning the disposition of the property. It is quite possible that it may be disposed of in a manner that would be contrary to what the couple would have preferred. For example, Mr. A buys stock and has it registered under his name and his wife's in joint tenancy. They are together on a plane that crashes, and both die. It is determined that the wife outlived him by a matter of an hour or two. There is no will. Before his second marriage to Mrs. A, Mr. A was a widower with two minor children from his first marriage. Under the laws of the state in which they reside, it is determined that the property must go to the second wife's closest blood relative, an aunt both of them hated.*
3. *The survivor of the joint ownership may lack the knowledge and ability to properly manage the property. While provisions to cover that possibility are available in wills and trusts, they are not available when property passes through joint ownership.*
4. *Joint ownership requires advance legal guidance to a greater extent than many other financial planning steps. Without it there is the possibility that serious tax and legal problems may arise involving substantial expense.*
5. *If the jointly owned property is a depreciable asset, there can be a real disadvantage when compared with the tax results of receiving the property as a beneficiary of a will. The beneficiary under a will, in establishing the cost base of an asset acquired prior to 1977, has the advantage of applying the "fresh start" adjustment. In other words, the inheritor is permitted to take the market value of the property as of December 31, 1976 as the cost basis. All depreciation taken before that date is automatically restored. This can increase the cost base materially. In contrast, the person coming into full possession of a depreciable asset as the survivor in joint ownership is not allowed to restore past depreciation. As a result the cost base can be very much*

lower, putting the recipient at a serious disadvantage when the property is sold. If the joint ownership was created after 1976, however, the joint ownership survivor and the person inheriting via a will are on equal footing. Both are required to reduce their cost bases to reflect past depreciation.

6. *When a joint interest is created, there may be a gift tax liability. These are the usual exceptions:*
   a. *a joint tenancy or tenancy by entirety, that is created by husband and wife when the property is real estate and the couple does not elect to treat the creation as a gift;*
   b. *the establishment of a joint bank account, provided that the one creating the joint account is free to withdraw without consent of the other;*
   c. *joint registration of U.S. saving bonds;*
   d. *joint brokerage accounts held in street name, provided that either may act as sole owner, and*
   e. *any joint ownership where both parties contribute equally to the original purchase. In such cases great stress must be placed on the absolute need to keep detailed records confirming the fact that each truly did make an equal contribution.*
7. *With certain exceptions, even when the establishment of the joint ownership is treated and reported as a gift and income is divided, the asset remains in the estate of the donor.*
8. *Mr. A has property and registers it in joint ownership with Mrs. A. She dies. Her taxable estate will include the value of the jointly held property, increasing her estate tax. In time Mr. A dies. Now the total value of the property becomes taxable in his estate. The tax on her half has been doubled, and, in addition, there is the possibility that he paid a gift tax when the joint ownership was created.*
9. *Unless careful records are kept on jointly held property where each contributed to the original investment, the full value can be taxed to the estate of the first to die—no matter how much or how little that person actually contributed. If each owned their own shares separately, this would be avoided.*
10. *In many ways joint ownership fails to be a substitute for a will.*
    a. *It is just about impossible for all of a person's assets to be held in joint ownership.*
    b. *State laws vary. In some states it is entirely possible that jointly held property may be distributed in keeping with that state's intestacy laws.*

c. *No provision is made for simultaneous deaths.*
d. *There can be way of directing and controlling the use of assets.*
e. *No provisions exist for the handling of debts, final expenses, and taxes.*

It might be a good idea, in light of what you have just read, to review the manner in which your various assets are registered. You may want to make some changes.

CANDIDATES FOR ACTION

- ☐ Freeing up some appreciated assets which
  - ☐ pay little or no income,
  - ☐ create an imbalance because too much of my capital is in a single investment, or
  - ☐ I am uneasy about the future of this investment.
- ☐ Use of an installment sale
- ☐ Use of a private annuity
- ☐ Sale of my home with tax on profit deferred
- ☐ Sale of my home, taking advantage of the over-age-55 privilege of paying no tax on as much as $100,000 capital gain.
- ☐ Review registration forms I now have for:
  - ☐ savings and checking accounts,
  - ☐ stocks,
  - ☐ real estate, and/or
  - ☐ residence.

11

The Riches in Real Estate

The attractiveness of real estate

Real estate investing has many attractions. For one thing, it is an investment you can *see,* visit, inspect, and keep an eye on. That is more than a superficial satisfaction. Many knowledgeable real estate specialists advise that you lean toward real estate investments close to home. If you are a city dweller, you know your area. You know which neighborhoods are likely to have a candidate for investment. You also have a sound basis for judging whether a neighborhood is on its way up or moving in the opposite direction. You know how traffic flows past a location being considered for a commercial enterprise. You know that certain parts of your town have a high crime rate and that others are regarded as relatively secure. You have a good idea of some of the things that may or may not occur in the future and that could have powerful positive or negative impact on a specific location. The point is that when you engage in real estate investing in your own backyard, you do not have to be an experienced, savvy real estate expert to be in a position to make a number of important judgments. And on the other side of the coin, when you put your money into a real estate investment far removed from your part of the world, you have no choice but to depend completely on the judgment and the integrity of others.

No type of investment has had kinder treatment from our

lawmakers than real estate. And few places where people put money have increased in value to the same extent. In a single investment, you have the best of current tax shelters and a powerful weapon in your battle against inflation. The things that make real estate investments so tax-gentle include:

- *It is the one investment where you have opportunities to take advantage of the immense benefit of nonrecourse loans. Just for illustration, you invest $10,000 in a project and are allowed to take tax deductions on $50,000 or $100,000. The difference reflects money borrowed, but* you have absolutely no obligation to repay any part of the loan even if the project fails. *That is what "nonrecourse" means.*
- *The unusually big tax deductions you are permitted to take will probably put you in a lower tax bracket. You pay a smaller tax on all your income, regardless of where it comes from.*
- *The market value of the property you invest in may grow, grow, grow, but you are allowed to take* depreciation *deductions as though the property is worth less, less, less. Thus you benefit from "phantom losses."*
- *Depreciation permits you to take deductions from otherwise taxable income, giving you tax-free cash flow.*
- *Any profit in the sale of the property is, of course, subject to tax at capital gain rates if you have held the property for more than one year. You are taxed on just 40 percent of the gain.*
- *If you sell at a loss you also get a break. On all other types of investment losses you are allowed to offset capital gains with as much as $3,000 of losses. When it is a real estate loss, however, there is no top limit. Deduct it all, and the IRS shares the loss with you at your top tax bracket. If you are at the 50-percent level, half your loss is taken off your back.*
- *When you borrow to finance any type of investment other than real estate, your interest deduction is generally held to a maximum of $10,000 plus your investment income. If the borrowing is for a real estate investment, there is no upper limit to your interest deduction.*

Aside from the tax advantages, the fact that you can enter a real estate venture with an investment representing just a small percentage of the overall value of the propertly greatly magnifies your profit potential. Were you to invest $50,000 in a

real estate venture and see it increase in value to $75,000, you would enjoy a 50-percent profit. But invest just $5,000 in the same venture and with the same percentage of ownership, the increase in value gives you 500-percent profit. With a nonrecourse loan, you do not expose yourself to any additional risk.

Why will any lender permit a nonrecourse loan? Because the property itself, plus your down payment, protects the lender against default. Keep in mind, too, that the leverage you get when you invest in this way has the same beneficial leveraging impact on your depreciation deduction. You take depreciation on the gross value of your interest in the property.

There are many ways to involve yourself in real estate. We will deal first with those requiring the most modest sums of money, and then we will move to the increasingly larger and more complex types of real estate ventures.

Investing in mortgages

One of the most direct ways of investing in a mortgage arises when you sell your own home.

The buyer needs help

You finally have found a potential buyer who is willing to pay your price. The only trouble is he has been unable to find a lender who will give him a big enough first mortgage. Any of three things can happen.

1. *You may agree to take a second mortgage.* A considerable risk is involved. To start with, the holder of the first mortgage—a bank or savings and loan institution in most cases—comes first, as the title of his mortgage suggests. If the buyer ever defaults on payments, the first mortgage holder can foreclose and put the house up for sale. If a sale is consummated, first mortgage holders take everything owed to them—the balance outstanding on the loan plus all accrued interest and foreclosing expenses. If anything remains, then it is your turn. But you do come second. So before you agree to take a second mortgage, you should know a good deal about the borrower and have good reason to be confident that he is not likely to fall behind in payments.

If you do take a second mortgage, the risk involved traditionally means that you are entitled to an interest rate in excess of that paid to the first mortgage holder. But a higher rate may be illegal in your state. The interest to be paid on the first mortgage is probably the maximum the law allows. It is entirely customary, under those circumstances, for you and the buyer to agree to increase the price for the house enough to compensate for the difference.

Incidentally, before you entertain the idea of giving your buyer a second mortgage make sure that the first mortgage lender permits you to do so. The first mortgage holder has the right to refuse to let the buyer take on the additional financial burden of paying off on another mortgage.

2. *You may take the first mortgage.* Your home is fully paid for, or close to it. Were you to sell, you might not have immediate need for all the money involved, that is, the buyer's down payment plus the balance of your sale price provided by the bank or savings and loan. The idea of having double-digit yield plus the gradual payment of principal flowing to you each month for a long period of time can be very appealing. Until

this time, the equity you have had in your home has been producing no income for you.

Once again, you will have to learn a great deal about the buyer, and, of course, you must also have the assistance of a knowledgeable lawyer, before you make this decision. One of the things to be considered is the capital gains tax you will owe on your profit in the sale. (As you saw in Chapter 10, there are ways to avoid or reduce the tax if you buy another home or are age 55 or older.) The chances are that the gain will be a lot of money even though you pay only 40 percent of the gain at whatever your tax bracket may be. If your top bracket is, for example, 50 percent and the profit is $80,000, you pay $16,000 in federal taxes alone in the year the sale is consummated and payment is received by you.

3. You may buy second mortgages. People have done quite well investing in individual second mortgages on private dwellings. If you have ready capital, it is not at all difficult to find homeowners and other people in the market to buy homes who are looking for second mortgage money. Real estate sales people welcome you. Your interest in supplying second mortgage money can make the difference in closing a sale. As the prices for homes go up and loan money becomes tighter, more and more welcome mats are laid out for second mortgage buyers.

Clearly, however, the increased demand for second mortgage money necessitates care on your part before you commit yourself. With sky-high prices and interest rates, the threat of loss goes just as high. For one thing there is the danger that the buyer may become overextended in order to meet inflated demands. And second, depressed economic conditions can have the twofold impact of putting the mortgage payer in a deteriorating position, and—should foreclosure become essential—property values could fall to a serious degree.

Given a secure situation, where you have excellent reasons to feel that the mortgagor will be able to weather any economic storms, a second mortgage can be unusually rewarding. Second mortgages normally range from five to ten years. They sell at discounts, which represent the premium paid for the higher risk that the second mortgage lender assumes. In most instances the discount amounts to 5 percent for each year in the life of the mortgage. If you take over a second mortgage for $5,000 and it has seven years to run, you buy the mortgage at a 35 percent discount—$3,250. But you collect interest on $5,000. In addition, the average second mortgage involves monthly payments of *interest only* with the payment of the principal sum—$5,000 in the example—at the end of the line. Thus, you are getting the agreed interest on the full $5,000 for the entire seven-year period. Assuming you are collecting a high rate of interest, that is a very desirable position to be in.

Ginnie Mae and Freddie Mac

While this heading may sound like a lead-in to social notes from all over, these Wall Street names refer to two government-sponsored ways of investing in mortgages.

Ginnie Mae. This is the playful abbreviation for Government National Mortgage Association. It is federally chartered to make more mortgage money available to the public. The association gives its approval to certain firms meeting its requirements, to issue securities backed by pools of FHA-insured or Veterans Administration loans on various types of dwellings. The firms issuing the securities, usually in $100,000 units, collect the mortgage payments and pass them along to the investors.

Two elements make Ginnie Maes interesting. First, the government guarantees that the mortgage payments will be made if the inhabitants of the dwellings fall behind or drop out completely. Second, in addition to the high income these mortgages generate—offering slightly higher yield than Treasury notes—the payments also include amortization of principal. Thus, in a single investment you have the strongest guarantee you can find plus excellent cash flow.

Freddie Mac. Similar to Ginnie Mae, Freddie Mac is the Federal Home Loan Mortgage Corporation, a U.S. government corporation. Freddie Mac creates portfolios of conventional nonguaranteed mortgages and sells them either as $100,000

Mortgage Participation Certificates or as Federal Home Loan Mortgage Corporation Guaranteed Mortgage Certificates, also in $100,000 denominations. Both certificates pass along interest and principal to you; the major difference between the two is that the latter has a fixed redemption date. Freddie Mac, while not guaranteed by the U.S. government directly, is guaranteed by FHLMC, an agency of the U.S. government. There is actually very little difference, but because of that difference the yields are slightly higher than Ginnie Mae's.

Since most interested investors are unlikely to have $100,000 to spare for investment, the mutual fund approach has been made. Mutual funds with portfolios of different Ginnie Mae issues make shares available for as little as $1,000. You pay a sales charge, but aside from that all other rights and benefits are the same as for those who invest directly. (Fewer funds have done the same with Freddie Mac, but some do exist.)

What attracts investors to Ginnie Mae and to Freddie Mac is that both combine very good cash flow and exceptional safety. The cash flow is high because it consists of generous interest plus some amortization of principal. A 9-percent yield from a Ginnie Mae investment, which is not unusual, amounts to something close to 10-percent cash flow thanks to the amortization element. The safety feature, as you have seen, is the guarantee of the United States government in the case of Ginnie Mae and of an agency of the United States government for Freddie Macs.

Real estate investment trusts

The "REITs," as they are best known, came onto the scene in 1960. Since then the REIT field has become fairly active, with nearly 200 active REITs in business. They patterned themselves after the mutual funds to a great extent. A REIT gives you the opportunity to invest in a variety of real estate items that are selected and supervised by professional managers. It is one way of investing in real estate projects that does not demand fairly sizable sums of money. It is a means of reducing risk by having your investment dollars spread over a number of properties. The REITs are *unlike* mutual funds in that the sponsor or distributor does not stand ready to repurchase your shares on request. Generally shares of an REIT are bought and sold through investment dealers in exactly the same way as you would deal with common stocks.

Types of REITs

There are three types of REITs:

1. *equity REITs,*
2. *mortgage REITs, and*
3. *combination REITs.*

Equity real estate investment trust. The managers of an equity REIT buy and manage properties such as apartment houses, office buildings, shopping centers (and the like)—properties that produce income. In addition to income, they try to handle their properties in ways that also create profits when they are sold. They could, of course, sell some of their properties at a loss. Loss or gain is passed on to the REIT shareholders, as is the income earned. Also passed along to shareholders is additional income made possible by the depreciation that management takes on its properties.

Mortgage real estate investment trust. This one subdivides into specialized categories. Some concentrate on short-term commitments, confining themselves to construction and development loans. Others deal strictly in long-term financing of major projects such as apartment and commercial buildings. A third category in this group is the leasebacks REIT.

Combination real estate investment trust. These, in most cases, are sponsored by major life insurance companies. The combination REIT buys and manages different kinds of income-producing properties and makes various kinds of mortgage loans as well. The underlying theory is that the REIT's managers are thus in a position to alter the trust's emphasis in keeping with changing economic condition.

Since the introduction of REITs, the equity type has done quite well. Thanks to the almost universal and vigorous growth of real estate values, these property-owning trusts have ridden on the crest of the inflation tide. It has not been true of all equity REITs for, as in all financial matters, so much depends on the experience, knowledge, skills, and integrity of those who are in charge. For the most part, however, the equity REITs have had excellent growth in both value and income.

On the other side of the scale, the mortgage REITs have suffered. This has been especially true of those concentrated in the short-term loan market, while some of long-term mortgage trusts managed to hold their heads above some rough water.

With the ability to walk on both sides of the street, the combination REITs come in between the two.

Vacation homes

For a long time, many people were lured to investments in vacation homes at beaches, lakes, and mountains, because they could use it for their vacation and then rent it the rest of the time. The assumption was that, because you rented the home to outsiders, even though you made some use of it yourself, the vacation home qualified as a business property. The heart of the tax saving was that owners of business properties are allowed to take deductions for depreciation, insurance, repairs, property taxes, and mortgage interest. Homeowners, however, were permitted to deduct from income only mortgage interest payments and property taxes. That much is still true.

If you did have a vacation home that you offered for rent, even for very brief periods of time, it was easy to show sizable tax losses. Most vacation homes are in areas that are attractive for only about three months a year, but depreciation, taxes, and interest are year-round affairs. The losses thus shown could be used to shelter income from a variety of sources.

The *1976 Tax Reform Act* drastically curbed this means of avoiding taxes. Rent your vacation home today, and you may deduct only mortgage interest and property taxes that exceed the rental income. No other deductions may be taken unless the rental income is greater than all expenses for the rental period. In that case depreciation and other expenses are includable, but there is no tax loss. If you, your family, and/or friends use the vacation home for less than fifteen days in the year or for 10 percent of the number of days the house is actually rented at fair rental value, whichever is greater, then you are not required to report the rental income at all, nor may you deduct as expenses anything other than interest and taxes.

The story is different if you buy a resort home and do not make any personal use of it, but offer it for rent throughout the year. This is a step you may take if you think in terms of using the home for yourself in years to come, perhaps at retirement. It is one way of attempting to provide yourself with an eventual vacation or retirement home at little or no real cost and possibly at a profit. Or you may buy such a home strictly as a side business venture for the rental income, the building of equity, and the eventual sale at a profit. In either case, since no personal use is involved, all expenses and full depreciation may be deducted from rental income. If the combined costs exceed income, you have a tax loss that you may apply to other earned income. However, if you don't show a profit in at least two out of five consecutive years, the losses may be disallowed as "hobby" losses.

Real estate limited partnerships

A real estate limited partnership is created by one or several people who are the general partners. The limited partners are passive investors. They take no part in the operation of the partnership, and they have no financial liability beyond the money they actually invest. The partnership form is used in preference to a corporation because a partnership pays no taxes and a corporation does. A partnership, therefore, is able to pass along to the individual partners all income, all losses, and all tax advantages. The partnership may involve the acquisition of a piece of land and the construction of an apartment house, an office building, a shopping center, or some similar income-producing venture. Or the partnership may be organized with the objective of buying existing income-producing properties. It may include joint ventures with other parties. It may be organized to build or purchase a single property, or it may have a variety of income-producing properties in different locations. Real estate limited partnerships, if of sufficient magnitude, are referred to as *syndications*; these are registered with the SEC and are offered only when the prospective investor is given a prospectus. Private placements generally, but not always, involve less capital and a tightly controlled number of limited partners. As a rule the limit is thirty-five. The costs of promoting and selling the syndications tend to reduce the net results, but the larger partnerships are more likely to offer the risk-reducing element of diversification. And many investors feel more secure with an investment registered with SEC.

Purposes and advantages. The objective of any real estate limited partnership is to provide the partners with cash distributions which, in the early years of operation, defer federal income tax until the property or properties are sold—to generate long-term capital gains and to build equity through the reduction of mortgage indebtedness. The most attractive feature is the fact that the mortgage loans are substantial and the limited partners enjoy tax deductions and tax-sheltered income based on the gross value of the properties, even though they have no liability for the partnership's borrowings. The lenders have recourse only to the property and cannot look to any of the partners for payment if there is a default.

There are risks. If a real estate venture does not work—due to serious vacancy problems, inexpert management of the properties, a challenge by taxing authorities regarding the structure of the partnership and their denial of some of the anticipated tax advantages, the eventual sale of the property at a loss—there can be losses greater than the income and the tax advantages.

Blind pool. In the case of many diversified syndications, the money invested by the limited partners goes into what is called a *blind pool.* The pool is "blind" if the general partners have no properties at the time of the offering. Not until the syndication has been sold out—which could involve the sale of many millions of dollars worth of limited partnership units to as many as one thousand or more individuals—do the general partners acquire properties. They cannot do so before having the money because negotiating for the purchase of a property and the securing of mortgage loans, prior to having the money for down payments and related costs, is difficult, if not impossible. Therefore, when you buy a limited partnership via a syndication you will probably not know what properties you are investing in or where they are geographically. This is normally compensated for, however, by the fact that the major syndicators are steeped in the knowledge of large real estate purchases and management. You may examine their records and see what they have previously accomplished. If you see reason to value their judgment, skills, financial strength, and integrity, the *blind pool* aspect is not a serious drawback.

Private placements. More often than not, these are based on a specific property. In that case you have the opportunity to know not only who the general partners are but also where your investment dollars are going. Before investing you should take a searching look at several important factors:

- *What percentage of your investment money goes to the general partners and to distribution expenses? Rule of thumb is that no more than 20 percent of your investment should be used for such purposes.*
- *Who is to have the contract to manage and maintain the properties? If the management is to be taken over by the general partners or by some organization in which one or more of the general partners have a direct or indirect interest; you should know that the fees going to management are fair and competitive with unrelated management organizations and that the proposed managers are experienced and competent.*
- *Is any property being bought from one of the general partners, directly or indirectly?*
- *Is it an arm's length deal with the price paid fully justified? Many private placements do involve property wholly or partly owned by a general partner. There is nothing wrong with such an aspect, provided the partnership does not pay an inflated price.*
- *Do the limited partners stand first in line for distributions of income profits and return of capital?*
- *Are general partners to get an inequitable percentage of distributions?*

Limited partnerships have limited lives. In most cases, after the major tax benefits have run their course, the property or properties are sold, the net proceeds are distributed to the partners, and the partnership comes to an end. On average, the life of real estate limited partnerships is between eight and twelve years. When properties are sold and the proceeds distributed, deferred taxes may become payable. Table 11-1 is an example that one real estate limited partnership syndicator has used to illustrate what a limited partner might anticipate. The example is extremely conservative, based on a hypothetical increase in the property value of just 2 percent a year. It covers a period of ten years and portrays the results for an investor with a top tax bracket of 40 percent. His investment is $10,000, and it is assumed that at the end of the tenth year the property is sold. Had the appreciation been 5 percent a year, the annual total return, after taxes, would have amounted to 20 percent.

Table 5. Example of Profitability of real estate limited partnership

Investment actually going into property after deduction of all fees	$ 8,000
Value added via mortgage	$16,000
Gross value of investment	24,000
Plus growth in value over the 10 years	5,000
Appreciated value	29,000
Less mortgage balance	−11,000
Net sales proceeds	18,000
Plus cash distribution received over the 10 years	10,000
Total return	28,000
Less original investment	10,000
Pre-tax profit	18,000
Taxes on distributions @ 405	4,000
After-tax profit	$14,000

or a total after-tax return of 14% a year.

Some limited partnerships permit the limited partners to spread the investments over a term of four or five years. This can be a great advantage. Not only does it reduce risk and ease the possible problem of having to raise a large amount of cash at one time, it creates the chance that the income you receive may be enough—even more than enough in some cases—to provide the cash needed for the investments to be made after the first year. This is a genuine possibility because of the very substantial tax deductions available in the early years.

An example of how this cash flow can work is detailed in the *Tax Shelter Desk Manual,* a publication of Executive Reports Corporation, Englewood Cliffs, New Jersey, and it is reprinted here:

Many big investors or builders find that their most pressing need is cash. And they're willing to trade off a good part of their ownership in exchange for that cash. Here's an—

EXAMPLE: Owner is in a severe cash crunch and must sell one of his properties for $1,100,000. It's an apartment house he's owned for some time. There's a first mortgage of $600,000 and a second of $300,000. That leaves $200,000 to be raised.

A limited partnership is formed with Owner as General Partner and ten investors as Limited Partners. (Naturally, each partner has his lawyer and accountant check things out very carefully before *putting up a penny and* **before** *signing anything.)*

The General Partner retains a 5% interest in the deal; ten investors share the other 95%.

The investors agree to put up the money. BUT *their advisors insist that the $200,000 (the Owner's equity) be put up over four years. That works out to $50,000 a year, or $5,000 per investor:*

Let's say financial projections show the project will sustain a $150,000 tax loss for four years running. The ten Limited Partners' share of these yearly losses (95%) is $142,500.

Split up the $142,500 writeoff among the ten investors (Limited Partners) and you come up with about a $14,250 annual writeoff per investor.

We're assuming all the Limited Partners in our example pay a tax of 50% on their top dollars. So the $14,250 annual writeoff is worth $7,125 in cold, hard cash to each of them. And since their cash investment each year is only $5,000, they actually net $2,125 in each of the first four years.

Here's how it works out:

Year	Writeoff	Cash	After-Tax Benefits	Cumulative
#1	$14,250	$5,000	$2,125	$2,125
#2	14,250	5,000	2,125	4,250
#3	14.250	5,000	2,125	6,375
#4	14,250	5,000	2,125	8,500

Installment sales to nonfamily members

In Chapter 10, dealing with locked-in capital gains, you saw how an installment sale made to a family member can solve a number of problems. If you own a real estate property that has grown in value to a considerable degree, an installment sale can be made to an outsider. Again the object is to avoid being hit with a big capital gains tax in the year of the sale. As in the case of dealing with someone in your family, the technique is to have the payments spread over a number of years so that the gain and the tax are also spread out, effectively reducing what you must give up to the tax collectors.

No more than 30 percent in the first year

The main thing is to be certain that you collect no more than 30 percent of the purchase price in the first year. Taking a 25 percent cash down payment from the buyer, with the buyer assuming responsibility for an existing mortgage, for example, can take you well over the 30 percent limitation. His acceptance of the mortgage reduces your cost. The reduction plus the down payment, should they add up to more than 30 percent, make the transaction a sale where your total capital gain becomes payable in the year of the sale. This is true even though you have not collected anything like the full amount of the agreed purchase price. You must examine the entire transaction with great care to be absolutely certain that, in no way, are you getting effective receipt of anything more than 30 percent. To play it safe, hold it to 28 percent or 29 percent. The help of a lawyer can be critically important in such matters.

Buying and improving residences

If you have the ability and the willingness to be carpenter, plumber, electrician, or painter, you may be able to build a real estate empire for yourself. The alternative is to work with a person or company willing to enter into some joint ventures with you. To succeed you must be a sharp negotiator and an innovative visualizer, and you must have cash, courage, and time.

Be sure of what you're buying

The cash may come from refinancing your own home if no other source of money is available to you. You start out by looking for a piece of property you can buy cheap because it *looks* bad. The emphasis is on the word *look*. The building you consider should not look "bad" to the extent that the plumbing is beyond redemption, the roof needs total replacement, the neighborhood is undesirable, and there is no sign of rapid improvement. In such a case, chances are that whatever you pay will not prove to be any bargain. Some buildings, however, have been neglected to the extent that they haven't been painted, windows may be broken, and no one has bothered to cut grass, trim away dead shrubbery or trees, repair the sidewalk or the sagging entrance door. The appearance is miserable; but the underlying structure is sound. Also, the neighborhood is at least acceptable from the standpoint that it is not a threatening area, and it is either stable or on its way up.

Look for opportunities

Having satisfied yourself that the building is basically sound and suitably situated, ask yourself if it is being used to its best economic advantage. Here is where your creativity comes to front stage. Beyond the fact that the rents obtainable from a neglected building can be increased considerably if the building is revitalized, look around to see if there are not some opportunities to turn non-income areas into dollar-makers. See if you can visualize how some low-cost but highly visible attractions may add appreciably to the appeal of the building.

A dark and cluttered basement might be converted to a bright and profitable use. An unused garage might become a usable garage, studio, or something else that could have strong drawing power.

Buying what you see

In negotiating with the owner, never let your eagerness to buy permit you to think and bargain in terms of what can be done. Concentrate on what is. The building is in a run-down condition, and that is what you are offering to buy—not future potential.

Let's assume we are talking about a four-family flat or a small rooming or apartment house. Before going into a bargaining session with the owner, make a decision as to what you want to do about the present occupants. You can either work around them in the process of refurbishing, or you can empty the building out and start from scratch. If the latter, include in your deal with the owner a provision that the tenants are terminated and that the building is delivered to you empty. If you are going to work around the tenants, you will be doing so with the firm intention of increasing their rents as much as you can. Try not to be "the enemy." Make the tenants your collaborators. Invite their ideas. What improvements would they like to see? As they share their ideas with you—and the ideas can be valuable, for tenants know the building far better than you do—they will expect and accept higher rents.

In contrast with your own home the residential property you buy for investment is, in the eyes of IRS, a business property. That gives you the advantage of being able to take depreciation on the property, which is a considerable tax advantage. It gives you paper losses without decreasing your cash flow.

Repairs and improvements

Repairs to the building are deductible items. Improvements are not. A *repair* is anything you do related to the efficient operation of the building that does not prolong its life or add to the property value. While *improvements* are not deductible from income, they do add to your cost base, and they can thus be an important means of reducing your taxable capital gain when you sell. To get the greatest benefit out of repairs and improvements and to avoid future problems with the taxing authorities, keep clear and careful records of what you spend for each. If you deal with one company or individual who does some repair and some improvement work for you, insist on separate bills so that the two are not intermingled in your files.

Return for a moment to the question of whether you are going to find the time, the energy, and the know-how to do all the rebuilding work yourself. Your labor has no value from a tax point of view. You cannot put a price on it and deduct it as a cost of repair, nor can you claim anything for your muscle work when you make capital improvements. If you hire labor for these jobs, however, you have the government sharing the cost with you. How much of the cost is taken over depends on your tax bracket. It is a consideration that can help you to make borderline decisions when you face the question, "Shall I do it myself or get outside help?"

Spreading your investments

Sell the property. Your big goal, if you want to make the buy-and-improve project an important part of your financial plan, is to move from an original venture to another and another and another until you have developed a broad-based, profitable business for yourself and not just a hobby. The surest way to do that is to buy, improve, and *sell.* The "sell" is imperative. Selling soon after you have done the improving and increased the income of the property is wise for several reasons. For one, your improvements are still fresh and at the height of their attractiveness, making a sale easier and commanding a better price. Second, you do not hang around waiting for unexpected problems with the building to arise. Third, to move on to the next and, hopefully, larger project requires the cash you get from selling the first one—and then the next—until you reach the point where you have enough capital or cash flow to permit you to have several projects going forward at the same time.

Borrow against your improvements. Having done the improving and having raised the rents, you are in a position to sell at a profit. But selling may not be your best way of moving along. If, as one possibility, the real estate market in general is in a slump at the time your property is up for sale, you not only may have good reason to be reluctant to put your building on the market, you may also see it as a particularly good time to pick up another property at a bargain price. But you need cash. On the strength of the improvements you have made to the building you own and of the increased income it provides, you are in an excellent position to go back to the bank for a larger loan. You will pay interest on the money borrowed, but it gives you tax-free dollars you can use for the down payment on your next venture.

Swap properties. A tax-free swap is the second alternative you have to selling, and it is a winner. Instead of making an outright sale, you exchange your property for another you like. The Internal Revenue says that if you exchange your property for another "of like kind" the deal is free of tax, and there is no recapture of the depreciation deductions you have taken. "Like kind" is interpreted quite generously. You are not compelled to exchange a four-family flat for another four-family flat. You may exchange an apartment house for a warehouse or an office building. What you are doing is exchanging one income-producing property for another income-producing property.

It isn't necessary to locate a property owner who wants your building and has something you want to exchange. You can make this idea work by finding a property you want. You then find a buyer interested in the property you are ready to dispose of. Have him buy the property you have your eye on and then exchange it with you. The details, satisfactory to both sides, can be worked out. You may sell a $50,000 building and take a $60,000 building in exchange. In that case the $50,000 exchange is tax-free, and you pay taxes on the cash portion as it relates to any capital gain you have realized.

Under other circumstances you might have a property worth $75,000 and exchange it for a building worth $200,000 with a $125,000 mortgage on it. You take the building and assume the mortgage. No cash changes hands, and there is no tax, even though your cost base for your building is only \$25,000. You now have a new cost base: your original cost of \$25,000 plus the \$125,000 mortgage, \$145,000. In this example you gain another material tax advantage. You have not put up any more money, but you can now take depreciation on a \$200,000 property.

Investing in commercial properties

Becoming a commercial property investor probably suggests really big money. It doesn't necessarily. Just as it is entirely possible to go into the ownership of residential properties with modest resources, there are approaches to commercial property investments with limited capital.

Many benefits

There are a number of pluses when you concentrate on commercial real estate. For one thing you can have tenants on much longer leases than are conceivable in the residential field. Twenty-year leases are not uncommon. Long leases can provide some protection for the owner by providing either an escalation clause involving automatic rent increases based on increased property taxes, increases in the Consumer Price Index, or increases from other sources. Another form of protection is a percentage factor, where lessees pay you an agreed percentage of their gross sales after they pass a certain plateau. Unlike residential leases, commercial leases generally are not subject to rent control. When a lease expires or if there is no lease, you are free to raise rents as you see fit. Commercial buildings involve many fewer management headaches. You escape the annoyance of late night phone calls because something has gone wrong, and there are fewer things to go wrong. Evictions are easier. The courts are extremely protective of individuals being evicted from their home, but a business tenant either pays the rent on time or you can take immediate action.

Finding the property

With modest capital resources you follow pretty much the same technique as if investing in residences. Look for neglected stores, for example. If you stay with familiar sections of your city you may have reason to know that some locations are on the way up—that new roads, bridges, or other transportation factors are likely to add to the value of a location because it will bring more people to the area. A neglected store in a location of that type holds considerable promise for a rapid increase in value in terms of the rental income it can produce and in terms of a profitable sale in the future. Concentrate on areas you know. Be in a position to have strong convictions about location, for in commercial real estate location is king.

A major problem with real estate ventures of this type is that banks are not very interested in such loans. If you find a property you want to buy and go to your bank, the probability is that you will be asked to make a 50 percent down payment—a far cry from the terms you can get when buying a home. You may find some appealing small properties you can buy for as little as $50,000 or $60,000, but if you do not have enough capital to make a 50 percent down payment you will do better to make personal loans than to ask a bank to lend money on the property. Savings and loan institutions have no interest: they are dedicated to making loans for home ownership.

Zoning can be important when looking for opportunities for investment. You might find an old home in what was once a good residential neighborhood. The qualities of the street may have deteriorated considerably for residential purposes, but it may be desirable from a commercial standpoint. Check the zoning. If the zoning permits, you might be able to do very well were you to buy the home and convert it to commercial use. Your imagination is challenged. Think of the types of business that might fare particularly well at that location, and then visualize ways in which you may restructure the home to accomodate the business ventures you have in mind. You have a good opportunity to develop an exceptionally original, inviting commercial quarters making it relatively easy to sign up appropriate tenants on excellent terms.

Buying a small office building or shopping center with tenants already on leases could work out well, provided that a painstaking study by your lawyer and/or accountant shows that the lease terms and rates are favorable in relation to the price you are to pay and the historic cost of maintenance. Deal in terms of what is, and not what might be. Avoid buying a commercial property in anticipation of a continuance of increasing value. If inflation does make the property more and more valuable as time goes by, wonderful—that is a welcome bonus. But stay away from buying unhappy surprises and disappointments.

One means of dealing with a commercial tenant that relieves you of many possibilities of unexpected bad and costly news is to enter into what is called a *net, net, net lease.* You settle for a somewhat lower rent, but the tenant accepts the full cost and responsibility for everything other than the exterior of the building. If the heating or air conditioning goes bad, that is the tenant's expense. If the roof leaks, you are responsible. Under a net, net, net lease, you provide no heat or any other utilities—just the bare building. Your only expenses are property taxes and insurance on the building itself, not the contents.

And the taxes . . .

The tax advantages you can enjoy are several. You may deduct from income all interest, taxes, and depreciation. In addition, if the building you buy is twenty years old or older and if you spend money rejuvenating it, you are allowed a 10-percent tax credit for what you spend. If your building qualifies as an historic preservation building and if you make an investment in its renovation within the guidelines for renovating historic preservation buildings, you may write off the full cost of the renovation over five years no matter how long a life may be realistic.

Depreciation. This deduction is extremely important. It is a deduction from income that would otherwise be taxable. It is a cost-free "expense" that increases your cash flow. You are *writing down* the building's value despite the fact that the value may be *going up* by leaps and bounds. You are allowed to take depreciation on the total cost of the building even though you may have bought it with only a small down payment. There are various ways to take depreciation.

Straight-line line depreciation is the simplest. If a property has an expected life of ten years, you just take 10 percent of the full value each year. A $100,000 property, therefore, would give you $10,000 a year as your depreciation deduction. (No form of depreciation allows a total writeoff. You may deduct down to a "salvage value.")

Accelerated depreciation gives you greatly increased deduction in the early years and decreasing deductions year by year. Accelerated depreciation can provide a big enough tax loss to shelter your equity and your income, and it can even shelter some of your income from other sources. Were you to take accelerated depreciation on the $100,000 property used in the straight-line depreciation example and use 150 percent declining balance (one form of accelerated depreciation), it would follow this pattern: first year, $15,000; second year, $12,500; third year, $10,875. What you are doing is taking 50 percent of the remaining value each year.

Your accoutant will be able to show you several approaches to accelerated depreciation. For residential property you may use 200-percent declining balance. On new commercial property, 150-percent declining balance may be employed. For used commercial property you must confine yourself to straight-line. But that is not bad news. There is another side to the depreciation story.

IRS has a *recapture rule.* Were you to buy a piece of commercial property and use the 150-percent declining method of taking depreciation, when you sell that property, the IRS calls on you to pay taxes on part of the depreciation you took. You pay ordinary income tax on whatever depreciation exceeded what you would have deducted had you used the straight-line method. There is no recapture at all on straight-line.

Investing in raw land

An investment in raw, undeveloped land can have interest for you if you are not looking for income. Not only are you willing to bypass income, you are in a position to sacrifice the income now being earned by whatever cash you put into raw land investment. Raw land is for you if you are seeking capital gains.

Buying a small tract of land offers little chance for interesting profits. Your greatest hope is that the property you buy will, in time, attract the biggest land-hungry buyers—commercial or residential developers. These people need a lot of ground. If your tract is less than ten acres, the chances are that they will have no interest.

Not only do you have to make the decision that you can forego income, but there are also continuing costs: You will have property taxes. There is interest on any money borrowed for the investment, and, in some cases, there is a further expense for maintaining the property in keeping with state or local regulations. The length of time you probably hold this nonincome-producing property before you can hope to realize the gain you want is a critical question, particularly in light of the fact that you cannot rely on a profit. For any of a variety of reasons you might find no interested buyers or have to sell for a lot less than the profit you visualized. You might even have to bail out with a loss. Nonincome-producing investments, therefore, demand an absence of need for income now and for a number of years into the future. They also call for skillful selection, able negotiating, courage, and luck.

Before you make a raw land investment, therefore, it is imperative that you employ some useful yardsticks in the property selection, that you take sensible steps available to overcome the negative income factor, and that you explore ways of acquiring the land with as little cash as possible.

Evaluating potential profit

Your evaluation of a potential investment must give in-depth consideration to a number of things.

Zoning. Is the property zoned for what you believe is its best ultimate use? If you are interested in the tract because you think it an ideal site for a factory or for an office building complex, does present zoning allow such use? If not, unless you have good reason to believe that you can prevail upon the zoning board to re-zone in your favor, you have a serious problem.

Topography and drainage. Does the tract lend itself to development without costly and difficult problems? A professional survey and appraisal will give you the answers to this important question.

Availability. Is the land on or close enough to major roads and/or highways? Is public transportation important for the eventual use you have in mind? Does it exist? How far is it from urban centers, from airports, from railroad sidings?

Can the land produce income until you sell? Is it so located that it will pay to make it a parking lot? Do you see sufficient demand to make the construction of a low-cost warehouse practical? What about a tent theater? A farmers' produce market? The nature of the vicinity and the character of the land suggest a number of possibilities.

Buying an option on the land

Having located a piece of property you have confidence in, because you can visualize one or more logical, effective uses for it, it is entirely possible that you may be able to induce the owner to sell you an option to buy. When you buy an option, you involve only a fraction of the cash that a purchase would require. Your risk is reduced. The loss of income from the use of the larger amount of your capital is reduced. Hence the percentage or profit you can realize is tremendously greater. You pay no interest for borrowed money. There are no property taxes, since you do not own the land. You have a capital gain if you win and a capital loss if you lose.

Raw land options take many forms, each with certain advantages and disadvantages. To be sure that you are adopting the most advantageous type of option for the land investment you wish, in keeping with your circumstances, the need for the help of a lawyer or real estate expert is evident.

Owners of land have various reasons to be interested in selling options. They may not feel as you do about the profit potential in the property and believe, therefore, that you will never exercise the option, leaving them with your option money. They may be prepared to take your option on one part of a larger parcel of land, because your option money covers their running expenses, and they will still enjoy any growth in value because of the balance of the property remaining in their hands.

CANDIDATES FOR ACTION

- ☐ Invest in mortgages
    - ☐ Taking second mortgage on sale of your home
    - ☐ Taking first mortgage on sale of your home
    - ☐ Buying second mortgages
    - ☐ Ginnie Mae and Freddie Mac
    - ☐ Real Estate Investment Trusts
        - ☐ Equity REIT
        - ☐ Mortgage REIT
        - ☐ Combination REIT
- ☐ Real estate limited partnerships
    - ☐ Syndicated
    - ☐ Private placement
- ☐ Nonfamily installment sale
- ☐ Buy and improve residences
- ☐ Commercial properties
- ☐ Raw land
    - ☐ Raw land options

12

I Will Have a Will

Where there is a will . . .

So many aspects of financial planning can have a serious impact on your financial well-being and the well-being of your family after you are gone, that it is difficult to assign priorities. But if any single element calls for early attention, it is an up-to-date will. It rates early attention because unless a firing squad is about to receive its orders, few of us have any way of knowing when our lives might end.

The great majority spend most of their adult lives working industriously to amass money and property, yet most of us fail to protect it. We cherish our assets. Most of us would knowingly risk our lives to protect them from unwarranted seizure. We want our capital for our own security and for the continuing security of our families after they are gone. But according to a survey reported by *U. S. News & World Report,* nine out of ten financially successful individuals do not have up-to-date wills. Still other studies show that eight out of ten people die without *ever* having had a will. Another way of expressing that is to say that eight out of ten are perfectly willing to surrender all direction and control of their hard-won property.

Why? The cost of going to a competent lawyer to have a will prepared cannot be the deterrent. Unless the will is one of unusual complexity, the cost of having a will prepared can be as little as $50. Time cannot be the obstacle, for it is not that time-consuming. The answer is . . . emotion.

Emotion and superstition. Because of them, people do not like to think about, talk about, or do anything about their own death. A lot of people are afraid to take any actions related to their own mortality. They believe that to do so might change their luck—put a "jinx" or a "hex" on themselves. Wives repel the invitation to discuss what arrangements should be made about financial affairs in the event that the husband might die. They simply close their ears and eyes. They walk away. They cannot bring themselves to think and talk about such matters. An old saying in the life insurance industry is, "Many wives are opposed to life insurance, but no widows are."

Facing the facts of death

Making a will entails admitting that you will not—cannot—live forever. Once you face up to the business of planning what should be in your will, you are confessing to the fact that you are not indestructible. Once you admit that shocking fact to yourself, you start to relax. You feel free of the burden of hiding from admitting the inevitable, and you are able to cheerfully, intelligently plan for the way you want your assets to be handled when you are no longer here. A. James Casner, a law professor at Harvard University, has said, "You can't die without your property going someplace. If you don't come up with instructions . . . the law makes the decision for you. And when you look at where the law sends your property, you may not like what you see."

Some say, "I don't need a will." The statement may be based on any of three assumptions: First, there aren't enough assets to bother. Second, the spouse will automatically get everything. Third, all their more substantial possessions are jointly held providing for immediate ownership by the surviving spouse. All three assumptions could be wrong.

Not enough assets?

First, unless someone has induced them to draw up personal financial statements, very few realize the extent of their own worth. The problems of paying the bills each month, the unfulfilled desire to trade in the old car for a modern one, the low levels of checking and savings accounts can give people the feeling that they don't have any substantial assets to leave behind. Inflationary forces are partly to blame. But if you are a homeowner, for example, the same inflationary force has probably increased the value of your home. The face value of life insurance policies do not represent cash you can spend, but it will eventually be spendable cash for your survivors. You may have more than you think.

Will the spouse get everything?

The second assumption, that the surviving spouse will get everything, is most unlikely. When a person dies without a will, the rigid laws of your state take over.

Each state has its own laws. In most states, where there is no will, a surviving wife gets one-third of the estate and the balance goes to the children or to other relatives. Take the case of a widow with a minor child. The state says the child's portion cannot be used by the widow as she sees fit, so the court appoints a guardian. She will probably be the guardian the court chooses, but she is then required to furnish a security bond, and she may make no expenditures of that money without court approval.

A court-appointed administrator is frequently faced with the need to secure a bond equal to or greater than the value of the estate. The bond and the step-by-step reporting mandates of the court all cost money—considerably more money, in many cases, than the fee of a lawyer for preparing a will. If all of the heirs agree, however, the bond may be waived. In some states the law require that the money set aside for minor children must be put into a trust until they come of age. In the meantime the mother of those children can have some needless difficulties.

You may check into your own state laws and be satisfied that the terms are in harmony with your own desires. But laws are not cast in bronze. They change. There can be no certainty that what seems to be in step with your thinking today will be moving in the same direction in the future.

A big consideration is the marital deduction (covered in detail in an earlier chapter). Essentially, the IRS permits $250,000 or half of the total estate, whichever is greater, of a married person to pass to the spouse free of any taxation. That can represent a great savings because the tax-free benefit applies no matter how much money is involved. Taking full advantage of this important means of saving taxes is simple through the proper wording of a will. When someone dies with no will, however, and the state laws stipulate that only one-third of the assets go to the surviving spouse, an important part of that big tax saving is lost.

Will joint ownership take care of everything?

The third assumption, that joint ownership replaces the need for a will, has its pitfalls. Should husband and wife be in an accident and both die at the same time, their property might pass on in a manner contrary to their own plans and desires. Again, the state prevails unless there is a will. In an accident, the wife, by way of illustration, might live an hour longer than the husband. If the couple happens to be childless, the couple's jointly held assets could end up in the hands of the wife's relatives, with nothing going to any of the husbands's family. This would happen even though her nearest relative may be a distant cousin that neither the husband or wife even knew, while the husband's parents are alive and in a tough financial bind. Joint ownership also brings the further possibility that there could be two estate taxes instead of one. Finally, wills are easy to change. To change from joint ownership, however, calls for the consent of both parties. That could cause problems.

To have a will written is the same as saying, "When I am gone, this is exactly what I want done with my possessions; these are the steps I want taken to make life as easy as possible for my family." A will can include burial instructions, state who is to be the executor, name the guardian for a minor child, even be used to tell some people off. One of the more famous of the latter type read:

To my wife I leave her lover and the knowledge that I wasn't the fool she thought I was. To my son, I leave the pleasure of earning a living. For 20 years he thought the pleasure was mine. He was mistaken. To my daughter, I leave $100,000. She will need it. The only good piece of business her husband ever did was to marry her. To my valet, I leave the clothes he has been stealing from me. To my partner, I leave the suggestion that he take some other clever man in with him at once if he expects to do any more business.

A will should be coordinated with all your other financial plans. It should reflect the facts revealed by your financial statement. It should conserve assets and protect people.

Despite the fact that a lawyer is the one who writes your

will, you are the one who must decide what the will says. You should have a clear understanding of what may be accomplished with a will. You need to be aware of its powers and limitations, of the things that should be included and of the things that should be avoided. You should know the language of wills, and you should be alert to the continuing need for a will to be updated. *But always remember that you are not a lawyer.* Don't try to write the will yourself.

Four parts to most wills

The average will has four major portions. After getting past the legal preamble about the soundness of your mind and the revocation of any former will, the typical will deals with cleaning up debts and funeral expenses and takes care of minor remembrance gifts and the parceling out of personal effects. The second part gets to the important disposition of assets to the spouse, children, and other close family members. In the third section, executors and guardians are named. Finally, the will often addresses itself to the subject of taxes.

1. Obligations and remembrances

The first portion requires little discussion. In taking care of all obligations, including funeral expenses, you should be aware that, on average, funeral and related expenses can easily amount to $5,000 or more. These items should be recognized when determining how much life insurance is needed. Also included in this part of the will are gifts and honorariums to friends, family members, servants, and others, plus specific gifts of personal items stating, for example, which child or grandchild should get a certain piece of jewelry, painting, or the stamp collection. Spelling out who gets which of your personal items is a good idea. Bitter family arguments can be avoided. Some authorities, however, believe that it is not a good idea to deal with gifts of personal property in the will. They prefer that everything be left to one person and that the testator write a personal letter to that person saying who should get what. There are good reasons for that approach. When specific items are detailed in a will, the IRS might assume they have more value than they would under other circumstances. Up goes their appraisal, and up go taxes. Second, if the testator has a change of mind about any of the gifts, it is easier to write a new letter than to change the will. A letter, however, does not bind the executor as do the terms of a will.

2. Major disposition of assets

The second part of the will is the big one. Here a testator must think of the things to provide for the surviving spouse as well as possible. The interests of minor children call for serious consideration, and, in the case of adult children, parents, and others who are part of the immediate family, there is a need to weigh special needs, ages, conditions of health, and the ability to provide for themselves. Is the spouse capable of handling large sums of money, security investments, real estate, a business interest? Is there a need to create safeguards to protect one or more of the beneficiaries from habitual reckless spending or blatant gullibility? Is there reason to protect any of the beneficiaries from other beneficiaries? Is there going to be an immediate or future tax problem that could wipe out a disturbingly large percentage of the assets. Can it be reduced or avoided?

These and a multiplicity of other possibilities all come into play when you are writing this portion of the will in ways calculated to pass along your assets in keeping with your plans and wishes. This complexity is one reason why an experienced lawyer must have the responsibility of writing a will. Legal training and background enable an attorney to foresee things that might occur in the future to twist, distort, or destroy what the testator wanted the assets to accomplish.

The principal questions and problems that are likely to arise in planning the average will include the marital deduction, the testamentary trust, the living trust, the A and B trusts, and other well tested and popularly used techniques that can enable you to distribute your possessions in exactly the way you think they should be distributed. These are the techniques you have been reading about as you journeyed through this book. In the planning of your will, you should turn back to those things you have checked off as "Candidates for Action" at the close of each chapter. Some you will discard in favor of later choices. Some will overlap. But these checklists bring all the elements together, as you consider how you want to control your financial life today and what you want to do to put your family in the strongest financial position possible when you are no longer on the scene. You will be able to spell out for your lawyer precisely what you want expressed by your will. Immediately following this chapter you will find a series of easy-to-use forms designed to help you to consolidate your "Candidates for Action" in a practical manner.

3. Executors and guardians

Naming executors and guardians involves a number of considerations.

Executors. When specifying the executor, you are saying, "This is the person who should take over the management of my affairs where I leave off." The executor could be a relative, a friend, a business associate, a lawyer, a bank, or a trust department.

A relative or close friend, knowing you and the family, is well-qualified to watch over family interests and to interpret what you wanted. The personal interest in the welfare of the family is an important factor. The question must be asked, however, if that individual has the capacity and the time to deal with the various duties and responsibilities involved. The size of the estate, of course, has an important bearing on the answer to that question. If your assets are large, the ability, the willingness, and the availability of the executor you have in mind require considerable examination. If a nonprofessional executor is chosen, you should name successor executors of your own choosing. This provides a degree of continuity should the original executor be unavailable, unable, or unwilling to serve at any time in the future.

Where assets are significant, you might do well to weigh the appointment of a personal friend, relative, or business associate to serve as co-trustee with a bank or trust company. This arrangement has a number of advantages. The person chosen can be counted on to represent the family and your wishes with genuine interest, knowledge, and empathy. The detailed, time-consuming work, however, will be in the hands of a well-staffed, experienced, professional organization.

A corporate executor or trustee, such as a bank or trust company, working alone or with a co-trustee, has several advantages to offer:

1. *It specializes in such activities and is completely equipped to handle all details.*
2. *It is experienced and has been qualified by the state and/or municipality where it is located to accept the responsibilities involved.*
3. *It is fair and impartial, pursuing its activities in a precise manner with the full knowledge that its acts are subject to detailed scrutiny at all times.*
4. *Being a corporation, its functions are not disrupted or terminated by illness, accident, or death.*

Guardians. If, at the time the will is written, there are minor children, the naming of a guardian is in order. To fail to name a guardian for minor children, particularly if a husband and wife should happen to die in a common disaster, means the future of the children may fall into the hands of the courts. This is not necessarily the outcome, for it is quite common for close relatives to take over without any formalities, and such an arrangement is not likely to be challenged unless another family member wants the children. The safest course under any circumstances is for the wills of the parents to express their own wishes as to the guardianship and to name alternates in case the guardian predeceases the parents or cannot or will not serve.

In actuality you do not appoint a guardian. The will expresses your wishes, and the court appoints. It would be an exceptional instance, however, when the court would fail to appoint the guardian named in the will.

In some situations, two types of guardians are named: a guardian of the person and a separate guardian of the property. For example, an aunt might be chosen as a proper guardian to raise a child, but if she is inexperienced in the handling of money, a second guardian, charged solely with the management of the child's assets, might be named. The guardian of the property may be an individual or a bank or trust company.

4. The tax instructions

The final part of the will may address itself to the subject of taxes. If there are estate taxes to be paid, the critical question is where the cash is to come from to meet those liabilities. The failure to put specific instructions in your will could lead to serious consequences. If your will neglects to state how the taxes should be paid, state law prevails. As you have seen, state law cannot be counted on to match your real wishes. Even if current state law seems in harmony with your ideas on the subject, there can be no assurance that the law will remain the same.

One factor that makes tax-paying instructions so vital is that there are two portions of property to be considered: (1) the portion that passes outside the will, such as jointly owned property and property in trust, and (2) the portion that is disposed of via the will itself, the *testamentary* portion. The will can say that all federal and state taxes are to be paid out of the testamentary portion, thus leaving intact the part going to the surviving spouse via jointly owned property or a trust. State law might otherwise say that the tax liability must be shared equally by the testamentary portion and the remainder of the estate, leaving the survivor with considerably less than you intended. On the other hand, a will may have bequests that are important to you, and the portion passing to the spouse may be so large that if the tax were taken entirely from those you wanted to have meaningful bequests, they could receive far less than you intended for them.

Liquidity is a big part of the problem. Executors might have no choice but to sell securities or real estate at a particularly unfavorable time. You might desire to leave controlling stock of a closely held corporation to one or more members of the family. What *could* happen, however, unless plans are made to avoid the possibility, is that the stock might have to be sold in order to raise the cash needed to meet the tax obligations. If a living trust exists, the liquidity problem is sometimes solved by stating in the trust that it may buy assets from the testamentary estate or lend money to it for the payment of taxes.

In any event, it is easy to visualize the complexities that could arise if the payment of taxes is left to chance.

Wives need wills too

The importance of having a will applies to husband and wife equally. If the wife dies before her husband, there are ample reasons for her to have dictated her wishes and to conserve assets for those she leaves behind, rather than idly tossing the decisions to disinterested state law. In the case of a common disaster taking both spouses' lives or the coincidental death of husband and wife within a short time of one another, the need for the wife to have a will, particularly if she outlives her mate for even minutes, is abundantly clear.

Joint wills

Some couples want joint wills for the implied sentiment involved. Couples, where one or both had been married and had children from an earlier marriage or marriages, lean toward a joint will. They see it as a possible means of safeguarding the rights they want for their children.

Joint wills, however, have very little flexibility. No changes can be made, for example, without mutual consent. They are considerably more vulnerable to litigation than separate wills, and they can put the important marital deduction at risk. It is always possible to cater to the wishes of both husband and wife with separate wills and, where needed, with the use of trusts.

And don't forget it

The most prudent place to keep a will is in your lawyer's possession. Copies should be kept at home, but the original in the lawyer's safe eliminates or reduces delays, searches, and questions as to whether the will produced is the most recent, and more.

The point about the will's being the most recent brings up a final, but absolute need: periodic, updating reviews. A will that has been written, forgotten, and allowed to age without review and change can do more harm than good. Many things that happen in a person's life or family situation can trigger the need for a will to be changed. Some of the more apparent factors include the death of a beneficiary, the birth of a child or grandchild, the sale of property, the establishment or sale of a business, inheritance, a change in your health or that of family members, changes in work status and/or finances, changes in law, a change of your residence to another state.

To safeguard against these or other elements bringing about undesirable results, it is advisable to have annual reviews with your lawyer. Once your lawyer has completed the writing of your will and you and the witnesses have signed it, never pick up a pen to make changes. It seems so easy to eliminate the name of someone who was to have received something through your will. All you do is ink out the name. But it is not that simple. When your will is examined by the court, and it is noted that there have been written changes—either additions or subtractions—and the witnesses testify that these were not present when they signed, whatever you tried to change will be thrown out. There have been many cases where such changes failed in their purpose.

The only proper, dependable way to alter a will is to have your lawyer write a codicil. It is easy, and quick, and it can be counted on to carry out your wishes.

Limitations on what may be passed along by a will

1. *The following states have community property laws: Arizona, California, Idaho, Louisiana, Nevada, New Mexico, Texas, and Washington. Community property is all property that was acquired during marriage. Usually neither husband nor wife can dispose of any community property without the consent of the other. There are some exceptions to this. Property owned by*

either spouse before marriage, for example, or received by either as a gift or inheritance, may be disposed of as the owner wishes.

2. *Property that is registered as jointly held passes to the survivor by law. There is no need to treat such property in the will, nor can the will alter the joint interest.*
3. *United States Saving Bonds registered as: "John and Helen Smith" or "Payable on death to ——" cannot be changed by will.*
4. *The beneficiary of a life insurance policy cannot be changed by instructions in a will unless the beneficiary is the person's estate.*
5. *Anticipated inheritances cannot be left by will on the simple premise that people cannot leave what they do not have.*
6. *In almost every state a husband is forbidden to deprive his wife of a certain specified share of his property. Most states do not permit a wife to disinherit the husband.*
7. *Because the states each have laws protecting the interests of the family of a deceased person, there are limits as to the amounts that may be given to charity.*

The language of wills

You have little or no reason to use legalistic, technical language when discussing your will with your lawyer or any other professional advisors. But since they and the will itself may use such terms, it pays to understand the language.

administrator. Where no executor has been designated in a will or when a named executor cannot or will not serve, the court appoints an administrator to carry out an executor's duties.

bequeath. To give personal property through a will.

bequest. The gift itself.

codicil. An instrument written after a will, changing or adding to instructions contained in the will. A codicil, to be legally binding, must be written with the same care and formality as the will.

demonstrative legacy. A gift of a specific amount intended to come from a specific source but to come out of the general estate if the source named is insufficient.

devise. To make a gift of real property. The recipient is known as the *devisee.*

executor. A person named in a will and charged with the responsibility of seeing to it that all the terms of the will are carried out.

general legacy. A gift of a precise amount of money out of the general assets of the estate.

guardian. A person who legally has the power and duty of managing the affairs of minors or incompetents.

holographic will. A will written entirely by hand by the testator.

intestate. When a person dies without having made a will, he or she is said to have died intestate.

legacy. A gift of personal property. The recipient is known as the *legatee.*

noncupative will. An oral will. State laws differ, but in general oral wills are accepted only when made as a death bed statement or by a member of the military during active combat.

ordinary will. One that has been put in writing, signed, and witnessed.

pecuniary legacy. Any gift of money.

personalty. Practically all property other than real estate.

probate. A will must be presented to probate court whose function is to determine that it is a valid will, not in conflict with state laws, and to evaluate all property embraced by the will.

real property. Real estate.

residuary estate. All remaining of a testator's property after specific devices, legacies, and outstanding bills and funeral expenses have been satisfied.

testator. Person making a will.

CANDIDATES FOR ACTION

- ☐ I do need a will
- ☐ We need two wills
- ☐ My will should be updated
- ☐ I will review my will annually

Consolidating your Candidates for Action

At the end of each chapter the Candidates for Action pages invited you to identify those ideas that seemed to fit you, your ideas and desires, and your emotional acceptance. You checked items that were worthy of further consideration.

There is no likelihood that you will, should, or can adopt everything you checked. You knew that when you ticked them off. They were purely candidates. Now is the time to eliminate and consolidate—the time to elect.

Your use of the following pages enable you to see where some of your preliminary choices overlap, where they are in conflict with one another, or where they are off-target. You are going to be in a position to see the full picture and to bring everything into sharp focus.

- Section A *is for a statement of your aims, to pinpoint your most important financial goals. It is a critical first step. Once you identify your goals, it is far easier to narrow down your action decisions. They must fit.*
- *In* Section B, *enter the action candidates that have survived your initial review. These are not your final choices. Those that do survive and are entered at this time are those coming closest to where you want to go financially—potential actions with which you feel comfortable.*
- Section C *takes you back to your financial inventory, the "This is Where I Stand" form on page 28. If you have completed that inventory and have done the analysis (and it is not too late if you*

Consolidating your candidates

have not done so already), you have a clear picture of what you have to work with. You can isolate the capital that can and should be transferred from places where it isn't doing all it can be doing to further your goals, to uses that are better identified to what you want to accomplish. You can see which part of your income can be channeled to building, to protection, to the increase of cash flow, and to decreases in taxes. Add to these the after-tax realizations that result from plans you now have to free-up any frozen assets or from the sale of your home and other sources.

- *Finally, in* **Section D**, *you will draft your specific battle plan for your personal attack on inflation, taxes, and the known and unknown threats to the financial future of yourself and of your family. With the facts at hand it can and should be a realistic plan tailored to what you have and where you are going.*

To complete **Section D** *on a completely practical basis you* *need help. Your knowledge of the exact costs and of the correctness of the things you aim to do are vital to the formation of your final decisions. The guidance of your lawyer, accountant, financial planner, broker, insurance agent, real estate broker—any or all of them—are essential.*

Your final action plan will not be perfect. You will probably have to cut back or postpone some actions you want to take. But moving forward with what is available now gives you the priceless advantage of using every day of time at your disposal. Time, unlike dollars, is irreplaceable. It is the priceless ingredient in any financial program.

Section A: MAJOR FINANCIAL GOALS

☐ Maximum income now

☐ Capital growth for:

☐ Future income ☐ Future needs of family

Specific objective:
☐ College costs ☐ Travel ☐ Own business

☐ Home purchase ☐ Other________________

Dollar amount needed $________________

Time until needed ________________

☐ Preserving what I have

☐ Financial independence by age _______

☐ Reduction of taxes now

☐ Reduction of estate taxes

Section B: TENTATIVE METHODS SELECTION

SAVINGS

☐ Bank ☐ Savings and loan Type of account______

☐ Money market fund

INVEST

☐ Securities

Type ______

☐ Gold or other precious metals

Type of investment ______

☐ Collectibles (Diamonds, rare coins, fine jewelry, art, antiques)

______

☐ Mutual funds

Type and nature of investment ______

☐ Tax-free municipal bonds

Nature of investment ______

☐ Annuity

Type and nature of investment ______

PROTECT

☐ Life insurance

Type of policy ______

☐ Disability

☐ Coverage of potential "income vacuum"

☐ Buy-sell agreement

TAX SAVING GIFTS

☐ Annual Exclusion

Uses ______

☐ Gifts of life insurance

Uses ______

☐ Gifts to minor children

Uses ______

☐ Short-term trusts

Uses ______

☐ Charitable gifts

Uses ______

TRUSTS	☐ Testamentary
	☐ Living trust
TAX SHELTERS	☐ Keogh
	☐ Keogh defined benefit
	☐ IRA
	☐ IRA rollover
	☐ EE and/or HH bonds
	☐ Real estate, oil & gas, other
	Uses ______
FROZEN GAINS	☐ Installment sale
	☐ Private annuity
REAL ESTATE	☐ Sale of home
	Method ______
	☐ Mortgage investments
	☐ Method ______
	☐ Real estate investment trust
	☐ Limited partnerships
	Type ______
	☐ Non-family installment sale
	☐ Buy and improve residences
	☐ Commercial properties
	☐ Raw land

Section C: RESOURCES

☐ Transfer capital out of: ______

______

______

making $______ available for action.

☐ Income from: ______________________________

____

making monthly income of $__________ available for action.

Section D: ACTIONS TO BE TAKEN NOW

SAVINGS

Immediate $__________ Monthly $__________

INVESTMENT

Immediate $__________ Monthly $__________

PROTECTION

Premiums of $__________ at (intervals) __________

TAX SAVING GIFTS

Immediate $__________ Other, $__________
at (intervals) __________

TRUSTS

Immediate $__________

TAX SHELTERS

Immediate $__________ Monthly $__________

REAL ESTATE

Immediate $__________

☐ Check or change registration of: ______________________________

____

____

☐ Make immediate arrangements to have will(s) prepared

☐ Review existing will(s)

☐ Review all current investments and insurance policies to determine if they are in harmony with my major financial goals

☐ Notes on calendar to remind myself of need for annual reviews of will, insurance policies, investments

Index

I

J

K

L

M

May all of your dreams come True

Best Wishes

"A Circle of Women"
Seen here are some of the many women and their families who have inspired this book. They demonstrate that disciplined planning is helping them gain control of their financial future.

WHAT PEOPLE ARE SAYING! . . .

I recommend this book for any man who provides financial services to women. Men will learn how women think when making buying decisions. I never realized there was a process for the middle class to accumulate wealth. This book tells women how.

Aggie Refice; Doylestown, Pennsylvania

The principles and situations described in this book have as many applications to men as to women. They reflect life as I see it everyday in my accounting practice. I recommend it as a reference to anyone who is concerned about the financial well-being of loved ones as well as for themselves.

Mike Fee, Certified Public Accountant

All companies should give this book to their female employees, . . . and all reputable life insurance companies should use this book in their sales training.

Nadine Johnson; Marietta, Georgia

All women should read this book, and I would recommend it to any man who loves his wife and family.

R. L. Vermeuel; CLU; Retired Executive; MetLife Insurance Company

This book will appeal to many women who have been in the dark about financial planning. It's easy reading and down to earth unlike other business books. As a single man, I learned from the solutions presented and could apply them to my own life.

Michael Palmer, Esq.; Dallas, Texas

I recommend that every CPA and attorney read this book. I use this book with women clients; they need to understand the consequences of not knowing how to satisfy their legal needs regarding wills and estate planning.

Susan McCabe, J.D.; Attorney; Trophy Club, Texas

This book is very easy to read; it teaches women how to establish trusting relationships and feel more comfortable and confident in their interactions with financial planning professionals.

Jane Sullivan; Euless, Texas

Every chapter is valuable. I wish I had it years ago to teach me the right questions to ask regarding financial planning. Each story offered something new to learn; I enjoyed the process of becoming enlightened.

Dr. Rita Fulop; Psychotherapist; Fair Lawn, New Jersey

A great book to make available for single women and couples. I would recommend the book for my wife, daughters and clients.

Jack Skryd; MDRT Producer; Glen Ellyn, Illinois

The book makes you think about life. You have to learn to play the hand you are dealt—sometimes you don't get a good one. So the importance of planning ahead is critical and the best way to deal yourself a few good cards.

Dr. Bob Parkhill; Chiropractor; Hurst, Texas

A terrific book. The parts about prenuptial agreements before second marriages give great ideas. I would recommend it to every bride and to any woman. I would recommend it as a gift to every young woman graduating from college.

Patrick Sullivan; Contract Administrator; Ft. Worth, Texas

I had a lawsuit with a firm that embezzled my money. I let dishonest people I trusted manage my money, and I lost it. After I had been widowed, then divorced, this author helped me salvage my financial affairs and rebuild my life as a single mother. Because of the advice in the chapters on remarriage concerning how to get a clear picture of prenuptials and wills, my divorce didn't cost me monetarily, even though it hurt me emotionally. She helped me conquer fear and become responsible on my own.

Judy Ruhland-Mertel; Colleyville, Texas

You never know when cancer, a debilitating disease or violent crime will befall you; then you still have a family to support and bills to pay and no or not enough income. These women's stories drive home the point and teach you to prepare for any possibility.

Diane Coxsey; Physician; North Richland, Texas

People don't plan to fail; they only fail to plan. This book addresses this very effectively and is a great tool for anyone.

John Claffey; Collections Executive; Menomonee Falls, Wisconsin

Seebeck certainly relates to women of the 90s and weaves a good tapestry of the feminine cares and concerns involved in women's needs for financial planning. A must read.

Dennis Claffey; Sales Executive; Menomonee Falls, Wisconsin

We hope that all people who read the stories in this book, as well as the one about our Mom, will grasp the message of why a young woman needs to have a secure financial plan in place to help those she loves continue to live to the fullest—after she's gone.

Brad, Chris, and Eric

AMERICAN DREAM WOMEN

INSURING WOMEN'S WEALTH

AMERICAN DREAM WOMEN

INSURING WOMEN'S WEALTH

MARY LYNN SEEBECK

TUNNEL PRESS, LTD.
LIGONIER, PENNSYLVANIA

Tunnel Press, Ltd., Post Office Box 933, Ligonier, Pennsylvania 15658-0933 USA 800.200.5278

American Dream Women: Insuring Women's Wealth
ISBN: 0-941461-08-4 Hardcover ISBN: 0-941461-07-6 Paper
Forthcoming: *American Dream Women: Workbook & Planning Guide*
ISBN: 0-941461-09-2

Edited by Kathleen M. Sewalk, BA, MS, ABC

Cover and Book Design by Suzette Johnson

Portrait Photography of Mary Lynn Seebeck by Gittings, Dallas

Library of Congress Cataloging-in-Publication Data:

Seebeck, Mary Lynn, 1939-
American dream women : insuring women's wealth / Mary Lynn Seebeck. —1st ed.
272 p. cm.
Includes bibliographical references (p. 239) and index.
ISBN 0-941461-08-4 (hard; alk. paper). — ISBN 0-941461-07-6 (pbk.; alk. paper).

1. Women—Finance, Personal. 2. Investments. I. Title.
HG179.S382 1997 97-67-23
332.024'042—dc21 CIP

Important Caution to the Reader: This book does not take the place of a personal review and financial needs analysis as performed by a professional for the purpose of determining financial or legal advice for a personal or business financial program. You are encouraged to seek advice from financial professionals who are licensed, experienced, and/ or certified.

The contents of this book represent the views of the author. Therefore, the information contained herein does not necessarily reflect the opinions of any insurance or financial services company. This book is for educational purposes only.

For instructional purposes throughout, the examples use compound interest tables, and average an assumed 9-percent annual rate of return over the time period. Due to market fluctuation, past performance is not a guarantee of future results, and there is no guarantee of future results.

First Edition Manufactured in the United States of America

Each woman measures wealth differently. Women have defined "being" wealthy as being: comfortable, well paid, financially independent, able to laugh all the way to the bank, able to spend without worry, able to have security for a rainy day, and able to run a profitable business. Tangibles associated with wealth include: a nest egg, financial resources, investment accounts, stocks and bonds, assets, property, and riches.

The women who have inspired this book have further defined their own wealth not in any dollar amount but as a future condition that improves life beyond what they experience today. Ideas women have shared include: knowing my freezer will always be full and my pantry will be diversified with essentials and goodies; outfitting children with more than one pair of shoes, clothing that fits them as they grow, and a wardrobe for each season; taking family vacations at will; being able to give children dance and music lessons; having no loans or credit card debt; living in a home that's paid for; paying for college without loans; living off an inheritance; maintaining my current lifestyle when I retire; being able to comfortably pay myself as well as my employees and to offer them excellent benefits; and leaving a legacy for children or a charitable institution.

Wealth encompasses a spirit and state of "being" as much as it refers to a condition of "having." This book is for all women striving and accomplishing wealth—on their own terms.

PREFACE

A Philosophy Based on Teaching

Throughout the course of life, women give their time and talents to make the world a better place—for loved ones, for communities and for humanity. As we prepare to enter the Third Millennium, American women enjoy educational, economic, political and social opportunities that are unequaled anywhere in the world. Such privilege is increasing women's capacity to give back to their families and communities—not only through humanitarian pursuits but financially as well.

I have watched my own daughters and women clients climb to levels of educational and career achievement which I never thought possible when I was growing up in the post-WW II era. Women are earning incomes at wonderful and staggering rates. Many women have made financial mistakes and have readjusted their strategies to gradually and definitely reach their goals. Women are now a majority in America by more than 7 million. With more women working and earning higher incomes than ever before, women's keen awareness of financial planning is imperative in order to accumulate wealth from such unprecedented income earning potential. The economic, insurance, investment and banking conditions that create this financial environment in the United States offer unique and unparalleled opportunities for us to accumulate wealth for ourselves and the children, parents, businesses, and employees who depend on us. To achieve the wealth that can come from disciplined savings and sound planning, we must attain knowledge, demonstrate creativity, exhibit courage, and assume accountability for determining our own financial futures.

In the 35 years that I've spent in sales and marketing while involved with my father's family business as well as my own insurance and financial planning practice, the majority of my women customers and clients have shared their life experiences in order that others may learn from their successes and failures. It is such a spirit that has driven the creation of this book.

TWELVE STEPS FOR SUCCESS

Part I provides 12 steps to help gain control of your financial future. Chapters focus on creating a comfort level and sense of urgency to take command of your personal finances and teaching you a step-by-step process by which to do so. The need for working with a professional team that will stay with you and assist you in monitoring your progress as your life needs change is explained and emphasized.

The 12 steps are: coordinating a team of advisors; selecting them; interviewing to find the right match for your personal style; learning how to identify unethical behavior; knowing what you want; assessing your present financial health; determining what you can afford; understanding your company benefits; coordinating company and personal planning; learning how to diversify savings, insurance, and investments for now and the future; controlling the buying process; selecting a company, products and progress updates. After reading the first part, you will have an insider's view of fundamentals of insurance and financial planning.

Part 2 features needs most prevalent among my clients and offers financial planning solutions to solve those needs. The family profiles, which are the core of this section are non-fictional accounts given by some of the 1,000 women and men who are served by my practice. Their stories tell about their lives alone, with a partner, with children, with businesses, and with parents. Names have been changed, but the experiences have not. The stories of women's lives address the circumstances and needs appealing to single women, recent college graduates beginning professional careers, women taking care of aging parents or special needs children, single parent moms, dual-income families, wives managing a wealthy husband's money, professionals, women business owners, widows, and self-made women wealthy in their own right.

Throughout my practice, I've serviced hundreds of women who have expressed common needs, wants and desires for the future. The personal stories they share in part 2 are organized according to life cycles. If you are like most members of our focus group, you will scan the table of contents to find the story which fits your current lifestyle and circumstances and go back to read the others as your life changes. Each story is independent and complete on its own and provides background, questions to ask, needs and possible solutions.

The objective of this book is not to teach you about technical products. The objective is to teach you how to attain knowledge; to ask the right questions of various types of professionals; to paint a larger picture of the many facets of accounting, legal provisions, insurance and investments and how they must work together if you ultimately to gain financial independence and achieve your financial goals.

This book is about heart and the core of how you can financially protect yourself and those you love—throughout your life, with or without a partner. It is not a technical treatise about the complex world of specific insurance or investment products. Every licensed professional is competent to teach you about these concepts or products on a face-to-face basis. **I do emphasize, however, that all women seeking financial planning counsel must be knowledgeable to ask the right questions, demand to be taught, and assure that the members of their professional team are licensed, experienced and/ or certified.**

When insurance agents, registered representatives, certified financial planners, attorneys, and certified public accountants approach these stories, they will see that the financial planning solutions proposed throughout are cross functional and interdisciplinary. Recommendations use mutual funds, investments such as stocks and bonds, annuities, certificates of deposit, and life insurance products, together with various legal provisions where appropriate, to satisfy short- and long-term goals.

A PHILOSOPHY BASED ON TEACHING

This book is based on a central psychological premise that the process used by women to make decisions about their future is markedly different than the process employed by men. My philosophy for working with clients advocates a relationship approach *vs. a transaction approach.* This relationship approach forms the foundation of my business practice as well as this book. The relationship approach poses a fundamental belief that women prefer to make decisions about their financial futures based on developing long-term relationships which will teach them and help them develop confidence over time.

As such, the approach I pose in this book precludes a transaction or product-oriented sale based on a one-time interaction or purchase which does not consider the total picture of a woman's financial plan (her current income and expenses relative to her wants, needs and desires for the future). My philosophy advocates that members of a woman's professional financial planning team provide her ongoing communication and knowledge through a teaching process. In fact, I am adamant that financial planning for women that is based on transaction selling rather than relationship selling is inappropriate for women because its methodology is contrary to women's decision making processes.

A PROCESS FOR CONTINUOUS IMPROVEMENT

Business or professional women active in corporate or private firms may recognize the thread of Total Quality Management (TQM) weaving a tapestry throughout this essay. Using a TQM approach offers a process by which personal financial planning can be adopted with ease until it becomes habit. A personal mission or goal is identified in terms of women's long-term desires. Assessment relative to selecting financial planning counsel, earning cycles, and saving cycles plays a major part in the process. Planning a financial program is followed by a disciplined commitment to implement the plan. Annual reviewing and adjusting the plan for incremental progress are a must if a program is to succeed in its mission of financial independence or accumulating wealth over time. The secret to accumulating wealth is to make the process dynamic, focused and ongoing so that it becomes habitual. For some women, this means a major shift in the way they have been conditioned to think *vs.* the way they *must* think and act if they are to prosper financially. The TQM model of defining goals, doing annual assessment, planning, implementing, and reviewing provides a track to run on that will adjust with personal circumstances through all cycles of life. It is a process which advocates an active relationship between a woman and all members on her team of professional advisors.

Neither a 12-step process nor the personal financial plan a woman creates can succeed without her commitment and discipline. A woman who expresses herself through athletics, music, art, dance, writing or other style of performance acknowledges the need for continuous development and determination if she is to succeed. If she has a vision or goal, she also needs the talent, skill and discipline to carry it out. She cannot rely on someone else to perform for her. Life will bring chaotic days, high-energy days, and low-energy days. All affect her ability to carry out her mission and vision and achieve her goal. But if she is focused on her goal, ultimately her athletic achievement, her performances, her paintings, her songs, her poems, or her sculptures are born and accumulate over time to build a collection that celebrates her discipline of achievement. I believe this discipline, if applied as a mindset and lifestyle can likewise yield financial wealth accumulation over time for American women disciplined enough to remain focused on the beauty and joy of their vision.

As American women of the New Age, we are exposed to many philosophies of thinking. Self actualization and spiritual well being come from achieving balance and control of the key dimensions of our lives. In *Anatomy of the Spirit*, medical intuitive Caroline Myss, Ph. D., explains how we manage power. She discusses how we become ill when we lose power due to imbalances among the essential physical and psycho-social dimensions of our life dealing with culture, ethnicity, politics, finance, family, partner, children, self-esteem, emotion, will power, intellect and spirituality. Myss concludes that how we manage and balance all these dimensions of our power determines our physical health, honor, and spiritual well being.

It is my heartfelt intent that this book will provide a step-by-step winning process as well as confidence and encouragement to all women who strive to control and balance their financial power. May you each achieve peace of mind and self determination to secure the future wealth that will provide for you and those who depend on you in the 21st Century.

Mary Lynn Seebeck *Ft. Worth, Texas*

CONTENTS

DEDICATION

Susie

HOLY ANGELS WAS AN ALL-GIRL CATHOLIC ACADEMY IN MILWAUKEE, Wisconsin. Here I met Susie as we entered our freshman year of high school in 1953. She was from a family of 10 children; I from a family of 5. We shared similar responsibilities for family chores and taking care of our younger brothers and sisters. But it was the Friday night dances, dates, and boys that sparked the bond that linked us in these tender years and ultimately—for life.

In high school, we were together all day. These were the times for poodle skirts, pony tails and saddle shoes, chatting, planning, dreaming and knowing every secret there was to know about each other—while a tiny transistor radio beat the Rock 'n Roll of the '50s.

Susie was the quiet one, and I was the spunky, spirited redhead most likely to get into trouble. At 16, we were driving around in my 1956 powder blue Ford convertible with a Thunderbird engine. We earned much attention from the boys back then!

After graduation, we proceeded to work in our family businesses. Susie was her father's clerical assistant in their dry cleaning business. My father's business consisted of 5 gas stations, and he made me do a little of everything including accounts receivable, administering fuel oil sales, and, of course, pumping gas. Susie and I believed our Dads loved us enough to keep us busy so that we had no time to get into trouble. We both eventually married our high school sweethearts.

Susie was married 10 years before adopting a son, Eric. Soon after, Christopher arrived and then Bradley. With a phone call or visit, we daily shared our happy times as we raised our families.

After 19 years, Susie's marriage ended in divorce. She faced the responsibilities of raising Eric, Christopher, and Bradley, who were ages 13, 10, and 7, respectively. She was overwhelmed, frightened, angry and stressed with worry as she juggled work, children and finances as a single mom. This was not the happily-forever-after story we had dreamed about as young teens.

We spent much time together then, playing games with the children, taking them to the park for picnics, and taking time as friends to lean on each other. It was tough to see my best friend giving so much of herself without direction or knowing where her life was going. I felt helpless to make a difference.

After 6 years as a single mom, Susie fell in love and married John in 1984. The three boys were in tuxedos at a quaint ceremony in a small country church; I was her attendant. The reception at a golf course, where she and John had courted, painted a lovely picture of a new secure future for her, and the expectation of many years of happiness.

Soon after her remarriage, my husband, Tom, and I moved to Texas to follow Tom's career. I signed a career contract as an agent and began my journey into the insurance business. Susie was my greatest supporter as we exchanged weekly updates about our lives. On numerous occasions she asked me to create an insurance program for her and explained that if anything ever happened to her, she did not want John to have the financial responsibility of raising the boys. Because she was my best friend, I felt that I needed to know absolutely everything about every product and the intricacies of insurance before I felt adequate to satisfy her request.

Ten months after I began selling life insurance, we were talking during one of our weekly updates on the phone; we discussed her concerns and determined that Susie needed $1,500 income each month in the event that she became disabled and $250,000 of life insurance protection to provide for her sons. I was planning a trip to Wisconsin the following May, and we would complete the paperwork at that time.

In April, a month before my scheduled trip, the call came. It was Susie telling me something a best friend never wants to hear. She was hospitalized with lung cancer. I was devastated; of course this did not make sense since I was the chain smoker.

Susie was hopeful for a full recovery, and knowing how important a patient's state of mind is, John and I joined the doctors in providing hope and encouragement.

I was overwhelmed and angry at myself for not having the self-confidence necessary to help her when she had originally asked for help. I had spent 1 year calling on businesses and strangers while letting my best friend go uncovered. I felt no sense of urgency, because I thought I would have her forever.

For the next 18 months, I shuttled back and forth from Texas to Wisconsin to be with Susie. We made visits to her doctor to hear his encouraging words. Praying that she would get better, I envisioned the possibility of her passing several years cancer free. If she was then in remission, hopefully she would be considered insurable, and I could fulfill the commitment that I was not confident enough to handle earlier.

During one visit on a clear and beautiful day, we drank tea in her back yard under the pines. We were alone and happy to have quiet time. She told me how happy she was with John and how good he was to her and to the boys. She also relayed the fears that she had of not being able to fight the cancer and that she was not yet ready to leave this world.

Susie was concerned about not being able to enjoy her sons' college days, their marriages, and the children she hoped they would have. We hugged and cried, fearful of the future. Neither one of us mentioned the insurance program that never came to fruition, but I knew Susie was disheartened. I was overwhelmed and without words; nothing I could say could ever fix my lack of responsiveness to her request.

Back in Texas, I prayed for Susie to be well again, for her family, and for the day she would again be insurable. I watched my dear friend struggle against cancer, emotionally giving her boys and John everything she had. However, the bitter truth was that during her disability, her income was not there to assist the family—because I had not taken care of her need when she was healthy. I had not been confident or ready enough to sell insurance to my best friend. In 1986, 18 months after being diagnosed with lung cancer, Susie was back in the hospital. After the call, I closed my office in Texas and flew to Wisconsin to be with her.

At the hospital, John asked me to break the news to Susie. Two and a half years after I entered the insurance business, I was faced with telling my best friend that she was dying. At 7:30 a.m., I closed the door to face her in her hospital room. This friend of mine, who had shared so many dreams with me, soon would not be around to share more. We looked at each other, and I said, "Susie, you are dying; I'm here." She nodded; she already knew it in her heart.

She thanked me for being with her and continued by adding that I was a great friend and that she was thankful for the memories. As her frail body lay in the hospital bed, she looked at me and said, "Mary, I've been fighting death because my affairs are not in order. I am running out of time, and I need your help. I want John to receive the little I have. Since you are my insurance agent and best friend, I know you will know how to do this." We set about getting Susie's financial affairs in order by appointing her husband, John, as beneficiary of the policy. I arranged for her to spend her last days in a hospice, so the boys and John could enjoy her time uninterrupted.

I wrote down her wishes about her assets and arranged for all to be notarized. Then, my dying friend said to me, "Mary, don't ever be ashamed of what you do. You have so much to give and so many people to talk to, for I have learned that insurance is the greatest gift anyone could give. I have forgiven you and myself, for failing to have my financial affairs in order." This is when I was able to tell Susie how sorry I was for not putting her insurance in place when she first asked me.

Even though she forgave me, it didn't change her family's financial position. I was feeling incredible guilt and never wanted to make the same mistake again. I never again wanted to say, "I'm sorry" for leaving a client unprotected. I was confused but knew that she would tell me the truth about what she would have done to protect her family if she could turn the clock back and do the planning all over again. We talked about insurance, disability protection, and investments. And I asked her what sequence and priority she felt each of these had when satisfying her goals for her family.

With a confidence that came with thinking about it over and over all these months, she explained in her frail voice, "Protect income first, Mary. With disability protection, I could have given so much more to John and the boys. It broke my heart to see them sacrifice when I could no longer work. It could have helped John with the medical expenses. The $1,500 monthly disability check we talked about would have gone a long way." She continued, " Life insurance coverage is second, Mary. The $250,000 life insurance policy could have provided a college fund. Investments should be considered last. The modest amount I received from my divorce settlement earned hardly anything, and what little it did earn I used for the boys. Just think how much life insurance that sum could have purchased."

She was getting tired but smiled; I could see a new calm beginning to settle over her. I knew at that moment that Susie's gift to me was to resolve this for me for the future. As Susie described what was important, she said nothing about how well known the insurance company was, nothing about any specific products, nothing about term insurance vs. whole life insurance, premiums or dividends—all concepts and phrases that agents get wrapped up in when they lose focus about the purpose of insurance. Susie explained that needs and feelings come first.

We held hands and continued to share our life's memories that morning. We cried and laughed, and I polished her nails for the last time. As we said our last Rosary together, she relaxed and found peace. Susie died soon after, at the age of 47, leaving Eric, Christopher, Bradley, and her dear love, John.

As I cried in the airplane on my trip back to Texas, I wrote my commitment about how I would serve my clients from that day forward. I would listen to their needs and goals, and review their income, expenses, and assets in relationship to their goals. I would recommend disability income coverage first, life insurance second, and investments, third—only after the insurance was in place.

It is Susie who is my motivation to dedicate my life to this great industry and the legacy it provides for families. She is truly beside me every day, and I remain ever committed to first satisfy the needs of women everywhere—especially those of friends and those who are dearest to me.

PART I

12 STEPS TO HELP GAIN CONTROL OF YOUR FINANCIAL FUTURE

Achieving the American Dream

AMERICA WAS BUILT ON A DREAM AND THE DREAM CONTINUES. THE vision of A promised land of opportunity where you can accomplish anything if you only work hard enough has been a driving force for generations of immigrant and American families.

In the latter half of the 20th Century, demographic changes in the American family and the American workplace have rewritten the rules of the American Dream. The number of women in the civilian labor force working outside the home increased from 23.2 million (38 percent of all women) in 1960 to 58.4 million (58 percent of all women) in 1993. Single and married working women with responsibilities for children increased from 8.1 million in 1960 to 31.5 million in 1993. Today, 6 million are single parents. More than ever, American women are facing responsibilities to pursue and achieve the American Dream—alone, and as heads of households, families, and businesses.[1]

The escalation of American women attaining undergraduate and post-graduate degrees has likewise created a new drive for American women to pursue higher paying jobs and to gain financial independence. Independence is a catalyst for self-actualization. The increase of women earning educational degrees has grown to heights unmatched anywhere in the world. In 1960, 5.8 million women graduated with bachelors', masters' or post-graduate degrees. That number grew to 19.2 million in 1993.[2]

However, women cannot rely on their success in academics or business to achieve success in the financial world. The successful behaviors that women have learned in their journey through academic life do not necessarily prepare us for what is necessary to accumulate financial wealth on our own. Studying hard, working hard, and giving a job 150 percent do not accumulate financial wealth.

I was born and raised in the *Ozzie and Harriet* generation when expectations were well-defined regarding my role as a wife and mother. My life then was not much different than that of many American women my age. I was responsible for making the house a home and taking care of the children. When I eventually entered the working world and pursued professional education after raising my family, *all* of this was fit in after I had my home and family responsibilities satisfied. The basics of daily family life such as grocery shopping, planning meals, doing laundry, keeping a clean and orderly home, and raising children were priorities *before* my career. All competed for my time. After I started my own business, the multiple responsibilities intensified.

Because there are only 24 hours in a day, my husband also shared with the family responsibilities. In my generation, it was the husband's role in the family to take care of the business of car insurance, home insurance and retirement, if any planning was done. For most families, assuring that the daily expenses and emergencies were covered was such a predominant concern that rarely could we even think about what we would need for retirement 40 years into the future.

In the 1960s, when the Women's Movement and the necessity of a two-income earning household brought women into the workplace in large numbers, many women were satisfied to assign the primary responsibility for family security to the husband's income. Women were content with whatever medical insurance and term life insurance was provided for their husbands by the companies where they worked; the husband's coverage was primary. Women relied on the company where their husbands worked to know what was right for them and were comfortable with the thought that as long as the company plans were available, families were in some way "safe and secure."

Today, educated, professional women working in corporate America or working in their own family businesses never dream that a day will come when their company benefits, dads, or husbands will not be there to help attend to these matters.

When the romance and beauty of marriage and raising young children become priorities for a woman, a loving, spirited and gentle hearted woman does not think that someday her life could be very different. Someday she could be alone. When marriage is good, and life is going according to plan, a woman does not want to plan for the worst. To do so seems like an act of doom or an admission of little faith or trust.

Women believe. We believe in trust and goodness and light. Living in the worlds we create, we believe that we have dominion over our homes, our families, and our lives. We believe that our lives are stories and that we can write our own chapters. That is how women write their American Dream. As women we believe that if we give all of our energy and love to make our marriages prosper, and if we give all of our time to our jobs and career, we will surely reap great rewards. We want it to be so.

When any woman wills positive energy into her home or family, she carries the expectation of positive results. Therefore, a woman will not believe that her positive efforts and energies can turn out wrong or take a turn for the worst. A woman will not believe that another woman could capture her husband's attention.

A woman will not believe that with her loyalty, creativity, flawless education, and prospective contributions to a company, the boss who hired her would stop believing in her one day. A woman will not believe that the company she gives her life to will let her go or outplace her, especially when she has put her career first and sacrificed a great deal in her family life to do so. When a woman is focused on climbing the ladder of success in corporate America, or medical institutions or academia, her focus is on doing her best job. Planning for the tables to turn in life is to accommodate negative thoughts that impair positive thinking.

The state of mind that many American women bring to life is a positive one. However, it does not prepare them to live or work in environments still dominated by patriarchal values and methods of learning. Women are often the last to learn that people don't have money or wealth by becoming educated and working hard. A college degree alone will not do it. Success can not do it. We must do it for ourselves. We can create wealth by implementing tactics and strategies for saving on a monthly basis.

DIFFERING VALUES ABOUT CONTROL

There is a great dichotomy between the values that women and men bring to living—values that affect the way they approach financial accumulation and values that affect the way buying decisions are made.

As young boys and growing adults, men are taught that life is war not a fairy tale. Competition and winning are keys for survival. Creativity assures supremacy. Life is a war to be won by tactics and strategies. That paradigm also defines how men create families and companies. It determines how men approach the accumulation of financial wealth. Someone is always there to challenge them; so they are forever ready with tactics and strategies in hand for winning. This is true whether they are being Boy Scouts, racing cars, playing sports, or building a corporate empire. Men believe that someone is always competing with them to sack the yardage they have gained; any jeopardy can happen. It must be controlled and protected with all options open. Options and strategies with the boss. Options and strategies with business associates. Options and strategies with women. Options and strategies with money. Men are taught that success comes from *being in control.*

For men, financial security is another priority on the chess board of life because they do not want to be held in check—caught unprotected. Their planning is a series of maneuvers through which they demonstrate an upper hand and by which they demonstrate superiority among their associates. Bits and pieces of information about the latest products and strategies are coveted as maneuvers for winning the war. Men revel at the game. Each maneuver or financial strategy is based on new and better intelligence or counter-intelligence provided by the agent or broker *du jour*. Therefore, with each step, a man gains confidence that the next strategy is the winning move—the one that will do it all for him. Men whom I have counseled, *appear* to be comfortable in the world of financial vehicles and money matters. Some buy: the stocks that are hot, the insurance where the premiums and company are the most competitive, mutual funds today, or bonds tomorrow.

By contrast, as I've seen with my clients, many women have been raised in families where they learn *how not to be in control* or *to abdicate control* to someone else regarding financial matters. Habits and behaviors for gaining control are something they must relearn after they leave home—sometimes the hard way. I firmly believe the greatest gift a parent can give a daughter is to teach her how to become financially responsible, knowledgeable, and accountable at an early age.

Many women's lives have vehicles—other than financial vehicles—as their priorities; they play taxi for car pools and soccer games. The successful professional women I've worked with do not revel in absorption of the latest and greatest technical data; they do not revel in playing the game. Their satisfaction comes from knowing that solutions are put in place to solve their emotional wants and needs for now and for the future.

When women decide to become involved in their own financial affairs, the process is markedly different than scouting for the latest financial hot tip of the week. **Women want to learn as they go. They want an extended educational process that demands complete explanations. They want to see solutions without complexity. Emotions, feelings, and a process of sharing are what matter.**

My experiences and perceptions gathered from working with women buyers since the early 1970s has been confirmed in more formal studies. Halya Doherty, an insurance marketing manager, participated in her firm's focus group of women buyers as well as women and men who sell insurance to women. The highlights were made public in *LIMRA'S MarketFACTS*, January/February 1995. According to Ms. Doherty:

> Findings reveal that [because] women live longer than men they tend to plan long-term for themselves and their children; whereas men tend to take a short-term approach and may spend their money on personal luxury items. Women spend more time during the interview process exploring options and building rapport with the agent. Men on the other hand are more bottom-line oriented and typically make decisions more quickly with less information. Women ask a lot of questions before making a purchase decision, whereas men are less detail oriented. Women are far more likely than men to give referrals if they are satisfied with the service they receive. And women are more likely than men to support each other when it comes to sharing helpful information and referring to reliable sources.[3]

EMOTIONAL *VS.* TECHNICAL ADVICE

The roles and behaviors that men and women learn create differences in how they approach financial planning. Because the banking, insurance, and finance industries are dominated by men, there is a dichotomy between the way women buy insurance or other financial products and the way these products are sold to women. It took me a long time to understand why I was having difficulty explaining to men the philosophy underlying the way I conduct my practice.

In the insurance industry, a company provides field agents with financial materials that illustrate cash values, and dividend accumulation, and computer enhancements. The support is technical. I have never found a questionnaire anywhere that addressed a woman's emotional desires, goals, and short- and long-term needs for her future. The questionnaires provided by companies are designed to elicit immediate answers from the prospective buyer. I don't believe that there are too many women who feel comfortable baring the truth about their lives until they understand a reason for doing so.

I've conducted joint sales work with many excellent agents; together we have come to the conclusion that there are distinct differences in the process that men and women use to make buying decisions for financial services products. Men are inclined to be technical. It's natural for them; they emphasize financial facts and bypass the world of emotion. Consider their process like this:

Need or Want Cash ➨ Review Data ➨ Make Decision Based on Price or Competitive Feature ➨ Trust Based on + or - Outcome of Financial Advice

A man develops trust with a financial professional based on the monetary outcome—win or lose.

We have found that a woman's process is more like this:

Emotional Expression of Qualitative Needs ➨ Sharing of Common Values ➨ Questions and Answers Based on Teaching and Learning ➨ Confidence, Comfort, and Mutual Respect ➨ Trust Grows ➨ Consideration of Products for Purchase

A woman's process begins with emotion, followed by sharing, teaching, learning, developing confidence and trust *before* any discussion of products occurs.

I've accompanied agents on interviews. They interact with prospective women clients as if they were a mother, a sister or a wife in a subordinate role. One item that creates discomfort when many agents approach women is that the agents conduct sales calls in women's homes rather than encouraging a sales call at the office. Some agents do not realize that many women may feel this to be an intrusion. Subconsciously, the women feel that the agent believes they belong in the home and are to be dealt with at the kitchen table. Working women want to be treated in a manner that affirms them but doesn't intrude into their valuable time. Women should be met at work or in a professional setting at the agent's office. It increases the sense of importance of the meeting, evokes a sense of safety, eliminates distractions, and confirms the professional credibility of the agent with whom they are doing business.

At the beginning of a sales interview, women are often approached with statements like: "I have a new life insurance product to show you." "I have a new disability policy to show you." "Do you need any more disability income insurance?" "Do you think you need any more life insurance?" "I have a great tip on a high paying mutual fund." "Let me take a look at your policies to see what they're like, maybe they aren't the best. Maybe the companies you've done business with aren't the best rated."

This approach is common. It isn't natural for the women I've worked with as clients; it doesn't address needs or emotions or build confidence or trust.

One client of mine, Carol, is 40-years old and married with two children. She recalls how it was years ago when she and her husband were meeting with agents. "All these years I sat and watched my husband with agents discussing life insurance around our dinner table. They looked and nodded at each other like they both knew what they were talking about. They didn't involve me in the discussion, and the agent was happy to discuss these things only with my husband. My husband never asked any questions. Now, my husband has openly admitted to me that he really doesn't know anything about life insurance; he just knew we needed some. I just looked at him dumbfounded; I couldn't believe it. My husband handled the life insurance, auto insurance, and house insurance. I handled everything else in our lives. I never understood life insurance and found that the agents did not talk to me but talked with my husband instead. I always thought my husband understood everything by the way he acted. Now 22 years later and 22 years older, I realize he is terribly underinsured, and I never had any policy of my own."

Some agents with whom I've worked have had difficulty asking women buyers simple questions like, "Tell me something about each of your children." "Do you see your marriage as being long term?" "Do you enjoy your career?" "Do you plan to change companies?" "Is the company you're working for growing or experiencing any downsizing or layoffs?" These questions get at the core of why women are making plans. These emotional questions and issues that I address easily, many agents find irrelevant to discuss. As a woman agent, I want to know and understand the emotional motivations that are driving my women clients toward their financial goals.

I believe a woman initially requires an emotional framework for her decision making that is based on a discussion of her wants, needs, and desires rather than a technical framework about product information.

The first time I was with a colleague on a sales call with a woman business owner, he talked about *split dollar* and *reverse split dollar*, which are technical terms involving the ownership and beneficiary arrangements of a cash value policy! I sat there amazed! I thought I was at a football game watching new plays I hadn't heard before. My understanding and discussion of such business insurance concepts is by the benefits they provide, not the technical jargon. I have found that discussing planning concepts with technical jargon doesn't fit comfortably into the language of the people I serve. My primary clients are business professionals, physicians, lawyers, certified public accountants, entrepreneurs, and the wealthy. I find that they want to be talked to in a way that will enable them to learn and understand rather than in a way that makes them feel they lack knowledge.

The difference between the emotional *vs.* the technical approach often causes frustration for women who seek to buy insurance or financial products. The availability of seasoned women agents does not meet the demand of the women's market. Most likely, women agents have not had any women as mentors. There are few women directing financial services companies. There are few women who are part of corporate technical teams. As a result, women buyers are being approached with technical information and marketing tactics that pre-suppose women think like men. I believe that this approach is not appropriate, adequate, or satisfying for women buyers.

Many financial professionals servicing women have a tendency to be preoccupied with illustrations, computer presentations, specific products, and all things analytical and technical during the sales call. This frustrates many women. When women buy insurance or investments, they need to demand that the products and policies are presented to them in a way that teaches them how the product addresses their emotional wants, needs, and desires. Women want plenty of time to tell their life stories, to analyze their mistakes, and to enjoy the successes they've made along the way. Focusing on technical support and data is not the way to begin developing a relationship that will last for the long term.

The financial services industry is making incremental progress toward developing a better understanding of the differences between how men and women approach a buying decision. Mimi Donaldson, a noted international communications consultant who trains corporate managers about improving relationships, addressed leading agents at the 1995 conference of the Million Dollar Round Table. She provided some of these key points in her discussion, *Men & Women—Can We Talk?* Ms. Donaldson asserts that women bond through stories and build relationships through stories.

For many women, stories are vital to sharing and understanding the type of relationships they are building. However, men are less inclined to share stories, and prefer to get to the bottom line of the sales process. Women are fixed on the larger picture and will focus their attention inward after they have bonded through telling their stories. Because men are less inclined to build relationsips by sharing emotional experiences, they do not encourage women to do so, and as a result, the women buyer can be offended.

John Savage and Ben Feldman have touched the lives of many and are greatly revered agents in the life insurance industry. Truthfully, what I've gained from them has not been technical information. John Savage or Ben Feldman never gave me technical advice. They spoke about addressing needs on an emotional level. This approach is even more appropriate and necessary for women who are buying and for those who are working with them.

NEGOTIATION: LET'S MAKE A DEAL

The last major difference I've observed between the way men and women approach planning for their financial futures is that men love a great game of negotiation and seek to master it—most women I work with do not. In fact, the majority of women clients I've worked with over the years have expressed that they detest any negotiation involved in a discussion of their serious financial issues. Yet, I've seen and heard that women continue to be approached during an interview with comments like, "Well, if you don't like the $150,000 whole life policy, I have a $200,000 term policy that would be cheaper."

When women embrace the commitment to gain control of their financial future and decide to put their financial affairs in order, they do not want to feel that they are playing *Let's Make a Deal*. Selling financial products to women and asking them to play to gamble about what's best is not appropriate given the way most women make decisions. Nor is it fun. Is the key to your financial future behind door number 1? Or is it door number 2? Or is it door number 3?

As a woman, gaining control, taking charge, getting confidence, showing courage, and being outspoken are the winning doors you must choose.

Liz

WHEN LIZ ENTERED MY OFFICE FOR THE FIRST TIME, SHE WAS 38—newly widowed with a pre-school daughter.

Liz was referred by one of my clients who was her friend. Liz relayed how difficult it was for her to make decisions after her husband's death. She was interrupted in the evenings by solicitations from agents and brokers calling her as a result of her husband's obituary notice. Liz was very frightened about managing money, about finances, and about being both Mom and Dad to her daughter. She had a difficult time getting her life back in order and needed time to build trust and confidence.

We talked woman to woman and began developing a relationship; I could sense she was not yet ready for a detailed discussion about how to invest the sizable amount of insurance proceeds she received after her husband's death. She happily showed me pictures of their daughter, Roxanne, and carefully described the details of their life over the last months.

Liz explained, "I had Roxanne when I was 34; neither Ron nor I had any other children previously." She proceeded to tell me of the joy they had with Roxanne who promised great happiness for both of them.

Only 6 months after Roxanne was born, Ron was diagnosed with lung cancer. It had metastasized to stage 4, and he was told he had between 1 month and 2 years to live; Ron was ill for 4 years. For the majority of that time, Ron remained strong and was able to handle many family responsibilities including the family finances.

Liz confided, "I knew I should get involved, and Ron tried to get me involved, but I had my hands full with a baby, a full-time job and the demands of his illness. I should have made myself develop a plan to learn about the family finances, in addition to attending to my priorities with Ron and Roxanne. I needed personal time for myself. Even before he became sick, he exclusively ran the household finances. I've never liked to hear women claim ignorance about family matters saying, . . .'My husband handles those things.'. . . I knew better and wanted my life to be different, but I just never made it happen. In my first marriage I was the one who handled everything and never liked it because it was stressful for me. When I married Ron, I felt lucky that we both shared similar values about maintaining good credit. The fact that Ron seemed so responsible and good at everything left me satisfied and complacent. His control of the finances made him feel he was participating in our family life during the illness. Therefore, while he was alive, I let him continue paying the bills, calling repairmen, and making decisions that I was not happy making. I didn't want to feel responsible for working outside the home, raising the child, taking care of all the domestic duties plus maintaining the household finances as well. As a result, I happily avoided the financial aspects."

Liz admitted, "Now I'm dragging myself, kicking and screaming, through all of this. Many times I wonder what Ron would be doing or how he would handle it. I'm not comfortable or confident about any of the advice I get. Learning how to deal with different business people, learning how to negotiate, and feeling comfortable enough to get 3 estimates for home repair projects should have been lessons learned much earlier than I did.

"Now, I'm also tired of hearing my friends and relatives tell me, after the fact, that I've paid too much. For instance, after getting pest control services, I had to get enough nerve to call the company back and say, 'Convince me that I didn't pay too much because my friends think that I did.' The person then explained how services and types of products vary depending on circumstances. After the explanation, I felt satisfied, but I want to feel satisfied *before* I buy the service, instead of justifying what I did afterwards. My friends admit that the pest control company I chose may make more visits to my house, but I still pay too much. To me the guarantees and the service are more important than the ultimate price. Because I do not feel that I have learned how to deal with these transactions, I am reluctant and not confident. Therefore, I'm delaying buying decisions.

"Also, as a widow I felt vulnerable when relatives wanted a share of the insurance proceeds following Ron's death. I'm an excellent example of not lending relatives money—any relative. Because I am very trusting, it is impossible for me to believe that someone would never pay a back a loan. I have a very trusted relative who currently owes me over $20,000. I don't regret loaning the money, but I do regret not learning the parameters for such types of personal notes and not learning how to carry them out. Roxanne and I are doing all right, but the learning process has been painful for me at this stage in my life. We women should have a set of parameters for making these business transactions in light of the values and priorities we establish for ourselves. Then we need to stick to them and feel confident to handle these financial affairs on our own and master being responsible."

After a year of being widowed, Liz is doing much better. She has sold a rental house that was demanding too much of her time and was creating added expense. She has updated her will and learned how mutual funds, annuities, investments and insurance work together to help shape her financial goals. Liz calls me frequently and visits to monitor the progress of her 401(k) portfolio and the growth of her mutual funds. She relies on our time together to continue her learning. She is feeling good about herself and her decisions. She has taken charge of her financial affairs; Liz has "mastered being responsible."

STEP1: COORDINATING A PROFESSIONAL TEAM TO INSURE SUCCESS

Tom

MIKE IS A CERTIFIED PUBLIC ACCOUNTANT WHOM I MET AT A MEETing in Dallas. We were both involved with the financial services industry and had a mutual acquaintance. As we theoretically discussed our working relationship as professionals advising clients, it was obvious from Mike's conversation that we had begun a topic about which he felt quite strongly. He proceeded to tell me a story about Tom, a client of his. It demonstrates how fragmented most clients' planning is and how professionals should work together when providing service to clients.

Tom was quite pleased with his life as he got into the car. Mary, his wife, had just told him that she was pregnant with their fourth child, and the kids were excited with the onset of school. Tom's business was having a record year. The stock tip that he received 3 weeks ago from Bud, his broker, had generated a handsome profit that reminded Tom that Bud had wanted to discuss another stock trade.

As he turned onto the busy thoroughfare, Tom may have been wondering how many of these tips he would need to fund a college education for each of his 4 children. The stock figures and his sales calls for the day were on his mind as he discussed these issues on his cellular phone with Bud. Bud recalled stress in Tom's voice when he caught a glimpse of something in his mirror. That was probably the last glimpse he remembered. The truck driver later told police that Tom swerved as though he didn't expect anyone to be in his lane.

Tom had always stated that he was a salesman and did not understand all the implications of his financial decisions. That was why he had an attorney to draft a will, a stock broker to purchase his stock trades, an insurance agent, and an accountant to assure his taxes were filed on time. Occasionally, Tom would talk to his certified public accountant about his will, or talk to his broker about tax concerns and investments. Yes, Tom had all the professionals in place to help him—but they never worked together on his behalf.

Tom was also aware that each of his professionals looked at him through very different eyes. To the attorney, Tom was a business owner who came in every other year and who seemed to have his business under control. To the stock broker, Tom was a wheeler-dealer who was interested in any kind of investment that could generate a quick return, yet he held other information about personal finances close to his vest. To the insurance agent, Tom was the wild and crazy guy he knew in college. To his certified public accountant, Tom maintained a very low profile.

Tom's situation is common. He had presented himself as a different person to each of those professionals whom he was trusting. Each accordingly developed different opinions about who Tom was, and what his goals and objectives were. Tom had a group of professionals in place, but he had not developed a team who communicated and planned together on his behalf.

People often use professionals in a limited fashion. In fact, often individuals take more time to plan for the future of their business or their employees than they do their own family. So it was for Tom. Instead of having a plan that all the professionals could implement as a team, Tom actually had no plan in place to orderly transfer his business, to address his estate for his family, or to minimize the expense of probate and taxation after he died.

Tom's wife Mary would have to contend with issues related to business continuation, succession, or sale. She would have to deal with issues regarding Tom's estate. As a widow, Mary would be administering these financial and legal matters for the first time. All of this would be present along with the emotional loss of a loving husband, her pregnancy, and the care of their children. When he was alive, Tom assumed that he would always be available and responsible to provide input to their financial and legal matters. In addition to not reaping the maximum benefits from his professionals, Tom had not told them his expectations and wishes so that they could assist during a period of catastrophe and transition until Mary could reasonably assume more of the responsibilities.

Tom needed to have a general idea about what his and Mary's goals were for the future. He needed to communicate those goals and objectives to the professionals he was going to use as a team. He needed to solicit their opinions about how to implement plans to attain those objectives, and then he needed to monitor them and revise them if necessary. If Tom had only taken the time to get his professionals together in the same room to hear his goals and objectives, he would have encouraged the professionals to develop a familiarity with each other that would improve communications among them. He would have better communicated with each of them about what his expectations were of them. He also would have begun bonds among them—bonds that would allow each of these professionals to feel as though they were part of a team—Tom and Mary's team. To get them together annually or semiannually nurtures their relationships as a team. It wouldn't have to be at the office; it could be done at a barbecue, at the pool or on the golf course.

Mike believes that as a certified public accountant who works with the attorney and agent on a client's behalf, a team approach is necessary to understand the client's goals and objectives and to focus on them. The members of the team are mutual resources to contact about items of importance regarding the others' areas of expertise. For instance, as a certified public accountant, Mike is concerned about whether or not clients have enough life or disability insurance. Such communication can help avert catastrophe for the client and the client's family. Working as a team allows each professional to perform to the best of his or her professional abilities as well as to be better focused on the client's needs. Every client deserves and should coordinate such a team approach.

Teamwork

CREATING A PROFESSIONAL TEAM AND COORDINATING ONGOING communication will build your confidence as well as give you emotional support that you are moving in the right direction to achieve your goals. Your culture and lifestyle demands dictate the type of relationships you maintain with your team as well as how frequently you meet. Many of my clients meet me semiannually along with their attorney and certified public accountant.

Rashinda, a divorced mother who recently began a small catering business explains, "It's not that I have transactions every 6 months; it's more that I want the agent, the broker, the certified public accountant, and the attorney to be speaking to one another, and I want them to have me at the top of their mind. This way when there are changes in the tax law or investment strategies, I know I am in the loop. I only have so much time to keep up with things. It's a great way for me to learn gradually instead of feeling pressured and in the dark when I do need to purchase some products or make changes. I want them to know that I expect them all to be in sync with my personal and business finances. I used the attorney at real estate closing, my divorce, setting up a will and trust accounts for my children as well as the employee contracts and lease contracts when I began my business. I also needed my accountant involved with the tax issues. The team is quite clear about what I expect."

Rashinda is like many women who are "in charge" today. There is a raised level of consumer expectation about coordination of her total life plan; it demands a synchronized team approach. Also, even though you have accepted accountability and control for your own long-term financial goals, you are not entirely alone as long as you communicate with your professional team. Nor are you blindly following the crowd conversation you may hear at the office water cooler. Your agent, registered representative and/or financial planner will advise you on your protection and accumulation goals. Your certified public accountant can help assure that you are taking advantage of all available tax savings personally—and for your business. The attorney's counsel is necessary regarding drafting wills, trusts, and contracts.

As we became aware through Tom's example, each team member needs to know the client's long-term goals and to update the other members of the professional team. The client needs to develop these relationships if they do not already exist. For example, if the agent feels that the client needs an overhead expense disability income policy, the certified public accountant could provide valuable information regarding the growth of the business and cash flow. This will enable the agent to be thorough when applying for the insurance and to give the underwriters in-depth information about the business. Proactive communication is good, because if the client goes on disability claim, the agent and the certified public accountant will be needed to help process the claim with the insurance company.

Personalities and expertise are needed to create a team of professionals with whom you are comfortable and who are comfortable working with each other. As Rashinda concludes, "I do not want 3 people going in separate directions. I want a coordinated team approach, which is working together on my behalf."

THE AGENT & INSURANCE

The agent specializes in given areas such as personal and family needs, business insurance, pension planning, or estate planning. The agent may represent 1 company or many companies offering an array of products needed for the insurance and financial needs of the client.

The agent should be trained and educated in how to use various products to satisfy specific needs—such as protecting a family, a business, an estate when someone dies, or creating a retirement program. An agent can specialize in auto and homeowners, worker's compensation, general liability, disability income coverage, or life insurance products. An agent may further specialize and work in a specific market such as payroll deduction; employee benefits including cancer plans, group life insurance, dental, vision, or health insurance. An agent may also specialize in using life insurance to help pay estate taxes or to help fund business succession programs. An agent who is a *registered representative* as well as being licensed to sell insurance, will also be knowledgeable about investments and able to discuss them with you.

An analogy is found within the medical profession. An orthopedic surgeon, general practitioner, and neurosurgeon each attended medical school, but each chose a different specialty. The orthopedic surgeon has education about the entire body but would most likely refer a head trauma injury to the neurosurgeon; they would work as a team if the trauma also included broken bones.

Here is an example of how insurance and investments coordinate. The agent is with the client discussing an annual review. While doing the updating of information, the agent discovers that the client needs a will updated because he or she is going to receive a sizable inheritance. The agent also discovers that the client plans to sell property that will have a large capital gain. The client also expects to receive a large bonus, because business has been very good. The agent has a responsibility to the client to coordinate a meeting with the attorney and certified public accountant to update them as to the clients' changes. The agent also needs to create a sense of urgency because the client needs counsel on tax and legal issues.

INVESTMENT & INSURANCE QUESTIONS

You can address these key questions to your insurance agent and registered representative.

- What type of life insurance should I have?
- How much life insurance do I need?
- What will happen to my insurance if I lose my job? How do I protect myself if this occurs?
- Where can I learn more about my insurance program?
- What is the difference between term, whole life, universal life, and variable life insurance?
- How does an annuity work?
- How do I know if I have the right kind of insurance?
- Is there anything I can do since I am no longer insurable?
- If I have no surviving relatives, what kind of insurance do I need?
- Should I have life insurance as a single woman without children?
- Do I need disability insurance since I have it at work?
- How much disability income protection should I have?
- Will my disability benefit be taxable at the time of my claim?
- How much money should I have as a reserve for emergencies?
- Should I pay more toward my mortgage monthly or invest in mutual funds instead?
- Should I pay off debt or invest more?
- What types of investments are suitable for me?
- How much can I contribute to my 401(k), 403(b) or IRA? Should I contribute more?
- When can I take income from my retirement plan?
- I have concerns regarding the size of my parents' estate and how much tax will be due when they die...What type of questions do I ask?
- What type of insurance should I have to take care of estate taxes?
- How do you know if insurance should be in a trust?
- Should I have a life insurance trust?
- What does asset protection mean?

- What is second-to-die insurance?
- Is the stability of my insurance company important?
- What does the rating of companies mean?

THE CERTIFIED PUBLIC ACCOUNTANT & TAX ISSUES

The certified public accountant is involved with the client at least once a year for tax preparation and reviewing income, expenses, profit and loss statements to assure all information is properly documented on tax returns. The certified public accountant is making sure the client takes advantage of ways to save taxes such as contributions to IRA, 401(k), 403(b), or contributions to other pension plans if available. The certified public accountant is astute to continued tax law changes and making sure proper deductions have been taken based on IRS rules. The certified public accountant is often asked legal or insurance questions.

For example, the certified public accountant has a client with high overhead in a business and is responsible for 4 children. The business has no disability program for the owner. The client asks if she should purchase a disability policy? How much does she need? How much would the premium be? The client may ask if $150,000 of life insurance enough? The client reveals she is considering making her key employee a partner for the purpose of succession planning. She asks how the change should be structured? What type of legal documents are needed? Should there be insurance protection for this? If so, how much and what type?

This is a classic example of the client feeling comfortable asking the certified public accountant the questions in the event he may not have a well-developed relationship with an insurance agent or an attorney. These questions may arise because the client is introspective about life goals because it is tax time. The certified public accountant should help the client by guiding the client to the agent, financial planner, or attorney. In the event the client does not have an agent or attorney, the certified public accountant should coordinate a team approach so all of the client's goals can be addressed.

TAX QUESTIONS

As an individual or a business owner, the following are frequently asked questions that you can address to your certified public accountant:

- What type of retirement program can I have?
- What will my capital gains tax be if I sell my home, farm, ranch or business?
- As my certified public accountant do you do business valuation?
- Should I consider incorporating? If so, what type of corporation would you recommend?

- Can I pay my children a salary out of the business?
- Can I tax deduct my life insurance premium?
- Can I tax deduct my disability premium?
- Can I tax deduct my health insurance premium?
- Should I consider looking at employee benefits for my staff or updating my business equipment with the profits of my business?
- Am I making use of all available income tax deductions?

THE ATTORNEY & LEGAL PROVISIONS

The attorney may specialize in tax planning, estate planning, or general practice such as family law, divorce, and custody issues. It is not likely that an attorney specializes in all of the above areas. For future financial strategies, the client would most likely seek out an attorney who specializes in tax planning, which would encompass business planning, estate planning, and personal tax planning.

This attorney specializes in implementation of contracts and legal documents such as business buy-sell agreements, setting up of corporations, many forms of trusts, wills, living wills and establishing various types of powers of attorney for the legal protection of the client.

For example, an attorney has been asked to draft a will, trust, and a family limited partnership for a client. The attorney needs to know the assets and liabilities of the client to complete family or business information, location of documents, and a complete analysis of the client's real estate and financial portfolio. Gathering and understanding of all the facts is necessary to properly diagnose the type of trust or legal documents best suited for the client based on the wants, needs, and desires of the client.

If the client or attorney chooses to bring in the team of specialists—in this case the certified public accountant and the insurance agent, the following would occur. If the certified public accountant and agent have a long-term relationship with the client, their knowledge would be valuable to the attorney and substantial time and money could be saved for the client. The certified public accountant would have full knowledge of the financial picture, regarding assets and liabilities personal and business profit and loss, and real estate values. The agent also has years of information shared by the client. The agent could provide all insurance and investment statements including ownership and beneficiary assignment information and help the attorney diagnose the need and solution based on the goals of the client.

The relationship among your attorney, certified public accountant, and insurance agent can coordinate and advance your goals by providing: 1) shared knowledge of goals and personal and financial facts; 2) an integrated and properly designed long-term protection and accumulation program; 3) a network of trust and mutual respect, and ultimately; 4) peace of mind regarding future planning.

LEGAL QUESTIONS

Here are common questions to address to your attorney:

- What is power of attorney?
- Do I need a trust? If so, what type of trust should I have?
- I had my will done years ago does it need to be updated?
- What is my estate value?
- How much tax will be due on my estate when I die?
- Should I consider a family limited partnership?
- What type of buy-sell agreement should my partners and I have for our business?
- What can I do to protect my special needs child?
- Should I have a prenuptial agreement?
- How does a living trust work?
- How does a living will work?
- What type of corporation should I have? What is the difference between a C-corporation and an S-corporation?

HOW THE TEAM WORKS TOGETHER

As a service to my clients, I have cultivated relationships with a number of attorneys and certified public accountants over the years. The most typical situation is that the tax planning attorneys review the needs of their clients and observe clients are underinsured or question if the policies are designed correctly for the intended purpose. The certified public accountants or attorneys request that I meet with clients either at their office or my business setting to discuss their insurance program. I am provided policies and all information pertaining to the coverage, why insurance was originally purchased, its objective, and how it has been updated.

We will organize the portfolio and prepare a completed spread sheet listing name of the company, contract number, current cash value, outstanding loans, owner and beneficiary of the policies, and premium amount. This is provided to the client, the attorney, and the certified public accountant in addition to an analysis and suggestions on how to coordinate additional coverage if needed in the present portfolio.

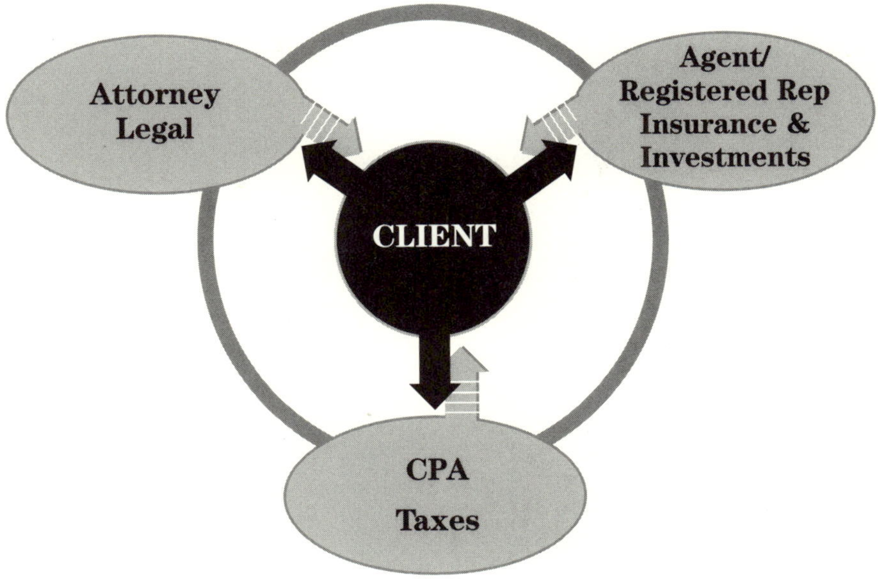

For my own clients, I coordinate a meeting with either an attorney or a certified public accountant. They provide 1 free hour consulting at my office if my clients are in need of estate or tax planning. This saves the client from visiting additional offices and helps the client focus on long-term goals while allowing the team of specialists to communicate solutions based on the need. I believe the agent should be the coordinator in providing information to the advisors along with coordinating meeting times and places. Once the team is in place, annual reviews and ongoing needs and solutions can be easily recommended for the client.

Many professionals have received interdisciplinary training in complementary areas and are much sought after. A few examples are:

- Certified Public Accountant and Chartered Financial Consultant (CPA, ChFC),
- Chartered Life Underwriter and Certified Public Accountant (CLU, CPA), and
- Attorney and Certified Financial Planner (JD, CFP).

There are a variety of possibilities for such credentials and training across legal, accounting, insurance and investment disciplines. The most important concept for you to realize is that **you do not want one professional "doing it all for you."** The legal, tax accounting, insurance, and investment worlds are extremely complex and various areas of specialty require years of continuing education and experience. As a result of using many professionals for counsel, **it is imperative that you set the stage to have them working as a coordinated team on your behalf.**

David

IN 1991, I CHOSE TO INVITE LOCAL ATTORNEYS, CERTIFIED PUBLIC accountants, and financial planners to my office for a seminar on insurance needs analyses and on the importance of a properly designed financial program encompassing health insurance, disability income insurance, life insurance, pension planning, and estate planning.

David was one of many attorneys who came to the session. As he was leaving, he asked if I would work with him regarding his own business and personal insurance needs. Later, when I arrived at his office, I received a warm welcome from his staff. His office setting was professional and inviting. I felt honored to be working with such a well-respected attorney who was also quite humble.

We reviewed his concerns and what he wanted to accomplish. I left the appointment with a box full of assorted papers, such as insurance contracts, retirement statements, mutual fund balances, and the like, which he had accumulated over the years.

My promise to David was that I would organize all his financial papers and return them on my next visit. I would organize his formal files according to: insurance, retirement, business, pension, and estate needs; plus each contract or policy would be accompanied with a full explanation.

David is a very giving person who lives his life for his wife and 2 children; he is active in the community and in his church. His overall desire is to create a financial legacy for all those people who are important to him. As I unraveled all of his insurance policies, I soon discovered that he had purchased various types of life insurance from different agents. But it was apparent that none of these agents had taken the time to properly design a total financial program based on David's income, expenses, wants, needs, and desires for his family. The entire box of papers did not contain any analysis of David's income relative to his expenses; therefore, it was difficult to determine whether David's policies and contracts would adequately cover his family income needs in the event of his death.

David recalls, "I admit that I had purchased insurance policies from assorted agents without too much thought being given as to specific overall needs. The coordination of my life, health and disability insurance programs transformed my efforts from a helter-skelter, hodgepodge mess into a coherent and coordinated program. Other agents had asked about current financial situation, debts, income and assets, but Mary wanted to know about my dreams for myself and my family. I related that I wanted to not only pay off debts at my death, but also to leave my family with enough money to cover living expenses, college and a legacy for future generations."

When we designed David's insurance program, I recommended that he be personally and actively involved in the process. I took the time to teach him how the different types of products would work for him and how they would provide solutions to what he wanted to accomplish financially. David's joint involvement and input made it very easy for us to make the most of this planning process. As we proceeded through the entire process, David explained that many of his clients had need of this type of thorough review and analysis to better understand their own financial affairs.

When his life insurance policies, investments and disability income protection contracts were reviewed as a whole in relation to his goals and what he wanted to accomplish, he felt there was a shortfall. As a result, David selected a whole life insurance policy with a special rider that enabled him to contribute additional amounts of money into the contract on an annual basis. Because he chose this option, the cash value and the death benefits can increase at a greater pace over time.[4] Also, because term insurance has a lower premium, he also chose additional term insurance. Buying term insurance enabled him to substantially increase his death benefit coverage while the policy is inforce. In the future, David can convert the term insurance into cash value life insurance when he is financially able to pay a higher premium.[5]

David had a business partner who died unexpectedly. There was no insurance to pay off debts in the event that one partner died prematurely. Because David had cosigned the loans, he was left to single-handedly pay off all the bank notes over time.

When David purchased disability income protection, he gained peace of mind; that in turn enabled him to muster all his financial resources to pay off debt. He remembers, "I was better able to intensely focus financial resources on paying off the bank notes, because I knew that my insurance would take care of my family if I died prematurely." By purchasing an individual disability income policy, David took the first step to protect his income earning potential in the event that he became disabled and qualified for benefits. Also, if David became disabled, he would still need to cover the expenses associated with running his law practice; therefore, he applied for an additional *business overhead disability income* insurance policy.[6]

David was satisfied with this process for analyzing and organizing his financial affairs. I agreed to perform an insurance needs analysis as well as help his clients understand how insurance, pensions, and investments work together. As a result, he agreed that I could refer my clients to him for consultation on wills and trust agreements.

This team concept between an insurance agent and an attorney has been an asset to our clients. David's clients' insurance programs are now coordinated with their overall financial program and estate planning, and my clients have properly drafted wills and trust agreements.

Life experiences such as divorce, custody, or settling the estates of loved ones affect us; but these do not affect only one segment of our lives. People working with attorneys to create prenuptial agreements, to settle divorce, or to handle estate issues have many questions about the impact that such legal milestones have on their financial life as well. As an attorney, David also assured that his statutory power of attorney, health care power of attorney and a living will were in order. Ideally, your attorney and agent should work together for the benefit of you and your family.

As David's financial situation improved and the debt was conquered, he entered phase 2 of his program. He began to concentrate on converting the term insurance into a permanent cash value policy, and he started a retirement planning program. The flexibility of the insurance allows David to make annual premium payments to help build up cash value for retirement or any other financial need.

David's goal is to keep funding the policies to leave a legacy. His desire is that when he dies, "I want [Mary] to show my family just how much I loved them when she delivers a check sufficient to cover all of their financial concerns. Buying life insurance is one of the ultimate acts of love and unselfishness. With insurance comes the peace of mind that your family will be taken care of financially. The love that we thrive on and share will continue to sustain them after I die."

STEP 2: SELECTING YOUR PROFESSIONAL TEAM

Finding an Agent

ONCE YOU UNDERSTAND THE VALUE OF COORDINATING a professional team, your next task becomes selecting your professional professionals.

From working with my clients, it seems that the most common pattern for people taking the first steps in protecting their assets is to begin with insurance. Indeed, many people do not even think of insurance as part of their future planning process. They must select car insurance in their teens, then renter's insurance, perhaps accident insurance when they fly, and home insurance. If they are employed by a corporation, they become introduced to the world of medical insurance, other employee benefits, and retirement planning. At this stage in life, most of their financial awareness revolves around insurance and protection needs. As they advance through marriage and business interests on their journey through life, they eventually build relationships with a certified public accountant and an attorney. This sequence is not the same for everyone, but it is one shared by a majority of women whom I serve in my practice.

For most, purchasing insurance through an agent is their initiation into the financial world. This initiation has been one where many women have been frustrated and frightened.

Women often tell me that they work with many professionals for separate purposes, yet no one coordinates their total financial picture. I see this approach as being like inviting people to a pot luck supper at your home. There are many interesting alternatives brought in to choose from, yet there is not necessarily a coordinated nutritional balance. The spontaneity of a pot luck supper may be fun for the weekend, but a daily diet wouldn't be healthy. In the same way, an uncoordinated smorgasbord of financial products as well as professionals isn't necessarily the best diet for the long-term. Ultimately, women buyers should demand that all of their financial vehicles and services be coordinated to the greatest extent possible. It is important that the planning for the future be in the hands of someone who knows and understands how to coordinate separate health, disability income, and life insurance protection as well as annuities, stocks, bonds, mutual funds, and various other investments. In addition, it is important to recognize risks to property that has accumulated. Agents should identify and recommend that sufficient amounts of auto insurance, homeowners or renters insurance be purchased to protect against liability.

The premise of my practice as an agent is that a very good insurance agent can and should be the catalyst to help you coordinate a professional team and suggest when it is time for you to seek counsel and begin establishing these other key relationships necessary for your future financial growth and wealth accumulation.

When you begin your planning, you should choose your insurance agent, financial planner, certified public accountant and/or attorney as carefully as you would select a life partner. Ideally, the relationship should grow more fulfilling over time.

Now let's look a process that will help you find and select an agent.

FRIENDS & REFERRALS

Women ask me how they can assure that the agent they chose is right for them. Where can they find someone for the long term? If I were to choose an agent today, I would spend a great deal of time talking with personal friends. Question friends whom you believe to be astute regarding the financial marketplace or those who seem to be actively involved in saving and planning. Their responses may be complete and helpful. Spend time asking some key questions:

- Are they happy with their present agent? Why or why not?

  You are looking for a quick response here. If it takes your friends time to answer this one, the agent probably isn't a key player in their financial decisions.

- What specifically has their agent accomplished for them?

  Here again, you are looking for a quick and concise answer. You want to hear responses like, "The agent put me on a program to help fund my children's education . . . or a program that can provide me with a certain monthly income when I retire." Responses such as these indicate two important principles: first, that the agent identified and created a solution to your friends' needs; and secondly, that the agent presented the sale in such a manner that your friends easily understand. If you hear, "The agent sold me a life insurance policy," that is not a stellar response. It indicates that your friends' needs have not been uncovered and that there is little, if any, connection between something your friends bought and goals they have for the future.

- Does their agent have a support staff that assists with service questions?

  Agents earn their living by new sales. Successful agents have made an investment in hiring staff to provide service to each client on a timely basis. An agent with staff is truly running a business and is more likely to be responsive.

It also means that the agent may have other professional associates with complementary expertise available easily to you.

- What does their agent specialize in?

  You are looking for an answer that is more specific than "insurance" or "investments" or "brokerage." If an agent does not totally disclose areas of expertise to clients, how do you know what you are buying? Think of it this way, you wouldn't hire someone who advertised that they did home repairs if you specifically needed an electrician, a plumber, or a roofer. You would have no professional guarantee that the house wouldn't burn, or the pipes and the roof wouldn't leak.

- Do they have more than one person handling their financial affairs: such as a stock broker, a property-casualty insurance agent; and a life, health, and disability income insurance agent?

  Why did they decide that having many people involved was an approach they preferred? Ultimately, the goal is coordination of all of your financial affairs. This means that eventually you will be dealing with a certified public accountant, an attorney, and two or more agents. You want the logistics and process of coordinating your team to be as simple as possible.

- Is their insurance agent one who handles multiple lines of business such as life, health, and disability income protection? Same as above.

- Is their agent building a relationship with them over time by sending newsletters, conducting periodic reviews of their program, or maintaining ongoing correspondence?

  You are looking for an answer that indicates that the agent is willing and able to invest in a long-term relationship.

- Do they receive annual review updates and service calls?

  The way of life is change. You want to find an agent who provides annual or bi-annual reviews to help assure that the coverage you have today meets your needs as the value of the dollar changes and as your family and income needs grow.

- Does the agent invite them to attend educational seminars of interest?

  This will demonstrate if the agent keeps up with changes in the industry and willingly seeks to make clients more knowledgeable.

- What is it that really stands out about the service their agent provides?

  A quick response is what you are looking for here. If your friends need to think long and hard about this question, then it is doubtful that a relationship has been built. Desirable answers are: the agent is easy to understand, or the agent teaches me until I understand everything, or the agent is always there for me.

- What character traits have they seen to be outstanding in their agent?

"Understanding," "trustworthy," "caring," and "sympathetic" are honorable responses here. "Drives a sporty car" may not be the answer you are looking for unless you are open for a ride.

Ask your friends all of these questions and ask if they conducted an interview with the prospective agent. Ultimately, determine what mattered in their final selection.

BY TELEPHONE BOOK OR DIRECTORY

If your questions to friends leave you feeling that you've not discovered what you're looking for, and if you've not yet established an ongoing relationship with a certified public accountant or attorney who can refer you to a reputable agent, working from a telephone book can tell a big story about an agent. First of all, if you've been given a referral on an agent who's not listed in any way, it could mean that the agent is new in the business, hasn't built a name yet, or is new in the area. The agent may work within a large *career agency* sales office, but even if this is the case, the agency should also have a phone number listed for the individual agent.

If you are trying to find an agent by looking in a telephone book or directory, look for specialty areas. These are based on your interest. For example under the "physicians" in the telephone book, you'll find "internal medicine," "family practice," and "pediatrics" as categories.

In your telephone book, insurance agents are listed by area of specialty as well. You want to refer to auto and homeowners insurance, known in the trade as property-casualty, or life, health, and disability income insurance. Some insurance agents are registered representatives who have also received advanced education or degrees and are licensed to sell variable annuities and mutual fund investments. Investigate about what services and types of insurance the agent advertises in the yellow pages. (Check the appendix for a list of abbreviations that explain what types of advanced credentials agents can earn.) As a woman, you may prefer working with a woman, just as many of us prefer doing business with a physician or attorney who is a woman.

If more than one agent is recommended, it's time to start the interviewing process yourself. If there is to be good chemistry between you and the professional you are choosing, I suggest you do your homework and begin an interviewing process. Selection by referrals is usually best. If you are pleased with your certified public accountant or attorney, ask for a reference for an agent. That's always a win-win method because, ultimately, if your planning is to serve your needs, your attorney, certified public accountant and insurance agent should and will inevitably work as a team—as you, your family, and/ or your business mature.

STEP 3: INTERVIEWING TO FIND THE RIGHT MATCH FOR YOU

The Right Stuff

YOUR NEXT STEP IS TO BEGIN AN INTERVIEWING PROCESS TO FIND an agent who is "right" for you. Credentials and experience of the agent are important. However, your comfort level is even more important—especially for women buyers. I cannot stress enough the importance of experiencing this essential step.

By interviewing several potential agents, you communicate and establish a respect for yourself; but equally important is the confidence this process gives you. Conducting interviews reaffirms that you are the prime mover and that you are actively taking charge of your financial affairs. If you are skeptical or believe that you can skip this step, approach it as you would a major purchase. You would not buy a car or a home without considerable discussion and review of the benefits and drawbacks of each option available to you. The relationship you develop should be a long-term commitment; your choice needs to be one with which you are happy and satisfied.

The American Council of Life Insurance (ACLI) has cooperated with the United States Office of Consumer Affairs and the Consumer Information Center to prepare many public service brochures listing guidelines for your expectations regarding reputable companies and agents. As a consumer, you can obtain a free copy of the materials by calling (800) 338-4471.

Usually you shouldn't need to interview more than 2 or 3 prospective agents. Visit their offices to see what type of business environments they have each created. Tell them that you are interviewing for an agent and would like to visit and ask some questions before you make a final selection. Ask the following:

- What lines of business is the agent licensed to sell?

  State departments of insurance require that all individuals selling life insurance be licensed; this also applies to individuals selling property and casualty insurance as well as health insurance. In addition to having state licenses, agents who sell securities products, variable annuities, and variable life insurance (which rely on a variety of risks and rewards due to their investment in stocks and bonds) must be appropriately licensed with a registered broker/dealer. Contact your state insurance department if you have any questions about the licensing status of an agent.

If an agent has a limited area of specialization, you will need to work with several people to cover all of your requirements. For example, if you have a need for any insurance—life, auto and homeowners, health, and disability income—or investments, it is not likely that one agent typically handles all. If this is the case, you can ask if the agent has supplementary staff associates or a network of other agents.

- Does the agent work with individuals and families, or small businesses, or professionals?

  This question enables you to understand the scope of the agent's practice. It is doubtful that an agent who works only in the family market will be able to assist you if you are starting a business or plan to be involved in a business in the near future.

- Does the agent have staff?

  An established agent is most likely aligned with other agents and can refer you to them for specialty areas. It is rare for one agent to keep up continued education in all areas; therefore, an agent will often hire a staff of specialists to assist you. As a result, all of your auto, homeowners, disability income, and life insurance needs can be coordinated. Also, having a staff to handle service calls means that there is always someone to handle your service needs and intercede with the insurance company on your behalf. Your service requests are more likely to be handled promptly if there is staff. You want to determine how readily available the agent is to you if you are in need. Ask how quickly your call will be returned—in an hour, in a day, in 2 days?

- How many years has the agent been in business?

  The first 4 years are critical in the insurance business, because this time is often the hardest period in an agent's career; it's the time when the agent is most likely to leave the business. An agent who has weathered these early years is more likely to be committed to the career for the long-term.

- What would happen to my insurance and investments if the agent becomes disabled or dies?

  It should be a real concern for you if something happens to the agent. This is a legitimate question. Many agents have prepared successor programs where a younger agent is planning to buy the senior agent's business or take over the practice. By the same token, an agent with 20 years or more in the business may be ready to retire or change careers. If you select an older seasoned agent, ask him or her if there is a business succession arrangement in place to assure continuity of service to you. You want someone who knows you, to be there as you grow older and your needs change. As a client, you need to know that the company is always behind the scene and maintaining permanent records of your account. It is important to remember that the insurer will be obligated to honor the terms of the insurance contract even if the agent is unable to continue to serve your needs.

- Is the agent licensed in many states?
  This will tell you whether the agent can continue to handle your affairs if there is a possibility that you and your career move geographically. If an agent is licensed in many states, it usually indicates a commitment to maintain service to clients after the clients move.
- Ask about the agent's training in the industry. You want to determine how much additional education the agent has earned and inquire about various professional designations as well as company or industry awards. There are many professional designations in various subject areas of the insurance industry. Common ones include Chartered Life Underwriter (CLU) and Life Underwriter Training Council Fellow (LUTCF). Agents may have earned designations such as Chartered Financial Consultant (ChFC), Certified Financial Planner (CFP), or Member of the Registry of Financial Planning Practitioners.[7] In your dialogue, ask about the agent's commitment to ongoing education in the industry.
- Ask about membership in the local Life and Health Underwriters Association. (The term NALU may be used; this is the National Association of Life Underwriters to which most professional agents belong.) These organizations assist agents' continuing education in the business. Similar training and services are provided through the American Society of CLU, the Institute of Certified Financial Planners (ICFP), and the International Association for Financial Planning (IAFP). Property/casualty agents have similar professional organizations and designations available to them.
  These are questions any established agent would feel comfortable answering in order to make you comfortable and confident to do business. The answers tell you about the level of commitment the agent has toward clients and the industry. Ask about Million Dollar Round Table (MDRT) qualification. Such membership with the MDRT indicates that the agent meets very high service and production standards in the industry. If the agent mentions personal involvement in the MDRT, it is another indication of her or his commitment to the industry and client service.
- How does the agent get paid?
  This indicates whether or not there will be a fee charged to you for service or whether commission on the sale funds the agent's salary. If the agent seems put off by this question, it is another clue that this agent may not be open with you. In planning for your financial future, private information is learned about your life and affairs; therefore, it is only fair that you be told how you will be expected to pay the agent for service.
- How many companies' products does the agent represent?
  Some agents are career agents loyal to selling the products of 1 company. That can be totally adequate to meet your needs if the company they represent has developed a full range of financial services products. All companies

select certain markets and products where they choose to be particularly competitive regarding product price or feature. Therefore, agents who represent multiple companies have a larger perspective on many companies vs. agents who are captive to one company. Many agents today choose to represent a large portfolio of products and companies based on the complexity of clients' needs. Some buyers, who are shopping only for price and for whom service is not a major selling point, prefer to buy from a brokerage firm or independent agents who shop for the best price. Make sure you learn why the agent represents multiple companies. Many women select loyalty over price as a major concern in a buying decision—this is another difference that distinguishes men and women buyers.

- How many claims has the agent handled with the insurer?
  This is an unusual question, but particularly in a disability income situation, you want to know that the agent you select has the experience of processing the paperwork and assisting with the claim settlement process. The insurer is responsible to protect you during rainy times. The last thing you need is an agent who does not know how or where to find the umbrella quickly when it starts raining.
- Does the agent have a fee-only certified financial planner, a certified public accountant or an attorney available to provide counsel if needed?
  This is often necessary. The agent may consider referrals to attorneys who wouldn't have a problem drawing up a will if creating a will is necessary. The agent should know attorneys and certified public accountants in the area who specialize in trusts and estates.

These are essential questions that will determine whether the chemistry is right and whether you will be comfortable with the agent you select. Upon closing your chat, feel confident to ask for more references. If initially you made it clear that your intention was to ask questions about business and suddenly find yourself seated across from someone trying to sell you a policy, consider this a lucky sign early on your journey. You have determined that the agent is not right for you, because it has been demonstrated that your priorities obviously do not come first and that the main goal of the appointment was to make a sale.(See Kay Ostberg, Alice Griffin and Phyllis Kaufman in selected bibliography for books that guide you in selecting an attorney and a certified public accountant.)

The time spent screening to select a professional is necessary when planning your financial future because your future is not a short-term need. It is a long-term commitment; you must feel comfortable with the professionals you choose. As a result, you want to take time initially to build a relationship that will stay with you and guide you through the years. You want a professional who will bring credibility to your financial alternatives. Ultimately, you need to select someone with whom you can build trust. Think of her as your guardian angel of finance.

Chemistry Quiz

THE OBJECTIVE QUESTIONS YOU'VE ASKED IN THE INTERVIEW determine if you feel that the agent you have selected has the fundamental credentials and experience to provide you sound advice. Now you must listen to your heart and ask yourself if you could trust whom you've selected and consider that person to **be among your best friends.** Each one of us has different needs. But if you feel the need to be taught, look for a person who is willing to take time to teach you. Learning from an agent willing to take the time to explain the hows and whys of insurance and investment products helps women to gain confidence and to enjoy the journey to attain dreams and financial goals.

Ultimately, try to imagine this. Picture yourself in a hospital; you have just been told you have cancer. You are frightened and need a friend who can take over processing a claim—someone who will be available to family members regarding financial needs and questions. You want someone willing to take time to be there as your friend because the best agent is a friend for life.

When you are interviewing potential agents, sometimes your intuition immediately tells you if the chemistry is right or wrong. You need to assess the chemistry of the individual with whom you'll be working. You need to find someone you are comfortable with socio-economically. You need to feel that you have something in common with this agent. As an agent, I'm a wife, mother, grandmother, sister, and a business owner. Many of my women clients can relate to this; we share similar experiences. I can talk about many problems and pose many solutions, because I've lived through many of the problems myself. And I can share solutions that have worked. This provides a great deal of comfort to my clients.

If you are feeling angry over the past—following the death of a loved one, divorce, loss of income, or financial failure—your agent should be someone who will understand your anger and who will care enough to help you get excited about your future by showing you options that will best fit your financial capabilities and goals. Maybe you've gone through a divorce, and you do not feel that the settlement was fair to you. Maybe you were a homemaker until your divorce; afterwards, for the first time in your life, you had to enter the working world. Drastic changes in lifestyle can build resentments. You may want to share all of these inner feelings.

I have been told by many women that they find it easier to share such concerns with another woman because she will listen.

Eventually, you reach a point in life when you realize it's time to be independent and accountable for the financial affairs that affect your life rather than rely solely on the information provided by your father, husband, boyfriend, children or employer. Women are emerging to take responsibility for their own financial affairs. That means their insurance and investment planning as well as buying a car or home. Ultimately, if there is insufficient planning done for our future, we have no one to blame but ourselves; we cannot blame someone else for negligence on our behalf. Remember, it is an actuarially based fact that women live longer than men. According to U. S. Bureau of Census data, on average women live approximately 7 years longer than men. Even though people will live longer in the future, data suggests that the 7-year spread is not expected to change by 2010. Therefore, if you are married, you should be proactive in the financial plans which will most likely support you after your husband is gone.

Also, when selecting the agent with the right emotional match for you, ask yourself if you are comfortable with a low-key approach or respond positively to a hard sell. There are different styles of individuals in this world. Some are more low key, there to help you when you need it but not repeatedly calling. However, if you are a person who needs to be called, encouraged and reminded, then you will need an agent whose staff can work this way for you. The agent will let you know whether the staff provides proactive service or reactive service.

STEP 4: IDENTIFYING UNETHICAL BEHAVIOR

The Good, the Bad & the Ugly

BY WORKING WITH WOMEN CLIENTS OVER THE YEARS, I'VE LEARNED **that the ethics, values, and integrity of the agent and the company are top priorities in women's decisions to buy**. Men I've worked with seem to place more value on competitive price and/ or product when making a buying decision. This further distinguishes how men will purchase and whether or not women will purchase at all.

I've known a woman to leave a 6-figure salary because the ethical and moral conditions of a company, its leadership and the job forced her to compromise personal integrity. Women will leave relationships if ethics and moral trust have been breached with their partners.

If situations or behaviors are unethical, some people may tend to be silent about them, detaching themselves from the problem. A woman in a relationship cringes at the memory of when her partner takes a vow of silence and avoids discussing anything with her—as if distancing eliminates accountability for any inappropriate conduct. Or if by discussing the issues, it is a demonstration that he has lost power and control. A woman wants to be open and direct. She wants to communicate with him and lay all the cards on the table. She wants to see him demonstrate by his speech and actions that his values are the same as her values. If there is silence or no demonstration of shared values, it is difficult for her to develop trust over time.

Women carry this attitude into business. **Women not only demand that the agent and the company they choose have ethics and integrity, but also that a definite communication and demonstration of these values exists.** More and more, women are demanding that these values be communicated on an ongoing basis.

When it comes to the sale of financial products, there are many ugly stories. The news media seek these with a pious vengeance. Insurance debacles in Pennsylvania, Florida, and Texas regarding agent misrepresentations have resulted in a renewed emphasis on and enforcement of professional ethics. Companies have always monitored their agents and registered representatives. However, during the last few years, corporate officers who serve on the American Council on Life Insurance have voluntarily heightened the internal monitoring of their ranks.

Companies are imposing and enforcing even more stringent guidelines and procedures that individual agents must follow regarding the advertising, description, and sale of insurance products, mutual funds, and securities to the consumer. Companies require that any and all marketing materials used by agents be formally approved to assure conformity with legal and compliance guidelines; this is being monitored in local sales offices, regional offices, and the corporate headquarters.

Interstate and intercompany monitoring is also in place. According to Eric Nordman of the National Association of Insurance Commissioners, "State insurance regulators have joined forces with interested insurers to compile a producer database so that rogue agents can be monitored and tracked. This will help states avoid licensing agents with dubious track records if their licenses have been lifted in other states. This is of great overall benefit to consumers who may not know these checks and balances are in place."

All financial professionals should demonstrate ethics and integrity, and my wish is that you do not encounter any unethical situations regarding your insurance or financial program. Here are some sales practices that can serve as red flags for you. These are all considered unethical in the insurance industry, because the end result of the action can be harmful to the client over the long term.

- Be wary if an agent offers to give you money as an incentive to buy a product. This is known as rebating, and it is illegal in **almost** all instances. (Check your state law.)
- Be wary if an agent tells you about a great new product that would be better for you if you cashed in your old policy.
- Be wary if an agent tells you that you can use the dividends or values in one policy to buy a new policy.
- Be wary if an agent collects a second premium payment and you still do not have a written policy for your files.
- Be wary if an agent delivers a policy to you that is different than your understanding of what you purchased.
- Be wary if an agent takes a payment from you in cash.
- Be wary if an agent takes a payment without completing a detailed written or computer automated application.
- Be wary if an agent asks for a payment and asks that you make the bank check payable to a name other than the name of the insurance company that is seen on the printed materials you are given.
- Be wary if an agent wants to replace an existing insurance policy while taking an application for new coverage. As a consumer, you should request that the agent obtain from your company written information that shows the death benefit, present cash value, and premium. The agent attempting to

replace your coverage should also obtain future values of your present contract. An agent should not discuss replacement under any condition whatsoever without this information. In many instances, it is not in the best interests of the insured to replace one life insurance policy with another. However, should you believe you want to do so, make certain you have all the facts.

The insurance industry isn't the only financial services sector that has experienced ethics violations. The banking industry and the securities industry have suffered from trustees who have embezzled or lost client's money through unsound or speculative investments that were inappropriate for the client's needs and risk tolerance. To protect yourself you should:

- Make sure your professional completes a risk tolerance questionnaire. She or he should explain and review it with you prior to making investment decisions. This will determine whether your investment portfolio is diversified according to conservative or aggressive goals.
- Be diligent in requesting and reviewing frequent performance statements. Be personally responsible for reading and understanding how to calculate the present value of your portfolio.

REPLACEMENT

Replacement of insurance policies is a serious issue—for the industry and for you as a consumer. You could have extensive debates with actuaries about the values of your policies, but as a consumer you are almost always better off to coordinate your insurance program around what you presently have rather than to seek replacement. If you are adamant and feel for some reason you need to replace a policy, the agent has the responsibility of explaining the negative consequences for that action. The agent also has the responsibility of showing you how your current policy is performing.

There is a philosophy in the marketplace which states "buy term and invest the difference." Agents for companies advocating this philosophy accomplish this tactic with a strategy that involves replacing people's whole life insurance policies that have been in force for many years and carry substantial cash value. It is not wise to fall for this type of sale. (See Jeanne's story.)

Replacement is the single most controversial ethical and legal issue currently in practice within the insurance and investment industries. Often the companies and agents that use replacement sales tactics attempt to cash in old whole life policies and use the money for other purposes. They satisfy insurance needs with temporary term insurance and place the extra money in mutual funds. The idea is that the investment portfolio will hypothetically grow so much in 20 years—or whatever the term was—that the insurance won't be needed anymore. If anyone could predict that they won't die or become uninsurable within that period of time, it could be a valid idea. However, in reality, such a strategy often turns out to be tragic for the consumer. In most cases, it will not solve the long-term needs that most people have because the term insurance may lapse or be too expensive to maintain as the insured gets older.

Many women have told me that husbands have been lured into this trap with the prospects of attractive and lucrative mutual fund returns. The wife who thinks her husband has everything under control is often devastated to find that he had succumbed to a replacement strategy and there is now no insurance at all, and the mutual funds he bought instead didn't perform as well as he thought they would.

STRATEGY TURNED TRAGEDY

Replacement in order to "buy term and invest the difference" has turned to tragedy for several of my clients. One 40-year-old gentleman cashed in his existing whole life policies to purchase term insurance from another company 5 years ago. He has since lost his insurability due to a heart attack and degenerating condition, and he will probably never get insurance again. The agent replaced $100,000 of whole life coverage with $75,000 of 20-year term insurance. When the whole life policy was 15-years old, if the original dividend scale had been maintained, the policy would have had enough cash value accumulated in it to offset the premium payments.

The term insurance that he bought was a 20-year level term. That means that his premium would stay the same for 20 years and the death benefit would never be more than $75,000—but only for that 20-year period, or when he becomes 60-years old. Most level term policies still provide coverage after the initial term just at a higher premium; this may be misleading.

A better strategy would have been to keep his whole life policy in force and (so long as the dividends were sufficient to continue to offset the premium payments) use the same premium amount to purchase mutual funds. Here are the consequences of the gamble he made:

- If he lives longer than age 60 and is uninsurable, the level term policy will allow continued coverage but at a premium that could be substantially higher.
- If he lives beyond age 60, he will have forfeited the cash value built up in his original whole life policy that could have provided him with living benefits and monthly supplemental income during his retirement years.
- If he lives to age 60 and tries to purchase insurance (for the purpose of helping to fund a buy-sell agreement on a business or additional insurance for his family, or to help pay estate taxes), he may not be able to because he may be uninsurable due to his heart attack.
- If he dies before age 60, his family receives less insurance. Plus, the mutual

funds he purchased may not have grown enough to compensate for the shortfall.

Replacing one policy with another means that you are starting over. You are starting over at an older age and at higher premiums, but the agent who replaced your policy receives a new commission for the sale. Replacement is often only to the benefit of the financial professional who is doing the replacement and is often at considerable cost and consequence to the consumer.

Unethical sales practices such as replacement are simple to counter and defend against. Just say no!

PROVIDING ANNUAL SERVICE & TEACHING

In addition to replacement, there are other non-desirable practices that deal with ways of selling women financial products. They are not illegal, but I am impassioned about them. I believe these practices extend the issue of what is appropriate when selling to women. I propose the following:

- It is inappropriate to sell financial products to women based on a transaction emphasizing price and product without relating them to a discussion of income, expenses, wants, needs, and desires for the future.
- It is inappropriate to sell financial products to women with any approach other than an approach that teaches women through a relationship that builds her knowledge and confidence over time.

One common ugly experience that clients have relayed occurs when women are being talked to in a manner that assumes they know all the definitions of financial jargon rather than in a manner that focuses on teaching. You might have had this experience in the past; it is a nightmare that women don't easily forget. The moment it happens again, it should send up red flags that working with this agent isn't working for you.

Women should demand to understand every aspect about a purchase. The purchase of a refrigerator provides an analogy. Most women are not concerned about the motor size, but women are concerned about the shelf space, freezer size, and self-defrosting unit. Capacity or function take priority over motor size. As buyers, women want to see more than one size or style and maybe more than one manufacturer. Typically, when women have an experience of buying a product that turns out to be unsuitable, it results from having minimal information or from being shown only 1 product.

Regarding insurance, often the frustration results when a relationship has not been developed (or will never develop) between the agent and the woman buyer. The agent emphasizes price or product but never understands truly what her goals are for her program. Making this type of "transaction" sale to a woman buyer is inappropriate because it is a tactic based on bottom-line product selling rather than in-depth client needs analysis, education, and ongoing client service over time.

The ability to learn by asking questions is crucial. No woman wants to deal with someone who is not willing to answer questions that she believes are relevant and sincere. In terms of selling financial services products to women, this involves avoiding financial jargon, teaching women at their level of understanding, and providing solutions to achieve their goals in terms they can understand. It means being responsible for ongoing service after the sale.

Another issue of utmost importance is the consequence of not providing annual service. The monetary value of the dollar changes as currency values change. Lifestyles change. Circumstances and responsibilities in family life change. Dependents change. Laws change. There are numerous stories about the consequences that result when beneficiaries are not updated.

As consumers, women must assume responsibility to demand annual or biannual service reviews. The agent will be responsible to show you what's available, and hopefully, the agent will be there to provide service whenever there is a need.

If you find yourself in a situation with an agent who hasn't taken the time to ask you extensive questions to determine your needs relative to your income and expenses, but instead asks for your old policy to replace coverage with a new and improved idea, run as fast as you can! Such an agent is not out for your best interests.

The establishment and enforcement of high ethical standards by insurance companies and securities and investment firms has done much to eliminate unethical sales practices. I firmly believe that these incidents will not be around 10 years from now. However, as a buyer—beware. I extend that thought to—as a buyer be demanding and aware. Knowledge is power. By knowing the rules of the game, you gain power and control.

STEP 5: KNOWING WHAT YOU WANT

Lahonda

I REMEMBER WHAT A STRIKING COUPLE LAHONDA AND RONNY WERE. They were both impeccably groomed. Ronny's shirt was hand-ironed and his boots newly polished. Lahonda was vibrant in her crisp cotton slacks and plaid blouse; she wore perfectly tailored clothes of fabrics that demanded much attention to look freshly pressed. Her nails were newly manicured, and her brown hair was salon-styled and curled to perfection. Every detail indicated that she and Ronny took special time to look their best and that great care was taken to prepare for the visit to my office. There was a look of firm resolve on her face.

She had an eternal smile, and she opened her arms to give me a huge hug the moment she entered my office. She wheeled in Ronny, who was disabled with multiple sclerosis. During our chat, it became easy to see that she was happy to have made the trip with her husband and happy to discuss their concerns. As I introduced Ronny and Lahonda to what services I would provide them, it was obvious that Lahonda was directing the conversation. Ronny sat relaxed in his wheel chair while Lahonda told me their story; she was 41 that Tuesday.

She explained that Ronny had lived with MS for over 20 years, and the severity of his condition required her strictest attention daily. Their son, Stephen, was 18-years old.

Lahonda had been battling cancer for 3 years and was in remission. She had solid hopes for the future. She worked a part-time job and was thankful for its flexible hours that enabled her to attend to Ronny.

Lahonda had 2 main concerns. First, she wanted to totally understand their current life insurance coverage. She was proud that she had purchased considerable individual whole life insurance when she was in her mid-30s. She had planned to purchase more, but she never thought she would become uninsurable at an early age. Lahonda sadly admitted, "You know Mary, a person can never ever know when they may lose their insurability; then it's too late." She wanted to know the current values of her policies and the benefits that would be left for Ronny and Stephen.

Second, because Lahonda and Ronny both had serious diseases and poor prognoses for the future, they had genetic concerns about Stephen's ability to obtain his own life insurance because of his parents' poor health. Stephen's future insurability as he became older was a passionate concern for Lahonda. She adamantly indicated that she wanted Stephen to have $350,000 of life insurance of his own if possible. He had been a loving and helpful son and was in excellent health at that time. Remembering that Ronny was only 27-years old when he contacted MS, Lahonda felt extreme urgency to help her son obtain insurance while he was young and healthy.

We proceeded to review their policies, monthly expenses, and any available assets. It was apparent they lived a lifestyle without debt, saved monthly, and enjoyed financial security in spite of their daily challenges. Through the entire process, Lahonda was strong and focused on her family's needs. As I reviewed their coverage, Lahonda would smile at Ronny. With his dark sparkling eyes, he returned her smile and occasionally embraced her arm as if he were really proud of what she had done. From their many years of struggle, a love and closeness emanated between them that I have witnessed only rarely in couples.

She asked that I explain differences, benefits, and drawbacks of both cash value and term life insurance; she was not certain about these. After considering all options, Lahonda confidently indicated that she preferred permanent insurance over term, because she wanted Stephen to have uninterrupted life insurance for the rest of his life. This was his mother's and father's bequest and legacy to him.

That meeting with Lahonda and Ronny was an inspiration about the power of life insurance. For Lahonda, it was clear that she was motivated by love to obtain insurance for Stephen, but she was also fearful of not having enough insurance on her own life in order to provide daily care for Ronny in the event she predeceased him. When they left my office that day, Ronny thanked me, and Lahonda was quick to offer another hug as she smiled an intense sigh of relief.

We applied for the coverage on Stephen as they wished. A few weeks later, I delivered their gift to their son—a $350,000 policy. As Lahonda wrote the check for the annual premium, her eyes gazed intently at Ronny. She said, "Promise me, Ronny, that if anything happens to me, you will always make sure this policy is secure. When Stephen is out of college and working, he can assume the payments on his own." Ronny took her hand in his and smiled at her affirming his vow that he would carry out her wishes.

Over the next few months, Lahonda called to keep me updated about what was happening with her family. In October, she notified me that her cancer returned and was moving very fast. She had been experiencing severe headaches and did not know how long she could communicate; her doctors were medicating her severely. We cried because we both knew we were losing a special relationship, and she was losing the battle. The last time I spoke with her, she reiterated how she appreciated the work we did together and asked if I would please stay in touch with Ronny and Stephen. Again indicating that she wished she had more life insurance to leave to her family, she said, "Mary, be proud of what you do, and tell my story whenever you feel a need so that it may help other women."

Lahonda died in December 1994, leaving Stephen and Ronny to carry on—with the memory of her eternal smile.

Wants, Needs & Desires

UNDERSTANDING THE HAPPY TIMES AS WELL AS OBSTACLES AND shattered dreams of my clients has been a major part of building the relationship we have. Relationship building with an agent ought to feel comfortable and open enough for you to honestly share or vent your fears. It should be as you remember when talking to your guardian angel as a child; your angel was someone who would know your worst fears, someone who would help you out of a mess and stay on your side forever.

If your relationship with your agent does not feel that way, then it will never stand the test of time. Perhaps you should continue your search. As consumers, American women have the benefits of choice to their advantage. With over 2000 life insurance companies and financial services companies with thousands of agents available, your chances of interviewing and selecting a professional who's right for you are very good.

In her best selling book, *The Popcorn Report*, futurist Faith Popcorn defines the customer of the future. Her track record with helping companies successfully focus their products and services to satisfy consumer trends is admirable. Ms. Popcorn makes 3 distinctions in consumer's motivations for buying. These are to satisfy wants, needs, and desires. Each rests on a continuum from providing basic necessities through satisfying self-actualization goals.[8]

Here are a few examples. If women are to secure their financial independence in America today, I consider food, clothing, shelter, transportation, education, and retirement to be basic needs. Desires are the emotional conditions that women define as important to their sense of success or self-actualization. Wants are the means to attain these ends. You may *desire to* educate your children through college, to own a business, to have a second vacation home, to buy a boat, or to attain financial independence. In order to achieve these desires, you may *want* a plan to become debt free or to save more money.

These goals are pleasant and fulfilling ones. Often, our lives can take a detour on the road to happiness, and women find themselves facing other unanticipated needs and desires. I often hear my women clients define other concerns and goals for themselves: "What happens to my security and insurance if my husband divorces me?" "What will happen with my husband's retirement if we should divorce?" "What happens to the grocery money I've saved over the past 10 years to put toward our retirement planning; am I going to get anything out of it if we are no longer married?"

PRENUPTIAL AGREEMENTS

First and foremost, women who are anticipating marriage or whose marriage may be strained, need to understand their state laws governing divorce, separate property, community property, and custody issues. In some states such as Texas, a community property state, property acquired during the course of marriage is usually owned equally by husband and wife regardless of title.

In America today, more and more women, who are entering second or third marriages, are taking a careful look at these issues. As one client told me, "Mary, it's not a matter of believing or not believing in 'till death do us part. If I didn't believe in the institution and the possibility of a happy marriage, I wouldn't be pursuing it again. Being single is socially acceptable in our society today, but I *want* to marry. My focus on financial safeguards has more to do with being accountable for my own actions. When you are in love and enraptured with the hope and possibility of a brighter future with someone you think you want to share your life with, you believe in the fairy tale and look at the world with rose colored glasses to such an extent that you do not protect yourself. I can see young women in their early years out of college getting married with stars in their eyes. Most of these young women have little to lose this early in life. A prenuptial agreement becomes imperative in a second or third marriage when women and men both have financial responsibilities for their own children. A prenuptial alone can't protect against all financial issues in the future, or from being 100 percent accountable for the joint debt that my new husband and I create together, but it can keep me from losing what little I have saved up to this point in time. Some women think of a prenuptial agreement as an admission of a belief that their marriage will not last. In America, the statistics prove that it probably won't. To me it seems smarter to have one and enjoy every anniversary year as a celebration that it wasn't necessary, rather than be in divorce court calling yourself naïve for dismissing the idea when you were in love and not thinking straight."

Not all generations of women with whom I deal have such strong feelings. In their work, *Preparing for Remarriage*, Lawrence Ganong and Marilyn Coleman cite a 55 percent divorce rate for second and third marriages as of 1989.[9] I've witnessed more women reconsidering the way they approach a second marriage. It seems that more new women clients come to me every year who have created prenuptial agreements and consider them to be "financial insurance of another kind." As one woman who is also an attorney explained, "This issue gets at the core of trust between a couple. If the future husband and wife cannot discuss matters as emotional and sensitive as an agreement of this kind, it probably means that they have not yet developed an ability to communicate with each other about serious real life issues. Such honest communication is imperative if the marriage *is to last*. Therefore, if the discussion about the prenuptial agreement doesn't get off on the right footing, it most likely indicates other serious flaws in the relationship. Most women have success with an agreement if a lawyer discusses the pros and cons with the couple together. The lawyer, as a neutral third party, can position the benefits of the agreements for both parties. This keeps the discussion on a non-confrontational basis. When it's all over, couples seem to welcome the experience, because it reveals the deep-seated feelings of their future partner."

Having dreams is necessary to achieve financial independence, but you must be able to save in a way that is flexible and protected to allow for the ups and downs of your life circumstances. **Specifically communicating goals and current circumstances is necessary if your financial professional is to make appropriate recommendations.** For instance, single women or single parents have much stress because their total earning capacity relies only on themselves. There is always a question about what happens if you start an insurance program and you can't maintain it if you lose a job or are outplaced. For single women in this cycle of life, disability income protection becomes of primary importance. Adequate disability income protection can help insure that cash is available to help pay the bills as well as maintain payments to retirement accounts. Women also ask about what happens if they cannot pay into their 401(k) or 403(b) retirement plan in the event of a financial crunch. Remember, if you don't pay into it, the retirement income may not be there at age 59 1/2.

If any of these issues are a concern or fear, you must relate them to the agent so the agent can explain the impact of these potential circumstances on the type of savings, insurance, or investment program you are considering. There are many insurance or financial accumulation products you can choose that would not have penalties or surrender charges if you need to access money to help you through a difficult time. There are also situations with many policies, such as universal life insurance, where you may be able to temporarily stop paying into them and the policy may continue as long as the fund value is sufficient to cover the monthly deductions.

As an example, if you are 35-years old and want to begin to save money for the future, yet you are uncertain about your status with your current employer, an annuity might not be the best choice for a retirement program. Tax deferred annuities are best used when you want to accumulate money beyond age 59 1/2. Prior to that time you can withdraw money from a tax deferred annuity, but you may be subject to income tax and a 10-percent penalty tax. If you think that there may be a rainy day or emergency that require you to borrow from this money you are accumulating, mutual funds may be better. Through your lifetime prior to age 59 as well as after age 59 1/2, you can withdraw money without penalty from these funds—that means the mutual funds are *liquid* for you when you need them. Also, there is no condition stating that you must deposit a prescribed amount into a mutual fund on a monthly or annual basis. Cash value life insurance is another strong contender. Your accumulation is tax deferred, plus you can borrow on its loan value without IRS penalties. However, the loan will reduce the death benefit and interest must be paid.

Ultimately, your appointment with your financial professional should reveal the core needs, wants, and desires that shape your attitudes. Without asking critical questions to identify your wants, needs, and desires relative to your current income and expenses, there are no guarantees that what you are buying will be suitable for your lifestyle, or financial condition in the future.

DEFINING YOUR WANTS, NEEDS & DESIRES

After you've finally selected your agent of choice and you're preparing for that first appointment to discuss your needs for the future, it is necessary for you to have your personal goals and objectives clearly identified and stated before that appointment. Here are qualitative questions that will help you define your own wants, needs and desires for the future:

- If you've already accumulated a sizeable estate, have you made provisions to protect your assets from exposure to lawsuits, estate taxes or inheritance taxes?
- If your spouse is a successful business owner, are you confident that your personal interests are protected in the event of his or her death, disability, or financial disaster?
- If your spouse is a successful business owner and should die, are you confident that you understand what happens to the ownership of the business and what effect that selling the business has on your daily lifestyle?
- What type of job or career do you envision for yourself in 5 years?
- What career values are important to you as you pursue a job in the marketplace?
- What values must the company you choose to work for demonstrate?
- Do you believe that you will remain with your present employer or do you feel that it is possible that you will change or be forced to change employers in the next 2 years? In the next 5 years? In the next 10 years?
- Do you plan to retire in the same field, or do you plan to begin a second career later in life?
- Do you see yourself owning or starting your own business some day? Do you think you will do this on your own or with a partner?

- Do you have any future educational goals for yourself or for members of your family?
- Do you plan to marry? Before your career takes off or after?
- Do you plan to have children?
- If you are responsible for the care of children, do you plan to remain at home or must you work to earn an income?
- Describe the type of education and schools you envision your children or grandchildren attending.
- Have you had thoughts of divorce?
- To what extent can genetic health issues impact your future?
- Is there a church, community, or art organization in which you are a dedicated and active member?
- How many times do you think you will move in the next 5 years? The next 10 years?
- Do you have an ideal place where you want to "settle down" or do you prefer to remain free to travel and relocate easily?
- Is it important for you to own your own home or condo? Is a vacation home or second residence in your plans?
- If you choose to raise a family, will you want to buy a larger home?
- After your children are raised and no longer living at home, will you plan to move into a smaller home?
- How old will you be when you retire? Where would you like to live? And what type of lifestyle will you require?
- Will you be financially responsible or personally involved in caring for special needs children, grandchildren, or aging parents in the future? Are you familiar with the decisions that need to be made when selecting an appropriate care facility?
- Do you plan to inherit any additional income, real estate or other holdings?
- What habits in life as you are living it right now would you be willing to "give up," if necessary, to attain your long-term goals?

These are critical and emotional questions whose answers carry lifestyle implications. If your financial planner, attorney, certified public accountant and insurance agent are to help you achieve the goals you've established in your life, you must consider life to be a step-by-step journey. Financial success and well being can not be accomplished in a day—not even by winning the lottery. **You must realize that achieving any goals generally requires a program that coordinates legal issues, insurance, savings, and investments. No one aspect will accomplish it for you.**

I believe the process of soul searching and defining personal goals for your life should be as important as the outcome itself. Thinking about your trials, blessings, dreams, and goals is an affirmation of your being. These define what you have been and what you have learned during the years you have been surrounded by the beauty of the world we have been given to play and work in.

These questions help you rekindle the motivation and commitment to achieve the milestones you have and will continue to set for yourself. While you do this, I encourage you to give yourself the luxury of quiet time to do your thinking. Perhaps it's a walk in the woods or along a stream while picking berries. Perhaps it's time musing at a window with the aroma of potpourri and tea or mulled cider steaming around you. Perhaps it's a long walk along the beach, alone and at peace. The time you spend in reviewing your life and setting new goals will be cherished for many years because it signifies again that you are assuming responsibility and control of your future. Determining your wants, needs and desires is another step along this financial journey of your life.

When it comes time for the appointment with your agent, registered representative, or financial planner, you will have spent a great deal of time soul searching about the wishes and dreams of your life. Any future planning must consider the ups and downs possible in life if it is to secure peace of mind, well being and financial success in the future.

Melva

MELVA ALWAYS KNEW HER WANTS AND DESIRES, BUT IT TOOK HER A long time to achieve them. Early in 1993, she came to visit me at the recommendation of her attorney. She was a petite grandmother with ash grey hair, cut short and tapered at the back. She had recently been widowed and felt a sincere need to get life insurance so that she could leave an inheritance for her children.

Our conversation revealed that she had a firm resolve for saving and that she and her husband had been focused on saving. She was in her mid-60s and healthy. As a result, Melva estimated that the insurance proceeds that she received following her husband's death would all be required to support her for the rest of her life. She talked about what a wonderful husband he had been and how much she truly missed his sparkle and their happy times together. She commended him for leaving her financially secure. However, because she was in excellent health, she had concerns about how far the amount would go if she was fortunate to live a long life.

In a tone of quiet reserve, Melva explained that her husband never felt she needed insurance. He believed that insurance was for the man as the head of the household, not for the woman. She said that he never understood her feelings or her desires when she realized that the amount of insurance he had for her would be needed to sustain her through life, but that she would not be able to leave an inheritance to their children and grandchildren when she died.

She anticipated entering a nursing home someday and knew that the nursing home might eventually assume the legal ownership of her home and real estate as payment for her residency. Therefore, she did not want to base her children's inheritance on the asset of her home when it could be reassigned to a nursing home before she died. She was concerned as she relayed a story to me about 2 of her friends. She explained that these women signed over their homes and moved to a nursing home only to "outlive" their arrangement. After 18 months, her friends were facing the end of the contracted agreement with the nursing home—alive with no place to call home, and nowhere to go.

Melva related to me that she had been a traditional homemaker all her life and did not work outside of the home as is customary for "this newer generation." She was with her children and grandchildren everyday; they were "her life." Melva explained that she had 2 wonderful children—a married daughter and a son who was divorced and raising a 10-year-old son. She felt comfortable with her daughter's future because her daughter's life seemed to be financially secure. She had genuine concerns for her son who was a single parent challenged to provide all the financial and emotional necessities for a growing child. As Melva described all the details of their lives, her gentleness and caring were apparent. Indeed, her children truly were the center of her world now that her husband had died.

Because Melva was not involved with the family's financial affairs while her husband was alive, she exuded a zeal to learn everything about insurance—something she had wanted a great deal but something that was denied to her. She vigorously asked questions and wanted to see proposals. She wanted to review, understand and analyze every option. I gave her an envelope of materials to study, and I can say that I cannot remember seeing anyone ever so excited about reviewing mounds of gray and unappealing paperwork as Melva—like a child in a candy store.

During her learning process, Melva was solicited for insurance by a direct mail company. Because direct mail companies do not carry the expenses associated with maintaining local offices to service policyholders or expenses associated with payments to agents, the cash values in this company's policy were higher in the early years. Ultimately, however, price was not a determining factor in Melva's choice. She was focused on the values of her policy at her death, and she was focused on service. She chose to work with an agent because of the value-added service and because she could ask questions and learn. She wanted me to be present at her funeral to be the financial strength for her family when she was gone.

At age 67, Melva's excellent health and vitality made it possible for her to obtain insurance affordably after a favorable medical exam. She felt an incredible sense of accomplishment to be able to provide this for her children. The excitement she felt about having her own insurance was unbelievable—even to me. Melva affirmed, "I have wanted this for a very long time as a testimony to my own personal worth as a woman and the love I have for my children. It enables me to financially give them much more after I'm gone than what I am able give them while I am alive."

By saving with her husband during his lifetime, Melva secured an income to satisfy her basic needs after he died. Her obtaining coverage on her own, at age 67, satisfied her desires to leave a substantial financial legacy to her children.

STEP 6: ASSESSING YOUR PRESENT FINANCIAL HEALTH

Telling All

WHEN YOU AND YOUR AGENT MEET TO BEGIN YOUR PLANNING, YOU must be ready to tell all. Many women feel uncomfortable providing financial data. Some even consider it to be an invasion of privacy. But for your agent, registered representative, or financial planner to complete a fact find that can thoroughly address your wants, needs, and desires, you must be prepared to tell all in this beginning stage of your planning interview.

I suggest you consider a thorough *fact find* as a critical and indispensable next step. (In the financial services industry, the terms *fact find* and *fact-finding interview* are used to describe a process by which your assets, income, expenses, and other family information are recorded, analyzed, and reviewed relative to your short-term and long-term goals.) It is necessary for a *diagnosis* of your present financial condition and must precede any recommendations for future planning.

There are many analogies found in the world of the other professionals with whom you work. For instance, a certified public accountant needs information about your earning and spending patterns to complete your tax documents. Your physician attempts to know all of your family's medical background as well as your own symptoms before prescribing a procedure or remedy. When creating a will, an attorney needs to know whom you want to care for your children in the event of your death. Similarly, the agent or financial professional needs information in order to provide for your financial welfare.

Because insurance is not an immediate or tangible product, its benefits often are misunderstood. Insurance is not only a benefit you can draw on in the long term, but it can also play a part in your overall lifestyle and goals. A professional should ask many questions about your monthly income and expenses. You should also be willing to provide family and employer data. Also, be leery if you are not asked extensive questions to provide this data. I cannot say enough about working with someone who is thorough in finding out the financial facts about your life.

If you are considering the purchase of securities, the SEC/ NASD require that a registered representative ask "suitability" questions under the NASD Rules of Fair Practice, rule 2310, "Know Your Customers." Ultimately, for your benefit and protection, make sure that the financial professional you choose to work with conducts a thorough fact find to obtain background information about your financial condition.

The ACLI, U. S. Office of Consumer Affairs and the Consumer Information Center concur that your agent is responsible for asking you questions about family income and net worth. They include the following:

> Using the information you have already assembled about your financial situation, you should be prepared to discuss your insurance options. You should be prepared to answer questions about your health, age, medical condition, medical history, family history, and personal lifestyle habits. [10]

The fact-find questionnaire is a document that should remain as part of your permanent record with your agent. It assists agents and staff when they service you. Some information never changes and remains permanent; but as the years go on, much information will change. If there should ever be a legal or ethical question about whether the financial vehicle you purchased was correct for you, the fact find can help document the facts at the time of your purchase. It is also important to have a written and updated document on file in the event that your agent becomes disabled or dies. A successor will have your full financial history. Therefore, I strongly recommend that you obtain 2 copies of the fact find signed by you and your agent—1 for the agent's company file and 1 for your personal records. The policy you will receive is a legal document; therefore, it is important that you know what it provides and how the agent determined that from your fact find.

BUILDING BLOCKS OF A FINANCIAL PORTFOLIO

Many of my women clients compare completion of the fact find to building a house. For the house you need an architectural plan, a foundation, lumber, brick, mortar, water, heat, electricity, and so on. You need to have all the components together to create a home that is strong, beautiful and satisfies your dreams. Similarly, a strong financial program that can accomplish your goals will include prenuptial agreements, wills, living wills, and trusts in addition to business agreements. Some if not all of these financial elements will also be included:

- Property and casualty insurance to help protect your home, possessions, and vehicle as assets and to help protect against unforeseen liabilities that may result from accidents or claims against you.
- Suitable individual disability income protection in the event that you can no longer provide monthly income for household needs.
- Business overhead expense coverage payable to your company to help cover monthly expenses such as rent, utilities, and employee salaries if you are a business owner who becomes disabled as described in the policy.

- Group life insurance as well as individual term or cash value life insurance proceeds can be used to help fund expenses of burial, food, clothing and housing for the remaining family members.
- Life insurance to fund a trust.
- Life insurance to help pay estate taxes.
- Tax deferred products such as life insurance and annuities.
- Liquid savings vehicles such as certificates of deposits and money market accounts.
- Securities such as mutual funds, stocks, bonds, variable life insurance, and variable annuities.

Caveat emptor! Let the buyer beware. Purchasing life insurance and sophisticated investment products is a paper-intensive and detail-oriented process. There should be an extensive amount of time spent on gathering information about you. Be wary of writing any checks or signing on the dotted line within an hour of meeting any new agent, registered representative or financial planner. Be proactive during the fact finding process and ask many questions. I cannot over emphasize to women, that in the midst of this data gathering session, if you are uncomfortable and seem to be the target of aggressive tactics or pressured sales—the agent you are working with is probably not right for you.

INFORMATION TO PROVIDE

Many companies and financial professionals have created their own written questionnaires to gather data as part of their fact-finding process. (A sample questionnaire is included in: *American Dream Women: A Workbook & Planning Guide.* Overall, any questionnaire will inquire about all necessary aspects of your finances. Be certain to provide:

- Auto, homeowners or renters, disability income, or life insurance policies.
- The last 2 year's Federal income tax statements.
- All interest or dividend earnings and account balance statements from: certificates of deposit, bank savings accounts, money market accounts, mutual funds, stocks, bonds, securities, annuities, 401(k), 403(b), or any other pension plans you may have started.
- *Handbook of Benefits* from your employer and any employee benefit statements.
- All of the above information that relates to any business interest.
- A detailed description of your monthly house and utility expenses, car loans and maintenance costs, credit card balances, home equity or other loans, medical bills, grocery receipts, entertainment expenses, average checking account activity on a monthly basis.

- Information about any legal wills or trust documents.
- Any other information that relates to what you have done in the past to provide for your financial future.

The agent will review this information and make recommendations based on your wants, needs, and desires. This gathering of your personal data is a way of cleaning house and getting all of your information—formal papers or informal notes—in order and in one place. (The *American Dream Women: Workbook & Planning Guide* offers an organized process to help assist you in this challenge.) Often, we go through life assuming that all of our affairs are in order only to find out in an emergency that they are not.

At this point, I'd like to address women business owners. Even more so than individuals, the business owner must plan to review and amend the fact-find data annually. You will see many changes that have taken place since the inception of your business. Changes in your employee benefit structure may cause you to consider profit sharing. Raising the deductibles on the employee health insurance plan could lower premiums and make dollars available to spend in other areas. Maybe it is time to consider a disability income protection program for your employees, or there may be a need for life insurance on key employees.

At times, a company will send you letters regarding updated information about your policy or other products you own (health insurance, disability income insurance, life insurance, mutual funds, annuities, stocks, bonds, certificates of deposit). The law requires that any significant changes affecting products or values be communicated in writing and mailed to the policyholder or owner directly from the company that issued the product. You should take care that this correspondence be filed with your important papers. Then you should demand that the agent or registered representative explain the changes to you and that the impact of these changes on the rest of your financial program be explained as well.

Life changes, and as a result, whether you are single, married with children, a single parent, or a woman business owner, the review and assessment of your financial program relative to the current interest rate environment, your current lifestyle and expenses, and your business needs is a process that never really ends. You owe it to yourself to review these financial affairs annually. Consider updates to your planning more important than updating your wardrobe. When this cycle repeats in your life, you know you are well underway to staying on top of it all—*you are* in control of your financial affairs.

STEP 7: DETERMINING WHAT YOU CAN AFFORD

Theresa

THERESA CAME TO INTERVIEW ME IN EARLY SPRING of 1985. She was a tall, gorgeous blonde. She was vivacious, with the smile and enthusiasm of a 21-year-old student, although she had turned 40 the previous November. Her poise made people watch her across a room; she commanded a second look. It was hard to believe that she was the mother of 3 college-age children. She wore a designer outfit, finely tailored of silk and linen with sandals of fabric and texture to match. Her 24-carat jewelry sparkled. Even her rouge and lipstick complemented the hues of her wardrobe. You couldn't help notice that her manicure and pedicure were fresh, and her accessories were carefully chosen as well. By the end of our first visit, it was apparent that everything in Theresa's life—her outings, her vacations, her parties, her clothes—was designed with great care, except her financial future.

Theresa was adamant about change. She explained that she was born and raised "in serenity" on a peaceful farm in the Tennessee horse country. Her tasks included early morning visits to the chicken coop to collect eggs for breakfast, while her younger brothers picked garden vegetables for the day's meals. The family farm provided an ample supply of meat from steers, pigs, and poultry. There was an ebullient pride in her story about how she had grown to accumulate a taste for knowledge about the finer things in life long after her humble beginnings.

She took special pride in explaining that when she was a young girl she learned to sew and tailor dresses from gingham and checkered pattern sacks that were a bonus on 100 pounds of flour. She felt special because the material was cut, washed, and creatively sewn "just for her" by her Mom. This was a real treat since she was from a family of 10 children.

The work ethic that was ingrained for Theresa's family became evident as she recalled the strength of her father, Jack, and her mother, Gayle. Her dad was also one of 10 children. He worked his way through college in Chattanooga by playing drums in a jazz band. Jack was determined to be successful and dreamed of having a chain of filling stations. America was taking to the new post-World War II freedom of the highway. Jack and Gayle saved and worked very hard on the farm until they had enough to lease their first filling station. His enterprise grew to a $1.7 million chain.

Gayle was a city girl from a prestigious family in Atlanta. Bred in high style and accustomed to gourmet butler service at every meal, she attended the famous Ward Belmont finishing school in Nashville and excelled as a ballerina. She was always picture perfect in her appearance—complete with hat and gloves for church.

In the '30s and '40s and '50s, a woman's "place" truly was at home. Gayle was adamant that the more time and nurturing given to children, the better-adjusted, well-mannered and responsible they would be as adults. With a full-time mother working at home, the children were trained to make their beds every morning, keep a perfectly clean and orderly room, do homework before supper, and enjoy friends and entertainment only after a rigorous regimen of household chores and family responsibilities. With a large family, Theresa's mother had her hands full with cooking, canning, cleaning, sewing and raising the little ones. The family was active in church and had a family pew in the front row where strict silence, behavior, and manners were required. The family was devout, religious, and prayed together daily while kneeling at the couch in thanksgiving for good health and blessings received. Their social life consisted of involvement in their rural community—pie socials, rummage sales, and church picnics. They generously gave to the community, and in addition to raising their children, they sponsored the education of 7 young men through the seminary.

As husband and wife, Jack and Gayle, felt that a woman's role was to be centered in the home and not involved with finances. These were not the days of dual incomes or dual income expectations; therefore, family finances were the husband's role. Mother's job was teacher and homemaker responsible for nurturing a family with social manners and solid morals. Jack gave Gayle a monthly allowance to cover grocery and household expenses. These were times of cash spending only. Nothing was bought unless it was bought with cash. Children were not privy to the financial affairs of the family, which Theresa later learned was critical behavior if a family today is to grow and live within its means.

As her story turned to her own family, Theresa's financial stress was revealed as she explained her early days after marrying Glenn, her high school sweetheart, in 1958. They both, along with her brothers, were molded by her father to someday run the family business. Theresa's goal was to learn the family business and enjoy home life and raising children. She never expected that her income would be necessary to support the family while Glenn's income was needed to put back into the family business.

Her father died, and the family watched the business quickly crumble because there was no life insurance that could have been used to help stabilize the business. Tears filled Theresa's eyes when she recalled that the funeral procession for her father was 3-miles long in tribute to this very well respected, gentle, and giving man. Theresa, Glenn, and her brothers involved in the business were not knowledgeable nor did they have ample funds to keep the business going. Without money to cover the cash flow, the business soon died.

With Theresa's and Glenn's goals and livelihood in jeopardy, they both sought other jobs. After 6 years of marriage, she had 3 children of her own and was raising her younger brothers and sisters because of her mother's illness and institutionalization. Theresa found herself in a dual-income world she had never experienced at home. She became resentful of trying to find ways to keep it all together, juggling a full-time job, sewing clothes for the children, having healthy meals on the table every evening, cleaning, doing laundry, being active in church, doing gardening and cutting grass. She was overwhelmed.

Their dual incomes also created expectations and demands for personal rewards for the sacrifices which were being made by both Theresa and Glenn. They wanted the luxuries of purchasing nicer clothes, dinner and dancing out. Things were starting to accumulate. Buying on credit with charge cards became a lifestyle. Both she and Glenn wanted new cars, furniture, carpeting, and vacations badly enough to undergo extreme financial stress to have them. Their friends created a peer pressure for accumulating things.

Theresa laughed as she described the typical family meals back then as they struggled to pay for the trappings of the household. Dinners were: pressure cooker Swiss steak or fried chicken with potatoes on Sunday, chicken and turkey pot pies with fruit cocktail throughout the week, grilled cheese and tomato soup on Thursday, macaroni and cheese with fish sticks on Friday, and jiffy steaks or beans and franks as a special treat on Saturday. The family couldn't wait for summer when they could have a cookout with hot dogs on the grill.

At that point in her life, Theresa's definition of wealth was to immediately have all the things that her mother took 30 years to struggle for; she "wanted it now" and "would pay for it over time." Whereas her parents didn't purchase anything unless they had cash, Theresa and Glenn began what she called "a period of debt addiction." They created an endless cycle of credit card buying and the payment stress that goes with it. The cycle of credit card buying and binge spending as a reward for hard work continued for Theresa and Glenn for more than 20 years.

It took Theresa 20 years to realize that as long as their life was dominated by debt addiction there could be no accumulation of wealth. She recalled "fear at 40" and explained, "Suddenly the lights went on. Things and stuff began losing their value while retirement concerns were becoming serious emotional issues looming for both of us." Together, Theresa and Glenn were committed to a lifestyle change in order to aggressively accumulate wealth over the next 25 years. They relocated to make a fresh start. They had used all their previous savings for the move and to sustain them for 1 year while their new careers were being established. When Glenn relocated, he lost his benefits and insurance.

Even though they were unemployed when they relocated, their long-term dream was to have a $2 million nest egg for retirement. They both chose commission jobs for the income potential: Glenn started in real estate; Theresa worked with cosmetics. When Theresa came to see me, she was determined. After a fact find to assess their financial condition, she began to put into action long-term goals so that some day she could go back to the uncomplicated serene life she remembered on the farm as a child.

She committed to put money away into her savings account with an obligation of no less than 10 percent of their combined gross income. She totaled their monthly credit card expenses and committed to paying double payments for three years until all were paid. As a couple they committed to refrain from purchasing anything unnecessary and started to follow a strict budget. Glenn was to receive a modest inheritance to be paid over 10 years as certificates of deposit became due. We created a program to put these deposits into mutual funds and diversify the money into 3 funds.

Theresa and Glenn made strict commitments to each other that money had to be put away for savings first. Each month they would write a check for savings "as if it were a bill" in order to "pay themselves first" as she called it. When the credit card debt was gone after the 3 years, they took the money that was being used to pay off the debt and applied it to their long-term wealth accumulation program. They also purchased a properly designed disability income and life insurance program to meet their needs by the time they reach age 65.[11] They took any bonuses and salary increases and put them into a liquid savings account so when premiums came due, they had the money to pay. Theresa quipped, "We went back to the early days of macaroni and cheese with fish sticks and started to laugh about how life had changed at 40. Instead of chicken pot pies to buy furniture and carpeting and stuff, we were eating macaroni and cheese so we could aggressively save."

After 10 years of committed and disciplined savings based on their dual incomes, they both no longer had a mindset controlled by short-term desires. It was replaced by an attitude focused on accumulation for retirement. To date they have accumulated over $600,000—which is on track for their goal of $2 million in another 15 years assuming a 9-percent interest rate is maintained.

On Theresa's last visit for her quarterly mutual fund update, she told me that she and Glenn had just purchased a dream house on a peaceful and serene fishing lake in the North Woods where they were planning to retire after they left the city. I knew how disciplined her savings had become, and I was amazed that she could still be able to purchase prime real estate. I asked her, "How did you ever manage that?"

She winked, "Macaroni and cheese with fish sticks."

Know What You Can Afford

AFTER THE AGENT OR FINANCIAL PROFESSIONAL LEAVES THE fact-finding interview with financial information to review, most women become concerned about their ability to pay for the recommendations that will come next. Hopefully, the days are past when agents took a quick look at your policies, told you what to buy, and you could not afford it over the long term.

You have done your homework. You've proceeded through your interviewing process. You've chosen your agent, registered representative, or financial planner. You've gathered all your financial information and turned it over for review.

All recommendations for insurance or investment plans must be understood in terms of your goals as well as your ability to save over the long term. Buying financial products is not like buying a winter wardrobe that would be forgotten or replaced next year. For a financial program to succeed over time, payments must be sustained over the long term. You must comfortably be able to afford payments.

Theresa and Glenn learned the process of wealth accumulation the hard way, but after 20 years, they realized that being **"wealthy" does not mean accumulating material "things" that symbolize a perception of what it means to be wealthy.** Accumulating wealth means accumulating savings over time. This is done by protecting your earning power to sustain cash flow into savings, insurance, and investments and by guarding against spending that drains cash flow.

A fundamental step in any financial strategy for the future is understanding your monthly overhead and living expenses. What women want in life is often a relentless driving force; yet they don't realize what they must do financially to accomplish their goals, or what short-term tradeoffs and sacrifices they must make to achieve financial success over the long term. Any professional to whom you are entrusting your planning cannot recommend a realistic program for you without knowledge of your income, all of your expenses and cash flow in relationship to what you need and want.

THE GENERATION OF ENTITLEMENT & DEBT ADDICTION

To achieve their dreams, many women have asked me, "Why must I be debt free? What will I have to do to become debt free? Will you help me with a budget?"

There are more college educated adults and couples in America today than ever. Since 1960, the number of women completing 4 or more years of college has quadrupled to more than 19 million annually. More than 103,968 million men and women have attained bachelor's degrees and live as married couples.[12] The sacrifices and time spent in attaining a technical, professional, trade and academic education in a post war economy have created an attitude of entitlement for the Baby Boomers and their children alike. The information age and the ease of advertising in a global marketplace have brought the allure of goods and services from around the world into our televisions at home and into our shopping malls. Time spent shopping at the mall constitutes a major pastime for American consumers. Our affluent society believes it must have the status of material wealth as a reward for arduous work or education. Status symbols such as luxury cars, designer clothing, jewelry, and fabulous vacations are all easily purchased at the mall, by phone, or on line with credit cards.

The ease of obtaining credit in our country has desensitized consumers to the long-term consequences of buy-now-pay-later spending. College coeds get credit cards; it's a sign that "they've arrived" into the adult world. She carries her department store cards; he carries his as well. When young couples marry today, they are eager for the revenue of two incomes, yet have seemed to lose focus that they both have brought a healthy stream of debt into their new marriage. Likewise, many couples are adamant about purchasing a home before they are married. They tell me, "After all—we've studied and worked hard, and we deserve it." What they don't realize is that they *do not deserve* the yoke of indebtedness that will sometimes prevent them from accumulating real wealth and saving for retirement until much too late. A large number of younger Americans, especially young married couples, live lifestyles beyond their means. They do it with the help of credit cards. Because they can afford the monthly credit card payments as a result of acquiring consumer goods, their credit card spending creates an illusion that they have material wealth. But they do not understand the short- and long-term costs of accumulating such debt. **There can be no long-term accumulation of future wealth if a couple carries debt that prevents them from saving 10-20 percent of their gross income.** This is true if the balance of a couples' disposable income after food, clothing, housing, and transportation, is used to pay credit card debt rather than saved to earn additional accumulation.

DEBT REDUCTION

If a client carries a heavy load of debt, my focus as an agent is to take time to understand the debt situation. My goal is a strict one: **I make removing debt the first priority.** This is accomplished as follows:

- A 2- or 3-year period is set aside with debt reduction as the priority before any disposable income is used for cash spending.

- Clients must agree not to make purchases unless they have the cash in hand. Buying habits that include purchasing with deferred payments are not an option to becoming debt-free. To believe a repetitive cycle of credit card debt will not hinder wealth accumulation is erroneous.
- Accelerated or double payments to pay off credit cards and/or consolidating them into an equity loan is necessary if possible.

The purpose of any financial program is to accomplish goals within a framework of consistently and methodically saving money. There are other reasons to make debt reduction a priority:

- It creates disciplined spending habits. It creates a new mindset based only on cash purchases. If focus is to eliminate $10,000 to $20,000 of credit card debt, it will be less likely to create new debt given the sacrifices which must be made to double payments.
- Concentration to pay off debt creates disciplined saving habits. Once the debt is paid, the $500 to $800 monthly payment is instantly available cash flow for investment. Gratification becomes swift and wonderful when this cycle begins.

Clients and I review how they can work toward removing debt, and during that time perhaps their insurance priorities are focused on disability income insurance protection and a term insurance program for death benefit protection. In the future, there can be a term conversion to cash value insurance and beginning considerations of mutual funds and various investments.

THE COST OF WAITING

When women begin careers in their early 20s and become more stable in their 30s, they enter what I call a "spending and debt cycle" as they acquire homes, expensive possessions, marry, and build families. It's usually not until age 40 that the fear of debt addiction or lost time becomes strong enough to force a change in attitude, lifestyle, buying habits and spending habits. For many women with whom I work, a realization about the cost of waiting is enough to catapult them into new savings habits with great zeal.

One client needed to remove debt. At age 42, she was depressed to realize that since college she had progressed in her career with 6 different jobs, had moved 10 times and had earned over $450,000. Yet she had accumulated no "real" savings to speak of and carried $25,000 in debt. As she viewed it, she "had nothing to show for 20 years in her career." She summed up her change in attitude this way: "I started to picture savings in terms of the long-term value of some of my excesses in spending. I used to love to buy new shoes—and only the best shoes. It wasn't difficult for me to spend $200 for a pair of designer shoes every month. I considered it a reward for my high stress job. When I realized that if I bought less expensive shoes and saved $200 each month over the 20 years since I've been out of college, today that "shoe money" would be worth over $130,000 assuming a 9-percent interest rate is maintained. How many pairs of shoes does a woman really need anyway!"[13]

Clients' credit card payment habits and spending habits have proven that very little wealth accumulation can occur in an aggressive savings approach if the majority of their income feeds a frenzied cycle of paying off old credit card debt and creating new credit card debt. Also, clients have demonstrated that modest regular savings will accumulate if any discipline to save can be achieved. One couple in their 20s was staggered to realize that by limiting eating out to once a week, and going out to the clubs twice a month rather than twice a week, they could save $100 a month. If that amount was saved in a disciplined fashion, their wealth accumulation at an average 9-percent rate of return by the time they were 40 would be almost $67,000.[14]

HOW TO ALLOCATE YOUR MONEY

Once you've satisfied your debt and attained the discipline of regular savings, you can determine what you can afford relative to your purchase of disability income and life insurance protection as well as your initiation of an investment strategy. It is necessary to understand the relationship between your checking account, short-term savings account, and future finances.

Imagine 3 circles or 3 reservoirs of money. The first is your checking account; the second is your short-term savings account; the third is for future accumulation.

Any future financial strategy needs to link these principles, and your financial focus on each of them should never waver. (See Figure 2.) Keeping in mind the relationship among these areas means that you will always be aware of your net income and expenses, that you always have a short-term savings in place to protect for unforeseen events, and that the first 2 be satisfied before any disciplined, long-term savings can accrue. If you are always being forced to borrow from what you consider a long-term savings account, then it will never grow or accumulate.

Based on the fact find and the expense analysis you completed earlier, by analyzing your *checking account*, you know the relationship of your expenses to your income, and what, if any, excess dollars are available. Your checking account ideally reflects 1 month's income and expenses. There are many young couples who have a checking account balance large enough to cover a year's worth of expenses. I do not recommend this because it is more difficult to remain focused on the 3 distinct budgets you have created for monthly expenses, short-term savings and future investments.

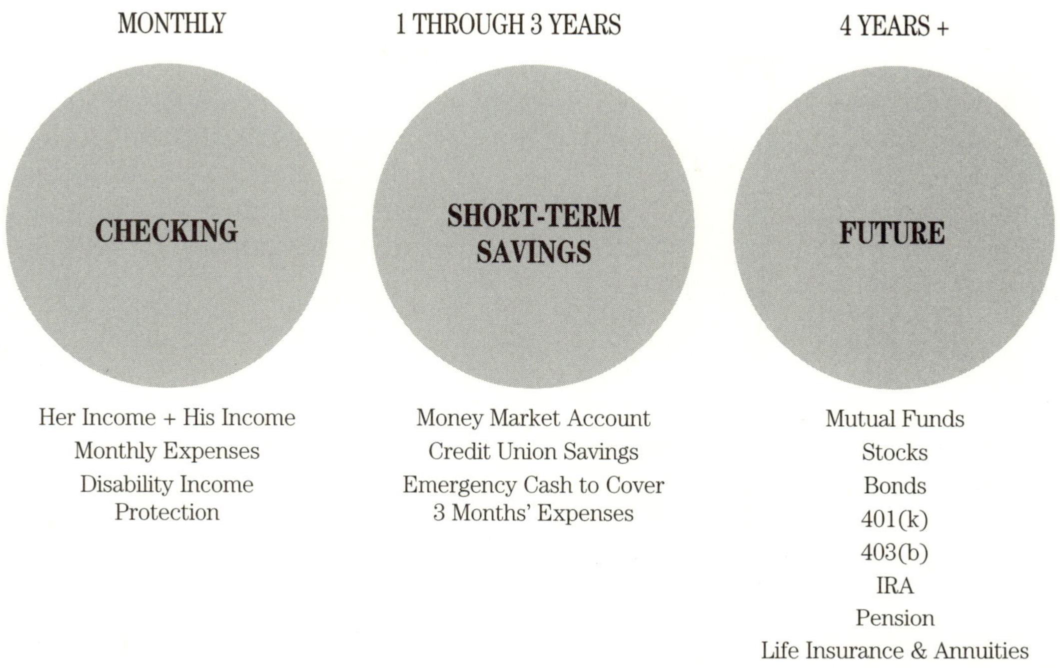

Figure 2. Relationship between checking, short-term savings and future accumulation.

The *short-term savings* circle is a short-term fund for liquid cash in an emergency—in case your furnace breaks, or your car needs major repair. This amount is typically enough to cover 1- to 6-months' expenses; a minimum of 3-month's expenses is a rule of thumb. This reserve of money is a must for several reasons. Not only is it available as a cushion in the event that you become disabled (in the interim before you receive any disability income payments), but also it creates a mental security blanket. I mandate this fund for my clients. The feeling of security of having it can help provide strong self-esteem and eliminate worry because any negative effect that an emergency or other binge spending may have on your long-term savings patterns has been diminished. A client who wants to eliminate this short-term savings fund has more difficulty living on a budget and maintaining regular and disciplined payments into a long-term savings vehicle because of "fear" of not having liquid cash available.

Savings vehicles for this type of short-term savings reserve may be a credit union, a bank savings account, or a money market account through a securities firm. Whatever vehicle you select, it should always be a reserve to satisfy short-term liquid cash needs rather than a reserve for long-term investment.

The *future accumulation* reservoir is considered for a 4-year period and longer. You are seeking long-term accumulation of cash in this reservoir. This typically includes any 401(k), 403(b), other pension or profit sharing plans and annuities which will be used at age 59 1/2 or later. Cash value life insurance is also included as an asset in this category. If the purpose is to provide an income to your family after you die, a rule of thumb is that you begin an insurance portfolio based on 8-15 times your annual income. The amount varies depending on what insurance companies will issue to you.

After you've eliminated your debt, have built a short-term emergency fund, and have begun saving in your future accumulation reservoir, the fun begins. Here is where your banker, certified public accountant, agent, registered representative or financial planner can help you calculate the nest egg you would like to accumulate for retirement and help you calculate how much you must contribute on a monthly or annual basis to achieve it. All professionals involved in the financial services industry have compound interest tables that can illustrate the growth potential of your savings over time based on various interest rates.

Everyone wants to save more money. One question I hear is how do I know the best way to save? How does a CD or certificate of deposit work? What will a money market do for me? What do mutual funds do? How does insurance work?

Saving more money can be accomplished in many different ways. You can save money on a *non-qualified basis* as well as a *qualified basis*. (*Qualified* generally refers to an IRA, pension, profit sharing, 401(k), 403(b), or similar retirement plan created by an employer for the benefit of eligible employees.) You generally cannot consider these funds to be liquid, which means that you cannot access them; they must remain untouched until age 59 1/2—or substantial IRS penalties and income tax will be incurred. Perhaps as you save your money, you want to have access to it quickly, that is you want it to be liquid and available to you in case of emergency. Vehicles that accomplish this are money market accounts, cash value life insurance, savings accounts, and mutual funds.

For a thorough understanding of these concepts relative to your personal circumstances, you must discuss these concepts with your certified public accountant, banker, agent, registered representative, or financial planner. Ultimately, the choice of products you choose must be yours—not theirs—based on your overall availability of funds and your needs.

The investment marketplace is dynamic, and interest rates are always changing. That is why it is imperative for you to quarterly or annually monitor values to assess how your projections have gone up or down from your previous monitoring. It's important that you realize that financial professionals cannot make investments on your behalf. **That is why it is your responsibility to require that your professional team continues to keep you aware of the marketplace**

and to determine if your portfolio is positioned for the highest potential of earnings based on your long-term objectives and risk tolerance.

After understanding the relationship among your monthly checking account, short-term savings account and future investment account, the next lesson in planning for your financial future is to learn how each relates to any employee benefits you have where you are employed.

STEP 8: UNDERSTANDING YOUR COMPANY BENEFITS

Maria

MARIA WAS A YOUNG WOMAN FROM AN UNEDUCATED working family; her mother and father expressed the work ethic with a stoic pride in their home, children, and jobs. To follow her dream meant that Maria worked her way through college washing dishes in a restaurant. Her grade point average was always at or near perfect. She was a petite brunette. Maria was not a beauty, but her warm heart, poise, and grace made people remember her—as well as her unusual hands that were large from years of masonry, roofing and carpentry work with her father. She was petite, not because she was diminutive, but because she was short. Maria was determined to work her way out of the old, dirty, blue collar industrial town where she was born and raised. She graduated *summa cum laude* from a prestigious college, received a scholarship to graduate school, married, and divorced early.

Since becoming my client, Maria had told me many times that her goal in those early years of her life and career was to achieve a superior education and a white collar job. She was a classic over achiever. Her creativity blossomed with her musical talent and writing ability. Nothing impaired her focus; for she believed strongly that if she was going to compete in a man's world, she needed to be well educated. She believed that women needed to have 3 times more education than men to earn respect in the American workplace. After several years working in corporations, her intuition seemed to be justified. At that time, Maria witnessed a working world where women having more credentials and experience in white collar corporate jobs earned less than men for doing the same work. That harsh reality fueled the fire of her drive and ambition "to be the best." Over the next few years, she went to night school and received a second master's degree in business management. Years of full-time work and night school continued until she had also earned the national board accreditation that she coveted so highly. In all, she brought 24 years of education to her career accompanied by over 20 years of full-time experience.

As she told me when she became my client, Maria was 33 when she had remarried—this time to an older man with children, ages 9, 10 and 13. His financial obligations to them in their formative years and impending college years meant that she was responsible for a major portion of their living expenses and those of her own children she hoped to have someday. This did not bother her because she was in love with someone who seemed to be more mature and stable—financially, it would all work out with time when his children were grown.

Three months after being married privately in judge's chambers, Maria's hopes for a new future and family of her own came to a halt. One night she had a dream of a serious illness. Her intuition had been right many times previously—enough to prompt her to seek medical testing. Within the week, medical examinations confirmed she had uterine cancer.

A life that had been focused on education and a career took the back seat to obtaining second medical opinions and checking with her employer about the types of medical benefits and disability benefits she would have. She learned that short-term salary continuation benefits for several weeks after surgery were provided for 90 days. But if she elected to consider additional post-operative procedures her finances would not be secure. The cost for the chemotherapy and radiology procedures would be covered, but if she grew ill and couldn't work in the following weeks, which was a certainty with such medical treatment, she would not be on full salary, and there would be some money **but not enough** money to pay the bills at home as well as help her husband with the financial needs of his 3 growing children.

In those bitter next few weeks, Maria also learned that in her state's legal system, Maria's good job and income actually made it possible for the birth mother of the children to request additional income from the children's father; his marriage to Maria increased his "ability to pay" to his ex-wife. Maria was disillusioned to learn that her sacrifices were empowering for another woman—and detrimental to her own financial condition at that time. According to the law, the father's obligations to his children came first before any obligations to his home or second wife.

Maria elected to have surgery. Her financial situation caused her to return to work after the 3-month short-term disability period ended. She refused the traditional therapies of Western medicine, and through reading and research, she embraced homeopathic remedies. The small town where she lived had no contact with such alternative medicine or doctors. Her physician insisted that full recovery was doubtful and pressured her to begin chemotherapy and radiation treatments.

For the first time since she began her journey on the fast track in high school, she felt vulnerable and alone. All of her education, career, and desires could not buy her health. She faced her hospital stay knowing she had no financial help from her second husband. To make matters emotionally worse, the hospital placed her in the maternity ward that intensified her anxiety at not being able to have children of her own. How had her life derailed to such an extent?

In our talks about those days, Maria could not stress enough how she wished that she had taken the time to understand the benefits of the plan she had at work. The details didn't seem to matter—until she learned she had cancer; then it was just too late.

Maria was hard on herself; she had felt "mortally naïve" as she called it. She trusted too many other people, insurance agents as well as her husband, to guide her when she did not totally understand the shortfall of her own benefits.

She knew how important insurance was, and she had religiously scheduled annual reviews with her agent. But she relied on the agent to tell her that everything was in order rather than asking him critical questions. She felt betrayed because the agent never taught her, and she felt angry with herself for not demanding to be taught—for delegating it to someone other than herself. She knew that she had short-term disability benefits at her job. But her agent never took the time to help her understand the 40-percent shortfall between the benefits and her income and monthly expenses in conjunction with her husband's financial commitments to his children. Maria never asked those critical questions.

Maria felt that no woman should go through the financial stress, physical pain, and emotional devastation that followed surgery. But with the inner grace that had been her strong suit, she was determined to "best this thing," as she called it. She embraced European and Asian therapies, macrobiotics, vegetarianism, and waited.

And she waited.

During her wait, Maria knew she would face an uphill battle with cancer. She would face a financial battle. She would face an emotional battle of not being able to have children of her own. She would face a larger battle with adoption agencies that would not consent to adoption because her health and the demanding hours of her career did not make her a suitable candidate at that time. She faced her company closing and losing her job. But she did not expect to face another woman in her husband's life—and the divorce that resulted.

She waited and would often joke to her closest friends how she "just couldn't wait to turn 40." Everybody else hated the thought of turning 40. Maria was eager for it because on that day it meant that she would have survived cancer 7 years in remission.

She dreamed of the 40th birthday. She had signs in her office and on her refrigerator door, "40 or Bust." Believing she would also face a mastectomy, she didn't know which would come first. Her humor was bizarre, yet always hopeful. She told me how she had planned the morning of her birthday. First, there would be Mass first as every day, followed by a breakfast meeting celebration. The breakfast meeting would be to purchase disability income insurance—for on that day she would again become insurable. And facing the world alone, she would never again rely on the minimum disability income protection provided by company benefits. Nor would she ever believe that a working husband would assure that the monthly mortgage and living expenses were paid in the event that she became unable to work.

In April 1992, Maria lived to have her breakfast.

She recalls, "I was smiling like a Cheshire cat the whole way to a breakfast buffet where I heaped bean sprouts and broccoli on my dish. I also placed an *a la carte* order for $3,000 of monthly disability income protection. I figured it was better for my future than a helping of blintzes."

Maria eventually moved to another position in the corporate world and was comfortable there with all of the benefits—401(k) retirement planning, long-term disability income protection, health insurance, $450,000 of life insurance, and a large salary providing her with $12,000 of monthly income. Her loyalties ran high. She tended to pursue a job and develop it on a track of excellence. She was not a corporate climber or job hopper; therefore, her style was not to pursue a high-profile, "Golden Wonder Boy" strategy up the corporate ladder. Because she was stable with a reputable track record, she believed in job security and envisioned being with the company for years. She had purchased and remodeled a home to her liking in a beautiful area near work.

Maria reached out to me and asked if I felt that she needed to do more, because she never again wanted "to be held hostage" by a passive attitude. I reviewed the individual life insurance and her individual disability income protection coverage that she had purchased 3 years earlier, and I reviewed the benefits she had with her employer.

During the interview, Maria told me of the cancer she had experienced and how happy she was to be once again "insurable" and qualify for disability income protection. We did an additional fact find to assess her income compared with her expenses. We both agreed that she had adequate disability income coverage provided through her employer plus the individual protection which she had purchased earlier. Yet, she did qualify for higher individual disability income protection based on the fact that her income had skyrocketed.

Before pursuing additional mutual funds and retirement planning, because she was a recovering cancer patient in a high stress job and totally on her own with enormous expenses, Maria was adamant about first obtaining even more individual disability income protection.

Three years later, Maria found herself in a management regime change that eventually forced her out of the position to which she had devoted her life. She was suddenly faced with no income, no benefits, and unable to pay a monthly fee of $400 for the Federally mandated extended COBRA health benefits. For months, Maria found it difficult to find any job let alone a position that would ever equal her previous salary.

She called to break the news to me the day that she was told to clean out her desk and leave the office. In the middle of the hurt and confusion of what was happening to her, I reminded her that the individual disability income coverage she had purchased while working cannot ever be canceled as long as she paid the annual premium every year.

Later, Maria told me more about the day she left the promises and benefits of the corporate world—carrying her career and life out the door in a white cardboard file box. In the midst of such confusion, she was proud.

Maria was proud of her sense of personal accountability for her own financial affairs. She was thankful that she knew that the disability income protection she had as an employee benefit was not portable and did not continue when she left the company. But even more, she was proud that when most people at her income level would have been content with one personal income disability policy and would have begun aggressive investing in long-term savings vehicles, Maria's priority instead was to maximize individual disability coverage. She was proud that she truly understood the implications this had for an educated, single women who was unemployed and facing a long road to find another equitable position.

Maria knew that in the near future if she pursued starting her own consulting business, most likely she could not immediately earn a salary at her previous level. Because she would be a start-up business with high expenses and no established track record of income over the next few years, she knew that she could not qualify for any disability coverage. She was gratified that she had such sizable individual disability income protection that would always stay with her.

As a player and pawn on the board of corporate chess, she had escaped capture. Maria was proud that this time in her life, when adversity confronted her, she had made a strategic winning move.

Understanding Your Company Benefits

BEFORE YOUR FINANCIAL PROFESSIONAL CAN TOTALLY ASSESS YOUR financial situation and determine strategies for financial growth, you both must understand the benefits you may or may not have with your company as well as what you can lose if you are no longer with the firm.

In America, the world of employee benefits is an industry all of its own. For example, it can cost a company 25 percent of your annual salary to provide you with employee benefits—on top of vacation and sick day packages. Another 3 percent can be spent on company match investment plans. That means if you receive an annual salary of $30,000 the company is spending at least another $7,500 on your behalf.

Employers continuously seek new ways to maximize employee benefits as well as cut expenses. They look for savings in health care and medical care. Some companies that seek aspiring top-notch employees will design extremely competitive benefit packages to lure the brightest talent away from their competition. They are looking for creative new ways to reward highly productive employees. Other companies look for ways of using greater numbers of part-time employees and fewer numbers of full-time employees with paid benefits. Every day, American companies face the pressures of off-shore and foreign companies manufacturing products with lower labor costs. The global economy is forcing American business to compete in ways that it never before dreamed.

At the same time, the risks we face every day are high. "Although women can live much longer than men, they tend to be sick more often. In fact, a woman is 15 percent more likely to have a short-term disease than a man of her age and socio-economic group," claims Larry Laudan in his *Book of Risks*. He continues to tell us that 70 percent of people between ages 20 and 74 have hypertension, 50 percent have diabetes but do not know it; 31 percent have maladies associated with high cholesterol; 20 percent will suffer some mental illness in their life, and of the U. S. working population between ages 18 to 64, 15 million are disabled and unable to work.[15] Given the high stress lifestyle of career-building Americans, the probability is above average that disability or hospitalization will jeopardize their income earning potential.

My women clients fall into 5 categories regarding employee benefits. The first are those wage earners with child or elder care responsibilities who can only work part-time and receive no benefits. The second do not work outside the home and rely on their husband's benefits. The third are from dual-income families who are full-time employees or professionals with paid benefits but who claim their spouse's employer as their primary carrier. The fourth are single wage earners who are full-time employees or professionals. Fifth, are women business owners with staffs. All agree that they do not fully understand the critical relationship and impact employee benefits have on their future financial planning.

During a job search campaign, job seekers place great emphasis on obtaining the best benefit package, and the choice of which company to work for is often based on the competitiveness of the benefits. However, the focus on the benefits often stops when the job is landed. Unfortunately, job seekers can often spend more time preparing the résumé and deciding which suit to wear on the interview than understanding their benefits afterwards. As new employees, women are often busy learning company procedures, position requirements, and company politics; they do not take the time to learn all the details of their benefit package. Once joining a new company, many women are satisfied that they have benefits and don't explore them fully until a need or emergency arises. Then it is sometimes too late. Career women often tell me that they consider their company as "family" and have been lulled into thinking of the company as "a father figure adequately taking care of them." Company benefits are sometimes not enough. One plan cannot possibly serve the needs of all.

Over the years, women clients, like Maria, have shared their life's lessons regarding employee benefits. Here are a few:

> . . . Except for the highest executive level positions in a corporation, benefit packages are usually not negotiable.
>
> —*TB*

> . . . For any woman to think that a company benefit package is designed to her personal advantage to help her accumulate wealth is erroneous.
>
> —*KLH*

> . . . For anyone to think that company insurance and disability benefits are all they need is naïve. That might only work if you can be at the same company for a lifetime—and those days are long gone in America.
>
> —*KMS*

> . . . For any woman to say that her husband's plan 'will take care of it' is short sighted. What if the husband or his job do not last?
>
> —*MS*

Disability, divorce, company mergers and consolidations, corporate downsizing, job outplacement, pre-existing conditions, changes in occupation, changes in job classification, leaving the corporate world to start your own business—all have a financial impact on the security of your future as well as your protection for the short-term. Laudan states that on average, people change employers every 5 years, and by the year 2010 people could change careers more than once. Whether you are staff or upper management, if you are employed with paid benefits through a partnership, small business, corporation, or professional firm, you owe it to yourself to completely understand what *group insurance* benefits you have, what you can lose, and the overall impact this has on your financial program over the long term.

Common basic ingredients in today's corporate benefit packages and their impact on your future planning follow.

SHORT-TERM DISABILITY

For Maria, life changed with a dream. Many people don't think they will ever become disabled. It's nothing you expect. Plus, if you're like most of us, you think accidents and disability are things which happen "to someone else." A recent National Safety Council study quoted by The American Council of Life Insurance tells us that for every 2 accidents there are 8 sicknesses. Every 3 seconds someone is injured in an accident. Every 10 seconds someone is injured at home. Every 17 seconds someone is injured at work. And an auto accident resulting in injury occurs every 19 seconds.[16] Obviously, the impact of illness or accident on your income and wealth accumulation could be disastrous.

With a short-term disability, your loss of earnings immediately affects cash flow into your checking account for monthly expenses. The provisions and amount of your short-term disability coverage with an employer determine the size of the short-term savings reservoir necessary for emergencies. Here are key questions that you must answer:

- How long after your illness or injury will it take for your monthly disability income payment to begin?
- What portion of your regular salary will you receive?
- How does the company define "short-term" and "disability"?
- Is the premium being paid by the company or are you paying for it by means of payroll deduction?
- Do you have sick days? If so, what portion of your salary is covered if you are out with a short-term illness?
- How are sick days accrued? Do you lose these sick days after a certain length of time if you haven't used them?

There are short-term policies available that go into effect on the first day of an accident or the eighth day of illness. The most common coverage provided by the insurance company will pay a percentage of your income up to 60 days, 90 days or 6 months. There are policies, however, that define short-term as being up to 12 months. It is very important that you know exactly what these provisions are and how that affects the amount you need in your short-term savings emergency reservoir relative to your monthly expenses for the period as well as unforeseen expenses that may occur due to the disability. It is not unusual for companies to have different levels of provisions based on a person's rank or position within the firm. It is also possible that if you are in a corporate or other non-union environment, there will be no provision for sick days. It is not unusual for only partial salary to be provided in the event that you are sick. **The oversight you can make is to have all of your money tied up in non-liquid investment funds and not have an ample liquid short-term savings reserve because you assume that your disability income payments will begin immediately or that you will receive full salary.**

How the company defines *disability* is also important. Typically, the definition states that as long as you are unable to perform the regular material duties of your position you are considered to be "disabled" as long as you are not working at any other occupation.

LONG-TERM DISABILITY

These programs are designed to begin when the maximum benefits period for short-term disability benefits has been reached and benefits are exhausted. Ask the following questions:

- What kind of paperwork is necessary and how long after your illness or injury will it take for your monthly disability income payment to be processed?
- How long after that will your first payment begin?
- What portion of your regular salary will you receive?
- Will bonus income be covered by your disability benefit?
- How does the company define "long-term" and "disability"?

If you have a short-term disability program that would have been in effect for 6 months, then typically the company will have the long-term disability program start after 6 months and continue anywhere from 5 years to age 65. How the company "defines" long-term disability again is very important. With *group disability income programs* through an employer, there are many stipulations and exclusions to these programs. Such stipulations are not as prevalent if you carry your own non-cancelable *personal disability income insurance* protection.

Often *group long-term disability programs* through employers will have a *2-year mental and nervous* benefit. This means that if you should have a nervous breakdown or any illness deriving from mental or nervous conditions, the company's insurance provider would only provide payments for 2 years.

As Maria learned so well, group disability income protection means that if you leave employment, you cannot take the benefit and protection with you; if it group coverage, it is not portable. If you become downsized or unemployed, or if you choose to start your own business as a result, you cannot carry the group benefit with you.

Many professional career women who understand this provision of their group coverage and realize the vulnerability of change in corporate America are considering supplementing their group disability income insurance protection coverage with an individual disability income policy of their own. A key provision on some policies is *a purchase option rider*. The purchase option rider will allow you to increase your disability benefit providing you have the necessary income qualifications. As an example, let's assume that you have a group disability program then leave the firm. You've lost your earning potential and your group disability income protection program. However, while you were with the firm, you also purchased an individual disability income protection policy for $1,000 or $2,000 of additional monthly payment (limited by whatever maximum was allowable by the insurance companies for someone of your position and income). That individual policy is a non-cancelable policy; it stays in effect; it is portable. You personally own your non-cancelable policy, and it states that the company cannot cancel that policy. By having your personal insurance program removed from the work setting, your individual non-cancelable policy will stay with you at least until you reach age 65 and continue to pay the annual premium.

Insurance companies are becoming keenly aware of the income shortfall left unprotected for many women who become disabled. Many companies are offering competitive individual or voluntary disability income protection suitable for women's needs.

Al Curnow at American United Life in Indianapolis claims, "There are many women . . . [who are dual income heads of households] who need to protect their incomes. . . . Many live from paycheck to paycheck and may not be able to get by for the first 90 or 180 days of a disability. They need income replacement right away." Guarantee Mutual Life in Omaha also addresses needs specific to women. Director Terry Reams adds, "If you look at basic demographics there are more female heads of household with dependents. Working women need [the supplementary] coverage much more than they ever did in the past. This is good for women because their needs may or may not be different from what a man's needs are."[17]

MEDICAL INSURANCE

As in the disability income protection discussion mentioned above, unforeseen medical expenses in addition to the loss of income if you are ill or disabled can lead to financial ruin. Many employers have clauses that preclude coverage based on pre-existing medical conditions. Some employers require a 6-month waiting period before medical benefits are provided. One client who was the wife of an engineer relayed a story about what happened within 6 months of her husband's starting his first "real" job following graduate school. At age 28, he had been having dizzy spells, fell over on the job and was hospitalized. He had tumors on his cranial nerves and needed brain surgery. He was in the hospital for 3 months, had 27 spinal taps and was unable to work for 18 months afterward. His illness occurred before the company medical coverage was in effect; their medical bills were over $250,000. They had been married for one year and lost everything of what little they had. Even if the 80 percent/ 20 percent co-pay insurance was available to them, their share of expenses and post-operative care would have totaled $43,000.

It takes a little homework, but learn what your benefits are before you need them. Questions to understand regarding your medical coverage are:

- What is your deductible payment before insurance payments begin?
- What is your co-payment arrangement? That is, what percent does the medical insurance coverage pay and what percent is your responsibility?
- Understand the definitions within the medical insurance policy—what it will cover and what it will not cover.
- What will the policy cover, and what will it not cover?
- Are you eligible for COBRA benefits if you should leave employment and how do you apply?[18]

Keep in mind that this COBRA individual medical coverage can be considerably more expensive than the group medical insurance coverage you were receiving while you were employed. If you are outplaced, you must also know that COBRA coverage is necessary in order to maintain an "uninterrupted break" in medical coverage. If you have no coverage, and it takes you 9 months to a year to find adequate employment, it could seriously impact you if you become disabled or develop a medical condition before your new company benefits are in effect; it would be considered a pre-existing condition and exempt from coverage in many cases. The financial consequences can be even larger if you are a long-tenured, high paid, technical or professional employee for whom it may take a considerable amount of time to secure a comparable position.

Your financial professional can help you calculate the impact these circumstances will have on your ability to pay expenses and what additional sums need to be placed in your short-term savings reserve.

SOCIAL SECURITY

You may not give much thought to Social Security if you are far from retirement age. Under Social Security, employees qualify for benefit payments based on a certain number of work credits. Once you have enough credits, your benefit amount depends on your average earnings over your working lifetime. Most adults need 40 credits to qualify for benefits, which means that they will need to have worked for 10 years. It is often easy to forget that employers and employees each pay Social Security taxes of 6.2 percent on the first $62,700 of covered wages. You each also pay Medicare taxes of 1.45 percent on all your covered wages. If you are a self-employed entrepreneur, your Social Security tax is 12.4 percent, and your Medicare tax is 2.9 percent on the same amount of earnings. [19]

Contemporary politicians and economists have created ample controversy about the long-term health and viability of Social Security. The Social Security Board of Trustees projects that the system will continue to have adequate resources to pay benefits in full for the next 34 years—year 2030.[20] But Social Security does provide more than retirement benefits; it also provides important disability, family and survivor benefits. It covers more than 141 million workers and pays monthly benefits to about 43 million people. Retirement benefits based on your average earnings over the years can begin at age 62. But the Social Security Amendments Act of 1983 gradually increases the normal retirement age from 65 to 67 by the year 2027. This increase will further lower the amount of your benefit if you retire at age 62. If you are divorced after at least 10 years of marriage, you will be entitled to Social Security benefits based on your spouse's earning record.

It is wise to check with the Social Security Administration every few years to verify that your earnings are accurately recorded. This can be done by obtaining a "Request for Earnings and Benefit Estimate Statement" from your local Social Security office.[21] It takes a few minutes to complete. You will receive a written statement for your records.

Social Security benefits are generally discounted as mythic among financial professionals who are serious about helping their clients achieve true financial success.

PENSIONS AND INVESTMENTS

More attention is paid to the accumulation benefits of an employer than the protection benefits—simply because these are more fun. Obtain answers to the following questions:

- Does your employer offer a 401(k), 403(b), or other type of retirement plan?
- With a 401(k), does the company match your contribution?
- If it is a matching situation, how much does the company match?

- Are you maximizing your employee contributions in your 401(k)?
- What is your account worth?
- In what type of funds are you presently investing?
- Are you monitoring the growth of your accounts quarterly and discussing it with your agent, registered representative, or financial planner?

Monitoring your quarterly reports or annual statements will help you feel the pleasure and witness the growth that can result from disciplined savings over time. Fully understanding your 401(k) or 403(b) plan is not only knowing the extent to which you are making contributions, but also understanding how the different funds are performing. Monitoring the growth of your account and the diversification of funds in which your dollars are distributed is just as important as the amounts you are putting into your account. Different rates of return are earned by different fund performances.

The *Rule of 72* is commonly used in the financial services industry. (It means if you want your money to double within a certain number of years, you take 72 and divide it by the number of years; it gives you the rate of interest you need to earn on your money. Then, if you divide 72 by the rate of interest you are already earning, it will tell you how long it will take to double your money.)

For example, assuming a 9-percent interest rate is maintained, your fund could double in 8 years. That means your dollars in your 401(k) or 403(b) as of today, with an assumed 9-percent rate of return, will double in 8 years. It is important to note that when dealing with investments there is no guarantee. Values will fluctuate.

Therefore, as you monitor your retirement account, you want to watch the rates of return you are getting on your various fund accounts as well as what funds you are choosing. The company pension accounts should be reviewed quarterly with your financial professional who can assist you in selecting the most appropriate funds for your 401(k) or 403(b) program to position your portfolio for maximum earnings based on your risk tolerance. It is your responsibility to be proactive.

LIFE INSURANCE

Group term insurance is an inexpensive benefit. A face amount 2- or 3-times your annual salary is common in the employee benefits arena. This type of insurance provides death benefit protection only. Plus, it is available to your beneficiary only if you die while you are working. (Some pension plans also continue term insurance benefits.) Group term insurance is not portable; if your firm downsizes and you become outplaced, or you develop an illness that makes you uninsurable, you cannot take the term insurance with you when you leave the firm. Some insurance companies may provide an opportunity for you to convert group life insurance into a permanent life insurance policy.

Here is what you should ask about your *group term insurance* program:

- How many times (1x, 2x, 3x) your salary is provided?
- What is the shortfall of death benefit protection between what you have with your group coverage *vs.* what you need to adequately protect your family?
- Calculate the difference to determine the extent to which you are under-insured.
- Is any type of life insurance part of the company retirement package?

Employee benefits are a detailed and complex arena of understanding. Make sure all questions you have about benefits are answered in writing by a officer of your firm, or are documented in your firm's benefit handbook published for associates of the company. Each time you change firms, it is necessary to address changes in your group benefits and determine any adjustments you need to make to your short-term liquid savings account as well as your long-term insurance and investment portfolios.

A summary of all group benefits that you have with your firm is necessary for a complete analysis of your financial program. Your financial professional can assess all your current funds in relationship to the future and, at your next meeting, take time to explain how these group benefits need to be coordinated with your individual insurance and investment programs to accomplish your long-term goals.

STEP 9: COORDINATING COMPANY & PERSONAL PLANNING

Critical Mix of Protection

THE CORPORATE, PRIVATE BUSINESS, AND PROFESSIONAL WORLDS bring great benefits. Now that you understand the value of risk protection and investment growth you have with your firm, it is time for you and your financial professional to help you understand and coordinate the critical mix of protection necessary between group benefits and what you have as an individual to accomplish your long-term goals.

When your long-term goal is wealth accumulation, a basic premise is that after you are free of significant debt, **protection comes first.** That means protection of your income stream as well as your personal or business assets. No real financial growth can occur if either cash flow or assets are in jeopardy. Let's look at areas of vulnerability where group benefits can fall short of your total needs and where private individual protection needs to be supplemented.

PROPERTY & CASUALTY INSURANCE

For most Americans, the first type of insurance they obtain is property and casualty insurance (P&C) to protect an auto; this is followed by renter's or homeowner's insurance. My clients normally do not consider property and casualty insurance to be a part of their long-term planning, nor do they feel that it has any relationship at all to the benefits they may have with their company. But here is one critical aspect to consider. No true long-term financial program can be secure if you are personally exposed to loss of assets because of exposure to liability.

Many property and casualty insurance companies offer *personal*, *professional* and/or *commercial umbrella policies* to provide very high limits of excess liability coverage. If you are a parent with teenage children who drive, it is wise to have maximum liability protection. There are scores of heartbreaking stories regarding a teenage son or daughter who is the driver in an auto or boating accident which disfigures, or kills a child, another teenager, or pedestrian. If alcohol or substance abuse are also involved, the personal lawsuits, court cases and financial liabilities can devastate and ruin growing families.

People with high profile positions can also be accused of defamation of character, invasion of privacy, libel, or slander against which they lack protection.

Professionals such as physicians, agents, teachers, lawyers, accountants, druggists, real estate agents and architects, just to name a few, can obtain professional umbrella policies. Liability insurance for these individuals is also known as *malpractice insurance* or *errors and omissions* insurance, and it seeks to indemnify the professional for malpractice, mistakes or errors committed or alleged to have been committed while performing professional duties.

Various types of commercial liability protection can be obtained if you are a business owner and the nature of your business exposes you to liability such as libel, slander, defamation, unfair competition, idea misappropriation and the like.

Various types of umbrella policies can offer additional protection. Not all umbrella policies are the same. You should work closely with your property and casualty agent to carefully determine what coverage and type of policy will be the most beneficial regarding your type of risk exposure.

Qualified employee retirement plans are protected from general creditors. Cash value life insurance and annuities (in some states) may also be entitled to protection. **Assets that are exposed to general creditors include mutual funds, stocks, bonds, and certificates of deposit that are not within a qualified employee retirement plan.** It is important that your professional team be in contact with your property and casualty agent to assure that the values of all of your assets, in addition to your home, are taken into consideration when considering the correct amount of liability coverage necessary for you. You should always check with your attorney regarding the types of property protected from creditors in your jurisdiction.

DISABILITY INCOME PROTECTION

Between individual and group coverage, you are allowed approximately 60-70 percent of your gross income to be protected by disability income insurance. This puts you at a 30-40 percent shortfall in the event that you experience illness or disability; if you are relying on 10 percent for savings, your ability to accumulate savings is immediately thrown into jeopardy. For example, with a $100,000 income, the insurance companies would allow you up to 70 percent of your annual income, or $70,000 of annual disability income coverage.

As a side note, you should be aware that major changes are currently afoot in the disability income insurance marketplace. Many companies no longer offer this coverage because a large volume of claims is causing them extraordinary losses. Therefore, contract language is changing dramatically. For instance, at one time individual disability income policies had a lifetime *mental and nervous* provision; today that has been altered by many companies to cover a 2-year maximum benefit period only.

If a long-term disability program is offered as an employment benefit, you would lose the income replacement protection if you lost your position or chose to leave the firm. Therefore, it is wise to consider having an additional individual disability policy in order to maximize what is allowed. Your individual disability income protection policy is controlled by you because you are personally paying the premium and you will never lose coverage or protection as long as you pay your annual premium.

If 70 percent is the maximum coverage allowable in the event of a disability, it is advisable to become accustomed to living on 70 percent of your gross income. Put the remaining 30 percent away on a monthly basis to have available for emergency needs and wealth accumulation.

Another advantage to individual disability income programs has to do with taxes. Employer paid coverage is taxable income to you. However, if you own a non-cancelable individual policy, your benefit will be tax free.

For entrepreneurs without group benefits, individual coverage can be vital. Jim was out with his family on a Sunday afternoon at the lake. He tripped and fell off the pier and crushed his right hip. A visit to the clinic determined that surgery was needed. Because Jim was self-employed, the business couldn't operate without his presence; the injury prevented him from working for 6 months. His family relied on his income for the house payment, food and clothing, and utilities. Jim and Ellen had enough in their short-term savings to carry the business overhead as well as the household for 3 months. Expenses for the following 3 months were supported by his individual disability income protection policy. Jim was lucky because he and Ellen planned. However, he and Ellen still faced the worry of losing contracts and customers because of his absence.

Another case concerns Ann who is a psychologist, single, with a full patient load. She was happy and secure with her life when she experienced a severe auto accident. After months of therapy and having to cut back on seeing patients due to severe back pain, she was advised to have back surgery followed by more rest. Ann was fortunate to have an individual disability income policy that helped replace her income and assisted her in paying her personal expenses. However, Ann did not have a disability overhead expense program to pay for expenses at her professional office. She needed to cash in her IRA accounts to support the business expenses of $1,500 per month for 7 months due to a lag time in receivables. Ann was fortunate to have a $20,000 IRA account to cover the $10,500. However, her penalties were substantial. If Ann had had a business overhead expense policy, she could have left her IRA in place. She had no spouse or family who could help her. She worried about not being available to her patients and about being healthy enough to resume her patient work. Ann's total time away from her practice was 5 months.

LIFE INSURANCE

Life insurance is such a common benefit that group term insurance can be overrated and misunderstood as well. It is important to realize that term insurance carries death benefit protection only and accumulates no cash values. It is a wonderful benefit—if you are working.

Let's consider these common scenarios that are witnessed in my practice every week. Your management position at your company is redefined and rewritten, as many are in corporate America. With no union or advocate to protect your interests, your position is eliminated; you no longer have the coverage. You are now looking for other work. Under the stress during the months of the outplacement process, you may develop a condition or illness that causes you to lose your insurability, and you cannot get insurance. Another common situation occurs if you have been working outside the home for 30 or 35 years. It may be close to retirement time; suddenly you realize that you will outlive your job and have no insurance, plus you discover that term insurance is not extended as part of your retirement package. At age 60 or 65 you would face a high insurance premium at a time when you have lost your earning power; perhaps you even may be uninsurable for health reasons.

These are only a few reasons why everyone needs to have a properly designed insurance program that mixes group and individual coverages. When women first visit me for counsel, it has been frightening to see how many women have insurance only through their employer or firm. If you have diabetes, or have heart or stress problems that are documented through your medical coverage, or have a major illness and lose insurability, you may not be able to get any more insurance at the time of leaving the firm.

The additional life insurance program needs to be diversified so the premium can be easily accommodated with your discretionary income. Also consider the peace of mind of having a completed life insurance program by the time you wish to retire, rather than just beginning one! It does not make sense to have term insurance without cash value at work and also have an individually owned term insurance policy—unless you are aggressively putting money away on a monthly basis outside of work as well. That is to say if your accumulation program has not reached the point where you are placing monthly contributions to additional mutual funds or other investment vehicles, cash value insurance that will accumulate cash values over time is preferred over additional term insurance.

With our American culture and lifestyle expectations, the need for life insurance never goes away. If life insurance is analyzed in terms of cost outlay and return of premium, cash value type life insurance will be better economically over the long term. If we knew when we were going to die, then term insurance would be a very good buy from an economic standpoint.

PENSION AND INVESTMENTS

Retirement plans such as 401(k) or 403(b) are excellent only if you take full advantage of them. Your benefit department will inform you of the amount of money you are allowed to contribute to this program on a *pre-tax basis*. (This means that you pay tax on your income after the contribution has been made.) If an employer is matching 3 percent in your 401(k) and you are saving 3 percent, that means that 6 percent of the gross income is being saved on a monthly basis for future retirement. Income that does not pass through your hands through such payroll deduction or deposit methods is unavailable for you to spend. That helps assure it will go toward your future goals.

Let's assume that you earn a $100,000 income. Six percent equals $6,000 on an annual basis, or $500 monthly. Assuming that a 9-interest rate is maintained, after 20 years the 401(k) would be worth $334,587. That's great accumulation from income that never passed through your hands.

Investments in 401(k) or 403(b) plans are portable if you lose your position or leave the firm. Whatever you have accumulated can be *rolled over* into an individual retirement (IRA) account for the purpose of avoiding taxes on the sum when you leave the firm. In the meantime, your investment reserve can continue to grow in a diversified portfolio and be available at age 59 1/2 or later. When you retire and are ready to use the monthly income, you then pay tax on the accumulated amount based on your income tax bracket. Such retirement plans are forced accumulation vehicles with distinct tax advantages.

At this point you understand what you can lose when you lose group benefits. You know why it is necessary for individual insurance and investment programs to coordinate with your group benefits. You know that you must calculate your short-term savings to cover shortfalls in personal and business cash flow which is left unprotected. If you are an entrepreneur, you also know that both your personal cash flow as well as your business overhead need to be protected. These are 3 important principles in protecting your earnings stream and existing assets and savings from jeopardy. When you have addressed these, you are well on your way to having the peace of mind that you are protected from financial jeopardy due to risk and that protection will enable you to begin **aggressively** pursuing your desire for wealth accumulation.

STEP 10: LEARNING HOW TO DIVERSIFY SAVINGS, INSURANCE & INVESTMENTS FOR NOW & THE FUTURE

Diversification

NOW YOU'RE AT THE POINT WHERE YOU UNDERSTAND THE NEED to protect your cash flow and assets while you plan an aggressive financial strategy. The next logical question is what do I do now? You're waiting for an analysis of your financial condition and recommendations.

All future planning must first consider the time period required to achieve a goal. *Short-term goals* are defined as 1- through 3-year goals. *Long-term goals* are 4 years and longer until the projected time when the money is needed.

As mentioned above, debt reduction and building short-term savings for emergency funds are generally considered short-term needs. Long-term needs are those such as retirement, funding a college education, paying off a mortgage, business succession arrangements, estate tax needs, leaving a legacy to heirs, insurance for the purpose of charitable giving to a religious, medical or art institution, and the like. It is key to select the proper funding vehicles so that you are not subject to surrender fees or sizable loss due to market fluctuations.

I am reminded of a client who told me a story about her plan to accumulate money for a 3- to 5-year period for a down payment to purchase her first home on her own. Karyn was young and out of college, totally trusting, and wasn't comfortable asking many questions. The agent who was selling her auto insurance suggested that she begin placing her money in an annuity; this Karyn did. The agent totally lost sight of Karyn's need to withdraw the money in 3 to 5 years. For her purpose, an annuity was an inappropriate product to accomplish her goal. As we have seen, annuities are designed as long-term products to be considered for income after the age of 59 1/2. When Karyn proceeded to take her money out of her annuity to buy her house, she was devastated to be charged substantial IRS withdrawal penalties; mutual funds would have been a better choice.

It's time for you to come to grips with the jargon you'll hear on that next interview with your financial professional. Don't worry! It's okay to be clueless. The insurance and the investment world is complicated. It takes years for your agent, registered representative, or financial planner to learn and apply knowledge. So do not be embarrassed about what you do not understand. It's a must for you to ask questions and share your feelings. Your counsel is there to teach you. After all, that's what you are paying for! If all you wanted was to purchase a product, you could do it by mail—as you do with catalogue purchases. Remember, you are in control. If it seems that the agent, registered representative, or financial planner is not explaining financial concepts in a way that you understand, just stop; slow down the conversation and ask questions—many questions. Even if you feel secure in knowing what's available in the financial marketplace for your personal needs, perhaps you are contemplating starting your own business. The world of insurance and investments for business needs is another world—equally complex.

People who have accumulated sizeable assets both understand and adhere to the concept of *portfolio diversification.* (It means that your total financial program incorporates life insurance, mutual funds, stocks, bonds, and/or other investments.) Diversification requires a fundamental understanding that each of the various products in the financial marketplace is designed differently to accomplish certain goals. Some are more appropriate for certain needs than others. Some are totally inappropriate.

So let's learn from Karyn and go back to the classroom. Our objective isn't to learn all the details and features about every product in the financial marketplace. That's the domain of your professional team. But you do want to acquire a broad understanding of the types of products available. One client used an analogy that I will remember forever. She equated the diversification process to learning about fabrics. Denim is strong, sturdy, and hot. It's great for western riding wear but you wouldn't wear it to work in a professional office setting. Pima cotton breathes and is absorbent; it's best suited for hot climates, but you wouldn't want a winter coat made of it. Polyester needs no ironing, wears well and is lightweight, but you wouldn't select it for your wedding dress. All fabrics work best for the purpose for which they are tailored. Chances are that your wardrobe contains denim, cotton, polyester, wool, silk, and linen to name a few—diverse fabrics for a variety of needs. The same holds true with tailoring a diversified financial portfolio.

Now, let's go to class. Diversification 101. Keep in mind, this is a quick survey about the types of vehicles on the market today.[22] Be certain to discuss them in detail with your financial professional who is qualified to teach you about how each product works and what it can or can not achieve relative to your individual needs.

There are many concepts to consider when making decisions about accumulating money based on your goal or purpose for having the money. Your personal or business needs determine how the portfolio should be diversified. There is not one single product or investment that is designed to be a total answer for short- and long-term needs, wants, and desires. If the goal is to have a short-term savings account that can be easily accessible for emergency needs, there are several ways to accomplish this. These include an interest-paying money market account with a checkbook, a bank savings account, saving through credit union payroll deduction, and a certificate of deposit.

Depending on your ability to pay and the time available to accomplish your goals, designing a properly diversified portfolio can satisfy your needs. When you begin to contribute to stocks, bonds, and mutual funds, a professional *risk tolerance questionnaire* must be completed to analyze how much you are willing to risk at various returns, with various levels of guarantee including no guarantee. (The *American Dream Woman: Handbook and Planning Guide* provides a detailed questionnaire and explanation.) The process of investing in mutual funds, stocks, and bonds differs from investing in certificates of deposit because CDs are FDIC insured and offer a guaranteed rate of return; however, investment in securities will fluctuate.

BANK SAVINGS ACCOUNTS

Checking accounts, money market accounts, NOW accounts, share draft accounts, and savings accounts are easily recognized as vehicles available to you through banks, savings and loan associations, and your credit union. On a trip to the bank, you can learn about the fees and interest rates of a variety of accounts. U. S. Government savings bonds are also readily available through these institutions as well as through payroll deduction. EE-bonds pay a variable rate of interest, tied to an index of Treasury bills if they are held at least 5 years. They are redeemable for cash at any time after the first 6 months.

SECURITIES: MUTUAL FUNDS, STOCKS & BONDS

Securities provide an opportunity to invest, for capital appreciation and for tax-free returns. **Understand that very few securities come with any insurance or any guarantee of return.** You should consider working with an experienced registered representative or financial planner to decide which investments are most appropriate for you. Always remember it is your personal responsibility to monitor the performance of these investments and make adjustments accordingly.

Mutual funds are commonly used vehicles for long-term investment goals such as retirement and college education. Remember, due to fluctuations in value, there is no guarantee that your goals will be reached. If your desire is strictly to invest to educate your children through college in 15 years, or to pay off your mortgage early, you may consider mutual fund investing. You can add to your mutual fund account monthly or do lump sum investing as bonuses or additional money come your way.

With a mutual fund, you can put your money into a variety of funds. These different funds may place money in common stocks, corporate bonds, tax-free bonds, or even in a fund that invests in short-term corporate debts. Mutual funds are pooled together (thus the term *mutual*) under professional management. A mutual fund provides ready access to your money although you may have to take a loss if you sell some shares when the market is down. A mutual fund also allows you to elect automatic reinvestment so that fund dividends which accrue are immediately put back into the fund to buy more shares.

Different mutual funds have different objectives—income, growth or aggressive growth. Your financial professional will review the mutual fund with you to point these out. (A *prospectus* is required with all securities purchases; it is the official document which describes the securities being offered for sale. When issued for a mutual fund, it describes the history, background of managers, fund objectives, charges and expenses, a financial statement, and other essential data to help you make an informed decision.)

Before you make a final selection, have answers to the following:

- Does the fund charge an initial *load*? (The financial services industry refers to this sales fee as a load. You may also hear the terms: *front-end load* and *back-end load*. These refer to when you pay the fee. Front-end load means it is paid at the time of your initial purchase. Back-end load means it is paid sometime in the future as defined in the prospectus.)
- What is the minimum amount you must purchase as well as the minimum increments required for additional purchases?
- Can you exchange or switch between funds with changing market conditions?

Treasury bills are fixed-income securities for large amounts that are issued by the U. S. Government. They can be purchased for a fee through your registered representative (licensed Series 7), a commercial bank, or a Federal Reserve Bank. Treasure bills are guaranteed by the U. S. Government, and if held to maturity, they offer a fixed rate of return.

Buying *common stock* is buying a portion of the corporation that issues the stock. You are becoming an owner, and your stock will grow or decline along with the performance of the company. Return on an investment is never guaranteed.

When you buy *bonds* you are becoming a creditor of the issuing corporation or government—thus the name corporate bonds or municipal bonds. You are lending money; in exchange, you receive periodic interest for the use of your money. When the bond is matured, you will receive the return of your original principal. Bonds are issued with maturity periods of varying lengths, and the market value can fluctuate until maturity. Bonds offer a fixed rate of return if held to maturity.

In the case of all securities purchases, seek a licensed and experienced financial professional who will teach you to understand what you are buying and communicate with you throughout the process.

LIFE INSURANCE

Insurance accomplishes what no other financial product can. Generally, the death benefit paid is higher than the amount of premiums paid regardless of when death occurs. Don't ever accept a stock broker telling you that you don't need insurance. Nor should you ever accept an insurance agent ever telling you that you don't need to purchase stock or mutual funds. Each vehicle has a role in a diversified portfolio.

Here are a just a few distinguishing principles about life insurance:

- Cash value life insurance provides *tax deferred growth.* (Life insurance is tax deferred, which means when your cash value life insurance accumulates, you do not pay current income taxes on that growth as you would with a CD or regular savings account.)
- Life insurance can create an income tax-free death benefit to those who are heirs or beneficiaries.
- Most personal life insurance policies provide a guaranteed death benefit as long as premiums have been paid according to the provisions of the policy.
- You can borrow on your cash value life insurance as you would a loan with an interest rate that is generally lower than the prevailing market rate. You can receive money tax-free unlike surrendering a policy for the cash values and paying tax on all money received above the basis amount (as long as the policy is not classified as a modified endowment and remains inforce.) A loan will also reduce the death benefit.
- You can also pay back the amount of money borrowed plus interest from the policy to reestablish the values of the policy.

Here are several practical applications of these principles. Cash value types of life insurance are commonly used for tax deferred growth. In some states, generally the cash value is considered a protected asset. In other words, if you were a high profile professional who is exposed to lawsuit, the cash values in your life insurance may be protected from creditors. (Check with local counsel.)

Life insurance is the only vehicle that has a higher face value than the dollars put into it. For example, depending on your circumstances, a $250,000 insurance policy may only have a $1,500 annual premium, but in the event of death, the beneficiaries receive the full $250,000 as long as premiums have been paid. The beneficiary also receives the face value amount as an income tax-free benefit. It may be subject to estate taxes, but it is not subject to federal income tax.

Participating whole life policies may declare dividends which are generally considered to be a return of premium and not subject to income tax until the amount received exceeds your premium dollars spent. Dividends are never guaranteed or estimates of future growth.

Life insurance also allows you to borrow the cash values in an emergency and pay the interest while not having to declare the values as income while the policy is inforce and as long as it is not a modified endowment. This can work well for liquid needs prior to age 59 1/2 unlike an annuity, 401(k), or 403(b) that carry IRS penalties for early withdrawal.

In addition to asset protection, the primary purpose of life insurance is to provide financial protection for the beneficiaries. If you are a working mother with young children, life insurance can help pay for child care and maintaining their standard of living in the event of your death. If you are a homemaker, life insurance could help pay the cost for the domestic services you provide to the family in the event of your death. If you are married in a dual income family, life insurance can help replace the income lost in the event of one of the wage earners. If you and your spouse were pooling income for a mortgage, life insurance could help the survivor to keep the property in the event the other dies. If you are single, cash value life insurance can help provide support to your aging parents if they survive you. Or if you are single and do not die, life insurance can be used to help fund your retirement years. If you are a partner in a business, life insurance can help assure the business will continue uninterrupted in the event that one partner dies.

There are many needs for life insurance; therefore, diversification is generally required when determining the type of product and the amount of insurance that is needed, the premium payment you can afford according to your budget, and what cash value you need for a particular goal. Also, there are many specific product names used by each company (like a brand name) for each of these products. It can be overwhelming. But think of it as analogous to various types of automobiles. Mercedes, Volvo, Volkswagen, Jeep, Corvette are brand names. In addition, there are generic style categories defined by the purpose for which the car was designed by which any car can be identified. These include luxury, family sedan, compact, sport utility, and high performance, respectively.

The following are the basic categories of life insurance for which each company is sure to have registered brand names. Whatever the name or the style, life insurance is also considered a long-term vehicle.

Term life insurance creates no cash build up and provides only death benefit life insurance for a specified period of time (thus the name *term*). Again, there are varieties of term for different purposes. It can be *convertible* into a cash value type without requiring that you have a medical examination. The premium is also based on your age and health when you purchase it, or it can have a level premium for a specified time such as 5, 10 or 15 years. After that, it can be *renewable*.

Whole life insurance offers long-term protection at a fixed premium while cash values build. The premium is based on your age and health when you purchase the policy. If you no longer need life insurance and you reach retirement age, you can use the cash value to buy an annuity that can provide monthly payments for as long as you live. There are many ways you can use whole life, and it is very versatile.

Traditional cash value insurance is conservative. As a result, to respond more quickly to attractive interest rates cycles, newer types of life insurance have been created in the last 20 years to offer yields that directly reflect interest rates and short-term investments.

Universal life insurance lets you pay premiums at any time, in any amount, subject to certain minimums. You can also change the amount of insurance or death benefit more easily than with traditional policies. The amount the cash value increases each year reflects the interest which is earned on the insurance company's investments. Because this is so flexible, universal life insurance can be used to meet changing lifelong needs.

Variable life insurance allows cash values to fluctuate according to the investment results of separate accounts. These can be equity securities, money market instruments, or bonds. There is a minimum invested in a guaranteed death benefit, but death benefit proceeds can be higher depending on the earnings of the separate accounts.

When teaching you about which life insurance products are best for your portfolio, the career life insurance agent's value becomes evident. Remember, in order to purchase the variable life products which have earnings driven by short-term market values, the agent needs to be a registered representative with a broker/ dealer as well as a licensed agent with the company whose products she or he is selling. A detailed prospectus must be provided to you when discussing variable life insurance.

ANNUITIES

Annuities are distinctive insurance products that provide income for a specified number of years or for life. They are frequently used to provide retirement income. Annuities typically are the vehicles used to pay out earnings for state lotteries. You can buy an annuity during your working years on an installment basis with regular annual payments. You can also buy an annuity with a single lump-sum premium with annuity payments to begin at the time of purchase, or at some future time such as retirement. (The latter is known as a *single premium deferred annuity.*) With any annuity, if owned by an individual, income accumulates tax deferred until it is withdrawn.

Annuities give you a choice of several pay-out options. A *straight-life annuity* pays you an income for life with no subsequent payment due to anyone else; these can have the largest payouts.

A *life annuity with installments certain* also pays you income for life, but if you die within a specified period of years, payments for the balance of the specified period are paid to your beneficiary.

The *refund annuity* guarantees payment for life or at least until the payments equal the premium paid into the contract. If you die before that time, a refund will be made to your beneficiary.

A *joint and survivor annuity* provides payments for as long as you and your designated survivor live.

A *fixed dollar annuity* is invested in fixed-income securities such as bonds and mortgages. You may receive more than expected but are guaranteed a minimum return.

A *variable annuity* differs from the others because it allows the contractholder to choose how purchase payments are allocated among subaccounts with a variety of investment objectives. A variable annuity is considered to be a security, and the contractholder bears the risk—both of return and loss of principal.

A variable annuity has your premiums invested in stock and bond portfolios. It can be more or less than you expect, but a minimum death benefit is guaranteed. Which one you choose depends on your resources and your risk tolerance profile. No variable annuity can be discussed without a prospectus, and you can purchase a variable annuity only from a registered representative.

Regardless of the type of annuity or payout you seek, here are questions your counsel should answer and help you understand before making your final selection:

- What are the penalties for early withdrawal of your money?
- Is there a minimum interest rate guaranteed in the contract?
- What are the administrative charges or fees?
- Can the interest rates fluctuate? If so, how often?

Some states have listed annuities along with life insurance as protected assets. That means that the values you contribute to an annuity may be protected from creditors; check with your local counsel. This becomes an excellent addition to your portfolio if you are exposed to lawsuit.

Annuities would not be recommended for a young couple who wants to fund their children's college education if they need to withdraw the money prior to the parents reaching age 59 1/2. They would be subject to additional IRS tax penalties upon surrender of the cash value.

STEP 11: CONTROLLING THE BUYING PROCESS

Being in the Know

SOME OF MY WOMEN CLIENTS WOULD TELL ME ABOUT THEIR FEAR of making a buying decision. Many just "freeze" when it comes time to decide. All agree that they rarely want "to sign anything" on a first interview and that they want "to take time to think about it." I often hear, "I've read and learned a little about mutual funds and insurance, but how do I know what my agent is recommending is right for me?"

DEMAND TO BE TAUGHT

Understanding key financial concepts goes a long way toward building your confidence. Demand study materials and start the process of learning. As mentioned at the outset, asking questions and learning before making decisions defines a key way women buy; so do not skip this process.

Instead, get excited and feel good because you have become responsible; you are in control. You are no longer a passenger; you are in the driver's seat. Consider it just as you do when buying a car. The research, the decision, and the final choice about how the vehicle fits your short-term and long-term needs are yours. You are going to be paying for the car, and you are going to own it. The same is true of each vehicle in your portfolio. It's time to get tough. Treat your financial future the same as if you were buying your car or your house—treat it like a major purchase that will have long-lasting consequences. In truth, your financial decisions have even longer consequences—far longer than any choice about your wardrobe, your house, your car, and yes, even the choice about your life partner.

Turn fright into might by being in the know. It's time women turn their timidity about financial affairs into action. An angry widow once told me, "For years men have been making decisions about family and retirement finances. Yet, women outlive men; therefore, we must live with those decisions."

At this point in the process, you are ready for a second interview to hear recommendations. You have considered your current situation as well as wants, needs and desires for your future. Recap the planning you have accomplished to this point and assure your final selection fits your goals.

- You know and have listed each of your monthly expenses and debt load for your household as well as your business.
- You have calculated your short-term savings for emergency protection needs to cover your overhead and expenses for a 3-to 6-month period.
- You have listed your personal short- and long-term desires.
- You understand what insurance protection you already have to protect your assets: home, personal property, earning and income stream, business cash flow, business continuation, life and estate (if your assets are worth $600,000 or more).
- You have assured that an up-to-date will has been prepared that states your wishes for your family and beneficiaries in the event of your death.
- You understand the results of your risk tolerance questionnaire.
- You understand what value the dollar might have when you are retirement age.
- You have begun to calculate the cost of your lifestyle needs at retirement.
- You have calculated how much you must save based on your expected rate of return to satisfy your wants, needs, and desires.
- You have determined if and how you need to alter your saving and spending patterns to accomplish your goals over the next 10, 15, 20, 25, or 30 years.
- You have demanded that your financial professional explains the role of each product in your **current** portfolio and how it addresses your goals for the long term.
- You have demanded that your financial professional explain any **additional** recommendations and products that you will purchase in terms of your plans for the future.

Whatever your time allows, it is necessary that you demand that your financial professional teach you about how the pieces in your portfolio work together to accomplish your protection and accumulation goals. This can help assure that your portfolio is diversified and in your best interests. The one most important thing you can do is ask questions, ask more questions and then ask again. You must demand that you be taught.

DEMAND COMMUNICATION AMONG YOUR PROFESSIONAL TEAM

Do not assume that what a financial professional recommends is what you feel you need. Perhaps an agent is not licensed to sell you what you really need. You must feel comfortable and certain that you are part of the sales process and that your life, your occupation, your expenses, what kinds of risks you are willing to take with your money, your dreams, and your desires have been considered. You must feel with great confidence that your financial program has been designed for only you. A single woman who has benefits as an employee in the corporate world has different needs than a married or divorced woman attempting to educate children through college. The right recommendations and proposed solutions to help assure asset protection and your accumulation goals depend on your lifestyle. Therefore, you should not get the feeling that your agent sells the same product and the same amount to everyone.

On the second interview, if your financial professional seems to be impatient with you for asking questions or gives you answers that you still do not understand, then most likely your best interests are not being met and the relationship will not last for the long term. Again, here is yet another step where you can feel lucky that you've seen the light before a buying decision has been made. As mentioned before, recommending that your agent, registered representative, or financial planner communicate decisions with your certified public accountant and your attorney creates another set of checks and balances and *professional accountability* among your professional team that is sure to serve *your* best interests.

If you are satisfied that your agent, registered representative, or financial planner in conjunction with your certified public accountant and attorney have attended to the items listed above, then you have developed a confidence that they are working in your best interests.

(. . . At this point, let's assume that you and your financial professional concur on what you need to secure your protection and accumulation needs and the appropriate products to consider based on those needs. We now complete the cycle of decision making and the final 2 steps in the process—purchasing a product, committing to review your progress over the long term, and making adjustments when necessary. . . .)

STEP 12: SELECTING A COMPANY & PRODUCT

Does the Company Really Matter?

WOMEN BUY BASED ON RELATIONSHIPS FIRST, AND THEN THEY MUST believe that the company whose product they choose is strong, stable and reputable. Men will follow the challenge of a "hot lead" to invest in a new product or maverick business venture. The majority of women I've serviced in my career take a more conservative approach.

You must feel comfortable about the company you choose. Many companies that have been around for 100 years or more have demonstrated that they can weather the strong currents, tides and storms of economic cycles. Whereas, a company that has been established for 10 years may not have yet demonstrated a similar ability to remain steadfast through economic hardship.

There are many questions to ask your financial professional about the company and the product you plan to purchase:

- Given the product you are purchasing, is there marketing information that discusses its performance over time and how it compares with similar products in the marketplace?
- If it is a company whose name you are not familiar with, have you checked with your state insurance department about whether the company is licensed in your state?
- If you are considering mutual funds or securities, what is their 3-, 5- or 10-year past performance, including sales charges?
- What is the company's philosophy about service? Can you call the company directly with questions or must you go through the local office?
- What is the company's main product emphasis? In what does the company excel?
- What technical expertise does the company offer your agent, registered representative or financial planner?
- How often will the company send you regular correspondence by which you can track or monitor the performance of the product you are buying?
- If you are making an insurance purchase, is the company you select a stock company or mutual company? As a policyholder of a *mutual life insurance*

company, you are considered to be an "owner" of the company. All policyholders share the profits by means of dividends, if one is declared.

- How is the company rated by Standard and Poor's, A. M. Best, Duff and Phelps, and Moody's ratings agencies?

ABOUT RATINGS

My experience has been that male clients and agents when placed in a competitive sales situation, tend to place more emphasis on the ratings of a company than do women buyers or women sellers. Ratings have certainly become a higher profile issue over the past few years as a result of failures and the financial difficulties of some companies in the financial services industry. As a result, the ratings agencies that had been more conservative are also looking at short-term performance or real estate performance rather than maintaining a past conservative posture based on performance over time.

AAA, A+ Superior, A-, B+, BBB . . . There is a wide variety in increments in the "ratings alphabet game" within a company as well as among ratings agencies. There are several ratings levels that will indicate whether or not the company you have chosen is "investment grade" or below. Remember, rating a mutual insurance company as if it were a company which performs in the capital markets is not comparing apples to apples. There are many A minus or B grade rated companies that are still considered "investment grade." It is equally important to review information about the past performance over time of the product you plan to purchase.

Also beware of the individual ratings agencies that have been in business less than 20 years—time has not yet enabled them to earn their wings, so it would be imprudent for you to base your decision exclusively on their opinion. If you are compelled to compare ratings, do so with the long-standing and established ratings agencies listed above. If you are reviewing insurance companies, keep in mind that A. M. Best is the ratings agency with the longest experience in rating insurance companies.

A. M. Best Company, Inc., the oldest rating agency for the life insurance industry, reviews more than 1,700 life insurers and assigns ratings to more than half of them. They have been doing so since 1905, and for many years, A. M. Best was the only rating agency evaluating insurers on a basis of financial performance and operating conditions.

Recently, additional rating agencies have begun looking at the insurance industry on the basis of claims paying ability. Each has a strong history of rating the financial soundness of bonds and other instruments across a broad range of industries.

Standard and Poor's rates about 150 companies. Moody's Investors Service issues ratings on about 75 insurers, and Duff & Phelps Credit Rating Co. issues ratings on about 50 insurers. [23]

The ratings review process by the ratings agencies is an annual or semi-annual cycle. The actuarial, financial, and investment data that the agencies review is slow to change. It is highly unlikely that ratings will drop or increase dramatically within a short 1- to 3-year period. Therefore, a consumer is more confident if a financial professional understands his or her company's investment strategies and financial management goals. Eric Nordman of the NAIC adds, "In addition, state insurance regulators audit an insurer's books and records on a regular basis to be sure that the insurer is complying with state laws and is carefully managing the funds entrusted to the insurer by its policyholders. In the event an insurer is declared insolvent, the state will take over the assets of the insurer and manage them for the benefit of policyholders. Certain protections are also provided by guaranty funds which serve as an extra layer of protection in the event of insurer insolvency."

DIRECT COMMUNICATION

Ratings and the inner workings of an insurance or financial institution's investments are an extremely complex dimension of the world of finance. By asking the questions listed above, you will ascertain how informed your financial professional is about the inner workings of the company. You will ascertain how well they have access and the opportunity for direct communication to the top management of the firm. Other members of your professional team—your certified public accountant and attorney—will likewise offer opinions. They are professionals in different fields, so keep their opinions in perspective with those of professionals in the insurance, finance, and investment industries.

It is important to understand the true direction of the insurance or investment company—above and beyond any media flurry that happens to hit the morning news. Be wary of uninformed lay people making emotional judgments without total knowledge or information about a company. Before you make a decision "to buy" or "not to buy" based on what you read in the newspaper, consider the following:

- Beware of incomplete or one-sided reporting and sensationalism.
- Verify the credentials and financial acumen of the reporter who prepared the coverage—not the big name anchor reading the report. If the reporter is not trained in the technical world of insurance and/or investments, chances are high that the story is not complete. Seek supplementary opinions from those professionals with credentials in finance, insurance or investments. This is yet another instance when having a financial professional with credentials is worth its weight in gold to you.
- Talk with your financial professional to understand the company's position and response to the issue.

In recent years, I've witnessed much media attention directed towards the financial services industry. Incomplete understanding of company long-term investment strategies and uninformed media coverage stirred by lay reporters aspiring for recognition can cause consumer panic. If you suspect that a company is in jeopardy, a sure sign of its financial strength and internal communication is to ask your professional about her/his own personal funds. It is likely that she/he is confident in the company and is not withdrawing personal funds. If she is moving her money, then it's time for you to reconsider your funds.

Ultimately, the company that is managing your money recognizes both moral and *fiduciary* responsibilities to manage your money according to sound business and investment practices. On the other hand, news reporters advocate a professional concern for the public's "need to know." Do not confuse the media's need to know with a financial institution's responsibility to do what's best for your money 40 years from now. By then the reporter will be covering another story.

Remember, your financial strategies for long-term accumulation rely on long-term performance over 10, 20, 30 or 40 years. Focusing on daily or weekly fluctuations in investments and markets is more appropriate if you are monitoring higher risk short-term vehicles. To make decisions about long-term performing vehicles based on day-to-day market fluctuations or semi-annual ratings changes does not fit with the purpose of a long-term goal of solid performance over time.

Application, Approval & Annual Review

HAVING SELECTED YOUR COMPANY OF CHOICE AND THE PRODUCT best suited to your protection and accumulation goals, you apply for the product. When purchasing a securities product, your registered representative should help you determine your suitability for that product. This is to safeguard that the vehicle you've selected for your long-term goal is appropriate for you. If you have the cash, there are no limits to the amount of mutual funds or securities you can choose. Life insurance is very different indeed.

If you have become uninsurable or currently suffer from a terminal or incurable disease, chances are high that no amount of cash in the world will enable you to purchase life insurance. Because the purchase of life insurance provides a payout that can exceed the premiums paid into it over time in the event that you die, there is more involved in the application and *underwriting* process by which an insurance company determines whether or not you are able to purchase its product. (The *underwriting* process is the means whereby the insurance company determines if you are an acceptable risk for the company at this point in your life. It determines the risk in terms of your medical history, income, credit history, and lifestyle.)

LIFE INSURANCE APPLICATION & UNDERWRITING

The underwriting process for the purchase of life insurance begins when you complete a detailed application. Group life insurance or payroll deduction life insurance programs through an employer can often have *simplified underwriting* that asks a limited number of health and risk related questions. However, an application for individual life insurance contains pages of detailed questions about your medical history; some companies ask about the health of your parents. It is imperative that you answer these questions truthfully. If on the application, you omit major surgery or an illness which is part of a physician's clinical or hospital records, it will likely be discovered later by means of the information systems used by most insurance companies. Forgetting or intentionally omitting information will only slow the underwriting process. Remember, the application itself carries your signature and is considered to be a legal document. If you omit medical information which is later discovered, and if you die within the *contestability period*

(2 years following issuance of the policy), falsification of information can nullify your beneficiaries' claim to the death benefit proceeds. It only stands to reason that the higher face amount of insurance you apply for the longer and more tedious the underwriting investigation is.

Do not be surprised if, after spending time with your agent to complete a detailed application, a representative of the insurance company calls you to verify the information. This again is part of a checks and balances procedure taken and paid for by the insurance companies on your behalf to assure that all the information on the application that you have signed is thorough and accurately represented by the agent who recorded the data.

In addition to the application, a medical or paramedical exam, weight check, urine specimen, and blood test are often routinely requested as part of the underwriting process. These are done at the insurance company's expense, and some companies will even provide you copies of the results. These tests help detect major medical conditions. It is not uncommon for clients to learn of their own medical conditions as a result of the insurance underwriting process! Circumstances which can affect your status of insurability and/or the premium rate charged to you are commonly discovered through the medical underwriting process. These may include HIV infection, diabetes, high cholesterol, smoking, and drug use.

Some companies will not issue insurance if you have a serious pre-existing condition; other companies will issue insurance but may do so with a higher premium. This is known as being issued a *rated policy*. Insurance companies have devised many rating levels depending on the condition and how advanced it is. Likewise, having surgery for a major illness such as cancer does not mean that you will never again qualify for insurance. After a period of 5 or more years, if you are in remission and show evidence of good health, it may be possible that you would be *insurable* again.

In addition to health risks, the underwriting process uncovers lifestyle risks. Clients with certain stressful or dangerous occupations or hobbies such as car racing, motorcycle riding, sky diving, flying, or boating are exposed to higher risks than the majority of the population. This, likewise, can affect premium rates. For an insurance company to obtain a motor vehicle report (MVR) from your state department or bureau of motor vehicles is a routine procedure in the insurance underwriting process. Evidence of speeding tickets, points on your record, moving violations, suspension of license, or driving while under the influence can impact not only whether or not a company will issue you life insurance, but also whether or not the policy is rated.

It is also common for an insurance company to review your credit report and income as part of the underwriting process. The standard credit reports also help a company assess whether you correctly stated your outstanding loans and debts on the application and whether your debt load is such that you will be able to make routine premium payments. This affects whether the policy may be likely to lapse due to unpaid premiums.

The professional underwriters at the insurance company are looking at your entire lifestyle. The more they know about each individual, the faster and easier is the underwriting process. The length of underwriting varies among companies and can be 5 days to 6 months depending on the complexity of the case, the number of people applying for insurance, and the amount of insurance being requested.

A group of business partners in a professional firm or corporation applying for life insurance on each other to protect the interests of the corporation would experience a more lengthy underwriting process than would an individual. If underwriters are underwriting a group life insurance policy, they no longer look at only one individual but assess the risk for everyone within the group. This also can take longer because there can be 20 or more people in the group. Each individual as well as the group as a whole determines whether the insurance company underwriters will make a decision to insure the group at all and whether or not the company will rate the premium for the group. Your agent's office staff will keep you informed about the progress of underwriting.

DISABILITY INCOME INSURANCE UNDERWRITING

Not all life insurance companies offer disability income insurance. For those that do, the underwriting process for disability income insurance is very different than underwriting for life insurance. You cannot apply for disability income unless you are employed in a full-time position. At application time, the insurance company will request your federal income tax returns for the past 2 years as proof of income.

Not all occupations qualify to be issued disability income insurance. The risk of the occupation and health of the insured are the most important factors in determining the premium amount charged. The type of coverage available differs based on occupational risk. For example, a certified public accountant will have a lower cost per thousand dollars of insurance than an electrician. Also, the certified public accountant will be able to receive a more liberal definition of coverage than the electrician. The certified public accountant can also have a longer benefit period —age 65. The electrician probably could only receive a maximum benefit payout for 5 years.

ABOUT BINDING AN APPLICATION

Binding an application is achieved when you pay the first month's premium at the time you apply for the coverage and meet all other requirements of the insurance company (which will be spelled out in the binder.) It is a further safeguard for your benefit.

A colleague told me a story about his client that illustrates why it is a good idea to pay the first premium when you submit an application for insurance. Tim wanted disability income protection, and based on company guidelines, he would qualify for a $3,000 monthly benefit based on his income. After completing the application with the agent, Tim chose not to pay 1 month's premium at the time. Tim did not have his checkbook handy, and he requested that he not pay until he knew the policy would be issued.

The agent arranged for blood testing, which Tim later canceled because he was busy traveling. He told the paramedics who were scheduling the blood test that he would not be available for a couple of weeks.

In the mean time, Tim had a serious automobile accident in which he sustained extensive back and leg injuries. If Tim had paid the first month's premium, completed the blood test, and had good health records, the insurance company would have most likely issued the disability policy. Instead, the agent notified the insurance company, and the insurance company stopped the underwriting process. Tim's coverage was not issued and according to industry practice, he had become *uninsurable*.

PRODUCT DELIVERY

Do not take for granted that the product you thought you were buying is the product that actually is delivered. Take special care to cross check all documents —whether you are buying life insurance, disability income protection, mutual funds or other securities. If you receive a contract or policy that is different than what you applied for or agreed to purchase, be certain to clarify this with your agent, registered representative or financial planner. It could have happened in error; it also could be done if your policy was rated. Do not accept or sign any documents unless you are totally comfortable.

If a life insurance company agrees to issue a rated policy, it is confirmation that your risk level is higher than normal. Accept the rated policy and consider the higher premium as worth the price. If the rating is due to a health problem, it may correct itself with time and someday the rating may be removed. Most companies are responsive about removing ratings in time if they see that a health condition has subsided or has been eliminated; however, you should take it upon yourself to notify your agent or your insurer if your condition improves. You should accept the rated policy—which may be your only chance to obtain life or disability income insurance. You could also invest your money in mutual funds at any time because you do not need to demonstrate positive health results to purchase mutual funds or securities. But if you do have a rated condition, your health could also degenerate to a point where you could be uninsurable and unable to purchase any life insurance at any cost—not even on a rated basis.

Disability policies are sometimes issued with a rider *excluding present health condition.* This means that the company is issuing the disability income protection policy, but it has chosen not to cover a health condition listed in the application. For instance, if you had fibroid breast tumors and became disabled due to a condition related to that, the coverage would not be paid; however, if you were in an accident and became disabled you would have the protection. In some instances, the company will add the rider and will agree to consider removing it after a 2-year review. That means if you pass 2 years and medical records prove that the condition has been eliminated, you could have the restriction removed from your policy. If you choose to accept the policy with the limitation, notify your agent or insurer if your condition improves.

Approach receiving an insurance policy as you would accepting your warranty on a new car purchase. Here are some checks and balances on your behalf:

- In most cases it is not recommended to have the agent mail the policy to you. To do so, you miss out on a face-to-face review of your policy relative to your needs.
- Verify that the coverage you received is the coverage you agreed to at a premium that is affordable to you.
- Check your policy before placing your signature on the policy delivery receipt.
- Never let an agent keep your policy or contract on file in the office.

Policy delivery is truly an exciting time. Not everyone can obtain insurance—if they are not healthy and no matter how rich they are. The policy is a legal contract between you and the life insurance company. The *delivery receipt* is also a legal document that confirms that you have the policy in your possession and that it is accurate according to your needs. If you are uncertain about anything, do not sign the delivery receipt. There is usually a *10-Day Free Look* period for you to review the coverage. Within this period you have the right to request a premium refund if you do not accept the coverage.

When you made a decision to purchase, you should have received and reviewed a number of *illustrations* with your financial professional. At policy delivery, if the policy that was issued is different than what you applied for, you should receive another revised illustration. (*Illustration* is an industry term for computer generated tables or charts which project future values based on certain assumptions defined in the illustration. Keep in mind that the monetary values shown on such illustrations are not to be construed as a company's guarantee or promise that the product will perform in that manner over time.)

Your professional has taken on the long-term responsibility to service your financial program. If you are truly pleased with her/his performance, do not hesitate to offer the names of others for referrals. You have chosen a representative who will be there on your behalf in the event of death or disability. You have chosen a person you feel comfortable enough with to share your ongoing goals, happy days and sad times.

ANNUAL REVIEWS FOR CONTINUOUS IMPROVEMENT

Your purchase means that you have made another step in planning for the future. At this point, you have succeeded in taking the 12 steps to gain control of your financial future!

- You have learned the importance of coordinating a team of professionals and how to make them work for you.
- You have a sound process for selecting them.
- You have a sound process for interviewing to find someone who is a right match for your personal style.
- You have parameters to identify unethical behavior.
- You have asked yourself introspective questions necessary for defining what you want in life.
- You understand all components necessary for assessing your present financial health and determining what you can afford.
- You understand your company benefits.
- You understand the elements necessary to coordinate company and personal planning.
- You understand the importance of diversifying savings, insurance, and investments for now and the future.
- You know how to control the buying process at a pace that's right for you by feeling confident to ask questions and demanding that your professionals teach you.
- You understand the essential aspects of selecting a company, and how products are underwritten and matched to your personal circumstances.
- You are committed to be personally responsible to monitor and update your program.

As we come to the close of the process, you can feel confident in knowing that you now have an insider's view of the fundamentals of a diversified planning process. It is a process that advocates an active relationship between you and your team of professionals.

Remember, neither a 12-step process nor the personal financial program a woman creates can succeed on its own. Success requires

personal accountability, commitment, discipline, and periodic review. Think of it as you would overseeing the maintenance of your car. There can be serious consequences if the oil and other vital fluids are not checked on a regular basis. There can be serious or fatal consequences if the tires are not properly inflated, rotated or changed. Waiting to attend to your vehicle until after it breaks makes you vulnerable and places you in jeopardy. The vehicle will not perform to its optimum without periodic monitoring and service. Your service station will oblige if you take the car in for servicing—they cannot help you unless you are proactive and request the service. Remember, you are in the driver's seat.

The analogy applies to monitoring the performance of your investment vehicles as well. Your financial portfolio requires frequent review. Because the investment marketplace is dynamic and fluctuating, if you are investing in a diversified portfolio, you must be involved and aware. Review each annual policy statement or fund statement when you receive it; don't just file it in a folder in your desk! You must understand how the funds are performing. Feel comfortable to call your financial professional to teach you how to read your statements if you are confused.

Investment values are just one aspect of your program needing frequent review. It is also necessary to make certain that the amount of insurance coverage increases to match the need. One example I have witnessed involved ABC Company that chose to have a buy-sell agreement created among 3 partners. They had $250,000 life insurance on each partner for the intent that if one partner should die, the $250,000 would help pay the family of the partner to buy-out the business interest. Because the partners were busy with the details of daily business, there was no time to have an annual review done. The partners did not increase the insurance amount or the buy-out price to keep pace with the value of the growing business. One partner died and the spouse received $250,000 instead of the current value of the partner's interest in the business which had grown to $750,000, which was the amount that the deceased partner would have hoped for the family.

I recommend that insurance be reviewed on an annual basis. Throughout the years of my insurance practice in an effort to keep my clients' future planning and insurance up-to-date and to provide the best possible service, I have developed materials to teach, communicate and service clients over the lifetime of our relationship. Since the '80s, my follow-up letters, ongoing teaching materials, and annual review checklists have helped many clients and families to stay focused on their goals and to update their programs for the future. It gives me great pride to have shared my "client for life" philosophy with my industry associates.

In order to assist you in the 12-step process to gain control of your financial future, THESeebeckSuccessSystem™ (included in *American Dream Women:*

Workbook & Planning Guide, [ISBN: 0-941061-09-2]), is designed to make the ongoing annual review and updating of your financial program a habit—one that will positively impact you for many years to come.

THE IMPORTANCE OF NAMING A BENEFICIARY

Another reason for the importance of annual review of your insurance program is to review the beneficiary designations on your policies. The people you name when you purchase your insurance do not necessarily remain your same choices throughout the years. Here are examples of circumstances that have occurred when clients do not update beneficiaries assigned to their insurance policies:

- The effect of divorce on the status of a named beneficiary will vary depending on state law. You should always contact your agent when the relationship of the beneficiary changes.
- If a business owner purchases a policy for the purpose of covering a business loan at the bank, there is a *collateral assignment* of the policy to the bank. If the loan is paid off, the agent has not been notified and the insured dies, and the bank never returned the policy, the family faces time and expense to prove that they are entitled to receive the proceeds of the life insurance policy. Legally, the insurance company must pay the bank as the named beneficiary or receive a signed note from the bank to surrender the money to the family.
- If you have a personal agent, but purchase insurance by mail or through an employer, you should notify the agent and your family about the policy. It is possible that because your agent does not know about the policy your family will never receive the proceeds because the mail-order company many not be aware of the death.
- If an "estate" is named as the beneficiary rather than a spouse or family member, it will delay the family's receipt of the benefit payment if no will was registered.
- A trust and legal will are put in order for a family. The attorney assumes the insured notified the agent to properly design the insurance program along with naming the trust as beneficiary of the policies. All beneficiary changes should be properly documented with the insurance company.

Having defined goals, assessed your current financial condition, created a financial program, implemented it in a series of steps, and committed yourself to periodic review, you now have a quality track to run on that is flexible to adjust with personal circumstances through all cycles of your life.

(. . .Now let us look at 12 needs and solutions that are common throughout various stages in the life of an American woman. . . .)

PART II

12 COMMON NEEDS & SOLUTIONS

Throughout my practice, I've serviced hundreds of women who have expressed common needs, wants, and desires for the future. Often women gain additional confidence by sharing and comparing their situation and goals with those of other women from similar life circumstances.

The second part of this book is dedicated exclusively to a discussion of the common desires of American women who have defined the American Dream in their own terms. These women's stories are organized according to common needs and their solutions. In these stories, which are composites of many experiences, women discuss their mistakes along the way, their new goals, and how they are accomplishing them. You are sure to find many parallels with the current stage of life you are in and what you choose for your future. The stories are also organized according to life cycles. If you are like most of our readers, you will read the story which fits your current lifestyle or concern for the future and go back to the others as your life changes.

Each story is independent and complete on its own; it provides background, gives questions to ask, discusses relevant financial needs and legal issues, and poses possible solutions. The need is a lack of something required or desirable in the pursuit of financial success. Necessity greatly intensifies urgency to the point that the need, obligation or requirement cannot be ignored. Exigency stresses great urgency brought about by particular circumstances which are imposed by external requirements rather than by an inner compulsion. The questions analyze or examine the problem and are those you should readily discuss with your financial professionals. The solution is a method or process of solving the need. There can be many solutions depending on your personal circumstances; however, these stories present those most common among the women I work with in my practice.

For instructional purposes throughout, my examples use compound interest tables, and average an assumed 9-percent annual rate of return over the time period. Due to market fluctuation, past performance is not a guarantee of future results, and there is no guarantee of future results.

#1: TO BECOME DEBT FREE

Single College Grad: Chen Li

CHEN LI HAS BEEN HAVING FUN. AT AGE 27, SHE IS A BRIGHT, petite, spirited, third-generation Asian American working her way up the career ladder in a professional firm where she earns a $60,000 starting salary as a promising attorney. Chen Li graduated *magna cum laude* from Catholic University of America and earned honors distinction and a law degree at Georgetown University in Washington D. C., where she served on the *Law Review* editorial board.

Chen Li was referred to me by her former professor and mentor, who is an attorney specializing in intellectual property law in New York. When Chen Li and I began our association, she was quick to point out, "My annual salary is far more than my father ever dreamed of making; if you don't count his car and mortgage, I've also accumulated more debt than he and mother ever had in their lives."

Chen Li explained that she enjoyed spending because her college days were a struggle without money from the family. After graduating from the rigors of law school, she took 3 months off with classmates from Georgetown to tour Europe and the Far East visiting her great grandparents' homeland in China and spending a great deal of time in Peking. The trip cost her $10,000, which she charged on credit cards. She said, "We worked hard for 7 years in college and were determined to enjoy the wonders of the world and go to places we always dreamed of."

Over an 18-month period after beginning her new job, Chen Li had accumulated $18,000 of debt. She rented a condominium in a "safe" up-scale Washington suburb and charged another $3,000 for furnishings. A designer wardrobe "that was of the caliber that the firm expected" cost her another $5,000, which she also deferred paying for with credit cards. She was thankful she had no student loans to repay.

By age 27, the thrill of having money and the duty of spending was no longer a reward. Chen Li recalled, "Already, I felt trapped by my own success. The money was there in black and white, but I didn't have any and started to feel suffocated, ashamed and hopelessly in debt. I couldn't imagine what it would be like if I were to marry. If both of us had debt along with student loans my fiancé might have to repay, we could face a potential of $75,000 to $100,000 of debt between us." Chen Li wanted to use the discipline that she had learned throughout her academic studies and at home to solve her financial worries. She needed to change her life, but did not know where or how to begin.

NEEDS

After our meeting, Chen Li realized she must begin at the beginning and first understand where her money was being spent by analyzing her expenses, debts, and savings habits; plus, she needed a budget. She also needed an attitude shift regarding her spending on items she felt "obligated to purchase." Like Chen Li, many women feel similar pressures to spend due to great urgency imposed by external job or peer requirements. Such exigency spending is justified intellectually, but creates a hidden debt addiction and interrupts personal cash flow each month. Chen Li needed to protect her income stream and grow an emergency fund. Plus, she needed to begin an aggressive approach to pay off her debt.

QUESTIONS TO ASK

If, like Chen Li, you are faced with similar circumstances and wish to aggressively eliminate debt, here are issues you must resolve:

- Are you willing to begin cash-only spending and put your credit cards away?
- Do you have any additional major expenses coming up such as a new car purchase?
- Do you know what is a realistic time frame for you to pay off your debt?
- Are you willing to cut back on spontaneous purchases and commit yourself to a monthly budget?
- Will you be receiving any additional salary increases, bonuses, or gifts?
- Do you have a disability income protection program? Do you know what percent of your salary will be covered? When do the benefits begin?
- Do you have short-term savings to use as an emergency fund?

SOLUTION

The irony in Chen Li's life is that "not having money" is not her dilemma. Her hurdle is having a mindset focused on short-term expenses that she feels obligated to make immediately. As a new attorney, she explained, "the exigencies of my job forced me into an upscale lifestyle, living in an affluent neighborhood, and maintaining an appropriate and honorable image." Her challenge was embracing cash only spending habits.

Chen Li desired to be debt free as soon as possible and was willing to sacrifice and adhere to cash only spending. Her 2 major credit cards were retained. To avoid binge spending, she literally froze her spending by placing the cards in a glass of water in the freezer.

Because of her salary, Chen Li has applied for her own disability income protection policy, knowing that if she is injured and qualifies for benefits, she will receive a monthly check to help pay her bills as well as cover the amount she hoped to begin saving. Her short-term disability income protection would cover her for the first 90 days. Chen Li also was committed to save her bonuses for 2 years to accumulate $10,000 in a short-term savings account for emergency needs. After that goal is accomplished, she will maximize contributions to her 401(k) retirement plan.

To eliminate her $18,000 debt, we identified her fixed monthly expenses of $3,600, of which $2,200 covered rent, utilities, car payment, and her insurance; she averaged $600 monthly for entertainment, new clothing purchases, *etc*. Also, $800 was spent each month on payments for 2 major credit cards as well as several smaller department store credit accounts. She had been spending $9,600 a year to pay off an $18,000 credit card debt. Unfortunately, a portion of her payments were applied to interest rather than paying off the principal.

Chen Li also needed a focused lifestyle change regarding her $600 monthly outlay for entertainment, clothing, and extras. She embraced cash only spending. She would limit her extras to enable her to apply an additional $500 each month to double credit card payments and to increase payments toward principal. As each card was paid off, she would apply that payment allocation toward increasing payments to another card. Her program would enable her to be debt free as well as accumulate a short-term money market account as an emergency fund in 2 1/2 to 3 years.

The greatest payoff for Chen Li will come after her debt is eliminated. She will then start aggressive long-term saving for she will have mastered disciplined spending habits to avoid debt accumulation. The $800 plus $500 she used monthly to pay off credit cards will begin accumulating as savings. If she maintains her discipline, her $15,600 annual contribution to a mutual fund could yield more than $874,288 in 20 years if she is fortunate enough to average an assumed 9-percent annual rate of return.

Chen Li admits that initially the discipline of cash only spending was hard because she "was accustomed to sharing the blessings" of a good salary to help her family and buying what was needed when it was needed. Such generosity was how she demonstrated honor to her parents as a result of achieving "the big job after law school." But when she learned a new definition of her financial power in terms of savings and wealth accumulation rather than spending, it "became easier." She remembered, "I felt good; for the first time, the control of my financial future was in my court."

#2: TO SAVE MORE MONEY

Holly

HOLLY'S FATHER WAS A HARD-WORKING, LARGE HUNK OF A MAN with thick black hair and huge hands of taut callused skin; he made a living as a Texas oil rigger. Her mother was a strawberry blonde beauty, thin and frail, who worked as a cook at the local Holiday Inn after their 3 children went off to grade school. When Holly and I first met, she was 20. She told me with great pride and sadness about how as her parents raised their family, they found that no matter how hard they worked, they were stretching paychecks from Friday to Friday but never getting ahead or able to save. She recalled that the whole family would sit on the porch swings at night telling stories and drinking her mother's homemade lemonade. On special nights, under the hot Texas moon, the kids would make pink lemonade by floating a maraschino cherry on their lemon. Her parents would tell of their dreams of owning a herd of mustangs on a little Texas ranch by the time they were 45. Holly's voice cracked as she told me that those dreams were getting more distant the older her parents became. Holly recalled how her parents called "being 45" a "magic age when everything would be easy," and they would sit back and raise horses and a few Texas longhorns.

At 20, Holly was determined to make her own dreams happen. She said, "I just don't know what to do or how to do it." Holly's strength was in knowing *what* she was capable of and doing that with a spirit "to be the best." Even more important at her age was that she knew what she did not know and sought help to make up for what she called her "short sights." Academics was not in her heart; after graduating from high school, Holly chose to "follow a path of beauty." She worked as a waitress as she put herself through cosmetology school with a goal of owning her own salon someday. She graduated with honors; her attitude and sights were set to be the best in her field. Our relationship began shortly thereafter when she started her first job in cosmetology.

Everything Holly does and every move she makes speaks of beauty and grace. Her glossy red hair is cut in a perfect bob that fits her face and freckles. She is a natural Irish beauty with a dazzling look that requires no make-up or time in front of the mirror. She tailors her own clothes; because they fit her lanky frame perfectly, she always looks impeccably groomed. Even her walk is focused and determined.

Her down-to-earth personality, which makes her a good listener, also makes her a natural for a customer oriented career such as a hairdresser. Customers like her and tip her generously. She makes customers feel special because she takes great pride in helping them have the right hair style for their type of hair, facial shape and personality, and she readily communicates these details to them.

Holly's initial financial goal was to continue to live modestly, at home with her parents and bring some money home to help with expenses. The arrangement she had at the salon was that she would earn minimum wage and would receive a commission on the portion of the business she generated. Tips were hers. Her strategy was to maintain a lifestyle based only on her minimum wage salary and immediately save what tips and commissions were net after taxes.

She zealously marketed herself and creatively hosted free workshops on Sunday evenings for women's groups in local churches and community organizations as a means of building clientele. She taught about selecting the right cut and style to complement facial features, as well as other points about tinting, painting and perming techniques. After 18 months, she had her schedule filled with 8 appointments each day—4 cuts and styles, 2 perms, and 2 tints or paints on average. Her tips averaged 20 percent or more, and she was able to save $250 each week on tips alone. Her goal was to try to save $1,000 a month as a minimum for a 6-year period, to give her at least $70,000 working capital to open a salon of her own. She visited my office often so I could keep her focused on saving and receive periodic feedback on the growth of her savings.

At age 26 Holly had her grand opening.

She has become an entrepreneur in her field, with an established clientele that eagerly followed her. When Holly opened her own salon, she had 2 other employees working for her. The salon is booked 2 weeks in advance and is the most desirable salon in Ft. Worth.

On one occasion of our meeting, Holly stated that she had concerns that her parents did not have enough money put aside for their retirement years. As the oldest daughter, she envisioned herself needing to help support them financially.

As disciplined and focused on her own goals as she was, I remember thinking how remarkable it was for such a young woman to be so concerned about her parents—at a time when her peers are focused on marriage, careers, or beginning families of their own. Holly stated that she felt she would like an insurance policy so that if something happened to her, the proceeds would help benefit her parents and create a small retirement income for them. She chose to put $100 a month into a cash value whole life insurance policy that would provide a $100,000 death benefit to her parents if she died. If she did not die by the time her parents could work no longer, she would borrow from the cash values in the whole life policy in the event that her parents needed financial help. Over the years, the cash value insurance would also supplement her retirement income.

At age 28, Holly married the man of her dreams, Dan, who has similar values regarding money and saving. She continues to save $100 for the purpose of helping her parents, and Holly and Dan have a pact to remain debt free. She and Dan are saving $250 monthly in contributions to mutual funds for retirement. Holly has increased her life insurance to also cover Dan. Dan's insurance program is, likewise, designed to be there for Holly in the event of his death.

Holly's and Dan's financial goals can become reality because they share similar values and are focused on saving rather than debt accumulation. Because they started their focused savings early as a married couple, by the time they are age 48, their $3000 annual contribution into a mutual fund has the potential of accumulating over $160,000 if they are fortunate enough to average an assumed 9-percent annual rate of return. Holly is quietly proud of what she has accomplished before age 30, but even more about providing for her parents and the life she is building with Dan.

She states her most recent joy, "My kids will *never* be burdened or have to worry about financially supporting me someday. . . . Now let's concentrate on what I need to do to provide benefits to my employees and to invest the profits from my business." Making up for her "short sights" she added, "I just don't know what to do or how to do these things. Let's begin again."

Single Professional Desires to Save: Ann

ANN IS A 30-YEAR-OLD OBSTETRICIAN WHO IS DEDICATED TO HER career and patients. She is a member of a professional firm in Dallas where her practice is thriving. When we first met, Ann told me that during her childhood she "lived a life of luxury," so much so that she felt guilty for her good fortune. It was this sensitivity to others less fortunate that led her to pursue a career in medicine to help mothers and their children.

Ann gave me splendid details of her family estate in Newport, Rhode Island, with its palatial grandeur and flower gardens overlooking the sea. She recalled her great joy at spending summers with her grandparents in Marblehead, Massachusetts. She described fondly that her Grandpap taught her all her marlinspike skills so she could tie any sailing or boating knot, and do it "faster and better than any bloke." She laughed when she remembered how her grandfather would let her steady the helm when they were on an easy run sailing out from Cape Ann. She recalls, "He'd tell me that the Cape was named after me, and I believed him of course!" She spent her teen years delivering boats for retiring New Englanders who were relocating to the warmer, bluer waters of the Caribbean. She made the run from the Cape, south through intercoastal waterways to Miami and sailed the final leg to the Bahamas or Virgin Islands.

For Ann, the exhilaration and courage of sailing was in her blood. She missed open water and felt the flat, dry, ranch lands around Dallas to be wanting. She always dreamed of owning a large sail boat like her grandfather's and someday circumnavigating the globe, or at least setting a challenging course that she could accommodate with her schedule.

Since medical school and beginning her practice in Dallas, where her family later moved, Ann truly has had little time—to dream, to sail, or to spend. Her demanding schedule as a physician makes it easy for Ann to focus on saving money. Since our work together, she has committed to save $75,000 annually which is 25 percent of her gross income of $250,000.

Ann is "on a mission" to save for and own a 44-foot ketch knowing that a preowned but relatively new craft will cost her about $120,000. As she explains, "Saving for the boat makes the joy and memories of my childhood come alive again.

With my hectic schedule, the memories *are* my recreation." She also wishes to accumulate wealth, because in her retirement years, she wants to live a lifestyle without worry as she had as a young girl. She would like to retire at age 60.

Protecting her assets is very important to her, and she fears a lawsuit but understands that as a physician she is vulnerable in this regard. She is also aware that she needs to be astute to tax planning because of her desirable income.

NEEDS

If, like Ann, you are newly beginning a professional practice, here are some key issues of concern:

- To maximize your disability income protection to help cover personal and business practice expenses in the event you become disabled and qualify for benefits.
- To build a short-term emergency reserve of liquid accessible funds before aggressive saving begins.
- To maximize malpractice insurance in the event of lawsuit.
- To help protect your accumulated savings and assets from exposure to lawsuit.
- To have a short-term savings program to buy a boat or achieve another goal in 5 years.
- To build a long-term tax deferred retirement program enabling you to retire at age 60.

QUESTIONS TO ASK

- What are your present savings that are liquid in the event of an emergency?
- Do you have disability income protection? When does it begin?
- What are your monthly expenses?
- Are you currently contributing to a 401(k), 403(b), SEP-IRA, or profit sharing?
- To date, how much have you been saving on a monthly basis?
- At what age do you wish to retire?
- How much can you save comfortably on a monthly basis?
- Do you presently have mutual funds, stocks, bonds, or annuities?

SOLUTION

Ann is committed to aggressively saving 25 percent of her annual income or $75,000. Here is how she diversifies her short-term and long-term savings to satisfy her needs and concerns for the future as well as her goals for saving.

Income Protection

The disability income protection Ann has at her professional firm begins its payout in the event of a covered disability after a 120-day elimination period, at 60 percent of salary to age 65. Also, we put into place an individual disability income policy to reduce the possibility that her income stream for savings could be jeopardized if she becomes disabled and qualifies for benefits. At her age, income level and excellent health, the premium is easily affordable for her.

Short-Term Savings for Emergency

Ann also needs an emergency cash account to cover her personal expenses as well as any expenses associated with her practice if she should become unable to work. (A complete explanation of disability income coverage to protect paying the cost of business overhead expenses is found in Rebecca's story.)

As a single woman without the additional income of a spouse, Ann's emergency fund should be 3- to 6- times her monthly expenses. In Ann's case, her monthly expenses were $5,300. She chose to have $32,500 as her goal for liquid savings in a money market account. This type of short-term savings gives her check writing privileges with a checkbook. These funds are available for use at any time without IRS penalties or costly surrender fees.

To create her short-term savings emergency fund, Ann saves $2,700 each month into an interest bearing money market account. She can use it for emergencies if needed or to purchase her boat when the time comes. After the first 12 months, Ann has secured $32,500 in her emergency fund.

Accumulate Short-Term Cash

Ann's other short-term need is to accumulate cash in 5 years to buy her boat. Ann chooses to invest $32,500 annually into a mutual fund portfolio. After contributing $2,700 each month for 4 years, Ann will be ready to purchase her boat if she is fortunate enough to average an assumed 9-percent annual rate of return.

Asset Protection

Ann's fear of lawsuit exposure can be addressed in 3 ways. The size of her money market short-term emergency fund can help pay for any legal fees she may incur. She has malpractice insurance for the maximum protection allowable. Third, she has a cash value life insurance policy. In Texas, life insurance and annuities are sheltered from exposure to lawsuit. (This is true in varying degrees in many other states as well.)

Ann chose to place $20,000 annually into a cash value life insurance policy. The potential growth of the cash value of the policy can help Ann fund a retirement program. Remember, cash value grows income tax deferred, and the owner can borrow it or *surrender to cost basis* (generally, this means total premiums paid) without income tax if the policy is not a modified endowment.

Borrowing requires interest to be paid and will reduce the death benefit. But, this may be unimportant for Ann who is primarily concerned about asset protection and supplementing retirement.

Long-Term Retirement

After she buys her boat at age 35, if Ann continues contributions to mutual funds, her cash accumulation in 25 years could be $3 million at age 60, with an average assumed 9-percent annual rate of return; however, she knows there is no guarantee of this over the long-term.

Ann's goal of accumulating retirement income can also be achieved by other savings strategies—individual retirement annuity, a 401(k) retirement program or a SEP-IRA. These vehicles are designed for long-term wealth accumulation and are available after age 59 1/2 for retirement income.

As a group, the professional corporation in which Ann is a principal has elected a SEP-IRA pension plan. They have also chosen to use mutual funds as the investment vehicle. The SEP-IRA contribution also provides her a tax deduction each year. Maximum allowable amounts are determined according to IRS law and are subject to change. Ann chose to invest an annual contribution of $22,500 over 30 years. If she is fortunate enough to average an assumed 9-percent annual rate of return, Ann could have an additional $3.3 million when she retires at age 60.

After creating her emergency fund, Ann's annual goal of saving $75,000 each year has been diversified into placing $32,500 in mutual funds, $20,000 for tax deferred growth in cash value life insurance and $22,500 into a SEP-IRA pension for retirement at age 60. Because her total accumulation in these 3 vehicles could be approximately $11 million, it will be necessary for Ann to do some serious estate planning, because the potential tax burden on her wealth would be $5.5 million in Federal estate tax.

Ann is young, with potential for marriage and children. So we will need to monitor her progress and wealth accumulation throughout her life stages. Ann diligently reviews her progress twice each year with her team of certified public accountant, attorney, agent and financial planner. When she came to review her fund values last fall, she was pleased and confident with her progress and liked "being steady at the helm with all the loose ends knotted and tied up." It's been 4 years since she began her program, and Ann is already checking out the ads in *Yachting* magazine hoping to find the right ketch.

#3: TO BUY A HOME

Single & Striving to Buy a Home: Farzana

FARZANA GRADUATED FROM RUTGERS WITH A BACHELOR'S degree in business. To most American women, this would be a rather normal expectation. However, for Farzana it was a symbol of liberation—fueled and given life by her mother's own desires. As the eldest born to a couple who emigrated from New Delhi to build a textile business in New York City after World War II, Farzana lived in a closed traditional Pakistani family where women served the home or the greater good of the family. Farzana explained that the endurance of dreams her mother had while "living behind the veil" were fueled by the venerated example of Indira Ghandi; this made it possible for Farzana to think of going to college and the community good that would come after her graduation.

Farzana's beauty was dominated by her gleaming, ebony, waist-length hair, and fig colored eyes. Her hair, which was never pulled back, cascaded over her face as she sat working at her computer. The weight of her hair caused her to walk erect, shoulders back, with great poise. She used a deep earth red lipstick that complemented her olive skin, and she had matching fingernails, so characteristic for New York women. She was striking and exotic. At 5' 8," she was tall as a bean; this she said was unusual for women of her culture and a trait which raised her in the eyes of her community. Even her father had to look up to her.

We met in 1990 when I had been in New York on company business. Farzana worked as a manager in an accounting department where a client of mine was vice president. I literally stumbled on Farzana in a private coffee room while she was kneeling on a mat prostrate in prayer. A devout Muslim, Farzana zealously maintained her cultural traditions in what she called, "an awkward corporate world where expressions of religious beliefs were as foreign as a smile." I was later amazed at her discipline to maintain a 40-day fast for Ramadan.

Farzana had worked for 13 years since college, and at her mother's wishes, was preparing to assist in operating her father's family business. Her father had become seriously ill, and Farzana's brothers were away at college and not able to run the business. Farzana was the one hope for the family. My client invited Farzana to join us for lunch to talk about future planning. At this point in her life, Farzana had accumulated no savings.

I recall Farzana as intense. She explained that her annual income had grown to $75,000 and anticipated that it would remain at that level for the next 3 years. The majority of her income was taken home to maintain the family and to help with necessary cash flow for her father's wholesale garment business on Seventh Avenue. The increase in synthetic fiber development was competitively eroding her father's textile business, and he chose not to change or modernize. Since Farzana had no savings, I was relieved to find that she had great medical and disability income protection benefits at the company where she worked. These included a comprehensive long-term disability income policy and a 401(k) investment plan, in which she was planning to maximize contributions to 10 percent of her income.

After graduating from college, Farzana's steady income had been a blessing to her family and her community. Her deep sense of duty led her to help all that she could. She was supporting her two younger brothers through medical school. Farzana's earnings also supported many bank loans for the family business—loans for which she was ultimately responsible. It had taken $500 per month for the last 5 years to pay off these loans. Her dream now was to purchase a home for her mother, father and the family so they could live in the suburbs and move out of their 3-bedroom apartment in the "jowls of the city" as she called it. Plus, at her income level, the mortgage interest deduction could benefit her when filing her Federal income taxes. Farzana was willing to do whatever was necessary on a monthly basis to buy a home in 3 to 5 years; then she would be 35-years old.

Farzana felt comfortable saving $500 each month because she was accustomed to paying that much on the various loans. She would save an additional $300 that had previously been spent on helping others outside the home. Even though she was earning a good income, Farzana was traditional, conservative and uncomfortable with financial risk—especially since her income benefited so many.

Farzana was committed to pay cash for family necessities and would cut back on giving money to people outside the family. She knew that if she was going to accomplish her goal to purchase the home, her role and obligation to share the wealth "as the family's financial savior" must change—money lent to outside family members was not considered a loan to be repaid. In fact, the money she gave for children's clothes and medicine for nieces and nephews was considered "a gift" never to be repaid.

NEEDS

If, like Farzana, you desire to own a home, you need to understand "how much house" you can afford and what relationship that has to your income. Specifically, you need:

- To save money for a down payment on a house as well as the closing costs.

The general rule is that mortgage lenders will require 10 percent to 20 percent as a down payment. First-time home buyers in many areas of the country can often find financing which is more liberal. Closing costs can vary between 2 percent and 5 percent of the mortgage depending on locality.

- To understand every monthly expense in order to determine what mortgage could be supported by monthly income.
- To know guidelines for financing. For example, Farzana's $75,000 gross income is $6,250 on a monthly basis; $6,250 x 33 percent equals $2,062. That is the amount that a bank or mortgage company will allow as a guideline for a monthly mortgage payment. Then all debt is added to the above amount. The next rule of thumb is that the total cannot exceed 38 percent of gross income.[24]
- To select a price range for houses by calculating the approximate monthly mortgage payment. On an annual basis, your house payments will be approximately 10 percent of the total mortgage, including taxes and interest. For example a $100,000 mortgage will have an annual payment of $10,000. That divided over 12 months would be approximately $833 each month.
- To select a well-known local realtor who will assist you in your search and financing.
- To help protect your ability to pay the mortgage in the event of disability or death.

QUESTIONS TO ASK

- How much money are you willing and able to save monthly?
- Will you have any bonuses or extra income in the future?
- Are you willing to take risks with your savings or do you want guaranteed interest rates with no risk attached?
- Will you pass the credit report that is part of your future mortgage loan application?
- Do you have credit card debt that you need to eliminate?
- Is your income protected in the event you become disabled?
- Does the bank or mortgage lending company require you to purchase *personal mortgage insurance* (PMI)?
- Do you now have, or will you need, additional life insurance to cover the mortgage payoff as well as other needs in the event of your death? (This is known as *individual mortgage protection life insurance.*)

You must understand that PMI insurance is **protection for the bank** or the mortgage lender only. In the event you default on your payments, the bank is protected until they foreclose on the property. **PMI does not pay off the**

mortgage on your behalf nor does it provide a death benefit to your family in the event of your death.

As a result, many dual-income homeowners elect to protect their ability to make mortgage payments in 2 ways. Some purchase individual disability income insurance to protect income if they become disabled and qualify for benefits. Some purchase individual mortgage protection life insurance equal to the amount of the outstanding mortgage. There are many ways and names by which companies sell or market this mortgage insurance idea, but it is very important to understand that this is life insurance. Many types of life insurance are used to accomplish paying off the mortgage (for example *decreasing term*, *level term*, *yearly renewable term*, *flexible premium whole life* and *variable life*). Life insurance can also be used creatively to accelerate the payoff of your mortgage earlier if you live (known as *mortgage acceleration*) or to pay off the bank if you die.

The important distinction between PMI and individual mortgage protection life insurance is that only your individual policy will benefit your beneficiaries in the event that you as breadwinner die before the mortgage is paid. The death benefit your family receives can then be used to satisfy the bank, after which your family receives clear title or deed to the house. After the struggle and sacrifice to buy a home, no one wants to be forced to lose their American Dream.

SOLUTION

To save for a down payment, Farzana wanted guaranteed interest rates without risk, so she selected a credit union savings account with a declared interest rate. She could also have purchased bank certificates of deposit or saved in a short-term money market account. Instead, she chose the payroll deduction benefit of credit union savings. She could not pledge to give away money outside the family if she did not have the money to spend each week when she received her paycheck. She was certain that the credit union approach would assure regular disciplined savings. For her, it was a matter of honor. With the payroll deduction approach, she truly did not have the money available to give away.

For Farzana, payments to annuities or life insurance, or maximizing contributions to her 401(k) at that time would not be appropriate vehicles for accumulating cash to be withdrawn before retirement for the purpose of purchasing a home.

In Farzana's case, her income and debt-free financial status could comfortably support a mortgage, tax and interest payment for a $150,000 mortgage or a $200,000 home.

Because she was the sole support of the mortgage, I felt it was necessary that Farzana not overextend herself with a mortgage payment that would prevent her from any other long-term retirement savings. As a result, she planned to purchase a less expensive home than she originally planned. She focused on a $150,000 maximum purchase price, because she wanted to keep her house payment around $1,200; she also wanted to begin contributions to her 401(k) retirement plan as soon as possible.

Based on Farzana's income she began saving $650 each month in a credit union savings for the house. She also opened a money market account into which she deposited $187.50 monthly; after 24 months, she had her short-term emergency fund of $4,500 secured.

Then Farzana saved $187.50 monthly as a 3-percent contribution to her 401(k) plan deducted from her payroll, and the company matched up to 3 percent, for a 6-percent total contribution on an annual basis.

After 5 years, Farzana had saved over $39,000 for her house; $30,000 was used as a down payment, and $9,000 went for closing costs, legal fees, and some new furniture for a "modest but large, old home in Ft. Lee, New Jersey."

When she bought the home in 1995, Farzana called me to purchase life insurance. Her desire was to provide cash to pay off the mortgage in the event of her death. She designated her mother and father as beneficiaries. Also, several months after her family moved into the home in Ft. Lee, Farzana started an investment portfolio with the $650 monthly payment she had been saving to buy the house. Her growing sense of confidence and pride at the accomplishment of purchasing the home for her parents and family, made her more willing to take on a measure of risk. With an annual contribution of $7,800, in 20 years she could pay off the mortgage early or have over $435,000 additional retirement income to complement her 401(k), if Farzana is fortunate enough to average an assumed 9-percent annual rate of return.

The day the family moved, Farzana phoned to tell me how her mother sat and cried—outside on the porch—all day. Farzana's voice beamed as she related how the large front room would be left empty for family prayer. The living room had a huge picture window. It faced East.

#4: TO PROTECT INDEPENDENCE

Single & Protecting Independence: Jody

JODY BEGAN VISITING MY OFFICE JUST TO SAY "HI." SHE PROCESSED a business loan for me in 1993, and I thought it was unusual for her to be stopping by so often, especially when my payments were current. I thought she was monitoring how the expansion and relocation of our office was progressing. She dropped by the office several times over a 6-month period and came to my teaching seminars.

Jody was 5'8" with ash blonde hair. She was an only child who portrayed a strong and sturdy image in her tailored business suits. Even though she had no children, she had the air of a confident matriarch who was always in control. She loved dogs and raised Boxers. She was raised with brindled Boxers in her family and favored the breed for its loyalty and strength. She said that Boxers kept fear at bay and gave her confidence and courage.

Every moment of her day was choreographed, and Jody "never took time to smell the roses." She was 35-years old and had spent all her years since college establishing herself in a banking career. She graduated from Rice in Houston with a degree in finance and business administration. She had worked her way up the ladder in the banking industry, beginning as a teller to her current position as a senior commercial loan officer in a prestigious private bank.

One day, I invited her to make an appointment to review her finances. She agreed, "just to have the confidence that all was in order," and felt that, as a banking officer, she owed it to herself to have "no loop holes for jeopardy." When we met to review income, expenses, and assets, she indicated that she carried a $150,000 mortgage on a home in a suburb of Ft. Worth. With her $85,000 income, she felt secure with her financial commitments as long as she remained healthy and could continue to receive a full paycheck. Her position at the bank provided her with $85,000 of term insurance coverage for which her estate was beneficiary. Jody did not feel that she would retire from her present employer, but anticipated changing companies because her expertise and education were constantly being sought. She was pleased to have disability income coverage totally paid by her employer.

Jody's major concern was an emotional one. She was slightly overweight and had reached the age where her mother and aunts on both sides of her family had experienced medical problems. Since turning age 35, Jody had become increasingly focused on health and knew that she could no longer be cavalier about it.

Even though her parents would have no legal obligation for her debts, Jody did not want them to be financially responsible or jeopardized in the event that she became disabled or died. She knew that her parents, who were retired and having difficulty maintaining their own standard of living, would always offer to help. Jody was increasingly concerned about her debt and had been focused on reducing it. Jody's desire was to have her program in order. Because she owned a home on her own, she was adamant about preserving her independence.

NEEDS

If, like Jody, you are rising in your career and have already purchased a home, you may want to eliminate any possibility or concern that your loved ones may feel responsible to help you if you are in need. You may also want to assure that in the event of your disability, that your monthly mortgage payment is not jeopardized, or in the event of your death, that your parents are able to live in your home with a paid-up mortgage. Consider the following.

- To protect your income and cash flow.
- To have adequate funds to pay off debt in the event of your disability or death.

QUESTIONS TO ASK

- What is your total monthly debt and income?
- What is available in short-term savings to pay off debt in the event of disability?
- What funds have been accumulated in 401(k), 403(b), and IRA accounts?
- How much life insurance is available and does it carry a waiver of premium provision?
- Could the family help or would they want to help in the event of your disability?
- Is the disability coverage adequate enough to pay monthly bills plus provide additional payments for debt reduction?

SOLUTION

Jody chose 2 courses of action to provide for debt reduction in the event of her death or disability. One was financial; the other was legal. She changed the beneficiary on her term insurance policy paid by her employer. Instead of naming her estate as beneficiary, she assigned her mother as beneficiary so that her mother would receive the benefits directly rather than going through legal procedures to receive the insurance proceeds. Jody discussed her wishes with her mother and her agent and also has created a will with an attorney.

A review of her disability income benefits at work revealed that the coverage will protect only 60 percent of Jody's gross salary in the event that she becomes disabled and qualifies for benefits, and it is not portable in the event that she leaves her job. Jody applied for an individual disability income policy with a purchase option rider so she has the maximum coverage allowed according to underwriting guidelines. This coverage will also stay with her in the event that she leaves her present position. Another shortfall in the disability income program at her employer was that it carried a 90-day elimination period. Jody's short-term savings amounted to only $4,000 of cash available for an emergency; but her monthly expenses were $2,800. Her goal was to save another $4,400 in a short-term money market account to serve as an emergency fund to secure her until her disability payment would be payable.

To this point in her career, Jody's attention has been on paying her college loans and saving for a down payment, closing costs and furnishings for her home. Jody had 2 more credit card debts to pay with a combined monthly payment of $200, which she planned to have paid in 6 more months. She has recently paid off several other credit card bills she created when she furnished her home.

To date she has not contributed to the 401(k) retirement plan she has at work but after her credit cards are paid, she will begin to place 6 percent of her monthly income, $425, in her 401(k) at the office. That amount plus the additional 3 percent match by her employer, $213, will grow her monthly savings to $638 or about $7,600 annually. At age 35, Jody still has 25 years to save for retirement and hopes to begin contributing more in the near future. Her $7,600 annual contribution has the potential of having more than $500,000 over 25 years, if Jody is fortunate enough to average an assumed 9-percent annual average rate of return.

Because Jody had little savings and only $85,000 in life insurance, her wish was to apply for additional life insurance to cover the amount of the mortgage on her house in the event of her death. (See Farzana's story for an explanation of the difference between PMI and individual mortgage insurance.) The term insurance she had through the bank had no waiver of premium option that would cover premium payments in the event she became disabled. Jody chose a $250,000 flexible premium cash value life insurance product. She named her mother as beneficiary. In the event Jody would die, her mother could pay the balance of the $150,000 mortgage and have the house as an asset which she could either choose to live in or sell. Another reason Jody selected cash value life insurance was for its loan potential from which she could borrow to pay off the mortgage early when cash values were sufficient. Once she pays her credit card debt, Jody will contribute as much as she can and is permissible in her life insurance policy for the purpose of increasing cash. The growth of cash value in her life insurance program is tax deferred as well as available for use prior to age 59 1/2. She also applied for the waiver of premium option which would continue to pay premiums after 6 months if Jody became disabled and qualified for benefits. Jody was pleased when she obtained the coverage.

Nine months after Jody set her goals, she had paid her remaining credit card debt and adopted a cash only method of spending. She remarked, "It's not that I cut up or stopped using credit cards. But the way I used them changed. When I paid my bills each month, I started a mindset that I must **pay myself first**—and wrote the checks for contributions to my savings goals. That meant that I had only $200 a month left for all discretionary expenses. I didn't use any credit cards unless the purchase fit within that budget, and I could pay the bill within that 30-day period. I actually thought of all my credit cards as if they were American Express cards, which had to be paid off immediately. But I just couldn't leave home without them."

Three years later, Jody was hospitalized with a heart attack. When I visited her in the hospital, Jody cried about what she had accomplished financially 3 years earlier. Cash was available to pay all her bills as well as continue contributions to her retirement. I processed her disability claim and agreed to meet with her mother to explain all that was covered and to discuss the bills and expenses. Jody is on a slow mend but has begun a promising recovery. Mom had to write the checks for her, but the money was there—there was even enough to pay a dog sitter over the 4 months Jody was in rehabilitation. Like her Boxers, her astute planning "has kept fear at bay and gave her confidence and strength."

#5: TO ACCUMULATE WEALTH

Single Professional Woman: Mercedes Chandler

I KNEW THE MOMENT SHE WALKED INTO MY OFFICE THAT THIS young woman was going places. Mercedes Chandler, who insisted that her compound proper name be used at all times, had a quality about her that commanded attention. She was a 5' 10" California beauty, blonde, and tall, built like a model. Raised in Santa Barbara and educated with a law degree from Stanford, her expectations for life were high. I recall a focus and ambition matched only by her sense of confidence. She made it quite clear that "while my brother and sister were squandering Dad's money, partying and drinking on the beach and in the canyons every night of the week, I was determined to make something of the opportunities I was given. After all, what's the sense of coming from wealthy parents if you never have any pride or wealth of your own. I can never go back."

She proceeded to tell me that by age 18 her brother had become an alcoholic and that her older sister had been in drug rehabilitation for the last 8 years. But for all of Mercedes Chandler's confidence, it was sweet to see that she was also humbly grateful for having her undergraduate and law school expenses paid. She declared, "when my parents were going through the stress of raising us, and when John and Amy were living a party life, my agreement with my Dad was that if I would stay straight, graduate with honors, and be accepted to law school, he would pay the bills. After all, it was costing him and Mom twice that much for private rehab for the other kids. . . . He agreed."

Mercedes Chandler also proudly recalled that her parents were so pleased with the way "she turned out," that after graduating from law school, they paid for a year off for her to travel through Europe and "buy stuff." She traveled, but saved most of the money.

She was focused and driven. At age 27, she landed a solid $65,000 job as a personal injury attorney with a firm in Dallas. She wanted to move as far away from California and her "dysfunctional siblings" as possible. Of her salary, she netted $48,000 and was rigorously saving $1,500 a month. Even though she fell short of her goal, she saved $26,000 in her first 2 years on the job. At age 29, she purchased a $120,000 condo and came to me to assist with what she called "an aggressive wealth accumulation strategy, so I can become a millionaire on my own like my Dad."

Given the curt descriptions about her brother and sister as worthless children, I remember being surprised when she became very serious about her need to marry and raise a family of her own. Mercedes Chandler confessed, "I know I come off as really assertive, and I am great at what I do; however, I do have a soft side that truly wants a family. We were a great family before we grew up. My parents loved each other and loved us so much. I can't stand to see my brother and sister hurt them so much with what they've done with their lives."

Mercedes Chandler was determined to make up for it—and make up for it all. She would be the one her "parents were proud of." She wanted a stable career and "to be established financially before she married."

NEEDS

Many young women who are children from wealthy families desire to make it on their own. If, like Mercedes Chandler, you are well educated, disciplined and driven to save at an early age, you'll want to have:

- Focused, consistent, and diversified savings.
- Knowledge about benefits available in disability income protection programs.
- Knowledge about ways of protecting your assets from potential liability exposure.
- Knowledge about what's available in the marketplace regarding tax deferred vehicles including life insurance and annuities.
- Knowledge about how to diversify investment vehicles.

QUESTIONS TO ASK

- Have your parents established a trust fund for you? If so, does it provide a monthly income? When will it be available to you?
- Is there a possibility that you will receive an inheritance?
- Are there any existing family assets in your name such as stocks or bonds?
- To what extent do you expect your income to grow?
- In addition to illness or disability, is your income exposed to any jeopardy relating to your profession?
- What are your monthly expenses and income?
- What are you presently doing to save for retirement?
- What are your balances for mutual funds, stocks and bonds?
- Do you understand all benefits available through your professional firm?
- What is the maximum potential of earnings for your career?
- Do you have an attorney, agent and an accountant working together as you plan for the future?

SOLUTION

Mercedes Chandler began working with me when she was 30-years old. She continues to build her public profile by being active in community and church organizations while practicing law.

When Mercedes began her planning she netted $4,000 income each month. Her mortgage and taxes on her condo were $1,500 monthly, with a budget of $1,000 to cover utilities, car expenses, insurance and any discretionary items she needed. She carried only short-term debt for which she paid the balance within 30-days. I took care to explain that even if she paid each credit card bill every month, it was still a monthly expense that needed to be totaled in her overall discretionary income.

Mercedes Chandler was disciplined and successful at keeping her expenses within the discretionary budget she has reserved because she considered her $1,500 monthly savings a priority. For 6 months after purchasing her condo, she continued to save the $1,500 monthly to accumulate $9,000 in a money market account for use as a short-term liquid savings fund.

Her employee benefits also included a great disability income program designed specifically for her needs. It carried an "own occupation" provision which means if she became disabled and no longer able to practice in court, but she was able to teach school, her policy would still pay her the benefit as long as she qualified.

Her basic life insurance protection needs had been satisfied with 3 times her annual salary (which has since grown to $100,000) or $300,000 of term insurance through her professional firm. Her intent was that this will be more than enough to satisfy the mortgage on her condo in the event of her death.

When Mercedes Chandler's income grew to net $6,000 monthly, she maintained her spending habits, but increased her discretionary income to save $2,500 each month. She continued to place $1,500 each month plus $4,000 in annual bonuses to maximize her 401(k) plan and begin personal mutual fund investing. Her $18,000 annual contribution can grow to $2.6 million by the time she is 60, if she is fortunate enough to average an assumed 9-percent annual rate of return.

When we reviewed her future goals and desires, Mercedes Chandler claimed that she also hoped to marry an attorney someday and to begin their own family practice together. For this reason, she became concerned when she realized that the $300,000 of term insurance she had with her firm would not be portable in the event she left the firm. She was also keenly aware that her age and excellent health were in her favor. As a result, she chose to apply for an individual cash value life insurance policy, which included a waiver of premium option; in the event she was disabled and qualified for benefits, the premium contributions would be paid. The insurance would provide her tax deferred cash value growth. The cash value could also help her fund future expenses such as college tuition or provide her with a retirement benefit.

Mercedes Chandler and I took time to organize her portfolio of benefits available through the firm, as well as her personal stocks, bonds, mutual funds, and life insurance statements. She maintains a close look at her portfolio binder and keeps focused on her quarterly profits and losses. She purchases stocks and mutual funds for future accumulation with any additional bonuses she earns.

At age 30, Mercedes Chandler was feeling the peer pressure of her colleagues whom she characterized as "heavy into the purchase of luxury cars and the like." I will always remember her response, "I guess my financial values are very different. I don't buy seasonal fashions or short-term luxury items that depreciate. I'm more oriented toward the long term and like when my purchases appreciate rather than depreciate like a car the moment you drive it out of the car dealership."

Mercedes Chandler has her own drive to create financial stability and aggressive long-term savings for accumulation. With or without a man, she is well on her way to her American Dream of becoming a millionaire in her own right by age 50—if not much sooner.

#6: TO RAISE A FAMILY

Jeanne

JEANNE WAS REFERRED TO ME IN 1990 TO BEGIN RETIREMENT planning. She intently told me her life story and how she came to her current financial situation.

Jeanne and Dan were married on May 5, 1973. She was a beautiful bride in a traditional white gown, and Dan was handsome beyond belief in his black tuxedo. She was careful to provide me with each and every detail of their wedding day—something that was as vivid as if it were yesterday. Jeanne told me about how gala the reception was with plenty of food and guests dancing under the moon as the band played on and on.

Jeanne mentioned that there was nothing unusual about their marriage. They were a typical American dual-income family, and they loved and respected each other. Their first son, Craig, was born in 1975, and Amy was born thereafter. Jeanne was quick to point out that she and Dan both shared the household chores and raised the children. He loved the kids and wanted to be active in their lives—even with “all the little things.” Dan was always protective of Jeanne. She said he “wore” his arm around her waist; she was 5' 1"; he stood at 5' 10". Weekends were spent having picnics and family gatherings. They lived for their family, and Monday morning usually meant going back to work so the bills could be paid.

In 1984, Dan was 34-years old when, as he and Craig were coming home from karate lessons, Dan experienced an aneurysm on the brain. Jeanne's world came to a halt. While Dan was in intensive care, the doctors doubted that he would live. Then, if he were to live, the question was to what extent he would have brain damage. The VA hospital had a coma center, and Jeanne wanted desperately for Dan's case to be on the waiting list so that someday he could be placed in the coma unit. After many weeks, Dan was moved to the VA hospital at Jeanne's relentless insistence.

At the time of Dan's seizure, his care at the VA was without cost to Jeanne. (This is not the case today.) During this time, Jeanne started to pull together her disability and life insurance policies along with becoming knowledgeable about Dan's benefits at work. She applied for Social Security 6 months after Dan's aneurysm, and later she started to receive the income for Craig and Amy along with a Social Security check for Dan.

Jeanne worked for the telephone company and was a member of the union when Dan became hospitalized. She had a boss who was compassionate, caring, and understanding. He encouraged her to take care of herself and the children and to work whatever hours she was able.

After some time, the VA hospital declared that because Dan's aneurysm was not caused by war, he must move out and into a nursing home. Jeanne was overwhelmed with having to care for the children, financially support the family and carry on with life. Not being able to share her feelings with her love and confidant incapacitated her. She could not talk, think or be responsible without him actively involved in her life.

The VA hospital helped her find a nursing home that was equipped to handle Dan's extreme and special needs. The VA also paid for the first 6 months of Dan's nursing home care. (The government benefits no longer provide this.) After 6 months, Jeanne needed to turn over Dan's Social Security check and the disability benefits which Dan received from his employer to the nursing home to pay for his care. Jeanne not only had lost her best friend and husband, but she also lost his income to help support their home and children.

Jeanne relayed to me the stress she had as she drove home one evening after a full day at work. She was ready to give up and to just continue driving. Thoughts of her children needing her and memories of happy times with Dan flashed before her. She knew she was ready to face the future.

Seventeen years after their wedding day and 6 years after his aneurysm, Dan died in 1990. Jeanne supported the family by working herself up the corporate ladder into a management position and the potential of higher earnings. When her employees experienced family problems, the impact of her own experience enabled Jeanne to show the compassion that was once given to her by her former boss.

When Jeanne began to work with me in 1990, we invested the money received from Dan's insurance, and she began saving in her 401(k) plan at work for retirement. She purchased life insurance for her and her children. She attended all the school functions for Craig and Amy. Her focus was to be both Mom and Dad to her children along with taking them on some great vacations throughout Texas to visit relatives. Craig is now in his fourth year of college and is studying sports fitness. His Social Security check stopped when he graduated from high school. Amy is a senior in high school and looking forward to college and accomplishing her dreams of becoming a physical therapist. Her Social Security check will stop too. There was a time when government assistance would have continued to help the children through 4 years of college.

Jeanne needed to support herself and her family for a long time. She received no Social Security for herself, but was thankful her children had some help after losing their father. Jeanne has accepted life for what it is, and when she prays, she remembers the good times and looks forward to the years ahead. She is aggressively saving for retirement—but only after the bills are paid.

Before Dan's accident, Dan was persuaded by another agent to cash in their insurance. The agent believed that there was no benefit to such cash value life insurance and that it was "inferior as an investment." Dan and Jeanne cashed in their $150,000 cash value life insurance policy in August 1982. It was replaced with a $100,000 decreasing term insurance policy—there was no waiver of premium placed on the new policy, which would have paid the premiums during the 6 years Dan was disabled. Plus, Jeanne was paying for a policy that was eventually worth much less than the amount originally purchased. A split-second decision to surrender cash value life insurance cost Jeanne over $60,000 when Dan died. Dan was convinced that "buy term invest the difference" was a great decision. Jeanne learned otherwise.

Protecting a Special Needs Child: Ellen

AT AGE 50, ELLEN WAS AN INDUSTRIOUS AND STUDIOUS WOMAN whose caring and sincerity were contagious. Ellen, who worked at building her career in the banking industry, waited until age 35 to marry. Her husband, Frank, had been previously married with children of his own. He was an attentive and financially responsible father. He had teenage sons and a younger daughter for whom he assiduously provided the best of everything. The boys excelled in football and gymnastics. His daughter was an Olympic caliber swimmer and hoped to someday become a concert pianist. He assisted his children's mother financially at every request. He was very proud of his children and that he intensely continued a supportive relationship with them after his divorce from their mother.

Ellen longed for the day she and Frank would have a child together. When Frank learned that their son would be born with Downs Syndrome, it created great emotional stress for him. Plus, his ex-wife continuously expressed her financial concerns. After Johnny's first birthday, Frank explained that the additional responsibilities were too great and much more than he had anticipated in a second marriage. Ellen and Frank separated, and Ellen was realistic enough not to expect that Frank would return.

Ellen had lived the next 13 years totally absorbed with caring for Johnny, who she considered to be "the total center and joy of her life." She received much happiness at watching him grow and had a heartfelt joy in the innocence and gentleness he would find in all that he saw and learned every day. The grandparents had a great love for Johnny whose smile was immense as he gave them a "big bear hug."

During our meeting, Ellen expressed concerns about what would happen to Johnny if she died first. Frank's heart and financial responsibilities were with the children of his first marriage, and he was mailing only sporadic financial support for Johnny at birthdays and the holidays. Ellen was resolved to this for she knew realistically that Frank truly was not financially capable of providing more, and she did not choose to pursue it and cause added stress in her life. She believed that, "going at it alone was definitely the easier alternative."

NEEDS

If you have a special needs child, your concerns are overwhelming. Like Ellen you need to make arrangements for your child's long-term care in the event of your death. Perhaps, you also need to explore options with halfway housing. Priority needs include the following.

- To have trust arrangements made for the child.
- To have a disability income program.
- To have life insurance and know who is named beneficiary.
- To know the value of your pension and who is named as beneficiary.
- To know what any potential inheritance will be.

QUESTIONS TO ASK

- Have any legal trust arrangements been made for your child?
- What is the value of your pension?
- Is your disability program employer-paid?
- How much life insurance are you carrying and who is named beneficiary?
- What is the value of your parents' estate?
- Do your parents have a long-term care policy?
- Have your parents made arrangements for the transfer of their assets by means of wills or trusts?

SOLUTION

Ellen has a $750,000 life insurance policy with benefit proceeds intended for Johnny's care. She named her parents as beneficiaries when she purchased the policy 10 years ago; then her parents were younger, and she felt they were capable of taking care of Johnny in the event of her death.

Ellen has worked in a corporate setting for years and has a $75,000 income and a superior benefit program. Her son is on her medical insurance program. Not knowing the future, this provides reassurance for Ellen. Johnny also receives a monthly Social Security check. Ellen has always used this for his special needs such as paying for a Nanny if necessary. Ellen's pension has accumulated to $350,000, and her parents are named as beneficiaries.

Her home, which she purchased when she was 29, was paid off last year; her parents' home was paid off as well. The value of Ellen's home is $150,000 and the value of her parents' home is $100,000, and there is a large parcel of land valued at $200,000. Her parents have set up their wills and trusts leaving all to Ellen.

For the sake of argument, if Ellen and her parents died in a car accident while traveling to pick up Johnny at school tomorrow, the total value of both estates, including Ellen's life insurance for Johnny, is valued at $1,675,000. An estate of this size carries an estate tax burden.

Ellen is thankful and proud that her father has his planning in order. However, Ellen wants to remove the stress and burden of Johnny's care from her aging parents. Ellen needs to meet with her attorney to structure a trust where she can direct her assets and remove her parents as beneficiary on all of her accounts. Based on Ellen's desires, her attorney can guide her about what type of trust to establish.

Ellen needs to have an organized written folder with her financial papers and policies in order in the event that she dies, and she needs to discuss her finances with her parents to give them peace of mind regarding what will happen to Johnny. There are several hypothetical situations that could occur.

- If Ellen predeceases Johnny, she needs a legal trust that will specify living arrangements and care for him as long as he lives.
- If Ellen predeceases Johnny, and Johnny dies soon after, Ellen needs to also specify in the trust that the balance of her assets will protect her parents until they die.
- Both her parents' and Ellen's legal trusts should be handled in tandem. Doing this will help assure that in the event Ellen and her parents die before Johnny, provisions will exist for his care. They also need to specify how to distribute the balance of funds, if any, in the event of Johnny's death.

As her insurance agent, I will join her certified public accountant and her attorney to continue to monitor Ellen's investment and insurance needs throughout the years.

The comfort of working with a professional team gave Ellen complete peace of mind. She was genuinely proud, thankful, and confident that Johnny's needs were provided for even if both she and her parents were not there to see him smile or give him his favorite "big bear hug."

Married Woman Raising a Family: Angela

ANGELA AND VINNIE ARE UPPER MIDDLE CLASS, second-generation Italian-Americans in their early 40s. They were high school sweethearts and are still married after 20 years. Vinnie is a salt-of-the-earth type, loving father, and "family man." His fun consists of playing a round of golf in a league each week, and he enjoys Dallas Cowboy football. Occasionally, there are late night poker games or bets in the football pool. Angela works as a loan officer in a prestigious bank, and Vinnie is a pilot with a well-known airline. They have two daughters; one is in college, and the other is in elementary school. Angela has a disability program as a benefit through the bank. Vinnie is also covered through the airline.

Together, they have a combined income of $125,000 and are underinsured considering that they hold a mortgage of $90,000 plus the responsibility of college education for 2 children. They are both contributing 10 percent to their 401(k) plans, and they understand very well the performance of the various funds. As a banker, Angela monitors their 401(k) plan performance and is astute to how the market is performing.

When Angela was referred to my office, she was stressed and exhausted—emotionally and financially. I remember her panic, "We are doing everything we can. The pressures to achieve it all are just too much. We are overwhelmed at times. As a parent, you wonder if it will come together. I'm here, because I'm afraid that we just can't do it all. We have many expenses now, another child to enter college in 10 years, and we just don't know how to juggle everything and still save for retirement."

Angela and Vinnie are "on track," but they both are looking forward to the day when the girls' college educations are paid. They want to build a dream home in the South, but don't think it will ever be possible. Angela is concerned with her high-stress position and its long hours. Expenses are high due to the needs and desires of a growing family. Because Vinnie works with the airline and the family can fly free, they have grown accustomed to the expectation of taking several, costly family vacations abroad each year. Angela's business responsibilities keep her wardrobe expenses high. Their daughters are Olympic hopefuls; therefore, gymnastic expenses are high, and there are music lessons, a third car for one daughter away at college and the college phone bills! All create a situation where their attractive dual-income is totally exhausted each month. Expenses equal net income.

NEEDS

Parents of dual-income families raising children have pressures that they cannot easily contain. If like Angela and Vinnie, you and your loved one are working hard and are torn in many directions—pulled by career, household expenses and chores—life is not fun.

The years when you should be enjoying your children rapidly pass with little quality time for the family. Providing taxi service and car pooling for children's activities sever critical family time together. Families are eating out more. Weekends bring even more stress to have fun. Family time is again diminished by errands that cannot be done during the week—laundry, dry cleaning, grocery shopping, mowing the lawn, gardening, painting, decorating, entertaining and shopping until you drop. The cycle is often vicious, and all you want to do is stop the train and get off!

There is even less time for long-term saving which is often viewed as "something you'll do later when you can afford it." It is seen as another burden rather than as a structured way to achieve peace of mind. Each year when you file your taxes you cringe and ask 'where did it all go?' You often have nothing to show for your hard work! These critical years of growing a family bring significant responsibilities. During these years, you can't afford not to plan. Here are common needs among dual-income families:

- Each spouse needs to maximize disability income coverage to help protect the mortgage payments, monthly expenses, and contributions to insurance and investments in the event he or she becomes disabled and qualifies for benefits.
- Each spouse needs life insurance protection on the other in an amount that can cover the mortgage expenses as well as help replace lost income.
- With a college student driving 85 miles one-way each weekend, the family will need personal excess liability protection in the event that she is in an auto accident with coeds or anyone else.
- They need to continue to save for the education of the second child who will be entering college in 10 years.

QUESTIONS TO ASK

- Do you have any debt?
- What are your monthly expenses?
- What is your combined gross and net income?

- Is your job secure?
- Do you have a short-term emergency savings or money market account?
- Do you and your spouse have income protection?
- How much life insurance are you carrying on each other?
- Do you have a will?
- What is the present value in each spouse's retirement account, and are you maximizing contributions, and attaining optimum growth?
- Is your auto insurance liability protection adequate for teenage drivers?
- Will you receive an inheritance?

SOLUTION

Vinnie and Angela can boost their peace of mind considerably by first helping insure that their protection needs are met in the event that either becomes disabled or dies—which is a high risk for Vinnie given his occupation as a pilot. The fact that the family is financially over-extended, demonstrates that the family lifestyle cannot be sustained if either income is jeopardized due to disability or death. In America, the realities and necessities of the dual-income family have put an end to the old myth that women do not need to have life insurance. Any dual-income family would be hard pressed, even with a male head of household, to retain its standard of living if the woman's income suddenly was not available due to death or disability.

Vinnie and Angela need to increase their life insurance on each other. Vinnie has $250,000 of life insurance, but his $90,000 income qualifies him for $900,000. Angela has $70,000 term insurance at work. Her $35,000 income should qualify her for $350,000. Vinnie should apply for $650,000 and Angela should apply for $280,000. It should be diversified using both term and permanent insurance based on a fact-find and cash flow analysis. Both Vinnie and Angela are fortunate to have disability income protection at work.

Beyond their current 401(k) contributions, it is unrealistic for this couple to believe they can do more. However, they can take charge of reducing their financial stress by focusing on monthly expenses and working at creating a new lifestyle with fewer expectations. Perhaps they can consider fewer vacations even though their airfare is paid. Each family member can't have it all. Together as a family they should discuss the financial facts of life and agree on limiting the added luxuries which become financial burdens as well.

I find that lifestyle issues are often the easiest for a family to resolve together as a team. Here are a few ideas my clients from dual-income families have shared as ways of simplifying life and cutting expenses:

- Assign times to do the household chores and errands—as a team; with everyone working, chores can get done quickly.

- Attempt to set aside some time during the week for the family to be together.
- Encourage teens to earn spending money to support their entertainment.
- Create a community youth exchange where the neighborhood kids do errands for other families. Often it increases their sense of self esteem and responsibility to work for someone else. Teach children and teens how to write checks and have a checking account. Teach children early that money comes as a result of working—not from a plastic card placed in the cash machine at the bank.
- Exercise your right as an American raising a strong healthy family to leave work at a reasonable hour. A steady habit of working late nights and weekends without other days off will not keep a family together.
- Eat out less.
- Limit student after-school activities to 1 day a week rather than 4 or 5. Get students focused on doing a few things very well rather than have the whole family scattered and running wild to keep up with the Joneses—who are also running wild.
- When they are in junior high school, begin to encourage students to learn about available college scholarships. By having a sports, an academic, or an art scholarship as a goal, students will have a specialized focus for their after school activities rather than having no direction until it's too late. Take advantage of your school tax dollars and consult your high school guidance counselor about scholarships.

I also encouraged Angela and Vinnie to meet with me along with their certified public accountant and attorney to help the family through these tough years. Their attorney needs to create or update a will. The fact that their professional team will meet with them together will give an enormous sense of self confidence and provide comfort for Angela and Vinnie. They will know that they are not struggling alone without support. After the second daughter graduates from college, Angela and Vinnie can begin aggressive savings for retirement and their dream home.

#7: TO DIVORCE & REMARRY WITH CHILDREN

Divorced Parent Starting Over: Dee

THE NUMBER OF AMERICAN WOMEN WHO ARE SINGLE PARENTS AND heads of households grows each year. In 1993, 31.5 million women were working single parents; this has grown from 8.1 million in 1960.[25] My divorced women clients share intensely personal and riveting stories. Divorced parents seem to have the most complicated set of factors at play in their efforts to put themselves on a solid course. They are uncertain about being able to save wealth for the future. They are dealing with their own economic and career influences, as well as the tenuous economic circumstances of an ex-spouse.

Issues of trust, of loyalty, of fear of failure, of fear of "doing it all alone," not to mention fear or anger, all arise to make divorced parents vulnerable, anxious and confused during the months following divorce. My clients who are divorced parents with growing children tell me they are so exhausted and overwhelmed about the present, that they cannot even begin to think about the future. They recall anxiety over parents, friends, and attorneys telling them what to do during the "rejection and divorce war." After divorce, many women claim that they are emotionally shattered, fearful, and incapable of making decisions on their own. Yet, divorced women feel a strong desire to be affirmed and to feel "fulfilled, attractive, and loved," which are feelings often coupled with a deep need to have a daily "father figure" in their children's lives. In a few years, life can become even more complicated and difficult when either a divorced father or mother contemplates remarriage. What I have witnessed in my practice is that the second marriage often cannot survive the emotional, financial and legal stress. Ultimately, more than half of second and third marriages fail.[26]

Women who have gone through the experience offer these insights.

> . . . I was totally blind sighted and ill prepared to be alone and face all the nurturing and financial responsibilities of my children. There was so much I didn't know—legally and financially. There should have been a seminar or course out there to teach me what not to do and what to do. I probably would have stuck it out in my first marriage and definitely not remarried. I was in such shell shock from the first divorce that I was hopeful that a second relationship would be a help.
>
> —*SEE*

. . . I think every woman who contemplates marriage owes it to herself to understand everything there is to know about the financial ramifications and legal issues involved with divorce. Once there are children in a marriage, the financial consequences and uncertainties of a divorce can set you back to square one. Actually, it's worse than starting over, because after divorce, you're older and everything is harder.

—MK

. . . I had 3 kids; the guy I was dating had 2. I felt we shared a common bond. Perhaps I remarried because I felt that it would be easier if we were both raising our kids together. . . . I was thinking of myself and my children and was totally unprepared for the realities associated with his ex-wife and her demands on him on behalf of her own children. Any single mother thinking about remarrying should take time to investigate all financial issues so she can be aware. Believe me, if you thought the end of the first marriage was no fairy tale, the second marriage can offer double jeopardy, especially if he has children of his own.

—MJS

. . . My friends had cautioned me about rebound relationships after I was divorced. I was devastated, lonely, and in need. But I did take the time to rediscover myself and to become more responsible. I was open to the possibility that I was also to blame in my failed marriage and took time to realize how I may have contributed to its demise. I joined a health club, became active in my church, and concentrated on quality time with the children. It took years, but I was satisfied that when I met my second husband I was mature, strong, and confident about what I had achieved on my own with my children. I was ready and whole to begin again.

—EJ

. . . I went through the ringer during my divorce, and I was determined to never let it happen to me again. Three years ago, I thought I had fallen in love and actually was planning to remarry. My best friend, who was a single parent and who was divorced twice, took me aside and strongly suggested that I take some time to totally analyze the situation. I met with my attorney and agent, and we spent time working out various scenarios for the future regarding my children, my parents and my retirement. It was the best thing I could have ever done. I realized that the understanding and common values that I thought I had with my future husband were all in my mind. When I started talking about a prenuptial agreement to protect my inheritance and assets, he was uncooperative and used mind games about "having no faith in our future together." I basically said that a prenuptial agreement encouraged open

> communication. When it came down to it, he never showed up. The hard dose of reality was really worth the effort because I diverted another disaster. The biggest lesson I learned was that it is *my* responsibility to plan and to provide a strategy for the future—no one else's. I ended up feeling much better and more confident about my own strength to take care of my children and my future. I may have been emotionally hurt again, but I avoided being hurt financially as well.
>
> —*ASK*

Dee was 34-years old and working as an executive secretary. She was proud of the opportunities she created for herself and readily admitted that with a $40,000 salary, many Americans coming from a small town would consider her successful for achieving such a salary without a college degree.

Dee was ambitious. She was a dark Mediterranean beauty with long brunette hair. She had been a social butterfly; she eventually married Brian, her high school sweetheart who had been captain of the football team.

Both were gregarious and popular; people told them they'd go far with their "good looks" and "great personalities." Brian attended a prominent university north of Milwaukee and became an engineer. Dee's front office poise and presence made her perfect for dealing with the public, and she easily obtained a position as a receptionist at the corporate office of a large local dairy and cheese product manufacturer in Wisconsin.

Dee was eager to move the marriage forward and to begin a family; many of her friends were enjoying pregnancy and motherhood. Brian, however, was just becoming established at the engineering firm, and he was not yet financially secure to begin a family; he wanted to pay off his student loans. Dee was convincing that she could work part-time, be a mom, and work within a budget. They had 2 sons within 2 years of Brian's graduation.

Dee told me her story. "I remember that I liked kids when I was growing up, and we had a few of our own because I felt as a woman it was the thing to do at that time in my life. I was a cheerleader; Brian played football; we were king and queen of the prom. When we were married, we looked like the little couple on top of the wedding cake. The exhilaration, attention and prominence Brian and I both had in high school just ended. He went on to college and grew as an individual; but my life just seemed to stop. All the happy high school times quickly became past memories as we started to fight over finances and whose responsibility it was to take out the trash as we were tripping over blocks and toys. Brian was devoted, loyal and a great father, but I wanted more. I blamed my own unhappiness on him. I thought he was responsible for making me happy. My attitude was childish. Brian just couldn't put up with it any more. He had this conservative image of how his mother and father ran a household—home cooked meals every night, home sewn clothes, a neat house to come home to, and his shirt freshly pressed each morning—everything I didn't do."

Dee and Brian both worked. Brian wanted to save and be responsible financially. Dee was unaware and unconcerned about the household finances and thought that her part-time job justified increased spending. She wasn't responsible and didn't accept the fact that she spent much more than what they both earned. They had different values about what was important in those early years.

Dee paid for the extras: designer clothing, European cosmetics, boutique decor for the house, and nightly dinners out. Brian paid for the mortgage, cars, household expenses, insurance, savings, and retirement.

The divorce was a struggle similar to what most couples face, but Dee was satisfied with the settlement. Her friends and family encouraged her to get the house. Dee was leery to pay for the upkeep on her own. Instead, her attorney negotiated for Brian to pay health care and to educate both sons through college. Dee "had realized too late how important it is for a husband and wife to share similar values about finances if a marriage is to grow and thrive." She also learned how valuable continued education was if she was to achieve higher earning potential.

NEEDS

If you are like Dee, and during your marriage you were out of touch with financial responsibility of the family, divorce probably means that you are starting over with a new commitment to be responsible in ways you may not have been in the past. If you have children, you will need:

- To obtain life insurance protection on each parent for the benefit of the children in the event that either parent dies.
- To obtain medical coverage for the children.
- To create a short-term savings fund that also provides cash flow in the event that child support payments are irregular.
- To select a professional team and begin serious planning.
- To analyze all expenses relative to net monthly income.
- To protect the income stream of both parents in the event of disability.

QUESTIONS TO ASK

- Do you have disability income protection coverage?
- What are your total monthly expenses?
- What is your net monthly income?

- Will you receive child support on a regular basis and how much will it be?
- Is your ex-spouse responsible to carry out the financial obligation of monthly support payments on an uninterrupted basis?
- Who is responsible for providing medical insurance coverage for the children?
- Does the ex-spouse carry life insurance? Who is designated as the beneficiary?
- Do you have life insurance?
- Do you and your ex-spouse have separate wills?
- Do you receive additional financial help from others in your family?
- What type of benefits do you have at work?
- Do you expect to inherit any money in the next 5 to 10 years?

SOLUTION

Brian's retirement remained intact after the divorce. Therefore, at age 34, Dee did not have a home, or any individual retirement program of her own except what she would receive from Social Security. Her divorce settlement also gave her the second car, which was older but paid off. She requested half of the 401(k) retirement, but instead, her attorney suggested Brian pay her $10,000 to be used as an emergency fund.

Dee realized too late the costs of not being financially responsible. She committed to become responsible and involved in her own retirement and financial future. She is looking forward to the day when she will be able to begin her own plan because the dairy company where she currently is employed has no retirement program.

Dee's children, Terry and Troy, were ages 14 and 12 at the time of her divorce. They are relying on her for emotional and financial security. She knows that they are growing up in Brian's footsteps with a love of football, sports—and their Dad. They resent being away from him.

After the divorce, Dee was pressured by her family to buy a small house of her own; they thought the mortgage interest deduction would be a significant benefit to her when filing her tax return. But Dee was afraid of the added responsibility, expenses, and unforeseen maintenance associated with owning a home. She met with her accountant to review the financials associated with owning *vs.* renting. Tax benefits of owning a home were not considerable enough for her. In relationship to the tax benefits, Dee's increased expenses and purchases associated with buying a home would be an encumbrance, and she would have no emergency savings if she used the $10,000 from her divorce settlement to purchase a home. Dee was resolved. She simplified her life and rented a town house to avoid such worries.

Instead, the $10,000 which Dee received was placed into a conservative mutual fund account; $6,000 was placed in a money market account for use as an emergency fund, and $4,000 was placed in a growth fund. The $6,000 money market account has a checkbook and is earning interest.

Dee then needed to address her $40,000 salary and how she could stretch her monthly net pay to cover rent, utilities, food, clothing and all the extras to which she had been accustomed and the extras for growing boys.

Dee needed to provide for income protection needs. In the event that he dies, Brian is carrying a life insurance policy to provide for child support until their sons are 21 and to cover the commitment for college. The divorce settlement provides for each son to attend a state college of his choice. (Insurance agents, registered representatives, financial planners, certified public accountants, and bank lending officers provide printed materials that project the cost of a college education in the future.) He also had to provide a disability income protection policy to help cover child support payments in the event that he becomes disabled and qualifies for benefits.

She applied for a personal disability income policy for $2,380 a month. She felt secure in knowing that if she became disabled and qualified for benefits, the policy would help her pay the bills and the groceries.

Dee also applied for a $400,000 term life insurance policy. Some day, she hopes to convert it to a cash value insurance to supplement her retirement, but due to her income, she is pleased with the amount of coverage she can purchase inexpensively.

She has met with the attorney to update her will and put a life insurance trust in order to help secure the children's support if she should die. By having a life insurance trust, she can designate how the money is to be used by those who would care for her sons in the event that she dies. She does not want to name Brian as beneficiary on the policy even though she knows if she dies he will have custody rights. With the help of her attorney, she can set the terms and guidelines for use of the life insurance proceeds within the trust. If Dee dies, the trust receives $400,000. If it averaged an assumed 10-percent annual rate of return, the trust could provide $40,000 annually for the housing and support of the boys in the event that the children are minors and the father dies.

Dee expects to receive an inheritance of approximately $150,000 when her parents and elderly aunt die. Her aunt is her godmother and has no one else to whom she can bequeath her estate. At that time, Dee would consider a diversified mutual fund account for the inheritance. This will help protect her income if she is in need; if life goes well, it can be considered a growth fund for the potential of retirement security. By considering this approach, Dee could truly think of her inheritance as the beginning of her retirement security.

POSSIBILITY OF REMARRIAGE

Two years after her divorce, Dee became financially concerned about the impact of a prospective remarriage in her life. Dee had always thrived on the attention that men gave her; she said it made her feel good, and she liked it when men were "nice to her." But nice is not enough. A divorced parent contemplating remarriage must approach any future relationship like a business. Dee was tired of being without a man in her life and vulnerable. It was hard for her to wipe the stars out of her eyes.

Dee needed to protect her personal assets. She needed to begin a discussion to determine her beau's income, his child support payments for his own children, as well as his total debt. She also was determined to talk to other divorced parents who had entered second marriages.

If Dee truly wants a long-term relationship, the total financial picture for both partners must be explained by each of them—not just verbally but—in black and white with both accountants present. It should be a time to review life insurance, and disability income protection policies, W2 statements, and retirement account statements. This is the time to ask questions as if your future depends upon it—because it does.

QUESTIONS TO ASK

- Do you each know the other's total financial status in terms of assets, gross and net income, and expenses?
- How much debt are you both bringing to the marriage?
- What is the extent of both parties' work benefits?
- Where do you each fall in the priority order of legal responsibilities to your own children and your own ex-spouses?
- What are the "unspoken or unwritten or informal" emotional, legal, financial, or other responsibilities each of you has made to your own children and to your own ex-spouse on their behalf? For instance: what are the monthly hidden costs beyond child support such as music, dance, or gymnastics lessons; recitals; musical instrument purchases; first car and insurance; exchange student opportunities; summer camps; other travel opportunities; vacations with friends; *etc.*?
- How do the unspoken commitments to ex-spouses and ex-grandparents impact the hierarchy of time, attention, and finances you can give to one another in this new emotional and financial relationship?
- Will you need to move into new housing to accommodate all the kids for vacations, weekends, and holidays?

- Does distance from step children of both families create other financial or time factors which will have a strong impact on your new family unit?
- If something happens to either in the remarriage, how do you want insurance proceeds to be addressed?
- What is the duration of child support—in terms of what is to be received and what is to be paid to another ex-spouse?
- If one of you becomes disabled, how is income and child support affected?
- If you are unable to work, his child support payments to his children are his first priority according to law. Will he also be able to support your joint living expenses together as a family when your full pay check is not there? (This is the 30 percent to 40 percent of your income which is uncovered by disability income insurance.)
- Will you both agree to a prenuptial agreement drafted by your attorneys?
- Do you know the child support and custody laws in the state or county that governs where the other's divorce decree was granted?
- According to applicable law, does the income you add to the joint family you create positively affect his "ability to pay" regarding additional demands by his ex-spouse on behalf of his children as they grow and the cost of living increases?
- Can you both afford life insurance with each other as the beneficiary, in addition to the policies which you each have for the benefit of your own children?
- Ultimately, do you both share the same values regarding raising children and finances?

SOLUTION

Dee and her beau can wait to remarry until their children are grown and on their own. In the meantime, they can find emotional support during romantic weekends alone. This could prove to be the least stressful financial alternative.

If Dee chooses to remarry while the kids are growing, she needs to first understand the financial and legal parameters and discuss a prenuptial agreement with her beau and attorney. Each needs to reveal total finances to each other, so if either dies, the surviving spouse is not left to deal with the other's ex-spouse. Each needs to define long-term goals.

Her beau needs to commit to a life insurance policy at 10 times his annual salary and name her as beneficiary. He needs to have a disability policy to cover his income.

He and she both must have properly written wills and trusts for the benefit of both sets of children and for the benefit of each other.

Dee's children's education is promised. But her beau also has obligations to his children. If he is responsible for them, he needs to put money aside to accumulate $70,000, which is the approximate estimated cost of a state college education in 10 years according to College Board tables. For instance, if Dee's beau is responsible for educating a child 10 years from now and if he is fortunate enough to average an assumed 9-percent annual rate of return, $350 a month or $4,200 annually needs to be placed in mutual funds or another investment vehicle.

If Dee's ex-husband, Brian, is responsible for a similar amount for her children, Dee needs to assure that money is being set aside in accounts in the children's name as a *uniform gift to minors with the parents as custodians.* Then she can request copies of the account statements to verify that the savings are accumulating.

Dee needs to assure that she will not cosign any loans for her beau's children in addition to the financial commitments she has to her own. **In the event of a second divorce and her beau is unable to pay a college loan that Dee cosigned, the bank holds Dee responsible to pay the loan—regardless of what the legal divorce settlement stipulates.**

As a newly remarried couple, Dee and her beau both must agree about how to save, for what purpose, how much, and who is paying for what! They must agree to keep their retirement funding separate. In the event the second marriage doesn't survive, their individual retirement savings will not be jeopardized; no one will be forced to make a lump sum payment in the event of a second divorce. The days are over when retirement accounts are considered applicable to only the husband in the household without any separate emphasis placed on the wife's retirement needs.

Both people in this remarriage have experienced the issues, the heartache, and the betrayal of divorce. From this point forward, they both should agree on open dialogue and insist that there will be no hidden agendas with ex-spouses. Each should consider that all debt as well as promised inheritances or savings belong to him and his children or her and her children. Secure this in a prenuptial agreement or other legal planning recommended by an attorney prior to remarriage. All future decisions about investments, home and retirement should be determined together by Dee and her new husband.

With all of their baggage checked, the couple is ready to embark on a new journey.

#8: TO CARE FOR AGING PARENTS

Single with Aged Parents: Pam

PAM, A SMILING BRUNETTE WHO LOVES INLAND FISHING, IS IN HER mid-40s and secure in a nursing career. She had been the department head in a large teaching hospital. In 1992, she sold her ranch in El Paso to take a new position on the Gulf Coast in Corpus Christie, Texas, near her father and mother, who are in their late 70s.

Pam has taken on a role as care giver for her parents; however, her parents have not been totally open with her about their wishes and plans for the future. Pam does not know the details of their life insurance program: how much they have, what company it is with, or how the beneficiaries are assigned. She has concerns about her parents becoming ill and whether she would need to consider nursing home or in-home care. She has heard her friends discuss concerns about the administrative fees associated with probate, and as a result, Pam wonders whether or not her parents have a current will.

When Pam was introduced to me, she was concerned about this new milestone in her life when she began worrying about her aging parents. Pam has a brother who is 10 years her senior, but she knows that because of his own lifestyle, business commitments and lack of closeness, he would share little if any participation in their elder parents' welfare—emotionally or financially. Matters were made worse when her brother told her that their mom and dad put $77,000 cash in little cigar boxes hidden under the floor boards of the linen closet. Both parents had deep memories of the Depression and recall the fears of their parents losing money when the banks closed.

Pam was confused about what to do first. She mentioned, "The worst part of all, is that as a family we never discussed these things with our parents. There was always silence when it came to issues such as money, death, and the future. Because there was no common discussion about this when we were growing up, we just can't discuss it comfortably now." Pam had no idea about what to do or what it was going to take for her parents to be responsible to communicate with her. Ultimately, it would be Pam who would be faced with their financial decisions in the future, and she was in a position of responsibility but had no idea about their net worth. Her father was a retired coal miner from Pennsylvania who moved to Texas in the late '70s because of his health. He had received a monetary payment because of his black lung disease.

NEEDS

If you have aging parents and find your situation similar to Pam's, you need to initiate discussion to uncover the facts. Parents who have experienced the Depression have deep feelings about their financial struggles and losses from that time. But they must understand that if their financial affairs are not in order and communicated to their children, the children could pay large legal fees and estate taxes, not to mention the time and frustration of getting matters in order after the parents are deceased. The irony for the family will be that lack of planning could cost what the parents have hidden and saved under the floor boards in their cigar boxes. Consider the following approach:

- Gather any pension statements and life insurance policies and understand their provisions to assure that beneficiary assignments are up-to-date.
- Be introduced to and begin to work with your parents' attorney and insurance agent.
- Understand the medical coverage and any outstanding medical bills which have accumulated with their illness.
- Investigate the local costs for *custodial care* within a nursing home and/ or in-home care.
- Work with an attorney to establish a *statutory power of attorney* to enable you to run the finances and monthly bills for your parents.
- Work with an attorney and your parents' physicians to establish a *health care power of attorney* to aid in making health care decisions for your parents in the event you are unable to do so.
- Work with an attorney to determine if your parents' will is current.
- Work with an attorney to establish a *living will* for your parents which includes their directives regarding whether they want to be kept alive by artificial means.
- Work with your parents to determine their wishes regarding burial or cremation services when they die. Join them in making final arrangements to put these affairs in order at an appropriate time.

QUESTIONS TO ASK

- If parents are on a fixed income, is there a shortfall in monthly income to cover increases in prescription expenses or medical expenses not covered by insurance?
- What are the provisions and how are the beneficiaries assigned on parent's life insurance policies, bank accounts etc.?
- In whose name are bank accounts, certificates of deposit, stocks, bonds, or mutual funds listed?

- If the family estate is valued at over $600,000, have there been provisions made to create a trust or otherwise provide cash to address the Federal estate tax potential?
- If your parents have elected custodial care, how will it affect the assignment of their assets? To the children? Or to the nursing home?
- If your parents face financial jeopardy, what portion of your discretionary income is available to assist them?

SOLUTION

I suggested that the attorney, Pam, and I meet together with her parents. I encouraged Pam to openly discuss her concerns. Having the attorney and I there made it easier for the issues to be discussed openly.

I analyzed the insurance policies and created a summary that explained each policy, contract numbers, company of issue, death benefit amounts and beneficiary designations.

I recommended long-term care coverage with an in-home provision for each parent. There were many types of policies for Pam to review. Many provided for nursing home care, others provided both in-home health care and nursing home care. The parents selected an appropriate plan based on their feelings.

The attorney reviewed the will and informed them that the will was outdated. It had not been reviewed since Pam was a little girl, and it had another family member who was deceased listed as a trustee. The attorney informed her parents that it was common practice to have *statutory power of attorney* documents drawn. The power of attorney would enable Pam to write checks, pay bills and make other financial decisions on their behalf if either parent should become incapacitated. An updated will was written. The attorney also suggested that her parents notify Pam about the location of their bank accounts, stock certificates and other financial papers; he had requested a summary of all accounts to organize all records. He would then review these and recommend actions to simplify matters for probate reasons. Having organized and properly assigned accounts prior to the death of each parent would minimize probate fees after the death of each.

Pam also brought her own insurance policies to the meeting for review. She was concerned whether she needed to provide financial help to her parents, her own disability income coverage and life insurance were properly designed if her parents would be relying on this income. Pam originally had her brother listed as the beneficiary of her insurance. She had genuine concerns that if she predeceased her parents and her brother received the death benefit, he would not necessarily share her same wishes to use the money to take care of their aging parents. The attorney suggested that Pam designate a trustee, because he recommended that her insurance be placed inside of a trust in order to secure the care of her parents if Pam predeceased them.

Even though Pam's parents would always consider Pam as their "little girl," I made them understand that a time would come when they may not be able to handle their own affairs. Her father was a proud man who had a hard time dealing with the fact that his daughter would someday be taking care of him. I communicated to her parents that the most important issue they needed to decide was whether they wanted the IRS and nursing home to potentially receive their assets or whether they wanted to leave a legacy to their son and daughter.

#9: TO OWN A BUSINESS

Starting a Business: Rebecca

"I'VE SPENT 15 YEARS WORKING FOR OTHER PEOPLE WHOM I FELT had lower standards than mine in this business." That was the first assertion I remember Rebecca making when we met. She was 37-years old and had "had enough of working for others."

I cannot forget how passionately Rebecca voiced her convictions when she exclaimed, "Doing what I love should not make me feel this miserable! I want to be in control of my destiny. I want to be as creative as I want and manage my daily hours according to the priorities which I set—rather than according to what someone else thinks I should be doing. And when my customer is happy, when my intentions are noble, when my work is excellent—it is fun. When I excel at what I love, this is my happiness. This is my measure of success."

Rebecca stated what other women believe in their hearts each day they go to work. She echoed the passions and beliefs that I hear again and again from many women who have launched private enterprises.

To say that Rebecca was driven and determined was an understatement. This woman was full of energy, and failure was not an option. Her fire was fueled by the realities of raising a daughter on her own after a very bitter divorce. She claims her dedication and long hours at work with a well-known public relations firm was "a strain on a marriage that just wasn't strong enough to survive a wife and mother working long hours outside the home."

Rebecca wanted a total overhaul of her life. Instead of retreating in self-doubt, she moved forward into even higher risk and uncertainty by starting her own business. She was attractive, creative, intellectual, sharp, and outspoken. Rebecca stated that she had been "through the muck of it and down on herself;" she wanted to shed 20 pounds that she attributed to stress and lack of appropriate exercise. Rebecca was a no-nonsense, sturdy, hard-working woman and a salt-of-the-earth type on whom everyone could depend to accomplish the impossible at the last hour.

Rebecca will face many issues and concerns throughout the life cycle of her business.

GENERAL NEEDS DURING THE LIFE CYCLE OF A BUSINESS

The life cycle of a business begins with the pride, motivation, and desire to start a venture that will succeed through various stages during its growth and development. The following concepts are what Rebecca learned during our association; her knowledge of what to expect built her confidence about her new venture.

For a moment, let's have you join Rebecca for an overview of Business 101.

Coordinating a Professional Team

I cannot encourage you enough to take the time to select and develop trusting relationships with a banker, certified public accountant, attorney, agent, registered representative, or financial planner as your professional team. Take the time to communicate with them quarterly. It is their input in the early months of starting your business that can give you the expertise and emotional support you need. That you receive education and attentiveness from every member of your professional team is absolutely essential. If months go by and you feel that one person just doesn't have the time to communicate with or teach you what you need to know, it's time for a change. Many women believe that unless they can communicate their concerns openly with a professional, they wouldn't be encouraged to develop a relationship where they can learn what they need to prosper.

Banker or Loan Officer

Your banker or loan officer will provide you a sample *business plan* to show you what is necessary in order to obtain financing. Establishing a business plan and learning how to predict business cycles and expenses is one of the primary fundamentals for a beginning entrepreneur who intends to market expertise and talent. There are many books on the market to assist you in developing a credible business plan.

Your banker or loan officer will then evaluate the loan potential of your business based on additional input from your accountant and the attorney. There are different types of loans the bank will consider. First is setting up a line of credit. A $50,000 *line of credit* requires that you complete a financial statement based on past record. The bank reviews the earnings power of the new business and will set the interest rate and payment conditions. A line of credit loan is designed to help only if you are in need of supplementing cash flow based on expenses. This type of loan is generally used for a young professional who will possibly need back-up financing in the early start-up months of the business.

A second type of loan, *a lump sum loan*, is often needed for the down payment or outright purchase of a business or building. The bank may be looking at business potential, book value, profit and loss. Collateral is often required for a lump sum loan; because of this, any cash value life insurance policy you have can be considered toward your collateral. The bank will also request term life insurance on the owners in order to be protected in the event of death of a loan holder. (This is known as a *collateral assignment* where your business pays the premium for a policy for the specific amount of the loan, and the bank is named as beneficiary as long as there is an outstanding loan balance for the amount owed.) The bank retains the policy and should return it to the owners after the debt has been paid.

Certified Public Accountant

Your certified public accountant will assist you in understanding the various types of business structures and how they impact taxation. Sole proprietorships, partnerships, S-corporations, and C-corporations all vary. Use your certified public accountant to help you decide what structure is best for you.

On an ongoing basis, your certified public accountant will also help you stay focused on your profit and loss to monitor growth of your business. If you should later decide to sell the business, the certified public accountant will determine its financial worth by providing a market analysis for the value of the building as well as your profit and loss over a period of time, usually 3 to 5 years.

Attorney

Early legal concerns for a start-up business involve purchasing and leasing agreements that must be drafted or reviewed by an attorney. The attorney will be concerned with all legal aspects of the business and will be your advocate regarding all clauses in your contracts.

Your attorney also is responsible for incorporation. The attorney assists you in establishing *bylaws* that are a key legal provision when establishing a new corporation; the bylaws establish rules to govern the internal affairs and regulations of your organization. If the building, leasing arrangements, business or professional practice is comprised of more than one individual, bylaws must be drafted and put in order. Bylaws are designed for the protection of everyone who is responsible for the growth of the business or who has signed their name to the purchase of the building or leasing commitment. The bylaws will require many conditions.

Insurance Agent

The insurance agent whom you select for your professional team should have expertise in business insurance planning and recommend other insurance agents who can provide liability and medical plans. Your primary agent should educate you about how to use insurance to protect the business and your employees.

PROTECTING THE BUSINESS

Liability insurance will be needed for the building and the business. It is designed to protect the building in the event of fire, theft or other catastrophe such as on-premises injury. Additional types of *errors or omissions insurance* or *personal excess liability* coverage can often be purchased to help safeguard against liability and exposure due to professional or technical performance of duties by you or your employees.

A new business that operates with more that one partner often purchases key man or *key person insurance*. This is for owners, partners or other contracted employees. This life insurance is for the purpose of paying the business a sum of money that would equate to the value of the person's contribution or expertise in operating the business. If the key person is responsible for one-third of the debt and cash flow to the business, then for the business to survive, it needs to be reassured that cash will be available in the event of the death of this person. The life insurance proceeds help in the replacement cost of hiring new talent to fill the loss.

The owners of the business often purchase *disability overhead expense* coverage to help cover business expenses. The purpose is to cover employee wages, utilities, outstanding loans, taxes, professional fees, and other monthly expenses. Subject to certain policy limitations, the policy will generally cover all expenses of a business except supplies. The insurance company will determine if it will insure the owners and the amount it is willing to insure depending on the nature of the occupation and the extent of expenses. The owner/s must be healthy and insurable without a major medical condition at the time of applying for the coverage. All members of the group will need this type of coverage to help insure that the mortgage payment and business expenses are covered in the event that one of the members becomes disabled and qualifies for benefits. For example, if there are 3 owners, and the expenses for the business are $6,000 per month, the program will provide that each owner has coverage for $2,000. This protects each owner and generally is a requirement for a bank loan.

The owner of a business corporation also can set up a formal *wage continuation* arrangement. As an employer, you need to set guidelines for yourself and for employees about how anyone would get paid in the event of a disability. If you **do not have** a formal wage continuation arrangement adopted as a resolution, any paycheck you receive if you become disabled may be considered an *ad hoc* dividend payment that is not deductible to the business. The IRS will allow a formal wage continuation arrangement drawn by your attorney to have parameters. For example, the owner will receive 100 percent of income for the first 90 days and then the disability policy will pay to age 65 if the owner becomes disabled and qualifies for benefits. The terms should be written and formally be part of the company resolutions prior to your disability.

There are many ways to use *business owned life insurance* to help the future success of a corporation if the principal owner dies. The corporation pays the premium and is beneficiary. The business owner is the insured. If the insured dies, the insurance company will pay the benefit to the business helping it to continue at a time when the business could have severe cash flow problems without the owner. This is similar to key person insurance. Your agent can help you determine the best type of policy for your business.

PROTECTING THE EMPLOYEES

Beyond establishing initial coverage to protect the key person and building, the continuing cycle of business development involves employee benefits. The following *group insurance* benefits are discussed in sequence according to order of importance for the employees and according to availability of cash flow of the growing business. These are the ones most commonly used by many small businesses.

Group health insurance comes in many forms and is available to as few as 1 employee including the owner, depending on the state. First, you determine what you want in the form of benefits and company rating. Health insurance can be purchased to cover costs associated with *medical, maternity, prescription, dental, vision and preventative care.*

Perhaps you will select a program such as—$500 deductible 80 /20 to $5,000. The employee would pay the first $500 then pay 20 percent of the $5,000. That would be $1,000 out of pocket for the employee, and the insurance company would pay the 80 percent of $5,000 and 100 percent after $5,000 up to a limit. (Some companies have no limit.) In this scenario, the total outlay for the employee would be $1,500. For example, if an employee had a $50,000 hospital bill for heart surgery, this coverage would work as follows. First, the patient pays the $500 deductible. The patient then pays 20 percent of the next $5,000 ($1,000) of the medical bill. The insurance company would pay 80 percent of $5,000 ($4,000) plus the remaining $44,500—if the charges were usual and customary and approved by the insurance company.

Maternity, prescription, dental, vision, and preventative care benefits are considered to be optional. Therefore, depending on the cost of the options, you can choose which is best. Health insurance requires an underwriting decision by the insurance company, so it is possible to have a group policy which is rated if health issues are prevalent among the employees. You would also have to follow the *pre-existing condition* guidelines of the insurance company. For instance, each company defines "pre-existing" differently. A common example is that any medical consultation or treatment within 1 year prior to applying for coverage would not be covered until 1 year after issue.

Once you have a group program in order, and if you choose to change carriers in a few years, in most instances the insurance carrier will entitle you to have *take over*. (Take over means that as long as you have met the inforce carrier's pre-existing guidelines, the new company will not make your employees satisfy them again.) The new carrier may also consider bills already paid by the employee in the year of the take over.

Group disability income insurance is another benefit for the employees that may be paid by the employer. There is a master certificate that defines the benefit, and each employee receives a summary page rather than a policy. The employer chooses the benefit of between 50 to 70 percent of the employee's gross salary plus options such as *partial disability, mental nervous, etc.* The employer creates a census listing employee name, gender, age, income, occupation, and smoker status and provides the listing to the insurance company. The company then determines the premium based on overall census risk. The disability coverage is in force for the employee as long as she is working full-time. Group disability insurance is not portable; therefore, if the employee chooses to leave your business, coverage is terminated assuming it cannot be converted into a personal policy.

Group life insurance can also be added to an employee benefit package in order to purchase insurance for employees and the owner. The price of this is actuarially determined by the ages of the group, but the premium is lower than the premium for cash value insurance because group life insurance is usually a term insurance product. Typically, an amount of $10,000, which is associated with the average cost of funeral expenses, can be purchased. Other options typically include amounts in multiples (1x, 2x, 3x) of an employee's salary. Often, the employer will pay for basic coverage (1x the salary) and offer an opportunity for the employee to increase the coverage (to 2x or 3x), which is done through payroll deduction.

Payroll deduction life insurance provides employees with a convenient opportunity to purchase additional individual life insurance coverage. As an employer, you have the peace of mind knowing that you are providing your employees a way to increase insurance protection that they may not be disciplined to purchase on their own. These programs provide ease of payment to obtain additional term or cash value insurance through payroll deduction. Depending on the program, premiums are deducted from their payroll, and your business makes the premium payments monthly. Also, each employee is the owner of the individual coverage; it can be taken with the employee and is portable in the event that the employee leaves your company. This contrasts with group life insurance mentioned above which is not portable but is generally convertible. Common payroll deduction programs offer cash value life insurance, individual disability income, dental, vision, and cancer plans.

A *Section 125* program provides benefits for both the employer and the employees. A plan needs to be administered according to an approved IRS document. The employee uses payroll deduction to select a product to fit needs. The premiums are *pre-taxed,* which means taxes are paid on a gross salary after the pre-tax amount has been subtracted.

The benefit of a Section 125 program to you as the employer is that you do not have to pay the FICA Social Security tax on the pre-tax amount for each employee. The benefit to the employees is that, within limits, they can apply the benefit to certain types of personal expense they choose such as eye care, dental care, cancer plans, group term, or life insurance. Child care or projected out-of-pocket health insurance expenses for the year are also options. The plan design determines what type of benefit the employee can choose.

LONG-TERM RETIREMENT PLANS

A variety of pension and retirement benefits are available for you to provide to employees. Often it is the retirement plan which helps your business to attract and to retain top notch talent. A *401(k) plan* is commonly used in settings of 10 or more employees. It allows employees to create a retirement plan by payroll deduction from their salary on a pre-tax basis. The amount is determined by the overall census and incomes. An employee can individually pick the investments for contributions based on risk tolerance generally with a family of funds. If you are interested in pursuing a 401(k) plan for your business, you'll need to seek a professional who is a registered representative offering securities through a broker/ dealer.

In addition to providing disciplined savings, the 401(k) plan can be taken with the employee if no longer employed at your business. The employee has the right to transfer the vested fund amount into an IRA upon leaving the company. Also, if any 401(k) or profit sharing plan is canceled due to lack of employee participation, the employer and employees retain their vested fund amounts and can transfer the amounts into IRA accounts, which they will personally own and monitor.

With *profit sharing* plans you, the employer, contribute to the plan on behalf of each employee as well as yourself as long as you are an employee. Generally, the employer contributes to this plan and the employees do not. Up to certain limits, you as the employer decide each year how much or how little to contribute. The benefit to the business owner is that if you are an employee you can contribute on your own behalf as well as your employees', and the money you contribute is tax deductible to the business.

As a business owner there are other retirement programs that can help provide retirement funds for you and your employees. *Deferred compensation* and *executive bonus* programs are among these. Your agent can explain these to you and help you diagnose the program that's best for your situation.

BUSINESS CONTINUATION

Eventually, you will retire. *Succession planning* will help you look for someone to continue the business which you began. To understand the options available and details to address when creating an arrangement, you need to meet with your agent, attorney and certified public accountant together as a team. (See Megan's, Boots's, and Anita's stories.)

A *buy-sell agreement* is a contract in which the business or the owners agree to purchase the business interest upon death, disability or some other occurrence of one of the owners. You enter into an agreement that is designed to protect the value of the business for the principals involved. Let's assume your business has a value of $3 million. Your partners cannot or do not want your family to be involved in running the business in the event of your death. Each partner is insured for $1 million dollars. When one dies, the business receives $1 million to buy out the interest from the family; the remaining partners reserve all future rights to run the business on their own.

A *buy-sell disability arrangement* is also available. These contracts can be designed to have a lump sum payout or monthly income determined by the amount to which each of your partners and you agree. The contracts and insurance policies will address how "total disability" is defined and you qualify for benefits under the terms of the policy, how much the payments will be, and how long the payments will be paid. Input and expertise from your attorney and agent are necessary because all partners need to agree on a 12-month, 18-month, or 24-month elimination period. The partners also need to determine parameters for activation of a buyout such as the length of time a partner must be disabled and the extent or degree of disability; these must be coordinated with the elimination period.

As your business grows, it is imperative that your professional team proactively communicate among themselves. It is imperative that the agent, certified public accountant and attorney each have expertise and experience in business issues—preferably with first-hand experience from running a business of their own. You want a team that's knowledgeable to advise you about pensions, benefits, legal issues, tax issues, and succession planning issues—everything involved in the life of your business.

Now that you have a broad understanding of key issues involved in establishing a business, let's return to Rebecca and see how she began. She was on a mission. From now on she would have her business, her rules, her profits, her headaches, and her losses.

NEEDS

If, like Rebecca, you are talented and motivated with the drive and ambition to begin your own business, here are critical items you must consider. You need:

- To determine if you will begin your enterprise alone, with a partner and/or with a staff of employees.
- To consult with business planning professionals to create a complete 3-year business plan that considers all expenses, income and staffing contingencies.
- To have adequate start-up capital to sustain your personal living expenses as well as business expenses for 3 years.
- To interview and select a certified public accountant, insurance agent, and attorney that suit your style and to develop working relationships with them. Preferably, you should seek professionals willing to take the time to teach you about what needs to be done and the reasons why. In order to assure that your team can relate to your concerns for the start-up business, you would probably select a professional team from among those who operate their own businesses with support staff. Associates who practice with large conglomerates often have not personally experienced the concerns of the sole proprietor or partnership.
- To select an appropriate site location and negotiate the lease. Have an attorney draft a contract for lease or purchase that is favorable to your needs, or have your attorney review the contract which is presented.
- To determine a suitable location that allows for future growth.
- To protect a partnership or corporation in the event of disability or death of the principals.
- To protect your income stream and cash flow as a sole proprietor in the event that you become disabled and qualify for benefits.
- To hire associates with expertise who will share your vision for the company.
- To minimize employee turnover by retaining associates with a benefit package.

QUESTIONS TO ASK

- Do you have a professional team in place whom you trust and who will teach you as your business grows?
- Will you need additional funding to run the business?
- What do you foresee your receivables to be on a monthly basis? Can you predict seasonal cycles for your business throughout the year?
- What was your last annual income prior to beginning your business?
- What are your personal monthly expenses?

- What does your business plan estimate your monthly business overhead expenses to be?
- How much life insurance do you have and who is beneficiary?
- Do you have a personal disability income protection policy?

SOLUTION

As confident as Rebecca was about her own skills, she was also keen enough to know that as a creative whiz she needed help with administrative skills and front-office expertise. She elected to begin her business as a partnership with a colleague. They agreed to "try it out together for 5 years."

Financing

Rebecca put a business plan in order because she had a long-time desire to open her own advertising agency and public relations consulting business. She felt confident with her technical skills, but she was concerned about what to do financially to run a business. While she was with her previous employer, she established a $50,000 line of credit. She had many satisfied clients who committed to keep their advertising services with her if she opened an agency of her own and hired staff to execute the work.

Rebecca used a $150,000 certificate of deposit that she received as an inheritance as collateral for her business loan and found a building to rent. She also made her shopping list for office equipment, computers and necessary materials to start the business.

Selecting a Professional Team

Rather than both partners using a variety of people, Rebecca and her partner chose to work with 1 professional team in order to simplify and coordinate all matters.

They had the attorney draw up a buy-sell contract assigning their individual value in the business to be $250,000. They each applied for $250,000 of insurance. If either were to die, the insurance company would pay $250,000 to their business, and the business would in-turn buy out the interest of the deceased partner.

I also advised Rebecca to have her attorney review the leasing contract. After review, Rebecca had the leasing company change the contract to include a disability clause that would allow her to end a 5-year lease in 3 months if she was considered to be totally disabled and could no longer operate the business.

Rebecca was also encouraged to meet with her attorney regarding her personal planning; these additional discussions considered updating her will. She needed to communicate her thoughts about what would happen to her daughter if

Rebecca were to die. Rebecca named her brother as executor of the estate, and her will designated the $250,000 death benefit to pay for her daughter's care.

Both Rebecca and her partner each applied for a disability income protection policy. The insurance company reviewed their income for the previous 2 years and determined a benefit amount based on the promise of the business and their past work performance. Rebecca also requested a purchase option rider on the policy to allow her to increase (without showing additional evidence of insurability) the amount of benefit, within limits, as her income increases.

Overhead expense disability income protection was also purchased for the business. The insurance company issued this coverage based on the business plan expenses and financial statement provided to the bank. If a bank loans a new business money, most likely the insurance company will issue an overhead expense policy assuming she meets medical requirements. Rebecca found that requirements vary among companies. With 2 partners in the business, and $12,000 in monthly expenses (not counting their income or supplies), each partner purchased an overhead expense policy to provide $6,000 per month to the business in the event that either became disabled and qualified for benefits.

After reviewing the business plan, we spent a great deal of time helping Rebecca and her partner become aware of how important it is to stay focused on cash flow and expenses. Their short-term goal was to accelerate cash flow and to monitor profit and loss. They learned how to draw a salary from the business as personal income. To do this, their first focus was to have enough receivables from continuous projects. They developed a 3-payment system which initiated receivables upon signing each job contract rather than waiting for projects to be completed and delivered before receiving payment.

Providing Benefits for Employees

Rebecca was excited about her new venture and wanted to consider offering a benefit package for herself, partner, and 2 employees. She chose a health insurance program after requiring 3 quotes. She limited the benefits to health insurance at the start, and offered an above-average, hourly wage to attract and keep employees and to compensate for not being able to provide a full benefit package because of cost. She was cautious with a start-up business.

As the business grows and the profit and loss statement indicates an increase in profits, Rebecca and her partner can begin to consider more employee benefits. A future benefit package can include payroll deduction life insurance, group disability income protection coverage, and a 401(k) or other pension plan.

Rebecca also needed to stay focused on her own personal retirement planning. She was busy and overwhelmed with beginning the new business, but that made it all the more necessary to stay focused on her personal long-term goals. It was her personal retirement planning goal as well as planning for her daughter's education in 8 years that assisted her in determining how much business profits needed to grow.

Rebecca and her partner had planned to re-evaluate their association after a 5-year period. At that time, Rebecca called to tell me that the partnership was dissolving, but it was for the better for both of them. When the partnership dissolved, the beneficiaries on all the insurance policies were changed and reassigned to personal family members.

Rebecca was proceeding on track. The partner was "going back" to work for someone else's profit.

Retiring Business Owner: Megan

MEGAN WAS SINGLE AND 62-YEARS OLD WHEN WE MET FOR THE first time. All her life she had idolized her father and studied "to be just like him." She and her brother were from a happy-go-lucky Irish-American family who loved life and dancing. Her older brother married the daughter of a department store owner; he went to work with her father and was molded to take over the business. That left Megan with a choice to help in her father's family business. It was a challenge that she accepted with great zeal and success. She followed in his footsteps and became a certified public accountant in Las Colinas, Texas, where she also employed 2 women. She never imagined that life would speed by so quickly. She had so much fun and loved doing what she did that she just "never had the time to get married."

Megan spent a great deal of time telling me about her needs and desires. She wanted to retire in 3 years, at age 65, and devote her life to working with Youth Groups at local churches. She knew that she needed to find another partner who could work side-by-side with her daily to gain knowledge about her clients. Hopefully, she would also purchase Megan's business.

Megan found a young, eager woman, Lisa, who appreciated the opportunity to learn from Megan. Because Megan had built her business through long-term relationships with her father's most trusted clients, she felt a pride and deep sense of responsibility to assure that the clients were comfortable with her successor. The 3 years they would work together would provide Megan with the confidence that Lisa was the right choice for the clients.

Megan's attorney and personal certified public accountant worked on the value of the business and put an arrangement in place that would allow Lisa to receive minimal income while learning from Megan. When Megan retired, Megan would continue to work 2 days a week to help with the continuity of the business for a year. Megan would also be available on a consulting basis to Lisa for a maximum of 5 years.

The business was to pay $3,000 monthly income to Megan for 2 years, and a $1,500 monthly income for the next 3 years. This arrangement was made instead of a lump sum buyout because Lisa did not have the financial resources nor did she feel comfortable with carrying the large debt. Megan wanted the arrangement to succeed for her, Lisa and the clients; so, she adjusted her retirement lifestyle based on the buyout arrangements.

Megan recalls, "After the initial planning, the time melted away quickly. It seemed to come overnight." She began receiving her individual pension and Social Security benefits as well as receiving the income from the business as agreed in the succession arrangement. Megan's household expenses were little because she had paid off her mortgage while she was working. She also retired without debt.

NEEDS

If, like Megan, you are a business owner facing retirement, you should consider the following:

- To have your attorney draft a formal succession arrangement stating: 1) terms, 2) conditions, 3) amount, and 4) duration of the monthly income you will receive from the business.
- To have your accountant determine the value of the business in order to assure that the purchase price the buyer is offering is realistic.
- To understand Social Security benefits and when to apply for them.
- If a pension plan had been funded throughout your active working business career, you need to determine its dollar amount so that you can have those figures to calculate the monthly income.
- A successor for the business will need to have in place a disability program that can help assure you of your monthly income in the event she becomes disabled and qualifies for benefits.
- The successor also needs to have a life insurance policy in place (with you named as beneficiary) for the value of the business in the event of her death.

QUESTIONS TO ASK

- When do you wish to retire?
- Do you want to sell the business outright?
- Do you want to have a lump sum buyout or a 1- to 5-year buyout program?
- How much money do you think your business is currently worth?
- What type of monthly payment is realistic?
- Do you have a retirement account, and what is it worth?
- What are your personal monthly household expenses?
- What are your retirement goals (travel, purchase retirement home, *etc.*)?
- Do you have life insurance? What is the value of the death benefit? Who is beneficiary?

SOLUTION

Megan planned well. Being debt-free allowed her flexibility in the way she sold and transferred her practice to a successor. Had she carried a large debt load, it may have been more difficult to accept the 5-year buyout arrangement she made with Lisa.

She needed Lisa to have a disability income protection policy on herself as well as a disability income overhead expense policy for the business. This would help protect Megan's monthly buyout payment over the 5-year period in the event that Lisa became disabled and qualified for benefits. This was reassuring for both women because if Lisa became disabled, the practice could remain open and Megan's promissory note could also be protected.

Lisa also applied for a $126,000 term life insurance policy to protect the total amount of the buy-out value of the business in the event of her death. Megan was named beneficiary on the policy.

In the event that Megan could no longer work, she kept her own disability policy in force for the first year of the business arrangement. This would help Lisa replace Megan's services that were promised 2 days a week.

Megan also had a $75,000 cash value life insurance policy that protected her earlier mortgage that was now paid off. Megan remembers how her brother questioned her about purchasing a cash value life insurance policy to cover the period of her mortgage; he was advocating that she purchase a term policy instead. She remembers her conviction to choose cash value insurance over the term. Now that the mortgage is paid, Megan is ecstatic to learn that the cash value life insurance has proven itself because the policy is worth more than the initial $75,000. She has changed the beneficiary and assigned the proceeds to her church.

A decision to purchase cash value insurance that was considered by her brother to be "foolhardy" many years ago today enables Megan to leave a proud legacy to support church Youth Programs. Even without children of her own, Megan's heartfelt wishes to make an impact will be felt long after her death.

Boots

"BY BEING BOTH A PHYSICIAN AND A TEACHER YOU CAN PROVIDE the greatest gifts to humanity. . . . I always considered teaching as the one profession that I hold higher than being a practicing physician. And I enjoyed teaching at a coed university. Don Meredith, who was a student at Southern Methodist University, was an All-American football player. The coach said that his team would be better players if they took modern dance, and Don was in my modern dance class. There he was, that clown, that wonderful person, going through the motions of modern dance—all influenced by a teacher. Teachers influence people to greatness. . . .That's how I got from Texas to the Women's Medical College in Philadelphia—through the direction of a teacher later in my life, after I had my bachelor's and master's degrees and had been teaching.

"I often wonder when someone goes to medical school at age 22, or enters any profession without having real people experience, if that doesn't contribute to their "mightier-than-thou" desire to direct someone's life. . . . It's been a different relationship for me with patients. I realized that I was a person long before I became a physician and that patients are people. You must first listen and address the humanness and concerns of people through teaching."[27]

Dr. Boots Cooper believed that a teaching process was integral for all women to learn about health, finances, and parenting. She believed women should demand that professionals "teach them" with the sincerity, caring, and patience of the best teacher they remember. Boots demanded that of herself as a physician helping people with their medical needs; she demanded it of me helping her with her financial needs.

I was in my agency one day when the office supervisor came to me and said that a woman physician, the "much respected Dr. Boots Cooper," called requesting help regarding her insurance program and overall planning. She asked that a woman return the call, preferably a woman who conducts her business by teaching—Boots didn't understand how financial programs and insurance worked. She didn't want someone who would just sell her a product but someone who would come out to see her and teach her. I called Boots and reassured her that I would explain all that I could.

On the appointment, I found a lady whom I instantly loved. Wearing her white lab coat, she appeared to be a small framed women and wore her gray hair, short, and stylish. Her staff was happy and cheerful. Her office was pleasant, non-medicinal, and comfortable. I saw an ashtray on her credenza, and I wondered if she smoked; there were no ashes.

As a physician, Boots had a $50,000 life insurance policy, and I explained what her policy would do for her. She had some cash value built up in the policy, and she had taken a small loan on the policy to purchase medical equipment. Her coverage was fine, and as we proceeded to discuss her needs and desires for the future, she could determine if she wanted to add to it. Through our interview, Boots said she wasn't sure if she needed the policy because she was not married and had no children of her own. In the event of her death, she wanted to give a tax-free benefit to her nurse who had been loyal for so many years. We completed the forms to assign the nurse as beneficiary.

I inquired if Boots had a disability income program, and she indicated that she needed help in this area because she hadn't done good planning. Proceeding with the fact find, we diagnosed that her practice had good receivables, but that what she took home was minimal. It didn't take long to realize that Boots had devoted her life to children and had given a great deal to the Girl Scouts of America. Much of her monthly income went to children whom she took in off the street because they needed a home.

She said it was a tough road to become a cardiologist, and her real love was helping other women become successful. I asked her what she meant by success. She defined it as "being happy doing what you're doing." As a teacher in her own right, Boots had an impact. As a physician, she spent her life teaching children and women that success comes from achieving inward happiness and from bringing happiness to others by helping them—rather than from material consumer wealth.

Boots recalled that another agent had called on her a year earlier and recommended that she use the dividends in her life insurance policy to buy more insurance. The agent didn't take the time to understand her values and concerns, and she had no intention to do further business with that agent. After that, Boots called my office searching for a "teacher" to solve her needs.

Boots and I researched what she needed for disability. When we had all the information about her personal and monthly business overhead expenses, my next question was to ask her if she smoked. She smiled and said she had 3 cigarettes a day—in private. We laughed because I smoked, too.

Because Boots was in her mid-50s, I was also concerned about business succession planning for her medical practice and asked if she had any plans for someone else coming into the business if anything happened to her or for someone taking over the practice so she could retire. Boots looked at me, smiled and said she thought about it but hadn't done anything. It would be a future need.

We worked out a disability income protection program. Boots's ability to afford it wasn't an issue. How much insurance she could obtain was. Her business expenses were $6,000 each month, in addition to her personal expenses. However, she had no debt.

The following week, we reviewed the disability application and further discussed her life and desires. She explained that she was called Boots because she grew up on a farm and always wore boots and jeans. As an accomplished and highly educated woman, her humility was astonishing; she truly preferred that everyone call her Boots.

We developed a great relationship. She would keep me updated, and I'd continue to encourage her to consider beginning a succession arrangement for her practice. We also discussed how she could leave a continuing legacy for charitable institutions through the gift of life insurance.

One day I received a call from her nurse saying that Boots had become ill and wasn't feeling well. Boots and I met, and she insisted that she would be okay. She was thrilled that the disability income program could help take care of her in the event that she couldn't work and qualified for benefits; the office would continue to run; the home bills could be paid. I continued to ask if she gave any more thought to bringing someone else into the business.

After a few months, Boots's health further deteriorated, and it was necessary for her to go on disability. It was hard for her because it meant backing down from her practice. Other doctors helped her, but no one could be found to take over.

One day she called and said she didn't have much time. She wanted me to review the $50,000 life insurance policy because she would like to give the benefit to the Girl Scouts of America. I told her it was a noble gesture.

She thanked me for my help and said she just wanted to say how important it was to her that I took the time to teach her. She said, "Being a physician I have always made it my practice to teach rather than just do. I gained patients with that approach over the years because patients seemed to understand the process of what I was doing for them." She said I did the same for her and insisted that women "never lose vision of requiring that they be taught." I was overwhelmed that this wonderful, humble lady, who was dying, was taking time to thank me.

After Boots's death, I kept involved. In her will, she gave her home to her nurse to enjoy the back yard with its magnolia trees, creek, and bird feeders. She had given to everyone. The terminal benefit on her disability policy was considered by the nurses to be the greatest gift of all because it paid one extra month after her death. The policy was in force 5 years before Boots became disabled. The $18,000 premium paid over that time enabled the business to run and personal expenses to be paid for 19 months. She received $9,000 each month for a total of more than $170,000 in benefits before she died.

I continue to provide service to the nurse. Developing our relationship means that the nurse calls me as her life changes. We get together again and again and continue to grow. We were still concerned about the future of the practice. The hospital made arrangements for another doctor to take it over. The successor had a different bedside manner, and this arrangement did not succeed.

Boots is gone, but her legacy is great. There was never a question of letting her down in any way. She called. I was available. She needed me. I was there. She fulfilled every dream and helped many women. Overall, her influence re-emphasized that as women we need and want to be taught. We want to go through a methodical process of learning. At each step, we want to understand what we are doing. We don't purchase without first acknowledging the emotional concerns that motivate us. Only then it is right for us. As a great teacher, that was Boots's greatest lesson of all.

#10: TO MANAGE WEALTH

Karen

KAREN WAS HOLDING HER INFANT DAUGHTER, AMY, IN HER ARMS the first time I met her. The baby was surrounded by toys and joy. Karen's husband, Juan, looked on with pride.

Karen is tall, with beautiful shoulder-length, chestnut hair. When she speaks, she speaks with compassion and confidence. Her laughter and smile are sincere. She is the type of woman everyone would want as a best friend. Juan is a tall, dark, and handsome physician who is driven to succeed.

Karen and Juan were new to Texas where Juan had recently started his neurosurgery practice. His first concern was to have a good disability income insurance program in place because he understood the need to protect his income stream. He wanted an *own occupation* disability program which would pay a monthly benefit if he could not perform surgery. (In Juan's case, *own occupation* means if he sustained injury to hands, eyes, legs, or back and could not perform as a surgeon, but he could teach, consult or perform patient care only, he would receive his disability income check, plus his earnings from his other work.)

As we conducted a thorough fact find about his personal and professional holdings, Juan explained that he wanted disability protection and proper life insurance for him and for Karen. I remember thinking how progressive he was because I did not have many male clients who readily understood the need for having separate life insurance protection on their wives. Juan explained that he had given Karen full authority in choosing what benefits and investments she felt were right for them based on their needs and goals. He also explained that he wanted an aggressive savings program that would enable him to accumulate wealth to an extent that he had the personal choice of when he wanted to retire in the future. He asked that Karen and I inform him when we accomplished the first $1 million savings toward his personal goal of $5 million.

As Karen and I reviewed their insurance needs and ability to pay, I took the time to explain and teach her how different products worked, and she in turn went home and explained the ideas to Juan.

Juan and Karen agreed that their first objective was to put the disability income and life insurance in place. The love they had for each other and their daughter was evident. Their first goal was achieved by a non-cancelable individual disability income protection policy with an own occupation definition as he had requested. They also chose a non-cancelable disability income overhead expense policy that would help pay the office bills in the event he became disabled and qualified for benefits. Cash value life insurance was also their choice. It provided tax deferred growth that is generally exempt from creditor claims, accumulation of cash to supplement Amy's college education, or a supplement for retirement.

It was clear that they intended to be serious and disciplined and would eventually accomplish additional goals that would provide for their long-term needs and desires.

COORDINATION AMONG THE PROFESSIONAL SUPPORT TEAM

Our next step was coordinating a team of professional support so that Juan could practice medicine, and Karen could stay focused on the financial needs of the business and personal financial growth. Their team consisted of certified public accountant, attorney, practice management advisors, pension administrator, and me as the agent. Each member committed to 3 things: to communicate with each other, to coordinate service, and to keep Karen updated on a quarterly basis.

The attorney assured that proper trust documents were written and in order, then she communicated with me so that we could make arrangements for the cash value life insurance to be placed inside of the trust.

The accountant informed me of the corporate year-end salaries of the physician and employees. I supplied information to their practice management team and pension administrator. The pension administrator prepared all documents for Juan's business profit sharing plan along with year-end statements and sent these to me. These values enabled me to inform Juan and his employees about the values in their retirement plans. The practice management team and my staff stay in close communication regarding health insurance, disability income insurance, and pension funding because the practice management team pays all bills and keeps ongoing records for the medical practice.

Karen has done what Juan has asked of her—to watch over their financial affairs. She proactively keeps in contact with each professional; each gives her updated information quarterly. Karen has been focused on the cash flow of the medical practice, funding their insurance protection, and saving aggressively in mutual funds, stocks and bonds to achieve their personal wealth accumulation goals. She is committed to and supportive of Juan's desire to reduce employees turnover by providing them superior benefits.

Karen is a woman to be greatly admired because she demanded to be taught about all legal, accounting, financial, and operations matters from the start. Nine years after we began working together, Karen is a very wealthy woman who takes an active part in managing the wealth of her husband for the benefit of her family and the medical practice.

Karen never lost focus of their wants, needs, and desires. Several years ago, she was able to tell Juan that he had accumulated his first $1 million of wealth. He responded with a smile, and it was obvious that he respected her abilities and her keen sense about money matters.

Married to a Wealthy Business Owner: Anita

ANITA, WHO IS 39-YEARS OLD, "HAS BEEN MARRIED FOREVER IT seems" to Jon. They grew up together in a Chicago suburb and were high school and college sweethearts. Anita describes them as a "comfortable team" because they grew up together and knew each other like a book. They shared similar drives and ambitions. Anita was an astute vice president with a public relations firm before she had their daughter. Jon was a graduate of a prominent business school and was on a fast track after completing his MBA.

Anita recalled, "Time had flown by; we were both engrossed in our careers, and Jon was concentrating on the business. I woke up one day realizing I wasn't getting any younger, and if there was a time to start a family, it was today. Nine months later Miriam was born. I was in my mid-30s then." Now Anita's life centers around "enjoying Miriam and doing things Moms do."

Jon has become very successful in their garment business, and they live in one of the prestigious villages outside Chicago. Anita also is involved with "obligatory society bashes at the club" although she would rather be home reading. Her humble beginnings make her conservative; she considers herself to be "a brunette with a brain" rather than "a showy bauble at the end of a husband's arm." Jon "gives her a hefty allowance each month," but Anita would rather spend money on antiques, the gardener, and other items "to create house beautiful" than spend money on expensive clothes and personal items. Jon buys her diamonds for each major occasion, and her collection is "to die for." Their daughter is growing, and Anita cannot believe how many years she has been out of the business world!

Anita describes Jon as "a good provider. He is the most intense and driven man I know." She cites, "his 'old world drive' is evidenced in everything he does. How he manipulates vendors, engineers processes to work, has his shoes shined, placates non-influential people, and controls influential ones. For Jon, the words "no" or "can't" do not exist. He is obsessed with money and power to the point that he truly believes that he can buy anything he needs or wants, anytime he wants it. He must have the best and biggest of everything—houses, cigars, wine, clothes, cars, and women."

Anita recalls incredulously, "It's the women that I never bargained for. And the wife is always the last to know. I knew about his secretary for a long time. But that was discreet and behind closed doors. But after he became successful and powerful, he didn't care what people thought anymore. He lost all discretion. Jon never thought I knew. His jilted secretary told me everything after she was replaced with another woman. 'Hell hath no fury like a woman scorned.'"

Anita had more courage and foresight regarding "the rich man/other woman syndrome" than any woman whom I have ever worked with. She resolved, "Power corrupts and absolute power corrupts absolutely. I'm just biding my time. The hardest thing I have to deal with is posing as the dutiful wife with the humiliation of everyone thinking that I don't know what Jon is doing, or thinking that I'm sitting back and accepting it. My time will come. But for now Miriam needs a father, and I have plenty of time. . . . But from this point forward, *I* am going to become very visible—in everything."

Anita respected her husband's business ability; he has devoted his life to it. She knows, however, that the details of succession planning have not been completed. His energy had been spent on making the business grow and not in the area of protecting the business or his family in case of his death or disability. He also drinks and smokes and truly believes his success and power in business in some way make him physically indestructible.

Anita began to review the financial details of her family and the business. The business has an outstanding loan of $750,000; it is secured by a life insurance policy assigned to the bank. Therefore, if Jon dies, the insurance will pay the loan.

Jon has no disability income protection because he truly believes the business could support him if he became disabled. What he does not realize is that if he is not actively working, the paycheck he receives from the business may be considered as a company dividend for income tax purposes. Therefore, the business may not deduct his paycheck, unless he has a formal wage continuation arrangement in place to explain how much he would receive and how long he would receive it. Neither his accountant nor agent has explained this.

Jon has a $1 million term life insurance policy of which Anita is beneficiary. Anita also learned that Jon also has two $500,000 cash value life insurance policies with other women named as beneficiaries.

There is no formal pension or other retirement plan at Jon's business. His old world ideas have instilled a mindset that truly believes that **the value of the business will be the retirement benefit**; it would be sold, and he would live off the proceeds. To this date, profits have been put back into the business for updating equipment, marketing efforts, and increasing staff to keep up with growth.

When Anita began to discuss finances and the business with Jon, he admitted that he wasn't personally involved in estate and pension planning; he made it known that he does not have the physical time to coordinate a financial program—"that's what he pays his attorney for." He also believed that he had enough life insurance; he's never sick; therefore, he doesn't need disability income protection, and he doesn't think he'll ever retire because he's "making too much money—why retire?"

When Anita told Jon she was going to get involved with the business finances, he wasn't overly receptive but did not deny her doing it either. She asked him to introduce her to the attorney, certified public accountant, and agent because there were "a few things [she] wanted to understand better." Jon also admitted to not being exact about the business value but estimated it at approximately $3 million.

NEEDS

If, like Anita, you are married to a wealthy business owner and desire to become more familiar than you have been about how you and your children are protected in addition to how the business is protected, you will want to become knowledgeable about the following:

- Ask to be introduced to the attorney, certified public accountant, and insurance agent and meet with them as a team. Ask them to come prepared to the meeting with copies of all wills, trust documents, corporate and personal tax returns and summaries for all insurance policies and investment statements.
- You want to understand the status of the business and your personal finances as a family. The purpose of this meeting is for you to tell them, "treat this visit as though I had just been widowed." You are asking them for their professional recommendations about any measures they should be taking to protect the business and personal or business assets.
- Ask the attorney how the business is structured and if your husband died what effect it would have on you, your family and the business.
- Learn from the attorney if there have been any trusts or wills written.
- Ask the attorney if there has been any estate tax planning done.
- Ask the attorney what type of exposure the business has to lawsuit.
- Ask the certified public accountant if there has been a business valuation done and to explain the last 5-year's corporate and personal tax returns.
- Ask the insurance agent, registered representative, or financial planner to provide a complete update regarding all insurance in place as well as to explain the benefits your husband presently has through the corporation.
- Ask the insurance agent to review all the insurance policies in place and who is beneficiary. You need to know how much there is for you as beneficiary. Oftentimes, a wife is told by her husband, "I have $3 million of life insurance." But he may not explain who is the owner and who is the beneficiary. The wife

believes that she has $3 million plus the business. This is often not the case because the insurance is assigned to the business.

- Ask the agent to explain what retirement planning has been done and how the investments have performed.

Often business owners have a grand idea that the value of the business *is* their retirement and that they will sell the business for $1 million to have security in their retirement years. Anita worried about this because she saw her uncle lose everything he had invested when the vinyl record industry collapsed to make way for new technology several years ago. She needs to anticipate what would happen if the business suffers great loss and the business loses its book values because its market or technology become obsolete overnight.

As a wife of a business owner, you should approach your understanding of the business as if you were widowed and left with the business and the responsibility of home and children. You need to know if there are employees who are trained and knowledgeable to run the business or if you will need to hire executive talent to help you to keep the business together. This is probably not realistic considering the fact that your husband's business was successful because of the successful relationships he built over the years. The business would suffer extreme losses while you try to begin new or to maintain those existing relationships on your own. In the meantime, there most likely would be a domestic or offshore competitor already knocking at the door of your customers while you are in mourning.

MARRIED TO A PRINCIPAL IN A PROFESSIONAL FIRM

When death occurs in businesses such as professional corporations involving doctors, lawyers or accountants, no one can step in and take over the role of the deceased partner other than a someone who is licensed in the business. As a wife and widow, you could be responsible for patient or client files, office expenses, and employees, and you could have no other choice but to sell the business. This process takes months, during which the business expenses must be paid. If you hope to sell the business and client base at a profit, the business must be a worthwhile investment to purchase, and, therefore, it must be operational and running while it is for sale. The employees, patients, or clients must be assured on a daily basis that there will be a new doctor, lawyer, or certified public accountant to provide the same care and skill as your husband once gave them. If not, they will all go elsewhere, leaving you as a widow without any business to sell.

QUESTIONS TO ASK

Anita's desire to become involved in understanding the financials of the business can begin by working with the attorney, certified public accountant, and agent who make up her husband's professional team. Anita's perseverance to obtain the necessary knowledge will prove to be an incredible asset. Here are specific questions to explore:

- In how many years does your husband wish to retire?
- Is there a succession arrangement in order at the business that provides for new management when he retires?
- Is there short- and long-term debt on the business?
- Has there been a business valuation done? What are the annual receivables?
- What income does your husband receive from the business?
- Is there a pension plan in order at the business?
- How much life insurance is there on your husband's life? How many separate policies exist?
- Who is listed as beneficiary of his life insurance?
- As a business owner, does your husband have an income protection policy?
- Does your husband have a disability overhead expense protection program that can help cover the cost of monthly business expenses in the event that he becomes disabled and qualifies for benefits? This is not available to all businesses.
- What type of wills and trusts are in order with your attorney?
- Are you knowledgeable about any estate planning that has been prepared for your family?
- Do you have your own life insurance?
- How long have you been married? Do you have a happy marriage? What would happen to you if he divorced you in order to marry his secretary?

SOLUTION

When Anita came to my office and shared her story and concerns, I suggested that she embark on this process as if she were a widow who is faced with these issues for real. Jon had given her full authority, and she was eager to begin. She stated, "It will be a tremendous learning curve, so I'll do it now while I am strong and before I'm faced with either death or divorce."

If Anita is widowed today, the total value of the estate needs to be known. Anita's attorney did a thorough study of potential estate tax issues and suggested an insurance trust for estate tax planning purposes. The attorney and the certified public accountant gave suggested ideas about succession planning for the business in the event that Jon dies. The manufacturing plant has an approximate $3 million valuation as long as he is there operating it. A great deal of the value is in equipment and inventory. But if these assets are sold to liquidate the business in the event of Jon's death, they may only earn 50 cents on the dollar. Therefore, in the event Jon dies, the value of the business is more likely $1.5 million. It is recommended that

Jon consider finding a talented, young, spirited successor to carry on the business operations to keep a steady flow of contracts and jobs producing revenue.

I recommended that a new life insurance policy be placed inside the insurance trust. The value of the business as well as home and other assets would create an estate tax issue. Life insurance inside the trust will help Anita to have an income and help pay estate taxes.

Anita must always remember that women generally outlive men. While planning, she needs to think as though she is a widow who will live with the plans that Jon put in place. Now is the opportunity to obtain the peace of mind and to verify that all issues have been addressed and satisfied.

By building relationships with the professional team of agent, certified public accountant, and attorney, Anita will stay involved and keep a keen eye on the growth of the business and its impact on her and Miriam's futures. She will also continue to keep a keen eye on Jon.

Wealthy in Your Own Right: Jane

WHEN THINKING ABOUT THE WEALTHY WOMEN I HAVE WORKED with over the years, I have great pride in those who have truly created and accumulated their own wealth. There are many successful entrepreneurs throughout the country whom I am concerned about as well. Have they spent the same amount of time being personally accountable for their financial affairs as they have spent time building their image and their empire? Do they have a trusting and loyal professional team? Do they have regular meetings with their attorneys, agents, registered representatives, and certified public accountants to review their personal finances as they have regular meetings to review their bookings and schedules? How many successful American women are earning wealth and losing it? How many models, actresses, TV personalities, singers, musicians, and athletes are turning over their financial futures to others because they themselves have no time to become knowledgeable and personally accountable for their financial affairs? Are they controlling their own assets, or have they delegated them "to their booking agent to handle?" Is someone else writing checks on her account and making decisions that will ultimately affect the wealthy woman's future long after retirement when she no longer has the benefit of her beauty, her body, her company, her product, or her pretty face?

There is shock when I read about beautiful, talented American women such as Margaux Hemingway, who seem "to have it all," yet reach an untimely death. Reports after Margaux's death recounted her turbulent career, marriages, and lack of successful money management. After reaching media fame and public success, her exploitation and loss of money at the hands of others left her broke—a situation that catapulted her into the $1 million lure of a nude magazine centerfold.

My client, Jane, is a successful actress who made her debut on *Dallas*. We met years after her career was solidly established. She had concerns about her money but did not know where or how to begin. The only person she had trusted in life had passed away; her father was her idol, her friend, and her confidant. Jane felt guilty about how she felt about her success. She discussed what she called "the fatal irony of her life." She confided, "I know that actresses are in the public and media eye. For it is the public, paparazzi, and the critics who make us or break us. Often our sense of self worth or whole identity is determined by whether our movie was well received by the public, the critics, or the media. We hate being owned by the public, and we desperately seek a very private life."

Her father knew the entertainment industry and taught her that there are ways to avoid *probate* (which is the process during which creditors are paid off and assets are distributed after a person's death.) The administrative fees of probate can be costly. Probate exposes the entire process to the world since all proceedings are a matter of public record and available to anyone at the local county courthouse. Jane recited the story as if her father had made her memorize it by rote. Marilyn Monroe's untimely death left an estate in probate for almost 18 years. After her death, royalties on her image and movies soared and earned her estate over $1.6 million dollars. During that time there were substantial expenses, and her beneficiaries only received a small portion of the original estate.[28]

We discussed Jane's concerns to the point where she felt comfortable with the understanding that putting insurance inside of a trust keeps its value from adding to the value of her estate. Insurance also can be used to help pay the taxes on her estate so her heirs would not experience a significant loss in the worth of the estate after the estate tax is paid 9 months after her death.

Jane also recited the Bing Crosby story her father told her. When Bing Crosby's first wife, Dixie, passed away in the 1950s, Bing had to sell some of their assets to pay the taxes. At that time, there was no unlimited marital deduction. Because of the community property laws, the probate records indicated the exact descriptions and amounts of all of Crosby's holdings. Bing was very upset by how the press seized the information and told the world. He later established a *living trust* that kept the value of his estate and holdings private when he died. In fact, to this day, no one but the family really knows how his assets were distributed or how large his estate was at the time of his death. Bing Crosby's estate planning goal was privacy, and a living trust enabled him to achieve that goal.

Jane's acting success, as well as the royalties and fees she earned on her movies and videos, had created a sizable revenue stream. Up to the time we met, Jane had designated the care of her income and investing to her talent agent. Her idea was that, "He assures me of the next job, so he has a vested interest to see that I make money."

Jane was comfortable with his guidance for the present. But she was uncomfortable with the idea for her long-term future. She was concerned about her later years when she was "80-years old and no longer working," after her beauty was gone and her image was "no longer a commodity that a newer, younger generation adored."

NEEDS

If, like Jane, you are blessed with talent, beauty, success, and the wealth these bring, do not be so busy with the trappings of everyday life that you delegate decisions about your personal financial future. **As a wealthy woman in your own right you must be personally involved because you more than anyone have the most to lose.** You need:

- To become knowledgeable of the financial world.
- To personally select your own professional team of a certified public accountant, attorney, and life insurance agent whom you know you can trust and who are willing to teach you as you grow and develop a long-term relationship.
- To begin to learn about investment vehicles, stocks, bonds, mutual funds, variable annuities, and the like.
- To determine goals and a greater purpose for your wealth.
- To understand how wealth creates significant tax issues. You need to become knowledgeable about estate tax planning, charitable remainder trusts, insurance trusts, family trusts, asset protection, and many others.
- To preserve the empire you have created.
- To be personally involved rather than delegate the responsibility of your future at an old age to any one other person. Do not let anyone sign checks without your approval.

QUESTIONS TO ASK

- Are you confident that the members of your professional team are available and willing to teach you?
- If you are single, where do you want your money to go when you die? Determine if you want to give cash to many non-productive relatives or would you prefer to set up a foundation or give to an existing charitable institution?
- If you are married or have children, have you done what is necessary to help preserve the empire for your children and minimize payment of estate taxes?
- What is your estate valued at today?
- What are your investment accounts worth? Who will receive the accounts when you die? Insist that your agent or registered representative give you quarterly or updated reports.
- What is the value of each of your real estate holdings?
- Is there a master record of all holdings including: address; name assigned to title, lease, or contract; present value; and, copy of the deed or title?
- How much life insurance do you have, and who are beneficiaries?
- What type of trusts are in order?
- If you died today, would your family or friends know what to do and who to call?

- Are all of your financial assets recorded with name of title, location, and account number?
- How long does your current contract guarantee your income?
- Is your income stream or wealth related to political or other power factors that can be easily jeopardized?
- Is your wealth related to athletic or physical performance which can be limited by a certain length of time when you are considered to be in the prime of your career?
- How much of your cash flow derives from investments in other business operations?

SOLUTION

Jane needed to begin at the beginning and was nervous about it. We detailed a list of action items that she needed to pursue once she was comfortable with assuming the responsibility.

She first needed to select a professional team with whom she would feel comfortable. She knew that in the future she wanted to have hands-on involvement regarding all financial decisions that will ultimately affect her estate and retirement.

Her certified public accountant would help in the valuation of her assets, real estate holdings, investments, rights, and royalties as well as be responsible for organizing a report summary.

She decided to select a new attorney, rather than retain her father's family attorney. She wanted someone experienced in the entertainment industry and in estate planning. The attorney would get her estate in order by drafting the proper trust so that estate taxes could be minimized.

CHECKS AND BALANCES AMONG PROFESSIONAL TEAM

As her insurance agent, I assisted in estate planning and asset protection. I suggested that we meet with the attorney to discuss a *charitable remainder trust* that offers creative tax advantages. Jane's estate was worth $18 million. Jane considered a series of concepts applicable to sizable estates: charitable remainder trusts, revocable and irrevocable life insurance trusts, asset protection for liability reasons, and family limited partnerships. Together, the attorney and I worked with Jane to diagnose her needs according to tax planning and wealth preservation priorities.

Jane has committed to meet with me, her certified public accountant, and attorney on a regular basis. We are her principal team who coordinate the rest of her financial professionals. We provide her with records of all of her holdings, teach her how her holdings and investments are diversified, coordinate and implement a properly designed insurance program, and provide updates on present investment values.

A checks and balances occurs among the professional team as we each discuss our perspectives on problems and solutions regarding Jane's estate. We meet each quarter prior to our group meeting with Jane. This enables us to prepare and present a cohesive approach to Jane regarding current and future issues impacting her wealth. Our opinions offer a wide range of expertise to create coordinated solutions and ways to implement her future plans. We also helped Jane to identify additional key players who are most likely to be involved during Jane's life and career. The attorney who specializes in contract rights, royalties, and the entertainment industry; the chief financial officer of her corporation; her tax planning attorney; and her investment portfolio manager are called upon as needed.

The woman with true wealth has a complexly detailed task in managing a course for her wealth. To simplify the course can mean the difference between her having or losing wealth. She needs to be at the helm, in control of the crew, steering the course—not the maiden figurehead or beautiful face along for the ride. For in a storm, she is first and hardest hit when the ship wrecks.

#11: TO RETIRE

Working Woman Retiring: Rea

"I WORKED HARD ALL MY LIFE; WITH NO ONE TO HELP ME, AND I'M looking forward to not working, so I can have time when I can make myself the main priority every day." That was Rea's admission when she came to my office for retirement planning at age 65. Rea was referred to me by her 50-year-old sister; I helped her understand her husband's pension and annuity benefit payout options.

Rea worked all her life as an executive secretary and administrative assistant for a large corporation. She is a tall and slender horsewoman who loved Texas, horses, and kids, in that order. Her reputation of teaching and mentoring kids to make them work well with animals was known far and wide. She had worked and championed 4-H programs in Ft. Worth and lived near her sister and brother-in-law. Rea's eyes danced when she talked about the riding students she had over the years—George was her favorite. "That good lookin' kid with that smile you'd remember forever; he learned that famous Texas two-step in a rodeo, and he's still singin' with it in his heart."

She was excited about retirement; however, she did not understand the pension materials her company provided. She was frightened because she never had financial guidance over the years. She did not feel she had the knowledge and expertise to make an informed decision regarding money matters that would affect the rest of her life.

Rea confided that she had no children or husband. Her lifestyle was modest and uncomplicated. Her social life consisted of equestrian and church activities and walking outdoors. She absolutely loved the subtle beauty of the high desert ranch lands of Texas and spent a great deal of time telling me about how she would paint watercolors of her favorite scenes so she could keep the image with her all year around—"fields of Texas bluebonnets; flocks of finches so plentiful, fine, and fair they'd turn a Cottonwood yellow."

"I've lived a simple life without too many sophisticated needs. But I want the perspective of someone who deals with these matters every day. Someone who can explain all the options to me," insisted Rea. She wanted to be taught; she wanted materials to read; she wanted explanations; she wanted to know all the reasons why something was recommended, and she wanted time to distill the information before making any decisions.

NEEDS

If, like Rea, you are approaching retirement, you'll want to consider the following:

- To become debt free.
- To have a mortgage paid.
- To have a complete understanding of your fixed expenses.
- To have a complete understanding of Social Security benefits.
- To have a full understanding of your pension and payout options.

QUESTIONS TO ASK

- Do you have an understanding of your Social Security and what your monthly benefits will be?
- Do you understand pension values and the amount you will receive?
- Can you take your pension in a lump sum?
- Do you understand all of your pension options?
- What are your fixed expenses?
- What are your plans and goals for your retirement years (*e.g.* write a book, travel, buy a vacation home)?

SOLUTION

Rea first needed an agent who was willing to review her company pension materials and explain them thoroughly.

The best years of Rea's career were the last 2 when she earned an annual salary of $45,000. Earlier, she had bought a Chevy Silverado pick-up truck knowing it would last her until she died. She paid it off and last year bought and paid for her Appaloosa and a horse trailer. Rea had been saving for 10 years and was proud to have her dream come true at last and to have it paid for in cash. Rea had paid the mortgage on her 1,500 sq. ft. Texas ranch house when she was in her 40s, so she was happy to be retiring without debt. Her monthly expenses were $1,500.

Upon review, her pension statement showed an annuity payout of $1,500 monthly and an $18,000 annual income for as long as Rea lives. If Rea had a spouse she could exercise an option to take less per month and guarantee an income to her spouse after she died. Since Rea is single, she will take the maximum allowed with the reassurance of having this monthly income for as long as she lives.

Let's look at her married sister's situation. Her husband wished to elect an annuity *payout option* upon retirement in 15 years. For a married couple, a

$3,000 monthly pension payment option can be handled in a number of ways.

- The employee monthly receives 100 percent of the annuity calculation, $3,000, for a lifetime. The benefit is the maximum monthly income. The drawback is that when her husband dies, the spouse has no income. Therefore, if a couple elects to receive the payout at 100 percent, they often purchase a life insurance policy that can provide the monthly income upon death of the employee (in this case the husband), that would have equaled the same amount as if the husband had elected the spousal payout option. (This concept is often referred to as *pension maximization*.)
- Another way is for the employee to take the *spousal annuity option*. This allows the couple to have less income than the 100 percent annuity calculation. Then, when the employee dies, the spouse will receive a calculated portion of the full amount—for instance, $2,500 per month while the employee lives and $1,250 per month for the spouse after the employee dies. In Rea's sister's case, at age 50, 15 years prior to retirement, the sister purchased a cash value life insurance policy on her husband that could provide her $3,000 monthly (the same amount as the 100-percent annuity calculation) after he died. Buying an adequate amount of cash value life insurance over the 15 years prior to retirement also enables the couple to consider taking the 100-percent payout amount when the employee is ready to retire.

Because Rea was alone, single, and without children who might look after her in her old age, she was concerned about her final years and elected to purchase a *long-term care* policy. She chose one with both nursing home and in-home health care benefits.

Rea chose to save her Social Security check of $600 per month and invest it in mutual funds. Her goal was to accumulate $10,000 in a money market account for emergency needs. After that, the monthly contributions were placed in growth and income funds.

We also made arrangements to transfer the $160,000 available in her 401(k) pension fund into a variable annuity which offers the opportunity of growth. Rea can access these funds any time when necessary later in life. In the event Rea became incapacitated, the annuity can provide for her care. A custodian or other individual may have to be designated in order for them to access the policy. Upon Rea's death, any balance will be bequeathed to the 4-H Club.

Rea was overjoyed to have her affairs "in order" as she called it. She was free to make time for what she loved—free to ride among flocks of finches in fields of Texas bluebonnets so fine and fair.

#12: TO PASS WEALTH ON TO HEIRS

Widow: Betty

BETTY NEVER THOUGHT SHE WOULD BE A WIDOW AT AGE 69—for a second time. Her young groom was killed in the Korean War, and she waited many years to remarry. At age 50, she married a younger man. She believed, "I wanted to marry someone younger whom I thought would outlive me because I never wanted to go through the pain of loss again. I never thought I would be widowed again."

At this point in her life, she did not have the emotional strength to remarry, even though she was "still young." She felt deeply about not ever being a burden to her daughter. She was very independent and lived on a fixed income.

She is doing fine financially because her husband had set up a trust from which she receives a monthly income. She likes the fact that she does not have to worry because he did a very good job of planning. She has 3 grandchildren, and she desires to live modestly, so that someday she will be able to pass on an inheritance to her daughter and grandchildren.

NEEDS

The months following the death of a faithful companion are heart wrenching, but eventually all the world becomes new again. If, like Betty, you are a widow, you will want to ask questions and consider these important next steps:

- To identify how assets are to be distributed after your death.
- To determine if estate taxes will be due.
- To have an updated will.
- To consider adding children to joint accounts.
- To obtain copies of trust and trust financial statements, life insurance company, address, agent/s, and phone number/s.
- To list names of attorney, certified public accountant, and agent.
- To locate the deed or title to your home.
- To enumerate your desires on a wish list. Designate jewelry, personal items, furnishings that are special as gifts to specific loved ones.

- To have a heart-to-heart discussion with your children, explain your desires and review what is in place, the location of important papers with summary pages explaining Social Security numbers, bank, bank location, account numbers, safety deposit box and numbers.

QUESTIONS TO ASK

- Do you have a long-term care program?
- Do you have a safety deposit box?
- Do you have any life insurance on yourself? If so, how much?
- Would you like to leave a legacy to your children or grandchildren?
- What investments do you have?
- Is your monthly income adequate?
- Do you have statutory or health care powers of attorney established?
- Have you updated your will since your husband's death? Do you have a living will drafted?
- Have you considered putting your children's names on any of your accounts?

SOLUTION

Betty has been taking interest from the trust fund her husband established. She has no debt and lives on $1,000 per month. Her husband made arrangements to provide her a lifetime income and pass the rest to her daughter upon Betty's death. Betty truly wants to leave the $175,000 trust fund to her daughter and grandchildren.

A portion of Betty's Social Security check has purchased a long-term care policy and has paid for the extras, gifts, and church contributions. Betty also had a cash value life insurance policy for $75,000 for which she has named her daughter beneficiary.

In addition, Betty has asked her daughter to purchase a $100,000 cash value life insurance policy on her mother. It is Betty's wish to leave $50,000 each to both grandchildren, and she is giving her daughter the money to pay the premiums. Life insurance at this stage in her life is a good way to provide her grandchildren this substantial sum of money on an income tax-free basis for less than $100,000.

In her heart, Betty knows that even though her mementos hold great importance to her, these will never have the same value to her heirs as $100,000 cash. The money will help the children in their financial direction in a way that mementos never will be able to help them. Her husband set affairs right for Betty, and it was her desire to do the same for her daughter and grandchildren.

Preserving Wealth for Children: Sharon

CRUCIAL LEGACY ISSUES ARISE WHEN A FAMILY GROWS AN EMPIRE and passes it from generation to generation. Some families have accumulated wealth by methodical cash savings; other families have acquired, nurtured, and developed various forms of standing wealth. Many families own standing wealth such as real estate, farms, or ranch lands.

Sharon and Rob were introduced to me by a friend who was aware of their concerns about their land holdings. Sharon and Rob grew up together on adjacent ranches and eventually married. Their union and inheritance created one of the largest spreads on the Great Plains.

Their 33,000-acre ranch has a meandering river where Sharon often sits on the bank to fish and to collect her thoughts. When we met there, Sharon had tears in her eyes as she told me about how she recently helped her best friend, Linda, the day that Linda's family was forced to auction off their ranch to pay estate taxes after her mother died. Linda's ranch had been in the family since 1805, and "nine generations of little ones had slept in grandma's feather bed." But the day had come when they lost it all. All of their possessions were on the front lawn, including tractors, machinery, a herd of Texas Longhorns, a herd of 200 wild mustangs that had sanctuary on the ranch, as well as work horses used for roundups. There were 24 ranch hands who watched their world come to an end. It all was auctioned—livestock, possessions, parcels of land, house—and grandma's feather bed. A legacy spanning almost 200 years was gone in 12 hours.

Sharon never wanted that to happen to her children. She was deeply concerned about one child who was suffering from drug addiction. The others were young and irresponsible and were taking the wealth of their land for granted.

Sharon and Rob live off the ranch and the land. They raise cattle for the stockyards; their garden and orchards provide all necessary foodstuffs. They work the land for survival—for themselves and 4 children. Sharon's wealth is the value of the land rather than any income it generates.

Sharon heard from a neighboring rancher about how his family had been working with an attorney to use *gifting* to give the land to the children in order to help reduce the estate value for tax purposes. This option didn't appeal to her because her children were not behaving responsibly. She had also heard about *family limited partnerships.* Therefore, she wanted to discuss these with her attorney as well as other estate planning concepts that would allow her and Rob to control the future of the estate during their lifetime and for generations to come long after she and Rob died.

NEEDS

If like Sharon, your livelihood is tied to standing wealth that is not generating income and is not easily liquidated, you need:

- To be involved in knowing the financials of the estate, particularly the profit and loss of goods and services at market to determine if ranching, farming, or other ventures are profitable.
- To have frequent communication with the real estate broker, attorney and certified public accountant regarding the value of the land or property.
- To select and use a local certified public accountant who is familiar with your type of property, holdings, and operations (such as ranch land, urban real estate, orchards, or vineyards), rather than rely on someone who may not be familiar with the local values of your ventures in other geographic locations.
- To work with the certified public accountant to understand the impact of estate taxes for children when parents die.
- To work with your attorney to create a family limited partnership and to explore additional gifting options.
- To work with your insurance agent to assure that adequate liability coverage exists and that proper life insurance is in place for estate planning purposes.

QUESTIONS TO ASK

- What is the total income projection from all sources?
- What is the present value of the land holdings?
- What, if any, estate planning has been done?
- Is there insurance in an insurance trust to cover estate taxes?
- Are you in the know and do you have a working relationship with the banker, attorney and agent?
- Have any liens been placed on the property over the years as collateral for loans on buildings, barns, equipment, livestock, seedlings? Have the liens been paid? Are more liens anticipated?
- What other personal debt are you holding?
- Is your marriage solid or do you fear a divorce?
- Have you created a will or discussed what you care to leave your children?

- Have you discussed family limited partnership arrangements with your attorney?

SOLUTION

Sharon and Rob have been coping with drug and alcohol dependency in their family. It is taking its toll on the family, and they have been focused on the turmoil of these present years and not had much time to think about the long-term future.

Sharon learned that their total holdings including land, ranch house, outbuildings and herds were valued at over $13 million, and the children would be faced with paying more than $6 million after the death of the second parent. After the outstanding liens were satisfied, there would be no money to pay the taxes; the children would have to parcel out the ranch and sell it. (If a property involves leaseholds, the issues are even more complex regarding Federal estate tax. It is imperative that a business valuation consultant be working with the attorney and tax specialist, in this case.)

FAMILY LIMITED PARTNERSHIP

The attorney proceeded to do estate tax planning and recommended that Sharon and Rob set up a family limited partnership. The first advantage of the family limited partnership is that the parents can give away wealth without giving up control over the assets. A second advantage is that the transfer (*i.e.*, gift) of the limited partnership interests to younger generations can often be valued at a discount which should be determined by your tax advisor. Finally, if stated in the partnership agreement, the limited partners cannot transfer their limited partnership interests except with the consent of the general partner and then only to other family members.[29]

I further recommended a *second-to die life insurance* policy for which the family limited partnership is owner and beneficiary. It would provide the benefit to the children, as limited partners, upon the death of the second parent. The father and the mother are insured together by the same life insurance contract. The underwriting process considers risk spread over the life expectancy of both individuals. Rob had been experiencing blood pressure problems, but Sharon's good health enabled them to receive a non-rated policy. Sharon and Rob purchased a $6 million second-to-die policy and will continue to monitor the value of the estate and the amount of insurance necessary to satisfy the estate taxes after the second insured dies.

Sharon and Rob, fearing "deep pockets syndrome," also increased their liability coverage because they feared exposure to lawsuit in the event that their teenagers involved with drugs and alcohol experienced driving accidents in which friends were injured or killed.

All of their planning with their professional team was to help realize the hope that no developers will ever divide the land, hunt the game, fish the rivers, or drill the oil on the ranch land they've had in their families for generations.

American lore is colored by tales of the great families of the Western Plains who have struggled to keep vast farmlands in the family for generations. There are families who have carved wealth from land rich with mineral rights or timberlands. Other great families have built and developed monumental estates and game preserves. Others have real estate, trading, banking, or industrial empires.

In America, the pioneer spirit and ability to homestead and live off the land evoke emotions and passions of epic proportions. Rich are the stories of families from the grasslands of the Great Plains; cattle ranches thick with mesquite and high chaparral westward from Texas to California; great timberlands of the Atlantic and Pacific north country; great tobacco and cotton plantations of the American South; fertile orchards and vineyards of the Pacific coast; and the ranches, pineapple groves, and sugar plantations on our island states and territories. Such standing American wealth was built on sweat, love and passion. It was built by blood and tears, war and conquest.

The spirit of wealth grows even stronger when families with large land holdings struggle to stem short-term economic trials in order to preserve the empire for their children and dream that their children marry to merge wealth. From *The Big Valley* to the *Ponderosa*, Americans have been excited about this fiction in books and movies for generations.

. . . Didi Devon is sassy, spirited, and attractive with a mind of her own. She knows what she wants and nothing will stop her from getting it. Her father is a rancher who owns half the valley over the Spring Mountains in western Nevada. She wants to paint and see the world. The dusty, arid ranch with its relentless heat and harsh winds is nice to visit, but no place to realize her dreams; she doesn't want to spend the rest of her life in a place with nothing but cattle, lizards, and jack rabbits.

Down the valley there's the Darling ranch. Dick Darling is lanky, blond, handsome, and ambitious. His hard working hands have talents to bring him the world and any woman he wants. He's leery of women gold diggers out for his land and his oil. He left his ranch to travel the world and seek fortune on his own. His grandfather owns the cattle ranch and oil rights. The parents want these two to marry and merge their joining lands; hopefully, it would settle these spirited youngsters down, keep them both closer to Nevada—for the good of the family. Their union would keep outside interests from buying the land in future years.

Together Didi and Dick could live happily ever after. They could own the whole valley; they could name their ranch the "Big Double D."

But after time with Dick, Didi realizes he's fun to be with, but she could never love him—a man who is always late and always has dirty hands, a man whose trucks, equipment, and business deals will always be more important that giving her the things she wants. Didi's mind and ambition are somewhere else. She wants a man with money, not a man who needs to work for it.

In his heart, Dick knows but won't admit that Didi can never give him the friendship, loyalty, love, and passion that he once had with Jane. Jane still adores him and is giving him all the time he needs to realize she is the only woman who truly loves him for what he is—not for what he can give her. His heart still remembers her dancing eyes and dark beauty in a phosphorescent tide on Horseshoe Bay along the pink sand in Bermuda, at another time. He quietly regrets buckling under family pressure to leave her. Jane was self-made with money of her own, not after his. She loved him honestly. Completely. She made him smile and made him happy. They were great for each other. With her, he could conquer the world, and together they could accomplish even more with a flame that consumes the darkness. . . .

Dick and Didi come close to marriage, but she admits he's not enough; she wants more, and Dick still can't get Jane out of his mind. The heart wants what the heart wants. Dick finally realizes that behind a successful man is a passionate woman and that Jane truly is the only woman who could ever love him exactly the way he is. No other woman can replace what he had with Jane. But would she wait? Would she still be there for him after all these years? . . .

You know the story. You've seen the movie. The parents are heartbroken and left angry to die among the tumbleweed. Without influx of new capital and new blood, the ranch is sold. Paradise is paved and outside interests put up a parking lot.

It will take more than marriage between the next generation to preserve the Devon and Darling legacies.

For large estates and families who have accumulated wealth, financial planning is essential. It is how the American Dream lives on—from generation to generation.

EPILOGUE
Barbara

BARBARA WAS 52-YEARS OLD WHEN SHE WAS REFERRED TO ME BY her attorney in 1993. In the early days of building her business, she had struggled as a single parent. Barbara was determined never to go backwards and began to tell me about how far she had really come to get to this point.

"I'll never forget the day in my small Oklahoma town, when I walked in tears from the courtroom; I was 37-years old and no longer a married woman. It was April 4, 1977, the day after my wedding anniversary. In one morning, I was suddenly a single parent with 2 teenage sons who needed a great deal of love, nurturing and guidance. An overwhelming sensation engulfed me—I would be doing this alone as well as exerting all my energies to live as a single woman. Back in 1977, the ERA had not yet emerged as a household word!

"As I drove to my apartment, my thoughts were on savings, college education, and retirement; however, the impending bills and everyday cost of living took over my imagination and quickly caused me to focus on the present. Important decisions needed to be made that would have an impact on all of us. The most important goal at that point was to be able to move home to Texas within a year. My parents lived there, and I thought it valuable to have family support nearby.

"The days ambled along, and I continued to work in a job that was interesting but had very little potential. My children were involved in school and community activities. Our lives were adjusting to the divorce as well as I could possibly expect. I labored diligently to meet my goal, and I saved whatever money I could by budgeting and by attempting several part-time jobs beyond my full-time employment. I could find no extra money to deposit in savings to meet emergency situations much less for anything beyond those.

"When we relocated to Texas, a position was offered to me. It increased my salary and produced a sense of security; nevertheless, it meant working for someone with less than a congenial attitude. Again my thoughts turned to providing for future needs, but how quickly these notions were diminished. I was overwhelmed from handling a new job, from establishing my sons in new schools, and from finding a place to live that we could call our own.

"On most evenings, the phone would ring and salesmen would inquire about my needs for insurance, financial planning, or burial plots. I dismissed these needs and took care of what I believed to be more urgent. It was the late '70s, and my main concentration was to be awarded credit in my own name! In those days, being single and a woman made this almost impossible. My vow to obtain as many credit cards as possible soon became an avocation. The importance for a woman, single or married, to develop her own identity in terms of financial credit became a priority.

"In 1979, within a year of moving to Texas, I seized an opportunity to purchase a small day care center. My parents agreed to aid in the financing that made another adventure possible. I happily put aside seeking credit card acceptance and thrust myself into what I considered to be a second job. The anticipation of the day when the day care center could become my sole support turned my thoughts to further establish goals. Unfortunately, my boss felt that my work with my day care center was a conflict of interest, and I was suddenly without primary employment. The new adventure of day care as an income supplement suddenly shifted to a battle for survival. It was another giant step for womankind!"

After starting a new business, Barbara felt that this is what she should have been doing for years. She had found her niche. Six months later, in 1980, she moved the day care center into larger quarters. Her next personal goal was to complete state certification requirements and obtain licensing. After she became licensed, the day care grew to 130 children by the end of 1981. Within 2 years, the center grew by 300 percent. Barbara was great at the day-to-day care of children and overseeing staff, but she lacked knowledge about how to run a business. She knew she needed to stay in touch with her insurance agent because it was important to increase coverage as her business grew. However, in 1986, 4 years after starting the business, the day care industry was dropped by all the top insurance companies.

Barbara remembered, "I was advised of the cancellation of my general liability policy and was told that several large insurance companies no longer insured day care centers. I panicked. My business would be unprotected. I could not lose what I had so diligently worked to build. Where would I go? Whom would I turn to? I joined a child care organization and started asking questions. Fortunately, I found people who knew what I was going through and what I needed. I was referred to a company and was able to be insured, but what a price I paid—both emotionally and financially!"

That incident changed Barbara's focus; she began to realize that she had to work with professionals who understood the needs of a small business owner. Barbara continued, "I did not feel that my certified public accountant was experienced in business issues nor did she keep me well informed. I stopped doing business with her, and I actively pursued a new certified public accountant and eventually found a tax attorney and insurance agent.

"In 1986, my new attorney recommended that I have a will in order because I had not had one created since moving to Texas. In 1990, the attorney also recommended incorporation; it would give me more leverage for banking purposes. Since a day care business has a high exposure to liability, being incorporated also protected me against personal liability in the event that the business was sued.

"As I continued the long trek of becoming a successful entrepreneur, the importance of having a financial program to face emergencies and to save money became immediate. I purchased whole life insurance policies for me and my sons. These policies were not large, but they gave me a feeling of security that I was protecting the future for my children. After the death of my parents, I received an inheritance and launched my first step into mutual funds. This money also enabled me to bestow money to each son to aid in his future plans. With the mutual funds in place and a certificate of deposit I gained years ago from my divorce settlement, my entrance into the world of savings finally had begun. I read about stocks, bonds, and different types of insurance. I bombarded my attorney with as many questions as possible on each appointment. My interest level peaked, and I began to feel that I would always be a woman, but no longer would I be an uninformed woman. I would continue my search for understanding, trust, and honesty in a business that tended to frighten women.

"By 1993, my son, Philip, received his master's degree in psychology and asked to join me in the business. This was my dream come true to know that one of my children wanted to share in the daily activities of the day care center—a business I loved. Besides, why should it be that only men can have their sons join them in business? Philip had been involved with the business since he was 15-years old, and it was a proud moment for both of us when he joined the staff as a certified psychologist. Since my son was interested in joining the business, my desire was for him to have partial ownership. After discussion with the attorney, I chose to keep 60 percent of the stock; Philip received 40 percent that was gifted over a 3-year period. My attorney also recommended that a buy-sell arrangement be created to protect the business and each other's family interests in the event one of us died."

Shortly after, the attorney referred Barbara to me in 1993. She recalls, "Now I don't know why I waited so long to discuss my financial affairs with anyone. Mary's office was a comfortable place where you could reach for a piece of candy. Antiques and a curio cabinet held a menagerie of personal memorabilia as well as professional honors and awards. It was different and exciting. This was not only a professional setting, but also a place where I found an answer to my search for understanding, trust and honesty in the world of insurance and investments."

Barbara's dreams turned into plans that were quickly brought into focus with goals and objectives. She made investments in lucrative mutual funds, and she actively began building a retirement fund. She continued an education process to learn important details and gained confidence. Barbara admits, "Never did I feel insignificant or unenlightened. The security I had worried about and longed for so desperately all these years suddenly became a reality. I arrived at that place in the least painful way I could have ever hoped or imagined. I became a stronger, better informed and happier individual, due in part to the care of a patient teacher. My peace of mind and life feel safe and secure now."

It has been 3 years since Barbara began a serious focus on her future planning. Barbara has mastered running the financial aspects of her business. She secured life insurance and disability income insurance protection for herself; she funded the buy-sell arrangement with insurance for her and Philip; she established overhead expense protection for her business which has grown by 1,000 percent in 10 years. Because of Barbara's genuine concern for her employees, she created an employee benefit package to protect 22 associates with health insurance, an employee sick-pay arrangement, and a bonus incentive. Barbara continues to zealously and methodically save for retirement, and she is on-target toward her goal of $1.5 million for retirement at age 65.

Now, the financial world is fun for her.

Barbara has indeed come a long way since her divorce in 1977 when she had "an overwhelming sensation engulf her," and she realized that she would be raising her sons "alone as well as exerting energy to live as a single woman." Her life alone has been a sensation and overwhelming with what she has accomplished—alone.

Another happy note is that Barbara has found love and has married a great Oklahoma gentleman of the highest order, who shares the same values and an ever blossoming love. She and Bob each have their busy lives and dreams. Occasionally, they must spend time away from each other, but when he comes home . . . there's the spin around the floor, the kick of the heels, a wink of the eye and "Hey Darlin,' Did Ya Miss Me?!"

ABOUT THE AUTHOR:

Mary Lynn Seebeck

AS AN ENTREPRENEUR, MARY BRINGS OVER 35 YEARS OF SALES AND marketing experience to Mary Seebeck & Associates, her insurance practice which she began in 1985. Mary's practice is a family business in which her son and two daughters play active roles.

Mary and her associates represent over 50 fine financial services companies and their affiliates in order to offer an array of products that address specific needs of clients. Included are: mutual funds as well as life insurance, annuity, health, and disability income insurance products to create financial strategies and solutions for professional, business, and individual clients' retirement and estate planning needs. More than 1,000 of her clients are women; many are celebrated in *American Dream Women* for their ability to meet the challenges of taking control of their financial futures.

Mark, Mary, Gayle, and Ellen of Mary Seebeck & Associates

Within the insurance industry, Mary is a Qualifying and Life member of the Million Dollar Round Table (MDRT). Annually, she achieves the National Quality Award, the National Sales Achievement Award, the Health Insurance Underwriters Award as well as numerous awards from the companies whose products she represents. Her industry affiliations include membership in the National Association of Life Underwriters and the Fort Worth Life Underwriters chapter, where she is a member of the Board of Directors. She is an active member of the Women Life Underwriters Confederation. Mary is a registered representative with MONY Securities, Corp. and an agent of the Mutual Life Insurance Company of New York, where she is a Hall of Fame member and a Top 50 and perennial President's Council qualifier.

Mary's community service is focused on active participation in the Ft. Worth Women's Haven that provides intervention counseling and housing services to battered women and their children. Mary serves as Treasurer of the Board of Directors and assists on the development committee with continuous fund raising efforts. Mary is a member of the American Business Women's Association, the organization of Business and Professional Women, and the National Association of Female Executives.

Mary's husband, Tom, is also a successful entrepreneur in real estate. Together Mary and Tom enjoy an active family life. They reside in Grapevine, a suburb of Ft. Worth and at Moss Lake, in northern Texas.

ACKNOWLEDGEMENTS

THIS BOOK SERVES AS A TESTIMONIAL TO OVER 1000 WOMEN WHOM I have had the opportunity of servicing throughout my practice. There have been hundreds who have participated, given support, and guided its message. To the families who inspired this book, I extend sincere and humble thanks for allowing us to step into their lives, and I thank them for the courage and insight they've provided. The stories add light to what can be a challenging journey through the world of investments, insurance, and financial planning. Through their stories and dreams, other women will better learn how to secure solid financial futures.

During the course of 2 years, a focus group, which was comprised of men and women ages 35 to 65 from all walks of life across America, was consulted prior to final publication. Their encouragement and written testimony indicate that 85 percent would recommend this book as required reading for the women they care about in their lives, especially mothers, wives, and daughters. Some believe this book should be placed next to the dictionary for use as a reference tool for life. I gratefully thank all members of the focus group who provided valuable insight.

Professionals directly involved with providing financial counsel to clients also gave support and expertise. Particularly, I would like to thank the following for their influence and their contributions representing their primary discipline: Steve Bethel, MF, CFA, MAI, business valuation consultant; Michael Palmer, Esq., attorney; Nancy Rackoff, JD and Susan McCabe, JD, estate planning attorneys; Jerry Jackson, CFP, RIA, tax and estate planning attorney; Dr. Bob Parkhill; Mike Fee, CPA; and Jack Skryd, agent and Million Dollar Round Table producer.

Many other professionals working in the insurance and investments industry gave their time and comments during the compliance and legal review of the text. I am indebted to: Eric Nordman, CPCU, CIE, of the National Association of Insurance Commissioners; officers of the National Association of Securities Dealers; David Waldman, JD and Frederick Tedeschi, JD, corporate attorneys; Bob Levy, JD, tax attorney; George Brenner, JD, estate planning attorney; Terry Howe and Ed Hill, compliance officers; and Evelyn Peos, FSA, actuary. The result of their efforts has created a synergy that spans many disciplines and a book reflecting multiple perspectives, beyond my own. In addition, their fastidious review of the text gives further assurance and confidence that this book can be readily used by other professionals in the financial services industry as they endeavor to teach their many clients about the roles that insurance, tax, and legal planning have in a thorough financial program that meets the many contingencies which can occur in the future. I thank them for their many hours and the value of their remarks.

Indeed, the experience of this group spans more than 200 years, which is longer than the life insurance industry has been in existence as we know it.

I cannot say enough how I am eternally grateful for the inspiration and personal mentoring I received early in my career from Ben Feldman and John Savage. Their attitude about the value of our great industry and its ability to change people's lives by assuring the peace of mind and financial well-being of families has been a guiding light for me as I service the needs of families and businesses.

It has been the zeal of Dr. Boots Cooper and her unwavering demand that people be taught by professionals which became the genesis of my dream to teach women everywhere to become financially responsible in terms they can understand and a language that is based on their emotions and desires to gain control of their financial independence.

Grateful acknowledgment is given to: John Wiley and Sons, Emerald, the Life Insurance Marketing Research Association, and the American Council of Life Insurance for permission to share facts, information, and summary definitions cited in their publications for the purpose of teaching the fundamentals and complexities of the various products and conditions in today's insurance and investments industry.

I acknowledge and pray for the many battered women and children we touch, teach, and help become whole at the Ft. Worth Women's Haven. It is their spirit to grow, gain confidence, and become all they can be that will continue to inspire women everywhere as they fight the obstacles which challenge them everyday.

Also, I give my heartfelt thanks to all of those whom I love in my immediate and extended family—my husband, children and their spouses, grandchildren, brothers, sister, and parents. They are the reason I continue to strive to become all I can be in order to leave my own legacy of love.

Mary Lynn Seebeck

APPENDIX A:
Million Dollar Round Table Professional Designations

ACAS	Associate of the Casualty Actuarial Society
ACS	Associate Customer Service
AEP	Accredited Estate Planner
AFP	Associate Financial Planner
ASA	Associate of the Society of Actuaries
CEBS	Certified Employee Benefits Specialist
CFP	Certified Financial Planner
ChFC	Chartered Financial Consultant
CIAM	Chartered Insurance Agency Manager
CIC	Certified Insurance Counselor
CLU	Chartered Life Underwriter
CPA	Certified Public Accountant
CPCU	Chartered Casualty/ Property Underwriter
CSSC	Certified Structured Settlement Consultant
FCAS	Fellow of the Casualty Actuarial Society
FIC	Fraternal Insurance Counselor
FICF	Fraternal Insurance Counselor-Fellow
FLMI	Fellow of the Life Office Management Institute
FSA	Fellow of the Society of Actuaries
FSPA	Fellow, Society of Pension Actuaries
JD	Juris Doctor
MSFS	Master of Science in Financial Services
MSPA	Member, Society of Pension Actuaries
RHU	Registered Health Underwriter
RIA	Registered Investment Advisor

APPENDIX B: Effects of Estate Taxation

Size of Estate	Federal Estate Tax	Unified Tax Credit	Net Estate Tax Due	Shrinkage
Estate				
$ 9,999	$ 0	$ 192,800	$ 0	0.00%
$ 10,000	$ 1,800	$ 192,800	$ 0	0.00%
$ 20,000	$ 3,800	$ 192,800	$ 0	0.00%
$ 40,000	$ 8,200	$ 192,800	$ 0	0.00%
$ 60,000	$ 13,000	$ 192,800	$ 0	0.00%
$ 80,000	$ 18,200	$ 192,800	$ 0	0.00%
$ 100,000	$ 23,800	$ 192,800	$ 0	0.00%
$ 150,000	$ 38,800	$ 192,800	$ 0	0.00%
$ 250,000	$ 70,800	$ 192,800	$ 0	0.00%
$ 500,000	$ 155,800	$ 192,800	$ 0	0.00%
$ 750,000	$ 248,300	$ 192,800	$ 55,500	7.40%
$ 1,000,000	$ 345,800	$ 192,800	$ 153,000	15.30%
$ 1,250,000	$ 448,300	$ 192,800	$ 255,500	20.44%
$ 1,500,000	$ 555,800	$ 192,800	$ 363,000	24.20%
$ 2,000,000	$ 780,800	$ 192,800	$ 588,000	29.40%
$ 2,500,000	$ 1,025,800	$ 192,800	$ 833,000	33.32%
$ 3,000,000	$ 1,290,800	$ 192,800	$ 1,098,000	36.60%
$ 4,000,000	$ 1,840,800	$ 192,800	$ 1,648,000	41.20%
$ 5,000,000	$ 2,390,800	$ 192,800	$ 2,198,000	43.96%
$ 6,000,000	$ 2,940,800	$ 192,800	$ 2,748,000	45.80%
$ 7,000,000	$ 3,490,800	$ 192,800	$ 3,298,000	47.11%
$ 8,000,000	$ 4,040,800	$ 192,800	$ 3,848,000	48.10%
$ 9,000,000	$ 4,590,800	$ 192,800	$ 4,398,000	48.87%
$10,000,000	$ 5,140,800	$ 192,800	$ 4,948,000	49.48%
$11,000,000	$ 5,690,800	$ 192,800	$ 5,498,000	49.98%
$12,000,000	$ 6,240,800	$ 192,800	$ 6,048,000	50.40%
$13,000,000	$ 6,790,800	$ 192,800	$ 6,598,000	50.75%
$14,000,000	$ 7,340,800	$ 192,800	$ 7,148,000	51.06%
$15,000,000	$ 7,890,800	$ 192,800	$ 7,698,000	51.32%
$16,000,000	$ 8,440,800	$ 192,800	$ 8,248,000	51.55%
$17,000,000	$ 8,990,800	$ 192,800	$ 8,798,000	51.75%
$18,000,000	$ 9,540,800	$ 192,800	$ 9,348,000	51.93%
$19,000,000	$10,090,800	$ 192,800	$ 9,898,000	52.09%
$20,000,000	$10,640,800	$ 192,800	$10,448,000	52.24%
$21,000,000	$11,190,800	$ 192,800	$10,998,000	52.37%
$22,000,000	$11,740,800	$ 192,800	$11,548,000	52.49%
$23,000,000	$12,290,800	$ 192,800	$12,098,000	52.60%
$24,000,000	$12,840,800	$ 192,800	$12,648,000	52.70%
$25,000,000	$13,390,800	$ 192,800	$13,198,000	52.79%

NOTES

1. U. S. Bureau of the Census, "Current Population Reports." *Statistical Abstracts of the United States,* 114th ed. (Washington, D.C.: U. S. Government Printing Office 1994): 137.

2. Ibid.

3. Halyna Doherty, "Women in Business: An Untapped Opportunity," *LIMRA's MarketFacts* (Jan-Feb 1995): 32-5.

4. Some insurance companies sell a whole life policy with a rider or option that enables you to make additional contributions to the policy if you choose. Such added payments can achieve two goals: additional cash value and increased death benefit. This is an attractive alternative to buying additional policies to meet growing family needs in the future. Advantages to this are that little or no evidence of insurability needs to be proven for additional benefit, and also the medical underwriting and application process to purchase more insurance are often eliminated. The third advantage is that you have more flexibility to add contributions when you are able to pay rather than what would be required if you purchased additional separate policies without such a rider.

5. Your agent may refer to this as a *term conversion option* or *term conversion privilege*. In the insurance industry, it is often the practice for companies to offer policyholders with term insurance an opportunity to later convert the term insurance to cash value insurance without additional evidence of insurability. This is a good reason for people to buy term insurance early in life when they are healthy and to convert it later. With term in the early years, a lower premium buys a certain amount of cash benefit upon death compared with a higher premium for the same amount of cash value insurance. Yet, if in the ensuing years after you buy the term policy, you would develop a medical condition that would make you a higher risk or even uninsurable, you might still have an opportunity to convert to permanent cash value insurance, which can also provide benefits to you while you are living. Check with the practices of your company and the laws governing insurance trade in your state.

6. Your agent may refer to this as *DI Business Overhead Expense.* Such a policy can cover rent, utilities, employee salaries, business loan payments, and professional dues subject to the terms of the policy. The benefit check is paid to the business. To cover your salary as a business owner, you would need a separate individual disability income protection policy.

7. American Council of Life Insurance, *What You Should Know About Buying Life Insurance* (Washington, D.C.: August 1995): 11.

8. Faith Popcorn, *The Popcorn Report.* (New York, N.Y.: Doubleday and Company, Inc., 1991).

9. Laurence Ganong and Marilyn Coleman, *Remarried Families* (Thousand Oaks, Calif.: Sage Publications, Inc. 1989).

10. American Council of Life Insurance, 13.

11. Theresa wanted to leave a legacy for her three children when she and Glenn died. She chose cash value life insurance rather than term insurance because she wanted to be able to have the premiums paid at age 65 offset by dividends (based on the current illustrative scale). If she had chosen term insurance because the premium was lower in those financially difficult years, she would have needed to continue making premium payments in the retirement years. By making a commitment to pay whole life premiums for 25 years, she accomplishes two things: 1) she committed herself to an accumulation program, and 2) she had a policy where the dividends, based on the current illustrative scale, would offset the premiums after 25 years.

12. U. S. Bureau of the Census, "Current Population Reports." *Statistical Abstracts of the United States,* 115th ed. (Washington: D.C.: U. S. Government Printing Office, 1995): 474.

13. Actually, the cost of waiting to begin her savings has cost her more than that. If she saved her shoe money and made a $2,400 annual contribution, at an assumed 9-percent rate of return after 20 years, it would have accumulated to $133,834.87. The Rule of 72 is a recognized economic concept

widely used in the finance and insurance industries. It calculates approximately how long it will take your savings to double based on the average rate of return. The equation is: 72 divided by the interest rate = the number of years to double your money.

14. At an assumed 9-percent rate of return, a $1,200 annual contribution will have grown to $66,917 after 20 years.

15. Larry Laudan, *Book of Risks: Fascinating Facts About the Chances We Take Every Day,* vol. 4 (New York, N.Y.: John Wiley and Sons, Inc., 1995), 125.

16. Ibid.

17. Brian Cox, "Women Are Good Prospects for Group Voluntary DI," *National Underwriter* (3 October 1994): 17.

18. This federal law mandates that outplaced employees be extended transition medical coverage that lasts up to 18 months after leaving employment. The employee benefits department of the company can provide details.

19. "Request for Earnings and Benefit Estimate Statement" (Washington, D.C.: U. S. Social Security Office 1996): 1.

20. Ibid., 2.

21. This Social Security form number is SSA-7004-SM OP-7. Be sure to list other names and Social Security numbers you have used in your work career.

22. Summary definitions of financial vehicles are by Grace W. Weinstein, *Financial Planning Especially for Women* (Washington, D.C.: American Council of Life Insurance 1989).

23. Consult the reference section in your library for publications by A. M. Best, Standard and Poor's, and Moody's Investor's Service, Inc. that provide details and current ratings of various financial institutions.

24. We thank American Western Mortgage for mortgage lending guideline tables: 33 percent of gross income is a guideline for a monthly mortgage payment; total debts along with the mortgage payment cannot exceed 38 percent of gross income. A bank lending officer or real estate agent can provide a copy of these tables.

25. U. S. Bureau of the Census, 115th ed., 114.

26. Ibid.

27. Boots Cooper was an honored woman of medicine and alumna of the Woman's Medical College Class of 1965 in Philadelphia, Pennsylvania. Her inspiration and influence has been most respected. See Janet Miller, *Oral History Interview with Boots Cooper, M. D.* (Philadelphia, Pa.: Medical College of Pennsylvania and Hahnemann University, 1992). In Women in Medicine Special Collection.

28. Probate accounts are a matter of public record. Emerald Publishing makes them available to the public.

29. Melvin Warshaw, Esq., "The Family Limited Partnership," *Investment Profiles* (May-June 1995): 99-100.

SELECTED BIBLIOGRAPHY

Ahmed, Nilufer R. "Marketing Opportunities." *Managers Magazine* 69, no. 6. (June 1994): 32.

Alexander, Sue. "Long Term Care: The Real Health Care Crisis." *Life & Health Insurance Sales* 137, no. 11. (November 1994): 30–3.

———. "Pat Phillips: Self Discipline from Career in Music Leads to Success in Life Insurance." *Life & Health Insurance Sales* 137, no. 11. (November 1994): 34–8.

———. "Phyllis Shelton: 'Road Less Traveled' Leads to Status as Long Term Care Guru." *Life & Health Insurance Sales* 137, no. 11. (November 1994): 22–8.

———. "Sally McClellan Provides Financial Strategies for Women." *Life & Health Insurance Sales* 137, no. 11. (November 1994): 14–8.

———. "Selling in the Women's Market is Relationship Building." *Life & Health Insurance Sales* 137, no. 11. (November 1994): 19–21.

———. "Women Business Owners: A Great Untapped Market." *Life & Health Insurance Sales* 137, no. 11. (November 1994): 40–5.

"American College, The." *Life & Health Insurance Sales* 138, no. 3. (March 1995): 16–20.

American Council of Life Insurance. *What You Should Know About Life Insurance.* Washington, D.C.: August 1995.

American Law Institute, The, and The American Bar Association. *The Practical Lawyer's Manual on Lawyer-Client Relations.* Philadelphia, Pa.: 1983.

"Are Women as Capable as Men in Handling Personal Finance Matters?" *LIMRA's MarketFacts*. (March/April 1995): 12.

Asch, Brian, CLU "Segmenting the Women's Market." *Security Life.* (July 1993): 5.

Bjerland, Karen, and Linda Doede-Sanderson. "Women: Still Your Neglected Market?" *Lutheran Life Bridge.* (August 1994): 4.

Bohigian, Valerie. *Ladybucks: Why Certain Women Turn Work Into Wealth.* North Tarrytown, N.Y.: Valian Associates, 1987.

Brenner, Lynn. "Retirement Planning: Three Case Studies." *Working Woman* 17, no. 5. (May 1992): 48–52.

Bryant, Pamela. "DIdeas." In *The Book of Risks: Fascinating Facts About the Chances We Take Every Day* by Larry Laudan. New York, N.Y.: John Wiley & Sons, Inc., 1994.

"Changes in the U.S." *Office* 118, no. 4. (October 1993): 18.

Cotton, Kathleen L., and Rachel W. Paysse. *Keys To Controlling Your Financial Destiny: Financial "Insider" Tips Every Woman Needs to Know.* Lynwood, Wash.: Wealth Books, April 1990.

Cox, Brian. "Women are Good Prospects for Group Voluntary DI." *National Underwriter.* (3 October 1994): 16–7.

Dempsey, Kay I. "Capturing the Nation's Largest Consumer Group." *Best's Review* 94, no. 10. (February 1994): 54.

———. "How to Sell Insurance to Women." *Life & Health Insurance Sales* 138, no. 5. (May 1995): 34–8.

Devine, Theresa J. "Characteristics of Self-Employed Women in the United States." *Monthly Labor Review.* (March 1994): 20.

"Dividend Options Summary Sheets." *MONY.* (15 January 1994).

Doherty, Halyna. "The Growing Market: Targeting Women in Business." *Managers Magazine* 70, no. 5. (May 1995): 9–12.

———. "Women in Business: An Untapped Opportunity." *LIMRA's MarketFacts* 14, no. 1. (January/February 1995): 32–5.

Dortch, Shannon. "What's Good for the Goose May Gag the Gander." *American Demographics.* (May 1994): 15.

Dunkin, Amy. "Buoying Women Investors." *Business Week.* 27 (February 1995): 126.

Emerald Publications. *Business Financial Management.* San Marcos, Calif.: 1989.

"Financial Decision Makers in Young Married Households 1965 vs. 1990 (i/r code 85.00)." *Life Insurance Marketing and Research Association Inc.* (23 September 1991).

Flach, Marlys. *For Women Only: Taking Charge of Your Life.* La Canada, Calif.: Freedom Productions, 1994.

Gaedeke, Andrea R. "Recruiting: Emerging Markets." *Managers Magazine* 67, no. 12. (December 1992): 26.

Ganong, Laurence, and Marilyn Coleman. *Remarried Families.* Thousand Oaks, Calif.: Sage Publications, Inc., 1989.

Gauches, Claudia. "Growth Opportunities Abound in Female Market." *National Underwriter* 97, no. 30. (26 July 1993): 16.

"Get to Grips With the Right Profile." *Marketing.* (3 February 1994): 3.

Gilbert, Evelyn. "M. O. M. Program Helps Deliver Healthy Babies." *National Underwriter* 96, no. 33. (17 August 1992): 25–6.

———. "Recruiting and Retention Tips for Associates." *National Underwriter* 98, no. 29. (18 July 1994): 17.

Gitter, Melissa. "Gender Trend: Equal Status, Unequal Strategies." *Financial Planning.* (October 1994): 36.

Greengard, Samuel. 'Saving for School the Smart Way.' *Life in Medicine.* (August 1994): 8.

Griffin, Alice. *How to Find the Right Lawyer.* New York, N.Y.: Cakewalk Press, 1996.

Grover, Mary Beth, and Jason Zweig. "Capital Research: Steak, No Sizzle." *Fund Families/ Fund Survey.* n.d.

Harris, Robert E. "Your Mission, If You Choose to Accept It…" *Texas Banking* 82, no. 6. (June 1993): 16.

"Health Briefs: Joint Marketing Projects to Examine Women's Needs in Life and Health Insurance Market." *National Underwriter* 96, no. 52. (28 December 1992 / 4 January 1993): 38.

Hedglon, Mead J., III. *How to Get the Best Legal Help for Your Business.* New York, N.Y.: McGraw-Hill Companies, 1992.

Intindola, Brendan. "New Software Calculates Dollars Lost From Death." *National Underwriter* 96, no. 5. (3 February 1992): 7.

———. "Poll: Women See Need for Savings, but Earn Less." *National Underwriter.* (5 April 1993): 49.

Jensen, Jeff. "What Golf Handicap?" *Advertising Age* 66, no. 22. (29 May 1995): 33.

Johnson, Kerry L., Ph.D. "The Gender Gap: How to Sell to the Opposite Sex." *Broker World.* (June 1991): 114.

Kaye, Steven D. with Kerry Hannon. "Wake Up, Baby Boomers." *U. S. News and World Report.* (13 June 1994): 84.

Katz, Deena. "Women in Transition Form Natural Market for Planning." *National Underwriter.* (19 June 1995): 7, 10.

Kaufman, Phyllis, and Arnold Corrigan. *How to Choose a Lawyer.* Ann Arbor, Mich.: Borders Press, 1987.

Knowles, Robert G. "Home Service Outpaces Others in Ethnic Minorities." *National Underwriter* 98, no. 24. (13 June 1994): 7, 15.

Koco, Linda. "Flex-Annuity Targets Older Seniors." *National Underwriter* 96, no. 25. (22 June 1992): 13.

Larson, Jan. "Understanding Stepfamilies." *American Demographics* 14, no. 7. (July 1992): 36–40.

Laudan, Larry *Book of Risks: Fascinating Facts About the Changes We Take Every Day*, 4 New York, N.Y.: John Wiley and Sons, Inc., 1994.

Levine, Joshua. "Italy's First Lady of the Factory." *Forbes* 150, no. 7. (28 September 1992): 154–6.

Lumsdon, Kevin. "Telecommunications: Hospitals Explore New Electronic Links to Reduce Costs, Increase Access." *Hospitals* 66, no. 18. (20 September 1992): 46–52.

Magill. *Professional Duties and Responsibilities.* Cincinnati, Ohio: South-Western Publishing Company, 1997.

Mahar, Maggie. "How the Sexes Save and Spend." *Working Woman* 18, no. 10. (October 1993): 20.

Mandola, Peg L. "The Female Force: Can You Afford to Overlook Nearly Half of Today's Work Force?" *LIMRA's MarketFacts* 12, no. 6. (November/ December 1993): 42.

Marenghi, Catherine. "There Are Cracks: But the Glass Ceiling is Still Mostly Intact." *Computerworld* 26, no. 5. (3 February 1992): 85.

McCoy, Thomas A. "Marketing to Women." *Rough Notes* 138, no. 9. (September 1995): 82–3.

Meisenheimer, Joseph R., II; Earl F. Mellor; and Leo G. Rydzewski. "Job Market Slid in Early 1991, then Struggled to Find Footing." *Monthly Labor Review* 115, no. 2. (February 1992): 3–17.

Meyers, Gerry. "Targeting the New Professional Woman." *Brandweek.* (31 January 1994): 1.

Miller, Janet. *Oral History Interview with Boots Cooper, M. D.* Philadelphia, Pa.: Medical College of Pennsylvania and Hahnemann University, 1992. In Women in Medicine Special Collection.

Mills, Joseph C. "Target Market: Single Professional Businesswoman." *Life Association News* 87, no. 9. (September 1992): 129–32.

Monroe, Stuart A., LLB., CLU., and The Bottom Line Task Force of the 1987 Million Dollar Round Table. *Estate Planning for the Agent.* Des Plaines, Ill.: 1987 Million Dollar Round Table, 1987.

Morrall, Katherine. "Banks Lend Support to Women Business Owners." *Bank Marketing* 25, no. 8. (August 1993): 22–7.

Mutual Life Insurance Company of New York, The. *Getting Started Toward a Financially Secure Future.* New York, N.Y.: n.d.

———. *Ratings: A Profile of MONY.* New York, N.Y.: 1991.

"Needs-Selling Agents Ignore Women." *National Underwriter* 98, no. 28. (11 July 1994): 7–8.

Nelson, Kristin L. "Against All Odds, Women Climb the Ladders." *Best's Review* 94, no. 10. (February 1994): 34.

———. "Finding and Keeping Women Clients." *Best's Review.* (September 1993): 88.

"New Era of Disabilities." *Life & Health Insurance Sales* 137, no. 12. (December 1994): 26–7.

O'Rourke, Tim. "It Won't Happen to Me!" *Broker World* 12, no. 12. (December 1992): 64–70.

Ostberg, Kay. *Using a Lawyer.* Washington, D.C.: HALT Publishing Company, 1990.

Petersen, Donald J., and Douglas P. Massengill. "Sexual Harassment Cases Five Years After Meritor Savings Bank v. Vinson." *Employee Relations Law Journal* 18, no. 3. (Winter 1992–3): 489–515.

Pillsbury, Dennis H. "Success Runs in the Family." *Life & Health Insurance Sales* 136, no. 4. (April 1993): 14.

———. "Tapping the Retirement Market." *Life & Health Insurance Sales* 136, no. 10. (October 1993): 27.

Pinson, Linda, and Jerry Jinnett. *Anatomy of a Business Plan: A Financial Planning Seminar.* 3d ed. Dover, N.H.: Upstart Publishing Company, Inc., 1996.

Popcorn, Faith. *The Popcorn Report.* New York, N.Y.: Doubleday and Company, Inc., 1991.

Priddy Patterson, Martha. "A Woman's Special Dilemma: Leaving the Work Force for Seven Years Can Cut Your Benefit in Half." *U. S. News and World Report.* (13 June 1994): 93.

Provident Life and Accident Insurance Company. *Section 105 Qualified Sick Pay Plan.* Chattanooga, Tenn.: n.d.

Retzloff, Cheryl D., ACS, LLIF. "Are Women Still Under-Insured?" *LIMRA's MarketFacts.* (January/ February 1995): 8.

Robert, Lee R. "Men Selling to Women and Women Selling to Women." *Life & Health Insurance Sales* 137, no. 11. (November 1994): 8–12.

Roberts, Sally. "A Conversation with: E. S. Leverett." *Business Insurance* 26, no. 44. (30 October 1992): 142.

Rodgers, Mary Augusta. "Stop Living from Paycheck to Paycheck." *Woman's Day.* (1 February 1995): 41.

Scanlon, James T. "The Female Market." *LIMRA's MarketFacts* 12, no. 4. (July/ August 1993): 40–1.

Sharp, Nancy. "Washington, D.C.: Fall 1992." *Nursing Management* 23, no. 10. (October 1992): 32–3.

Sullivan, Aline. "E. C. Court Cuts Retroactive Pension Liability." *Business Insurance* 27, no. 43. (18 October 1993): 71–2.

Sullivan, Michael P. "Marketing to the Mature Woman." *The Banker's Magazine.* (July/ August 1993): 68.

Sykes, Tanisha A. "Business Lunch." *Black Enterprise* 24, no. 4. (November 1993): 34.

Thomas, Vicki. "Filling the Information Gap." *Bank Marketing* 27, no. 4. (April 1995): 23–6.

U. S. Bureau of the Census. "Current Population Reports." *Statistical Abstracts of the United States.* 114th ed. Washington, D.C.: 1994.

———. "Current Population Reports." *Statistical Abstracts of the United States.* 115th ed. Washington, D.C.: 1995.

Vatter, Robert H. "Women in the Labor Force." *Statistical Bulletin.* (July–September 1994): 2.

Warshaw, Melvin A., Esq. "The Family Limited Partnership." *Investment Profiles.* (May/ June 1994): 99.

Washer, Louise. "The Best Franchises for Women." *Working Woman* 17, no. 11. (November 1992): 73–5.

Weinstein, Grace. *Financial Planning Especially for Women.* Washington, D.C.: American Council of Life Insurance, 1989.

West, Robin. *How to Find the Right Divorce Lawyer.* Chicago, Ill.: Contemporary Books, Inc., 1997.

Western and Southern Life Insurance Company. "Women as Buyers of Life Insurance." *Western and Southern Field News.* (October 1993): 5.

Weylman, C. Richard. "Seminar Spade Work is as Important as [the] Event." *National Underwriter* 96, no. 52. (28 December 1992 / 4 January 1993): 20–1.

"Where the Boys Aren't." *American Demographics..* (December 1992): 8.

"Women's View of Money Driven by Personality: Study." *National Underwriter.* (3 April 1995): 23.

Zellner, Wendy. "Pioneer: The Race Battle Never Ends." *Business Week* 98, no. 33. (17 October 1994): 98–100.

INDEX

NEUROCIRCUITRY OF ADDICTION

NEUROCIRCUITRY OF ADDICTION

Edited by

NICHOLAS W. GILPIN
LSU Health Sciences Center, USA

ELSEVIER

ACADEMIC PRESS
An imprint of Elsevier

Academic Press is an imprint of Elsevier
125 London Wall, London EC2Y 5AS, United Kingdom
525 B Street, Suite 1650, San Diego, CA 92101, United States
50 Hampshire Street, 5th Floor, Cambridge, MA 02139, United States
The Boulevard, Langford Lane, Kidlington, Oxford OX5 1GB, United Kingdom

ISBN: 978-0-12-823453-2

For information on all Academic Press publications visit our website at https://www.elsevier.com/books-and-journals

Publisher: Nikki P. Levy
Acquisitions Editor: Joslyn T. Chaiprasert-Paguio
Editorial Project Manager: Sara Pianavilla
Production Project Manager: Fahmida Sultana
Cover Designer: Christian J. Bilbow

Typeset by TNQ Technologies

Contents

5. Insular Cortical circuits

Christine Ibrahim and Bernard Le Foll

6. Thalamic circuits

Alessandra Matzeu, Francisco J. Flores-Ramirez and Rémi Martin-Fardon

7. Hippocampal circuits

Chitra D. Mandyam

8. Amygdala circuits

Lieselot L.G. Carrette, Elizabeth A. Sneddon and Olivier George

9. Bed Nucleus of Stria Terminalis (BNST) circuits

Samuel W. Centanni, Jordan A. Brown, Kellie M. Williford, Elizabeth A. Flook, Joseph R. Luchsinger and Danny G. Winder

10. Noradrenergic circuits

Zoé A. McElligott, Madigan L. Bedard, Sara Y. Conley, Isabel M. Bravo, Elizabeth S. Cogan and Anthony M. Downs

11. Cholinergic modulation of circuits

Nii A. Addy, Christie D. Fowler and Robert J. Wickham

Contributors

Kelly M. Abshire Clinical Psychoneuroendocrinology and Neuropsychopharmacology Section, Translational Addiction Medicine Branch, National Institute on Drug Abuse and National Institute on Alcohol Abuse and Alcoholism, National Institutes of Health, Baltimore, MD, United States

Nii A. Addy Department of Psychiatry, Yale School of Medicine, New Haven, CT, United States; Yale Tobacco Center of Regulatory Science, Yale School of Medicine, New Haven, CT, United States; Department of Cellular and Molecular Physiology, Yale School of Medicine, New Haven, CT, United States; Interdepartmental Neuroscience Program, Yale University, New Haven, CT, United States; Wu Tsai Institute, Yale University, New Haven, CT, United States

Madigan L. Bedard Department of Pharmacology, University of North Carolina at Chapel Hill, Chapel Hill, NC, United States

Isabel M. Bravo Bowles Center for Alcohol Studies, University of North Carolina at Chapel Hill, Chapel Hill, NC, United States

Jordan A. Brown Vanderbilt Center for Addiction Research, Vanderbilt University School of Medicine, Nashville, TN, United States

Lieselot L.G. Carrette Department of Psychiatry, University of California San Diego, La Jolla, CA, United States

Samuel W. Centanni Vanderbilt Center for Addiction Research, Vanderbilt University School of Medicine, Nashville, TN, United States

Elizabeth S. Cogan Bowles Center for Alcohol Studies, University of North Carolina at Chapel Hill, Chapel Hill, NC, United States

Sara Y. Conley Neuroscience Curriculum, University of North Carolina at Chapel Hill, Chapel Hill, NC, United States

Anthony M. Downs Bowles Center for Alcohol Studies, University of North Carolina at Chapel Hill, Chapel Hill, NC, United States

M. Flavia Barbano National Institute on Drug Abuse (NIDA/NIH), Baltimore, MD, United States

Elizabeth A. Flook Vanderbilt Center for Addiction Research, Vanderbilt University School of Medicine, Nashville, TN, United States

Francisco J. Flores-Ramirez Department of Molecular Medicine, The Scripps Research Institute, La Jolla, CA, United States

Christie D. Fowler Department of Neurobiology and Behavior, University of California, Irvine, Irvine, CA, United States

Mackenzie C. Gamble Molecular and Translational Medicine, Graduate Medical Sciences, Department of Medicine, Boston University School of Medicine, Boston, MA, United States; Department of Pharmacology and Experimental Therapeutics, Boston University School of Medicine, Boston, MA, United States

Olivier George Department of Psychiatry, University of California San Diego, La Jolla, CA, United States

Matthew C. Hearing Department of Biomedical Sciences, Marquette University, Milwaukee, WI, United States

Christine Ibrahim Translational Addiction Research Laboratory, Centre for Addiction and Mental Health, Toronto, ON, Canada; Department of Pharmacology and Toxicology, Faculty of Medicine, University of Toronto, Toronto, ON, Canada

Bernard Le Foll Translational Addiction Research Laboratory, Centre for Addiction and Mental Health, Toronto, ON, Canada; Department of Pharmacology and Toxicology, Faculty of Medicine, University of Toronto, Toronto, ON, Canada; Addictions Division, Centre for Addiction and Mental Health, Toronto, ON, Canada; Campbell Family Mental Health Research Institute, Centre for Addiction and Mental Health, Toronto, ON, Canada; Department of Psychiatry, Faculty of Medicine, University of Toronto, Toronto, ON, Canada; Institute of Medical Sciences, University of Toronto, Toronto, ON, Canada; Department of Family and Community Medicine, University of Toronto, Toronto, ON, Canada

Lorenzo Leggio Clinical Psychoneuroendocrinology and Neuropsychopharmacology Section, Translational Addiction Medicine Branch, National Institute on Drug Abuse and National Institute on Alcohol Abuse and Alcoholism, National Institutes of Health, Baltimore, MD, United States; Medication Development Program, National Institute on Drug Abuse Intramural Research Program, National Institutes of Health, Baltimore, MD, United States; Center for Alcohol and Addiction Studies, Department of Behavioral and Social Sciences, School of Public Health, Brown University, Providence, RI, United States; Division of Addiction Medicine, Department of Medicine, School of Medicine, Johns Hopkins University, Baltimore, MD, United States; Department of Neuroscience, Georgetown University Medical Center, Washington, DC, United States

Ryan W. Logan Department of Pharmacology and Experimental Therapeutics, Boston University School of Medicine, Boston, MA, United States; Center for Systems Neuroscience, Boston University, Boston, MA, United States

Joseph R. Luchsinger Vanderbilt Center for Addiction Research, Vanderbilt University School of Medicine, Nashville, TN, United States

Chitra D. Mandyam VA San Diego Healthcare System, San Diego, CA, United States; Department of Anesthesiology, University of California San Diego, San Diego, CA, United States

John R. Mantsch Department of Pharmacology & Toxicology, Medical College of Wisconsin, Milwaukee, WI, United States

Rémi Martin-Fardon Department of Molecular Medicine, The Scripps Research Institute, La Jolla, CA, United States

Brian N. Mathur Department of Pharmacology, University of Maryland School of Medicine Baltimore, MD, United States

Alessandra Matzeu Department of Molecular Medicine, The Scripps Research Institute, La Jolla, CA, United States

Zoé A. McElligott Bowles Center for Alcohol Studies, University of North Carolina at Chapel Hill, Chapel Hill, NC, United States; Department of Psychiatry, University of North Carolina at Chapel Hill, Chapel Hill, NC, United States; Department of Pharmacology, University of North Carolina at Chapel Hill, Chapel Hill, NC, United States

Marisela Morales National Institute on Drug Abuse (NIDA/NIH), Baltimore, MD, United States

Michael S. Patton Department of Pharmacology, University of Maryland School of Medicine Baltimore, MD, United States

Michael C. Salling Louisiana State University Health Sciences Center, New Orleans, LA, United States

Elizabeth A. Sneddon Department of Psychology and Center for Neuroscience and Behavior, Miami University, Oxford, OH, United States

Robert J. Wickham Department of Psychology, Lafayette College, Easton, PA, United States

Kellie M. Williford Vanderbilt Center for Addiction Research, Vanderbilt University School of Medicine, Nashville, TN, United States

Danny G. Winder Vanderbilt Center for Addiction Research, Vanderbilt University School of Medicine, Nashville, TN, United States

Preface

Nicholas W. Gilpin, Ph.D.

Humans have consumed substances with psychoactive effects for many thousands of years. Direct evidence for or documentation of the use of drugs dates back at least 9000 years and includes production of fermented beverages and cultivation of opium poppies and coca leaves. It is likely that drug and alcohol addiction has been around just as long.

People use drugs and alcohol for countless different reasons that include, but are not limited to, cultural and social norms, achieving the "high" associated with drug use, and treatment of medical conditions under direction from medical professionals, as well as via self-medication of undiagnosed physical and mental health conditions. A wide array of physical and mental health issues can also be *caused* by either acute drug use (e.g., respiratory depression resulting from acute opioid overdose) or chronic drug use (e.g., lung cancer resulting from cigarette use or liver cirrhosis from alcohol use).

Over the last few centuries, governments have regulated drug production, distribution, and use, but this has always been a dynamic process in which greater or lesser regulation of specific drugs changes over time based on political, cultural, and social realities. One example of these changes is the prohibition of alcohol in the United States in 1920 followed by the repeal of prohibition 13 years later. Another example is the categorization of marijuana as a Schedule 1 substance throughout the United States by the Controlled Substances Act of 1970, as compared to the current-day mixed bag of medical and recreational legalization of THC products at the state level, even while THC products remain illegal at the federal level in the United States.

The diagnosis of addiction itself, as a health problem with a defined etiology and symptomatology, has undergone many iterations over the past 100 or so years. Definitions of addiction, used for the diagnosis and treatment of the disorder, have evolved from a primary basis on physical manifestations (e.g., functional and physiological tolerance to acute drug effects, and a withdrawal syndrome in the absence of the drug) to greater emphasis on behavioral manifestations in the current edition of the *Diagnostic and Statistical Manual of Mental Disorders*, the principal guide used by medical professionals. In the DSM-V, addiction is no longer called addiction, but instead is referred to as a collection of substance use disorders (SUDs) (e.g., alcohol use disorder, cocaine use disorder, etc.). The purpose of this change in terminology was at least twofold: first, to allow for quantification of addiction-related phenotypes along a spectrum of severity based on the number of symptoms that are identified in a patient, and second, to reduce stigma associated with an SUD diagnosis (e.g., by avoiding the use of terms that suggest a moral failing in those with an SUD).

Doctors and researchers have worked to understand the causes and mediators of drug and alcohol addiction ever since addiction was acknowledged as having medical, social, and economic consequences.

In the United States, two of the National Institutes of Health (NIH) are devoted entirely to this mission: the National Institute on Drug Abuse (NIDA) and the National Institute on Alcohol Abuse and Alcoholism (NIAAA) fund a large percentage of the addiction research being conducted globally. A major area of focus for these institutes, and for the addiction science field at large, is to identify the neurobiological mechanisms underlying drug and alcohol addiction, and to use this knowledge for the treatment of substance use disorders.

Until about 15 years ago, addiction neuroscientists were limited to asking scientific questions at the level of "nodes" in the brain (or in the whole organism). For studies employing brain manipulations, most preclinical work conducted prior to the 21st century tested the effects of stimulation or lesion or drug injection in one brain area at a time—this radically changed with the advent and widespread adoption of circuit-based technologies (introduced extensively in the first chapter of this book). These new approaches allowed researchers to manipulate circuits, rather than single "nodes," with remarkable spatial and temporal resolution. Since that time, the technology has evolved to allow for selective manipulations of specific cell types, allowing for a level of resolution previously inconceivable in addiction neuroscience. Now, the major challenge facing the field is to bring this increasingly granular knowledge back to the clinic in a way that improves human lives.

This book is tailored to provide the reader with the state of the science in the field of addiction neuroscience today. This book is tailored for individuals with a basic understanding of neuroscience. No prior in-depth knowledge of addiction neuroscience is required, as the book includes primers that will help the reader navigate the specialized material. Chapters are organized by circuits, each of them placing a specific brain region or neuromodulatory system at the "center of the neural universe" so to speak, then goes on to describe major inputs and outputs to these neural hubs. Each chapter then summarizes the literature as it pertains to the roles of specific neural circuits in mediating drug effects, paying special mind to the diversity of effects observed with different drug classes, as well as the roles of those circuits in controlling addiction-related behaviors.

My hope is that this book will inspire some in the next generation to pursue a career in addiction neuroscience and to carry the mantle forward as the field determines how to improve human health based on a circuit approach to the addiction problem.

CHAPTER

1

Leveraging circuits to understand addiction

Michael C. Salling

Louisiana State University Health Sciences Center, New Orleans, LA, United States

Introduction

Advancements in neuroscientific methods often drive new waves of insight into our understanding of addiction. While addiction research questions persist, technical improvements can augment our observational sensitivity, allowing us to update and extend existing addiction models through method development, creative application, and scientific discovery. As a result of this iterative process, we have reached the point where neuroscientists can now readily identify, monitor, and control specific neural circuits during behavior, thereby opening new windows of inquiry into the neurobiology of addiction. The objective of this chapter is to familiarize the reader with standard and emerging techniques used to observe and interrogate neural circuitry that are prevalent in contemporary clinical and preclinical addiction neuroscience labs and that are presented throughout the book. This chapter will further discuss the historical context, benefits, and limitations of these techniques with a look forward into how they can be applied to questions of addiction neurocircuitry.

Perhaps the most common analogy used to describe the central nervous system is to say it is like a computer. This a useful comparison for many reasons. For instance, the brain signals electrically along insulated pathways that are "wired" for a particular function. These connections are referred to as neural circuits and they have powerful processing abilities that include input/output functions, memory storage and information processing that can even exist within compartments of single neurons. While there is no other known entity that can process complex information quite like a brain, computers are the closest comparator. Yet, unlike our computers, we did not ourselves design the human brain and therefore are not privy to its inner workings. Imagine discovering a computer built by another civilization that is orders of magnitude more complex and efficient than what we know and then being tasked with having to reverse engineer it. Neuroscientists have been embarking on this puzzle for

Neurocircuitry of Addiction
https://doi.org/10.1016/B978-0-12-823453-2.00002-3

centuries, learning how this "alien computer" is organized, how it transmits information, and how it is able to interact with the environment to produce behavior. Untangling wires and breaking them into individual circuits has emerged as a leading strategy toward this goal and thus new waves of neuroscience tools have been developed out of this strategy.

The current prevailing view in the addiction neuroscience field is that the behaviors that define substance use disorders (SUDs) result from drug-induced alterations to specific neurocircuitry in an individual's brain (Koob and Volkow, 2010). Initial acute drug exposure acts on select neural circuits to create experiences that are often euphoric, anxiolytic and overall rewarding. As the effects of the drug wear off after exposure, there are counter adaptations in the CNS that hang over and are experienced as drug withdrawal. Repeated cycling of drug use and withdrawal, which occurs during chronic drug use, can cause physiological adaptations in systems initially affected by the drug and/or recruit activity in other brain systems—collectively, these circuits are responsible for associative learning (Hyman et al., 2006), affective internal states (Koob and Le Moal, 2001), and cognition (Dalley et al., 2011). Circuits underlying these brain processes are dysregulated by chronic drug exposure and eventually drug-related cues and drug withdrawal states drive an organism to seek the drug, often despite increasingly negative consequences associated with drug seeking and drug use. While there is no doubt that the probability of becoming addicted is affected by one's genetic predisposition and environmental conditions, the onset of addiction is subject to drug by neural circuit interactions in all individuals, but perhaps on different time scales. Treatment of SUDs often include behavioral therapy approaches alongside strategies aimed at mitigating hazardous drug use or attenuating symptoms that are thought to be driven by dysregulated neural systems (Volkow and Boyle, 2018). Optimization of pharmacotherapies or brain stimulation treatments that target affected neural systems require a clearer understanding of the underlying neural circuits and physiological adaptions that occur (Salling and Martinez, 2016).

In the field of addiction research, circuit-based approaches have been highly prevalent and fruitful for enriching our understanding of the neurobiology underlying addiction. Relative to other psychiatric disorders, a major strength of addiction research lies in the validity and breadth of the animal models to which circuit-based inquiry can be applied. For instance, animal species used in laboratories include fruit flies (Devineni and Heberlein, 2009), rodents (Sanchis-Segura and Spanagel, 2006), and nonhuman primates (Goldberg et al., 1969), each of which will voluntarily consume addictive drugs and/or show preference for drug taking environments (Foltin and Evans, 2001; Kaun et al., 2011; Mucha et al., 1982). This remarkable commonality among such diverse species demonstrates the existence of conserved circuits that are sensitive to addictive drugs and can be investigated using species-specific neuroscience tools. Furthermore, addiction-related behaviors and processes that are used to define and diagnose SUDs can be modeled in research animals and include sensitization, tolerance, withdrawal, and drug seeking (Koob, 2011; Fredriksson et al., 2021). Clever experimental paradigms that allow for the monitoring and causal testing of neural circuit function during these behaviors are constantly being devised, optimized, and implemented (Vollmer et al., 2021; Mazza et al., 2021). Fortunately, addiction research is heavily rooted in the discipline of behavioral pharmacology and as a result, many behavioral neuroscience labs have been investigating, replicating, and improving upon drug self-administration paradigms for decades, often alongside neural systems-based approaches. For instance, targeted brain lesions or site-specific drug infusions have continuously narrowed down specific areas and neurotransmitter systems of the brain that influence drug seeking and other addictive behaviors particularly in rats and mice (Caprioli et al., 2018; Ikemoto and Bonci, 2014). As a result of this past and continuing work, the field of addiction neuroscience has gained an understanding of the major neurotransmitter systems and brain regions involved in addictive behavior in animal models, creating an entry point for teasing apart the contribution of individual neural circuits.

Due to the immense complexity of neural circuitry in the human brain, influence of environmental factors, and behavioral sequalae of SUDs, establishing a comprehensive understanding of the neurobiology of addiction requires a multidisciplinary, "all tools in the toolbox" strategy. In this chapter, research methods in clinical studies including postmortem investigation and non-invasive imaging will be introduced as well as their limitations in studying neural circuitry. Preclinical methods in animal models that can identify specific neural circuits through chemical and genetic targeting to measure physiological adaptations to addictive drugs will be discussed. Finally, *in vivo* methods increasingly used in preclinical addiction labs that enable the researcher to monitor and manipulate neural activity in select circuits during addiction-related behaviors will be presented. Collectively, these techniques can be used to identify the neural substrates implicated in SUDs, the underlying mechanisms that cause circuit dysregulation, and the causal role of the affected neural circuits in addictive behavior.

Identification of neural circuits implicated in addiction: where to start?

Human beings have cultivated, developed, and shared psychoactive substances since prehistorical times. How cultures perceive substance use and what is defined as a problematic substance use has changed over that time and will continue to change alongside social contexts (Durrant et al., 2009). Nevertheless, the production, distribution, and consumption of drugs like heroin, cocaine, and alcohol across the world over many generations have demonstrated that there are specific and unambiguous behavioral patterns common to individuals that use and misuse these substances. They include harmful and hazardous behaviors that can result in severe negative health consequences including mortality. As far as we know, problematic drug use is a uniquely human phenomenon and therefore the human nervous system must serve as the starting point for any inquiry into what makes an addicted brain biologically different from a non-addicted one. Human studies are largely limited to investigations of postmortem brain tissue, genetic association studies and noninvasive neuroimaging techniques. These approaches have been successful in illuminating key differences in the structural and functional neurobiology of drug users, yet many gaps in the knowledge of how drug use specifically affects circuit function remain.

Human histopathological techniques

Observing what "your brain on drugs" looks like has been less obvious than advertised. To the naked eye, gross neuroanatomical examinations of the human brains of substance users have revealed that major systematic and pathologic changes are not the rule. Some of the exceptions include higher propensities of brain atrophy in late-stage alcohol use disorder (AUD) (Harper et al., 1985), ischemic lesions in methamphetamine users, and cerebral edema in opioid users (Pelletier and Andrew, 2017). Rather than evidence of a recognizable brain disease as seen in neurodegenerative diseases like Parkinson's, these findings are more likely grim reminders of the severe consequences of addiction including malnutrition in severe AUD, tolerance to neurotoxic doses of methamphetamine, and respiratory failure during opioid overdose. Instead of a lesion, the pathology underlying addictive behavior is thought to occur from repeated pharmacological interactions with brain systems that lead to long-term, neuroplastic changes to circuitry (Kalivas and O'Brien, 2008; Heilig et al., 2021). A higher resolution lens is needed to observe the type of neurobiological changes that are responsible for addiction and that should be evident earlier in the addiction process alongside the presence of the behaviors that are used to define it.

At the microscopic level, histological processing of postmortem human brains can assess more subtle features of neurons including neurotoxicity, neuron morphology, white matter tracts, and protein expression. Traditional histological methods like Nissl stain which labels ribosomal bodies enriched in neurons can be used for mapping the distribution and counts of neurons in brain regions. Brain cells that have initiated programmed cell death, or apoptosis, can be identified using cytotoxic markers like deoxynucleotidyl transferase-mediated dUTP nick end (TUNEL) staining, a chemical dye that signals the presence of DNA breaks. The Golgi-Cox method which indiscriminately stains the entirety of 1−3% of neurons in brain samples is used to visualize and compare aspects of neuronal morphology including dendritic arborization and spines, indicative of synapse density. Myelin-based stains, for instance Weigert's method, can identify axonal fiber tracts and map regional connectivity. Findings from these traditional staining methods have revealed that loss of frontal cortical neuron numbers occurs in stimulant and heavy alcohol users and an increased presence of apoptotic cells in select brain regions including the cortex, hippocampus and cerebellum (Buttner, 2011). In chronic alcohol users, loss of white matter tracts in the genu of the corpus callosum and reductions in neuronal spine density in the frontal cortex have been observed indicating decreased connectivity in brain regions that influence higher cognition and likely control over drug seeking behaviors (Harper and Corbett, 1990; Ferrer et al., 1986). These findings implicate brain regions that are vulnerable to addictive drugs and by identifying microstructural changes, can complement and confirm findings from brain imaging.

Immunohistochemistry is widely used across labs to assess the expression and localization of select proteins in tissue. This method involves labeling of proteins using specific antibodies to native antigens that are generated by inoculating whole animals or *in vitro* systems to specific protein fragments and collecting the antibody rich serum or media. When experimental tissue is incubated in these primary antibodies, they will bind to a specific protein target. Secondary antibodies which are generated to recognize common fragments of primary antibodies often are designed to have a chemical dye conjugated to them and thus the presence of the specific protein can be visualized in neurons or other cells under light or fluorescence microscopy. Some examples of findings from these studies have revealed drug-specific brain changes that include increased expression of activated microglia (a marker of neuroinflammation) and reductions in dopamine transporter expression in humans that misuse stimulants (Buttner, 2011; He and Crews, 2008). In general, examination of human

Open Books Ltd
905 W. 19th St.
Chicago, IL 60608
UNITED STATES
orders@open-books.org

Open Books Ltd
905 W. 19th St.
Chicago, IL 60608
UNITED STATES

To: Alibris APEX DC 76926317-49 - APEX
800 Avondale Ave.

Grandview Heights, OH 43212-3473
UNITED STATES

If this order is shipping from the US to an international buyer, remember to attach proper documentation. Complete and attach USPS Form CN-22 for all Priority Mail International Envelopes or First-Class Mail International shipments (available at your post office).

Order Number:	2180446
Ship Method:	Standard
Customer Name:	Alibris APEX DC 76926317-49 - APEX
Order Date:	9/15/2026
Alibris Order #:	76926317-49
Email:	

Items:

brains using histological methods are challenging due to availability of donors and the need to rapidly collect and process postmortem human brain tissue before neuronal morphology and proteins are degraded (Lewis, 2002).

Application of molecular biology techniques to human samples

At the molecular level, drug effects on regional gene and protein expression may reveal neuroadaptations that occur in individuals with SUDs. Common techniques used in molecular biology labs have been applied to human brain tissue. For instance, brain regions can be dissected from postmortem samples and gene expression in the brain can be measured following homogenization of tissue and cell lyses (Fig. 1.1A). RNA transcription can be

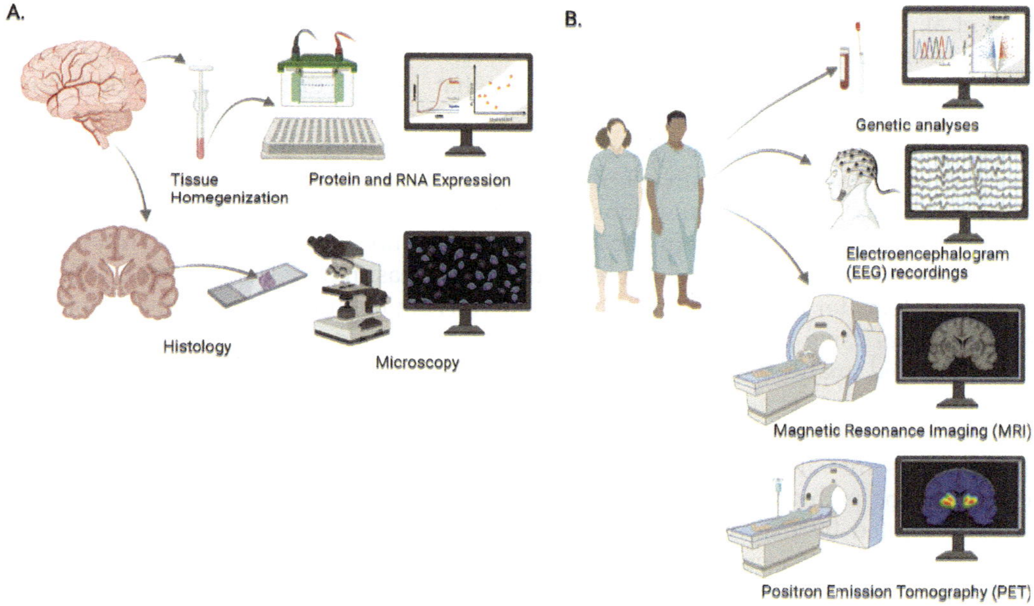

FIGURE 1.1 **Human research methods to study of neurobiology of addiction.** (A) Assessing the neurobiological differences in brains of individuals that displayed symptoms of SUDs can be compared using molecular biology techniques. Top: Postmortem brain tissue collected from donated specimens is amenable to messenger RNA or protein expression studies where brain regions can be dissected out, homogenized and probed for targeted RNA transcript and protein expression using RT PCR and Western blot methods. More unbiased and comprehensive approaches to include transcriptomic and proteomic methodologies. Bottom: Microstructural changes to neurons can be assessed using histological stains and immunohistochemistry to assess the impact of substance use on neuronal morphology and protein expression in individual neurons. (B) Top: Clinical studies of individuals with SUDs often include collecting genetic material from the subject and DNA sequencing to assess the existence of gene variants that may be associated with SUDs. Second from top: EEG setup where brain activity can be measured noninvasively on the scalp with EEG during behavioral states or tasks. Third from top: MRI scanners can measure structural changes in gray and white matter due to substance use. Bottom: In PET studies, radioactive compounds like specific receptor ligands are delivered to the subject intravenously. A PET scan is able to measure the location of radioligand binding to demonstrate the expression and location of a radioligand target. *Created with Biorender.*

measured for a selected number of genes using quantitative real time PCR (qT-PCR) or larger subsets through hybridization assays on microarrays. For comparing entire genomes, termed transcriptomics, RNA-sequencing (RNA-seq) has emerged as a powerful technique where RNA can be isolated and sequenced to determine the presence and the number of copies of gene transcripts in brain samples. RNA-seq studies have been performed in tissue collected from individuals with SUDs, including those that achieve single-cell resolution following cell-sorting procedures (Huggett and Stallings, 2020; Brenner et al., 2020). New methods for comprehensive transcript identification in single cells preserves unique gene expression profiles that can be used to identify and probe changes to neuronal subpopulations in clinical SUD samples. For instance, there are specific genes only expressed in excitatory or inhibitory neurons, which can be used to segregate and delineate transcript differences in these subtypes of neurons. Further application of *in situ* RNA hybridization using RNA transcript probes or spatial transcriptomics in postmortem histological preparations can provide anatomical dimensions that confirm or complement findings from quantitative RNA analyses (Tran et al., 2021; Maynard et al., 2021).

Protein expression is the business end of the central dogma of molecular biology as functional proteins, rather than nucleotides, are what largely dictate physiological function *in vivo*. Several techniques can be used to measure specific protein levels from brain samples including Western Blot analyses, a common technique where proteins are separated using gel electrophoresis and probed with specific antibodies to reveal their relative expression. Unbiased proteomics techniques are a more comprehensive and objective approach to compare proteomes of brain regions from substance users and non-substance users. In this method, all proteins that reach a detectable threshold can be measured by isolating and radioactively tagging proteins for quantification and then identifying them using mass spectrometry. Proteomic studies using brains of humans with SUDs have identified a wealth of targets, and pathway-based analyses have revealed that proteins involved in synaptic transmission are often affected (Wang et al., 2011). Regional brain dissection and homogenization of tissue precludes confirmation of specific neural circuits involved, but ultimately, these techniques and their analyses are valuable as they provide the depth and molecular context that can lead to novel signaling pathways to be explored in hypothesis-driven experiments. These studies are similarly limited by the availability and quality of tissue resources. The omission of non-white and female subjects in earlier studies have greatly limited their significance. Further muddying the waters, human gene transcription and protein expression studies can be difficult to interpret due to unknown and uncontrolled environmental factors of brain donors. Complicated medical histories are common in addiction and include a higher prevalence of underlying health issues, polydrug use and comorbidity of psychiatric disorders which may each elicit gene expression changes. Without knowing comprehenssive autobiographical and medical histories of subjects, it is challenging to differentiate what other underlying neurobiological differences have occurred due to substance use (Lewis, 2002) which may confound results and limit interpretation. Continuous improvements in donor-to-lab workflow, expansion of subject inclusion, integration of datasets and application of new molecular techniques are aimed at revitalizing this important field of research (Lewis, 2002; Salvatore et al., 2019).

SUDs are known to be heritable and so it is expected that specific genes and gene variants are more likely to be carried by affected individuals (Goldman et al., 2005). For insights into the genetic risk factors underlying SUDs, genomic DNA can be easily collected from routine sampling like a blood draw or cheek swab and an individual's major genetic risk factors or even entire genome can be identified and/or sequenced. Proliferation of human genomic studies following the mapping of the human genome have produced several genetic libraries that serve as databases to be queried for the presence of gene variants and single nucleotide polymorphisms (SNP)s that may be associated with SUDs. Genome-wide association studies (GWASs) for addictive drugs have been carried out for several decades and hundreds of genes have been identified (Gelernter and Polimanti, 2021). An inherent challenge for the application of genomics to addiction is the polygenic nature of SUDs, meaning that multiple genes contribute to a psychiatric phenotype, which makes it difficult for specific genes to reach significance in statistically powered samples. Further complicating matters, SUDs have high rates of comorbidity with other psychiatric disorders like depression and anxiety which each have their own subsets of genetic risk factors, creating additional sources of variability. Gene by environment interactions are another important factor that cannot be fully accounted for in genetic studies. Epigenetic regulation of gene expression, for instance methylation of genetic material which can alter gene expression, is influenced by environmental factors, inherited from parents, associated with addictive behaviors, and can modify neural circuits (Nestler and Lüscher, 2019). Recent studies that include epigenetic modifications and characterization have provided new insights into environmental interactions with genetic risk factors of SUDs (Egervari et al., 2019).

Neuroimaging techniques in clinical studies

Non-invasive imaging technologies likely have the most potential for advancing clinical research and treatment of SUDs. In an ideal scenario for SUDs, brain imaging would be able to diagnose and measure responses to treatment non-invasively, akin to how X-rays are used to observe the presence and healing of broken bones. Unfortunately, the drug-exposed brain is defined by subtle changes in neural processes and protein expression rather than definitive damage to structures the size of bones. Computerized Tomography (CT), which integrates multiple X-ray scans, can typically only discern blood vessels in the brain (500-μm diameter) with the help of contrast agents that cannot be used to image neurons and their processes (Inoue et al., 2018). For more detailed structural brain imaging, the superior technology is magnetic resonance imaging (MRI) which uses a large magnetic coil to create oscillating magnetic fields directed into sections of tissue. When the magnetic field is present, hydrogen atoms, which have a single proton nucleus, cease their natural rotation, and become aligned to the magnetic field. Radio waves are then beamed at these tacit protons at frequencies that cause them to resonate and when those magnetic pulses are stopped, they generate their own radio frequencies that are captured in a radiofrequency receiver along the coil. Choreographed programs using different magnetic pulse rhythms generate signals in a structure-specific manner that can be used to reconstruct a 3D image of soft tissue. The structural resolution of these images is typically measured in voxels which is a calculation from the field of view size, segmentation, and pixel resolution. Voxel size is inversely proportional to the strength of the magnetic field coil which is measured in Teslas (T). Clinical MRI coils can range from 0.1 to 3 T with voxel sizes of $\sim 3\ mm^3$, while research MRIs use higher power magnetic coils that can reach ~ 7 to 11.7 T and produce higher resolution images with voxel sizes below 1 mm^3. High-resolution structural MRI has been used to show that alcohol and cocaine dependence result in gray matter reductions in several cortical regions, most notably the insula, frontal cortex, and cingulate compared to controls (Mackey et al., 2019).

To address questions related to connectivity, advances in MRI methodology allow for more targeted and refined imaging of white matter tracts. This is achieved by magnetic pulse programs that vary direction and allow for monitoring diffusion of water molecules into the thin spaces of axons. The directionality of the water diffusion or fractional anisotropy (FA) can be leveraged to identify bundles of axons called fibers. This technique is known as Diffusion Tensor Imaging (DTI) and the mapping of these fiber bundles is called tractography. Using high magnetic fields, DTI has given researchers the ability to observe fiber bundles in individual brains and can be used to generate a detailed whole-brain white matter tract map. Whole-brain connectivity is extremely valuable as it can assess the extent to which different brain regions communicate, as the density of an axon fiber correlates with the number and speed of inputs. SUDs and other psychiatric disorders likely alter inter-regional communication and connectivity, which can be measured using DTI. While this method is still relatively early in its application to addictive disorders, results from multiple DTI studies have revealed that alcohol, opiate, and cocaine users show reductions in FA, particularly in the genu of the corpus callosum (Ottino-Gonzalez et al., 2022; Beard et al., 2019). Like findings from structural MRI, single snapshots of connectivity are not able to indicate which changes are specifically due to drug use, as these studies often lack pre-drug baseline measurements. This issue is being addressed through ongoing, large multi-faceted longitudinal imaging studies supported by the European Commission, and also by the National Institute of Drug Abuse (NIDA) and the National Institute of Alcohol Abuse and Alcoholism (NIAAA): these studies take repeated measurements from a large cohort of subjects as they enter their teenage years, initiate or refrain from drug use, and continue or discontinue drug use during adulthood (Brown et al., 2015; Volkow et al., 2018; Mascarell Maričić et al., 2020), Using complementary MRI and DTI studies along with neuropsychological, genetic and psychiatric testing (among many other measures), these studies have the potential to elucidate neurobiological changes that occur during the development of an SUD, and also identify which social and genetic factors predispose and bias individuals toward this outcome.

In addition to structural changes, the ability to image and analyze neurotransmitter systems and their dysregulation is another critical layer to understanding addiction. A variation of MRI termed Magnetic Resonance Spectroscopy (MRS) can be used to measure abundant metabolites in the brain noninvasively. These include the ability to measure glutamate and GABA, the primary excitatory and inhibitory neurotransmitters of the brain. While these neurotransmitter levels are challenging to measure and not all brain regions are accessible, MRS studies applied to addiction have generated meaningful datasets including ones that show that stimulant users have reductions in glutamate/glutamine in the frontal cortex compared to controls (Hellem et al., 2015). A more common and powerful technique that can measure neurotransmitter function is Positron Emission Tomography (PET). PET imaging uses radiolabeled biological agents or radiotracers in which a radionuclide, often carbon-11 or fluorine-18, is incorporated into a small molecule so that it can transiently emit measurable, but safe levels of gamma ray radioactivity for collection during brain imaging. In a typical PET experiment, a subject will be administered a vehicle followed by a radiotracer intravenously while being scanned in the PET scanner to produce an image of where that radiotracer binds. This image is overlayed on a structural scan of the subject, for instance a 3D CT or MRI image to localize the radiotracer signal to an individual's neuroanatomy. In addition to metabolic signals, radiotracers are often radiolabeled ligands that target specific neurotransmitter receptors. For example, radiolabeled raclopride ([11C]-raclopride) which is a specific antagonist to dopamine receptor 2-like receptors (D2Rs) can indicate dopamine receptor expression and activity. Drugs themselves can be radiolabeled to demonstrate where drugs act in the brain (Fowler et al., 2001). Raclopride studies have had arguably the most impactful and replicable findings in human addiction research. They have consistently shown that humans that misuse drugs have reduced rates of raclopride binding, interpreted as less D2R availability, in the ventral striatum, an area of the brain implicated in reward (Volkow et al., 1990, 2009). There is a vast number of receptor-specific pharmacological compounds and other biological targets like neuroinflammatory markers that have the potential to become radiotracers, which contributes to the immense potential of PET imaging as a diagnostic tool for different aspects of addiction, including personalized treatment response. Unfortunately, radiotracer development is a long and arduous process that requires extensive pharmaceutical validation and safety testing. Ultimately, the cost-prohibitive nature of running sufficiently powered PET experiments limits it potential impact in research and clinical practice despite its successful track record.

The imaging techniques described above are primarily used for generating temporally distinct snapshots of brain states and do not directly evaluate how the brain is functioning during behavior. Linking an individual's brain activity with external stimuli or behaviors is a critical next step in understanding the brain processes underlying addictive behavior. In another variation of MRI called functional MRI (fMRI), the strategy is to detect dynamic states of blood oxygenation or hemodynamic response as indirect measures of neuronal activity. This can be accomplished because sustained neural activity requires glucose metabolism which quickly increases levels of deoxygenated hemoglobin. This triggers vasodilation of adjacent blood vessels to bring in more oxygenated hemoglobin. Since deoxygenated hemoglobin is more responsive to magnetic pulses and because these differences can be rapidly detected with MRI, a temporally relevant signal called the blood oxygen level dependent (BOLD) signal can be extracted that indicates areas of increased brain activity. Importantly, in fMRI studies, computer screens and response devices can be placed within the scanner, and visual stimuli or neuropsychological testing batteries can be administered while imaging brain activity. During active and resting states, correlated brain activity can be used to understand what regions are co-active and probablistically connected (Wilcox et al., 2019). In addiction research, fMRI studies have frequently reported differences in the BOLD signal elicited by substance-related visual cues or cue reactivity in the striatum and cortex of humans that misuse drugs relative to controls (Tapert et al., 2003; Goldstein et al., 2007). Important limitations of fMRI imaging are that observing increased blood flow within a brain region does not directly measure the activity of specific cells and circuits, and that transformation of the imaging signal can produce false positives. To reconcile criticisms of fMRI, standardized analyses, data sharing and larger group sizes are increasingly required for publication of findings.

Additional functional imaging approaches that can measure brain activity during behavior include functional PET imaging and electroencephalography. In functional PET imaging studies, radiotracer displacement can be measured during a behavioral task. For instance, dopamine activity can be assessed using raclopride displacement, a proxy of dopamine release, and following presentation of visual drug cues, differences in dopamine release can be observed using PET (Parvaz et al., 2011). Electroencephalography (EEG) directly measures brain electrical activity by situating passive electrodes on the scalp of a subject to measure voltage differences. This is made possible due to small but reliable changes in neuronal activity transmitted through the dura, cranium, and skin that can be amplified, recorded, and localized to specific brain areas. EEG can detect consistent changes in the magnitude of voltage differences during presentation of external stimuli or during active psychological testing called event related potentials (ERPs). Additionally, waves of neural activity, called oscillations, can be computationally isolated by their frequency, which is useful because different frequency bands reflect different arousal and attentive states. Circuit level inquiries in these type of recordings are made possible by the fact that separate brain regions with coherent frequencies allows for inference of circuit engagement, and EEG signatures can be computationally linked to specific sources in the brain (Cohen, 2014).

Ultimately, the most convincing approach in human-based research that avoids forlorn conclusions is to collect sound data on as many levels of inquiry as possible. Cross-validation of findings through combinations of analyses of postmortem cytoarchitecture, structural and functional imaging, and genetic influence on substance use symptomology can solidify a foundation for future studies. Equally important to the characterization of neural systems in addiction is the assessment of effective treatments and what systems they act upon (Venniro et al., 2020). Of course, there are many gaps that human addiction research simply cannot bridge: for example, monitoring of neural activity at mesoscale resolution, establishing causality of specific neural circuits, or manipulating gene expression, all of which limit hypothesis-driven experiments at the circuit, cellular and molecular level. Fortunately, preclinical research in nonhuman primates and other laboratory animals are poised to complement and confirm our growing understanding of SUDs.

Preclinical research methods to identify circuits and their adaptations to addictive drugs

Our inability to resolve specific neural circuits and how they are affected by addictive drugs is an inherent obstacle in human research that can be better addressed using animal models. The complexity of any mammalian brain remains a significant challenge to overcome and can seem incomprehensible when considering the number of neurons multiplied by the number of synaptic connections within even a subregion of a mouse brain (Cizeron et al., 2020). Fortunately, neuroscientists are aided by an ever-increasing repertoire of instruments including diverse chemical and genetic tools for unraveling individual circuits into neuroanatomical units and testing their biological function. Specific neuroadaptations in response to drug exposure can be measured using controlled drug exposures and *ex vivo* measurements of gene expression, neuronal activity, and neurotransmission. This level of granularity can help resolve circuit-specific neuroadaptations to addictive drugs that are candidate mechanisms underlying SUDs.

Neural tracing techniques

The identification of neural circuits can be achieved through selective tracing techniques where individual neurons are labeled and their connectivity is resolved. Practically speaking, this is achieved by infusing a bolus of tracer through a cannula into a target brain region under stereotaxic surgical conditions and subsequent imaging of filled neurons once the label has been absorbed (Fig. 1.2A). If the label is taken up by the soma or dendrites at the site of injection and continues to label the efferent axons, this is known as an anterograde tracer. Conversely, retrograde tracers are taken up by axons or their terminals and travel back to label the soma and dendrites of a neuron. Some tracers traverse synapses and label neurons that form synaptic connections with the initially labeled neuron in either a monosynaptic (labels neurons one synapse away) or polysynaptic (labels neurons more than one synapse away) fashion (Fig. 1.2B). Successful visualization of a filled neuron's location and morphology, including the distribution of its dendrites, soma, and axons, can inform connectivity, signal directionality and the extent to which it processes specific signals. Our current understanding of the major roles of brain regions help scientists to infer the type of information being carried in specific circuits, yet when used in combination with putative markers of cell identity and with functional assays, circuit function can provide insights into the mode of neurotransmission and timing of neural circuit engagement (Lanciego and Wouterlood, 2020).

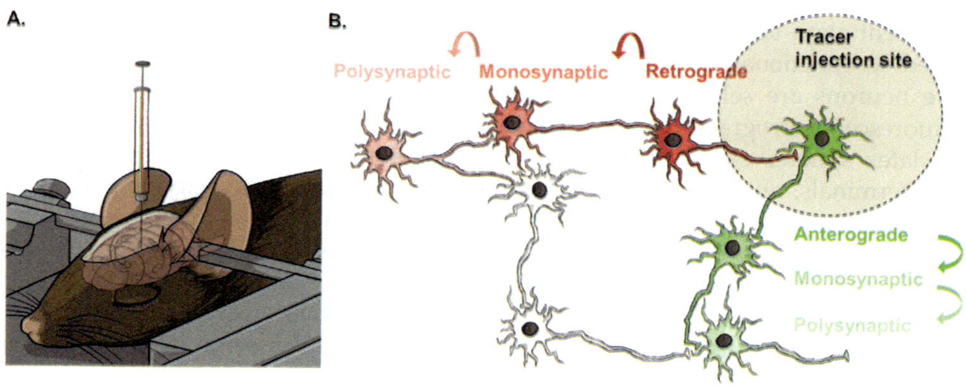

FIGURE 1.2 **Identifying neural circuits with tracers.** (A) Under stereotaxic surgical conditions including anesthesia and ear bars to stabilize the head, neurotracers can be infused into a desired brain region of a mouse through using a microsyringe or other small diameter infusion system. In this example, hypothetical anterograde and retrograde tracers are delivered into the mediodorsal thalamus. (B) At the tracer injection site, an anterograde tracer is taken up by the cell bodies and travels to the axon terminals. Retrograde tracers selectively enter the axon terminals and are transported to the cell body and dendrites. Tracers are available that are able to transverse synapses and be endocytosed into neurons that share synapses with the starter neuron are referred to as monosynaptic and more than one synapse away as polysynaptic. *Illustrated by Faith Maxwell, M.S.*

Conventional tracers

Conventional tracers have unique properties that allow them to be selectively taken up and dispersed within neurons and then visualized. Several organic and inorganic compounds have these tracer properties, with the most utilized tracers being the easiest to implement and to improve upon (Lanciego and Wouterlood, 2011). A good example is the use of horseradish peroxidase (HRP) which is an enzyme that can be readily extracted from the horseradish plant and reacted with hydrogen peroxide and chemical agents to produce a chromogen, usually a dark colored product. In addition to numerous biochemistry assays across academic, industrial and commercial fields, it was discovered that HRP can be taken up by cells through endocytosis of neurons, which are typically the only cells that would be connected between distant brain regions (Kristensson and Olsson, 1971). HRP can be used for retrograde labeling because the clathrin-coated endosomes that envelop the injected HRP are trafficked back to the soma on the saddle of retrograde axonal transport proteins. A major drawback of HRP is that endocytosis is rather inefficient for filling a neuron, relying on a weak signal to visualize. To improve the uptake of the HRP into neurons it can be conjugated to other molecules including wheat germ agluttin (WGA) or the nontoxic subunit of the bacterial cholera toxin referred to as cholera toxin B (CtB). These modifications allow HRP to be more selectively and efficiently internalized into neurons for neuroanatomical tracing (Gerfen and Sawchenko, 1984; Stoeckel et al., 1977; Trojanowski et al., 1981). Improvements in HRP uptake have resulted in a higher signal-to-noise ratio, thereby allowing for more accurate labeling and identification of afferent projection neurons. Use of HRP flourished during original brain-mapping experiments and has been instrumental in demonstrating the connective organization of many brain regions and neurotransmitter systems. Yet, another drawback of HRP is that it can only be processed and visualized in fixed tissue, limiting its use to postmortem histological studies. To further improve retrograde tracing, HRP can be swapped with fluorescent dyes referred to as fluorophores that can also be directly conjugated to CtB, preserving efficient axon targeting and uptake. As a result, they can be visualized in live tissue and used in functional assays like slice electrophysiology experiments, in which tracer-positive neurons are selectively targeted for neural activity recordings. Other commonly used fluorescent retrograde dyes include hydroxystilbamadine or "Fluorogold™" and fluorescent latex spheres called "Retrobeads™" each of which have shown robust selectivity for axon terminals, retrograde transport, stable fluorescence, low toxicity, live tissue compatibility and have made major contributions to our understanding of brain connectivity (Katz and Iarovici, 1990). The history of HRP including its replacement by other methods is highlighted because its story arc is typical of how research tools are discovered and optimized, then re-thought to meet the demands of researchers and their emerging questions.

The application of fluorescence dyes and fluorescence microscopy were instrumental in adding dimensionality to biological signals like tracers. A major advantage of fluorophore-based tracers is that they can absorb light in a confined range of wavelengths and emit light, or fluoresce, in a separate longer wavelength range permitting optical separation of fluorescent probes. There are a variety of chemical and genetically encoded fluorophores in routine lab use that have different excitation and emission spectral windows which can be leveraged using fluorescence microscopy where fluorescent signals are filtered by their known wavelengths and imaged. Fluorescent tracers can be combined with other fluorescent cellular markers in the same tissue and queried for cellular co-labeling. For instance, a red fluorescent tracer can be combined with a green fluorescent stain or histochemical tags that identify the major neurotransmitters that are released by the tracer labeled neuron. Another example is the use of multiple tracers with different fluorescent signals that can be visualized separately or together. Injecting green and red fluorescent retrograde tracers in separate brain regions can inform the regional distribution of efferent neurons. Cell bodies from neurons that terminate in separate tracer-injected brain regions will occasionally appear as co-labeled, indicating that there are multiple axon targets emanating from a single neuron. This phenomenon is referred to as axon collaterals, an underappreciated factor of neuronal connectivity.

Anterograde tracer compounds have also been developed and improved along similar lines. One of the most widely used is dextran amine, which is a polysaccharide that enters neurons through disrupted cell membranes at an injection site and can fill the cytoplasm in a primarily anterograde fashion. Often these dextran amines are either tagged with a fluorescent dyes like rhodamine or are attached to biotin. Biotinylated dextran amine (BDA) is processed with streptavidin, a protein which rapidly and reliably forms high affinity complexes with biotin and can be conjugated to a fluorophore or chromophore. An advantage of using the biotin-streptavidin complex is that there are multiple biotins per dextran amine which amplifies the signal compared to background and can be processed in parallel with immunohistochemistry. Since anterograde tracers are often used to trace axons that are notably smaller than the cell soma (~1%), a high signal-to-noize ratio is preferred when resolving efferent regional inputs. Another commonly used anterograde tracer is phaseus vulgaris lecoagluttinin (PHA-L), a lectin product derived from the red kidney bean. PHA-L extensively fills neurons, can be processed with additional cell markers and used to resolve small morphological features like axon terminals and dendritic spines. In addition, while they are not solely anterograde tracers, carbocyanine dyes including DiI (red) and DiO (green) have been frequently used in neuroanatomical studies including addiction research. These fluorescent dyes are lipophilic, meaning they can enter and travel along phospholipid bilayer of the membrane in the anterograde and retrograde direction and are excellent for resolving the morphological features of neurons. A unique application using DiO is to use them for ballistic labeling, referred to as DIOlistic labeling (Gan et al., 2000). This technique uses a high-pressure gene gun to scatter-shoot tungsten particles coated with DIO into neurons located in slices of brain tissue. Sparse labeling, exploited in the Golgi-cox method, is highly preferred in imaging applications as it allows for detailed morphological reconstruction of neuronal processes including dendritic spines without optical interference from a neighboring neuron. Addiction studies using DIOlistic labeling have been able to demonstrate that exposure to drugs impacts the formation and maintenance of spines, for instance following cocaine or alcohol exposure (Dobi et al., 2011; Kroener et al., 2012).

Characterization of circuits through cell type identification

Many of the chemical neuroanatomical tracers described above benefit from being able to be co-labeled with immunohistochemical markers that can provide important information regarding neuronal identity and function. A bevy of antibodies have been generated against protein markers of neuronal cell types including the neurotransmitters and neuropeptides they release. For instance, there are antibodies to vesicular glutamate transporters (VGLUTs) that exclusively label excitatory neurons and antibodies to vesicular GABA transporter (VGAT) that label inhibitory neurons. Additional neurotransmitter system markers include acetylcholinesterase (ACH), the enzyme used in the synthesis of acetylcholine and tyrosine hydroxylase (TH), the latter of which is a limiting enzymatic step for dopamine and norepinephrine synthesis and is often used to identify dopaminergic neurons. The dopamine transporter (DAT) can also be used label dopamine-releasing neurons. Co-labeling of tracer labeled neurons with neurotransmitter markers has been instrumental in establishing boundaries of the cholinergic, serotonergic and dopaminergic systems of the brain and have provided the foundation upon which many addiction studies are built (Björklund and Dunnett, 2007). Often, other proteins can be labeled that are indicative of a particular neuronal subclass which may not always have a clear and relevant functional role. For example, there are subcategories of interneurons including fast spiking basket cells that can be labeled with antibodies toward the calcium buffer protein, parvalbumin. Parvalbumin-containing neurons (PV+) have a specific type of neural firing pattern and in the cortex, target their inhibitory synapses to specific locations on the neuron, primarily the soma, and represent a unique neuronal subclass. Other major subclasses of inhibitory neurons with their own morphologic and electrical features can be identified through the expression of somatostatin (SST) or serotonin receptor 3A (5HT3A) (Rudy et al., 2011). Identifying and categorizing neurons that share features and properties allows circuits to be deconstructed both anatomically and functionally, increasing the ability to identify specific neuroadaptations related to drug exposures.

In addition to neuronal subtype, some protein targets can indicate levels of neuronal activity and are associated with brain states occurring directly prior to collection. This approach uses antibodies that recognize immediate early genes (IEGs), which are genes that don't require new protein synthesis for their expression and are rapidly transcribed and translated following changes in cellular activity. The most commonly targeted IEG is c-fos, a proto-oncogene that is highly responsive to sustained neuronal depolarization or synaptic excitation (Benito and Barco, 2015). When neurons are highly active, c-fos is transcribed within 5–10 min and measurably translated into its protein target Fos within 15 min. The expression of Fos is elevated for up to up to ~3 h in highly active neurons, creating a supra-threshold signal that can be detected with antibodies. When Fos expression is used in combination with tracers or other methods to identify cell types the activity of specific circuits can be discerned (Benito and Barco, 2015; Barnes et al., 2015).

The effects of acute and chronic administration of opiate, cocaine, alcohol, and nicotine on Fos expression in select brain regions have been extensively studied and used to identify drug relevant brain regions. Addictive behaviors like drug sensitization, craving and relapse-like drug seeking have also been able to associate specific brain regions with these behaviors (Cruz et al., 2015; Salery et al., 2021). When combined with neural tracers that have a separate fluorophore, highly active neural circuits can be labeled to demonstrate that the preceding stimulus or behavior led to the engagement of a particular circuit. In a hypothetical cocaine experiment, let's say the ventral striatum in a group of rats was injected with red fluorescent CtB tracer, then following recovery from surgery, rats were trained in a 15-minute cocaine-seeking paradigm. Next, after a cocaine-seeking session, brains were collected and processed for Fos immunohistochemistry with a fluorescent green secondary antibody. Higher numbers of Fos+/CtB+ co-labeled neurons in the ventral tegmental area (VTA) in cocaine-seeking rats compared to co-labeled neurons outside the VTA and in cocaine-naïve rats would indicate that VTA neurons that project to the ventral striatum are highly active during cocaine-seeking. Cell bodies in the ventral striatum may also demonstrate increased Fos expression as a co-activated downstream brain region. New studies using brain clearing methods and light sheet microscopy for whole-brain imaging are able identify comprehensive c-fos-activated networks and enable researchers to identify and map functional circuits related to specific addiction-related behaviors (Simpson et al., 2021).

Immunohistochemistry methods are accessible and widely used in neuroscience labs, but there are some noteworthy drawbacks that limit its many applications. Antibodies are widely available from commercial vendors for most protein targets common in neuroscience research. Quite often, the quality and specificity of the antibody can vary considerably, and extensive validation of new antibodies should be performed by the researcher prior to their use to obtain accurate results. The methods described here have been primarily related to counting cell numbers and co-labeling, but often immunohistochemistry can be applied to measure semi-quantitative differences in protein expression in regions and circuits. A major caveat of this method is that the quality of tissue fixation can also significantly affect antibody binding, creating another source of variability across animals that may lead to false positive or negative results (Fritschy, 2008). The best way to address this variability is through careful fixation procedures and controls, unbiased stereology in quantification, replication of results, and confirmation with other molecular techniques.

In situ hybridization is another common technique for identification of cell types that does not depend on the quality of an antibody. In this method, synthesized RNA probes are designed to bind to specific RNA sequences. Experimental tissue incubated with these probes in the presence of heat causes a hybridization of the probe to its RNA target. The probes are then amplified and bound to either a chromogen or a fluorophore for detection of the gene target in tissue and is used to demonstrate the spatial distribution of gene transcripts across the brain. Fluorescent *in situ* hybridization (FISH) has become more widely available which allows for co-labeling with multiple RNA targets and tracers that can tolerate FISH processing. The use of RNA probes provides a more reliable method for the identification of specific neuronal types including VGLUT1, VGLUT2, VGAT, TH, PV, SST, 5HT3A and immediate early genes like c-fos. *In situ* hybridization can additionally be used for measuring differential gene transcription between experimental groups, and probes can even be developed to bind to splice variants of a gene due to the high specificity of the probes. Some caveats with this method include that detection of transcript may not indicate expression of functional protein, the method does not demonstrate location of translated proteins, and quantification of newer ISH techniques (e.g., RNAscope) is in its early stages and not yet standardized across the field. Experiments directed at assessing levels of transcript need to also be appropriately performed with controls for tissue quality, background fluorescent signals as well as systematic cell counting procedures.

Genetic approaches to identifying circuits

Techniques used to modify genes have been widely adopted across biological disciplines and are highly prevalent in research geared at understanding the neurocircuitry of addiction.

The ability to read and reproduce sequences of all genes that are expressed in the brain provides the bill of materials for its construction. Perhaps more importantly, it allows for genetic material to be modified experimentally by the researcher to selectively target specific neural circuits and probe their function. The application of these strategies essentially hands over the keys to the car for driving biological systems and demonstrating their causality in physiological and behavioral assays related to addiction.

Genetic targeting approaches

Homologous recombination is the transfer of genetic material across strands of nucleic acids that have similar sequences and is the same process that occurs when parental DNA is exchanged across chromosomes. Gene modification strategies using homologous gene transfer are designed to align and to either remove a wild type gene or switch it out with a synthesized gene (Fig. 1.3A). In the lab, this typically starts with cloning a gene of interest within flanking DNA sequences that are known to exist alongside a native or wild type gene. When the new DNA plasmid is introduced into the nucleus of cell, it can align with the wild type gene along the matching, flanking sequences and permit homologous recombination to produce a cell with a new genetic insert, or transgene. To create a genetically modified mouse using homologous recombination, stem cells are collected from a blastocyst of pregnant mouse called a dam. The plasmid DNA is then introduced into the stem cells *in vitro* which are then selected for and transferred into a blastocyst for reinsertion into the dam. With some luck, this process can yield offspring with the new genetic code in their gametes leading to germline transmission of the mutation to their offspring and the establishment of a new genetic mouse line which are often made available for the research community. These methods are used to generate mouse lines with either a genetic knockout (KO) in which the target gene is fully or partially removed to make it functionally obsolete or a genetic knock-in (KI) where the wild type gene is replaced with a transgene generated synthetically or from another organism's DNA. Mice have been more accessible for this type of technique because their stem cells are more easily maintained prior to implantation, however new gene editing techniques including the CRISPR-Cas9 system have made rats and some nonhuman primates more accessible for whole organism genetic modification. More detailed descriptions of the wide array of related genetic techniques used in neuroscience labs are available (Navabpour et al., 2020; Heidenreich and Zhang, 2016).

A large proportion of transgenic animal colonies maintained and used in addiction neuroscience labs are reporter mice. They have been quite valuable for identifying specific cell types via the insertion of gene that encodes a protein that can be easily visualized behind a chosen promoter. A promoter is the DNA sequence that recruits proteins to transcribe a downstream gene. Reporter proteins are commonly ones that have native bioluminescent or fluorescent properties previously observed in other organisms in which the encoding gene was sequenced and optimized for experimental applications. They include proteins like luciferase taken from fireflies or green fluorescent protein (GFP) developed from jellyfish. GFP was further modified into many derivative fluorescent reporters using protein engineering approaches that cause targeted or random mutations and then subsequent screening for shifts in excitation and emission spectrums as well as improvements in fluorescence brightness and

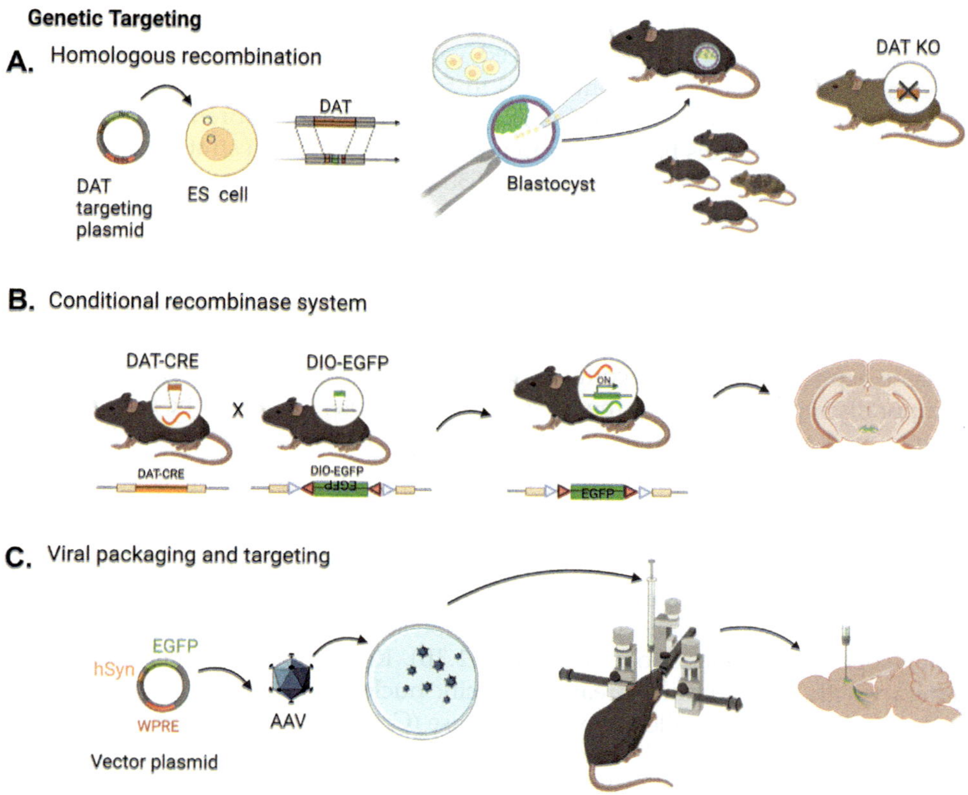

FIGURE 1.3 **Genetic modification strategies.** (A) Genetic knockout mice are traditionally generated using homologous recombination strategies. A plasmid containing a transgene is flanked by nucleotide sequences that complement the sequences surrounding a target gene. In this example, the dopamine transporter gene Slc6a3, referred to as DAT is targeted for genetic deletion. Instead of the DAT gene, the plasmid contains a neomycin resistant gene and probe sequence for confirmation of expression. Embryonic stem cells are collected from a pregnant mouse and transfected with the plasmid. The plasmid flanking sequences align with the DAT gene and it is replaced with the transgene. Surviving ES cells treated with neomycin in culture indicate successful recombination. These cells are injected into a blastocyst of a pregnant dam of a different coat, producing a chimeric mouse that can be selected for breeding to generate a mouse with a heterozygous genetic KO of the DAT gene. Further breeding strategies for mice homozygous for the KO allow for an assessment of that gene's function. (B) Conditional transgenic approaches utilize expression of the endonuclease Cre recombinase to excise DNA at lox sites, known as the Cre/lox conditional system. In this example, Cre recombinase is downstream of the DAT promoter and should only be expressed in neurons that express the DAT gene, which would be nearly all dopaminergic neurons. EGFP is inverted so that it doesn't make a function protein, but is flanked by double lox sites, loxp and lox2722, so that in the presence of Cre the gene is flipped over and expressed in DAT cells. When a DAT-Cre mouse is crossed with a DIO-EGFP mouse the offspring expressed EGFP in dopaminergic neurons. (C) Illustration of the generation and use of viral vectors like the AAV9 serotype. Initially a plasmid is made from the AAV backbone that contains a transgene of interest like EGFP behind a promoter like hSyn which is only expressed in neurons. Once packaged in an AAV9 capsid, the virus can be grown *in vitro* with the help of HEK cells and helper viruses. When the viral titer is sufficiently concentrated, the virus can be collected and used *in vivo*. For instance, in the right panel, AAV9 containing hSyn-EGFP is injected into the frontal cortex and terminals from transduced neurons can be seen in downstream regions. *Created with Biorender.*

stability. Common fluorescent proteins (FPs) generated from jellyfish include enhanced blue FP (EBFP), enhanced GFP (EGFP), enhanced yellow FP (EYFP) and their offshoots which cover emission spectrum peaks from ~440 to 530 nm. Other organisms like coral and sea anemones express fluorescence proteins in longer wavelengths (orange to red and far red respectively). These proteins have undergone similar optimization strategies to produce common red FPs like mCherry and TdTomato (~550 to 630 nm) and far-red FPs like mRuby and mKate (~630 to 680 nm). Currently, there exists a nearly full spectrum of fluorescent proteins that can be inserted for selective expression and multiplexed with other fluorescent proteins for neuroscience applications (Lambert, 2019).

One of the challenges of deleting or replacing genes within a whole animal is that the modification exists across the lifespan of the animal in all cells that express the promoter. Often, gene expression can have complex roles in an organism that are dynamic, multiorgan and temporally regulated during the lifespan. For example, there may be a protein that exists in the brain and appears to influence tolerance to opiates. This same protein may also be an important regulator in the development of the heart. A genetic knockout mouse that constitutively and permanently removes this gene would likely result in heart malformation and embryonic lethality well before any studies of its role in opiates can be understood in a mature mouse when the behavior occurs. Even when animals survive to adulthood, gene deletion from embryonic stages can lead to compensatory effects during development. To meet these challenges, *conditional* gene modification strategies using restriction endonucleases were developed (Tian and Zhou, 2021) (Fig. 1.3B). Restriction endonucleases are enzymes that interact with DNA to cause breaks at specific nucleic acid sequences. A restriction endonuclease found in bacteria called Cre recombinase (Cre) has been the most prominently used in this strategy as it is well understood, efficient and is not expressed in mammalian species. It recognizes a 34 base pair nucleotide sequence referred to as a loxp site. When loxp sites are cloned around a gene of interest, that gene becomes a floxed allele which can be selectively removed in the presence of Cre. When a mouse with a floxed allele is crossed with a mouse with Cre downstream a promoter region, the floxed allele is removed in cells that express that specific promoter. This strategy is referred to as a conditional genetic system, meaning that the gene is not affected and transcribed normally until Cre is introduced and expressed. In the previous example, inserting Cre behind a promoter that is only expressed in neurons localizes the gene deletion to the central nervous system, thereby avoiding the lethal effects of constitutive gene deletion on heart development. As a result, its role in opioid tolerance can be more reasonably studied.

Now, let us imagine that the gene is also important for neuronal differentiation during early development and without it, certain neuronal populations are lost. In this case, there is a need to restrict neuronal gene deletion in a temporally selective manner following early stages of brain development and neuronal differentiation. *Inducible* gene expression systems have been created, in which the activity of Cre or other factors that influence gene expression can be triggered using an exogenous factor like a ligand or even fluorescent light. A prominent example is the CreERT2 system, where Cre is fused to the ligand binding domain of the estrogen receptor (ER). The binding domain of ER sequesters Cre outside of the nucleus and away from its DNA targets. When tamoxifen is administered, typically through a systemic injection, it's metabolite 4-hydroxytamoxifen (4-OHT) binds to the ER domain causing a translocation of the CreERT2 complex to the nucleus where Cre can then bind to loxp sites and excise the floxed allele. Inducible and conditional systems allow for selective and temporal gene modification that can target specific neuronal subtypes. In addition to conditional and inducible systems, other approaches have been applied to tease apart circuits using additional recombinases. Other Cre strategies include floxing a stop sequence upstream or inverting the transgene to prevent the expression of the transgene in the absence of Cre, so that when Cre is introduced, the gene is "turned on." More complex strategies include recombinases/restriction site pairs of FLP/FRT and Dre/rox, and vCre/Vloxp which can be multiplexed for targeting multiple genetic modification outcomes in different cell types within the same animal. This strategy requires insertion of multiple restriction sites that require more than one restriction enzyme to be expressed for genetic recombination, a strategy termed INTERSECT (Fenno et al., 2014). These tools are emerging as neuronal cell type databases are being expanded and higher selectivity of neuronal subpopulations through the presence of multiple promoters is required to target specific sets of neurons.

To limit expression of a reporter protein, recombinase, or other desired protein to a specific cell type or neural circuit, the choice of promoter region is a critical feature to consider. Some promoters that are nearly ubiquitously expressed in all cell types include cytomegalovirus (CMVs) developed from the herpes virus and the CAG promoter, a synthetic promoter that combines elements of the CMV and chicken *ß*-actin and can robustly express recombinases or reporters at high levels. Of course, a major advantage of gaining access to the organism's genome is the ability to target specific subclasses of neurons using promoters that restrict expression of the transgene. Other common promoters that limit expression to neurons include the human synapsin-1 (HSYN1) promoter (a pan-neuronal promoter) as well as those that lead to selective expression in broad classes of neurons like excitatory (e.g. VGLUT1-3, CAMK2A in cortex) or inhibitory neurons (VGAT, DLX). Other neurotransmitter systems can be selectively targeted, for instance, promoters specific for the dopaminergic system like tyrosine hydroxylase (TH) and the dopamine transporter protein (DAT, gene name SLC6A3) expressed in dopamine releasing neurons. On the receptor end, promoters for the dopamine receptor subclasses D1 (DRD1) and D2 (DRD2, but also ADORA) have been available to tease apart selective dopamine receptor subclasses in multiple brain regions (Gerfen and Surmeier, 2011). Other interneuron populations can be targeted using promoters for cholinergic neurons (ChAT) and other interneuron classes described previously like parvalbumin (PV), somatostatin (SST), and the serotonin 3A receptor (5HT3RA). The-wide availability of promoter lines that increasingly restrict expression of recombinases to facilitate the expression or removal of select proteins provides researchers with the flexibility to systematically or specifically probe the function of specific neuronal populations based on their experimental needs.

Genetically defined promoters are not limited to neurotransmitter type and anatomical location. Promoters for c-fos and other immediate early genes can be used to rapidly express a transgene selectively in active neurons. For instance, the DNA sequence for EGFP can be inserted downstream of the c-fos promoter in knockin mice and rats. As a result, highly active neurons will express EGFP for up to 6 h after a specific stimulus which can be visualized in fixed or live tissue preparations (Barth et al., 2004; Cifani et al., 2012). A collection of neurons that are highly active by a specific stimulus or behavior is known as a neuronal ensemble. Neuronal ensembles were originally described after being observed during *in vivo* electrophysiology recordings in which a subset of neurons firing together during a specific stimuli could be temporally segregated. The use of activity-dependent labeling approaches can effectively capture the full anatomical distribution of a neuronal ensemble circuit, albeit with less temporal specificity. IEGs like c-fos, Arc and synthetic activity-dependent promoters have been placed upstream from inducible systems to probe ensemble function. In one strategy, the enzyme ß-galactosidase is placed downstream from the c-fos promoter and when expressed it can convert the pro-drug Daun02 to daunorubicin which can inactivate the c-fos expressing neuronal ensembles. In another, more modular strategy recombinases like Cre-ERT2 and other inducible gene expression strategies that uses tetracycline (e.g Tet-tag) are placed downstream from immediate early gene promoters. In these systems, activated neuronal ensembles can be orthogonally captured for genetic targeting during a defined window of behavior (Guenthner et al., 2013; Reijmers et al., 2007). Neuronal ensembles captured during a memory recall, like from a context or cue that elicits a behavioral response, are called engrams, and are purported to be the physiological representation of memories. In addition to labeling, insertion of protein actuators discussed later in the chapter can be used to selectively, stimulate or inhibit neuronal ensembles during behavior giving the researcher the capability to transiently activate or erase engrams. Identification of drug-related engrams is an emerging area in addiction research poised to greatly contribute to how we understand the specific neurobiological processes underlying addiction and how drug-related cues are encoded to drive addictive behavior (Josselyn et al., 2015). While these studies are early in their application to addiction research, they have been used to capture drug-specific neuronal ensembles and manipulate drug-related memories (Pfarr et al., 2015; Cruz et al., 2014).

Conditional and inducible gene modification systems and related strategies have been highly impactful in elucidating the role of specific genes in biological functions, but they are not perfect and require validation and optimization. One of the potential caveats of these systems is that promoter expression is not always where we expect it will be and expression can vary across the same neuronal population. Our understanding of what regulates the location, timing and extent of promoter expression is often incomplete and as a result, genetic knockout or transgene expression may have unexpected consequences. Another common issue with transgenic lines is that in inducible and conditional systems, the expression of Cre under a chosen promoter can be turned on in gametes leading to unintended gene deletion or transgenic expression constitutively in the offspring, known as germline transmission. To avoid the problem, there are guidelines for appropriate breeding, genotyping, and validation for common neuroscience promoters (Luo et al., 2020). For inducible systems like CreERT2, when there is high expression of CreERT2, there is the potential for unregulated travel to the nucleus referred to as Cre leakiness and a loss of control of Cre activity which has been improved in subsequent versions (e.g. improved Cre-ERT2 (iCreERT2). In general, confirmation of genotype, gene expression patterns, and control over inducible systems should be carefully carried out using appropriate controls within any experiment where transgenic lines are used.

Viral vector approaches to dissecting neural circuits

Identification and characterization of select neural circuits have greatly benefited from recent advancements in virology that have complemented existing genetic modification strategies. Viruses exist as relatively simple infectious agents that are made up of a protein envelope called a capsid with external features that allow them to bind to particular cell types called host cells (Fig. 1.3C). Once bound, they can transfer their viral genetic material inside the host cell, a process called transduction. Viral genomes are either RNA- or DNA-based and carry sequences that encode the replication of new viruses with the help of the host cell. The ability to efficiently transfer recombinant genetic material into specific cells using viral approaches has been leveraged across research labs to create unique tools for neurobiological applications that allow their use for viral tracing, circuit-specific gene modification, and for expression of protein-based biosensors and effectors that monitor cellular activity and inhibit or activate specific neural circuits.

An increasing number of neurobiological tools are becoming viral due to their modularity and availability and therefore a familiarity of viral vector design is important to understanding and performing neurocircuitry research. Some major parameters of viral design in neuroscience applications include the (1) *genetic payload*, or the amount and type of genetic material that can be effectively inserted into viral genomes, (2) *viral tropism*, or what types of cells and cell compartments the virus transduces, (3) *toxicity*, or the impact a viral infection has on cell activity and viability, and (4) *expression profile*, meaning the rate and level of transgene expression following viral transduction (Nectow and Nestler, 2020). These properties naturally vary across viral species but can also be altered through genetic modification of the viral genome creating a diverse viral toolkit for different experimental questions. Importantly, genes within the native virus that render them as potential biosafety hazards can be removed including replication sequences or those that are toxic to host cells resulting in viral tools that are more practical for routine bench lab work under standard lab safety procedures.

Each viral class or species has advantages and disadvantages that make them useful for certain experiments. Commonly used viruses in neuroscience labs are adeno-associated viruses (AAVs), lentiviruses, canine adenovirus 2 (CAV2), Herpes-simplex viruses (HSVs), and rabies viruses (RVs). AAVs are the most widely used in neuroscience research due to their low biosafety level and ability to be used in diverse applications. Viral engineering has produced a variety of AAV seryotypes with different tropisms and expression levels including several anterograde AAVs (AAV1, AAV2, AAV5, AAV8, AAV9, AAVDJ), retrograde AAVs (rgAAVs), and AAVs that can be delivered to the central (AAV-PhP.eB) and peripheral nervous system (AAV-PHP.S) without the use of stereotaxic surgery, for instance through intraocular or intravenous injection. AAVs are DNA-based which allows their transgene to be accessed by recombinases for conditional gene expression. A drawback of AAVs is that they have a small packaging capacity (~4.3 kb) and thus large genes or multiple genes may not fit inside the vector. Lentiviruses are RNA-based, anterograde viruses that have a large packaging capacity (8–10 kb) for the insertion of large or multiple recombinant genes, but do need additional biosafety measures, have lower rates of transduction, and are not able to be targeted by common recombinase strategies. CAV2 is a DNA-based vector that preferentially transduces axon terminals and can be used for primarily for retrograde tracing or Cre expression. HSVs are available for anterograde or retrograde transport and express the viral package rapidly. They can be designed for either monosynaptic or polysynaptic transport and expression. RVs have been designed to label neurons that form monosynaptic connections with an infected cell enabling researchers to map inputs into a single neuron (Wickersham et al., 2007). To increase the specificity of viral targeting, dual-virus injections using conditional approaches can be applied. For instance, the Cre recombinase gene can be packaged in CAV2 and combined with an anterograde virus, like an AAV with a floxed protein. In a more specific example, injection of CAV2 into the ventral striatum will transduce Cre plasmid into neurons that project there, and injection of AAV-DIO-GFP into the VTA will result in expression EGFP in VTA neurons that specifically project to the ventral striatum. This approach allows for the singling out of region to region circuits. Viral strategies have been wildly successful and are a result of major efforts to optimize and invent new tools as well as widespread availability of those tools to many neuroscience labs via academic, commercial, and non-profit production pipelines. As a result, there now exists an expanding arsenal of viral techniques that can be used in neuroscience labs to study neural circuits.

Identifying neuroadaptations in neural circuits

Within the neuroscience toolkit, there are several techniques for measuring functional changes to select neural circuits. In the context of addiction research, identifying how circuits respond to acute drugs, as well as specific neuroadaptations caused by addictive drugs, provides evidence for the roles individual circuits play in the drug experience, and which circuits are likely important for addiction-related behaviors. In the past, whole brain regions hypothesized to mediate these effects were investigated and many drug-induced changes were identified across drug classes. The shifting focus toward targeting specific brain circuits and cells that has occurred alongside technological advances that allow for measurement of circuit function and circuit manipulation has refined our understanding of drug effects on the brain while overcoming, accounting for, and leveraging neuronal heterogeneity in specific brain regions.

Electrophysiology techniques

One of the most versatile tools for studying the effects of drugs on the brain is electrophysiology. This branch of physiology refers to the group of electrical recording techniques and strategies used to study the electrical properties of live tissue. Using different preparations and recording configurations, recordings of electrical events can be amplified and filtered to measure the activity of single ion channels, single neurons, or populations of neurons. Electrophysiological techniques are highly prevalent in addiction neuroscience labs because they can be applied to many questions regarding how addictive drugs affect the functional properties of neurons including how acute drug exposure affects neural activity, the effects of chronic drug exposure on neurotransmission, and how addictive drugs influence neural plasticity. A major advantage of electrophysiology over other methods is that electrical activity is the primary language of the neuron and can be directly measured at sampling rates that outpace neural activity and therefore, are observed in real time.

The membrane is a critical feature in cellular design and without it, biological communication as we know it would not be possible. A neuron's membrane is composed of a phospholipid bilayer that is hydrophobic, allowing it to separate the cytoplasm of neurons from the cerebrospinal fluid in the extracellular space. Charged atoms in solution known

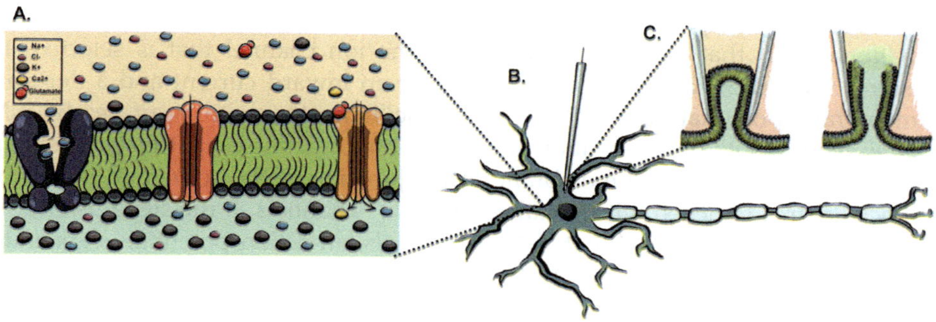

FIGURE 1.4 **Electrophysiology of a neuron.** (A) Illustration of a neuronal membrane with Na^+/K^+ pump (*navy blue*) that helps establish the ionic gradient that makes action potentials by exchanging Na^+ extracellularly and K^+ intracellularly to bring the membrane voltage to resting membrane potential. A voltage-gated Na^+ channel (*light pink*) is shown that opens following depolarization to the action potential threshold initiated by a voltage sensor within the channel. A calcium permeable AMPA receptor is also shown that when bound to glutamate (*red*) opens to allow in Na^+ and Ca^{2+} which contributes to a excitatory postsynaptic potential or EPSP. (B) Multipolar neuron that has been targeted with a micropipette for electrical recording. (C) Illustration of whole cell patch clamping technique where the tip of a glass micropipette has been placed on the neuronal membrane under negative pressure that pulls in the membrane within the micropipette and creates a tight seal. Quick suction into the pipette ruptures the membrane while maintaining the seal, creating electrical access to the intracellular environment. *Illustrated by Faith Maxwell, M.S.*

as ions like sodium (Na^+), potassium (K^+), calcium (Ca^{2+}), and chloride (Cl^-) exist in the intracellular and extracellular environment and their composition is regulated by proteins that function as ion pumps or channels embedded throughout the membrane (Fig. 1.4A). Ion pumps exchange cations and anions in order set up an ionic gradient, meaning some ions are shuttled from the cytoplasm to the extracellular space and vice versa shifting their intracellular and extracellular concentration; for example, the Na^+/K^+ pump which uses ATP (ATP) to exchange the shuttling of Na^+ outside the neuron and K^+ inside. The buildup of differentially charged ions on each side of the membrane creates a difference in voltage, called the membrane potential and sets the stage for an excitable membrane. Voltage gated ion channels (VGICs) are located strategically within the membrane where they can sense fluctuations in membrane potential through voltage sensors that exists within the ion channel. If triggered by a large enough change in membrane potential, most often a depolarization or increase in voltage, the voltage sensor will cause a conformational change to the channel and a gate located inside will open. The pore size of the channel, along with charged amino acids that line the pore, allow it to filter which ions pass through, primarily Na^+, Cl^-, K^+, or Ca^{2+}, which differ in charge and size. As ion channels open, and ions are permitted through, an electrical current is generated which can be sensed and transmitted passively along the membrane and actively when additional ion channels are triggered and opened in a process called propagation.

In a typical multipolar neuron, the propagation of an electrical signal often starts in synapses along the dendrites and soma of a postsynaptic neuron. At these synapses, neurotransmitter is released from presynaptic neurons and binds to ligand gated ion channels (LGICs) embedded within the postsynaptic neuronal membrane. Excitatory neurotransmission is primarily communicated through ionotropic glutamate receptors (iGluRs) that include *a*-amino-3-hydroxy-5-methyl-4-isoxazoleporprionic acid receptors (AMPARs) and N-methyl-D-Aspartate receptors (NMDARs). When bound to glutamate, AMPARs undergo a conformational shift that causes an opening of the ion channel that is selective for Na^+ and in some AMPARS, Na^+ and Ca^{2+}, generating an inward current and a depolarization of the membrane potential. AMPAR activation facilitates the opening of nearby NMDARs which often require both depolarization and ligand binding. The excitatory postysynaptic potential (EPSP) travels along the membrane to the junction of the soma and axon called the axon hillock an area enriched with voltage-gated Na^+ channels. If the signal is large enough to reach the threshold of voltage-gated Na^+ channels, an action potential is generated. The action potential waveform starts when the mass of Na^+ enters the neuron, followed by activation of voltage-gated K^+ channels which open and due to their ionic gradient, K^+ exits the neuron to bring the membrane back toward resting membrane potential. Na^+ channels next enter an inactivation state channels followed by K^+ channels and the membrane becomes repolarized. The action potential signal is further propagated down the axon with the help of segments insulated by myelin sheaths until it reaches the axon terminal. The axon terminal has a high density of voltage-gated Ca^{2+} channels and when triggered by the membrane depolarization, open to allow Ca^{2+} to enter the terminal where it binds to docking proteins to release vesicles filled with neurotransmitter. The vesicles fuse with the terminal membrane and neurotransmitter is released into the synaptic cleft to diffuse toward nearby receptors onto the synaptically coupled neuron. If the neurotransmitter is GABA (gamma-aminobutyric acid), it will oppose membrane depolarization by binding to ionotropic GABA receptors ($GABA_ARs$) leading to an outward current generated by Cl^- entering the postsynaptic neuron generating an inhibitory postsynaptic potential (IPSP). Importantly, these are the very basic aspects electrical communication in neurons which greatly simplifies the process. In all neurons, there are a myriad of additional LGICs, VGICs, intracellular signaling mechanisms, and other sources of extracellular electrical input that shape and modulate action potential waveforms and synaptic transmission. These polymorphic modes of neural activity vary across neurons and can serve as signatures to identify neuronal subtypes.

In addition to excitatory and inhibitory synaptic transmission, other neurotransmitter receptors called G-protein coupled receptors (GPCRs) indirectly modulate the membrane potential through activation of a group of intracellular signaling pathways that involve specific G-proteins, which require guanosine triphosphate (GTP). Glutamate GPCRs are referred to as metabotropic glutamate receptors (mGluRs) and GABAergic GPCRs are known as $GABA_B$ receptors. Both classes have slower effects on neuron excitability due to their indirect signaling mechanisms. Dopamine receptors are solely GPCRs and they affect neuronal excitability in opposing fashion. For instance, when dopamine is released, it binds to 2 classes of GPCRs: D1-like receptors (D1R, D5R) signal through $G_{\alpha s/olf}$ to increase membrane excitability via cyclic AMP and protein kinase A (PKA). D2-like receptors (D2R, D3R D4R) signal through $G_{\alpha i}$ to oppose membrane depolarization through inhibition of cAMP and opening of K^+ channels. Neurons with different expression of these dopamine receptor classes can have their own projection targets and as a result neurons expressing D1-like or D2-like receptors have differential responses to dopamine release and activity on the downstream regions where they project.

Electrophysiologists use a variety of different sample preparations and electrode configurations to measure neuronal activity. Some of the most common preparations include primary neurons that are cultured *in vitro*, *ex vivo* slices of brain tissue, and *in vivo* recordings where electrodes are implanted in the brain of whole, intact animals. In most *in vitro* and *ex vivo* preparations, neuronal viability is maintained during recordings by placing them in oxygenated artificial cerebrospinal fluid (aCSF) composed of glucose and salts that approximate the ion composition, pH, temperature, and osmolality of the extracellular brain environment. Altering the compositions of these factors can be used experimentally to affect neuronal function. For instance, increasing the normal concentration of extracellular Ca^{2+} can promote the release of neurotransmitters in the synapse and decreasing extracellular K^{+} can dampen neural activity. To block or stimulate receptor activity, pharmacological agents can be applied generally as a wash-on to the preparation or locally by being spritzed on a specific area of a neuron or groups of neurons. For *in vivo* recordings, the preparation involves the implanting of an electrode or array of electrodes into an animal brain (typically a rodent or nonhuman primate) during surgery and attaching the electrode interface to the skull. Wires are then connected to the interface and the signal is amplified and digitized to generate the recording (Fig. 1.5E and F). This allows the recordings to take place with the whole brain intact and during behavioral actions.

Electrophysiological measurements of neurons are obtained by giving the primary electrode(s) electrical access to either the extracellular or intracellular space relative to a ground electrode. In extracellular field recordings, electrodes are fabricated from low impedance simple wire or a designed array of contacts that can be placed within the extracellular space of a neuronal preparation, often cultured neurons, brain slices, or within the brain. Passive recordings of generalized neural activity called local field potentials (LFPs) are made of low voltage, primarily synaptic events from the electrode where the field of measurement includes the electrical currents generated from many neurons at the same time with the nearest neurons geometrically aligned having the greatest signal contribution (Buzsáki et al., 2012). Offline computational analyses of the recorded traces can decompose the cocktail of activity using a high pass filter to detect spike frequency and a low pass filter to isolate population level oscillations of the neural activity signal. Extracellular electrodes can also be designed to record from individual neurons by using high impedance microelectrodes that are placed close enough to a single neuron's membrane that it can detect primarily that neuron's activity. These recordings are called single unit recordings and can detect the presence of APs as well as pre and postsynaptic events when properly isolated. For other types of single neuron and single channel recordings, micropipettes are fabricated by melting glass borosilicate capillaries to form tapered, open tips. The wire electrode can be inserted into a glass micropipette and filled with a conductive ionic solution like aCSF. The insulation of the glass and small opening allows for electrical access and specific targeting of the electrode to a neuron. The smooth tip can be placed directly on a neuronal membrane and given slight negative pressure to create as seal and gently bring in the membrane into the pipette without rupturing it, a technique called cell-attached recording which is primarily used to measure firing frequency and postsynaptic potentials (Perkins, 2006). Pulling the attached micropipette away from the cell can collect a small patch of membrane called an inside-out patch permitting extracellular access to the ion channels within the membrane patch. Intracellular recordings can be performed by creating a micropipette with a very small opening called a sharp electrode that can pierce the neuronal membrane without lysing the cell. This technique allows for the membrane potential to be accurately measured between the sharp electrode and an extracellular

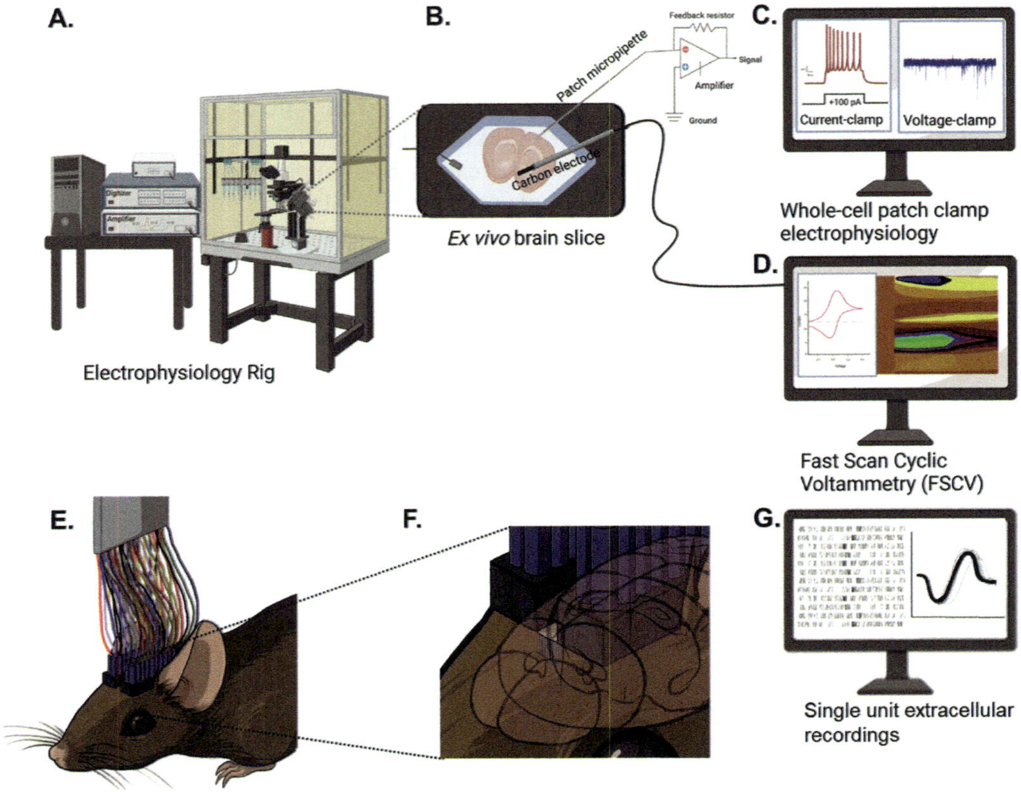

FIGURE 1.5 **Electrophysiology configurations.** (A) Slice electrophysiology rig that consists of Faraday cage on top of an air table. A microscope is placed on the table that is focused on a brain slice that is being continuously perfused with oxygenated artificial cerebrospinal fluid (aCSF). Inset shows bath holding an *ex vivo* brain coronal slice containing the striatum. For whole cell recordings a reference electrode is placed in the bath and micropipette is moved using a micromanipulator to the membrane of a neuron that is visualized using microscope under near infrared or fluorescent light conditions. The micropipette contains an electrode that connected to an amplifier and digitizer. (C) Computer screen demonstrating a recording of neuronal firing following a square pulse positive current injection through the electrode (*left*) or a recording of synaptic inward currents when neuron is held at −70 mV in the voltage clamp configuration (*right*). (D) Example of a fast scan cyclic voltammetry (FSCV) study where a carbon fiber electrode is also placed in the ventral striatum of the brain slice and recordings of dopamine are performed following rapid cycling of a voltage ramp that to cause oxidation and reduction of dopamine. The connected computer screen illustrates a graph, created from the voltammogram demonstrating the following the voltage ramp (left) and heat map showing a dopamine response following a stimulation that releases dopamine (*right*). (E) Illustration of a mouse with multielectrode headstage attached to wiring for *in vivo* single unit recordings where the mouse is tethered, but can move sufficiently for behvaioral experiments. (F) Zoomed in illustration showing placement of an array of tetrodes within the frontal cortex of a mouse. (G) Computer screen showing spike timing from individual single units and a overlayed image of the spike waveform that are time stamped to a behavioral event. *Fig. 5A-B Created with Biorender; Fig 5D-G Illustrated by Faith Maxwell, M.S.*

reference electrode without significantly affecting the composition of the cytoplasm. To perform whole-cell recordings, micropipettes can be pulled with larger openings and, similar to a cell-attached approach, negative pressure is used to attach to the neuron. Once the neuronal membrane forms a tight enough seal with the micropipette, indicated by measuring the resistance at the tip (>1 GΩ), known as a gigaseal, a short burst of stronger negative pressure created by the experimenter's mouth, or a syringe can rupture the membrane so that the intracellular space is continuous with the solution of the micropipette and internal electrode (Fig. 1.4C). Importantly, to maintain normal cell activity and health, the solution in the micropipette needs to include ionic concentrations found in the cytoplasm as well as ATP, GTP, and other factors to preserve the function of ion pumps, calcium buffering, GPCRs and changes in pH. Like the extracellular solutions, deliberately altering ion concentrations can be used probe cellular function. Furthermore, access to the isolated intracellular environment permits the testing of internal channel sites and signaling cascades through peptides and compounds that can be experimentally included in the intracellular solution. One caveat of whole cell recording is that the internal solution will never perfectly match the cytoplasmic contents and some important factors for neuronal activity will be functionally lost or overcompensated for following dialysation of the neuron with the internal solution. Perforated patch clamp strategies which create pores in the attached membrane using antibiotic compounds as opposed to fully rupturing can better preserve cytoplasmic contents while attaining whole cell electrical access, however the tradeoff is typically lower throughput. Collectively, electrophysiological techniques offer multiple levels of examination including measuring activity and function from large populations of brain cells, individual neurons, and even single ion channels.

Our understanding of how acute and chronic drug exposures impact neuronal function has been greatly aided by the development and proliferation of the whole cell patch clamp technique across neuroscience labs and its application to brain slice electrophysiology. In this preparation, brains are removed from live animals under anesthesia and slices are collected using a vibratome or other microtome that limits cellular damage and then incubated and recorded from in oxygenated aCSF. Neurons can be visualized for micropipette targeting under a light microscope typically using infrared light illumination and differential interference contrast optics (Fig. 1.5A and B). Fluorescently labeled neurons either from genetically defined neuron populations using transgenic reporter mice, rats or other methods to anatomically define neuronal populations like conventional or viral tracers can be identified within the live slice. Patch micropipettes are then advanced to the neuron, usually the soma for the whole cell recording, but also can be performed on dendrites with smaller tipped pipettes. Following break-in, recordings are collected by clamping the current to measure the voltage or clamping the voltage to measure current (Fig. 1.5C). Voltage-clamping refers to the clever method where the input voltage that is being measured from the electrode is opposed using a voltage following amplifier to "clamp" the membrane potential at a specific (Covey and Carter, 2015) voltage by passing and adjusting the appropriate amount of "counter" current. The current is then measured at the feedback resistor where opposing voltage changes are calculated using Ohm's law: voltage = current x resistance ($V = IR$). In current clamp configuration, the voltage is allowed to vary and is directly measured. Rather than responding to voltage changes, negative or positive current can be passed from the electrode to stimulate the neuron. The electrical signals recorded from the amplifier are analog and transformed for analyses with the use of a digitizer. For further reading, there are several excellent guides and books available the describe patch clamping in greater detail (Covey and Carter, 2015; Okada, 2012).

Whole cell patch-clamp measurements are performed in individual neurons with the purpose of measuring the intrinsic and extrinsic electrical properties of the neuron. The intrinsic properties are primarily measured in current clamp configuration and include passive membrane properties like *resting membrane potential (mV)*, but also measurements following subthreshold square pulse current injections like *input resistance (MΩ)*: the amount of current needed to change the voltage, *membrane capacitance*: the electrical output needed to charge the membrane, proportional to the neuron's size and *time constant (msec)*: the time needed for a cell to return to resting membrane potential following cessation of a current pulse. Active membrane properties are measured following larger sustained current injections that allow the membrane to reach its action potential threshold and include aspects of the action potential (AP) initiation and waveform. Active membrane properties commonly measured are *rheobase (pA)*: the minimal amount of current needed illicit an AP, the *AP-threshold (mV)*, *peak (mV)*, *half-width (msec)*, *frequency (Hz)* and *accommodation* ratio calculated from the ratio of the first inter spike interval (ms) to subsequent inter spike intervals (ms). While not an exhaustive list of intrinsic measurements, many of these can profile aspects of the neuron's excitability. In addiction neuroscience, repeated exposures to drugs have been responsible for changes in passive and active membrane properties, and often this is due to changes in ion channel function or expression which can confirmed by isolating and measuring specific ion channel currents in voltage clamp (Kourrich et al., 2015). For instance, holding or stepping the membrane potential to the activation range of VGICs and LGICs and/or applying pharmacological agents can directly measure the channel current and conductance. In addition, voltage clamp configuration is frequently used to measure extrinsic activity like spontaneous excitatory and inhibitory postsynaptic currents (sEPSCs and sIPSCs) which preserves the spontaneous firing of neurons in the brain slice. Quantal synaptic release of neurotransmitter and postsynaptic receptor effects can be better estimated when tetrodotoxin, a Na^+ channel blocker, is included in the aCSF to block all APs in the slice. The remaining synaptic activity is referred to as *miniature* excitatory and inhibitory postsynaptic currents (mEPSCs and mIPSCS) and can be used to further characterize alterations in synaptic activity. Measurements of intrinsic and extrinsic electrophysiological properties can be systematically walked along a desired neural circuit in both upstream and downstream directions using fluorescent neural tracers or reporter mice. While individual neurons can create rich datasets, a major limitation of the whole-cell patch clamp technique is that it is low throughput: preparation of viable slices takes considerable time and effort, neurons are typically patched one at a time often with low yield and researchers require years of training to become proficient.

Many concepts related to how addictive drugs cause long-term effects on behavior are attributed to alterations in synaptic connectivity. Alterations in the synaptic strength of neural circuits known as synaptic plasticity are a dynamic feature of the brain and are the neural basis of learning and memory. In the slice preparation, measurements of synaptic strength and synaptic plasticity can be performed by adding a stimulation electrode into the slice and using stimulation paradigms thought to mimic neural activity that recruit mechanisms of synaptic plasticity. Electrical stimulation can be applied through what are typically bipolar or concentric electrodes connected to a stimulation generator that are placed in areas that have high concentrations of afferents to the targeted neuronal population. Experimentally determined stimulation ranges are applied that can cause electrically evoked release of neurotransmitter to the postsynaptic neuron. These can be performed in single stimulus experiments to solely measure the evoked release of neurotransmitter or following stimulation trains that can lead to plastic changes in cellular response to stimulation. For excitatory transmission, synaptic strength can be measured by isolating and comparing the relative contribution of AMPA receptor current to NMDA receptor current ratio (Kauer and Malenka, 2007). In this experiment, the electrodes are positioned to stimulate release of glutamate onto a postsynaptic neuron being held near resting membrane potential and then at depolarized potentials that relieve the magnesium block to NMDAR activation. To further isolate the response, pharmacological agents like antagonists to $GABA_ARs$, NMDARs and AMPARs can be applied. A very influential finding using the AMPA/NMDA ratio has been that multiple addictive drugs and other highly rewarding substances can cause a sustained increase in the AMPA/NMDA ratio of dopamine neurons in the VTA and this can occur even after a single drug exposure (Stuber et al., 2010). Plastic changes in synaptic strength can be observed directly using stimulation protocols that enhance the magnitude of synaptic events, for instance measurements of synaptic plasticity termed long-term potentiation (LTP) (Bliss and Collingridge, 1993). In LTP experiments, afferents are stimulated at frequencies above 50 Hz which causes a lasting potentiation of EPSP magnitudes which can be observed either through extracellular or whole cell recordings. Alternatively, long-term depression (LTD) can be observed in a similar preparation, but with frequencies below 10 Hz. LTD protocols lead to lasting synaptic weakening or scaling down of post stimulation EPSP magnitudes. A stimulation protocol thought to be a more biologically relevant measure of synaptic plasticity is spike-timing dependent plasticity (STDP) where the order of stimulation of the presynaptic neuron related to the postsynaptic neuron determines the synaptic strengthening. For instance, if the presynaptic neuron is stimulated shortly before the postsynaptic neurons, the synaptic response is increased while the opposite order leads to decreased synaptic strength. A loss of plastic mechanisms following drug exposure might be interpreted as circuits that are unable to dynamically strengthen or weaken their communication and may represent potential mechanisms for maladaptive behaviors associated with addiction.

In addition to recording neural activity in an *ex vivo* brain slice, neurotransmitter release can be measured using an electrochemical technique called fast scan cyclic voltammetry (FSCV). By applying cyclical voltage ramps from a carbon-tipped electrode that is placed in the extracellular space of brain tissue, oxidation and reduction of readily oxidizable molecules like dopamine can be detected and measured in the resulting current waveform called a voltammogram. Rapidly cycling steep voltage ramps (>10 Hz at $100\ V\,s^{-1}$) samples concentrations of neurotransmitter (e.g., dopamine) at sub-second resolution within the nanomolar concentration range, thereby allowing the tracking of neurotransmitter release, for example when dopamine neurons are phasically activated or are electrically stimulated (Fig. 1.5D). Other neurotransmitters can also be detected during FSCV including adenosine, norepinephrine and serotonin, although their waveforms are more difficult to distinguish (Shin et al., 2019). FSCV can also be used *in vivo* by implanting carbon electrodes within the brain and is able to track neurotransmitter release during behavior (Robinson et al., 2008). In addiction research, FSCV has contributed to our understanding of how drugs of abuse increase dopamine release as well as the reward prediction error (RPE). In a series of experiments, RPE was developed to explain data where peak levels of dopamine release measured using FSCV are observed during unexpected rewards like during initial administration of a drug of abuse like cocaine. Following repeated exposures of cocaine, the peak dopamine signal shifts to cues that predict the presence of cocaine and this dopamine signal is thought to stimulate drug-seeking (Phillips et al., 2003) (Redish, 2004). Sexually dimorphic differences in the actions of cocaine on dopamine release that explain sex-specific addiction vulnerability have been revealed using FSCV (Calipari et al., 2017).

In vivo techniques for measuring cellular activity

Single-unit recordings are often used for *in vivo* recordings in awake behaving rodents or nonhuman primates. When recording neuronal activity, *in vivo* electrophysiology techniques have many clear advantages in temporal resolution, dynamic range and the duration and fidelity of the active signal to other methods (Fig. 1.5B). However, when used on their own, *in vivo* electrophysiology techniques do not inform the researcher of the specific circuit or neuronal subclass being recorded from unless additional techniques are added. Furthermore, the passive electrical signal from the electrode is the net result of the actions of many neurotransmitter and effector molecules, and cannot achieve the spatial and genetic clarity that newly devised biosensors can provide. Biosensors have followed a similar technology development pathway in neuroscience applications, starting with primarily chemical compounds and leading to engineered proteins that can be selectively expressed in genetically defined circuits and cells.

Monitoring cellular activity can be achieved through the optical imaging of fluctuations in free calcium levels, called Ca^{2+} imaging. It has emerged as the one of most prominent techniques applied in contemporary neuroscience and addiction research is no exception. Ca^{2+} has diverse roles within a neuron including affecting membrane excitability and acting as second messenger for intracellular signaling pathways. The release, uptake, and binding of calcium is highly regulated across many spatiotemporal domains including the cytoplasm, organelles, and axon terminals. The dynamic activity of Ca^{2+} during action potentials make it particularly useful for neuroscience applications. Voltage-gated calcium channels play a prominent role in generating the AP waveform. Due to the higher concentration of calcium extracellularly, calcium enters the cell which can stimulate additional release of calcium stores from the endoplasm. Elevated cytoplasmic calcium levels are then reset by being sequestered by intracellular signaling cascades, organelle reuptake, or extracellular release via pumps or channels. While the concentration of calcium does not directly track the membrane voltage, the timing of its rise and fall make it a very tractable, but indirect measure of action potentials when using calcium indicators.

Initial successful calcium indicators were primarily based on calcium chelators conjugated to light sensitive organic dyes. For instance, rhodamine was bound to BAPTA, which allowed for absorption and emission of photons upon calcium binding. In dye-loaded cells, increases in cytoplasmic calcium concentration caused increases in fluorescence intensity which can be measured using live imaging microscopy. Chemical dyes have a wide range of calcium detection including indicators with low and high affinities for calcium (Paredes et al., 2008). These indicators have led to many rich discoveries and insights into the spatial dynamics of calcium activity across many cell types, yet there were several drawbacks to chemical-based methods that limited their use to monitor neural circuits *in vivo*. For many years, they lacked ratiometric, or 1:1 ratio, of fluorescent intensity to calcium concentration affecting precision of the measure. They also were challenging to use and required incubations or single-cell filling, and non-standardized imaging techniques that limited their widespread adoption. As a result, they were used primarily with *in vitro* preparations, which prevented them being used to track calcium levels during behavioral experiments. Perhaps most importantly for neurocircuitry research, they lacked the ability to be targeted to genetically or in anatomically defined neuronal cell types and it was technically challenging to observe their activity *in vivo* using standard microscopy.

A major advancement in monitoring the activity of select neural circuits occurred when proteins were engineered to optically respond to calcium. This was accomplished by fusing GFP to calmodulin, a protein that binds calcium at low concentrations through a linker peptide called a domain light chain. The result was GCaMP (from GFP-Calmodulin-Peptide), a relatively inert exogenous protein that exhibits increases in green fluorescence when cytosolic Ca^{2+} levels are elevated. As in the previous examples of protein based reporters, GCaMP was a clear step forward as it could then be encoded and expressed into specific cell types using transgenic mice and/or viral strategies. These proteins were termed genetically encoded calcium indicators (GECIs). To further optimize GECIs in terms of signal to noise ratio, photostability and temporal precision, the GCaMP molecule has been continuously tinkered with using mutational approaches and selection of new features. The most recent GCaMPs are the generations GCaMP6-8 and they include several variants with different tradeoffs of kinetics, calcium affinity and brightness. For instance, GCaMP7f has the fastest kinetics of the seventh generation but has a lower signal to noise than the slower kinetics version (GCaMP7s) (Dana et al., 2019). In addition to a green fluorescent indicators, red fluorescent calcium indicators have also been developed and include RCaMP and jRGECO which, when properly stimulated and filtered, can be imaged simultaneously alongside GCaMP in other cell populations or combined with other green fluorescent emitting signals including other biosensors (Akerboom et al., 2013; Labouesse and Patriarchi, 2021).

The experimental methods and principles that were successful in generating the many varied and robust fluorescent GECIs could also be applied to other biological signals. For instance, many genetically encoded neurotransmitter indicators (GENIs) have been developed by fusing native receptors to FPs. There are currently GENIs developed from receptors for dopamine (e.g. Dlight and GRAB-DA), glutamate (iGluSnFr), GABA (iGABASnFr), serotonin (Psychlight, GRAB-5HT), endocannabinoids (eCB-GRAB) and norepinephrine (GRAB-NE) (Labouesse and Patriarchi, 2021; Wu et al., 2022). An advantage of *in vivo* GENIs over *in vivo* FSCV and microdialysis is that their use enables the visualization of neurotransmitter release by monitoring fluorescent activity in genetically targeted cell populations. Additional biosensor tools have been developed that can monitor the activity of intracellular signaling pathways including PKA and cAMP (Kim et al., 2021). A major caveat of these emerging biosensors is that the signal-to-noize ratio and kinetics are currently much lower and slower than the GECIs creating technical and computational challenges that not all laboratories are able to overcome using strategies optimized for GECIs. Based on the inherent experimental value of these emerging genetically encoded biosensor classes to addiction neuroscience and the groundwork laid out by the optimization of GECIs, there is little doubt that new waves of biosensors will become increasingly accessible and impactful.

GCaMP and other biosensors can be used in neuronal cultures and *ex vivo* slice imaging, but their most prominent contemporary application is *in vivo*, and this has expanded due to technological advancements in imaging technologies. In order to collect photons emitted from GCaMP and other biosensors *in vivo*, there must be optical access in the brain so that the fluorophore can be excited by fluorescent light either through a laser or LED and the emitted light received by a photodetector or camera. There are three primary ways of gaining optical access to an awake and behaving brain, each with their own advantages and limitations, as described below in order of increasing spatial resolution (Tye and Deisseroth, 2012; Siciliano and Tye, 2019).

The first technique is fiber-based photometry, in which a fiber optic ferrule is implanted into a specific brain region that expresses a biosensor. During *in vivo* recordings, the ferrule is connected to a fiber optic patch cord which is a fiber optic cable that can attach against the ferrule end and is long enough to connect the animal to the fiber photometry system composed of the light source, filters and dichroic mirrors to direct the optical path to and from the ferrule, and to a light receiver (Fig. 1.6A). In single site recordings, light can be collected using a photodetector capable of measuring emitted photons from neurons expressing the specific biosensor FP. More recently, scientific CMOS cameras have been used as they can capture the light of multiple fiber optic cables from multiple brain regions and separate wavelengths on separate spots of a wider chip-based sensor. Fiber photometry has the advantage of being relatively easy to implement compared to other *in vivo* optical approaches as the equipment used has simpler design and requires less technical training and analyses. It also is less constrictive of animal movement and behavior enabling more complex behavioral assays. To control for background fluorescence, a separate ultraviolet light ($\sim$400 nm) is also emitted in the brain where it can be used as an isosbestic point to which the biosensor signal can be normalized. The major disadvantage of fiber photometry is that the optical field of fiber optic ferrule is typically a small flat circle 100–300 μM in diameter that lacks the spatial resolution to resolve the activity of single cells in a single focal plane. Fiber photometry has been successfully used across many addiction neuroscience labs primarily in the monitoring of calcium activity using GECIs. For instance, expression of GCaMP in D1 or D2 neurons in the ventral striatum and monitoring Ca^{2+} activity during the development of cocaine conditioned place preference using fiber photometry revealed a specific role of D1 neurons in cue encoding and drug-seeking behavior (Calipari et al., 2016). Fiber photometry has been applied to studies of multiple drugs of abuse, biosensors, and experimental paradigms (Wei et al., 2018). One caveat of fiber photometry is that when used as a single measure of neural activity, the interpretation of the biosensor data is limited as it is not a direct measure of electrical activity. Implantation of electrodes to measure electrical activity in the target brain region can be used to validate the nature of the GCaMP signal.

In vivo cellular resolution can be achieved by a second technique, which involves attachment of miniaturized microscopes to the heads of animals. The head fixed endoscope known as a miniscope, comes complete with an LED light source, objective, CMOS sensor, and optical components for the separation of the excitation and emission spectra (Fig. 1.6B). To extend the focal plane within the brain, a Gradient Refractive Index (GRIN) lens which is a 0.5–2 mm diameter cylindric lens with a convex end is implanted into the brain above the targeted brain region and secured to the skull. The miniscope can then be attached and coupled to the lens and secured to the head for recording. This configuration allows emitted

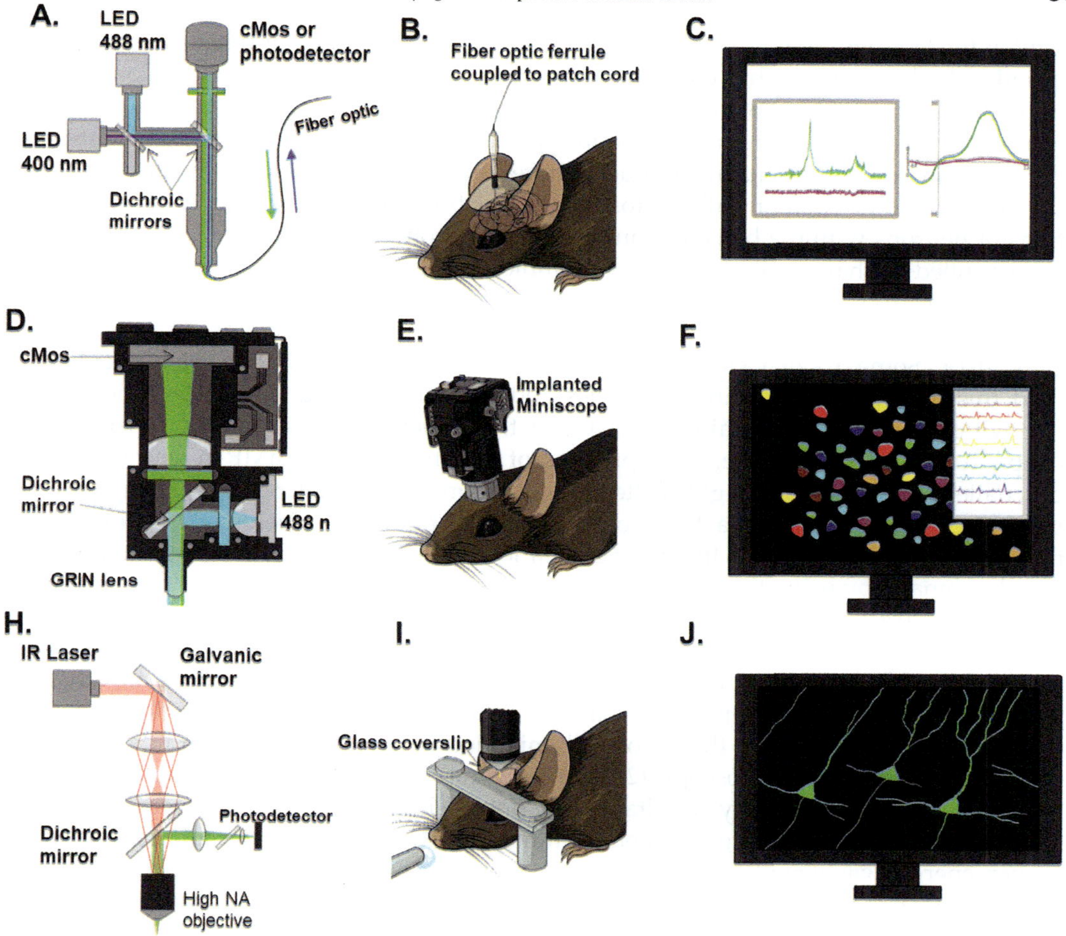

FIGURE 1.6 ***In vivo* biosensor imaging:** (A) Illustration of the major components of a typical fiber photometry system and it's light path. A 488 and 400 nm LED are directed by dichroic mirror toward the collimator and fiber patch cord. The blue 488 stimulating light is directed toward the fiber patch cord an into the brain to stimulate biosensors like GCaMP that produce a green emission light that is directed back toward a photodetector in the case of a single fiber system or a CMOS camera that can measure multiple fibers and emission wavelengths. A 400 nm light is additionally directed into the brain and its emitted light serves as a isosbestic point that controls for motion and native tissue fluorescence. (B) Illustration of a mouse with a fiber ferrule implant into the brain that is secured by epoxy to the skull. (C) Computer screen showing a hypothetical recording of green fluorescence signal and purple isosbestic point during an *in vivo* behavioral experiment on the left and a transformed signal aligned with a behavioral event. (D) Illustration of miniscope system and light path that demonstrates the LED source, CMOS camera, GRIN lens lowered into the brain and dichroic mirrors and filters used to direct the light path. (E) Depiction of mouse with miniscope attached allowing animal to perform behavior which can be timestamped for neuronal ensemble recordings. (E) Visualization of hypothetical neuronal ensembles where individual neurons are have separated by color and their corresponding GCaMP waveform is shown on the right. (F) Illustration of a two-photon system that uses rapid pulses of an infrared laser directed at a single point to fluorescently excite a biosenser like GCaMP and collect light in a photodetector, often a photomultiplier tube. A galvanic mirror is used to scan the field of view to create a higher resolution image that can discern the localized GCaMP signal in processes like dendrites. (G) Cartooned image of neurons on a screen imaged using 2-photon stimulation. *Illustrated by Faith Maxwell, M.S.*

light at the lens end to reflect onto the CMOS sensor to track GECI or other biosensor activity in individual neurons. What emerges from these recordings is a two-dimensional window into the activity of neuronal ensembles during defined behaviors that can capture the complexity of neuronal communication in spatially and temporally ordered segments. Multiplexing with other biosensors or fluorophores that are from genetically or anatomically defined neuron populations allows for the dissociation biosensor activity in known populations of neurons within a behaving animal. In addiction neuroscience labs, miniscopes have been applied to characterizing neuron ensembles in the hippocampus activated during nicotine reward, frontal cortex projections during aversive-resistant alcohol self-administration and motivations to self-administer cocaine (Xia et al., 2017; Siciliano et al., 2019; Cameron et al., 2019). Some drawbacks of miniscopes are the size of the miniscope can hinder behavior (and this may differ according to species and animal size) and the implantation requires removing large areas of brain tissue above the target region, especially when targeting deep structures. Furthermore, the expression of biosensors like GCaMP in neurites and optical challenges due to tissue light scatter are compounded by challenges in placing the lens in view of GCaMP cells using a 1-photon system. Cell population yields can be improved by attaching GCaMP to proteins that restrict their localization to specific neuronal compartments like the soma or by using the end of the GRIN lens to deliver the virus to the focal plane (Shemesh et al., 2020). Another important aspect and potential source of error comes from offline analyses of activity that require additional expertize in deconvolution and mathematical transformation of the signal to precisely measure biosensor activity (Zhou et al., 2018).

Two-photon imaging of biosensors has emerged as technology that offers the highest level of spatial resolution. Rather than broad illumination of a specimen as seen in single photon microscopy, 2-photon microscopy (2PM) uses a rapid-pulsing infrared laser (>800 nm) to emit 2 photons of light nearly simultaneously onto a single point. When directed at a fluorescent protein, the lower energy photons summate to stimulate the fluorophore at its native, higher energy wavelength. The focal point is then scanned across the specimen using a rotating galvanic mirror and reflected to a photomultiplier tube (PMT) to measure the subsequent fluorescence. This approach creates a high-resolution image scan that is free from many of the artifacts caused by light scatter above and below a focal plane observed in 1-photon illumination preparations. Another advantage of the 2P system is that infrared light travels deeper into tissue compared to blue light allowing 2P to reach deeper structures (~1 mm) through a cover glass that sits on top of the exposed brain or through a thinned skull without having to implant lenses or fibers into the brain. On the other hand, 2P imaging rigs are typically bulkier and more expensive, preventing them from being reduced to a size that could be fixed to the head of rodents and interfaced with a computer. The workaround is restraining the head movement of the animal by attaching hard structures to the skull and attaching them to posts to restrain the head of the animal during recordings (Fig. 1.6I). While this would appear to greatly limit 2P use in behavioral experiments, rodents can be habituated to being head-restrained and trained to use licks, paw touches, running on a ball and whisker movement to respond to experimental stimuli (Guo et al., 2014). While relatively new in its application to addiction neuroscience, *in vivo* 2P imaging has impacted our understanding of reward-related learning and is poised to transform the resolution with which we can observe circuits during addictive behavior (Otis et al., 2017; Li et al., 2021).

Interrogating neural circuit function *in vivo*

Capturing neural activity *in vivo* during behavioral tasks helps the researcher understand circuit dynamics, yet in passive recording behavioral experiments, the measured activity is mostly correlative with a somewhat limited interpretation. To conclude that a brain region or circuit is causal for a behavior or physiological response requires evidence of *necessity* of the neural circuit for the complete behavior, and/or *sufficiency* of circuit activation for generation of the specific behavior in question. Historically, these have been tested using chemical lesions to brain regions or selected circuits or site-specific drug infusions. Currently, there are established and emerging tools that have been developed from protein engineering approaches that allow for determination of the necessity and sufficiency of select circuits for specific behaviors in awake behaving animals at high spatial and temporal resolutions. Common terms used to describe these experiments are neural circuit "interrogation" and the molecular tools used to interrogate circuit function are often called neural *actuators*. Keep in mind that neural circuits often contain diverse cell types that elicit excitatory, inhibitory, and neuromodulatory effects on other neurons, therefore the terms "activation" and "inhibition" in these experiments refer to promoting and attenuating the natural physiological process of a specified neuron population.

Experiments designed to better understand the function of a selected brain system or circuit have traditionally relied upon targeted lesions into brain regions or transections of neuronal fibers. Targeted infusions of toxins, epileptic agents or mechanical means were used disrupt neural communication and subsequent observation of a specific change in a behavior using appropriate controls would be that the damaged area plays a role in that behavior. Of course, these types of lesions are permanent, non-specific, and often destroy fibers of passage leading to deleterious effects outside of the lesion. Drug infusions emerged as a more convincing and sophisticated technique as they allowed for targeting of cells in transient and selective fashion. For instance, pharmacological agents like the $GABA_AR$ receptor agonist muscimol or the sodium channel blockers TTX or lidocaine can be infused through a cannula prior to or during behavior and are more likely to transiently inhibit somatodendritic neural activity and less likely to affect fibers of passage (Majchrzak and Di Scala, 2000). The dissociation of specific behaviors by comparing inactivation of separate brain regions was a fruitful approach that produced many of the major findings in behavior—brain relationships in systems addiction neuroscience (Everitt and Robbins, 2005) Furthermore, drug infusions could also impact specific neurotransmitter systems and ion channels within a brain region to probe their involvement in behavior, for instance, targeting dopaminergic or cholinergic receptor activity with agonists or antagonists. Similar to previous techniques, the major drawbacks of these strategies are the inability to selectively alter genetically defined neuronal populations and/or anatomically-defined neural circuits. Fortunately, new approaches afforded by genetic modification strategies and viral targeting of neural circuits can reach this level of selectivity.

A largely successful enterprise in the neuroscience toolkit for the interrogation of neural circuits *in vivo* has been the development of chemogenetic strategies where exogenously administered ligands can influence the activity of select neural circuits. This is achieved by engineering a receptor that can be expressed in genetically defined neurons to influence neuronal excitability following administration of an exogenous, typically inert ligand. The first generation of chemogenetic proteins were named RASSLs which were used in the heart, but were not as useful in the brain (Conklin et al., 2008). A breakthrough occurred when designer receptors exclusively activated by designer drugs (DREADDs) were developed for selective neural circuit manipulation (Armbruster et al., 2007). DREADDs are muscarinic receptors that have undergone mutations that make them unable to respond to their native ligand, acetylcholine, but are instead activated by inert ligands like clozapine-N-oxide (CNO) which would not have direct actions on native receptors in the brain. Muscarinic receptors are cholinergic GPCRs that primarily signal though Gαq or Gαs to increase excitability in the case of engineered M4 receptors or decrease excitability through Gαi signaling in engineered M3 receptors (Fig. 1.7A). Through drug-screening assays, these receptors were optimized to respond only to CNO and could therefore be activated following administration of CNO. Additional chemogenetic tools were developed from the kappa opioid receptor and are able to inhibit neural activity through another inert ligand, salvinorin B allowing for bidirectional chemogenetic control over neurons when co-expressed with hM3Dq (Vardy et al., 2015). Expression of DREADDs can be targeted using selected promoters and conditional transgenic mouse lines or packaged and administered in viruses like AAVs to target neural circuits in selected brain regions.

While DREADDS and other chemogenetic actuators have generated many impactful studies that were successful in interrogating and providing functional insight in a myriad of neural circuits, there are important experimental factors to consider when designing these experiments. CNO is not completely inert in all animal species (e.g., nonhuman primates), and there have been reports of back metabolism into the active compound clozapine leading to behavioral effects in rodents that lack DREADD expression especially at higher doses (Gomez et al., 2017). Therefore, dose-dependent effects and proper controls should always be used when applying chemogenetic strategies. For instance, when virally expressing DREADD receptors, a control virus group that expresses just the reporter fluorophore can be used to separate out DREADD specific effects (Smith et al., 2021). New DREADD ligands that are more selective, efficacious and brain penetrant have been developed that can avoid unintended CNO effects and can be additionally used in primates (Oyama et al., 2022) (Fig. 1.7A).

Another breakthrough for *in vivo* neural circuit research over the last two decades has been the discovery and development of optogenetics. Optogenetics refers to the technique of using light to stimulate the activity of genetically defined cell populations. While the idea of optogenetics has existed for some time (Crick, 1999), the rapid emergence of optogenetics in neuroscience took place following the coalescing of several advancements that enabled the targeted expression of channelrhodopsin into neurons using viruses and the ability to optically stimulate these populations *in vivo* for circuit manipulation (Deisseroth, 2015). Channelrhodopsins are nonselective cation channels found in algae that are rapidly activated by light to stimulate flagella motility. After many years of characterization and development, channelrhodopsin 2 (Chr2) emerged as the marquee optogenetics tool. *Ex vivo* whole cell recordings demonstrated its ability to illicit action potentials using short pulses (msec) of 480–490 nm light in expressed neurons as well as stimulation of axon terminals to cause synaptic release. Initial versions of Chr2 required robust expression levels and light intensity to stimulate action potentials which could be achieved by using a concentrated viral titer and laser stimulation. To transfer the technology *in vivo*, fiber optic ferrules were implanted above

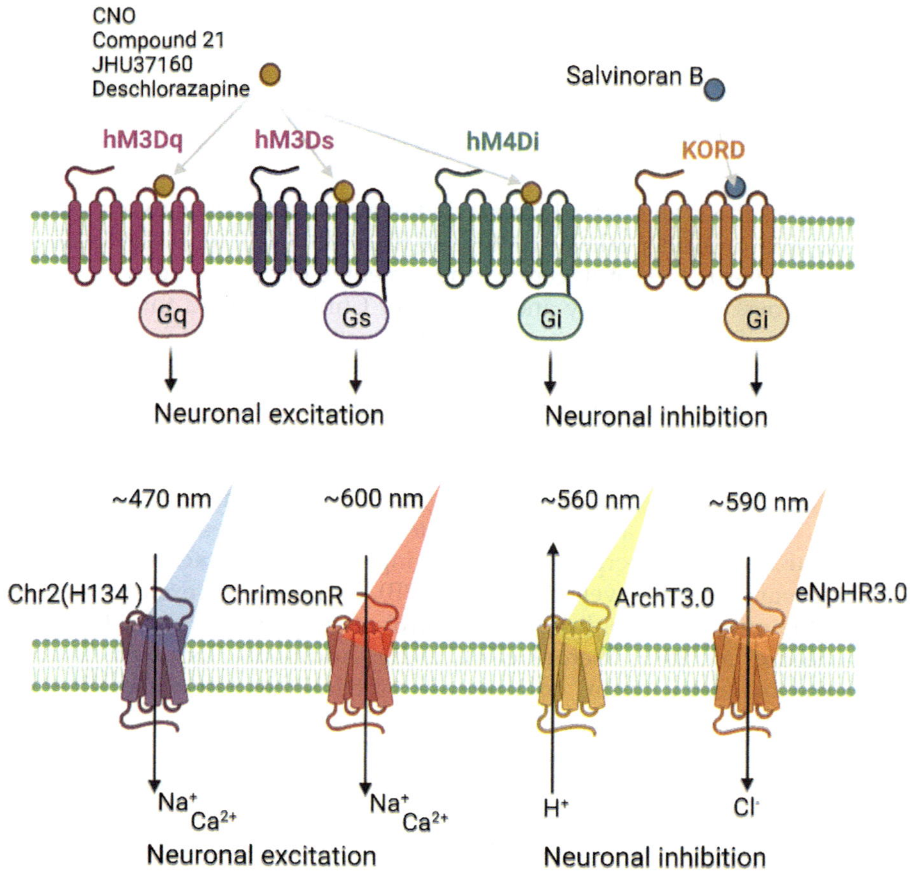

FIGURE 1.7 **Chemogenetic and optogenetic strategies:** (A) DREADD receptors expressed in the membrane that are based on muscarinic receptors (hM3Dq, hMD3Ds, hM3Di) or kappa receptor (KORD). Muscarinic based DREADDs and that are selectively activated by inert compounds CNO, Compound 21, JHU, and DCZ and KORDs are activated by salvinorin B Activation of hM3Dq and hMD3Ds cause an increase in excitability through G-protein signaling pathways (Gq and Gs). hM4Di and KORD decrease neuronal activity primarily through Gi signaling pathways. (B) Frequently used optogenetic constructs that include Chr2(H134) activated by *blue light* and ChrimsonR activated by *red light* that can cause a depolarization via the influx of cations into the neuron after light stimulation opens the channel. Other opsins shown are inhibitory and can be stimulated by other light wavelengths. For instance, ArchT3.0 inhibits the neuron by pumping hydrogen out of the neuron and Enphr3.0 inhibits the neuron by increasing intracellular Cl^- levels. *Created with Biorender.*

neurons expressing Chr2 and fiber optic patch cords were connected to laser stimulation sources for spatially restricted light stimulation. Light stimulation of Chr2 targeted to the cell body can lead to action potentials and neurotransmitter release in all downstream connected regions. Alternatively, placing the ferrule above the afferent axons restricts the release of neurotransmitter and stimulation to the specific circuit from the location of viral injection to where the ferrule is placed. This approach has been highly successful in identifying and probing the function of specific neural circuits leading to many new insights into how these circuits communicate to control behavior (Tye and Deisseroth, 2012). For instance, many of these initial studies were used to demonstrate the role of dopamine neurons in reward and the frontal cortex in executive control over drug seeking (Chen et al., 2013; Adamantidis et al., 2011). A major advantage of optogenetics comes from the use of light stimulation, endowing the technique the temporal and spatial precision required to remotely control neural circuits during behavior.

The optogenetics toolkit has greatly expanded over the last decade due to major efforts in protein engineering to further take advantage of these powerful tools. Once the structure of Chr2 was solved, site-directed mutagenesis and screening of new optogenetic tools had more guidance to improve the sensitivity and kinetics of Chr2 which led to variants with larger photocurrents (e.g., Chr2 [H134 R]) and red-shifted activation (e.g. ChrimsonR) (Deisseroth and Hegemann, 2017). Other variants of Chr2 called stabilized step function opsins (SSFOs) were generated that could cause long-term depolarization of the membrane potential with a pulse of blue light and reversal with a pulse of orange light (Yizhar et al., 2011). Several inhibitory optogenetic rhodopsins were developed from other biological sources that can depress neural activity. These include the creation of light activated chloride pumps based on halorhodopsins (e.g., ENpHR 3.0) and outward proton pumps derived from Archearhodopsins (e.g. ArchT3.0) that could hyperpolarize the resting membrane potential and inhibit neural activity using separate light wavelengths (Fig. 1.7B). By packaging excitatory and inhibitory opsins within the same virus, bidirectional control of single neurons can be made possible (Carus-Cadavieco et al., 2017; Vierock et al., 2021). Additional, localized neuronal control can be achieved by fusing opsins to accessory proteins that target their insertion in the neuronal membrane to specific compartments including the soma, axon terminal or dendrites (Shemesh et al., 2017; Rost et al., 2022). Furthermore, GPCRs have been developed to respond to optical stimulation to stimulate G-protein pathways called Opto-XRs (Airan et al., 2009). New light-sensitive tools have been able to further specify intracellular signaling pathways including light responsive kinases CaMKII2, PKA that can lead to potentiation or depression of synaptic strength (Shibata et al., 2021; Murakoshi et al., 2017). Continued development, sharing, and application of optogenetic tools will no doubt lead the addiction field to new insights into circuit function, yet, with any new tool, there are often unexpected consequences related to their use that may not be observed in initial characterization experiments. For instance, the heat from high-powered light stimulation in the brain may produce off-target effects (Owen et al., 2019). Furthermore, in some neural populations, expression of inhibitory opsins in axons can lead to an unintended depolarization of axon terminals during sustained light stimulation (Mahn et al., 2016). Again, careful control experiments and proof-of-principle studies should be carried out in the experimenter's chosen system prior to the application of optogenetic strategies. The optogenetic actuators listed here do not fully encompass their full diversity and breadth, and new optogenetic tools are introduced into the field every year.

Conclusions

Human and preclinical addiction neuroscience labs use a diverse array of experimental strategies to identify and understand the specific neural circuits that control addictive behavior. Our knowledge of the underlying neurobiological factors and environmental conditions that contribute to the development of SUDs is guided by human psychiatric, genetic, postmortem, and clinical neuroimaging studies that are beginning to resolve contributing factors at the circuit level. Preclinical labs have an important role in providing comprehensive anatomical, physiological, and functional characterization of neural circuits in animal models of addiction. They have been greatly aided by recent advancements in microscopy and genetically encoded tools that can monitor and manipulate select neural circuits with high spatial and temporal resolution. As the volume, diversity, and complexity of these varied datasets grow, sophisticated computational approaches will undoubtedly be needed if we are to make sense of how addiction manifests itself in the "alien computer". This chapter was intended as a neurocircuitry primer, and the above-described methods will be repeatedly referred to in the following chapters.

References

Airan, R.D., et al., 2009. Temporally precise in vivo control of intracellular signalling. Nature 458 (7241), 1025–1029.

Akerboom, J., et al., 2013. Genetically encoded calcium indicators for multi-color neural activity imaging and combination with optogenetics. Front. Mol. Neurosci. 6.

Armbruster, B.N., et al., 2007. Evolving the lock to fit the key to create a family of G protein-coupled receptors potently activated by an inert ligand. Proc. Natl. Acad. Sci. U. S. A. 104 (12), 5163–5168.

Barnes, S.J., et al., 2015. Subnetwork-specific homeostatic plasticity in mouse visual cortex in vivo. Neuron 86 (5), 1290–1303.

Barth, A.L., Gerkin, R.C., Dean, K.L., 2004. Alteration of neuronal firing properties after in vivo experience in a FosGFP transgenic mouse. J. Neurosci. 24 (29), 6466–6475.

Beard, C.L., et al., 2019. Regional differences in white matter integrity in stimulant use disorders: a meta-analysis of diffusion tensor imaging studies. Drug Alcohol Depend. 201, 29–37.

Benito, E., Barco, A., 2015. The neuronal activity-driven transcriptome. Mol. Neurobiol. 51 (3), 1071–1088.

Björklund, A., Dunnett, S.B., 2007. Dopamine neuron systems in the brain: an update. Trends Neurosci. 30 (5), 194–202.

Bliss, T.V., Collingridge, G.L., 1993. A synaptic model of memory: long-term potentiation in the hippocampus. Nature 361 (6407), 31–39.

Brenner, E., et al., 2020. Single cell transcriptome profiling of the human alcohol-dependent brain. Hum. Mol. Genet. 29 (7), 1144–1153.

Brown, S.A., et al., 2015. The national consortium on alcohol and NeuroDevelopment in adolescence (NCANDA): a multisite study of adolescent development and substance use. J. Stud. Alcohol Drugs 76 (6), 895–908.

Buttner, A., 2011. Review: the neuropathology of drug abuse. Neuropathol. Appl. Neurobiol. 37 (2), 118–134.

Buzsáki, G., Anastassiou, C.A., Koch, C., 2012. The origin of extracellular fields and currents-EEG, ECoG, LFP and spikes. Nat. Rev. Neurosci. 13 (6), 407–420.

Calipari, E.S., et al., 2016. In vivo imaging identifies temporal signature of D1 and D2 medium spiny neurons in cocaine reward. Proc. Natl. Acad. Sci. U. S. A. 113 (10), 2726–2731.

Calipari, E.S., et al., 2017. Dopaminergic dynamics underlying sex-specific cocaine reward. Nat. Commun. 8, 13877.

Cameron, C.M., et al., 2019. Increased cocaine motivation is associated with degraded spatial and temporal representations in IL-NAc neurons. Neuron 103 (1), 80–91 e7.

Caprioli, D., et al., 2018. Effect of novel allosteric modulators of metabotropic glutamate receptors on drug self-administration and relapse: a review of preclinical studies and their clinical implications. Biol. Psychiatr. 84 (3), 180–192.

Carus-Cadavieco, M., et al., 2017. Gamma oscillations organize top-down signalling to hypothalamus and enable food seeking. Nature 542 (7640), 232–236.

Chen, B.T., et al., 2013. Rescuing cocaine-induced prefrontal cortex hypoactivity prevents compulsive cocaine seeking. Nature 496 (7445), 359–362.

Cifani, C., et al., 2012. Medial prefrontal cortex neuronal activation and synaptic alterations after stress-induced reinstatement of palatable food seeking: a study using c-fos-GFP transgenic female rats. J. Neurosci. 32 (25), 8480–8490.
Cizeron, M., et al., 2020. A brainwide atlas of synapses across the mouse life span. Science 369 (6501), 270–275.
Cohen, M.X., 2014. Analyzing Neural Time Series Data: Theory and Practice. MIT press.
Conklin, B.R., et al., 2008. Engineering GPCR signaling pathways with RASSLs. Nat. Methods 5 (8), 673–678.
Covey, E., Carter, M., 2015. Basic Electrophysiological Methods.
Crick, F., 1999. The impact of molecular biology on neuroscience. Philos. Trans. R. Soc. Lond. B Biol. Sci. 354 (1392), 2021–2025.
Cruz, F.C., et al., 2014. Role of nucleus accumbens shell neuronal ensembles in context-induced reinstatement of cocaine-seeking. J. Neurosci. 34 (22), 7437–7446.
Cruz, F.C., Javier Rubio, F., Hope, B.T., 2015. Using c-fos to study neuronal ensembles in corticostriatal circuitry of addiction. Brain Res. 1628 (Pt A), 157–173.
Dalley, J.W., Everitt, B.J., Robbins, T.W., 2011. Impulsivity, compulsivity, and top-down cognitive control. Neuron 69 (4), 680–694.
Adamantidis, A.R., et al., 2011. Optogenetic interrogation of dopaminergic modulation of the multiple phases of reward-seeking behavior. J. Neurosci. 31 (30), 10829–10835.
Dana, H., et al., 2019. High-performance calcium sensors for imaging activity in neuronal populations and microcompartments. Nat. Methods 16 (7), 649–657.
Deisseroth, K., 2015. Optogenetics: 10 years of microbial opsins in neuroscience. Nat. Neurosci. 18 (9), 1213–1225.
Deisseroth, K., Hegemann, P., 2017. The form and function of channelrhodopsin. Science 357 (6356).
Devineni, A.V., Heberlein, U., 2009. Preferential ethanol consumption in Drosophila models features of addiction. Curr. Biol. 19 (24), 2126–2132.
Dobi, A., et al., 2011. Cocaine-induced plasticity in the nucleus accumbens is cell specific and develops without prolonged withdrawal. J. Neurosci. 31 (5), 1895–1904.
Durrant, R., et al., 2009. Drug use and addiction: evolutionary perspective. Aust. N. Z. J. Psychiatr. 43 (11), 1049–1056.
Egervari, G., et al., 2019. Molecular windows into the human brain for psychiatric disorders. Mol. Psychiatr. 24 (5), 653–673.
Everitt, B.J., Robbins, T.W., 2005. Neural systems of reinforcement for drug addiction: from actions to habits to compulsion. Nat. Neurosci. 8 (11), 1481–1489.
Fenno, L.E., et al., 2014. Targeting cells with single vectors using multiple-feature Boolean logic. Nat. Methods 11 (7), 763–772.
Ferrer, I., et al., 1986. Decreased numbers of dendritic spines on cortical pyramidal neurons in human chronic alcoholism. Neurosci. Lett. 69 (1), 115–119.
Foltin, R.W., Evans, S.M., 2001. Location preference related to smoked heroin self-administration by rhesus monkeys. Psychopharmacology (Berl) 155 (4), 419–425.
Fowler, J.S., et al., 2001. [(11)]Cocaine: PET studies of cocaine pharmacokinetics, dopamine transporter availability and dopamine transporter occupancy. Nucl. Med. Biol. 28 (5), 561–572.
Fredriksson, I., et al., 2021. Animal models of drug relapse and craving after voluntary abstinence: a review. Pharmacol. Rev. 73 (3), 1050–1083.
Fritschy, J.M., 2008. Is my antibody-staining specific? How to deal with pitfalls of immunohistochemistry. Eur. J. Neurosci. 28 (12), 2365–2370.
Gan, W.B., et al., 2000. Multicolor "DiOlistic" labeling of the nervous system using lipophilic dye combinations. Neuron 27 (2), 219–225.
Gelernter, J., Polimanti, R., 2021. Genetics of substance use disorders in the era of big data. Nat. Rev. Genet. 22 (11), 712–729.
Gerfen, C.R., Sawchenko, P.E., 1984. An anterograde neuroanatomical tracing method that shows the detailed morphology of neurons, their axons and terminals: immunohistochemical localization of an axonally transported plant lectin, Phaseolus vulgaris leucoagglutinin (PHA-L). Brain Res. 290 (2), 219–238.
Gerfen, C.R., Surmeier, D.J., 2011. Modulation of striatal projection systems by dopamine. Annu. Rev. Neurosci. 34, 441–466.

Goldberg, S.R., Woods, J.H., Schuster, C.R., 1969. Morphine: conditioned increases in self-administration in rhesus monkeys. Science 166 (3910), 1306–1307.

Goldman, D., Oroszi, G., Ducci, F., 2005. The genetics of addictions: uncovering the genes. Nat. Rev. Genet. 6 (7), 521–532.

Goldstein, R.Z., et al., 2007. Role of the anterior cingulate and medial orbitofrontal cortex in processing drug cues in cocaine addiction. Neuroscience 144 (4), 1153–1159.

Gomez, J.L., et al., 2017. Chemogenetics revealed: DREADD occupancy and activation via converted clozapine. Science 357 (6350), 503–507.

Guenthner, C.J., et al., 2013. Permanent genetic access to transiently active neurons via TRAP: targeted recombination in active populations. Neuron 78 (5), 773–784.

Guo, Z.V., et al., 2014. Procedures for behavioral experiments in head-fixed mice. PLoS One 9 (2), e88678.

Harper, C., Corbett, D., 1990. Changes in the basal dendrites of cortical pyramidal cells from alcoholic patients—a quantitative Golgi study. J. Neurol. Neurosurg. Psychiatry 53 (10), 856–861.

Harper, C.G., Kril, J.J., Holloway, R.L., 1985. Brain shrinkage in chronic alcoholics: a pathological study. Br. Med. J. 290 (6467), 501–504.

He, J., Crews, F.T., 2008. Increased MCP-1 and microglia in various regions of the human alcoholic brain. Exp. Neurol. 210 (2), 349–358.

Heidenreich, M., Zhang, F., 2016. Applications of CRISPR-Cas systems in neuroscience. Nat. Rev. Neurosci. 17 (1), 36–44.

Heilig, M., et al., 2021. Addiction as a brain disease revised: why it still matters, and the need for consilience. Neuropsychopharmacology 46 (10), 1715–1723.

Hellem, T., et al., 2015. The utility of magnetic resonance spectroscopy for understanding substance use disorders: a systematic review of the literature. J. Am. Psychiatr. Nurses Assoc. 21 (4), 244–275.

Huggett, S.B., Stallings, M.C., 2020. Genetic architecture and molecular neuropathology of human cocaine addiction. J. Neurosci. 40 (27), 5300–5313.

Hyman, S.E., Malenka, R.C., Nestler, E.J., 2006. Neural mechanisms of addiction: the role of reward-related learning and memory. Annu. Rev. Neurosci. 29, 565–598.

Ikemoto, S., Bonci, A., 2014. Neurocircuitry of drug reward. Neuropharmacology 76 Pt B, 329–341.

Inoue, T., et al., 2018. Brain computed tomography using iterative reconstruction to diagnose acute middle cerebral artery stroke: usefulness in combination of narrow window setting and thin slice reconstruction. Neuroradiology 60 (4), 373–379.

Josselyn, S.A., Köhler, S., Frankland, P.W., 2015. Finding the engram. Nat. Rev. Neurosci. 16 (9), 521–534.

Kalivas, P.W., O'Brien, C., 2008. Drug addiction as a pathology of staged neuroplasticity. Neuropsychopharmacology 33 (1), 166–180.

Katz, L.C., Iarovici, D.M., 1990. Green fluorescent latex microspheres: a new retrograde tracer. Neuroscience 34 (2), 511–520.

Kauer, J.A., Malenka, R.C., 2007. Synaptic plasticity and addiction. Nat. Rev. Neurosci. 8 (11), 844–858.

Kaun, K.R., et al., 2011. A Drosophila model for alcohol reward. Nat. Neurosci. 14 (5), 612–619.

Kim, N., Shin, S., Bae, S.W., 2021. cAMP biosensors based on genetically encoded fluorescent/luminescent proteins. Biosensors 11 (2).

Koob, G.F., 2011. Animal models of drug dependence: motivational perspective. In: Johnson, B.A. (Ed.), Addiction Medicine: Science and Practice. Springer New York, New York, NY, pp. 333–357.

Koob, G.F., Le Moal, M., 2001. Drug addiction, dysregulation of reward, and allostasis. Neuropsychopharmacology 24 (2), 97–129.

Koob, G.F., Volkow, N.D., 2010. Neurocircuitry of addiction. Neuropsychopharmacology 35 (1), 217–238.

Kourrich, S., Calu, D.J., Bonci, A., 2015. Intrinsic plasticity: an emerging player in addiction. Nat. Rev. Neurosci. 16 (3), 173–184.

Kristensson, K., Olsson, Y., 1971. Uptake and retrograde axonal transport of peroxidase in hypoglossal neurons. Electron microscopical localization in the neuronal perikaryon. Acta Neuropathol. 19 (1), 1–9.

Kroener, S., et al., 2012. Chronic alcohol exposure alters behavioral and synaptic plasticity of the rodent prefrontal cortex. PLoS One 7 (5), e37541.

Labouesse, M.A., Patriarchi, T., 2021. A versatile GPCR toolkit to track in vivo neuromodulation: not a one-size-fits-all sensor. Neuropsychopharmacology 46 (12), 2043–2047.

Lambert, T.J., 2019. FPbase: a community-editable fluorescent protein database. Nat. Methods 16 (4), 277–278.

Lanciego, J.L., Wouterlood, F.G., 2011. A half century of experimental neuroanatomical tracing. J. Chem. Neuroanat. 42 (3), 157–183.

Lanciego, J.L., Wouterlood, F.G., 2020. Neuroanatomical tract-tracing techniques that did go viral. Brain Struct. Funct. 225 (4), 1193–1224.

Lewis, D.A., 2002. The human brain revisited: opportunities and challenges in postmortem studies of psychiatric disorders. Neuropsychopharmacology 26 (2), 143–154.

Li, M., et al., 2021. Alcohol reduces the activity of somatostatin interneurons in the mouse prefrontal cortex: a neural basis for its disinhibitory effect? Neuropharmacology 188, 108501.

Luo, L., et al., 2020. Optimizing nervous system-specific gene targeting with Cre driver lines: prevalence of germline recombination and influencing factors. Neuron 106 (1), 37–65 e5.

Mackey, S., et al., 2019. Mega-analysis of gray matter volume in substance dependence: general and substance-specific regional effects. Am. J. Psychiatr. 176 (2), 119–128.

Mahn, M., et al., 2016. Biophysical constraints of optogenetic inhibition at presynaptic terminals. Nat. Neurosci. 19 (4), 554–556.

Majchrzak, M., Di Scala, G., 2000. GABA and muscimol as reversible inactivation tools in learning and memory. Neural Plast. 7 (1–2), 19–29.

Mascarell Maričić, L., et al., 2020. The IMAGEN study: a decade of imaging genetics in adolescents. Mol. Psychiatr. 25 (11), 2648–2671.

Maynard, K.R., et al., 2021. Transcriptome-scale spatial gene expression in the human dorsolateral prefrontal cortex. Nat. Neurosci. 24 (3), 425–436.

Mazza, M., et al., 2021. Virtual reality: a powerful technology to provide novel insight into treatment mechanisms of addiction. Transl. Psychiatry 11 (1), 617.

Mucha, R.F., et al., 1982. Drug reinforcement studied by the use of place conditioning in rat. Brain Res. 243 (1), 91–105.

Murakoshi, H., et al., 2017. Kinetics of endogenous CaMKII required for synaptic plasticity revealed by optogenetic kinase inhibitor. Neuron 94 (1), 37–47 e5.

Navabpour, S., Kwapis, J.L., Jarome, T.J., 2020. A neuroscientist's guide to transgenic mice and other genetic tools. Neurosci. Biobehav. Rev. 108, 732–748.

Nectow, A.R., Nestler, E.J., 2020. Viral tools for neuroscience. Nat. Rev. Neurosci. 21 (12), 669–681.

Nestler, E.J., Lüscher, C., 2019. The molecular basis of drug addiction: linking epigenetic to synaptic and circuit mechanisms. Neuron 102 (1), 48–59.

Okada, Y., 2012. Patch Clamp Techniques : From Beginning to Advanced Protocols. In: Springer Protocols Handbooks. Springer. xi, Tokyo; New York, p. 439.

Otis, J.M., et al., 2017. Prefrontal cortex output circuits guide reward seeking through divergent cue encoding. Nature 543 (7643), 103–107.

Ottino-Gonzalez, J., et al., 2022. White matter microstructure differences in individuals with dependence on cocaine, methamphetamine, and nicotine: findings from the ENIGMA-Addiction working group. Drug Alcohol Depend. 230, 109185.

Owen, S.F., Liu, M.H., Kreitzer, A.C., 2019. Thermal constraints on in vivo optogenetic manipulations. Nat. Neurosci. 22 (7), 1061–1065.

Oyama, K., et al., 2022. Chronic behavioral manipulation via orally delivered chemogenetic actuator in macaques. J. Neurosci. 42 (12), 2552–2561.

Paredes, R.M., et al., 2008. Chemical calcium indicators. Methods 46 (3), 143–151.

Parvaz, M.A., et al., 2011. Neuroimaging for drug addiction and related behaviors. Rev. Neurosci. 22 (6), 609–624.

Pelletier, D.E., Andrew, T.A., 2017. Common findings and predictive measures of opioid overdoses. Acad Forensic Pathol 7 (1), 91–98.

Perkins, K.L., 2006. Cell-attached voltage-clamp and current-clamp recording and stimulation techniques in brain slices. J. Neurosci. Methods 154 (1–2), 1–18.

Pfarr, S., et al., 2015. Losing control: excessive alcohol seeking after selective inactivation of cue-responsive neurons in the infralimbic cortex. J. Neurosci. 35 (30), 10750–10761.

Phillips, P.E., et al., 2003. Subsecond dopamine release promotes cocaine seeking. Nature 422 (6932), 614–618.

Redish, A.D., 2004. Addiction as a computational process gone awry. Science 306 (5703), 1944–1947.

Reijmers, L.G., et al., 2007. Localization of a stable neural correlate of associative memory. Science 317 (5842), 1230–1233.

Robinson, D.L., et al., 2008. Monitoring rapid chemical communication in the brain. Chem. Rev. 108 (7), 2554–2584.

Rost, B.R., et al., 2022. Optogenetics at the presynapse. Nat. Neurosci. 25, 984–998.

Rudy, B., et al., 2011. Three groups of interneurons account for nearly 100% of neocortical GABAergic neurons. Dev Neurobiol 71 (1), 45–61.

Salery, M., Godino, A., Nestler, E.J., 2021. Drug-activated cells: from immediate early genes to neuronal ensembles in addiction. Adv. Pharmacol. 90, 173–216.

Salling, M.C., Martinez, D., 2016. Brain stimulation in addiction. Neuropsychopharmacology 41 (12), 2798–2809.

Salvatore, J.E., et al., 2019. Beyond genome-wide significance: integrative approaches to the interpretation and extension of GWAS findings for alcohol use disorder. Addiction Biol. 24 (2), 275–289.

Sanchis-Segura, C., Spanagel, R., 2006. Behavioural assessment of drug reinforcement and addictive features in rodents: an overview. Addiction Biol. 11 (1), 2–38.

Shemesh, O.A., et al., 2017. Temporally precise single-cell-resolution optogenetics. Nat. Neurosci. 20 (12), 1796–1806.

Shemesh, O.A., et al., 2020. Precision calcium imaging of dense neural populations via a cell-body-targeted calcium indicator. Neuron 107 (3), 470–486 e11.

Shibata, A.C.E., et al., 2021. Photoactivatable CaMKII induces synaptic plasticity in single synapses. Nat. Commun. 12 (1), 751.

Shin, M., et al., 2019. Electrochemistry at the synapse. Annu. Rev. Anal. Chem. 12 (1), 297–321.

Siciliano, C.A., et al., 2019. A cortical-brainstem circuit predicts and governs compulsive alcohol drinking. Science 366 (6468), 1008–1012.

Siciliano, C.A., Tye, K.M., 2019. Leveraging calcium imaging to illuminate circuit dysfunction in addiction. Alcohol 74, 47–63.

Simpson, S., et al., 2021. The hidden brain: uncovering previously overlooked brain regions by employing novel preclinical unbiased network approaches. Front. Syst. Neurosci. 15, 595507.

Smith, K.S., et al., 2021. Dreadds: use and application in behavioral neuroscience. Behav. Neurosci. 135 (2), 89–107.

Stoeckel, K., Schwab, M., Thoenen, H., 1977. Role of gangliosides in the uptake and retrograde axonal transport of cholera and tetanus toxin as compared to nerve growth factor and wheat germ agglutinin. Brain Res. 132 (2), 273–285.

Stuber, G.D., et al., 2010. Neuroplastic alterations in the limbic system following cocaine or alcohol exposure. In: Self, D.W., Staley Gottschalk, J.K. (Eds.), Behavioral Neuroscience of Drug Addiction. Springer Berlin Heidelberg, Berlin, Heidelberg, pp. 3–27.

Tapert, S.F., et al., 2003. Neural response to alcohol stimuli in adolescents with alcohol use disorder. Arch. Gen. Psychiatr. 60 (7), 727–735.

Tian, X., Zhou, B., 2021. Strategies for site-specific recombination with high efficiency and precise spatiotemporal resolution. J. Biol. Chem. 296, 100509.

Tran, M.N., et al., 2021. Single-nucleus transcriptome analysis reveals cell-type-specific molecular signatures across reward circuitry in the human brain. Neuron 109 (19), 3088–3103 e5.

Trojanowski, J.Q., Gonatas, J.O., Gonatas, N.K., 1981. Conjugates of horseradish peroxidase (HRP) with cholera toxin and wheat germ agglutinin are superior to free HRP as orthogradely transported markers. Brain Res. 223 (2), 381–385.

Tye, K.M., Deisseroth, K., 2012. Optogenetic investigation of neural circuits underlying brain disease in animal models. Nat. Rev. Neurosci. 13 (4), 251–266.

Vardy, E., et al., 2015. A new DREADD facilitates the multiplexed chemogenetic interrogation of behavior. Neuron 86 (4), 936–946.

Venniro, M., et al., 2020. Improving translation of animal models of addiction and relapse by reverse translation. Nat. Rev. Neurosci. 21 (11), 625–643.

Vierock, J., et al., 2021. BiPOLES is an optogenetic tool developed for bidirectional dual-color control of neurons. Nat. Commun. 12 (1), 4527.

Volkow, N.D., Boyle, M., 2018. Neuroscience of addiction: relevance to prevention and treatment. Am. J. Psychiatr. 175 (8), 729–740.

Volkow, N.D., et al., 1990. Effects of chronic cocaine abuse on postsynaptic dopamine receptors. Am. J. Psychiatr. 147 (6), 719–724.

Volkow, N.D., et al., 2009. Imaging dopamine's role in drug abuse and addiction. Neuropharmacology 56 (Suppl. 1), 3–8.

Volkow, N.D., et al., 2018. The conception of the ABCD study: from substance use to a broad NIH collaboration. Dev. Cogn. Neurosci. 32, 4–7.

Vollmer, K.M., et al., 2021. A novel assay allowing drug self-administration, extinction, and reinstatement testing in head-restrained mice. Front. Behav. Neurosci. 15, 744715.

Wang, J., Yuan, W., Li, M.D., 2011. Genes and pathways co-associated with the exposure to multiple drugs of abuse, including alcohol, amphetamine/methamphetamine, cocaine, marijuana, morphine, and/or nicotine: a review of proteomics analyses. Mol. Neurobiol. 44 (3), 269–286.

Wei, C., et al., 2018. Response dynamics of midbrain dopamine neurons and serotonin neurons to heroin, nicotine, cocaine, and MDMA. Cell Discov. 4, 60.

Wickersham, I.R., et al., 2007. Monosynaptic restriction of transsynaptic tracing from single, genetically targeted neurons. Neuron 53 (5), 639–647.

Wilcox, C.E., Abbott, C.C., Calhoun, V.D., 2019. Alterations in resting-state functional connectivity in substance use disorders and treatment implications. Prog. Neuro-Psychopharmacol. Biol. Psychiatry 91, 79–93.

Wu, Z., Lin, D., Li, Y., 2022. Pushing the frontiers: tools for monitoring neurotransmitters and neuromodulators. Nat. Rev. Neurosci. 23 (5), 257–274.

Xia, L., et al., 2017. Dorsal-CA1 hippocampal neuronal ensembles encode nicotine-reward contextual associations. Cell Rep. 19 (10), 2143–2156.

Yizhar, O., et al., 2011. Neocortical excitation/inhibition balance in information processing and social dysfunction. Nature 477 (7363), 171–178.

Zhou, P., et al., 2018. Efficient and accurate extraction of in vivo calcium signals from microendoscopic video data. Elife 7.

CHAPTER

2

Midbrain (VTA) circuits

Marisela Morales and M. Flavia Barbano

National Institute on Drug Abuse (NIDA/NIH), Baltimore, MD, United States

The involvement of dopamine (DA) in drug addiction was proposed more than 40 years ago based on the effects that pharmacological manipulations of the DA system had on drug intake (Dackis and Gold, 1985; Yokel and Wise, 1975), and based on lesions of DA neurons within ventral tegmental area (VTA) that resulted in reduction of conditioned place preference or instrumental responding induced by psychostimulants (cocaine or methamphetamine). Subsequently, it was shown by brain microdialysis that all addictive drugs, regardless of their specific mechanisms of action and diverse pharmacological molecular targets, induce strong increases of DA release in the nucleus accumbens (NAc; Di Chiara and Imperato, 1986, 1988). Since these initial observations, clinical studies and findings from animal models have provided evidence that supports the crucial role of the VTA DA system in the development, maintenance, withdrawal and relapse phases of drug addiction (Di Chiara and Bassareo, 2007; Everitt and Robbins, 2005; Hyman et al., 2006; Koob and Volkow, 2010, 2016; Robinson and Berridge, 2008; Shultz, 2011), and converging evidence has established that NAc drug-induced DA vesicular release derives from the axons of VTA DA neurons. Regarding the distinct cellular mechanisms that account for the increase of NAc DA release associated with the intake of drugs of abuse, three cellular mechanisms have been proposed (Lüscher and Ungless, 2006), including a direct effect of drugs on the depolarization of DA neurons, as in the case of nicotine and alcohol (Gessa et al., 1985; Pidoplichko et al., 1997; Tateno and Robinson, 2011); a blockade of the DA reuptake mechanisms, as in the case of cocaine, amphetamine and ecstasy (Brodie and Dunwiddie, 1990; Colado et al., 2004; Giros et al., 1996); and a disinhibition of DA neurons induced by drug inhibition of VTA GABA neurons synapsing on DA neurons, as in the case of opioids, alcohol, cannabis, benzodiazepines and GHB (Kaupmann et al., 2003; O'Brien and White, 1987; Szabo et al., 2002; Tateno and Robinson, 2011; Vaughan et al., 1997). Each of these cellular mechanisms implicates changes in the neuronal activity of VTA DA neurons, as well as regulation of DA neurotransmission by their axon terminals that are critical for mediating drug effects on NAc neurotransmission.

While VTA DA neurons play a role in the rewarding effects of drugs of abuse (Koob and Volkow, 2010, 2016), it is widely recognized that VTA DA neurons play a more general and

Neurocircuitry of Addiction
https://doi.org/10.1016/B978-0-12-823453-2.00008-4

crucial role in motivated behaviors that are essential for animal survival. For instance, it is well established that consumption of natural rewards, such as food, water and sex, increases DA release in the NAc, especially in the case of novel, unexpected rewards (Pfaus and Phillips, 1991; Schultz et al., 1997; Yoshida et al., 1992). This increment is viewed as a reward prediction signal that reinforces the behaviors that preceded the obtention of the reward, thus, increasing the probability to repeat the same behavioral actions in the future so the reward can be obtained again (Schultz, 1998). In addition, DA release in the NAc increases the "salience" of environmental stimuli that are associated with, and predictive of the reward, and this promotes learning and optimizes behavior. Once an environmental stimulus becomes a certain predictor of reward availability, consumption of the reward no longer induces NAc DA release, but presentation of the predictive environmental cues does; in this case, the behavior can be considered as fully optimized. If resources are no longer available, the environmental stimuli become inaccurate predictors of reward availability, triggering a decrease in NAc DA release in response to the absence of the expected reward that will promote new learning about the changing conditions of the environment (Schultz, 1998). The ability to produce appropriate responses that maximize reward acquisition is evolutionarily important for fitness, reproduction, and survival. However, in the case of drugs of abuse, these homeostatic processes are disrupted due to the intrinsic pharmacological properties of drugs, which promote an elevated tone of extracellular NAc DA during both the presentation of cues associated with drug delivery and the consumption of the drug (Koob and Volkow, 2010, 2016; Volkow and Morales, 2015). Through these higher than natural drug-induced increases of DA release in the NAc, the environmental cues predicting drug delivery trigger craving for the drug concomitant with drug consumption, and will, therefore, maintain the motivation to further seek and consume the drug. These alterations in reward processing induced by drugs of abuse may explain the heightened probability of developing compulsive patterns of drug consumption when compared to patterns of natural reward consumption.

Recreational use of licit or illicit drugs is not an inevitable step towards loss of control in drug intake and chronic addiction. Indeed, only a small proportion of drug users become addicted (Anthony et al., 1994; Seedall and Anthony, 2013), a finding that has also been observed in animal models (Deroche-Gamonet et al., 2004), suggesting the existence of individual vulnerability in the transition to compulsive drug taking and to drug addiction. In this framework, addiction appears to emerge gradually and has been conceptualized as a three-stage recurring cycle (Koob and Volkow, 2010, 2016), in which the binge/intoxication stage precedes the withdrawal/negative affect stage that in turn triggers preoccupation with/anticipation of obtaining the drug. Midbrain DA neurotransmission is differentially implicated in these various stages of the addiction cycle. During early experiences with drugs of abuse, the mesolimbic DA system is activated, resulting in increases of DA release in the medial shell of the NAc, as measured by microdialysis and electrochemical technology (Fast-Scan Cyclic Voltammetry, FSCV; Di Chiara and Imperato, 1988; Phillips et al., 2003). Some early studies questioned the involvement of the mesolimbic system in mediating the rewarding effects of certain drugs of abuse. These studies showed that either lesions of VTA DA neurons by the DA neurotoxin 6-OHDA or NAc blockade of DA receptors did not prevent the acquisition of heroin self-administration in rats (Ettenberg et al., 1982; Pettit et al., 1984) and also that mice genetically deficient in DA still exhibited conditioned place preference (CPP) for morphine (Hnasko et al., 2005). In contrast with these findings, recent observations applying genetically encoded DA sensors show transient increases in NAc DA release in mice after injections of heroin (Corre et al., 2018), suggesting that opiate reinforcement is indeed supported by NAc DA neurotransmission. Drugs of abuse also increase nigrostriatal dopamine release in the dorsal striatum (Robinson and Becker, 1982; Sharp et al. 1987; Zahniser et al., 1998), which is accompanied by stereotypic behavior (Robinson and Becker, 1982; Sharp et al. 1987).

In order for a drug to support reinforced behavior, drug-induced increases in NAc DA release need to be large enough to stimulate the low-affinity DA type 1 (D1) receptors expressed in NAc medium spiny neurons (MSNs). Axons from these D1-MSNs target the VTA and mediate drug reward (Caine et al., 2007). High-affinity DA type 2 (D2) receptors are also activated by drug-induced DA release in the NAc, leading to inhibition of NAc D2-MSNs that target the ventral pallidum, which does not induce drug reward *per se* (Caine et al., 2002; Durieux et al., 2009). Drug-induced maximal increase in reinforced behavior, as measured by nose-poking or time spent in a chamber previously associated with the drug, requires concomitant activation of both D1 and D2 receptors in the NAc (Steinberg et al., 2014; Welter et al., 2007). Increases in NAc DA release must be not only of high magnitude, but they must also occur quickly in order to induce the subjective sensation of "high" after drug intake. As such, human studies using brain imaging show that stable increases in striatal dopamine achieved over 60 min fail to induce the sensation of "high", while fast increases achieved in less than 10 min do promote this "high" sensation (Volkow et al., 2008). Interestingly, occupancy of D2 receptors by DA was directly linked to the perceived "high" when humans with no prior history of drug consumption received intravenous methylphenidate (Volkow et al., 1999). In addition, fast and steep increases in striatal DA release confer incentive salient properties to previously neutral stimuli, reinforcing the learned associations between them and drugs of abuse that, in turn, creates a strong motivation to seek the drug once those stimuli are presented again.

VTA heterogenous neuronal composition

The VTA, best known for containing DA neurons, harbors a highly heterogeneous group of neurons located in the midline of the ventral mesencephalon of the midbrain (Fig. 2.1). The VTA was originally described in the opossum by Tsai in 1925 (Tsai, 1925), and it was later equated to the DA cell group referred as A10 DA neurons based on histofluorescence detection of DA and connectivity studies (Dahlstrom and Fuxe, 1964). VTA DA neurons are adjacent to DA neurons located in the substantia nigra compacta (SNC; A9 DA neurons) (Dahlstrom and Fuxe, 1964); and, while VTA DA neurons send projections to several limbic structures (for instance, the ventral striatum, also known as NAc) and medial prefrontal cortex (mPFC), the SNC DA neurons innervate the dorsal striatum (Fig. 2.1). The VTA has several nuclei, including the parabrachial pigmented nucleus, PBP; paranigral nucleus, PN; interfascicular nucleus, IF; caudal linear nucleus and CLi; rostral linear nucleus of the raphe, RLi (Oades and Halliday, 1987; Phillipson, 1979). The PBP and PN nuclei are located in the lateral and lateromedial parts of the VTA, while the CLi, RLi and IF nuclei are located in the medial aspect of the VTA (Fig. 2.2). The different nuclei within the VTA were initially characterized based mostly on DA neuronal morphology, but further anatomical, biochemical, and electrophysiological studies have shown that there is heterogeneity among VTA DA and non-DA neuron within each of these nuclei. The heterogeneity among VTA DA neurons includes the co-expression of DA transporters (DAT) or D2 receptors in DA neurons within the lateral VTA (Fig. 2.3; Li et al., 2013), which innervate the NAc, and their absence in DA

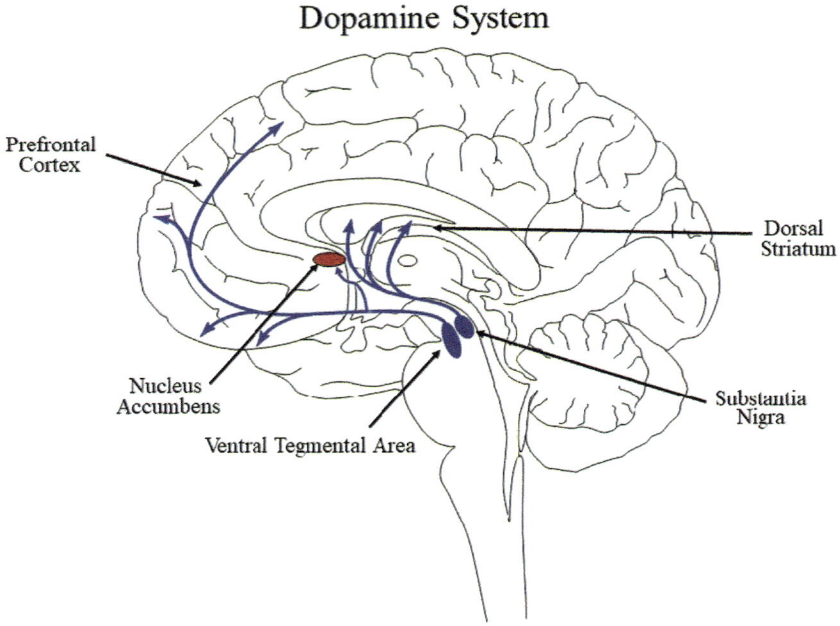

FIGURE 2.1 **Dopamine system.** Dopamine neurons (in blue) are distributed within the Ventral Tegmental Area that sends inputs to the ventral striatum (Nucleus Accumbens) and the Prefrontal Cortex, and the Substantia Nigra that sends inputs to the Dorsal Striatum.

FIGURE 2.2 **Ventral Tegmental Area subnuclei.** The Ventral Tegmental Area is divided into several subnuclei, including the parabrachial pigmented nucleus (PBP), paranigral nucleus (PN), caudal linear nucleus (CLi), interfascicular nucleus (IF), and rostral linear nucleus of the raphe (RLi, not shown). The PBN and PN are part of the lateral and lateromedial VTA, the CLi, IF and RLi are part of the medial VTA. mt, medial terminal nucleus of the accessory optic tract; SNC, substantia nigra pars compacta.

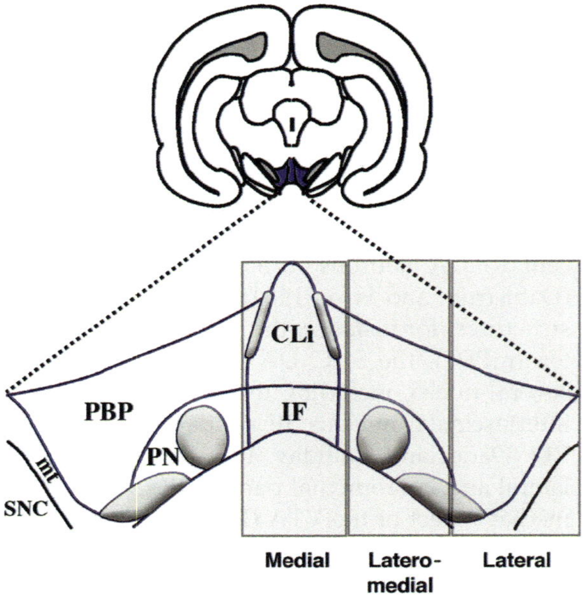

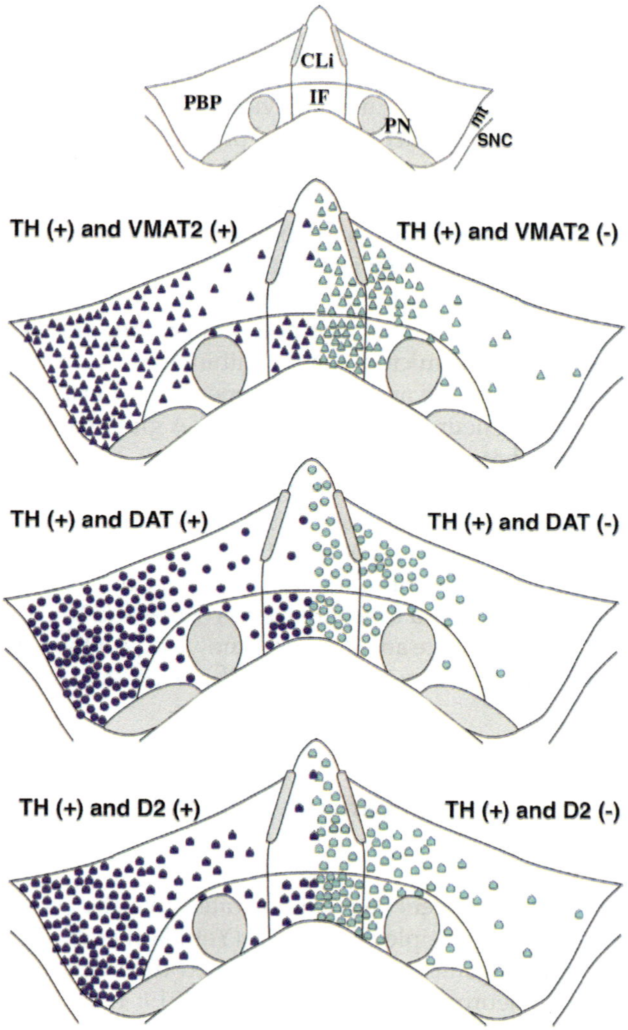

FIGURE 2.3 **Dopamine neurons expressing different levels of dopamine markers.** Latero-medial distribution of neurons expressing [indicated by (+)] tyrosine hydroxylase (TH; a marker of dopamine production) and expressing or lacking [indicated by (−)] mRNA transcripts encoding vesicular monoamine transporter 2 (VMAT2), dopamine transporters (DAT) or the dopamine D2 receptors in the rat ventral tegmental area (VTA). TH-positive neurons co-expressing mRNA for VMAT2, DAT or D2 receptors are more concentrated within the lateral aspect of the VTA. In contrast, TH-positive neurons lacking mRNA transcripts encoding VMAT2, DAT or D2 receptors are more common within the medial and lateromedial aspects of the VTA. About half of TH-positive neurons in the paranigral nucleus (PN) and interfascicular nucleus (IF), as well as most TH-positive neurons in the rostral linear nucleus of the raphe (RLi; not shown), lack mRNA encoding VMAT2, DAT or D2 receptors.

neurons within the middle portion of the VTA (Fig. 2.3; Li et al., 2013), which innervate the mPFC (Bannon and Roth, 1983; Lammel et al., 2012; Sesack and Grace, 2010). Some of the VTA DA neurons innervating the NAc have axons with micro-domains for either DA or glutamate signaling (Zhang et al., 2015). In addition, electrophysiological recordings indicate that administration of cocaine differentially activates DA neurons located in the lateral or the medial aspects of the VTA (Lammel et al., 2011). Thus, to better compare findings, extract information and reach conclusions across different studies, it is important to report where in the VTA the experiments have been performed. Based on recent findings on the molecular composition of VTA neurons, we have been proposing to delineate the VTA into 'medial' 'lateromedial' and 'lateral' (Fig. 2.2), which also roughly corresponds to the distribution of different VTA cellular phenotypes (Miranda-Barrientos et al., 2021; Mongia et al., 2019; Root et al., 2016, 2018; Yamaguchi et al., 2015).

For decades, VTA and area A10 were used in the literature as synonymous, and consequently, most early research focused on VTA DA neurons, but accumulating evidence indicates that an increasing diversity on the cellular types, cytoarchitecture, neurochemical profiles and connectivity has been shown within the VTA, and even within a same cellular type (Morales and Margolis, 2017; Lammel et al., 2014). It is now recognized that in addition to DA neurons, the VTA has gamma-amino butyric acid (GABA) and glutamate neurons, and combinatorial neurons that co-release more than one type of neurotransmitter (for a review, see Morales and Margolis, 2017), which are present in the VTA of rats, mouse, non-human primates and humans (Root et al., 2016). Among VTA neurons that co-release more than one neurotransmitter are those DA neurons that co-release glutamate from different microdomains within a common axon (Zhang et al., 2015). Different VTA neurons have unique and shared properties, for instance a recent study demonstrated that similar to VTA DA neurons, the activity of VTA glutamate neurons increases in response to rewards or the cues that predict them (Root et al., 2020). VTA GABA and glutamate neurons send long-range projections to different brain areas, but they also form local microcircuits that regulate the function of VTA DA neurons, including the regulation of firing of certain VTA neurons that innervate the NAc (Wang et al., 2015). Given that the VTA DA system is associated with specific phases of drug addiction, and that brain exposure to drugs of abuse affects this system at the molecular, structural and functional levels (Koob and Volkow, 2010, 2016; Volkow and Morales, 2015), it is crucial to have an integrated knowledge of the ways in which drugs of abuse affect the diverse neuronal pathways that regulate the DA system in general, and VTA DA neurons in particular.

VTA neuronal activity is regulated by converging inputs from multiple brain areas

Application of classical chemical neuronal tract tracers has demonstrated that the activity of neurons within the VTA is under the control of multiple brain areas (Yetnikoff et al., 2014, 2015), and combination of viral vectors and transgenic mice have facilitated the mapping of afferents that specifically target the VTA DA neurons (Beier et al., 2015, 2019; Faget el al., 2016; Menegas et al., 2015; Ogawa et al., 2014; Watabe-Uchida et al., 2012). Furthermore, the synaptic connectivity between VTA DA neurons and neurons from different brain areas has been demonstrated by the ultrastructural visualization of their synapses (by electron microscopy analysis) or by inference of the synapses by application of optogenetics in conjunction with ex vivo electrophysiology. Findings from these ultrastructural and functional studies have shown that the activation of VTA DA neurons is under the regulation of excitatory inputs from glutamatergic neurons distributed within the mPFC (Carr and Sesack, 2000), pedunculopontine tegmentum (PPTg; Charara et al., 1996), laterodorsal tegmentum nucleus (LDTg; Omelchenko and Sesack, 2005), lateral habenula (LHb; Omelchenko et al., 2009), periaqueductal gray (PAG; Omelchenko and Sesack, 2010), bed nucleus of the stria terminalis (BNST; Georges and Aston-Jones, 2001) and dorsal raphe nucleus (DRN; Qi et al., 2014). In turn, inhibition of VTA DA neurons is controlled by inhibitory inputs from GABA neurons distributed within the NAc (Bocklisch et al., 2013; Yang et al., 2018), rostromedial mesopontine tegmental nucleus (RMTg; also known as the tail of the VTA; Jhou et al., 2009; Kaufling et al., 2010), PAG (Omelchenko and Sesack, 2010), DRN (Beier et al., 2015,

2019), lateral hypothalamus (LH; Nieh et al., 2015, 2016), and ventral pallidum (VP; Hjelmstad et al., 2013). The activity of VTA DA neurons is also regulated by local GABA (Bocklisch et al., 2013; Tan et al., 2012; van Zessen et al., 2012) and glutamate (Dobi et al., 2010; Wang et al., 2015) neurons (Fig. 2.4).

Plastic changes associated with drug intake in midbrain dopamine circuits

The initial increase in NAc DA release after a single dose of several drugs of abuse (such as psychostimulants, opioids, nicotine, or alcohol) induces changes in excitatory synapses onto VTA DA neurons that outlast the presence of the drug in the body (Saal et al., 2003; Ungless et al., 2001). This phenomenon, called drug-induced synaptic plasticity, has been shown in other brain areas, as well as at GABAergic synapses (Bocklisch et al., 2013), and involves the N-methyl-D-aspartate (NMDA) receptors, α-amino-3-hydroxy-5-methyl-4-isozazolepropionic acid (AMPA) receptors and D1 receptors. Excitatory synapses in the VTA are potentiated (strengthened) by drug administration and this potentiation was originally suggested to result from the insertion of additional AMPA receptors in the neuronal membrane because the ratio of amplitude of AMPA receptor/NMDA receptor-mediated postsynaptic currents is higher than normal after drug exposure (Ungless et al., 2001). Current findings indicate that drug-induced plasticity in the VTA results from membrane insertion of calcium-permeable AMPA receptors that lack the GluA2 subunit (Bellone and Lüscher, 2006) and membrane insertion of calcium-impermeable NMDA receptors that contain the GluN3 subunit (Mameli et al., 2011; Yuan et al., 2013). Optogenetic activation of VTA DA neurons mimics drug-induced synaptic plasticity (Brown et al., 2010), indicating that strong stimulation of the mesolimbic dopamine system is sufficient to induce the membrane insertion of calcium-permeable AMPA and calcium-impermeable NMDA receptors.

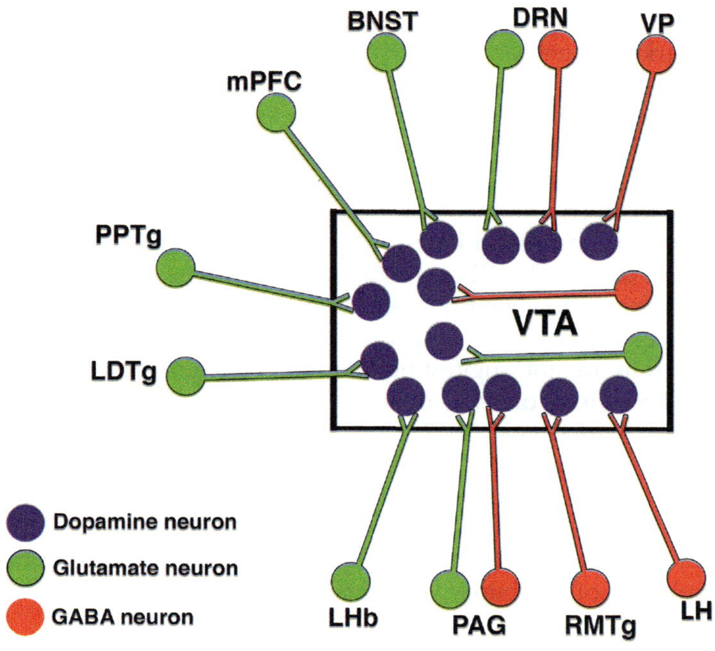

FIGURE 2.4 **Inputs to Ventral Tegmental Area dopamine neurons.** VTA DA neurons receive glutamatergic inputs from the medial prefrontal cortex (mPFC), pedunculopontine tegmentum (PPTg), laterodorsal tegmentum nucleus (LDTg), lateral habenula (LHb), periaqueductal gray (PAG), bed nucleus of the stria terminalis (BNST), and dorsal raphe nucleus (DRN). VTA DA neurons receive GABAergic inputs from the rostromedial mesopontine tegmental nucleus (RMTg; also known as the tail of the VTA), PAG, DRN, lateral hypothalamus (LH), and ventral pallidum (VP). There are also local glutamate and GABA neurons making synapses onto VTA dopamine neurons.

In general, MSN subtypes in the NAc exhibit opposite changes in synaptic plasticity in response to DA release, with long-term potentiation occurring in D1-MSNs and long-term depression occurring in D2-MSNs (Gerfen and Surmeier, 2011). Particularly, cocaine-induced synaptic plasticity is observed in excitatory afferents onto NAc MSNs, but this plasticity is delayed when compared with plasticity processes induced by cocaine in the VTA, requiring extended drug exposure to develop (Mameli et al., 2009; Thomas et al., 2001). In this case, chronic cocaine administration first induces depression of synaptic transmission that reverts to potentiation some weeks after the last administration of the drug, which, in turn, can be reduced by re-administering cocaine (Kourrich et al., 2007; Thomas et al., 2001). Cocaine-induced potentiation of excitatory synapses arising from the mPFC or the ventral hippocampus and synapsing onto D1-MSNs has been linked to cue-induced reinstatement of cocaine seeking behavior and locomotor sensitization (Pascoli et al., 2014; Terrier et al., 2016), while cocaine-induced potentiation of excitatory synapses arising from the basolateral amygdala (BLA) and synapsing onto D2-MSNs has been linked to incubation of cocaine craving (Terrier et al., 2016). In addition, synaptic plasticity induced by cocaine self-administration in D1-MSNs is similar to that observed after optogenetic self-stimulation of VTA DA neurons (Pascoli et al., 2015), suggesting that strong stimulation of VTA DA neurons resulting in high levels of NAc DA release induces synaptic plasticity in NAc MSNs.

VTA DA neurons and pathways involved in the reinforcing effects of drugs of abuse

In addition to the DA-induced plastic changes at the synaptic level demonstrated by ex vivo electrophysiology and detailed above, the role of interactions between VTA DA neurons and other brain regions in drug abuse at the circuitry level has been demonstrated by combination of anatomical, pharmacological, optogenetics, chemogenetics, behavior and in vivo neuronal recordings. Some of these interactions have been identified after observing increases of cFos (an anatomical marker for neuronal activity) in response to drugs of abuse in brain areas known to innervate the VTA.

Neurons within the ventral pallidum (VP) that project to the VTA express cFos in response to psychostimulants, such as cocaine or methamphetamine (Colussi-Mas et al., 2007; Geisler et al., 2008). Within the LH, neurons expressing the neuropeptide orexin (hypocretin) showed increased levels of cFos in response to an environment previously associated with cocaine or morphine (Harris et al., 2005; Richardson and Aston-Jones, 2012), and some of those hypothalamic neurons were shown to project to the VTA (Richardson and Aston-Jones, 2012). While VTA-projecting hypothalamic non-orexinergic neurons are heavily activated during cue-induced reinstatement of cocaine seeking behavior, as shown by enhanced cFos expression, VTA-projecting LH orexinergic neurons are not, suggesting that this particular hypothalamic subpopulation mediates the rewarding effects of drugs of abuse, but it is not involved in cue-induced reinstatement (Mahler and Aston-Jones, 2012). Acute administration of amphetamine also increases cFos expression in VTA-projecting hypothalamic neurons, irrespective of their intrinsic phenotype (Colussi-Mas et al., 2007). No significant differences in hypothalamic cFos expression are observed in mice after an acute injection of saline or nicotine (Dehkordi et al., 2017), indicating that drug-mediated activation in the LH may depend on the type of drug. Optogenetic stimulation of inhibitory afferents to VTA, such as RMTg or

NAc, reduces cFos expression in DA neurons that is correlated with a reduction in cocaine CPP (Weitz et al., 2021). High levels of cFos are observed in neurons within the RMTg and the LHb during extinction sessions or after presentation of cues that do not predict cocaine availability in rats trained to self-administer cocaine (Mahler and Aston-Jones, 2012), suggesting that both structures may mediate the suppression of cocaine-seeking behavior. In contrast, low doses of alcohol injected intraperitoneally increase cFos expression in VTA-projecting LHb neurons (Fu et al., 2017), and while both short- and long-term exposure to cocaine induced higher levels of cFos in the lateral part of the LHb, only long-term exposure induces significant increases in cFos expression in the medial LHb (Gao et al., 2018). Other brain areas that project to the VTA and that are activated by psychostimulants include the PFC, lateral septum (LS), BNST, lateral preoptic area, globus pallidus, posterior hypothalamus, PPTg and LDTg, among others (Colussi-Mas et al., 2007; Geisler et al., 2008).

As detailed above, drugs of abuse induce increases in DA release within the NAc, which results in plastic changes at the synaptic level, and several studies have been focused on the analysis of drug-induced changes within the NAc at the anatomical, molecular, and functional levels. The NAc has been broadly divided into two anatomically and functionally diverse divisions, the core and the shell (Herkenham et al., 1984), which receive differential innervation from VTA DA neurons (Lammel et al., 2008) and have distinct participation in drug-induced reinforcement. As such, NAc core mediates conditioned reinforcement for psychostimulants while NAc shell mediates their psychomotor stimulant effects (Everitt and Robbins, 2005; Parkinson et al., 1999). Unexpected presentation of stimuli associated with cocaine administration promotes DA release in the NAc core but not in the shell (Ito et al., 2000), and chronic cocaine exposure alters the DA release pattern induced by VTA electric stimulation, with a reduction in the peak of release, as well as slower release and reuptake kinetics in the core and a relative insensitivity to the stimulation range in the shell (Saddoris, 2016). Chronic administration of psychostimulants or morphine induces differential synaptic plasticity in the NAc core and shell, and this heterogeneity in the observed effects appears to be drug dependent (Jedynak et al., 2016; Madayag et al., 2019).

The central nucleus of the amygdala (CeA) is another brain area in which DA release from VTA inputs mediates the reinforcing effects of drugs of abuse. Microdialysis studies have shown that intraperitoneal injection of ethanol or co-perfusion with ethanol increases DA release in the CeA in rats (Yoshimotot et al., 2000). While blockade of D1receptors in the CeA increases cocaine self-administration in rats (Alleweireldt et al., 2006; Caine et al., 1995; McGregor and Roberts, 1993), microinjections of a D2/3 receptor agonist in the CeA reduces cocaine self-administration, as well as cue- and priming-induced reinstatement (Thiel et al., 2010); and intra-CeA blockade of D3 receptor antagonists reduces the incubation of cocaine craving in rats (Xi et al., 2013). In addition, alcohol-dependent mice and rats showed increased activation of CeA-projecting VTA neurons during withdrawal, as measured by higher levels of cFos and by higher percentage of spontaneously active neurons, suggesting involvement of the VTA-CeA pathway in alcohol dependence (Avegno et al., 2021).

The BLA plays a role in the way in which stimulus-associated information is translated into drug-seeking behavior, as shown by its involvement in cue-induced reinstatement of extinguished cocaine-seeking behavior (Meil and See, 1997). Microdialysis measurements have shown increases of DA release in the BLA after the presentation of a cocaine-associated stimulus (Weiss et al., 2000). While intra-BLA blockade of D1 receptors significantly reduces cue-induced reinstatement without affecting cocaine self-administration (See et al., 2001), intra-BLA administration of amphetamine promotes cue-induced reinstatement without affecting extinction (Ledford et al., 2003), suggesting that DA tone in the BLA potentiates the salience or motivational effects of drug-associated stimuli that is translated into enhanced drug-seeking behavior. In addition, a role of VTA dopamine release on the regulation of BLA glutamatergic neurons projecting to NAc in mediating cue-induced cocaine seeking has been demonstrated by a "pharmacological disconnection" procedure. In these disconnection studies, BLA unilateral infusion of a dopamine receptor antagonist together with NAc core contralateral infusion of an AMPA-kainate receptor antagonists prevented cue-induced cocaine seeking (Di Ciano and Everitt, 2004).

In contrast to the role of the amygdala in conditioning mediated by discrete cues, the hippocampus plays a role in conditioning mediated by contextual or spatial stimuli (Selden et al., 1991). In particular, the dorsal hippocampus participates in encoding the associations between drugs and the context in which they are taken (Kramar et al., 2014a, b) and receives sparse, yet significant, innervation from VTA DA neurons (Broussard et al., 2016; Gasbarri et al., 1994; Kramar et al., 2021). Microdialysis measurements have shown that acute administration of cocaine, alcohol, nicotine, or amphetamine increases DA release in the hippocampus (Borgkvist et al., 2012; Kalinichenko et al., 2019; Kramar et al., 2014a; Toth et al., 1992). The involvement of DA neurotransmission acting at the hippocampal level in drug addiction has been mainly studied in contextual paradigms, such as CPP, in which the rewarding effects of drugs are associated with a given context while a different context is associated with drug vehicle. Disrupting DA neurotransmission by intra-hippocampal microinjections of D1/D5 receptor antagonists immediately before training impairs cocaine-associated short- and long-term memory (Kramar et al., 2014b). In contrast, cocaine-associated long-term memory is not affected when the disruption occurs immediately or 12 h after training (Kramar et al., 2014b). In addition, blockade of D1/D5 receptors immediately before test completely abolishes the expression of cocaine CPP memory, suggesting that VTA DA is necessary for acquisition and expression of cocaine-related memories (Kramar et al., 2014b). Similar results have been found for intra-VTA morphine-induced CPP in which administration of both D1 and D2 receptor antagonists into the dorsal hippocampus impairs the acquisition of morphine CPP memory (Esmaeili et al., 2012), but only the blockade of hippocampal D2 receptors suppresses the expression of this type of memory (Haghparast et al., 2013).

The VP is another brain area that receives DA inputs from the VTA that are susceptible to be modulated by drugs of abuse. By FSCV, a differential DA release pattern in the rostral versus caudal VP was demonstrated in naïve mice, with higher release occurring in the rostral VP. This difference was selectively enhanced after chronic administration of methamphetamine, which correlated with sensitized behavior, defined as an enhanced locomotor response to additional drug administration following a period of withdrawal (Stout et al., 2016). In addition, microdialysis studies showed that systemic or intra-VP injections of cocaine increase extracellular DA levels in the VP, and that 6-OHDA lesions of DA inputs within the VP prevent the development of cocaine CPP (Gong et al., 1997). DA release in the VP is also induced by anticipation, consumption, and post-consumption of ethanol in a strain of alcohol-preferring rats (Melendez et al., 2004), indicating a role of mesopallidal DA in mediating the reinforcing properties of alcohol.

Imaging studies in humans show that methylphenidate doses within a therapeutic range induced increases in thalamic dopamine release (Montgomery et al., 2007). Moreover, people with cocaine use disorder, but not healthy controls, challenged with methylphenidate had a thalamic increased neuronal response, as measured by distribution volume and DA D2 receptor availability, which was correlated with higher craving and could be mediated by D3R

(Volkow et al., 1997). In contrast to the NAc that receives DA inputs from the VTA, the dorsal striatum that receives DA inputs from the SNC does not seem to play a role during acute intoxication with drugs of abuse, but it plays a major role in the transition between recreational controlled drug use to compulsive drug seeking and taking. In this context, blockade of DA receptors in the dorsal striatum reduces established cocaine seeking in a second-order schedule in rats (Vanderschuren et al., 2005). Moreover, studies combining intra-dorsal striatum DA receptor blockade with selective lesions of the NAc core demonstrated decreases in cocaine seeking under conditions in which the behavior was well-established (Belin and Everitt, 2008). Other studies have shown that dorsal striatum DA release is elicited by contingent presentation of cocaine-associated cues after extensive training, but it is not elicited by noncontingent presentation of these cues or by the presentation of neutral cues (Ito et al., 2002).

VTA DA neurons and withdrawal

The withdrawal/negative affect state in the addiction cycle comprises aversive motivational elements, such as dysphoria, emotional pain, stress, chronic irritability, and decreased motivation for natural rewards that arise after termination of drug use. It is believed that people with drug use disorder will continue to use drugs to mitigate these negative affective states, even though they are less sensitive to the reinforcing properties of such drugs (Volkow et al., 1997). The opponent-process theory of motivation (Solomon and Corbit, 1974) proposes that the body will produce adaptations that counteract and oppose drug effects. In this framework, the increases in NAc DA release observed after drug administration would be counteracted by decreases below basal levels when the drug is no longer available, which would result in negative emotional states. This conceptualization has been developed into the allostatic theory of addiction (Koob and Le Moal, 2001), which postulates that after repeated cycles of intoxication and withdrawal, the reward system in the brain fails to return to a normal homeostatic range and reaches instead an allostatic state through opponent processes. The allostatic state is characterized by a chronic deviation from the normal reward set point, which would promote or facilitate negative affective states, thereby leading to an increased vulnerability to relapse in response to stressors or to motivationally relevant stimuli associated with drug use.

Microdialysis studies combined with animal behavioral models have shown a decrease in the basal level of DA in the NAc during acute withdrawal for a variety of drugs, such as alcohol, nicotine, amphetamine, cocaine, morphine, and the active compound of marijuana, tetrahydrocannabinol (Hildebrand et al., 1998; Rossetti et al., 1992; Weiss et al., 1996). In addition, brain imaging techniques used in animal models identified reduced metabolic activity during withdrawal in the NAc of rats that escalate their intake during cocaine self-administration (Gozzi et al., 2011; Nicolas et al., 2017). Reduced striatal DA signaling has also been observed in mice chronically exposed to cocaine after an acute cocaine challenge (Park et al., 2013). Similar findings were found in humans by using brain imaging techniques, where the DA release by drugs was blunted by 50% in detoxified people who had previously experienced drug use disorder and by 80% in people with current drug use disorder, when compared to people without drug use disorder (Martinez et al., 2007; Volkow et al., 1997, 2007, 2014). The negative affective state induced by chronic drug use has been modeled in animals by using a taste reactivity test associated with drug administration. In this model, a sweet solution that originally elicited appetitive oromotor reactions when injected in the mouth of rats is devalued and eventually elicits aversive oromotor reactions after several pairings with administration of cocaine (Wheeler et al., 2008). The observed shift in the hedonic properties of the sweet taste is associated with reductions in DA concentrations in the NAc and indicates drug-related negative affect (Roitman et al., 2008; Wheeler et al., 2011). The participation of DA in the emergence of this negative state was further emphasized by recent findings showing that optogenetic stimulation of VTA DA inputs to the rostral part of the NAc shell, which increases DA release during the intra-oral administration of the sweet taste prevented the development of the aversive state as measured by the taste reactivity test (Hurley et al., 2017). In contrast, the same stimulation in the caudal part of the NAc shell aggravated the aversive state measured by taste reactivity, indicating that dysregulations of VTA DA release along the rostro-caudal axis of the NAc shell may promote the appearance of a dysphoric state, which could contribute to drug craving and relapse.

Another classical observation during the withdrawal/negative affect state of the addiction cycle is the increase in brain reward thresholds using animal models of intracranial self-stimulation, a measure that evaluates the sensitivity of the reward system. Such increases in brain reward thresholds have been observed after withdrawal from several drugs of abuse, and this observation is often interpreted as being indicative of an anhedonic state (Epping-Jordan et al., 1998; Markou and Koob, 1991; Schulteis et al., 1994, 1995; Wise and Munn, 1995). Similarly, people with drug use disorders have reported disruptions in the sensitivity of the reward system during withdrawal, with less intense "high" and "restlessness" sensations described after methylphenidate exposure, when compared to controls (Volkow et al., 1997). Alterations in the neurocircuits that mediate the reinforcing effects of drugs of abuse are called within-system neuroadaptations. However, brain systems that mediate stress and aversion also get dysregulated by chronic drug use, and these changes are called between-system neuroadaptations. Increases in stress and aversion are homeostatic attempts to overcome the non-physiological hyperactivation of the reward system by drugs of abuse and to restore brain normal function. In fact, withdrawal from chronic administration of most abused drugs induces a hyperactivation of stress-related systems, such as the hypothalamic-pituitary-adrenal axis or the ones mediated by corticotropin-releasing factor, noradrenaline or dynorphin (Koob, 2008; Koob and Kreek, 2007). In this regard, chronic activation of the DA system by drugs of abuse increases the expression of pro-dynorphin in the striatum of both animals and humans (Brandon and Steiner, 2003; Daunais et al., 1993; Di Benedetto et al., 2006; Hurd and Herkenham, 1993), and activation of κ-opioid receptors (KOR) by selective agonists decreases DA release in the NAc (Chefer et al., 2005; Spanagel et al., 1992). In addition, mutant mice lacking KOR show increased release of DA in the NAc after cocaine challenges, a behavioral phenotype consistent with drug sensitization (Chefer et al., 2005). A decrease in the release of DA in the striatum has also been demonstrated after administration of dynorphin in the SNC (Reid et al., 1988). Collectively, these findings suggest that chronic drug use induces an upregulation of the dynorphin/KOR system, which in turn would promote an hypodopaminergic state consistent with the motivational deficits associated with addiction.

Clinical studies have shown that, while DA increases triggered by drugs are significantly blunted in people with chronic drug use disorder (Martinez et al., 2007; Volkow et al., 1997, 2007, 2014), sensitivity to drug-associated cues is enhanced and correlates with craving (Volkow et al., 2006a, 2014). Similarly, heavy smokers showed a potentiated neuronal response to smoking-associated cues in the dorsal striatum and cortical areas when compared with neutral cues during abstinence (McClernon et al., 2009). This hypersensitivity to stimuli associated with drugs is mediated, in part, by DA release in the striatum, amygdala and hippocampus (Fotros et al., 2013; Volkow et al., 2006a, 2014) and may contribute to relapse, perpetuating the intoxication-withdrawal-relapse cycle characteristic of addiction (Koob and Volkow, 2010, 2016). Other studies have shown that chronic exposure to drugs of abuse is linked to substantial reductions of D2 receptor availability in the striatum of rodents (Park et al., 2013), non-human primates (Nader et al., 2006; Porrino et al., 2004a) and humans (Volkow et al., 1997, 2001); and this imbalance may underlie behavioral changes observed in addiction. As such, chronic administration of cocaine attenuates signaling through D1 and D2 receptors after an acute challenge with cocaine in mice, with a higher attenuation observed for D2 receptors (Park et al., 2013). In this context, signaling during the intoxication state is biased toward D1 receptors, establishing a higher D1-to-D2 receptor signaling ratio. Given that enhanced sensitivity to drug reward is mediated by D1 receptors (Caine et al., 2007), the higher D1-to-D2 receptor ratio during drug intoxication may confer increased sensitivity to craving and compulsive drug taking in people with chronic drug use disorder (Thompson et al., 2010). Based on D2 receptor occupancy observed in clinical studies, it has been proposed that this occupancy mediates the "high" sensation after drug administration in humans (Volkow et al., 1999), and thus, a decrease in D2 receptors could contribute to the perceived decrease in the reinforcing effects of drugs during withdrawal.

Several studies have provided evidence supporting the idea that low levels of D2 receptors may represent a risk factor to develop addicted traits and high levels of D2 receptors may protect against vulnerability to consume drugs. For example, studies have shown that socially-housed dominant monkeys have increased levels of D2 receptors compared to individually-housed or socially-housed subordinate monkeys, and that this is associated with lower rates of cocaine self-administration (Morgan et al., 2002). Other studies in rodents showed that impulsive rats without cocaine history had a lower than normal availability of D2/3 receptors in the NAc, which correlated with a marked propensity to escalate cocaine intake (Dalley et al., 2007). Moreover, overexpressing D2 receptors in the NAc by viral transfection reduced alcohol preference and total alcohol intake in strains of rats selectively bred to prefer and not to prefer alcohol (i.e., alcohol preferring and non-preferring rats; Thanos et al., 2001). In addition, clinical studies have shown that non-alcoholic individuals with heavy family history of alcoholism have higher than normal striatal D2 receptor expression, suggesting that D2 receptor overexpression could be a protective factor against alcoholism (Volkow et al., 2006b). Furthermore, striatal D2 receptor availability within normal ranges predicted a better treatment outcome (completed detoxification treatment without relapse) in people with methylphenidate use disorder, but a worst outcome (relapse episodes) in subjects with lower than normal striatal D2 receptor availability (Wang et al., 2012). Likewise, people with cocaine use disorder that achieved extended abstinence had higher striatal D2/3 receptor binding and DA release compared with people with cocaine use disorder that did not achieve extended abstinence (Martinez et al., 2011). As DA exerts an inhibitory effect in the indirect pathway through D2-MSNs (Gerfen and Surmeier, 2011), low striatal levels of D2 receptors would reduce DA-mediated inhibition of the indirect pathway, resulting in reduced thalamo-cortical stimulation, which, in turn, will reduce activity in PFC (Volkow and Morales, 2015). It has been proposed that the risk for compulsive drug taking associated with low levels of striatal D2 receptors may reside in this reduced PFC activity, which will prevent cortical executive control over behavior (Volkow et al., 2007; see Prefrontal Cortical Circuits chapter).

Transition to compulsion in addiction

One of the hallmarks of addiction is its compulsive nature. It has been proposed that the transition from controlled to compulsive drug taking implicates a change in the participation of striatal subregions mediating drug reward (Everitt and Robbins, 2005; Everitt et al., 2008; Lüscher et al., 2020). During initial experience with drugs, the NAc, as well as the dorsomedial striatum, a brain region mediating action-outcome learning, are engaged. However, after extensive training (or chronic use in humans), the dorsolateral striatum, a brain region mediating habit formation, becomes increasingly involved (Murray et al., 2012; Porrino et al., 2004b, 2007; Veeneman et al., 2012; Volkow et al., 2006a). Initial studies with monkeys demonstrated a downregulation of D2 receptors in the NAc after chronic administration of cocaine, which transition to the dorsal striatum as the exposure to cocaine continues (Porrino et al., 2004a). The D2 receptor decrease that initiates in the NAc and continues into the dorsal striatum depended more on the duration of exposure than on the dose of cocaine (Porrino et al., 2004a). This switch from NAc to dorsal striatal regions has been also found in rodents after chronic consumption of cocaine, heroin, or alcohol (Belin and Everitt, 2008; Giuliano et al., 2019; Hodebourg et al. 2019; Murray et al., 2012; Vanderschuren et al., 2005). A proposed anatomical base underling the transition from voluntary (goal-directed) to compulsive (habitual) drug use postulates that the switch between striatal ventromedial to dorsolateral circuits (Everitt and Robbins, 2005; Lüscher et al., 2020) relies on the cascading loop circuitry by which inputs from the NAc shell modulate VTA DA neurons, which project to the NAc core, which innervates the substantia nigra compacta, which sends DA inputs to the dorsal striatum (Haber and Knutson 2010; Haber et al., 2000).

Drug addiction and long-term memory

One of the key features of addiction is its relapsing nature, even after years of abstinence. Many drug users experience urgent, unavoidable cravings after undergoing negative emotional states, acute stress or when they are confronted with stimuli paired with drug-taking or the drug itself, making their attempts to reduce or stop drug consumption unsuccessful. This stage of addiction is believed to be mediated by activation of cortical brain regions and DA release in areas associated with emotions and memory, such as the amygdala and the hippocampus (Koob and Volkow, 2010; Robbins et al., 2008; Stewart, 2010; Wolf, 2016). The molecular mechanisms by which drug memory traces are formed involve activity-dependent processes by which synapses are strengthened (long-term potentiation or LTP) or weakened (long-term depression or LTD). LTP and LTD happen when glutamate is released by presynaptic neurons concomitantly with depolarization of the postsynaptic neurons; and they are induced by changes in the phosphorylation state or the activation of several signaling molecules, such as kinases, phosphatases, immediate early genes or proteins involved in DNA methylation or acetylation. After drug memories are acquired, they undergo a process of stabilization known as memory consolidation by which a physical representation of the memory is created in the brain. Memory consolidation can last hours or even days and it is a process that is independent of memory acquisition. It has been proposed that the mnemonic trace is formed in the hippocampus, but it later migrates to cortical areas, where it can be evoked during retrieval. However, retrieval can also occur when the mnemonic trace still resides in the hippocampus, leading to a process known as reconsolidation, where the trace becomes again labile and susceptible to manipulation (Haubrich and Nader, 2018; Izquierdo and Medina, 1997; Squire et al., 2015). Research focused on the long-term storage of drug-associated memories identified a late consolidation period (12 h after training) in which hippocampal disruption of VTA DA neurotransmission acted to extend the duration of an otherwise short-living memory, while decreased the duration of an otherwise long-living memory. This modulation appears to be mediated by VTA DA acting through D5 receptors, but not D2 receptors, and the phospholipase C signaling cascade, but not the protein kinase A signaling cascade (Kramar et al., 2014a). While heavily implicated in memory processing, the hippocampus has been historically disregarded as a brain structure playing a role in the reward circuitry, specifically the circuitry concerning drug addiction. This may be due to the hypothesis posing that VTA DA innervation of the hippocampus is too sparse to be physiologically relevant and that hippocampal DA is released by the locus coeruleus (Kempadoo et al., 2016). The controversy has yet to be resolved but recent findings using optogenetics to selectively target specific neuronal populations indicate that VTA DA neurons play a key role in modulating hippocampal function and promoting the long-term storage of memories (Kramar et al., 2021; McNamara et al., 2014; Rosen et al., 2015).

VTA dopamine neurons and relapse to seeking drugs of abuse

Relapse to drug seeking after a period of extinction or abstinence remains a key impediment to successful treatment, and accumulating evidence indicates that VTA DA neurons participate in the reinstatement of drug seeking behavior. Towards having a better understanding of the role of VTA DA neurons and their inputs and outputs in promoting drug seeking behavior in animal models and relapse in humans, several experimental approaches have been implemented. These experimental approaches have included anatomy, pharmacology, electrophysiology, molecular biology, optogenetics, chemogenetics, and human brain imaging, and have applied conditions known to lead to reinstatement following periods of abstinence: presentation of cues previously associated with drug intake, re-exposure to the drug itself (priming), and exposure to acute stress (Stewart, 2000) or context (Crombag and Shaham, 2002).

VTA DA neurons and their outputs in reinstatement to drug seeking

The role of VTA DA neurons in reinstatement of cocaine seeking behavior has been determined by studies showing that the selective chemogenetic activation of VTA DA neurons induces cocaine seeking in rats following self-administration and extinction (Mahler et al., 2019). Other studies have demonstrated that the selective inactivation of VTA DA neurons prevents reinstatement of cue-induced (Valyear et al., 2020) or context-induced (Liu et al., 2020) alcohol-seeking behavior. Recent studies have shown that the involvement of VTA DA in reinstatement of drug seeking behavior have a topographical distribution, as in vivo calcium imaging of VTA DA neurons demonstrated that reacquisition of alcohol-seeking is associated with activity in VTA DA neurons located in the medial lateral aspect of the VTA, adjacent to the SNC (Liu et al., 2020). In contrast, activity of lateral, but not medial, VTA DA neurons is associated with context-induced alcohol-seeking (Liu et al., 2020). Consistent with these observations, context-induced reinstatement of alcohol-seeking is prevented by optogenetic inhibition of lateral, but not medial VTA DA neurons, whereas reacquisition is prevented by optogenetic inhibition of either lateral or medial VTA DA neurons (Liu et al., 2020). These observations further strength the notion of great diversity among latero-medial VTA DA neurons (Morales and Margolis, 2017), indicating that while VTA DA neurons play a role in reinstatement of drug seeking, different populations of VTA DA neurons have distinct activity profiles and different causal roles in different forms of relapse.

At the circuitry level, observations based on microinjections of DA receptor antagonists or measurements of DA release had shown that VTA DA inputs contributes to reinstatement of drug-seeking by releasing DA in several brain structures, including the NAc (Bossert et al., 2007; Chaudhri et al., 2009; Phillips et al., 2003), BLA (See et al., 2001; Tran-Nguyen et al., 1998) and mPFC (Capriles et al., 2003; Lin et al., 2007; McFarland et al., 2004; See, 2009). Application of chemogenetic and optogenetic approaches has further provided evidence for the specific participation of VTA DA inputs in mediating reinstatement of drug seeking behavior by releasing DA within the NAc, mPFC or BLA. By site-specific control of DA release from VTA DA inputs, it has been established that release of DA in the NAc core induces cocaine seeking behavior, whereas the release of DA in mPFC or BLA increases cue-induced cocaine seeking behavior (Mahler et al., 2019). In addition to cocaine, DA release from VTA inputs in the NAc core mediates cue-induced alcohol seeking, whereas VTA DA inputs to NAc shell mediate context-induced alcohol seeking (Valyear et al., 2020). Furthermore, pharmacological studies have demonstrated that micro-infusions of D1 receptor antagonists into the prelimbic cortex block shock-induced cocaine seeking behavior (Capriles et al., 2003; McFarland et al., 2004). More recent studies had established that shock-triggered cocaine seeking in rats is associated with increases of cFos in VTA neurons innervating the prelimbic cortex (Vranjkovic et al., 2018), and that chemogenetic inhibition of VTA neurons projecting to the prelimbic cortex prevents shock-induced reinstatement of cocaine seeking behavior (Vranjkovic et al., 2018). These converging observations indicate that VTA DA inputs to the prelimbic cortex play a role in the reinstatement of drug seeking.

Other studies had addressed the dynamic of NAc DA release during reinstatement of drug seeking behavior (Liu et al., 2020; Phillips et al., 2003). Pioneer measurements of NAc DA release by FSCV established that the initiation of drug-seeking behavior coincides with a rapid DA signaling (transients, duration of 1–2 s; Phillips et al., 2003). In addition to FSCV, DA transients have been increasingly evaluated by photometry measurements of fluorescent signal derived from the genetically encoded DA sensor dLight (Patriarchi et al., 2018). Recent use of the DA sensor dLight has shown that context-induced reinstatement of alcohol seeking behavior is associated with increases in DA transients in medial NAc shell and NAc core, but not in lateral NAc shell (Liu et al., 2020), stressing the notion of diversity among VTA DA neurons and their projection targets (Morales and Margolis, 2017). While the use of recent developed methodology allows the measuring and manipulation of DA function in real-time during reinstatement, the combination of these emerging technologies together with well stablished methods (such as pharmacology and ultrastructural analysis) will provide important insights into how DA actions in different brain regions contribute to different aspects of relapse to drug consumption.

Inputs to VTA DA neurons and reinstatement to drug seeking

Given that the activity of VTA DA neurons is regulated by inputs from multiple brain structures (as detailed above), it is important to determine the type of inputs that, by acting on VTA DA neurons, mediate different forms of reinstatement of drug seeking behavior. In a pioneer anatomical study, a combination of detection of cFos and neuronal tract tracing identified neurons that send inputs to VTA and expressed cFos in response to cue-induced cocaine seeking (Mahler and Aston-Jones, 2012). These cFos VTA projecting neurons were found mainly in the NAc shell, VP, extended amygdala, and LS, suggesting their recruitment during cue-induced reinstatement and cocaine seeking (Mahler and Aston-Jones, 2012). Further studies had characterized the functional participation of VTA inputs from the NAc, VP and LS in reinstatement of drug-seeking behavior. **NAc inputs to VTA.** The NAc D1-MSNs provides a major GABAergic input to the VTA, and a recent study demonstrated that the GABA inhibitory input of D1-MSNs to VTA participates in the reinstatement of alcohol seeking behavior (Gibson et al., 2018). Given that context-induced reinstatement of alcohol-seeking is suppressed by either VTA optogenetic inhibition of inputs from D1-MSNs or by VTA chemogenetic excitation of local GABA neurons, it has been suggested that context-induced reinstatement of alcohol-seeking involves GABA inputs from D1-MSNs that inhibit VTA GABA neurons synapsing on VTA DA neurons (Gibson et al., 2018). **VP inputs to VTA.** VP inputs to the VTA participate in the reinstatement of cocaine (Mahler et al., 2014) or alcohol seeking (Prasad and McNally, 2020; Prasad et al., 2020). Some of these studies included the anatomical demonstration that VP projections to VTA from the rostral VP, but not from the caudal VP, induces expression of cFos during cue-induced reinstatement of cocaine seeking (Mahler et al., 2014). In addition to the observed anatomical cFos differences between rostral and caudal VP, there is a functional dissociation between them as shown by site chemogenetic experiments in which inhibition of rostral VP inputs, but not those from caudal VP, to VTA neurons blocks cue-induced cocaine seeking (Mahler et al., 2014). These observations together with findings from VTA ex vivo recordings and neuronal disconnection of VTA DA neurons suggest that cue-induced cocaine seeking involves the release of GABA from rostral VP inputs onto VTA DA and non-DA neurons (Mahler et al., 2014). Another study revealed a cell specific role of VP neurons expressing the calcium binding protein parvalbumin in the reinstatement of alcohol seeking. In this study, anatomical results showed that the induced expression of cFos within the VP population of parvalbumin neurons is associated with reinstatement of alcohol seeking. In follow-up chemogenetic functional studies, it was shown that VP parvalbumin inputs to VTA control reinstatement of alcohol-seeking behavior (Prasad et al., 2020). Collectively, these findings demonstrate that the reinstatement of drug-seeking mediated by inputs from VP to the VTA involves selective interactions between different types of VP neurons synapsing on both VTA DA and non-DA neurons. **LS inputs to VTA.** The LS is a trans-synaptic relay between the dorsal hippocampus and the VTA that plays a role in the reinstatement of cocaine seeking; and electrical stimulation of the hippocampus has been found to elicit cocaine-seeking (Vorel et al., 2001; Luo et al., 2011). Pharmacological disconnection of inputs from the LS to VTA prevents context-induced reinstatement of cocaine seeking, suggesting that hippocampal contextual information is relayed to the VTA by LS inputs (hippocampus → LS → VTA; Luo et al., 2011).

Given that the VTA DA neurons are intermixed with glutamate and GABA neurons (Morales and Margolis, 2017), including neurons that co-release glutamate and GABA (Root et la., 2014), and some of them regulate the activity of neighboring DA neurons, it is necessary to determine the extent to which local VTA GABA and glutamate neurons participate in drug addiction. For instance, emerging evidence indicates that VTA GABA neurons receiving inhibitory GABA inputs from the NAc shell promotes alcohol seeking behavior by regulating the activity of DA neurons (Gibson et al., 2018). In addition, cocaine promotes VTA DA neuronal firing by potentiation of inhibitory neurotransmission from NAc D1-expressing MSNs to VTA GABA neurons (Bocklisch et al., 2013).

Acknowledgments

This research was supported by the Intramural Research Program of the NIH, NIDA.

References

Alleweireldt, A.T., Hobbs, R.J., Taylor, A.R., Neisewander, J.L., 2006. Effects of SCH-23390 infused into the amygdala or adjacent cortex and basal ganglia on cocaine seeking and self-administration in rats. Neuropsychopharmacology 31, 363–374.

Anthony, J.C., Warner, L.A., Kessler, R.C., 1994. Comparative epidemiology of dependence on tobacco, alcohol, controlled substances, and inhalants: basic findings from the National Comorbidity Survey. Exp. Clin. Psychopharmacol. 2, 244–268.

Avegno, E.M., Kasten, C.R., Snyder 3rd, W.B., Kelley, L.K., Lobell, T.D., Templeton, T.J., Constans, M., Wills, T.A., Middleton, J.W., Gilpin, N.W., 2021. Alcohol dependence activates ventral tegmental area projections to central amygdala in male mice and rats. Addiction Biol. 16, e12990.

Bannon, M.J., Roth, R.H., 1983. Pharmacology of mesocortical dopamine neurons. Pharmacol. Rev. 35, 53–68.

Beier, K.T., Steinberg, E.E., DeLoach, K.E., Xie, S., Miyamichi, K., Schwarz, L., Gao, X.J., Kremer, E.J., Malenka, R.C., Luo, L., 2015. Circuit architecture of VTA dopamine neurons revealed by systematic input-output mapping. Cell 162, 622–634.

Beier, K.T., Gao, X.J., Xie, S., DeLoach, K.E., Malenka, R.C., Luo, L., 2019. Topological organization of ventral tegmental area connectivity revealed by viral-genetic dissection of input-output relations. Cell Rep. 26, 159–167.

Belin, D., Everitt, B.J., 2008. Cocaine seeking habits depend upon dopamine-dependent serial connectivity linking the ventral with the dorsal striatum. Neuron 57, 432–441.

Bellone, C., Lüscher, C., 2006. Cocaine triggered AMPA receptor redistribution is reversed in vivo by mGluR-dependent long-term depression. Nat. Neurosci. 9, 636–641.

Bocklisch, C., Pascoli, V., Wong, J.C., House, D.R., Yvon, C., de Roo, M., Tan, K.R., Lüscher, C., 2013. Cocaine disinhibits dopamine neurons by potentiation of GABA transmission in the ventral tegmental area. Science 341, 1521–1525.

Borgkvist, A., Malmlöf, T., Feltmann, K., Lindskog, M., Schilström, B., 2012. Dopamine in the hippocampus is cleared by the norepinephrine transporter. Int. J. Neuropsychopharmacol. 15, 531–540.

Bossert, J.M., Poles, G.C., Wihbey, K.A., Koya, E., Shaham, Y., 2007. Differential effects of blockade of dopamine D1-family receptors in nucleus accumbens core or shell on reinstatement of heroin seeking induced by contextual and discrete cues. J. Neurosci. 27, 12655–12663.

Brandon, C.L., Steiner, H., 2003. Repeated methylphenidate treatment in adolescent rats alters gene regulation in the striatum. Eur. J. Neurosci. 18, 1584–1592.

Brodie, M.S., Dunwiddie, T.V., 1990. Cocaine effects in the ventral tegmental area: evidence for an indirect dopaminergic mechanism of action. Naunyn-Schmiedebergs Arch. Pharmacol. 342, 660–665.

Broussard, J.I., Yang, K., Levine, A.T., Tsetsenis, T., Jenson, D., Cao, F., Garcia, I., Arenkiel, B.R., Zhou, F.-M., De Biasi, M., Dani, J.A., 2016. Dopamine regulates aversive contextual learning and associated in vivo synaptic plasticity in the hippocampus. Cell Rep. 14, 1930–1939.

Brown, M.T., Bellone, C., Mameli, M., Labouèbe, G., Bocklisch, C., Balland, B., Dahan, L., Luján, R., Deisseroth, K., Lüscher, C., 2010. Drug-driven AMPA receptor redistribution mimicked by selective dopamine neuron stimulation. PLoS One 5, e15870.

Caine, S.B., Heinrichs, S.C., Coffin, V.L., Koob, G.F., 1995. Effects of the dopamine D-1 antagonist SCH 23390 microinjected into the accumbens, amygdala or striatum on cocaine self-administration in the rat. Brain Res. 692, 47–56.

Caine, S.B., Negus, S.S., Mello, N.K., Patel, S., Bristow, L., Kulagowski, J., Vallone, D., Saiardi, A., Borrelli, E., 2002. Role of dopamine D2-like receptors in cocaine self-administration: studies with D2 receptor mutant mice and novel D2 receptor antagonists. J. Neurosci. 22, 2977–2988.

Caine, S.B., Thomsen, M., Gabriel, K.I., Berkowitz, J.S., Gold, L.H., Koob, G.F., Tonegawa, S., Zhang, J., Xu, M., 2007. Lack of self-administration of cocaine in dopamine D1 receptor knock-out mice. J. Neurosci. 27, 13140–13150.

Capriles, N., Rodaros, D., Sorge, R.E., Stewart, J., 2003. A role for the prefrontal cortex in stress- and cocaine-induced reinstatement of cocaine seeking in rats. Psychopharmacology 168, 66–74.

Carr, D.B., Sesack, S.R., 2000. Projections from the rat prefrontal cortex to the ventral tegmental area: target specificity in the synaptic associations with mesoaccumbens and mesocortical neurons. J. Neurosci. 20, 3864–3873.

Charara, A., Smith, Y., Parent, A., 1996. Glutamatergic inputs from the pedunculopontine nucleus to midbrain dopaminergic neurons in primates: phaseolus vulgaris-leucoagglutinin anterograde labeling combined with postembedding glutamate and GABA immunohistochemistry. J. Comp. Neurol. 364, 254–266.

Chaudhri, N., Sahuque, L.L., Janak, P.H., 2009. Ethanol seeking triggered by environmental context is attenuated by blocking dopamine D1 receptors in the nucleus accumbens core and shell in rats. Psychopharmacology 207, 303–314.

Chefer, V.I., Czyzyk, T., Bolan, E.A., Moron, J., Pintar, J.E., Shippenberg, T.S., 2005. Endogenous kappa-opioid receptor systems regulate mesoaccumbal dopamine dynamics and vulnerability to cocaine. J. Neurosci. 25, 5029–5037.

Colado, M.I., O'Shea, E., Green, A.R., 2004. Acute and long-term of MDMA on cerebral dopamine biochemistry and function. Psychopharmacology 173, 249–263.

Colussi-Mas, J., Geisler, S., Zimmer, L., Zahm, D.S., Bérod, A., 2007. Activation of afferents to the ventral tegmental area in response to acute amphetamine: a double-labelling study. Eur. J. Neurosci. 26, 1011–1025.

Corre, J., van Zessen, R., Loureiro, M., Patriarchi, T., Tian, L., Pascoli, V., Lüscher, C., 2018. Dopamine neurons projecting to medial shell of the nucleus accumbens drive heroin reinforcement. Elife 7, e39945.

Crombag, H.S., Shaham, Y., 2002. Renewal of drug seeking by contextual cues after prolonged extinction in rats. Behav. Neurosci. 116, 169–173.

Dackis, C.A., Gold, M.S., 1985. New concepts in cocaine addiction: the dopamine depletion hypothesis. Neurosci. Biobehav. Rev. 9, 469–477.

Dahlstrom, A., Fuxe, K., 1964. Evidence for the existence of monoamine containing neurons in the central nervous system. I. Demonstration of monoamines in the cell bodies of brain stem neurons. Acta Physiol. Scand. 62, 1–55.

Dalley, J.W., Fryer, T.D., Brichard, L., Robinson, E.S., Theobald, D.E., Lääne, K., Peña, Y., Murphy, E.R., Shah, Y., Probst, K., Abakumova, I., Aigbirhio, F.I., Richards, H.K., Hong, Y., Baron, J.C., Everitt, B.J., Robbins, T.W., 2007. Nucleus accumbens D2/3 receptors predict trait impulsivity and cocaine reinforcement. Science 315, 1267–1270.

Daunais, J.B., Roberts, D.C., McGinty, J.F., 1993. Cocaine self-administration increases preprodynorphin, but not c-fos, mRNA in rat striatum. Neuroreport 4, 543–546.

Dehkordi, O., Rose, J.E., Dávila-García, M.I., Millis, R.M., Mirzaei, S.A., Manaye, K.F., Jayam-Trouth, A., 2017. Neuroanatomical relationships between orexin/hypocretin-containing neurons/nerve fibers and nicotine-induced c-Fos-activated cells of the reward-addiction neurocircuitry. J. Alcohol Drug Depend 5, 273.

Deroche-Gamonet, V., Belin, D., Piazza, P.V., 2004. Evidence for addiction-like behavior in the rat. Science 305, 1014–1017.

Di Benedetto, M., D'addario, C., Candeletti, S., Romualdi, P., 2006. Chronic and acute effects of 3,4-methylenedioxy-N-methylamphetamine ("ecstasy") administration on the dynorphinergic system in the rat brain. Mol. Neurosci. 137, 187–196.

Di Chiara, G., Bassareo, V., 2007. Reward system and addiction: what dopamine does and doesn't do. Curr. Opin. Pharmacol. 7, 69–76.

Di Chiara, G., Imperato, A., 1986. Preferential stimulation of dopamine release in the nucleus accumbens by opiates, alcohol, and barbiturates: studies with transcerebral dialysis in freely moving rats. Ann. N. Y. Acad. Sci. 473, 367–381.

Di Chiara, G., Imperato, A., 1988. Drugs abused by humans preferentially increase synaptic dopamine concentrations in the mesolimbic system of freely moving rats. Proc. Natl. Acad. Sci. U.S.A. 85, 5274–5278.

Di Ciano, P., Everitt, B.J., 2004. Direct interactions between the basolateral amygdala and nucleus accumbens core underlie cocaine-seeking behavior by rats. J. Neurosci. 24, 7167–7173.

Dobi, A., Margolis, E.B., Wang, H.L., Harvey, B.K., Morales, M., 2010. Glutamatergic and nonglutamatergic neurons of the ventral tegmental area establish local synaptic contacts with dopaminergic and nondopaminergic neurons. J. Neurosci. 30, 218–229.

Durieux, P.F., Bearzatto, B., Guiducci, S., Buch, T., Waisman, A., Zoli, M., Schiffmann, S.N., de Kerchove d'Exaerde, A., 2009. D2R striatopallidal neurons inhibit both locomotor and drug reward processes. Nat. Neurosci. 12, 393–395.

Epping-Jordan, M.P., Watkins, S.S., Koob, G.F., Markou, A., 1998. Dramatic decreases in brain reward function during nicotine withdrawal. Nature 393, 76–79.

Esmaeili, M.H., Kermani, M., Parvishan, A., Haghparast, A., 2012. Role of D1/D2 dopamine receptors in the CA1 region of the rat hippocampus in the rewarding effects of morphine administered into the ventral tegmental area. Behav. Brain Res. 231, 111–115.

Ettenberg, A., Pettit, H.O., Bloom, F.E., Koob, G.F., 1982. Heroin and cocaine intravenous self-administration in rats: mediation by separate neural systems. Psychopharmacology 78, 204–209.

Everitt, B.J., Robbins, T.W., 2005. Neural systems of reinforcement for drug addiction: from actions to habits to compulsion. Nat. Neurosci. 8, 1481–1489.

Everitt, B.J., Belin, D., Economidou, D., Pelloux, Y., Dalley, J.W., Robbins, T.W., 2008. Neural mechanisms underlying the vulnerability to develop compulsive drug-seeking habits and addiction. Philos. Trans. R. Soc. Lond. B. Biol. Sci. 363 (1507), 3125–3135.

Faget, L., Osakada, F., Duan, J., Ressler, R., Johnson, A.B., Proudfoot, J.A., Yoo, J.H., Callaway, E.M., Hnasko, T.S., 2016. Afferent inputs to neurotransmitter-defined cell types in the ventral tegmental area. Cell Rep. 15, 2796–2808.

Fotros, A., Casey, K.F., Larcher, K., Verhaeghe, J.A., Cox, S.M., Gravel, P., Reader, A.J., Dagher, A., Benkelfat, C., Leyton, M., 2013. Cocaine cue-induced dopamine release in amygdala and hippocampus: a high-resolution PET [^{18}F]fallypride study in cocaine dependent participants. Neuropsychopharmacology 38, 1780–1788.

Fu, R., Mei, Q., Zuo, W., Li, J., Gregor, D., Bekker, A., Ye, J., 2017. Low-dose ethanol excites lateral habenula neurons projecting to VTA, RMTg, and raphe. Int. J. Physiol. Pathophysiol. Pharmacol. 9, 217–230.

Gao, P., Groenewegen, H.J., Vanderschuren, L.J.M.J., Voorn, P., 2018. Heterogeneous neuronal activity in the lateral habenula after short- and long-term cocaine self-administration in rats. Eur. J. Neurosci. 47, 83–94.

Gasbarri, A., Vernew, C., Innocensi, R., Campana, E., Pacitti, C., 1994. Mesolimbic dopaminergic neurons innervating the hippocampal formation in the rat: a combined retrograde tracing and immunohistochemical study. Brain Res. 668, 71–79.

Geisler, S., Marinelli, M., Degarmo, B., Becker, M.L., Freiman, A.J., Beales, M., Meredith, G.E., Zahm, D.S., 2008. Prominent activation of brainstem and pallidal afferents of the ventral tegmental area by cocaine. Neuropsychopharmacology 33, 2688–2700.

Georges, F., Aston-Jones, G., 2001. Potent regulation of midbrain dopamine neurons by the bed nucleus of the stria terminalis. J. Neurosci. 21, RC160.

Gerfen, C.R., Surmeier, D.J., 2011. Modulation of striatal projection systems by dopamine. Annu. Rev. Neurosci. 34, 441–466.

Gessa, G.L., Muntoni, F., Collu, M., Vargiu, L., Mereu, G., 1985. Low doses of ethanol activate dopaminergic neurons in the ventral tegmental area. Brain Res. 348, 201–203.

Gibson, G.D., Prasad, A.A., Jean-Richard-Dit-Bressel, P., Yau, J.O.Y., Millan, E.Z., Liu, Y., Campbell, E.J., Lim, J., Marchant, N.J., Power, J.M., Killcross, S., Lawrence, A.J., McNally, G.P., 2018. Distinct accumbens shell output pathways promote versus prevent relapse to alcohol seeking. Neuron 98, 512–520.

Giros, B., Jaber, M., Jones, S.R., Wightman, R.M., Caron, M.G., 1996. Hyperlocomotion and indifference to cocaine and amphetamine in mice lacking the dopamine transporter. Nature 379, 606–612.

Giuliano, C., Belin, D., Everitt, B.J., 2019. Compulsive alcohol seeking results from a failure to disengage dorsolateral striatal control over behavior. J. Neurosci. 39, 1744–1754.

Gong, W., Neill, D., Justice Jr., J.B., 1997. 6-Hydroxydopamine lesion of ventral pallidum blocks acquisition of place preference conditioning to cocaine. Brain Res. 754, 103–112.

Gozzi, A., Tessari, M., Dacome, L., Agosta, F., Lepore, S., Lanzoni, A., Cristofori, P., Pich, E.M., Corsi, M., Bifone, A., 2011. Neuroimaging evidence of altered fronto-cortical and striatal function after prolonged cocaine self-administration in the rat. Neuropsychopharmacology 36, 2431–2440.

Haber, S.N., Knutson, B., 2010. The reward circuit: linking primate anatomy and human imaging. Neuropsychopharmacology 35, 4–26.

Haber, S.N., Fudge, J.L., McFarland, N.R., 2000. Striatonigrostriatal pathways in primates form an ascending spiral from the shell to the dorsolateral striatum. J. Neurosci. 20, 2369–2382.

Haghparast, A., Esmaeili, M.H., Taslimi, Z., Kermani, M., Yazdi-Ravandi, S., Alizadeh, A.M., 2013. Intrahippocampal administration of D2 but not D1 dopamine receptor antagonist suppresses the expression of conditioned place preference induced by morphine in the ventral tegmental area. Neurosci. Lett. 541, 138–143.

Harris, G.C., Wimmer, M., Aston-Jones, G., 2005. A role for lateral hypothalamic orexin neurons in reward seeking. Nature 437, 556–559.

Haubrich, J., Nader, K., 2018. Memory reconsolidation. Curr. Top. Behav. Neurosci. 37, 151–176.

Herkenham, M., Edley, S.M., Stuart, J., 1984. Cell clusters in the nucleus accumbens of the rat, and the mosaic relationship of opiate receptors, acetylcholinesterase and subcortical afferent terminations. Neuroscience 11, 561–593.

Hildebrand, B.E., Nomikos, G.G., Hertel, P., Schilström, B., Svensson, T.H., 1998. Reduced dopamine output in the nucleus accumbens but not in the medial prefrontal cortex in rats displaying a mecamylamine-precipitated nicotine withdrawal syndrome. Brain Res. 779, 214–225.

Hjelmstad, G.O., Xia, Y., Margolis, E.B., Fields, H.L., 2013. Opioid modulation of ventral pallidal afferents to ventral tegmental area neurons. J. Neurosci. 33, 6454–6459.

Hnasko, T.S., Sotak, B.N., Palmiter, R.D., 2005. Morphine reward in dopamine-deficient mice. Nature 438, 854–857.

Hodebourg, R., Murray, J.E., Fouyssac, M., Puaud, M., Everitt, B.J., Belin, D., 2019. Heroin seeking becomes dependent on dorsal striatal dopaminergic mechanisms and can be decreased by N-acetylcysteine. Eur. J. Neurosci. 50, 2036–2044.

Hurd, Y.L., Herkenham, M., 1993. Molecular alterations in the neostriatum of human cocaine addicts. Synapse 13, 357–369.

Hurley, S.W., West, E.A., Carelli, R.M., 2017. Opposing roles of rapid dopamine signaling across the rostral-caudal axis of the nucleus accumbens shell in drug-induced negative affect. Biol. Psychiatr. 82, 839–846.

Hyman, S.E., Malenka, R.C., Nestler, E.J., 2006. Neural mechanisms of addiction: the role of reward-related learning and memory. Annu. Rev. Neurosci. 29, 565–598.

Ito, R., Dalley, J.W., Howes, S.R., Robbins, T.W., Everitt, B.J., 2000. Dissociation in conditioned dopamine release in the nucleus accumbens core and shell in response to cocaine cues and during cocaine-seeking behavior in rats. J. Neurosci. 20, 7489–7495.

Ito, R., Dalley, J.W., Robbins, T.W., Everitt, B.J., 2002. Dopamine release in the dorsal striatum during cocaine-seeking behavior under the control of a drug-associated cue. J. Neurosci. 22, 6247–6253.

Izquierdo, I., Medina, J.H., 1997. Memory formation: the sequence of biochemical events in the hippocampus and its connection to activity in other brain structures. Neurobiol. Learn. Mem. 68, 285–316.

Jedynak, J., Hearing, M., Ingebretson, A., Ebner, S.R., Kelly, M., Fischer, R.A., Kourrich, S., Thomas, M.J., 2016. Cocaine and amphetamine induce overlapping but distinct patterns of AMPAR plasticity in nucleus accumbens medium spiny neurons. Neuropsychopharmacology 41, 464–476.

Jhou, T.C., Fields, H.L., Baxter, M.G., Saper, C.B., Holland, P.C., 2009. The rostromedial tegmental nucleus (RMTg), a GABAergic afferent to midbrain dopamine neurons, encodes aversive stimuli and inhibits motor responses. Neuron 61, 786–800.

Kalinichenko, L.S., Hammad, L., Reichel, M., Kohl, Z., Gulbins, E., Kornhuber, J., Müller, C.P., 2019. Acid sphingomyelinase controls dopamine activity and responses to appetitive stimuli in mice. Brain Res. Bull. 146, 310–319.

Kaufling, J., Veinante, P., Pawlowski, S.A., Freund-Mercier, M.J., Barrot, M., 2010. γ-Aminobutyric acid cells with cocaine-induced ΔFosB in the ventral tegmental area innervate mesolimbic neurons. Biol. Psychiatr. 67, 88–92.

Kaupmann, K., Cryan, J.F., Wellendroph, P., Mombereau, C., Sansig, G., Klebs, K., Schmutz, M., Froestl, W., van der Putten, H., Mosbacher, J., Bräuner-Osborne, H., Waldmeier, P., Bettler, B., 2003. Specific gamma-hydroxybutyrate-binding sites but loss of pharmacological effects of gamma-hydroxybutyrate in GABA(B)(1)-deficient mice. Eur. J. Neurosci. 18, 2722–2730.

Kempadoo, K.A., Mosharov, E.V., Choi, S.J., Sulzer, D., Kandel, E.R., 2016. Dopamine release from the locus coeruleus to the dorsal hippocampus promotes spatial learning and memory. Proc. Natl. Acad. Sci. U.S.A. 113, 14835–14840.

Koob, G.F., 2008. A role for brain stress systems in addiction. Neuron 59, 11–34.

Koob, G.F., Kreek, M.J., 2007. Stress, dysregulation of drug reward pathways, and the transition to drug dependence. Am. J. Psychiatr. 164, 1149–1159.

Koob, G.F., Le Moal, M., 2001. Drug addiction, dysregulation of reward, and allostasis. Neuropsychopharmacology 24, 97–129.

Koob, G.F., Volkow, N.D., 2010. Neurocircuitry of addiction. Neuropsychopharmacology 35, 217–238.

Koob, G.F., Volkow, N.D., 2016. Neurobiology of addiction: a neurocircuitry analysis. Lancet Psychiatr. 3, 760–773.

Kourrich, S., Rothwell, P.E., Klug, J.R., Thomas, M.J., 2007. Cocaine experience controls bidirectional synaptic plasticity in the nucleus accumbens. J. Neurosci. 27, 7921–7928.

Kramar, C.P., Chefer, V.I., Wise, R.A., Medina, J.H., Barbano, M.F., 2014a. Dopamine in the dorsal hippocampus impairs the late consolidation of cocaine-associated memory. Neuropsychopharmacology 39, 1645–1653.

Kramar, C.P., Barbano, M.F., Medina, J.H., 2014b. Dopamine D1/D5 receptors in the dorsal hippocampus are required for the acquisition and expression of a single trial cocaine-associated memory. Neurobiol. Learn. Mem. 116, 172–180.

Kramar, C.P., Castillo-Díaz, F., Gigante, E.D., Medina, J.H., Barbano, M.F., 2021. The late consolidation of an aversive memory is promoted by VTA dopamine release in the dorsal hippocampus. Eur. J. Neurosci. 53, 841–851.

Lammel, S., Hetzel, A., Häckel, O., Jones, I., Liss, B., Roeper, J., 2008. Unique properties of mesoprefrontal neurons within a dual mesocorticolimbic dopamine system. Neuron 57, 760–773.

Lammel, S., Ion, D.I., Roeper, J., Malenka, R.C., 2011. Projection-specific modulation of dopamine neuron synapses by aversive and rewarding stimuli. Neuron 70, 855–862.

Lammel, S., Lim, B.K., Ran, C., Huang, K.W., Betley, M.J., Tye, K.M., Deisseroth, K., Malenka, R.C., 2012. Input-specific control of reward and aversion in the ventral tegmental area. Nature 491, 212–217.

Lammel, S., Lim, B.K., Malenka, R.C., 2014. Reward and aversion in a heterogeneous midbrain dopamine system. Neuropharmacology 76, 351–359.

Ledford, C.C., Fuchs, R.A., See, R.E., 2003. Potentiated reinstatement of cocaine-seeking behavior following D-amphetamine infusion into the basolateral amygdala. Neuropsychopharmacology 28, 1721–1729.

Li, X., Qi, J., Yamaguchi, T., Wang, H.L., Morales, M., 2013. Heterogeneous composition of dopamine neurons of the rat A10 region: molecular evidence for diverse signaling properties. Brain Struct. Funct. 218, 1159–1176.

Lin, S.K., Pan, W.H., Yeh, P.H., 2007. Prefrontal dopamine efflux during exposure to drug-associated contextual cues in rats with prior repeated methamphetamine. Brain Res. Bull. 71, 365–371.

Liu, Y., Jean-Richard-Dit-Bressel, P., Yau, J.O., Willing, A., Prasad, A.A., Power, J.M., Killcross, S., Clifford, C.W.G., McNally, G.P., 2020. The mesolimbic dopamine activity signatures of relapse to alcohol-seeking. J. Neurosci. 40, 6409–6427.

Luo, A.H., Tahsili-Fahadan, P., Wise, R.A., Lupica, C.R., Aston-Jones, G., 2011. Linking context with reward: a functional circuit from hippocampal CA3 to ventral tegmental area. Science 333, 353–357.

Lüscher, C., Ungless, M.A., 2006. The mechanistic classification of addictive drugs. PLoS Med. 3, e437.

Lüscher, C., Robbins, T.W., Everitt, B.J., 2020. The transition to compulsion in addiction. Nat. Rev. Neurosci. 21, 247–263.

Madayag, A.C., Gomez, D., Anderson, E.M., Ingebretson, A.E., Thomas, M.J., Hearing, M.C., 2019. Cell-type and region-specific nucleus accumbens AMPAR plasticity associated with morphine reward, reinstatement, and spontaneous withdrawal. Brain Struct. Funct. 224, 2311–2324.

Mahler, S.V., Aston-Jones, G.S., 2012. Fos activation of selective afferents to ventral tegmental area during cue-induced reinstatement of cocaine seeking in rats. J. Neurosci. 32, 13309–13326.

Mahler, S.V., Vazey, E.M., Beckley, J.T., Keistler, C.R., McGlinchey, E.M., Kaufling, J., Wilson, S.P., Deisseroth, K., Woodward, J.J., Aston-Jones, G., 2014. Designer receptors show role for ventral pallidum input to ventral tegmental area in cocaine seeking. Nat. Neurosci. 17, 577–585.

Mahler, S.V., Brodnik, Z.D., Cox, B.M., Buchta, W.C., Bentzley, B.S., Quintanilla, J., Cope, Z.A., Lin, E.C., Riedy, M.D., Scofield, M.D., Messinger, J., Ruiz, C.M., Riegel, A.C., España, R.A., Aston-Jones, G., 2019. Chemogenetic manipulations of ventral tegmental area dopamine neurons reveal multifaceted roles in cocaine abuse. J. Neurosci. 39, 503–518.

Mameli, M., Halbout, B., Creton, C., Engblom, D., Parkitna, J.R., Spanagel, R., Lüscher, C., 2009. Cocaine-evoked synaptic plasticity: persistence in the VTA triggers adaptations in the NAc. Nat. Neurosci. 12, 1036–1041.

Mameli, M., Bellone, C., Brown, M.T., Lüscher, C., 2011. Cocaine inverts rules for synaptic plasticity of glutamate transmission in the ventral tegmental area. Nat. Neurosci. 14, 414–416.

Markou, A., Koob, G.F., 1991. Postcocaine anhedonia. An animal model of cocaine withdrawal. Neuropsychopharmacology 4, 17–26.

Martinez, D., Narendran, R., Foltin, R.W., Slifstein, M., Hwang, D.R., Broft, A., Huang, Y., Cooper, T.B., Fischman, M.W., Kleber, H.D., Laruelle, M., 2007. Amphetamine-induced dopamine release: markedly blunted in cocaine dependence and predictive of the choice to self-administer cocaine. Am. J. Psychiatr. 164, 622–629.

Martinez, D., Carpenter, K.M., Liu, F., Slifstein, M., Broft, A., Friedman, A.C., Kumar, D., Van Heertum, R., Kleber, H.D., Nunes, E., 2011. Imaging dopamine transmission in cocaine dependence: link between neurochemistry and response to treatment. Am. J. Psychiatr. 168, 634–641.

McClernon, F.J., Kozink, R.V., Lutz, A.M., Rose, J.E., 2009. 24-h smoking abstinence potentiates fMRI-BOLD activation to smoking cues in cerebral cortex and dorsal striatum. Psychopharmacology 204, 25–35.

McFarland, K., Davidge, S.B., Lapish, C.C., Kalivas, P.W., 2004. Limbic and motor circuitry underlying footshock-induced reinstatement of cocaine-seeking behavior. J. Neurosci. 24, 1551–1560.

McGregor, A., Roberts, D.C., 1993. Dopaminergic antagonism within the nucleus accumbens or the amygdala produces differential effects on intravenous cocaine self-administration under fixed and progressive ratio schedules of reinforcement. Brain Res. 624, 245–252.

McNamara, C.G., Tejero-Cantero, A., Trouche, S., Campo-Urriza, N., Dupret, D., 2014. Dopaminergic neurons promote hippocampal reactivation and spatial memory persistence. Nat. Neurosci. 17, 1658–1660.

Meil, W.M., See, R.E., 1997. Lesions of the basolateral amygdala abolish the ability of drug associated cues to reinstate responding during withdrawal from self-administered cocaine. Behav. Brain Res. 87, 139–148.

Melendez, R.I., Rodd, Z.A., McBride, W.J., Murphy, J.M., 2004. Involvement of the mesopallidal dopamine system in ethanol reinforcement. Alcohol 32, 137–144.

Menegas, W., Bergan, J.F., Ogawa, S.K., Isogai, Y., Umadevi Venkataraju, K., Osten, P., Uchida, N., Watabe-Uchida, M., 2015. Dopamine neurons projecting to the posterior striatum form an anatomically distinct subclass. Elife 4, e10032.

Miranda-Barrientos, J., Chambers, I., Mongia, S., Liu, B., Wang, H.L., Mateo-Semidey, G.E., Margolis, E.B., Zhang, S., Morales, M., 2021. Ventral tegmental area GABA, glutamate, and glutamate-GABA neurons are heterogeneous in their electrophysiological and pharmacological properties. Eur. J. Neurosci. 54, 4061–4084. Feb 22. Epub ahead of print.

Mongia, S., Yamaguchi, T., Liu, B., Zhang, S., Wang, H., Morales, M., 2019. The ventral tegmental area has calbindin neurons with the capability to co-release glutamate and dopamine into the nucleus accumbens. Eur. J. Neurosci. 50, 3968–3984.

Montgomery, A.J., Asselin, M.C., Farde, L., Grasby, P.M., 2007. Measurement of methylphenidate-induced change in extrastriatal dopamine concentration using [11C]FLB 457 PET. J. Cerebr. Blood Flow Metabol. 27, 369–377.

Morales, M., Margolis, E.B., 2017. Ventral tegmental area: cellular heterogeneity, connectivity and behaviour. Nat. Neurosci. 18, 73–85.

Morgan, D., Grant, K.A., Gage, H.D., Mach, R.H., Kaplan, J.R., Prioleau, O., Nader, S.H., Buchheimer, N., Ehrenkaufer, R.L., Nader, M.A., 2002. Social dominance in monkeys: dopamine D2 receptors and cocaine self-administration. Nat. Neurosci. 5, 169–174.

Murray, J.E., Belin, D., Everitt, B.J., 2012. Double dissociation of the dorsomedial and dorsolateral striatal control over the acquisition and performance of cocaine seeking. Neuropsychopharmacology 37, 2456–2466.

Nader, M.A., Morgan, D., Gage, H.D., Nader, S.H., Calhoun, T.L., Buchheimer, N., Ehrenkaufer, R., Mach, R.H., 2006. PET imaging of dopamine D2 receptors during chronic cocaine self-administration in monkeys. Nat. Neurosci. 9, 1050–1056.

Nicolas, C., Tauber, C., Lepelletier, F.X., Chalon, S., Belujon, P., Galineau, L., Solinas, M., 2017. Longitudinal changes in brain metabolic activity after withdrawal from escalation of cocaine self-administration. Neuropsychopharmacology 42, 1981–1990.

Nieh, E.H., Matthews, G.A., Allsop, S.A., Presbrey, K.N., Leppla, C.A., Wichmann, R., Neve, R., Wildes, C.P., Tye, K.M., 2015. Decoding neural circuits that control compulsive sucrose seeking. Cell 160, 528–541.

Nieh, E.H., Vander Weele, C.M., Matthews, G.A., Presbrey, K.N., Wichmann, R., Leppla, C.A., Izadmehr, E.M., Tye, K.M., 2016. Inhibitory input from the lateral hypothalamus to the ventral tegmental area disinhibits dopamine neurons and promotes behavioral activation. Neuron 90, 1286–1298.

Oades, R.D., Halliday, G.M., 1987. Ventral tegmental (A10) system: neurobiology. 1. Anatomy and connectivity. Brain Res. 434, 117–165.

O'Brien, D.P., White, F.J., 1987. Inhibition of non-dopamine cells in the ventral tegmental area by benzodiazepines: relationship to A10 dopamine cell activity. Eur. J. Pharmacol. 142, 343–354.

Ogawa, S.K., Cohen, J.Y., Hwang, D., Uchida, N., Watabe-Uchida, M., 2014. Organization of monosynaptic inputs to the serotonin and dopamine neuromodulatory systems. Cell Rep. 8, 1105–1118.

Omelchenko, N., Sesack, S.R., 2005. Laterodorsal tegmental projections to identified cell populations in the rat ventral tegmental area. J. Comp. Neurol. 483, 217–235.

Omelchenko, N., Bell, R., Sesack, S.R., 2009. Lateral habenula projections to dopamine and GABA neurons in the rat ventral tegmental area. Eur. J. Neurosci. 30, 1239–1250.

Omelchenko, N., Sesack, S.R., 2010. Periaqueductal gray afferents synapse onto dopamine and GABA neurons in the rat ventral tegmental area. J. Neurosci. Res. 88, 981–991.

Park, K., Volkow, N.D., Pan, Y., Du, C., 2013. Chronic cocaine dampens dopamine signaling during cocaine intoxication and unbalances D1 over D2 receptor signaling. J. Neurosci. 33, 15827–15836.

Parkinson, J.A., Olmstead, M.C., Burns, L.H., Robbins, T.W., Everitt, B.J., 1999. Dissociation in effects of lesions of the nucleus accumbens core and shell on appetitve Pavlovian approach behavior and the potentiation of conditioned reinforcement and locomotor activity by D-amphetamine. J. Neurosci. 19, 2401–2411.

Pascoli, V., Terrier, J., Espallergues, J., Valjent, E., O'Connor, E.C., Lüscher, C., 2014. Contrasting forms of cocaine-evoked plasticity control components of relapse. Nature 509, 459–464.

Pascoli, V., Terrier, J., Hiver, A., Lüscher, C., 2015. Sufficiency of mesolimbic dopamine neuron stimulation for the progression to addiction. Neuron 88, 1054–1066.

Patriarchi, T., Cho, J.R., Merten, K., Howe, M.W., Marley, A., Xiong, W.H., Folk, R.W., Broussard, G.J., Liang, R., Jang, M.J., Zhong, H., Dombeck, D., von Zastrow, M., Nimmerjahn, A., Gradinaru, V., Williams, J.T., Tian, L., 2018. Ultrafast neuronal imaging of dopamine dynamics with designed genetically encoded sensors. Science 360, eaat4422.

Pettit, H.O., Ettenberg, A., Bloom, F.E., Koob, G.F., 1984. Destruction of dopamine in the nucleus accumbens selectively attenuates cocaine but not heroin self-administration in rats. Psychopharmacology 84, 167–173.

Pfaus, J.G., Phillips, A.G., 1991. Role of dopamine in the anticipatory and consummatory aspects of sexual behavior in the male rat. Behav. Neurosci. 105, 727–743.

Phillips, P.E., Stuber, G.D., Heien, M.L., Wightman, R.M., Carelli, R.M., 2003. Subsecond dopamine release promotes cocaine seeking. Nature 422, 614–618.

Phillipson, O.T., 1979. The cytoarchitecture of the interfascicular nucleus and ventral tegmental area of Tsai in the rat. J. Comp. Neurol. 187, 85–98.

Pidoplichko, V.I., DeBiasi, M., Williams, J.T., Dani, J.A., 1997. Nicotine activates and desensitizes midbrain dopamine neurons. Nature 390, 401–404.

Porrino, L.J., Daunais, J.B., Smith, H.R., Nader, M.A., 2004a. The expanding effects of cocaine: studies in a nonhuman primate model of cocaine self-administration. Neurosci. Biobehav. Rev. 27, 813–820.

Porrino, L.J., Lyons, D., Smith, H.R., Daunais, J.B., Nader, M.A., 2004b. Cocaine self-administration produces a progressive involvement of limbic, association, and sensorimotor striatal domains. J. Neurosci. 24, 3554–3562.

Porrino, L.J., Smith, H.R., Nader, M.A., Beveridge, T.J., 2007. The effects of cocaine: a shifting target over the course of addiction. Prog. Neuro-Psychopharmacol. Biol. Psychiatry 31, 1593–1600.

Prasad, A.A., McNally, G.P., 2020. The ventral pallidum and relapse in alcohol seeking. Br. J. Pharmacol. 177, 3855–3864.

Prasad, A.A., Xie, C., Chaichim, C., Nguyen, J.H., McClusky, H.E., Killcross, S., Power, J.M., McNally, G.P., 2020. Complementary roles for ventral pallidum cell types and their projections in relapse. J. Neurosci. 40, 880–893.

Qi, J., Zhang, S., Wang, H.L., Wang, H., de Jesus Aceves Buendia, J., Hoffman, A.F., Lupica, C.R., Seal, R.P., Morales, M., 2014. A glutamatergic reward input from the dorsal raphe to ventral tegmental area dopamine neurons. Nat. Commun. 5, 5390.

Reid, M., Herrera-Marschitz, M., Hokfelt, T., Terenius, L., Ungerstedt, U., 1988. Differential modulation of striatal dopamine release by intranigral injection of gamma-aminobutyric acid (GABA), dynorphin A and substance P. Eur. J. Pharmacol. 147, 411–420.

Richardson, K.A., Aston-Jones, G., 2012. Lateral hypothalamic orexin/hypocretin neurons that project to ventral tegmental area are differentially activated with morphine preference. J. Neurosci. 32, 3809–3817.

Robbins, T.W., Ersche, K.D., Everitt, B.J., 2008. Drug addiction and the memory systems of the brain. Ann. NY Acad. Sci. 1141, 1–21.

Robinson, T.E., Becker, J.B., 1982. Behavioral sensitization is accompanied by an enhancement in amphetamine-stimulated dopamine release from striatal tissue in vitro. Eur. J. Pharmacol. 85, 253–254.

Robinson, T.E., Berridge, K.C., 2008. The incentive sensitization theory of addiction: some current issues. Philos. Trans. R. Soc. Lond. B Biol. Sci. 363, 3137–3146.

Roitman, M.F., Wheeler, R.A., Wightman, R.M., Carelli, R.M., 2008. Real-time chemical responses in the nucleus accumbens differentiate rewarding and aversive stimuli. Nat. Neurosci. 11, 1376–1377.

Root, D.H., Mejias-Aponte, C.A., Zhang, S., Wang, H.L., Hoffman, A.F., Lupica, C.R., Morales, M., 2014. Single rodent mesohabenular axons release glutamate and GABA. Nat. Neurosci. 17, 1543–1551.

Root, D.H., Wang, H.L., Liu, B., Barker, D.J., Mód, L., Szocsics, P., Silva, A.C., Maglóczky, Z., Morales, M., 2016. Glutamate neurons are intermixed with midbrain dopamine neurons in nonhuman primates and humans. Sci. Rep. 6, 30615.

Root, D.H., Zhang, S., Barker, D.J., Miranda-Barrientos, J., Liu, B., Wang, H.L., Morales, M., 2018. Selective brain distribution and distinctive synaptic architecture of dual glutamatergic-GABAergic neurons. Cell Rep. 23, 3465–3479.

Root, D.H., Barker, D.J., Estrin, D.J., Miranda-Barrientos, J.A., Liu, B., Zhang, S., Wang, H.L., Vautier, F., Ramakrishnan, C., Kim, Y.S., Fenno, L., Deisseroth, K., Morales, M., 2020. Distinct signaling by ventral tegmental area glutamate, GABA, and combinatorial glutamate-GABA neurons in motivated behavior. Cell Rep. 32, 108094.

Rosen, Z.B., Cheung, S., Siegelbaum, S.A., 2015. Midbrain dopamine neurons bidirectionally regulate CA3-CA1 synaptic drive. Nat. Neurosci. 18, 1763–1771.

Rossetti, Z.L., Hmaidan, Y., Gessa, G.L., 1992. Marked inhibition of mesolimbic dopamine release: a common feature of ethanol, morphine, cocaine and amphetamine abstinence in rats. Eur. J. Pharmacol. 221, 227–234.

Saal, D., Dong, Y., Bonci, A., Malenka, R.C., 2003. Drugs of abuse and stress trigger a common synaptic adaptation in dopamine neurons. Neuron 37, 577–582.

Saddoris, M.P., 2016. Terminal dopamine release kinetics in the accumbens core and shell are distinctly altered after withdrawal from cocaine self-administration. eNeuro 3. ENEURO.0274-16.2016.

Schulteis, G., Markou, A., Gold, L.H., Stinus, L., Koob, G.F., 1994. Relative sensitivity to naloxone of multiple indices of opiate withdrawal: a quantitative dose-response analysis. J. Pharmacol. Exp. Therapeut. 271, 1391–1398.

Schulteis, G., Markou, A., Cole, M., Koob, G.F., 1995. Decreased brain reward produced by ethanol withdrawal. Proc. Natl. Acad. Sci. U.S.A. 92, 5880–5884.

Schultz, W., Dayan, P., Montague, P.R., 1997. A neural substrate of prediction and reward. Science 275, 1593–1599.

Schultz, W., 1998. Predictive reward signal of dopamine neurons. J. Neurophysiol. 80, 1–27.

Schultz, W., 2011. Potential vulnerabilities of neuronal reward, risk, and decision mechanisms to addictive drugs. Neuron 69, 603–617.

See, R.E., 2009. Dopamine D1 receptor antagonism in the prelimbic cortex blocks the reinstatement of heroin-seeking in an animal model of relapse. Int. J. Neuropsychopharmacol. 12, 431–436.

See, R.E., Kruzich, P.J., Grimm, J.W., 2001. Dopamine, but not glutamate, receptor blockade in the basolateral amygdala attenuates conditioned reward in a rat model of relapse to cocaine-seeking behavior. Psychopharmacology 154, 301–310.

Seedall, R.B., Anthony, J.C., 2013. Risk estimates for starting tobacco, alcohol, and other drug use in the United States: male-female differences and the possibility that 'limiting time with friends' is protective. Drug Alcohol Depend. 133, 751–753.

Selden, N.R., Everitt, B.J., Jarrard, L.E., Robbins, T.W., 1991. Complementary roles for the amygdala and hippocampus in aversive conditioning to explicit and contextual cues. Neuroscience 42, 335–350.

Sesack, S.R., Grace, A.A., 2010. Cortico-Basal Ganglia reward network: microcircuitry. Neuropsychopharmacology 35, 27–47.

Sharp, T., Zetterström, T., Ljungberg, T., Ungerstedt, U., 1987. A direct comparison of amphetamine-induced behaviours and regional brain dopamine release in the rat using intracerebral dialysis. Brain Res. 401, 322–330.

Solomon, R.L., Corbit, J.D., 1974. An opponent-process theory of motivation. I. Temporal dynamics of affect. Psychol. Rev. 81, 119–145.

Spanagel, R., Herz, A., Shippenberg, T.S., 1992. Opposing tonically active endogenous opioid systems modulate the mesolimbic dopaminergic pathway. Proc. Natl. Acad. Sci. U.S.A. 89, 2046–2050.

Squire, L.R., Genzel, L., Wixted, J.T., Morris, R.G., 2015. Memory consolidation. Cold Spring Harbor Perspect. Biol. 7 (8), a021766.

Steinberg, E.E., Boivin, J.R., Saunders, B.T., Witten, I.B., Deisseroth, K., Janak, P.H., 2014. Positive reinforcement mediated by midbrain dopamine neurons requires D1 and D2 receptor activation in the nucleus accumbens. PLoS One 9, e94771.

Stewart, J., 2000. Pathways to relapse: the neurobiology of drug- and stress-induced relapse to drug-taking. J. Psychiatr. Neurosci. 25, 125–136.

Stewart, J., 2010. The neurobiology of relapse. In: Robbins, T.W., Everitt, B.J., Nutt, D. (Eds.), The Neurobiology of Addiction: New Vistas. Oxford University Press, Oxford, pp. 61–82.

Stout, K.A., Dunn, A.R., Lohr, K.M., Alter, S.P., Cliburn, R.A., Guillot, T.S., Miller, G.W., 2016. Selective enhancement of dopamine release in the ventral pallidum of methamphetamine-sensitized mice. ACS Chem. Neurosci. 7, 1364–1373.

Szabo, B., Siemes, S., Wallmichrath, I., 2002. Inhibition of GABAergic neurotransmission in the ventral tegmental area by cannabinoids. Eur. J. Neurosci. 15, 2057–2061.

Tan, K.R., Yvon, C., Turiault, M., Mirzabekov, J.J., Doehner, J., Labouèbe, G., Deisseroth, K., Tye, K.M., Lüscher, C., 2012. GABA neurons of the VTA drive conditioned place aversion. Neuron 73, 1173–1183.

Tateno, T., Robinson, H.P.C., 2011. The mechanism of ethanol action on midbrain dopaminergic neuron firing: a dynamic-clamp study of the role of I(h) and GABAergic synaptic integration. J. Neurophysiol. 106, 1901–1922.

Terrier, J., Lüscher, C., Pascoli, V., 2016. Cell-type specific insertion of GluA2-lacking AMPARs with cocaine exposure leading to sensitization, cue-induced seeking, and incubation of craving. Neuropsychopharmacology 41, 1779–1789.

Thanos, P.K., Volkow, N.D., Freimuth, P., Umegaki, H., Ikari, H., Roth, G., Ingram, D.K., Hitzemann, R., 2001. Overexpression of dopamine D2 receptors reduces alcohol self-administration. J. Neurochem. 78, 1094–1103.

Thiel, K.J., Wenzel, J.M., Pentkowski, N.S., Hobbs, R.J., Alleweireldt, A.T., Neisewander, J.L., 2010. Stimulation of dopamine D2/D3 but not D1 receptors in the central amygdala decreases cocaine-seeking behavior. Behav. Brain Res. 214, 386–394.

Thomas, M.J., Beurrier, C., Bonci, A., Malenka, R.C., 2001. Long-term depression in the nucleus accumbens: a neural correlate of behavioral sensitization to cocaine. Nat. Neurosci. 4, 1217–1223.

Thompson, D., Martini, L., Whistler, J.L., 2010. Altered ratio of D1 and D2 dopamine receptors in mouse striatum is associated with behavioral sensitization to cocaine. PLoS One 5, e11038.

Toth, E., Sershen, H., Hashim, A., Vizi, E.S., Lajtha, A., 1992. Effect of nicotine on extracellular levels of neurotransmitters assessed by microdialysis in various brain regions: role of glutamic acid. Neurochem. Res. 17, 265–271.

Tsai, C., 1925. The optic tract and centers of the opossum, *Didelphis virginiana*. J. Comp. Neurol. 39, 173–216.

Tran-Nguyen, L.T., Fuchs, R.A., Coffey, G.P., Baker, D.A., O'Dell, L.E., Neisewander, J.L., 1998. Time-dependent changes in cocaine-seeking behavior and extracellular dopamine levels in the amygdala during cocaine withdrawal. Neuropsychopharmacology 19, 48–59.

Ungless, M.A., Whistler, J.L., Malenka, R.C., Bonci, A., 2001. Single cocaine exposure in vivo induces long-term potentiation in dopamine neurons. Nature 411, 583–587.

Valyear, M.D., Glovaci, I., Zaari, A., Lahlou, S., Trujillo-Pisanty, I., Andrew Chapman, C., Chaudhri, N., 2020. Dissociable mesolimbic dopamine circuits control responding triggered by alcohol-predictive discrete cues and contexts. Nat. Commun. 11, 3764.

Vanderschuren, L.J., Di Ciano, P., Everitt, B.J., 2005. Involvement of the dorsal striatum in cue-controlled cocaine seeking. J. Neurosci. 25, 8665–8670.

van Zessen, R., Phillips, J.L., Budygin, E.A., Stuber, G.D., 2012. Activation of VTA GABA neurons disrupts reward consumption. Neuron 73, 1184–1194.

Vaughan, C.W., Ingram, S.L., Connor, M.A., Christie, M.J., 1997. How opioids inhibit GABA-mediated neurotransmission. Nature 390, 611–614.

Veeneman, M.M., Broekhoven, M.H., Damsteegt, R., Vanderschuren, L.J., 2012. Distinct contributions of dopamine in the dorsolateral striatum and nucleus accumbens shell to the reinforcing properties of cocaine. Neuropsychopharmacology 37, 487–498.

Volkow, N.D., Morales, M., 2015. The brain on drugs: from reward to addiction. Cell 162, 712–725.

Volkow, N.D., Wang, G.J., Fowler, J.S., Logan, J., Gatley, S.J., Hitzemann, R., Chen, A.D., Dewey, S.L., Pappas, N., 1997. Decreased striatal dopaminergic responsiveness in detoxified cocaine-dependent subjects. Nature 386, 830–833.

Volkow, N.D., Wang, G.J., Fowler, J.S., Logan, J., Gatley, S.J., Wong, C., Hitzemann, R., Pappas, N.R., 1999. Reinforcing effects of psychostimulants in humans are associated with increases in brain dopamine and occupancy of D(2) receptors. J. Pharmacol. Exp. Therapeut. 291, 409–415.

Volkow, N.D., Chang, L., Wang, G.J., Fowler, J.S., Ding, Y.S., Sedler, M., Logan, J., Franceschi, D., Gatley, J., Hitzemann, R., Gifford, A., Wong, C., Pappas, N., 2001. Low level of brain dopamine D2 receptors in methamphetamine abusers: association with metabolism in the orbitofrontal cortex. Am. J. Psychiatr. 158, 2015–2021.

Volkow, N.D., Wang, G.J., Telang, F., Fowler, J.S., Logan, J., Childress, A.R., Jayne, M., Ma, Y., Wong, C., 2006a. Cocaine cues and dopamine in dorsal striatum: mechanism of craving in cocaine addiction. J. Neurosci. 26, 6583–6588.

Volkow, N.D., Wang, G.J., Begleiter, H., Porjesz, B., Fowler, J.S., Telang, F., Wong, C., Ma, Y., Logan, J., Goldstein, R., Alexoff, D., Thanos, P.K., 2006b. High levels of dopamine D2 receptors in unaffected members of alcoholic families: possible protective factors. Arch. Gen. Psychiatr. 63, 999–1008.

Volkow, N.D., Wang, G.J., Telang, F., Fowler, J.S., Logan, J., Jayne, M., Ma, Y., Pradhan, K., Wong, C., 2007. Profound decreases in dopamine release in striatum in detoxified alcoholics: possible orbitofrontal involvement. J. Neurosci. 27, 12700–12706.

Volkow, N.D., Wang, G.J., Telang, F., Fowler, J.S., Logan, J., Childress, A.R., Jayne, M., Ma, Y., Wong, C., 2008. Dopamine increases in striatum do not elicit craving in cocaine abusers unless they are coupled with cocaine cues. Neuroimage 39, 1266–1273.

Volkow, N.D., Tomasi, D., Wang, G.J., Logan, J., Alexoff, D.L., Jayne, M., Fowler, J.S., Wong, C., Yin, P., Du, C., 2014. Stimulant-induced dopamine increases are markedly blunted in active cocaine abusers. Mol. Psychiatr. 19, 1037–1043.

Vorel, S.R., Liu, X., Hayes, R.J., Spector, J.A., Gardner, E.L., 2001. Relapse to cocaine-seeking after hippocampal theta burst stimulation. Science 292, 1175–1178.

Vranjkovic, O., Van Newenhizen, E.C., Nordness, M.E., Blacktop, J.M., Urbanik, L.A., Mathy, J.C., McReynolds, J.R., Miller, A.M., Doncheck, E.M., Kloehn, T.M., Stinnett, G.S., Gerndt, C.H., Ketchesin, K.D., Baker, D.A., Seasholtz, A.F., Mantsch, J.R., 2018. Enhanced CRFR1-dependent regulation of a ventral tegmental area to prelimbic cortex projection establishes susceptibility to stress-induced cocaine seeking. J. Neurosci. 38, 10657–10671.

Wang, G.J., Smith, L., Volkow, N.D., Telang, F., Logan, J., Tomasi, D., Wong, C.T., Hoffman, W., Jayne, M., Alia-Klein, N., Thanos, P., Fowler, J.S., 2012. Decreased dopamine activity predicts relapse in methamphetamine abusers. Mol. Psychiatr. 17, 918–925.

Wang, H.L., Qi, J., Zhang, S., Wang, H., Morales, M., 2015. Rewarding effects of optical stimulation of ventral tegmental area glutamatergic neurons. J. Neurosci. 35, 15948–15954.

Watabe-Uchida, M., Zhu, L., Ogawa, S.K., Vamanrao, A., Uchida, N., 2012. Whole-brain mapping of direct inputs to midbrain dopamine neurons. Neuron 74, 858–873.

Weiss, F., Parsons, L.H., Schulteis, G., Hyytiä, P., Lorang, M.T., Bloom, F.E., Koob, G.F., 1996. Ethanol self-administration restores withdrawal-associated deficiencies in accumbal dopamine and 5-hydroxytryptamine release in dependent rats. J. Neurosci. 16, 3474–3485.

Weiss, F., Maldonado-Vlaar, C.S., Parsons, L.H., Kerr, T.M., Smith, D.L., Ben-Shahar, O., 2000. Control of cocaine-seeking behavior by drug-associated stimuli in rats: effects on recovery of extinguished operant-responding and extracellular dopamine levels in amygdala and nucleus accumbens. Proc. Natl. Acad. Sci. U.S.A. 97, 4321–4326.

Weitz, M., Khayat, A., Yaka, R., 2021. GABAergic projections to the ventral tegmental area govern cocaine-conditioned reward. Addiction Biol. 26, e13026.

Welter, M., Vallone, D., Samad, T.A., Meziane, H., Usiello, A., Borrelli, E., 2007. Absence of dopamine D2 receptors unmasks an inhibitory control over the brain circuitries activated by cocaine. Proc. Natl. Acad. Sci. USA 104, 6840–6845.

Wheeler, R.A., Twining, R.C., Jones, J.L., Slater, J.M., Grigson, P.S., Carelli, R.M., 2008. Behavioral and electrophysiological indices of negative affect predict cocaine self-administration. Neuron 57, 774–785.

Wheeler, R.A., Aragona, B.J., Fuhrmann, K.A., Jones, J.L., Day, J.J., Cacciapaglia, F., Wightman, R.M., Carelli, R.M., 2011. Cocaine cues drive opposing context-dependent shifts in reward processing and emotional state. Biol. Psychiatr. 69, 1067–1074.

Wise, R.A., Munn, E., 1995. Withdrawal from chronic amphetamine elevates baseline intracranial self-stimulation thresholds. Psychopharmacology 117, 130–136.

Wolf, M.E., 2016. Synaptic mechanisms underlying persistent cocaine craving. Nat. Rev. Neurosci. 17, 351–365.

Xi, Z.X., Li, X., Li, J., Peng, X.Q., Song, R., Gaál, J., Gardner, E.L., 2013. Blockade of dopamine D3 receptors in the nucleus accumbens and central amygdala inhibits incubation of cocaine craving in rats. Addiction Biol. 18, 665–677.

Yamaguchi, T., Qi, J., Wang, H.L., Zhang, S., Morales, M., 2015. Glutamatergic and dopaminergic neurons in the mouse ventral tegmental area. Eur. J. Neurosci. 41, 760–772.

Yang, H., de Jong, J.W., Tak, Y., Peck, J., Bateup, H.S., Lammel, S., 2018. Nucleus accumbens subnuclei regulate motivated behavior via direct inhibition and disinhibition of VTA dopamine subpopulations. Neuron 97, 434–449.

Yetnikoff, L., Lavezzi, H.N., Reichard, R.A., Zahm, D.S., 2014. An update on the connections of the ventral mesencephalic dopaminergic complex. Neuroscience 282, 23–48.

Yetnikoff, L., Cheng, A.Y., Lavezzi, H.N., Parsley, K.P., Zahm, D.S., 2015. Sources of input to the rostromedial tegmental nucleus, ventral tegmental area, and lateral habenula compared: a study in rat. J. Comp. Neurol. 523, 2426–2456.

Yokel, R.A., Wise, R.A., 1975. Increased lever pressing for amphetamine after pimozide in rats: implications for a dopamine theory of reward. Science 187, 547–549.

Yoshida, M., Yokoo, H., Mizoguchi, K., Kawahara, H., Tsuda, A., Nishikawa, T., Tanaka, M., 1992. Eating and drinking cause increased dopamine release in the nucleus accumbens and ventral tegmental area in the rat: measurements by in vivo microdyalisis. Neurosci. Lett. 139, 73–76.

Yoshimoto, K., Ueda, S., Kato, B., Takeuchi, Y., Kawai, Y., Noritake, K., Yasuhara, M., 2000. Alcohol enhances characteristic releases of dopamine and serotonin in the central nucleus of the amygdala. Neurochem. Int. 37, 369–376.

Yuan, T., Mameli, M., O'Connor, E.C., Dey, P.N., Verpelli, C., Sala, C., Perez-Otano, I., Lüscher, C., Bellone, C., 2013. Expression of cocaine-evoked synaptic plasticity by GluN3A-containing NMDA receptors. Neuron 80, 1025–1038.

Zhang, S., Qi, J., Li, X., Wang, H.L., Britt, J.P., Hoffman, A.F., Bonci, A., Lupica, C.R., Morales, M., 2015. Dopaminergic and glutamatergic microdomains in a subset of rodent mesoaccumbens axons. Nat. Neurosci. 18, 386–392.

Zahniser, N.R., Peris, J., Dwoskin, L.P., Curella, P., Yasuda, R.P., O'Keefe, L., Boyson, S.J., 1998. Sensitization to cocaine in the nigrostriatal dopamine system. NIDA Res. Monogr. 88, 55–77.

CHAPTER

3

Striatal circuits

Michael S. Patton and Brian N. Mathur

Department of Pharmacology, University of Maryland School of Medicine Baltimore, MD, United States

Introduction

The striatum is a subcortical structure that serves as the primary input nucleus of the basal ganglia. Through its diverse arrangement of afferent and efferent connections, the striatum regulates the expression of actions by integrating motor commands with cognitive, motivational, and emotional input (Haber, 2016). By merging internal value with external cues, the striatum learns which actions, and in which context, result in the acquisition of a reward and reinforces those actions to guide future reward-driven behavior. If the reward being sought is a drug of abuse, the striatum pathologically promotes actions that lead to acquisition of the substance. Consider the process of drinking a few beers after a stressful week of work. Execution of this behavior requires the selection of a motor plan motivated by an internal drive (e.g., to reduce stress) and the integration of the reward history of that motor action (e.g., drinking previously was rewarding). Once this motor program is learned, through repeated execution and reinforcement, this behavior becomes engrained in striatal circuits and can be elicited almost automatically by sensory cues in the environment—even in the face of known negative consequences (e.g., drinking previously led to poor work performance). As such, the striatum plays a fundamental role in the decisions and actions we make every day, and by extension how we define ourselves through those actions.

As an action leading to the acquisition of a drug is learned and repeatedly executed, the recurring exposure of the brain to drugs of abuse induces maladaptive neuroplastic changes to discrete striatal circuits that ultimately promotes compulsive drug use, which is a core feature of addiction. As such, striatal pathology is a core component of addiction. Therefore, it is critical to understand how drugs of abuse affect striatal circuits. In this chapter, we will discuss striatal cellular composition, anatomical subdivisions and the afferent and efferent striatal circuits that underlie specific components of action. Finally, we provide empirical evidence demonstrating that drugs of abuse, including alcohol, amphetamine, opiates, nicotine, and cocaine disrupt striatal circuitry to promote drug addiction.

https://doi.org/10.1016/B978-0-12-823453-2.00010-2

Anatomy of the striatum

The striatal complex is divided into dorsal and ventral regions. These subdivisions have distinct afferent and efferent anatomical connections and contribute to specific aspects of motivated behavior. The ventral striatum, also referred to as the nucleus accumbens, is a critical structure in the reward system, receiving dopaminergic signals from the ventral tegmental area (VTA) and providing feedback to the VTA in the form of the so-called "direct" striatal output pathway. Through these reciprocal connections, the nucleus accumbens plays an important role in the motivational drive underlying instrumental learning. The nucleus accumbens is further divided into the core and shell regions based on neurochemical staining and specific connections to limbic and cortical brain regions (Zahm, 1989). For example, the nucleus accumbens core receives excitatory input from the prelimbic prefrontal cortex (PFC) and sends inhibitory projections to the ventral pallidum, while the nucleus accumbens shell receives excitatory input from the infralimbic PFC and relays information to the VTA (Zahm and Brog, 1992). Nucleus accumbens core and shell subcomponents uniquely contribute to motivational learning: the nucleus accumbens core drives reward seeking and acquisition while the nucleus accumbens shell encodes associations between rewards and sensory cues (Rodd-Henricks et al., 2002; Sellings and Clarke, 2003).

While the nucleus accumbens provides the incentive value for goal-directed actions, the dorsal striatum encodes the motor programs that allow us to perform complex actions required for reward acquisition in complex environments. Working together, the nucleus accumbens communicates reward incentive information to the dorsal striatum to shape the expression of goal-relevant motor skills (Fig. 3.1). For example, as an action is initially learned, the nucleus accumbens recruits the involvement of dorsal striatum through recurrent connections with midbrain dopamine neurons (Haber et al., 2000). The nucleus accumbens continues to influence the dorsal striatum as a motor skill is learned and mastered, at which point the activity in the dorsal striatum eventually dominates behavioral expression (Everitt and Robbins, 2016). This concept follows an early reinforcement learning model that likens the role of the nucleus accumbens to a critic that directs an actor's actions to acquire a reward (O'Doherty et al., 2004). In addition to the shift in activity from the ventral to dorsal striatum, there is a medial to lateral shift in activity within the dorsal striatum as actions transition from initial learning to mastery (Fig. 3.1). The dorsomedial striatum (DMS), or the caudate nucleus in humans and primates, initially dominates behavioral expression and encodes motor programs that allow us to perform complex, yet reversible, actions for the acquisition of a reward. However, as an action is repeatedly executed and reinforced, the motor program is stored in the dorsolateral striatum (DLS) (putamen in humans and non-human primates) (Wolf et al., 2019; Dhawale et al., 2019) and DLS activity dominates behavioral expression (Fig. 3.1; Everitt and Robbins, 2016).

In the context of drug use, addictive substances reinforce behavior, in part, by positively modulating VTA dopamine release into the nucleus accumbens. For example, cocaine inhibits dopamine re-uptake by blocking the dopamine transporter at dopaminergic axon terminals (Kuhar et al., 1991), nicotine directly depolarizes dopamine neurons in male rats (Lüscher and Ungless, 2006), and ethanol facilitates action potential firing of VTA dopamine neurons in male rats likely through modulation of G protein-coupled inwardly-rectifying potassium

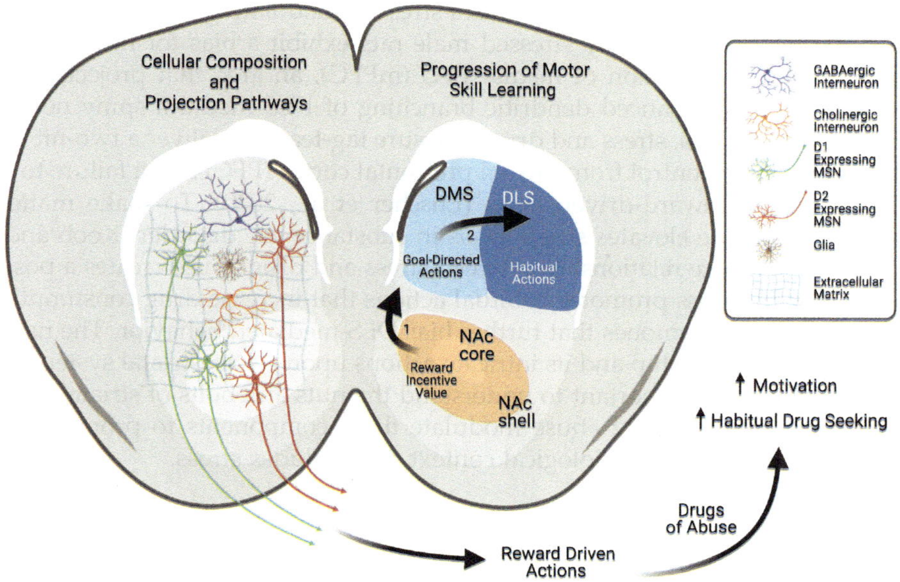

FIGURE 3.1 Cellular composition and projection pathways of the nucleus accumbens (NAc) dorsomedial striatum (DMS) and dorsolateral striatum (DLS) (left). D1 dopamine receptor-expressing medium spiny neurons (MSNs) transmit 'go' signals through the basal ganglia along the direct pathway (green). D2 dopamine receptor-expressing MSNs transmit 'no go' signals through the basal ganglia along the indirect pathway (red). The activity of striatal MSNs are locally modulated by striatal interneurons (blue, orange), glia (brown), and the dynamic regulation of the extracellular matrix. Coinciding output signals from both direct and indirect pathway MSNs enable activation of goal-directed actions and the simultaneous suppression of unwanted actions. The progression of activity in the striatum during motor skill learning (right). In the initial stages of motor skill learning, the nucleus accumbens (Nac) integrates reward information to incentivize and shape motor actions. This reward information is then relayed to the dorsal striatum (1) to produce learned goal-directed actions. Through repeated execution, motor sequences are refined to efficiently acquire reward as activity shifts from the dorsomedial to the dorsolateral striatum (2). Once mastered, these motor skills are habitually expressed with little executive oversight. Activity between these striatal subregions is highly dynamic and enables adaptive behavioral responses to sensory feedback from the environment. However, drugs of abuse impair this dynamic activity resulting in increased motivation for drug reward and an overreliance for habitual actions aimed to acquire drugs.

(GIRK) channels and hyperpolarization-activated cyclic nucleotide gated (HCN) channels (Deehan et al., 2016; Abrahao et al., 2017). In part by increasing synaptic concentrations of dopamine in the striatum, these drugs of abuse reinforce drug acquisition-related actions. Significant evidence from clinical and preclinical studies indicates that as recreational drug use transitions to addiction (i.e., alcohol and drug use disorders), there is a coinciding shift toward DLS-mediated behaviors and an increase in DLS neural activity (Lüscher et al., 2020). This bias toward DLS output (relative to DMS and ventral striatum output) indicates that chronic drug exposure alters the balance of neural activity in striatal subregions, resulting in preferential engagement of the DLS encoding habitual behaviors that support highly efficient, compulsive drug acquisition.

Compulsive drug-seeking and -taking behavior, hallmarks of substance use disorder, manifest, at least in part, by profound drug-induced adaptations to broader corticostriatal circuitry. Exacerbating this effect is the role of stress in modulating corticostriatal circuits and associated behaviors. Chronically stressed male rats exhibit a bias for habitual responding and a corresponding reduction of medial PFC (mPFC), an area that projects to the DMS, neuronal volume and enhanced dendritic branching of DLS medium spiny neurons (Dias-Ferreira et al., 2009). Thus, stress and drug exposure tag-team to deliver a two-hit blow exerting a loss of top-down control from medial prefrontal cortex (PFC) and a failure to disengage DLS circuits during reward-driven tasks (Lüscher et al., 2020). To make matters worse, repeated drug exposure elevates stress levels in substance use disorder (Koob and Volkow, 2016). Thus, the intimate relationship between stress and drug abuse creates a positive feedback loop, whereby stress promotes habitual actions that increase drug consumption, which in turn elevates stress hormones that further bias DLS-mediated behavior. The nature of this positive feedback relationship and its intricate actions upon corticostriatal systems are highly complex. Therefore, it is important to understand the nuts and bolts of striatal anatomy and physiology, and how drugs of abuse modulate these components to promote compulsive drug use within a broader physiological context that includes stress.

The striatum: cells and circuits

The striatum integrates cortical and limbic signals and relays these signals to downstream basal ganglia nuclei to guide motivated behavior. Processing this input in the striatum are multiple neuron types that are categorized into two distinct groups: the projection neurons and the interneurons. The projection neurons are the most prominent cell type and account for approximately 90–95% of the neuronal population (Haber, 2016). These projection neurons are the so-called medium spiny neurons (MSNs) that possess relatively medium-sized somata (15–20 μM) and dendrites studded with spines. MSNs are further categorized into two subpopulations based on the expression of neuropeptides, dopamine receptor subtypes, and their axonal projections that course either directly or indirectly to the output nucleus of the basal ganglia. Ultimately, these two MSN subpopulations serve distinct roles that collectively allow for proper execution of motivated behavior.

While MSNs express GABA as their primary neurotransmitter, the MSN subpopulation that forms the direct pathway contains the neuropeptides substance P and dynorphin, and preferentially expresses the D1 dopamine receptor. In contrast, the indirect pathway neurons express enkephalin and the D2 dopamine receptor (Gerfen et al., 1990; Le Moine et al., 1990, 1991; Surmeier et al., 1996; Lobo et al., 2006). D1 dopamine receptors are coupled to the $G_{\alpha s/olf}$ family of G proteins that activate adenylyl cyclase to stimulate cAMP production. cAMP production subsequently activates downstream signaling cascades through cAMP-dependent protein kinases that ultimately regulate MSN synaptic strength and gene expression (Sassone-Corsi, 2012). The D2 dopamine receptors are coupled to $G_{\alpha i/o}$ proteins that inhibit adenylyl cyclase and cAMP production, thereby also exerting effects on synaptic strength and an opposing influence on gene transcription. It is important to note that while MSNs generally fall into these two neurochemical subcategories, there is a small subpopulation of neurons that express both D1 and D2 dopamine receptors (Surmeier et al., 1996).

In the dorsal striatum, D1 dopamine receptor-expressing MSNs send axonal projections directly to the basal ganglia output nucleus, the substantia nigra pars reticulata (SNr), while

D2 dopamine receptor-expressing MSNs send their projections indirectly to the output nucleus through the globus pallidus external segment and, subsequently, the subthalamic nucleus. In the classical basal ganglia model, activation of the direct pathway inhibits the SNr to, in turn, disinhibit the thalamus, thereby activating the cortex. In contrast, indirect pathway activation leads to (indirect) activation of the SNr and, therefore, inhibition of the thalamus, leading to decreased cortical drive. Ultimately this striato-thalamo-cortical circuit results in the activation of cortical neurons that send projections along the pyramidal tract to the brainstem and spinal cord to control the muscles of the body, neck, and face. Basal ganglia output from the SNr additionally projects to the superior colliculus to influence orienting movements of the head, eyes, and body (Liu and Basso, 2008; Hikosaka 2007; Hikosaka et al., 2019; Lee and Sabatini, 2021), to the pedunculopontine nucleus to influence cholinergic neurons projecting to the cortex, thalamus, the basal ganglia, the cerebellum and spinal cord (French and Muthusamy, 2018), and to the brainstem reticular formation to affect muscle tone (Manetto and Lidsky, 1987). There is an additional pathway called the 'hyper-direct pathway' where cortical neurons bypass the striatum and project to the subthalamic nucleus (Kita, 1992). This hyper-direct pathway likely enables general inhibition of movement (Mink, 1996; Nambu et al., 2002).

Initial models of basal ganglia function proposed that the striatum is composed of a homogenous pool of projection neurons that provide a single output signal to control motor actions. While this model served as a useful neurological framework for early studies of basal ganglia disorders, closer examination of this model revealed contradictions in the predicted outcomes of specific basal ganglia manipulations (Albin et al., 1989). Upon presentation of the histochemical and fiber tracing data previously mentioned, the model was updated to include two separate subpopulations of projection neurons that are differentially regulated by dopamine (Albin et al., 1989). These two populations, as mentioned above, form the direct and indirect pathways and provide signals to initiate and suppress motor actions (Fig. 3.1; Kravitz et al., 2010). These two pathways, referred to as the "go" and "no-go" pathways, collectively coordinate the initiation of task-relevant behavior and simultaneous suppression of unwanted actions (Cui et al., 2013). One significant way in which drugs of abuse alter striatal function is by shifting the balance in activity of the go and no-go pathways to promote reward-related behavior. In the classic model, synaptic dopamine binds to and activates D1 dopamine receptor-expressing MSNs and suppresses D2 dopamine receptor-expressing MSNs through their respective G-protein signaling cascades. The net result is preferential activation of the 'go' pathway and suppression of the 'no go' pathway, which strongly biases the striatum to engage in reward-driven behavior including drug seeking and consumption. While this model is not without merit, we shall see later that the picture is much more complex than this.

In rats (Kawaguchi et al., 1990) and in monkeys (Parent et al., 1995), dorsal striatum MSNs do not exclusively send their axons to either the globus pallidus or to the substantia nigra, but rather the density of the axonal arbor is greater in one of these targets and the collaterals to the other region is sparse. For example, direct pathway neurons send the majority of their axon fibers to the substantia nigra and only sparsely innervate the globus pallidus. However, the difference in density of these projections suggests that activation of direct pathway neurons still ultimately leads to activation of thalamus and cortex, while activation of the indirect pathway neurons predominantly suppresses activity of the thalamus and cortex. Additional regulatory control of action may arise from the more sparse collateral fibers as well as collateral MSN projections within the striatum forming synapses on other MSNs and interneurons (Smith et al., 1998).

In the ventral striatum, it was originally assumed that the nucleus accumbens core exhibits a similar projection pattern, where D1 dopamine receptor-expressing MSNs project directly to the ventral tegmental area (VTA), while D2 dopamine receptor-expressing MSNs project indirectly through the ventral pallidum to the VTA. However, further investigation of these projection pathways indicates that there is considerably more convergence of D1 and D2 dopamine receptor-expressing MSNs with regard to their output projections as compared to the dorsal striatum in mice (Kupchik and Kalivas, 2017). Retrograde tracing studies demonstrate that both D1 and D2 dopamine receptor expressing nucleus accumbens MSNs project to the ventral pallidum (Lu et al., 1998). Following this study, Kupchik et al. (2015) demonstrated that ventral pallidum neurons respond to optical stimulation of both D1 and D2 dopamine receptor-expressing nucleus accumbens MSNs, though the majority of D2 dopamine receptor-expressing MSNs and only a subset of D1 dopamine receptor-expressing MSNs elicited responses. While these data indicate a significant convergence of projection fibers from D1 and D2 dopamine receptor expressing MSNs, the electrophysiology data suggests that, like the dorsal striatum, information from D1 and D2 dopamine receptor-expressing MSNs are predominately relayed through the direct and indirect pathways, respectively. Thus, conventional models of the direct and indirect pathway hold value in the nucleus accumbens. However, further investigation into the functional significance of these collateral projections will likely reveal novel regulatory actions on the expression of motivated behavior.

In the nucleus accumbens shell, there is a similar proposed projection scheme where D1 dopamine receptor-expressing MSNs of the shell project directly to VTA while D2 dopamine receptor-expressing neurons project indirectly through the ventral pallidum (Heimer et al., 1991; Scofield et al., 2016). The classical interpretation of this projection model posits that D1 dopamine receptor-expressing MSNs convey reward signals by increasing VTA-derived accumbal dopamine release, while D2 dopamine receptor-expressing MSNs encode aversion by inhibiting VTA-derived accumbal dopamine release via the indirect pathway (Soares-Cunha et al., 2019). Modulation of VTA dopamine neuron activity occurs through MSN projections onto VTA interneurons whereby direct pathway activation disinhibits VTA dopamine neurons, and indirect pathway activation inhibits VTA dopamine neurons (Xia et al., 2011). Supporting the reward/aversion model of the nucleus accumbens, Lobo et al. (2010) demonstrated that optogenetic stimulation of D1 dopamine receptor-expressing MSNs enhances cocaine-conditioned place preference in male mice, while optogenetic stimulation of D2 dopamine receptor-expressing MSNs decreases cocaine-conditioned place preference. While this study supports the notion that reward and aversion are encoded through selective activation of direct and indirect pathways, respectively, Soares-Cunha et al. (2019) demonstrated that both D1 and D2 dopamine receptor-expressing MSNs drive both reward and aversion in male and female mice depending on the pattern of neuronal stimulation. An important consideration of these data, again, is the potential interaction of MSN output pathways through their collateral inhibitory projections.

Beyond MSNs, the remaining 5%–10% of neurons in the striatal complex are interneurons and can be categorized into several subclasses by their neurochemical profiles

(Kawaguchi et al., 1995). Classically there are three distinct populations of GABAergic interneurons in the striatum: the parvalbumin expressing fast-spiking interneurons; the somatostatin/neuropeptide Y expressing low-threshold spiking interneurons; and the calretinin expressing interneurons (Tepper and Bolam, 2004). An additional subset of GABAergic interneurons, first identified in the primate brain (Dubach et al., 1987) has recently received considerable attention because of their expression of tyrosine hydroxylase (TH), the rate-limiting enzyme for the synthesis of dopamine. These striatal TH-positive interneurons do not release dopamine (Ibáñez-Sandoval et al., 2010; Xenias et al., 2015), but instead release GABA to provide widespread inhibition of both D1 and D2 dopamine receptor-expressing MSNs. The other major class of interneuron is the tonically active cholinergic interneuron. These cholinergic interneurons provide the primary source of acetylcholine in the striatum and are by far the most studied striatal interneuron population (Calabresi et al., 2000). Collectively, these interneurons shape striatal function by modulating presynaptic input to MSNs, as well as MSN output (Ding et al., 2010; Koós and Tepper, 1999).

In addition to neurons, glial cells, which are approximately three times as abundant as neurons in the brain (von Bartheld et al., 2016), play a critical role in striatal function (Khakh, 2019). While the exact role of glial cells in striatal microcircuits is only now beginning to unfold, initial studies clearly demonstrate that astrocyte function regulates striatal MSN activity and shape striatal dependent behavior. Astrocytes regulate neuronal function, in part, through fluxes in intracellular calcium at distal astrocytic processes causing release of transmitters that act on neighboring neurons (Bazargani and Atwell, 2016). For example, Yu et al. (2018) demonstrated that selectively altering astrocyte calcium influx impacts neighboring MSN activity and the expression of a repetitive motor action sequence, self-grooming, in male and female mice. This mechanism likely involves GABAergic transmission, as the effect was reversed by blocking astrocyte GABA transporter 3 (GAT-3). Notably, GABAergic communication between astrocytes and striatal MSNs is bi-directional, as Nagai et al. (2019) demonstrated that MSNs communicate with astrocytes through $GABA_B$ receptors to modulate the influx of astrocyte calcium. Selectively activating the Gi pathway in striatal astrocytes with DREADDS, thereby mimicking the signaling cascade induced by $GABA_B$ receptor activation, induces hyperactivity and attentional deficits in male and female mice.

Astrocytes additionally modulate neuronal function by regulating the concentration of extracellular glutamate through their dynamic expression of glutamate transporters (Williams et al., 2005) and cystine-glutamate exchangers (Malarkey and Parpura, 2008). In the striatum, the expression level of these astrocytic proteins significantly impacts MSN function and striatum-dependent behavior. For example, Boender et al. (2020) recently demonstrated that after repeated instrumental training, the glutamate transporter EAAT-2 is upregulated in the DLS, and that preventing this upregulation blocks habitual responding for food reward in male mice. The promotion of habitual behavior through EAAT-2 expression likely occurs through modifications in glutamatergic synaptic plasticity, as EAAT-2 function modulates spike time-dependent plasticity in the dorsal striatum (Valtcheva and Venance, 2015). Drugs of abuse, including psychostimulants and opioids disrupt astrocytic regulation of striatal glutamate resulting in shifts in striatal glutamate levels that promote addiction-like behavior (Kruyer and Kalivas, 2021). For example, chronic heroin and cocaine exposure each downregulate the expression of EAAT-2 on astrocytes in the nucleus accumbens of male rats (Roberts-Wolfe and Kalivas, 2015; Kim et al., 2018), resulting in increased synaptic glutamate spillover. Notably, this increase in nucleus accumbens glutamate promotes drug-seeking behavior (Shen et al., 2014) that can be reversed by pharmacological treatments that upregulate EAAT-2 expression in male rats (Kruyer and Kalivas, 2021). Collectively, these studies demonstrate the significant, but understudied, role that striatal glia play in drug addiction. Further research will likely broaden the depth of their contribution to include modulation of other transmitter systems, including dopamine (Fouyssac and Belin, 2019).

Lastly, the extracellular matrix, a collection of structural molecules that surround and support the branched network of neurons and glia cells is modulated by drugs of abuse to influence striatal-dependent behavior. The extracellular matrix comprises approximately 20% of the volume of the mature rat brain (Nicholson and Sykova, 1998) that in addition to providing structural support for neurons and glia, acts as a signaling domain that regulates neurotransmission, plasticity and cellular apoptosis (Barros et al., 2011). The extracellular matrix consists of two main classes of proteins: proteoglycans and fibrous proteins including laminin, collagen, elastin, and fibronectin. Communication between neurons and this extracellular matrix is bidirectional, whereby changes in the extracellular space are signaled to the neuron and changes in the internal state of the neuron can be transmitted to the extracellular matrix. For example, pharmacologically blocking neuronal activity, including action potential firing and synaptic transmission through calcium permeable AMPA receptors, dramatically decreases extracellular matrix structures *in vitro*, suggesting that extracellular matrix formation is dependent on neuronal activity (Dityatev et al., 2006). Additionally, changes in synaptic strength signal structural modifications to the extracellular matrix to enable morphological plasticity of dendritic spines (Lu et al., 2011). Communication is transmitted in part through cell adhesion molecules, which are transmembrane proteins expressed on neurons that bind to extracellular matrix glycoproteins (Shinoe and Goda, 2015). Collectively, this bidirectional communication between neurons and the extracellular matrix help to maintain neuronal homeostasis and promote dynamic synaptic transmission.

This raises the possibility that drugs of abuse may influence the extracellular matrix to alter striatal circuit function and, therefore, drug-seeking behavior. Indeed, emerging evidence indicates that drugs of abuse alter extracellular matrix proteins to influence striatal synaptic transmission in rodents (Smith et al., 2015). For example, heroin reinstatement transiently increases matrix metalloproteinase-9 activity, an enzyme that degrades the extracellular matrix, around D1 dopamine receptor-expressing MSNs in the accumbens of male and female rats (Chioma et al., 2021). Similarly, cocaine withdrawal increases nucleus accumbens matrix metalloproteinase activity, which is necessary for cocaine relapse in male rats (Smith et al., 2014). In line with these preclinical studies, RNA sequencing data from men and women diagnosed with opioid use disorder depict an enrichment of transcripts that regulate extracellular matrix signaling in the nucleus accumbens (Seney et al., 2021). Collectively, these data indicate that multiple drugs of abuse impact striatal extracellular matrix. Continued exploration of these drug-induced changes will expand our understanding of the pathophysiology of addiction and may lead to the identification of novel therapeutic targets for substance use disorder.

The striatum in action selection

So, with knowledge of these molecular, cellular and circuit components intact, what does the striatum do? The striatum integrates executive and sensorimotor information from cortical centers with ascending reinforcement signals from midbrain dopamine neurons to allow for selection of actions that result in reward. Thus, while excitatory input to the striatum informs the content of the action, dopamine input provides an action selection and vigor signal (Klaus et al., 2017). An early model of basal ganglia function posited that activation of, particularly dorsal striatal, direct pathway MSNs produces pro-kinetic effects, while activation of indirect pathway MSNs produces anti-kinetic effects (Albin et al., 1995; Nelson and Kreitzer, 2014). In support of this model, optogenetic activation of D1 dopamine receptor-expressing MSNs results in action expression, while activating D2 dopamine receptor-expressing MSNs results in action inhibition in male and female mice (Kravitz et al., 2010). This along with other data support the "rate model": that is, the striatum serves as the gas and brake pedals of the motor system whereby the degree of activation of the direct pathway concomitantly drives action, while the degree of activation of the indirect pathway concomitantly inhibits action.

However, the rate model does not fully explain how specific actions are encoded and elicited by the striatum. Addressing this, Mink (1996) and, later, Hikosaka et al. (2000) proposed a model where direct and indirect pathway MSNs are concurrently activated to initiate a specific action and simultaneously suppress unwanted actions. This model is described as the support/suppress model and gained support by advances in genetic engineering that enable simultaneous measurement of direct and indirect MSN activity during motor behavior. Using two different optical indicators specifically expressed in D1 and D2 dopamine receptor-expressing MSNs, Cui et al. (2013) revealed that both direct and indirect pathway neurons are activated in male and female mice during a given action. This discovery supports the notion that both neuron populations are necessary for the proper execution of a motor behavior. Additional evidence for the support/suppress model came from data demonstrating that ensembles of MSNs activate in male and female mice for specific components of a motor action (Klaus et al., 2017; Parker et al., 2018): for example, a neural ensemble consisting of both direct and indirect pathway MSNs encode leftward head movement while a separate MSN ensemble encode rightward head movements.

These neural ensembles likely develop as a motor behavior is learned and refined over time, as chronic striatal electrophysiology recordings in male rats reveal that MSN activity becomes more organized as a motor skill is learned (Barnes, 2005). Again, activity of both direct and indirect pathway MSNs would be required for this refinement. One can imagine that to perform a particularly refined action, such as playing a scale on a piano, the motor movements unnecessary for accurate performance of the action must be inhibited just as the motor movements necessary for the action itself must be promoted. In summary, as a motor skill is acquired, dynamic events in the striatum result in the organization of neuronal ensembles consisting of direct and indirect pathway MSNs that harmoniously activate to properly execute a motor skill. Significant changes to this balance result in overt motor impairments, exemplified by Parkinson's disease and Huntington's disease patients, but as we will discuss in the next section, changes induced by drugs of abuse selectively promote actions related to drug seeking and acquisition.

The nucleus accumbens: motivated behavior and addiction

A prominent view of the nucleus accumbens is that it serves as the pleasure center of the brain, a notion that stems from numerous studies implicating the nucleus accumbens in the acquisition of rewarding stimuli, such as food, sex, or drugs of abuse. Indeed, animals will elect to press a lever that electrically stimulates the nucleus accumbens (Mogenson, 1979). In humans, the nucleus accumbens activates in response to the presentation of rewarding stimuli, including monetary gain (Knutson et al., 2001), a pleasant taste (O'Doherty, 2004) and smiling faces (Spreckelmeyer et al., 2009). Collectively, these studies support the notion that the nucleus accumbens is simply the area of brain that encodes reward. However, this notion deviates from the original idea put forth by Mogenson, who proposed that the nucleus accumbens serves as a limbic–motor interface that integrates emotional signals from the limbic system to bias the direction and intensity of behavior to obtain a reward.

Many of these early studies describing the rewarding effects of nucleus accumbens activation led the field to believe that the nucleus accumbens is responsible for encoding positive valence, while other limbic structures, like the amygdala, are responsible for negative emotional processing. However, subsequent studies revealed that the nucleus accumbens also plays a role in aversive behavior and negative reinforcement learning (Reynolds and Berridge, 2002). This has led to an updated model of the nucleus accumbens where both rewarding and aversive information are integrated to promote an appropriate behavioral response, particularly one that reduces the likelihood of negative outcomes and increases the likelihood of positive rewards. For example, activation of D1 dopamine receptor-expressing MSNs drives reward-related behaviors while activation of D2 dopamine receptor-expressing MSNs drives aversion in male mice (Lobo et al., 2010). Further supporting this idea, inactivation of D1 dopamine receptor-expressing MSNs in the nucleus accumbens with Designer Receptors Exclusively Activated by Designer Drugs (DREADDs) prevents reward-seeking behavior in male mice (Calipari et al., 2016). These studies provide an important foundation to understand how parallel MSN circuits are influenced by drugs of abuse to, in turn, influence drug-seeking behavior.

Looking into the mechanism underlying incentivized behavior, the nucleus accumbens integrates reward signals from midbrain dopamine neurons to regulate the association of a motor action with a rewarding outcome (Dickinson and Balleine, 1994). A core associative learning type requiring this system is Pavlovian learning (also referred to as classical conditioning), which involves associating a sensory cue with the delivery of a reward. If an animal initially trained to associate a sensory cue with a reward is then trained to perform an action (e.g., a lever press) in order obtain the associated reward, the reward incentive from the original conditioned stimulus is transferred to the motor action required to receive the reward. This process is referred to as Pavlovian instrumental transfer and lesioning the nucleus accumbens in male rats significantly impairs the acquisition of this lever behavior (Balleine and Killcross, 1994; Chang et al., 2012). In other words, the nucleus accumbens encodes the reward value of an outcome and provides the incentive for an animal to perform an action in order to receive the reward.

In addition to mediating the association of cues, rewards, and the actions that elicit rewards, the nucleus accumbens also encodes information about the context in which cues are presented. This contextual information is relayed from the hippocampus fibers that project to the nucleus accumbens and will be covered in more detail later in this chapter. This reward–context association is evidenced by a commonly used behavioral paradigm that utilizes classical Pavlovian conditioning to study the rewarding effects of abused drugs called conditioned place preference (CPP). In this paradigm an animal is placed in a two-chamber arena and is administered a dose of a rewarding substance on only one side of the chamber. The animal learns that being in that side results in a reward, and given the chance to explore either side of the arena, the animal will exhibit a preference for the drug-associated side. Most drugs of abuse, including cocaine, amphetamines, nicotine, and ethanol induce a dose dependent, and sometimes species dependent, conditioned place preference (Tzschentke, 2007). In line with the role of D1 dopamine receptor-expressing MSNs, but not D2 dopamine receptor-expressing MSNs, in reward-related behavior, Cervo and Samanin (1995) demonstrated that cocaine CPP is blocked in male rats by administration of a D1 receptor antagonist, but not a D2 dopamine receptor antagonist. Additionally, nicotine CPP is prevented by blocking D1 dopamine receptors in the nucleus accumbens in male rats (Spina et al., 2006). This drug pairing is attributed to release of dopamine in the nucleus accumbens from VTA projections, as selective activation of these dopaminergic terminals enhances conditioned place preference for morphine in male mice (Koo et al., 2012). These studies demonstrate that drugs of abuse result in preferential activation of D1 dopamine receptor-expressing MSNs in the nucleus accumbens and that this activation underlies reward-related behavior.

The cyclical nature of repeated drug use and withdrawal activates the brain's stress response system, which in turn impacts how the nucleus accumbens encodes reward/aversion. For example, Lemos et al. (2012) demonstrated that corticotropin-releasing factor (CRF), a neuropeptide released in response to arousing environmental stimuli and stress, acutely enhances dopamine release in the nucleus accumbens to promote reward-cue associations, as measured by CPP. This enhanced dopamine release is mediated by CRF activating cholinergic interneurons through the CRF type 1 receptors, which increases their firing rate of cholinergic interneurons (Lemos et al., 2019). The resulting release of acetylcholine activates local type 5 muscarinic acetylcholine receptors in the nucleus accumbens that is necessary for the enhanced dopamine release induced by CRF (Lemos et al., 2019). However, chronic stress, which elevates CRF levels in the nucleus accumbens (Zorilla et al. 2014) prevents acute CRF-mediated potentiation of dopamine release and diminishes CRF-induced CPP in male mice (Lemos et al., 2012). This stress induced transition from reward signaling to aversion likely underlies the negative affective state seen in substance use disorder that promotes drug seeking and consumption aimed at alleviating negative affective symptoms of drug withdrawal (Zorilla et al., 2014).

As mentioned above, the nucleus accumbens can be divided into core and shell regions based on neurochemical staining, connections to limbic and cortical structures, and their role in distinct components of motivated behavior (Zahm,1989). The nucleus accumbens core, which comprises the population of MSNs closely encompassing the anterior commissure, receives more dense projections from prelimbic, anterior cingulate, and insular cortices. On the other hand, the shell, which surrounds the core, receives projections from infralimbic prefrontal cortex and piriform cortex (Zahm and Brog, 1992). Evidence of behavioral distinctions between these sub-compartments come from site-specific lesion studies (Corbit et al., 2001) and site-specific intracranial self-administration studies (Rodd-Henricks et al., 2002; Engleman et al., 2009). For example, female rats will self-administer cocaine or ethanol directly into the accumbens shell, but not the accumbens core (Rodd-Henricks et al., 2002; Engleman et al., 2009). Additionally, lesions to the nucleus accumbens shell produce a deficit in stimulus-guided action selection in female rats (Corbit et al., 2001), which taken together with the self-administration studies demonstrates its role in cue–reward associations. In contrast, lesions to the nucleus accumbens core, but not the shell, reduce the acquisition rate of lever-pressing behavior, indicating its role in reward acquisition (Corbit et al., 2001). The division between the nucleus accumbens core and shell is further characterized by the expression of distinct classes of opioid receptors, where the core predominately expresses the mu opioid receptor, and the shell predominately expresses the delta opioid receptor (Mansour et al., 1995; Hipólito et al., 2008). Delivering a mu opioid receptor antagonist into the nucleus accumbens core decreases outcome-guided responses, while a delta opioid receptor antagonist administered into the nucleus accumbens shell impairs cue-guided actions in male mice (Laurent et al., 2012).

Recent investigation into the anatomical divisions of the nucleus accumbens has revealed that the story is, in fact, more complex with further sub-compartmental organization evident (Gangarossa et al., 2013; Yang et al., 2018). This warrants further characterization to better understand how these sub-compartments specifically contribute to motivated behavior. However, while it is likely that each nucleus accumbens circuit encodes a distinct component of motivated behavior, the nucleus accumbens core and shell work in concert to properly integrate reward information to guide goal-directed actions.

The dorsal striatum: motivated behavior and addiction

The nucleus accumbens encodes reward incentive and, through a series of circuit loops, transfers information to the dorsal striatum to guide and refine the complex motor actions necessary to acquire rewards (Fig. 3.1). The dorsal striatum is divided into medial and lateral regions based on distinct excitatory inputs and the specific function each region contributes to motivated behavior (Burton et al., 2015). Again, these subregions are the dorsomedial (DMS) and dorsolateral striatum (DLS), which in the human and primate brain are referred to as the caudate and putamen, respectively. The DMS receives excitatory input from the orbitofrontal cortex, the medial prefrontal cortex, and the intralaminar nuclei of the thalamus (Gerfen, 1988; Hunnicutt et al., 2016). Integrating these inputs, the DMS subserves the expression of reversible, goal-directed action strategies that require executive oversight (Yin et al., 2005b, 2009). DMS circuit activity is critical for the formation of action-outcome associations during initial drug use and ingrain the actions performed for that drug reward (Everitt and Robbins, 2013). On the other hand, the DLS receives excitatory input from somatosensory and motor cortices as well as the intralaminar thalamus (Gerfen, 1988; Hunnicutt et al., 2016) and plays a critical role in organizing motor elements into complex action sequences (Bailey and Mair, 2006; Yin, 2010). These action sequences are executed in response to sensory cues with high precision and efficiency under low executive oversight. These so-called stimulus-response behaviors underlie habitual action strategies that may lead to compulsive behavior (Graybiel, 2008; Everitt and Robbins, 2016).

As an action is learned, activation of the DMS predominates to reversibly associate a reward outcome with an action (Yin, 2010). The presentation of a reward reinforces that action and thereby encourages repeated execution of that action. If, however, the reward is devalued, by satiation, a noxious additive, omission of the reward or increased effort to perform the task, then the action is no longer reinforced and, thus, not performed. This goal-directed behavior is said to be *sensitive* to reward feedback, which is attributed to the upstream prefrontal cortex (Laskowski et al., 2016; Le Merre et al., 2018). This reward sensitivity benefits an organism by promoting behavioral flexibility to respond accordingly to changes in the environment. Consider the following example: you are hungry so decide to drive to your local fast-food restaurant. Your goal is to purchase a savory cheeseburger with fries, but, along the way, you hear on the radio that the fast-food restaurant received a poor cleanliness rating so you decide to head home, still hungry. In this example, consciously and flexibly changing your actions away from food seeking due to reward devaluation (e.g., tainted food), allowed for a scenario ensuring optimal chances at survival, albeit at the expense of time. When this flexible behavior is disrupted however, due to dysregulation of the medial prefrontal cortex or the DMS, for example, individuals struggle to flexibly change their behavior to match a change in the environment and instead exhibit rigid, perseverative behavior. Examples of this include obsessive compulsive disorder (Vaghi et al., 2017; Remijnse et al., 2013) and the persistent negative thoughts seen in major depressive disorder (Remijnse et al., 2013; Miranda et al., 2013).

While goal-directed behavior is influenced by the outcome of an action, repeated training shifts the association from an action-outcome pairing (e.g., press lever = reward) to a stimulus-response association (cue light signaling the action = press lever), where now the actions are performed in response to the presentation of sensory cues. In this state, these actions may continue to be expressed despite changes in the reward outcome, such as devaluation. This is operationally defined as habitual behavior. Take, for example, typing on a keyboard. When one first learns to type, one must identify where each letter is placed on the keyboard and, subsequently, slowly type each letter to construct a word. However, after many hours of practice, the sequenced finger movements necessary to generate each word improve in speed and accuracy. After years of practice, the DLS can package these individual motor elements into readily releasable motor sequences (Yin et al., 2004, 2005a). Thus, the DLS saves considerable cognitive energy that can be used instead for more demanding, parallel tasks (e.g., maintaining a conversation as you type your name). These automated behaviors play a significant role in our daily lives, and are engaged when we brush our teeth, tie our shoes, or drive a car to work.

The specific contribution of the DMS and DLS to goal-directed and habitual behavior was originally discovered through site-specific lesion studies revealing the respective contributions of each striatal subregion to motivated behavior (Yin et al., 2004; 2005a, b). Following these foundational studies, chronic electrophysiology recordings from the dorsal striatum of rats learning to perform a motor task revealed that as an animal initially learns an operant task, activity in the DMS predominates and this behavior is sensitive to reward devaluation. However, after repeated training, the behavior becomes habitual and activity in the DMS diminishes while the DLS remains active (Thorn et al., 2010). As the striatum is driven by excitatory projections from the cortex, one might predict that transitioning from early to late skill learning is met with concomitant changes in cortical afferents. Indeed, Yin et al. (2009) demonstrated that corticostriatal LTD is enhanced in the DLS of male rats that have mastered a motor skill compared to naïve rats and those that are in the early stages of motor training. Supporting this result, Kupferschmidt et al. (2017) demonstrated that cortical terminals from the medial prefrontal cortex are robustly active during the acquisition of a new motor skill, but as the motor skill is learned, this activity is reduced. Importantly, recordings from the cell bodies of the cortical neurons projecting to the striatum revealed that while the terminals experienced learning-dependent changes in activity, the response of cell bodies in the cortex did not change during the learning paradigm. These studies indicate that synaptic plasticity in the striatum may subserve the mastery of a motor skill and subsequently the transition from goal-directed to habitual behaviors. Notably, drugs of abuse hijack these synaptic mechanisms (and others) to ultimately tip the balance of behavior toward habitual action strategy expression.

It is now evident that in both humans and rodent models of substance use disorder that chronic drug exposure promotes hyperactivation of the DLS and subsequently biases behavior from goal-directed to habitual action strategies on instrumental tasks. For example, the duration of alcohol dependence correlates with alcohol-cue induced responses in the putamen (i.e., DLS) in women and men (Sjoerds et al., 2014) and alcohol dependent men and women exhibit an overreliance on habitual responses on a computer-based instrumental learning task (Sjoerds et al., 2013). In rodent models of addiction, the same pattern of habitual behavior is present (Everitt and Robbins, 2016). Chronic cocaine exposure, for example, produces habitual cocaine seeking in male rats (Zapata et al., 2010). Ethanol seeking behavior is driven by stimulus-response action strategies in male rats (Dickinson et al., 2002). Additionally, habitual responding occurs in male rats self-administering nicotine (Clemens et al., 2014). Notably, chronic drug exposure does not simply produce habitual actions for the drug itself, but also generalizes habitual responding to natural rewards and facilitates the habit-learning process. For example, repeated amphetamine treatment rapidly produces habitual responding for sucrose in male rats (Nelson and Killcrose, 2006); chronic ethanol exposure accelerates habitual control of natural reward seeking in male rats (Corbit et al., 2012); and cocaine administration facilitates habitual responding for a natural reward in male rats (Schmitzer-Torbert et al., 2015). Together, these studies demonstrate that drugs of abuse broadly impact habit circuitry to promote a dominance of habitual responding for both drugs and natural rewards (Everitt and Robins, 2016).

This notion is supported by a diffusion tensor imaging study of healthy men and women showing that white matter connectivity within these corticostriatal pathways predicts individual differences in the balance of goal-directed and habitual control (de Wit et al., 2012). For example, tract strength between the medial prefrontal cortex and the caudate (i.e., DMS) predicts goal-directed action, while tract strength between the premotor cortex and the putamen (i.e., DLS) predicts habitual behavior (de Wit et al., 2012). Additionally, brain imaging studies reveal that chronic drug abuse negatively impacts the function of the prefrontal cortex (Perry et al., 2011). For example, male cocaine-dependent individuals exhibit reduced prefrontal cortical volume and functional deficits (Fein et al., 2002). Even an acute alcohol exposure reduces prefrontal cortical activity in healthy male subjects (Kähkönen et al., 2003), while chronic exposure results in a significant reduction in gray matter in the prefrontal cortex of men and women (Yang et al., 2016). Provided the importance of the prefrontal cortex in DMS-mediated behavior, these studies suggest chronic drug abuse promotes habitual behaviors by disengaging prefrontal cortex thereby shifting the balance toward DLS-driven habitual behavior.

Stress, habits, and addiction

Further biasing striatal function toward habitual actions is stress. This occurs through the action of stress hormones and catecholamine transmitters that bind to and activate their respective receptors that are expressed throughout the brain. Notably, stress hormone receptors are expressed in high density within the prefrontal cortex, as evidenced in male and female squirrel monkey brains (Patel et al., 2000). Indeed, stress produces dramatic deficits in prefrontal cortex driven behavior (Moghaddam and Jackson 2004), including cognitive flexibility in male rats (Bondi et al., 2008). This deficit likely arises from stress-induced morphological changes in the prefrontal cortex, as chronically stressed male rats exhibit dendritic atrophy on pyramidal neurons in the medial prefrontal cortex (Cook and Wellman, 2004). Thus, stress may profoundly dysregulate prefrontal cortex function and reduce executive control over goal-directed actions, therefore biasing DLS-mediated habitual behaviors.

The stress-induced enhancement of DLS-dependent behaviors is evident from several studies. For example, male and female participants exposed to a stress protocol that combines physical and psychosocial stressors exhibit a shift from goal-directed action to habitual control on an instrumental learning task (Schwabe and Wolf, 2009, 2011). Expanding on this work, Zerbes et al. (2020) demonstrated that the level of the stress response to an acute stressor, measured by cortisol, correlates with the activity in the dorsal striatum and the relative bias toward habitual actions in healthy men and women. These findings from human fMRI studies are further supported by preclinical models revealing that chronic stress accelerates DSL-dependent response learning and impairs hippocampus-dependent place learning in male rats, indicating that stress biases habitual actions over more cognitive-based learning strategies (Goodman and McIntyre, 2017). This bias is mediated by the action of stress hormones acting locally in the striatum, as local administration of glucocorticoids into the DLS, but not the DMS, accelerates habit learning in male rats (Siller-Pérez et al., 2017). Glucocorticoid signaling in the striatum likely promotes chronic stress-induced medium spiny neuron dendritic atrophy in the DMS but enhanced dendritic complexity in DLS medium spiny neurons in male rats (Dias-Ferreira et al., 2009).

In addition to the corticosteroid response, stress also elicits an acute surge of norepinephrine in the brain. This norepinephrine response plays an important role in promoting habitual actions. For example, healthy men and women carrying a loss of function variant of the gene encoding the a2b-adrenoceptor (ADRA2B) exhibit a reduced bias toward habit memories after stress (Wirz et al., 2017). In rats, stress cues bias DLS-driven habitual actions over hippocampus-dependent 'cognitive' actions in a procedural memory task, which can be blocked by systemic administration of the beta-adrenergic receptor antagonist propranolol in male rats (Goode et al., 2016). Providing further interest in the adrenergic stress mechanism, Goodman et al. (2015) revealed that glucocorticoid enhancement of habitual behavior in male rats requires concurrent activation of the beta-adrenergic system, suggesting that norepinephrine receptors are important therapeutic targets for stress-related disorders.

In addition to dysregulating corticostriatal function, chronic stress impacts functional connectivity between the amygdala and striatum to further promote habitual actions. For example, healthy men and women exposed to an acute stressor exhibit increased functional connectivity between the amygdala and the putamen (Wirz et al., 2017). Notably, acute administration of the mineralocorticoid receptor antagonist spironolactone prevents this increased connectivity and blocks the shift toward habitual actions in healthy men (Vogel et al., 2017). In male rats, stress-induced habitual responding is blocked by administering the beta-adrenergic receptor antagonist propranolol into the basolateral amygdala (Goode et al., 2016). These studies have led many in the field to believe that stress induced changes in the amygdala orchestrate the shift to habitual actions through its connections with the striatum. Supporting this claim, individuals carrying the aforementioned a2b-adenoceptor mutation, which prevents stress-induced habitual bias, exhibit increased functional connectivity between the amygdala and entorhinal cortex instead of the increased connectivity between the amygdala and the putamen seen in healthy controls (Wirz et al., 2017). Thus, a complex interaction of glucocorticoid, noradrenergic, and extended striatal circuitry mediate a shift toward habitual action strategy selection in the face of stress.

When drugs of abuse are added to the equation, stress-induced habitual action strategy selection is kicked into high gear. In substance use disorder, forced abstinence induces negative affective states including anxiety, irritability, emotional pain, and a loss of motivation for natural rewards that escalate drug intake (Koob et al., 2014; Uhl et al., 2019). These negative states motivate continued drug use to achieve an alleviation of these negative feelings (i.e., negative reinforcement) and are incited by drug withdrawal induced stress. Indeed, chronic administration of all major drugs of abuse elevate stress hormone responses, including adrenocorticotropic hormone, corticosterone, and corticotropin releasing factor (CRF) during acute withdrawal (Koob et al., 2014). Accordingly, administration of a CRF receptor antagonist blocks escalated self-administration of cocaine (Specio et al., 2008), nicotine (George et al., 2007) heroin (Greenwell et al., 2009), and alcohol in male rats (Funk et al., 2007). Therefore, the cycle of drug use and acute withdrawal induce key neuroadaptations within striatal circuits that ultimately promote continued, elevating drug use that traps an individual in a cycle of stress-fueled habitual drug use.

Striatal circuits in motivated behavior and addiction

Orbitofrontal cortex→dorsal striatum

The orbitofrontal cortex (OFC) regulates cognitive flexibility, or the ability to change behavior in response to a change in reward contingency. Dysfunction of the OFC is implicated in the pathophysiology of obsessive-compulsive disorder and other compulsive behaviors (Saxena et al., 1998; Joel et al., 2005a, b; Remijnse et al., 2006) including compulsive drug use (Everitt and Robins, 2005). Here we focus on the excitatory projections from OFC to the striatum, discuss how this circuit regulates goal-directed actions, and describe how drugs of abuse disrupt this circuit to promote continued drug use despite a desire to achieve sobriety.

The OFC sends direct projections to the DMS (Pan et al., 2010; Hoover and Vertes, 2011; Schilman et al., 2008) that predominantly arise from ventral/ventrolateral orbital areas (Fig. 3.2). Additionally, projections from lateral/dorsolateral orbital areas sparsely terminate in DLS and lateral regions of the nucleus accumbens (Schilman et al., 2008). Independent lesion studies of both the OFC or the DMS shed light on the functional role of this corticostriatal circuit. As inactivating the DMS results in impaired goal-directed behavior (Yin et al., 2005a),

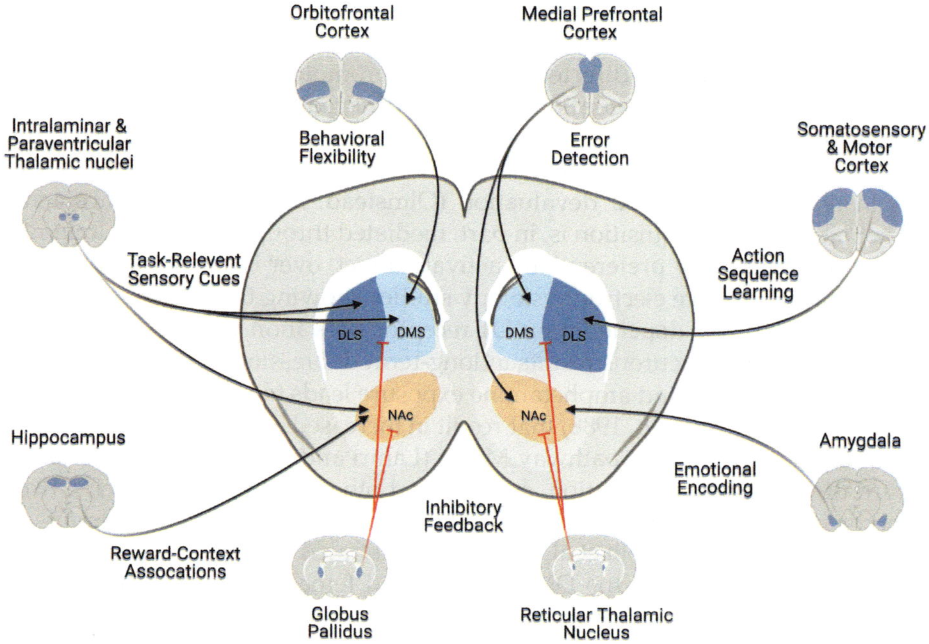

FIGURE 3.2 Circuit diagram of excitatory and inhibitory projections to the striatum and their respective behavioral correlates. The medial prefrontal cortex sends excitatory afferents to the DMS to encode error detection during motivated behavior. The orbitofrontal cortex sends excitatory afferents to the DMS and DLS to promote flexible actions to attain a reward. The somatosensory and motor cortices provide excitatory projections that import action sequence information to be stored in the DLS, while thalamic structures including the intralaminar nuclei and the paraventricular thalamus, send excitatory, integrated sensory inputs to all subregions of the striatum to update goal-directed actions (NAc and DMS) or initiate learned actions (DLS). The amygdala sends excitatory projections to the NAc to provide emotional context for goal-directed actions. The hippocampus sends excitatory projections to the NAc to form associations with environmental cues with reward. The globus pallidus and reticula thalamic nuclei both send inhibitory signals to all subregions of the striatum to suppress motor actions.

lesioning the OFC in male rats results in compulsive lever-pressing behavior (Schilman et al., 2010), where an animal will continue to press an incorrect lever even though the reward is not delivered. These results suggest that the OFC→striatum circuit regulates the ability to shift behavior in response to updated environmental signals that enable an organism to maintain a goal-directed action. Recall the example of the late-night drive to the fast-food restaurant. In this scenario, the tainted food report is likely processed by the OFC and updated information is imported to the DMS to alter the action plan to return home. What we have learned from simultaneous *in vivo* electrophysiology recordings from both OFC and DMS is that indeed both of these structures become more active during goal-directed behavior, but also that activating this circuit optogenetically results in goal-directed action expression (Gremel and Costa, 2013). Interestingly, the ability to dissect the roles of specific OFC-striatum circuits has shed light on the unique contributions of OFC sub-circuits to flexible or adaptive decision making. For example, OFC projections onto basolateral amygdala neurons that, in turn, project to the striatum mediate stabilization of action values, and ablating this circuit enhances reversal learning performance (Groman et al., 2019). Further investigation of these sub-circuits will undoubtedly clarify the broader mechanisms that collectively shape goal-directed actions.

Drugs of abuse engage goal-directed circuitry to promote further acquisition of drugs and the corresponding rewarding sensation. This goal-directed action can be recapitulated in rodent models in which rodents are administered a drug reward acutely. For example, male rats robustly self-administer acute doses of cocaine that, like sucrose self-administration, diminishes in response to reward devaluation (Olmstead, 2001). The enhancement of goal-directed actions for drug acquisition is, in part, mediated through increased dopamine release in the striatum, which may preferentially activate direct, over indirect, pathway MSNs. This notion is supported by slice electrophysiology studies showing that long-term potentiation of corticostriatal synapses is dependent on D1 receptor activation whereas D2 receptor activation on indirect pathway neurons results in long-term depression (Shen et al., 2008; Surmeier et al., 2009). Acute cocaine and amphetamine exposure leads to increases in striatal dopamine levels (Di Chiara and Imperato, 1988) that result in increased activity of direct pathway MSNs and the suppression of indirect pathway MSNs (Lahiri and Bevan, 2020). By biasing the system toward direct pathway activation, cocaine, and other dopamine-enhancing drugs, act as psychomotor stimulants to increase motor activity. Examining the specific circuits mediating these stimulatory effects, Bariselli et al. (2020) demonstrated that acute cocaine administration enhances OFC transmission to the DMS in male and female mice, and that optogenetically inducing long-term depression of local field potential responses *in vivo* attenuates cocaine-induced hyperactivity.

While initial drug use is characterized by goal-directed actions, repeated drug exposure impairs goal-directed behavior and biases toward habitual action expression mediated by the DLS. This phenomenon is thought to arise, in part, through a decrease in prefrontal cortical control of the DMS. For example, men and women with substance use disorder exhibit inflexible behavior on decision-making tasks (Bechara et al., 2001; Everitt et al., 2008) that parallel the cognitive deficits seen in patients with damage to the OFC (Bechara et al., 2000, 2004). This cognitive dysfunction diminishes the control over flexible goal-directed actions that would otherwise enable an individual to discontinue maladaptive behaviors such as drug taking. Instead, chronic drug exposure produces dysfunction of the OFC, which promotes impulsive decision making and perseverative actions for stimuli with diminishing reward value. For example, chronic cocaine use reduces gray matter volume in the OFC of men (Franklin et al., 2002), a phenomenon that correlates with the extent of drug use (Ersche et al., 2011). In addition to the structural damage induced by chronic drug use, OFC function, measured by fMRI, is markedly reduced in men and women that chronically abuse alcohol or cocaine (Goldstein and Volkow, 2002). Notably, hypofunction of the OFC can, in some cases, persist up to 10 years following the last drug exposure (Moorman, 2018), illustrating the profound impact chronic drug exposure has on the brain.

Focusing on the projection from the OFC to the striatum, Renteria et al. (2018) demonstrated that chronic ethanol exposure decreases excitatory synaptic transmission from the OFC to the DMS in male and female mice. Specifically, chronic ethanol exposure reduces OFC excitatory transmission onto direct pathway MSNs but not indirect pathway MSNs through an unknown pre-synaptic mechanism. In line with previous studies, these chronically exposed mice exhibit perseverative lever-pressing behavior for natural rewards, suggesting a disruption in top-down control over goal-directed actions. The authors also demonstrate that goal-directed behavior is restored by activating the OFC with excitatory DREADDS (Renteria et al., 2018). Similarly, chronic amphetamine exposure reduces activity in direct pathway MSNs, but not indirect pathway MSNs, in male rats (Furlon et al., 2015). This shift in MSN activity is associated with deficits in goal-directed behavior. As expected, restoring the balance in direct versus indirect pathway MSNs by inhibiting indirect pathway MSNs with an adenosine 2A receptor antagonist restores goal-directed behavior (Furlong et al., 2017). These studies not only identify specific impairments in OFC-striatum circuit function induced by chronic drug exposure, but they also implicate the OFC→DMS circuit as a potential target for therapeutic intervention in substance abuse disorders.

Medial prefrontal cortex→nucleus accumbens/dorsomedial striatum

The medial prefrontal cortex (mPFC) is in the frontal lobe of the brain and has a prominent role in executive functions including decision making, error detection, and cognitive control (Bahlmann et al., 2015; Euston et al., 2012; Modirrousta and Fellows, 2008). In rodents, the mPFC includes the infralimbic prefrontal cortex, the prelimbic prefrontal cortex, and the anterior cingulate cortex. Early neuronal tract-tracing studies reveal that the mPFC sends dense excitatory projections to both the DMS and the nucleus accumbens (Fig. 3.2; Sesack et al., 1989) where they synapse onto and excite MSNs (O'Donnel and Grace, 1995). These corticostriatal projections predominantly arise from layer V/VI and, to some extent, deep layer III pyramidal neurons (Goldman-Rakic and Selemon, 1986; McFarland and Haber, 2000). However, the nucleus accumbens core additionally receives cortical input from layer II (Ding et al., 2001).

To determine the functional role of corticostriatal transmission, initial studies utilized *ex vivo* slice electrophysiology to characterized synaptic plasticity and elucidate key molecules driving striatal dependent behaviors. The mPFC pathway to the DMS is the predominant glutamatergic input to this area and, post-synaptically, both AMPA and NMDA receptors are expressed on MSNs. These seminal studies revealed that the predominant form of plasticity in the DMS, presumably at corticostriatal synapses, is long-term synaptic potentiation (LTP) that is dependent on NMDA glutamate receptors (Partridge et al., 2000; Dang et al., 2006). Notably, blocking the NMDA receptor, specifically in the DMS, impairs instrumental learning (Yin et al., 2005a). Later, with the advent of circuit-specific monitoring and manipulation tools such as fiber photometry and optogenetics, respectively, scientists began to investigate how exactly this corticostriatal system governs goal-directed behavior *in vivo*. We now know that as an animal learns an instrumental task, the mPFC→DMS circuit becomes engaged (Kupferschmidt et al., 2017) and through positive reinforcement, synaptic transmission from the cortex to the striatum is potentiated (Reynolds et al., 2001). Additionally, the degree to which this synaptic potentiation occurs correlates with the acquisition of the instrumental task (Reynolds et al., 2001), suggesting that potentiation of corticostriatal synaptic transmission may serve as an important biological mechanism driving goal-directed actions. Testing this hypothesis, Ma et al. (2018) optogenetically stimulated cortical inputs to the DMS in a manner that produced synaptic potentiation or synaptic depression. When corticostriatal synapses were potentiated, this produced long-lasting reward-seeking behavior, but depression of these synapses prevented reward-seeking behavior. This corticostriatal plasticity may be specifically expressed on direct and indirect pathway neurons, as Shan et al. (2014) demonstrated that acquisition of a goal-directed action elicits potentiation of cortical synapses onto direct pathway neurons, and depression at cortical synapses onto indirect pathway neurons.

The NMDA receptor is critical for mediating the ability of drugs of abuse, especially ethanol, to shape action strategies that enhance drug seeking. For example, as ethanol enters the brain, it interacts with NMDA receptors to modulate ion conductance, thereby impacting forms of glutamatergic synaptic transmission that is critical for striatal based learning (Lovinger et al., 1989). While modulation of NMDA receptor function varies across brain regions and likely depends on ethanol exposure duration and receptor subunit composition (Kumari and Ticku, 2000; Ron, 2004), acute ethanol administration in the dorsal striatum facilitates NR2B-NMDA receptor function in male rodents (Wang et al., 2007). In contrast, chronic ethanol exposure converts NMDA receptor-dependent LTP to LTD, which likely underlies the deficits in goal-directed behavior seen in chronic alcohol users (Yin et al., 2007).

In addition to the effects of ethanol on NMDA receptor function in the striatum, opiate exposure indirectly modulates striatal NMDA receptor function by acting on neighboring opioid receptors inducing G-protein signaling mechanisms that regulate NMDA receptor function, a mechanism referred to as receptor crosstalk (Martin et al., 1997). For example, application of a mu-opioid agonist increases the amplitude of postsynaptic NMDA currents through G-protein activation of protein kinase C (Chartoff and Connery, 2014). Additionally, activation of kappa-opioid receptors in the dorsal striatum prevents LTP in direct pathway neurons (Hawes et al., 2017) while activation of mu-opioid receptor produces lasting synaptic depression (Muñoz et al., 2020). Notably, this so-called mu-opioid-LTD is sensitive to ethanol exposure, suggesting a convergent effect of ethanol and the endogenous opioid system or, possibly, an interaction of ethanol and opiates. Therefore, the crosstalk between opioid and NMDA receptors may have important implications for opiate and alcohol dependence (Glass, 2011).

In addition to opiates, amphetamine exerts behavioral effects through NMDA receptor function. For example, Kelley and Throne (1992) demonstrated that inhibiting NMDA receptors in the nucleus accumbens reduces amphetamine-induced hyper-locomotion and conditioned lever responding in male rats. Additionally, chronic amphetamine exposure reduces corticostriatal transmission onto direct pathway MSNs in male mice, an effect that is normalized by acute amphetamine exposure; this indicates a potential source of drug motivation during abstinence (Wang et al., 2013). Thus, multiple drugs of abuse disrupt native striatal plasticity mechanisms that underlie goal-directed behavior.

The exact functional role of the mPFC projection to the nucleus accumbens is less clear than that of the DMS projection. This is due in part to the additional projections made by mPFC neurons to the VTA that ultimately modulate dopamine release in both the cortex and nucleus accumbens (Tzschentke and Schmidt, 2000). While considerable attention is paid to the influence of mPFC activity on dopamine release in the nucleus accumbens and the subsequent impact on motivated behavior (Thompson and Moss, 1995), few studies have delineated the influence of the direct mPFC → nucleus accumbens projection. However, recently it was discovered that this circuit plays an important role in integrating internal body cues, or interoceptive cues, for drug-seeking behavior (Randall et al., 2019). Interoception, or sensation of one's self, enables an individual to maintain a homeostatic balance with the environment. For example, a person will approach a heat source when they feel cold but avoid one if they are too warm. Similarly, rewarding stimuli, including drugs of abuse, elicit an interoceptive response that guides future motivated behavior (Paulus and Stewart, 2014). In preclinical models, interoceptive responses to drugs of abuse can be studied using a drug discrimination task, where an animal learns to press one lever when it feels the effects of a drug, or a second lever when it feels a vehicle injection. Through this task, the animal demonstrates the ability to discriminate the interoceptive feeling of a drug over a vehicle injection. Chemogenetically inhibiting mPFC projections to the nucleus accumbens prevents nicotine and ethanol discrimination responding in male rats (Randall et al., 2019). This interoceptive response to drug administration is thought to arise from increased glutamate release from cortical afferents into the nucleus accumbens, which then activate local glutamate receptors. Supporting this idea, cocaine administration increases glutamate release in the nucleus accumbens, which is prevented by lesioning the mPFC (Pierce et al., 1998). This drug-induced surge in glutamate release binds to glutamate receptors in the nucleus accumbens, including mGluR5, to elicit an interoceptive response. For example, Besheer et al. (2009) demonstrated that as inhibiting mGluR5 in the nucleus accumbens prevents ethanol discrimination while activating mGluR5 receptors enhance discrimination of a sub-threshold ethanol dose.

Hippocampus → nucleus accumbens

The hippocampus, located in the medial temporal lobe of the brain, is one of the most well-studied systems in the brain (Bird and Burgess, 2008). Dating back to early clinical studies of patients with damage to the temporal lobe, we learned that the hippocampus plays a fundamental role in binding memories to form complex representations that are necessary for spatial and contextual memory (Kutlu and Gould, 2016). In the context of drug addiction, the hippocampus promotes maladaptive drug—context associations that enable an individual to navigate toward a known drug source. This likely occurs through excitatory projections from the hippocampus to the nucleus accumbens, which synapse onto and excite accumbal MSNs (Fig. 3.2; Groenewegen et al., 1982, 1996; Kelley and Domesick, 1982). Additionally, the hippocampus indirectly influences the dorsal striatum through its connections with the mPFC and OFC and provides important spatial information to help overcome multiple possible actions related to a specific location in order to maintain accurate goal-directed behavior (Goodroe et al., 2018).

Subsequent neuronal tract-tracing studies demonstrate that the hippocampus and mPFC send excitatory projections that converge onto nucleus accumbens MSNs (French and Totterdell, 2002), giving rise to the idea that hippocampal input influences and possibly gates information from the cortex. Provided that MSNs do not fire spontaneously but instead require a significant amount of excitatory input to reach spike threshold (Pennartz et al., 1994), convergent excitatory input may be necessary to elicit MSN spike firing. Supporting this idea, excitation of only hippocampal inputs brings MSNs to a depolarized state (O'Donnell and Grace, 1995), and only in this depolarized state can inputs from the mPFC evoke spike firing (French and Totterdell, 2002). Hippocampal gating of cortical input to the nucleus accumbens is likely the phenomenon underlying the ability to use contextual cues to maintain goal-directed action despite changes in, or in response to, spatial context.

Chronic drug exposure has a dramatic impact on hippocampal function, disrupting hippocampal neurogenesis (Eisch and Harburg, 2006) and synaptic plasticity in rodents (Thompson et al., 2002) that collectively contribute to maladaptive behavior in addiction. For instance, amphetamines, after their release as a prescription drug in 1935, were marketed for their ability to enhance memory recall (Zeeuws and Soetens, 2007) attention (Johnson et al., 2000) and working memory (Mattay et al., 2000) in men and women. In contrast, chronic amphetamine use produces dramatic deficits in memory, attention and decision making in men and women (Ornstein et al., 2000; Nordahl et al., 2003; Simon et al., 2010). Preclinical studies demonstrate the specific impact of chronic amphetamine use on hippocampal-dependent learning tasks, including deficits in spatial object recognition and spatial navigation on the Morris water maze in male mice (Mandillo et al., 2003). This suggests an enhancement of hippocampal→nucleus accumbens activity, particularly in early stages of addiction, that serves to strengthen contextual memories associated with drug use that are later triggered by environmental stimuli signaling drug availability.

Further supporting this concept, acute cocaine exposure enhances hippocampus→nucleus accumbens synaptic strength in male mice (Britt et al., 2012). This occurs by increasing postsynaptic AMPA receptor expression in MSNs, specifically onto direct pathway MSNs (Pascoli et al., 2014). Following the go/no-go model of striatal function, such hippocampus-to-accumbens cocaine-induced enhancement of direct pathway output would foster drug reinforcement. Indeed, Pascoli et al. (2014) demonstrated that reversing plasticity from these hippocampal inputs abolishes drug-seeking behavior in male and female mice. Similarly, acute ethanol exposure enhances glutamatergic synaptic transmission from hippocampus to direct pathway MSNs and abolishes LTD at these synapses by increasing the insertion of calcium permeable AMPA receptors into the postsynaptic membrane (Kircher et al., 2019). These preclinical studies demonstrate that acute drug exposure facilitates hippocampal drive of nucleus accumbens that likely subserves context-dependent drug reinforcement. However, chronic drug exposure impairs hippocampal function and disrupts hippocampus-dependent learning that likely facilitates continued drug use despite attempts to learn new reward associations related to sobriety (Kutlu and Gould, 2016).

Somatosensory and motor cortex→dorsolateral striatum

Pyramidal neurons in the deep layers of the somatosensory and motor cortices send excitatory projections to the DLS to integrate and transpose cortical information into selected actions (Fig. 3.2). These excitatory inputs converge onto the same MSNs to elicit action potential firing (Charpier et al., 2020), suggesting that somatosensory and motor information integrate to produce a selected motor response. The topographical organization seen in the somatosensory and motor cortices extend to the striatum in primates (Flaherty and Graybiel, 1994; McFarland and Haber, 2000), rats (Berendse et al., 1992) and mice (Hintiryan et al., 2016). However, more recent evidence suggests that the topographic compartmentalization in the striatum is more complicated and varies across cell type and cortical area (Hooks et al., 2018).

High frequency activation of somatomotor cortical afferents to the DLS elicits LTD onto MSNs (Calabresi et al., 1992; Lovinger et al., 1993). This is a phenomenon that likely underlies the learning adaptations governing action automatization and, if taken further, habit formation. Supporting this notion, Yin et al. (2009) and Hawes et al. (2015) demonstrated that as a motor skill is learned, corticostriatal LTP is enhanced in the DMS, but as a motor skill is automatized, through repeated training, corticostriatal LTD in the DLS is augmented. This highlights the fundamental role that plasticity plays in the myriad actions expressed in our daily lives, and it should come as no surprise that aberrant corticostriatal synaptic plasticity contributes to the compulsive behavior seen in obsessive compulsive disorder (Graybiel and Rauch, 2000) and addiction (Gerdeman et al., 2003).

These corticostriatal plasticity mechanisms do not exist in a glutamate-only vacuum. Corticostriatal LTD is dependent on local dopamine release that activates D2 dopamine receptors on MSNS and cholinergic interneurons (Wang et al., 2006; Lerner and Kreitzer, 2012; Augustin et al., 2018). This orchestrated corticostriatal and dopamine signaling mobilizes the release of endocannabinoids that act on presynaptic cannabinoid type-1 (CB1) receptors to reduce synaptic transmission from cortical terminals onto MSNs (Gerdeman and Lovinger, 2000). The complex interplay of acetylcholine, dopamine, endocannabinoid neuromodulatory signaling underlying this glutamatergic corticostriatal plasticity leads to potential LTD perturbation by several abused substances that target these component neurotransmitter systems (e.g., nicotine, stimulants, cannabinoids, and ethanol).

As the corticostriatal synapse is the most abundant synapse type on MSNs and corticostriatal LTD is linked to action learning (Yin et al., 2009), corticostriatal LTD represents a key mechanism by which drugs of abuse expedite the automatization of actions leading to drug reward. Accordingly, manipulation of the underlying neurotransmitter systems with drugs of abuse or experimental manipulations modulates habit formation. For example, chronic cocaine exposure biases the use of habitual action strategies for drug reward in male rats (Schmitzer-Torbert et al., 2015; Zapata et al., 2010). Inactivation of the dopamine neurons that project to the DLS abolishes habitual lever pressing behavior in male rats (Faure et al., 2005). Additionally, Murray et al. (2012) demonstrated that simply inhibiting dopamine receptors in the DLS is sufficient to abolish habitual cocaine-seeking behavior in male rats. Thus, psychostimulants are positioned to disrupt corticostriatal synaptic transmission to promote habitual drug-seeking and -taking behavior. Chronic drug exposure may have more generalized effects on reward-related behavior, as chronic ethanol exposure (Corbit et al., 2012) and amphetamine exposure (Nelson and Killcross, 2006) both enhance habitual responding for natural rewards in male rats. Indeed, clinical reports indicate that individuals with substance use disorder feel overpowered by habitual actions, including but not limited to habitual drug use (Seo and Sinha, 2014).

Provided the critical role of cholinergic neurons in DLS LTD, it is likely that nicotine, an acetylcholine nicotinic receptor agonist, significantly impacts this form of plasticity and, therefore, could have a dramatic impact on habitual behavior. In a recent human study, it was shown that that the degree of nicotine dependence in men and women was positively correlated to habitual responding on a stimulus-response task (Luijten et al., 2019). The authors noted that this effect was accompanied by reductions in goal-directed responding, resulting in a shift toward predominantly habitual responses. In line with these results, preclinical studies of nicotine use demonstrate that, initially, nicotine seeking is goal-directed (Clemens et al., 2014), but with additional training and exposure, responding for nicotine becomes habitual in male rats (Loughlin et al., 2017). As discussed above, this transition from goal-directed behavior to habitual responding involves corticostriatal plasticity and this process is certainly modulated by repeated nicotine exposure. For example, in brain slices, nicotine exposure depresses excitatory transmission onto MSNs, an effect that is dependent on D2 dopamine receptor activation (Licheri et al., 2018). Additionally, Partridge et al. (2002) demonstrated that activation of nicotinic receptors facilitates corticostriatal LTD in the DLS. Collectively, these results suggest that the chronic nicotine exposure may dramatically influence striatal plasticity to underlie habitual behaviors that emerge with repeated drug use.

In addition to drugs that act directly on the transmitter systems underlying corticostriatal LTD, such as nicotine on acetylcholine receptors, chronic ethanol also disrupts striatal LTD by modulating cannabinoid signaling. For example, chronic ethanol exposure impairs striatal LTD in male rats (Adermark et al., 2011) and mice (Depoy et al., 2013), which is recovered by a high dose application of a CB1 receptor agonist (Adermark et al., 2011). Additionally, even acute ethanol exposure can disrupt endocannabinoid mediated LTD in the dorsal striatum in male rats (Clarke and Adermark, 2010). The chronic ethanol effect is likely due to changes in CB1 receptor expression, as Adermark et al. (2011) revealed a decrease in CB1 mRNA expression in the striatum of rats chronically exposed to ethanol. Additionally, men with alcohol use disorder exhibit significantly reduced CB1 receptor binding, a proxy for CB1 receptor expression, across multiple brain regions including the dorsal and ventral striatum (Hirvonen et al., 2013). Notably, these authors revealed that the degree of CB1 receptor binding negatively correlates with the duration of alcohol abuse, further supporting the relationship between ethanol exposure and CB1 receptor expression (Hirvonen et al., 2013).

The effects of chronic ethanol exposure on striatal endocannabinoid signaling and corticostriatal plasticity likely impact subsequent ethanol consumption, as systemically administered CB1 receptor agonists increase (Colombo et al., 2002), and CB1 receptor antagonists decrease, voluntary ethanol consumption in male rats (Serra et al., 2001). While subsequent studies demonstrated that delivery of a CB1 receptor antagonist into the nucleus accumbens reduces ethanol self-administration in male rats (Caillé et al., 2007; Alvarez-Jaimes et al., 2009), future studies are needed to determine if these effects are replicated in the dorsal striatum. Regardless, these studies collectively demonstrate that multiple drugs of abuse significantly impact DLS synaptic plasticity, which is a key mechanism for action learning. Therefore, dissecting the mechanisms underlying various forms of striatal glutamatergic plasticity and how drugs of abuse hijack them may lead to new treatment avenues.

Thalamus → nucleus accumbens/dorsal striatum

The thalamus is a collection of nuclei supporting a multitude of functions. Some of these nuclei can be characterized as sensory relay nuclei, as they receive primary sensory input from the periphery and relay this information to the cortex. Another set of thalamic nuclei are categorized as association nuclei, which integrate information from a variety of cortical and subcortical sources and output to multiple cortical and subcortical areas (Cover and Mathur, 2021; Sherman, 2016). Specifically, the striatum receives glutamatergic projections from a subset of association thalamic nuclei, called the intralaminar nuclei of the thalamus, which is anatomically divided into rostral and caudal regions (Fig. 3.2; Parent et al., 1983; Matsumoto et al., 2000). The caudal region of the intralaminar nuclei contains the center median (CM) and parafascicular (Pf) nuclei in primates, while in rodents the caudal region only consists of the Pf nucleus (Groenewegen and Berendse, 1994; Van der Werf et al., 2002). The rostral intralaminar nuclei (rILN) consists of the central medial, the paracentral, and the central lateral nuclei (Cover and Mathur, 2021; Fisher and Reynolds, 2014). Additionally, the midline thalamus, consisting of the paraventricular nucleus (PVN) and paratenial nucleus, sends projections to the dorsal striatum and nucleus accumbens in the rat (Fig. 3.2; Vertes and Hoover, 2008). These excitatory afferents synapse onto striatal MSNs and exhibit greater projection density onto direct pathway neurons, as measured by electron microscopy (Sidibé and Smith, 1996). The information traveling through this thalamostriatal circuit depolarizes MSNs to a subthreshold "up state" (Shulz et al., 2009) that likely informs the striatum of salient events that, in conjunction with dopamine signals, reinforces action learning (Fisher and Reynolds, 2014). Notably, there is considerable convergence of thalamostriatal and corticostriatal projections onto striatal MSNs (Hunnicutt et al., 2016) that likely interact to influence striatal function and action expression.

A key driver of drug addiction is the conditioned response to drug-related stimuli that persists despite negative feedback, suggesting aberrant thalamic function in chronic users (Huang et al., 2017). Supporting this hypothesis, chronic drug exposure increases nonspecific thalamic activity in response to drug cues in men and women (Zilverstand et al., 2018). For example, fMRI studies demonstrate hyperresponsivity of the thalamus to drug cues in male and female cocaine users (Ray et al., 2015), heroin users (Li et al., 2013), and alcohol-dependent individuals (Feldstein Ewing et al., 2010). An understanding of the interaction between thalamic structures and the striatum is required to conceptualize how this aberrant activity in the thalamus in response to drug-related cues shapes drug-seeking behavior.

Early models of basal ganglia function suggest that the striatum regulates appropriate actions by providing start and stop commands to downstream control circuits (Graybiel, 1998; Jin and Costa, 2015). This hypothesis is supported by electrophysiology recordings from rodents (Barnes et al., 2005; Jin and Costa, 2010) and primates (Desrochers et al., 2015) showing that activity in the striatum aligns with the initiation and termination of trained motor behaviors. Within this model, the striatum is activated by cortical projections from motor cortex that dictate which striatal motor program is executed. However, more recent studies demonstrate that the striatum encodes important kinematic information for the elements that comprise an action sequence, including action speed (Wolf et al., 2019; Roberts et al., 2019).

Recently it was demonstrated that once learned, an action can be executed without the participation of motor cortex (Kawai et al., 2015). This suggests that a motor program is potentially acquired from the cortex and stored in the dorsal striatum where it is then re-activated by an alternative source. Since MSNs require excitatory input to fire action potentials, re-activation of a stored motor program would theoretically require drive from an excitatory structure outside the cortex. A candidate that would meet the necessary requirements to drive MSN activity and, therefore, learned actions that are stored in the dorsal striatum, is the intralaminar thalamus. The intralaminar thalamus provides extensive excitatory projections to the striatum. Supporting the role of intralaminar thalamostriatal circuitry in motor learning, Wolff et al. (2019) demonstrated that initial motor learning requires cortical drive of the DLS, but once a motor skill is learned these actions are evoked by thalamic inputs to the DLS. The authors suggest that the motor cortex transfers relevant motor information to the intralaminar thalamus through convergent activation of MSNs in a manner that requires synaptic plasticity. Testing this hypothesis, the authors demonstrate that inhibiting long-term synaptic plasticity with PKM zeta inhibitor ZIP in the striatum, but not the cortex, disrupts motor skill learning. This work suggests that thalamostriatal circuits play a critical role in the expression of, at least, well-learned actions that support drug-seeking behavior.

Given this role of the intralaminar thalamus, inputs from these nuclei to the striatum unsurprisingly play an important role in drug-seeking behavior: inactivation of the rostral grouping of the intralaminar nuclei (including central lateral, central medial, and paracentral nuclei) projections to the DMS decreases methamphetamine-seeking behavior after 30 days of withdrawal in male rats (Li et al., 2018). As such, these thalamostriatal circuits likely play a key role in the so-called incubation of craving for drug reward during extended withdrawal. Despite the apparent importance of this thalamostriatal circuit in mediating drug-seeking behavior, very little is known about how drugs of abuse modulate thalamostriatal signaling. While a simple assumption would be that both cortical and thalamic excitatory synapses function similarly, slice electrophysiology studies demonstrate that these inputs exhibit different glutamate release probabilities (Ding et al., 2008) and that thalamostriatal inputs, but not cortical inputs, undergo synaptic depression by activation of mu-opioid receptors (Atwood et al., 2014). Importantly, this mu-opioid dependent LTD was lost after acute injection of oxycodone, suggesting that opiate exposure selectively impacts thalamostriatal transmission.

In addition to direct contacts onto striatal MSNs, thalamic terminals arising from intralaminar nuclei also innervate striatal cholinergic interneurons (Lapper and Bolam, 1992; Aosaki et al., 1994). This circuit has received considerable attention since cholinergic signaling plays a central role in striatal-dependent learning (Diaz del Guante et al., 1991). Striatal cholinergic interneurons are tonically active (Wilson et al., 1990; Aosaki et al., 1994; Kawaguchi et al., 1995), but exhibit burst-pause firing behavior in response to salient reward and aversive sensory input in monkeys (Yamada et al., 2004). This burst-pause behavior is abolished by pharmacological inactivation of the monkey CM/Pf (Matsumoto et al., 2000). Additionally, optogenetically activating intralaminar nucleus terminals produces burst firing in cholinergic interneurons (Ding et al., 2010). This burst activity was coupled to a decrease in MSN activity, followed by a selective increase in sensitivity of indirect pathway MSNs to cortical stimulation (Ding et al., 2010). This suggests that by resetting cortical input, this thalamic input facilitates shifting behavior to respond to updated information about a reward contingency. Supporting this idea, in a reversal learning task where an animal learns that a previously rewarding stimulus is no longer rewarding, there is an increase in striatal acetylcholine that arises with Pf activation in rats (Brown et al., 2010). Moreover, inactivating Pf inputs to the striatum produces a learning deficit in rats when action-outcome contingencies have changed (Bradfield et al., 2013). Thus, the Pf-to-cholinergic interneuron circuit may update new and existing information to enable accurate goal-directed actions.

As striatal acetylcholine and dopamine act in concert to mediate behavioral reinforcement and drug-related behavior, it stands to reason that thalamostriatal inputs arising from the intralaminar nuclei may also modulate dopamine release in the striatum. Indeed, Threlfell et al. (2012) showed in the dorsal striatum of mice that activation of Pf inputs elicits dopamine release in a cholinergic interneuron-dependent manner. In addition, the rILN also display this ability: activation of these afferents in the dorsal striatum elicits stable dopamine release

(Cover et al., 2019). Thus, intralaminar thalamic afferent activation drives cholinergic interneuron release of acetylcholine, which in turn, activates nicotinic receptors on nigrostriatal terminals to release dopamine (Threlfell et al., 2012; Cover et al., 2019). This suggests a possible mechanism for how nicotine may modulate striatal dopamine and promote reward-driven behaviors. For example, Cover et al. (2019) demonstrated that mice will self-stimulate the rILN → dorsal striatum circuit, which is dependent on D1 dopamine receptor activation. Considering that the rILN are required for incubation of methamphetamine craving in a D1 dopamine receptor-dependent manner in male rats (Li et al., 2018), the rILN are positioned as an emerging target for therapeutic intervention in addiction.

In addition to the intralaminar nuclei, the PVN has also received considerable attention for its role in reinstatement of drug-seeking behavior, which is thought to manifest from associations between drug cues and the resulting drug reward (Huang et al., 2017). Indeed, PVN inactivation studies demonstrate that this structure is necessary for reinstatement of drug-seeking behavior, including cocaine-seeking behavior in male rats (Matzeu et al., 2015; Hamlin et al., 2009). PVN neurons that project to the nucleus accumbens appear to be critical for reinstatement of drug-seeking behavior, as reinstatement of ethanol seeking results in greater activation of striatal-projecting PVN neurons (Hamlin et al., 2009) and selective inhibition of this circuit attenuates the acquisition of cocaine self-administration behaviors in male rats (Neuman et al., 2016). Taken together, these studies suggest that several thalamic nuclei projecting to the striatal complex act in concert to prime behavioral engagement in drug-seeking behavior once these behaviors are learned, and stored, in ensembles of striatal MSNs (Cover and Mathur 2021).

Amygdala → nucleus accumbens/dorsal striatum

The amygdala is a limbic structure that plays a key role in emotional coding of environmental stimuli (Kaada, 1972). The collection of nuclei forming the amygdaloid complex consists of three distinct subregions, the basolateral amygdala (BLA), the medial amygdala, and the central amygdala (CeA), each of which play unique roles in emotional processing (Hyrbouski et al., 2016). The striatum receives inputs predominantly from the BLA (Christie et al., 1987; McDonald 1991, 1992; Pan et al., 2010) that specifically arise from glutamatergic pyramidal (class I) BLA neurons but not GABAergic (class II and III) BLA neurons (Christie et al., 1987; McDonald 1992; Zorilla and Koob, 2012). These BLA projections primarily innervate the nucleus accumbens (Fig. 3.2; Krettek and Price, 1978, Kelley et al., 1982), but also more sparsely innervate the dorsal striatum (Pan et al., 2010; Cho et al., 2013).

The BLA is of particular interest for this chapter as it receives robust sensory information from prefrontal cortex and thalamus and relays this information to the striatum to influence motivational learning (Wassum and Izquierdo, 2016). Structurally, Cho et al. (2013) revealed that the topographical organization in the cortex is maintained throughout the cortico-amygdala-striatal circuit, which the authors suggest promotes the integration of internal emotional states with external social and sensory information to inform emotionally complex behaviors. Zooming in on the BLA projections to the nucleus accumbens, Ambroggi et al. (2008) demonstrated that cue-evoked excitation of accumbens MSNs depends on the BLA and that inactivating the BLA diminishes lever-pressing performance on a discriminative stimulus task in male rats. Additionally, projections from the BLA and the mPFC converge in the nucleus accumbens, suggesting that the BLA may also influence motivated behavior by modulating cortical drive of nucleus accumbens MSNs (McGinty and Grace, 2009). For example, train stimulating of BLA inputs to the nucleus accumbens depresses cortically-evoked spiking of striatal MSNs (McGinty and Grace, 2009). Conversely, Popescu et al. (2007) demonstrated that BLA inputs to the accumbens potentiate corticostriatal LTP through NMDA receptor activation. While the direction of these two forms of modulation are inconsistent, perhaps due to different stimulation conditions of amygdala projection neurons, these two studies clearly demonstrate the ability of the amygdala to modulate cortical drive of the nucleus accumbens. This likely serves an important mechanism by which the amygdala provides emotional incentive to shape motivated behavior that is driven by the cortex.

In addition to the major input to the nucleus accumbens, the BLA also sends projections to the medial and posterior regions of the DMS (Kelley et al., 1982). This circuit may encode emotional significance to guide goal-directed actions to a reward (Corbit et al., 2012). This contribution may additionally require communication with cortical structures, as Fisher et al. (2020) recently demonstrated that amygdala projections to the mPFC, but not the DMS, are critical for goal-directed learning in male and female mice. However further investigation of this specific BLA projection is needed to further characterize its functional contributions to motivated behavior.

Drugs of abuse dramatically impact BLA function impairing its ability to properly update reward incentive values from environmental cues. This results in maladaptive behavioral responses including the propensity to express habitual actions (Wassum and Izquierdo, 2016). Functional imaging studies demonstrate amygdala dysfunction in nicotine addicted men and women (Mihov and Hurlemann, 2012), where smoking cues elicit increased amygdala activity in abstinent smokers but not in nonsmokers (Due et al., 2002). Additionally, the amygdala response to unpleasant stimuli is decreased in nicotine using men and women, indicating impaired encoding of emotional stimuli (Kobiella et al., 2010). Similarly, alcohol intoxication dysregulates amygdala response to emotional cues in men and women (Gilman et al., 2008). In cocaine-dependent men and women there is elevated activity in the amygdala (Kilts et al., 2001; Bonson et al., 2002) and these effects last for months after termination of drug use, which demonstrates the long-lasting effects of drug use on brain function (Schoenbaum and Setlow, 2005). Unfortunately, these functional imaging studies could not specify the exact location of activation within the amygdaloid complex. However, considering the rodent studies that will be discussed in this section, it is likely that BLA dysfunction is integral to substance use disorder. A prevailing concept is that a dysfunctional BLA response to normal emotional cues may predispose one to ignore salient, emotionally laden cues in the environment that would normally shift behavior away from drug seeking.

Another view is supported by Parkes and Balleine (2013) who reported that the BLA encodes outcome values forming an "incentive memory" that influences future actions in male rats. In the context of addiction, actions that result in the acquisition of drug are similarly encoded by the BLA to form "drug memories" that guide future behavior toward a known drug reward (Luo et al., 2013). Supporting this, inactivating the BLA prevents the formation of these drug memories including cocaine- (Fuchs et al., 2002) and morphine-induced conditioned place preference in male rodents (Rezayof et al., 2002). Furthermore, inactivating the BLA abolishes cocaine-seeking behavior in male rats (Whitelaw et al., 1996).

The process of encoding drug–reward associations likely occurs through dopamine release from VTA dopamine neurons that send extensive projections to the BLA and nucleus accumbens (Loughlin and Fallon, 1982; Haber and Fudge, 1997). For example, male rats self-administering cocaine exhibit a dopamine surge in the amygdala and nucleus accumbens while pressing for the cocaine-paired lever but not the unpaired lever (Weiss et al., 2000). Following this result, infusion of a D1 but not D2 dopamine receptor antagonist into the BLA prevents cue-induced reinstatement of cocaine-seeking behavior in male rats (See et al., 2001). Subsequent studies revealed that BLA projections to the nucleus accumbens drive cue-induced reinstatement of cocaine-seeking behavior, as inhibiting this circuit pharmacologically (Di Ciano and Everitt, 2004) or chemogenetically (Puaud et al., 2021) prevents reinstatement of cocaine-seeking behavior in male rats.

The BLA also plays a key role in value encoding for ethanol reward that is critical for ethanol-seeking behavior (Gremel and Cunningham, 2009). Several mechanisms may be at play to underlie this effect. In a mechanically isolated neuron/bouton preparation, acute ethanol exposure increases GABAergic transmission from local interneurons in male rats (Zhu and Lovinger, 2006; Silberman et al., 2009), while chronic ethanol exposure increases glutamatergic signaling onto BLA pyramidal neurons in male and female rats (Läck et al., 2007; Morales et al., 2018). Providing a possible mechanism underlying this effect, it was recently demonstrated that chronic ethanol exposure upregulates acetylcholine release in the BLA that activates presynaptic alpha-7 nicotinic acetylcholine receptors to enhance glutamatergic transmission (Sizer et al., 2021). Additionally, withdrawal from chronic ethanol exposure robustly decreases GABA release from interneurons in the BLA of male rats (Diaz et al., 2011) and increases glutamatergic transmission through increased AMPA receptor expression (Christian et al., 2012). These authors suggested that by reducing inhibitory tone and increasing excitation of the BLA, chronic ethanol exposure produces long-lasting changes of amygdala function that ultimately shape incentive learning. For example, Gass et al. (2011) recorded simultaneous glutamate release in the BLA and nucleus accumbens in chronic ethanol-treated male rats and demonstrated increased glutamate release in both structures during cue-induced reinstatement of ethanol-seeking behavior. This would suggest that the BLA drives nucleus accumbens projection neurons to promote ethanol-seeking behavior. Supporting this idea, pharmacologically inactivating the BLA or the nucleus accumbens reduces Pavlovian responses for ethanol reward in male rats (Chaudhri et al., 2013; Millan et al., 2015). Following these results, Millan et al. (2017) demonstrated that specifically disrupting synaptic transmission from the BLA to the nucleus accumbens using optogenetics reduces conditioned ethanol consumption in rats, supporting the role of this circuit in ethanol reward associative learning (Millan et al., 2017).

Relapse is a significant obstacle in recovering substance users that is thought to arise from conditioned responses to drug-cues in the environment that illicit drug seeking behavior (Weiss, 2005). Examining the role of the BLA → nucleus accumbens circuit in ethanol relapse, Keistler et al. (2017) ablated BLA projection to the accumbens in male rats self-administering ethanol and tested cue-induced reinstatement following ethanol extinction. The authors found that ablating the BLA → nucleus accumbens projection attenuates cue-induced ethanol reinstatement, but also that ethanol reinstatement is completely blocked when inputs from the mPFC → nucleus accumbens are ablated. Considering the electrophysiology data previously discussed, where inputs from the BLA modulate cortical excitation of accumbens

MSNs (McGinty and Grace, 2009), these data collectively demonstrate that the BLA encodes important reward cues from the environment, including drug-associated cues, and relays this information to the nucleus accumbens to guide behavior toward drug acquisition.

As an individual with substance use disorder cycles through episodes of repeated drug use and withdrawal, the stress response system adapts by becoming hyperactive. This produces anxiety and reward deficits that promote further drug use in order to alleviate these negative symptoms (Koob et al., 2014; Koob and Volkow, 2016). Contributing to this viscous cycle, stress negatively impacts the function of both the amygdala and the nucleus accumbens, which play a key role in the negative affective state seen in addiction. Specifically, the amygdala and nucleus accumbens exhibit aberrant responses to reward and aversive cues, respectively, where the degree of this aberrant response predicts a greater risk of alcohol abuse in young men and women (Nikolova et al., 2016). This dysregulated activity is associated with increased stimulus-response behavior in men (Vogel et al., 2016), which as we mentioned previously contributes to compulsive drug seeking and consumption in addiction. Notably, administration of an antagonist to the receptor for the stress hormone mineralocorticoid, corrects aberrant amygdala activity and stimulus-response behavior in men (Vogel et al., 2016). The dysregulated activity of the amygdala and nucleus accumbens may arise from a loss of top-down control from the mPFC, as chronic stress decreases activity in the mPFC and increases activity in the BLA in male rats (Piggott et al., 2019).

Inhibitory striatal circuits in motivated behavior and addiction

In addition to excitatory projections driving MSN activity, the striatum receives inhibitory signals from extrinsic and intrinsic sources. For example, the dorsal pallidum sends inhibitory projections that terminate in the dorsal striatum (Staines et al., 1981; Staines and Fibiger, 1984) and the ventral pallidum sends inhibitory projections to the nucleus accumbens (Fig. 3.2; Churchill and Kalivas, 1994). These projections provide the largest extrinsic source of GABAergic inhibition to the striatum and synapse onto striatal MSNs, cholinergic interneurons and parvalbumin expressing fast-spiking interneurons (Mallet et al., 2012). The reticular thalamic nucleus, a thin shell of neurons surrounding the dorsal thalamus, provides an additional source of extrinsic GABAergic inhibition to the striatum (Fig. 3.2; Minderhound, 1971). These projections synapse onto and inhibit parvalbumin-expressing GABAergic fast-spiking striatal interneurons (Klug et al., 2018). In addition to these early studied sources of extrinsic inhibition, cortical somatostatin-expressing interneurons send inhibitory projections to the striatum that directly inhibit MSNs, thereby providing an addition source of extrinsic inhibitory control (Rock et al., 2016).

Locally, the striatum receives strong inhibitory control from interneurons, which includes the fast-spiking interneurons, the low-threshold spiking interneurons, the calretinin expressing interneurons, and the TH-expressing interneurons (Dubach et al., 1987; Koós and Tepper, 1999; Ibáñez-Sandoval et al., 2010; Tepper et al., 2010). The most well-studied inhibitory interneuron in the striatum is the fast-spiking interneuron (Tepper et al., 2010) that synapses onto proximal MSN dendrites and somata (Kita et al., 1990) and evokes large-amplitude inhibitory postsynaptic potentials (Koós and Tepper, 1999, 2002). Fast-spiking interneurons synapse onto both direct and indirect MSNs as well as other fast-spiking interneurons, but do not synapse onto cholinergic interneurons or low-threshold spiking interneurons (Gittis et al., 2010). In addition to the reciprocal synaptic connections between pairs of fast-spiking interneurons, these neurons form an interconnected network through dendro-dendritic gap junctions (Kita et al., 1990; Koós and Tepper, 1999). Together, fast-spiking interneurons delay or entirely blocking action potentials in many MSNs simultaneously (Koós and Tepper, 1999). Through this network, striatal fast-spiking interneurons provide a strong feedforward inhibition that regulates MSN spike timing to shape the striatal output signal (Koós and Tepper, 1999; Tepper, 2010).

The low-threshold spiking interneurons were characterized, in part, by the presence of a low-threshold calcium spike (Kawaguchi, 1993), and a significant portion of recorded neurons exhibit spontaneous activity (Tepper et al., 2010). The low-threshold spiking interneurons synapse onto distal dendrites of MSNs (DiFiglia and Aronin, 1982; Kubota and Kawaguchi, 2000) and form synaptic contacts with cholinergic interneurons (Vuillet et al., 1989a, b). The inhibitory input from these neurons produces relatively weak GABAergic inhibitory postsynaptic currents in MSNs (Gittis et al., 2010). This may be due to low expression of the GABA synthetic enzyme glutamate decarboxylase expressed in these neurons (Chesselet and Robbins, 1989; Kubota and Kawaguchi, 2000).

The calretinin-expressing interneurons are much less studied, and our knowledge of this cell type depends on immunostaining, as these cells have not been knowingly recorded electrophysiologically (Tepper et al., 2010). These morphological studies indicate that calretinin-expressing interneurons extend aspiny dendrites and can be categorized into three distinct subtypes in the mouse striatum (Tepper et al., 2010). Lastly the TH-expressing interneurons are comprised of a heterogenous class that has been characterized into four types based on intrinsic electrophysiological properties and morphology (Ibáñez-Sandoval et al., 2010). Type I, II, and III neurons innervate striatal MSNs and elicit large amplitude inhibitory post-synaptic potentials that are strong enough to delay MSN action potential firing (Ibáñez-Sandoval et al., 2010). Thus, these TH-positive interneurons provide an additional source of inhibitory control of MSNs.

Although less studied than glutamatergic transmission, there is significant evidence demonstrating that drugs of abuse modulate striatal GABAergic transmission, which likely contributes to maladaptive behaviors seen in substance use disorder. For example, acute cocaine and amphetamine exposure depresses GABAergic inhibitory postsynaptic currents on striatal MSNs, which is mediated by activation of the D2 dopamine receptor in male rats (Centonze et al., 2002). Additionally, opiates, including morphine and heroin, elevate VTA dopaminergic neuron activity by inhibiting presynaptic GABAergic interneurons (Xi and Stein, 2002). For example, acute opiate administration decreases the firing rate of interneurons while increasing the firing rate of VTA dopamine neurons in male rats (Kelley et al., 1980). Additionally, administering gamma-vinyl GABA in to the VTA, an irreversible GABA-transaminase inhibitor, completely blocks heroin-induced dopamine release in the nucleus accumbens and heroin self-administration in male rats (Xi and Stein, 2000). This opiate-induced dopamine release is mediated by $GABA_B$ receptors in the VTA, as administering a $GABA_B$ agonist blocks heroin self-administration and nucleus accumbens dopamine release in male rats (Xi and Stein, 1989, 1999). Further supporting for the involvement of the $GABA_B$ receptor in opiate reward, Tsuji et al. (1996) demonstrated that administering a $GABA_B$ agonist also inhibits morphine conditioned place preference in male rats.

Arguably the most well studied drug-mediated change of GABAergic transmission in the brain, including in the striatum, is by ethanol (Davis and Wu, 2001). While ethanol directly interacts with $GABA_A$ receptors to enhance GABA responses in dorsal root ganglion preparations (Lobo and Harris, 2008), ethanol actions on GABAergic synapses in the striatum is more complicated. In the nucleus accumbens, ethanol does not alter baseline GABAergic synaptic transmission (Patton et al., 2019). Instead, a TrkB-dependent form of long-term synaptic depression of inhibitory inputs to the nucleus accumbens is enhanced by ethanol exposure in male and female mice, which may serve as a physiological substrate for ethanol modulation of nucleus accumbens-mediated reward encoding (Patton et al., 2019). In the dorsal striatum, chronic ethanol exposure selectively reduces the frequency and amplitude of spontaneous GABAergic transmission onto MSNs in the putamen of male cynomolgus monkeys (Cuzon Carlson et al., 2011) and decreases the frequency of inhibitory transmission onto dorsal striatum MSNs in male mice (Willcox et al., 2014). Notably, this effect was more prominent in the DLS compared to the DMS, and this difference may be due to differential effects of chronic alcohol exposure on D1 versus D2 MSNs, as Cheng et al. (2017) demonstrated that chronic ethanol consumption strengthens inhibitory transmission onto D2 neurons in the DMS of male mice. However, a more detailed investigation using transgenic mouse lines is needed to determine whether inhibitory transmission is altered by alcohol exposure specifically onto D1 or D2 MSNs in both subregions of the dorsal striatum. Interestingly, acute ethanol exposure does not directly impact MSN physiology, but instead indirectly influences MSN activity through its actions on striatal interneurons. For example, acute alcohol exposure increases intrinsic excitability of FSIs in male and female rats by suppressing potassium currents (Blomeley et al., 2011). Furthermore, acute ethanol exposure reduces inhibitory transmission from striatal fast-spiking interneurons onto MSNs by activating presynaptic delta-opioid receptors in male and female mice (Patton et al., 2016). Notably, these striatal fast-spiking interneurons are critical for habit formation (O'Hare et al., 2017) and support the formation of habitual action strategies that drive compulsive ethanol consumption (Patton et al., 2020). Continued investigation into the effects of abused substances on GABAergic transmission in the striatum will benefit from technologies that allow circuit-specific manipulations to reveal the specific sources of GABAergic transmission that are impacted by acute and chronic exposure to various drugs of abuse.

Sex differences in substance use disorder

It is important to note that many, if not most, of the studies examining the effects of abused substances on striatal function were conducted in either men, or male rodent models. Therefore, much of our current understanding of how drugs of abuse impact the striatum are viewed from the perspective of the male brain. This historical trend of male-centric research presents a significant obstacle for the development of effective treatment for women with substance use disorder, as drug use and relapse behavior manifests differently in women than in men (Becker and Hu, 2008). Historically, men are two-to-three times more likely to develop a substance use disorder (Becker and Hu, 2008), historically drink larger amounts of alcohol, and exhibit more frequent binge drinking episodes than women (Becker and Koob, 2016). This difference may lie in biological differences as well as cultural influences.

Indeed, as our cultural perspective of gender stereotypes has evolved and the opportunities for women have increased, the gap in alcohol consumption between the sexes has narrowed. Keyes et al. (2008) found that women born between 1912–1932 only reported a 2% prevalence of binge drinking, whereas women born between 1968–1984 reported a 16% prevalence of binge drinking. Further, the 2019 National Survey on Drug Use and Health (NSDUH) found that 29.7% of men and 22.2% of women ages 18 and older reported that they engaged in binge drinking in the past month. In contrast, women are more likely than men: to begin cocaine use at an earlier age (Chen and Kandel, 2002); to consume greater amounts of cocaine; and to exhibit a longer duration of cocaine use (Kosten et al., 1993). Provided these differences in drug consumption between men and women, it is important to understand the biological mechanisms underlying these sex differences in order to develop more personalized therapies for substance use disorder.

While cultural influences significantly impact the likelihood and the onset of initial drug exposure, how an individual responds to and continues using a drug is, in part, influenced by sex hormones (Anker and Carroll, 2010). In a clinical study, the subjective effects of acute amphetamine were self-reported in women across menstrual cycle; revealing that the positive sensation of amphetamine increased during the follicular phase of the menstrual cycle, where estradiol levels slowly rise, and progesterone levels decrease (Becker and Hu, 2008). Further, administration of estradiol increases the positive sensation of acute amphetamine treatment in women (Justice and de Wit, 2000). These studies suggest that ovarian hormones positively modulate the subjective effects of stimulants, which likely contributes to the higher stimulant abuse rates seen in women compared to men. In line with this hypothesis, female rats exhibit a greater locomotor response to amphetamine (Becker et al., 1982) and cocaine compared to male rats (Segarra et al., 2010). Additionally, cocaine-induced CPP is mediated by estradiol in female rats (Segarra et al., 2014) and mice (Satta et al., 2018). One mechanism by which estradiol enhances the rewarding effects of stimulant use is through the modulation of dopamine signaling in the striatum. For example, acute administration of cocaine produces higher levels of electrically-evoked dopamine release events in the DMS in female rats compared to male rats (Walker et al., 2006) and this affect is attenuated in ovariectomized female rats but reinstated by a physiological dose of estrogen (Becker et al., 1999). Additionally, amphetamine-induced CPP is accompanied by a greater increase in dopamine release in the nucleus accumbens of female rats compared to male rats (Robinson and Becker, 1982). Not surprisingly then, the rewarding effects of stimulant use are due, in part, to activation of estrogen receptors in the mesolimbic system. Indeed, knockdown of the estrogen beta receptor prevents cocaine-induced CPP in female mice (Satta et al., 2018).

As we previously mentioned, men historically drink alcohol more than women. However, women are more likely to develop medical problems from excessive drinking (Erol and Karpyak, 2015). As such, examining sex differences in animal models of alcohol drinking is critical. In nonhuman primates, male (cynomolgus) monkeys drink more than females (Vivian et al., 2001). However, in rodents female mice (Eriksson and Pikkarainen, 1968; Sneddon et al., 2019) and rats (Li and Lumeng, 1984) drink more ethanol than males. Similar to cocaine use, sex differences in ethanol consumption are also linked to ovarian hormones, as Almeida et al. (1998) demonstrated that ethanol consumption in neonatally estrogenized female rats, which confers a masculinized adult brain, is reduced to levels similar to male rats. Potentially underlying this difference are the fluctuations in sex hormones evident during critical developmental periods and across the estrous cycle that modulate the nucleus accumbens to promote drug consumption (Tonn Eisinger et al., 2018). For example, while adult female rats drink more than males, and ethanol-induced dopamine release into the nucleus accumbens is greater in adult female rats (Blanchard et al., 1993), adolescent male rats drink more ethanol compared to females (Vetter O'Hagen et al., 2009). Collectively, these studies demonstrate the profound impact that sex hormones, specifically estradiol, exert on drug consumption. It is therefore imperative that we continue exploring at a more detailed circuit level the biological mechanisms underlying sex differences in drug consumption, withdrawal, and relapse to inform sex-specific therapies for substance use disorder.

Conclusions

The striatal complex plays a critical role in the expression of reward-driven actions. As we explore the environment, cues predicting rewards are encoded in the nucleus accumbens. As this occurs, internal emotional information from the amygdala and external contextual information from the hippocampus is integrated in the nucleus accumbens to motivate behavior toward further reward acquisition. As reward acquisition continues, the actions that achieve rewards are encoded in the DMS. During this stage, information about the reward outcome is continuously updated through projections from the medial prefrontal cortex and orbitofrontal cortex to the DMS, and if an action no longer results in a reward, behavior flexibly adapts to this feedback. If an action continues to be reinforced through reward acquisition, an automatized action becomes encoded in the DLS by incoming information from somatosensory and motor cortices. Drugs of abuse modulate each step of this dynamic and parallel processing to facilitate enhanced motivation to perform highly automatized, compulsive drug-seeking behavior.

Drugs of abuse exert these effects on the striatal complex largely by interacting with the rich neurotransmitter systems that orchestrate synaptic plasticity events. Drug-induced neural circuit-specific synaptic plasticity ultimately affects what information is stored in the striatal complex, which includes a pathologically strong motivation to perform habitual actions geared toward compulsive drug-seeking and -taking behaviors. These stored action sequences, consisting of ensembles of striatal interneurons and projection neurons alike, are engaged by thalamic structures to elicit stimulus-response strategies that underlie compulsive drug seeking and consumption, a key feature of addiction that thwarts efforts to limit drug use. Clearly, the circuit-specific mechanisms underlying this transition to compulsive drug use is intimidatingly multidimensional. While the task to devise novel addiction treatments appears daunting, the complexity of the problem also presents a plethora of mechanisms to target for therapeutic strategy development that should be considered through a sex-specific lens.

Bibliography

Abrahao, K.P., Sallnas, A.G., Lovinger, D.M., 2017. Alcohol and the brain: neuronal molecular targets, synapses, and circuits. Neuron 20, 1223–1238.

Adermark, L., Jonsson, S., Ericson, M., Bo, S., 2011. Intermittent ethanol consumption depresses endocannabinoid-signaling in the dorsolateral striatum of rat. Neuropharmacology 61, 1160–1165.

Albin, R.L., 1995. The pathophysiology of chorea/ballism and Parkinsonism. Park. Relat. Disord. 1, 3–11.

Albin, R.L., Young, A.B., Penney, J.B., 1989. The functional anatomy of basal ganglia disorders. TINS (Trends Neurosci.) 12, 366–375.

Almeida, O.F.X., Shoaib, M., Deicke, J., Fischer, D., Darwish, M.H., et al., 1998. Gender differences in ethanol preference and ingestion in rats. J. Clin. Invest. 10, 2677–2685.

Alvarez-Jaimes, L., Polis, I., Parsons, L.H., 2009. Regional influence of cannabinoid CB_1 receptors in the regulation of ethanol self-administration by wistar rats. Open Neuropsychopharmacol. J. 2, 77–85. https://doi.org/10.2174/1876523800902020077. PMID: 27974944; PMCID: PMC5152943.

Ambroggi, F., Ishikawa, A., Fields, H.L., Nicola, S.M., 2008. Basolateral amygdala neurons facilitate reward-seeking behavior by exciting nucleus accumbens neurons. Neuron 59, 648–661.

Anker, J.J., Carroll, M.E., 2010. Females are more vulnerable to drug abuse than males: evidence from preclinical studies and the role of ovarian hormones. Biol. Basis Sex Diff. Psychopharmacol. 8, 73–96.

Aosaki, T., Tsubokawa, H., Ishida, A., Watanabe, K., Graybiel, A.M., Kimura, M., 1994. Responses of tonically active neurons in the primate's striatum undergo systematic changes during behavioral sensorimotor conditioning. J. Neurosci. 14, 3969–3984.

Atwood, B.K., Kupferschmidt, D.A., Lovinger, D.M., 2014. Opioids induce dissociable forms of long-term depression of excitatory inputs to the dorsal striatum. Nat. Neurosci. 17, 540–548.

Augustin, S.M., Chancey, J.H., Lovinger, D.M., 2018. Dual dopaminergic regulation of corticostriatal plasticity by cholinergic interneurons and indirect pathway medium spiny neurons. Cell Rep. 24, 2883–2893.

Bahlmann, J., Aarts, E., D'Esposito, M., 2015. Influence of motivation on control hierarchy in the human frontal cortex. J. Neurosci. 35, 3207–3217.

Bailey, K.R., Mair, R.G., 2006. The role of striatum in initiation and execution of learned action sequences in rats. J. Neurosci. 26, 1016–1025.

Balleine, B., Killcross, S., 1994. Effects of ibotenic acid lesions of the nucleus accumbens on instrumental action. Behav. Brain Res. 65, 181–193.

Bariselli, S., Miyazaki, N.L., Creed, M.C., Kravitz, A.V., 2020. Orbitofrontal-striatal potentiation underlies cocaine-induced hyperactivity. Nat. Commun. 11, 3996.

Barnes, T.D., Kubota, Y., Hu, D., Jin, D.Z., Graybiel, A.M., 2005. Activity of striatal neurons reflects dynamic encoding and recoding of procedural memories. Nature 437, 1158–1161.

Barros, C.S., Franco, S.J., Müller, U., 2011. Extracellular matrix: functions in the nervous system. Cold Spring Harbor Perspect. Biol. 3, a005108.

Bazargani, N., Attwell, D., 2016. Astrocyte calcium signaling: the third wave. Nat. Neurosci. 19, 182–189.

Bechara, A., 2004. The role of emotion in decision making: evidence from neurological patients with orbitofrontal damage. Brain Cognit. 55, 30–40.

Bechara, A., Dolan, S., Denburg, N., Hindes, A., Anderson, S.W., Nathan, P.E., 2000. Decision-making deficits, linked to a dysfunctional ventromedial prefrontal cortex, revealed in alcohol and stimulant abusers. Neuropsychologia 39, 376–389.

Bechara, A., Dolan, S., Denburg, N., Hindes, A., Anderson, S.W., Nathan, P.E., 2001. Decision-making deficits, linked to a dysfunctional ventromedial prefrontal cortex, revealed in alcohol and stimulant abusers. Neuropsychologia 39 (4), 376–389. https://doi.org/10.1016/s0028-3932(00)00136-6. PMID: 11164876.

Becker, J.B., Hu, M., 2008. Sex differences in drug abuse. Front Neuroendocrinol 29 (1), 36–47. https://doi.org/10.1016/j.yfrne.2007.07.003. Epub 2007 Aug 24. PMID: 17904621; PMCID: PMC2235192.

Becker, J.B., Koob, G.F., 2016. Sex differences in animal models: focus on addiction. Pharmacol. Rev. 68, 242–263.

Becker, J.B., Rudick, C.N., 1999. Rapid effects of estrogen or progesterone on amphetamine-induced increase in striatal dopamine are enhanced by estrogen priming: a microdialysis study. Pharmacol. Biochem. Behav. 64, 53–57.

Becker, J.B., Robinson, T.E., Lorenz, K.A., 1982. Sex differences and estrous cycle variations in amphetamine-elicited rotational behavior. Eur. J. Pharmacol. 80, 65–72.

Berendse, H.W., Glias-de Graaf, Y., Groenewegen, H.J., 1992. Topographical organization and relationship with ventral striatal compartments of prefrontal corticostriatal projections in the rat. J. Comp. Neurol. 316, 314–347.

Besheer, J., Grondin, J., Salling, M.C., Spanos, M., Stevenson, R.A., Hodge, C.W., 2009. Interoceptive effects of alcohol require mGlu5 receptor activity in the nucleus accumbens. J. Neurosci. 29, 9582–9591.

Bird, C.M., Burgess, N., 2008. The hippocampus and memory: insights from spatial processing. Nat. Rev. 9, 182–194.

Blanchard, B.A., Steindorf, S., Glick, S.D., 1993. Sex differences in ethanol-induced dopamine release in nucleus accumbens and in ethanol consumption in rats. Alcohol Clin. Exp. Res. 17, 968–973.

Blomeley, C.P., Cains, S., Smith, R., Bracci, E., 2011. Ethanol affects striatal interneurons directly and projection neurons through a reduction in cholinergic tone. Neuropsychopharmacology 36, 1033–1046.

Boender, A.J., Bontempi, L., Nava, L., Pelloux, Y., Tonini, R., 2020. Striatal astrocytes shape behavioral flexibility via regulation of the glutamate transporter EAAT2. Biol. Psychiatr. 89, 1045–1057.

Bondi, C.O., Rodriguez, G., Gould, G.G., Frazer, A., Morilak, D.A., 2008. Chronic unpredictable stress induces a cognitive deficit and anxiety-like behavior in rats that is prevented by chronic antidepressant drug treatment. Neuropsychopharmacology 33 (2), 320–331. https://doi.org/10.1038/sj.npp.1301410. Epub 2007 Apr 4. PMID: 17406647.

Bonson, K.R., Grant, S.J., Contoreggi, C.S., Links, J.M., Metcalfe, J., Weyl, H.L., et al., 2002. Neural systems and cue-induced cocaine craving. Neuropsychopharmacology 26, 376–386.

Bradfield, L.A., Bertran-Gonzalez, J., Chieng, B., Balleine, B.W., 2013. The thalamo-striatal pathway and cholinergic control of goal direct action: interlacing new and existing learning in the striatum. Neuron 79, 1–25.

Britt, J.P., Benaliouad, F., McDevitt, R.A., Stuber, G.D., Wise, R.A., Bonci, A., 2012. Synaptic and behavioral profile of multiple glutamatergic inputs to the nucleus accumbens. Neuron 76, 790–803.

Brown, H.D., Baker, P.M., Ragozzino, M.E., 2010. The parafascicular thalamic nucleus concomitantly influences behavioral flexibility and dorsomedial striatal acetylcholine output in rats. J. Neurosci. 30, 14390–14398.

Burton, A.C., Nakamura, K., Roesch, M.R., 2015. From ventral-medial to dorsal-lateral striatum: neural correlates of reward-guided decision-making. Neurobiol. Learn. Mem. 117, 51–59.

Caillé, S., Alvarez-Jaimes, L., Polis, I., Stouffer, D.G., Parsons, L.H., 2007. Specific alterations of extracellular endocannabinoid levels in the nucleus accumbens by ethanol, heroin, and cocaine self- administration. J. Neurosci. Off. J. Soc. Neurosci. 27 (14), 3695–3702.

Calabresi, P., Maj, R., Pisani, A., Mercuri, N.B., Bernardi, G., 1992. Long-term synaptic depression in the striatum: physiological and pharmacological characterization. J. Neurosci. 12, 4224–4233.

Calabresi, P., Centoze, D., Gubellini, P., Marfia, G.A., Pisani, A., Sancesario, G., et al., 2000. Synaptic transmission in the striatum: from plasticity to neurodegeneration. Prog. Neurobiol. 61, 231–265.

Calipari, E.S., Bagot, R.C., Purushothaman, I., Davidson, T.J., Yorgason, J.T., Peña, C.J., et al., 2016. In vivo imaging identifies temporal signatures of D1 and D2 medium spiny neurons in cocaine reward. Proc. Natl. Acad. Sci. USA 113, 2726–2731.

Centonze, D., Picconi, B., Baunez, C., Borrelli, E., Pisani, A., Bernardi, G., Calabresi, P., 2002. Cocaine and amphetamine depress striatal GABAergic synaptic transmission through D2 dopamine receptors. Neuropsychopharmacology 26, 164–175.

Cervo, L., Samanin, R., 1995. Effects of dopaminergic and glutamatergic receptor antagonists on the acquisition and expression of cocaine conditioning place preference. Brain Res. 673, 8502–8511.

Chang, S.E., Wheeler, D.S., Holland, P.C., 2012. Roles of nucleus accumbens and basolateral amygdala in autoshaped lever pressing. Neurobiol. Learn. Mem. 97, 441–451.

Charpier, S., Pidoux, M., Mahon, S., 2020. Converging sensory and motor cortical inputs onto the same striatal neurons: An in vivo intracellular investigation. PLoS One 15 (2), e0228260. https://doi.org/10.1371/journal.pone.0228260. PMID: 32023274; PMCID: PMC7001913.

Chartoff, E.H., Connery, H.S., 2014. It's MORe exciting than mu: crosstalk between mu opioid receptors and glutamatergic transmission in the mesolimbic dopamine system. Front. Pharmacol. 5, 116.

Chaudhri, N., Woods, C.A., Sahuque, L.L., Gill, T.M., Janak, P.H., 2013. Unilateral inactivation of the basolateral amygdala attenuates context-induced renewal of Pavlovian-conditioned alcohol-seeking. Eur. J. Neurosci. 38 (5), 2751–2761. https://doi.org/10.1111/ejn.12278. Epub 2013 Jun 12. PMID: 23758059; PMCID: PMC4079556.

Chen, K., Kandel, D., 2002. Relationship between extent of cocaine use and dependence among adolescents and adults in the United States. Drug Alcohol Depend. 68, 65–85.

Cheng, Y., Huang, C.C.Y., Ma, T., Wei, X., Wang, X., Lu, J., Wang, J., 2017. Distinct synaptic strengthening of the striatal direct and indirect pathways drives alcohol consumption. Biol. Psychiatr. 81, 918–929.

Chesselet, M.F., Robbins, E., 1989. Characterization of striatal neurons expressing high levels of glutamic acid decarboxylase messenger RNA. Brain Res. 492, 237–244.

Chioma, V.C., Kruyer, A., Bobadilla, A., Angelis, A., Ellison, Z., et al., 2021. Heroin seeking and extinction from seeking activate matrix metalloproteinases at synapses on distinct subpopulations of accumbens cells. Biol. Psychiatr. 89, 947–958.

Cho, Y.T., Erns, M., Fudge, J.L., 2013. Cortico-amygdala-striatal circuits are organized as hierarchical subsystems through the primate amygdala. J. Neurosci. 33, 14017–14030.

Christian, D.T., Alexander, N.J., Diaz, M.R., Robinson, S., McCool, B.A., 2012. Chronic intermittent ethanol and withdrawal differentially modulate basolateral amygdala AMPA-type glutamate receptor function and trafficking. Neuropharmacology 62, 2430–2439.

Christie, M.J., Summers, R.J., Stephenson, J.A., Cook, C.J., Beart, P.M., 1987. Excitatory amino acid projections to the nucleus accumbens septi in the rat: a retrograde transport study utilizing D[3H]aspartate and [3H]GABA. Neuroscience 2, 425–439.

Churchill, L., Kalivas, P.W., 1994. A topographically organized gamma-aminobutyric acid projection from the ventral pallidum to the nucleus accumbens in the rat. J. Comp. Neurol. 345, 579–595.

Clarke, R.B., Adermark, L., 2010. Acute ethanol treatment prevents endocannabinoid-mediated long-lasting disinhibition of striatal output. Neuropharmacology 58 (4-5), 799–805. https://doi.org/10.1016/j.neuropharm.2009.12.006. Epub 2009 Dec 21. PMID: 20026138.

Clemens, K.J., Castino, R.M., Corish, J.L., Goodchild, A.K., Holmes, N.M., 2014. Behavioral and neural substrates of habit formation in rats intravenously self-administering nicotine. Neuropsychopharmacology 39, 2584–2593.

Colombo, G., Serra, S., Brunetti, G., Gomes, R., Melis, S., Vacca, G., et al., 2002. Stimulation of voluntary ethanol intake by cannabinoid receptor agonists in ethanol-preferring sP rats. Psychopharmacology 159, 181–187.

Cook, S.C., Wellman, C.L., 2004. Chronic stress alters dendritic morphology in rat medial prefrontal cortex. J. Neurobiol. 60, 236–248.

Corbit, L.H., Muir, J.L., Balleine, B.W., 2001. The role of the nucleus accumbens in instrumental conditioning: evidence of a functional dissociation between accumbens core and shell. J. Neurosci. 21, 3251–3260.

Corbit, L.H., Nie, H., Janak, P.H., 2012. Habitual alcohol seeking: time course and the contribution of subregions of the dorsal striatum. Biol. Psychiatr. 72, 389–395.

Cover, K.K., Mathur, B.N., 2021. Rostral intralaminar thalamus engagement in cognition and behavior. Front. Behav. Neurosci. 15, 652764.

Cover, K.K., Gyawali, U., Kerkhoff, W.G., Patton, M.H., Mu, C., White, M.G., et al., 2019. Activation of the rostral intralaminar thalamus drives reinforcement through striatal dopamine release. Cell Rep. 26, 1389–1398.

Cui, G., Jun, S.B., Pham, M.D., Vogel, S.S., Lovinger, D.M., Costa, R.M., 2013. Concurrent activation of striatal direct and indirect pathways during action initiation. Nature 494, 238–245.

Cuzon Carlson, V.C., Seabold, G.K., Helms, C.M., Garg, N., Odagiri, M., Rau, A.R., et al., 2011. Synaptic and morphological neuroadaptations in the putamen associated with long-term, relapsing alcohol drinking in primates. Neuropsychopharmacology 26, 2513–2528.

Davis, K.M., Wu, J.Y., 2001. Role of glutamatergic and GABAergic systems in alcoholism. J. Biomed. Sci. 8, 7–19.

Dang, M.T., Yokoi, F., Yin, H.H., Lovinger, D.M., Wang, Y., Li, Y., 2006. Disrupted motor learning and long-term synaptic plasticity in mice lacking NMDAR1 in the striatum. Proc. Natl. Acad. Sci. U S A. 103 (41), 15254–15259. https://doi.org/10.1073/pnas.0601758103. Epub 2006 Oct 2. PMID: 17015831; PMCID: PMC1622809.

de Wit, S., Watson, P., Harsay, H.A., Cohen, M.X., van de Vijver, I., Ridderinkhof, R.K., 2012. Corticostriatal connectivity underlies individual differences in the balance between habitual and goal-directed action control. J. Neurosci. 32, 12066–12075.

Deehan Jr., G.A., Knight, C.P., Waeiss, R.A., Engleman, E.A., Toalston, J.E., McBride, W.J., et al., 2016. Peripheral administration of ethanol results in a correlated increase in dopamine and serotonin within the posterior ventral tegmental area. Alcohol 51 (5), 535–540.

DePoy, L., Daut, R., Brigman, J., MacPherson, K., Crowley, N., Gunduz-Cinar, O., et al., 2013. Chronic alcohol produces neuroadaptations to prime dorsal striatal learning. Proc. Natl. Acad. Sci. USA 110, 14783–14788.

Desrochers, T.M., Amemori, K., Graybiel, A.M., 2015. Habit learning by naïve macaques is marked by response sharpening of striatal neurons representing the cost and outcome of acquired action sequences. Neuron 87, 853–868.

Dhawale, A.K., Wolff, S.B.E., Ko, R., Ölveczky, B.P., 2019. The Basal Ganglia Can Control Learned Motor Sequences Independently of Motor Cortex. bioRxiv.

Di Chiara, G., Imperato, A., 1988. Drugs abused by humans preferentially increase synaptic dopamine concentrations in the mesolimbic system of freely moving rats. Proc. Natl. Acad. Sci. U.S.A. 85, 5274–5278.

Di Ciano, P., Everitt, B.J., 2004. Direct Interactions between the basolateral amygdala and nucleus accumbens core underlie cocaine-seeking behavior by rats. J. Neurosci. 24, 7167–7173.

Dias-Ferreira, E., Sousa, J.C., Melo, I., Morgado, P., Mesquita, A.R., Cerquira, J.J., et al., 2009. Chronic stress causes frontostriatal reorganization and affects decision-making. Science 325, 621–625.

Diaz del Guante, M.A., Cruz-Morales, S.E., Prado-Alcalá, R.A., 1991. Time-dependent effects of cholinergic blockade of the striatum on memory. Neurosci. Lett. 122, 79–82.

Diaz, M.R., Christain, D.T., Anderson, N.J., McCool, B.A., 2011. Chronic ethanol and withdrawal differentially modulate latera/basolateral amygdala paracapsular and local GABAergic synapses. J. Pharmacol. Exp. Therapeut. 337, 162–170.

Dickinson, A., Balleine, B., 1994. Motivational control of goal-directed action. Anim. Learn. Behav. 22, 1–18.

Dickinson, A., Wood, N., Smith, J.W., 2002. Alcohol seeking by rats: action of habit? Q. J. Exp. Psychol. B 55, 331–348.

DiFiglia, M., Aronin, N., 1982. Ultrastructural features of immunoreactive somatostatin neurons in the rat caudate nucleus. J. Neurosci. 2, 1267–1274.

Ding, D.C.D., Gabbott, P.L.A., totterdell, S., 2001. Difference in the laminar origin of projections from the prefrontal cortex to the nucleus accumbens shell and core regions in the rat. Brain Res. 917, 81–89.

Ding, J., Peterson, J.D., Surmeier, J.D., 2008. Corticostriatal and thalamostriatal synapses have distinct properties. J. Neurosci. 28, 6483–6492.

Ding, J.B., Guzman, J.N., Peterson, J.D., Goldberg, J.A., Surmeier, J.D., 2010. Thalamic gating of corticostriatal signaling by cholinergic interneurons. Neuron 67, 294–307.

Dityatev, A., Brückner, G., Dityateva, G., Grosche, J., Kleene, R., Schachner, M., 2007. Activity-dependent formation and functions of chondroitin sulfate-rich extracellular matrix of perineuronal nets. Dev. Neurobiol. 67 (5), 570–588.

Dubach, M., Schmidt, R., Kunkel, D., Bowden, D.M., Martin, R., German, D.C., 1987. Primate neostriatal neurons containing tyrosine hydroxylase. Immunohistochemical evidence. Neurosci. Lett. 75, 205–210.

Due, D., Huettel, S., Hall, W., Rubin, D., 2002. Activation in mesolimbic and visuospatial neural circuits elicited by smoking cues: evidence from functional magnetic resonance imaging. Am. J. Psychiatr. 159, 954–960.

Eisch, A.J., Harburg, G.C., 2006. Opiates, psychostimulants, and adult hippocampal neurogenesis: insights for addiction and stem cell biology. Hippocampus 16, 271–286.

Engleman, E.A., Ding, Z., Oster, S.M., Toalston, J.E., Bell, R.L., Murphy, J.M., et al., 2009. Ethanol is self-administered into the nucleus accumbens shell but not the core: evidence of genetic sensitivity. Alcohol Clin. Exp. Res. 33, 2162–2171.

Eriksson, K., Pikkarainen, P.H., 1968. Differences between the sexes in voluntary alcohol consumption and liver ADH-activity in inbred strains of mice. Metabolism 17, 1037–1042.

Erol, A., Karpyak, V.M., 2015. Sex and gender-related differences in alcohol use and its consequences: Contemporary knowledge and future research considerations. Drug Alcohol Depend 156, 1–13. https://doi.org/10.1016/j.drugalcdep.2015.08.023. Epub 2015 Sep 5. PMID: 26371405.

Ersche, K.D., Barnes, A., Jones, P.S., Morein-Zamin, S., Robbins, T.W., Bullmore, E.T., 2011. Abnormal structure of frontostriatal brain systems is associated with aspects of impulsivity and compulsivity in cocaine dependence. Brain 134, 2013–2024.

Euston, D.R., Gruber, A.J., McNaughton, B.L., 2012. The role of medial prefrontal cortex in memory and decision making. Neuron 76, 1057–1070.

Everitt, B.J., Robbins, T.W., 2005. Neural systems of reinforcement for drug addiction: from actions to habits to compulsion. Nat. Neurosci. 8, 1481–1489.

Everitt, B.J., Robbins, T.W., 2013. From the ventral to the dorsal striatum: devolving views of their roles in drug addiction. Neurosci. Biobehav. Rev. 37, 1946–1954.

Everitt, B.J., Robbins, T.W., 2016. Drug addictions. Updating actions to habits to compulsions ten years on. Annu. Rev. Psychol. 67, 23–50.

Everitt, B.J., Wolf, M.E., 2002. Psychomotor stimulant addiction: a neural systems perspective. J. Neurosci. 22, 3312–3320.

Everitt, B.J., Belin, D., Economidou, D., Pelloux, Y., Dalley, J.W., Robbins, T.W., 2008. Neural mechanisms underlying vulnerability to develop compulsive drug-seek habits and addiction. Phil. Trans. Royal Soc. B 363, 3125–3135.

Faure, A., Haberland, U., Condé, F., El Massioui, N., 2005. Lesions to the nigrostriatal dopamine system disrupts stimulus-response habit formation. J. Neurosci. 25, 2771–2780.

Fein, G., Di Sclafani, V., Meyerhoff, D.J., 2002. Prefrontal cortical volume reduction associated with frontal cortex function deficit in 6-week abstinent crack-cocaine dependent men. Drug Alcohol Depend. 68, 87–93.

Feldstein Ewing, S.W., Filbey, F.M., Chandler, L.D., Hutchison, K.E., 2010. Exploring the relationship between depressive and anxiety symptoms and neuronal response to alcohol cues. Alcohol Clin. Exp. Res. 34 (3), 396–403. https://doi.org/10.1111/j.1530-0277.2009.01104.x. Epub 2009 Dec 17. PMID: 20028366; PMCID: PMC2911356.

Feldstein Ewing, S.W., Filbey, F.M., Sabbineni, A., Chandler, L.D., Hutchinson, K.E., 2011. How psychosocial alcohol interventions work: a preliminary look at what fMRI can tell us. Alcohol Clin. Exp. Res. 35, 643–651.

Fisher, S.D., Reynolds, J.N.J., 2014. The intralaminar thalamus- an expressway linking visual stimuli to circuits determining agency and action selection. Front. Behav. Neurosci. 8, 1–7.

Fisher, S.D., Ferguson, L.A., Bertran-Gonzales, J., Balleine, B.W., 2020. Amygdala-cortical control of striatal plasticity drives the acquisition of goal-directed action. bioRxiv. https://doi.org/10.1016/j.cub.2020.08.090.

Flaherty, A.W., Graybiel, A.M., 1994. Input-output organization of the sensorimotor striatum in the squirrel monkey. J. Neurosci. 14, 599–610.

Floresco, S.B., 2015. The nucleus accumbens: an interface between cognition, emotion, and action. Annu. Rev. Psychol. 66, 25–52.

Fouyssac, M., Belin, D., 2019. Beyond drug-induced alteration of glutamate homeostasis, astrocytes may contribute to dopamine-dependent intrastriatal functional shifts that underlie the development of drug addiction: A working hypothesis. Eur. J. Neurosci. 50 (6), 3014–3027. https://doi.org/10.1111/ejn.14416. Epub 2019 May 14. PMID: 30968489; PMCID: PMC6852203.

Franklin, T.R., Acton, P.D., Maldjian, J.A., Gray, J.D., Croft, J.R., Dackis, C.A., et al., 2002. Decreased gray matter concentrations in the insular, orbitofrontal, cingulate, and temporal cortices of cocaine patients. Biol. Psychiatr. 51, 134–142.

French, I.T., Muthusamy, K.A., 2018. A review of pedunculopontine nucleus in Parkinson's disease. Front. Aging Neurosci. 10, 1–16.

French, S.J., Totterdell, S., 2002. Hippocampal and prefrontal cortical inputs monosynaptically converge with individual projection neurons of the nucleus accumbens. J. Comp. Neurol. 446, 151–165.

Fuchs, R.A., weber, S.M., Rice, H.J., Neisewander, J.L., 2002. Effects of excitotoxic lesions of the basolateral amygdala on cocaine-seeking behavior and cocaine conditioned place preference in rats. Brain Res. 929, 15–25.

Fudge, J.L., Kunishio, K., Walsh, P., Richard, C., Haber, S.N., 2002. Amygdaloid projections to ventromedial striatal subterritories in the primate. Neuroscience 110, 257–275.

Funk, C.K., Zorrilla, E.P., Lee, M.J., Rice, K.C., Koob, G.F., 2007. Corticotropin-releasing factor 1 antagonists selectively reduce ethanol self-administration in ethanol-dependent rats. Biol. Psychiatr. 61, 78–86.

Furlon, T.M., Alva, S.A., Corbit, L.H., Killcross, S., Balleine, B.W., 2015. Pulling habits out of rats: adenosine 2A receptor antagonism in dorsomedial striatum rescues methamphetamine-induced deficits in goal-directed action. Addiction Biol. 22, 172–183.

Furlong, T.M., Supit, A.S., Corbit, L.H., Killcross, S., Balleine, B.W., 2017. Pulling habits out of rats: adenosine 2A receptor antagonism in dorsomedial striatum rescues meth-amphetamine-induced deficits in goal-directed action. Addict. Biol. 22 (1), 172–183. https://doi.org/10.1111/adb.12316. Epub 2015 Oct 30. PMID: 26515740; PMCID: PMC4851927.

Gangarossa, G., Espallergues, J., d'Exaerde, A., Mestikawy, S., Gerfen, C.R., Girault, J., Valjent, E., 2013. Distribution and compartmental organization of GABAergic medium-sized spiny neurons in the mouse nucleus accumbens. Front. Neural Circ. 7, 1–20.

Gass, J.T., Sinclair, C.M., cleva, R.M., Widholm, J.J., Olive, F.M., 2011. Alcohol-seeking behavior is associated with increased glutamate transmission in basolateral amygdala and nucleus accumbens as measured by glutamate-oxidase coated biosensors. Addiction Biol. 16, 215–228.

George, O., Ghozland, S., Azar, M.R., Cottone, P., Zorrilla, E.P., et al., 2007. CRF-CRF1 system activation mediates withdrawal-induced increases in nicotine self-administration in nicotine-dependent rats. Proc. Natl. Acad. Sci. U.S.A. 104, 17198–17203.

Gerdeman, G., Lovinger, D.M., 2000. CB1 cannabinoid receptor inhibits synaptic release of glutamate in rat dorsolateral striatum. Am. Physiol. Soc. 85, 468–471.

Gerdeman, G.L., Partridge, J.G., Lupica, C.R., Lovinger, D.M., 2003. It could be habit forming drugs of abuse and striatal synaptic plasticity. Trends Neurosci. 26, 184–192.

Gerfen, C.R., 1988. Synaptic organization of the striatum. J. Electron. Microsc. Tech. 10, 265–281.

Gerfen, C.R., Engber, T.M., Mahan, L.C., Susel, Z., Chase, T.N., Monsma, F.J., Sibley, D.R., 1990. D1 and D2 dopamine receptor-regulated gene expression of striatonigral and striatopallidal neurons. Science 250, 1429–1432.

Gilman, J.M., Ramchandani, V.A., Davis, M.G., Bjork, J.M., Hommer, D.W., 2008. Why we like to drink: a functional magnetic resonance study of the rewarding and anxiolytic effects of alcohol. J. Neurosci. 28, 4583–4591.

Gittis, A.H., Nelson, A.B., Thwin, M.T., Palop, J.J., Kreitzer, A.C., 2010. Distinct roles of GABAergic interneurons in the regulation of striatal output pathways. J. Neurosci. 30, 2223–2234.

Glass, M.J., 2011. Opioid dependence and NMDA receptors. ILAR J. 42, 342–351.

Goldman-Rakic, P.S., Selemon, L.D., 1986. Topography of corticostriatal projections in nonhuman primates and implications for functional parcellation of the neostriatum. Cerebr. Cortex 5. https://doi.org/10.1007/978-1-4613-2149-1_12.

Goldstein, R.Z., Volkow, N.D., 2002. Drug addiction and its underlying neurobiological basis: neuroimaging evidence for the involvement of the frontal cortex. Am. J. Psychiatr. 159, 1642–1652.

Goodan, J., Leong, K., Packard, M.G., 2015. Glucocorticoid enhancement of dorsolateral striatum-dependent habit memory requires concurrent noradrenergic activity. Neuroscience 311, 1–8. https://doi.org/10.1016/j.neuroscience.2015.10.014. Epub 2015 Oct 22. PMID: 26470808.

Goode, T.D., Leong, K., Goodman, J., Maren, S., Packard, M.G., 2016. Enhancement of striatum-dependent memory by conditioned fear is mediated by beta-adrenergic receptors in the basolateral amygdala. Neurobiol Stress 3, 74–82.

Goodman, J., McIntyre, C.K., 2017. Impaired spatial memory and enhanced habit memory in a rat model of post-traumatic stress disorder. Front. Pharmacol. 8, 663.

Goodman, J., Leong, K.C., Packard, M.G., 2015. Glucocorticoid enhancement of dorsolateral striatum-dependent habit memory requires concurrent noradrenergic activity. Neuroscience 311, 1–8. https://doi.org/10.1016/j.neuroscience.2015.10.014. Epub 2015 Oct 22. PMID: 26470808.

Goodroe, S.C., Starnes, J., Brown, T.I., 2018. The complex nature of hippocampal-striatal interactions in spatial navigation. Front. Hum. Neurosci. 12, 250.

Graybiel, A.M., 1998. The basal ganglia and chunking of action repertoires. Neurobiol. Learn. Mem. 70, 119–136.

Graybiel, A.M., 2008. Habits, rituals and the evaluative brain. Annu. Rev. Neurosci. 31, 359–387.

Graybiel, A.M., Rauch, S.L., 2000. Toward a neurobiology of obsessive-compulsive disorder. Neuron 28, 343–347.

Greenwell, T.N., Funk, C.K., Cottone, P., Richardson, H.N., Chen, S.A., et al., 2009. Corticotropin-releasing factor-1 receptor antagonists decrease heroin self-administration in long-but not short- access rats. Addiction Biol. 14, 130–143.

Gremel, C.M., Costa, R.M., 2013. Orbitofrontal and striatal circuits dynamically encode the shift between goal-directed and habitual actions. Nat. Commun. 4, 2264.

Gremel, C.M., Cunningham, C.L., 2009. Involvement of amygdala dopamine and nucleus accumbens NMDA receptors in ethanol-seeking behavior in mice. Neuropsychopharmacology 34, 1443–1453.

Groenewegen, H.J., Berendse, H.W., 1994. The specificity of the 'nonspecific' midline and intralaminar thalamic nuclei. Trends Neurosci. 17, 52–57.

Groenewegen, H.J., Room, P., Witter, M.P., Loham, A.H., 1982. Cortical afferents of the nucleus accumbens in the cat, studied with anterograde and retrograde transport techniques. Neuroscience 7, 977–996.

Groenewegen, H.J., Wright, C.I., Beijer, A.V., 1996. The nucleus accumbens: gateway for limbic structures to reach the motor system? Prog. Brain Res. 107, 485–511.

Groman, S.M., Keistler, C., Keip, A.J., Pittenger, C., Lee, D., Taylor, J.R., 2019. Orbitofrontal circuits control multiple reinforcement-learning processes. Neuron 103, 734–746.

Haber, S.N., 2016. Corticostriatal circuitry. Dialogues Clin. Neurosci. 18, 7–21.

Haber, S.N., Fudge, J.L., 1997. The interface between dopamine neurons and the amygdala: implications for schizophrenia. Schizophr. Bull. 23, 471–482.

Haber, S.N., Fudge, J.L., McFarland, N.R., 2000. Striatonigrostriatal pathways in primates form an ascending spiral from the shell to the dorsolateral striatum. J. Neurosci. 20, 2369–2382.

Hamlin, A.S., Clemens, K.J., Choi, E.A., McNally, G.P., 2009. Paraventricular thalamus mediates context-induced reinstatement (renewal) of extinguished reward seeking. Eur. J. Neurosci. 29, 802–812.

Hawes, S.L., Evans, R.C., Unruh, B.A., Benkert, E.E., Gillani, F., Dumans, T.C., Blackwell, K.T., 2015. Multimodal plasticity in dorsal striatum while learning a lateralized navigation task. J. Neurosci. 35, 10535–10549.

Hawes, S.L., Salinas, A.G., Lovinger, D.M., Blackwell, K.T., 2017. Long-term plasticity of corticostriatal synapses is modulated by pathway-specific co-release of opioids through kappa-opioid receptors. J. Physiol. 16, 5637–5652.

Heimer, L., Zahm, D.S., Churchill, L., Kalivas, P.W., Wohltmann, C., 1991. Specificity in the projection patterns of accumbal core and shell in the rat. Neuroscience 41, 89–125.

Hikosaka, O., 2007. Basal ganglia mechanisms of reward-oriented eye movement. Ann. N. Y. Acad. Sci. https://doi.org/10.1196/annals.1390.012.

Hikosaka, O., Takikawa, Y., Kawagoe, R., 2000. Role of the basal ganglia in the control of purposive saccadic eye movements. Physiol. Rev. 80, 953–970.

Hikosaka, O., Kim, H.F., Amita, H., Yasuda, M., Isoda, M., Tachibana, Y., Yoshida, A., 2019. Direct and indirect pathways for choosing objects and actions. Eur. J. Neurosci. 49, 637–645.

Hintiryan, H., Foster, N.N., Bowman, I., Bay, M., Song, M.Y., Gou, L., et al., 2016. The mouse cortico-striatal projectome. Nat. Neurosci. 19, 1100–1114.

Hipólito, L., Sánche-Catalán, M.J., Zanolini, S., Polache, A., Granero, L., 2008. Shell/core differences in mu- and delta-opioid receptor modulation of dopamine efflux in nucleus accumbens. Neuropharmacology 55, 183–189.

Hirvonen, J., Zanotti-Fregonara, P., Umhau, J.C., George, D.T., Rallis-Frutos, D., Lyoo, C.H., Li, C.T., Hines, C.S., Sun, H., Terry, G.E., Morse, C., Zoghbi, S.S., Pike, V.W., Innis, R.B., Heilig, M., 2013. Reduced cannabinoid CB1 receptor binding in alcohol dependence measured with positron emission tomography. Mol. Psychiatry. 18 (8), 916–921. https://doi.org/10.1038/mp.2012.100. Epub 2012 Jul 10. PMID: 22776901; PMCID: PMC3594469.

Hooks, B.M., Papale, A.E., Paletzki, R.F., Feroze, M.W., Eastwood, B.S., Couey, J.J., Winnubst, J., Chandrashekar, J., Gerfen, C.R., 2018. Topographic precision in sensory and motor corticostriatal projections varies across cell type and cortical area. Nat. Commun. 9 (1), 3549. https://doi.org/10.1038/s41467-018-05780-7. Erratum in: Nat Commun. 2018 Oct 12;9(1):4317. PMID: 30177709; PMCID: PMC6120881.

Hoover, W.B., Vertes, R.P., 2011. Projections of the medial orbital and ventral orbital cortex in the rat. J. Comp. Neurol. 519, 3766–3801.

Huang, A.S., Mitchel, J.A., Haber, S.N., Alia-Klein, N., Goldstein, R.Z., 2017. The thalamus in drug addiction: from rodents to humans. Phil. Trans. R Soc. B 373, 20170028.

Hunnicutt, B.J., Jongbloets, B.C., Birdson, W.T., Gertz, K.J., Zhon, H., Mao, T., 2016. A comprehensive excitatory input map of the striatum reveals novel functional organization. elife 5, e19103.

Hyrbouski, S., Aghamohammadi-Sereshki, A., Madan, C.R., Shafer, A.T., Baron, C.A., Seres, P., et al., 2016. Amygdala subnuclei response and connectivity during emotional processing. NeuroImage 133, 98–110.

Ibáñez-Sandoval, O., Tecuapetla, F., Unal, B., Shah, F., Koós, T., Tepper, J.M., 2010. Electrophysiological and morphological characteristics and synaptic connectivity of tyrosine hydroxylase-expressing neurons in adult mouse striatum. J. Neurosci. 30, 6999–7016.

Jin, X., Costa, R.M., 2010. Start/stop signals emerge in nigrostriatal circuits during sequence learning. Nature 466, 457–462.

Jin, X., Costa, R.M., 2015. Shaping action sequences in basal ganglia circuits. Curr. Opin. Neurobiol. 33, 188–196. https://doi.org/10.1016/j.conb.2015.06.011. Epub 2015 Jul 17. PMID: 26189204; PMCID: PMC4523429.

Joel, D., Doljansky, J., Roz, N., Rehavi, M., 2005a. Role of the orbital cortex and of the serotonergic system in a rat model of obsessive-compulsive disorder. Neuroscience 130, 25–36.

Joel, D., Doljansky, J., Schiller, D., 2005b. 'Compulsive' lever pressing in rats is enhanced following lesions to the orbital cortex, but not to the basolateral nucleus of the amygdala or to the dorsal medial prefrontal cortex. Eur. J. Neurosci. 21, 2252–2262.

Johnson, B.A., Ait-Daoud, N., Wells, L.T., 2000. Effects of israpidine, a dihydropyridine-class calcium channel antagonist, on D-methamphetamine-induced cognitive and physiological changes in humans. Neuropsychopharmacology 22, 504–512.

Justice, A.J.H., de Wit, H., 2000. Acute effects of estradiol pretreatment on the response to d-amphetamine in women. Clin. Neuroendocrinol. 71, 51–59.

Kaada, B.R., 1972. Stimulation and regional ablation of the amygdaloid complex with reference to functional representations. In: Eleftheriou, B.E. (Ed.), The Neurobiology of Amygdala. Plenum, New York, pp. 205–281.

Kähkönen, S., Wilenius, J., Nikulkn, V.V., Olikainen, M., Ilmoniemi, R.J., 2003. Alcohol reduces prefrontal cortical excitability in humans: a combined TMS and EEG study. Neuropsychopharmacology 28, 747–754.

Kawaguchi, Y., 1993. Physiological, morphological, and histochemical characterization of three classes of interneurons in rat neostriatum. J. Neurosci. 13 (11), 4908–4923. https://doi.org/10.1523/JNEUROSCI.13-11-04908.1993. PMID: 7693897; PMCID: PMC6576359.

Kawaguchi, Y., Wilson, C.J., Emson, P.C., 1990. Projection subtypes of rat neostriatal matrix cells revealed by intracellular injection of biocytin. J. Neurosci. 10, 3421–3438.

Kawaguchi, Y., Wilson, C.J., Augood, S.J., Emson, P.C., 1995. Striatal interneurons. Chemical, physiological and morphological characterization. Trends Neurosci. 18, 527–535.

Kawai, R., Markman, T., Poddar, R., Ko, R., Fantan, A., Dhawale, A.K., et al., 2015. Motor cortex is required for learning but not for executing a motor skill. Neuron 86, 800–812.

Keistler, C.R., Hammarlund, E., Barker, J., Bond, C.W., DiLeone, R.J., Pittenge, C., Taylor, J.R., 2017. Regulation of alcohol extinction and cue-induced reinstatement by specific projections among medial prefrontal cortex, nucleus accumbens, and basolateral amygdala. J. Neurosci. 37, 4462–4471.

Kelley, A.E., Throne, L.C., 1992. NMDA receptors mediate the behavioral effects of amphetamine infused into the nucleus accumbens. Brain Res. Bull. 29, 247–254.

Kelley, A.E., Stinus, L., Iversen, S.D., 1980. Interactions between D-ala-met-enkephalin, A10 dopaminergic neurones, and spontaneous behaviour in the rat. Behav. Brain Res. 1 (1), 3–24. https://doi.org/10.1016/0166-4328(80)90043-1. PMID: 6269560.

Kelley, A.E., Domesick, V.B., Nauta, W.J.H., 1982. The amygdalo-striatal projection in the rat- an anatomical study by anterograde and retrograde tracing methods. Neuroscience 7, 615–630.

Keyes, K.M., Grant, B.F., Hasin, D.S., 2008. Evidence for a closing gender gap in alcohol use, abuse, and dependence in the United States population. Drug Alcohol Depend. 93, 21–29.

Khakh, B.S., 2019. Astrocyte-neuron interactions in the striatum: insights on identity, form, and function. Trends Neurosci. 42, 617–630.

Kilts, C.D., Schqeitzer, J.B., Quinn, C.K., Gross, R.E., Faber, T.L., et al., 2001. Neural activity related to drug craving in cocaine addiction. Arch. Gen. Psychiatr. 58, 334–341.

Kim, R., Sepulveda-Orengo, M.T., Healey, K.L., Williams, E.A., Reissner, K.J., 2018. Regulation of glutamate transporter 1 (GLT-1) gene expression by cocaine self-administration and withdrawal. Neuropharmacology 128, 1–10.

Kircher, D.M., Aziz, H.C., Mangieri, R.A., Morrisett, R.A., 2019. Ethanol experience enhances glutamatergic ventral hippocampal inputs to D1 receptor-expressing medium spiny neurons in the nucleus accumbens shell. J. Neurosci. 39, 2459–2469.

Kita, H., 1992. Responses of globus pallidus neurons to cortical stimulation. Intracellular study in the rat. Brain Res. 589, 84–90.

Kita, H., Kosaka, T., Heizmann, C.W., 1990. Parvalbumin-immunoreactive neurons in the rat neostriatum: a light and electron microscopic study. Brain Res. 536, 1–15.

Klaus, A., Martins, G.J., Paixao, V.B., Zhou, P., Paninski, L., Costa, R.M., 2017. The spatiotemporal organization of the striatum encodes action space. Neuron 95, 1171–1180.

Klug, J.R., Engelhardt, M.D., Cadman, C.N., Li, H., Smith, J.B., Ayala, S., et al., 2018. Differential inputs to striatal cholinergic and parvalbumin interneurons imply functional distinctions. elife 7, e35657.

Knutson, B., Adams, C.M., Fong, G.W., Hommer, D., 2001. Anticipation of increased monetary reward selectively recruits nucleus accumbens. J. Neurosci. 21, 1–5.

Kobiella, A., Ulshöfer, D., Vollmert, C., Vollstâdt-Klein, S., Bühler, M., Esslinger, C., et al., 2010. Nicotine increases neural responses to unpleasant stimuli and anxiety in non-smokers. Addiction Biol. 6, 285–295.

Koo, J.W., Mazei-Robison, M.S., Chaudhury, D., Juarez, B., LaPlant, Q., Ferguson, D., et al., 2012. BDNF is a negative modulator of morphine action. Science 338, 124–128.

Koob, G.F., Volkow, N.D., 2016. Neurobiology of addiction: a neurocircuitry analysis. Lancet Psychiatr. 3, 760–773.

Koob, G.F., Buck, C.L., Cohen, A., Edwards, S., Park, P.E., et al., 2014. Addition as a stress surfeit disorder. Neuropharmacology 76, 370–382.

Koós, T., Tepper, J.M., 1999. Inhibitory control of neostriatal projection neurons by GABAergic interneurons. Nat. Neurosci. 2, 467–472.

Koós, T., Tepper, J.M., 2002. Dual cholinergic control of fast-spiking interneurons in the neostriatum. J. Neurosci. 22, 529–535.

Kosten, T.A., Gawin, F.H., Kosten, T.R., Rounsaville, B.J., 1993. Gender differences in cocaine use and treatment response. J. Subst. Abuse Treat. 10, 63–66.

Kravitz, A.V., Freeze, B.S., Parker, P.R.L., Kay, K., Thwin, M.T., Deisseroth, K., Kreitzer, A.C., 2010. Regulation of parkinsonian motor behaviors by optogenetic control of basal ganglia circuitry. Nature 466, 622–626.

Krettek, J.E., Price, J.L., 1978. Amygdaloid projections to subcortical structures within the basal forebrain and brainstem in the rat and cat. J. Comp. Neurobiol. 178, 225–254.

Kruyer, A., Kalivas, P.W., 2021. Astrocytes as cellular mediators of cue reactivity in addiction. Curr. Opin. Pharmacol. 56, 1–6.

Kubota, Y., Kawaguchi, Y., 2000. Dependence of GABAergic synaptic areas on the interneuron type and target size. J. Neurosci. 20, 375–386.

Kuhar, M.J., Ritz, M.C., Boja, J.W., 1991. The dopamine hypothesis of the reinforcing properties of cocaine. Trends Neurosci. 14, 299–302.

Kumari, M., Ticku, M., 2000. Regulation of NMDA receptors by ethanol. Prog. Drug Res. 54, 152–189.

Kupchik, Y., Kalivas, P.W., 2017. The direct and indirect pathways of the nucleus accumbens are not what you think. Neuropsychopharmacol. Rev. 42, 369–370.

Kupchik, Y.M., Brown, R.M., Heinsbroek, J.A., Lobo, M.K., Schwartz, D.J., Kalivas, P.W., 2015. Coding the direct/indirect pathways by D1 and D2 receptors is not valid for accumbens projections. Nat. Neurosci. 18, 1230–1232.

Kupferschmidt, D.A., Juczewski, K., Cui, G., Johnson, K.A., Lovinger, D.M., 2017. Parallel but dissociable processing in discrete corticostriatal inputs encodes skill learning. Neuron 96, 476–489.

Kutlu, M.G., Gould, T.J., 2016. Effects of drugs of abuse on hippocampal plasticity and hippocampus-dependent learning and memory: contributions to development and maintenance of addiction. Learn. Mem. 23, 515–533.

Läck, A.K., Diaz, M.R., Chappell, A., DuBois, D.W., McCool, B.A., 2007. Chronic ethanol and withdrawal differentially modulate pre and postsynaptic function at glutamatergic synapses in rat basolateral amygdala. J. Neurophysiol. 98, 3185–3196.

Lahiri, A.K., Bevan, M.D., 2020. Dopaminergic transmission rapidly and persistently enhances excitability of D1 receptor-expressing striatal projection neurons. Neuron 106, 277–290.

Lapper, S.R., Bolam, J.P., 1992. Input from the frontal cortex and the parafascicular nucleus to cholinergic interneurons in the dorsal striatum of the rat. Neuroscience 51, 533–545.

Laskowski, C.S., Williams, R.J., Martens, K.M., Gruber, A.J., Fisher, K.G., Euston, D.R., 2016. The role of the medial prefrontal cortex in updating reward value and avoiding perseveration. Behav. Brain Res. 306, 52–63.

Laurent, V., Leung, B., Maidment, N., Balleine, B.W., 2012. Mu-and delta-opioid-related processing in the core and shell differentially mediate the influence of reward-guided and stimulus-guided decisions on choice. J. Neurosci. 32, 1875–1883.

Le Merre, P., Esmaeili, V., Charrière, E., Galan, K., Salin, P., Petersen, C.C.H., Crochet, S., 2018. Reward-based learning drives rapid sensory signals in medial prefrontal cortex and dorsal hippocampus necessary for goal-directed behavior. Neuron 97, 83–91.

Le Moine, C., Normand, E., Guitteny, A.F., Fouque, B., Teoule, R., Bloch, B., 1990. Dopamine receptor gene expression by enkephalin neurons in rate forebrain. Proc. Natl. Acad. Sci. U.S.A. 87, 230–234.

Le Moine, C., Normand, E., Bloch, B., 1991. Phenotypical characterization of the rat striatal neurons expressing D1 dopamine receptor gene. Proc. Natl. Acad. Sci. U.S.A. 88, 4205–4209.

Lee, J., Sabatinia, B., 2021. Striatal indirect pathway mediates exploration via collicular competition. Nature. https://doi.org/10.1038/s41586-021-04055-4.

Lemos, J.C., Wanat, M.J., Smith, J.S., Reyes, B.A.S., Hollon, N.G., Van Bockstaele, E.J., et al., 2012. Sever stress switches CRF action in the nucleus accumbens from appetitive to aversive. Nature 18, 402–406.

Lemos, J.C., Shin, J.H., Alvarez, V.A., 2019. Striatal cholinergic interneurons are a novel target of corticotropin releasing factor. J. Neurosci. 39, 5647–5661.

Lerner, T.N., Kreitzer, A.C., 2012. RGS4 is required for dopaminergic control of striatal LTD and susceptibility to parkinsonian motor deficits. Neuron 73, 347–359.

Li, T.K., Lumeng, L., 1984. Alcohol preference and voluntary alcohol intakes of inbred rat strains and the NIH heterogeneous stock rats. Clin. Exp. Res. 8, 485–487.

Li, Q., Wang, Y., Zhang, Y., Li, W., Shu, J., Sheng, Y., et al., 2013. Assessing cue-induced brain response as a function of abstinence duration in heroin-dependent individuals: an event-related fMRI study. PLoS One 8, e62911.

Li, X., Witonsky, K.R., Lofaro, O.M., Surjono, F., Zhang, J., Bossert, J.M., Shaham, Y., 2018. Role of anterior intralaminar nuclei of thalamus projections to dorsomedial striatum in incubation of methamphetamine craving. J. Neurosci. 38, 2270–2282.

Licheri, V., Lagström, O., Lotfi, A., Patton, M.H., Wigström, H., Mathur, B., Adermark, L., 2018. Complex control of striatal neurotransmission by nicotinic acetylcholine receptors via excitatory inputs onto medium spiny neurons. J. Neurosci. 38, 6597–6607.

Liu, P., Basso, M.A., 2008. Substantia nigra stimulation influences monkey superior colliculus neuronal activity bilaterally. J. Neurophsyiol. 100, 1098–1112.

Lobo, I.A., Harris, R.A., 2008. $GABA_A$ receptors and alcohol. Pharmacol. Biochem. Behav. 90, 90–94.

Lobo, M.K., Karsten, S.L., Gray, M., Geschwind, D.H., Yang, X.W., 2006. FACS-array profiling of striatal projection neuron subtypes in juvenile and adult mouse brains. Nat. Neurosci. 9, 443–452.

Lobo, M.K., Covington III, H.E., Chaudhury, D., et al., 2010. Cell type-specific loss of BDNF signaling mimics optogenetic control of cocaine reward. Science 330, 385–390.

Loughlin, S., Fallon, J.H., 1982. Dopaminergic and non-dopaminergic projections to amygdala from substantia nigra and ventral tegmental area. Brain Res. 262, 334–338.

Loughlin, A., Funk, D., Coen, K., Lê, A.D., 2017. Habitual nicotine-seeking in rats following limited training. Psychopharmacology (Berl) 234 (17), 2619–2629. https://doi.org/10.1007/s00213-017-4655-0. Epub 2017 Jun 7. PMID: 28589264.

Lovinger, D.W., White, G., Weight, F.F., 1989. Ethanol inhibits NMDA-activated ion currents in hippocampal neurons. Science 31, 1721–1724.

Lovinger, D.M., Tyler, E.C., Merritt, A., 1993. short- and long-term synaptic depression in rat neostriatum. J. Neurophysiol. 70, 1937–1949.

Lu, X.Y., Chasemzadeh, M.B., Kalivas, P.W., 1989. Expression of D1 receptor, D2 receptor, substance P and enkephalin messenger RNAs in the neurons projecting from the nucleus accumbens. Neuroscience 82, 767–780.

Lu, X.Y., Ghasemzadeh, M.B., Kalivas, P.W., 1998. Expression of D1 receptor, D2 receptor, substance P and enkephalin messenger RNAs in the neurons projecting from the nucleus accumbens. Neuroscience 82 (3), 767–780. https://doi.org/10.1016/s0306-4522(97)00327-8. PMID: 9483534.

Lu, P., Takai, K., Weaver, V.M., Werb, Z., 2011. Extracellular matrix degeneration and remodeling in development and disease. Cold Spring Harbor Perspect. Biol. 3, a005058.

Lu, X.Y., Ghasemzadeh, M.B., Kalivas, P.W., 1998. Expression of D1 receptor, D2 receptor, substance P and enkeph alin messenger RNAs in the neurons projecting from the nucleus accumbens. Neuroscience 82, 767–780. In press.

Luijten, M., Gillan, C.M., de Wit, S., Franken, I.H.A., Robbins, T.W., Ersche, K.D., 2019. Goal-directed and habitual control in smokers. Nicotine Tob. Res. 2020, 188–195.

Luo, Y., Xue, Y., Shen, H., Lu, L., 2013. Role of amygdala in drug memory. Neurobiol. Learn. Mem. http://dx.oid.org/10.1016/j.nlm.2013.06.017.

Lüscher, C., Ungless, M.A., 2006. The mechanistic classification of addictive drugs. PLoS Med. 3, 2005–2010.

Lüscher, C., Robbins, T.W., Everitt, B.J., 2020. The transitions to compulsion in addiction. Nat. Rev. 21, 247–263.

Ma, T., Cheng, Y., Hellard, E.R., Wang, X., Lu, J., Gao, X., et al., 2018. Bidirectional and long-lasting control of alcohol-seeking behavior by corticostriatal LTP and LTD. Nat. Neurosci. 21, 373–383.

Malarkey, E.B., Parpura, V., 2008. Mechanisms of glutamate release from astrocytes. Neurochem. Int. 52, 142–154.

Mallet, N., Micklem, B., Henny, P., Brown, M.T., Williams, C., Bolam, P.J., et al., 2012. Dichotomous organization of the external globus pallidus. Neuron 74, 1075–1086.

Mandillo, S., Rinaldi, A., Oliverio, A., Mele, A., 2003. Repeated administration of phencyclidine, amphetamine and MK-801 selectively impairs spatial learning in mice: a possible model of psychotomimetic drug-induced cognitive deficits. Behav. Pharmacol. 14, 533–544.

Manetto, C., Lidsky, T.I., 1987. Influences of the basal ganglia on the medullary reticular formation. Neurosci. Lett. 75, 278–282.

Mansour, A., Fox, C.A., Burke, S., Akil, H., Watson, S.J., 1995. Immunohistochemical localization of the cloned u opioid receptor in the rat CNS. J. Chem. Neuroanat. 8, 283–305.

Martin, G., Nie, Z., Siggins, G.R., 1997. mu-Opioid receptors modulate NMDA receptor-mediated responses in nucleus accumbens neurons. J. Neurosci. 17 (1), 11–22. https://doi.org/10.1523/JNEUROSCI.17-01-00011.1997. PMID: 8987732; PMCID: PMC6793696.

Martinez, L.A., Paterson, B.M., Meisel, R.L., Mermelstein, P.G., 2014. Estradiol facilitation of cocaine-induced locomotor sensitization in female rats requires activation of mGLuR5. Behav. Brain Res. 271, 39–42.

Matsumoto, N., Minamimoto, T., Graybiel, A.M., Kimura, M., 2000. Neurons in the thalamic CM-Pf complex supply striatal neurons with information about behaviorally significant sensory events. J. Physiol. 85, 960–976.

Mattay, V.S., Callicott, J.H., Bertolino, A., Heaton, I., Frank, J.A., Coppola, R., et al., 2000. Effects of Dextroamphetamine on Cognitive Performance and Cortical Activation.

Matzeu, A., Weiss, F., Martin-Fardon, R., 2015. Transient inactivation of the posterior paraventricular nucleus of the thalamus blocks cocaine-seeking behavior. Neurosci. Lett. 608, 34–39. https://doi.org/10.1016/j.neulet.2015.10.016. Epub 2015 Oct 9. PMID: 26455867; PMCID: PMC4639449.

Matzeu, A., Cauvi, G., Kerr, T.M., Weiss, F., Martin-Fardon, R., 2017. The paraventricular nucleus of the thalamus is differentially recruited by stimuli conditioned to the availability of cocaine vs. palatable food. Addiction Biol. 22, 70–77.

McDonald, A.J., 1991. Topographical organization of amygdaloid projections to the caudatoputamen, nucleus accumbens, and related striatal-like areas of the rat brain. Neuroscience 44, 15–33.

McDonald, A.J., 1992. Projection neurons of the basolateral amygdala: a correlative Golgi and retrograde tract tracing study. Brain Res. Bull. 28, 179–185.

McFarland, N.R., Haber, S.N., 2000. Convergent inputs from thalamic motor nuclei and frontal cortical areas to the dorsal striatum in the primate. J. Neurosci. 20, 3798–3813.

McGinty, V.B., Grace, A.A., 2009. Activity-dependent depression of medial prefrontal cortex inputs to accumbens neurons by the basolateral amygdala. Neuroscience 162 (4), 1429–1436. https://doi.org/10.1016/j.neuroscience.2009.05.028. Epub 2009 May 19. PMID: 19460420; PMCID: PMC2884401.

Mihov, Y., Hurlemann, R., 2012. Altered amygdala function in nicotine addiction: insights from human neuroimaging studies. Neuropsychologia 50, 1719–1729.

Millan, E.Z., Reese, R.M., Grossman, C.D., Chaudhri, N., Janak, P.H., 2015. Nucleus accumbens and posterior amygdala mediate cue-triggered alcohol seeking and suppress behavior during the omission of alcohol-predictive cues. Neuropsychopharmacology 40 (11), 2555–2565.

Millan, E.Z., Kim, A.H., Janak, P.H., 2017. Optogenetic activation of amygdala projections to nucleus accumbens can arrest conditioned and unconditioned alcohol consummatory behavior. Neuroscience 360, 106–117.

Minderhound, J.M., 1971. An anatomical study of the efferent connections of the thalamic reticular nucleus. Exp. Brain Res. 12, 435–446.

Mink, J.W., 1996. The basal ganglia. Focused selection and inhibition of competing motor programs. Prog. Neurobiol. 50, 381–425.

Miranda, R., Valderrama, J., Tsypes, A., Gadol, E., Gallagher, M., 2013. Cognitive inflexibility and suicidal ideation: mediating role of brooding and hopelessness. Psychiatr. Res. 210, 174–181.

Modirrousta, M., Fellows, L.K., 2008. Dorsal medial prefrontal cortex plays a necessary role in rapid error predictions in humans. J. Neurosci. 28, 14000–14005.

Mogenson, G.J., Takigawa, M., Robertson, A., Wu, M., 1979. Self-stimulation of the nucleus accumbens and ventral tegmental area of tsai attenuated by microinjections of spiroperidol into the nucleus accumbens. Brain Res. 171, 247–259.

Moghaddam, B., Jackson, M., 2004. Effect of stress on prefrontal cortex function. Neurotox. Res. 6, 73–78.

Moorman, D.E., 2018. The role of the orbitofrontal cortex in alcohol use, abuse, and dependence. Prog. Neuropsychopharmacol. Biol. Psychiatry 20, 85–107.

Morales, M., McGinnis, M.M., Robinson, S.L., Chappell, A.M., McCool, B.A., 2018. Chronic intermittent ethanol exposure modulation of glutamatergic neurotransmission in rat lateral/basolateral amygdala is duration- input- and sex-dependent. Neuroscience 371, 277–287.

Muñoz, B., Haggerty, D.L., Atwood, B.K., 2020. Synapse-specific expression of mu opioid receptor long-term depression in the dorsomedial striatum. Sci. Rep. 10, 7234.

Murray, J.E., Belin, D., Everitt, B.J., 2012. Double dissociation of the dorsomedial and dorsolateral striatal control over the acquisition and performance of cocaine seeking. Neuropsychopharmacology 37, 2456–2466.

Nagai, J., Rajbhandari, A.K., Gangwani, M.R., Hachisuaka, A., Giovanni, C., Masmanidis, S.C., et al., 2019. Hyperactivity with disrupted attention by activation of an astrocyte synaptogenic cue. Cell 177, 1280–1292.

Nambu, A., Tokuno, H., Takada, M., 2002. Functional significance of the cortico-subthalamo-pallidal 'hyperdirect' pathway. Neurosci. Res. 43, 111–117.

Nelson, A., Killcross, S., 2006. Amphetamine exposure enhances habit formation. J. Neurosci. 26, 3805–3812.

Nelson, A.B., Kreitzer, A.C., 2014. Reassessing models of basal ganglia function and dysfunction. Annu. Rev. Neurosci. 37, 117–135.

Neumann, P.A., Wang, Y., Yan, Y., Wang, Y., Ishikawa, M., Cui, R., et al., 2016. Cocaine-induced synaptic alterations in thalamus to nucleus accumbens projection. Neuropsychopharmacology 41, 2399–2410.

Nicholson, C., Sykova, E., 1998. Extracellular space structure revealed by diffusion analysis. Trends Neurosci. 21, 207–215.

Nikolova, Y.S., Knodt, A.R., Radtke, S.R., Hariri, A.R., 2015. Divergent responses of the amygdala and ventral striatum predict stress-related problem drinking in young adults: possible differential markers of affective and impulsive pathways of risk for alcohol use dirosrder. Mol. Psychiatry 21, 348–356.

Nikolova, Y.S., Knodt, A.R., Radtke, S.R., Hariri, A.R., 2016. Divergent responses of the amygdala and ventral striatum predict stress-related problem drinking in young adults: possible differential markers of affective and impulsive pathways of risk for alcohol use disorder. Mol. Psychiatry 21 (3), 348–356. https://doi.org/10.1038/mp.2015.85. Epub 2015 Jun 30. PMID: 26122584; PMCID: PMC4696925.

Nordahl, T.E., Salo, R., Leamon, M., 2003. Neuropsychological effects of chronic methamphetamine use on neurotransmitters and cognition: a review. J. Neuropsychiatry Clin. Neurosci. 15, 317–325.

Olmstead, M.C., Lafond, M.V., Everitt, B.J., Dickinson, A., 2001. Cocaine seeking by rats is a goal-directed action. Behav. Neurosci. 115, 394–402.

Ornstein, T.J., Iddon, J.L., Baldacchino, A.M., Sahakian, B.J., London, M., Everitt, B.J., Robbins, T.W., 2000. Profiles of cognitive dysfunction in chronic amphetamine and heroin abusers. Neuropsychopharmacology 23, 113–126.

O'Doherty, J., Dayan, P., Schultz, J., Deichmann, R., Friston, K., Dolan, R.J., 2004. Dissociable roles of ventral and dorsal striatum in instrumental conditioning. Science 304, 452–454.

O'Donnell, P., Grace, A.A., 1995. Synaptic Interactions among excitatory afferents to nucleus accumbens neurons: hippocampal gating of prefrontal cortical input. J. Neurosci. 15, 3622–3639.

O'Hare, J.K., Li, H., Kim, N., Gaidis, E., Ade, K., Beck, J., Yin, H., Calakos, N., 2017. Striatal fast-spiking interneurons selectively modulate circuit output and are required for habitual behavior. elife. https://doi.org/10.7554/eLife.26231.001.

Pan, W.X., Mao, T., Dudman, J.T., 2010. Inputs to the dorsal striatum of the mouse reflect the parallel circuit architecture of the forebrain. Front. Neuroanat. 4, 1–14.

Parent, A., Hazrati, L.N., 1995. Functional anatomy of basal ganglia I. The cortico-basal ganglia-thalamo-cortical loop. Brain Res. Rev. 20, 91–127.

Parent, A., Mackey, A., De Bellefeuille, L., 1983. The subcortical afferents to caudate nucleus and putamen in primate: a fluorescence retrograde double labeling study. Neuroscience 10, 1137–1150.

Parker, J.G., Marshall, J.D., Ahanonu, B., Wu, Y.W., Kim, T.H., Grewe, B.F., et al., 2018. Diametric neural ensembles dynamics in parkinsonian and dyskinetic states. Nature 557, 177–182.

Parkes, S.L., Balleine, B.W., 2013. Incentive memory: evidence the basolateral amygdala encodes and the insular cortex retrieves outcome values to guide choice between goal-directed actions. J. Neurosci. 33, 8753–8763.

Partridge, J.G., Tang, K.C., Lovinger, D.M., 2000. Regional and postnatal heterogeneity of activity-dependent long-term changes in synaptic efficacy in the dorsal striatum. J Neurophysiol 84 (3), 1422–1429. https://doi.org/10.1152/jn.2000.84.3.1422. PMID: 10980015.

Partridge, J.G., Apparsundaram, S., Gerhardt, G.A., Ronesi, J., Lovinger, D.M., 2002. Nicotinic acetylcholine receptors interact with dopamine in induction of striatal long-term depression. J. Neurosci. 22, 2541–2549.

Pascoli, V., Terrier, J., Espallergues, J., Valjen, E., O'Connor, E.C., Lüscher, C., 2014. Contrasting forms of cocaine-evoked plasticity control components of relapse. Nature 509, 459–464.

Patel, P.D., Lopez, J.F., Lyons, D.M., Burke, S., Wallace, M., Schatzberg, A.F., 2000. Glucocorticoid and mineralocorticoid receptor mRNA expression in squirrel monkey brain. J. Psychiatr. Res. 34, 383–392.

Patton, M.H., Roberts, B.M., Lovinger, D.M., Mathur, B.N., 2016. Ethanol disinhibits dorsolateral striatum medium spiny neurons through activation of a presynaptic opioid receptor. Neuropsychopharmacology 41, 1831–1840.

Patton, M.P., Padgett, K.E., McKeon, P.N., Qadir, H., Patton, M.S., Mu, C., et al., 2019. TrkB-dependent disinhibition of the nucleus accumbens is enhanced by ethanol. Neuropsychopharmacology 44, 1114–1122.

Patton, M.S., Heckman, M., Kim, C., Mu, C., Mathur, B.N., 2020. Compulsive alcohol consumption is regulated by dorsal striatum fast-spiking interneurons. Neuropsychopharmacology 46, 351–359.

Paulus, M.P., Steward, J.L., 2014. Interoception and drug addiction. Neuropharmacology 76. https://doi.org/10.1016/j.neuropharm.2013.07.002.

Pennartz, C.M., Groenewegen, H.J., Lopes da Silva, F.H., 1994. The nucleus accumbens as a complex of functionally distinct neuronal ensembles: an integration of behavioural, electrophysiological and anatomical data. Prog Neurobiol 42 (6), 719–761. https://doi.org/10.1016/0301-0082(94)90025-6. PMID: 7938546.

Perry, J.L., Joseph, J.E., Jiang, Y., Zimmerman, R.S., Kelly, T.H., Darna, M., et al., 2011. Prefrontal cortex and drug abuse vulnerability: translation to prevention and treatment interventions. Brain Res. Rev. 65, 124–149.

Pierce, R.C., Reeder, D.C., Hicks, R.J., Morgan, Z.R., Kalivas, P.W., 1997. Ibotenic acid lesions of the dorsal prefrontal cortex disrupts the expression of behavioral sensitization to cocaine. Neuroscience 82, 1103–1114.

Pierce, R.C., Reeder, D.C., Hicks, J., Morgan, Z.R., Kalivas, P.W., 1998. Ibotenic acid lesions of the dorsal prefrontal cortex disrupt the expression of behavioral sensitization to cocaine. Neuroscience 82 (4), 1103–1114. https://doi.org/10.1016/s0306-4522(97)00366-7. PMID: 9466434.

Piggott, V.M., Bosse, K.E., Lisieski, M.J., Strader, J.A., Stanley, J.A., et al., 2019. Single-prolonged stress impairs prefrontal cortex control of amygdala and striatum in rats. Front. Behav. Neurosci. 13, 1–18.

Popescu, A.T., Saghyan, A.A., Paré, D., 2007. NMDA-dependent facilitation of corticostriatal plasticity by the amygdala. Proc. Natl. Acad. Sci. USA 104, 341–346.

Puaud, M., Higuera-Matas, A., Brunault, P., Everitt, B.J., Belin, D., 2021. The basolateral amygdala to nucleus accumbens core circuit mediates the conditioned reinforcing effects of cocaine-paired cues on cocaine seeking. Biol. Psychiatr. 89, 356–365.

Randall, P.A., McElligott, Z.A., Besheer, J., 2019. Role of mPFC and nucleus accumbens circuitry in modulation of nicotine plus alcohol compound drug state. Addiction Biol. 25, e12782.

Ray, S., Haney, M., Hanson, C., Biswal, B., Hanson, S.J., 2015. Modeling causal relationships between brain regions within the drug-cue processing network in chronic cocaine smokers. Neuropsychopharmacology 40, 2960–2968.

Remijnse, P.L., Nielen, M.M.A., van Balkom, A.J.L.M., Cath, D.C., van Oppen, P., Uylings, H.B.M., Veltman, D.J., 2006. Reduced orbitofrontal-striatal activity on a reversal learning task in obsessive-compulsive disorder. Arch. Gen. Psychiatr. 63, 1125–1136.

Remijnse, P.L., van den Heuvel, O.A., Nielen, M.M.A., Vriend, C., Hendriks, G., Hoogendijk, W.J.G., et al., 2013. Cognitive inflexibility in obsessive-compulsive disorder and major depression is associated with distinct neural correlates. PLoS One 8, e59600.

Renteria, R., Baltz, E.T., Gremel, C.M., 2018. Chronic alcohol exposure disrupts top-down control over basal ganglia action selection to produce habits. Nat. Commun. 9, 211.

Reynolds, S.M., Berridge, K.C., 2002. Positive and negative motivation in nucleus accumbens shell: bivalent rostrocaudal gradients for GABA-elicited eating, taste "liking"/"disliking" reactions, place preference/avoidance, and fear. J. Neurosci. 22, 7308–7320.

Reynolds, J.N., Hyland, B.I., Wickens, J.R., 2001. A cellular mechanism of reward-related learning. Nature 413, 67–70.

Rezayof, A., Sarrindast, M.R., Sahraei, H., Haeri-Rohanni, A.H., 2002. Involvement of dopamine D2 receptors of the central amygdala on the acquisition and expression of morphine-induced place preference in rat. Pharmacol. Biochem. Behav. 74, 187–197.

Roberts-Wolfe, D.J., Kalivas, P.W., 2015. Glutamate transporter GLT-1 as a therapeutic target for substance use disorder. CNS Neurol. Disord. Drug Targets 14, 745–756.

Roberts, B.M., White, M.G., Patton, M.H., Chen, R., Mathur, B.N., 2019. Ensemble encoding of action speed by striatal fast-spiking interneurons. Brain Struct. Funct. 224 (7), 2567–2576. https://doi.org/10.1007/s00429-019-01908-7. Epub 2019 Jun 26. PMID: 31243530; PMCID: PMC6698421.

Robinson, T.E., Becker, J.B., 1982. Behavioral sensitization is accompanied by an enhancement in amphetamine- stimulated dopamine release from striatal tissue in vitro. Eur. J. Pharmacol. 85, 253–254.

Rock, C., Zurita, H., Wilson, C., Apicella, A.J., 2016. An inhibitory corticostriatal pathway. elife 5, e15890.

Rodd-Henricks, Z.A., McKinzie, D.L., Li, T.K., Murhpy, J.M., McBride, W.J., 2002. Cocaine is self-administered into the shell but not the core of the nucleus accumbens of wistar rats. J. Pharmacol. Exp. Therapeut. 303, 1216–1226.

Ron, D., 2004. Signaling cascades regulating NMDA receptor sensitivity to ethanol. Neuroscientist 10, 325–336.

Sassone-Corsi, P., 2012. The cylclic AMP pathway. Cold Spring Harbor Perspect. Biol. 4, 1–3.

Satta, R., Certa, B., He, D., Lasek, A.W., 2018. Estrogen receptor beta in the nucleus accumbens regulates the rewarding properties of cocaine in female mice. Int. J. Neuropsychopharmacol. 21, 382–392.

Saxena, S., Brody, A.L., Schwartz, J.M., Baxter, L.R., 1998. Neuroimaging and frontal-subcortical circuitry in obsessive-compulsive disorder. Br. J. Psychiatr. Suppl. 26, 26–37.

Schilman, E.A., Uylings, H.B.M., Galis-de Graaf, Y., Joel, D., Groenewegen, H.J., 2008. The orbital cortex in rats topographically projects to central parts of the caudate-putamen complex. Neurosci. Lett. 432, 40–45.

Schilman, E.A., Klavir, O., Winter, C., Sohr, R., Joel, D., 2010. The role of the striatum in compulsive behavior in intact and orbitofrontal-cortex-lesioned rats: possible involvement of the serotonergic system. Neuropsychopharmacology 35, 1026–1039.

Schmitzer-Torbert, N., Apostolidis, S., Amoa, R., O'Rear, C., Kaster, M., Stowers, J., Ritz, R., 2015. Post-training cocaine administration facilitates habit learning and requires the infralimbic cortex and dorsolateral striatum. Neurobiol. Learn Mem. 118, 105–112. https://doi.org/10.1016/j.nlm.2014.11.007. Epub 2014 Nov 21. PMID: 25460040; PMCID: PMC4331257.

Schoenbaum, G., Setlow, B., 2005. Cocaine makes actions insensitive to outcomes but not extinction: implications for altered orbitofrontal-amygdalar function. Cerebr. Cortex 15, 1162–1169.

Schwabe, L., Wolf, O.T., 2009. Stress prompts habit behavior in humans. J. Neurosci. 29, 7191–7198.

Schwabe, L., Wolf, O.T., 2011. Stress-induced modulation of instrumental behavior: from goal-directed to habitual control of action. Behav. Brain Res. 219, 321–328.

Scofield, M.D., Heinsbroek, J.A., Gipson, C.D., Kupchik, Y.M., Spencer, S., Smith, A.C.W.W., et al., 2016. The nucleus accumbens. Mechanisms of addiction across drug classes reflect the importance of glutamate homeostasis. Pharmacol. Rev. 68, 816–871.

See, R.E., Kruzich, P.J., Grimm, J.W., 2001. Dopamine, but not glutamate, receptor blockade in the basolateral amygdala attenuates conditioned reward in a rat model of relapse to cocaine-seeking behavior. Psychopharmacology 154, 301–310.

Seeuws, I., Soetens, E., 2007. Verbal memory performance improved via an acute administration of D- amphetamine. Hum. Psychopharmacol. Clin. Exp. 22, 279–287.

Segarra, A.C., Agosto-Rivera, J.L., Febo, M., Lugo-Escobar, N., Menéndez-Delmestre, R., et al., 2010. Estradiol: a key biological substrate mediating the response to cocaine in female rats. Horm. Behav. 58, 33–43.

Segarra, A.C., Torres-Diaz, Y.M., Silva, R.D., Puig-Ramos, A., Menéndez-Delmestre, R., et al., 2014. Estrogen receptors mediate estradiol's effect on sensitization and CPP to cocaine in female rates: role of contextual cues. Horm. Behav. 65, 77–87.

Sellings, L.H.L., Clarke, P.B.S., 2003. Segregation of amphetamine reward and locomotor stimulation between nucleus accumbens medial shell and core. J. Neurosci. 21, 6295–6303.

Seney, M.L., Kim, S., Glausier, J.R., Hildebrand, M.A., Xue, X., et al., 2021. Transcriptional alterations in dorsolateral prefrontal cortex and nucleus accumbens implicate neuroinflammation and synaptic remodeling in opioid use disorder. Biol. Psychiatr. 90, 550–562.

Seo, D., Sinha, R., 2014. The neurobiology of alcohol craving and relapse. Handb. Clin. Neurol. 125, 355–368.

Serra, S., Carai, M., Brunetti, G., Gomes, R., Melis, S., Vacca, G., et al., 2001. The cannabinoid receptor antagonist SR 141716 prevents acquisition of drinking behavior in alcohol-preferring rats. Eur. J. Pharmacol. 430, 369–371.

Sesack, S.R., Deutch, A.Y., Roth, R.H., Bunney, B.J., 1989. Topographical organization of the efferent projections of the medial prefrontal cortex in the rat: an anterograde tract-tracing study with *Phaseolus vulgaris* leucoagglutinin. J. Comp. Neurol. 290, 213–242.

Shan, Q., Christie, M.J., Balleiene, B.W., 2014. The acquisition of goal-directed actions generates opposing plasticity in direct and indirect pathways in dorsomedial striatum. J. Neurosci. 34, 9196–9201.

Sharpier, S., Pidoux, M., Mahon, S., 2020. Converging sensory and motor cortical inputs onto the same striatal neurons: an *in vivo* intracellular investigation. PLoS One 15, e0228260.

Shen, W., Flajolet, M., Greengard, P., Surmeier, J.D., 2008. Dichotomous dopaminergic control of striatal synaptic plasticity. Science 321, 848–851.

Shen, H.W., Scofield, M.D., Boger, H., Hensley, M., Kalivas, P.W., 2014. Synaptic glutamate spillover due to impaired glutamate uptake mediates heroin relapse. J. Neurosci. 34 (16), 5649–5657. https://doi.org/10.1523/JNEUROSCI.4564-13.2014. PMID: 24741055; PMCID: PMC3988415.

Sherman, S.M., 2016. Thalamus plays a central role in ongoing cortical function. Nat. Neurosci. 19, 533–541.

Shinoe, T., Goda, Y., 2015. Tuning synapses by proteolytic remodeling of the adhesive surface. Curr. Opin. Neurobiol. 35, 148–155.

Shulz, J.M., Redgrave, P., Mehring, C., Aertsen, A., Clements, K.M., Wickens, J.R., Reynolds, J.N.J., 2009. Short-latency activation of striatal spiny neurons via subcortical visual pathways. J. Neurosci. 29, 6336–6347.

Sidibé, M., Smith, Y., 1996. Differential synaptic innervation of striatofugal neurons projecting to the internal or external segments of the globus pallidus by thalamic afferents in the squirrel monkey. J. Comp. Neurol. 365, 445–465.

Silberman, Y., Bajo, M., Chappel, A.M., Christian, D.T., Cruz, M., Dias, M.R., et al., 2009. Neurobiological mechanism contributing to alcohol-stress-anxiety interactions. Alcohol 43, 509–519.

Siller-Pérez, C., Serafín, N., Prado-Alcalá, R.A., Roozendaal, B., Quirarte, G.L., 2017. Glucocorticoid administration into the dorsolateral but not dorsomedial striatum accelerates the shift from a spatial toward procedural memory. Neurobiol. Learn. Mem. 141, 124–133.

Simon, S.L., Dean, A.C., Cordova, X., Monterosso, J.R., London, E.D., 2010. Methamphetamine dependence and neuropsychological functioning: evaluating change during early abstinence. J. Stud. Alcohol Drugs 71, 335–344.

Sizer, S.E., Parrish, B.C., McCool, B.A., 2021. Chronic ethanol exposure potentiates cholinergic neurotransmission in the basolateral amygdala. Neuroscience 455, 165–176.

Sjoerds, Z., van den Brink, W., Beekman, A.T.F., Penninx, B.W.J.H., Veltman, D.J., 2013. Cue reactivity is associated with duration and severity of alcohol dependence: an fMRI study. PLoS One 9, e84560.

Sjoerds, Z., van den Brink, W., Beekman, A.T., Penninx, B.W., Veltman, D.J., 2014. Cue reactivity is associated with duration and severity of alcohol dependence: an FMRI study. PLoS One 9 (1), e84560. https://doi.org/10.1371/journal.pone.0084560. PMID: 24400099; PMCID: PMC3882248.

Smith, Y., Bevan, M.D., Shink, E., Bolam, J.P., 1998. Microcircuitry of the direct and indirect pathways of the basal ganglia. Neuroscience 86, 353–387.

Smith, A.C.W., Kupchik, Y.M., Scofield, M.D., Gipson, C.D., Wiggins, A., et al., 2014. Synaptic plasticity mediating cocaine relapse requires matrix metalloproteinases. Nat. Neurosci. 17, 1655–1657.

Smith, A.C.W., Scofield, M.D., Kalivas, P.W., 2015. The tetrapartite synapse: extracellular matrix remodeling contributes to corticoaccumbens plasticity underlying drug addiction. Brain Res. 1628, 29–39.

Sneddon, E.A., White, R.D., Radke, A.K., 2019. Sex differences in binge-like and aversion-resistant alcohol drinking in C57BL/6J mice. Alcohol Clin. Exp. Res. 43, 243–249.

Soares-Cunha, C., de Vasconcelos, N.A.P., Coimbra, B., et al., 2019. Nucleus accumbens medium spiny neurons subtypes signal both reward and aversion. Mol. Psychiatr. 25, 3241–3255.

Specio, S.E., Wee, S., O'Dell, L.E., Boutrel, B., Zorrilla, E.P., Koob, G.F., 2008. CRF(1) receptor antagonists attenuate escalated cocaine self-administration in rats. Psychopharmacology (Berl) 196 (3), 473–482. https://doi.org/10.1007/s00213-007-0983-9. Epub 2007 Oct 30. PMID: 17965976; PMCID: PMC2769571.

Speco, S.E., Wee, S., O'Dell, L.E., Boutrel, B., Zorilla, E.P., et al., 2007. CRF1 receptor antagonists attenuate escalated cocaine self-administration in rats. Psychopharmacology 196, 473–482.

Spina, L., Fenu, S., Longoni, R., Rivas, E., Chiara, G., 2006. Nicotine-conditioned single-trial place preference: selective role of nucleus accumbens shell dopamine D1 receptors in acquisition. Psychopharmacology 184, 477. -455.

Spreckelmeyer, K.N., Krach, S., Kohls, G., Rademacher, L., Kircher, T., Gründer, G., 2009. Anticipation of monetary and social reward differently activates mesolimbic brain structures in men and women. Scan 4, 158–165.

Staines, W.A., Fibiger, H.C., 1984. Collateral projections of neurons of the rat globus pallidus to the striatum and substantia nigra. Exp. Brain Res. 56, 217–220.

Staines, W.A., Atmadja, S., Fibiger, H.C., 1981. Demonstration of a pallidostriatal pathway by retrograde transport of HRP-labeled lectin. Brain Res. 206, 446–450.

Surmeier, D.J., Song, W.J., Yan, Z., 1996. Coordinated expression of dopamine receptors in neostriatal medium spiny neurons. J. Neurosci. 16, 6579–6591.

Surmeier, J.D., Plotkin, J., Shen, W., 2009. Dopamine and synaptic plasticity in dorsal striatal circuits controlling action selection. Curr. Opin. Neurobiol. 19, 621–628.

Tang, D.W., Fellows, L.K., Small, D.M., Dagher, A., 2012. Food and drug cues activate similar brain regions: a meta-analysis of function MRI studies. Physiol. Behav. 106, 317–324.

Tepper, J.M., Bolam, J.P., 2004. Functional diversity and specificity of neostriatal interneurons. Curr. Opin. Neurobiol. 14, 685–692.

Tepper, J.M., Tecuapetla, F., Koós, T., Ibáñez-Sandoval, O., 2010. Heterogeneity and diversity of striatal GABAergic interneurons. Front. Neuroanat. 4, 1–18.

Thompson, T.L., Moss, R.L., 1995. In vivo stimulated dopamine release in the nucleus accumbens: modulation by the prefrontal cortex. Brain Res. 686, 93–98.

Thompson, A.M., Gosnell, B.A., Wagner, J.J., 2002. Enhancement of long-term potentiation in the rat hippocampus following cocaine exposure. Neuropharmacology 42, 1039–1042.

Thorn, C.A., Atallah, H., Howe, M., Graybiel, A.M., 2010. Differential dynamics of activity changes in dorsolateral and dorsomedial striatal loops during learning. Neuron 66, 781–795.

Threlfell, S., Lalic, T., Platt, N.J., Jennings, K.A., Diesseroth, K., Cragg, S.J., 2012. Striatal dopamine release is triggered by synchronized activity in cholinergic interneurons. Neuron 75, 58–64.

Tonn Eisinger, K.R., Larson, E.B., Boulware, M.I., Thomas, M.J., Mermelstein, P.G., 2018. Membrane estrogen receptor signaling impacts the reward circuitry of the female brain to influence motivated behaviors. Steroids 133, 53–59.

Tsuji, M., Nakagaw, Y., Ishibashi, Y., Yoshii, T., Takashima, T., Shimada, M., Suzuki, T., 1996. Activation of ventral tegmental $GABA_B$ receptors inhibits morphine-induced place preference in rats. Eur. J. Pharmacol. 313, 169–173.

Tzschentke, T.M., 2007. Measuring reward with the conditioned place preference (CPP) paradigm: update of the last decade. Addiction Biol. 12, 227–462.

Tzschentke, T.M., Schmidt, W.J., 2000. Functional relationship among medial prefrontal cortex, nucleus accumbens, and ventral tegmental area in locomotion and reward. Crit. Rev. Neurobiol. 14, 131–142.

Uhl, G.R., Koob, G.F., Cable, J., 2019. The neurobiology of addiction. Ann. N. Y. Acad. Sci. 1451, 5–28.

Vaghi, M.M., Vértes, P.E., Kitzbichler, M.G., Apergis-Schoute, A.M., van der Flier, F.E., Fineberg, N.A., et al., 2017. Specific frontosriatal circuits for impaired cognitive flexibility of goal-directed planning in obsessive-compulsive disorder: evidence from resting-state functional connectivity. Biol. Psychiatr. 81, 708–717.

Valtcheva, S., Venance, L., 2015. Astrocytes gate Hebbian synaptic plasticity in the striatum. Nat. Commun. 7, 1–17.

Van der Werf, Y.D., Witter, M.P., Groenewegen, H.J., 2002. The intralaminar and midline nuclei of the thalamus. Anatomical and function evidence for participation in processes of arousal and awareness. Brain Res. Rev. 39, 107–140.

Vertes, R.P., Hoover, W.B., 2008. Projections of the paraventricular and paratenial nuclei of the dorsal midline thalamus in the rat. J. Comp. Neurol. 508, 212–237.

Vetter-O' Hagen, C., Varlinskaya, E., Spear, L., 2009. Sex differences in ethanol intake and sensitivity to aversion affects during adolescence and adulthood. Alcohol Alcohol 44, 547–554.

Vivian, J.A., Green, H.L., Young, J.E., Majerksy, L.S., Thomas, B.W., et al., 2001. Induction and maintenance of ethanol self-administration in cynomolgus monkeys (macaca fascicularis): long-term characterization of sex and individual differences. Alcohol Clin. Exp. Res. 25, 1087–1097.

Vogel, S., Klumpers, F., Schröder, T.N., Oplaat, K.T., Krigers, H.J., et al., 2016. Stress induces a shift towards striatum dependent stimulus-response learning via the mineralocorticoid receptor. Neuropsychopharmacology 42, 1262–1271.

Vogel, S., Klumpers, F., Schröder, T.N., Oplaat, K.T., Krugers, H.J., Oitzl, M.S., Joëls, M., Doeller, C.F., Fernández, G., 2017. Stress induces a shift towards striatum-dependent stimulus-response learning via the mineralocorticoid receptor. Neuropsychopharmacology 42 (6), 1262–1271. https://doi.org/10.1038/npp.2016.262. Epub 2016 Nov 23. PMID: 27876790; PMCID: PMC5437884.

Von Bartheld, C.S., Bahney, J., Herculano-Houzel, S., 2016. The search for true numbers of neurons and glial cells in the human brain: a review of 150 years of cell counting. J. Comp. Neurol. 15, 3865–3895.

Vuillet, J., Kerkerian, L., Salin, P., Nieoullon, A., 1989a. Ultrastructural features of NPY-containing neurons in the rat striatum. Brain Res. 477, 241–251.

Vuillet, J., Kerkerian, L., Kachidian, P., Bosler, O., Nieoullon, A., 1989b. Ultrastructural correlates of functional relationships between nigral dopaminergic or cortical afferent fivers and neuropeptide Y-containing neurons in the rat striatum. Neurosci. Lett. 100, 99–104.

Walker, D.Q., Ray, R., Kuhn, C.M., 2006. Sex differences in neurochemical effects of dopaminergic drugs in rat striatum. Neuropsychopharmacology 31, 1193–1202.

Wang, Z., Ka, L., Day, M., Ronesi, J., Yin, H.H., Ding, J., et al., 2006. Dopaminergic control of corticostriatal long-term synaptic depression in medium spiny neurons is mediated by cholinergic interneurons. Neuron 50, 443–452.

Wang, J., Carnicella, S., Phamluong, K., Jeanblanc, J., Ronesi, J.A., Chaudhri, N., et al., 2007. Ethanol induces long-term facilitation of NR2B-NMDA receptor activity in the dorsal striatum: implications for alcohol drinking behavior. J. Neurosci. 27, 3593–3602.

Wang, W., Darvas, M., Storey, G.P., Bamford, I.J., Gibbs, J.T., Palmiter, R.D., et al., 2013. Acetylcholine encodes long-lasting presynaptic plasticity at glutamatergic synapses in the dorsal striatum after repeated amphetamine exposure. J. Neurosci. 33, 10405–10426.

Wassum, K.M., Izquierdo, A., 2016. The basolateral amygdala in reward learning and addiction. Neurosci. Biobehav. Rev. 57, 271–283.

Weiss, F., 2005. Neurobiology of craving, conditioned reward and relapse. Curr. Opin. Pharmacol. 5 (1), 9–19. https://doi.org/10.1016/j.coph.2004.11.001. PMID: 15661620.

Weiss, F., Maldonado-Vlaar, C.S., Parsons, L.H., Kerr, T.M., Smith, D.L., Ben-Shahar, O., 2000. Control of cocaine-seeking behavior by drug-associated stimuli in rats: effects on recovery of extinguished operant-responding and extracellular dopamine levels in amygdala and nucleus accumbens. Proc. Natl. Acad. Sci. U.S.A. 97, 4321–4326.

Whitelaw, R.B., Markou, A., Robbins, T.W., Everitt, B.J., 1996. Excitotoxic lesions of the basolateral amygdala impair the acquisition of cocaine-seeking behavior under a second-order schedule of reinforcement. Psychopharmacology 127, 213–224.

Willcox, M.V., Cuzon Carlson, V.C., Sherazee, N., Sprow, G.M., Bock RThiele, T.E., et al., 2014. Repeated binge-like ethanol drinking alters ethanol drinking patterns and depresses striatal GABAergic transmission. Neuropsychopharmacology 39, 579–594.

Williams, S.M., Sullican, R.K.P., Scott, H.L., Finkelstein, D.I., Colditz, P.B., Lingwood, B.E., et al., 2005. Glial glutamate transporter expression patterns in brains from multiple mammalian species. GLIA 49, 520–541.

Wilson, C.J., Chang, H.T., Kitai, S.T., 1990. Firing patterns and synaptic potentials of identified giant aspiny interneurons in the rat neostriatum. J. Neurosci. 10, 508–519.

Wirz, L., Wacker, J., Felten, A., Reuter, M., Schwabe, L., 2017. A deletion variant of the a2b-adrenoceptor modulates the stress-induced shift from "cognitive" to "habit" memory. J. Neurosci. 37, 2149–2160.

Wolff, S.B.E., Ko, R., Ölveczky, B.P., 2019. Distinct roles for motor cortical and thalamic inputs to striatum during motor learning and execution. bioRxiv. https://dio.org/10.1101/825810.

Xenias, H.S., Ibáñez-Sandoval, O., Koós, T., Tepper, J.M., 2015. Are striatal tyrosine hydroxylase interneurons dopaminergic. J. Neurosci. 35, 6584–6599.

Xi, Z.X., Stein, E.A., 1989. Nucleus accumbens dopamine release modulation by mesolimbic $GABA_A$ receptors- an *in vivo* electrochemical study. Brain Res. 798, 156–165.

Xi, Z.X., Stein, E.A., 1999. Baclofen inhibits heroin self-administration and mesolimbic dopamine release. J. Pharmacol. Exp. Therapeut. 290, 1360–1374.

Xi, Z.X., Stein, E.A., 2000. Increased mesolimbic GABA concentration blocks heroin self-administration in the rat. J. Pharmacol. Exp. Therapeut. 294 (2), 613–619.

Xi, Z.X., Stein, E.A., 2002. GABAergic mechanisms of opiate reinforcement. Alcohol Alcohol 37, 485–494.

Xia, Y., Driscoll, J.R., Wilbrecht, L., Margolis, E.B., Fields, H.L., Hjelmstad, G.O., 2011. Nucleus accumbens medium spiny neurons target non-dopaminergic neurons in the ventral tegmental area. J. Neurosci. 31, 7811–7816.

Yamada, H., Matumoto, N., Kimura, M., 2004. Tonically active neurons in the primate caudate nucleus and putamen differentially encode instructed motivational outcomes of action. J. Neurosci. 24, 3500–3510.

Yang, X., Tian, F., Zhang, H., Zeng, J., Chen, T., Wang, S., et al., 2016. Cortical and subcortical gray matter shrinkage in alcohol-use disorders: a voxel-based meta-analysis. Neurosci. Biobehav. Rev. 66, 92–103.

Yang, H., de Jong, J.W., Tak, Y., Peck, J., Bateup, H.S., Lammel, S., 2018. Nucleus accumbens subnuclei regulate motivated behavior via direct inhibition and disinhibition of VTA dopamine subpopulations. Neuron 97 (2). https://doi.org/10.1016/j.neuron.2017.12.022, 434-449.e4. Epub 2018 Jan 4. PMID: 29307710; PMCID: PMC5773387.

Yang, H., de Jong, J., Tak, Y., Peck, J., Bateup, H.S., Lammel, S., 2019. Nucleus accumbens subnuclei regulate motivated behavior via direct inhibition and disinhibition of VTA dopamine subpopulation. Neuron 97, 434–449.

Yin, H.H., 2010. The sensorimotor striatum is necessary for serial order learning. J. Neurosci. 30, 14719–14723.

Yin, H.H., Knowlton, B.J., Balleine, B.W., 2004. Lesions of dorsolateral striatum preserve outcome expectancy but disrupt habit formation in instrumental learning. Eur. J. Neurosci. 19, 181–189.

Yin, H.H., Knowlton, B.J., Balleiene, B.W., 2005a. Inactivation of dorsolateral striatum enhances sensitivity to changes in the action-outcome contingency in instrumental conditioning. Behav. Brain Res. 166, 189–196.

Yin, H.H., Pstlund, S.B., Knowlton, B.J., Balleine, B.W., 2005b. The role of dorsomedial striatum in instrumental conditioning. Eur. J. Neurosci. 22, 513–523.

Yin, H.H., Park, B.S., Adermark, L., Lovinger, D.M., 2007. Ethanol reverses the direction of long-term synaptic plasticity in the dorsomedial striatum. Eur. J. Neurosci. 25, 3226–3232.

Yin, H.H., Mulcare, S.P., Hilário, M.R.F., Clouse, E., Holloway, T., Davis, M.I., et al., 2009. Dynamic reorganization of striatal circuits during the acquisition and consolidation of a skill. Nat. Neurosci. 12, 333–341.

Yu, X., Taylor, A.M.W., Nagai, J., Golshani, P., Evans, C.J., Coppola, G., Khakh, B.S., 2018. Reducing astrocyte calcium signaling in vivo alters striatal microcircuits and causes repetitive behavior. Neuron 99, 1170–1187.

Zahm, D.S., 1989. The ventral striatopallidal parts of the basal ganglia in the rat -II. Compartmentation of ventral pallidal efferents. Neuroscience 30, 33–50.

Zahm, D.S., Brog, J.S., 1992. On the significance of subterritories in the "accumbens" part of the rat ventral striatum. Neuroscience 50, 751–767.

Zapata, A., Minney, V.L., Shippenberg, T.S., 2010. Shift from goal-directed to habitual cocaine seeking after prolonged experience in rats. J. Neurosci. 30, 15457–15463.

Zeeuws, I., Soetens, E., 2007. Verbal memory performance improved via an acute administration of D-amphetamine. Hum. Psychopharmacol. 22 (5), 279–287. https://doi.org/10.1002/hup.848. PMID: 17599332.

Zerbes, G., Kausche, F.M., Schwabe, L., 2020. Stress-induced cortisol modulates the control of memory retrieval towards the dorsal striatum. Eur. J. Neurosci. https://doi.org/10.1111/ejn.14942.

Zhu, P.J., Lovinger, D.M., 2006. Ethanol potentiates GABAergic synaptic transmission in a postsynaptic neuron/synaptic bouton preparation from basolateral amygdala. J. Neurophysiol. 96, 433–441.

Zilverstand, A., Huang, A.S., Alia-Klein, N., Goldstein, R.Z., 2018. Neuroimaging impaired response inhibition and salience attribution inhuman drug addiction: a systematic review. Neuron 98, 886–903.

Zorilla, E.P., Koob, G.F., 2012. Amygdalostriatal projections in the neurocircuitry for motivation: a neuroanatomical thread through the career of Ann Kelley. Neurosci. Biobehav. Rev. 37. https://doi.org/10.1016/j.neubiorev.2012.11.019.

Zorilla, E.P., Logrip, M.L., Koob, G.F., 2014. Corticotropin releasing factor: a key role in the neurobiology of addiction. Front. Neuroendocrinol. 35, 234–244.

CHAPTER

4

Prefrontal Cortical (PFC) circuits

Matthew C. Hearing[a] *and John R. Mantsch*[b]

[a]Department of Biomedical Sciences, Marquette University, Milwaukee, WI, United States; [b]Department of Pharmacology & Toxicology, Medical College of Wisconsin, Milwaukee, WI, United States

Introduction

Theories in neuropsychology increasingly define addiction as a progressive disorder that involves a transition from social use to a compulsive relapsing state. A prevailing model in the addiction field is that this transition results from genetic, developmental, and sociological vulnerabilities, that are compounded by pharmacodynamically-induced adaptations in neurochemistry and cellular physiology within brain regions responsible for cognitive control. Although the range of cognitive problems in addiction is diverse, the most consistently documented deficits include uncontrollable drug seeking and drug taking, inflexibility in decision making, impulsivity, and attentional biases toward drug use. Deficits in one or more of these constructs can ostensibly promote a pathological strengthening of well-learned drug-related behaviors and impair one's capacity to effectively monitor, suppress, or override behaviors triggered by drugs and drug-associated stimuli, thus leaving individuals in a state of chronic relapse or relapse vulnerability (Hyman et al., 2006; Kalivas and O'Brien, 2008; Lupien et al., 2009; Diamond, 2013; Etkin et al., 2013; Spronk et al., 2013; Jentsch and Pennington, 2014; Bangasser et al., 2018).

Notably, the above-mentioned behaviors are not universally diagnosed in all people who misuse substances or across all substance use disorders (SUDs). Further, these behaviors often emerge in distinct temporal patterns. For example, deficits in cognitive flexibility may precede and perhaps facilitate the subsequent emergence of compulsive drug use. Moreover, comorbidity involving these behaviors likely exerts unique and/or synergistic influences on addiction severity based on the individual or drug. Nonetheless, commonalities in addictive behaviors have led to a push for a unified theory of addiction that includes most addictive substances, as increasing evidence indicates that misuse of many drugs exerts overlapping effects on the brain and behavior to promote addiction.

Neurocircuitry of Addiction
https://doi.org/10.1016/B978-0-12-823453-2.00001-1

Early work exploring the neurobiology of addiction focused heavily on changes in mesolimbic regions such as the nucleus accumbens (NAc) and ventral tegmental area (VTA), however research over the past two decades has made it increasingly clear that addiction-based behavioral constructs likely involve modifications within prefrontal cortical (PFC) circuits, as substantial clinical and preclinical evidence points to the PFC as a critical substrate for governing numerous cognitive functions including strategy shifting, behavioral inhibition, reinforcement learning, attention, acquisition of drug self-administration, and relapse to drug seeking (Everitt and Robbins 2005; Kalivas and O'Brien, 2008; Kalivas, 2009; Van den Oever et al., 2010; Badiani et al., 2011; Goldstein and Volkow 2011).

This chapter will focus on the contribution of PFC dysfunction in terms of cognitive constructs thought to promote the emergence of addiction behavior through a transition from goal-directed (controlled) social use to excessive use and ultimately uncontrollable use. We will highlight the purported underlying neurobiology of this dysfunction with a focus on temporal dynamics as well as brain region- and circuit-specific neuroadaptations, as we know that distinct brain circuits are differently regulated during different phases of use and abstinence. Finally, we will briefly discuss how factors such as stress and biological sex significantly influence PFC function and vulnerability to addiction.

Functional neuroanatomy of the PFC

Human anatomy

Comprising the most rostral aspects of the mammalian frontal lobe, the human PFC is commonly defined based on its cytoarchitecture (i.e., the presence of a granular layer IV) and afferent projections (from the mediodorsal nucleus of the thalamus) and includes Brodmann areas 8, 9, 10, 11, 12, 24, 25, 32, 33, 44, 45, 46, and 47. In humans, the PFC can be generally divided into *medial* (areas 12, 24, 25, 32, and 33), *orbital* (areas 10, 11 and 47; note—we have chosen to segregate the medial and orbital prefrontal cortices for this chapter), and *lateral* (areas 8, 9, 44, 45, 46 and 47) subregions. The collective actions of these regions mediate what is commonly referred to as "executive function" (Fig. 4.1). In general terms, the PFC is responsible for the mental representation of abstract information so that it can be used to guide thoughts, emotion, and behavior. These functions, which include goal representation, planning, decision making, attention, working memory and inhibitory control, enable what Fuster (2015) terms "perception–action cycles." These cycles require the coordinated activity of prefrontal cortical subregions many of which provide outputs to striatal structures, including the basal ganglia and nucleus accumbens. Notably, these striatal projections are part of a closed loop system which, via the globus pallidus and thalamus, feeds back to the PFC.

The human *medial prefrontal cortex (mPFC)* includes the dorsal (area 32) and ventral (area 24) cingulate cortex and the pregenual (area 33) and subgenual (area 25) regions. The *dorsal anterior cingulate cortex* is often considered to be functionally homologous with the rodent prelimbic cortex and integrates task-relevant information to create representations that guide value-based decision making. Accordingly, projection targets from the dorsal anterior cingulate cortex are widespread and include brain regions implicated in emotion (e.g., amygdala,

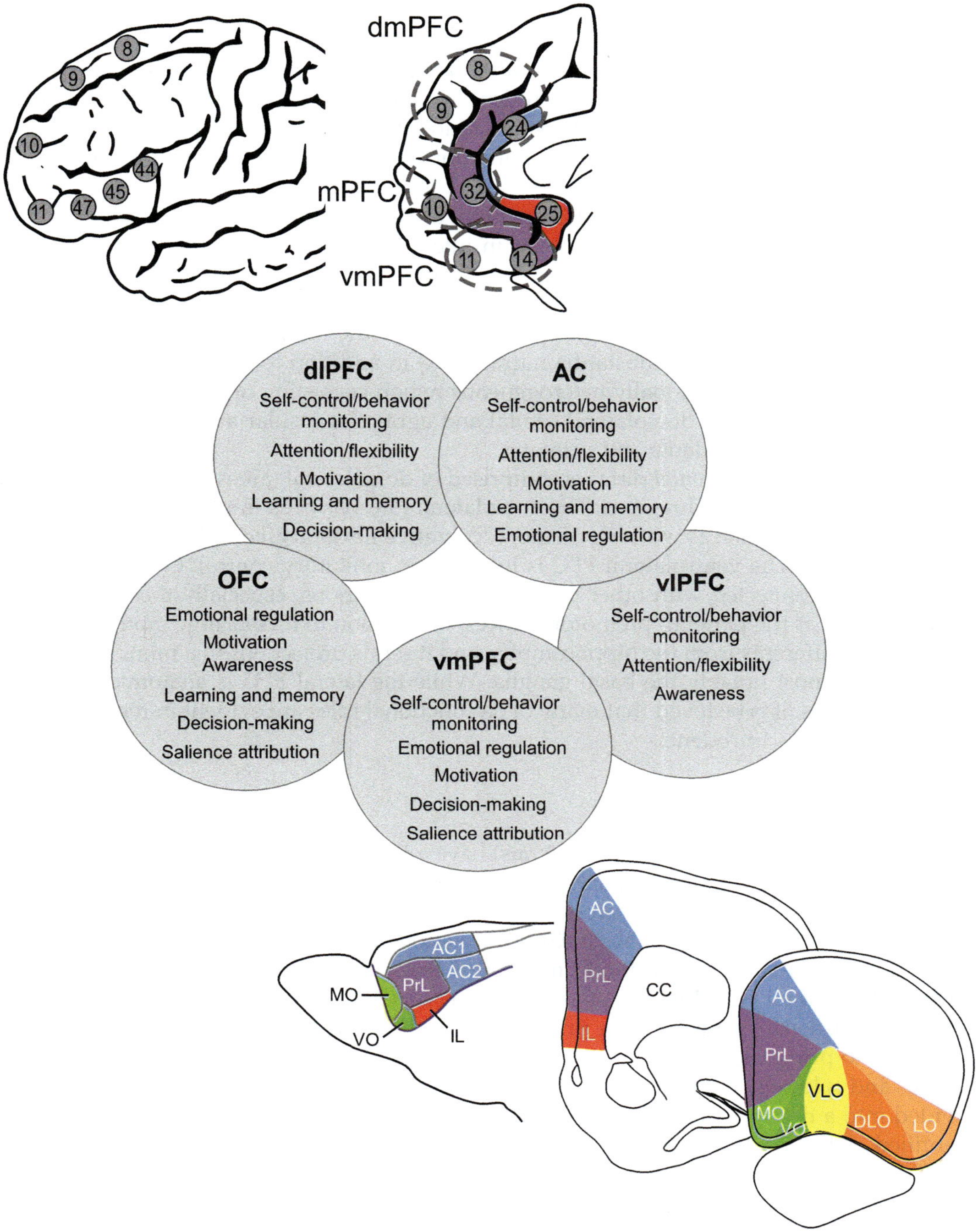

FIGURE 4.1 Anatomical layout of the human and rodent frontal cortex and associated behavioral control.

hypothalamus, ventromedial prefrontal cortex, insula, ventral striatum/nucleus accumbens), cognition and executive control (e.g., dorsal prefrontal cortex), and motor control (basal ganglia). The more *ventral* aspects of the mPFC, including the subgenual region, are thought to be functionally homologous with the rodent infralimbic cortex and appear to play important roles in emotional regulation and response inhibition. Other dorsal regions in the human medial prefrontal cortex (e.g., the ventral anterior cingulate cortex and pregenual area) are involved in social cognition.

The human *orbital frontal cortex* (OFC) includes areas 11, 13 and 47 (and according to some, area 10—the frontal pole) and is involved in integrating external and internal information into cognitive maps of value relationships that can be used to establish goals and guide decision making. In line with this function, the OFC is highly connected with other prefrontal areas and sends projections to various components of the mesocorticostriatal system (e.g., dorsal and ventral striatum, substantia nigra, VTA) in addition to the amygdala and lateral hypothalamus. It is a functionally heterogeneous region consisting of medial orbital, ventral, ventrolateral, lateral, and dorsolateral orbital and agranular insular areas with some degree of homology between rodents and primates.

The human *lateral prefrontal cortex* is comprised of dorsolateral (areas 9 and 46) and ventrolateral (areas 44 and 45) subregions. The dorsolateral PFC has been implicated in higher order executive functions such as working memory, cognitive flexibility, complex planning, and abstract reasoning. The ventrolateral PFC is involved in inhibitory control. Overall, the lateral PFC is highly connected with other prefrontal cortical regions, especially the orbital frontal cortex, as well as the parietal/premotor cortices. In addition to its thalamic inputs, the lateral PFC receives afferents from the hippocampus, and it sends projections to a number of subcortical regions, most notably the basal ganglia. While the lateral PFC is anatomically present only in primates, it is believed that many of its functional roles are evident in medial prefrontal cortical regions in rodents.

Rodent PFC

The extent to which rodents (mice and rats) have a PFC has been the subject of much debate (Uylings et al., 2003), with the primary issue reflecting whether rodents have a prefrontal region that is comparable with the dorsolateral PFC of primates. Although this debate lies outside the scope of this chapter, Ulyings et al. (2003) made a strong argument that rodents do in fact have functionally divided regions of the frontal cortex that can be defined both anatomically and functionally as the PFC. More recently, Seamans et al. (2008) suggested that the rodent mPFC combines functional elements of the primate dlPFC and ACC (Seamans et al., 2008).

Similar to primates, the rodent PFC (Fig. 4.1) is located at the anterior pole of the frontal cortices and is loosely defined as the mPFC, the ACC, and the OFC. The mPFC is further subdivided into a dorsal region designated as the prelimbic cortex (PrLC) and a ventral region identified as the infralimbic cortex (ILC). Notably, the mPFC is also often referred to as the dmPFC that is comprised of the dorsal PrLC and cg1/cg2 regions versus the vmPFC, comprised of the ventral PrLC and dorsal ILC. Similarly, the OFC is subdivided into medial, ventral, lateral, and dorsolateral regions. Much like primates, the rodent PFC displays topographical connectivity that includes a dorsal-to-ventral projection pattern. For instance, the PrLC densely innervates the dorsal striatum and gradually transitions to the ventral striatum (i.e., core subdivision of the NAc) and subsequently to the shell region of the NAc through the ILC and OFC (Fig. 4.3).

PFC dysfunction and addiction

A dimensional or construct approach is often applied to the examination of individuals with behavioral addictions, including gambling, the internet, food, sex, and substance misuse as it allows an operationalization of maladaptive behavior. Behavioral constructs that are often viewed as the most relevant are based on applicability toward treatment of addiction. Importantly, cognitive deficits are not universally diagnosed across all individuals with SUDs and may emerge on distinct temporal patterns and exert unique and/or synergistic influences on addiction severity based on the individual. Further, while SUDs appear to share a number of core pathologies (Bossert et al., 2006; Bossert et al., 2007; Rogers et al., 2008; Bossert et al., 2009; Bossert et al., 2012), there is also literature that contentiously supports behavioral and neurobiological distinctions across drug classes (Dalley et al., 2005; McNamara et al., 2010; Badiani et al., 2011; Hearing et al., 2018). Thus, while commonalities have pushed for a unified theory of substance misuse, we cannot assume that the same neural and psychological mechanisms underlie the emergence of SUDs across drug classes (for reviews, see (Badiani et al., 2011; Hearing et al., 2018; Hearing, 2019)—highlighting a need to identify overlap and divergence to improve and tailor treatment.

In general, the consequences of structural (Franklin et al., 2002; Tanabe et al., 2009), transcriptomal (Walker et al., 2018) and functional (Goldstein and Volkow, 2011) alterations in the PFC that contribute to SUDs are evident in three inter-related domains. First, PFC dysfunction can lead to a *loss of inhibitory control* that may manifest as increased impulsivity and heightened stressor reactivity (Fig. 4.2). Second, changes in *attentional bias* resulting from altered PFC function contribute to the exaggerated salience/influence of drug-associated cues observed in SUDs. Third, *impaired decision making* in individuals with SUDs can fuel persistent use and contribute to many of the deleterious effects of SUDs on other aspects of life. Alterations in PFC function that contribute to SUDs can emerge situationally (i.e., acutely with drug use or upon exposure to stressful stimuli) or may be the result of persistent deficits that are pre-existing due to genetic, environmental, or developmental factors and/or are attributable to neuroadaptations stemming from repeated drug use. Indeed, it has been reported that cortical thickness in PFC regions (Makris et al., 2008) and resting state connectivity in corticostriatal circuits (Ersche et al., 2021) predict risk for and resilience against SUDs. While it is likely that many drug-induced alterations in PFC structure and function persist, some of them (i.e., gray matter volume) appear to resolve over time in those seeking treatment (Parvaz et al., 2017). Moreover, restoring PFC function using non-invasive approaches such as transcranial magnetic stimulation (TMS) can rescue deficits in decision making (West et al., 2021) and reduce drug seeking/craving and use (Chen et al., 2013; Bolloni et al., 2016; Hanlon et al., 2016).

Drug self-administration and seeking

While PFC hypofunction emerges with chronic drug use, neuroimaging studies of individuals with SUDs report that exposure to drug-associated cues or drug use is associated with

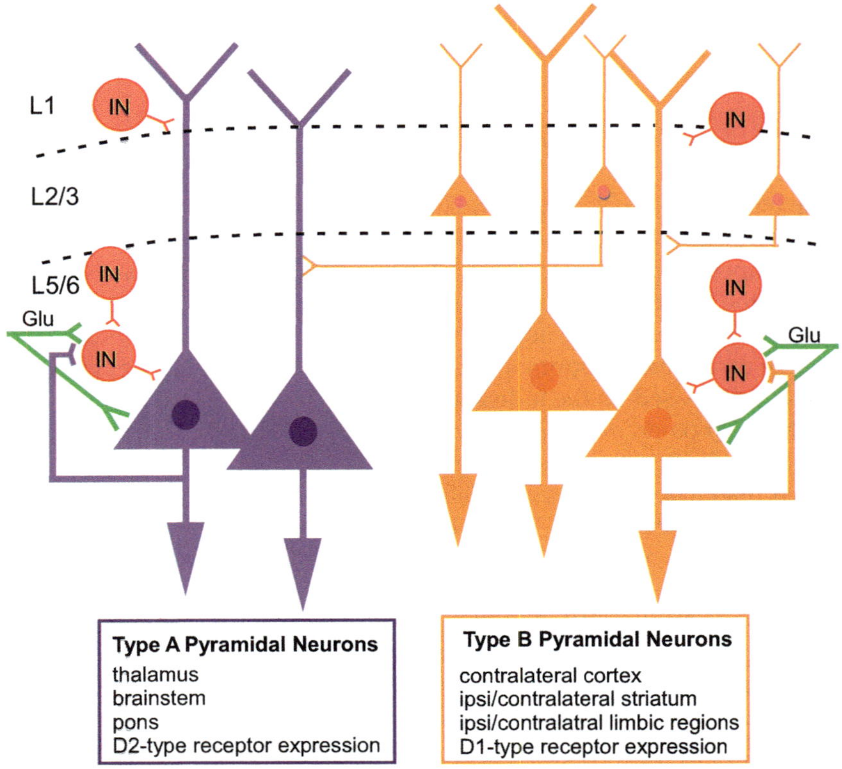

FIGURE 4.2 Microcircuitry of cortical pyramidal neuron subpopulations.

activation of subregions of the PFC, particularly the DLPFC, OFC, and ACC (Grant et al., 1996; Maas et al., 1998; Childress et al., 1999; Volkow et al., 1999; Daglish et al., 2001; George et al., 2001; Bonson et al., 2002). Thus, in contrast to general deficits in PFC function and diminished responsiveness to non-drug stimuli, PFC activation in response to drugs and drug-associated cues is intensified in addiction. Indeed, it has been proposed that cue-evoked fMRI BOLD signal in the mPFC may serve as a transdiagnostic marker of drug addiction (Hanlon et al., 2019). These observations in people are paralleled by findings in rodents. Repeated drug self-administration disrupts PFC activity (Sun and Rebec, 2006; Anderson et al., 2021), but drug exposure and drug cues evoke robust responses in PFC subregions that encode drug seeking (Ciccocioppo et al., 2001; Koya et al., 2006; Dayas et al., 2007; Kufahl et al., 2009; Bossert et al., 2012; Bal et al., 2019). Moreover, it has been reported that delivery of cocaine directly into the rodent PFC can induce cocaine seeking (Park et al., 2002) and support self-administration (Goeders and Smith, 1983), while inhibition of the PFC using pharmacological (baclofen/muscimol or tetrodotoxin), optogenetic, or DREADD (designer receptor exclusively activated by designer drugs) based approaches attenuates cocaine (Capriles et al., 2003; McFarland et al., 2003; McFarland et al., 2004; Stefanik et al., 2013), heroin (Rogers et al., 2008), methamphetamine (Rocha and Kalivas, 2010) or alcohol seeking (Palombo et al., 2017) in rats. Furthermore, micro-infusions of dopamine receptor antagonists into PFC subregions (i.e., PrLC or OFC) attenuates cocaine seeking in rats (Capriles et al., 2003; Vranjkovic et al., 2018).

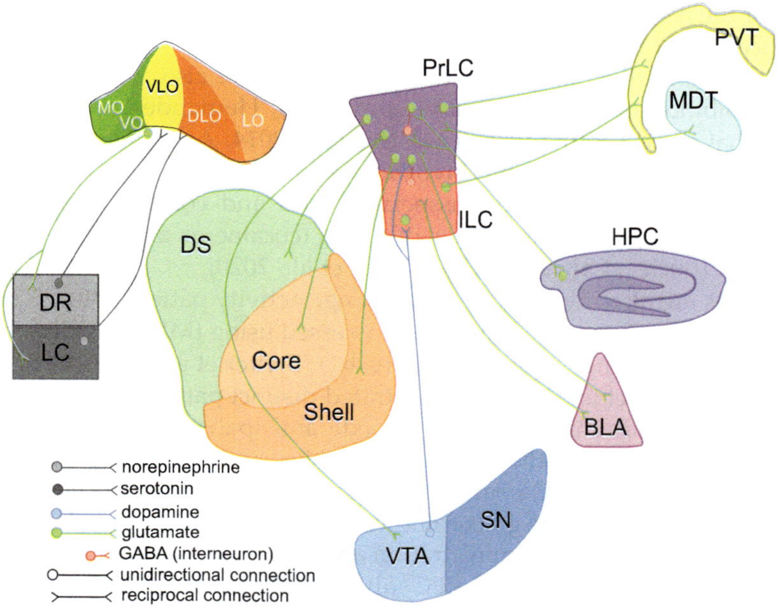

FIGURE 4.3 Schematic of important connections of frontal cortex connections thought to be involved in addiction behavior. Abbreviations: *BLA*, basolateral amygdala; *Core*, nucleus accumbens core; *DLO*, dorsolateral orbital; *DR*, dorsal raphe; *DS*, dorsolateral striatum; *HPC*, hippocampus; *MO*, medial orbital; *LO*, lateral orbital; *MDT*, medi-odorsal thalamus; *PVT*, paraventricular thalamus; *Shell*, nucleus accumbens shell; *SN*, substantia nigra; *VO*, ventral orbital; *VTA*, ventral tegmental area.

Although PFC pyramidal neuron outputs to the thalamus (Giannotti et al., 2018) and midbrain (Cruz et al., 2021) regulate drug seeking, corticostriatal projections appear to be particularly important for drug craving and relapse (Kalivas and Volkow, 2005). Most notably, it has been demonstrated in rats that the activation of pyramidal neurons in the dorsomedial PFC (e.g., PrLC) that project to the NAc core promote cocaine seeking (McFarland et al., 2003; McLaughlin and See, 2003; Stefanik et al., 2013; Kerstetter et al., 2016; McGlinchey et al., 2016), heroin seeking (LaLumiere and Kalivas, 2008), and methamphetamine seeking (Rocha and Kalivas 2010). For other drugs (e.g., alcohol, nicotine, and THC), the contribution of this pathway to drug seeking has not been well-studied. By contrast, activation of pyramidal neurons in the ventromedial PFC (e.g., ILC) that project to the NAc shell, has been proposed to provide a stop signal to inhibit drug seeking under conditions of extinction or signaled drug reinforcement omission (Peters et al., 2008; Augur et al., 2016; Lague et al., 2019). This simplified view has been challenged by observations that inhibition of the ILC pathway to the NAc shell attenuates context-induced reinstatement of heroin seeking (Bossert et al., 2012), while pharmacological inhibition of the ILC prevents cue-induced reinstatement of cocaine seeking (Madangopal et al., 2021). Moreover, neuronal activity in the ILC encodes cocaine seeking (Kane et al., 2021). While factors such as the type of self-administered drug and experimental context likely contribute to these discordant observations, one potential explanation for the disparate findings is that specific ensembles of neurons in both the PL and IL cortices encode and mediate drug seeking.

Neuronal ensembles that contribute to drug seeking are also found in the OFC (Fanous et al., 2012). Inhibition of the OFC (Fuchs et al., 2004; Hernandez et al., 2020), specifically OFC neurons that project to the BLA (Lasseter et al., 2014; Arguello et al., 2017), attenuates cocaine seeking in rats. Notably, the involvement of the OFC in drug seeking is selective for that which is triggered by drug-associated cues and context; reinstatement of drug seeking in response to priming injections of drugs (cocaine or alcohol) is not prevented by OFC inactivation (Fuchs et al., 2004; Hernandez et al., 2020).

PFC subregions are also involved in drug taking. Activity patterns of PFC subregions during cocaine self-administration by humans, as assessed using fMRI, encode subjective aspects of cocaine use (e.g., "craving", "high", and "rush") (Breiter et al., 1997; Risinger et al., 2005). Similarly, in rats, Chang et al. (1998) demonstrated distinct patterns on neuronal firing in the PFC during drug self-administration that encode anticipation of drug infusions and post-infusion drug effects. Notably, they found that while there was some overlap, there was a high degree of variability in PFC neuronal firing patterns and affected neuronal populations across self-administered drugs (e.g., cocaine vs. heroin). Distinct ensembles of PFC neurons also appear to encode drug self-administration and extinction during drug omission (Warren et al., 2019). Manipulations of the PFC also influence progressive ratio cocaine self-administration (McGregor and Roberts, 1995; McGregor et al., 1996) and appear to be particularly effective in the presence of drug-associated cues (Weissenborn et al., 1997). Indeed, rats will self-administer cocaine directly into the mPFC (Goeders and Smith, 1983). Consistent with the role of the PFC in "top-down" regulation of behavior, escalating patterns of drug self-administration, which emerge after "excessive" use (e.g., self-administration under conditions of longer daily access), are associated with altered PFC gene expression (Ploense et al., 2018), glutamate signaling (Ben-Shahar et al., 2012), and cell composition (George et al., 2008) as well as ischemia in the PFC (Du et al., 2020), but not with altered dendritic spine characteristics (Ferrario et al., 2005). While a clear causal role for PFC dysfunction in loss of control over drug use that leads to escalation has not been established, escalated alcohol seeking has been observed after ablation of select cue-responsive neurons in the rat ILC (Pfarr et al., 2015).

Inhibitory control

In humans, deficits in inhibitory control can be studied using a range of approaches that assess the ability to people to withhold behavior, including the Stroop, Flanker, Go/No-Go, and Stop Signal Tasks. SUDs are associated with deficits in each of these tasks (Verdejo-García et al., 2007; Franken et al., 2007; Lane et al., 2007; Smith et al., 2014; Prisciandaro et al., 2014). Moreover, while there is some task-dependent variation across PFC subregions, populations of drug users, and drug classes, a number of studies have reported that, in people with SUDs, the PFC is disengaged during tasks where inhibitory control is required (Goldstein et al., 2001; Kaufman et al., 2003; Bolla et al., 2004). In those with SUDs, impaired inhibitory control can manifest as an inability to withhold drug seeking (Prisciandaro et al., 2013) and may permeate other aspects of life, leading to harmful behaviors. Impaired PFC function can also lead to emotional dysregulation, thus exaggerating responses to stressful stimuli and promoting aggression and other socially inappropriate responses (Goldstein et al., 2005). Indeed, negative urgency, or the tendency to act rashly when distressed (Settles et al., 2012) has been identified as a key construct in SUD (see e.g., Atkinson et al., 2021) and has been associated with PFC dysfunction (Um et al., 2019; Irizar et al., 2020).

Impaired inhibitory control is also evident in rodents with a history of drug exposure. As is the case with humans, the rodent PFC is critical for inhibitory control, and deficits in PFC function can lead to increases in drug seeking, inefficient behavior, and fear-like behaviors (see e.g., Floresco et al., 2008; Minhindou et al., 2013; Moorman and Aston-Jones, 2015; Gourley and Taylor, 2016; Goode and Maren, 2019; Singewald and Holmes, 2019). In particular, the rodent infralimbic cortex is important for inhibition of drug seeking (e.g., during extinction) (Peters et al., 2008; Augur et al., 2016; Lague et al., 2019); however, recent studies have demonstrated that this function is likely encoded by neuronal ensembles that are distributed across the infralimbic and prelimbic regions of the PFC (Suto et al., 2016; Warren et al., 2019). Activating these neurons can suppress drug seeking, while inhibition can promote drug seeking/use. The PFC also suppresses compulsive behaviors, thus promoting purposeful, goal-directed behavior. In people with SUDs, PFC dysfunction may promote perseverative, habitual drug use that persists in the absence of drug-associated cues and context (Everitt and Robbins, 2016). As with humans, repeated drug exposure in rodents can more broadly disrupt inhibitory control, suggesting that the impact of drug-induced cortical deficits can extend beyond drug seeking and use.

Attentional bias

In those with SUDs, exposure to cues associated with drug use typically precipitate craving, thereby increasing the risk for relapse to drug use. The influence of drug cues is exacerbated by the establishment of attentional bias (Field and Cox, 2008) such that the salience and value of drug-associated cues is enhanced while the responses to non-drug cues are diminished. In humans, this can be observed as disproportionately large subjective and physiological reactivity to and preference for drug-related cues (Moeller et al., 2009; Wilcox et al., 2011; Waters et al., 2012; Garland et al., 2013; Kennedy et al., 2014) and by heightened drug cue-induced recruitment of neural networks associated with salience and reward processing accompanied by blunted non-drug related responses (Zilverstrand et al., 2018). Prefrontal regions, including the OFC and ACC represent key nodes in these networks. Thus, altered attentional bias attributable to PFC dysfunction can account for a defining feature of SUDs: that is, a fixation on drug pursuit/use that supplants other non-drug-related behavioral alternatives. Not surprisingly, the degree of attentional bias for drug-related cues and the corresponding pattern of PFC activation are predictive of risk for drug misuse and relapse (Garland et al., 2014; Li et al., 2015).

There is also evidence for drug-related attentional bias in rodents. As is the case with other reinforcers, drugs promote motivational salience of predictive cues, as illustrated by the emergence of sign-tracking behavior (i.e., the propensity to attend to reward-associated stimuli) in Pavlovian conditioning designs (Uslaner et al., 2006). However, sign tracking manifests differently across primary reinforcers making direct comparison problematic. Moreover, in contrast to non-human primates, it is difficult in rats to establish choice of drugs or drug cues over non-drug reinforcers or non-drug cues (Madsen and Ahmed, 2015), although this can be achieved in a subpopulation of animals, akin to the observation that only a small percentage of humans who initially use drugs transition to addiction (Guillem and Ahmed, 2018, but see Townsend et al., 2021). Comparison between rats that choose cocaine and those that choose non-drug reinforcers reveals that non-overlapping populations of OFC neurons encode drug versus non-drug choice (Guillem and Ahmed, 2018). Acute cocaine preexposure promotes cocaine choice and the activity of OFC neurons that encode this preference (Vandaele et al., 2016). It is likely that chronic cocaine-induced perturbances in the OFC (Lucantonio et al., 2012) and other prefrontal regions also produce lasting alterations in attentional bias that amplify drug valuation and salience, thereby promoting pathological drug-seeking behavior. Interestingly, there is evidence in rats that PFC plasticity associated with cue-induced drug and non-drug seeking is distinct: specifically, cue-induced cocaine seeking but not sucrose seeking is associated with synaptic depotentiation (i.e., the loss of long-term potentiation) at synapses in the prelimbic cortex (Koya et al., 2006; Gipson et al., 2013). Similarly, in rats, cue-induced cocaine seeking but not sucrose seeking requires PFC dopamine signaling (James et al., 2018), and these two behaviors involve at least partially distinct output pathways (James et al., 2018) as well as unique downstream neuronal ensembles in the NAc core (Bobadilla et al., 2020). PrLC neurons that project to the contralateral nucleus accumbens core are activated during cue-induced reinstatement of cocaine seeking, but not sucrose seeking (James et al., 2018) and micro-infusions of the D1/D2 dopamine receptor antagonist, fluphenazine into the PrLC blocks cue-induced cocaine seeking without affecting sucrose seeking (James et al., 2018). Moreover, using a TRAP2 transgenic mouse line to tag cells activated by cocaine and sucrose seeking according to Fos expression, it has been demonstrated that only about 30% of nucleus accumbens core neurons are active during both cocaine and sucrose seeking (Bobadilla et al., 2020). Notably, while there is some divergence in the PFC ensembles activated by drug and non-drug rewards, there is also a large amount of overlap. Using dual *in situ* hybridization for simultaneous detection nascent and mature c-fos transcripts, thus permitting examination of overlapping neuronal reactivity in the rat ILC in response to consecutive cue-induced alcohol and saccharin seeking sessions, close to 50% overlap was observed (Pfarr et al., 2018).

Decision making

Drug-induced alterations in PFC function can also lead to cognitive deficits that interfere with decision making. Individuals with SUDs display cognitive deficits in a number of domains that have been associated with PFC subregion dysfunction (Rotheram-Fuller et al., 2004; Hester et al., 2007; Verdejo-García et al., 2007; Chen et al., 2020). Indeed, impaired performance in many decision making tasks has been associated with disrupted PFC function (Bechara et al., 2001; Moeller et al., 2014; Lucantonio et al., 2014, 2015; Gowin et al., 2017; Worhunsky et al., 2017; Hobkirk et al., 2019), and, in some cases, predicts risk for drug misuse and relapse (Bowden-Jones et al., 2005; Paulus et al., 2005; Verdejo-Garcia et al., 2007; Sebold et al., 2017; Huhn et al., 2019; but see Adinoff et al., 2016). Such deficits can also promote other harmful behaviors in those with SUDs (see e.g., Koffarnus et al., 2016). While there is some variation, it is notable that many of these deficits generalize across classes of addictive drugs (Gowin et al., 2018).

Drug-induced cognitive deficits related to decision making can also be observed in rodents following non-contingent drug administration and may manifest as increases in risky behavior, economically unfavorable decision making, insensitivity to gains and losses, impaired deliberation and reevaluation, over-expectancy, and inflexibility (Schoenbaum and Setlow, 2005; Simon et al., 2007; Roesch et al., 2007; Setlow et al., 2009; Mendez et al., 2010; Anderson et al., 2021). These effects can also be observed in animals following repeated drug self-administration (Calu et al., 2007; George et al., 2008; Mendez et al., 2010; Parsegian et al., 2011; Wied et al., 2013; Mitchell et al., 2014; Zhukovsky et al., 2019; Cocker et al., 2020). Using rodent models, Schoenbaum and colleagues identified deficits in the ability to effectively incorporate value-based information into a cognitive map that can guide decision making (Lucantonio et al., 2014; Schoenbaum et al., 2016). These deficits are closely associated with dysfunction of the OFC (Lucantonio et al., 2012; Schoenbaum et al., 2016). For example, cocaine-experienced rats exhibit alterations in OFC neuronal encoding associated with decision making tasks (Stalnaker et al., 2006). These findings align with observations that there are functional and structural deficits in the OFC of human drug users (Franklin et al., 2002; Goldstein et al., 2007; Tanabe et al., 2009; Smith et al., 2015; Ersche et al., 2021).

Summary

In summary, the PFC subserves key functions that contribute to inhibitory control, attentional bias, and decision making. Deficits in each of these cognitive domains can contribute directly to the development and maintenance of SUDs and are problematic for other aspects of the lives of drug users. Accordingly, SUD risk and outcomes are closely aligned with PFC dysfunction. While pre-existing or environmentally-induced deficits in PFC function can contribute to SUDs, many of the cortical alterations related to drug addiction emerge with repeated drug use. The next section will summarize what we know about drug-induced neuroadaptations in the PFC that are associated with addiction.

Structure and physiology of the PFC

Principal pyramidal neurons

Pyramidal neurons in frontal cortical regions are glutamate (excitatory) neurons located in layers 2/3 and 5/6 and comprise ~85% of the total neuronal composition. These neurons in combination with local-circuit GABAergic (inhibitory) neurons (often termed interneurons; INs) are the building blocks of PFC microcircuits (Kawaguchi, 1993; Kawaguchi and Kubota, 1993). A complex network of collateral connections between pyramidal neurons as well as direct and reciprocal connections between GABA interneurons work in conjunction to provide a dynamic balance of excitation and inhibition that is critical for cortical information processing and function (Fig. 4.2) (Isaacson and Scanziani, 2011). These microcircuits are modulated by a number of afferent projections, including dopamine and GABA arising from the ventral tegmental area, and excitatory inputs from a variety of cortical and subcortical regions (Petreanu et al., 2009; Hearing et al., 2012; Hooks et al., 2013). Notably, these excitatory inputs can exert effects on pyramidal neurons through direct synaptic connections or indirectly through pronounced "feed forward" inhibitory responses via local GABA interneurons (Goldman-Rakic et al., 1989; Sesack et al., 1995; Seamans et al., 2001; Cruikshank et al., 2007; Cruikshank et al., 2010; Sotres-Bayon et al., 2012; Rock and Apicella, 2015) (Fig. 4.3).

Cortical pyramidal neurons, in particular those located in layer 5/6, are the principal output cells and represent a major source of excitatory input to addiction-relevant brain regions such as the ventral tegmental area, NAc, amygdala and hippocampus that permits direct and indirect top-down regulation of these structures (Sesack et al., 1989; Sesack and Pickel, 1992; Taber et al., 1995; Taber and Fibiger 1995). It remains unknown to what degree a single pyramidal neuron may send collateral projections to multiple downstream targets, however increasing evidence suggests that anatomical connectivity amongst subtypes of pyramidal neurons often aligns with distinctions in molecular profiles. These distinctions include differences in cell morphology, intrinsic membrane properties (e.g., membrane resistance and ionic conductance) as well as the degree of excitatory versus inhibitory presynaptic input that combine to influence synaptic responsivity, neuronal firing properties, and integration of incoming information (Hattox and Nelson, 2007; Brown and Hestrin, 2009; Dembrow et al., 2010; Gee et al., 2012; Little and Carter 2013; Lee et al., 2014; Dembrow et al., 2015; Suter and Shepherd, 2015).

In general, layer 5/6 pyramidal neurons can be defined as thick-tufted, subcortically-projecting type A (also referred to as Type I) neurons, with a robust hyperpolarization-activated cation current (h-current) that influences the size and duration (decay) of synaptic responses and primarily express dopamine type 2 receptors (D2Rs). Alternatively, thin-tufted type B (or Type II) neurons heavily innervate the contralateral cortex, largely lack h-currents, and primarily express dopamine type 1 receptors (D1R) (Fig. 4.2). These subpopulations of cortical cells provide an anatomical framework for regulation of complex behavioral control through processing distinct aspects of information and for defining experience-induced plasticity in cortical circuits (Anderson et al., 2019). Thus, drug-induced adaptations in cortical sub-regions or cell subpopulations may have distinct implications for drug-seeking behavior and impaired control of drug intake, and drugs may exhibit varying degrees of overlap in these effects on the cortex and related behaviors.

Interneurons

Cortical information processing relies on a delicate balance of excitation and inhibition (E/I balance) that when disrupted under pathological conditions is thought to underlie impaired cognition associated with neurological and psychological disorders as well as substance misuse (Rubenstein and Merzenich, 2003; Yizhar et al., 2011; Lewis 2012; Lewis et al., 2012; Lisman, 2012; Van Snellenberg, Girgis et al., 2016; Ferguson and Gao, 2018). GABAergic interneurons are critical for gating incoming long-range inputs (Fig. 4.2). There are more than 20 molecularly-, morphologically- or physiologically-defined interneuron subpopulations that are often identified based on the selective expression of neuropeptides such as somatostatin, parvalbumin, cholecystokinin, and vasopressin. Further, each subpopulation appears to make unique contributions to regulating pyramidal neuron outputs and thus may make distinct contributions to regulatory functions in controlling specific behaviors (Rudy et al., 2011; Murray et al., 2015; Kim, Jeong et al., 2016; Kim, Ahrlund-Richter et al., 2016; Yang et al., 2022).

For example, soma-targeting parvalbumin-expressing fast-spiking interneurons (PV-IN) comprise approximately 50% of cortical interneurons (Kawaguchi and Kubota, 1997), often target somatodendritic regions of pyramidal neurons, and are highly recruited by afferent excitatory drive to regulate excitatory/inhibitory balance and synchronized firing (Atallah et al., 2012; Kvitsiani et al., 2013; Hu et al., 2014) that is necessary for higher order cognitive processes (Markram et al., 2004; Sohal et al., 2009; Anastasiades and Butt, 2011; Rudy et al., 2011; Murray et al., 2015; Kim, Jeong et al., 2016; Kim, Ahrlund-Richter et al., 2016; Anderson et al., 2019). Alternatively, somatostatin-expressing interneurons (SST-IN) heavily influence cell membrane excitability and enhance excitatory inputs selectivity by forming inhibitory synapses on distal dendritic branches of pyramidal neurons (Markram et al., 2004). In contrast to PV-IN, SST-IN appear to play a more prominent role in processing information related to affect (i.e., emotion). As with pyramidal neurons, drug-induced adaptations in cortical interneuron subpopulations may have distinct implications for drug-seeking behavior and impaired control of drug intake, and drugs may have different on these subsets of cells.

Drug-induced adaptations

Clinical and preclinical evidence in rats and mice indicates that, in general, chronic exposure to drugs such as cocaine, opioids (heroin, remifentanil), and alcohol promotes a persistent reduction in the activity and overall function of the dorsal PFC (Dao-Castellana et al., 1998; Childress et al., 1999; Goldstein and Volkow 2002; Sun and Rebec, 2005; Botelho et al., 2006; Sun and Rebec, 2006; Couey et al., 2007; Langleben et al., 2008; Rogers et al., 2008; Abernathy et al., 2010; McGinty et al., 2010; Goldstein and Volkow 2011; Shen et al., 2011; Peters and De Vries 2012; Chen et al., 2013; Peters et al., 2013; Anderson et al., 2021; West et al., 2021). In contrast, initial intoxication and exposure to drug-associated information (e.g., cues), but not naturally rewarding stimuli, are associated with increased activation of these regions (Grant et al., 1996; Chang et al., 1998; Childress et al., 1999; Garavan et al., 2000; Neisewander et al., 2000; Schmidt et al., 2005; Sun and Rebec, 2005; Koya et al., 2006; Zavala et al., 2007; Hearing et al., 2008; Leriche et al., 2008; Avchalumov et al., 2021). Preclinical evidence suggests that this reduction in activity underlies impaired behavioral control while activation of this region is likely required for facilitating acquisition of drug use behavior and engaging in relapse to drug seeking. Alternatively, more ventral PFC regions may exhibit reduced activation during exposure to drugs, as has been shown with cocaine use (Bonson et al., 2002). This finding may have behavioral significance, as unlike more dorsal mPFC regions, activation of the ventral mPFC promotes inflexible behavior and exerts an inhibitory effect on drug seeking (Weissenborn et al., 1997; Rogers et al., 2008; Rocha and Kalivas 2010; Badiani et al., 2011; Peters et al., 2013). Notably, this anatomical divide may not apply to opioids, as activity in both the dorsal and ventral PFC facilitate opioid seeking in rodents (Peters, LaLumiere et al., 2008a; Peters, Vallone et al., 2008b; Bossert, Stern et al. 2011, 2012). These adaptations are thought to contribute to alterations in motivational behavior whereby preferences for drugs is elevated over non-drug rewards (i.e. food, social interaction) and increased responsivity to drug-conditioned cues that drive craving and reduced inhibitory control over abstaining from use (Dole et al., 1966; Martin and Jasinski, 1969; Koob and Le Moal, 1997; Harris and Aston-Jones 2003; Zijlstra et al., 2009).

In this section, we will provide an overview of how drug exposure alters the activity of the PFC, the underlying excitatory and inhibitory neural plasticity, and how these adaptations equate to current theories of addiction. Using largely insight from rodent studies, we will focus primarily on the more medial PrL and IL cortices, as these regions govern various cognitive functions, including encoding of flexible decision-making, inhibitory control, goal-directed (i.e., motivated) behavior, assigning value to rewarding stimuli, and restoration of drug-seeking following abstinence (Sesack et al., 1989; Sesack and Pickel, 1992; Taber et al., 1995; Taber and Fibiger 1995; Kalivas and Volkow 2005; Rogers et al., 2008; Goldstein and Volkow 2011; Bissonette and Roesch, 2017).

Effects on pyramidal neuron activity

Although relatively few in number, studies in both humans and rodents show that acute (i.e. immediate) effects prefrontal cortical regions and tha neuron activity show that cocaine and nicotine administration increases cortical activity and promotes a transient depolarization and/or firing of cortical pyramidal cells (Stein et al., 1998; Lambe et al., 2003; Woodward and Pava, 2009; Trantham-Davidson et al., 2012). Alternatively, initial exposure to morphine (in vivo) in rats appears to attenuate the excitatory response of pyramidal neurons to locally applied and afferent-evoked glutamate. Interestingly, this effect of morphine was reported to be more pronounced at thalamic inputs compared to those arising from the amygdala or hippocampus—suggesting the possibility of pathway- or cell-type specific regulation by mu opioid receptors (Giacchino and Henriksen, 1998; James et al., 2013; Jiang et al., 2021). With cocaine, this initial activation is followed shortly after by an overall reduction in firing rates in anesthetized and self-administering rats (Trantham-Davidson and Lavin, 2004; Sun and Rebec, 2006). *In vitro* electrophysiology studies in acute mouse brain slices have shown that intrinsic excitability of these neurons is not altered 24 h following a single cocaine exposure (Dong et al., 2005; Hearing et al., 2013), however a single exposure to morphine in mice at a similar timepoint promotes disinhibition of pyramidal neurons in the PrLC (Jiang et al., 2021), suggesting that the threshold for initiating acute plasticity in this region varies with drug class. Similar to morphine, ethanol/alcohol exposure also appears to have inhibitory effect, with acute application of ethanol ex vivo rat brain slices or in vivo i.p. injection in anesthetized rats promoting an overall suppression of prefrontal nextwork activity (Tu et al., 2007; Woodward and Pava, 2009; Avchalumov et al., 2021). Similar reductions in metabolic activity observed with alcohol misuse (Dao-Castellana et al., 1998). Although unclear, it is possible that these reductions in activity are driven by upregulation of inhibitory interneurons, as increased Fos expression has been observed in mPFC neurons positive for the GABA marker, glutamic acid decarboxylase (GAD), in rats following acute gavage administration of ethanol shown to increase (Leriche et al., 2008).

In vivo work has shown that repeated self-administration of cocaine augments putative pyramidal neuron responsivity to cocaine and cocaine-related stimuli in the mPFC. Similarly, the dmPFC has been shown in rats to encode incentive value of nicotine-associated cues during relapse tests (Struik et al., 2019), whereas exposure to environmental cues linked to morphine reward is strongly associated with increased activity of PrLC neurons and reinstatement of heroin-seeking increases neuronal markers of activity. *In vitro* slice work has shown that repeated experimenter-administered cocaine or self-administration of the opioid, remifentanil, in male mice triggers an enduring increase in pyramidal neuron membrane excitability in PrLC, but not ILC layer 5/6 pyramidal neurons that persists up to 45 and 14 days post exposure, respectively (Dong et al., 2005; Nasif, Hu et al., 2005a; Huang, Lin et al., 2007; Huang, Yang et al., 2007; Hearing et al., 2013). It remains unknown whether non-contingent opioids and contingent cocaine self-administration produce similar effects, or if these adaptations extend to other stimulant drugs (e.g. methamphetamine). Notably, this increase in excitability following short-term remifentanil exposure is only present in male mice, as females exhibit reduced excitability following 5 or 10 to 14 days of self-administration (Anderson et al., 2021) after 14 day withdrawal (see below discussion of sex differences). However, increasing evidence indicates in rats that neurons in the same region of the mPFC exhibit a gradual reduction in basal activity, indicative of a hyperactive frontal cortical state during drug seeking and reduced activity under conditions where animals are not engaged in drug-related behavior (Sun and Rebec, 2006; West et al., 2021). This decreased activity state is thought to reflect reductions in PFC function, often referred to as a' hypofrontality' and is thought to drive reduced control over limiting drug intake.

This ostensible dichotomy in activity states is reinforced by functional magnetic resonance imaging (fMRI) studies in abstinent individuals abusing cocaine (Jentsch and Taylor, 1999; Tomasi et al., 2007; Goldstein and Volkow, 2011), heroin (Daglish et al., 2001; Rapeli et al., 2006; Fu et al., 2008; Yuan et al., 2009), and methamphetamine (Paulus et al., 2002; Paulus et al., 2005; Kim et al., 2011), whereby individuals show reduced baseline metabolic activity but increased responsivity to drug- and drug-associated cues. Similar observations have been made in rats. For example, extended cocaine self-administration promotes an enduring reduction in excitability of PrLC pyramidal neurons that is significantly more pronounced in a subpopulation of aversion-resistant rats (Chen et al., 2013). Such reductions in rat pyramidal cell excitability following cocaine exposure are characterized by a reduced ability to enter "up-states," whereby action potentials are promoted by synchronous excitatory inputs (Trantham et al., 2002) and have been causally linked to compulsive-like drug-intake and reduced flexibility in behavior (Chen et al., 2013; West et al., 2021).

It is worth noting that while individuals that misuse heroin and cocaine exhibit relatively similar profiles in PFC activity states, studies on the effects of opioid exposure on rodent PFC function are few in number. leads Reductions in the activity-regulated gene, c-fos, have been observed in the orbitofrontal cortex following a two-week chronic escalating-dose regimen of non-contingent morphine, whereas c-fos was elevated in subregions of the mPFC at this time point (Piao et al., 2017). Notably, no changes in c-fos were observed in these regions following 6 weeks of withdrawal. In mice, following a 14–21 days abstinence period from two weeks of daily remifentanil self-administration, pyramidal neurons in the PrLC (but not ILC) show increased excitability and spike firing in male mice that progressively shifts to a dichotomous state in which cells exhibit reduced excitability but increased firing capacity at more depolarized potentials (Anderson et al., 2021). Notably, these divergent phenotypes appear to be more prevalent in a subpopulation of cells. While it is unclear what defines these subpopulations, these data indicate that subsets of PFC neurons may undergo unique forms of plasticity, which may be akin to human reports of a hypoactive PFC basal state with retention of increased firing potential under certain conditions. In support of this notion immediately following repeated experimenter administered drug exposure (i.e., during intoxification) in rats, cocaine, heroin, and methamphetamine all reduce excitability of Type B pyramidal neurons whereas ethanol selectively increased excitability of Type A neurons (Leyrer-Jackson et al., 2021). While these data highlight potential sub-population effects of drug exposure, interpretation of these data should be taken with care as time point of abstinence (acute vs. protracted vs. immediately following drug exposure) when dependent measures are taken, route of administration (contingent vs. non-contingent) and drug class all likely impact the results.

Alterations in ionic conductance in mPFC neurons

Modifications in ion channel function, localization, and expression have profound effects on intrinsic cell physiology. These changes can include modifications in membrane excitability, action potential amplitude or duration, action potential firing interval, and after-hyperpolarization currents. Although distinct from synaptic adaptations, intrinsic plasticity alters how a cell responds to excitatory and inhibitory input. For example, a cell that exhibits increased excitability will likely have a lower threshold for activation in response to glutamate release. While identifying a change in a particular membrane or firing trait is an important first step, identifying the cause of a given change is often difficult given the interactive nature of intracellular signaling.

Reductions in D2R expression and binding is observed in the frontal cortex of cocaine-dependent humans and in the mPFC and OFC of rodents following cocaine self-administration, the latter of which correlates with deficits in mPFC-dependent cognitive function (Volkow and Fowler 2000; Bowers et al., 2004; Briand et al., 2008). Similar reductions in the level of D2 receptors have also been observed in methamphetamine, alcohol- and heroin-dependent individuals (Volkow et al., 2001), however it remains unclear if similar adaptations occur with marijuana/cannabis use. Thus, reductions in mPFC pyramidal neuron basal activation, as well as augmented responsivity to drug stimuli may in part be driven by a drug-induced shift toward preferential activation of intracellular signaling via D1R over D2R. Although it is not clear whether these changes occur in specific subsets of cells, studies in rats indicate reductions in D2R-mediated inhibition of local GABA signaling may result in unopposed D1R-mediated enhancement of local GABA release and an overall reduction in evoked pyramidal neuron firing (Jayaram and Steketee, 2005, 2006; Nogueira et al., 2006; Couey et al., 2007; Kroener and Lavin, 2010; Van den Oever et al., 2010). This shift toward increased D1R activity in GABA neurons may also underlie observed reductions in voltage-sensitive sodium channels (VSSC) activity and decreased intracellular Ca^{2+} release in pyramidal neurons (Hu, 2007) that may reduce basal state activity and excitability of pyramidal neurons. Together these adaptations would be predicted to reduce basal state activity and excitability of pyramidal neurons, and reduce behavioral flexibility, resulting in a state where only strong stimuli (e.g., drugs or conditioned cues) are capable of guiding behavior (Seamans and Yang, 2004).

Drug-induced shifts toward D1R-signaling may also directly increase pyramidal neuron excitability and thus responsivity to drug-related information (Dong et al., 2005; Nasif, Hu et al., 2005; Nasif, Sidiropoulou et al., 2005; Hearing et al., 2013). Increases in D1R activation during early drug exposure appears to be an essential step in triggering reductions in mPFC pyramidal neuron $GABA_BR$-dependent activation of G protein-inwardly rectifying K+ (GIRK) channels that act as a neuronal "off switch" (Hearing et al., 2013; Anderson et al., 2021). This reduction increases excitability and spike firing of PrLC pyramidal neurons and promotes increased sensitivity to the behavioral effects of drugs (Witkowski et al., 2008; Witkowski et al., 2012; Hearing et al., 2013). While numerous factors likely contribute to increased D1R-dependent signaling in the PFC, it may reflect increases or decreases in proteins that regulate signaling of inhibitory metabotropic G protein-coupled receptors like D2Rs and $GABA_BRs$ (Bowers et al., 2004; Hearing et al., 2012). For example, cocaine self-administration in rats increases expression of the protein activator of G-protein signaling 3 (AGS3) in the mPFC for up to 8 weeks post drug exposure (Bowers et al., 2004), whereas preventing cocaine withdrawal-induced AGS3 expression with antisense oligonucleotides blocked post abstinence drug seeking. As a negative regulator of $G_{i/o}$-dependent signaling, this may in turn lead to an upregulation in signaling cascades that are usually inhibited by $G_{i/o}$-dependent signaling, such as the cAMP/PKA pathway (Dong and White, 2003; Dong et al., 2005; Hearing et al., 2013), increase Ca^{2+} influx, and reduce voltage-sensitive K^+ currents (Dong et al., 2005; Nasif, Hu et al., 2005a; Nasif, Sidiropoulou et al., 2005b; Hearing et al., 2013), collectively leading to an overall increase in pyramidal neuron excitation and activation that drive cocaine seeking.

Excitatory and inhibitory plasticity

Changes in behavior related to drug use are thought to be mediated, at least in part, by drug-induced plasticity in multiple brain areas, including the PFC. This notion is supported by findings that drugs alter the dynamics and microstructure of both dendrites and dendritic spines of neurons that may contribute to learning of drug-related associations, escalation of drug use, and sustained susceptibility to relapse (DePoy et al., 2016). With the exception of heroin, most drugs (amphetamine, cocaine, ethanol, nicotine) promote increases in mPFC dendritic arborization and spine density in adult rodents (Brown and Kolb, 2001; Crombag et al., 2005; Kroener et al., 2012; Klenowski et al., 2016) but see (Robinson, Gorny et al. 2001, 2002; Radley et al., 2015). Notably, this increase in complexity is not likely universal across age and/or frontal cortical regions, as repeated exposure to cocaine during early adolescence produces lasting reductions in OFC pyramidal cell dendritic arbor length and complexity (DePoy et al., 2014).

Alterations in dendritic complexity may reflect alterations in both inhibitory or excitatory synapses, or both, as numerous studies have shown that exposure to drugs alter pre- and/or post-synaptic GABA and glutamate neurotransmission. For instance, cocaine- and ethanol-induced alterations in spine density are associated with increased activity-dependent excitatory synaptic strength through upregulation of NMDA-type (GluN) and AMPA-type

(GluA) receptors in the mPFC (Tang et al., 2004; Ben-Shahar et al., 2009; Kroener et al., 2012; Klenowski et al., 2016; Otis et al., 2017). Thus, increases in excitatory synapse density appears to reflect elevated excitatory drive in pyramidal neurons that may in turn contribute to observed increases in mPFC excitability and activity during early drug exposure. Further, during the first 3 to 5 days of cocaine exposure, there is an increased ability to induce long-term potentiation of glutamate signaling (Huang, Yang et al., 2007; Lu et al., 2010). This facilitation of LTP is reliant on signaling through D1Rs and appears to reflect in part, a reduction in GABAergic inhibition mediated by the fast-conducting $GABA_A$ receptor (Huang, Lin et al., 2007; Lu et al., 2010). These adaptations are not universal across drug classes however, as self-administration of heroin or remifentanil does not alter postsynaptic glutamate signaling in mPFC pyramidal neurons following approximately two-weeks of abstinence with or without extinction (Van den Oever et al., 2008; Anderson et al., 2021). However, this may be unique to males, as remifentanil self-administration in females promotes a reduction in AMPAR-signaling as well as an increase in $GABA_AR$-mediated signaling after 14 days of abstinence in mice, whereas males exhibit reduced and increased GABA signaling mediated by metabotropic $GABA_BRs$ at a similar abstinence time point after 14 and 30 days of remifenanil exposure, respectively (Anderson et al., 2021). Thus, while changes in mPFC pyramidal neuron activity may occur similarly across multiple drug classes and biological sex, the underlying mechanisms may be distinct.

PFC circuit-specific plasticity

In rodents, the PrL subdivision of the PFC has emerged as the primary cortical region that promotes relapse to drug-seeking, as pharmacological or optogenetic inactivation of this region reduces seeking for cocaine, heroin, methamphetamine, and ethanol (McFarland and Kalivas 2001; Kalivas and Volkow 2005; Rogers et al., 2008; Rocha and Kalivas 2010; Stefanik and Kalivas 2013; Palombo et al., 2017). As discussed earlier in the chapter, the mPFC governs behavior through connections with thalamic, cortical, striatal, and limbic brain regions. Of these targets, glutamate projections to the NAc has been most frequently implicated in goal-directed behavior and all major forms of drug seeking during early (e.g. 10–14 days) of drug self-administration in rat models (Sun and Rebec, 2006; Bossert et al., 2007; Couey et al., 2007; LaLumiere and Kalivas 2008; Rogers et al., 2008; Shen et al., 2011; Peters and De Vries 2012; Peters et al., 2013).

Activation of PrLC projections to the NAc core appears essential for cue- and drug-induced reinstatement of cocaine seeking (McFarland and Kalivas, 2001; Kalivas, 2009; McCutcheon et al., 2011; Peters et al., 2013; Stefanik et al., 2013; Ma et al., 2014; Scofield et al., 2016). Direct evidence of this specific circuit remains lacking for other drugs such as methamphetamine and heroin, however activation of the NAc core is necessary for these behaviors (Rocha and Kalivas, 2010; Shen et al., 2011; Shen et al., 2014). Numerous adaptations are known to occur throughout the PrLC-to-NAc core circuit. These include changes in intrinsic cell membrane physiology in PrLC pyramidal neurons and principal medium spiny neurons (MSNs) in the NAc as well as alterations in synaptic input to PrLC pyramidal neurons and PrLC-to-NAc core synaptic connections. Notably, adaptations may occur during progressive drug exposure or require a period of post drug abstinence to manifest. In rats, cocaine reduces basal glutamate tone on presynaptic glutamate autoreceptors on PrL glutamate terminals in the NAc core (Baker et al., 2003; Kalivas, 2009), resulting in a reduction presynaptic "brake" systems in place to reduce glutamate release during high levels of activity that results in glutamate "spillover" outside of the synaptic cleft. Both cocaine and opioids (remifentanil) increase excitability of PrLC-to-Core Layer 5/6 pyramidal neurons in mice (Hearing et al., 2013; Anderson et al., 2021), resulting in an overall increased likelihood of being activated in response to drug and drug-related stimuli. Further, exposure to drugs such as cocaine in rats, elevate postsynaptic signaling via AMPA-type glutamate receptors in NAc core medium spiny neurons (Conrad et al., 2008; McCutcheon et al., 2011), with recent data showing that that this occurs at PrLC synaptic inputs to NAc core following self-administration of remifentanil in mice (Anderson et al., unpublished observation). Together, these adaptations may lead to strengthened glutamate responses in PrLC-NAc circuits that drive drug seeking (Conrad et al., 2008; McCutcheon et al., 2011; Ma et al., 2014). This notion is supported by findings cocaine self-administering male rats in which reversal of withdrawal-induced increases in silent synapse expression at PrLC-to-NAc core synapses exert an inhibitory effect on subsequent relapse behavior (Ma et al., 2014).

Although numerous studies have failed to identify global drug-induced alterations in synaptic signaling and cell excitability of pyramidal neurons of the ILC (Van den Over et al., 2008; Anderson et al., 2021), increases in AMPAR-mediated synaptic strength have been observed at ILC-to-NAc shell synapses following non-contingent morphine and cocaine exposure in mice (Hearing et al., 2016; Hearing et al., 2018; Benneyworth et al., 2019), suggesting that plasticity in ILC pyramidal neurons may be more pathway-specific than those observed in the PrLC. However, the functional relevance of altered synaptic strength within this circuit may serve distinct purposes depending on the drug class. For example, separate findings in mice show that AMPAR signaling is elevated at ILC-to-NAc shell synapses two-weeks following drug exposure and that re-exposure to the drug triggers a rapid reduction in synaptic strength in the NAc akin to LTD (Hearing et al., 2016; Benneyworth et al., 2019; Madayag et al., 2019). With cocaine, this short-term plasticity was necessary to promote reinstatement of conditioned place, as optogentic stimulation and inhibition alone was sufficient to reinsate and inhibit preference, respectively (Benneyworth et al., 2019). Alternatively, blockade of this short-term plasticity during morphine re-exposure augmented reinstatement of place preference (Madayag et al., 2019).

On the other hand, accumulating evidence suggests that experiences leading to transient depotentiation (i.e. weakening) of ILC-to-NAc shell MSN synapses may reduce the ability of this pathway to inhibit relapse-associated behavior and thereby facilitate reinstatement (Kourrich et al., 2007; Pascoli et al., 2011; Rothwell et al., 2011; Ma et al., 2014). This pro-versus anti-relapse circuitry is substantiated by evidence showing that reducing basal glutamate transmission during extinction/abstinence, particularly in the NAc shell, enhances reinstatement of drug seeking (Self and Choi, 2004; Bachtell et al., 2008). For example, blocking endocytosis of GluA2-containing AMPARs in the ILC reduces reinstatement of heroin seeking (Van den Oever et al., 2008). Similar mechanisms may promote relapse to other addictive drugs, as re-exposure to heroin-as well as cocaine-conditioned cues both increase expression of proteins associated with endocytosis of GluA2-containing AMPARs in the mPFC (Koya et al., 2006; Hearing et al., 2008a). Much like the ILC, re-exposure to cocaine and/or a cocaine-associated context triggers a transient (24–48 h long) depotentiation of synaptic strength at NAc shell MSNs that is reliant on AMPAR endocytosis and is necessary and sufficient to promote reinstatement of cocaine-induced CPP. Further, direct activation of the ILC-NAc shell circuit using optogenetic stimulation triggers this depotentiation and reinstates conditioned reward behavior, whereas inhibition of this circuit as well as preventing the initial development of potentiated synaptic strength during early withdrawal prevents depotentiation and reinstatement (Benneyworth and Hearing et al., 2019; Ma et al., 2014). Thus, it appears that potentiation and subsequent activation of this circuit is necessary to "trigger" the depotentiation and thus behavior.

The dense reciprocal connectivity of the mPFC with numerous subcortical regions suggests that plasticity in other prefrontal-based circuits are likely to play an important role in addiction as well, however data are far more sparse. For example, the basolateral amygdala (BLA) is heavily innervated by both the PrLC and IL subdivisions, with evidence suggesting these circuits play a role in driving cue-induced reinstatement of cocaine seeking as well as extinguishing that response to cocaine and heroin (McDonald, 1987; Sesack, et al. 1989; See et al., 2003; Crombag et al., 2008; Ovari and Leri, 2008; Van den Oever et al., 2010; Peters et al., 2013). For instance, inactivation of the ILC-BLA circuit PrLC projections to the PVT are also important for drug seeking, as inhibition of this pathway reduces cocaine seeking, while mPFC-to-VTA projections appear to gate excitation of a subset of dopamine neurons that may be important for conditioned learning underlying drug-seeking behavior (Liu et al., 2015).

Relevance of drug-induced changes in mPFC plasticity

The functional implications of co-occurring increased responsivity to drug-associated cues and reduced basal activation of the mPFC remains a vital question toward understanding how addictive drugs impair cognitive control and increase drug use. Studies in humans and animals suggest that early drug use leads to increases in excitability of mPFC pyramidal neurons that aligns with heightened activity in prefrontal circuits in response to drug-related information during drug taking and withdrawal (Childress et al., 1999; Dong et al., 2005; Sun and Rebec, 2006; Hearing et al., 2013; Anderson et al., 2021). Increased excitation may lower the threshold for induction of longer-lasting plasticity in PFC circuits necessary for reinforcement learning related to the development of drug–cue associations responsible for precipitating craving and drug-seeking behavior. This notion is supported by preclinical work showing that sparsely distributed neurons (i.e., neuronal ensembles) encode learned associations between heroin reward and heroin-associated stimuli that drive relapse behavior (Bossert et al., 2012; Van den Oever et al., 2013).

On the other hand, reductions in excitability following repeated drug exposure in animals match well with reduced basal activation of similar regions in dependent humans. As drug cues have the ability to precipitate craving and activate the PFC, reductions in basal activity states may amplify responsiveness of the mPFC to drug and drug-conditioned cues, while simultaneous increases in the activation threshold of these circuits (e.g., reduced excitability) may allow only drug-associated cues to activate PFC networks and thus exert undue control over behavior. However, with further use, this dichotomous prefrontal state may progress toward an overall hypoactive basal and activity state. Emergence of this hypofunction appears to underlie impairments in cognitive flexibility, increased impulsivity, and habit-like drug use as well as a reduced role of the PFC in drug seeking, perhaps reflecting a shift toward control by habit-based neural circuits (Jentsch and Taylor 1999; Everitt and Robbins 2005; Fuchs et al., 2006; See et al., 2007; Pacchioni et al., 2011; Chen et al., 2013; Anderson et al., 2021; West et al., 2021). In support of this, non-human primates exhibit increased activation of striatal circuits associated with habitual behavior following 100 days of cocaine self-administration compared to the first day (Porrino et al., 2004). Further, recent studies show that co-occurring hypoactive basal excitability and hyperactive firing observed in PrLC pyramidal neurons produced by global remifentanil self-administration progressively shift toward a hypoactive basal excitability *and* firing after approximately two additional weeks of self-administration (Anderson et al., 2021). Regardless of how these data are interpreted, they clearly show that repeated drug exposure produces progressive, exposure-dependent alterations in pyramidal neuron responsivity, reflecting a combination of modified synaptic transmission, as well as intrinsic synaptic structure and physiology.

Impact of biological sex, stress, and preexisting differences on addiction and PFC function

Sex differences in prevalence, progression, and neural mechanisms

Biological sex dictates drug-related behavioral and neurobiological outcomes (Becker et al., 2012), as women are at heightened risk for developing SUDs, and exposure to illicit substances leads women to transition to addiction more rapidly than men (Becker and Hu, 2008; Becker et al., 2012). Although the basic neural systems involved in positive and negative reinforcement as well PFC-dependent behavioral control are largely similar in males and females, sex differences have been observed in PFC organization, activation patterns, and anatomical connectivity. These differences are thought to underlie sex-specific brain responses to experiences such as stress and drug exposure, and thus the path to addiction. An encompassing discussion of sex differences in addiction is outside the scope of this chapter, however many excellent reviews have been published on quantitative, population, and mechanistic sex differences in addiction and drug misuse (Becker and Koob, 2016; Becker et al., 2016; Becker and Chartoff, 2019; Nicolas et al., 2021). Below, we will briefly touch on known sex differences in addiction prevalence and progression followed by a discussion of clinical and preclinical studies that highlight mechanistic sex differences in the underlying neurobiology of addiction.

Clinical reports indicate that, overall, cocaine, opioid, and alcohol use disorders are more prevalent in men than women, with men reporting more lifetime and past-year use of cocaine, all opioid drugs, and alcohol. However, women generally exhibit a more rapid progression from initial intermittent drug use to dependence (Kosten et al., 1993; Brady and Randall, 1999; Agabio et al., 2017). Notably, women are more likely to report lifetime use of prescription opioids as the primarily (mis)used drug (Serdarevic et al., 2017), which may reflect greater prevalence of non-neuropathic chronic pain conditions in women (Berkley, 1997; Gureje et al., 1998; Fillingim et al., 2009; Mogil, 2012), and an increased incidence of prescriptions written for women (Darnall and Stacey, 2012; Darnall et al., 2012), or reduced efficacy of opioid analgesics in women versus men (Kest et al., 2000; Fillingim and Gear, 2004). Women also report experiencing greater feelings of euphoria during cocaine use than men, which may contribute to faster progression toward dependence. During periods of abstinence, women self-report experiencing enhanced drug craving for cocaine and opioids that likely to contributes to greater incidence of relapse. During bouts of relapse, women often consume larger amounts of drug and resume use for longer periods (Kosten et al., 1993; Brady and Randall, 1999; Robbins et al., 1999; Chen and Kandel, 2002; Gallop et al., 2007; Ignjatova and Raleva, 2009; Soldin et al., 2011; Kennedy et al., 2013; Bobzean, Dennis et al., 2014; Bobzean, DeNobrega et al., 2014; Fernandez-Montalvo et al., 2017).

Work in animals has revealed similar trends in females versus males. For example, female rats develop conditioned place preference for lower doses of cocaine compared to males, indicating that females are more sensitive to the rewarding effects of the drug (Russo, Festa et al., 2003; Russo, Jenab et al., 2003; Zakharova et al., 2009). Moreover, female rats acquire cocaine and heroin self-administration behavior more rapidly than males, and they self-administer more drug at a faster rate than do male rats (Lynch and Carroll, 1999; Cicero et al., 2003). Females are also more sensitive to cocaine-primed reinstatement of cocaine-seeking behavior (Doncheck et al., 2020), in part due to the influence of estrogen in the PFC (Doncheck et al., 2021). However, several notable studies have shown no evidence for increased acquisition and maintenance of opioid self-administration in female rats (Bossert et al., 2020; Reiner et al., 2020), and also indicate that males exhibit higher fentanyl choice than females while (Townsend et al., 2019). Finally, recent evidence indicates that remifentanil self-administration in females promotes a more rapid emergence of impaired flexibility in decision-making behavior that may contribute to more rapid loss of control of drug use in females (Anderson et al., 2021) (Figs. 4.4 and 4.5).

In humans, positron emission tomography (PET) and fMRI studies have been used to identify brain regions activated (or inhibited) during craving induced by exposure to drugs, drug cues, or stress. However, most human and animal studies have exclusively used men/males or included women/females but were not designed (lacked power) to assess sex differences (Becker and Hu, 2008; Becker et al., 2012; Becker and Koob, 2016; Becker and Chartoff, 2019). The few studies that aimed to investigate the role of sex in cocaine use disorder (CUD) have shown lower activity levels within the dorsal and ventral portions of the medial PFC in females compared to male cocaine-dependent individuals when viewing drug-related imagery (Kilts et al., 2004; Volkow et al., 2012; Canterberry et al., 2016) as well as negative emotional stimuli. Similar to studies in humans, preclinical studies have largely focused on males or not sufficiently powered studies to directly compare behavior or plasticity observed in males versus females. However, it should not be assumed that every aspect of addiction is distinct based on sex. Moreover, caution should be taken when assuming that even though a similar behavior (e.g., deficits in cognitive function) or change in neural activity (e.g., hypoactivity) is observed in both sexes that the underlying neural mechanisms are the same (for a review, see Becker and Chartoff, 2019).

Cognitive Processing:	Disruption in Addiction:	Brain Region(s):
Self-control/behavior monitoring: Response inhibition Behavior Coordination Conflict and error	Impulsivity, compulsiveness, risk taking, impaired self-monitoring (habitual, inflexible behavior)	dlPFC, dAC, vlPFC
Emotional Regulation: cognitive/affective suppression of emotion	Increased stress response; inability to suppress intense emotions (anxiety, anhedonia, irritability)	mOFC, vmPFC, AC
Motivation: initiative, drive, persistence towards goals	Increased motivation to obtain and use drugs and reduced motivation for non-drug/appetitive rewards	OFC, AC, vmPFC, dlPFC
Awareness: one's physical and subjective state; insight	Reduced satiety for drug use; inability to acknowledge illness and need for treatment	AC, mPC, OFC, vlPFC
Attention and flexibility:	Increased attentional bias towards drug-related stimuli; inflexibility in goals to obtain drug; increased relapse due to reduced maintenance of abstinence	dlPFC, AC, vlPFC
Learning and memory: associative learning, reward devaluation, extinction, conditioned reward, long-term memory	Conditioned associations between drug-related stimuli and reward that trigger craving; over learning of behaviors associated with procuring and using drug; inability to alter (increase) value of non-drug rewards	dlPFC, OFC, AC
Decision making: planning and goal formation, probability estimation and expected outcome, choice versus valuation	Choice of immediate reward over delayed gratification; discounting future (negative) consequences; drug-related anticipation; reduced prediction of outcomes	lOFC, mOFC, vmPFC, dlPFC
Salience attribution: reward valuation/appraisal, incentive salience	Increased (sensitized) value given to drugs/drug-cue/reduced value to non-drug reinforcers; impaired ability to perceive a gradient in reward value	mOFC and vmPFC

FIGURE 4.4 PFC cognitive constructs disrupted in addiction.

In summary, data indicate that the neural mechanisms underlying the transition to addiction is distinct between sexes and that impairments in cognitive control and the underlying neural adaptations arise more rapidly in females. However, key empirical evidence for this contention is lacking, as most studies focusing on mechanisms of cognitive impairment and compulsive drug taking have used males only (Becker and Hu, 2008; Becker et al., 2012; Becker and Koob, 2016; Becker and Chartoff, 2019). Thus, it is imperative that we identify core behavioral and neural adaptations shared across sexes, as they likely represent important focal points of treatment, but also points of divergence between the sexes, as these likely represent opportunities to tailor treatment of SUDs to the individual.

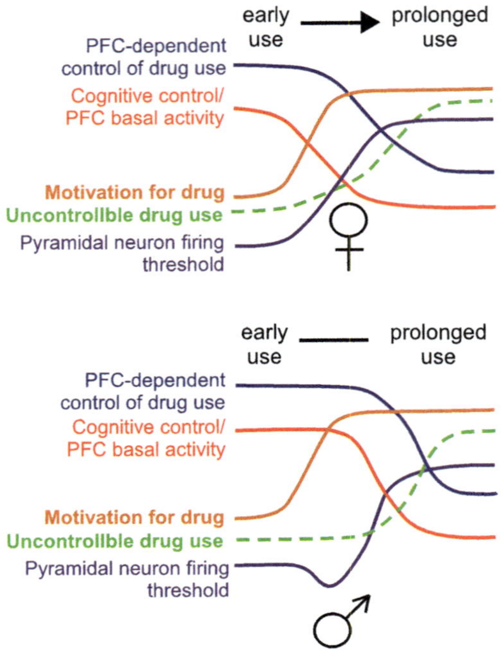

FIGURE 4.5 Theoretical timeline of addiction progression in males versus females.

Impact of stress

The PFC is heavily influenced by stressful stimuli, largely via regulation by monoaminergic systems (Arnsten, 2009, 2015). Changes in prefrontal cortical processing are important for adaptive responses to stressors, and stress effects often involve a removal of top-down control of reflexive behaviors that support survival in the face of threats. As drug-seeking behaviors involve many of the same circuits and networks that are subject to top-down regulation by the PFC, it is not surprising that acute stress-induced dysregulation of PFC function can promote or trigger drug seeking. In humans, craving elicited by personalized stress imagery is associated with a reduced BOLD signal in various regions of the PFC (Sinha and Li, 2007; Li and Sinha, 2008; Seo et al., 2013). Moreover, chronic stress can lead to persistent PFC hypofunction (Radley et al., 2004; Cook and Wellman, 2004; Liston et al., 2006, 2009; Shansky et al., 2009; Goldwater et al., 2009; McKlveen et al., 2016; Wellman et al., 2020), which is also evident in individuals with major depressive disorder (Soares and Mann, 1997; Diener et al., 2012; McEwen et al., 2016; Drysdale et al., 2017; Belleau et al., 2019), thus promoting long-term risk for heightened patterns of drug use and relapse. The impact of stress on PFC function varies across development with apparent windows of "opportunity," such that stress may have exaggerated effects on drug (mis)use during adolescence (see Noschang et al., 2021 for review).

As is the case with drug priming injections and drug-associated cues, the PrLC and prelimbic projections to the nucleus accumbens core have been implicated in stress-induced cocaine seeking in rats (see Mantsch et al., 2016 for review). Inhibition of the prelimbic

PFC prevents stress-induced cocaine seeking (Capriles et al., 2003; McFarland et al., 2004) and stress-induced reinstatement is associated with Fos immunoreactivity in the PrLC (Schank et al., 2015; Vranjkovic et al., 2018; Walker et al., 2020). PFC mechanisms are likely important for stress effects on processing of drug-related information. Indeed, we have found that stress can promote or potentiate cocaine seeking in response to cocaine priming injections via disruption of inhibitory regulation of PrLC pyramidal neuron output pathways (Graf et al., 2011; McReynolds et al., 2018; Doncheck et al., 2020). This effect involves elevated corticosterone and mobilization of endocannabinoid signaling which attenuates GABA release from PFC interneurons and removes inhibition of output pathways that mediate drug seeking. Stress effects in the PrLC intensify with drug exposure, as we have found that stress effects on dopaminergic signaling in the PrLC and cocaine seeking are recruited with daily cocaine self-administration under long-access/high intake conditions as a result of enhanced corticotropin releasing factor (CRF) signaling in the VTA via upregulation of CRFR1 receptors (Blacktop et al., 2011; Vranjkovic et., 2018).

Pre-existing differences

Recognition that long-term alterations in PFC function promote risk for drug use and seeking allows for the possibility that such deficits, whether drug-induced, environmentally established (e.g., via stress), or pre-existing may serve as vulnerability factors for SUDs. As noted above, cortical thickness in PFC regions (Makris et al., 2008) and resting state connectivity in corticostriatal circuits (Ersche et al., 2021) can predict risk for and resilience against SUDs. These alterations are likely aligned with traits that may render people susceptible to developing SUDs (Ersche et al., 2012). Understanding the transcriptional, functional, and psychometric markers that that link PFC deficits to SUD risk and outcomes will have great relevance for guiding effective interventions. Indeed, work in rodents has identified transcriptional (Navandar et al., 2021), synaptic (Kasanetz et al., 2013) and neurochemical (see e.g., Piazza et al., 1991) profiles that predict individual differences in susceptibility to addiction-like behaviors.

Conclusions

In conclusion, because of its critical role in cognition, alterations in the function of the PFC can have profound effects on inhibitory control, attentional bias, decision making and other related constructs that fundamentally contribute to SUDs. Deficits in PFC function can account for susceptibility to drug use, relapse, and addiction, as well as the progression and severity of SUDs, and can pre-exist or emerge with repeated cycles of drug use. Elucidating the relationship between PFC dysfunction at the cellular, microcircuit, and network level and SUDs has important implications for more precise diagnosis and the development of more effective and targeted interventions. Indeed, the accessibility of the PFC to non-invasive transcranial approaches for functional manipulation as well as its responsiveness to pharmacological and behavioral/cognitive approaches provides hope and opportunity that better understanding PFC circuits will lead to better outcomes for those burdened with addiction.

References

Abernathy, K., Chandler, L.J., Woodward, J.J., 2010. Alcohol and the prefrontal cortex. Int. Rev. Neurobiol. 91, 289–320.

Adinoff, B., Carmody, T.J., Walker, R., Donovan, D.M., Brigham, G.S., Winhusen, T.M., 2016. Decision-making processes as predictors of relapse and subsequent use in stimulant-dependent patients. Am. J. Drug Alcohol Abuse 42 (1), 88–97. https://doi.org/10.3109/00952990.2015.1106550.

Agabio, R., Pisanu, C., Gessa, G.L., Franconi, F., 2017. Sex differences in alcohol use disorder. Curr. Med. Chem. 24 (24), 2661–2670.

Anastasiades, P.G., Butt, S.J., 2011. Decoding the transcriptional basis for GABAergic interneuron diversity in the mouse neocortex. Eur. J. Neurosci. 34 (10), 1542–1552. https://doi.org/10.1111/j.1460-9568.2011.07904.x.

Anderson, E.M., Gomez, D., Caccamise, A., McPhail, D., Hearing, M., 2019. Chronic unpredictable stress promotes cell-specific plasticity in prefrontal cortex D1 and D2 pyramidal neurons. Neurobiol. Stress 10, 100152. https://doi.org/10.1016/j.ynstr.2019.100152.

Anderson, E.M., Engelhardt, A., Demis, S., Porath, E., Hearing, M.C., 2021. Remifentanil self-administration in mice promotes sex-specific prefrontal cortex dysfunction underlying deficits in cognitive flexibility. Neuropsychopharmacology. https://doi.org/10.1038/s41386-021-01028-z.

Arguello, A.A., Richardson, B.D., Hall, J.L., Wang, R., Hodges, M.A., Mitchell, M.P., Fuchs, R.A., 2017. Role of a lateral orbital frontal cortex-basolateral amygdala circuit in cue-induced cocaine-seeking behavior. Neuropsychopharmacology 42 (3), 727–735. https://doi.org/10.1038/npp.2016.157.

Arnsten, A.F., 2009. Stress signalling pathways that impair prefrontal cortex structure and function. Nat. Rev. Neurosci. 10 (6), 410–422. https://doi.org/10.1038/nrn2648.

Arnsten, A.F., 2015. Stress weakens prefrontal networks: molecular insults to higher cognition. Nat. Neurosci. 18 (10), 1376–1385. https://doi.org/10.1038/nn.4087.

Atallah, B.V., Bruns, W., Carandini, M., Scanziani, M., 2012. Parvalbumin-expressing interneurons linearly transform cortical responses to visual stimuli. Neuron 73 (1), 159–170. https://doi.org/10.1016/j.neuron.2011.12.013.

Atkinson, E.A., Peterson, S.J., Riley, E.N., Davis, H.A., Smith, G.T., 2021. How people experience and respond to their distress predicts problem drinking more than does the amount of distress. Addict. Behav. 120, 106959. https://doi.org/10.1016/j.addbeh.2021.106959.

Augur, I.F., Wyckoff, A.R., Aston-Jones, G., Kalivas, P.W., Peters, J., 2016. Chemogenetic activation of an extinction neural circuit reduces cue-induced reinstatement of cocaine seeking. J. Neurosci. 36 (39), 10174–10180. https://doi.org/10.1523/jneurosci.0773-16.2016.

Avchalumov, Y., Oliver, R.J., Trenet, W., Heyer Osorno, R.E., Sibley, B.D., Purohit, D.C., Contet, C., Roberto, M., Woodward, J.J., Mandyam, C.D., 2021. Chronic ethanol exposure differentially alters neuronal function in the medial prefrontal cortex and dentate gyrus. Neuropharmacology 185, 108438.

Bachtell, R.K., Choi, K.H., Simmons, D.L., Falcon, E., Monteggia, L.M., Neve, R.L., Self, D.W., 2008. Role of GluR1 expression in nucleus accumbens neurons in cocaine sensitization and cocaine-seeking behavior. Eur. J. Neurosci. 27 (9), 2229–2240. https://doi.org/10.1111/j.1460-9568.2008.06199.x.

Badiani, A., Belin, D., Epstein, D., Calu, D., Shaham, Y., 2011. Opiate versus psychostimulant addiction: the differences do matter. Nat. Rev. Neurosci. 12 (11), 685–700. https://doi.org/10.1038/nrn3104.

Baker, D.A., McFarland, K., Lake, R.W., Shen, H., Tang, X.C., Toda, S., Kalivas, P.W., 2003. Neuroadaptations in cystine-glutamate exchange underlie cocaine relapse. Nat. Neurosci. 6 (7), 743–749. https://doi.org/10.1038/nn1069.

Bal, A., Gerena, J., Olekanma, D.I., Arguello, A.A., 2019. Neuronal activation in orbitofrontal cortex subregions: Cfos expression following cue-induced reinstatement of cocaine-seeking behavior. Behav. Neurosci. 133 (5), 489–495.

Bangasser, D.A., Eck, S.R., Telenson, A.M., Salvatore, M., 2018. Sex differences in stress regulation of arousal and cognition. Physiol. Behav. 187, 42–50. https://doi.org/10.1016/j.physbeh.2017.09.025.

Bechara, A., Dolan, S., Denburg, N., Hindes, A., Anderson, S.W., Nathan, P.E., 2001. Decision-making deficits, linked to a dysfunctional ventromedial prefrontal cortex, revealed in alcohol and stimulant abusers. Neuropsychologia 39 (4), 376–389. https://doi.org/10.1016/s0028-3932(00)00136-6.

Becker, J.B., Chartoff, E., 2019. Sex differences in neural mechanisms mediating reward and addiction. Neuropsychopharmacology 44 (1), 166–183. https://doi.org/10.1038/s41386-018-0125-6.

Becker, J.B., Hu, M., 2008. Sex differences in drug abuse. Front. Neuroendocrinol. 29 (1), 36–47. https://doi.org/10.1016/j.yfrne.2007.07.003.

Becker, J.B., Koob, G.F., 2016. Sex differences in animal models: focus on addiction. Pharmacol. Rev. 68 (2), 242–263. https://doi.org/10.1124/pr.115.011163.

Becker, J.B., Perry, A.N., Westenbroek, C., 2012. Sex differences in the neural mechanisms mediating addiction: a new synthesis and hypothesis. Biol. Sex Differ. 3 (1), 14. https://doi.org/10.1186/2042-6410-3-14.

Becker, J.B., McClellan, M., Reed, B.G., 2016. Sociocultural context for sex differences in addiction. Addiction Biol. 21 (5), 1052–1059.

Belleau, E.L., Treadway, M.T., Pizzagalli, D.A., 2019. The impact of stress and major depressive disorder on hippocampal and medial prefrontal cortex morphology. Biol. Psychiatr. 85 (6), 443–453. https://doi.org/10.1016/j.biopsych.2018.09.031.

Ben-Shahar, O., Obara, I., Ary, A.W., Ma, N., Mangiardi, M.A., Medina, R.L., Szumlinski, K.K., 2009. Extended daily access to cocaine results in distinct alterations in Homer 1b/c and NMDA receptor subunit expression within the medial prefrontal cortex. Synapse 63 (7), 598–609. https://doi.org/10.1002/syn.20640.

Ben-Shahar, O.M., Szumlinski, K.K., Lominac, K.D., Cohen, A., Gordon, E., Ploense, K.L., DeMartini, J., Bernstein, N., Rudy, N.M., Nabhan, A.N., Sacramento, A., Pagano, K., Carosso, G.A., Woodward, N., 2012. Extended access to cocaine self-administration results in reduced glutamate function within the medial prefrontal cortex. Addiction Biol. 17 (4), 746–757.

Benneyworth, M.A., Hearing, M.C., Asp, A.J., Madayag, A., Ingebretson, A.E., Schmidt, C.E., Silvis, K.A., Larson, E.B., Ebner, S.R., Thomas, M.J., 2019. Synaptic depotentiation and mGluR5 activity in the nucleus accumbens drive cocaine-primed reinstatement of place preference. J. Neurosci. 39 (24), 4785–4796. https://doi.org/10.1523/JNEUROSCI.3020-17.2019.

Berkley, K.J., 1997. Sex differences in pain. Behav. Brain Sci. 20 (3), 371–380 discussion 435-513.

Bissonette, G.B., Roesch, M.R., 2017. Neurophysiology of rule switching in the corticostriatal circuit. Neuroscience 345, 64–76. https://doi.org/10.1016/j.neuroscience.2016.01.062.

Blacktop, J.M., Seubert, C., Baker, D.A., Ferda, N., Lee, G., Graf, E.N., Mantsch, J.R., 2011. Augmented cocaine seeking in response to stress or CRF delivered into the ventral tegmental area following long-access self-administration is mediated by CRF receptor type 1 but not CRF receptor type 2. J. Neurosci. 31 (31), 11396–11403. https://doi.org/10.1523/jneurosci.1393-11.2011.

Bobadilla, A.C., Dereschewitz, E., Vaccaro, L., Heinsbroek, J.A., Scofield, M.D., Kalivas, P.W., 2020. Cocaine and sucrose rewards recruit different seeking ensembles in the nucleus accumbens core. Mol. Psychiatr. 25 (12), 3150–3163. https://doi.org/10.1038/s41380-020-00888-z.

Bobzean, S.A., Dennis, T.S., Perrotti, L.I., 2014. Acute estradiol treatment affects the expression of cocaine-induced conditioned place preference in ovariectomized female rats. Brain Res. Bull. 103, 49–53.

Bobzean, S.A., DeNobrega, A.K., Perrotti, L.I., 2014b. Sex differences in the neurobiology of drug addiction. Exp. Neurol. 259, 64–74.

Bolla, K., Ernst, M., Kiehl, K., Mouratidis, M., Eldreth, D., Contoreggi, C., London, E., 2004. Prefrontal cortical dysfunction in abstinent cocaine abusers. J. Neuropsychiatry Clin. Neurosci. 16 (4), 456–464. https://doi.org/10.1176/jnp.16.4.456.

Bolloni, C., Panella, R., Pedetti, M., Frascella, A.G., Gambelunghe, C., Piccoli, T., Maniaci, G., Brancato, A., Cannizzaro, C., Diana, M., 2016. Bilateral transcranial magnetic stimulation of the prefrontal cortex reduces cocaine intake: a pilot study. Front. Psychiatr. 7, 133.

Bonson, K.R., Grant, S.J., Contoreggi, C.S., Links, J.M., Metcalfe, J., Weyl, H.L., Kurian, V., Ernst, M., London, E.D., 2002. Neural systems and cue-induced cocaine craving. Neuropsychopharmacology 26 (3), 376–386. https://doi.org/10.1016/s0893-133x(01)00371-2.

Bossert, J.M., Gray, S.M., Lu, L., Shaham, Y., 2006. Activation of group II metabotropic glutamate receptors in the nucleus accumbens shell attenuates context-induced relapse to heroin seeking. Neuropsychopharmacology 31 (10), 2197–2209. https://doi.org/10.1038/sj.npp.1300977.

Bossert, J.M., Poles, G.C., Wihbey, K.A., Koya, E., Shaham, Y., 2007. Differential effects of blockade of dopamine D1-family receptors in nucleus accumbens core or shell on reinstatement of heroin seeking induced by contextual and discrete cues. J. Neurosci. 27 (46), 12655–12663. https://doi.org/10.1523/JNEUROSCI.3926-07.2007.

Bossert, J.M., Wihbey, K.A., Pickens, C.L., Nair, S.G., Shaham, Y., 2009. Role of dopamine D(1)-family receptors in dorsolateral striatum in context-induced reinstatement of heroin seeking in rats. Psychopharmacology (Berl) 206 (1), 51–60. https://doi.org/10.1007/s00213-009-1580-x.

Bossert, J.M., Stern, A.L., Theberge, F.R., Cifani, C., Koya, E., Hope, B.T., Shaham, Y., 2011. Ventral medial prefrontal cortex neuronal ensembles mediate context-induced relapse to heroin. Nat. Neurosci. 14 (4), 420–422.

Bossert, J.M., Stern, A.L., Theberge, F.R., Marchant, N.J., Wang, H.L., Morales, M., Shaham, Y., 2012. Role of projections from ventral medial prefrontal cortex to nucleus accumbens shell in context-induced reinstatement of heroin seeking. J. Neurosci. 32 (14), 4982–4991. https://doi.org/10.1523/jneurosci.0005-12.2012.

Bossert, J.M., Kiyatkin, E.A., Korah, H., Hoots, J.K., Afzal, A., Perekopskiy, D., Thomas, S., Fredriksson, I., Blough, B.E., Negus, S.S., Epstein, D.H., Shaham, Y., 2020. In a rat model of opioid maintenance, the G protein-biased mu opioid receptor agonist TRV130 decreases relapse to Oxycodone seeking and taking and prevents oxycodone-induced brain hypoxia. Biol. Psychiatr. 88 (12), 935–944. https://doi.org/10.1016/j.biopsych.2020.02.014.

Botelho, M.F., Relvas, J.S., Abrantes, M., Cunha, M.J., Marques, T.R., Rovira, E., Fontes Ribeiro, C.A., Macedo, T., 2006. Brain blood flow SPET imaging in heroin abusers. Ann. N. Y. Acad. Sci. 1074, 466–477. https://doi.org/10.1196/annals.1369.047.

Bowden-Jones, H., McPhillips, M., Rogers, R., Hutton, S., Joyce, E., 2005. Risk-taking on tests sensitive to ventromedial prefrontal cortex dysfunction predicts early relapse in alcohol dependency: a pilot study. J. Neuropsychiatry Clin. Neurosci. 17 (3), 417–420. https://doi.org/10.1176/jnp.17.3.417.

Bowers, M.S., McFarland, K., Lake, R.W., Peterson, Y.K., Lapish, C.C., Gregory, M.L., Lanier, S.M., Kalivas, P.W., 2004. Activator of G protein signaling 3: a gatekeeper of cocaine sensitization and drug seeking. Neuron 42 (2), 269–281.

Brady, K.T., Randall, C.L., 1999. Gender differences in substance use disorders. Psychiatr. Clin. 22 (2), 241–252.

Breiter, H.C., Gollub, R.L., Weisskoff, R.M., Kennedy, D.N., Makris, N., Berke, J.D., Hyman, S.E., 1997. Acute effects of cocaine on human brain activity and emotion. Neuron 19 (3), 591–611. https://doi.org/10.1016/s0896-6273(00)80374-8.

Briand, L.A., Flagel, S.B., Garcia-Fuster, M.J., Watson, S.J., Akil, H., Sarter, M., Robinson, T.E., 2008. Persistent alterations in cognitive function and prefrontal dopamine D2 receptors following extended, but not limited, access to self-administered cocaine. Neuropsychopharmacology 33 (12), 2969–2980. https://doi.org/10.1038/npp.2008.18.

Brown, S.P., Hestrin, S., 2009. Intracortical circuits of pyramidal neurons reflect their long-range axonal targets. Nature 457 (7233), 1133–1136.

Brown, R.W., Kolb, B., 2001. Nicotine sensitization increases dendritic length and spine density in the nucleus accumbens and cingulate cortex. Brain Res. 899 (1–2), 94–100.

Calu, D.J., Stalnaker, T.A., Franz, T.M., Singh, T., Shaham, Y., Schoenbaum, G., 2007. Withdrawal from cocaine self-administration produces long-lasting deficits in orbitofrontal-dependent reversal learning in rats. Learn. Mem. 14 (5), 325–328. https://doi.org/10.1101/lm.534807.

Canterberry, M., Peltier, M.R., Brady, K.T., Hanlon, C.A., 2016. Attenuated neural response to emotional cues in cocaine-dependence: a preliminary analysis of gender differences. Am. J. Drug Alcohol Abuse 42 (5), 577–586.

Capriles, N., Rodaros, D., Sorge, R.E., Stewart, J., 2003. A role for the prefrontal cortex in stress- and cocaine-induced reinstatement of cocaine seeking in rats. Psychopharmacology (Berl) 168 (1–2), 66–74.

Chang, J.Y., Janak, P.H., Woodward, D.J., 1998. Comparison of mesocorticolimbic neuronal responses during cocaine and heroin self-administration in freely moving rats. J. Neurosci. 18 (8), 3098–3115. https://doi.org/10.1523/jneurosci.18-08-03098.1998.

Chen, K., Kandel, D., 2002. Relationship between extent of cocaine use and dependence among adolescents and adults in the United States. Drug Alcohol Depend. 68 (1), 65–85.

Chen, B.T., Yau, H.J., Hatch, C., Kusumoto-Yoshida, I., Cho, S.L., Hopf, F.W., Bonci, A., 2013. Rescuing cocaine-induced prefrontal cortex hypoactivity prevents compulsive cocaine seeking. Nature 496 (7445), 359–362. https://doi.org/10.1038/nature12024.

Chen, S., Yang, P., Chen, T., Su, H., Jiang, H., Zhao, M., 2020. Risky decision-making in individuals with substance use disorder: a meta-analysis and meta-regression review. Psychopharmacology (Berl) 237 (7), 1893–1908. https://doi.org/10.1007/s00213-020-05506-y.

Childress, A.R., Mozley, P.D., McElgin, W., Fitzgerald, J., Reivich, M., O'Brien, C.P., 1999. Limbic activation during cue-induced cocaine craving. Am. J. Psychiatr. 156 (1), 11–18. https://doi.org/10.1176/ajp.156.1.11.

Ciccocioppo, R., Sanna, P.P., Weiss, F., 2001. Cocaine-predictive stimulus induces drug-seeking behavior and neural activation in limbic brain regions after multiple months of abstinence: reversal by D(1) antagonists. Proc. Natl. Acad. Sci. U. S. A. 98 (4), 1976–1981.

Cicero, T.J., Aylward, S.C., Meyer, E.R., 2003. Gender differences in the intravenous self-administration of mu opiate agonists. Pharmacol. Biochem. Behav. 74 (3), 541–549.

Cocker, P.J., Rotge, J.Y., Daniel, M.L., Belin-Rauscent, A., Belin, D., 2020. Impaired decision making following escalation of cocaine self-administration predicts vulnerability to relapse in rats. Addiction Biol. 25 (3), e12738. https://doi.org/10.1111/adb.12738.

Conrad, K.L., Tseng, K.Y., Uejima, J.L., Reimers, J.M., Heng, L.J., Shaham, Y., Marinelli, M., Wolf, M.E., 2008. Formation of accumbens GluR2-lacking AMPA receptors mediates incubation of cocaine craving. Nature 454 (7200), 118–121. https://doi.org/10.1038/nature06995.

Cook, S.C., Wellman, C.L., 2004. Chronic stress alters dendritic morphology in rat medial prefrontal cortex. J. Neurobiol. 60 (2), 236–248. https://doi.org/10.1002/neu.20025.

Couey, J.J., Meredith, R.M., Spijker, S., Poorthuis, R.B., Smit, A.B., Brussaard, A.B., Mansvelder, H.D., 2007. Distributed network actions by nicotine increase the threshold for spike-timing-dependent plasticity in prefrontal cortex. Neuron 54 (1), 73–87. https://doi.org/10.1016/j.neuron.2007.03.006.

Crombag, H.S., Gorny, G., Li, Y., Kolb, B., Robinson, T.E., 2005. Opposite effects of amphetamine self-administration experience on dendritic spines in the medial and orbital prefrontal cortex. Cerebr. Cortex 15 (3), 341–348. https://doi.org/10.1093/cercor/bhh136.

Crombag, H.S., Bossert, J.M., Koya, E., Shaham, Y., 2008. Review. Context-induced relapse to drug seeking: a review. Philos. Trans. R. Soc. Lond. B Biol. Sci. 363 (1507), 3233–3243. https://doi.org/10.1098/rstb.2008.0090.

Cruikshank, S.J., Lewis, T.J., Connors, B.W., 2007. Synaptic basis for intense thalamocortical activation of feedforward inhibitory cells in neocortex. Nat. Neurosci. 10 (4), 462–468.

Cruikshank, S.J., Urabe, H., Nurmikko, A.V., Connors, B.W., 2010. Pathway-specific feedforward circuits between thalamus and neocortex revealed by selective optical stimulation of axons. Neuron 65 (2), 230–245.

Cruz, A.M., Spencer, H.F., Kim, T.H., Jhou, T.C., Smith, R.J., 2021. Prelimbic cortical projections to rostromedial tegmental nucleus play a suppressive role in cue-induced reinstatement of cocaine seeking. Neuropsychopharmacology 46 (8), 1399–1406. https://doi.org/10.1038/s41386-020-00909-z.

Daglish, M.R., Weinstein, A., Malizia, A.L., Wilson, S., Melichar, J.K., Britten, S., Brewer, C., Lingford-Hughes, A., Myles, J.S., Grasby, P., Nutt, D.J., 2001. Changes in regional cerebral blood flow elicited by craving memories in abstinent opiate-dependent subjects. Am. J. Psychiatr. 158 (10), 1680–1686.

Dalley, J.W., Laane, K., Pena, Y., Theobald, D.E., Everitt, B.J., Robbins, T.W., 2005. Attentional and motivational deficits in rats withdrawn from intravenous self-administration of cocaine or heroin. Psychopharmacology (Berl) 182 (4), 579–587. https://doi.org/10.1007/s00213-005-0107-3.

Dao-Castellana, M.H., Samson, Y., Legault, F., Martinot, J.L., Aubin, H.J., Crouzel, C., Feldman, L., Barrucand, D., Rancurel, G., Feline, A., Syrota, A., 1998. Frontal dysfunction in neurologically normal chronic alcoholic subjects: metabolic and neuropsychological findings. Psychol. Med. 28 (5), 1039–1048.

Darnall, B.D., Stacey, B.R., 2012. Sex differences in long-term opioid use: cautionary notes for prescribing in women. Arch. Intern. Med. 172 (5), 431–432.

Darnall, B.D., Stacey, B.R., Chou, R., 2012. Medical and psychological risks and consequences of long-term opioid therapy in women. Pain Med. 13 (9), 1181–1211.

Dayas, C.V., Liu, X., Simms, J.A., Weiss, F., 2007. Distinct patterns of neural activation associated with ethanol seeking: effects of naltrexone. Biol. Psychiatr. 61 (8), 979–989.

Dembrow, N.C., Chitwood, R.A., Johnston, D., 2010. Projection-specific neuromodulation of medial prefrontal cortex neurons. J. Neurosci. 30 (50), 16922–16937.

Dembrow, N.C., Zemelman, B.V., Johnston, D., 2015. Temporal dynamics of L5 dendrites in medial prefrontal cortex regulate integration versus coincidence detection of afferent inputs. J. Neurosci. 35 (11), 4501–4514.

DePoy, L.M., Perszyk, R.E., Zimmermann, K.S., Koleske, A.J., Gourley, S.L., 2014. Adolescent cocaine exposure simplifies orbitofrontal cortical dendritic arbors. Front. Pharmacol. 5, 228.

DePoy, L.M., Allen, A.G., Gourley, S.L., 2016. Adolescent cocaine self-administration induces habit behavior in adulthood: sex differences and structural consequences. Transl. Psychiatry 6 (8), e875.

Diamond, A., 2013. Executive functions. Annu. Rev. Psychol. 64, 135–168. https://doi.org/10.1146/annurev-psych-113011-143750.

Diener, C., Kuehner, C., Brusniak, W., Ubl, B., Wessa, M., Flor, H., 2012. A meta-analysis of neurofunctional imaging studies of emotion and cognition in major depression. Neuroimage 61 (3), 677–685. https://doi.org/10.1016/j.neuroimage.2012.04.005.

Dole, V.P., Nyswander, M.E., Kreek, M.J., 1966. Narcotic blockade. Arch. Intern. Med. 118 (4), 304–309. Retrieved from. https://www.ncbi.nlm.nih.gov/pubmed/4162686.

Doncheck, E.M., Liddiard, G.T., Konrath, C.D., Liu, X., Yu, L., Urbanik, L.A., Herbst, M.R., DeBaker, M.C., Raddatz, N., Van Newenhizen, E.C., Mathy, J., Gilmartin, M.R., Liu, Q.S., Hillard, C.J., Mantsch, J.R., 2020. Sex, stress, and prefrontal cortex: influence of biological sex on stress-promoted cocaine seeking. Neuropsychopharmacology 45 (12), 1974–1985. https://doi.org/10.1038/s41386-020-0674-3.

Doncheck, E.M., Anderson, E.M., Konrath, C.D., Liddiard, G.T., DeBaker, M.C., Urbanik, L.A., Hearing, M.C., Mantsch, J.R., 2021. Estradiol regulation of the prelimbic cortex and the reinstatement of cocaine seeking in female rats. J. Neurosci. 41 (24), 5303–5314. https://doi.org/10.1523/JNEUROSCI.3086-20.2021.

Dong, Y., White, F.J., 2003. Dopamine D1-class receptors selectively modulate a slowly inactivating potassium current in rat medial prefrontal cortex pyramidal neurons. J. Neurosci. 23 (7), 2686–2695.

Dong, Y., Nasif, F.J., Tsui, J.J., Ju, W.Y., Cooper, D.C., Hu, X.T., Malenka, R.C., White, F.J., 2005. Cocaine-induced plasticity of intrinsic membrane properties in prefrontal cortex pyramidal neurons: adaptations in potassium currents. J. Neurosci. 25 (4), 936–940. https://doi.org/10.1523/jneurosci.4715-04.2005.

Drysdale, A.T., Grosenick, L., Downar, J., Dunlop, K., Mansouri, F., Meng, Y., Liston, C., 2017. Resting-state connectivity biomarkers define neurophysiological subtypes of depression. Nat. Med. 23 (1), 28–38. https://doi.org/10.1038/nm.4246.

Du, C., Volkow, N.D., You, J., Park, K., Allen, C.P., Koob, G.F., Pan, Y., 2020. Cocaine-induced ischemia in prefrontal cortex is associated with escalation of cocaine intake in rodents. Mol. Psychiatr. 25 (8), 1759–1776. https://doi.org/10.1038/s41380-018-0261-8.

Ersche, K.D., Turton, A.J., Chamberlain, S.R., Müller, U., Bullmore, E.T., Robbins, T.W., 2012. Cognitive dysfunction and anxious-impulsive personality traits are endophenotypes for drug dependence. Am. J. Psychiatr. 169 (9), 926–936. https://doi.org/10.1176/appi.ajp.2012.11091421.

Ersche, K.D., Lim, T.V., Murley, A.G., Rua, C., Vaghi, M.M., White, T.L., Williams, G.B., Robbins, T.W., 2021. Reduced glutamate turnover in the putamen is linked with automatic habits in human cocaine addiction. Biol. Psychiatr. 89 (10), 970–979.

Etkin, A., Gyurak, A., O'Hara, R., 2013. A neurobiological approach to the cognitive deficits of psychiatric disorders. Dialogues Clin. Neurosci. 15 (4), 419–429. Retrieved from. https://www.ncbi.nlm.nih.gov/pubmed/24459409.

Everitt, B.J., Robbins, T.W., 2005. Neural systems of reinforcement for drug addiction: from actions to habits to compulsion. Nat. Neurosci. 8 (11), 1481–1489. https://doi.org/10.1038/nn1579.

Everitt, B.J., Robbins, T.W., 2016. Drug addiction: updating actions to habits to compulsions ten years on. Annu. Rev. Psychol. 67, 23–50. https://doi.org/10.1146/annurev-psych-122414-033457.

Fanous, S., Goldart, E.M., Theberge, F.R., Bossert, J.M., Shaham, Y., Hope, B.T., 2012. Role of orbitofrontal cortex neuronal ensembles in the expression of incubation of heroin craving. J. Neurosci. 32 (34), 11600–11609. https://doi.org/10.1523/jneurosci.1914-12.2012.

Ferguson, B.R., Gao, W.J., 2018. PV interneurons: critical regulators of E/I balance for prefrontal cortex-dependent behavior and psychiatric disorders. Front. Neural Circ. 12, 37. https://doi.org/10.3389/fncir.2018.00037.

Fernandez-Montalvo, J., Lopez-Goni, J.J., Azanza, P., Arteaga, A., Cacho, R., 2017. Gender differences in treatment progress of drug-addicted patients. Women Health 57 (3), 358–376.

Ferrario, C.R., Gorny, G., Crombag, H.S., Li, Y., Kolb, B., Robinson, T.E., 2005. Neural and behavioral plasticity associated with the transition from controlled to escalated cocaine use. Biol. Psychiatr. 58 (9), 751–759. https://doi.org/10.1016/j.biopsych.2005.04.046.

Field, M., Cox, W.M., 2008. Attentional bias in addictive behaviors: a review of its development, causes, and consequences. Drug Alcohol Depend. 97 (1–2), 1–20. https://doi.org/10.1016/j.drugalcdep.2008.03.030.

Fillingim, R.B., Gear, R.W., 2004. Sex differences in opioid analgesia: clinical and experimental findings. Eur. J. Pain 8 (5), 413–425.

Fillingim, R.B., King, C.D., Ribeiro-Dasilva, M.C., Rahim-Williams, B., Riley 3rd, J.L., 2009. Sex, gender, and pain: a review of recent clinical and experimental findings. J. Pain 10 (5), 447–485.

Floresco, S.B., St Onge, J.R., Ghods-Sharifi, S., Winstanley, C.A., 2008. Cortico-limbic-striatal circuits subserving different forms of cost-benefit decision making. Cognit. Affect Behav. Neurosci. 8 (4), 375–389. https://doi.org/10.3758/cabn.8.4.375.

Franken, I.H., van Strien, J.W., Franzek, E.J., van de Wetering, B.J., 2007. Error-processing deficits in patients with cocaine dependence. Biol. Psychol. 75 (1), 45–51. https://doi.org/10.1016/j.biopsycho.2006.11.003.

Franklin, T.R., Acton, P.D., Maldjian, J.A., Gray, J.D., Croft, J.R., Dackis, C.A., O'Brien, C.P., Childress, A.R., 2002. Decreased gray matter concentration in the insular, orbitofrontal, cingulate, and temporal cortices of cocaine patients. Biol. Psychiatr. 51 (2), 134–142.

Fu, L.P., Bi, G.H., Zou, Z.T., Wang, Y., Ye, E.M., Ma, L., Ming, F., Yang, Z., 2008. Impaired response inhibition function in abstinent heroin dependents: an fMRI study. Neurosci. Lett. 438 (3), 322–326.

Fuchs, R.A., Evans, K.A., Parker, M.P., See, R.E., 2004. Differential involvement of orbitofrontal cortex subregions in conditioned cue-induced and cocaine-primed reinstatement of cocaine seeking in rats. J. Neurosci. 24 (29), 6600–6610. https://doi.org/10.1523/jneurosci.1924-04.2004.

Fuchs, R.A., Branham, R.K., See, R.E., 2006. Different neural substrates mediate cocaine seeking after abstinence versus extinction training: a critical role for the dorsolateral caudate-putamen. J. Neurosci. 26 (13), 3584–3588. https://doi.org/10.1523/JNEUROSCI.5146-05.2006.

Fuster, J.M., 2015. The Prefrontal Cortex, fifth ed. Elsevier.

Gallop, R.J., Crits-Christoph, P., Ten Have, T.R., Barber, J.P., Frank, A., Griffin, M.L., Thase, M.E., 2007. Differential transitions between cocaine use and abstinence for men and women. J. Consult. Clin. Psychol. 75 (1), 95–103.

Garavan, H., Pankiewicz, J., Bloom, A., Cho, J.K., Sperry, L., Ross, T.J., Salmeron, B.J., Risinger, R., Kelley, D., Stein, E.A., 2000. Cue-induced cocaine craving: neuroanatomical specificity for drug users and drug stimuli. Am. J. Psychiatr. 157 (11), 1789–1798. https://doi.org/10.1176/appi.ajp.157.11.1789.

Garland, E.L., Howard, M.O., 2014. Opioid attentional bias and cue-elicited craving predict future risk of prescription opioid misuse among chronic pain patients. Drug Alcohol Depend. 144, 283–287. https://doi.org/10.1016/j.drugalcdep.2014.09.014.

Garland, E.L., Froeliger, B.E., Passik, S.D., Howard, M.O., 2013. Attentional bias for prescription opioid cues among opioid dependent chronic pain patients. J. Behav. Med. 36 (6), 611–620. https://doi.org/10.1007/s10865-012-9455-8.

Gee, S., Ellwood, I., Patel, T., Luongo, F., Deisseroth, K., Sohal, V.S., 2012. Synaptic activity unmasks dopamine D2 receptor modulation of a specific class of layer V pyramidal neurons in prefrontal cortex. J. Neurosci. 32 (14), 4959–4971.

George, M.S., Anton, R.F., Bloomer, C., Teneback, C., Drobes, D.J., Lorberbaum, J.P., Nahas, Z., Vincent, D.J., 2001. Activation of prefrontal cortex and anterior thalamus in alcoholic subjects on exposure to alcohol-specific cues. Arch. Gen. Psychiatr. 58 (4), 345–352.

George, O., Mandyam, C.D., Wee, S., Koob, G.F., 2008. Extended access to cocaine self-administration produces long-lasting prefrontal cortex-dependent working memory impairments. Neuropsychopharmacology 33 (10), 2474–2482. https://doi.org/10.1038/sj.npp.1301626.

Giacchino, J.L., Henriksen, S.J., 1998. Opioid effects on activation of neurons in the medial prefrontal cortex. Prog. Neuro-Psychopharmacol. Biol. Psychiatry 22 (7), 1157–1178.

Giannotti, G., Barry, S.M., Siemsen, B.M., Peters, J., McGinty, J.F., 2018. Divergent prelimbic cortical pathways interact with BDNF to regulate cocaine-seeking. J. Neurosci. 38 (42), 8956–8966. https://doi.org/10.1523/JNEUROSCI.1332-18.2018.

Gipson, C.D., Kupchik, Y.M., Shen, H., Reissner, K.J., Thomas, C.A., Kalivas, P.W., 2013. Relapse induced by cues predicting cocaine depends on rapid, transient synaptic potentiation. Neuron 77 (5), 867–872. https://doi.org/10.1016/j.neuron.2013.01.005.

Goeders, N.E., Smith, J.E., 1983. Cortical dopaminergic involvement in cocaine reinforcement. Science 221 (4612), 773–775. https://doi.org/10.1126/science.6879176.

Goldman-Rakic, P.S., Leranth, C., Williams, S.M., Mons, N., Geffard, M., 1989. Dopamine synaptic complex with pyramidal neurons in primate cerebral cortex. Proc. Natl. Acad. Sci. U. S. A. 86 (22), 9015–9019.

Goldstein, R.Z., Volkow, N.D., 2002. Drug addiction and its underlying neurobiological basis: neuroimaging evidence for the involvement of the frontal cortex. Am. J. Psychiatr. 159 (10), 1642–1652. https://doi.org/10.1176/appi.ajp.159.10.1642.

Goldstein, R.Z., Volkow, N.D., 2011. Dysfunction of the prefrontal cortex in addiction: neuroimaging findings and clinical implications. Nat. Rev. Neurosci. 12 (11), 652–669. https://doi.org/10.1038/nrn3119.

Goldstein, R.Z., Volkow, N.D., Wang, G.J., Fowler, J.S., Rajaram, S., 2001. Addiction changes orbitofrontal gyrus function: involvement in response inhibition. Neuroreport 12 (11), 2595–2599. https://doi.org/10.1097/00001756-200108080-00060.

Goldstein, R.Z., Alia-Klein, N., Leskovjan, A.C., Fowler, J.S., Wang, G.J., Gur, R.C., Volkow, N.D., 2005. Anger and depression in cocaine addiction: association with the orbitofrontal cortex. Psychiatr. Res. 138 (1), 13–22. https://doi.org/10.1016/j.pscychresns.2004.10.002.

Goldstein, R.Z., Tomasi, D., Rajaram, S., Cottone, L.A., Zhang, L., Maloney, T., Telang, F., Alia-Klein, N., Volkow, N.D., 2007. Role of the anterior cingulate and medial orbitofrontal cortex in processing drug cues in cocaine addiction. Neuroscience 144 (4), 1153–1159.

Goldwater, D.S., Pavlides, C., Hunter, R.G., Bloss, E.B., Hof, P.R., McEwen, B.S., Morrison, J.H., 2009. Structural and functional alterations to rat medial prefrontal cortex following chronic restraint stress and recovery. Neuroscience 164 (2), 798–808. https://doi.org/10.1016/j.neuroscience.2009.08.053.

Goode, T.D., Maren, S., 2019. Common neurocircuitry mediating drug and fear relapse in preclinical models. Psychopharmacology (Berl) 236 (1), 415–437. https://doi.org/10.1007/s00213-018-5024-3.

Gourley, S.L., Taylor, J.R., 2016. Going and stopping: dichotomies in behavioral control by the prefrontal cortex. Nat. Neurosci. 19 (6), 656–664. https://doi.org/10.1038/nn.4275.

Gowin, J.L., May, A.C., Wittmann, M., Tapert, S.F., Paulus, M.P., 2017. Doubling down: increased risk-taking behavior following a loss by individuals with cocaine use disorder is associated with striatal and anterior cingulate dysfunction. Biol. Psychiatry Cogn. Neurosci. Neuroimaging 2 (1), 94–103. https://doi.org/10.1016/j.bpsc.2016.02.002.

Gowin, J.L., Sloan, M.E., Ramchandani, V.A., Paulus, M.P., Lane, S.D., 2018. Differences in decision-making as a function of drug of choice. Pharmacol. Biochem. Behav. 164, 118–124. https://doi.org/10.1016/j.pbb.2017.09.007.

Graf, E.N., Hoks, M.A., Baumgardner, J., Sierra, J., Vranjkovic, O., Bohr, C., Baker, D.A., Mantsch, J.R., 2011. Adrenal activity during repeated long-access cocaine self-administration is required for later CRF-Induced and CRF-dependent stressor-induced reinstatement in rats. Neuropsychopharmacology 36 (7), 1444–1454.

Grant, S., London, E.D., Newlin, D.B., Villemagne, V.L., Liu, X., Contoreggi, C., Phillips, R.L., Kimes, A.S., Margolin, A., 1996. Activation of memory circuits during cue-elicited cocaine craving. Proc. Natl. Acad. Sci. U. S. A. 93 (21), 12040–12045.

Guillem, K., Ahmed, S.H., 2018. Preference for cocaine is represented in the orbitofrontal cortex by an increased proportion of cocaine use-coding neurons. Cerebr. Cortex 28 (3), 819–832. https://doi.org/10.1093/cercor/bhw398.

Gureje, O., Von Korff, M., Simon, G.E., Gater, R., 1998. Persistent pain and well-being: a world health organization study in primary care. JAMA 280 (2), 147–151.

Hanlon, C.A., Dowdle, L.T., Moss, H., Canterberry, M., George, M.S., 2016. Mobilization of medial and lateral frontal-striatal circuits in cocaine users and controls: an interleaved TMS/BOLD functional connectivity study. Neuropsychopharmacology 41 (13), 3032–3041.

Hanlon, C.A., Shannon, E.E., Porrino, L.J., 2019. Brain activity associated with social exclusion overlaps with drug-related frontal-striatal circuitry in cocaine users: a pilot study. Neurobiol. Stress 10, 100137.

Harris, G.C., Aston-Jones, G., 2003. Altered motivation and learning following opiate withdrawal: evidence for prolonged dysregulation of reward processing. Neuropsychopharmacology 28 (5), 865–871. https://doi.org/10.1038/sj.npp.1300122.

Hattox, A.M., Nelson, S.B., 2007. Layer V neurons in mouse cortex projecting to different targets have distinct physiological properties. J. Neurophysiol. 98 (6), 3330–3340.

Hearing, M., 2019. Prefrontal-accumbens opioid plasticity: implications for relapse and dependence. Pharmacol. Res. 139, 158–165. https://doi.org/10.1016/j.phrs.2018.11.012.

Hearing, M.C., Miller, S.W., See, R.E., McGinty, J.F., 2008. Relapse to cocaine seeking increases activity-regulated gene expression differentially in the prefrontal cortex of abstinent rats. Psychopharmacology (Berl) 198 (1), 77–91. https://doi.org/10.1007/s00213-008-1090-2.

Hearing, M.C., Zink, A.N., Wickman, K., 2012. Cocaine-induced adaptations in metabotropic inhibitory signaling in the mesocorticolimbic system. Rev. Neurosci. 23 (4), 325–351. https://doi.org/10.1515/revneuro-2012-0045.

Hearing, M., Kotecki, L., Marron Fernandez de Velasco, E., Fajardo-Serrano, A., Chung, H.J., Lujan, R., Wickman, K., 2013. Repeated cocaine weakens GABA(B)-Girk signaling in layer 5/6 pyramidal neurons in the prelimbic cortex. Neuron 80 (1), 159–170. https://doi.org/10.1016/j.neuron.2013.07.019.

Hearing, M.C., Jedynak, J., Ebner, S.R., Ingebretson, A., Asp, A.J., Fischer, R.A., Schmidt, C., Larson, E.B., Thomas, M.J., 2016. Reversal of morphine-induced cell-type-specific synaptic plasticity in the nucleus accumbens shell blocks reinstatement. Proc. Natl. Acad. Sci. U. S. A. 113 (3), 757–762.

Hearing, M., Graziane, N., Dong, Y., Thomas, M.J., 2018. Opioid and psychostimulant plasticity: targeting overlap in nucleus accumbens glutamate signaling. Trends Pharmacol. Sci. 39 (3), 276–294. https://doi.org/10.1016/j.tips.2017.12.004.

Hernandez, J.S., Binette, A.N., Rahman, T., Tarantino, J.D., Moorman, D.E., 2020. Chemogenetic inactivation of orbitofrontal cortex decreases cue-induced reinstatement of ethanol and sucrose seeking in male and female wistar rats. Alcohol Clin. Exp. Res. 44 (9), 1769–1782. https://doi.org/10.1111/acer.14407.

Hester, R., Simões-Franklin, C., Garavan, H., 2007. Post-error behavior in active cocaine users: poor awareness of errors in the presence of intact performance adjustments. Neuropsychopharmacology 32 (9), 1974–1984. https://doi.org/10.1038/sj.npp.1301326.

Hobkirk, A.L., Bell, R.P., Utevsky, A.V., Huettel, S., Meade, C.S., 2019. Reward and executive control network resting-state functional connectivity is associated with impulsivity during reward-based decision making for cocaine users. Drug Alcohol Depend. 194, 32–39. https://doi.org/10.1016/j.drugalcdep.2018.09.013.

Hooks, B.M., Mao, T., Gutnisky, D.A., Yamawaki, N., Svoboda, K., Shepherd, G.M., 2013. Organization of cortical and thalamic input to pyramidal neurons in mouse motor cortex. J. Neurosci. 33 (2), 748–760.

Hu, X.T., 2007. Cocaine withdrawal and neuro-adaptations in ion channel function. Mol. Neurobiol. 35 (1), 95–112.

Hu, H., Gan, J., Jonas, P., 2014. Interneurons. Fast-spiking, parvalbumin(+) GABAergic interneurons: from cellular design to microcircuit function. Science 345 (6196), 1255263. https://doi.org/10.1126/science.1255263.

Huang, C.C., Lin, H.J., Hsu, K.S., 2007a. Repeated cocaine administration promotes long-term potentiation induction in rat medial prefrontal cortex. Cerebr. Cortex 17 (8), 1877–1888. https://doi.org/10.1093/cercor/bhl096.

Huang, C.C., Yang, P.C., Lin, H.J., Hsu, K.S., 2007. Repeated cocaine administration impairs group II metabotropic glutamate receptor-mediated long-term depression in rat medial prefrontal cortex. J. Neurosci. 27 (11), 2958–2968. https://doi.org/10.1523/jneurosci.4247-06.2007.

Huhn, A.S., Brooner, R.K., Sweeney, M.M., Yip, S.W., Ayaz, H., Dunn, K.E., 2019. Increased neural activity in the right dorsolateral prefrontal cortex during a risky decision-making task is associated with cocaine use in methadone-maintained patients. Drug Alcohol Depend. 205, 107650. https://doi.org/10.1016/j.drugalcdep.2019.107650.

Hyman, S.E., Malenka, R.C., Nestler, E.J., 2006. Neural mechanisms of addiction: the role of reward-related learning and memory. Annu. Rev. Neurosci. 29, 565–598. https://doi.org/10.1146/annurev.neuro.29.051605.113009.

Ignjatova, L., Raleva, M., 2009. Gender difference in the treatment outcome of patients served in the mixed-gender program. Bratisl. Lek. Listy 110 (5), 285–289.

Irizar, P., Albein-Urios, N., Martínez-González, J.M., Verdejo-Garcia, A., Lorenzetti, V., 2020. Unpacking common and distinct neuroanatomical alterations in cocaine dependent versus pathological gambling. Eur. Neuropsychopharmacol 33, 81–88. https://doi.org/10.1016/j.euroneuro.2020.01.019.

Isaacson, J.S., Scanziani, M., 2011. How inhibition shapes cortical activity. Neuron 72 (2), 231–243. https://doi.org/10.1016/j.neuron.2011.09.027.

James, A.S., Chen, J.Y., Cepeda, C., Mittal, N., Jentsch, J.D., Levine, M.S., Evans, C.J., Walwyn, W., 2013. Opioid self-administration results in cell-type specific adaptations of striatal medium spiny neurons. Behav. Brain Res. 256, 279–283.

James, M.H., McGlinchey, E.M., Vattikonda, A., Mahler, S.V., Aston-Jones, G., 2018. Cued reinstatement of cocaine but not sucrose seeking is dependent on dopamine signaling in prelimbic cortex and is associated with recruitment of prelimbic neurons that project to contralateral nucleus accumbens core. Int. J. Neuropsychopharmacol. 21 (1), 89–94. https://doi.org/10.1093/ijnp/pyx107.

Jayaram, P., Steketee, J.D., 2005. Effects of cocaine-induced behavioural sensitization on GABA transmission within rat medial prefrontal cortex. Eur. J. Neurosci. 21 (7), 2035–2039. https://doi.org/10.1111/j.1460-9568.2005.04000.x.

Jayaram, P., Steketee, J.D., 2006. Cocaine-induced increases in medial prefrontal cortical GABA transmission involves glutamatergic receptors. Eur. J. Pharmacol. 531 (1–3), 74–79. https://doi.org/10.1016/j.ejphar.2005.11.056.

Jentsch, J.D., Pennington, Z.T., 2014. Reward, interrupted: inhibitory control and its relevance to addictions. Neuropharmacology 76 Pt B, 479–486. https://doi.org/10.1016/j.neuropharm.2013.05.022.

Jentsch, J.D., Taylor, J.R., 1999. Impulsivity resulting from frontostriatal dysfunction in drug abuse: implications for the control of behavior by reward-related stimuli. Psychopharmacology (Berl) 146 (4), 373–390.

Jiang, C., Wang, X., Le, Q., Liu, P., Liu, C., Wang, Z., He, G., Zheng, P., Wang, F., Ma, L., 2021. Morphine coordinates SST and PV interneurons in the prelimbic cortex to disinhibit pyramidal neurons and enhance reward. Mol. Psychiatr. 26 (4), 1178–1193.

Kalivas, P.W., 2009. The glutamate homeostasis hypothesis of addiction. Nat. Rev. Neurosci. 10 (8), 561–572. https://doi.org/10.1038/nrn2515.

Kalivas, P.W., O'Brien, C., 2008. Drug addiction as a pathology of staged neuroplasticity. Neuropsychopharmacology 33 (1), 166–180. https://doi.org/10.1038/sj.npp.1301564.

Kalivas, P.W., Volkow, N.D., 2005. The neural basis of addiction: a pathology of motivation and choice. Am. J. Psychiatr. 162 (8), 1403–1413. https://doi.org/10.1176/appi.ajp.162.8.1403.

Kane, L., Venniro, M., Quintana-Feliciano, R., Madangopal, R., Rubio, F.J., Bossert, J.M., Warren, B.L., 2021. Fos-expressing neuronal ensemble in rat ventromedial prefrontal cortex encodes cocaine seeking but not food seeking in rats. Addiction Biol. 26 (3), e12943. https://doi.org/10.1111/adb.12943.

Kasanetz, F., Lafourcade, M., Deroche-Gamonet, V., Revest, J.M., Berson, N., Balado, E., Manzoni, O.J., 2013. Prefrontal synaptic markers of cocaine addiction-like behavior in rats. Mol. Psychiatr. 18 (6), 729–737. https://doi.org/10.1038/mp.2012.59.

Kaufman, J.N., Ross, T.J., Stein, E.A., Garavan, H., 2003. Cingulate hypoactivity in cocaine users during a GO-NOGO task as revealed by event-related functional magnetic resonance imaging. J. Neurosci. 23 (21), 7839–7843. https://doi.org/10.1523/jneurosci.23-21-07839.2003.

Kawaguchi, Y., 1993. Groupings of nonpyramidal and pyramidal cells with specific physiological and morphological characteristics in rat frontal cortex. J. Neurophysiol. 69 (2), 416–431.

Kawaguchi, Y., Kubota, Y., 1993. Correlation of physiological subgroupings of nonpyramidal cells with parvalbumin- and calbindinD28k-immunoreactive neurons in layer V of rat frontal cortex. J. Neurophysiol. 70 (1), 387–396.

Kawaguchi, Y., Kubota, Y., 1997. GABAergic cell subtypes and their synaptic connections in rat frontal cortex. Cerebr. Cortex 7 (6), 476–486. Retrieved from. https://www.ncbi.nlm.nih.gov/pubmed/9276173.

Kennedy, A.P., Epstein, D.H., Phillips, K.A., Preston, K.L., 2013. Sex differences in cocaine/heroin users: drug-use triggers and craving in daily life. Drug Alcohol Depend. 132 (1–2), 29–37. https://doi.org/10.1016/j.drugalcdep.2012.12.025.

Kennedy, A.P., Gross, R.E., Ely, T., Drexler, K.P., Kilts, C.D., 2014. Clinical correlates of attentional bias to drug cues associated with cocaine dependence. Am. J. Addict. 23 (5), 478–484. https://doi.org/10.1111/j.1521-0391.2014.12134.x.

Kerstetter, K.A., Wunsch, A.M., Nakata, K.G., Donckels, E., Neumaier, J.F., Ferguson, S.M., 2016. Corticostriatal afferents modulate responsiveness to psychostimulant drugs and drug-associated stimuli. Neuropsychopharmacology 41 (4), 1128–1137. https://doi.org/10.1038/npp.2015.253.

Kest, B., Sarton, E., Dahan, A., 2000. Gender differences in opioid-mediated analgesia: animal and human studies. Anesthesiology 93 (2), 539–547.

Kilts, C.D., Gross, R.E., Ely, T.D., Drexler, K.P., 2004. The neural correlates of cue-induced craving in cocaine-dependent women. Am. J. Psychiatr. 161 (2), 233–241.

Kim, J., Park, B.H., Lee, J.H., Park, S.K., Kim, J.H., 2011. Cell type-specific alterations in the nucleus accumbens by repeated exposures to cocaine. Biol. Psychiatr. 69 (11), 1026–1034. https://doi.org/10.1016/j.cell.2015.11.038.

Kim, D., Jeong, H., Lee, J., Ghim, J.W., Her, E.S., Lee, S.H., Jung, M.W., 2016. Distinct roles of parvalbumin- and somatostatin-expressing interneurons in working memory. Neuron 92 (4), 902–915. https://doi.org/10.1016/j.neuron.2016.09.023.

Kim, H., Ahrlund-Richter, S., Wang, X., Deisseroth, K., Carlen, M., 2016b. Prefrontal parvalbumin neurons in control of attention. Cell 164 (1–2), 208–218. https://doi.org/10.1016/j.cell.2015.11.038.

Klenowski, P.M., Fogarty, M.J., Shariff, M., Belmer, A., Bellingham, M.C., Bartlett, S.E., 2016. Increased synaptic excitation and abnormal dendritic structure of prefrontal cortex layer V pyramidal neurons following prolonged binge-like consumption of ethanol. eNeuro 3 (6). https://doi.org/10.1523/eneuro.0248-16.2016.

Koffarnus, M.N., Johnson, M.W., Thompson-Lake, D.G., Wesley, M.J., Lohrenz, T., Montague, P.R., Bickel, W.K., 2016. Cocaine-dependent adults and recreational cocaine users are more likely than controls to choose immediate unsafe sex over delayed safer sex. Exp. Clin. Psychopharmacol 24 (4), 297–304. https://doi.org/10.1037/pha0000080.

Koob, G.F., Le Moal, M., 1997. Drug abuse: hedonic homeostatic dysregulation. Science 278 (5335), 52–58. https://doi.org/10.1126/science.278.5335.52.

Kosten, T.A., Gawin, F.H., Kosten, T.R., Rounsaville, B.J., 1993. Gender differences in cocaine use and treatment response. J. Subst. Abuse Treat. 10 (1), 63–66.

Kourrich, S., Rothwell, P.E., Klug, J.R., Thomas, M.J., 2007. Cocaine experience controls bidirectional synaptic plasticity in the nucleus accumbens. J. Neurosci. 27 (30), 7921–7928. https://doi.org/10.1523/jneurosci.1859-07.2007.

Koya, E., Spijker, S., Voorn, P., Binnekade, R., Schmidt, E.D., Schoffelmeer, A.N., De Vries, T.J., Smit, A.B., 2006. Enhanced cortical and accumbal molecular reactivity associated with conditioned heroin, but not sucrose-seeking behaviour. J. Neurochem. 98 (3), 905–915. https://doi.org/10.1111/j.1471-4159.2006.03917.x.

Kroener, S., Lavin, A., 2010. Altered dopamine modulation of inhibition in the prefrontal cortex of cocaine-sensitized rats. Neuropsychopharmacology 35 (11), 2292–2304. https://doi.org/10.1038/npp.2010.107.

Kroener, S., Mulholland, P.J., New, N.N., Gass, J.T., Becker, H.C., Chandler, L.J., 2012. Chronic alcohol exposure alters behavioral and synaptic plasticity of the rodent prefrontal cortex. PLoS One 7 (5), e37541. https://doi.org/10.1371/journal.pone.0037541.

Kufahl, P.R., Zavala, A.R., Singh, A., Thiel, K.J., Dickey, E.D., Joyce, J.N., Neisewander, J.L., 2009. c-Fos expression associated with reinstatement of cocaine-seeking behavior by response-contingent conditioned cues. Synapse 63 (10), 823–835.

Kvitsiani, D., Ranade, S., Hangya, B., Taniguchi, H., Huang, J.Z., Kepecs, A., 2013. Distinct behavioural and network correlates of two interneuron types in prefrontal cortex. Nature 498 (7454), 363–366. https://doi.org/10.1038/nature12176.

LaLumiere, R.T., Kalivas, P.W., 2008. Glutamate release in the nucleus accumbens core is necessary for heroin seeking. J. Neurosci. 28 (12), 3170–3177. https://doi.org/10.1523/JNEUROSCI.5129-07.2008.

Lambe, E.K., Picciotto, M.R., Aghajanian, G.K., 2003. Nicotine induces glutamate release from thalamocortical terminals in prefrontal cortex. Neuropsychopharmacology 28 (2), 216–225. https://doi.org/10.1038/sj.npp.1300032.

Lane, S.D., Moeller, F.G., Steinberg, J.L., Buzby, M., Kosten, T.R., 2007. Performance of cocaine dependent individuals and controls on a response inhibition task with varying levels of difficulty. Am. J. Drug Alcohol Abuse 33 (5), 717–726. https://doi.org/10.1080/00952990701522724.

Langleben, D.D., Ruparel, K., Elman, I., Busch-Winokur, S., Pratiwadi, R., Loughead, J., O'Brien, C.P., Childress, A.R., 2008. Acute effect of methadone maintenance dose on brain FMRI response to heroin-related cues. Am. J. Psychiatr. 165 (3), 390–394. https://doi.org/10.1176/appi.ajp.2007.07010070.

Laque, A., De Ness, G.,L., Wagner, G.E., Nedelescu, H., Carroll, A., Watry, D., Suto, N., 2019. Anti-relapse neurons in the infralimbic cortex of rats drive relapse-suppression by drug omission cues. Nat. Commun. 10 (1), 3934. https://doi.org/10.1038/s41467-019-11799-1.

Lasseter, H.C., Xie, X., Arguello, A.A., Wells, A.M., Hodges, M.A., Fuchs, R.A., 2014. Contribution of a mesocorticolimbic subcircuit to drug context-induced reinstatement of cocaine-seeking behavior in rats. Neuropsychopharmacology 39 (3), 660–669. https://doi.org/10.1038/npp.2013.249.

Lee, A.T., Gee, S.M., Vogt, D., Patel, T., Rubenstein, J.L., Sohal, V.S., 2014. Pyramidal neurons in prefrontal cortex receive subtype-specific forms of excitation and inhibition. Neuron 81 (1), 61–68.

Leriche, M., Mendez, M., Zimmer, L., Berod, A., 2008. Acute ethanol induces Fos in GABAergic and non-GABAergic forebrain neurons: a double-labeling study in the medial prefrontal cortex and extended amygdala. Neuroscience 153 (1), 259–267.

Lewis, D.A., 2012. Cortical circuit dysfunction and cognitive deficits in schizophrenia–implications for preemptive interventions. Eur. J. Neurosci. 35 (12), 1871–1878. https://doi.org/10.1111/j.1460-9568.2012.08156.x.

Lewis, D.A., Curley, A.A., Glausier, J.R., Volk, D.W., 2012. Cortical parvalbumin interneurons and cognitive dysfunction in schizophrenia. Trends Neurosci. 35 (1), 57–67. https://doi.org/10.1016/j.tins.2011.10.004.

Leyrer-Jackson, J.M., Hood, L.E., Olive, M.F., 2021. Drugs of abuse differentially alter the neuronal excitability of prefrontal layer V pyramidal cell subtypes. Front. Cell. Neurosci. 15, 703655.

Li, C.S., Sinha, R., 2008. Inhibitory control and emotional stress regulation: neuroimaging evidence for frontal-limbic dysfunction in psycho-stimulant addiction. Neurosci. Biobehav. Rev. 32 (3), 581–597. https://doi.org/10.1016/j.neubiorev.2007.10.003.

Li, Q., Li, W., Wang, H., Wang, Y., Zhang, Y., Zhu, J., Liu, Y., 2015. Predicting subsequent relapse by drug-related cue-induced brain activation in heroin addiction: an event-related functional magnetic resonance imaging study. Addiction Biol. 20 (5), 968–978. https://doi.org/10.1111/adb.12182.

Lisman, J., 2012. Excitation, inhibition, local oscillations, or large-scale loops: what causes the symptoms of schizophrenia? Curr. Opin. Neurobiol. 22 (3), 537–544. https://doi.org/10.1016/j.conb.2011.10.018.

Liston, C., Miller, M.M., Goldwater, D.S., Radley, J.J., Rocher, A.B., Hof, P.R., McEwen, B.S., 2006. Stress-induced alterations in prefrontal cortical dendritic morphology predict selective impairments in perceptual attentional set-shifting. J. Neurosci. 26 (30), 7870–7874. https://doi.org/10.1523/jneurosci.1184-06.2006.

Liston, C., McEwen, B.S., Casey, B.J., 2009. Psychosocial stress reversibly disrupts prefrontal processing and attentional control. Proc. Natl. Acad. Sci. U. S. A. 106 (3), 912–917. https://doi.org/10.1073/pnas.0807041106.

Little, J.P., Carter, A.G., 2013. Synaptic mechanisms underlying strong reciprocal connectivity between the medial prefrontal cortex and basolateral amygdala. J. Neurosci. 33 (39), 15333–15342.

Liu, C., Fang, X., Wu, Q., Jin, G., Zhen, X., 2015. Prefrontal cortex gates acute morphine action on dopamine neurons in the ventral tegmental area. Neuropharmacology 95, 299–308. https://doi.org/10.1016/j.neuropharm.2015.03.037.

Lu, H., Cheng, P.L., Lim, B.K., Khoshnevisrad, N., Poo, M.M., 2010. Elevated BDNF after cocaine withdrawal facilitates LTP in medial prefrontal cortex by suppressing GABA inhibition. Neuron 67 (5), 821–833. https://doi.org/10.1016/j.neuron.2010.08.012.

Lucantonio, F., Stalnaker, T.A., Shaham, Y., Niv, Y., Schoenbaum, G., 2012. The impact of orbitofrontal dysfunction on cocaine addiction. Nat. Neurosci. 15 (3), 358–366. https://doi.org/10.1038/nn.3014.

Lucantonio, F., Caprioli, D., Schoenbaum, G., 2014. Transition from 'model-based' to 'model-free' behavioral control in addiction: involvement of the orbitofrontal cortex and dorsolateral striatum. Neuropharmacology 76 Pt B (0 0), 407–415. https://doi.org/10.1016/j.neuropharm.2013.05.033.

Lucantonio, F., Takahashi, Y.K., Hoffman, A.F., Chang, C.Y., Bali-Chaudhary, S., Shaham, Y., Schoenbaum, G., 2014b. Orbitofrontal activation restores insight lost after cocaine use. Nat. Neurosci. 17 (8), 1092–1099. https://doi.org/10.1038/nn.3763.

Lucantonio, F., Kambhampati, S., Haney, R.Z., Atalayer, D., Rowland, N.E., Shaham, Y., Schoenbaum, G., 2015. Effects of prior cocaine versus morphine or heroin self-administration on extinction learning driven by overexpectation versus omission of reward. Biol. Psychiatr. 77 (10), 912–920. https://doi.org/10.1016/j.biopsych.2014.11.017.

Lupien, S.J., McEwen, B.S., Gunnar, M.R., Heim, C., 2009. Effects of stress throughout the lifespan on the brain, behaviour and cognition. Nat. Rev. Neurosci. 10 (6), 434–445. https://doi.org/10.1038/nrn2639.

Lynch, W.J., Carroll, M.E., 1999. Sex differences in the acquisition of intravenously self-administered cocaine and heroin in rats. Psychopharmacology (Berl) 144 (1), 77–82.

Ma, Y.Y., Lee, B.R., Wang, X., Guo, C., Liu, L., Cui, R., Lan, Y., Balcita-Pedicino, J.J., Wolf, M.E., Sesack, S.R., Shaham, Y., Schluter, O.M., Huang, Y.H., Dong, Y., 2014. Bidirectional modulation of incubation of cocaine craving by silent synapse-based remodeling of prefrontal cortex to accumbens projections. Neuron 83 (6), 1453–1467. https://doi.org/10.1016/j.neuron.2014.08.023.

Maas, L.C., Lukas, S.E., Kaufman, M.J., Weiss, R.D., Daniels, S.L., Rogers, V.W., Kukes, T.J., Renshaw, P.F., 1998. Functional magnetic resonance imaging of human brain activation during cue-induced cocaine craving. Am. J. Psychiatr. 155 (1), 124–126.

Madangopal, R., Ramsey, L.A., Weber, S.J., Brenner, M.B., Lennon, V.A., Drake, O.R., Hope, B.T., 2021. Inactivation of the infralimbic cortex decreases discriminative stimulus-controlled relapse to cocaine seeking in rats. Neuropsychopharmacology 46 (11), 1969–1980. https://doi.org/10.1038/s41386-021-01067-6.

Madayag, A.C., Gomez, D., Anderson, E.M., Ingebretson, A.E., Thomas, M.J., Hearing, M.C., 2019. Cell-type and region-specific nucleus accumbens AMPAR plasticity associated with morphine reward, reinstatement, and spontaneous withdrawal. Brain Struct. Funct. 224 (7), 2311–2324.

Madsen, H.B., Ahmed, S.H., 2015. Drug versus sweet reward: greater attraction to and preference for sweet versus drug cues. Addiction Biol. 20 (3), 433–444. https://doi.org/10.1111/adb.12134.

Makris, N., Gasic, G.P., Kennedy, D.N., Hodge, S.M., Kaiser, J.R., Lee, M.J., Kim, B.W., Blood, A.J., Evins, A.E., Seidman, L.J., Iosifescu, D.V., Lee, S., Baxter, C., Perlis, R.H., Smoller, J.W., Fava, M., Breiter, H.C., 2008. Cortical thickness abnormalities in cocaine addiction–a reflection of both drug use and a pre-existing disposition to drug abuse? Neuron 60 (1), 174–188.

Mantsch, J.R., Baker, D.A., Funk, D., Lê, A.D., Shaham, Y., 2016. Stress-induced reinstatement of drug seeking: 20 years of progress. Neuropsychopharmacology 41 (1), 335–356. https://doi.org/10.1038/npp.2015.142.

Markram, H., Toledo-Rodriguez, M., Wang, Y., Gupta, A., Silberberg, G., Wu, C., 2004. Interneurons of the neocortical inhibitory system. Nat. Rev. Neurosci. 5 (10), 793–807. https://doi.org/10.1038/nrn1519.

Martin, W.R., Jasinski, D.R., 1969. Physiological parameters of morphine dependence in man–tolerance, early abstinence, protracted abstinence. J. Psychiatr. Res. 7 (1), 9–17. https://doi.org/10.1016/0022-3956(69)90007-7.

McCutcheon, J.E., Wang, X., Tseng, K.Y., Wolf, M.E., Marinelli, M., 2011. Calcium-permeable AMPA receptors are present in nucleus accumbens synapses after prolonged withdrawal from cocaine self-administration but not experimenter-administered cocaine. J. Neurosci. 31 (15), 5737–5743. https://doi.org/10.1523/jneurosci.0350-11.2011.

McDonald, A.J., 1987. Organization of amygdaloid projections to the mediodorsal thalamus and prefrontal cortex: a fluorescence retrograde transport study in the rat. J. Comp. Neurol. 262 (1), 46–58. https://doi.org/10.1002/cne.902620105.

McEwen, B.S., Nasca, C., Gray, J.D., 2016. Stress effects on neuronal structure: Hippocampus, amygdala, and prefrontal cortex. Neuropsychopharmacology 41 (1), 3–23. https://doi.org/10.1038/npp.2015.171.

McFarland, K., Kalivas, P.W., 2001. The circuitry mediating cocaine-induced reinstatement of drug-seeking behavior. J. Neurosci. 21 (21), 8655–8663.

McFarland, K., Lapish, C.C., Kalivas, P.W., 2003. Prefrontal glutamate release into the core of the nucleus accumbens mediates cocaine-induced reinstatement of drug-seeking behavior. J. Neurosci. 23 (8), 3531–3537.

McFarland, K., Davidge, S.B., Lapish, C.C., Kalivas, P.W., 2004. Limbic and motor circuitry underlying footshock-induced reinstatement of cocaine-seeking behavior. J. Neurosci. 24 (7), 1551–1560.

McGinty, J.F., Whitfield Jr., T.W., Berglind, W.J., 2010. Brain-derived neurotrophic factor and cocaine addiction. Brain Res. 1314, 183–193. https://doi.org/10.1016/j.brainres.2009.08.078.

McGlinchey, E.M., James, M.H., Mahler, S.V., Pantazis, C., Aston-Jones, G., 2016. Prelimbic to accumbens core pathway is recruited in a dopamine-dependent manner to drive cued reinstatement of cocaine seeking. J. Neurosci. 36 (33), 8700–8711. https://doi.org/10.1523/jneurosci.1291-15.2016.

McGregor, A., Roberts, D.C., 1995. Effect of medial prefrontal cortex injections of SCH 23390 on intravenous cocaine self-administration under both a fixed and progressive ratio schedule of reinforcement. Behav. Brain Res. 67 (1), 75–80. https://doi.org/10.1016/0166-4328(94)00106-p.

McGregor, A., Baker, G., Roberts, D.C., 1996. Effect of 6-hydroxydopamine lesions of the medial prefrontal cortex on intravenous cocaine self-administration under a progressive ratio schedule of reinforcement. Pharmacol. Biochem. Behav. 53 (1), 5–9. https://doi.org/10.1016/0091-3057(95)00192-1.

McKlveen, J.M., Morano, R.L., Fitzgerald, M., Zoubovsky, S., Cassella, S.N., Scheimann, J.R., Herman, J.P., 2016. Chronic stress increases prefrontal inhibition: a mechanism for stress-induced prefrontal dysfunction. Biol. Psychiatr. 80 (10), 754–764. https://doi.org/10.1016/j.biopsych.2016.03.2101.

McLaughlin, J., See, R.E., 2003. Selective inactivation of the dorsomedial prefrontal cortex and the basolateral amygdala attenuates conditioned-cued reinstatement of extinguished cocaine-seeking behavior in rats. Psychopharmacology (Berl) 168 (1–2), 57–65. https://doi.org/10.1007/s00213-002-1196-x.

McNamara, R., Dalley, J.W., Robbins, T.W., Everitt, B.J., Belin, D., 2010. Trait-like impulsivity does not predict escalation of heroin self-administration in the rat. Psychopharmacology (Berl) 212 (4), 453–464. https://doi.org/10.1007/s00213-010-1974-9.

McReynolds, J.R., Doncheck, E.M., Li, Y., Vranjkovic, O., Graf, E.N., Ogasawara, D., Cravatt, B.F., Baker, D.A., Liu, Q.S., Hillard, C.J., Mantsch, J.R., 2018. Stress promotes drug seeking through glucocorticoid-dependent endocannabinoid mobilization in the prelimbic cortex. Biol. Psychiatr. 84 (2), 85–94. https://doi.org/10.1016/j.biopsych.2017.09.024.

Mendez, I.A., Simon, N.W., Hart, N., Mitchell, M.R., Nation, J.R., Wellman, P.J., Setlow, B., 2010. Self-administered cocaine causes long-lasting increases in impulsive choice in a delay discounting task. Behav. Neurosci. 124 (4), 470–477. https://doi.org/10.1037/a0020458.

Mihindou, C., Guillem, K., Navailles, S., Vouillac, C., Ahmed, S.H., 2013. Discriminative inhibitory control of cocaine seeking involves the prelimbic prefrontal cortex. Biol. Psychiatr. 73 (3), 271–279. https://doi.org/10.1016/j.biopsych.2012.08.011.

Mitchell, M.R., Weiss, V.G., Ouimet, D.J., Fuchs, R.A., Morgan, D., Setlow, B., 2014. Intake-dependent effects of cocaine self-administration on impulsive choice in a delay discounting task. Behav. Neurosci. 128 (4), 419–429. https://doi.org/10.1037/a0036742.

Moeller, S.J., Maloney, T., Parvaz, M.A., Dunning, J.P., Alia-Klein, N., Woicik, P.A., Goldstein, R.Z., 2009. Enhanced choice for viewing cocaine pictures in cocaine addiction. Biol. Psychiatr. 66 (2), 169–176. https://doi.org/10.1016/j.biopsych.2009.02.015.

Moeller, S.J., Froböse, M.I., Konova, A.B., Misyrlis, M., Parvaz, M.A., Goldstein, R.Z., Alia-Klein, N., 2014. Common and distinct neural correlates of inhibitory dysregulation: stroop fMRI study of cocaine addiction and intermittent explosive disorder. J. Psychiatr. Res. 58, 55–62. https://doi.org/10.1016/j.jpsychires.2014.07.016.

Mogil, J.S., 2012. The etiology and symptomatology of spontaneous pain. J. Pain 13 (10), 932–933 discussion 934–935.

Moorman, D.E., Aston-Jones, G., 2015. Prefrontal neurons encode context-based response execution and inhibition in reward seeking and extinction. Proc. Natl. Acad. Sci. U. S. A. 112 (30), 9472–9477. https://doi.org/10.1073/pnas.1507611112.

Murray, A.J., Woloszynowska-Fraser, M.U., Ansel-Bollepalli, L., Cole, K.L., Foggetti, A., Crouch, B., Riedel, G., Wulff, P., 2015. Parvalbumin-positive interneurons of the prefrontal cortex support working memory and cognitive flexibility. Sci. Rep. 5, 16778. https://doi.org/10.1038/srep16778.

Nasif, F.J., Hu, X.T., White, F.J., 2005. Repeated cocaine administration increases voltage-sensitive calcium currents in response to membrane depolarization in medial prefrontal cortex pyramidal neurons. J. Neurosci. 25 (14), 3674–3679. https://doi.org/10.1523/jneurosci.0010-05.2005.

Nasif, F.J., Sidiropoulou, K., Hu, X.T., White, F.J., 2005. Repeated cocaine administration increases membrane excitability of pyramidal neurons in the rat medial prefrontal cortex. J. Pharmacol. Exp. Therapeut. 312 (3), 1305–1313. https://doi.org/10.1124/jpet.104.075184.

Navandar, M., Martín-García, E., Maldonado, R., Lutz, B., Gerber, S., Ruiz de Azua, I., 2021. Transcriptional signatures in prefrontal cortex confer vulnerability versus resilience to food and cocaine addiction-like behavior. Sci. Rep. 11 (1), 9076. https://doi.org/10.1038/s41598-021-88363-9.

Neisewander, J.L., Baker, D.A., Fuchs, R.A., Tran-Nguyen, L.T., Palmer, A., Marshall, J.F., 2000. Fos protein expression and cocaine-seeking behavior in rats after exposure to a cocaine self-administration environment. J. Neurosci. 20 (2), 798–805.

Nicolas, J., Claessen, B.E., Cao, D., Chiarito, M., Sartori, S., Qiu, H., Goel, R., Nardin, M., Roumeliotis, A., Vogel, B., Turfah, A., Chandiramani, R., Baber, U., Barman, N., Sweeny, J., Krishnan, P., Kini, A., Sharma, S.K., Dangas, G.D., Mehran, R., 2021. A sex paradox in clinical outcomes following complex percutaneous coronary intervention. Int. J. Cardiol. 329, 67–73.

Nogueira, L., Kalivas, P.W., Lavin, A., 2006. Long-term neuroadaptations produced by withdrawal from repeated cocaine treatment: role of dopaminergic receptors in modulating cortical excitability. J. Neurosci. 26 (47), 12308–12313. https://doi.org/10.1523/jneurosci.3206-06.2006.

Noschang, C., Lampert, C., Krolow, R., de Almeida, R.M.M., 2021. Social isolation at adolescence: a systematic review on behaviour related to cocaine, amphetamine and nicotine use in rats and mice. Psychopharmacology (Berl) 238 (4), 927–947. https://doi.org/10.1007/s00213-021-05777-z.

Otis, J.M., Namboodiri, V.M., Matan, A.M., Voets, E.S., Mohorn, E.P., Kosyk, O., McHenry, J.A., Robinson, J.E., Resendez, S.L., Rossi, M.A., Stuber, G.D., 2017. Prefrontal cortex output circuits guide reward seeking through divergent cue encoding. Nature 543 (7643), 103–107.

Ovari, J., Leri, F., 2008. Inactivation of the ventromedial prefrontal cortex mimics re-emergence of heroin seeking caused by heroin reconditioning. Neurosci. Lett. 444 (1), 52–55. https://doi.org/10.1016/j.neulet.2008.08.015.

Pacchioni, A.M., Gabriele, A., See, R.E., 2011. Dorsal striatum mediation of cocaine-seeking after withdrawal from short or long daily access cocaine self-administration in rats. Behav. Brain Res. 218 (2), 296–300. https://doi.org/10.1016/j.bbr.2010.12.014.

Palombo, P., Leao, R.M., Bianchi, P.C., de Oliveira, P.E.C., Planeta, C.D.S., Cruz, F.C., 2017. Inactivation of the prelimbic cortex impairs the context-induced reinstatement of ethanol seeking. Front. Pharmacol. 8, 725.

Park, W.K., Bari, A.A., Jey, A.R., Anderson, S.M., Spealman, R.D., Rowlett, J.K., Pierce, R.C., 2002. Cocaine administered into the medial prefrontal cortex reinstates cocaine-seeking behavior by increasing AMPA receptor-mediated glutamate transmission in the nucleus accumbens. J. Neurosci. 22 (7), 2916–2925.

Parsegian, A., Glen Jr., W.B., Lavin, A., See, R.E., 2011. Methamphetamine self-administration produces attentional set-shifting deficits and alters prefrontal cortical neurophysiology in rats. Biol. Psychiatr. 69 (3), 253–259. https://doi.org/10.1016/j.biopsych.2010.09.003.

Parvaz, M.A., Moeller, S.J., d'Oleire Uquillas, F., Pflumm, A., Maloney, T., Alia-Klein, N., Goldstein, R.Z., 2017. Prefrontal gray matter volume recovery in treatment-seeking cocaine-addicted individuals: a longitudinal study. Addiction Biol. 22 (5), 1391–1401.

Pascoli, V., Turiault, M., Luscher, C., 2011. Reversal of cocaine-evoked synaptic potentiation resets drug-induced adaptive behaviour. Nature 481 (7379), 71–75. https://doi.org/10.1038/nature10709.

Paulus, M.P., Hozack, N.E., Zauscher, B.E., Frank, L., Brown, G.G., Braff, D.L., Schuckit, M.A., 2002. Behavioral and functional neuroimaging evidence for prefrontal dysfunction in methamphetamine-dependent subjects. Neuropsychopharmacology 26 (1), 53–63.

Paulus, M.P., Tapert, S.F., Schuckit, M.A., 2005. Neural activation patterns of methamphetamine-dependent subjects during decision making predict relapse. Arch. Gen. Psychiatr. 62 (7), 761–768. https://doi.org/10.1001/archpsyc.62.7.761.

Peters, J., De Vries, T.J., 2012. Glutamate mechanisms underlying opiate memories. Cold Spring Harb. Perspect. Med. 2 (9), a012088. https://doi.org/10.1101/cshperspect.a012088.

Peters, J., LaLumiere, R.T., Kalivas, P.W., 2008. Infralimbic prefrontal cortex is responsible for inhibiting cocaine seeking in extinguished rats. J. Neurosci. 28 (23), 6046–6053. https://doi.org/10.1523/jneurosci.1045-08.2008.

Peters, J., Vallone, J., Laurendi, K., Kalivas, P.W., 2008. Opposing roles for the ventral prefrontal cortex and the basolateral amygdala on the spontaneous recovery of cocaine-seeking in rats. Psychopharmacology (Berl) 197 (2), 319–326.

Peters, J., Pattij, T., De Vries, T.J., 2013. Targeting cocaine versus heroin memories: divergent roles within ventromedial prefrontal cortex. Trends Pharmacol. Sci. 34 (12), 689–695.

Petreanu, L., Mao, T., Sternson, S.M., Svoboda, K., 2009. The subcellular organization of neocortical excitatory connections. Nature 457 (7233), 1142–1145.

Pfarr, S., Meinhardt, M.W., Klee, M.L., Hansson, A.C., Vengeliene, V., Schönig, K., Sommer, W.H., 2015. Losing control: excessive alcohol seeking after selective inactivation of cue-responsive neurons in the infralimbic cortex. J. Neurosci. 35 (30), 10750–10761. https://doi.org/10.1523/jneurosci.0684-15.2015.

Pfarr, S., Schaaf, L., Reinert, J.K., Paul, E., Herrmannsdörfer, F., Roßmanith, M., Sommer, W.H., 2018. Choice for drug or natural reward engages largely overlapping neuronal ensembles in the infralimbic prefrontal cortex. J. Neurosci. 38 (14), 3507–3519. https://doi.org/10.1523/jneurosci.0026-18.2018.

Piao, C., Liu, T., Ma, L., Ding, X., Wang, X., Chen, X., Duan, Y., Sui, N., Liang, J., 2017. Alterations in brain activation in response to prolonged morphine withdrawal-induced behavioral inflexibility in rats. Psychopharmacology (Berl) 234 (19), 2941–2953.

Piazza, P.V., Rougé-Pont, F., Deminière, J.M., Kharoubi, M., Le Moal, M., Simon, H., 1991. Dopaminergic activity is reduced in the prefrontal cortex and increased in the nucleus accumbens of rats predisposed to develop amphetamine self-administration. Brain Res. 567 (1), 169–174. https://doi.org/10.1016/0006-8993(91)91452-7.

Ploense, K.L., Vieira, P., Bubalo, L., Olivarria, G., Carr, A.E., Szumlinski, K.K., Kippin, T.E., 2018. Contributions of prolonged contingent and non-contingent cocaine exposure to escalation of cocaine intake and glutamatergic gene expression. Psychopharmacology (Berl) 235 (5), 1347–1359. https://doi.org/10.1007/s00213-017-4798-z.

Porrino, L.J., Lyons, D., Smith, H.R., Daunais, J.B., Nader, M.A., 2004. Cocaine self-administration produces a progressive involvement of limbic, association, and sensorimotor striatal domains. J. Neurosci. 24 (14), 3554–3562.

Prisciandaro, J.J., Myrick, H., Henderson, S., McRae-Clark, A.L., Brady, K.T., 2013. Prospective associations between brain activation to cocaine and no-go cues and cocaine relapse. Drug Alcohol Depend. 131 (1–2), 44–49. https://doi.org/10.1016/j.drugalcdep.2013.04.008.

Prisciandaro, J.J., Joseph, J.E., Myrick, H., McRae-Clark, A.L., Henderson, S., Pfeifer, J., Brady, K.T., 2014. The relationship between years of cocaine use and brain activation to cocaine and response inhibition cues. Addiction 109 (12), 2062–2070. https://doi.org/10.1111/add.12666.

Radley, J.J., Sisti, H.M., Hao, J., Rocher, A.B., McCall, T., Hof, P.R., Morrison, J.H., 2004. Chronic behavioral stress induces apical dendritic reorganization in pyramidal neurons of the medial prefrontal cortex. Neuroscience 125 (1), 1–6. https://doi.org/10.1016/j.neuroscience.2004.01.006.

Radley, J.J., Anderson, R.M., Cosme, C.V., Glanz, R.M., Miller, M.C., Romig-Martin, S.A., LaLumiere, R.T., 2015. The contingency of cocaine administration accounts for structural and functional medial prefrontal deficits and increased adrenocortical activation. J. Neurosci. 35 (34), 11897–11910. https://doi.org/10.1523/jneurosci.4961-14.2015.

Rapeli, P., Kivisaari, R., Autti, T., Kahkonen, S., Puuskari, V., Jokela, O., Kalska, H., 2006. Cognitive function during early abstinence from opioid dependence: a comparison to age, gender, and verbal intelligence matched controls. BMC Psychiatr. 6, 9.

Reiner, D.J., Lofaro, O.M., Applebey, S.V., Korah, H., Venniro, M., Cifani, C., Bossert, J.M., Shaham, Y., 2020. Role of projections between piriform cortex and orbitofrontal cortex in relapse to fentanyl seeking after palatable food choice-induced voluntary abstinence. J. Neurosci. 40 (12), 2485–2497. https://doi.org/10.1523/jneurosci.2693-19.2020.

Risinger, R.C., Salmeron, B.J., Ross, T.J., Amen, S.L., Sanfilipo, M., Hoffmann, R.G., Stein, E.A., 2005. Neural correlates of high and craving during cocaine self-administration using BOLD fMRI. Neuroimage 26 (4), 1097–1108. https://doi.org/10.1016/j.neuroimage.2005.03.030.

Robbins, S.J., Ehrman, R.N., Childress, A.R., O'Brien, C.P., 1999. Comparing levels of cocaine cue reactivity in male and female outpatients. Drug Alcohol Depend. 53 (3), 223–230.

Robinson, T.E., Gorny, G., Mitton, E., Kolb, B., 2001. Cocaine self-administration alters the morphology of dendrites and dendritic spines in the nucleus accumbens and neocortex. Synapse 39 (3), 257–266. https://doi.org/10.1002/1098-2396(20010301)39:3<257::aid-syn1007>3.0.co;2-1.

Robinson, T.E., Gorny, G., Savage, V.R., Kolb, B., 2002. Widespread but regionally specific effects of experimenter- versus self-administered morphine on dendritic spines in the nucleus accumbens, hippocampus, and neocortex of adult rats. Synapse 46 (4), 271–279. https://doi.org/10.1002/syn.10146.

Rocha, A., Kalivas, P.W., 2010. Role of the prefrontal cortex and nucleus accumbens in reinstating methamphetamine seeking. Eur. J. Neurosci. 31 (5), 903–909. https://doi.org/10.1111/j.1460-9568.2010.07134.x.

Rock, C., Apicella, A.J., 2015. Callosal projections drive neuronal-specific responses in the mouse auditory cortex. J. Neurosci. 35 (17), 6703–6713.

Roesch, M.R., Takahashi, Y., Gugsa, N., Bissonette, G.B., Schoenbaum, G., 2007. Previous cocaine exposure makes rats hypersensitive to both delay and reward magnitude. J. Neurosci. 27 (1), 245–250. https://doi.org/10.1523/jneurosci.4080-06.2007.

Rogers, J.L., Ghee, S., See, R.E., 2008. The neural circuitry underlying reinstatement of heroin-seeking behavior in an animal model of relapse. Neuroscience 151 (2), 579–588. https://doi.org/10.1016/j.neuroscience.2007.10.012.

Rotheram-Fuller, E., Shoptaw, S., Berman, S.M., London, E.D., 2004. Impaired performance in a test of decision-making by opiate-dependent tobacco smokers. Drug Alcohol Depend. 73 (1), 79–86. https://doi.org/10.1016/j.drugalcdep.2003.10.003.

Rothwell, P.E., Kourrich, S., Thomas, M.J., 2011. Synaptic adaptations in the nucleus accumbens caused by experiences linked to relapse. Biol. Psychiatr. 69 (11), 1124–1126. https://doi.org/10.1016/j.biopsych.2010.12.028.

Rubenstein, J.L., Merzenich, M.M., 2003. Model of autism: increased ratio of excitation/inhibition in key neural systems. Gene Brain Behav. 2 (5), 255–267. https://doi.org/10.1034/j.1601-183x.2003.00037.x.

Rudy, B., Fishell, G., Lee, S., Hjerling-Leffler, J., 2011. Three groups of interneurons account for nearly 100% of neocortical GABAergic neurons. Dev. Neurobiol. 71 (1), 45–61. https://doi.org/10.1002/dneu.20853.

Russo, S.J., Festa, E.D., Fabian, S.J., Gazi, F.M., Kraish, M., Jenab, S., Quinones-Jenab, V., 2003. Gonadal hormones differentially modulate cocaine-induced conditioned place preference in male and female rats. Neuroscience 120 (2), 523–533.

Russo, S.J., Jenab, S., Fabian, S.J., Festa, E.D., Kemen, L.M., Quinones-Jenab, V., 2003b. Sex differences in the conditioned rewarding effects of cocaine. Brain Res. 970 (1–2), 214–220.

Schank, J.R., Nelson, B.S., Damadzic, R., Tapocik, J.D., Yao, M., King, C.E., Heilig, M., 2015. Neurokinin-1 receptor antagonism attenuates neuronal activity triggered by stress-induced reinstatement of alcohol seeking. Neuropharmacology 99, 106–114. https://doi.org/10.1016/j.neuropharm.2015.07.009.

Schmidt, E.D., Voorn, P., Binnekade, R., Schoffelmeer, A.N., De Vries, T.J., 2005. Differential involvement of the prelimbic cortex and striatum in conditioned heroin and sucrose seeking following long-term extinction. Eur. J. Neurosci. 22 (9), 2347–2356. https://doi.org/10.1111/j.1460-9568.2005.04435.x.

Schoenbaum, G., Setlow, B., 2005. Cocaine makes actions insensitive to outcomes but not extinction: implications for altered orbitofrontal-amygdalar function. Cerebr. Cortex 15 (8), 1162–1169. https://doi.org/10.1093/cercor/bhh216.

Schoenbaum, G., Chang, C.Y., Lucantonio, F., Takahashi, Y.K., 2016. Thinking outside the box: orbitofrontal cortex, imagination, and how we can treat addiction. Neuropsychopharmacology 41 (13), 2966–2976. https://doi.org/10.1038/npp.2016.147.

Scofield, M.D., Heinsbroek, J.A., Gipson, C.D., Kupchik, Y.M., Spencer, S., Smith, A.C., Roberts-Wolfe, D., Kalivas, P.W., 2016. The nucleus accumbens: mechanisms of addiction across drug classes reflect the importance of glutamate homeostasis. Pharmacol. Rev. 68 (3), 816–871. https://doi.org/10.1124/pr.116.012484.

Seamans, J.K., Yang, C.R., 2004. The principal features and mechanisms of dopamine modulation in the prefrontal cortex. Prog. Neurobiol. 74 (1), 1–58. https://doi.org/10.1016/j.pneurobio.2004.05.006.

Seamans, J.K., Gorelova, N., Durstewitz, D., Yang, C.R., 2001. Bidirectional dopamine modulation of GABAergic inhibition in prefrontal cortical pyramidal neurons. J. Neurosci. 21 (10), 3628–3638.

Seamans, J.K., Lapish, C.C., Durstewitz, D., 2008. Comparing the prefrontal cortex of rats and primates: insights from electrophysiology. Neurotox. Res. 14 (2–3), 249–262.

Sebold, M., Nebe, S., Garbusow, M., Guggenmos, M., Schad, D.J., Beck, A., Heinz, A., 2017. When habits are dangerous: alcohol expectancies and habitual decision making predict relapse in alcohol dependence. Biol. Psychiatr. 82 (11), 847–856. https://doi.org/10.1016/j.biopsych.2017.04.019.

See, R.E., Fuchs, R.A., Ledford, C.C., McLaughlin, J., 2003. Drug addiction, relapse, and the amygdala. Ann. N. Y. Acad. Sci. 985, 294–307.

See, R.E., Elliott, J.C., Feltenstein, M.W., 2007. The role of dorsal vs ventral striatal pathways in cocaine-seeking behavior after prolonged abstinence in rats. Psychopharmacology (Berl) 194 (3), 321–331. https://doi.org/10.1007/s00213-007-0850-8.

Self, D.W., Choi, K.H., 2004. Extinction-induced neuroplasticity attenuates stress-induced cocaine seeking: a state-dependent learning hypothesis. Stress 7 (3), 145–155. https://doi.org/10.1080/10253890400012677.

Seo, D., Lacadie, C.M., Tuit, K., Hong, K.I., Constable, R.T., Sinha, R., 2013. Disrupted ventromedial prefrontal function, alcohol craving, and subsequent relapse risk. JAMA Psychiatr. 70 (7), 727–739. https://doi.org/10.1001/jamapsychiatry.2013.762.

Serdarevic, M., Striley, C.W., Cottler, L.B., 2017. Sex differences in prescription opioid use. Curr. Opin. Psychiatr. 30 (4), 238–246. https://doi.org/10.1097/yco.0000000000000337.

Sesack, S.R., Pickel, V.M., 1992. Prefrontal cortical efferents in the rat synapse on unlabeled neuronal targets of catecholamine terminals in the nucleus accumbens septi and on dopamine neurons in the ventral tegmental area. J. Comp. Neurol. 320 (2), 145–160. https://doi.org/10.1002/cne.903200202.

Sesack, S.R., Deutch, A.Y., Roth, R.H., Bunney, B.S., 1989. Topographical organization of the efferent projections of the medial prefrontal cortex in the rat: an anterograde tract-tracing study with Phaseolus vulgaris leucoagglutinin. J. Comp. Neurol. 290 (2), 213–242. https://doi.org/10.1002/cne.902900205.

Sesack, S.R., Snyder, C.L., Lewis, D.A., 1995. Axon terminals immunolabeled for dopamine or tyrosine hydroxylase synapse on GABA-immunoreactive dendrites in rat and monkey cortex. J. Comp. Neurol. 363 (2), 264–280. https://doi.org/10.1002/cne.903630208.

Setlow, B., Mendez, I.A., Mitchell, M.R., Simon, N.W., 2009. Effects of chronic administration of drugs of abuse on impulsive choice (delay discounting) in animal models. Behav. Pharmacol. 20 (5–6), 380–389. https://doi.org/10.1097/FBP.0b013e3283305eb4.

Settles, R.E., Fischer, S., Cyders, M.A., Combs, J.L., Gunn, R.L., Smith, G.T., 2012. Negative urgency: a personality predictor of externalizing behavior characterized by neuroticism, low conscientiousness, and disagreeableness. J. Abnorm. Psychol. 121 (1), 160–172. https://doi.org/10.1037/a0024948.

Shansky, R.M., Hamo, C., Hof, P.R., McEwen, B.S., Morrison, J.H., 2009. Stress-induced dendritic remodeling in the prefrontal cortex is circuit specific. Cerebr. Cortex 19 (10), 2479–2484. https://doi.org/10.1093/cercor/bhp003.

Shen, H., Moussawi, K., Zhou, W., Toda, S., Kalivas, P.W., 2011. Heroin relapse requires long-term potentiation-like plasticity mediated by NMDA2b-containing receptors. Proc. Natl. Acad. Sci. U. S. A. 108 (48), 19407–19412. https://doi.org/10.1073/pnas.1112052108.

Shen, H.W., Gipson, C.D., Huits, M., Kalivas, P.W., 2014. Prelimbic cortex and ventral tegmental area modulate synaptic plasticity differentially in nucleus accumbens during cocaine-reinstated drug seeking. Neuropsychopharmacology 39 (5), 1169–1177.

Simon, N.W., Mendez, I.A., Setlow, B., 2007. Cocaine exposure causes long-term increases in impulsive choice. Behav. Neurosci. 121 (3), 543–549. https://doi.org/10.1037/0735-7044.121.3.543.

Singewald, N., Holmes, A., 2019. Rodent models of impaired fear extinction. Psychopharmacology (Berl) 236 (1), 21–32. https://doi.org/10.1007/s00213-018-5054-x.

Sinha, R., Li, C.S., 2007. Imaging stress- and cue-induced drug and alcohol craving: association with relapse and clinical implications. Drug Alcohol Rev. 26 (1), 25–31. https://doi.org/10.1080/09595230601036960.

Smith, J.L., Mattick, R.P., Jamadar, S.D., Iredale, J.M., 2014. Deficits in behavioural inhibition in substance abuse and addiction: a meta-analysis. Drug Alcohol Depend. 145, 1–33. https://doi.org/10.1016/j.drugalcdep.2014.08.009.

Smith, D.G., Jones, P.S., Williams, G.B., Bullmore, E.T., Robbins, T.W., Ersche, K.D., 2015. Overlapping decline in orbitofrontal gray matter volume related to cocaine use and body mass index. Addiction Biol. 20 (1), 194–196. https://doi.org/10.1111/adb.12081.

Soares, J.C., Mann, J.J., 1997. The anatomy of mood disorders–review of structural neuroimaging studies. Biol. Psychiatr. 41 (1), 86–106. https://doi.org/10.1016/s0006-3223(96)00006-6.

Sohal, V.S., Zhang, F., Yizhar, O., Deisseroth, K., 2009. Parvalbumin neurons and gamma rhythms enhance cortical circuit performance. Nature 459 (7247), 698–702. https://doi.org/10.1038/nature07991.

Soldin, O.P., Chung, S.H., Mattison, D.R., 2011. Sex differences in drug disposition. J. Biomed. Biotechnol. 2011, 187103.

Sotres-Bayon, F., Sierra-Mercado, D., Pardilla-Delgado, E., Quirk, G.J., 2012. Gating of fear in prelimbic cortex by hippocampal and amygdala inputs. Neuron 76 (4), 804–812. https://doi.org/10.1016/j.neuron.2012.09.028.

Spronk, D.B., van Wel, J.H., Ramaekers, J.G., Verkes, R.J., 2013. Characterizing the cognitive effects of cocaine: a comprehensive review. Neurosci. Biobehav. Rev. 37 (8), 1838–1859. https://doi.org/10.1016/j.neubiorev.2013.07.003.

Stalnaker, T.A., Roesch, M.R., Franz, T.M., Burke, K.A., Schoenbaum, G., 2006. Abnormal associative encoding in orbitofrontal neurons in cocaine-experienced rats during decision-making. Eur. J. Neurosci. 24 (9), 2643–2653. https://doi.org/10.1111/j.1460-9568.2006.05128.x.

Stefanik, M.T., Kalivas, P.W., 2013. Optogenetic dissection of basolateral amygdala projections during cue-induced reinstatement of cocaine seeking. Front. Behav. Neurosci. 7, 213.

Stefanik, M.T., Kupchik, Y.M., Brown, R.M., Kalivas, P.W., 2013. Optogenetic evidence that pallidal projections, not nigral projections, from the nucleus accumbens core are necessary for reinstating cocaine seeking. J. Neurosci. 33 (34), 13654–13662. https://doi.org/10.1523/jneurosci.1570-13.2013.

Stein, E.A., Pankiewicz, J., Harsch, H.H., Cho, J.K., Fuller, S.A., Hoffmann, R.G., Hawkins, M., Rao, S.M., Bandettini, P.A., Bloom, A.S., 1998. Nicotine-induced limbic cortical activation in the human brain: a functional MRI study. Am. J. Psychiatr. 155 (8), 1009–1015. https://doi.org/10.1176/ajp.155.8.1009.

Struik, R.F., Marchant, N.J., de Haan, R., Terra, H., van Mourik, Y., Schetters, D., Carr, M.R., van der Roest, M., Heistek, T.S., De Vries, T.J., 2019. Dorsomedial prefrontal cortex neurons encode nicotine-cue associations. Neuropsychopharmacology 44 (12), 2011–2021.

Sun, W., Rebec, G.V., 2005. The role of prefrontal cortex D1-like and D2-like receptors in cocaine-seeking behavior in rats. Psychopharmacology (Berl) 177 (3), 315–323. https://doi.org/10.1007/s00213-004-1956-x.

Sun, W., Rebec, G.V., 2006. Repeated cocaine self-administration alters processing of cocaine-related information in rat prefrontal cortex. J. Neurosci. 26 (30), 8004–8008. https://doi.org/10.1523/jneurosci.1413-06.2006.

Suter, B.A., Shepherd, G.M., 2015. Reciprocal interareal connections to corticospinal neurons in mouse M1 and S2. J. Neurosci. 35 (7), 2959–2974.

Suto, N., Laque, A., De Ness, G.L., Wagner, G.E., Watry, D., Kerr, T., Weiss, F., 2016. Distinct memory engrams in the infralimbic cortex of rats control opposing environmental actions on a learned behavior. Elife 5. https://doi.org/10.7554/eLife.21920.

Taber, M.T., Fibiger, H.C., 1995. Electrical stimulation of the prefrontal cortex increases dopamine release in the nucleus accumbens of the rat: modulation by metabotropic glutamate receptors. J. Neurosci. 15 (5 Pt 2), 3896–3904.

Taber, M.T., Das, S., Fibiger, H.C., 1995. Cortical regulation of subcortical dopamine release: mediation via the ventral tegmental area. J. Neurochem. 65 (3), 1407–1410.

Tanabe, J., Tregellas, J.R., Dalwani, M., Thompson, L., Owens, E., Crowley, T., Banich, M., 2009. Medial orbitofrontal cortex gray matter is reduced in abstinent substance-dependent individuals. Biol. Psychiatr. 65 (2), 160–164. https://doi.org/10.1016/j.biopsych.2008.07.030.

Tang, W., Wesley, M., Freeman, W.M., Liang, B., Hemby, S.E., 2004. Alterations in ionotropic glutamate receptor subunits during binge cocaine self-administration and withdrawal in rats. J. Neurochem. 89 (4), 1021–1033. https://doi.org/10.1111/j.1471-4159.2004.02392.x.

Tomasi, D., Goldstein, R.Z., Telang, F., Maloney, T., Alia-Klein, N., Caparelli, E.C., Volkow, N.D., 2007. Widespread disruption in brain activation patterns to a working memory task during cocaine abstinence. Brain Res. 1171, 83–92.

Townsend, E.A., Negus, S.S., Caine, S.B., Thomsen, M., Banks, M.L., 2019. Sex differences in opioid reinforcement under a fentanyl vs. food choice procedure in rats. Neuropsychopharmacology 44 (12), 2022–2029. https://doi.org/10.1038/s41386-019-0356-1.

Townsend, E.A., Schwienteck, K.L., Robinson, H.L., Lawson, S.T., Banks, M.L., 2021. A drug-vs-food "choice" self-administration procedure in rats to investigate pharmacological and environmental mechanisms of substance use disorders. J. Neurosci. Methods 354, 109110. https://doi.org/10.1016/j.jneumeth.2021.109110.

Trantham, H., Szumlinski, K.K., McFarland, K., Kalivas, P.W., Lavin, A., 2002. Repeated cocaine administration alters the electrophysiological properties of prefrontal cortical neurons. Neuroscience 113 (4), 749–753.

Trantham-Davidson, H., Lavin, A., 2004. Acute cocaine administration depresses cortical activity. Neuropsychopharmacology 29 (11), 2046–2051. https://doi.org/10.1038/sj.npp.1300482.

Trantham-Davidson, H., LaLumiere, R.T., Reissner, K.J., Kalivas, P.W., Knackstedt, L.A., 2012. Ceftriaxone normalizes nucleus accumbens synaptic transmission, glutamate transport, and export following cocaine self-administration and extinction training. J. Neurosci. 32 (36), 12406–12410. https://doi.org/10.1523/jneurosci.1976-12.2012.

Tu, Y., Kroener, S., Abernathy, K., Lapish, C., Seamans, J., Chandler, L.J., Woodward, J.J., 2007. Ethanol inhibits persistent activity in prefrontal cortical neurons. J. Neurosci. 27 (17), 4765–4775.

Um, M., Whitt, Z.T., Revilla, R., Hunton, T., Cyders, M.A., 2019. Shared neural correlates underlying addictive disorders and negative urgency. Brain Sci. 9 (2). https://doi.org/10.3390/brainsci9020036.

Uslaner, J.M., Acerbo, M.J., Jones, S.A., Robinson, T.E., 2006. The attribution of incentive salience to a stimulus that signals an intravenous injection of cocaine. Behav. Brain Res. 169 (2), 320–324. https://doi.org/10.1016/j.bbr.2006.02.001.

Uylings, H.B., Groenewegen, H.J., Kolb, B., 2003. Do rats have a prefrontal cortex? Behav. Brain Res. 146 (1–2), 3–17.

Van den Oever, M.C., Goriounova, N.A., Li, K.W., Van der Schors, R.C., Binnekade, R., Schoffelmeer, A.N., De Vries, T.J., 2008. Prefrontal cortex AMPA receptor plasticity is crucial for cue-induced relapse to heroin-seeking. Nat. Neurosci. 11 (9), 1053–1058. https://doi.org/10.1038/nn.2165.

Van den Oever, M.C., Spijker, S., Smit, A.B., De Vries, T.J., 2010. Prefrontal cortex plasticity mechanisms in drug seeking and relapse. Neurosci. Biobehav. Rev. 35 (2), 276–284. https://doi.org/10.1016/j.neubiorev.2009.11.016.

Van den Oever, M.C., Rotaru, D.C., Heinsbroek, J.A., Gouwenberg, Y., Deisseroth, K., Stuber, G.D., Mansvelder, H.D., Smit, A.B., 2013. Ventromedial prefrontal cortex pyramidal cells have a temporal dynamic role in recall and extinction of cocaine-associated memory. J. Neurosci. 33 (46), 18225–18233. https://doi.org/10.1523/jneurosci.2412-13.2013.

Van Snellenberg, J.X., Girgis, R.R., Horga, G., van de Giessen, E., Slifstein, M., Ojeil, N., Weinstein, J.J., Moore, H., Lieberman, J.A., Shohamy, D., Smith, E.E., Abi-Dargham, A., 2016. Mechanisms of working memory impairment in schizophrenia. Biol. Psychiatr. 80 (8), 617–626. https://doi.org/10.1016/j.biopsych.2016.02.017.

Vandaele, Y., Cantin, L., Serre, F., Vouillac-Mendoza, C., Ahmed, S.H., 2016. Choosing under the influence: a drug-specific mechanism by which the setting controls drug choices in rats. Neuropsychopharmacology 41 (2), 646–657. https://doi.org/10.1038/npp.2015.195.

Verdejo-García, A., Bechara, A., Recknor, E.C., Pérez-García, M., 2007. Negative emotion-driven impulsivity predicts substance dependence problems. Drug Alcohol Depend. 91 (2–3), 213–219. https://doi.org/10.1016/j.drugalcdep.2007.05.025.

Verdejo-García, A.J., Perales, J.C., Pérez-García, M., 2007. Cognitive impulsivity in cocaine and heroin polysubstance abusers. Addict. Behav. 32 (5), 950–966. https://doi.org/10.1016/j.addbeh.2006.06.032.

Volkow, N.D., Fowler, J.S., 2000. Addiction, a disease of compulsion and drive: involvement of the orbitofrontal cortex. Cerebr. Cortex 10 (3), 318–325.

Volkow, N.D., Wang, G.J., Fowler, J.S., Hitzemann, R., Angrist, B., Gatley, S.J., Logan, J., Ding, Y.S., Pappas, N., 1999. Association of methylphenidate-induced craving with changes in right striato-orbitofrontal metabolism in cocaine abusers: implications in addiction. Am. J. Psychiatr. 156 (1), 19–26.

Volkow, N.D., Chang, L., Wang, G.J., Fowler, J.S., Ding, Y.S., Sedler, M., Logan, J., Franceschi, D., Gatley, J., Hitzemann, R., Gifford, A., Wong, C., Pappas, N., 2001. Low level of brain dopamine D2 receptors in methamphetamine abusers: association with metabolism in the orbitofrontal cortex. Am. J. Psychiatr. 158 (12), 2015–2021.

Volkow, N.D., Wang, G.J., Fowler, J.S., Tomasi, D., 2012. Addiction circuitry in the human brain. Annu. Rev. Pharmacol. Toxicol. 52, 321–336.

Vranjkovic, O., Van Newenhizen, E.C., Nordness, M.E., Blacktop, J.M., Urbanik, L.A., Mathy, J.C., Mantsch, J.R., 2018. Enhanced CRFR1-dependent regulation of a ventral tegmental area to prelimbic cortex projection establishes susceptibility to stress-induced cocaine seeking. J. Neurosci. 38 (50), 10657–10671. https://doi.org/10.1523/jneurosci.2080-18.2018.

Walker, D.M., Cates, H.M., Loh, Y.E., Purushothaman, I., Ramakrishnan, A., Cahill, K.M., Lardner, C.K., Godino, A., Kronman, H.G., Rabkin, J., Lorsch, Z.S., Mews, P., Doyle, M.A., Feng, J., Labonte, B., Koo, J.W., Bagot, R.C.,

Logan, R.W., Seney, M.L., Calipari, E.S., Shen, L., Nestler, E.J., 2018. Cocaine self-administration alters transcriptome-wide responses in the brain's reward circuitry. Biol. Psychiatr. 84 (12), 867–880.

Walker, L.C., Kastman, H.E., Lawrence, A.J., 2020. Pattern of neural activation following yohimbine-induced reinstatement of alcohol seeking in rats. Eur. J. Neurosci. 51 (3), 706–720. https://doi.org/10.1111/ejn.14431.

Warren, B.L., Kane, L., Venniro, M., Selvam, P., Quintana-Feliciano, R., Mendoza, M.P., Hope, B.T., 2019. Separate vmPFC ensembles control cocaine self-administration versus extinction in rats. J. Neurosci. 39 (37), 7394–7407. https://doi.org/10.1523/jneurosci.0918-19.2019.

Waters, A.J., Marhe, R., Franken, I.H., 2012. Attentional bias to drug cues is elevated before and during temptations to use heroin and cocaine. Psychopharmacology (Berl) 219 (3), 909–921. https://doi.org/10.1007/s00213-011-2424-z.

Weissenborn, R., Robbins, T.W., Everitt, B.J., 1997. Effects of medial prefrontal or anterior cingulate cortex lesions on responding for cocaine under fixed-ratio and second-order schedules of reinforcement in rats. Psychopharmacology (Berl) 134 (3), 242–257. https://doi.org/10.1007/s002130050447.

Wellman, C.L., Bollinger, J.L., Moench, K.M., 2020. Effects of stress on the structure and function of the medial prefrontal cortex: insights from animal models. Int. Rev. Neurobiol. 150, 129–153. https://doi.org/10.1016/bs.irn.2019.11.007.

West, E.A., Niedringhaus, M., Ortega, H.K., Haake, R.M., Frohlich, F., Carelli, R.M., 2021. Noninvasive brain stimulation rescues cocaine-induced prefrontal hypoactivity and restores flexible behavior. Biol. Psychiatr. 89 (10), 1001–1011. https://doi.org/10.1016/j.biopsych.2020.12.027.

Wied, H.M., Jones, J.L., Cooch, N.K., Berg, B.A., Schoenbaum, G., 2013. Disruption of model-based behavior and learning by cocaine self-administration in rats. Psychopharmacology (Berl) 229 (3), 493–501. https://doi.org/10.1007/s00213-013-3222-6.

Wilcox, C.E., Teshiba, T.M., Merideth, F., Ling, J., Mayer, A.R., 2011. Enhanced cue reactivity and fronto-striatal functional connectivity in cocaine use disorders. Drug Alcohol Depend. 115 (1–2), 137–144. https://doi.org/10.1016/j.drugalcdep.2011.01.009.

Witkowski, G., Szulczyk, B., Rola, R., Szulczyk, P., 2008. D(1) dopaminergic control of G protein-dependent inward rectifier K(+) (GIRK)-like channel current in pyramidal neurons of the medial prefrontal cortex. Neuroscience 155 (1), 53–63.

Witkowski, G., Rola, R., Szulczyk, P., 2012. Effect of cyclic adenosine monophosphate on the G protein-dependent inward rectifier K(+)-like channel current in medial prefrontal cortex pyramidal neurons. J. Physiol. Pharmacol. 63 (5), 457–462.

Woodward, J.J., Pava, M.J., 2009. Effects of ethanol on persistent activity and up-States in excitatory and inhibitory neurons in prefrontal cortex. Alcohol Clin. Exp. Res. 33 (12), 2134–2140. https://doi.org/10.1111/j.1530-0277.2009.01059.x.

Worhunsky, P.D., Potenza, M.N., Rogers, R.D., 2017. Alterations in functional brain networks associated with loss-chasing in gambling disorder and cocaine-use disorder. Drug Alcohol Depend. 178, 363–371. https://doi.org/10.1016/j.drugalcdep.2017.05.025.

Yang, J., Yang, X., Tang, K., 2022. Interneuron development and dysfunction. FEBS J. 289 (8), 2318–2336.

Yizhar, O., Fenno, L.E., Prigge, M., Schneider, F., Davidson, T.J., O'Shea, D.J., Sohal, V.S., Goshen, I., Finkelstein, J., Paz, J.T., Stehfest, K., Fudim, R., Ramakrishnan, C., Huguenard, J.R., Hegemann, P., Deisseroth, K., 2011. Neocortical excitation/inhibition balance in information processing and social dysfunction. Nature 477 (7363), 171–178. https://doi.org/10.1038/nature10360.

Yuan, Y., Zhu, Z., Shi, J., Zou, Z., Yuan, F., Liu, Y., Lee, T.M., Weng, X., 2009. Gray matter density negatively correlates with duration of heroin use in young lifetime heroin-dependent individuals. Brain Cognit. 71 (3), 223–228.

Zakharova, E., Wade, D., Izenwasser, S., 2009. Sensitivity to cocaine conditioned reward depends on sex and age. Pharmacol. Biochem. Behav. 92 (1), 131–134.

Zavala, A.R., Biswas, S., Harlan, R.E., Neisewander, J.L., 2007. Fos and glutamate AMPA receptor subunit coexpression associated with cue-elicited cocaine-seeking behavior in abstinent rats. Neuroscience 145 (2), 438–452. https://doi.org/10.1016/j.neuroscience.2006.12.038.

Zhukovsky, P., Puaud, M., Jupp, B., Sala-Bayo, J., Alsiö, J., Xia, J., Dalley, J.W., 2019. Withdrawal from escalated cocaine self-administration impairs reversal learning by disrupting the effects of negative feedback on reward exploitation: a behavioral and computational analysis. Neuropsychopharmacology 44 (13), 2163–2173. https://doi.org/10.1038/s41386-019-0381-0.

Zijlstra, F., Veltman, D.J., Booij, J., van den Brink, W., Franken, I.H., 2009. Neurobiological substrates of cue-elicited craving and anhedonia in recently abstinent opioid-dependent males. Drug Alcohol Depend. 99 (1–3), 183–192. https://doi.org/10.1016/j.drugalcdep.2008.07.012.

Zilverstand, A., Huang, A.S., Alia-Klein, N., Goldstein, R.Z., 2018. Neuroimaging impaired response inhibition and salience attribution in human drug addiction: a systematic review. Neuron 98 (5), 886–903. https://doi.org/10.1016/j.neuron.2018.03.048.

CHAPTER

5

Insular Cortical circuits

Christine Ibrahim[a,b] *and Bernard Le Foll*[a,b,c,d,e,f,g]

[a]Translational Addiction Research Laboratory, Centre for Addiction and Mental Health, Toronto, ON, Canada; [b]Department of Pharmacology and Toxicology, Faculty of Medicine, University of Toronto, Toronto, ON, Canada; [c]Addictions Division, Centre for Addiction and Mental Health, Toronto, ON, Canada; [d]Campbell Family Mental Health Research Institute, Centre for Addiction and Mental Health, Toronto, ON, Canada; [e]Department of Psychiatry, Faculty of Medicine, University of Toronto, Toronto, ON, Canada; [f]Institute of Medical Sciences, University of Toronto, Toronto, ON, Canada; [g]Department of Family and Community Medicine, University of Toronto, Toronto, ON, Canada

In this chapter, we will discuss the insula and insular brain circuits that pertain to drug addiction. We will begin with an overview of the insula and its functions, as well as its link with other brain areas involved in addiction. We will also present a large body of preclinical and clinical evidence implicating the insula in addiction to substances such as nicotine, alcohol, amphetamines and more, citing studies ranging from lesion research to neuroimaging research to brain stimulation research. It should be noted that this chapter is an extension of a previously published review paper by our group (Ibrahim, Rubin-Kahana et al., 2019), as such we have included work from the paper along with new advancements in this research area since the time of that publication.

Insula neuroanatomy and structure

The insula, also known as the insular cortex, Island of Reil or insular lobe, is part of the cerebral cortex. In humans, it is located deep within the lateral sulcus and can be accessed anatomically by removing the opercula that covers it. Previous reviews have covered in detail the neuro-anatomy and cellular structure of the insula (Augustine, 1996; Nieuwenhuys, 2012) and we will summarize here the main findings (Naidich et al., 2004; Türe et al., 1999). Studies performed in primates (non-humans and humans) describe three subregions: a rostro-ventral (anterior insular cortex, aIC) agranular area, a caudo-dorsal (posterior insular cortex, pIC) granular area and an intermediate dysgranular area (in between aIC and pIC). As with other

Neurocircuitry of Addiction
https://doi.org/10.1016/B978-0-12-823453-2.00005-9

cortical areas, the insular cortex presents multiple layers. The presence (granular) or absence (agranular) of granular cells in the layer IV is the reason of the classification of aIC and pIC, while the term dysgranular is due to the moderate presence of those granular cells in layer IV in the intermediate area. Many studies have been performed in non-human primates and it is usually agreed that there is good analogy between insular cortex anatomy in human and non-human primates (the reader is referred to the review the following review (Nieuwenhuys, 2012) that discuss the anatomical results obtained in various primate species). However, it should be noted that there is large variability in the morphology of the insula between mammal species. Most studies have been performed in rodents and non-human primates. Early work from Broadmann reported on the anatomy of the insular cortex in various species. In addition, more recently, some description of the anatomy of the insula has been reported in other species such as walrus, hippopotamus, beluga whales and the Florida manatee (Butti and Hof, 2010). Interestingly, it has been described in advanced species (like non-human primates, humans) that the layer V of the aIC contains some large spindled-shaped cells, which have been described as von Economo neurons (Allman et al., 2011).

The insular cortex has numerous connections with various parts of the brain. The majority of the afferent fibers come from the dorsal thalamus and from sensory cortical areas (Nieuwenhuys, 2012). The insular cortex also has bidirectional connections with the orbitofrontal cortex (OFC), anterior cingulate cortex (ACC), supplementary motor areas, primary and secondary somatosensory areas, temporal cortices, amygdala, globus pallidus and thalamus. There are also local intra-insular connections. There are fibers projecting from the insular cortex to the premotor cortex and the ventral striatum (Friedman et al., 1986). The connections are further characterized based on the two parts of the insula, whereby the aIC has more connectivity to the frontal lobe and the pIC has more connectivity to the parietal lobe (Gasquoine, 2014). More specifically, the aIC sends projections to the caudate-putamen, nucleus accumbens (NAcc) and extended amygdala (McDonald et al., 1999; McGeorge and Faull, 1989; Shi and Cassell, 1998b; Wright and Groenewegen, 1996), but also has mutual connections with the basolateral amygdala (BLA) and the prelimbic cortex (Gerfen and Clavier, 1979; Saper, 1982; Vertes, 2004). The aIC in turn also receives connections from the medial subdivision of the mediodorsal thalamic nucleus and other medial thalamic nuclei (Krettek and Price, 1977; Van der Werf et al., 2002). On the other hand, the pIC sends projections to the caudate-putamen, thalamus and somatosensory cortex (Shi and Cassell, 1998a) and receives general viscerosensory unimodal inputs (Cechetto and Saper, 1987), nociceptive thalamic inputs (Gauriau and Bernard, 2004) and somatosensory cortex inputs. In addition, the areas that the insula has connectivity to have been shown to be circuits implicated in addiction (Fig. 5.1) (Strang et al., 2020). It has been proposed that there are three stages of addiction: binge/intoxication, negative affect/withdrawal, and preoccupation/anticipation. Each stage is associated with plasticity in specific neural circuits.

Afferent projections to the insular cortex have been summarized by Nieuwenhuys (2012). Understanding these projections allow the understanding of the various functions that get integrated by the insula. We will summarize the main findings as synthetized previously (Nieuwenhuys, 2012):

- The vestibular nuclear complex projects to various thalamic nuclei (ventral posterior superior nucleus and the ventral posterior inferior nucleus) and then projects to a

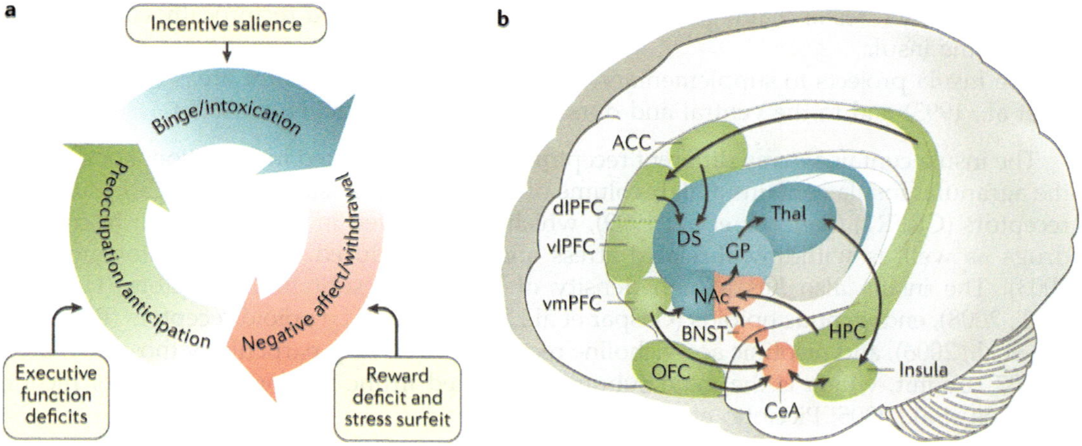

FIGURE 5.1 (A) The three-stage cycle of addiction (B) The brain circuits involved in each stage of the cycle of addiction. The binge/intoxication stage is mediated by the basal ganglia and nucleus accumbens (NAc). The negative affect/withdrawal stage is mediated by the extended amygdala. The preoccupation/anticipation stage is mediated by the prefrontal cortex (PFC). The insula is implicated in all three stages. *ACC*, anterior cingulate cortex; *BNST*, bed nucleus of the stria terminalis; *CeA*, central nucleus of the amygdala; *dlPFC*, dorsolateral PFC; *DS*, dorsal striatum; *GP*, globus pallidus; *HPC*, hippocampus; *OFC*, orbitofrontal cortex; *Thal*, thalamus; *vlPFC*, ventrolateral PFC; *vmPFC*, ventromedial PFC. *Image from Strang et al., 2020.*

posterosuperior part of the insula, which is part of the *parietoinsular vestibular cortex* (Büttner-Ennever and Gerrits, 2004).

- Nociceptive and thermoreceptive spinothalamic lamina I neurons (Craig et al., 1994) project to the posterosuperior part of the insular cortex, which can be designated as the *insular nociceptive and thermoreceptive cortex* (Brooks et al., 2005).
- Gustatory projections from the nucleus of the solitary tract project through the parvocellular part of the ventral posteromedial nucleus of the thalamus to the granular anterosuperior part of the insula (designated as a part of the *primary gustatory cortex*), which projects to the dysgranular insular cortex (which is designated as the *secondary gustatory cortex*).
- Visceral information from the caudal part of the nucleus of the solitary tract projects through the lateral part of the parvocellular part of the ventral posteromedial nucleus of the thalamus to an area of the insular cortex that is located posterior to the gustatory areas. This area is known as the insular viscerosensory cortex (IVSC). This area receives input from gastrointestinal, respiratory or cardiovascular (Saper, 2002).
- An anterior zone of the insula receives projections from olfactory, gustatory cortices and from the primary viscerosensory insular cortex. This zone processes information about food-related stimuli (Carmichael and Price, 1996).
- The posteriosuperior portion of the insula has been called the *insular somatic association cortex,* receiving input from somatosensory, primary vestibular areas and auditory association areas.
- Some high-order association areas, such as area 11 of anterior orbitofrontal cortex and areas 45 and 46 of prefrontal cortex and polymodal association cortex in superior temporal sulcus are also connected with the insula (Seltzer and Pandya, 1991).

- Limbic structures and amygdaloid nuclei are importantly and reciprocally connected with the insula.
- The insula projects to supplementary and presupplementary motor areas (Luppino et al., 1993) and to the ventral and dorsal striatum (Chikama et al., 1997).

The insula contains many different receptors that are implicated in addiction. For example, the agranular insula contains a high volume of corticotropin-releasing factor (CRF) subtype 1 receptors (CRFR1) (Sánchez et al., 1999), which are involved in the motivation to consume drugs as well as withdrawal-related stress and stress-induced relapse (Contoreggi et al., 2003). The insula also has a high density of hypocretin subtype-1 receptors (Hollander et al., 2008), endogenous opioids (Gaspar et al., 1989), μ-subtype opioid receptors (Baumgärtner et al., 2006), and nicotinic acetylcholine receptors (nAChRs), particularly those containing the β2 subunit, which is the main subunit implicated in the reinforcing effects of nicotine (Maskos et al., 2005; Picciotto et al., 1998).

Functions of the insula

The insula is involved in a multitude of functions. Those functions have been reviewed previously (for example Augustine (1996), Nieuwenhuys (2012), and in a special issue of Brain Structure and Function edited by Craig (2010)). Here, we will present a short summary of those reviews:

Interoception

AD Craig has described the insula as a region crucial to interoception (Craig, 2002). He defined interoception as the integration of body signals and external stimuli to guide behavior towards or away from said stimuli with the goal of maintaining homeostasis. The current state of the body is accounted for by the pIC, which then sends information to the dysgranular insular cortex and thalamus, which integrate this information with information related to external stimuli (Craig, 2004). The current state of the body and environment is compared to previous states and environments by the aIC, leading to certain behaviors aimed at the maintenance of homeostasis.

Self-recognition

Neuroimaging studies indicate that the aIC along with the ACC is activated in humans when they recognize their own image. Authors suggest that these two regions could be involved in maintaining sense of self (see for review (Craig, 2009)).

Body awareness

Lesion of the insula can lead an individual to believe that their limbs do not belong to them, suggesting that the insula is critical for representation of body awareness (Karnath and Baier, 2010).

Emotions

The aIC is implicated in some aspects of emotional regulation such as fear, disgust, happiness and sadness (see Phan et al. (2002) for a review).

Taste

The insula was originally viewed as the area responsible for taste perception (Penfield and Faulk, 1955; Pritchard et al. 1999). This was demonstrated by studies in non-human primates (Bagshaw and Pribram, 1953). In humans, the gustatory center is located in the central part of the insula (Stephani et al., 2011) (see Rolls (2019) for a recent review).

Olfaction

The seminal studies of Penfield and Faulk had identified that electrical stimulation of the insula can produce olfactory sensations (Penfield and Faulk, 1955). Imaging studies indicate that the insula is activated by olfactory stimuli (Roy-Côté et al., 2021).

Viscero-sensation

We now know that the functions of the insula include not only taste perception, but also integration of visceral sensations from viscera (Allen et al., 1991; Cechetto and Saper, 1987). The seminal experiments from Penfield and Faulk indicated that electrical stimulation of the insula produced nausea and gastro-intestinal sensations (Penfield and Faulk, 1955). Sensory stimuli from the gut (e.g., rectal distension) also activates the insula and processes that may be dysfunctional in some gastroenterological diseases (see Nisticò et al. (2022) for a recent review of functional neuroimaging studies in irritable bowel syndrome).

Visceromotor control

Initial electrical stimulation studies by Penfield and Faulk and others showed that the insula could elicit gastro-intestinal symptoms as well as changes in cardiovascular and respiratory systems (Penfield and Faulk, 1955). Some of this central control is mediated by the parasympathetic and the sympatheric limbs of the autonomic nervous system. A recent study performed in male Sprague-Dawley rats used retrograde transneuronal transport of rabies virus to identify the cortical areas involved in controlling rat stomach function (Levinthal and Strick, 2020). Control of parasympathetic output to the stomach relies on the activity of neurons in the rostral insula and medical PFC (whereas sympathetic output is under control of neurons in primary and secondary motor cortex and primary somatosensory cortex) (Levinthal and Strick, 2020). Lesions of the insula has been associated with arrythmia, diurnal blood pressure variation disruption and myocardial injury (Nagai et al., 2010; Ruggiero et al., 1987).

Somatosensory functions

In nonhuman primates, neurons in the granular part of the insula get activated by cutaneous stimulation (Schneider et al., 1993). Similarly, in humans, an earlier PET study showed that tactile-vibration stimuli activates the insular cortex (Burton et al., 1993).

Auditory functions

Functional imaging studies have implicated the insula in auditory functions. The insula appears to allow one to pay attention to novel auditory stimuli. Lesioning of the insula may also produce auditory agnosia (see Bamiou et al. (2003) for a review).

Vestibular functions

Vestibular stimuli activates parieto-insular vestibular cortex (Grüsser et al., 1990a, b). The insular cortex has long been described as a vestibular area, initially due to its connection with the vestibular thalamic relay nucleus in non-human primates (Augustine, 1985). The insula is involved in perception of verticality and is involved in some vestibular balance problems (Dieterich and Brandt, 2019).

Pain

Lesions involving the insula may modulate pain perception (Birklein et al., 2005). Imaging studies clearly implicate the insula in pain processes (Wager et al., 2013). The posterior insula is activated by pain and there is correlation of this activation with pain intensity (Segerdahl et al., 2015). Various imaging studies have shown that pain is associated with increased activity of the insular cortex. Electrical stimulation of the insula in humans can also induce pain or affect pain threshold (Mazzola et al., 2009; Mazzola et al., 2012).

Temperature perception

Lesions involving the insula eliminated contralateral cold perception (Birklein et al., 2005). Thermal stimuli activates the dorsal posterior insular cortex in humans (Hua et al., 2005).

Somatomotor control

Hand and foot motor tasks activate the insular cortex (Mutschler et al., 2009).

Speech

The insula is one of the brain areas that is involved in speech motor control (Bohland and Guenther, 2006).

Cognition

The insula is involved in a variety of cognitive tasks. The aIC is the subregion of the insula most commonly found to be activated during auditory, visual and task-free condition cognitive tasks (Uddin et al., 2017). Insula lesion studies have demonstrated the importance of this brain region in recognizing pleasant and unpleasant emotions during a social cognition task (Lerner et al., 2015). More generally, researchers have defined a cognitive control network in the brain that is composed of the aIC along with the ACC, pre-supplementary motor area, dorsal lateral prefrontal cortex (dlPFC), inferior frontal junction, posterior parietal cortex (PPC) and dorsal pre-motor cortex (Cole and Schneider, 2007).

Empathy and compassion

The insula plays a critical part in empathy and compassion and appears to be involved in various social emotions (Lamm and Singer, 2010).

Decision making and gambling

The insula is important for decision-making processes (Droutman et al., 2015). It is also involved in evaluating the value of reward and risk. It seems that agranular and granular cortex have different roles in choice behavior, as assessed by rodent gambling tasks (Pushparaj, Kim, Musiol, Zangen, et al., 2015). In humans, the insula is evidently activated by anticipation and delivery of monetary reward (Jauhar et al., 2021).

Addiction

A large number of studies have implicated the insula in addiction and those studies will be reviewed in the next section.

Evidence implicating the insula in addiction

Evidence will be presented in the sections below regarding the insula and its involvement in addiction. It will be evident that the insula does not work alone. In fact, there are currently three well established intrinsic networks in the addiction field. There is the default mode network (DMN) comprised of the vmPFC and the posterior cingulate cortex (PCC), the executive control network (ECN) comprised of the dlPFC and PPC, and the salience network (SN) comprised of the aIC and ACC. Each network has been proposed to have a different role in addiction. The DMN is active when a person is not concentrating on external tasks (e.g., daydreaming), in terms of addiction it is active during rumination of drug use. Meanwhile, the ECN is active when a person is focusing on external tasks that demand cognitive functioning. The SN works as a bridge between the two, it dynamically switches between the two networks after detection of a relevant stimulation or condition (Menon and Uddin, 2010). One group of researchers proposed an explanation to understand how these networks work in addictions using nicotine as the substance of abuse. They explained that under conditions of nicotine deprivation (i.e., abstinence), the SN would switch to DNM, thereby directing the individuals' attention towards internal withdrawal symptoms. Under nicotine administration, the SN would switch to the ECN causing the attention to be directed towards external stimuli and executive functions (Lerman et al., 2014; Sutherland et al., 2012; Sutherland and Stein, 2018). Therefore, if the SN (which includes the insula) was not functioning this would affect both the DMN and ECN, thus affecting a number of brain functions including addiction.

The section below provides evidence of the involvement of the insula and its related circuits in addiction. We have separated the evidence by substance of abuse and present both preclinical and clinical studies. With preclinical studies, researchers usually target the anterior agranular subregion (aAgIC) or posterior granular subregion (pGIC). Targeting the dysgranular subregion is more complex and is not often done due to difficulty precisely targeting it with local infusion. We also present clinical data based on lesion, neuroimaging, and brain stimulation studies, that implicates the insula in various drug addictions. A summary of functional connectivity studies is provided in Table 5.1.

Nicotine

The majority of research on the insula and addiction tends to focus on nicotine. Noncontingent nicotine exposure (2 mg kg^{-1} day for two weeks administered by experimenter) in male Long Evans rats increases dendritic complexity, both in terms of length and bifurcations, in the aAgIC (Ehlinger et al., 2012). In addition, noncontingent nicotine pyrrolidine methiodide administration (30 μg kg^{-1}) in CD-1 mice resulted in increases in c-Fos immunoreactivity (a marker for neuronal activity) of the aAgIC and other areas involved in brain reward circuitry such as the hypothalamus, amygdala, hippocampus, nucleus accumbens and medial prefrontal cortex (Dehkordi et al., 2015). Lesioning the aIC in male C57BL/6J mice disrupted the acquisition of nicotine-induced conditioned place preference (CPP), and this was specific to nicotine as food was not affected (Scott and Hiroi, 2011), but it had no effect on avoidance of withdrawal associated cues in conditioned place aversion (CPA), whereas inactivation of the orbitofrontal cortex did affect withdrawal (and not craving). Furthermore, our laboratory showed that chemical inactivation of the aAgIC or pGIC significantly decreases nicotine (30 μg kg^{-1} infusion) taking and seeking in male Long Evans rats (Forget et al., 2010; Pushparaj, Kim, Musiol, Trigo, et al., 2015). Our laboratory also found the same decrease when electrically inactivating the pGIC in male Long Evans rats (Pushparaj et al., 2013). Of importance, food intake was not affected by the inactivation, thus showing once again that it is specific to nicotine. Blockade of hypocretin-1 receptors in the pGIC attenuates nicotine self-administration (0.03 mg kg^{-1} per infusion) and motivation to acquire nicotine in male Wistar rats, as well as the stimulatory effects of nicotine on brain reward circuits, but these effects were not observed after blockade of these receptors in the somatosensory cortex, suggesting these effects are brain region-specific (Hollander et al., 2008). Similarly, blocking dopamine D1 receptors (not D2) receptors in the aAgIC resulted in a more than 50% decrease in nicotine self-administration (0.03 mg kg^{-1} infusion) in female Sprague-Dawley rats (Kutlu et al., 2013). Of note, it has also been observed that food intake is affected by high doses of D1 antagonists (Di Pietro et al., 2008). The incubation (defined as an increase in drug seeking after a period of abstinence) of nicotine seeking after 7 days of abstinence compared to 1 day of abstinence was found to lead to higher levels of dopamine and cyclic adenosine monophosphate-regulated phosphoprotein of 32 kDa (this phosphoprotein is enriched in dopamine neurons that contain D1 receptors) in both the aAgIC and pGIC in male Sprague Dawley rats (Abdolahi et al., 2010). Interestingly, a group sought to investigate if brain connectivity is a predictor of nicotine dependence severity. They found that in male Sprague Dawley rats the strength of the insular-frontal connectivity prior to any nicotine

TABLE 5.1 Summary of functional connectivity neuroimaging studies

Reference	Substance	Sample size	Design	Results
Fedota et al. (2016)	Nicotine	$N = 35$ smokers $N = 21$ non-smokers	rsFC	- ↓ connectivity: right aIC and right superior frontal gyrus
Zhou et al. (2017)	Nicotine	$N = 37$ smokers $N = 37$ non-smokers	rsFC	- ↓ connectivity: insula, superior frontal gyrus, OFC and temporal lobe - Positive correlation between insula, OFC, temporal lobe and inferior parietal cortex with FTND scores - Negative correlation between insula and ACC with FTND scores
Faulkner et al. (2019)	Nicotine	$N = 21$ smokers	Nicotine administration rsFC	- High nicotine (0.763 mg) led to ↓ connectivity: aIC and ACC
Bi et al. (2017)	Nicotine	$N = 33$ smokers	rsFC	- Abstinence led to ↑ connectivity: right aIC, right OFC and vmPFC; aIC and ACC
Huang et al. (2014)	Nicotine	$N = 11$ smokers $N = 10$ non-smokers	rsFC	- Abstinence led to ↑ connectivity: insula and ACC
Fedota et al. (2018)	Nicotine	$N = 20$ smokers	rsFC	- Abstinence led to ↑ connectivity: pIC and dorsal insula to the DMN and SN; ↓ connectivity: ventral insula and ECN - Positive correlation during satiety with connectivity between pIC and SN with certain subscales of withdrawal - Negative correlation during abstinence with connectivity between ventral insula and ECN with craving
Li, Yang et al. (2017)	Nicotine	$N = 66$ smokers $N = 92$ non-smokers	rsFC	- Slow metabolizers of CYP2A6 have ↓ connectivity between dorsal ACC and ventral striatum driven by insula
Perry et al. (2019)	Nicotine	$N = 26$ smokers	Nicotine administration rsFC	- Actual nicotine led to ↓ connectivity: aIC and dorsal ACC; aIC and NAcc - Perceived nicotine led to ↑ connectivity: insula and dorsal ACC - Withdrawal and craving associated with connectivity between insula and NAcc
Wei et al. (2016)	Nicotine	$N = 21$ smokers	rsFC	- Risky decision making correlated with ↑ connectivity: aIC dorsal ACC; left and right aIC

(*Continued*)

TABLE 5.1 Summary of functional connectivity neuroimaging studies—cont'd

Reference	Substance	Sample size	Design	Results
Sutherland, Carroll, Salmeron, Ross, and Stein (2013)	Nicotine	$N = 24$ smokers $N = 20$ non-smokers	rsFC	- Alexithymia in smokers correlated with ↓ connectivity: right aIC and vmPFC. This correlated with increased craving after abstinence
Addicott et al. (2015)	Nicotine	$N = 41$ relapsed smokers $N = 44$ non-relapsed smokers	rsFC	- Relapsed smokers had ↓ connectivity: insula and primary sensorimotor cortices
Janes et al. (2010)	Nicotine	$N = 9$ relapsed smoker $N = 12$ non-relapsed smoker	rsFC	- Relapsed smokers had ↓ connectivity: insula, dlPFC and dorsal ACC
Wang, Shen et al. (2020)	Nicotine	$N = 16$ quitters $N = 14$ relapsed smokers	rsFC	- Quitters had ↑ connectivity: aIC, left precuneus, and medial frontal gyrus - Relapsed smokers had ↓ connectivity
Janes et al. (2020)	Nicotine	$N = 36$ smokers	rsFC Cue reactivity fMRI	- Craving correlated with ↑ rsFC: ventral aIC to rostral ACC, medial PFC, superior parietal lobule and agranular gyrus - Smoking cues ↑ activation in dorsal aIC
Claus et al. (2013)	Nicotine	$N = 116$ smokers	Cue reactivity fMRI	- Smoking cues led to ↑ connectivity: left insula, right insula, somatosensory cortex, OFC, and striatum - Connectivity correlated with FTND scores
Janes et al. (2015)	Nicotine	$N = 18$ smokers	Memory retrieval fMRI	- Smoking cues led to ↑ activation: left insula and inferior frontal gyrus
Moran-Santa Maria et al. (2015)	Nicotine	$N = 63$ smokers	Cue reactivity fMRI	- Smokers with increased craving when viewing smoking cues had ↑ connectivity: right aIC and precuneus
Stippekohl et al. (2012)	Nicotine	$N = 16$ content smokers $N = 16$ discontent smokers	Cue reactivity fMRI	- Discontent smokers when viewing smoking initiation cues had ↑ activation: insula, amygdala, and left hippocampus

TABLE 5.1 Summary of functional connectivity neuroimaging studies—cont'd

Reference	Substance	Sample size	Design	Results
Kim et al. (2020)	Nicotine	$N = 30$ smokers $N = 30$ non-smokers	Cue reactivity Mental simulation fMRI	- Smokers during smoking mental simulation had ↑ connectivity: insula, PCC, and rostro-lateral PFC
Moran et al. (2018)	Nicotine	$N = 11$ non-smokers	Nicotine administration Monetary delay task fMRI	- Nicotine patch when viewing reward/loss cues led to ↑ activation: right aIC and striatal regions
Wang, Zegel et al. (2020)	Nicotine	$N = 18$ non-smokers	Nicotine administration Reward task fMRI	- Acute nicotine administration led to ↑ activation during monetary reward anticipation: NAcc - ↓ activation to outcome: insula, ACC, and OFC
Gilman et al. (2018)	Nicotine	$N = 22$ smokers $N = 19$ non-smokers	Go/No Go task fMRI	- Inhibition task led to ↑ activation: insula
Lesage et al. (2020)	Nicotine	$N = 24$ smokers $N = 20$ non-smokers	Go/No Go task fMRI	- Inhibition task led to ↑ activity in the SN, presupplementary motor areas, striatum and thalamus
Sullivan et al. (2013)	Alcohol	$N = 12$ alcohol users $N = 12$ non-users	Cerebral blood flow	- ↓ connectivity: SN - ↓ blood flow to insula
Gorka et al. (2018)	Alcohol	$N = 39$ regular binge drinkers	Alcohol administration fMRI	- Alcohol administration led to ↓ connectivity: SN - ↓connectivity correlated with feelings of calmness
Ihssen et al. (2011)	Alcohol	$N = 12$ light drinkers $N = 11$ heavy drinkers	Cue reactivity fMRI	- Heavy drinkers when viewing alcohol cues had ↑ BOLD: left insula and ventral striatum
Wisner et al. (2013)	Cocaine	$N = 33$ cocaine users $N = 32$ non-users	rsFC	- ↑ connectivity: aIC and ACC - ↓ connectivity: SN and striatum; correlated with greater impulsivity but not craving
Geng et al. (2017)	Cocaine	$N = 64$ cocaine users $N = 67$ non-users	rsFC	- ↓ connectivity: right insula, left insula and ACC

(*Continued*)

TABLE 5.1 Summary of functional connectivity neuroimaging studies—cont'd

Reference	Substance	Sample size	Design	Results
McHugh et al. (2013)	Cocaine	$N = 45$ cocaine users $N = 22$ non-users	rsFC	- Relapsed users had ↑ connectivity: pIC and bilateral putamen
Hanlon et al. (2017)	Cocaine, nicotine, alcohol	$N = 45$ cocaine users $N = 48$ nicotine users $N = 53$ alcohol users	Cue reactivity fMRI	- Substance cues led to ↑ activity: insula and left inferior frontal gyrus; right premotor cortex; and medial PFC and ACC - Not affected by type of substance
Stewart et al. (2017)	Cocaine amphetamine	$N = 184$ occasional stimulant users	Decision making task fMRI	- During a decision-making task, users that developed substance use disorder had baseline ↑ activation: insula, ACC, superior temporal, precuneus, inferior parietal and cerebellum
Stewart et al. (2014)	Methamphetamine	$N = 42$ abstinent users $N = 18$ relapsed users	Reinforcement learning task fMRI	- Relapsed users during a reinforcement learning task had ↓ activation: insula, striatum, left ACC and left inferior frontal gyrus
Gowin et al. (2015)	Methamphetamine	$N = 50$ abstinent users $N = 18$ relapsed users	Reward processing fMRI	- Successful abstinent users during reward processing for large/risky rewards had ↑ activation: left aIC and right striatum - No difference in reward type for relapsed users
Langenecker et al. (2020)	Amphetamine	$N = 73$ non-users	Amphetamine administration Monetary reward task fMRI	- Liking d-amphetamine associated with ↓ activation: insula and caudate putamen and ↑ activation: amygdala
Shollenbarger et al. (2019)	Cannabis	$N = 79$ cannabis users $N = 80$ non-users	rsFC	- Users had ↑ connectivity: left insula, left rostral ACC, right rostral ACC, and left amygdala
Koenis et al. (2020)	Cannabis	$N = 57$ cannabis users	rsFC	- Users had ↓ connectivity: right insula and superior parietal gyrus - Controlling for nicotine use made findings no longer significant

TABLE 5.1 Summary of functional connectivity neuroimaging studies—cont'd

Reference	Substance	Sample size	Design	Results
Filbey et al. (2009)	Cannabis	$N = 38$ cannabis users	Cue reactivity fMRI	- Abstinence when viewing cannabis cues led to ↑ activation: insula, amygdala, ACC, thalamus and VTA
Kleinhans et al. (2020)	Cannabis	$N = 28$ cannabis users	Cue reactivity fMRI	- Those at risk of developing cannabis use disorder had ↑ activation: insula, VTA, and pallidum - Cannabis odor cues led to ↑ activation: aIC, NAcc, putamen, pallidum, supplementary motor area, angular gyrus and superior frontal gyrus

administration (1.2 mg kg^{-1} day or 4.8 mg kg^{-1} day) predicted nicotine dependence severity (Hsu et al., 2019). Thereby demonstrating that some individuals may be more at risk of nicotine dependence.

An even larger amount of evidence exists in the clinical research linking the insula to nicotine. Although research had been done prior, it was not until 2007 that people really started to see the implication of the insula in addiction. Naqvi and colleagues found that smokers who suffered damage to the insula were more likely to undergo a smoking disruption than those with damage elsewhere (Naqvi et al., 2007). They defined a disruption of smoking as someone who quit smoking easily, quickly (less than 1 day after the lesion), without relapse and without any urge to smoke since quitting. Others began to look into this as well and found that damage to the insula predicts smoking cessation and increases the probability of quitting by five times (Suñer-Soler et al., 2012). It also was associated with full abstinence of all nicotine products (e.g., other forms of tobacco, nicotine replacement therapy) (Abdolahi et al., 2015b), less frequent and severe withdrawal symptoms (Abdolahi et al., 2015a), and less smoking urges (Abdolahi et al., 2017). In quitters who did relapse, those that had damage to the insula were more likely to remain abstinent for longer periods than those with damage elsewhere (Abdolahi et al., 2015b). Some differences have been found when investigating left versus right insular damage. Those with left insular damage were found to have more decreases in acute urges to smoke and less withdrawal symptoms than those with right insula damage. However, no differences were found in chronic changes (Abdolahi et al., 2019). In addition, it has been found that damage to the basal ganglia also increases rates of smoking cessation, but when that damage also included the insula, it led to an even higher percentage of smoking abstinence (Gaznick et al., 2014). However, one group of researchers in Poland found no relationship between damage to the insula and smoking cessation (Bienkowski et al., 2010). It has been suggested that this difference in findings may be due to the location of where the study took place, since the harmful effects of smoking are not recognized as well in Poland (Naqvi et al., 2014).

These lesions studies led the way to further research investigating the role of the insula in addiction using neuroimaging. Researchers have found that cortical thickness and gray matter density of the insula is significantly decreased in smokers compared to non-smokers

(Fritz et al., 2014; Hanlon et al., 2016; Li et al., 2015; Stoeckel et al., 2016). A meta-analysis using 761 smokers and 1182 non-smokers demonstrated that smoking was linked with decreased gray matter in the left insula, cerebellum, PFC, thalamus and parahippocampus. They also found that the left insula showed co-activation with the right insula, posterior medial PFC, ACC, thalamus, parietal cortex and cerebellum (Sutherland et al., 2016). The general consensus is that smoking is associated with decreased gray matter density, yet one study showed that smokers actually have increased gray matter density in the left insula (Zhang et al., 2011). Another study found that although smokers compared to non-smokers had decreased gray matter in the insula, precuneus, superior temporal gyrus, inferior and middle frontal gyrus, cerebellum and anterior lobe, those who had severe nicotine dependence had less of a decrease in gray matter than those with moderate nicotine dependence (Peng et al., 2018). However, others have found no difference in structural changes to the insula between smokers who quit, smokers who relapsed and non-smokers (Wang et al., 2019). It has been suggested these structural changes may be due to chronic exposure to smoking since young smokers were found to have no difference in insula thickness compared to non-smokers (Morales et al., 2014). Whereas, older smokers had more evident changes in insular density than younger smokers (Hanlon et al., 2016). In addition, there is evidence of correlations between measures of smoking and gray matter density of the insula, whereby the density is negatively correlated with daily cigarettes smoked (Stoeckel et al., 2016), pack year smoking (Morales et al., 2014) and Fagerström Test for Nicotine Dependence (FTND) scores (a measure widely used to assess nicotine dependence severity) (Wang et al., 2019). With regards to white matter, smokers compared to non-smokers were found to have decreased fractional anisotropy (measure of white matter integrity) between the aIC to NAcc and the pIC to NAcc. They also had lower axial diffusivity, radial diffusivity, and mean diffusivity, which are all measures of white matter integrity, between the aIC to medial OFC, pIC to medial OFC and pIC to NAcc. However, no difference was found between smokers who relapsed after a 12-week course of treatment of varenicline compared to those who did not relapse (Wang, Wang et al., 2020).

Functional imaging, such as the resting state functional connectivity (rsFC), provide researchers important information about the neurocircuitry of addiction. This method uses a resting state (i.e., no tasks being administered) to measure the activity between brain regions. Many of these studies have implicated the insula as part of a circuit in addiction. There is decreased rsFC between the right aIC and the right superior frontal gyrus in smokers. This alludes to decreased rsFC between the SN and the ECN since both of these regions are part of the two large scale brain networks (Fedota et al., 2016). Smokers were also found to have decreased rsFC between the insula and the OFC, temporal lobe and superior frontal gyrus as compared to non-smokers (Zhou et al., 2017). The region of the insula also presents different connectivity. In smokers who recently smoked, the ventral aIC had connectivity to the DMN and the dorsal aIC had connectivity to the frontoparietal network. In addition, craving at baseline was correlated with increased ventral aIC connectivity to the midline rostral ACC, medial PFC, superior parietal lobule and agranular gyrus (Janes et al., 2020). Interestingly, one group administered cigarettes to smokers of different nicotine amounts (0.027−0.763 mg) and found that only the high nicotine cigarette (0.763 mg) led to a decrease in connectivity between aIC and ACC. Although cigarettes typically have higher amount than that of nicotine, thereby leading to the decreased connectivity, this study demonstrates that lower doses of nicotine may aid in alleviating this altered connectivity (Faulkner et al., 2019). Moreover, a 12-hour abstinence led to an increase in rsFC between the right aIC, right OFC, vmPFC and within the SN (Bi et al., 2017). Similarly, another group found that smokers who abstained from smoking for 11 h had an increased rsFC between the insula and ACC when compared to when they were in a satiated state (Huang et al., 2014). After 48 h of abstinence from smoking, blood oxygenation level-dependent (BOLD) imaging indicated that the overall rsFC decreased after abstinence. However, the posterior and dorsal insula connections were increased to the DMN and SN, while the ventral insula and ECN connection was decreased (Fedota et al., 2018). Evidence from a meta-analysis demonstrated that for smokers, administration of a nAChR agonist or smoking a cigarette was associated with a decrease in activity between the insula, vmPFC, and PCC (regions associated with the SN and DMN), but was associated with an increase in activity in the thalamus, cuneus, dorsal ACC and lateral PFC (regions associated with the ECN) (Sutherland et al., 2015). In addition, we know that there are genetic variations that can affect the rate of nicotine metabolism such as *CYP2A6*. Researchers have found that smokers that are slow metabolizers of *CYP2A6* have a decreased connection between the dorsal ACC and the ventral striatum and that this is driven by the insula (Li, Yang et al., 2017). This is interesting as it alludes to the many layers and depth of factors that affect the connectivity of the insula and other brain regions in smokers. Furthermore, one group demonstrated the importance between actual and perceived nicotine administration (Perry et al., 2019). Actual nicotine administration in smokers led to decreased connectivity between the aIC and dorsal ACC, as well as between the aIC and NAcc. However, perceived nicotine administration (i.e., using a nicotine-free inhaler) increased connectivity between the insula and dorsal ACC. Withdrawal and craving were also found to be associated with the connectivity between the insula and NAcc (Perry et al., 2019).

Correlations between rsFC and nicotine measures have also been demonstrated, whereby rsFC between the insula, OFC, temporal lobe, inferior parietal cortex, and occipital lobe were positively correlated with FTND scores, while the rsFC between the insula and ACC were negatively correlated with FTND scores (Zhou et al., 2017). Correlations have also been reported between aversive affect and withdrawal symptoms and the rsFC of the posterior and ventral insula circuits with the ECN and SN (Fedota et al., 2018). More specifically, when sated there was a positive correlation between the pIC and SN with the sadness and anger subscale of the Wisconsin Withdrawal Scale (WSWS). During abstinence, there was a negative correlation between the ventral insula and ECN with the craving subscale of the WSWS (Fedota et al., 2018). One group looked to see the effect of risky decision making in smokers, since this is associated with increased nicotine dependence, and found that it was associated with an increased rsFC between the aIC and dorsal ACC and between the left and right aIC (Wei et al., 2016). Furthermore, smokers with alexithymia (a personality trait whereby a person has trouble identifying and explaining emotional experiences) tend to have decreased rsFC between the right aIC and vmPFC. This decreased rsFC then in turn predicted increased craving following an overnight abstinence (Sutherland, Carroll, Salmeron, Ross and Stein, 2013). Research has also been done with regards to relapse, whereby relapsed smokers compared to non-relapsed smokers were found to have decreased connectivity between the insula and primary sensorimotor cortices (Addicott et al., 2015), as well as between the insula, dlPFC and dorsal ACC (Janes et al., 2010). Thereby suggesting that this decreased connectivity could be a predictor of relapse. Others have also found similar findings such that successful quitters in a treatment study had increased connectivity between the aIC and left precuneus and medial frontal gyrus after treatment, while those who relapsed had decreased connectivity (Wang, Shen et al., 2020). Sutherland and Stein proposed that insula centered circuits might represent a biomarker for acute withdrawal (Sutherland and Stein, 2018). For instance, abstinent smokers had increased connectivity between the insula and amygdala (a connection underlying negative affect) (Koob and Le Moal, 2005; Koob and Volkow, 2010), but when nicotine or varenicline (smoking cessation medication) were administered the connectivity decreased (Sutherland, Carroll, Salmeron, Ross, Hong, et al., 2013).

Although resting state studies provide insightful information about what occurs under a neutral setting, non-resting state studies also allow researchers to gain valuable knowledge when participants are undergoing tasks. For instance, when smokers were presented with smoking cues and food cues, the smoking cues led to increased connectivity between the left insula and the right insula, somatosensory cortex, OFC, and striatum (Claus et al., 2013). This connectivity was also correlated with nicotine dependence severity as measured by FTND scores. When a memory retrieval task using smoking and neutral cues was administered to smokers, it showed that when smoking cues were present the left insula and inferior frontal gyrus were significantly more active (Janes et al., 2015). Craving was also reported when viewing the smoking cues, thus suggesting the insula's activation in craving. In another study, smokers with higher craving ratings had increased connectivity between the right aIC and the precuneus when presented with smoking cues as compared to neutral cues (Moran-Santa Maria et al., 2015). Both these regions are recognized as having a role in self-awareness and interoception. The specific region of the aIC also have different activations to smoking cues, whereby the dorsal aIC compared to the ventral aIC showed increased connectivity when smokers were presented smoking cues (Janes et al., 2020). Numerous studies have been done using smoking cue reactivity tasks combined with functional magnetic resonance imaging (fMRI). This is a non-invasive imaging technique widely used to indirectly measure brain activity via direct measurement of changes in brain region-specific blood flow. The most common form of fMRI is done with blood-oxygen-level dependent (BOLD) contrast. The magnetic properties of oxygenated and deoxygenated blood are different and therefore can be detected with fMRI. After neuronal activation, blood oxygenation levels increase and where that signal stems from in the brain can be mapped (Glover, 2011). This technique is particularly useful for cue-related tasks because it allows researchers to identify which brain areas are activated during exposure to a particular type of cue. A meta-analysis concluded that smoking cues compare to neutral cues do in fact lead to a larger fMRI response in the insula, precuneus, cingulate gyrus, extended visual system, dorsal striatum and medial PFC (Engelmann et al., 2012). The type of smoking cue, such as those relating to smoking-initiation (e.g., lighter) and those relating to smoking conclusion (e.g., cigarette butt in ashtray), evoke different fMRI responses when presented to smokers. This response is also different depending on if the smoker is content with drug taking or discontent. Research has shown that discontent smokers compared to content smokers had larger responses in the insula, amygdala and left hippocampus when viewing smoking initiation cues (Stippekohl et al., 2012). It has also been observed that the aIC is activated during intrinsic motivation as opposed to extrinsic motivation in healthy individuals (Lee and Reeve, 2013), thus potentially explaining this difference in activation with the smoking initiation cues. Not only do smoking cues lead to different activation patterns, but so does mentally simulating smoking hand movements. Research found that smokers compared to non-smokers had increased connectivity between the PCC, insula and rostro-lateral PFC during smoking mental simulation (Kim et al., 2020). One group of researchers conducted a study on non-smokers and gave them a nicotine patch or placebo patch. They found that the nicotine patch was associated with enhanced activation of the right aIC and striatal regions when presented with cues pertaining to rewards or losses (Moran et al., 2018). In another study using non-smokers, acute nicotine administration compared to placebo resulted in more NAcc activation to monetary reward anticipation, but decreased activation to the insula, ACC, OFC during outcome (Wang, Zegel et al., 2020). These studies are important as they demonstrate that an effect occurs even when there is acute nicotine exposure and not just with chronic smoking. Research on abstinent smokers undergoing an inhibitory control task found that there is greater activation in the aIC, thus a decrease in the activation of the insula leads to decreased inhibitory control (Gilman et al., 2018). A more recent study also found similar results showing that smokers undergoing an inhibition task (Go-No Go task) have increased activity in the SN, presupplementary motor areas, striatum and thalamus (Lesage et al., 2020). This is of importance because it could be an indicator of relapse.

Brain stimulation is a powerful tool that can allow researchers to investigate the role a brain region has on a particular matter. For addiction, this can be particularly useful, especially in the areas which we have a lot of evidence for their involvement in addiction. The challenge with targeting the insula with brain stimulation is that this was not possible up until recent years. The insula is more deeply embedded in the brain and the non-invasive brain stimulation techniques that were available only allowed for stimulation of surface areas (Ibrahim, Rubin-Kahana et al., 2019). However, with the advancement of technology we are now able to target the insula through deep repetitive transcranial magnetic stimulation (rTMS). Deep rTMS is a non-invasive technique that alters the magnetic fields of a targeted brain region in order to generate an electrical current (Barker et al., 1985). Individuals have a magnetic coil placed over their head, and upon stimulation, a discharge passes through the scalp, skull and meninges leading to the facilitation or suppression of neurons underneath the coil (Barker et al., 1985; Diana et al., 2017; Lefaucheur et al., 2014). This technique is currently approved by the FDA for the treatment of depression, obsessive compulsive disorder and most recently, for smoking cessation. Two studies to date have targeted the insula in smokers, which led to its FDA approval as a new smoking cessation treatment. In the first study, smokers received 13 sessions of high frequency (10 Hz), low frequency (1 Hz) or sham stimulation to the insula and PFC. Those receiving high frequency stimulation were found to have reduced cigarette consumption and nicotine dependence after treatment. Those receiving high frequency and had smoking cues presented during treatment had the most promising results with an abstinence rate of 44% at the end of treatment and 33% at the 6-month follow-up (Dinur-Klein et al., 2014). More recently, a multicenter, randomized, double-blind, sham-controlled trial was completed. Participants received 15 daily deep rTMS sessions to the insula and PFC of high-frequency active or sham stimulation after being presented with smoking cues. The primary end point was continuous quit rate (CQR), which they found to be 28.4% in those who received active stimulation compared to 11.7% in those who received sham stimulation (Zangen and George, 2020). Nonetheless, it is not possible to attribute all the affects to the insula alone since the PFC was stimulated as well in both studies. Interestingly, one group of researchers published preliminary results for a trial investigating the effects of deep rTMS targeting the insula and PFC, however the results were not as positive as the previous two studies. Out of the 45 participants who were randomized, 8 stopped smoking, 22 completed treatment but did not stop smoking, and the dropout rate was 31.8% (Bellini et al., 2020). However, these are preliminary results, and the study is still blinded, thus there is limited information available about the details of the study and findings. Meanwhile, our laboratory is currently running a trial testing a combined treatment approach for smoking cessation using deep rTMS to the insula (without the PFC) and varenicline. This will potentially provide more insight on the insula's role in smoking addiction.

From the evidence presented above, it is clear that brain regions do not work alone, but rather work in connection with other areas. Even with brain stimulation, the area stimulated may not be the only area affected due to secondary activations. Secondary activations can occur from neurotransmitter release or back propagation of action potentials originating from the initial site of stimulation (Diana et al., 2017). In fact, it may not just activate the networks associated specifically with the primary site, but could also have widespread activation (Gratton et al., 2013). Studies combining both brain stimulation and brain imaging are able to demonstrate this effect. One study examined the effect of rTMS to the insula on dopamine levels in healthy individuals. They found that low-frequency stimulation decreased dopamine levels in the sensorimotor striatum, associative striatum and substantia nigra (Malik et al., 2018). Researcher has also been done in addicted individuals, such that smokers who underwent one session of high frequency rTMS to the left dorsal PFC had inhibition of activity in the right insula and thalamus (measured by fractional amplitude of low-frequency fluctuation) (Li, Du et al., 2017). Thus, even when targeting one specific area, the effect can occur to numerous areas.

Alcohol

Alcohol exposure (1 g kg^{-1}) decreases neuronal activity, measured using c-Fos immunoreactivity, in aIC, medial prefrontal cortex (PFC), and rhomboid thalamic nucleus neurons, all of which project to the NAcc, of male Long Evans rats (Jaramillo et al., 2016). Anterior AgIC brain slices from *Drd1a*-tdTomato BAC transgenic adult mice (who were naïve to alcohol) revealed that bath-applied ethanol of different concentrations (20, 40, 60 mM) inhibits electrically evoked N-methyl-D-aspartate (NMDA) receptor-mediated excitatory post-synaptic currents, thus demonstrating that glutamatergic transmission in the aAgIC is affected by ethanol (Shillinglaw et al., 2018). Furthermore, long-term synaptic depression in the dorsolateral striatum (DLS) occurs exclusively at inputs from the aIC, which is disrupted by acute alcohol exposure (intraperitoneal injection, 2 g kg^{-1} ethanol) in male C57BL/6J mice (Muñoz et al., 2018). Inactivation studies have also been done and have shown that inactivation of the aAgIC and thalamic nucleus lead to a partial substitution for the discriminative stimulus effects of alcohol (1 g kg^{-1}) in male Long Evans rats, whereas inactivation of the medial prefrontal cortex leads to full substitution for the discriminative stimulus effects of alcohol (Jaramillo et al., 2016). Similarly, silencing of the aIC or the aIC projections to the NAcc via a chemogenic technique resulted in decreased sensitivity to the interoceptive effects of alcohol (1 g kg^{-1}) in male Long Evans rats (Jaramillo et al., 2018a). On the other hand, another group found that chemogenic stimulation of the aIC and amygdala suppressed alcohol intake in male Alko Alcohol rats, but chemogenic inhibition did not have an effect. They did find that manipulating the insula projections to the amygdala and NAcc stimulated alcohol taking, but inhibiting these projections had no effect (Haaranen et al., 2020). Meanwhile, inhibition, using optogenetics, of aIC glutamatergic input to the NAcc core reduced aversion-resistant alcohol intake in male Wistsar rats, but only in the presence of aversive stimuli (quinine or footshock) (Seif et al., 2013). However, others found that chemogenic partial inhibition of the aIC resulted in an increase in alcohol intake, but when the aIC projections to the NAcc core were inhibited, there was a decrease in alcohol intake male Long Evans (Jaramillo et al. 2018b, c). Although the majority of research has focused on the aIC, our laboratory showed that even the inactivation of the pGIC attenuates alcohol taking under a fixed ratio-3 in male Long Evans rats (Pushparaj and Le Foll, 2015). Others have investigated negative affect symptoms after prolonged alcohol abstinence, since relapse often occurs during this period, using a model of chronic alcohol consumption (42 days of drinking, 10% ethanol) followed by forced abstinence (15 days). That study reported that abstinence increases c-fos expression and glutamatergic neurotransmission in the dorsal bed nucleus of the stria terminalis (dBNST) in male and female C57BL/6J mice. Further investigation was done to determine which brain regions are sending inputs to the dBNST and therefore contributing to the observed negative affect. Using a channelrhodopsin-assisted mapping strategy, that study reported that it was the insula that strongly affected the neuronal activity of the dBNST (Centanni et al., 2019). This study thereby shows that an insula-dBNST circuit is important for negative affect after alcohol abstinence, which in turn is important in relapse.

In humans, alcohol users exhibit structural changes to the insula. For instance, adolescents with alcohol use disorder had increased white matter volume in the left insula (Chung and Clark, 2014). This was correlated with enhancement motives (hedonic feelings associated with use) and frequency of binge drinking at baseline and at 1-year follow up. In addition, white matter in the right insula was positively correlated with alcohol craving and obsession (Chung and Clark, 2014). On the other hand, gray matter volume in the right insula was decreased in young adult heavy alcohol drinkers compared to light drinkers (Heikkinen et al., 2017). One group looked at the change in surface area in the insula and OFC in adolescents who initiated alcohol use, alcohol use and cannabis use or no substance use over a 6-year period. Although they found a decrease in surface area in both the insula and OFC for all three groups after a 6-year period, the most substantial decrease was found in the adolescents who started using alcohol, thus demonstrating the effect alcohol has on brain development (Infante et al., 2018). A meta-analysis has been conducted that looked at dependence in general as well as dependence based on specific substances. They found that dependent participants compared to non-dependent participants had lower cortical thickness in the insula, precentral and supramarginal gyrus, and the right medial OFC. However, when looking at the substance specific (alcohol, nicotine, methamphetamine, cocaine or cannabis) differences, alcohol dependence was the only one that showed significant differences in cortical thickness, and this included the insula. Interestingly, when looking at dependence when removing alcohol, the insula and inferior parietal cortex were still significantly thinner than the non-dependent group (Mackey et al., 2019).

In terms of brain connectivity in alcohol users, men with alcohol use disorder have been found to have lower SN connectivity and decreased blood flow to the insula compared to non-users (Sullivan et al., 2013). Similarly, in an alcohol administration study, regular binge drinkers had decreased connectivity within the SN when given alcohol compared to placebo. Interestingly, the more the connection decreased, the more the participants felt calm, thereby alluding to the fact that a decreased connection between the aIC and dorsal ACC could be linked to the relaxing effects of alcohol (Gorka et al., 2018). There is also a difference between heavy and light drinkers, whereby heavy alcohol drinkers showed increased BOLD signal in the left insula (only a trend was found in the right insula) and the ventral striatum when viewing alcohol cues compared to light drinkers. Heavy drinkers also had decreased responses in frontal brain areas when viewing pictures relating to higher-order life goals and in the cingulate cortex when viewing food stimuli, thus suggesting they have more trouble finding alternative goals. The researchers were able to distinguish between heavy and light drinkers to great precision by using this activation pattern (Ihssen et al., 2011).

In terms of brain stimulation studies, one group found that a single session of continuous theta burst stimulation to the left frontal pole led to a decrease in the evoked BOLD signal in the insula, as well as the left OFC and lateral sensorimotor cortex in alcohol users. However, no effect was found on subjective craving (Hanlon et al., 2017). On the other hand, a group of researchers reported that in one patient with alcohol dependence, the patient had a temporary suppression of alcohol craving after a single session of rTMS to the dorsal ACC. The suppression of craving was correlated with a decrease in beta electroencephalogram activity in the right insula (De Ridder et al., 2011). More recently, a 12-week clinical trial using rTMS targeting the insula and overlaying regions for alcohol addiction was completed. They found no differences between alcohol dependent individuals receiving active treatment and those receiving sham treatment. They found that those receiving active treatment did have altered resting state connectivity in the insula after treatment, thus showing the ability to alter the area. However, they reported no efficacy in targeting the insula for treatment of alcohol dependence (Perini et al., 2020).

Cocaine

Lesions the aAgIC does not affect acquisition of cocaine-taking behavior in male Lister hooded rats, but it does facilitate cocaine relapse-like behavior, whereas lesions of the BLA increase cocaine seeking and lesions of the prelimbic cortex reduce relapse-like behavior, and lesions of the ACC, OFC and infralimbic cortex have no effect on either cocaine taking or relapse-like behavior, again demonstrating the cortical subregion-specific effects on drug-taking and -seeking behaviors (Pelloux et al., 2013). In addition, inactivation using lidocaine of the aAgIC or the prelimbic PFC does not affect established cocaine-taking ($1\ mg\ kg^{-1}$) or seeking in male Wistar rats (Di Pietro et al., 2006). Lesions of the aIC prior to training actually has the opposite effect whereby it increases subsequent cocaine intake in male Sprague Dawley rats, whereas post-training (3 weeks, 12-h extended self-administration) lesions reduce cocaine intake (Rotge et al., 2017). Extended access self-administration of cocaine ($1\ mg\ kg^{-1}$, fixed ratio-5), but not noncontingent exposure, affects performance in an insular cortex/orbital PFC-related task (odor guided delayed win shift task) in male Wistar rats (Kantak et al., 2005). Furthermore, cocaine self-administration ($0.3\ mg\ kg^{-1}$) in male rhesus monkeys leads to a decrease in glucose utilization in the aAgIC, ventral tegmental area (VTA), medial PFC and ventral striatum (Porrino et al., 2002).

Although it was found that blocking dopamine D1 receptors in the aAgIC decreased cocaine intake (1 mg kg^{-1}, fixed interval ratio 5) in male Wistar rats, food intake also decreased, thus it was not specific to cocaine (Di Pietro et al., 2008). Finally, sex differences have been reported for cocaine-related increases in neuronal activity in the aAgIC, dorsal medial caudate-putamen, NAcc, VTA and hippocampus of male and female Sprague Dawley rats (Zhou et al., 2014).

In terms of cue-induced cocaine seeking, inactivation of the aAgIC (using baclofen and muscimol) in male Sprague Dawley rats led to a reduction of seeking without having any effects on drug priming-induced cocaine seeking or food seeking induced by cue and/or priming. Interestingly, inactivation of the pGIC had no effect, thus demonstrating that even within the insular cortex, different subregions have different levels of involvement in cocaine use behaviors (Cosme et al., 2015). Cue-induced cocaine seeking is also attenuated by CRF receptor-1 blockade in the aAgIC of male Sprague Dawley rats (Cosme et al., 2015). In addition, inactivation of the aAgIC (using baclofen and muscimol), but not the somatosensory cortex, attenuates context-induced reinstatement of cocaine seeking without affecting locomotor activity in male Sprague Dawley rats. Conversely, when the inactivation occurs immediately after re-exposure to drug context, there is no effect on cocaine-seeking (i.e., memory reconsolidation) (Arguello et al., 2017). Meanwhile, inactivation of the aAgIC leads to attenuation of cue and context induced cocaine seeking in male Wistar rats, specifically when the context is associated with odor cues rather than sound cues (Di Pietro et al., 2006). One possible explanation could be that the insula is part of the gustatory cortex, which in turn is influenced by odor (Pritchard et al. 1999). On the other hand, one group of researchers found that lesioning the aAgIC in male Lister hooded rats led to an increase in cocaine seeking (Pelloux et al., 2013). This may be due to the fact that the lesioning occurred prior to the acquisition of cocaine taking, which as previously mentioned has an effect on cocaine intake (Rotge et al., 2017). One study using c-fos and Fos protein to measure neuronal activation found that cue-induced cocaine seeking led to an increase in expression in the PFC, VTA, dorsal striatum and NAcc in male Sprague Dawley rats, as well as a correlation between cocaine-seeking behavior and Fos expression in the aAgIC and BLA (Kufahl et al., 2009). More recently, a group found that inhibiting the BLA projections to the NAcc is what abolishes cocaine seeking in male Sprague Dawley rats, while chemogenic inhibition of the aIC had no effect (Puaud et al., 2021).

In male rhesus monkeys, chronic cocaine self-administration (12 months; cumulative dose of approximately 600 mg kg^{-1}) compared to water self-administration led to a decrease in gray matter density in the insula, OFC, amygdala and temporal cortex. More importantly, this decreased gray matter in the insula, OFC and amygdala persisted even after 2 years of forced abstinence (Jedema et al., 2021). This demonstrates that the structural brain effects caused by cocaine may be long term and therefore may present as a risk of relapse.

With cocaine, decreased gray matter volume of the insula has been reported in human cocaine abusers (Gardini and Venneri, 2012). This was confirmed by other researchers who also found cocaine dependent individuals to have decreased gray matter volume in the insula compared to healthy controls (Ersche et al., 2011). This decrease was also correlated with the duration of dependence; the longer the dependence has been occurring, the more we see a decrease in insula gray matter volume (Barrós-Loscertales et al., 2011; Ersche et al., 2011). In turn, the decreased gray matter of the insula is associated with greater impulsivity (Ersche et al., 2011), which is a trait seen in cocaine users (García-Marchena et al., 2018). Interestingly, a gender interaction has been reported with women potentially driving this difference in decreased gray matter volume of the left aIC in cocaine dependent individuals (Rabin et al., 2020). Cortical thickness of the insula was also found to be decreased in cocaine users compared to healthy controls (Geng et al., 2017). These studies compared users with a random sample of healthy controls, but with addiction we know brain structures can be heritable. This raises the question that maybe these users had a predisposition to these structural differences in the insula, thus one group sought to investigate this by using sibling pairs with one sibling being a stimulant user (94% were cocaine users and 6% were amphetamine users) and the other being a non-user (Ersche et al., 2012). They also had one unrelated group of healthy controls. They found that some structural changes were common between the siblings (e.g., increases in gray matter in the amygdala, hippocampus and putamen), but the decrease in the insula was specific to the stimulant users and it was also correlated with duration of cocaine use (Ersche et al., 2012). Thus, providing more evidence that the insula change is related to the drug use. Meta-analyses have supported the evidence that cocaine users have significantly decreased gray matter in the insula as compared to non-users (Ersche et al., 2013; Hall et al., 2015). We have also conducted the transcriptomic characterization of the insula in humans and found that the insula had enrichment of cocaine associated genes. This was the only drug of abuse that survived multiple test correction. Although that is surprising, we did find that the insula was the second highest brain region that had the most enrichment of genes relating to the dopamine signaling pathway (Ibrahim, Le Foll and French, 2019). This is of importance as it is known that dopamine is linked with addiction and all drugs tend to affect dopamine levels (Nestler, 2005).

Brain connectivity is also altered in cocaine users. Research shows that there is greater connectivity between the aIC and ACC (i.e., SN), but reduced connectivity between the SN and the striatum (Wisner et al., 2013). Moreover, the weaker connection correlated with greater impulsivity but not with craving. However, others have found a decreased connection between the right and left insula and to the dorsal ACC in cocaine users (Geng et al., 2017). Therefore, there is less consensus in cocaine users as to whether it leads to decreased or increased connectivity within the SN. However, individuals who relapsed from cocaine showed decreased connectivity between the pIC and bilateral putamen, which plays a minor role in higher impulsivity (McHugh et al., 2013). With regards to cue reactivity, a task conducted on cocaine, alcohol or nicotine users demonstrated that substance cues compared to neutral cues resulted in increased BOLD activity in three clusters: insula/left inferior frontal gyrus, right premotor cortex and the medial PFC/ACC. This finding was not affected by drug of abuse as it was seen in all three groups of users (Hanlon et al., 2018). In addition, occasional stimulant users (cocaine or amphetamine) that developed stimulant use disorder at the 3 year follow up showed decreased activation during a decision-making task in the insula, ACC, superior temporal, precuneus, inferior parietal and cerebellum at baseline compared to those who stopped their drug use (Stewart et al., 2017).

Therefore, although the preclinical evidence for cocaine and insula was not strong, the clinical evidence shows otherwise. There is clear evidence here presenting that cocaine does in fact lead to changes in both the structural aspects of the insula and the connectivity of the insula.

Amphetamine

Injections of amphetamine (1.5 mg kg; 5 injections over 10 days) that produce a conditioned place preference (i.e., reward) lead to activation (measured using Fos expression) of the pGIC and inactivating that region prevents this conditioned place preference in male Sprague Dawley rats. This was specific to the insula because inactivation of the somatosensory cortex did not produce the same effect (Contreras et al., 2007). A similar effect occurred when anisomycin (a protein synthesis inhibitor) was injected into the pGIC following reactivation of CPP, and this effect lasted even longer when anisomycin was injected into the aAgIC in male Sprague Dawley rats (Contreras et al., 2012). Studies using *in vivo* microdialysis of the aAgIC revealed that methamphetamine-treated male Wistar rats (4 mg kg^{-1} daily for 30 days) exhibit decreased depolarization-evoked gamma-Aminobutyric acid (GABA) release in that brain region. Furthermore, during a decision making task, the methamphetamine-treated rats selected more high risk/high reward options and this coincided with increased c-Fos expression in the insula, striatum and NAcc (Mizoguchi et al., 2015). Contingency management is an effective treatment for drug addiction but when it is stopped, many individuals relapse. Research has been done using a rat model, which showed that inactivation of the aIC prolongs abstinence of methamphetamine even after the removal of contingency management (using palatable food pellets) in male Sprague Dawley rats. In addition, they demonstrated that chemogenic inhibition of monosynaptic glutamatergic projections from aIC to the central amygdala decreases relapse-like behavior in rats (Venniro et al., 2017), suggesting that this circuit may hold promise as a novel target for relapse prevention. Methamphetamine seeking after 10 days of self-administration and 26 days of abstinence demonstrated, via fos expression, increased neuronal activity in the aIC, ACC, OFC, anterior intralaminar nucleus of thalamus lateral and medial (AIT-L, AIT-M), and parafascicular nucleus (PF) in female Sprague Dawley rats (Davis et al., 2021), which was similar but not identical to activation levels observed in male Sprague Dawley rats (Li et al., 2018). In females, projections from the AIT to the DLS are important for methamphetamine seeking, and projections from ACC to DLS, aIC to DLS, and OFC to DLS also play a role in mediating this behavior (Davis et al., 2021).

Methamphetamine users who have recently remained abstinent (between 14–160 days) were found to have lower gray matter density of the insula compared to healthy controls (Schwartz et al., 2010). However, a meta-analysis found the opposite, such that duration of abstinence was associated with increased gray matter of the left insula (Hall et al., 2015). Meta-analyses have also indicated that amphetamine users have decreased gray matter volumes in the insula, particularly the left insula (Ersche et al., 2013; Hall et al., 2015), but there was also an association between duration of use and increased gray matter volume of the right insula (Hall et al., 2015).

Connectivity studies have shown that insula related circuits may be a tool used for prognosis and relapse prediction. Relapsed methamphetamine-dependent individuals conducting a reinforcement learning task exhibit decreased activation in the insula, striatum, left ACC and left inferior frontal gyrus in outcomes pertaining to winning, tying or losing compared to non-relapsed users (Stewart et al., 2014). Furthermore, abstinent methamphetamine users demonstrate increased activation in the left aIC and right striatum in reward processing for large/risky rewards compared to small/safe rewards, while relapsed users exhibit no difference in activation between reward types (Gowin et al., 2015). In healthy participants, liking of d-amphetamine was associated with decreased activation of the insula and caudate putamen and increased activation of the amygdala (Langenecker et al., 2020). Therefore, even in individuals without a history of substance abuse, a single dose of amphetamine affects brain connectivity.

With regards to brain stimulation, abstinent methamphetamine users who underwent one session of transcranial direct current stimulation (another type of non-invasive stimulation but cannot reaches deep brain areas and cannot lead to neuron firing) to the dlPFC showed a decrease in subjective craving. The craving was correlated with a decrease in DMN connectivity and with an increase in ECN and SN connectivity (Shahbabaie et al., 2018). Another study on participants with severe methamphetamine use disorder underwent 20 sessions of rTMS to the dlPFC. Active TMS decreased craving and led to a decrease in functional connectivity between the insula, inferior parietal lobule, medial temporal lobe and precuneus (Su et al., 2020).

Opioids

Inactivation of the pGIC in male Sprague Dawley rats prevents the acquisition of morphine-induced CPP (15 mg kg^{-1} over 6 days), but inactivation of the aAgIC does not affect this outcome measure (Li et al., 2013). Others have shown that lesioning the aIC or pIC does not produce any effect on the acquisition of CPP induced by morphine (15 mg kg^{-1} over 6 days) in male Wistar rats (Mackey et al., 1986; Sun et al., 2018). However, one group found that inhibition of nitric oxide in the pIC reduced the acquisition of morphine-induced (15 mg kg^{-1} over 6 days) CPP in male Sprague Dawley rats, thereby demonstrating the role of the insula in drug reward memory (Ma et al., 2014). In addition, lesioning the aIC prevented the acquisition of CPA from morphine (300 mg kg^{-1} over 5 days) withdrawal in male Swiss-Kumming mice (Wang et al., 2016). This was also found when inactivating the pGIC or aAgIC in male Sprague Dawley rats (Li et al., 2013).

Extended morphine (400 mg kg^{-1} over 6 days) withdrawal (28 days) in male C57BL/6 mice leads to increased activation of glutamatergic neurons in the medial insula. Furthermore, lesioning the medial insula reduces the anxiety-like behaviors observed during morphine withdrawal (Ma et al., 2018). In male Sprague Dawley rats, morphine dependence using implanted morphine pellets followed by naloxone-precipitated withdrawal leads to an increase in c-fos expression in dopaminergic, noradrenergic and opioidergic neurons in the aAgIC, cingulate cortex and motor cortex (Georges et al., 2000). Work on the endocannabinoid system in this brain region has revealed that inhibition of monoacylglycerol lipase (leads to an elevation of the endocannabinoid 2-arachidonyl glycerol) in the pGIC and the BLA prevents acquisition of CPA associated with morphine withdrawal, and that this effect is blocked by cannabinoid-1 receptors (CB1R) male Sprague Dawley rats (Wills et al., 2016).

Although there has not been as much clinical research done with opioids and the insula, one study showed that heroin abusers compared to healthy controls had decreased gray matter volume in the right insula (Gardini and Venneri, 2012). There is also greater connectivity within the SN in heroin abusers compared to healthy controls (Wang et al., 2010). In terms of abstinence, one group looked to see the difference between heroin addicts with long term abstinence

(6–12 months), short term abstinence (7–15 days) and healthy controls with regards to brain connectivity in the large-scale brain networks. They found that both the short- and long-term abstinence groups compared to the healthy controls had decreased connectivity between the left aIC (area in the SN) and the dlPFC (area in the ECN) (Chen et al., 2020). Craving in heroin users has also been negatively correlated with rsFC between the occipital thalamus and insula, NAcc and hippocampus (Zhang et al., 2021). In heroin dependent individuals who are receiving methadone maintenance treatment, relapse frequency was negativity correlated with the functionality between the right insula and left NAcc (Wang et al., 2021).

Cannabis

There are few insula-related animal studies on cannabis and THC. One group investigated c-fos expression after a single treatment with Δ9-tetrahydrocannabinol (THC) (10 mg kg^{-1}, i.p.) in male Wistar rats. They found that 21 out of the 26 regions examined exhibited increases in fos expression after THC treatment; the insula was one of these 21 regions but was not one of the regions expressing the highest density of fos (Allen et al., 2003). Clearly, more studies are needed to determine if there is a role for the insula in mediating acute and chronic THC effects.

With regards to human studies, regular cannabis users have less gray matter volume in the left insula than occasional cannabis users, and this volume is inversely correlated with frequency of use in the past 3 months (Battistella et al., 2014). With regards to age of onset of cannabis use, heavy use shows decreased gray matter volume in the insula regardless of age. However, there was a significant difference in occasional users who started using late compared to regular users (early or late users), whereby the occasional users had higher gray matter volume of the insula (Battistella et al., 2014).

In terms of brain connectivity, cannabis users compared to non-users exhibit greater connectivity between the left rostral ACC and the left insula, right rostral ACC, and left amygdala (Shollenbarger et al., 2019). Individuals with cannabis use disorder have less functional connectivity between the right insula and superior parietal gyrus. Factoring in alcohol use and substance use disorders (not including cannabis and nicotine) did not explain the relationship as findings remained significant when controlling for them. However, when controlling for nicotine dependence, the findings were no longer significant, thus suggesting the decreased connectivity may be in fact due to nicotine and not cannabis (Koenis et al., 2020). Users who were abstinent from cannabis for 72 h showed increased BOLD activation in the insula, amygdala, ACC, thalamus, and VTA when viewing cannabis cues compared to neutral cues (Filbey et al., 2009). Cannabis users at risk of developing cannabis use disorder were found to have increased activation in the insula, VTA, and pallidum compared to non-users. Also, presenting the users with cannabis odor cues led to greater activation in the aIC, NAcc, putamen, pallidum, supplementary motor area, angular gyrus and superior frontal gyrus (Kleinhans et al., 2020).

Conclusions

All of the data discussed above implicate the insula and insular circuits as having important roles in human addiction and animal models of addiction.

An important factor to consider is that the insula does not work alone. For instance, the insula contains dopaminergic neuron terminals that originate in the VTA and substantia nigra (see Chapter 2) and have a key role in drug addiction (Kalivas and Volkow, 2005). The agranular insula is noted as having high dopamine utilization, due to it having a high density of dopamine D1-subtype receptors that surround dopaminergic terminals from the substantia nigra and VTA (Gaspar et al., 1989; Hurd et al., 2001). There are also midbrain dopamine terminals in the agranular insula, which contains large pyramidal neurons in layer 5 with gamma-Aminobutyric acid (GABA) B-subtype receptors on their dendrites (Margeta-Mitrovic et al., 1999) that project to the amygdala and NAcc (Ohara et al., 2003). These neurons may be important for mediating addiction-related behavior since, for example, injection of GABA receptor agonists into the insula attenuates nicotine-taking and -seeking behaviors in rats (Forget et al., 2010). Therefore, the insula is innervated by and projects to various brain regions implicated in addiction. Human neuroimaging studies provide further evidence that insular circuits are important in mediating drug effects and addiction-related behaviors.

There may appear to be some contradictions in the evidence presented above. For instance, neuroimaging studies show that addiction leads to increased activation of the insula, which would suggest a gain of function in this brain area whereas structural studies typically show that addiction leads to loss of gray matter in the insula, which would suggest a loss of function of the area. Some have suggested that decreased gray matter actually leads to an overactive insula via compensatory mechanisms that increase function in cases where insula volume is reduced. Similar results have been observed in some cases in which lower cortical volume is associated with increased task performance (Droutman et al., 2015; Turel et al., 2018). Furthermore, Naqvi et al. (2014) proposed that, with respect to addiction, the function that is being investigated affects whether the insula exhibits gain or loss of function. When an individual takes a drug, insula activity contributes to create the internal state produced by the consumed drug. This is related to its role in interoception and likely contributes to continued seeking of the drug, such that an individual may pursue drug with the goal of achieving a prior internal state encoded by the insula. Meanwhile, a person living with drug addiction may have difficulties stopping drug seeking behavior because of impaired ability to consider the negative consequences of drug use, which may also be related to activity of the insula and insular circuits. Although both factors are crucial to addiction, it may be the gain of function that is most important since we know that insula lesions increase the probability of cessation of drug use.

Much work remains to be done in this area. Preclinical evidence is quite strong and demonstrated how the insula and insula circuits affects drug taking and drug seeking in animals, but the clinical evidence is not as conclusive. There are many contradictory findings, whereby some researchers find that the insula is critical in addiction and others find that it does not seem to have a major role. For instance, a meta-analysis (although somewhat outdated now) concluded that the insula did not play a role in drug cue-induced activity or craving-related activity, although this negative finding may be attributable to the use of rigid exclusion criteria in that study (Chase et al., 2011). A more recent study using brain stimulation targeting the insula in individuals with AUD found no evidence of any efficacy of the treatment (Perini et al., 2020). On the other hand, in smokers, rTMS in the insula and PFC leads to improved abstinence rates (Dinur-Klein et al., 2014; Zangen and George, 2020). It may be that the insula plays a more prominent role in the use, misuse and effects of some specific drugs of abuse relative to others, but more work is needed to determine if this is indeed the case.

Lastly, it should be noted that the studies presented are not without limitations. For starters, most of the clinical studies discussed above had small sample sizes and the majority of the study samples were composed mostly or entirely of men. Also, the clinical studies described above examined different phases of the addiction cycle (i.e., current users, abstinent users, etc.), making general conclusions more elusive. Differences in technical approaches across studies may also contribute to variable or seemingly discrepant findings. Finally and most importantly, all the neuroimaging studies presented are correlational, not causational.

In conclusion, the insula is a critical component of brain circuits that mediate processes (e.g., decision making, interoception) that are critical for the onset and maintenance of drug addiction. Based on the evidence presented above, future work should examine the potential utility of using non-invasive brain stimulation techniques (e.g., TMS) in the insula as a treatment option for substance use disorders. Furthermore, researchers should seek to combine TMS with BOLD imaging in order to better understand the circuits affected by stimulation of the insula in individuals living with an SUD.

References

Abdolahi, A., Acosta, G., Breslin, F.J., Hemby, S.E., Lynch, W.J., 2010. Incubation of nicotine seeking is associated with enhanced protein kinase A-regulated signaling of dopamine- and cAMP-regulated phosphoprotein of 32 kDa in the insular cortex. Eur. J. Neurosci. 31 (4), 733–741. https://doi.org/10.1111/j.1460-9568.2010.07114.x.

Abdolahi, A., Williams, G.C., Benesch, C.G., Wang, H.Z., Spitzer, E.M., Scott, B.E., van Wijngaarden, E., 2015a. Damage to the insula leads to decreased nicotine withdrawal during abstinence. Addiction 110 (12), 1994–2003. https://doi.org/10.1111/add.13061.

Abdolahi, A., Williams, G.C., Benesch, C.G., Wang, H.Z., Spitzer, E.M., Scott, B.E., van Wijngaarden, E., 2015b. Smoking cessation behaviors three months following acute insular damage from stroke. Addict. Behav. 51, 24–30. https://doi.org/10.1016/j.addbeh.2015.07.001.

Abdolahi, A., Williams, G.C., Benesch, C.G., Wang, H.Z., Spitzer, E.M., Scott, B.E., van Wijngaarden, E., 2017. Immediate and sustained decrease in smoking urges after acute insular cortex damage. Nicotine Tob. Res. Off. J. Soc. Res. Nicotine Tobacco 19 (6), 756–762. https://doi.org/10.1093/ntr/ntx046.

Abdolahi, A., Williams, G.C., van Wijngaarden, E., 2019. Implications of insular cortex laterality for treatment of nicotine addiction. Drug Alcohol Depend. 201, 178–181. https://doi.org/10.1016/j.drugalcdep.2019.04.017.

Addicott, M.A., Sweitzer, M.M., Froeliger, B., Rose, J.E., McClernon, F.J., 2015. Increased functional connectivity in an insula-based network is associated with improved smoking cessation outcomes. Neuropsychopharmacology 40 (11), 2648–2656. https://doi.org/10.1038/npp.2015.114.

Allen, G.V., Saper, C.B., Hurley, K.M., Cechetto, D.F., 1991. Organization of visceral and limbic connections in the insular cortex of the rat. J. Comp. Neurol. 311 (1), 1–16. https://doi.org/10.1002/cne.903110102.

Allen, K.V., McGregor, I.S., Hunt, G.E., Singh, M.E., Mallet, P.E., 2003. Regional differences in naloxone modulation of Δ9-THC induced Fos expression in rat brain. Neuropharmacology 44 (2), 264–274. https://doi.org/10.1016/S0028-3908(02)00364-7.

Allman, J.M., Tetreault, N.A., Hakeem, A.Y., Manaye, K.F., Semendeferi, K., Erwin, J.M., Hof, P.R., 2011. The von Economo neurons in the frontoinsular and anterior cingulate cortex. Ann. N. Y. Acad. Sci. 1225, 59–71. https://doi.org/10.1111/j.1749-6632.2011.06011.x.

Arguello, A.A., Wang, R., Lyons, C.M., Higginbotham, J.A., Hodges, M.A., Fuchs, R.A., 2017. Role of the agranular insular cortex in contextual control over cocaine-seeking behavior in rats. Psychopharmacology 234 (16), 2431–2441. https://doi.org/10.1007/s00213-017-4632-7.

Augustine, J.R., 1985. The insular lobe in primates including humans. Neurol. Res. 7 (1), 2–10. https://doi.org/10.1080/01616412.1985.11739692.

Augustine, J.R., 1996. Circuitry and functional aspects of the insular lobe in primates including humans. Brain Res. Rev. 22 (3), 229–244. https://doi.org/10.1016/s0165-0173(96)00011-2.

Bagshaw, M.H., Pribram, K.H., 1953. Cortical organization in gustation (Macaca mulatta.). J. Neurophysiol. 16, 499–508.

Bamiou, D.E., Musiek, F.E., Luxon, L.M., 2003. The insula (Island of Reil) and its role in auditory processing. Literature review. Brain Res. Rev. 42 (2), 143–154. https://doi.org/10.1016/s0165-0173(03)00172-3.

Barker, A.T., Jalinous, R., Freeston, I.L., 1985. Non-invasive magnetic stimulation of human motor cortex. Lancet 325 (8437), 1106–1107. https://doi.org/10.1016/S0140-6736(85)92413-4.

Barrós-Loscertales, A., Garavan, H., Bustamante, J.C., Ventura-Campos, N., Llopis, J.J., Belloch, V., Avila, C., 2011. Reduced striatal volume in cocaine-dependent patients. Neuroimage 56 (3), 1021–1026. https://doi.org/10.1016/j.neuroimage.2011.02.035.

Battistella, G., Fornari, E., Annoni, J.-M., Chtioui, H., Dao, K., Fabritius, M., Giroud, C., 2014. Long-term effects of cannabis on brain structure. Neuropsychopharmacology Off. Publ. Am. Coll. Neuropsychopharmacol. 39 (9), 2041–2048. https://doi.org/10.1038/npp.2014.67.

Baumgärtner, U., Buchholz, H.-G., Bellosevich, A., Magerl, W., Siessmeier, T., Rolke, R., Schreckenberger, M., 2006. High opiate receptor binding potential in the human lateral pain system. Neuroimage 30 (3), 692–699. https://doi.org/10.1016/j.neuroimage.2005.10.033.

Bellini, B., Scholz, J.R., Arnaut, D., Abe, T.M.O., Alberto, R.L., Ferrari, C.L., Marcolin, M.A., 2020. Preliminary characteristic of 45 patient of the study placebo-controlled, randomized, double-blind clinical trial to assess the safety and efficacy of using Deep Transcranial Magnetic Stimulation (EMTp) in smoking cessation. Brain Stimul. Basic Transl. Clin. Res. Neuromodul. 13 (6), 1844–1845. https://doi.org/10.1016/j.brs.2020.06.025.

Bi, Y., Zhang, Y., Li, Y., Yu, D., Yuan, K., Tian, J., 2017. 12h abstinence-induced right anterior insula network pattern changes in young smokers. Drug Alcohol Depend. 176, 162–168. https://doi.org/10.1016/j.drugalcdep.2017.02.019.

Bienkowski, P., Zatorski, P., Baranowska, A., Ryglewiczc, D., Sienkiewicz-Jarosz, H., 2010. Insular lesions and smoking cessation after first-ever ischemic stroke: a 3-month follow-up. Neurosci. Lett. 478, 161–164.

Birklein, F., Rolke, R., Müller-Forell, W., 2005. Isolated insular infarction eliminates contralateral cold, cold pain, and pinprick perception. Neurology 65 (9), 1381. https://doi.org/10.1212/01.wnl.0000181351.82772.b3.

Bohland, J.W., Guenther, F.H., 2006. An fMRI investigation of syllable sequence production. Neuroimage 32 (2), 821–841. https://doi.org/10.1016/j.neuroimage.2006.04.173.

Brooks, J.C., Zambreanu, L., Godinez, A., Craig, A.D., Tracey, I., 2005. Somatotopic organisation of the human insula to painful heat studied with high resolution functional imaging. Neuroimage 27 (1), 201–209. https://doi.org/10.1016/j.neuroimage.2005.03.041.

Burton, H., Videen, T.O., Raichle, M.E., 1993. Tactile-vibration-activated foci in insular and parietal-opercular cortex studied with positron emission tomography: mapping the second somatosensory area in humans. Somatosens. Mot. Res. 10 (3), 297–308. https://doi.org/10.3109/08990229309028839.

Butti, C., Hof, P.R., 2010. The insular cortex: a comparative perspective. Brain Struct. Funct. 214 (5–6), 477–493. https://doi.org/10.1007/s00429-010-0264-y.

Büttner-Ennever, J.A., Gerrits, N.M., 2004. The Human Bervous System. Elsevier, Amsterdam.

Carmichael, S.T., Price, J.L., 1996. Connectional networks within the orbital and medial prefrontal cortex of macaque monkeys. J. Comp. Neurol. 371 (2), 179–207. https://doi.org/10.1002/(sici)1096-9861(19960722)371:2<179::Aid-cne1>3.0.Co;2-#.

Cechetto, D.F., Saper, C.B., 1987. Evidence for a viscerotopic sensory representation in the cortex and thalamus in the rat. J. Comp. Neurol. 262 (1), 27–45. https://doi.org/10.1002/cne.902620104.

Centanni, S.W., Morris, B.D., Luchsinger, J.R., Bedse, G., Fetterly, T.L., Patel, S., Winder, D.G., 2019. Endocannabinoid control of the insular-bed nucleus of the stria terminalis circuit regulates negative affective behavior associated with alcohol abstinence. Neuropsychopharmacology 44 (3), 526–537. https://doi.org/10.1038/s41386-018-0257-8.

Chase, H.W., Eickhoff, S.B., Laird, A.R., Hogarth, L., 2011. The neural basis of drug stimulus processing and craving: an activation likelihood estimation meta-analysis. Biol. Psychiatry 70 (8), 785–793. https://doi.org/10.1016/j.biopsych.2011.05.025.

Chen, J., Wang, F., Zhu, J., Li, Y., Liu, W., Xue, J., Wang, W., 2020. Assessing effect of long-term abstinence on coupling of three core brain networks in male heroin addicts: a resting-state functional magnetic resonance imaging study. Addiction Biol. e12982. https://doi.org/10.1111/adb.12982.

Chikama, M., McFarland, N.R., Amaral, D.G., Haber, S.N., 1997. Insular cortical projections to functional regions of the striatum correlate with cortical cytoarchitectonic organization in the primate. J. Neurosci. 17 (24), 9686–9705. https://doi.org/10.1523/jneurosci.17-24-09686.1997.

Chung, T., Clark, D.B., 2014. Insula white matter volume linked to binge drinking frequency through enhancement motives in treated adolescents. Alcohol. Clin. Exp. Res. 38 (7), 1932–1940. https://doi.org/10.1111/acer.12461.

Claus, E.D., Blaine, S.K., Filbey, F.M., Mayer, A.R., Hutchison, K.E., 2013. Association between nicotine dependence severity, BOLD response to smoking cues, and functional connectivity. Neuropsychopharmacology Off. Publ. Am. Coll. Neuropsychopharmacol. 38 (12), 2363–2372. https://doi.org/10.1038/npp.2013.134.

Cole, M.W., Schneider, W., 2007. The cognitive control network: integrated cortical regions with dissociable functions. Neuroimage 37 (1), 343–360. https://doi.org/10.1016/j.neuroimage.2007.03.071.

Contoreggi, C., Herning, R.I., Na, P., Gold, P.W., Chrousos, G., Negro, P.J., Cadet, J.L., 2003. Stress hormone responses to corticotropin-releasing hormone in substance abusers without severe comorbid psychiatric disease. Biol. Psychiatry 54 (9), 873–878. https://doi.org/10.1016/S0006-3223(03)00167-7.

Contreras, M., Billeke, P., Vicencio, S., Madrid, C., Perdomo, G., González, M., Torrealba, F., 2012. A role for the insular cortex in long-term memory for context-evoked drug craving in rats. Neuropsychopharmacology Off. Publ. Am. Coll. Neuropsychopharmacol. 37 (9), 2101–2108. https://doi.org/10.1038/npp.2012.59.

Contreras, M., Ceric, F., Torrealba, F., 2007. Inactivation of the interoceptive insula disrupts drug craving and malaise induced by lithium. Science 318 (5850), 655–658. https://doi.org/10.1126/science.1145590.

Cosme, C.V., Gutman, A.L., LaLumiere, R.T., 2015. The dorsal agranular insular cortex regulates the cued reinstatement of cocaine-seeking, but not food-seeking, behavior in rats. Neuropsychopharmacology 40 (10), 2425–2433. https://doi.org/10.1038/npp.2015.92.

Craig, A.D., 2002. How do you feel? Interoception: the sense of the physiological condition of the body. Nat. Rev. Neurosci. 3 (8), 655–666. https://doi.org/10.1038/nrn894.

Craig, A.D., 2004. Human feelings: why are some more aware than others? Trends Cognit. Sci. 8 (6), 239–241. https://doi.org/10.1016/j.tics.2004.04.004.

Craig, A.D., 2009. How do you feel — now? The anterior insula and human awareness. Nat. Rev. Neurosci. 10, 59–70.

Craig, A.D., 2010. Once an island, now the focus of attention. Brain Struct Funct. 214, 395–396.

Craig, A.D., Bushnell, M.C., Zhang, E.T., Blomqvist, A., 1994. A thalamic nucleus specific for pain and temperature sensation. Nature 372 (6508), 770–773. https://doi.org/10.1038/372770a0.

Davis, I.R., Coldren, S.A., Li, X., 2021. Methamphetamine seeking after prolonged abstinence is associated with activated projections from anterior intralaminar nucleus of thalamus to dorsolateral striatum in female rats. Pharmacol. Biochem. Behav. 200, 173087. https://doi.org/10.1016/j.pbb.2020.173087.

De Ridder, D., Vanneste, S., Kovacs, S., Sunaert, S., Dom, G., 2011. Transient alcohol craving suppression by rTMS of dorsal anterior cingulate: an fMRI and LORETA EEG study. Neurosci. Lett. 496 (1), 5–10. https://doi.org/10.1016/j.neulet.2011.03.074.

Dehkordi, O., Rose, J.E., Asadi, S., Manaye, K.F., Millis, R.M., Jayam-Trouth, A., 2015. Neuroanatomical circuitry mediating the sensory impact of nicotine in the central nervous system. J. Neurosci. Res. 93 (2), 230–243. https://doi.org/10.1002/jnr.23477.

Di Pietro, N.C., Black, Y.D., Kantak, K.M., 2006. Context-dependent prefrontal cortex regulation of cocaine self-administration and reinstatement behaviors in rats. Eur. J. Neurosci. 24 (11), 3285–3298. https://doi.org/10.1111/j.1460-9568.2006.05193.x.

Di Pietro, N.C., Mashhoon, Y., Heaney, C., Yager, L.M., Kantak, K.M., 2008. Role of dopamine D1 receptors in the prefrontal dorsal agranular insular cortex in mediating cocaine self-administration in rats. Psychopharmacology 200 (1), 81–91. https://doi.org/10.1007/s00213-008-1149-0.

Diana, M., Raij, T., Melis, M., Nummenmaa, A., Leggio, L., Bonci, A., 2017. Rehabilitating the addicted brain with transcranial magnetic stimulation. Nat. Rev. Neurosci. 18 (11), 685–693. https://doi.org/10.1038/nrn.2017.113.

Dieterich, M., Brandt, T., 2019. Perception of verticality and vestibular disorders of balance and falls. Front. Neurol. 10, 172. https://doi.org/10.3389/fneur.2019.00172.

Dinur-Klein, L., Dannon, P., Hadar, A., Rosenberg, O., Roth, Y., Kotler, M., Zangen, A., 2014. Smoking cessation induced by deep repetitive transcranial magnetic stimulation of the prefrontal and insular cortices: a prospective, randomized controlled trial. Biol. Psychiatry 76 (9), 742–749. https://doi.org/10.1016/j.biopsych.2014.05.020.

Droutman, V., Read, S.J., Bechara, A., 2015. Revisiting the role of the insula in addiction. Trends Cognit. Sci. 19 (7), 414–420. https://doi.org/10.1016/j.tics.2015.05.005.

Ehlinger, D.G., Bergstrom, H.C., McDonald, C.G., Smith, R.F., 2012. Nicotine-induced dendritic remodeling in the insular cortex. Neurosci. Lett. 516 (1), 89–93. https://doi.org/10.1016/j.neulet.2012.03.064.

Engelmann, J.M., Versace, F., Robinson, J.D., Minnix, J.A., Lam, C.Y., Cui, Y., Cinciripini, P.M., 2012. Neural substrates of smoking cue reactivity: a meta-analysis of fMRI studies. Neuroimage 60 (1), 252–262. https://doi.org/10.1016/j.neuroimage.2011.12.024.

Ersche, K.D., Barnes, A., Jones, P.S., Morein-Zamir, S., Robbins, T.W., Bullmore, E.T., 2011. Abnormal structure of frontostriatal brain systems is associated with aspects of impulsivity and compulsivity in cocaine dependence. Brain 134 (Pt 7), 2013–2024. https://doi.org/10.1093/brain/awr138.

Ersche, K.D., Jones, P.S., Williams, G.B., Turton, A.J., Robbins, T.W., Bullmore, E.T., 2012. Abnormal brain structure implicated in stimulant drug addiction. Science 335 (6068), 601–604. https://doi.org/10.1126/science.1214463.

Ersche, K.D., Williams, G.B., Robbins, T.W., Bullmore, E.T., 2013. Meta-analysis of structural brain abnormalities associated with stimulant drug dependence and neuroimaging of addiction vulnerability and resilience. Curr. Opin. Neurobiol. 23 (4), 615–624. https://doi.org/10.1016/j.conb.2013.02.017.

Faulkner, P., Ghahremani, D.G., Tyndale, R.F., Paterson, N.E., Cox, C., Ginder, N., London, E.D., 2019. Neural basis of smoking-induced relief of craving and negative affect: contribution of nicotine. Addiction Biol. 24 (5), 1087–1095. https://doi.org/10.1111/adb.12679.

Fedota, J.R., Ding, X., Matous, A.L., Salmeron, B.J., McKenna, M.R., Gu, H., Stein, E.A., 2018. Nicotine abstinence influences the calculation of salience in discrete insular circuits. Biol. Psychiatry Cogn. Neurosci. Neuroimaging 3 (2), 150–159. https://doi.org/10.1016/j.bpsc.2017.09.010.

Fedota, J.R., Matous, A.L., Salmeron, B.J., Gu, H., Ross, T.J., Stein, E.A., 2016. Insula demonstrates a non-linear response to varying demand for cognitive control and weaker resting connectivity with the executive control network in smokers. Neuropsychopharmacology 41 (10), 2557–2565. https://doi.org/10.1038/npp.2016.62.

Filbey, F.M., Schacht, J.P., Myers, U.S., Chavez, R.S., Hutchison, K.E., 2009. Marijuana craving in the brain. Proc. Natl. Acad. Sci. U. S. A. 106 (31), 13016–13021. https://doi.org/10.1073/pnas.0903863106.

Forget, B., Pushparaj, A., Le Foll, B., 2010. Granular insular cortex inactivation as a novel therapeutic strategy for nicotine addiction. Biol. Psychiatry 68 (3), 265–271. https://doi.org/10.1016/j.biopsych.2010.01.029.

Friedman, D.P., Murray, E.A., O'Neill, J.B., Mishkin, M., 1986. Cortical connections of the somatosensory fields of the lateral sulcus of macaques: evidence for a corticolimbic pathway for touch. J. Comp. Neurol. 252 (3), 323–347. https://doi.org/10.1002/cne.902520304.

Fritz, H.C., Wittfeld, K., Schmidt, C.O., Domin, M., Grabe, H.J., Hegenscheid, K., Lotze, M., 2014. Current smoking and reduced gray matter volume-a voxel-based morphometry study. Neuropsychopharmacology 39 (11), 2594–2600. https://doi.org/10.1038/npp.2014.112.

García-Marchena, N., Ladrón de Guevara-Miranda, D., Pedraz, M., Araos, P.F., Rubio, G., Ruiz, J.J., Rodríguez de Fonseca, F., 2018. Higher impulsivity as a distinctive trait of severe cocaine addiction among individuals treated for cocaine or alcohol use disorders. Front. Psychiatry 9, 26. https://doi.org/10.3389/fpsyt.2018.00026.

Gardini, S., Venneri, A., 2012. Reduced grey matter in the posterior insula as a structural vulnerability or diathesis to addiction. Brain Res. Bull. 87 (2–3), 205–211. https://doi.org/10.1016/j.brainresbull.2011.11.021.

Gaspar, P., Berger, B., Febvret, A., Vigny, A., Henry, J.P., 1989. Catecholamine innervation of the human cerebral cortex as revealed by comparative immunohistochemistry of tyrosine hydroxylase and dopamine-beta-hydroxylase. J. Comp. Neurol. 279 (2), 249–271. https://doi.org/10.1002/cne.902790208.

Gasquoine, P.G., 2014. Contributions of the insula to cognition and emotion. Neuropsychol. Rev. 24 (2), 77–87. https://doi.org/10.1007/s11065-014-9246-9.

Gauriau, C., Bernard, J.F., 2004. Posterior triangular thalamic neurons convey nociceptive messages to the secondary somatosensory and insular cortices in the rat. J. Neurosci. 24 (3), 752–761. https://doi.org/10.1523/JNEUROSCI.3272-03.2004.

Gaznick, N., Tranel, D., McNutt, A., Bechara, A., 2014. Basal ganglia plus insula damage yields stronger disruption of smoking addiction than basal ganglia damage alone. Nicotine Tob. Res. 16 (4), 445–453. https://doi.org/10.1093/ntr/ntt172.

Geng, X., Hu, Y., Gu, H., Salmeron, B.J., Adinoff, B., Stein, E.A., Yang, Y., 2017. Salience and default mode network dysregulation in chronic cocaine users predict treatment outcome. Brain 140 (5), 1513–1524. https://doi.org/10.1093/brain/awx036.

Georges, F., Stinus, L., Le Moine, C., 2000 Mapping of c-fos gene expression in the brain during morphine dependence and precipitated withdrawal, and phenotypic identification of the striatal neurons involved. Eur. J. Neurosci. 12 (12), 4475–4486. https://doi.org/10.1046/j.0953-816X.2000.01334.x.

Gerfen, C.R., Clavier, R.M., 1979. Neural inputs to the prefrontal agranular insular cortex in the rat: horseradish peroxidase study. Brain Res. Bull. 4 (3), 347–353. https://doi.org/10.1016/S0361-9230(79)80012-X.

Gilman, J.M., Radoman, M., Schuster, R.M., Pachas, G., Azzouz, N., Fava, M., Evins, A.E., 2018. Anterior insula activation during inhibition to smoking cues is associated with ability to maintain tobacco abstinence. Addictive Behaviors Reports 7, 40–46. https://doi.org/10.1016/j.abrep.2018.01.002.

Glover, G.H., 2011. Overview of functional magnetic resonance imaging. Neurosurg. Clin. 22 (2), 133–vii. https://doi.org/10.1016/j.nec.2010.11.001.

Gorka, S.M., Phan, K.L., Childs, E., 2018. Acute calming effects of alcohol are associated with disruption of the salience network. Addiction Biol. 23 (3), 921–930. https://doi.org/10.1111/adb.12537.

Gowin, J.L., Ball, T.M., Wittmann, M., Tapert, S.F., Paulus, M.P., 2015. Individualized relapse prediction: personality measures and striatal and insular activity during reward-processing robustly predict relapse. Drug Alcohol Depend. 152, 93–101. https://doi.org/10.1016/j.drugalcdep.2015.04.018.

Gratton, C., Lee, T., Nomura, E., D'Esposito, M., 2013. The effect of theta-burst TMS on cognitive control networks measured with resting state fMRI. Front. Syst. Neurosci. 7 (124). https://doi.org/10.3389/fnsys.2013.00124.

Grüsser, O.J., Pause, M., Schreiter, U., 1990a. Localization and responses of neurones in the parieto-insular vestibular cortex of awake monkeys (Macaca fascicularis). J. Physiol. 430, 537–557. https://doi.org/10.1113/jphysiol.1990.sp018306.

Grüsser, O.J., Pause, M., Schreiter, U., 1990b. Vestibular neurones in the parieto-insular cortex of monkeys (Macaca fascicularis): visual and neck receptor responses. J. Physiol. 430, 559–583. https://doi.org/10.1113/jphysiol.1990.sp018307.

Haaranen, M., Schäfer, A., Järvi, V., Hyytiä, P., 2020. Chemogenetic stimulation and silencing of the insula, amygdala, nucleus accumbens, and their connections differentially modulate alcohol drinking in rats. Front. Behav. Neurosci. 14, 580849. https://doi.org/10.3389/fnbeh.2020.580849.

Hall, M.G., Alhassoon, O.M., Stern, M.J., Wollman, S.C., Kimmel, C.L., Perez-Figueroa, A., Radua, J., 2015. Gray matter abnormalities in cocaine versus methamphetamine-dependent patients: a neuroimaging meta-analysis. Am. J. Drug Alcohol Abuse 41 (4), 290–299. https://doi.org/10.3109/00952990.2015.1044607.

Hanlon, C.A., Dowdle, L.T., Correia, B., Mithoefer, O., Kearney-Ramos, T., Lench, D., George, M.S., 2017. Left frontal pole theta burst stimulation decreases orbitofrontal and insula activity in cocaine users and alcohol users. Drug Alcohol Depend. 178, 310–317. https://doi.org/10.1016/j.drugalcdep.2017.03.039.

Hanlon, C.A., Dowdle, L.T., Gibson, N.B., Li, X., Hamilton, S., Canterberry, M., Hoffman, M., 2018. Cortical substrates of cue-reactivity in multiple substance dependent populations: transdiagnostic relevance of the medial prefrontal cortex. Transl. Psychiatry 8 (1). https://doi.org/10.1038/s41398-018-0220-9, 186-186.

Hanlon, C.A., Owens, M.M., Joseph, J.E., Zhu, X., George, M.S., Brady, K.T., Hartwell, K.J., 2016. Lower subcortical gray matter volume in both younger smokers and established smokers relative to non-smokers. Addiction Biol. 21 (1), 185–195. https://doi.org/10.1111/adb.12171.

Heikkinen, N., Niskanen, E., Könönen, M., Tolmunen, T., Kekkonen, V., Kivimäki, P., Vanninen, R., 2017. Alcohol consumption during adolescence is associated with reduced grey matter volumes. Addiction 112 (4), 604–613. https://doi.org/10.1111/add.13697.

Hollander, J.A., Lu, Q., Cameron, M.D., Kamenecka, T.M., Kenny, P.J., 2008. Insular hypocretin transmission regulates nicotine reward. Proc. Natl. Acad. Sci. U. S. A. 105 (49), 19480–19485. https://doi.org/10.1073/pnas.0808023105.

Hsu, L.M., Keeley, R.J., Liang, X., Brynildsen, J.K., Lu, H., Yang, Y., Stein, E.A., 2019. Intrinsic insular-frontal networks predict future nicotine dependence severity. J. Neurosci. 39 (25), 5028–5037. https://doi.org/10.1523/jneurosci.0140-19.2019.

Hua, L.H., Strigo, I.A., Baxter, L.C., Johnson, S.C., Craig, A.D., 2005. Anteroposterior somatotopy of innocuous cooling activation focus in human dorsal posterior insular cortex. Am. J. Physiol. Regul. Integr. Comp. Physiol. 289 (2), R319–R325. https://doi.org/10.1152/ajpregu.00123.2005.

Huang, W., King, J.A., Ursprung, W.W.S., Zheng, S., Zhang, N., Kennedy, D.N., DiFranza, J.R., 2014. The development and expression of physical nicotine dependence corresponds to structural and functional alterations in the anterior cingulate-precuneus pathway. Brain Behav. 4 (3), 408–417. https://doi.org/10.1002/brb3.227.

Hurd, Y.L., Suzuki, M., Sedvall, G.C., 2001. D1 and D2 dopamine receptor mRNA expression in whole hemisphere sections of the human brain. J. Chem. Neuroanat. 22 (1–2), 127–137. https://doi.org/10.1016/s0891-0618(01)00122-3.

Ibrahim, C., Le Foll, B., French, L., 2019a. Transcriptomic characterization of the human insular cortex and claustrum. Front. Neuroanat. 13 (94). https://doi.org/10.3389/fnana.2019.00094.

Ibrahim, C., Rubin-Kahana, D.S., Pushparaj, A., Musiol, M., Blumberger, D.M., Daskalakis, Z.J., Le Foll, B., 2019b. The insula: a brain stimulation target for the treatment of addiction. Front. Pharmacol. 10 (720). https://doi.org/10.3389/fphar.2019.00720.

Ihssen, N., Cox, W.M., Wiggett, A., Fadardi, J.S., Linden, D.E., 2011. Differentiating heavy from light drinkers by neural responses to visual alcohol cues and other motivational stimuli. Cerebr. Cortex 21 (6), 1408–1415. https://doi.org/10.1093/cercor/bhq220.

Infante, M.A., Courtney, K.E., Castro, N., Squeglia, L.M., Jacobus, J., 2018. Adolescent brain surface area pre- and post-cannabis and alcohol initiation. J. Stud. Alcohol Drugs 79 (6), 835–843. https://doi.org/10.15288/jsad.2018.79.835.

Janes, A.C., Krantz, N.L., Nickerson, L.D., Frederick, B.B., Lukas, S.E., 2020. Craving and cue reactivity in nicotine-dependent tobacco smokers is associated with different insula networks. Biol. Psychiatry Cogn. Neurosci. Neuroimaging 5 (1), 76–83. https://doi.org/10.1016/j.bpsc.2019.09.005.

Janes, A.C., Pizzagalli, D.A., Richardt, S., deB Frederick, B., Chuzi, S., Pachas, G., Kaufman, M.J., 2010. Brain reactivity to smoking cues prior to smoking cessation predicts ability to maintain tobacco abstinence. Biol. Psychiatry 67 (8), 722–729. https://doi.org/10.1016/j.biopsych.2009.12.034.

Janes, A.C., Ross, R.S., Farmer, S., Frederick, B.B., Nickerson, L.D., Lukas, S.E., Stern, C.E., 2015. Memory retrieval of smoking-related images induce greater insula activation as revealed by an fMRI-based delayed matching to sample task. Addiction Biol. 20 (2), 349–356. https://doi.org/10.1111/adb.12112.

Jaramillo, A.A., Agan, V.E., Makhijani, V.H., Pedroza, S., McElligott, Z.A., Besheer, J., 2018a. Functional role for suppression of the insular-striatal circuit in modulating interoceptive effects of alcohol. Addiction Biol. 23 (5), 1020–1031. https://doi.org/10.1111/adb.12551.

Jaramillo, A.A., Randall, P.A., Frisbee, S., Besheer, J., 2016. Modulation of sensitivity to alcohol by cortical and thalamic brain regions. Eur. J. Neurosci. 44 (8), 2569–2580. https://doi.org/10.1111/ejn.13374.

Jaramillo, A.A., Randall, P.A., Stewart, S., Fortino, B., Van Voorhies, K., Besheer, J., 2018b. Functional role for cortical-striatal circuitry in modulating alcohol self-administration. Neuropharmacology 130, 42–53. https://doi.org/10.1016/j.neuropharm.2017.11.035.

Jaramillo, A.A., Van Voorhies, K., Randall, P.A., Besheer, J., 2018c. Silencing the insular-striatal circuit decreases alcohol self-administration and increases sensitivity to alcohol. Behav. Brain Res. 348, 74–81. https://doi.org/10.1016/j.bbr.2018.04.007.

Jauhar, S., Fortea, L., Solanes, A., Albajes-Eizagirre, A., McKenna, P.J., Radua, J., 2021. Brain activations associated with anticipation and delivery of monetary reward: a systematic review and meta-analysis of fMRI studies. PLoS One 16 (8), e0255292. https://doi.org/10.1371/journal.pone.0255292.

Jedema, H.P., Song, X., Aizenstein, H.J., Bonner, A.R., Stein, E.A., Yang, Y., Bradberry, C.W., 2021. Long-term cocaine self-administration produces structural brain changes that correlate with altered cognition. Biol. Psychiatry 89 (4), 376–385. https://doi.org/10.1016/j.biopsych.2020.08.008.

Kalivas, P.W., Volkow, N.D., 2005. The neural basis of addiction: a pathology of motivation and choice. Am. J. Psychiatry 162 (8), 1403–1413. https://doi.org/10.1176/appi.ajp.162.8.1403.

Kantak, K.M., Udo, T., Ugalde, F., Luzzo, C., Di Pietro, N., Eichenbaum, H.B., 2005. Influence of cocaine self-administration on learning related to prefrontal cortex or hippocampus functioning in rats. Psychopharmacology 181 (2), 227–236. https://doi.org/10.1007/s00213-005-2243-1.

Karnath, H.O., Baier, B., 2010. Right insula for our sense of limb ownership and self-awareness of actions. Brain Struct. Funct. 214 (5–6), 411–417. https://doi.org/10.1007/s00429-010-0250-4.

Kim, J.I., Lee, J.D., Hwang, H.J., Ki, S.W., Park, I.H., Park, T.Y., 2020. Altered subcallosal and posterior cingulate cortex-based functional connectivity during smoking cue and mental simulation processing in smokers. Prog. Neuro-Psychopharmacol. Biol. Psychiatry 97, 109772. https://doi.org/10.1016/j.pnpbp.2019.109772.

Kleinhans, N.M., Sweigert, J., Blake, M., Douglass, B., Doane, B., Reitz, F., Larimer, M., 2020. FMRI activation to cannabis odor cues is altered in individuals at risk for a cannabis use disorder. Brain Behav. 10 (10), e01764. https://doi.org/10.1002/brb3.1764.

Koenis, M.M.G., Durnez, J., Rodrigue, A.L., Mathias, S.R., Alexander-Bloch, A.F., Barrett, J.A., Glahn, D.C., 2020. Associations of cannabis use disorder with cognition, brain structure, and brain function in African Americans. Hum. Brain Mapp. https://doi.org/10.1002/hbm.25324.

Koob, G.F., Le Moal, M., 2005. Plasticity of reward neurocircuitry and the 'dark side' of drug addiction. Nat. Neurosci. 8 (11), 1442–1444. https://doi.org/10.1038/nn1105-1442.

Koob, G.F., Volkow, N.D., 2010. Neurocircuitry of addiction. Neuropsychopharmacology 35 (1), 217–238. https://doi.org/10.1038/npp.2009.110.

Krettek, J.E., Price, J.L., 1977. The cortical projections of the mediodorsal nucleus and adjacent thalamic nuclei in the rat. J. Comp. Neurol. 171 (2), 157–191. https://doi.org/10.1002/cne.901710204.

Kufahl, P.R., Zavala, A.R., Singh, A., Thiel, K.J., Dickey, E.D., Joyce, J.N., Neisewander, J.L., 2009. c-Fos expression associated with reinstatement of cocaine-seeking behavior by response-contingent conditioned cues. Synapse 63 (10), 823–835. https://doi.org/10.1002/syn.20666.

Kutlu, M.G., Burke, D., Slade, S., Hall, B.J., Rose, J.E., Levin, E.D., 2013. Role of insular cortex D1 and D2 dopamine receptors in nicotine self-administration in rats. Behav. Brain Res. 256, 273–278. https://doi.org/10.1016/j.bbr.2013.08.005.

Lamm, C., Singer, T., 2010. The role of anterior insular cortex in social emotions. Brain Struct. Funct. 214 (5–6), 579–591. https://doi.org/10.1007/s00429-010-0251-3.

Langenecker, S.A., Kling, L.R., Crane, N.A., Gorka, S.M., Nusslock, R., Damme, K.S.F., Phan, K.L., 2020. Anticipation of monetary reward in amygdala, insula, caudate are predictors of pleasure sensitivity to d-Amphetamine administration. Drug Alcohol Depend. 206, 107725. https://doi.org/10.1016/j.drugalcdep.2019.107725.

Lee, W., Reeve, J., 2013. Self-determined, but not non-self-determined, motivation predicts activations in the anterior insular cortex: an fMRI study of personal agency. Soc. Cognit. Affect Neurosci. 8 (5), 538–545. https://doi.org/10.1093/scan/nss029.

Lefaucheur, J.-P., André-Obadia, N., Antal, A., Ayache, S.S., Baeken, C., Benninger, D.H., Garcia-Larrea, L., 2014. Evidence-based guidelines on the therapeutic use of repetitive transcranial magnetic stimulation (rTMS). Clin. Neurophysiol. 125 (11), 2150–2206. https://doi.org/10.1016/j.clinph.2014.05.021.

Lerman, C., Gu, H., Loughead, J., Ruparel, K., Yang, Y., Stein, E.A., 2014. Large-scale brain network coupling predicts acute nicotine abstinence effects on craving and cognitive function. JAMA Psychiatry 71 (5), 523–530. https://doi.org/10.1001/jamapsychiatry.2013.4091.

Lerner, J.S., Li, Y., Valdesolo, P., Kassam, K.S., 2015. Emotion and decision making. Annu. Rev. Psychol. 66, 799–823. https://doi.org/10.1146/annurev-psych-010213-115043.

Lesage, E., Sutherland, M.T., Ross, T.J., Salmeron, B.J., Stein, E.A., 2020. Nicotine dependence (trait) and acute nicotinic stimulation (state) modulate attention but not inhibitory control: converging fMRI evidence from Go-Nogo and Flanker tasks. Neuropsychopharmacology 45 (5), 857–865. https://doi.org/10.1038/s41386-020-0623-1.

Levinthal, D.J., Strick, P.L., 2020. Multiple areas of the cerebral cortex influence the stomach. Proc. Natl. Acad. Sci. U. S. A. 117 (23), 13078–13083. https://doi.org/10.1073/pnas.2002737117.

Li, C.-L., Zhu, N., Meng, X.-L., Li, Y.-H., Sui, N., 2013. Effects of inactivating the agranular or granular insular cortex on the acquisition of the morphine-induced conditioned place preference and naloxone-precipitated conditioned place aversion in rats. J. Psychopharmacol. 27 (9), 837–844. https://doi.org/10.1177/0269881113492028.

Li, S., Yang, Y., Hoffmann, E., Tyndale, R.F., Stein, E.A., 2017a. CYP2A6 genetic variation alters striatal-cingulate circuits, network hubs, and executive processing in smokers. Biol. Psychiatry 81 (7), 554–563. https://doi.org/10.1016/j.biopsych.2016.09.013.

Li, X., Du, L., Sahlem, G.L., Badran, B.W., Henderson, S., George, M.S., 2017b. Repetitive transcranial magnetic stimulation (rTMS) of the dorsolateral prefrontal cortex reduces resting-state insula activity and modulates functional connectivity of the orbitofrontal cortex in cigarette smokers. Drug Alcohol Depend. 174, 98–105. https://doi.org/10.1016/j.drugalcdep.2017.02.002.

Li, X., Witonsky, K.R., Lofaro, O.M., Surjono, F., Zhang, J., Bossert, J.M., Shaham, Y., 2018. Role of anterior intralaminar nuclei of thalamus projections to dorsomedial striatum in incubation of methamphetamine craving. J. Neurosci. 38 (9), 2270. https://doi.org/10.1523/JNEUROSCI.2873-17.2018.

Li, Y., Yuan, K., Cai, C., Feng, D., Yin, J., Bi, Y., Tian, J., 2015. Reduced frontal cortical thickness and increased caudate volume within fronto-striatal circuits in young adult smokers. Drug Alcohol Depend. 151, 211–219. https://doi.org/10.1016/j.drugalcdep.2015.03.023.

Luppino, G., Matelli, M., Camarda, R., Rizzolatti, G., 1993. Corticocortical connections of area F3 (SMA-proper) and area F6 (pre-SMA) in the macaque monkey. J. Comp. Neurol. 338 (1), 114–140. https://doi.org/10.1002/cne.903380109.

Ma, H., Wang, N., Wang, X., Jia, M., Li, Y., Cui, C., 2018. Wnt7a in mouse insular cortex contributes to anxiety-like behavior during protracted abstinence from morphine. Neuroscience 394, 164–176. https://doi.org/10.1016/j.neuroscience.2018.10.032.

Ma, P., Liu, H., Li, H., Huang, X., Chen, L., Zhai, H., 2014. Involvement of the insular nitric oxide signaling pathway in the expression of morphine-induced conditioned place preference in rats. Neuroreport Rapid Commun. Neurosci. Res. 25 (9), 641–646. https://doi.org/10.1097/WNR.0000000000000146.

Mackey, S., Allgaier, N., Chaarani, B., Spechler, P., Orr, C., Bunn, J., Garavan, H., 2019. Mega-analysis of gray matter volume in substance dependence: general and substance-specific regional effects. Am. J. Psychiatry 176 (2), 119–128. https://doi.org/10.1176/appi.ajp.2018.17040415.

Mackey, W.B., Keller, J., Van der Kooy, D., 1986. Visceral cortex lesions block conditioned taste aversions induced by morphine. Pharmacol. Biochem. Behav. 24 (1), 71–78. https://doi.org/10.1016/0091-3057(86)90047-X.

Malik, S., Jacobs, M., Cho, S.-S., Boileau, I., Blumberger, D., Heilig, M., Le Foll, B., 2018. Deep TMS of the insula using the H-coil modulates dopamine release: a crossover [11C] PHNO-PET pilot trial in healthy humans. Brain Imag. Behav. 12 (5), 1306–1317. https://doi.org/10.1007/s11682-017-9800-1.

Margeta-Mitrovic, M., Mitrovic, I., Riley, R.C., Jan, L.Y., Basbaum, A.I., 1999. Immunohistochemical localization of GABAB receptors in the rat central nervous system. J. Comp. Neurol. 405 (3), 299–321. https://doi.org/10.1002/(SICI)1096-9861(19990315)405:3<299::AID-CNE2>3.0.CO;2-6.

Maskos, U., Molles, B.E., Pons, S., Besson, M., Guiard, B.P., Guilloux, J.P., Changeux, J.P., 2005. Nicotine reinforcement and cognition restored by targeted expression of nicotinic receptors. Nature 436 (7047), 103–107. https://doi.org/10.1038/nature03694.

Mazzola, L., Isnard, J., Peyron, R., Guénot, M., Mauguière, F., 2009. Somatotopic organization of pain responses to direct electrical stimulation of the human insular cortex. Pain 146 (1–2), 99–104. https://doi.org/10.1016/j.pain.2009.07.014.

Mazzola, L., Isnard, J., Peyron, R., Mauguière, F., 2012. Stimulation of the human cortex and the experience of pain: wilder Penfield's observations revisited. Brain 135 (Pt 2), 631–640. https://doi.org/10.1093/brain/awr265.

McDonald, A.J., Shammah-Lagnado, S.J., Shi, C., Davis, M., 1999. Cortical afferents to the extended amygdala. Ann. N. Y. Acad. Sci. 877, 309–338. https://doi.org/10.1111/j.1749-6632.1999.tb09275.x.

McGeorge, A.J., Faull, R.L., 1989. The organization of the projection from the cerebral cortex to the striatum in the rat. Neuroscience 29 (3), 503–537. https://doi.org/10.1016/0306-4522(89)90128-0.

McHugh, M.J., Demers, C.H., Braud, J., Briggs, R., Adinoff, B., Stein, E.A., 2013. Striatal-insula circuits in cocaine addiction: implications for impulsivity and relapse risk. Am. J. Drug Alcohol Abuse 39 (6), 424–432. https://doi.org/10.3109/00952990.2013.847446.

Menon, V., Uddin, L.Q., 2010. Saliency, switching, attention and control: a network model of insula function. Brain Struct. Funct. 214 (5), 655–667. https://doi.org/10.1007/s00429-010-0262-0.

Mizoguchi, H., Katahira, K., Inutsuka, A., Fukumoto, K., Nakamura, A., Wang, T., Yamada, K., 2015. Insular neural system controls decision-making in healthy and methamphetamine-treated rats. Proc. Natl. Acad. Sci. USA 112 (29), E3930. https://doi.org/10.1073/pnas.1418014112.

Morales, A.M., Ghahremani, D., Kohno, M., Hellemann, G.S., London, E.D., 2014. Cigarette exposure, dependence, and craving are related to insula thickness in young adult smokers. Neuropsychopharmacology 39 (8), 1816–1822. https://doi.org/10.1038/npp.2014.48.

Moran, L.V., Stoeckel, L.E., Wang, K., Caine, C.E., Villafuerte, R., Calderon, V., Evins, A.E., 2018. Nicotine increases activation to anticipatory valence cues in anterior insula and striatum. Nicotine Tob. Res. Off. J. Soc. Res. Nicotine Tobacco 20 (7), 851–858. https://doi.org/10.1093/ntr/ntx217.

Moran-Santa Maria, M.M., Hartwell, K.J., Hanlon, C.A., Canterberry, M., Lematty, T., Owens, M., George, M.S., 2015. Right anterior insula connectivity is important for cue-induced craving in nicotine-dependent smokers. Addiction Biol. 20 (2), 407–414. https://doi.org/10.1111/adb.12124.

Muñoz, B., Fritz, B.M., Yin, F., Atwood, B.K., 2018. Alcohol exposure disrupts mu opioid receptor-mediated long-term depression at insular cortex inputs to dorsolateral striatum. Nat. Commun. 9 (1). https://doi.org/10.1038/s41467-018-03683-1, 1318-1318.

Mutschler, I., Wieckhorst, B., Kowalevski, S., Derix, J., Wentlandt, J., Schulze-Bonhage, A., Ball, T., 2009. Functional organization of the human anterior insular cortex. Neurosci. Lett. 457 (2), 66–70. https://doi.org/10.1016/j.neulet.2009.03.101.

Nagai, M., Hoshide, S., Kario, K., 2010. The insular cortex and cardiovascular system: a new insight into the brain-heart axis. J. Am. Soc. Hypertens. 4 (4), 174–182. https://doi.org/10.1016/j.jash.2010.05.001.

Naidich, T.P., Kang, E., Fatterpekar, G.M., Delman, B.N., Gultekin, S.H., Wolfe, D., Yousry, T.A., 2004. The insula: anatomic study and MR imaging display at 1.5 T. AJNR Am. J. Neuroradiol. 25 (2), 222–232.

Naqvi, N.H., Gaznick, N., Tranel, D., Bechara, A., 2014. The insula: a critical neural substrate for craving and drug seeking under conflict and risk. Ann. N. Y. Acad. Sci. 1316, 53–70. https://doi.org/10.1111/nyas.12415.

Naqvi, N.H., Rudrauf, D., Damasio, H., Bechara, A., 2007. Damage to the insula disrupts addiction to cigarette smoking. Science 315 (5811), 531–534. https://doi.org/10.1126/science.1135926.

Nestler, E.J., 2005. Is there a common molecular pathway for addiction? Nat. Neurosci. 8 (11), 1445–1449. https://doi.org/10.1038/nn1578.

Nieuwenhuys, R., 2012. The insular cortex: a review. Prog. Brain Res. 195, 123–163. https://doi.org/10.1016/b978-0-444-53860-4.00007-6.

Nisticò, V., Rossi, R.E., D'Arrigo, A.M., Priori, A., Gambini, O., Demartini, B., 2022. Functional neuroimaging in irritable bowel syndrome: a systematic review highlights common brain alterations with functional movement disorders. J. Neurogastroenterol. Motil. 28 (2), 185–203. https://doi.org/10.5056/jnm21079.

Ohara, P.T., Granato, A., Moallem, T.M., Wang, B.-R., Tillet, Y., Jasmin, L., 2003. Dopaminergic input to GABAergic neurons in the rostral agranular insular cortex of the rat. J. Neurocytol. 32 (2), 131–141. https://doi.org/10.1023/B:NEUR.0000005598.09647.7f.

Pelloux, Y., Murray, J.E., Everitt, B.J., 2013. Differential roles of the prefrontal cortical subregions and basolateral amygdala in compulsive cocaine seeking and relapse after voluntary abstinence in rats. Eur. J. Neurosci. 38 (7), 3018–3026. https://doi.org/10.1111/ejn.12289.

Penfield, W., Faulk, M.E., 1955. The insula: further observations on its function. Brain 78 (4), 445–470.

Peng, P., Li, M., Liu, H., Tian, Y.R., Chu, S.L., Van Halm-Lutterodt, N., Jiang, T., 2018. Brain structure alterations in respect to tobacco consumption and nicotine dependence: a comparative voxel-based morphometry study. Front. Neuroanat. 12, 43. https://doi.org/10.3389/fnana.2018.00043.

Perini, I., Kämpe, R., Arlestig, T., Karlsson, H., Löfberg, A., Pietrzak, M., Heilig, M., 2020. Repetitive transcranial magnetic stimulation targeting the insular cortex for reduction of heavy drinking in treatment-seeking alcohol-dependent subjects: a randomized controlled trial. Neuropsychopharmacology 45 (5), 842–850. https://doi.org/10.1038/s41386-019-0565-7.

Perry, R.N., Schlagintweit, H.E., Darredeau, C., Helmick, C., Newman, A.J., Good, K.P., Barrett, S.P., 2019. The impacts of actual and perceived nicotine administration on insula functional connectivity with the anterior cingulate cortex and nucleus accumbens. J. Psychopharmacol. 33 (12), 1600–1609. https://doi.org/10.1177/0269881119872205.

Phan, K.L., Wager, T., Taylor, S.F., Liberzon, I., 2002. Functional neuroanatomy of emotion: a meta-analysis of emotion activation studies in PET and fMRI. Neuroimage 16 (2), 331–348. https://doi.org/10.1006/nimg.2002.1087.

Picciotto, M.R., Zoli, M., Rimondini, R., Léna, C., Marubio, L.M., Pich, E.M., Changeux, J.P., 1998. Acetylcholine receptors containing the beta2 subunit are involved in the reinforcing properties of nicotine. Nature 391 (6663), 173–177. https://doi.org/10.1038/34413.

Porrino, L.J., Lyons, D., Miller, M.D., Smith, H.R., Friedman, D.P., Daunais, J.B., Nader, M.A., 2002. Metabolic mapping of the effects of cocaine during the initial phases of self-administration in the nonhuman primate. J. Neurosci. 22 (17), 7687. https://doi.org/10.1523/JNEUROSCI.22-17-07687.2002.

Pritchard, T.C., Macaluso, D.A., Eslinger, P.J., 1999. Taste perception in patients with insular cortex lesions. Behav. Neurosci. 113 (4), 663–671.

Puaud, M., Higuera-Matas, A., Brunault, P., Everitt, B.J., Belin, D., 2021. The basolateral amygdala to nucleus accumbens core circuit mediates the conditioned reinforcing effects of cocaine-paired cues on cocaine seeking. Biol. Psychiatry 89 (4), 356–365. https://doi.org/10.1016/j.biopsych.2020.07.022.

Pushparaj, A., Hamani, C., Yu, W., Shin, D.S., Kang, B., Nobrega, J.N., Le Foll, B., 2013. Electrical stimulation of the insular region attenuates nicotine-taking and nicotine-seeking behaviors. Neuropsychopharmacol. Off. Publ. Am. Coll. Neuropsychopharmacol. 38 (4), 690–698. https://doi.org/10.1038/npp.2012.235.

Pushparaj, A., Kim, A.S., Musiol, M., Trigo, J.M., Le Foll, B., 2015. Involvement of the rostral agranular insular cortex in nicotine self-administration in rats. Behav. Brain Res. 290, 77–83. https://doi.org/10.1016/j.bbr.2015.04.039.

Pushparaj, A., Kim, A.S., Musiol, M., Zangen, A., Daskalakis, Z.J., Zack, M., Le Foll, B., 2015. Differential involvement of the agranular vs granular insular cortex in the acquisition and performance of choice behavior in a rodent gambling task. Neuropsychopharmacology 40, 2832–2842.

Pushparaj, A., Le Foll, B., 2015. Involvement of the caudal granular insular cortex in alcohol self-administration in rats. Behav. Brain Res. 293, 203–207. https://doi.org/10.1016/j.bbr.2015.07.044.

Rabin, R.A., Mackey, S., Parvaz, M.A., Cousijn, J., Li, C.S., Pearlson, G., Goldstein, R.Z., 2020. Common and gender-specific associations with cocaine use on gray matter volume: data from the ENIGMA addiction working group. Hum. Brain Mapp. https://doi.org/10.1002/hbm.25141.

Rolls, E.T., 2019. Taste and smell processing in the brain. Handb. Clin. Neurol. 164, 97–118. https://doi.org/10.1016/b978-0-444-63855-7.00007-1.

Rotge, J.-Y., Cocker, P.J., Daniel, M.-L., Belin-Rauscent, A., Everitt, B.J., Belin, D., 2017. Bidirectional regulation over the development and expression of loss of control over cocaine intake by the anterior insula. Psychopharmacology 234 (9–10), 1623–1631. https://doi.org/10.1007/s00213-017-4593-x.

Roy-Côté, F., Zahal, R., Frasnelli, J., Nguyen, D.K., Boucher, O., 2021. Insula and olfaction: a literature review and case report. Brain Sci. 11 (2). https://doi.org/10.3390/brainsci11020198.

Ruggiero, D.A., Mraovitch, S., Granata, A.R., Anwar, M., Reis, D.J., 1987. A role of insular cortex in cardiovascular function. J. Comp. Neurol. 257 (2), 189–207. https://doi.org/10.1002/cne.902570206.

Sánchez, M.M., Young, L.J., Plotsky, P.M., Insel, T.R., 1999. Autoradiographic and in situ hybridization localization of corticotropin-releasing factor 1 and 2 receptors in nonhuman primate brain. J. Comp. Neurol. 408 (3), 365–377. https://doi.org/10.1002/(SICI)1096-9861(19990607)408:3<365::AID-CNE5>3.0.CO;2-N.

Saper, C.B., 1982. Convergence of autonomic and limbic connections in the insular cortex of the rat. J. Comp. Neurol. 210 (2), 163–173. https://doi.org/10.1002/cne.902100207.

Saper, C.B., 2002. The central autonomic nervous system: conscious visceral perception and autonomic pattern generation. Annu. Rev. Neurosci. 25 (1), 433–469. https://doi.org/10.1146/annurev.neuro.25.032502.111311.

Schneider, R.J., Friedman, D.P., Mishkin, M., 1993. A modality-specific somatosensory area within the insula of the rhesus monkey. Brain Res. 621 (1), 116–120. https://doi.org/10.1016/0006-8993(93)90305-7.

Schwartz, D.L., Mitchell, A.D., Lahna, D.L., Luber, H.S., Huckans, M.S., Mitchell, S.H., Hoffman, W.F., 2010. Global and local morphometric differences in recently abstinent methamphetamine-dependent individuals. Neuroimage 50 (4), 1392–1401. https://doi.org/10.1016/j.neuroimage.2010.01.056.

Scott, D., Hiroi, N., 2011. Deconstructing craving: dissociable cortical control of cue reactivity in nicotine addiction. Biol. Psychiatry 69 (11), 1052–1059. https://doi.org/10.1016/j.biopsych.2011.01.023.

Segerdahl, A.R., Mezue, M., Okell, T.W., Farrar, J.T., Tracey, I., 2015. The dorsal posterior insula subserves a fundamental role in human pain. Nat. Neurosci. 18 (4), 499–500. https://doi.org/10.1038/nn.3969.

Seif, T., Chang, S.-J., Simms, J.A., Gibb, S.L., Dadgar, J., Chen, B.T., Hopf, F.W., 2013. Cortical activation of accumbens hyperpolarization-active NMDARs mediates aversion-resistant alcohol intake. Nat. Neurosci. 16 (8), 1094–1100. https://doi.org/10.1038/nn.3445.

Seltzer, B., Pandya, D.N., 1991. Post-rolandic cortical projections of the superior temporal sulcus in the rhesus monkey. J. Comp. Neurol. 312 (4), 625–640. https://doi.org/10.1002/cne.903120412.

Shahbabaie, A., Ebrahimpoor, M., Hariri, A., Nitsche, M.A., Hatami, J., Fatemizadeh, E., Ekhtiari, H., 2018. Transcranial DC stimulation modifies functional connectivity of large-scale brain networks in abstinent methamphetamine users. Brain Behav. 8 (3), e00922. https://doi.org/10.1002/brb3.922.

Shi, C.J., Cassell, M.D., 1998a. Cascade projections from somatosensory cortex to the rat basolateral amygdala via the parietal insular cortex. J. Comp. Neurol. 399 (4), 469–491. https://doi.org/10.1002/(sici)1096-9861(19981005)399:4<469::aid-cne3>3.0.co;2-#.

Shi, C.J., Cassell, M.D., 1998b. Cortical, thalamic, and amygdaloid connections of the anterior and posterior insular cortices. J. Comp. Neurol. 399 (4), 440–468. https://doi.org/10.1002/(sici)1096-9861(19981005)399:4<440::aid-cne2>3.0.co;2-1.

Shillinglaw, J.E., Morrisett, R.A., Mangieri, R.A., 2018. Ethanol modulates glutamatergic transmission and NMDAR-mediated synaptic plasticity in the agranular insular cortex. Front. Pharmacol. 9 (1458). https://doi.org/10.3389/fphar.2018.01458.

Shollenbarger, S., Thomas, A.M., Wade, N.E., Gruber, S.A., Tapert, S.F., Filbey, F.M., Lisdahl, K.M., 2019. Intrinsic frontolimbic connectivity and mood symptoms in young adult cannabis users. Front. Public Health 7, 311. https://doi.org/10.3389/fpubh.2019.00311.

Stephani, C., Fernandez-Baca Vaca, G., Maciunas, R., Koubeissi, M., Lüders, H.O., 2011. Functional neuroanatomy of the insular lobe. Brain Struct. Funct. 216 (2), 137–149. https://doi.org/10.1007/s00429-010-0296-3.

Stewart, J.L., Butt, M., May, A.C., Tapert, S.F., Paulus, M.P., 2017. Insular and cingulate attenuation during decision making is associated with future transition to stimulant use disorder. Addiction (Abingdon, England) 112 (9), 1567–1577. https://doi.org/10.1111/add.13839.

Stewart, J.L., Connolly, C.G., May, A.C., Tapert, S.F., Wittmann, M., Paulus, M.P., 2014. Striatum and insula dysfunction during reinforcement learning differentiates abstinent and relapsed methamphetamine dependent individuals. Addiction 109, 460–471.

Stippekohl, B., Winkler, M.H., Walter, B., Kagerer, S., Mucha, R.F., Pauli, P., Stark, R., 2012. Neural responses to smoking stimuli are influenced by smokers' attitudes towards their own smoking behaviour. PLoS One 7 (11). https://doi.org/10.1371/journal.pone.0046782 e46782-e46782.

Stoeckel, L.E., Chai, X.J., Zhang, J., Whitfield-Gabrieli, S., Evins, A.E., 2016. Lower gray matter density and functional connectivity in the anterior insula in smokers compared with never smokers. Addiction Biol. 21 (4), 972–981. https://doi.org/10.1111/adb.12262.

Strang, J., Volkow, N.D., Degenhardt, L., Hickman, M., Johnson, K., Koob, G.F., Walsh, S.L., 2020. Opioid use disorder. Nat. Rev. Dis. Prim. 6 (1), 3. https://doi.org/10.1038/s41572-019-0137-5.

Su, H., Liu, Y., Yin, D., Chen, T., Li, X., Zhong, N., Zhao, M., 2020. Neuroplastic changes in resting-state functional connectivity after rTMS intervention for methamphetamine craving. Neuropharmacology 175, 108177. https://doi.org/10.1016/j.neuropharm.2020.108177.

Sullivan, E.V., Müller-Oehring, E., Pitel, A.-L., Chanraud, S., Shankaranarayanan, A., Alsop, D.C., Pfefferbaum, A., 2013. A selective insular perfusion deficit contributes to compromised salience network connectivity in recovering alcoholic men. Biol. Psychiatry 74 (7), 547–555. https://doi.org/10.1016/j.biopsych.2013.02.026.

Sun, Y.-M., Chen, R.-X., Li, Z.-F., Spijker, S., Zhai, R.-W., Yang, S.-C., 2018. The caudal part of the posterior insula of rats participates in the maintenance but not the acquisition of morphine conditioned place preference. CNS Neurosci. Ther. 24 (5), 420–428. https://doi.org/10.1111/cns.12799.

Suñer-Soler, R., Grau, A., Gras, M.E., Font-Mayolas, S., Silva, Y., Dávalos, A., Serena, J., 2012. Smoking cessation 1 year poststroke and damage to the insular cortex. Stroke 43 (1), 131–136. https://doi.org/10.1161/strokeaha.111.630004.

Sutherland, M.T., Carroll, A.J., Salmeron, B.J., Ross, T.J., Hong, L.E., Stein, E.A., 2013a. Down-regulation of amygdala and insula functional circuits by varenicline and nicotine in abstinent cigarette smokers. Biol. Psychiatry 74 (7), 538–546. https://doi.org/10.1016/j.biopsych.2013.01.035.

Sutherland, M.T., Carroll, A.J., Salmeron, B.J., Ross, T.J., Stein, E.A., 2013b. Insula's functional connectivity with ventromedial prefrontal cortex mediates the impact of trait alexithymia on state tobacco craving. Psychopharmacology 228 (1), 143–155. https://doi.org/10.1007/s00213-013-3018-8.

Sutherland, M.T., McHugh, M.J., Pariyadath, V., Stein, E.A., 2012. Resting state functional connectivity in addiction: lessons learned and a road ahead. Neuroimage 62 (4), 2281–2295. https://doi.org/10.1016/j.neuroimage.2012.01.117.

Sutherland, M.T., Ray, K.L., Riedel, M.C., Yanes, J.A., Stein, E.A., Laird, A.R., 2015. Neurobiological impact of nicotinic acetylcholine receptor agonists: an activation likelihood estimation meta-analysis of pharmacologic neuroimaging studies. Biol. Psychiatry 78 (10), 711–720. https://doi.org/10.1016/j.biopsych.2014.12.021.

Sutherland, M.T., Riedel, M.C., Flannery, J.S., Yanes, J.A., Fox, P.T., Stein, E.A., Laird, A.R., 2016. Chronic cigarette smoking is linked with structural alterations in brain regions showing acute nicotinic drug-induced functional modulations. Behav. Brain Funct. BBF 12 (1). https://doi.org/10.1186/s12993-016-0100-5, 16-16.

Sutherland, M.T., Stein, E.A., 2018. Functional neurocircuits and neuroimaging biomarkers of tobacco use disorder. Trends Mol. Med. 24 (2), 129–143. https://doi.org/10.1016/j.molmed.2017.12.002.

Türe, U., Yasargil, D.C., Al-Mefty, O., Yasargil, M.G., 1999. Topographic anatomy of the insular region. J. Neurosurg. 90 (4), 720–733. https://doi.org/10.3171/jns.1999.90.4.0720.

Turel, O., He, Q., Brevers, D., Bechara, A., 2018. Delay discounting mediates the association between posterior insular cortex volume and social media addiction symptoms. Cognit. Affect Behav. Neurosci. 18 (4), 694–704. https://doi.org/10.3758/s13415-018-0597-1.

Uddin, L.Q., Nomi, J.S., Hébert-Seropian, B., Ghaziri, J., Boucher, O., 2017. Structure and function of the human insula. J. Clin. Neurophysiol. Off. Publ. Am. Electroencephalographic Soc. 34 (4), 300–306. https://doi.org/10.1097/WNP.0000000000000377.

Van der Werf, Y.D., Witter, M.P., Groenewegen, H.J., 2002. The intralaminar and midline nuclei of the thalamus. Anatomical and functional evidence for participation in processes of arousal and awareness. Brain Res. Rev. 39 (2–3), 107–140. https://doi.org/10.1016/s0165-0173(02)00181-9.

Venniro, M., Caprioli, D., Zhang, M., Whitaker, L.R., Zhang, S., Warren, B.L., Shaham, Y., 2017. The anterior insular cortex→central amygdala glutamatergic pathway is critical to relapse after contingency management. Neuron 96 (2), 414–427.e418. https://doi.org/10.1016/j.neuron.2017.09.024.

Vertes, R.P., 2004. Differential projections of the infralimbic and prelimbic cortex in the rat. Synapse 51 (1), 32–58. https://doi.org/10.1002/syn.10279.

Wager, T.D., Atlas, L.Y., Lindquist, M.A., Roy, M., Woo, C.-W., Kross, E., 2013. An fMRI-based neurologic signature of physical pain. N. Engl. J. Med. 368 (15), 1388–1397. https://doi.org/10.1056/NEJMoa1204471.

Wang, C., Huang, P., Shen, Z., Qian, W., Li, K., Luo, X., Zhang, M., 2019. Gray matter volumes of insular subregions are not correlated with smoking cessation outcomes but negatively correlated with nicotine dependence severity in chronic smokers. Neurosci. Lett. 696, 7–12.

Wang, C., Shen, Z., Huang, P., Qian, W., Zhou, C., Li, K., Zhang, M., 2020a. Increased interregional functional connectivity of anterior insula is associated with improved smoking cessation outcome. Brain Imaging Behav. 14 (2), 408–415. https://doi.org/10.1007/s11682-019-00197-2.

Wang, C., Wang, S., Huang, P., Shen, Z., Qian, W., Luo, X., Zhang, M., 2020b. Abnormal white matter tracts of insula in smokers. Brain Imaging Behav. https://doi.org/10.1007/s11682-020-00389-1.

Wang, F., Jing, X., Yang, J., Wang, H., Xiang, R., Han, W., Wu, C., 2016. The role of the insular cortex in naloxone-induced conditioned place aversion in morphine-dependent mice. Physiol. Res. 65 (4), 701–709. https://doi.org/10.33549/physiolres.933106.

Wang, K.S., Zegel, M., Molokotos, E., Moran, L.V., Olson, D.P., Pizzagalli, D.A., Janes, A.C., 2020c. The acute effects of nicotine on corticostriatal responses to distinct phases of reward processing. Neuropsychopharmacology 45 (7), 1207–1214. https://doi.org/10.1038/s41386-020-0611-5.

Wang, L., Hu, F., Wang, W., Li, Q., Li, Y., Zhu, J., Wang, Y., 2021. Altered brain intrinsic functional hubs and connectivity associated with relapse risk in heroin dependents undergoing methadone maintenance treatment: a resting-state fMRI study. Drug Alcohol Depend. 219, 108503. https://doi.org/10.1016/j.drugalcdep.2020.108503.

Wang, W., Wang, Y.R., Qin, W., Yuan, K., Tian, J., Li, Q., Guo, Y.M., 2010. Changes in functional connectivity of ventral anterior cingulate cortex in heroin abusers. Chin. Med. J. (Engl) 123 (12), 1582–1588.

Wei, Z., Yang, N., Liu, Y., Yang, L., Wang, Y., Han, L., Zhang, X., 2016. Resting-state functional connectivity between the dorsal anterior cingulate cortex and thalamus is associated with risky decision-making in nicotine addicts. Sci. Rep. 6, 21778. https://doi.org/10.1038/srep21778.

Wills, K.L., Petrie, G.N., Millett, G., Limebeer, C.L., Rock, E.M., Niphakis, M.J., Parker, L.A., 2016. Double dissociation of monoacylglycerol lipase inhibition and CB1 antagonism in the central amygdala, basolateral amygdala, and the interoceptive insular cortex on the affective properties of acute naloxone-precipitated morphine withdrawal in rats. Neuropsychopharmacology 41 (7), 1865–1873. https://doi.org/10.1038/npp.2015.356.

Wisner, K.M., Patzelt, E.H., Lim, K.O., MacDonald 3rd, A.W., 2013. An intrinsic connectivity network approach to insula-derived dysfunctions among cocaine users. Am. J. Drug Alcohol Abuse 39 (6), 403–413. https://doi.org/10.3109/00952990.2013.848211.

Wright, C.I., Groenewegen, H.J., 1996. Patterns of overlap and segregation between insular cortical, intermediodorsal thalamic and basal amygdaloid afferents in the nucleus accumbens of the rat. Neuroscience 73 (2), 359–373. https://doi.org/10.1016/0306-4522(95)00592-7.

Zangen, A., George, M., 2020. 3-Weeks of prefrontal and insular deep TMS combined with cue-induced craving significantly increases smoking abstinence: results from an international, multi-site, randomized, sham controlled trial. Biol. Psychiatry 87 (9), S129. https://doi.org/10.1016/j.biopsych.2020.02.348.

Zhang, M., Liu, S., Wang, S., Xu, Y., Chen, L., Shao, Z., Yuan, K., 2021. Reduced thalamic resting-state functional connectivity and impaired cognition in acute abstinent heroin users. Hum. Brain Mapp. https://doi.org/10.1002/hbm.25346.

Zhang, X., Salmeron, B.J., Ross, T.J., Geng, X., Yang, Y., Stein, E.A., 2011. Factors underlying prefrontal and insula structural alterations in smokers. Neuroimage 54 (1), 42–48. https://doi.org/10.1016/j.neuroimage.2010.08.008.

Zhou, L., Pruitt, C., Shin, C.B., Garcia, A.D., Zavala, A.R., See, R.E., 2014. Fos expression induced by cocaine-conditioned cues in male and female rats. Brain Struct. Funct. 219 (5), 1831–1840. https://doi.org/10.1007/s00429-013-0605-8.

Zhou, S., Xiao, D., Peng, P., Wang, S.K., Liu, Z., Qin, H.Y., Wang, C., 2017. Effect of smoking on resting-state functional connectivity in smokers: an fMRI study. Respirology 22 (6), 1118–1124. https://doi.org/10.1111/resp.13048.

CHAPTER

6

Thalamic circuits

Alessandra Matzeu, Francisco J. Flores-Ramirez and Rémi Martin-Fardon

Department of Molecular Medicine, The Scripps Research Institute, La Jolla, CA, United States

Overview of the thalamus

The thalamus is a mostly gray matter structure in the diencephalon in the brain that plays many essential roles and is involved in several neural functions. It is composed of various nuclei that each serve a unique role, ranging from relaying sensory and motor signals to regulating consciousness and alertness. The thalamus is a paired gray matter structure deep within the brain, thereby reflecting its primordial function, that is located adjacent to the third ventricle. Each member of the pair is roughly the size of a walnut (Fig. 6.1). Although the thalamus mostly consists of gray matter (i.e., cell bodies of neurons), it also has some areas of white matter (i.e., axons). The thalamus is above the midbrain or mesencephalon, allowing fiber connections to the cerebral cortex in all directions. Each thalamus connects to the other thalamus via interthalamic adhesion. One unique function of the thalamus is to gate or control the flow of information to the cortex (Scheibel, 1997; Sherman, 2017). The thalamus is the largest part of the diencephalon in mammals. It is composed of a collection of nuclei that are primarily composed of excitatory neurons that project to the cortex in a highly organized fashion, as well as other subcortical structures, including the striatum, amygdala, and hippocampus (Fig. 6.2). Thalamic structures receive important inputs from subcortical nuclei, including the lateral hypothalamus, brainstem, and amygdala. As a general rule, thalamic nuclei project to one or more well-defined areas of the cortex (i.e., "specific thalamus") or send diffuse projections (i.e., "nonspecific thalamus" (Bentivoglio et al., 1991; Halassa and Sherman, 2019; Pereira de Vasconcelos and Cassel, 2015). Thalamocortical neurons receive sensory or motor information from the rest of the body and send select information via nerve fibers (i.e., thalamocortical radiations) to the cortex. It also has connections with the hippocampus, mammillary bodies, and the fornix via the mammillothalamic tract (Stein et al., 2000). Structures of the limbic system (e.g., the amygdala; Fig. 6.2) are connected to anterior

Neurocircuitry of Addiction
https://doi.org/10.1016/B978-0-12-823453-2.00012-6

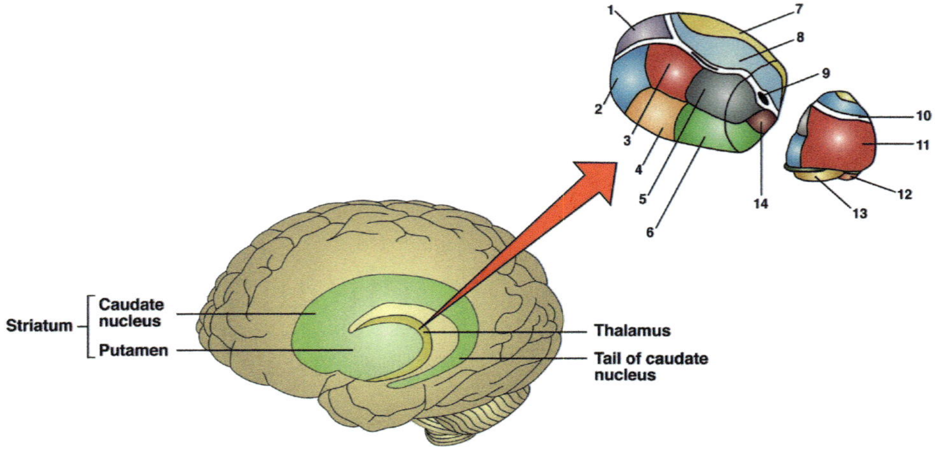

FIGURE 6.1 Simplified schematic diagram of the human brain and various thalamic nuclei. 1. Anterior nucleus. 2. Ventral anterior nucleus. 3. Lateral dorsal nucleus. 4. Ventrolateral nucleus. 5. Lateral posterior nucleus. 6. Ventral posterior lateral nucleus. 7. Midline thalamic nuclei. 8. Medial nucleus. 9. Intralaminar nuclei. 10. Internal medullary lamina. 11. Pulvinar nucleus. 12. Medial geniculate nucleus. 13. Lateral geniculate nucleus. 14. Ventral posteromedial nucleus.

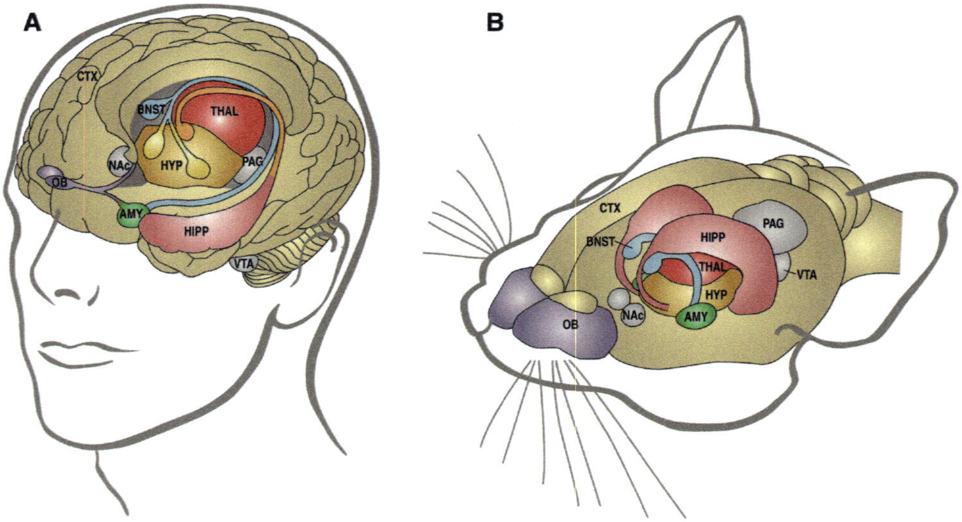

FIGURE 6.2 Simplified representation of the human (A) and rodent (B) brain with common structures that are found in both species, including the thalamus. *AMY*, amygdala; *BSNT*, bed nucleus of the stria terminalis; *CTX*, cortex; *HIPP*, hippocampus; *HYP*, hypothalamus; *NAc*, nucleus accumbens; *OB*, olfactory bulbs; *PAG*, periaqueductal gray; *THAL*, thalamus; *VTA*, ventral tegmental area.

nuclei of the thalamus, thereby allowing the thalamus to be involved in learning and episodic memory processes (Child and Benarroch, 2013). The thalamus is involved in regulating sleep and wakefulness (Steriade and Llinas, 1988; Gent et al., 2018; Vantomme et al., 2019).

Put simply, the thalamus acts as a relay station that filters information between the brain and body. In fact, with the exception of olfaction, every sensory system has a thalamic nucleus that receives, processes, and sends information to an associated cortical area (Scheibel, 1997). Fig. 6.1 presents a schematic diagram of different thalamic nuclei. For example, the lateral geniculate nucleus of the thalamus receives visual sensory inputs from the retina directly to the visual cortex of the occipital lobe. The medial geniculate nucleus receives auditory sensory information from the inferior colliculus and projects this information to the primary auditory cortex in the temporal lobe. The ventral posterior nucleus of the thalamus is further subdivided into three subregions. The spinothalamic tract is the sensory pathway for pain, temperature, and crude touch that originates in the spinal cord and feeds to the ventral posterior lateral nucleus of the thalamus for further processing. The ventral posteromedial nucleus receives sensory facial information from the trigeminal nerve (Torrico and Munakomi, 2021). The thalamus is classically known for its roles as a sensory relay for visual, auditory, somatosensory, and gustatory systems. It also plays important roles in motor activity, emotion, memory, arousal, and other sensorimotor association functions. Specifically, the thalamus can be divided into five major functional components. Reticular and intralaminar nuclei are involved in arousal and the regulation of pain. Sensory nuclei are implicated in all sensory domains, with the exception of olfaction. Effector nuclei are pivotal for the control of motor function and language function. Associative nuclei participate in higher-level cognitive functions. Limbic nuclei encompass mood and motivation (Schmahmann, 2003).

Thalamic lesions—importantly in the context of the present chapter, lesions that are induced by drugs of abuse—can have serious clinical consequences. Recently, accumulating evidence has shown that the thalamus is both affected by, and implicated in, substance use disorders, which is discussed in further detail below.

The thalamus and substance use disorder: overview

The thalamus has traditionally been characterized by its relay functions and multinuclear structure (Sherman, 2007; Sommer, 2003). Abundant thalamic circuitries and its diverse functions suggest that this structure is widely involved in several physiological and pathological processes. Numerous studies have sought to clarify the neuronal substrates that regulate compulsive behavioral characteristics of addiction. Brain regions that have been shown to be involved in drug addiction include the medial prefrontal cortex, basolateral amygdala, central nucleus of the amygdala, bed nucleus of the stria terminalis, hippocampus, nucleus accumbens, dorsal striatum, and ventral tegmental area (Belin and Everitt, 2008; Cardinal et al., 2002; Everitt et al., 2001; Goldstein and Volkow, 2002; Ito et al., 2002; Kalivas and Volkow, 2005; McFarland and Kalivas, 2001; See, 2002; Steketee and Kalivas, 2011; Weiss, 2005). Recently, emerging evidence has suggested that the thalamus could also be an integral part of the neurocircuitry of addiction. Indeed, it is considered an important key relay between the ventral striato-pallidum and dorsal striatum and may contribute to the development and persistence of compulsive drug-seeking behavior (Pierce and Vanderschuren, 2010). The thalamus is now considered an integral structure within brain reward circuitry, and findings from both animal and human studies suggest that this brain region plays an important role in both drug self-administration and the reinstatement of drug-seeking behavior (Huang et al., 2018).

Before introducing and discussing further the wide scientific literature that supports the pivotal participation of the thalamus in substance use disorder, it is important to note some important methodological considerations. Animal and human studies differ dramatically in their experimental approaches. Animal studies most often focus on targeting specific thalamic nuclei, whereas human studies investigate the structure and function of the thalamus more comprehensively as a whole. Animal studies can look at the role of different thalamic nuclei in different phases of the addiction cycle. Animal studies are also able to examine behavioral outcomes of site-specific manipulations of discrete thalamic nuclei, whereas human studies can better examine the relationship (e.g., connectivity; see **Human studies** section below for details) between the thalamus and other system changes across the whole brain. For example, human neuroimaging studies indicate that the thalamus exhibits a baseline reduction in the volume of both gray and white matter. White matter integrity has been linked to a reduction of baseline thalamic metabolism and functional connectivity in addicted individuals at rest. However, despite this baseline reduction of activation, thalamus hyperactivity was observed upon the presentation of drug-associated stimuli, indicating that the thalamic response to salient drug stimuli overcomes a general reduction of thalamic activation. Many studies of the thalamus in animals, specifically rodents, have focused on the role of the paraventricular nucleus of the thalamus (PVT), likely because of its extensive connections with the ventral and dorsal striatum (Everitt et al., 2001; S. Li and Kirouac, 2008; Moga et al., 1995; Vertes and Hoover, 2008; Wise, 1996). Although not a part of the thalamus proper but instead part of the epithalamus, the lateral and medial habenula have also received research attention in studies of addiction in rodents, mainly because of their connections with the ventral tegmental area and the interpeduncular nucleus respectively. Animal studies suggest that different thalamic nuclei may be involved in different aspects of drug addiction. Evidence suggests the involvement of the paraventricular nucleus of the thalamus and habenula in the reinstatement of drug-seeking behavior, which might mimic the increase in salience value that abstinent subjects experience in the presence of stimuli that are previously associated with drugs. The mediodorsal nucleus of the thalamus has also gained some attention because of its involvement in drug-seeking behavior in animals that are trained to self-administer drugs, further suggesting that the thalamus plays an essential role in the association between drug-associated stimuli and drug-seeking behavior.

The present chapter reviews and discusses scientific evidence from human studies of the critical involvement of the thalamus in addiction. We then present and examine the preclinical literature in rodents that demonstrate the involvement of the thalamus and thalamic circuits in animal models of drug addiction.

The thalamus: human studies

The thalamus is a relay center that promotes both sensory and motor mechanisms (Fig. 6.2A). A large number of thalamic nuclei project to one or a few well-defined cortical areas, and several cortical areas receive afferents from a single thalamic nucleus and send information back to different thalamic nuclei. The thalamus relays information between cortical regions and other brain areas, including the striatum, and it plays a key role in processing and integrating sensory information that is relevant to emotional and cognitive functions (e.g de Bourbon-Teles et al., 2014; Lawrence et al., 2003; Scheibel, 1997; Halassa and Kastner, 2017; Halassa and Sherman, 2019). Therefore, any lesion or dysfunction of the thalamus, such as by drugs of abuse, can have severe consequences on emotions and cognition. The compromising effects of drugs of abuse on thalamic function have been known for decades (e.g Gaudreau and Gagnon, 2005). Below we provide a short overview of the effects of cocaine, opioid, and alcohol use disorders on the thalamus, followed by a brief discussion of the consequences of polysubstance use.

The thalamus and cocaine misuse in humans

Cocaine dependence is associated with deficits in cognitive control and believed to be a critical psychological factor that contributes to continued compulsive cocaine use in individuals with cocaine use disorder (de Wit, 2009; Garavan and Hester, 2007; Li and Sinha, 2008; Porrino et al., 2007). Imaging studies have reported cortical and subcortical dysfunction in individuals with cocaine dependence (Aron and Paulus, 2007; Goldstein et al., 2007, 2009; Hanlon et al., 2009; Hanlon et al., 2011; Hester and Garavan, 2004; Kaufman et al., 2003; Moeller et al., 2005), suggesting that a decrease in the activation of brain regions in the "control network" (e.g., prefrontal cortex and thalamus) increases the vulnerability to relapse because it interferes with executive function (i.e., cognitive inhibition).

Cocaine-dependent subjects were reported to have lower gray matter volume in cerebellar hemispheres, the frontal cortex, the temporal cortex, and the thalamus (e.g. Ide et al., 2014; Sim et al., 2007), and a reduction of white matter integrity throughout and around the thalamus (Bell et al., 2011; Yip et al., 2017). Cocaine abusers, compared with controls, exhibited hypoactivation of the thalamus during a visual spatial attention task (Tomasi et al., 2007). A recent longitudinal study reported that lower error-related activation of the thalamus predicted both relapse and an earlier time to relapse to cocaine use in cocaine-dependent subjects (Luo et al., 2013). Cocaine use disorder has been associated with impulsivity and deficits in visual learning and memory, executive function, verbal learning, visuospatial ability, and working memory that could be the result of thalamic dysfunction (Potvin et al., 2014). In early imaging studies, the thalamus was suggested to mediate cocaine craving (Volkow et al., 1997a, b). Although a reduction of gray matter volume was observed in the thalamus in cocaine addicts (Sim et al., 2007), an increase in thalamic activation was observed in cocaine-dependent subjects who were presented with cocaine-related stimuli (Ray et al., 2015), possibly because of functional heterogeneity of the thalamus (e.g Scheibel, 1997; Bentivoglio et al., 1991; Groenewegen and Berendse, 1994).

Several studies have demonstrated alterations of cerebral functional connectivity in subjects with cocaine use disorder (Cisler et al., 2013; Ding and Lee, 2013; Gu et al., 2010; Kelly et al., 2011; Li et al., 2000; Tomasi et al., 2010; Verdejo-Garcia et al., 2014; Wilcox et al., 2011; Zhang et al., 2014). In active cocaine users, a decrease in connectivity was observed between the thalamus and midbrain (Tomasi et al., 2010), putamen and ventral tegmental area (Gu et al., 2010), and anterior cingulate cortex (Verdejo-Garcia et al., 2014). Furthermore, connectivity between the thalamus and midbrain (Tomasi et al., 2010) and ventral tegmental area (Gu et al., 2010) negatively correlated with the number of years of cocaine use, suggesting that cocaine use affects both activity of the thalamus and its connectivity. Altogether, these findings support thalamic circuit dysfunction in cognitive control as an important neural marker of cocaine use disorder.

The thalamus and opioid abuse in humans

Neuroimaging approaches have shown that impairments in cognitive function/control in individuals with opioid use disorder may be attributable to abnormal prefrontal brain activity (Lee and Pau, 2002; Pau et al., 2002). The thalamic-cortical system is critical for synchronizing activity of the thalamus and prefrontal cortex and thus plays a key role in orchestrating and integrating functions across different brain regions (Jones, 2002; Steriade, 2006). Beyond prefrontal brain regions, the thalamus is also critically implicated in cognitive control and plays a pivotal role in the attention process (de Bourbon-Teles et al., 2014; Lawrence et al., 2003). The effects of heroin are mostly mediated by μ-opioid receptors. One brain region where μ-opioid receptors are particularly densely expressed is the thalamus (Maurer et al., 1983; Pfeiffer et al., 1982). In the thalamus, μ-opioid receptors are densest in the dorsomedial, lateroposterior, and laterodorsal thalamus, demonstrated by *in situ* hybridization in post-mortem human brains (Peckys and Landwehrmeyer, 1999) and consistent with earlier studies that performed μ-opioid receptor binding assays (Pilapil et al., 1987; Voorn et al., 1996).

Opioid receptors are highly expressed in the thalamus (Apkarian et al., 2005; Lever, 2007). Reductions of glucose metabolism were observed in subjects with opioid use disorder who were maintained on methadone treatment (Galynker et al., 2000; Prosser et al., 2009), and a reduction of resting-state regional homogeneity of the thalamus was found in heroin-dependent subjects (Qiu et al., 2011). These findings strongly suggest that heroin use is associated with abnormal thalamic activity. More recently, acute heroin treatment in heroin-dependent individuals reduced functional connectivity between the thalamus and cortical regions (Denier et al., 2015). This study showed that the acute administration of heroin in the heroin-dependent group led to a decrease in functional connectivity and an increase in intrinsic thalamic resting-state oscillation, assessed by analyses of regional homogeneity and the fractional amplitude of low-frequency fluctuations, compared with placebo and healthy control groups. These abnormalities were partially related to clinical characteristics and plasma levels of morphine (the main metabolite of heroin). A reduction of thalamocortical functional connectivity to cortical regions and alterations of intrinsic thalamic oscillation characteristics may explain some deficits in cognitive function in heroin-dependent subjects (Denier et al., 2015). Importantly, gray matter abnormalities and numerous functional and neurometabolic deficits have been reported in individuals with opioid use disorder. Subjects with a history of opioid dependence have a higher level of opioid receptor availability in the thalamus at 10 days of abstinence, most likely because of an increase in opioid receptor number immediately following detoxification from opioids (Williams et al., 2007). Neuroimaging studies reported that the thalamus undergoes marked gray matter reductions in individuals with opioid use disorder (Reid et al., 2008; Tolomeo et al., 2016). Furthermore, a significant decrease in functional connectivity, reflected by a significant reduction of white matter, was found between the central nucleus of the amygdala and thalamus in prescription opioid-dependent patients (Upadhyay et al., 2010). In abstinent heroin-dependent individuals, higher impulsivity scores and a significant enhancement of intrinsic amygdala functional connectivity network activity were found in the thalamus (Xie et al., 2011). Overall, these findings clearly demonstrate that, similar to cocaine use disorder, thalamic circuit dysfunction is an important neural marker of opioid use disorder.

The thalamus and alcohol use disorder in humans

White matter abnormalities and numerous functional and neurometabolic deficits have been reported in heavy consumers of alcohol (Buhler and Mann, 2011). The effects of alcohol use disorder on the thalamus have been known for decades. Several studies have reported reductions of the volume of the thalamus in alcohol-dependent individuals (Fein and Fein, 2013; Grodin and Momenan, 2017; Kril et al., 1997; Mon et al., 2014). Additionally, the volume of the thalamus negatively correlated with alcohol consumption (Kril et al., 1997). Neuroimaging studies demonstrated that the thalamus undergoes marked volume reductions that result in characteristic cognitive impairments in individuals with severe alcohol use disorder (Mann et al., 2001; Mann et al., 1999; Pitel et al., 2015; Tedstone and Coyle, 2004). Early studies suggested that the thalamus is strongly implicated in alcohol craving in individual with alcohol use disorder (Modell et al., 1990). When exposed to alcohol-related cues, alcohol-dependent subjects exhibited increases in brain activity in the thalamus (George et al., 2001). Alcohol-dependent subjects with a smaller thalamus tended to resume heavy alcohol consumption (Segobin et al., 2014) and exhibited greater thalamus activation in response to an alcohol taste cue (Monnig et al., 2014). Importantly, such shrinkage of the thalamus has also been observed in animals. Marchigian-Sardinian (msP) alcohol-preferring rats exhibited a decrease in thalamus volume, suggesting that the predisposition to alcohol dependence in msP rats may be associated with brain abnormalities that are reminiscent of those that are observed in alcohol-dependent patients (Gozzi et al., 2013).

Any condition that leads to chronic thiamine (vitamin B1) deficiency can lead to Wernicke's encephalopathy and, if untreated, Korsakoff syndrome (Sharp et al., 2016). Wernicke's encephalopathy is characterized by ataxia, abnormal eye movements, a confusional state, blurred and double vision, tremor, and nystagmus; it is often associated with chronic alcoholism and inadequate nutrition. The neurological symptoms of Wernicke's encephalopathy (e.g., ataxia, ophthalmoplegia, and nystagmus) can be reversed in its early stages by thiamine supplementation but learning and memory deficits respond more slowly and only incompletely (Day et al., 2013; Thomson, 2000). The most common cause of Korsakoff syndrome is chronic alcohol abuse. Although Korsakoff syndrome can be caused by long-lasting starvation and a nutritionally deprived state, it is widely accepted that alcohol abuse is the most frequent etiology (Hammoud and Jimenez-Shahed, 2019; Zahr and Pfefferbaum, 2017; Covell and Siddiqui, 2020). Alcohol-related Korsakoff syndrome results from the combination of chronic and excessive alcohol consumption and thiamine deficiency. Individuals with alcohol use disorder are at risk for thiamine deficiency because of a poor diet that is associated with malnutrition, compromised thiamine absorption from the gastrointestinal tract, impairments in thiamine storage, and lower thiamine phosphorylation (Thomson, 2000). Cognitive impairments that are specific to Korsakoff syndrome include anterograde amnesia, profoundly limiting learning capacity, retrograde amnesia, and executive deficits, resulting in lower inhibition and difficulties with judgment, planning, and problem-solving (Arts et al., 2017; Oudman et al., 2015). Anterograde amnesia can result in the symptom of confabulations (i.e., patching up "blanks" in memory with fabricated information without the intention of deception (Johnson and Fox, 2018; Wiggins and Bunin, 2020).

The entire brain is clearly affected by alcohol use disorder. However, notable regional differences are observed in the deleterious effects of chronic and heavy alcohol consumption. The thalamus is a target for the combined effects of alcohol and thiamine deficiency, which in turn causes severe thalamic dysfunction that is characteristic of Korsakoff's syndrome (Pitel et al., 2012). Particularly relevant to the present chapter, Korsakoff's syndrome can be described as a "model" for study thalamus damage. In individuals who suffer from alcohol use disorder, two brain networks are particularly affected by excessive and chronic alcohol consumption, namely Papez's circuit and the frontocerebellar circuit. The thalamus plays a central connecting role in both of these circuits (Pitel et al., 2015). Papez's circuit has been implicated in episodic memory (i.e., remembering prior events by mentally traveling back in time to re-experience those events (Wheeler et al., 1997). This memory system is thought to be in charge of encoding, storing, and retrieving personally experienced events that are associated with a precise spatial and temporal context of encoding. The frontocerebellar circuit is involved in working memory and executive function. All of these functions are affected in individuals with alcohol use disorder (Pitel et al., 2014). Therefore, the reduction of volume of the thalamus that is induced by chronic and heavy alcohol use has dramatic consequences on both Papez's circuit and the frontocerebellar circuit, reflected by severe cognitive impairments in individuals with alcohol use disorder.

Although it is now widely recognized that the thalamus is a critical node in neural circuits that are compromised by alcohol use disorder, remaining to be thoroughly investigated are the effects of alcohol on specific thalamic nuclei that may likely help provide a better understanding of the evolution of different cognitive and motor impairments that are associated with alcohol use disorder. A recent study began to address this issue by showing differential ventral posterior lateral thalamic-based functional connectivity in individuals with alcohol use disorder compared with controls. Specifically, the negative correlation between the ventral posterior lateral thalamus (see Fig. 6.1) and bilateral middle temporal lobe region in controls became a positive correlation in individuals with alcohol use disorder. Furthermore, the negative correlation between the ventral posterior lateral thalamus and cerebellum was stronger in individual with alcohol use disorder compared with controls (Honnorat et al., 2021).

Although data are still limited on the effect of alcohol on specific thalamic nuclei, the above findings suggest that the volume of the thalamus might serve as a good indicator of the severity of alcohol use disorder but be useful for evaluating the likelihood that an abstinent individual with alcohol use disorder will resume drinking (relapse).

The thalamus and polysubstance use disorder

The previous three sections focused on the effects of three substances separately on the thalamus. However, an important feature of substance use disorder is the use of multiple substances in combination (e.g., cocaine, heroin, nicotine, and alcohol), referred to as polysubstance use disorder. Although any combination of drugs may be used, studies have shown that alcohol is commonly used with another substance (Culverhouse et al., 2005;

Malcolm et al., 2006). For example, people who drink alcohol are more likely to smoke, and people who drink larger amounts of alcohol tend to smoke more cigarettes (Bobo and Husten, 2000). Patients who are diagnosed with dependence on one of the drugs are also commonly diagnosed with dependence on the other (Zacny, 1990). Approximately 85% of individuals with alcohol use disorder smoke. Common genes have been suggested to control the development of both alcohol and nicotine dependence (Swan et al., 1997). Heavy drinkers tend to be heavy smokers, and alcohol influences nicotine dependence (Dani and Harris, 2005). Human studies also suggest that a smaller volume of the thalamus (i.e., a decrease in gray matter) is correlated with nicotine dependence severity in smokers (Sutherland et al., 2016; Yu et al., 2017), and lesions of the thalamus resulted in the cessation of smoking and drinking (Najeeb et al., 2016).

Similar to what is observed with alcohol use disorder, neurobiological abnormalities in individuals with polysubstance use disorder are associated by impairments in cognitive function (Block et al., 2002; Medina et al., 2004). In fact, comorbid alcohol and substance use disorders are extremely common and associated with morphological abnormalities in the brain (Grodin and Momenan, 2017; Mon et al., 2014). For example, earlier studies showed that individuals with polysubstance use disorder (i.e., cocaine, alcohol, heroin, and marijuana) who were abstinent for 15 days exhibited smaller volumes of the prefrontal lobe compared with the control group, reflected by a smaller volume of gray matter but not white matter (Liu et al., 1998). Another study reported that individuals with polysubstance use disorder (i.e., cocaine, amphetamine, and alcohol) who were abstinent for over 2 years presented a significant reduction of gray matter volume in the bilateral medial orbitofrontal cortex (Tanabe et al., 2009), suggesting that the combination of several substances can cause more dramatic neurobiological changes. Numerous neuroimaging studies have investigated the effects of individual substances on brain biology. To our knowledge, however, only a few studies have investigated the consequences of polysubstance use disorder on the thalamus. Individuals with polysubstance use disorder exhibited significantly smaller gray matter volume in the thalamus (Mon et al., 2014; Noyan et al., 2016).

Each class of substances alters neuronal integrity and neurotransmission via different mechanisms (Buttner, 2011; Licata and Renshaw, 2010), and their co-abuse can have unique, even different adverse effects on the brain relative to any one substance alone (Abe et al., 2013). Therefore, further investigations of structural abnormalities that are caused by polysubstance use disorder and consequences on cognitive function will help identify potential pharmacological and behavioral treatment targets that are specific to polysubstance use disorder to decrease high relapse rates.

The thalamus: preclinical studies

The following sections present and discuss scientific findings from animal studies, mainly rodents, that indicate the involvement of thalamic nuclei and thalamic circuits in animal models (Fig. 6.2B) of drug addiction. Particular attention is given to the paraventricular nucleus of the thalamus (PVT), the mediodorsal thalamic nucleus, and epithalamic structures, including the lateral and medial habenula.

The paraventricular nucleus of the thalamus: preclinical studies

The PVT, a part of dorsal midline thalamic nuclei, lies adjacent to the dorsal side of the third ventricle and has been shown to play a significant role in functions that are related to arousal, attention, reward, and awareness (Bentivoglio et al., 1991; Groenewegen and Berendse, 1994; Van der Werf, Witter and Groenewegen, 2002). The dorsoventral spatial distribution of the PVT is limited, but it is remarkably extended along the anterior–posterior axis. Because of its extension along the anterior–posterior dimension, the PVT has at least two anatomical subdivisions: anterior (aPVT) and posterior (pPVT) (Vertes and Hoover, 2008). Importantly, some differences in the projections and functions of these subregions have been reported based on distinct efferents of these two subregions. Some examples of the characteristics of the aPVT versus pPVT are discussed further below. Here, we refer to the PVT simply as a whole without distinguishing the anatomical subdivisions. Midline and intralaminar thalamic nuclei have widespread connections throughout the brain, such as innervating distinct areas of the cortex and striatum (Groenewegen and Berendse, 1994; Smith et al., 2004; Van der Werf et al., 2002). Early studies suggested that these thalamic nuclei are mainly involved in processing non-discriminative nociceptive inputs (Berendse and Groenewegen, 1991). However, over the last two decades, studies of thalamic nuclei in general and the PVT in particular have become more numerous in the literature on preclinical studies of drug addiction. This broad literature has suggested that the PVT is a key structure in brain circuitries that control drug intake and relapse, shaping the notion that the PVT should be further elucidated as part of the neurocircuitry of drug addiction (Hamlin et al., 2009; James and Dayas, 2013; Martin-Fardon and Boutrel, 2012; Millan et al., 2017; Zhou and Zhu, 2019).

Neuroanatomical studies have shown that the PVT receives projections from brainstem regions, particularly the periaqueductal gray, the parabrachial nucleus, the nucleus of the solitary tract, the locus coeruleus, the laterodorsal tegmental nucleus, the pedunculopontine tegmental nucleus, and raphe nuclei (Kirouac, 2015; Vertes et al., 2015), regions that are associated with arousal and autonomic nervous system function (Chen and Su, 1990; Cornwall and Phillipson, 1988b; Hsu and Price, 2009; Krout et al., 2002; Krout and Loewy, 2000; Ruggiero et al., 1998). The PVT, similar to other thalamic nuclei, does not have γ-aminobutyric acid (GABA)ergic interneurons and instead receives inhibitory signaling from other neuronal structures, such as the zona incerta and thalamic reticular nucleus (Kirouac, 2015; Zhang and van den Pol, 2017). The medial prefrontal cortex represents another major source of input to the PVT (Li and Kirouac, 2012; Vertes, 2002, 2004) and is thought to contribute to reward-seeking behavior (Otis et al., 2017). Moreover, the PVT receives large and distinct inputs from several areas of the hypothalamus, including suprachiasmatic, arcuate, dorsomedial, and ventromedial nuclei and preoptic and lateral hypothalamic areas (Chen and Su, 1990; Cornwall and Phillipson, 1988a; Hsu and Price, 2009; Kirouac et al., 2005, 2006; Novak et al., 2000a; Otake, 2005; Peng and Bentivoglio, 2004). These structures are critical for the expression of motivated behavior (Swanson, 2000). Notably, the PVT is a target of hypothalamic peptidergic innervation (Kirouac, 2015; Kirouac et al., 2005) and has been shown to function as an interface between the hypothalamus and cortical-striatal projections that are essential for the integration of energy balance and arousal to control appetitive behavior (Kelley et al., 2005).

Paraventricular nucleus of the thalamus neurons project to the ventral striatum (Dong et al., 2017; Hoover and Vertes, 2007; Ligorio et al., 2009), central nucleus of the amygdala, basolateral amygdala, bed nucleus of the stria terminalis (Dong et al., 2017; Li and Kirouac, 2008), and prefrontal cortex (Berendse and Groenewegen, 1991; Hoover and Vertes, 2007; Kirouac, 2015). Particularly interesting for the present chapter are PVT connections with the prefrontal cortex and nucleus accumbens (Berendse and Groenewegen, 1990; Brog et al., 1993; Bubser and Deutch, 1998; Freedman and Cassell, 1994; Hsu and Price, 2009; S. Li and Kirouac, 2008; Moga et al., 1995; Otake and Nakamura, 1998; Parsons et al., 2007; Su and Bentivoglio, 1990; Vertes and Hoover, 2008), placing this thalamic structure in a strategic position that influences cortico-striatal mechanisms that are involved in reward and motivation (Cardinal et al., 2002; Pennartz et al., 1994; Walker et al., 2003).

Studies that investigated neuronal activity in the PVT in rodents have shown that PVT neurons express diurnal changes (i.e., changes in intrinsic electrical properties throughout the day). Specifically, PVT neurons are more excitable during the dark (i.e., at nighttime when rodents are active) compared with the light (i.e., at daytime when rodents are less active (Challet et al., 1997; Kolaj et al., 2014), suggesting that PVT neurons are sensitive to circadian rhythm. Paraventricular nucleus of the thalamus neurons are also activated during periods of arousal, food intake, and stressful conditions (Bhatnagar and Dallman, 1998; Bubser and Deutch, 1999; Novak and Nunez, 1998; Novak et al., 2000b; Otake et al., 2002; Peng et al., 1995; Timofeeva et al., 2002). The PVT has indeed been implicated in the regulation of food consumption, hypothalamic-pituitary-adrenal activity in response to chronic stress, and energy balance (Bhatnagar and Dallman, 1998, 1999; Jaferi et al., 2003). Paraventricular of the thalamus neurons are activated following the systemic passive (i.e., involuntary) administration of various drugs of abuse, including opioids, psychostimulants, nicotine, alcohol, and cannabinoids (Allen et al., 2003; Deutch et al., 1998; Garcia et al., 1995; Gutstein et al., 1998; Ren and Sagar, 1992; Ryabinin and Wang, 1998). Interestingly however, excitotoxic lesions of the PVT did not interfere with alcohol or cocaine self-administration (Hamlin et al., 2009; Neumann et al., 2016), suggesting that the functionality of this thalamic structure is not essential for voluntary drug intake, at least for alcohol and cocaine. Importantly, other findings demonstrated that PVT neurons are recruited during alcohol seeking (Dayas et al., 2008; Hamlin et al., 2009; Marchant et al., 2016; Perry and McNally, 2013) and during cocaine seeking (James et al., 2011a).

The PVT appears to be sensitive to the effects of alcohol withdrawal (Smith et al., 2020). This study showed dynamic changes in Fos expression (i.e., a marker of neuronal activity) in the PVT at different time points of withdrawal from chronic intermittent alcohol vapor exposure. Specifically, the PVT exhibited an initial decrease in Fos expression at 2 h of withdrawal, followed by an increase at 26 h and then another decrease at 72 h that then persisted until 7 days into withdrawal (Smith et al., 2020). This study indicated that alcohol dependence and withdrawal drove long-lasting neuroadaptations in the PVT. The PVT also appears to be important for some behavioral aspects of drugs of abuse. For example, lesions of the PVT blocked cocaine sensitization (Young and Deutch, 1998), and transient inactivation of the PVT prevented cue-induced (Matzeu et al., 2015) and prime-induced (James et al., 2010) cocaine-seeking behavior and the expression of cocaine-induced conditioned place preference (Browning et al., 2014), without affecting the motivation to seek a palatable food reward (Matzeu et al., 2015). Paraventricular nucleus of the thalamus activity is also involved in heroin seeking. A recent study showed that PVT activation using a chemogenetic approach reduced heroin-seeking behavior in chronically food-restricted rats (Chisholm et al., 2020). Recruitment of the PVT and the importance of its functionality for the expression of drug-seeking behavior strongly demonstrate a pivotal role for the PVT in relapse.

Drug exposure might also induce alterations of electrophysiological properties of PVT neurons. Paraventricular nucleus of the thalamus neurons exhibit firing patterns and ionic conductance that vary throughout the day (Kolaj et al., 2012); for review, see (Kolaj et al., 2014). The resting membrane potential of PVT neurons is maintained by several ionic conductances, whereas firing patterns are regulated by high and low voltage-activated Ca^+ conductances. The electrophysiological profiling of PVT neurons revealed two predominant firing patterns: tonic (prevalent) and bursting (Kolaj et al., 2007, 2012, 2014; Wong et al., 2013). Paraventricular nucleus of the thalamus neuron excitability is also modulated by the activation of receptors that are activated by GABA, glutamate, monoamines, and several neuropeptides (e.g., arginine vasopressin, gastrin-releasing peptide, thyrotropin-releasing hormone, and orexin) that are associated with afferent pathways to the PVT. Cocaine administration increases the percentage of PVT neurons that exhibit tonic firing (Yeoh et al., 2014), suggesting that cocaine exposure shifts PVT neurons to a more excitable state that could be attributable to the enhancement of function of the orexin system by cocaine that in turn increases the ratio of tonic *vs.* burst firing (Heydendael et al., 2011; Yeoh et al., 2012). Indeed, orexin increases glutamate release in the PVT and increases the input resistance of PVT neurons through potassium channel closure (Ishibashi et al., 2005; Matzeu et al., 2018). Cocaine might also alter PVT neuron excitability by increasing the release of norepinephrine or serotonin in the PVT (Goaillard and Vincent, 2002; Hadfield and Milio, 1992; Zhang et al., 2009). In contrast, opioids appear to have an inhibitory action on PVT neurons (Brunton and Charpak, 1998), and dynorphin hyperpolarizes PVT neurons (Chen et al., 2015; Matzeu et al., 2018). Drugs of abuse might also perturb neural physiology by altering gene expression (Heydendael et al., 2011, 2012; Winrow et al., 2010). For example, alcohol intake increased relative mRNA expression of the orexin receptor 2 (*OrxR2*) gene in the aPVT (Barson et al., 2015). Relative mRNA expression of the orexin receptor 1 (*OrxR1*) and *OrxR2* genes in the pPVT was upregulated in alcohol-dependent rats at early (8 h) withdrawal (Matzeu and Martin-Fardon, 2020). Cocaine-dependent rats exhibited an higher number of OrxR2-expressing cells in the pPVT, with no changes in the number of OrxR1-expressing cells at 2 to 3 weeks of abstinence (Matzeu and Martin-Fardon, 2021a). Additionally, cocaine-induced conditioned place preference and exposure to a cocaine-associated context increased AT-rich sequence binding protein 2 the PVT (Salti et al., 2018). SATB2 is a DNA binding protein that specifically binds nuclear matrix attachment regions involved in transcriptional regulation and chromatin remodeling. Drugs of abuse induce changes in the physiology (intrinsic excitability) and organization of the PVT, including both gene and protein expression, which together might contribute to drug-induced neuroadaptations and thus the "addiction" phenotype.

The following sections present and discuss preclinical studies, mainly rodent studies, that demonstrate the involvement of PVT-specific interconnections in drug taking, withdrawal, and relapse. Among the drugs of abuse, particular attention is given to alcohol, cocaine, opioids, and nicotine. Because of the involvement of the PVT in feeding behavior, this section will further discuss the involvement of the PVT in behaviors that are motivated by food reward, which is often used as a comparison control for behaviors that are motivated by drug reward.

Hypothalamic → PVT circuitry: preclinical studies

As mentioned above, the PVT receives dense innervation through peptidergic fibers. Several neuromodulatory peptidergic fibers originate from the hypothalamus, including orexin, dynorphin, cocaine- and amphetamine-regulated transcript (CART), agouti-related peptide, neuropeptide Y, enkephalin, and neurotensin (for review, see Kirouac, 2015). Among the hypothalamic peptidergic projections to the PVT, hypothalamic orexin, dynorphin and CART projections (Fig. 6.3) have received great attention in the addiction field and have been implicated in drug intake and relapse. A wide body of literature has documented the involvement of this peptidergic hypothalamic projection to the PVT in drug of abuse-related behaviors.

Infusions of orexin in the pPVT reinstated extinguished cocaine-seeking behavior in an OrxR2-dependent manner (Matzeu et al., 2016). However, the observation that orexin injections in the pPVT also effectively induced seeking behavior for a palatable food reward, such as sweetened condensed milk (Matzeu et al., 2018; Matzeu and Martin-Fardon, 2021b), suggests that hypothalamic orexin inputs to the PVT might play a general role in reward seeking, consistent with earlier studies in the feeding field (for review, see (Kelley et al., 2005). Orexin infusion in the aPVT promoted alcohol drinking in an OrxR2-dependent manner (Barson et al., 2015), suggesting differential specialization of the aPVT (drug intake) *vs.* pPVT (drug seeking). However, the actions of orexin in the PVT during intake are linked specifically to the aPVT subregion, but actions that promote the reinstatement of reward seeking that are linked to the pPVT remain to be fully investigated.

Studies that investigated the role of endogenous orexin transmission in the PVT and the implication of OrxR1 *vs.* OrxR2 during cue-, stress-, and prime-induced drug-seeking behavior

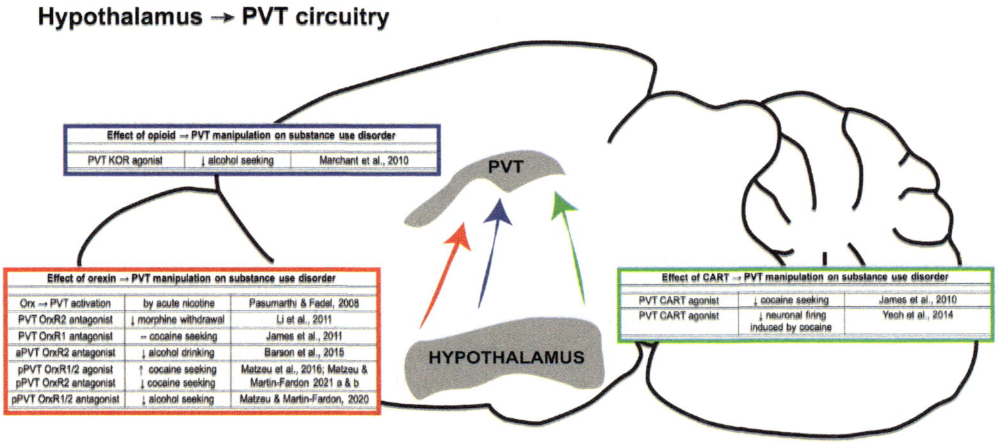

FIGURE 6.3 Schematic summary of hypothalamic → PVT circuitry involvement in substance use disorders. *Red arrow* and table indicate the orexin → PVT pathway. *Blue arrow* and table indicate the opioid → PVT pathway. *Green arrow* and table indicate the CART → PVT pathway. PVT, paraventricular nucleus of the thalamus; pPVT, posterior paraventricular nucleus of the thalamus; aPVT, anterior paraventricular nucleus of the thalamus; Orx, orexin; OrxR1, orexin receptor 1; OrxR2, orexin receptor 2; KOR, κ-opioid receptor; CART, cocaine- and amphetamine-regulated transcript.

are limited. The mechanisms by which orexin's action in the PVT trigger the reinstatement of reward-seeking behavior are difficult to explain. Infusions of an OrxR1 antagonist in the PVT had no effect on cocaine conditioned reinstatement, suggesting that OrxR1 signaling is not essential for the cue-induced reinstatement of cocaine-seeking behavior (James et al., 2011b). However, because this study did not test the involvement of OrxR2, a possible role for PVT orexin release in the conditioned reinstatement of drug-seeking behavior cannot be completely excluded, especially because the PVT is also known to strongly express OrxR2 (Marcus et al., 2001; Trivedi et al., 1998). For alcohol, however, orexin transmission via OrxR1/OrxR2 signaling appears to play a prominent role in the stress-induced reinstatement of alcohol seeking in alcohol-dependent rats (Matzeu and Martin-Fardon, 2020). Although a role for orexin transmission in the PVT in the reinstatement of drug-seeking behavior has been suggested by several studies, remaining to be shown is that cue-, stress-, or priming-induced seeking behavior are actually attributable to actions of endogenous orexins at their receptors in the PVT. Beyond findings that are related to cocaine and alcohol, other studies suggest that orexin in the PVT might mediate the aversive effects of morphine withdrawal. Indeed, the PVT application of an OrxR2 antagonist significantly attenuated the expression of naloxone-induced conditioned place aversion (Li et al., 2011), which is consistent with cocaine and alcohol studies that investigated OrxR2-dependent mechanisms of action (Barson et al., 2015; Matzeu et al., 2016). Orexin transmission in the PVT also appears to be involved in the behavioral effects of nicotine. Orexin projections to the PVT are robustly activated by acute nicotine treatment, suggesting that orexin-projecting neurons to the PVT are components of neural substrates that may contribute to the effects of nicotine on arousal and cognition (Pasumarthi and Fadel, 2008).

Hypothalamic neurons also express dynorphin, and orexin neurons co-express dynorphin (Chou et al., 2001). Both peptides are released during electrical stimulation of the hypothalamus (Li and van den Pol, 2006). Evidence suggests that these peptides act in tandem and play opposing roles in cocaine self-administration, brain stimulation reward, impulsivity, and cocaine-seeking behavior (Matzeu et al., 2018; Muschamp et al., 2014). In the PVT, dynorphin may prevent drug-seeking behavior while orexin may promote it (Matzeu et al., 2018). Dynorphin preferentially binds to κ-opioid receptors, and κ-opioid receptor mRNA is highly expressed in the PVT (Mansour et al., 1994a, b). The activation of opioidergic projections from the hypothalamus to the PVT prevented the context-induced reinstatement of alcohol seeking (Marchant et al., 2010), suggesting that the contribution of the PVT to relapse is under inhibitory control from the hypothalamic opioidergic projections, in addition to excitatory control that is implied by the effects of PVT orexin manipulations. Therefore, the contribution of hypothalamus → PVT circuitry to relapse may be under the inhibitory control of dynorphin and excitatory actions of orexin. The balance between these two systems might be perturbed by drug experience and significantly contribute to compulsive drug seeking.

The PVT also receives a dense innervation by CART from the hypothalamus (Kirouac et al., 2006). Microinjections of CART in the PVT significantly attenuated cocaine prime-induced reinstatement (James et al., 2010) and attenuated PVT neuron firing in cocaine-exposed animals (Yeoh et al., 2014). CART signaling in the PVT might represent another inhibitory control that the hypothalamus exerts over the PVT to influence drug-seeking behavior.

Paraventricular nucleus of the thalamus → nucleus accumbens circuitry: preclinical studies

The nucleus accumbens receives major projections from the PVT (Fig. 6.4), particularly from the nucleus accumbens shell (Millan et al., 2017). In 1998, Deutch et al. were the first to report that among PVT neurons that were recruited (i.e., higher Fos expression) by an acute injection of amphetamine were neurons that project to the nucleus accumbens shell (Deutch et al., 1998), providing evidence that the PVT → nucleus accumbens shell circuit is involved in the stimulant effects of amphetamine. A decade later, Hamlin et al. were the first to link PVT → nucleus accumbens shell projections to drug self-administration and relapse (Hamlin et al., 2009), showing that PVT neurons that project to the nucleus accumbens shell are recruited during the context-induced reinstatement of alcohol-seeking behavior. Consistent with these findings, subsequent work showed that cocaine exposure and withdrawal induced complex and profound alterations of the PVT → nucleus accumbens projection at the synaptic level (Neumann et al., 2016). Chronic cocaine increased silent synapses, although their levels returned to baseline after prolonged withdrawal. Moreover, the disruption of PVT → nucleus accumbens synaptic transmission decreased cocaine self-administration in rats, suggesting a faciliatory role for this pathway in cocaine intake (Neumann et al., 2016).

Another study identified the PVT as a prominent input to the nucleus accumbens that mediates the expression of opioid withdrawal and activity of the PVT → nucleus accumbens circuit that is necessary and sufficient to mediate behavioral aversion that is observed during withdrawal from morphine (Zhu et al., 2016). Injections of naloxone in chronic morphine-treated mice elicited robust Fos expression in PVT → nucleus accumbens projection neurons (Zhu et al., 2016). Selective silencing of the PVT → nucleus accumbens pathway using an

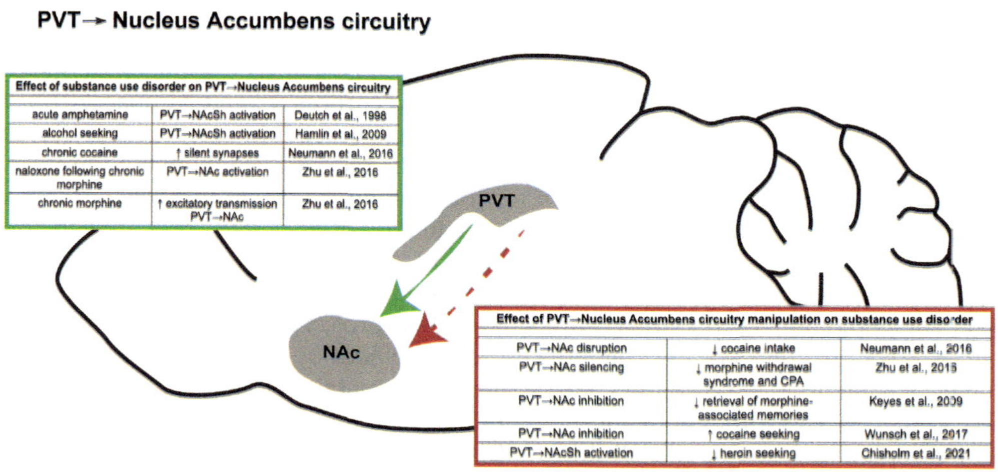

FIGURE 6.4 Schematic summary of PVT → nucleus accumbens circuitry involvement in substance use disorders. *Green arrow* and table summarize the effects of substance use disorders on PVT → nucleus accumbens circuitry activity. *Red dotted arrow* and *red* table indicate effects of the exogenous manipulation of PVT → nucleus accumbens circuitry on substance use disorders. *CPA*, conditioned place aversion; *NAc*, nucleus accumbens; *NAcSh*, nucleus accumbens shell; *PVT*, paraventricular nucleus of the thalamus.

optogenetic approach reduced the expression of both the somatic opioid withdrawal syndrome and conditioned place aversion that was precipitated by an injection of naloxone in opioid-dependent mice. This study also showed that chronic opioid (i.e., morphine) exposure selectively potentiated excitatory transmission between the PVT and dopamine D_2 receptor-expressing medium spiny neurons in the nucleus accumbens. Moreover, the *in vivo* optogenetic restoration of normal synaptic transmission in PVT → D_2 receptor-expressing medium spiny neuron synapses robustly reduced the expression of behavioral symptoms of withdrawal and conditioned aversive memory of the withdrawal-paired chamber (Zhu et al., 2016). A recent study showed that chemogenetic inhibition of the PVT → nucleus accumbens pathway prevented the retrieval of morphine-associated memories in a conditioned place preference model (Keyes et al., 2020).

However, the role of the PVT → nucleus accumbens pathway in drug-seeking behavior appears to be complex and sometimes controversial. Site-specific manipulation experiments revealed that the PVT → nucleus accumbens circuit plays an inhibitory role in regulating drug seeking, supported by evidence that the inhibition of this circuit enhanced the cue-induced reinstatement of cocaine seeking (Wunsch et al., 2017). The chemogenetic activation of PVT → nucleus accumbens shell projections attenuated heroin seeking in food-restricted rats (Chisholm et al., 2021), suggesting an important role for this projection in the enhancement of heroin seeking that is induced by chronic food restriction.

These findings are important because they suggest a fundamental role for the PVT → nucleus accumbens pathway in addiction-related behaviors across a variety of drugs of abuse. Future studies that dissect the molecular mechanism of this pathway and shed light on its role in different aspects addiction are warranted.

Other PVT circuits in drug addiction: preclinical studies

The PVT receives dense innervations from medial prefrontal cortex glutamatergic projections that arise from prelimbic, infralimbic, and insular cortices (Li and Kirouac, 2012). These cortical subregions are also critical components of the neurocircuitry of addiction (Koob and Volkow, 2016). The role of prelimbic transmission to the PVT (prelimbic cortex → PVT, Fig. 6.5) has gained attention in studies of reward seeking. However, the role of this cortical projection to the PVT is still ambiguous. Exposure to reward-associated cues appears to result in an inhibitory response of prelimbic cortex → PVT neurons. Activation of this pathway suppressed the acquisition and expression of conditioned reward seeking (Otis et al., 2019). The inhibition of prelimbic cortex → pPVT projection neurons attenuated post-abstinence context-induced and cue-induced reinstatement of extinguished cocaine-seeking behavior (Giannotti et al., 2018). In contrast, the chemogenetic activation or inhibition of prelimbic cortex → PVT projections did not alter heroin-seeking behavior in chronically food-restricted rats after a period of withdrawal (Chisholm et al., 2021).

The PVT might influence drug-associative memories through its connection to the central nucleus of the amygdala (Fig. 6.5). Indeed, the central nucleus of the amygdala is important for associating cues with both appetitive and aversive outcomes (Fadok et al., 2018), and the PVT → central nucleus of the amygdala pathway is required for fear conditioning (Do-Monte et al., 2015; Penzo et al., 2015). The functionality of this circuit is required for associating drug

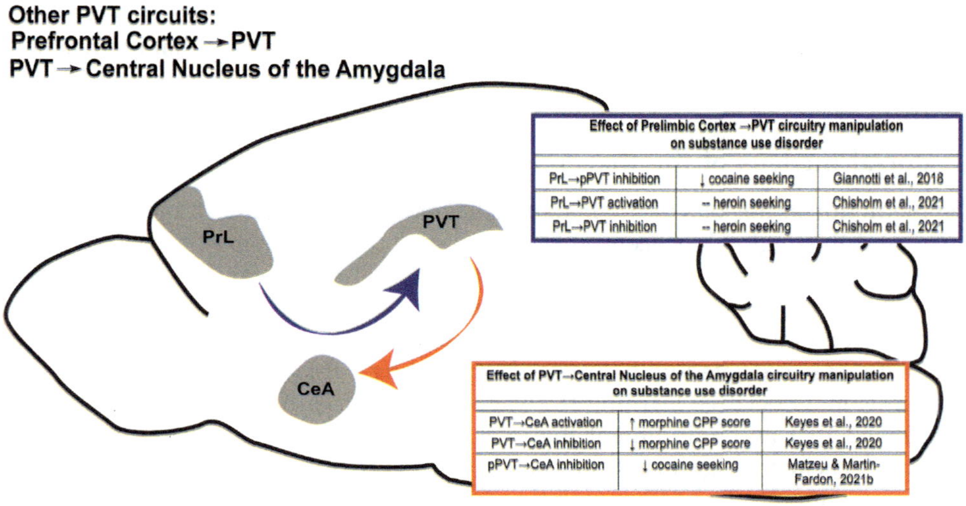

FIGURE 6.5 Schematic summary of the involvement of other PVT circuits and manipulations in substance use disorders. *Blue arrow* and table summarize effects of the exogenous manipulation of prelimbic cortex → PVT circuitry on substance use disorders. *Orange arrow* and table indicate effects of the exogenous manipulation of PVT → central nucleus of the amygdala circuitry on substance use disorders. PVT, paraventricular nucleus of the thalamus; pPVT, posterior paraventricular nucleus of the thalamus; PrL, prelimbic cortex; CeA, central nucleus of the amygdala; CPP, conditioned place preference.

(e.g., morphine) reward with environmental cues (Keyes et al., 2020). A role for the PVT → central nucleus of the amygdala circuit in cocaine seeking behavior was suggested in a recent study. Using a rodent model of cocaine dependence (i.e., self-administration under long-access conditions), hypothalamic orexin inputs to the pPVT → central nucleus of the amygdala pathway were shown to be essential for inducing cocaine-seeking behavior, and pPVT orexin-induced cocaine-seeking behavior was driven by activation of the central nucleus of the amygdala via corticotropin-releasing factor-1 receptor signaling (Matzeu and Martin-Fardon, 2021b).

Further investigations of PVT connections with other addiction-related brain regions, including the bed nucleus of the stria terminalis and locus coeruleus, are necessary.

Other thalamic nuclei

The majority of preclinical literature on thalamic nuclei focuses on the contribution of the PVT. However, emerging evidence has also implicated other thalamic nuclei, such as the mediodorsal nucleus of the thalamus, and other brains regions that are not specific to the thalamus proper, such as the lateral and medial habenula, which may also play an influential role in the expression, extinction, and reinstatement of drug-seeking behavior (Baxter and Murray, 2002; Brown et al., 2010; Zhang et al., 2005). Importantly, the architecture and circuitry of the thalamus is vast and complex. In simple terms, nuclei that may be found in the thalamus have both input and output functions. The mediodorsal nucleus of the thalamus and ventral lateral thalamic complex are terminal subcortical regions that are reached before giving rise to projections back to the frontal cortex (Haber and McFarland, 2001).

Mediodorsal nucleus of the thalamus and drug addiction: preclinical studies

The mediodorsal nucleus of the thalamus has been recognized as a part of limbic-cortical circuitry, and this region has been previously shown to mediate motor, cognitive, and motivational aspects of behavior (for review, see (Baxter and Murray, 2002). In a rodent study, rats were trained to discriminate olfactory cues that were associated with either a reward or non-reward. Approximately 10% of mediodorsal thalamic neurons responded to the presentation of cues that were associated with a reward, suggesting a role for the mediodorsal nucleus of the thalamus in associative learning (Kawagoe et al., 2007). A conditioned place preference study showed that an environment that was previously paired with morphine, compared with vehicle, elicited a significant increase in Fos expression in the mediodorsal nucleus of the thalamus (Guo et al., 2008), suggesting that neural activity within this nucleus may be induced by environmental contexts that are associated with drugs of abuse (Fig. 6.6). Excitotoxic, axon-sparing lesions of the mediodorsal nucleus of the thalamus significantly reduced cocaine self-administration during 14 days of acquisition training and attenuated responses to lower doses of cocaine, thus indicating an increase in sensitivity to the reinforcing properties of cocaine in rats that were subjected to lesions of the mediodorsal nucleus of the thalamus compared with their respective control counterparts (Weissenborn et al., 1998).

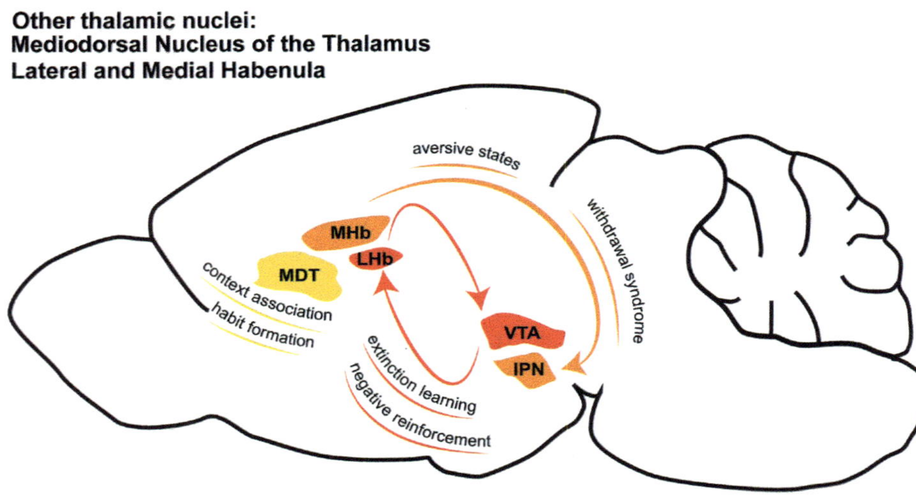

FIGURE 6.6 Schematic summary of roles of the mediodorsal nucleus of the thalamus (*yellow*), lateral habenula (*red*), and medial habenula (*orange*) in substance use disorders. *IPN*, interpeduncular nucleus; *LHb*, lateral habenula; *MDTs*, mediodorsal nucleus of the thalamus; *MHb*, medial habenula; *VTA*, ventral tegmental area.

Further demonstrating the role that the mediodorsal nucleus of the thalamus plays in reward-related processes, axon-sparing lesions of mediodorsal nucleus cell bodies abolished the acquisition of sucrose-induced conditioned place preference in food-restricted rats (McAlonan et al., 1993). Similarly, transient inactivation of the mediodorsal nucleus of the thalamus by lidocaine disrupted the expression of methamphetamine-induced conditioned place preference in rats, an effect that lasted only 24 h (Kuo et al., 2011). More recently, the cue-induced reinstatement of alcohol seeking during a 1-day test in mice was associated with increases in the immunoreactivity of phosphorylated calcium/calmodulin-dependent protein kinase II (CaMKII) at threonine 286 (i.e., a molecular component that is required for plasticity events) in different brain regions, including the mediodorsal nucleus of the thalamus (Salling et al., 2017). Collectively, these finding suggest that the mediodorsal nucleus of the thalamus plays a specific role in the expression of behaviors that are related to habitual drug use (Fig. 6.6). The mediodorsal nucleus of the thalamus may be a key player in the development of learning contextual associations, thereby contributing to habit formation with regard to drug use and abuse.

Lateral habenula and drug addiction: preclinical studies

Although the lateral habenula does not correspond to the thalamus proper, and it does not play a significant role in cortico-striato-thalamo-cortical loops, this particular epithalamic brain region has gained attention in recent years because of its potential role in such disorders as depression (Li et al., 2011a; Sartorius et al., 2010), psychosis (Shepard et al., 2006), and more importantly disruptions of reward-seeking behavior and drug addiction (Brown et al., 2010; Velasquez et al., 2014; Zhang et al., 2005). Such involvement is unsurprising because the lateral habenula has well-established connections with the ventral tegmental area (Fig. 6.6). The ventral tegmental area sends major dopaminergic projections to the lateral habenula (Beckstead et al., 1979). This dopaminergic input arrives via the fasciculus retroflexus, with some of these inputs also innervating the medial habenula. Interestingly, lesions of the ventral tegmental area resulted in an approximately 75% loss of dopamine in the lateral habenula (Oades and Halliday, 1987). Notably, the lateral habenula projects glutaminergic (inhibitory) innervations back to the ventral tegmental area (Araki et al., 1988; Gruber et al., 2007; Phillipson and Pycock, 1982), suggesting that neurons in the lateral habenula may modulate both the activity and release of dopamine, which could ultimately influence goal-directed behaviors. Disturbances of the lateral habenula, regardless of the experimental approach, have been hypothesized to influence drug-seeking behavior, given dopaminergic connections between the lateral habenula and ventral tegmental area. Empirical data have shown that the inhibition of midbrain nuclei decreases dopaminergic cell firing, ultimately reducing motivation and reward (Ji and Shepard, 2007).

An early study showed that bilateral electrolytic lesions of the lateral habenula increased dopamine utilization in the prefrontal cortex but not nucleus accumbens, tuberculum olfactorium, or striatum. Interestingly, subsequent studies found that electrical stimulation of the lateral habenula exerted an inhibitory effect in up to 97% of the dopaminergic neuronal population in the substantia nigra and ventral tegmental area (Christoph et al., 1986; Ji and Shepard, 2007). These findings led researchers to propose that the lateral habenula plays a fundamental role in modulating negative reinforcement, punishment, and aversive responses, in part via a pathway where excitatory neurons that originate in the lateral habenula innervate GABAergic neurons in the rostromedial tegmental area, also known as the ventral tegmental area tail, which ultimately inhibit downstream dopaminergic neurons (Jhou et al., 2009). Additionally, a study that assessed the synaptic plasticity of neurons in the lateral habenula found that cocaine administration for two consecutive days strengthened *a*-amino-3-hydroxy-5-methyl-4-isoxazolepropionic acid (AMPA) receptor-mediated synaptic transmission in neurons that connected the lateral habenula to the rostromedial tegmental area. This is a rather seminal finding because it may have uncovered a potential mechanism by which the brain forms memories that are particularly associated with drugs (Maroteaux and Mameli, 2012).

Deep-brain stimulation studies in rodent demonstrated that low-frequency stimulation of the lateral habenula reduced cocaine self-administration and reinstatement while also improving extinction and reducing cocaine cravings (Friedman et al., 2010). Interestingly, lesions of the lateral habenula increased cocaine-seeking behavior, which was hypothesized to have resulted from the weakening of cocaine-induced glutamate inputs to the ventral tegmental area. Importantly, combined frequency stimulation during extinction caused animals to reach extinction criteria faster than controls, and deep brain stimulation decreased drug-induced reinstatement (Friedman et al., 2010). Furthermore, an injection of a dopamine D_3 receptor antagonist in the lateral habenula attenuated the cue-induced reinstatement of nicotine seeking but not food self-administration (Khaled et al., 2014).

Preclinical studies that employed cue- and cocaine-induced reinstatement protocols showed greater Fos activity in the lateral habenula in high-reinstatement rats and mice compared with low-reinstatement rats and mice (Brown et al., 2010; James et al., 2011a; Zhang et al., 2005). Animals with lesions of the lateral habenula escalated their alcohol consumption faster that animals that received sham lesions. Lateral habenula-lesioned animals also maintained higher stable rates of alcohol intake. Lesions of the lateral habenula also blocked the reinstatement of alcohol-seeking behavior after extinction that was induced by yohimbine administration (Haack et al., 2014). However, these effects were not replicated in lesioned rats that were trained to self-administer heroin (Wang et al., 2009). Lesion studies also found that in rats that were trained to self-administer cocaine, a permanent lesion of the lateral habenula before extinction (i.e., during cocaine self-administration training) caused the rats to fail to reach the extinction criterion (Friedman et al., 2010). In contrast, another study showed that transient inactivation of the lateral habenula with combined baclofen + muscimol administration before the first cocaine extinction session (i.e., after cocaine self-administration training) did not affect day 1 extinction responding or subsequent extinction responding (Gill et al., 2013). Overall, these findings suggest that integrity of the lateral habenula is required to achieve extinction, and the timing when the lateral habenula is lesioned (e.g., pre-extinction vs. at extinction) results in different outcomes. These findings support the implication of habenular circuitry in learning that is driven by undesirable outcomes. Nevertheless, this role of the lateral habenula is complex and may depend on the type of drug that is administered and the time at which lesions of this area occur within the self-administration cycle.

Dopamine levels in the brain are directly related to reward, and increases in dopamine are an important factor that should be considered when assessing the abuse potential of various drugs (Di Chiara and Imperato, 1988). Recent evidence indicates that dopamine's role may be more complex than simply reflecting a stimulus response. In a seminal study, nonhuman primates learned to associate a reward (i.e., juice) with a predictive cue. Interestingly, after the juice–cue association was established, the juice itself stopped inducing dopamine activation, whereas withholding the expected reward (juice) resulted in a decrease in dopaminergic activity. This implies that dopamine may play a larger role in reward prediction, rather than the feeling of reward itself, particularly after a negative prediction error (Montague et al., 1996; Schultz et al., 1997), which is thought to mediate learning from mistakes. Empirical data suggest that the lateral habenula may be responsible for this decrease in dopaminergic activation (Matsumoto and Hikosaka, 2007). This study reported an increase in dopaminergic activation in the lateral habenula when an expected reward was not received, whereas a decrease in dopaminergic activation was observed when an unexpected reward was received. These findings indicate that the habenula may be activated by negative events. Collectively, activation of the habenula after negative events may result in downstream decreases in dopaminergic activation via the GABAergic inhibition of brain regions that form circuits with the habenula (such as the ventral tegmental area), ultimately resulting in negative affect (Matsumoto and Hikosaka, 2007).

Medial habenula and drug addiction: preclinical studies

Importantly, the habenula is divided into two distinct regions: lateral habenula and medial habenula (Klemm, 2004). Structurally, the medial habenula gives rise to projections to the interpeduncular nucleus (Fig. 6.6) via the core of the fasciculus retroflexus, which itself innervates various structures within the mid- and hindbrain that underlie affective state regulation (Herkenham and Nauta, 1979). Importantly, the interpeduncular nucleus projects to several structures, including the lateral habenula (Morley, 1986). In a study that employed escalating doses of morphine, a reduction of acetylcholinesterase activity was observed in the medial habenula after chronic exposure. Interestingly, this reduction returned to normal levels during morphine withdrawal, reflecting a need to return to homeostasis (Neugebauer et al., 2013). In contrast to cocaine exposure, which results in an increase in the expression of Fos in the habenula (Brown et al., 2010), long-term exposure to morphine decreases Fos activity specifically in the medial habenula (Neugebauer et al., 2013). Additionally, an increase in glucose metabolism has been observed in different limbic and thalamic regions in rats, including the medial habenula during morphine withdrawal (Kimes et al., 1990). Interestingly, this effect contrasts with the lateral habenula, which exhibits an increase in Fos expression during withdrawal (Brown et al., 2010; James et al., 2011a). Altogether, these findings support the assertion that the interplay between the medial and lateral habenula is important for the organism to reach homeostasis.

Notably, withdrawal syndrome may be precipitated in mice with a history of chronic alcohol administration via intraperitoneal injections of mecamylamine, a nonselective nicotinic acetylcholine receptor (nAChR) antagonist. Interestingly, these withdrawal symptoms were also exhibited in mice that received central infusions of mecamylamine to the medial habenula and interpeduncular nucleus but not when they received mecamylamine infusions to the ventral tegmental area or hippocampus (Perez et al., 2015). These findings demonstrate that medial habenula–interpeduncular nucleus circuitry may be involved in modulating withdrawal syndrome (Fig. 6.6). Furthermore, rats that preferred alcohol exhibited the loss of neuropeptide Y mRNA (i.e., a neuropeptide that has been shown to be involved in the regulation of alcohol intake) in the medial habenula, in contrast to non-alcohol-preferring rats that exhibited an enhanced neuropeptide Y mRNA signal (Hwang et al., 1999). Indeed, the acute administration of 18-methoxycoronaride, an α3β4 nAChR antagonist, decreased signs of naltrexone-induced morphine withdrawal (Rho and Glick, 1998), an effect that has been characterized as being mediated by activity of the interpeduncular nucleus and medial habenula (Panchal et al., 2005; Taraschenko et al., 2007). Importantly, central infusions of 18-methoxycoronaride in the medial habenula and interpeduncular nucleus decreased morphine self-administration (Glick et al., 2006). Collectively, these findings demonstrate that both the medial habenula and interpeduncular nucleus, as well as the neural pathway that connects them, are involved in the regulation of drug addiction-related behavior, particularly withdrawal (Fig. 6.6).

Most preclinical evidence that implicates the medial habenula in drug use and abuse has derived from studies of its contribution to mediating nicotine withdrawal symptoms following chronic exposure. This is unsurprising, given the large density of various nAChRs that are known to populate the medial habenula–interpeduncular nucleus pathway (Mugnaini et al., 2002). Additionally, the generation of nAChR subunit transgenic mice gave researchers the ability to more thoroughly investigate the ways in which specific receptor subunits, such as α2 and β4, among others, mediate nicotine addiction (Kedmi et al., 2004; Maskos et al., 2005; Rosenkranz et al., 2003; Salas et al., 2009). Researchers have been particularly interested in revealing the ways in which these specific receptor subunits in the medial habenula influence nicotine intake and withdrawal. For example, the α5 subunit, which is believed to be expressed in about 20% of medial habenula neurons that project to the interpeduncular nucleus (Picciotto and Kenny, 2013), has been shown to play a significant role in modulating nicotine intake. Mutant mice with knockout of the α5 subtype exhibited higher levels of self-administration compared with their wildtype counterparts, suggesting that the α5 subunit may be necessary for nicotine's aversive outcomes (Fowler et al., 2011). Additionally, mice that lacked the α5 subunit exhibited lower interpeduncular nucleus activation after exposure to nicotine compared with their wildtype counterparts (Fowler et al., 2013). Transgenic mice with α2 subunit knockdown exhibited increases in glutamate and GABA in the interpeduncular nucleus, which may indicate that this subunit is involved in modulating nicotine's effects (Lotfipour et al., 2013). Supporting this possibility, an increase in GABAergic neuronal activation was observed in the interpeduncular nucleus during nicotine withdrawal, which may be enhanced by an increase in glutamate release from the medial habenula (Zhao-Shea et al., 2013). Interestingly, a recent study of α3β4 receptor subunit blockade in the medial habenula via microinjections of *a*-conotoxin AulB or 18-methoxycoronaride prevented increases in dopamine in the nucleus accumbens, further suggesting that the medial habenula may play a role in modulating mesolimbic dopamine (McCallum et al., 2012).

The mechanism of action by which the medial habenula modulates dopaminergic activity is not thoroughly understood, but two major hypotheses have been proposed. Given its major connection with the interpeduncular nucleus, which sends direct innervations to major dopaminergic regions, one hypothesis proposes that activity of the medial habenula may influence dopamine levels in the striatum, regardless of activity in the lateral habenula

(Klemm, 2004). The second hypothesis theorizes direct connections from the medial to lateral habenula but not conversely from the lateral to medial habenula, raising the possibility that one of the functions of the medial habenula is to provide additional inputs to the lateral habenula (Kim and Chang, 2005).

There is a dearth of literature on the contribution of different thalamic nuclei to drug addiction and abuse. Nonetheless, these nuclei represent an exciting avenue of research. Indeed, as discussed in this chapter, emerging evidence highlights the mediodorsal nucleus of the thalamus as a potential mediator of context-associated drug-seeking behavior, a fundamental aspect of drug addiction that warrants further investigation. Similarly, increasing evidence links the habenula to cocaine and morphine addiction and withdrawal. Studies have shown that deep brain stimulation decreases cocaine self-administration in rats, which could potentially open the door to the development of more effective therapeutic approaches for cocaine use disorder in humans. Interestingly, the habenula's specific contribution to addiction may involve the encoding of reward states, in which habenula activation increases if the reward is negative and decreases if the reward is positive. Future research on the medial habenula–interpeduncular nucleus pathway will allow us to better understand the effects of other psychomotor stimulants and the ways in which this specific pathway is involved mechanisms of withdrawal and relapse. Additionally, worthy lines of investigation are to further elucidate connections between the lateral and medial habenula and better understand the ways in which this assembly affects downstream structures that have been shown to be key players in drug addiction and other human behaviors.

Conclusions

Clinical studies have proven that the thalamus in humans is significantly compromised by drugs of abuse. Preclinical studies that employed various animal models of addiction corroborate evidence from human studies that specific thalamic and epithalamic nuclei play key roles in different aspects of drug addiction across several drug classes. Human studies have the ability to investigate the structure and functionality of the thalamus more systematically, whereas animal studies have the ability to target specific thalamic nuclei. Bringing together clinical and preclinical studies is essential for further investigating and understanding the neurobiology of drug addiction and ultimately discovering promising therapeutical targets to treat substance use disorder.

Acknowledgments

This is publication number 30078 from The Scripps Research Institute. The authors thank Michael Arends for proofreading the manuscript. This study was supported by the National Institute on Alcohol Abuse and Alcoholism (grant no. AA006420, AA026999, AA028549 to RM-F and T32 AA007456) and the Merck Investigator Studies Program (grant no. MISP59371 to AM).

References

Abe, C., Mon, A., Durazzo, T.C., Pennington, D.L., Schmidt, T.P., Meyerhoff, D.J., 2013. Polysubstance and alcohol dependence: unique abnormalities of magnetic resonance-derived brain metabolite levels. Drug Alcohol Depend. 130 (1–3), 30–37. https://doi.org/10.1016/j.drugalcdep.2012.10.004.

Allen, K.V., McGregor, I.S., Hunt, G.E., Singh, M.E., Mallet, P.E., 2003. Regional differences in naloxone modulation of Delta(9)-THC induced Fos expression in rat brain. Neuropharmacology 44 (2), 264–274. https://doi.org/10.1016/s0028-3908(02)00364-7.

Apkarian, A.V., Bushnell, M.C., Treede, R.D., Zubieta, J.K., 2005. Human brain mechanisms of pain perception and regulation in health and disease. Eur. J. Pain 9 (4), 463–484. https://doi.org/10.1016/j.ejpain.2004.11.001.

Araki, M., McGeer, P.L., Kimura, H., 1988. The efferent projections of the rat lateral habenular nucleus revealed by the PHA-L anterograde tracing method. Brain Res. 441 (1–2), 319–330. https://doi.org/10.1016/0006-8993(88)91410-2.

Aron, J.L., Paulus, M.P., 2007. Location, location: using functional magnetic resonance imaging to pinpoint brain differences relevant to stimulant use. Addiction 102 (Suppl. 1), 33–43. https://doi.org/10.1111/j.1360-0443.2006.01778.x.

Arts, N.J., Walvoort, S.J., Kessels, R.P., 2017. Korsakoff's syndrome: a critical review. Neuropsychiatric Dis. Treat. 13, 2875–2890. https://doi.org/10.2147/NDT.S130078.

Barson, J.R., Ho, H.T., Leibowitz, S.F., 2015. Anterior thalamic paraventricular nucleus is involved in intermittent access ethanol drinking: role of orexin receptor 2. Addiction Biol. 20 (3), 469–481. https://doi.org/10.1111/adb.12139.

Baxter, M.G., Murray, E.A., 2002. The amygdala and reward. Nat. Rev. Neurosci. 3 (7), 563–573. https://doi.org/10.1038/nrn875.

Beckstead, R.M., Domesick, V.B., Nauta, W.J., 1979. Efferent connections of the substantia nigra and ventral tegmental area in the rat. Brain Res. 175 (2), 191–217. https://doi.org/10.1016/0006-8993(79)91001-1.

Belin, D., Everitt, B.J., 2008. Cocaine seeking habits depend upon dopamine-dependent serial connectivity linking the ventral with the dorsal striatum. Neuron 57 (3), 432–441. https://doi.org/10.1016/j.neuron.2007.12.019. S0896-6273(07)01032-X [pii].

Bell, R.P., Foxe, J.J., Nierenberg, J., Hoptman, M.J., Garavan, H., 2011. Assessing white matter integrity as a function of abstinence duration in former cocaine-dependent individuals. Drug Alcohol Depend. 114 (2–3), 159–168. https://doi.org/10.1016/j.drugalcdep.2010.10.001.

Bentivoglio, M., Balercia, G., Kruger, L., 1991. The specificity of the nonspecific thalamus: the midline nuclei. Prog. Brain Res. 87, 53–80. https://doi.org/10.1016/s0079-6123(08)63047-2.

Berendse, H.W., Groenewegen, H.J., 1990. Organization of the thalamostriatal projections in the rat, with special emphasis on the ventral striatum. J. Comp. Neurol. 299 (2), 187–228. https://doi.org/10.1002/cne.902990206.

Berendse, H.W., Groenewegen, H.J., 1991. Restricted cortical termination fields of the midline and intralaminar thalamic nuclei in the rat. Neuroscience 42 (1), 73–102. https://doi.org/10.1016/0306-4522(91)90151-d.

Bhatnagar, S., Dallman, M., 1998. Neuroanatomical basis for facilitation of hypothalamic-pituitary-adrenal responses to a novel stressor after chronic stress. Neuroscience 84 (4), 1025–1039. Retrieved from. http://www.ncbi.nlm.nih.gov/entrez/query.fcgi?cmd=Retrieve&db=PubMed&dopt=Citation&list_uids=9578393.

Bhatnagar, S., Dallman, M.F., 1999. The paraventricular nucleus of the thalamus alters rhythms in core temperature and energy balance in a state-dependent manner. Brain Res. 851 (1–2), 66–75. S0006-8993(99)02108-3 [pii].

Block, R.I., Erwin, W.J., Ghoneim, M.M., 2002. Chronic drug use and cognitive impairments. Pharmacol. Biochem. Behav. 73 (3), 491–504. https://doi.org/10.1016/s0091-3057(02)00816-x.

Bobo, J.K., Husten, C., 2000. Sociocultural influences on smoking and drinking. Alcohol Res. Health 24 (4), 225–232. Retrieved from. https://www.ncbi.nlm.nih.gov/pubmed/15986717.

Brog, J.S., Salyapongse, A., Deutch, A.Y., Zahm, D.S., 1993. The patterns of afferent innervation of the core and shell in the "accumbens" part of the rat ventral striatum: immunohistochemical detection of retrogradely transported fluoro-gold. J. Comp. Neurol. 338 (2), 255–278. https://doi.org/10.1002/cne.903380209.

Brown, R.M., Short, J.L., Lawrence, A.J., 2010. Identification of brain nuclei implicated in cocaine-primed reinstatement of conditioned place preference: a behaviour dissociable from sensitization. PLoS One 5 (12), e15889. https://doi.org/10.1371/journal.pone.0015889.

Browning, J.R., Jansen, H.T., Sorg, B.A., 2014. Inactivation of the paraventricular thalamus abolishes the expression of cocaine conditioned place preference in rats. Drug Alcohol Depend. 134, 387–390. https://doi.org/10.1016/j.drugalcdep.2013.09.021.

Brunton, J., Charpak, S., 1998. mu-Opioid peptides inhibit thalamic neurons. J. Neurosci. 18 (5), 1671–1678. Retrieved from. https://www.ncbi.nlm.nih.gov/pubmed/9464992.

Bubser, M., Deutch, A.Y., 1998. Thalamic paraventricular nucleus neurons collateralize to innervate the prefrontal cortex and nucleus accumbens. Brain Res. 787 (2), 304–310. Retrieved from. http://www.ncbi.nlm.nih.gov/pubmed/9518661.

Bubser, M., Deutch, A.Y., 1999. Stress induces Fos expression in neurons of the thalamic paraventricular nucleus that innervate limbic forebrain sites. Synapse 32 (1), 13–22. https://doi.org/10.1002/(SICI)1098-2396(199904)32:1<13::AID-SYN2>3.0.CO;2-R.

Buhler, M., Mann, K., 2011. Alcohol and the human brain: a systematic review of different neuroimaging methods. Alcohol Clin. Exp. Res. 35 (10), 1771–1793. https://doi.org/10.1111/j.1530-0277.2011.01540.x.

Buttner, A., 2011. Review: the neuropathology of drug abuse. Neuropathol. Appl. Neurobiol. 37 (2), 118–134. https://doi.org/10.1111/j.1365-2990.2010.01131.x.

Cardinal, R.N., Parkinson, J.A., Hall, J., Everitt, B.J., 2002. Emotion and motivation: the role of the amygdala, ventral striatum, and prefrontal cortex. Neurosci. Biobehav. Rev. 26 (3), 321–352. S0149763402000076 [pii].

Challet, E., Jacob, N., Vuillez, P., Pevet, P., Malan, A., 1997. Fos-like immunoreactivity in the circadian timing system of calorie-restricted rats fed at dawn: daily rhythms and light pulse-induced changes. Brain Res. 770 (1–2), 228–236. https://doi.org/10.1016/s0006-8993(97)00796-8.

Chen, S., Su, H.S., 1990. Afferent connections of the thalamic paraventricular and parataenial nuclei in the rat—a retrograde tracing study with iontophoretic application of Fluoro-Gold. Brain Res. 522 (1), 1–6. Retrieved from. http://www.ncbi.nlm.nih.gov/pubmed/2224500.

Chen, Z., Tang, Y., Tao, H., Li, C., Zhang, X., Liu, Y., 2015. Dynorphin activation of kappa opioid receptor reduces neuronal excitability in the paraventricular nucleus of mouse thalamus. Neuropharmacology 97, 259–269. https://doi.org/10.1016/j.neuropharm.2015.05.030.

Child, N.D., Benarroch, E.E., 2013. Anterior nucleus of the thalamus: functional organization and clinical implications. Neurology 81 (21), 1869–1876. https://doi.org/10.1212/01.wnl.0000436078.95856.56.

Chisholm, A., Iannuzzi, J., Rizzo, D., Gonzalez, N., Fortin, E., Bumbu, A., Shalev, U., 2020. The role of the paraventricular nucleus of the thalamus in the augmentation of heroin seeking induced by chronic food restriction. Addiction Biol. 25 (2), e12708. https://doi.org/10.1111/adb.12708.

Chisholm, A., Rizzo, D., Fortin, E., Moman, V., Quteishat, N., Romano, A., Shalev, U., 2021. Assessing the role of corticothalamic and thalamo-accumbens projections in the augmentation of heroin seeking in chronically food-restricted rats. J. Neurosci. 41 (2), 354–365. https://doi.org/10.1523/JNEUROSCI.2103-20.2020.

Chou, T.C., Lee, C.E., Lu, J., Elmquist, J.K., Hara, J., Willie, J.T., Scammell, T.E., 2001. Orexin (hypocretin) neurons contain dynorphin. J. Neurosci. 21 (19), RC168. Retrieved from. http://www.ncbi.nlm.nih.gov/pubmed/11567079.

Christoph, G.R., Leonzio, R.J., Wilcox, K.S., 1986. Stimulation of the lateral habenula inhibits dopamine-containing neurons in the substantia Nigra and ventral tegmental area of the rat. J. Neurosci. 6 (3), 613–619. Retrieved from. https://www.ncbi.nlm.nih.gov/pubmed/3958786.

Cisler, J.M., Elton, A., Kennedy, A.P., Young, J., Smitherman, S., Andrew James, G., Kilts, C.D., 2013. Altered functional connectivity of the insular cortex across prefrontal networks in cocaine addiction. Psychiatr. Res. 213 (1), 39–46. https://doi.org/10.1016/j.pscychresns.2013.02.007.

Cornwall, J., Phillipson, O.T., 1988a. Afferent projections to the dorsal thalamus of the rat as shown by retrograde lectin transport—I. The mediodorsal nucleus. Neuroscience 24 (3), 1035–1049. Retrieved from. http://www.ncbi.nlm.nih.gov/pubmed/3380295.

Cornwall, J., Phillipson, O.T., 1988b. Afferent projections to the dorsal thalamus of the rat as shown by retrograde lectin transport. II. The midline nuclei. Brain Res. Bull. 21 (2), 147–161. Retrieved from. http://www.ncbi.nlm.nih.gov/pubmed/3191403.

Covell, T., Siddiqui, W., 2020. Korsakoff syndrome. In: StatPearls. Treasure Island, FL.

Culverhouse, R., Bucholz, K.K., Crowe, R.R., Hesselbrock, V., Nurnberger Jr., J.I., Porjesz, B., Bierut, L.J., 2005. Long-term stability of alcohol and other substance dependence diagnoses and habitual smoking: an evaluation after 5 years. Arch. Gen. Psychiatr. 62 (7), 753–760. https://doi.org/10.1001/archpsyc.62.7.753.

Dani, J.A., Harris, R.A., 2005. Nicotine addiction and comorbidity with alcohol abuse and mental illness. Nat. Neurosci. 8 (11), 1465–1470. https://doi.org/10.1038/nn1580.

Day, E., Bentham, P.W., Callaghan, R., Kuruvilla, T., George, S., 2013. Thiamine for prevention and treatment of Wernicke-Korsakoff Syndrome in people who abuse alcohol. Cochrane Database Syst. Rev. 7, CD004033. https://doi.org/10.1002/14651858.CD004033.pub3.

Dayas, C.V., McGranahan, T.M., Martin-Fardon, R., Weiss, F., 2008. Stimuli linked to ethanol availability activate hypothalamic CART and orexin neurons in a reinstatement model of relapse. Biol. Psychiatr. 63 (2), 152–157. Retrieved from. http://www.ncbi.nlm.nih.gov/entrez/query.fcgi?cmd=Retrieve&db=PubMed&dopt=Citation&list_uids=17570346.

de Bourbon-Teles, J., Bentley, P., Koshino, S., Shah, K., Dutta, A., Malhotra, P., Soto, D., 2014. Thalamic control of human attention driven by memory and learning. Curr. Biol. 24 (9), 993–999. https://doi.org/10.1016/j.cub.2014.03.024.

de Wit, H., 2009. Impulsivity as a determinant and consequence of drug use: a review of underlying processes. Addiction Biol. 14 (1), 22–31. https://doi.org/10.1111/j.1369-1600.2008.00129.x.

Denier, N., Schmidt, A., Gerber, H., Vogel, M., Huber, C.G., Lang, U.E., Borgwardt, S., 2015. Abnormal functional integration of thalamic low frequency oscillation in the BOLD signal after acute heroin treatment. Hum. Brain Mapp. 36 (12), 5287–5300. https://doi.org/10.1002/hbm.23011.

Deutch, A.Y., Bubser, M., Young, C.D., 1998. Psychostimulant-induced Fos protein expression in the thalamic paraventricular nucleus. J. Neurosci. 18 (24), 10680–10687. Retrieved from. https://www.ncbi.nlm.nih.gov/pubmed/9852603.

Di Chiara, G., Imperato, A., 1988. Drugs abused by humans preferentially increase synaptic dopamine concentrations in the mesolimbic system of freely moving rats. Proc. Natl. Acad. Sci. U. S. A. 85 (14), 5274–5278. https://doi.org/10.1073/pnas.85.14.5274.

Ding, X., Lee, S.W., 2013. Cocaine addiction related reproducible brain regions of abnormal default-mode network functional connectivity: a group ICA study with different model orders. Neurosci. Lett. 548, 110–114. https://doi.org/10.1016/j.neulet.2013.05.029.

Do-Monte, F.H., Quinones-Laracuente, K., Quirk, G.J., 2015. A temporal shift in the circuits mediating retrieval of fear memory. Nature 519 (7544), 460–463. https://doi.org/10.1038/nature14030.

Dong, X., Li, S., Kirouac, G.J., 2017. Collateralization of projections from the paraventricular nucleus of the thalamus to the nucleus accumbens, bed nucleus of the stria terminalis, and central nucleus of the amygdala. Brain Struct. Funct. 222 (9), 3927–3943. https://doi.org/10.1007/s00429-017-1445-8.

Everitt, B.J., Dickinson, A., Robbins, T.W., 2001. The neuropsychological basis of addictive behaviour. Brain Res Brain Res Rev 36 (2–3), 129–138. S0165017301000881 [pii].

Fadok, J.P., Markovic, M., Tovote, P., Luthi, A., 2018. New perspectives on central amygdala function. Curr. Opin. Neurobiol. 49, 141–147. https://doi.org/10.1016/j.conb.2018.02.009.

Fein, G., Fein, D., 2013. Subcortical volumes are reduced in short-term and long-term abstinent alcoholics but not those with a comorbid stimulant disorder. Neuroimage Clin 3, 47–53. https://doi.org/10.1016/j.nicl.2013.06.018.

Fowler, C.D., Lu, Q., Johnson, P.M., Marks, M.J., Kenny, P.J., 2011. Habenular alpha5 nicotinic receptor subunit signalling controls nicotine intake. Nature 471 (7340), 597–601. https://doi.org/10.1038/nature09797.

Fowler, C.D., Tuesta, L., Kenny, P.J., 2013. Role of alpha5* nicotinic acetylcholine receptors in the effects of acute and chronic nicotine treatment on brain reward function in mice. Psychopharmacology (Berl). https://doi.org/10.1007/s00213-013-3235-1.

Freedman, L.J., Cassell, M.D., 1994. Relationship of thalamic basal forebrain projection neurons to the peptidergic innervation of the midline thalamus. J. Comp. Neurol. 348 (3), 321–342. https://doi.org/10.1002/cne.903480302.

Friedman, A., Lax, E., Dikshtein, Y., Abraham, L., Flaumenhaft, Y., Sudai, E., Yadid, G., 2010. Electrical stimulation of the lateral habenula produces enduring inhibitory effect on cocaine seeking behavior. Neuropharmacology 59 (6), 452–459. https://doi.org/10.1016/j.neuropharm.2010.06.008.

Galynker II, Watras-Ganz, S., Miner, C., Rosenthal, R.N., Des Jarlais, D.C., Richman, B.L., London, E., 2000. Cerebral metabolism in opiate-dependent subjects: effects of methadone maintenance. Mt. Sinai J. Med. 67 (5–6), 381–387. Retrieved from. https://www.ncbi.nlm.nih.gov/pubmed/11064488.

Garavan, H., Hester, R., 2007. The role of cognitive control in cocaine dependence. Neuropsychol. Rev. 17 (3), 337–345. https://doi.org/10.1007/s11065-007-9034-x.

Garcia, M.M., Brown, H.E., Harlan, R.E., 1995. Alterations in immediate-early gene proteins in the rat forebrain induced by acute morphine injection. Brain Res. 692 (1–2), 23–40. https://doi.org/10.1016/0006-8993(95)00625-z.

Gaudreau, J.D., Gagnon, P., 2005. Psychotogenic drugs and delirium pathogenesis: the central role of the thalamus. Med. Hypotheses 64 (3), 471–475. https://doi.org/10.1016/j.mehy.2004.08.007.

Gent, T.C., Bassetti, C., Adamantidis, A.R., 2018. Sleep-wake control and the thalamus. Curr. Opin. Neurobiol. 52, 188–197. https://doi.org/10.1016/j.conb.2018.08.002.

George, M.S., Anton, R.F., Bloomer, C., Teneback, C., Drobes, D.J., Lorberbaum, J.P., Vincent, D.J., 2001. Activation of prefrontal cortex and anterior thalamus in alcoholic subjects on exposure to alcohol-specific cues. Arch. Gen. Psychiatr. 58 (4), 345–352. Retrieved from. http://www.ncbi.nlm.nih.gov/htbin-post/Entrez/query?db=m&form=6&dopt=r&uid=11296095.

Giannotti, G., Barry, S.M., Siemsen, B.M., Peters, J., McGinty, J.F., 2018. Divergent prelimbic cortical pathways interact with BDNF to regulate cocaine-seeking. J. Neurosci. 38 (42), 8956–8966. https://doi.org/10.1523/JNEUROSCI.1332-18.2018.

Gill, M.J., Ghee, S.M., Harper, S.M., See, R.E., 2013. Inactivation of the lateral habenula reduces anxiogenic behavior and cocaine seeking under conditions of heightened stress. Pharmacol. Biochem. Behav. 111, 24–29. https://doi.org/10.1016/j.pbb.2013.08.002.

Glick, S.D., Ramirez, R.L., Livi, J.M., Maisonneuve, I.M., 2006. 18-Methoxycoronaridine acts in the medial habenula and/or interpeduncular nucleus to decrease morphine self-administration in rats. Eur. J. Pharmacol. 537 (1–3), 94–98. https://doi.org/10.1016/j.ejphar.2006.03.045.

Goaillard, J.M., Vincent, P., 2002. Serotonin suppresses the slow after hyperpolarization in rat intralaminar and midline thalamic neurones by activating 5-HT(7) receptors. J. Physiol. 541 (Pt 2), 453–465. https://doi.org/10.1113/jphysiol.2001.013896.

Goldstein, R.Z., Alia-Klein, N., Tomasi, D., Carrillo, J.H., Maloney, T., Woicik, P.A., Volkow, N.D., 2009. Anterior cingulate cortex hypoactivations to an emotionally salient task in cocaine addiction. Proc. Natl. Acad. Sci. U. S. A. 106 (23), 9453–9458. https://doi.org/10.1073/pnas.0900491106.

Goldstein, R.Z., Tomasi, D., Alia-Klein, N., Zhang, L., Telang, F., Volkow, N.D., 2007. The effect of practice on a sustained attention task in cocaine abusers. Neuroimage 35 (1), 194–206. https://doi.org/10.1016/j.neuroimage.2006.12.004.

Goldstein, R.Z., Volkow, N.D., 2002. Drug addiction and its underlying neurobiological basis: neuroimaging evidence for the involvement of the frontal cortex. Am. J. Psychiatr. 159 (10), 1642–1652. Retrieved from. http://www.ncbi.nlm.nih.gov/entrez/query.fcgi?cmd=Retrieve&db=PubMed&dopt=Citation&list_uids=12359667.

Gozzi, A., Agosta, F., Massi, M., Ciccocioppo, R., Bifone, A., 2013. Reduced limbic metabolism and fronto-cortical volume in rats vulnerable to alcohol addiction. Neuroimage 69, 112–119. https://doi.org/10.1016/j.neuroimage.2012.12.015.

Grodin, E.N., Momenan, R., 2017. Decreased subcortical volumes in alcohol dependent individuals: effect of polysubstance use disorder. Addiction Biol. 22 (5), 1426–1437. https://doi.org/10.1111/adb.12421.

Groenewegen, H.J., Berendse, H.W., 1994. The specificity of the 'nonspecific' midline and intralaminar thalamic nuclei. Trends Neurosci. 17 (2), 52–57. Retrieved from. http://www.ncbi.nlm.nih.gov/pubmed/7512768.

Gruber, C., Kahl, A., Lebenheim, L., Kowski, A., Dittgen, A., Veh, R.W., 2007. Dopaminergic projections from the VTA substantially contribute to the mesohabenular pathway in the rat. Neurosci. Lett. 427 (3), 165–170. https://doi.org/10.1016/j.neulet.2007.09.016.

Gu, H., Salmeron, B.J., Ross, T.J., Geng, X., Zhan, W., Stein, E.A., Yang, Y., 2010. Mesocorticolimbic circuits are impaired in chronic cocaine users as demonstrated by resting-state functional connectivity. Neuroimage 53 (2), 593–601. https://doi.org/10.1016/j.neuroimage.2010.06.066.

Guo, N., Garcia, M.M., Harlan, R.E., 2008. A morphine-paired environment alters c-Fos expression in the forebrain of rats displaying conditioned place preference or aversion. Behav. Neurosci. 122 (5), 1078–1086. https://doi.org/10.1037/a0012595.

Gutstein, H.B., Thome, J.L., Fine, J.L., Watson, S.J., Akil, H., 1998. Pattern of c-fos mRNA induction in rat brain by acute morphine. Can. J. Physiol. Pharmacol. 76 (3), 294–303. Retrieved from. https://www.ncbi.nlm.nih.gov/pubmed/9673793.

Haack, A.K., Sheth, C., Schwager, A.L., Sinclair, M.S., Tandon, S., Taha, S.A., 2014. Lesions of the lateral habenula increase voluntary ethanol consumption and operant self-administration, block yohimbine-induced reinstatement of ethanol seeking, and attenuate ethanol-induced conditioned taste aversion. PLoS One 9 (4), e92701. https://doi.org/10.1371/journal.pone.0092701.

Haber, S., McFarland, N.R., 2001. The place of the thalamus in frontal cortical-basal ganglia circuits. Neuroscientist 7 (4), 315–324. https://doi.org/10.1177/107385840100700408.

Hadfield, M.G., Milio, C., 1992. Cocaine and regional brain monoamines in mice. Pharmacol. Biochem. Behav. 43 (2), 395–403. https://doi.org/10.1016/0091-3057(92)90168-f.

Halassa, M.M., Kastner, S., 2017. Thalamic functions in distributed cognitive control. Nat. Neurosci. 20 (12), 1669–1679. https://doi.org/10.1038/s41593-017-0020-1.

Halassa, M.M., Sherman, S.M., 2019. Thalamocortical circuit motifs: a general framework. Neuron 103 (5), 762–770. https://doi.org/10.1016/j.neuron.2019.06.005.

Hamlin, A.S., Clemens, K.J., Choi, E.A., McNally, G.P., 2009. Paraventricular thalamus mediates context-induced reinstatement (renewal) of extinguished reward seeking. Eur. J. Neurosci. 29 (4), 802–812. https://doi.org/10.1111/j.1460-9568.2009.06623.x.

Hammoud, N., Jimenez-Shahed, J., 2019. Chronic neurologic effects of alcohol. Clin. Liver Dis. 23 (1), 141–155. https://doi.org/10.1016/j.cld.2018.09.010.

Hanlon, C.A., Wesley, M.J., Porrino, L.J., 2009. Loss of functional specificity in the dorsal striatum of chronic cocaine users. Drug Alcohol Depend. 102 (1–3), 88–94. https://doi.org/10.1016/j.drugalcdep.2009.01.005.

Hanlon, C.A., Wesley, M.J., Stapleton, J.R., Laurienti, P.J., Porrino, L.J., 2011. The association between frontal-striatal connectivity and sensorimotor control in cocaine users. Drug Alcohol Depend. 115 (3), 240–243. https://doi.org/10.1016/j.drugalcdep.2010.11.008.

Herkenham, M., Nauta, W.J., 1979. Efferent connections of the habenular nuclei in the rat. J. Comp. Neurol. 187 (1), 19–47. https://doi.org/10.1002/cne.901870103.

Hester, R., Garavan, H., 2004. Executive dysfunction in cocaine addiction: evidence for discordant frontal, cingulate, and cerebellar activity. J. Neurosci. 24 (49), 11017–11022. https://doi.org/10.1523/JNEUROSCI.3321-04.2004.

Heydendael, W., Sengupta, A., Bhatnagar, S., 2012. Putative genes mediating the effects of orexins in the posterior paraventricular thalamus on neuroendocrine and behavioral adaptations to repeated stress. Brain Res. Bull. 89 (5–6), 203–210. https://doi.org/10.1016/j.brainresbull.2012.09.002.

Heydendael, W., Sharma, K., Iyer, V., Luz, S., Piel, D., Beck, S., Bhatnagar, S., 2011. Orexins/hypocretins act in the posterior paraventricular thalamic nucleus during repeated stress to regulate facilitation to novel stress. Endocrinology 152 (12), 4738–4752. https://doi.org/10.1210/en.2011-1652.

Honnorat, N., Saranathan, M., Sullivan, E.V., Pfefferbaum, A., Pohl, K.M., Zahr, N.M., 2021. Performance ramifications of abnormal functional connectivity of ventral posterior lateral thalamus with cerebellum in abstinent individuals with Alcohol Use Disorder. Drug Alcohol Depend. 220, 108509. https://doi.org/10.1016/j.drugalcdep.2021.108509.

Hoover, W.B., Vertes, R.P., 2007. Anatomical analysis of afferent projections to the medial prefrontal cortex in the rat. Brain Struct. Funct. 212 (2), 149–179. https://doi.org/10.1007/s00429-007-0150-4.

Hsu, D.T., Price, J.L., 2009. Paraventricular thalamic nucleus: subcortical connections and innervation by serotonin, orexin, and corticotropin-releasing hormone in macaque monkeys. J. Comp. Neurol. 512 (6), 825–848. https://doi.org/10.1002/cne.21934.

Huang, A.S., Mitchell, J.A., Haber, S.N., Alia-Klein, N., Goldstein, R.Z., 2018. The thalamus in drug addiction: from rodents to humans. Philos. Trans. R. Soc. Lond. B Biol. Sci. 373 (1742). https://doi.org/10.1098/rstb.2017.0028.

Hwang, B.H., Zhang, J.K., Ehlers, C.L., Lumeng, L., Li, T.K., 1999. Innate differences of neuropeptide Y (NPY) in hypothalamic nuclei and central nucleus of the amygdala between selectively bred rats with high and low alcohol preference. Alcohol Clin. Exp. Res. 23 (6), 1023–1030. Retrieved from. https://www.ncbi.nlm.nih.gov/pubmed/10397286.

Ide, J.S., Zhang, S., Hu, S., Sinha, R., Mazure, C.M., Li, C.R., 2014. Cerebral gray matter volumes and low-frequency fluctuation of BOLD signals in cocaine dependence: duration of use and gender difference. Drug Alcohol Depend. 134, 51–62. https://doi.org/10.1016/j.drugalcdep.2013.09.004.

Ishibashi, M., Takano, S., Yanagida, H., Takatsuna, M., Nakajima, K., Oomura, Y., Sasaki, K., 2005. Effects of orexins/hypocretins on neuronal activity in the paraventricular nucleus of the thalamus in rats in vitro. Peptides 26 (3), 471–481. https://doi.org/10.1016/j.peptides.2004.10.014. S0196-9781(04)00474-7 [pii].

Ito, R., Dalley, J.W., Robbins, T.W., Everitt, B.J., 2002. Dopamine release in the dorsal striatum during cocaine-seeking behavior under the control of a drug-associated cue. J. Neurosci. 22 (14), 6247–6253. Retrieved from. http://www.ncbi.nlm.nih.gov/entrez/query.fcgi?cmd=Retrieve&db=PubMed&dopt=Citation&list_uids=12122083.

Jaferi, A., Nowak, N., Bhatnagar, S., 2003. Negative feedback functions in chronically stressed rats: role of the posterior paraventricular thalamus. Physiol. Behav. 78 (3), 365–373. Retrieved from. http://www.ncbi.nlm.nih.gov/pubmed/12676271.

James, M.H., Charnley, J.L., Flynn, J.R., Smith, D.W., Dayas, C.V., 2011a. Propensity to 'relapse' following exposure to cocaine cues is associated with the recruitment of specific thalamic and epithalamic nuclei. Neuroscience 199, 235–242. https://doi.org/10.1016/j.neuroscience.2011.09.047. S0306-4522(11)01132-8 [pii].

James, M.H., Charnley, J.L., Jones, E., Levi, E.M., Yeoh, J.W., Flynn, J.R., Dayas, C.V., 2010. Cocaine- and amphetamine-regulated transcript (CART) signaling within the paraventricular thalamus modulates cocaine-seeking behaviour. PLoS One 5 (9), e12980. https://doi.org/10.1371/journal.pone.0012980.

James, M.H., Charnley, J.L., Levi, E.M., Jones, E., Yeoh, J.W., Smith, D.W., Dayas, C.V., 2011b. Orexin-1 receptor signalling within the ventral tegmental area, but not the paraventricular thalamus, is critical to regulating cue-induced reinstatement of cocaine-seeking. Int. J. Neuropsychopharmacol. 14 (5), 684–690. https://doi.org/10.1017/S1461145711000423.

James, M.H., Dayas, C.V., 2013. What about me...? The PVT: a role for the paraventricular thalamus (PVT) in drug-seeking behavior. Front. Behav. Neurosci. 7, 18. https://doi.org/10.3389/fnbeh.2013.00018.

Jhou, T.C., Fields, H.L., Baxter, M.G., Saper, C.B., Holland, P.C., 2009. The rostromedial tegmental nucleus (RMTg), a GABAergic afferent to midbrain dopamine neurons, encodes aversive stimuli and inhibits motor responses. Neuron 61 (5), 786–800. https://doi.org/10.1016/j.neuron.2009.02.001.

Ji, H., Shepard, P.D., 2007. Lateral habenula stimulation inhibits rat midbrain dopamine neurons through a GABA(A) receptor-mediated mechanism. J. Neurosci. 27 (26), 6923–6930. https://doi.org/10.1523/JNEUROSCI.0958-07.2007.

Johnson, J.M., Fox, V., 2018. Beyond thiamine: treatment for cognitive impairment in Korsakoff's syndrome. Psychosomatics 59 (4), 311–317. https://doi.org/10.1016/j.psym.2018.03.011.

Jones, E.G., 2002. Thalamic circuitry and thalamocortical synchrony. Philos. Trans. R. Soc. Lond. B Biol. Sci. 357 (1428), 1659–1673. https://doi.org/10.1098/rstb.2002.1168.

Kalivas, P.W., Volkow, N.D., 2005. The neural basis of addiction: a pathology of motivation and choice. Am. J. Psychiatr. 162 (8), 1403–1413. Retrieved from. http://www.ncbi.nlm.nih.gov/entrez/query.fcgi?cmd=Retrieve&db=PubMed&dopt=Citation&list_uids=16055761.

Kaufman, J.N., Ross, T.J., Stein, E.A., Garavan, H., 2003. Cingulate hypoactivity in cocaine users during a GO-NOGO task as revealed by event-related functional magnetic resonance imaging. J. Neurosci. 23 (21), 7839–7843. Retrieved from. https://www.ncbi.nlm.nih.gov/pubmed/12944513.

Kawagoe, T., Tamura, R., Uwano, T., Asahi, T., Nishijo, H., Eifuku, S., Ono, T., 2007. Neural correlates of stimulus-reward association in the rat mediodorsal thalamus. Neuroreport 18 (7), 683–688. https://doi.org/10.1097/WNR.0b013e3280bef9a6.

Kedmi, M., Beaudet, A.L., Orr-Urtreger, A., 2004. Mice lacking neuronal nicotinic acetylcholine receptor beta4-subunit and mice lacking both alpha5- and beta4-subunits are highly resistant to nicotine-induced seizures. Physiol. Genom. 17 (2), 221–229. https://doi.org/10.1152/physiolgenomics.00202.2003.

Kelley, A.E., Baldo, B.A., Pratt, W.E., 2005. A proposed hypothalamic-thalamic-striatal axis for the integration of energy balance, arousal, and food reward. J. Comp. Neurol. 493 (1), 72–85. Retrieved from. http://www.ncbi.nlm.nih.gov/entrez/query.fcgi?cmd=Retrieve&db=PubMed&dopt=Citation&list_uids=16255002.

Kelly, C., Zuo, X.N., Gotimer, K., Cox, C.L., Lynch, L., Brock, D., Milham, M.P., 2011. Reduced interhemispheric resting state functional connectivity in cocaine addiction. Biol. Psychiatr. 69 (7), 684–692. https://doi.org/10.1016/j.biopsych.2010.11.022.

Keyes, P.C., Adams, E.L., Chen, Z., Bi, L., Nachtrab, G., Wang, V.J., Chen, X., 2020. Orchestrating opiate-associated memories in thalamic circuits. Neuron 107 (6), 1113–1123 e1114. https://doi.org/10.1016/j.neuron.2020.06.028.

Khaled, M.A., Pushparaj, A., Di Ciano, P., Diaz, J., Le Foll, B., 2014. Dopamine D3 receptors in the basolateral amygdala and the lateral habenula modulate cue-induced reinstatement of nicotine seeking. Neuropsychopharmacology 39 (13), 3049–3058. https://doi.org/10.1038/npp.2014.158.

Kim, U., Chang, S.Y., 2005. Dendritic morphology, local circuitry, and intrinsic electrophysiology of neurons in the rat medial and lateral habenular nuclei of the epithalamus. J. Comp. Neurol. 483 (2), 236–250. https://doi.org/10.1002/cne.20410.

Kimes, A.S., Bell, J.A., London, E.D., 1990. Clonidine attenuates increased brain glucose metabolism during naloxone-precipitated morphine withdrawal. Neuroscience 34 (3), 633–644. https://doi.org/10.1016/0306-4522(90)90170-9.

Kirouac, G.J., 2015. Placing the paraventricular nucleus of the thalamus within the brain circuits that control behavior. Neurosci. Biobehav. Rev. 56, 315–329. https://doi.org/10.1016/j.neubiorev.2015.08.005.

Kirouac, G.J., Parsons, M.P., Li, S., 2005. Orexin (hypocretin) innervation of the paraventricular nucleus of the thalamus. Brain Res. 1059 (2), 179–188. Retrieved from. http://www.ncbi.nlm.nih.gov/entrez/query.fcgi?cmd=Retrieve&db=PubMed&dopt=Citation&list_uids=16168969.

Kirouac, G.J., Parsons, M.P., Li, S., 2006. Innervation of the paraventricular nucleus of the thalamus from cocaine- and amphetamine-regulated transcript (CART) containing neurons of the hypothalamus. J. Comp. Neurol. 497 (2), 155–165. Retrieved from. http://www.ncbi.nlm.nih.gov/entrez/query.fcgi?cmd=Retrieve&db=PubMed&dopt=Citation&list_uids=16705679.

Klemm, W.R., 2004. Habenular and interpeduncularis nuclei: shared components in multiple-function networks. Med. Sci. Mon. Int. Med. J. Exp. Clin. Res. 10 (11), RA261–273. Retrieved from. https://www.ncbi.nlm.nih.gov/pubmed/15507867.

Kolaj, M., Doroshenko, P., Yan Cao, X., Coderre, E., Renaud, L.P., 2007. Orexin-induced modulation of state-dependent intrinsic properties in thalamic paraventricular nucleus neurons attenuates action potential patterning and frequency. Neuroscience 147 (4), 1066–1075. https://doi.org/10.1016/j.neuroscience.2007.05.018.

Kolaj, M., Zhang, L., Hermes, M.L., Renaud, L.P., 2014. Intrinsic properties and neuropharmacology of midline paraventricular thalamic nucleus neurons. Front. Behav. Neurosci. 8, 132. https://doi.org/10.3389/fnbeh.2014.00132.

Kolaj, M., Zhang, L., Ronnekleiv, O.K., Renaud, L.P., 2012. Midline thalamic paraventricular nucleus neurons display diurnal variation in resting membrane potentials, conductances, and firing patterns in vitro. J. Neurophysiol. 107 (7), 1835–1844. https://doi.org/10.1152/jn.00974.2011.

Koob, G.F., Volkow, N.D., 2016. Neurobiology of addiction: a neurocircuitry analysis. Lancet Psychiatr. 3 (8), 760–773. https://doi.org/10.1016/S2215-0366(16)00104-8.

Kril, J.J., Halliday, G.M., Svoboda, M.D., Cartwright, H., 1997. The cerebral cortex is damaged in chronic alcoholics. Neuroscience 79 (4), 983–998. https://doi.org/10.1016/s0306-4522(97)00083-3.

Krout, K.E., Belzer, R.E., Loewy, A.D., 2002. Brainstem projections to midline and intralaminar thalamic nuclei of the rat. J. Comp. Neurol. 448 (1), 53–101. https://doi.org/10.1002/cne.10236.

Krout, K.E., Loewy, A.D., 2000. Parabrachial nucleus projections to midline and intralaminar thalamic nuclei of the rat. J. Comp. Neurol. 428 (3), 475–494. Retrieved from. http://www.ncbi.nlm.nih.gov/pubmed/11074446.

Kuo, C.S., Chai, S.C., Chen, H.H., 2011. Mediodorsal nucleus of the thalamus is critical for the expression of memory of methamphetamine-produced conditioned place preference in rats. Neuroscience 178, 138–146. https://doi.org/10.1016/j.neuroscience.2010.12.021.

Lawrence, N.S., Ross, T.J., Hoffmann, R., Garavan, H., Stein, E.A., 2003. Multiple neuronal networks mediate sustained attention. J. Cognit. Neurosci. 15 (7), 1028–1038. https://doi.org/10.1162/089892903770007416.

Lee, T.M., Pau, C.W., 2002. Impulse control differences between abstinent heroin users and matched controls. Brain Inj. 16 (10), 885–889. https://doi.org/10.1080/02699050210128915.

Lever, J.R., 2007. PET and SPECT imaging of the opioid system: receptors, radioligands and avenues for drug discovery and development. Curr. Pharmaceut. Des. 13 (1), 33–49. https://doi.org/10.2174/138161207779313821.

Li, B., Piriz, J., Mirrione, M., Chung, C., Proulx, C.D., Schulz, D., Malinow, R., 2011a. Synaptic potentiation onto habenula neurons in the learned helplessness model of depression. Nature 470 (7335), 535–539. https://doi.org/10.1038/nature09742.

Li, C.S., Sinha, R., 2008. Inhibitory control and emotional stress regulation: neuroimaging evidence for frontal-limbic dysfunction in psycho-stimulant addiction. Neurosci. Biobehav. Rev. 32 (3), 581–597. https://doi.org/10.1016/j.neubiorev.2007.10.003.

Li, S., Kirouac, G.J., 2008. Projections from the paraventricular nucleus of the thalamus to the forebrain, with special emphasis on the extended amygdala. J. Comp. Neurol. 506 (2), 263–287. https://doi.org/10.1002/cne.21502.

Li, S., Kirouac, G.J., 2012. Sources of inputs to the anterior and posterior aspects of the paraventricular nucleus of the thalamus. Brain Struct. Funct. 217 (2), 257–273. https://doi.org/10.1007/s00429-011-0360-7.

Li, S.J., Biswal, B., Li, Z., Risinger, R., Rainey, C., Cho, J.K., Stein, E.A., 2000. Cocaine administration decreases functional connectivity in human primary visual and motor cortex as detected by functional MRI. Magn. Reson. Med. 43 (1), 45–51. https://doi.org/10.1002/(sici)1522-2594(200001)43:1<45::aid-mrm6>3.0.co;2-0.

Li, Y., van den Pol, A.N., 2006. Differential target-dependent actions of coexpressed inhibitory dynorphin and excitatory hypocretin/orexin neuropeptides. J. Neurosci. 26 (50), 13037–13047. https://doi.org/10.1523/JNEUROSCI.3380-06.2006.

Li, Y., Wang, H., Qi, K., Chen, X., Li, S., Sui, N., Kirouac, G.J., 2011b. Orexins in the midline thalamus are involved in the expression of conditioned place aversion to morphine withdrawal. Physiol. Behav. 102 (1), 42–50. https://doi.org/10.1016/j.physbeh.2010.10.006. S0031-9384(10)00359-8 [pii].

Licata, S.C., Renshaw, P.F., 2010. Neurochemistry of drug action: insights from proton magnetic resonance spectroscopic imaging and their relevance to addiction. Ann. N. Y. Acad. Sci. 1187, 148–171. https://doi.org/10.1111/j.1749-6632.2009.05143.x.

Ligorio, M., Descarries, L., Warren, R.A., 2009. Cholinergic innervation and thalamic input in rat nucleus accumbens. J. Chem. Neuroanat. 37 (1), 33–45. https://doi.org/10.1016/j.jchemneu.2008.08.003.

Liu, X., Matochik, J.A., Cadet, J.L., London, E.D., 1998. Smaller volume of prefrontal lobe in polysubstance abusers: a magnetic resonance imaging study. Neuropsychopharmacology 18 (4), 243–252. https://doi.org/10.1016/S0893-133X(97)00143-7.

Lotfipour, S., Byun, J.S., Leach, P., Fowler, C.D., Murphy, N.P., Kenny, P.J., Boulter, J., 2013. Targeted deletion of the mouse alpha2 nicotinic acetylcholine receptor subunit gene (Chrna2) potentiates nicotine-modulated behaviors. J. Neurosci. 33 (18), 7728–7741. https://doi.org/10.1523/JNEUROSCI.4731-12.2013.

Luo, X., Zhang, S., Hu, S., Bednarski, S.R., Erdman, E., Farr, O.M., Li, C.S., 2013. Error processing and gender-shared and -specific neural predictors of relapse in cocaine dependence. Brain 136 (Pt 4), 1231–1244. https://doi.org/10.1093/brain/awt040.

Malcolm, B.P., Hesselbrock, M.N., Segal, B., 2006. Multiple substance dependence and course of alcoholism among Alaska native men and women. Subst. Use Misuse 41 (5), 729–741. https://doi.org/10.1080/10826080500391803.

Mann, K., Agartz, I., Harper, C., Shoaf, S., Rawlings, R.R., Momenan, R., Heinz, A., 2001. Neuroimaging in alcoholism: ethanol and brain damage. Alcohol Clin. Exp. Res. 25 (5 Suppl. ISBRA), 104S–109S. Retrieved from. http://www.ncbi.nlm.nih.gov/htbin-post/Entrez/query?db=m&form=6&dopt=r&uid=11391058.

Mann, K., Gunther, A., Stetter, F., Ackermann, K., 1999. Rapid recovery from cognitive deficits in abstinent alcoholics: a controlled test-retest study. Alcohol Alcohol 34 (4), 567–574. Retrieved from. http://www.ncbi.nlm.nih.gov/pubmed/10456585.

Mansour, A., Fox, C.A., Burke, S., Meng, F., Thompson, R.C., Akil, H., Watson, S.J., 1994. Mu, delta, and kappa opioid receptor mRNA expression in the rat CNS: an in situ hybridization study. J. Comp. Neurol. 350 (3), 412–438. https://doi.org/10.1002/cne.903500307.

Mansour, A., Fox, C.A., Meng, F., Akil, H., Watson, S.J., 1994. Kappa 1 receptor mRNA distribution in the rat CNS: comparison to kappa receptor binding and prodynorphin mRNA. Mol. Cell. Neurosci. 5 (2), 124–144. https://doi.org/10.1006/mcne.1994.1015.

Marchant, N.J., Campbell, E.J., Whitaker, L.R., Harvey, B.K., Kaganovsky, K., Adhikary, S., Shaham, Y., 2016. Role of ventral subiculum in context-induced relapse to alcohol seeking after punishment-imposed abstinence. J. Neurosci. 36 (11), 3281–3294. https://doi.org/10.1523/JNEUROSCI.4299-15.2016.

Marchant, N.J., Furlong, T.M., McNally, G.P., 2010. Medial dorsal hypothalamus mediates the inhibition of reward seeking after extinction. J. Neurosci. 30 (42), 14102–14115. https://doi.org/10.1523/JNEUROSCI.4079-10.2010, 30/42/14102 [pii].

Marcus, J.N., Aschkenasi, C.J., Lee, C.E., Chemelli, R.M., Saper, C.B., Yanagisawa, M., Elmquist, J.K., 2001. Differential expression of orexin receptors 1 and 2 in the rat brain. J. Comp. Neurol. 435 (1), 6–25. https://doi.org/10.1002/cne.1190.

Maroteaux, M., Mameli, M., 2012. Cocaine evokes projection-specific synaptic plasticity of lateral habenula neurons. J. Neurosci. 32 (36), 12641–12646. https://doi.org/10.1523/JNEUROSCI.2405-12.2012.

Martin-Fardon, R., Boutrel, B., 2012. Orexin/hypocretin (Orx/Hcrt) transmission and drug-seeking behavior: is the paraventricular nucleus of the thalamus (PVT) part of the drug seeking circuitry? Front. Behav. Neurosci. 6, 75. https://doi.org/10.3389/fnbeh.2012.00075.

Maskos, U., Molles, B.E., Pons, S., Besson, M., Guiard, B.P., Guilloux, J.P., Changeux, J.P., 2005. Nicotine reinforcement and cognition restored by targeted expression of nicotinic receptors. Nature 436 (7047), 103–107. https://doi.org/10.1038/nature03694.

Matsumoto, M., Hikosaka, O., 2007. Lateral habenula as a source of negative reward signals in dopamine neurons. Nature 447 (7148), 1111–1115. https://doi.org/10.1038/nature05860.

Matzeu, A., Kallupi, M., George, O., Schweitzer, P., Martin-Fardon, R., 2018. Dynorphin counteracts orexin in the paraventricular nucleus of the thalamus: cellular and behavioral evidence. Neuropsychopharmacology 43 (5), 1010–1020. https://doi.org/10.1038/npp.2017.250.

Matzeu, A., Kerr, T.M., Weiss, F., Martin-Fardon, R., 2016. Orexin-A/Hypocretin-1 mediates cocaine-seeking behavior in the posterior paraventricular nucleus of the thalamus via orexin/hypocretin receptor-2. J. Pharmacol. Exp. Therapeut. 359 (2), 273–279. https://doi.org/10.1124/jpet.116.235945.

Matzeu, A., Martin-Fardon, R., 2020. Blockade of orexin receptors in the posterior paraventricular nucleus of the thalamus prevents stress-induced reinstatement of reward-seeking behavior in rats with a history of ethanol dependence. Front. Integr. Neurosci. 14, 599710. https://doi.org/10.3389/fnint.2020.599710.

Matzeu, A., Martin-Fardon, R., 2021a. Cocaine-seeking behavior induced by orexin A administration in the posterior paraventricular nucleus of the thalamus is not long-lasting: neuroadaptation of the orexin system during cocaine abstinence. Front. Behav. Neurosci. 15, 620868. https://doi.org/10.3389/fnbeh.2021.620868.

Matzeu, A., Martin-Fardon, R., 2021b. Blockade of the corticotropin-releasing factor receptor 1 in the central amygdala prevents cocaine-seeking behavior induced by orexin-A administered into the posterior paraventricular nucleus of the thalamus in male rats. J. Psychiatry Neurosci. (in press).

Matzeu, A., Weiss, F., Martin-Fardon, R., 2015. Transient inactivation of the posterior paraventricular nucleus of the thalamus blocks cocaine-seeking behavior. Neurosci. Lett. 608, 34–39. https://doi.org/10.1016/j.neulet.2015.10.016.

Maurer, R., Cortes, R., Probst, A., Palacios, J.M., 1983. Multiple opiate receptor in human brain: an autoradiographic investigation. Life Sci. 33 (Suppl. 1), 231–234. https://doi.org/10.1016/0024-3205(83)90485-x.

McAlonan, G.M., Robbins, T.W., Everitt, B.J., 1993. Effects of medial dorsal thalamic and ventral pallidal lesions on the acquisition of a conditioned place preference: further evidence for the involvement of the ventral striatopallidal system in reward-related processes. Neuroscience 52 (3), 605–620. https://doi.org/10.1016/0306-4522(93)90410-h.

McCallum, S.E., Cowe, M.A., Lewis, S.W., Glick, S.D., 2012. alpha3beta4 nicotinic acetylcholine receptors in the medial habenula modulate the mesolimbic dopaminergic response to acute nicotine in vivo. Neuropharmacology 63 (3), 434–440. https://doi.org/10.1016/j.neuropharm.2012.04.015.

McFarland, K., Kalivas, P.W., 2001. The circuitry mediating cocaine-induced reinstatement of drug-seeking behavior. J. Neurosci. 21 (21), 8655–8663, 21/21/8655 [pii].

Medina, K.L., Shear, P.K., Schafer, J., Armstrong, T.G., Dyer, P., 2004. Cognitive functioning and length of abstinence in polysubstance dependent men. Arch. Clin. Neuropsychol. 19 (2), 245–258. https://doi.org/10.1016/S0887-6177(03)00043-X.

Millan, E.Z., Ong, Z., McNally, G.P., 2017. Paraventricular thalamus: gateway to feeding, appetitive motivation, and drug addiction. Prog. Brain Res. 235, 113–137. https://doi.org/10.1016/bs.pbr.2017.07.006.

Modell, J.G., Mountz, J.M., Beresford, T.P., 1990. Basal ganglia/limbic striatal and thalamocortical involvement in craving and loss of control in alcoholism. J. Neuropsychiatry Clin. Neurosci. 2 (2), 123–144. https://doi.org/10.1176/jnp.2.2.123.

Moeller, F.G., Hasan, K.M., Steinberg, J.L., Kramer, L.A., Dougherty, D.M., Santos, R.M., Narayana, P.A., 2005. Reduced anterior corpus callosum white matter integrity is related to increased impulsivity and reduced discriminability in cocaine-dependent subjects: diffusion tensor imaging. Neuropsychopharmacology 30 (3), 610–617. https://doi.org/10.1038/sj.npp.1300617.

Moga, M.M., Weis, R.P., Moore, R.Y., 1995. Efferent projections of the paraventricular thalamic nucleus in the rat. J. Comp. Neurol. 359 (2), 221–238. https://doi.org/10.1002/cne.903590204.

Mon, A., Durazzo, T.C., Abe, C., Gazdzinski, S., Pennington, D., Schmidt, T., Meyerhoff, D.J., 2014. Structural brain differences in alcohol-dependent individuals with and without comorbid substance dependence. Drug Alcohol Depend. 144, 170–177. https://doi.org/10.1016/j.drugalcdep.2014.09.010.

Monnig, M.A., Thayer, R.E., Caprihan, A., Claus, E.D., Yeo, R.A., Calhoun, V.D., Hutchison, K.E., 2014. White matter integrity is associated with alcohol cue reactivity in heavy drinkers. Brain Behav 4 (2), 158–170. https://doi.org/10.1002/brb3.204.

Montague, P.R., Dayan, P., Sejnowski, T.J., 1996. A framework for mesencephalic dopamine systems based on predictive Hebbian learning. J. Neurosci. 16 (5), 1936–1947. Retrieved from. https://www.ncbi.nlm.nih.gov/pubmed/8774460.

Morley, B.J., 1986. The interpeduncular nucleus. Int. Rev. Neurobiol. 28, 157–182. https://doi.org/10.1016/s0074-7742(08)60108-7.

Mugnaini, M., Tessari, M., Tarter, G., Merlo Pich, E., Chiamulera, C., Bunnemann, B., 2002. Upregulation of [3H] methyllycaconitine binding sites following continuous infusion of nicotine, without changes of alpha7 or alpha6 subunit mRNA: an autoradiography and in situ hybridization study in rat brain. Eur. J. Neurosci. 16 (9), 1633–1646. https://doi.org/10.1046/j.1460-9568.2002.02220.x.

Muschamp, J.W., Hollander, J.A., Thompson, J.L., Voren, G., Hassinger, L.C., Onvani, S., Carlezon Jr., W.A., 2014. Hypocretin (orexin) facilitates reward by attenuating the antireward effects of its cotransmitter dynorphin in ventral tegmental area. Proc. Natl. Acad. Sci. U. S. A. 111 (16), E1648–E1655. https://doi.org/10.1073/pnas.1315542111.

Najeeb, F., Silver, B., Khan, M., 2016. Cessation of smoking and alcohol addiction following thalamic hemorrhage. Neurol. 21 (6), 91–92. https://doi.org/10.1097/NRL.0000000000000091.

Neugebauer, N.M., Einstein, E.B., Lopez, M.B., McClure-Begley, T.D., Mineur, Y.S., Picciotto, M.R., 2013. Morphine dependence and withdrawal induced changes in cholinergic signaling. Pharmacol. Biochem. Behav. 109, 77–83. https://doi.org/10.1016/j.pbb.2013.04.015.

Neumann, P.A., Wang, Y., Yan, Y., Wang, Y., Ishikawa, M., Cui, R., Dong, Y., 2016. Cocaine-induced synaptic alterations in thalamus to nucleus accumbens projection. Neuropsychopharmacology 41 (9), 2399–2410. https://doi.org/10.1038/npp.2016.52.

Novak, C.M., Harris, J.A., Smale, L., Nunez, A.A., 2000. Suprachiasmatic nucleus projections to the paraventricular thalamic nucleus in nocturnal rats (*Rattus norvegicus*) and diurnal nile grass rats (Arviacanthis niloticus). Brain Res. 874 (2), 147–157. Retrieved from. https://www.ncbi.nlm.nih.gov/pubmed/10960599.

Novak, C.M., Nunez, A.A., 1998. Daily rhythms in Fos activity in the rat ventrolateral preoptic area and midline thalamic nuclei. Am. J. Physiol. 275 (5 Pt 2), R1620–R1626. Retrieved from. https://www.ncbi.nlm.nih.gov/pubmed/9791082.

Novak, C.M., Smale, L., Nunez, A.A., 2000. Rhythms in Fos expression in brain areas related to the sleep-wake cycle in the diurnal Arvicanthis niloticus. Am. J. Physiol. Regul. Integr. Comp. Physiol. 278 (5), R1267–R1274. https://doi.org/10.1152/ajpregu.2000.278.5.R1267.

Noyan, C.O., Kose, S., Nurmedov, S., Metin, B., Darcin, A.E., Dilbaz, N., 2016. Volumetric brain abnormalities in polysubstance use disorder patients. Neuropsychiatric Dis. Treat. 12, 1355–1363. https://doi.org/10.2147/NDT.S107733.

Oades, R.D., Halliday, G.M., 1987. Ventral tegmental (A10) system: neurobiology. 1. Anatomy and connectivity. Brain Res. 434 (2), 117–165. https://doi.org/10.1016/0165-0173(87)90011-7.

Otake, K., 2005. Cholecystokinin and substance P immunoreactive projections to the paraventricular thalamic nucleus in the rat. Neurosci. Res. 51 (4), 383–394. https://doi.org/10.1016/j.neures.2004.12.009. S0168-0102(04)00313-X [pii].

Otake, K., Kin, K., Nakamura, Y., 2002. Fos expression in afferents to the rat midline thalamus following immobilization stress. Neurosci. Res. 43 (3), 269–282. Retrieved from. https://www.ncbi.nlm.nih.gov/pubmed/12103445.

Otake, K., Nakamura, Y., 1998. Single midline thalamic neurons projecting to both the ventral striatum and the prefrontal cortex in the rat. Neuroscience 86 (2), 635–649. Retrieved from. http://www.ncbi.nlm.nih.gov/pubmed/9881876.

Otis, J.M., Namboodiri, V.M., Matan, A.M., Voets, E.S., Mohorn, E.P., Kosyk, O., Stuber, G.D., 2017. Prefrontal cortex output circuits guide reward seeking through divergent cue encoding. Nature 543 (7643), 103–107. https://doi.org/10.1038/nature21376.

Otis, J.M., Zhu, M., Namboodiri, V.M.K., Cook, C.A., Kosyk, O., Matan, A.M., Stuber, G.D., 2019. Paraventricular Thalamus Projection Neurons Integrate Cortical and Hypothalamic Signals for Cue-Reward Processing. Neuron 103 (3), 423–431 e424. https://doi.org/10.1016/j.neuron.2019.05.018.

Oudman, E., Nijboer, T.C., Postma, A., Wijnia, J.W., Van der Stigchel, S., 2015. Procedural learning and memory rehabilitation in Korsakoff's syndrome—a review of the literature. Neuropsychol. Rev. 25 (2), 134–148. https://doi.org/10.1007/s11065-015-9288-7.

Panchal, V., Taraschenko, O.D., Maisonneuve, I.M., Glick, S.D., 2005. Attenuation of morphine withdrawal signs by intracerebral administration of 18-methoxycoronaridine. Eur. J. Pharmacol. 525 (1–3), 98–104. https://doi.org/10.1016/j.ejphar.2005.09.060.

Parsons, M.P., Li, S., Kirouac, G.J., 2007. Functional and anatomical connection between the paraventricular nucleus of the thalamus and dopamine fibers of the nucleus accumbens. J. Comp. Neurol. 500 (6), 1050–1063. https://doi.org/10.1002/cne.21224.

Pasumarthi, R.K., Fadel, J., 2008. Activation of orexin/hypocretin projections to basal forebrain and paraventricular thalamus by acute nicotine. Brain Res. Bull. 77 (6), 367–373. https://doi.org/10.1016/j.brainresbull.2008.09.014. S0361-9230(08)00333-X [pii].

Pau, C.W., Lee, T.M., Chan, S.F., 2002. The impact of heroin on frontal executive functions. Arch. Clin. Neuropsychol. 17 (7), 663–670. Retrieved from. https://www.ncbi.nlm.nih.gov/pubmed/14591849.

Peckys, D., Landwehrmeyer, G.B., 1999. Expression of mu, kappa, and delta opioid receptor messenger RNA in the human CNS: a 33P in situ hybridization study. Neuroscience 88 (4), 1093–1135. https://doi.org/10.1016/s0306-4522(98)00251-6.

Peng, Z.C., Bentivoglio, M., 2004. The thalamic paraventricular nucleus relays information from the suprachiasmatic nucleus to the amygdala: a combined anterograde and retrograde tracing study in the rat at the light and electron microscopic levels. J. Neurocytol. 33 (1), 101–116. https://doi.org/10.1023/B:NEUR.0000029651.51195.f9.

Peng, Z.C., Grassi-Zucconi, G., Bentivoglio, M., 1995. Fos-related protein expression in the midline paraventricular nucleus of the rat thalamus: basal oscillation and relationship with limbic efferents. Exp. Brain Res. 104 (1), 21–29. Retrieved from. https://www.ncbi.nlm.nih.gov/pubmed/7621938.

Pennartz, C.M., Groenewegen, H.J., Lopes da Silva, F.H., 1994. The nucleus accumbens as a complex of functionally distinct neuronal ensembles: an integration of behavioural, electrophysiological and anatomical data. Prog. Neurobiol. 42 (6), 719–761. Retrieved from. http://www.ncbi.nlm.nih.gov/pubmed/7938546.

Penzo, M.A., Robert, V., Tucciarone, J., De Bundel, D., Wang, M., Van Aelst, L., Li, B., 2015. The paraventricular thalamus controls a central amygdala fear circuit. Nature 519 (7544), 455–459. https://doi.org/10.1038/nature13978.

Pereira de Vasconcelos, A., Cassel, J.C., 2015. The nonspecific thalamus: a place in a wedding bed for making memories last? Neurosci. Biobehav. Rev. 54, 175–196. https://doi.org/10.1016/j.neubiorev.2014.10.021.

Perez, E., Quijano-Carde, N., De Biasi, M., 2015. Nicotinic mechanisms modulate ethanol withdrawal and modify time course and symptoms severity of simultaneous withdrawal from alcohol and nicotine. Neuropsychopharmacology 40 (10), 2327–2336. https://doi.org/10.1038/npp.2015.80.

Perry, C.J., McNally, G.P., 2013. A role for the ventral pallidum in context-induced and primed reinstatement of alcohol seeking. Eur. J. Neurosci. 38 (5), 2762–2773. https://doi.org/10.1111/ejn.12283.

Pfeiffer, A., Pasi, A., Mehraein, P., Herz, A., 1982. Opiate receptor binding sites in human brain. Brain Res. 248 (1), 87–96. https://doi.org/10.1016/0006-8993(82)91150-7.

Phillipson, O.T., Pycock, C.J., 1982. Dopamine neurones of the ventral tegmentum project to both medial and lateral habenula. Some implications for habenular function. Exp. Brain Res. 45 (1–2), 89–94. https://doi.org/10.1007/BF00235766.

Picciotto, M.R., Kenny, P.J., 2013. Molecular mechanisms underlying behaviors related to nicotine addiction. Cold Spring Harb. Perspect. Med. 3 (1), a012112. https://doi.org/10.1101/cshperspect.a012112.

Pierce, R.C., Vanderschuren, L.J., 2010. Kicking the habit: the neural basis of ingrained behaviors in cocaine addiction. Neurosci. Biobehav. Rev. 35 (2), 212–219. https://doi.org/10.1016/j.neubiorev.2010.01.007.

Pilapil, C., Welner, S., Magnan, J., Gauthier, S., Quirion, R., 1987. Autoradiographic distribution of multiple classes of opioid receptor binding sites in human forebrain. Brain Res. Bull. 19 (5), 611–615. https://doi.org/10.1016/0361-9230(87)90080-3.

Pitel, A.L., Chetelat, G., Le Berre, A.P., Desgranges, B., Eustache, F., Beaunieux, H., 2012. Macrostructural abnormalities in Korsakoff syndrome compared with uncomplicated alcoholism. Neurology 78 (17), 1330–1333. https://doi.org/10.1212/WNL.0b013e318251834e.

Pitel, A.L., Eustache, F., Beaunieux, H., 2014. Component processes of memory in alcoholism: pattern of compromise and neural substrates. Handb. Clin. Neurol. 125, 211–225. https://doi.org/10.1016/B978-0-444-62619-6.00013-6.

Pitel, A.L., Segobin, S.H., Ritz, L., Eustache, F., Beaunieux, H., 2015. Thalamic abnormalities are a cardinal feature of alcohol-related brain dysfunction. Neurosci. Biobehav. Rev. 54, 38–45. https://doi.org/10.1016/j.neubiorev.2014.07.023.

Porrino, L.J., Smith, H.R., Nader, M.A., Beveridge, T.J., 2007. The effects of cocaine: a shifting target over the course of addiction. Prog. Neuro-Psychopharmacol. Biol. Psychiatry 31 (8), 1593–1600. https://doi.org/10.1016/j.pnpbp.2007.08.040.

Potvin, S., Stavro, K., Rizkallah, E., Pelletier, J., 2014. Cocaine and cognition: a systematic quantitative review. J. Addiction Med. 8 (5), 368–376. https://doi.org/10.1097/ADM.0000000000000066.

Prosser, J., London, E.D., Galynker, I.I., 2009. Sustained attention in patients receiving and abstinent following methadone maintenance treatment for opiate dependence: performance and neuroimaging results. Drug Alcohol Depend. 104 (3), 228–240. https://doi.org/10.1016/j.drugalcdep.2009.04.022.

Qiu, Y.W., Han, L.J., Lv, X.F., Jiang, G.H., Tian, J.Z., Zhuo, F.Z., Zhang, X.L., 2011. Regional homogeneity changes in heroin-dependent individuals: resting-state functional MR imaging study. Radiology 261 (2), 551–559. https://doi.org/10.1148/radiol.11102466.

Ray, S., Haney, M., Hanson, C., Biswal, B., Hanson, S.J., 2015. Modeling causal relationship between brain regions within the drug-cue processing network in chronic cocaine smokers. Neuropsychopharmacology 40 (13), 2960–2968. https://doi.org/10.1038/npp.2015.150.

Reid, A.G., Daglish, M.R., Kempton, M.J., Williams, T.M., Watson, B., Nutt, D.J., Lingford-Hughes, A.R., 2008. Reduced thalamic grey matter volume in opioid dependence is influenced by degree of alcohol use: a voxel-based morphometry study. J. Psychopharmacol. 22 (1), 7–10. https://doi.org/10.1177/0269881107080795.

Ren, T., Sagar, S.M., 1992. Induction of c-fos immunostaining in the rat brain after the systemic administration of nicotine. Brain Res. Bull. 29 (5), 589–597. https://doi.org/10.1016/0361-9230(92)90127-j.

Rho, B., Glick, S.D., 1998. Effects of 18-methoxycoronaridine on acute signs of morphine withdrawal in rats. Neuroreport 9 (7), 1283–1285. https://doi.org/10.1097/00001756-199805110-00004.

Rosenkranz, J.A., Moore, H., Grace, A.A., 2003. The prefrontal cortex regulates lateral amygdala neuronal plasticity and responses to previously conditioned stimuli. J. Neurosci. 23 (35), 11054–11064. Retrieved from. https://www.ncbi.nlm.nih.gov/pubmed/14657162.

Ruggiero, D.A., Anwar, S., Kim, J., Glickstein, S.B., 1998. Visceral afferent pathways to the thalamus and olfactory tubercle: behavioral implications. Brain Res. 799 (1), 159–171. Retrieved from. http://www.ncbi.nlm.nih.gov/pubmed/9666113.

Ryabinin, A.E., Wang, Y.M., 1998. Repeated alcohol administration differentially affects c-Fos and FosB protein immunoreactivity in DBA/2J mice. Alcohol Clin. Exp. Res. 22 (8), 1646–1654. Retrieved from. https://www.ncbi.nlm.nih.gov/pubmed/9835277.

Salas, R., Sturm, R., Boulter, J., De Biasi, M., 2009. Nicotinic receptors in the habenulo-interpeduncular system are necessary for nicotine withdrawal in mice. J. Neurosci. 29 (10), 3014–3018. https://doi.org/10.1523/JNEUROSCI.4934-08.2009.

Salling, M.C., Hodge, C.J., Psilos, K.E., Eastman, V.R., Faccidomo, S.P., Hodge, C.W., 2017. Cue-induced reinstatement of alcohol-seeking behavior is associated with increased CaMKII T286 phosphorylation in the reward pathway of mice. Pharmacol. Biochem. Behav. 163, 20–29. https://doi.org/10.1016/j.pbb.2017.10.011.

Salti, A., Apostolova, G., Kummer, K.K., Lemos, C., Dechant, G., El Rawas, R., 2018. Cocaine paired environment increases SATB2 levels in the rat paraventricular thalamus. Front. Behav. Neurosci. 12, 224. https://doi.org/10.3389/fnbeh.2018.00224.

Sartorius, A., Kiening, K.L., Kirsch, P., von Gall, C.C., Haberkorn, U., Unterberg, A.W., Meyer-Lindenberg, A., 2010. Remission of major depression under deep brain stimulation of the lateral habenula in a therapy-refractory patient. Biol. Psychiatr. 67 (2), e9–e11. https://doi.org/10.1016/j.biopsych.2009.08.027.

Scheibel, A.B., 1997. The thalamus and neuropsychiatric illness. J. Neuropsychiatry Clin. Neurosci. 9 (3), 342–353. https://doi.org/10.1176/jnp.9.3.342.

Schmahmann, J.D., 2003. Vascular syndromes of the thalamus. Stroke 34 (9), 2264–2278. https://doi.org/10.1161/01.STR.0000087786.38997.9E.

Schultz, W., Dayan, P., Montague, P.R., 1997. A neural substrate of prediction and reward. Science 275 (5306), 1593–1599. https://doi.org/10.1126/science.275.5306.1593.

See, R.E., 2002. Neural substrates of conditioned-cued relapse to drug-seeking behavior. Pharmacol. Biochem. Behav. 71 (3), 517–529. Retrieved from. http://www.ncbi.nlm.nih.gov/pubmed/11830186.

Segobin, S.H., Chetelat, G., Le Berre, A.P., Lannuzel, C., Boudehent, C., Vabret, F., Pitel, A.L., 2014. Relationship between brain volumetric changes and interim drinking at six months in alcohol-dependent patients. Alcohol Clin. Exp. Res. 38 (3), 739–748. https://doi.org/10.1111/acer.12300.

Sharp, C.S., Wilson, M.P., Nordstrom, K., 2016. Psychiatric emergencies for clinicians: emergency department management of Wernicke-Korsakoff syndrome. J. Emerg. Med. 51 (4), 401–404. https://doi.org/10.1016/j.jemermed.2016.05.044.

Shepard, P.D., Holcomb, H.H., Gold, J.M., 2006. Schizophrenia in translation: the presence of absence: habenular regulation of dopamine neurons and the encoding of negative outcomes. Schizophr. Bull. 32 (3), 417–421. https://doi.org/10.1093/schbul/sbj083.

Sherman, S.M., 2007. The thalamus is more than just a relay. Curr. Opin. Neurobiol. 17 (4), 417–422. https://doi.org/10.1016/j.conb.2007.07.003.

Sherman, S.M., 2017. Functioning of circuits connecting thalamus and cortex. Compr. Physiol. 7 (2), 713–739. https://doi.org/10.1002/cphy.c160032.

Sim, M.E., Lyoo, I.K., Streeter, C.C., Covell, J., Sarid-Segal, O., Ciraulo, D.A., Renshaw, P.F., 2007. Cerebellar gray matter volume correlates with duration of cocaine use in cocaine-dependent subjects. Neuropsychopharmacology 32 (10), 2229–2237. https://doi.org/10.1038/sj.npp.1301346.

Smith, R.J., Anderson, R.I., Haun, H.L., Mulholland, P.J., Griffin 3rd, W.C., Lopez, M.F., Becker, H.C., 2020. Dynamic c-Fos changes in mouse brain during acute and protracted withdrawal from chronic intermittent ethanol exposure and relapse drinking. Addiction Biol. 25 (6), e12804. https://doi.org/10.1111/adb.12804.

Smith, Y., Raju, D.V., Pare, J.F., Sidibe, M., 2004. The thalamostriatal system: a highly specific network of the basal ganglia circuitry. Trends Neurosci. 27 (9), 520–527. https://doi.org/10.1016/j.tins.2004.07.004.

Sommer, M.A., 2003. The role of the thalamus in motor control. Curr. Opin. Neurobiol. 13 (6), 663–670. https://doi.org/10.1016/j.conb.2003.10.014.

Stein, T., Moritz, C., Quigley, M., Cordes, D., Haughton, V., Meyerand, E., 2000. Functional connectivity in the thalamus and hippocampus studied with functional MR imaging. AJNR Am. J. Neuroradiol. 21 (8), 1397–1401. Retrieved from. https://www.ncbi.nlm.nih.gov/pubmed/11003270.

Steketee, J.D., Kalivas, P.W., 2011. Drug Wanting: behavioral sensitization and relapse to drug-seeking behavior. Pharmacol. Rev. 63 (2), 348–365. https://doi.org/10.1124/pr.109.001933 pr.109.001933 [pii].

Steriade, M., 2006. Grouping of brain rhythms in corticothalamic systems. Neuroscience 137 (4), 1087–1106. https://doi.org/10.1016/j.neuroscience.2005.10.029.

Steriade, M., Llinas, R.R., 1988. The functional states of the thalamus and the associated neuronal interplay. Physiol. Rev. 68 (3), 649–742. https://doi.org/10.1152/physrev.1988.68.3.649.

Su, H.S., Bentivoglio, M., 1990. Thalamic midline cell populations projecting to the nucleus accumbens, amygdala, and hippocampus in the rat. J. Comp. Neurol. 297 (4), 582–593. https://doi.org/10.1002/cne.902970410.

Sutherland, M.T., Riedel, M.C., Flannery, J.S., Yanes, J.A., Fox, P.T., Stein, E.A., Laird, A.R., 2016. Chronic cigarette smoking is linked with structural alterations in brain regions showing acute nicotinic drug-induced functional modulations. Behav. Brain Funct. 12 (1), 16. https://doi.org/10.1186/s12993-016-0100-5.

Swan, G.E., Carmelli, D., Cardon, L.R., 1997. Heavy consumption of cigarettes, alcohol and coffee in male twins. J. Stud. Alcohol 58 (2), 182–190. Retrieved from. https://www.ncbi.nlm.nih.gov/pubmed/9065896.

Swanson, L.W., 2000. Cerebral hemisphere regulation of motivated behavior. Brain Res. 886 (1–2), 113–164. Retrieved from. http://www.ncbi.nlm.nih.gov/pubmed/11119693.

Tanabe, J., Tregellas, J.R., Dalwani, M., Thompson, L., Owens, E., Crowley, T., Banich, M., 2009. Medial orbitofrontal cortex gray matter is reduced in abstinent substance-dependent individuals. Biol. Psychiatr. 65 (2), 160–164. https://doi.org/10.1016/j.biopsych.2008.07.030.

Taraschenko, O.D., Shulan, J.M., Maisonneuve, I.M., Glick, S.D., 2007. 18-MC acts in the medial habenula and interpeduncular nucleus to attenuate dopamine sensitization to morphine in the nucleus accumbens. Synapse 61 (7), 547–560. https://doi.org/10.1002/syn.20396.

Tedstone, D., Coyle, K., 2004. Cognitive impairments in sober alcoholics: performance on selective and divided attention tasks. Drug Alcohol Depend. 75 (3), 277–286. https://doi.org/10.1016/j.drugalcdep.2004.03.005.

Thomson, A.D., 2000. Mechanisms of vitamin deficiency in chronic alcohol misusers and the development of the Wernicke-Korsakoff syndrome. Alcohol Alcohol Suppl. 35 (1), 2–7. https://doi.org/10.1093/alcalc/35.supplement_1.2.

Timofeeva, E., Picard, F., Duclos, M., Deshaies, Y., Richard, D., 2002. Neuronal activation and corticotropin-releasing hormone expression in the brain of obese (fa/fa) and lean (fa/?) Zucker rats in response to refeeding. Eur. J. Neurosci. 15 (6), 1013–1029. https://doi.org/10.1046/j.1460-9568.2002.01942.x.

Tolomeo, S., Gray, S., Matthews, K., Steele, J.D., Baldacchino, A., 2016. Multifaceted impairments in impulsivity and brain structural abnormalities in opioid dependence and abstinence. Psychol. Med. 46 (13), 2841–2853. https://doi.org/10.1017/S0033291716001513.

Tomasi, D., Goldstein, R.Z., Telang, F., Maloney, T., Alia-Klein, N., Caparelli, E.C., Volkow, N.D., 2007. Thalamo-cortical dysfunction in cocaine abusers: implications in attention and perception. Psychiatr. Res. 155 (3), 189–201. https://doi.org/10.1016/j.pscychresns.2007.03.002.

Tomasi, D., Volkow, N.D., Wang, R., Carrillo, J.H., Maloney, T., Alia-Klein, N., Goldstein, R.Z., 2010. Disrupted functional connectivity with dopaminergic midbrain in cocaine abusers. PLoS One 5 (5), e10815. https://doi.org/10.1371/journal.pone.0010815.

Torrico, T.J., Munakomi, S., 2021. Neuroanatomy, thalamus. In: StatPearls. Treasure Island. FL.

Trivedi, P., Yu, H., MacNeil, D.J., Van der Ploeg, L.H., Guan, X.M., 1998. Distribution of orexin receptor mRNA in the rat brain. FEBS Lett. 438 (1–2), 71–75. https://doi.org/10.1016/s0014-5793(98)01266-6.

Upadhyay, J., Maleki, N., Potter, J., Elman, I., Rudrauf, D., Knudsen, J., Borsook, D., 2010. Alterations in brain structure and functional connectivity in prescription opioid-dependent patients. Brain 133 (Pt 7), 2098–2114. https://doi.org/10.1093/brain/awq138.

Van der Werf, Y.D., Witter, M.P., Groenewegen, H.J., 2002. The intralaminar and midline nuclei of the thalamus. Anatomical and functional evidence for participation in processes of arousal and awareness. Brain Res. Brain Res. Rev. 39 (2–3), 107–140. https://doi.org/10.1016/s0165-0173(02)00181-9.

Vantomme, G., Osorio-Forero, A., Luthi, A., Fernandez, L.M.J., 2019. Regulation of local sleep by the thalamic reticular nucleus. Front. Neurosci. 13, 576. https://doi.org/10.3389/fnins.2019.00576.

Velasquez, K.M., Molfese, D.L., Salas, R., 2014. The role of the habenula in drug addiction. Front. Hum. Neurosci. 8, 174. https://doi.org/10.3389/fnhum.2014.00174.

Verdejo-Garcia, A., Contreras-Rodriguez, O., Fonseca, F., Cuenca, A., Soriano-Mas, C., Rodriguez, J., de la Torre, R., 2014. Functional alteration in frontolimbic systems relevant to moral judgment in cocaine-dependent subjects. Addiction Biol. 19 (2), 272–281. https://doi.org/10.1111/j.1369-1600.2012.00472.x.

Vertes, R.P., 2002. Analysis of projections from the medial prefrontal cortex to the thalamus in the rat, with emphasis on nucleus reuniens. J. Comp. Neurol. 442 (2), 163–187. https://doi.org/10.1002/cne.10083.

Vertes, R.P., 2004. Differential projections of the infralimbic and prelimbic cortex in the rat. Synapse 51 (1), 32–58. https://doi.org/10.1002/syn.10279.

Vertes, R.P., Hoover, W.B., 2008. Projections of the paraventricular and paratenial nuclei of the dorsal midline thalamus in the rat. J. Comp. Neurol. 508 (2), 212–237. https://doi.org/10.1002/cne.21679.

Vertes, R.P., Linley, S.B., Hoover, W.B., 2015. Limbic circuitry of the midline thalamus. Neurosci. Biobehav. Rev. 54, 89–107. https://doi.org/10.1016/j.neubiorev.2015.01.014.

Volkow, N.D., Wang, G.J., Fowler, J.S., Logan, J., Gatley, S.J., Hitzemann, R., Pappas, N., 1997a. Decreased striatal and enhanced thalamic dopaminergic responsivity in detoxified cocaine abusers. J. Nucl. Med. 38 (5), 126, 126. Retrieved from <Go to ISI>://WOS:A1997WY98000126.

Volkow, N.D., Wang, G.J., Fowler, J.S., Logan, J., Gatley, S.J., Hitzemann, R., Pappas, N., 1997b. Decreased striatal dopaminergic responsiveness in detoxified cocaine-dependent subjects. Nature 386 (6627), 830–833. https://doi.org/10.1038/386830a0.

Voorn, P., Brady, L.S., Berendse, H.W., Richfield, E.K., 1996. Densitometrical analysis of opioid receptor ligand binding in the human striatum—I. Distribution of mu opioid receptor defines shell and core of the ventral striatum. Neuroscience 75 (3), 777–792. https://doi.org/10.1016/0306-4522(96)00271-0.

Walker, D.L., Toufexis, D.J., Davis, M., 2003. Role of the bed nucleus of the stria terminalis versus the amygdala in fear, stress, and anxiety. Eur. J. Pharmacol. 463 (1–3), 199–216. Retrieved from. http://www.ncbi.nlm.nih.gov/entrez/query.fcgi?cmd=Retrieve&db=PubMed&dopt=Citation&list_uids=12600711.

Wang, Y., Zhang, F., Tang, S., Lai, M., Hao, W., Zhang, Y., Zhou, W., 2009. Lack of effect of habenula lesion on heroin self-administration in rats. Neurosci. Lett. 461 (2), 167–171. https://doi.org/10.1016/j.neulet.2009.06.029.

Weiss, F., 2005. Neurobiology of craving, conditioned reward and relapse. Curr. Opin. Pharmacol. 5 (1), 9–19. Retrieved from. http://www.ncbi.nlm.nih.gov/entrez/query.fcgi?cmd=Retrieve&db=PubMed&dopt=Citation&list_uids=15661620.

Weissenborn, R., Whitelaw, R.B., Robbins, T.W., Everitt, B.J., 1998. Excitotoxic lesions of the mediodorsal thalamic nucleus attenuate intravenous cocaine self-administration. Psychopharmacology (Berl) 140 (2), 225–232. https://doi.org/10.1007/s002130050761.

Wheeler, M.A., Stuss, D.T., Tulving, E., 1997. Toward a theory of episodic memory: the frontal lobes and autonoetic consciousness. Psychol. Bull. 121 (3), 331–354. https://doi.org/10.1037/0033-2909.121.3.331.

Wiggins, A., Bunin, J.L., 2020. Confabulation. In: StatPearls. Treasure Island, FL.

Wilcox, C.E., Teshiba, T.M., Merideth, F., Ling, J., Mayer, A.R., 2011. Enhanced cue reactivity and fronto-striatal functional connectivity in cocaine use disorders. Drug Alcohol Depend. 115 (1–2), 137–144. https://doi.org/10.1016/j.drugalcdep.2011.01.009.

Williams, T.M., Daglish, M.R., Lingford-Hughes, A., Taylor, L.G., Hammers, A., Brooks, D.J., Nutt, D.J., 2007. Brain opioid receptor binding in early abstinence from opioid dependence: positron emission tomography study. Br. J. Psychiatry 191, 63–69. https://doi.org/10.1192/bjp.bp.106.031120.

Winrow, C.J., Tanis, K.Q., Reiss, D.R., Rigby, A.M., Uslaner, J.M., Uebele, V.N., Renger, J.J., 2010. Orexin receptor antagonism prevents transcriptional and behavioral plasticity resulting from stimulant exposure. Neuropharmacology 58 (1), 185–194. https://doi.org/10.1016/j.neuropharm.2009.07.008. S0028-3908(09)00215-9 [pii].

Wise, R.A., 1996. Neurobiology of addiction. Curr. Opin. Neurobiol. 6 (2), 243–251.

Wong, A.Y., Borduas, J.F., Clarke, S., Lee, K.F., Beique, J.C., Bergeron, R., 2013. Calcium influx through N-type channels and activation of SK and TRP-like channels regulates tonic firing of neurons in rat paraventricular thalamus. J. Neurophysiol. 110 (10), 2450–2464. https://doi.org/10.1152/jn.00363.2013.

Wunsch, A.M., Yager, L.M., Donckels, E.A., Le, C.T., Neumaier, J.F., Ferguson, S.M., 2017. Chemogenetic inhibition reveals midline thalamic nuclei and thalamo-accumbens projections mediate cocaine-seeking in rats. Eur. J. Neurosci. 46 (3), 1850–1862. https://doi.org/10.1111/ejn.13631.

Xie, C., Shao, Y., Fu, L., Goveas, J., Ye, E., Li, W., Yang, Z., 2011. Identification of hyperactive intrinsic amygdala network connectivity associated with impulsivity in abstinent heroin addicts. Behav. Brain Res. 216 (2), 639–646. https://doi.org/10.1016/j.bbr.2010.09.004.

Yeoh, J.W., James, M.H., Graham, B.A., Dayas, C.V., 2014. Electrophysiological characteristics of paraventricular thalamic (PVT) neurons in response to cocaine and cocaine- and amphetamine-regulated transcript (CART). Front. Behav. Neurosci. 8, 280. https://doi.org/10.3389/fnbeh.2014.00280.

Yeoh, J.W., James, M.H., Jobling, P., Bains, J.S., Graham, B.A., Dayas, C.V., 2012. Cocaine potentiates excitatory drive in the perifornical/lateral hypothalamus. J. Physiol. 590 (16), 3677–3689. https://doi.org/10.1113/jphysiol.2012.230268.

Yip, S.W., Morie, K.P., Xu, J., Constable, R.T., Malison, R.T., Carroll, K.M., Potenza, M.N., 2017. Shared microstructural features of behavioral and substance addictions revealed in areas of crossing fibers. Biol Psychiatry Cogn Neurosci Neuroimaging 2 (2), 188–195. https://doi.org/10.1016/j.bpsc.2016.03.001.

Young, C.D., Deutch, A.Y., 1998. The effects of thalamic paraventricular nucleus lesions on cocaine-induced locomotor activity and sensitization. Pharmacol. Biochem. Behav. 60 (3), 753–758. https://doi.org/10.1016/s0091-3057(98)00051-3.

Yu, D., Yuan, K., Cheng, J., Guan, Y., Li, Y., Bi, Y., Lu, X., 2017. Reduced thalamus volume may reflect nicotine severity in young male smokers. Nicotine Tob. Res. https://doi.org/10.1093/ntr/ntx146.

Zacny, J.P., 1990. Behavioral aspects of alcohol-tobacco interactions. Recent Dev. Alcohol 8, 205–219. Retrieved from. https://www.ncbi.nlm.nih.gov/pubmed/2185518.

Zahr, N.M., Pfefferbaum, A., 2017. Alcohol's effects on the brain: neuroimaging results in humans and animal models. Alcohol Res. 38 (2), 183–206. Retrieved from. https://www.ncbi.nlm.nih.gov/pubmed/28988573.

Zhang, F., Zhou, W., Liu, H., Zhu, H., Tang, S., Lai, M., Yang, G., 2005. Increased c-Fos expression in the medial part of the lateral habenula during cue-evoked heroin-seeking in rats. Neurosci. Lett. 386 (2), 133–137. https://doi.org/10.1016/j.neulet.2005.06.008.

Zhang, L., Renaud, L.P., Kolaj, M., 2009. Properties of a T-type Ca2+channel-activated slow afterhyperpolarization in thalamic paraventricular nucleus and other thalamic midline neurons. J. Neurophysiol. 101 (6), 2741–2750. https://doi.org/10.1152/jn.91183.2008.

Zhang, S., Hu, S., Bednarski, S.R., Erdman, E., Li, C.S., 2014. Error-related functional connectivity of the thalamus in cocaine dependence. Neuroimage Clin 4, 585–592. https://doi.org/10.1016/j.nicl.2014.01.015.

Zhang, X., van den Pol, A.N., 2017. Rapid binge-like eating and body weight gain driven by zona incerta GABA neuron activation. Science 356 (6340), 853–859. https://doi.org/10.1126/science.aam7100.

Zhao-Shea, R., Liu, L., Pang, X., Gardner, P.D., Tapper, A.R., 2013. Activation of GABAergic neurons in the interpeduncular nucleus triggers physical nicotine withdrawal symptoms. Curr. Biol. 23 (23), 2327–2335. https://doi.org/10.1016/j.cub.2013.09.041.

Zhou, K., Zhu, Y., 2019. The paraventricular thalamic nucleus: a key hub of neural circuits underlying drug addiction. Pharmacol. Res. 142, 70–76. https://doi.org/10.1016/j.phrs.2019.02.014.

Zhu, Y., Wienecke, C.F., Nachtrab, G., Chen, X., 2016. A thalamic input to the nucleus accumbens mediates opiate dependence. Nature 530 (7589), 219–222. https://doi.org/10.1038/nature16954.

CHAPTER

7

Hippocampal circuits

Chitra D. Mandyam

VA San Diego Healthcare System, San Diego, CA, United States; Department of Anesthesiology, University of California San Diego, San Diego, CA, United States

Introduction

Substance use disorder (SUD) is a chronic, relapsing disorder characterized by uncontrollable drug use, which is associated with recurrent thoughts and actions aimed at compulsively taking the drugs, loss of control over drug consumption and relapse to drug taking (Altman et al., 1996; Koob et al., 1998). SUD continues to be a public health issue. It results in maladaptive behavioral changes, some that can last a lifetime. For example, addiction to illicit drugs is linked to disrupted learning, with the development of strong but maladaptive memories that contribute to drug-seeking behavior. This is based on the premise that initial or acute drug experience can facilitate the development of memories between drug effects and environmental stimuli, and that these associated memories can exert strong behavioral control and facilitate drug-seeking behavior and relapse. With continued and chronic use of drugs, learning deficits emerge along with cognitive inflexibility. These learning deficits and cognitive inflexibility combined with previously formed maladaptive drug-context/ drug–cue associations contribute to the maintenance of addiction. Alterations in neural ensembles and neural plasticity is associated with and predicts these behavioral changes, suggesting that there is a high degree of overlap between the neurobiology of learning and memory and the neurobiology of addiction (White, 1996; Volkow et al., 2013; Volkow and Morales, 2015; Goodman and Packard, 2016). In the last several decades the mechanistic studies in animal models of addiction have mainly focused on the mesolimbic as well as on mesocortical dopamine pathways and their telencephalic projection targets and their role in development and maintenance of addiction (Pierce and Kalivas, 1997; Robinson and Berridge, 2000; Kelley, 2004; Koob and Volkow, 2016). However, recent studies on the link between rewarding properties of addictive drugs and drug memories (facilitated by drug context, cues) demonstrate that the conditioning mechanisms involved during drug

Neurocircuitry of Addiction
https://doi.org/10.1016/B978-0-12-823453-2.00006-0

experience facilitate the transition from initial drug use into eventual drug dependency (Hyman et al., 2006; Goodman and Packard, 2016). More importantly, these studies support the involvement of the hippocampus in the development and maintenance of addiction.

This chapter provides an overview of the hippocampus focusing on learning and memory functions, anatomy, plasticity, and circuitry, and discusses research that supports the involvement of the hippocampus in the development and maintenance of drug addiction. Based on several preclinical studies and supporting clinical findings, it is becoming clear that initial exposure to stimulants (cocaine and amphetamines) and alcohol may enhance hippocampal function and, therefore, the engagement of learning and memory functions to support drug–context associations that contribute to the development of addiction. On the contrary, studies on forced withdrawal and abstinence from stimulants, ethanol, and cannabis in animal and human studies reveal hippocampus-dependent learning and memory deficits. These findings overall suggest that individuals may choose to engage in continued drug use in an attempt to alleviate withdrawal-induced deficits, and that these maladaptive behaviors may contribute to relapse to drug use and maintenance of addiction. Taken together, preclinical and clinical research thus far supports the further evaluation of the role of the hippocampus in drug addiction and that added discoveries may help to formulate a better understanding of addiction and underlying neural substrates assisting with maintenance of drug use.

Hippocampal formation

The hippocampus is a brain region that is important for the formation and storage of episodic and semantic declarative memories. In addition, the hippocampus is one of the most thoroughly investigated regions in the brain for learning and memory functions. Since the 1957 report of the famous H.M., a case study subject who lost the ability to form new declarative memories after surgical removal of the hippocampus to treat epilepsy, the hippocampus has been at the forefront of research into the biological bases of learning and memory (Squire and Wixted, 2011). Our understanding of the neurophysiological bases of hippocampal function were greatly enhanced by the finding of activity-dependent synaptic plasticity in the hippocampus (Bliss and Lomo, 1973), and the discovery of hippocampal place cells—neurons that are important for spatial position of an animal (O'Keefe and Dostrovsky, 1971). These important discoveries steered many scientists and researchers around the world to investigate and subsequently advance knowledge in our understanding of different forms of synaptic plasticity in hippocampal circuits, and in particular how different forms of synaptic plasticity contribute to different types of memories and learning dependent on the hippocampus.

Synaptic plasticity in the hippocampus

Understanding and deciphering learning and memory mechanisms is one of the major tasks for neuroscientists. To understand cellular mechanisms of learning and memory, neuronal or synaptic plasticity in the hippocampus are often studied (Bliss and

Collingridge, 1993). Synaptic plasticity can be defined as the ability of neurons to change their activity in response to external or internal stimuli by reorganizing their morphology, connections or function. The term "plastic" originates from the Latin-word "plasticus" which comes from the Greek-word "plastos" originally meaning "formed". In the last century, several scientists made important contributions to our understanding of synaptic plasticity, including Santiago Ramon y Cajal who first defined a neuron as the anatomical, physiological, genetic unit of the nervous system in his "Neuron Doctrine" (Jones, 1994). Synaptic plasticity indicates either strengthening or weakening of synaptic connections. One-form of strengthened plasticity is long-term potentiation (LTP), whereas one-form of weakened plasticity is long-term depression (LTD (Bliss and Lomo, 1973; Malenka and Nicoll, 1999; Collingridge et al., 2010)). Long-lasting changes in synaptic plasticity are key mechanisms underlying learning and long-term memory (Kandel and Tauc, 1965). Another-form of plasticity is short-term plasticity, which can indicate either short-term facilitation and short-term depression that lasts from milliseconds to several minutes, and can be elicited by high or low frequency stimulations. This-form of plasticity is considered to be important for short-term memory. The exact cellular and molecular mechanisms underlying short-term plasticity are not fully understood and are currently being investigated in several laboratories (Zucker and Regehr, 2002; Citri and Malenka, 2008).

During the 20th century, the question—how is information stored in the brain—generated an enormous body of work that concentrated on the properties of synaptic transmission and synaptic plasticity. For example, Canadian psychologist Donald Hebb postulated a theory regarding the possible neuronal mechanisms of learning and memory (Hebb, 1949). Hebbian plasticity is a widely used model in neuroscience to study synaptic plasticity in the hippocampus of mammals. However, the first true evidence linking plasticity (short-term plasticity) to behavioral modification came from studies in Aplysia (a marine gastropod mollusk (Kandel and Tauc, 1965)). Research on synaptic transmission and synaptic plasticity moved beyond using invertebrates in the late 60s and early 70s due to discovery of novel techniques that allowed the use of mammalian brain slice preparation for electrophysiology studies (Skrede and Westgaard, 1971). This-type of preparation from mammalian brain tissue was used in Andersen's lab to discover LTP in the dentate gyrus of the rabbit hippocampus (Andersen, 1975; Lomo, 2003). Researchers have continued using slice preparation from hippocampal tissue in the last four decades to enhance our understanding of neuronal plasticity.

Another-form of synaptic plasticity, LTD was also discovered in the 70s with use of slice preparation from mammalian brain tissue (Lynch et al., 1977). Furthermore, the development of patch clamp electrophysiology techniques as well as other types of intracellular recording techniques led to discovery of different types of plasticity in the hippocampus as well as in other regions of the brain (Gray and Johnston, 1985). For example, during the 1990s, a new form of plasticity was discovered using intracellular recording techniques. In this form, the relative timing of active backpropagation of sodium-dependent action potential into the dendrites generated by pre- and postsynaptic neurons at monosynaptic connections was demonstrated when measured in pairs of cortical neurons (Stuart and Sakmann, 1994; Markram et al., 2011). This feature is important for a type of synaptic modification, called spike timing-dependent plasticity (STDP). STDP can be induced by timing-dependent repetitive activations of multiple spikes or even by single spikes in pre- and post-synaptic neurons, and it was shown to occur in several brain regions (Dan and Poo, 2006; Feldman, 2012; Markram et al., 2012).

STDP was also described for hippocampal synapses, and in particular, in mossy fiber-cornu ammonis (CA)3 and CA1 Schaffer-collaterals (Debanne et al., 1994; Letzkus et al., 2006; Fino et al., 2009; Hunt et al., 2013; Brandalise and Gerber, 2014; Pang et al., 2019). Additional forms of plasticity, such as metaplasticity, were also discovered in the hippocampus (Abraham and Bear, 1996). This-form of plasticity is also termed as "the plasticity of synaptic plasticity," and it is a phenomenon that involves activity-dependent changes in neuronal function that modulate synaptic plasticity. At this moment, the precise role of metaplasticity in learning and memory functions is not clear, but several reports have indicated that it may serve to stabilize synapses within a dynamic range of activity (Yang et al., 2014; Baione et al., 2019; Crestani et al., 2019; Gebhardt et al., 2019; Hegemann and Abraham, 2019; Lutzu and Castillo, 2021).

In the past two decades, another form of plasticity was defined that regulated the total synaptic strength of a neuron and operated over longer time scales. This was termed homeostatic plasticity (Turrigiano and Nelson, 2004). This-type of plasticity increases or decreases the strength of all of a neuron's synaptic inputs as a function of its activity, to maintain homeostasis over a wide range of spatial and temporal scales. This homeostatic plasticity regulates synaptic scaling and is thought to stabilize synaptic strength at the level of a single neuron (Turrigiano et al., 1998; Turrigiano, 2012). The exact relationship between STDP and homeostatic plasticity is not yet understood. Structural plasticity can be visualized postmortem in several regions of the brain. Here, changes in synaptic strength are measured as structural modification of axons, dendrites and spine morphology. Different studies have shown that increases in spine size occur during the induction of LTP (Matsuzaki et al., 2004), whereas spine shrinkage occurs during LTD (Nagerl et al., 2004; Zhou et al., 2004). Taken together, decades of research has made it clear that the mammalian brain, and particularly the hippocampus, harbors several forms of plasticity, and that hippocampal plasticity is critical for determining hippocampal function and hippocampal circuit activity, as well as the relevance of both of these for behavioral outcomes.

Intra-hippocampal circuitry

The hippocampus is a region in the mammalian brain that is essential for learning, including acquisition of new memories and retention of acquired memories (Scoville and Milner, 1957; Squire et al., 2004). It consists of three sub-divisions: dentate gyrus (DGs), cornu ammonis (CAs) 1, and CA3 (Fig. 7.1). Information via neurotransmission is propagated from the entorhinal cortex (EC) to the DG, CA1 and CA3 (via perforant path fibers), DG to CA3 pyramidal neurons (via mossy fibers), from CA3 to CA1 pyramidal neurons (via Schaffer collaterals), and CA1 in turn projects back to cortex in unidirectional, feed-forward excitation manner forming the "tri-synaptic hippocampal circuit" ((Swanson et al., 1978; Amaral and Witter, 1989); Figs. 7.1 and 7.2). Each sub-division plays a critical role in regulating the tri-synaptic circuit, with each neuronal subtype contributing to synaptic transmission and plasticity in the hippocampus, which contribute to the storage, consolidation, retrieval of declarative, spatial, and associative long-term memory (Nakazawa et al., 2001, 2006; Burgess et al., 2002; Squire et al., 2004; Gold and Kesner, 2005). Excitatory perforant path fibers from the EC are the major afferents projecting to the DG; therefore the DG serves as a gateway to the hippocampus by filtering and processing neurotransmission from the cortical areas (Andersen et al., 1966). In

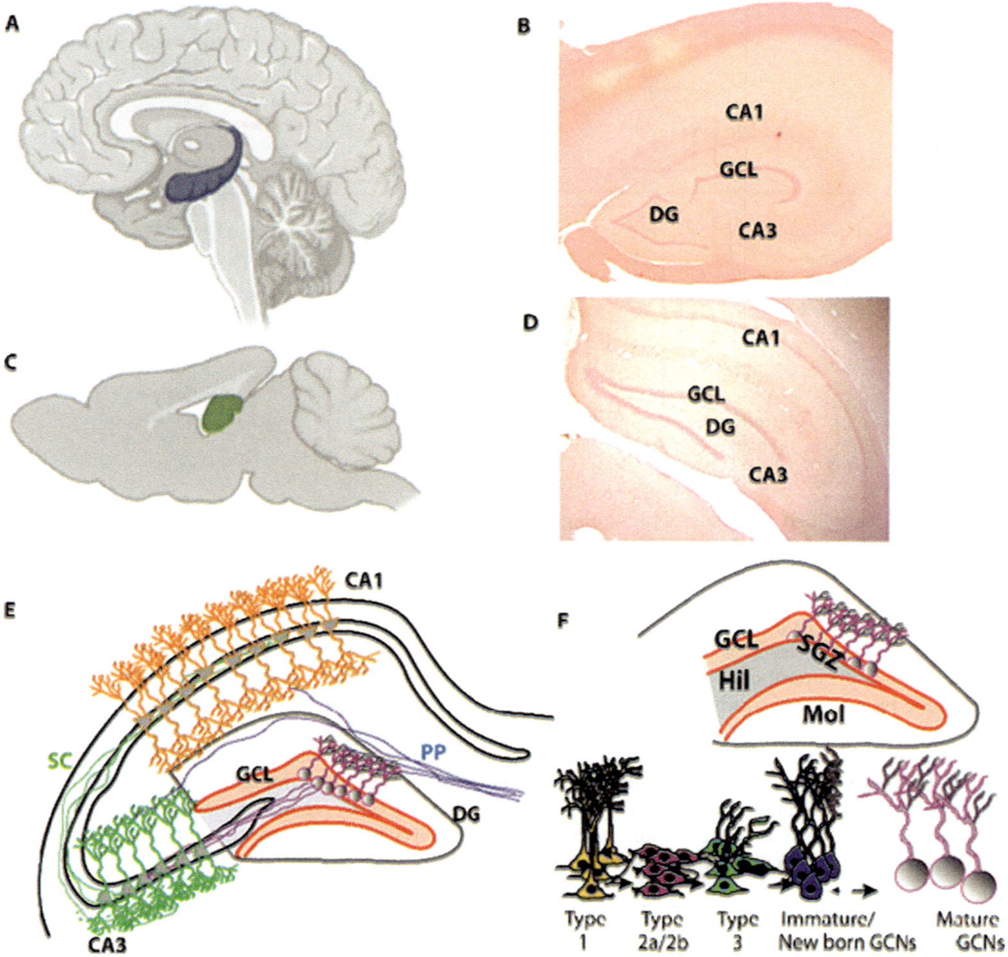

FIGURE 7.1 Sagital view of the entire human (A) and rodent brain (C) exposing the hippocampus. These images were made with BioRender basic version. (B, D) 40× magnification of coronal sections through the hippocampus stained with FastRed to reveal neuroanatomical arrangement within the hippocampus. The regions CA1, CA3 and DG are indicated. GCL, granule cell layer; SGZ, subgranular zone; Hil, hilus or polymorphic layer; Mol, molecylar layer. (E) Within the hippocampal subregions, neurons participate in synaptic transmission and synaptic plasticity. Pyramidal neurons in the CA1 region are colored in *orange*, pyramidal neurons in the CA3 region are colored in *green*. Granule cell neurons in the DG are colored in *purple*. Axons from the entorhinal cortex synapse onto neurons in the DG, CA1 and CA3 to form the perforant pathway (PP). Axons from the CA3 synapse onto neurons in the CA1 to form the schafer collaterals (SCs). (F) Within the DG another form of plasticity is evident, termed as neurogenesis. Neurogenesis occurs as a process with type 1 stem-like cells dividing to produce type 2 and 3 progenitors and these cells differentiating into immature granule cell neurons and finally surviving as mature granule cell neurons.

the following sections, we define the circuitry and plasticity in the hippocampus, and expand the information on plasticity in the CA1, CA3 and DG regions. In the subsequent sections, we introduce adult neurogenesis in the DG as a form of plasticity, and discuss how addictive drugs affect synaptic plasticity in the hippocampus.

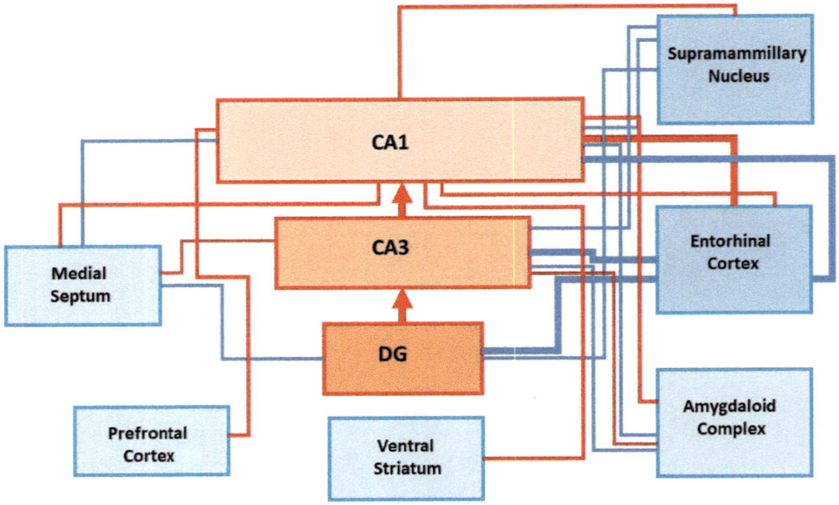

FIGURE 7.2 Simplified schematic representing projections in the hippocampus with emphasis on the inter- and intra-hippocampal circuits. Subregions of the hippocampus; CA, Cornu Ammonis; CA1, CA2 and dentate gyru, DG. Inputs to the hippocamapal subregions are colored in *blue* and outputs from the hippocampal region are colored in *red*. Trisynaptic circuitry in the hippocampus is indicated with axons from the entorhinal cortex (EC) projecting unidirectionally to the DG, CA1 and CA3 neurons (perforant path projection; very thick blue lines); DG neurons project to the apical dendrites of the CA3 pyramidal neurons (mossy fiber projection, very thick red arrow); CA3 neurons project to the apical dendrites of the CA1 neurons (schaffer collateral projection, very thick red arrow). The CA1 from the hippocampus sends major projections to the EC (thick red line). The CA1 neurons have bidirectional projections to and from the amgydaloid complex. The DG and CA1 also receive direct inputs from the medial septum. The DG, CA3 and CA1 receive direct inputs from the supramammillary nucleus. CA1 projects to the prefrontal cortex and ventral striatum. The efferent projections from the hippocampus (CA1, CA3, DG) to the other regions is indicated by red lines, and the afferent projections from the other regions to the hippocampus is indiccated by blue lines. The author would like to indicate that a simplified circuit and other inputs and outputs to and from the hippocampal subregions to several other subnuclei in the brain is not included.

In the rat hippocampus, there are estimated to be almost 1,000,000 DG granule cell neurons (GCNs), 300,000 CA3 pyramidal neurons, 30,000 CA2 pyramidal neurons, and about 300,000 CA1 pyramidal neurons (Amaral and Witter, 1989; Witter et al., 1989). In addition to these principal excitatory neurons, there are many different types of inhibitory neurons in the hippocampus, and they constitute to about 10%–20% of the principal neurons. We limit our discussion to the excitatory neurons in this review, and direct the readers to other publications for more information on the inhibitory neurons (Klausberger and Somogyi, 2008; Pelkey et al., 2017). The major source of the inputs to the excitatory neurons in the hippocampus come from the EC. The EC conveys spatial and non-spatial information to the hippocampus via direct and indirect pathways (van Strien et al., 2009). Neurons in layers II and III of EC give rise to projections to the sub-regions in the hippocampus (van Strien et al., 2009). For example, layer II cells of EC project to DG and CA3, whereas layer III cells project to CA1 and the subiculum (Kerr et al., 2007). The layer II cells of the EC give rise to the well-characterized indirect route of information that flows through the tri-synaptic circuit. In addition to the tri-synaptic circuit, other circuits have been discovered that assist with communications between the EC and hippocampal subregions. For example, the CA1 region of hippocampus also receives a direct glutamatergic input from EC layer III pyramidal neurons and this pathway is known as the temporoammonic pathway (Soltesz and Jones, 1995). Another important indirect input to the hippocampus is through the nucleus reuniens of the thalamus, which forms a relay between the prefrontal cortex and the CA1 (Brun et al., 2008; Nakashiba et al., 2008; Suh et al., 2011; Xu and Sudhof, 2013).

Recently, additional within-hippocampal circuits have been identified, with studies demonstrating connections between the CA1 and the CA2 region of the hippocampus (Chevaleyre and Siegelbaum, 2010). The CA2 region of the hippocampus is a small area which is located between the CA3 and CA1 regions (Benoy et al., 2018). Currently, the CA2 region remains largely unexplored, due to its small size and transitional location between CA3 and CA1 regions, although recent studies clearly show an important identity of the CA2 region (Piskorowski and Chevaleyre, 2012). Taken together, we have discussed the hippocampal circuitry as a within region function. Furthermore, the within region circuitry in the hippocampus is the most captivating feature of this brain region, and researchers have coined it a functional brain system called the hippocampal formation. In some ways, the neuroanatomical organization of the hippocampus, namely pyramidal shaped CA1 projection neurons and smaller interneurons resembles other cortical regions. However, distinct from other cortical regions is the organization in the hippocampus, which is the largely unidirectional passage of information through intrahippocampal circuits. There are several extrinsic connections between other brain nuclei and the hippocampus (Fig. 7.2). The next section of this chapter will highlight the connections in brief.

Hippocampal circuit connections with other brain regions

Dentate gyrus

EC projections to the hippocampus initiate at the DG, as discussed in the previous section. The perforant pathway fibers terminate exclusively in the molecular layer therefore, innervating the GCNs of the DG. Therefore, the other neuronal types in the DG (neurons exclusive to the polymorphic layer of the DG-mossy cells, basket cells) do not receive EC inputs (van Groen et al., 2002). In addition to the EC, GCNs receive inputs from the presubiculum and parasubiculum, where the axons innervate the molecular layer and ramify in a zone that is interspaced between the perforant path fibers (Köhler, 1985). Compared with the extensive inputs from the EC, the GCNs receive relatively few inputs from subcortical structures, the most robust and longest studied is the projection from the septal nuclei (medial septal nucleus and the nucleus of the diagonal band of Broca) a major portion of these being cholinergic (Andersen et al., 1961). GCNs receive glutamatergic inputs from the hypothalamus, largely from the supramammillary area (Kiss et al., 2000). The DG also receives prominent noradrenergic inputs from the pontine nucleus of the locus coeruleus, minor dopaminergic input from the ventral tegmental area, and serotonergic inputs from the raphe nucleus (Loughlin et al., 1986; Vertes et al., 1999). These fibers mainly terminate in the polymorphic layer of the DG, often targeting pyramidal basket cells. The functional significance of these inputs are yet to be explored.

CA1, CA2 and CA3

EC inputs also target CA1, CA2 and CA3 neurons. The difference in that EC projections to the CA2/CA3 originate from layer II in the EC and the EC projections to the CA1 originate from layer III in the EC. Next, while CA2/CA3 and CA1 receive substantial inputs from the

EC, only CA1 sends projections to the EC (Witter, 1993). With respect to the neocortex, only the CA1 region has bidirectional connections, with CA2/CA3 fields of the hippocampus not known to have any direct connections (Rolls, 2015). Regarding the amygdaloid complex, it was previously thought that only CA1 region received direct inputs, but anatomical tracing studies indicate that the CA3 also receives direct inputs from the amygdala (Pitkänen et al., 2000). CA3 and CA1 neurons also have bidirectional connections to and from the septal nuclei contributing extensively to the septo-hippocampal pathway (Müller and Remy, 2018). As for the hypothalamic connections, weak inputs to the CA2/CA3/CA1 originate from the supramammillary region (Maglóczky et al., 1994). Un-like the hypothalamic inputs targeting all the CA regions, thalamic inputs and inputs from the brain stem nuclei, mostly monoaminergic, innervate the CA1 region (Swanson et al., 1987; Dolleman-Van der Weel and Witter, 2000). Monoaminergic inputs to the hippocampus are sparse but are thought to regulate synaptic plasticity in the hippocampus.

In addition to receiving inputs from cortical and limbic regions, the CA1 region also provides a major output from the hippocampus, sending projections to several parts of the brain, including the subiculum, lateral septum via fornix, ventral striatum, amygdala and prefrontal cortex (van Groen and Wyss, 1990; Wyss and Van Groen, 1992; McNaughton et al., 1996; Friedman et al., 2002; Squire et al., 2004). A small subset of pyramidal neurons from the CA1 also project to the retrosplenial cortex (Wyss and Van Groen, 1992). Taken together, these neurobiological circuits within the hippocampus and between the hippocampus and other brain regions indicate that hippocampal circuitry is complex, and that multiple other brain regions are likely involved in the regulation of hippocampus-dependent learning and memory functions (Lisman and Grace, 2005; Duncan et al., 2012).

Synaptic plasticity in hippocampal sub-regions

CA1

The key molecule that underlies plasticity in the CA1 is glutamate via its actions at glutamate receptors (Collingridge et al., 1983; Elgersma and Silva, 1999). Support for this comes from seminal studies that have indicated causation between glutamatergic receptors and LTP, in that the selective antagonist DL-2-amino-5-phosphononvalerate (APV) of the *N*-methyl-D-aspartate (NMDA)-type glutamatergic receptor (GluNs) blocks the induction of LTP, but it has no effect on basal synaptic potentials following stimulation of the SC of the CA1 region of the hippocampus (Collingridge et al., 1983; Harris et al., 1984; Wigstrom et al., 1986). These initial studies were followed by additional studies that determined the mechanism underlying the activation of GluNs to produce long-lasting enhancement of synaptic efficacy. For example, modulation of calcium entry by these receptors were thought to play a major role in regulating synaptic plasticity (Lynch et al., 1983; Kauer et al., 1988; Malenka et al., 1988; Malenka and Bear, 2004). Support for this came from a report which showed that intracellular injection of the calcium chelator N, N, N′, N′-tetraacetic acid (EGTA) into pyramidal cells of the CA1 region blocks the induction of LTP in the CA1 region of the hippocampus (Lynch et al., 1983). Later studies determined the subunit of the GluN receptors that played a dominant role in regulating LTP. For example, both GluN2A and GluN2B subunits activate signaling pathways that are required for initiation and maintenance of LTP and

LTD in the CA1 (Hrabetova et al., 2000; Kohr et al., 2003; Liu et al., 2004; Fox et al., 2006; Morishita et al., 2007). It is also conceptualized that differential kinetics of GluN2A and GluN2B-mediated excitatory post synaptic currents and the resulting differences in calcium influx may contribute to their roles in LTP versus LTD (Lisman, 1989; Cull-Candy et al., 2001). Furthermore, it is believed that different intracellular signaling pathways may contribute to the direction of synaptic changes, including LTP and LTD (Sheng and Pak, 2000). For example, phosphorylation of calcium/calmodulin-dependent protein kinase ll, protein kinase A (PKA), protein kinase B, extracellular signal-regulated kinases are mediators for GluN-dependent LTP (Malinow et al., 1989; Barria et al., 1997; Blitzer et al., 1998; Malenka and Nicoll, 1999; Yasuda et al., 2003; Lynch, 2004; Sweatt, 2004). However, activation of protein phosphatases, low calcium concentrations, and dephosphorylation of PKA and protein kinase B mediate GluN-dependent LTD (Mulkey and Malenka, 1992; Kirkwood and Bear, 1994; Kameyama et al., 1998; Lee et al., 1998; Hrabetova and Sacktor, 2001; van Dam et al., 2002). Therefore, it appears that LTP and LTD are extensively studied in the CA1 region, and multiple mechanisms assist with and regulate plasticity in the CA1 region.

CA3

Un-like the GluN-dependent mechanisms in the CA1 for induction and maintenance of LTP and LTD, GluN-independent mechanisms underlie induction of LTP in the CA3 in the mossy fiber synapses (Harris and Cotman, 1986; Weisskopf et al., 1994; Nicoll and Malenka, 1995). Mossy fiber LTP does not require postsynaptic activation and it is induced purely by presynaptic activation of intracellular calcium in presynaptic terminals (Weisskopf et al., 1994; Mellor and Nicoll, 2001). For example, it seems that this form of LTP requires activation of presynaptic kainite receptors by endogenous glutamate (Contractor et al., 2001). Furthermore, it is becoming clear that activation of PKA and presynaptic substrates that activate PKA are probably essential in mediating this form of long-term synaptic plasticity (Sudhof et al., 1989; Schluter et al., 1999; Castillo et al., 2002). Additionally, mechanistic studies indicate that hyperpolarization-activated cation channels provide long-lasting control of transmitter release to regulate mossy fiber LTP (Chevaleyre and Castillo, 2002; Mellor et al., 2002). Taken together, it can be conceptualized that significant molecular heterogeneity exists between LTP in the CA1 and mossy fiber LTP in the CA3 region, and that synaptic vesicle proteins are ultimately responsible for both the short-term and long-term regulation of neurotransmitter release in mossy fiber LTP to regulate plasticity in the CA3 region.

Dentate gyrus

The DG is well characterized anatomically and functionally. GCNs, the principal neurons of the DG, receive their primary excitatory input from stellate cells in the EC, whose axons form the perforant pathway (Amaral et al., 2007). All EC projections to DG make glutamatergic synapses onto GCNs but with different functional properties depending on the afferents coming from the lateral perforant path (LPP) or medial perforant path (MPP) (Min et al., 1998). Therefore, LTP in the DG is very similar to the LTP in the CA1 region of the hippocampus, given that they are both GluN dependent (Bliss and Gardner-Medwin, 1973; Bliss and Lomo, 1973; Bliss and Collingridge, 1993). In addition to glutamate, several other molecules have been implicated in modulating LTP in the DG. For example, neuroligins (NL) are transmembrane cell adhesion proteins that are involved in the regulation of synaptic plasticity in the DG (Krueger et al., 2012). Mechanistic studies show that hippocampal knockdown of NL1 decreases perforant path-granule cell LTP in acute slices of the adult rat DG (Shipman and Nicoll, 2012). Furthermore, global knockdown of NL1 reduces excitatory transmission and diminishes LTP in the DG (Jedlicka et al., 2015). Other molecules, such as brain specific guanine nucleotide exchange factor collybistin (Cb), interacts with the synaptic scaffolding protein gephyrin to regulate LTP in the DG (Papadopoulos and Soykan, 2011). Mechanistically, it has been demonstrated that Cb knock out mice exhibit impairment in LTP in the DG, and that it is most likely mediated by altered function of GABAergic inhibitory synapses (Papadopoulos et al., 2007). In addition to the dependency of LTP in the DG on the glutamatergic system, LTD in the DG is also dependent on activation of GluNs as well as L type calcium channels (Trommer et al., 1996). In addition to GluNs, a role for the cannabinoid system is implicated in mediating LTD in the DG (Penasco et al., 2019). For example, activation of cannabinoid type 1 receptor at medial perforant path mediates LTD, and the activation of the cannabinoid receptor requires activation of metabotropic glutamate receptors (Penasco et al., 2019). These findings support the distinct mechanisms in the hippocampus subregions in regulating long-term plasticity, and emphasize the complex cellular heterogeneity in synaptic plasticity mechanisms that could differentially regulate behaviors dependent on the hippocampus.

Neurogenesis as a form of plasticity in the DG

The DG is of particular interest as newly born GCNs are continuously generated via a process called neurogenesis (Altman and Das, 1965; Cameron and McKay, 1998; Ming and Song, 2011). While this form of plasticity in the DG is now being recognized as functionally significant, the presence of neurogenesis was discovered several decades ago. As indicated by Santiago Ramon y Cajal in 1913—the adult brain was initially thought to be static, the nerve paths fixed and completed; the adult brain not capable of regeneration (Ramon y Cajal, 1928). This led to the most important dogma in neuroscience in that neurogenesis was restricted to prenatal and early postnatal development, and that the adult mammalian brain was unable to facilitate neurogenesis. However, around the same time, Ezra Allen (1912) proposed that cell proliferation can occur in the adult mammalian brain (Allen, 1912). It was only in the 1960s Joseph Altman provided the first autoradiographic evidence for the production of new neurons in the DG of the hippocampus in the adult mammalian brain (Altman, 1963). In the recent years, based on consistent findings from several laboratories, it is confirmed that in the adult mammalian brain, there are two regions in which active neurogenesis occur: the olfactory system and the hippocampus. In the olfactory system, neural progenitor cells are born in the subventricular zone of the lateral ventricles and these cells migrate and differentiate into newborn neurons in the olfactory bulb (Ernst et al., 2014). In the hippocampus, neural progenitor cells are born in the subgranular zone of the DG, where they migrate into the granule cell layer and differentiate and mature into functional excitatory GCNs (Ming and Song, 2011) (Fig. 7.1E and F). The authors would like to direct the readers to reviews that discuss distinct steps of neuronal development during olfactory bulb adult neurogenesis (Gheusi et al., 2013; Lepousez et al., 2013), and DG neurogenesis (Enikolopov et al., 2015; Kempermann et al., 2015; Goncalves et al., 2016).

Adult neurogenesis in the DG influences synaptic plasticity in the DG

It is now established that the DG harbors a large number of newly generated GCNs in the adult mammalian brain (Altman and Das, 1967; Gould et al., 1999; Ihunwo et al., 2016). GCNs are the principal cell types in the DG, and they project to the CA3 region of the hippocampus via mossy fiber axons (Amaral et al., 2007). The first description of long-lasting potentiation in the hippocampus was described in the DG, in particular in the perforant path DG synapses by Bliss and Lomo (Bliss and Lomo, 1973). Because certain types of learning and memory, and in particular, associative learning and memory increases neurogenesis (Martinez and Derrick, 1996), and because LTP is thought to represent synaptic model of learning and memory, current research is focused on how synaptic plasticity in the DG is influenced by neurogenesis. Here, we provide a brief update on the recent studies that have evaluated the effects of adult neurogenesis on synaptic plasticity in DG.

With respect to adult-born GCNs (GCNs born via neurogenesis in the proliferative zone), there is an initial critical period (days to weeks postmitosis), during which the survival and integration of adult-born GCNs is dependent on both GABAergic and glutamatergic input (Ge et al., 2006; Zhao et al., 2008). For example, data from DG slices from adult-born GCNs and developmentally born GCNs or pre-existing GCNs from superficial layers show that high frequency stimulation induced robust LTP in both types of GCNs (Wang et al., 2000). Interestingly, mechanistic studies with different LTP paradigms show that LTP induction occurs at a lower threshold in adult-born GCNs. In addition, LTP induction in adult-born GCNs is insensitive to GABAergic transmission, whereas LTP induction in pre-existing GCNs is blocked when GABAergic transmission is intact. With respect to glutamatergic influence on adult-born GCNs, in particular, survival of adult-born GCNs (weeks to months postmitosis) requires GluN receptor activation (Tashiro et al., 2006). Notably, LTP in adult-born GCNs is blocked by GluN2B subtype-specific antagonists or genetic deletion of GluN2Bs, demonstrating that GluN2Bs are essential for DG synaptic plasticity driven by adult-born GCNs (Snyder et al., 2001; Ge et al., 2007; Kheirbek et al., 2012). Consistently, ablation of neurogenesis prevents the induction of LTP evoked by medial perforant path stimulation in the DG of slices with intact GABAergic transmission, suggesting that synaptic plasticity in the DG is supported by adult-born GCNs via a GluN dependent mechanism (Snyder et al., 2001; Saxe et al., 2006; Massa et al., 2011). Additional mechanistic studies have indicated that stimulation of granule cell mossy fibers is sufficient to induce LTP in the DG, as well as increase the number of adult-born GCNs, indicating that neurogenesis in the DG is regulated by synaptic plasticity in the hippocampus, as well as by efferent stimulation (Derrick et al., 2000). Furthermore, studies from conditional knockdown of neurogenesis show that adult-born GCNs also play a role in DG LTD (Massa et al., 2011). Notably, restoring neurogenesis provides complete rescue of LTP, at a much faster rate than LTD (Massa et al., 2011). These results demonstrate that both LTP and LTD in the DG are influenced by adult-born GCNs and that their integration into the pre-existing network effects the ability of pre-existing GCNs to express bidirectional synaptic plasticity. In addition to effecting the expression of synaptic plasticity in the DG, adult-born GCNs also play a role in the gradual decay of hippocampal LTP (a feature assisting with the gradual decay of hippocampal dependency of associative memory over time, or memory clearance (Kitamura et al., 2009)). In summary, there is now strong evidence to demonstrate that synaptic plasticity in the DG is regulated by neurogenesis. Together, these data indicate that adult-born GCNs are hyperplastic and may as a result make unique contributions to DG circuits and hippocampal function.

Regulation of plasticity in the hippocampus by addictive drugs

The motivational and emotional aspects of hippocampal-dependent learning and memory functions are influenced by the reciprocal interactions between the hippocampus and the limbic and reward areas (McNamara et al., 2014). As such, alterations in these interactions may subserve a pathologic function in the context of SUDs, where these behavioral domains are profoundly altered (Koob and Volkow, 2016). In this context, the hippocampus plays a prominent role in memory acquisition, and contextual Pavlovian conditioning for drug-related memories (Phillips and LeDoux, 1992). Therefore, neuronal activity and plasticity in the hippocampus may be important for acquisition and expression of drug context memories.

Preclinical studies suggest that initial exposure to stimulants (e.g. cocaine, amphetamines, nicotine) and alcohol may enhance hippocampal function and, therefore, the formation of augmented drug–context associations that contribute to the development of addiction. In the context of this hypothesis, reinforcing doses of cocaine and nicotine enhance, whereas, neurotoxic doses of methamphetamine reduce LTP in the CA1 region of the hippocampus (Thompson et al., 2004; Yamazaki et al., 2006; North et al., 2013). These studies indicate that synaptic alterations in the hippocampus by stimulants could facilitate the learning of drug-associated memories and eventual addiction to the drug. Whereas stimulants enhance CA1 LTP, alcohol and drugs (opiates, cannabinoids) that are central nervous system depressants lead to reduced CA1 LTP. For example, evidence from studies using animal models of moderate to severe alcohol use disorder demonstrate that chronic ethanol experience inhibits hippocampal CA1 LTP (Durand and Carlen, 1984; Roberto et al., 2002), and that this inhibition fails to recover after prolonged period of forced abstinence (Tremwel and Hunter, 1994). Reduced CA1 LTP is also evident in animals made dependent to morphine or heroin (Pu et al., 2002; Salmanzadeh et al., 2003); however, enhanced DG LTP is observed after chronic morphine treatment (Ito et al., 2001). These studies clearly demonstrate that chronic misuse of opiates produces severe alteration in hippocampal LTP, and reveals the interesting differences between morphine in its effects on the differential modulation of hippocampal sub-region specific synaptic plasticity. With respect to cannabinoids, acute treatment with synthetic cannabinoid receptor (CB1/CB2) agonists reduces CA1 LTP (Barbieri et al., 2016). Similar effects on CA1 LTP were observed in animals chronically treated with delta(9)-tetrahydrocannabinol (delta-9-THC), the psychoactive component of marijuana (Hoffman et al., 2007). More interesting is the fact that the reduced CA1 LTP with chronic delta-9-THC was not recovered after weeks of withdrawal (Hoffman et al., 2007), suggesting that the effects of CB1 agonists on synaptic depression is not transient.

In addition to altering synaptic plasticity in the CA1 and DG of the hippocampus, addictive drugs and alcohol also affect adult neurogenesis in the DG. Based on several groundbreaking studies, it is demonstrated that reinforcing doses of stimulants, alcohol, opiates and cannabinoids reduce the number of adult-born GCNs ((Eisch et al., 2000; Abrous et al., 2002; Eisch and Harburg, 2006; Mandyam et al., 2008; Noonan et al., 2008; Richardson et al., 2009; Brown et al., 2010; Catlow et al., 2010; Garcia-Fuster et al., 2010; Sudai et al., 2011) and reviewed in (Crews and Nixon, 2003; Eisch and Mandyam, 2004; Powrozek et al., 2004; Eisch and Harburg, 2006; Mandyam and Koob, 2012; Castilla-Ortega and Santin, 2020). Mechanistic studies have shown that addictive drugs and alcohol reduce several aspects of neurogenesis, including reducing the number of actively dividing progenitor cells, reducing the number of proliferating cells maturing and differentiating into adult-born GCNs. However, the exact functional implication of such impairment in adult-born GCNs is largely unknown.

Emerging mechanistic studies from rodent models indicate that manipulating adult neurogenesis could be a promising bio-behavioral target in several neuropathologies, including drug addiction (Akers et al., 2014; Hill et al., 2015; Danielson et al., 2016; Yun et al., 2016). The most clearly demonstrated examples are increased neurogenesis by antidepressants and decreased neurogenesis by addictive drugs (Dranovsky and Hen, 2006; Canales, 2013; Mahar et al., 2014; Hill et al., 2015; Kyzar et al., 2016; Anacker and Hen, 2017; Castilla-Ortega et al., 2017). However, several unanswered questions need to be addressed before recalibration of DG function by hippocampal neurogenesis can be utilized as a therapeutic strategy in such neuropsychiatric conditions. For example, are GCNs born during or after chronic stress and/or drug experience different (electrophysiological and biochemical properties) from those born in age-matched controls? If so, are these differences adaptive and help with recovery or are they maladaptive and contribute to the long-term perpetuation of deficits? Recent mechanistic studies suggest that a subset of newly born GCNs in a model of methamphetamine addiction directly contribute to compulsive methamphetamine seeking behavior (Galinato et al., 2018a,b), thus raising new questions about the role of neurogenesis in recovery from addiction. However, technologies to address such nuanced questions are still in their nascent stages of development. For example, single-cell RNA sequencing (RNA-seq) methods have demonstrated transcriptome-level differences between individual quiescent stem cells (Shin et al., 2015) and mature DG neurons (Lacar et al., 2016), suggesting that progenitors in the DG could be harnessed for therapeutic purposes. Furthermore, new transgenic rodent models that support conditional knockdown of adult neurogenesis will be invaluable for determining differences between new hippocampal neurons born under physiological conditions and those following pathopharmacological challenges (Lepousez et al., 2015). For example, the Nestin-TK and GFAP-TK mice that expressed thymidine kinase (TK) under neuronal stem cell specific promoter allowed temporal regulation of level of neurogenesis without affecting any other neuronal or non-neuronal cell population (Dhaliwal and Lagace, 2011). These pharmacogenetic models helped ascertain that adult-born GCNs played a role in contextual fear conditioning, spatial memory retrieval and spatial pattern separation, all behaviors dependent on an intact hippocampus (Saxe et al., 2006; Deng et al., 2009; Niibori et al., 2012). The more recent availability of transgenic GFAP-TK rats opened up the possibility of investigating even more complex neurobehavioral questions (Snyder et al., 2016). Specifically, hippocampal neurogenesis was found to regulate sucrose preference, reward-related behavior (Snyder et al., 2016), and buffered changes in social preference during social stress, thereby contributing to reliance following a disruption in the social-dominance hierarchy (Opendak et al., 2016). These new tools can help better understand the specific role of the natural regenerative capacity of DG, and may thereby facilitate the much-needed expansion of the treatment toolkit for the underserved patients with neuropsychiatric conditions.

Supporting this hypothesis, newly born GCNs can modify excitatory synaptic transmission to mature GCNs, specifically those excitatory perforant path fibers input from the EC to the mature GCNs. For example, enhanced number of newly generated GCNs is associated with reduced excitatory synaptic transmission to mature GCNs-mediated by fewer functional synapses, whereas ablation of newly born GCNs is accompanied by increased excitatory synaptic transmission to mature GCNs with no change in intrinsic properties and inhibition (Adlaf et al., 2017). Given that newly born GCNs could function to enable animals to distinguish related stimuli and events rapidly, and support contextual discrimination, and participate in hippocampal memory clearance (Akers et al., 2014; Epp et al., 2016), it is tempting to speculate that endogenous alterations in the number of newly born GCNs and DG excitability could contribute to drug memories and addiction (Frankland and Josselyn, 2016). It will be an interesting and exciting possibility for future research to link the alterations in adult-born GCNs by addictive drugs and the synaptic plasticity in the hippocampus. Such research may open up new therapeutic strategies to treat drug addiction.

The following two sections will discuss the effects of cocaine and alcohol on the function and plasticity of hippocampal sub-regions and circuits, as well as the role of those sub-regions and circuits in modulating addiction-related behaviors. Specifically, cocaine and alcohol are reviewed because these two drugs have distinct mechanistic effects on hippocampal plasticity. It should be noted that, even though we focus here on cocaine and alcohol, the use and effects of other addictive drugs have also been linked to hippocampal function and plasticity.

Cocaine

Cocaine and hippocampal plasticity

Superfusion of cocaine on hippocampal slices alters LTP in the CA1 region, with lower doses (5−10 mM) (Thompson et al., 2005; Stramiello and Wagner, 2010) enhancing and higher doses ((30−60 mM) (Smith et al., 1993; Thompson et al., 2005)) reducing LTP. More importantly, acute cocaine-induced alterations in synaptic plasticity in the CA1 region were dependent on intact dopaminergic and glutamatergic activity. Superfusion of cocaine does not alter LTP in the DG region (Huang et al., 2014), and the acute effects of cocaine on CA3 synaptic plasticity are unknown. The effects on CA1 LTP by experimenter delivered cocaine is varied, where, short-term treatment with lower dose enhances LTP, whereas, long-term treatment with higher dose does not alter LTP (Thompson et al., 2002; Guan et al., 2009). It is interesting to note that while long-term treatment with higher dose of cocaine did not alter CA1 LTP, early withdrawal from this paradigm increased CA1 LTP. In contrast to the effects in the CA1 region, experimenter delivered cocaine reduces the threshold of LTP induction in the DG without altering the magnitude of LTP (Perez et al., 2010). The findings from experimenter delivered cocaine were replicated with self-administered cocaine, where LTP in the CA1 region was enhanced (Thompson et al., 2004). Surprisingly, the in vivo effects of self-administered cocaine was transient as this effect was not evident weeks into forced abstinence and in fact, showed an opposite effect of suppressed LTP in the CA1 region months into forced abstinence (Thompson et al., 2004). These findings demonstrate that acute cocaine generates a high efficiency of hippocampal synaptic plasticity that may be transient and lead into the aberrant engagement of learning processes that may support cocaine addiction.

With chronic cocaine exposure in animals that self-administered cocaine under extended access conditions, studies reveal strengthening of synaptic plasticity in the CA1 region of the hippocampus, an effect that was seen days to weeks after abstinence, however, diminished and revealed as weakening of synaptic plasticity months after abstinence (Thompson et al., 2004; del Olmo et al., 2006; Werner et al., 2020). In parallel, behavioral studies indicate disrupted learning and memory functions dependent on the hippocampus in animals that self-administered cocaine under extended access conditions, an effect that persisted in to protracted abstinence (George et al., 2008; Fijał et al., 2015; Gobin and Schwendt, 2017). These data suggest that chronic cocaine continues to stimulate hippocampal plasticity and these cellular effects may initiate formation of cocaine memories and assist with cocaine taking and seeking behaviors.

Assessment of signaling molecules in the hippocampus post cocaine experience demonstrate that there is a positive relationship between the direction of synaptic plasticity and activation of the proteins within the cell signaling cascades that support long-term memory formation. For example, phosphorylation of extracellular signal regulated kinases −1 and −2 (ERK1/2) was elevated in the dorsal hippocampus following cocaine CPP (Tropea et al., 2008). Similarly, phosphorylation of hippocampal cAMP-response element binding protein (CREB) was increased following cocaine CPP (Tropea et al., 2008). In addition to correlative changes with ERK1/2 and CREB, mechanistic studies support the role of cAMP-dependent protein kinase (PKA) in the formation and maintenance of cocaine-context memories, as post-training intracerebroventricular injections of a PKA inhibitor disrupted the consolidation of cocaine CPP (Cervo et al., 1997). Few studies have focused on withdrawal-induced changes in signaling proteins, and one study found that phosphorylated CREB levels in the hippocampus were enhanced weeks into forced abstinence from experimenter delivered cocaine (Valzachi et al., 2013).

It has been demonstrated that cocaine is a potent suppressor of neurogenesis, mainly by reducing proliferation of neural progenitor cells (Castilla-Ortega et al., 2016b). While reduction in other aspects of neurogenesis, such as differentiation of progenitors and maturation into granule cell neurons is evident during cocaine experience, these effects are compensated during withdrawal from cocaine (Mandyam and Koob, 2012). These findings suggest that the suppressive effects of cocaine on neurogenesis is temporary and that withdrawal-induced rebound effects on neurogenesis could assist with cocaine-specific memories (Castilla-Ortega et al., 2016b).

Cocaine reward and reinforcement

Initial exposure to cocaine produces procognitive effects in humans (Garavan et al., 2008) and rodents (Wood et al., 2007). It can be hypothesized that the actions of cocaine on cognitive performance could be prelude to continued cocaine experience-induced formation of strong cocaine context/cue associations that may facilitate the development of cocaine addiction. Several studies conducted in animal models of cocaine reward and cocaine addiction support this hypothesis, as animals demonstrate a faster latency to acquire and maintain cocaine self-administration compared with non reward substances (Richardson and Roberts, 1996; España et al., 2010), associate cocaine reward with specific context/cue (Spyraki et al., 1982; Vidal-Infer et al., 2012) and prefer cocaine taking compared with other rewarding activities despite adverse consequences (Deneau et al., 1969; Lenoir et al., 2007; Kerstetter et al., 2012; Perry et al., 2013).

The behavioral effects of cocaine can be attributed to altered functioning of several circuits in the brain. For example, the mesolimbic and mesocortical circuit is effected by cocaine experience and contributes to aspects of cocaine taking and seeking behaviors (Bardo, 1998; Thomas et al., 2008). In addition to these circuits, the hippocampus is also effected by cocaine exposure (Castilla-Ortega et al., 2016b) and plays a role in maladaptive cocaine context associations that assist with cocaine addiction (Grant et al., 1996; Childress et al., 1999; Kilts et al., 2001; Wexler et al., 2001). For example, inactivation of the hippocampal CA1 prior to cocaine CPP conditioning disrupts learning, indicating that the hippocampus is important for the formation and expression of cocaine memories (Meyers et al., 2006; Hernandez-Rabaza et al., 2008). Additionally, inactivation of the hippocampal CA1 after CPP expression impairs retrieval of cocaine CPP memory (Hitchcock and Lattal, 2018). Furthermore, inactivation of the hippocampal CA1 prior to extinction or after extinction of cocaine memories impairs extinction and retrieval of extinguished memories (Hitchcock and Lattal, 2018). However, the role of the hippocampus in cocaine memory consolidation is less clear as inactivation of the hippocampal CA1 after acquisition of cocaine CPP leaves consolidation of context–cocaine associations intact (Meyers et al., 2006). In addition to neuronal activity, epigenetic mechanisms in the hippocampus also play an important role in cocaine associative memories (Itzhak et al., 2013). For example, systemic administration of the HDAC inhibitor sodium butyrate prior to cocaine CPP conditioning leads to increased histone acetylation in the hippocampus, and this correlates with enhanced recall of cocaine–context memories. Furthermore, site specific injection of a DNMT inhibitor into the hippocampal CA1 delayed acquisition of the cocaine–context associative memory (Han et al., 2010). These findings indicate that mechanisms in the hippocampal CA1 such as neuronal activation, DNA methylation and acetylation are important for acquisition and consolidation of cocaine specific memories. The role of hippocampal CA3 in cocaine reward and reinforcement has rarely been explored and recent findings demonstrate a role for CA3 neurons in reinstatement of cocaine seeking behaviors (Luo et al., 2011; Qi et al., 2022). Additional findings using chemogenetic strategies show that the projections of CA3 neurons to the lateral septum selectively control context driven reinstatement of cocaine seeking behaviors (McGlinchey and Aston-Jones, 2018). Leision studies restricted to the DG of the hippocampus show that the DG plays a role in cocaine reward (Hernández-Rabaza et al., 2008), however, additional findings indicate that the DG may be less important for context-driven reinstatement of cocaine seeking behaviors (Lasseter et al., 2010). These results indicate that the hippocampus contributes to cocaine context-induced cocaine seeking in a subregion-specific manner, with the functional integrity of the entire hippocampus being necessary for memory or motivational aspects of cocaine-paired environmental stimuli.

Additional mechanistic studies comparing dorsal versus ventral hippocampus by performing permanent lesions of the dorsal, but not ventral hippocampus, or causing temporary inactivation of the dorsal hippocampus by local muscimol infusions show impairment in cocaine

CPP (Meyers et al., 2003, 2006), supporting a role for the dorsal hippocampus in cocaine reward. Furthermore, studies using approaches to inactivate the dorsal hippocampus show that this subregion also controls context-induced reinstatement of cocaine seeking behavior (Fuchs et al., 2005, 2007; Xie et al., 2010; Wells et al., 2011), supporting a role for the dorsal hippocampus in cocaine craving. Mechanistic studies have also demonstrated a role for the ventral hippocampus in cocaine seeking behavior when triggered by cues and cocaine itself and in animals that were trained to extinguish cocaine self-administration behavior (Vorel et al., 2001; Rogers and See, 2007; Ramirez et al., 2009). Therefore it appears that the ventral hippocampus plays a role in cocaine craving under high demand conditions.

With respect to hippocampal neurogenesis and cocaine reward, taking and seeking behaviors, preclinical studies have been conducted with various strategies to reduce or ablate proliferating progenitors or neurogenesis in the hippocampus. For example, studies have used the DNA alkylating agent temozolomide (TMZ (Garthe et al., 2009)), cranial irradiation (Snyder et al., 2005) or inducible transgenic strategy (Dupret et al., 2008) to reduce proliferation of progenitors, and the associated cohort of newly born GCNs to determine their roles in behavioral responses to cocaine. Reducing the number of newly born GCNs with TMZ prior to acquisition of cocaine CPP did not disrupt acquisition, however enhanced the latency to extinguish cocaine-seeking behavior (Castilla-Ortega et al., 2016a). Notably, reducing the number of newly born GCNs after acquisition of cocaine CPP did not alter latency to extinguish cocaine-seeking behaviors, however enhanced recall of cocaine-context memories (Castilla-Ortega et al., 2016a). Ablating the newly born GCNs with irradiation prior to cocaine self-administration enhanced cocaine taking and motivation to seek cocaine, whereas ablating newly born GCNs after acquisition of cocaine self-administration enhances latency to extinguish cocaine seeking without effecting reinstatement of cocaine seeking triggered by cocaine cues or cocaine itself (Noonan et al., 2010). Reducing the number of newly born GCNs with an inducible transgenic approach prior to cocaine self-administration did not effect acquisition of cocaine self-administration and did not alter cocaine intake, however enhanced motivational responses to cocaine and reinstatement of cocaine seeking triggered by cocaine cues (Deroche-Gamonet et al., 2019). While these studies indicate the importance of different techniques in modulating the number of newly generated GCNs, the general consensus is that newly born GCNs assist with extinguishing cocaine memories and reduce motivation to seek cocaine. While these outcomes are based on preclinical studies, investigations of neurogenesis in cocaine addicts and the relevance to craving is still lacking. If the benefits of newly born GCNs in cocaine memories can be confirmed in human subjects, stimuli that potentiate adult neurogenesis in humans (Kempermann et al., 2018; Moreno-Jiménez et al., 2021) could be harnessed for their potential therapeutic options to reduce cocaine craving in humans suffering from cocaine use disorder.

Cocaine and hippocampus-dependent behaviors

Preclinical studies show that the procognitive effects of cocaine are evident after low dose of cocaine, however, cognitive dysfunction is noted with moderate to higher doses of cocaine in animals tested for contextual and cued fear conditioning (Wood et al., 2007). In addition, hippocampal dependent spatial learning is impaired in rodents experiencing chronic cocaine during adolescence or adulthood (Santucci et al., 2004; Mendez et al., 2008; Santucci, 2008), suggesting that deficits in learning by cocaine are evident in all age groups. It is also notable that chronic cocaine-induced learning deficits are long-lasting, as learning deficits persist in animals that were withdrawn from cocaine for months after exposure (Kelley et al., 2005; Mendez et al., 2008). In support of the preclinical studies, clinical findings also support the procognitive effects of acute cocaine administration, visualized as enhancement of response inhibition and psychomotor speed (Spronk et al., 2013). Similar to findings in animal studies, neuropsychological deficits are observed in chronic cocaine users, and more importantly the deficits correlated positively with the severity of the disorder (Ardila et al., 1991; Mittenberg and Motta, 1993; Bolla et al., 1999). These deficits may be due to loss of hippocampal function in chronic cocaine users (London et al., 1990; Beveridge et al., 2006; Gu et al., 2010), visualized as altered functional connectivity in the hippocampus (Gu et al., 2010; Ma et al., 2018). The neuropsychological deficits observed after chronic cocaine experience may disrupt cognitive flexibility and assist with craving for cocaine, hinder the ability of behavioral therapeutic strategies that involve extinction of cocaine memories or acquisition of non drug context memories, and reversal of cocaine memories.

Based on the studies discussed above, it is clear that initial cocaine experience enhances hippocampus-dependent learning and memory resulting in strong cocaine-context associations, which may facilitate cocaine-seeking behavior and chronic cocaine misuse. In turn, chronic cocaine exposure alters hippocampus function and results in hippocampal cognitive deficits during withdrawal and abstinence, which may contribute to impaired cognitive flexibility and inability to reverse cocaine-context associations, contributing to relapse.

Alcohol

There are several *in vitro* and in vivo preclinical model systems representing various stages of alcohol intoxication, addiction and dependence. For example, findings from *in vitro* organotypic hippocampal cell culture model, intragastric intubation model and chronic ethanol vapor induced dependence (CEID) model have allowed us to determine the toxic and neuromodulatory effects of ethanol in specific brain regions and reward systems. The *in vitro* organotypic hippocampal cell culture model is commonly used to study hippocampal excitotoxicity associated with alcoholism, because the *in vitro* model harbors critical hippocampal heterogeneity necessary for neuron–neuron and neuron–glia interactions to occur, thus maintaining structural and functional integrity of hippocampal circuitry and pharmacology (Gutierrez and Heinemann, 1999; Martens and Wree, 2001). Notably, the *in vitro* model has been extensively used to study the effects of chronic ethanol and withdrawal from ethanol on hippocampal neurotoxicity and excitotoxicity (Gibson et al., 2003; Prendergast et al., 2004; Wilkins et al., 2006), and studies indicate that ethanol excitotoxicity is dependent on the concentration of ethanol and duration of withdrawal after ethanol exposure. The intragastric intubation model has been widely used to study hippocampal neurotoxicity associated with alcoholism, because the model produces observable signs of prodromal detoxication and physiological dependence (Majchrowicz, 1975), and these extreme signs of ethanol intoxication and dependence have been correlated with reduced neuroplasticity, and enhanced neurodegeneration (Nixon and

Crews, 2002; Crews and Nixon, 2009). CEID model of alcohol dependence links chronic ethanol exposure regimens with self-administration procedures; this model is based on the idea that dependence (and withdrawal experience during dependence) drives excessive drinking during withdrawal through altered motivational processes (e.g., negative reinforcement) (O'Dell et al., 2004; Lopez and Becker, 2005; Gehlert et al., 2007; Griffin et al., 2009). CEID model has several advantages compared with intragastric intubation model of alcohol dependence as it causes increases in ethanol self-administration and enhanced responsiveness to the environmental stimuli that lead to excessive drinking in humans (Valdez et al., 2002; O'Dell et al., 2004). Importantly, CEID produces relatively high blood alcohol levels (BALs) during a short period of time, making this approach advantageous for studying the somatic aspects, motivational aspects, and neurobiological consequences of alcohol dependence (Macey et al., 1996; Liu and Weiss, 2002, 2003; Moore et al., 2004; Budygin et al., 2007; Miki et al., 2008; Gilpin et al., 2009; Richardson et al., 2009; Zahr et al., 2009). Taken together, investigating the neurobiological effects of chronic ethanol in CEID models has helped identify other vulnerability factors contributing to the pathology of alcoholism in humans (Macey et al., 1996; Liu and Weiss, 2002, 2003; Moore et al., 2004; Budygin et al., 2007; Miki et al., 2008; Gilpin et al., 2009; Richardson et al., 2009; Zahr et al., 2009; Hansson et al., 2010; Vendruscolo and Roberts, 2014; Vendruscolo et al., 2015; Kramer et al., 2020).

Alcohol and hippocampal plasticity

Using the *in vitro* organotypic hippocampal cell culture model it has been demonstrated that hippocampal CA1 excitotoxicity is evident after withdrawal from chronic ethanol exposure and not during ethanol exposure (Mulholland et al., 2003; Prendergast et al., 2004; Wilkins et al., 2006); and that withdrawal associated effects are due to the release of excessive glutamate and polyamines and corresponding activation of GluN receptors in the hippocampal region (Gibson et al., 2003). Importantly, the ethanol studies in this *in vitro* model reflect the importance of the glutamatergic system as a final common pathway mediating neurotoxicity and excitotoxicity.

Acute ethanol in hippocampal slices decreases hippocampal synaptic activity (decreases GluN and alpha-amino-3-hydroxy-5-methyl-4-isoxazole-propionic acid (GluA) receptor-mediated currents and increases γ-aminobutyric acid (GABA)A receptor-mediated currents) and decreases synaptic plasticity in the hippocampal CA1 and DG, evident as reduced LTP (Lovinger et al., 1989; Blitzer et al., 1990; Wayner et al., 1997; Weiner et al., 1999; Wright et al., 2003; Izumi et al., 2005; Fujii et al., 2008). Chronic in vivo ethanol exposure oppositely effects hippocampal CA1 synaptic activity compared with acute ethanol effects (seen as increases in GluN and decreases in GABAA receptor-mediated activity) and produces tolerance to acute ethanol mediated impairment of GluN activity (Sanna et al., 1993; Wu et al., 1993; Nelson et al., 2005; Sheela Rani and Ticku, 2006; Fujii et al., 2008). Notably, chronic in vivo ethanol exposure similarly impairs hippocampal plasticity as seen with acute effects, observed as reduced (CA1) LTP through a presynaptic LTP mechanism (Durand and Carlen, 1984; Roberto et al., 2002). Chronic in vivo ethanol exposure also alters excitability of DG GCNs, seen as increases in the number of action potentials generated in GCNs hours after cessation of CEID, an effect that persists into protracted abstinence (Avchalumov et al.,

2021). These findings suggest re-organization of hippocampal networking after chronic in vivo ethanol exposure and indicate that the cellular mechanisms that maintain hippocampal plasticity are compensated in chronic ethanol exposed animals and these maladaptive changes could contribute to the impairment of hippocampal dependent behaviors in alcohol dependent animals (Lukoyanov et al., 1999; Cippitelli et al., 2010; George et al., 2012). Chronic ethanol exposure produces dendritic retraction of CA1 and CA3 pyramidal neurons and DG GCNs (McMullen et al., 1984; Cadete-Leite et al., 1989; Staples et al., 2015), suggesting concomitant structural re-organization of hippocampal neurons compared with functional changes in hippocampal circuitry. Support of the involvement of the glutamatergic system in chronic in vivo ethanol-induced hippocampal neurotoxicity comes from several preclinical studies (Claus et al., 1982; Keller et al., 1983; Wilce et al., 1993; Snell et al., 1996; Wirkner et al., 1999). For example, glutamate release is increased in the hippocampus during ethanol withdrawal (Claus et al., 1982; Keller et al., 1983), and the changes in glutamate levels are also associated with enhanced polyamine levels in combination with increased number of functional GluN receptors (Davidson et al., 1993, 1995), suggesting that these effects may induce ethanol withdrawal hyperexcitability and may also lead to increased susceptibility to hippocampal excitotoxicity (Hoffman, 2003).

Evidence from studies examining the molecular mechanisms underlying ethanol's effects on hippocampal plasticity suggests that chonic in vivo ethanol-induced inhibition of CA1 LTP may result from decreased excitability of hippocampal neurons due to blockage of GluNs, specifically GluN1/GluN2A or GluN1/GluN2B subtypes (Hoffman et al., 1989; Lovinger et al., 1989; Schummers and Browning, 2001; Izumi et al., 2005) as well as activation of inhibitory GABAA receptors (Allan and Harris, 1986; Aguayo, 1990; Reynolds et al., 1992). In addition, ethanol-induced suppression of CA1 LTP has been associated with reduced ERK1/2 activity and signaling, reduced CREB activity and enhanced cannabinoid receptor 1 activity (Sanna et al., 2002; Bison and Crews, 2003; Roberto et al., 2003; Chandler and Sutton, 2005; Basavarajappa et al., 2008; Wang et al., 2012). These molecular changes associated with reduced synaptic plasticity in the hippocampus by ethanol could suggest that these mechanisms could also play a role in the leaning and memory deficits seen with chronic in vivo ethanol exposure (Atkins et al., 1998; Vianna et al., 2000; Riedel and Davies, 2005).

Additional findings indicate that ethanol exposure alters DG neurogenesis (reviewed in (Nixon, 2006; Mandyam and Koob, 2012)), an effect that has been observed in rodents, nonhuman primates and human subjects (Taffe et al., 2010; Dhanabalan et al., 2018; Le Maître et al., 2018). Ethanol exposure in rodents (intragastric intubation, two-bottle choice, ethanol liquid diet and CEID paradigms) alters every stage of DG neurogenesis (proliferation, differentiation, maturation, and survival of neural stem cells), and these effects vary by the dose, duration, and pattern of ethanol exposure or timing of ethanol exposure before labeling the neural progenitors (Nixon and Crews, 2002; Crews et al., 2004; Rice et al., 2004; He et al., 2005; Ieraci and Herrera, 2007; Richardson et al., 2009; Contet et al., 2014; Somkuwar et al., 2016). Therefore, the inhibitory effect of ethanol on the regenerative capacity of the adult hippocampus is now being considered a precursor for ethanol-induced neurodegeneration in the hippocampus (Nixon, 2006; Wooden et al., 2021).

Very few studies have explored how forced withdrawal from drug exposure alters DG neurogenesis (Nixon and Crews, 2004; Nixon et al., 2008; Noonan et al., 2008; Barr et al., 2010; Hansson et al., 2010; Taffe et al., 2010; Garcia-Fuster et al., 2011; Deschaux et al., 2014; Recinto et al., 2012).

With respect to alcohol, withdrawal from ethanol exposure (intragastric intubation and CEID paradigms) enhances cell proliferation in the hippocampus (Nixon and Crews, 2004; Hansson et al., 2010) which results in initial microglial proliferation (Nixon et al., 2008) followed by production of immature neurons and eventual neurogenesis (Nixon and Crews, 2004). Aberrant neurogenesis during abstinence is thought to be from central nervous system hyperexcitability that is associated with ethanol withdrawal symptomatology, such as whole-body tremors resulting from termination of ethanol exposure. Particularly interesting is the increases in GluN2B subunit expression in the hippocampus during CEID (Pian et al., 2010) and corticotropin releasing factor (CRF) levels in the hippocampus during withdrawal (Criado et al., 2011) which parallels the increased GluN2B subunit and CRF expression in the hippocampus during epileptogenesis (Smith et al., 1997; Frasca et al., 2011). Taken together, it appears that the hyperactivity stemming from the neurocircuitry underlying the ethanol withdrawal-induced kindling-like behaviors causes a hyperglutamatergic state and produces hippocampal excitotoxicity, which may be decisive factors for the maintenance of dependence in the long term (Baram et al., 1992; Smith et al., 1997; Wilkins et al., 2006; Frasca et al., 2011; Prior and Galduroz, 2011). However, the cellular mechanisms regulating ethanol withdrawal-induced aberrant neurogenesis in the DG have not been identified (Staples et al., 2015; Somkuwar et al., 2016; Nawarawong et al., 2021), and future mechanistic studies are needed to address the contribution of aberrant DG neurogenesis to brain changes associated with alcohol dependence.

Alcohol reward and reinforcement

The hippocampus is involved in ethanol reward and relapse to ethanol seeking (Koob and Volkow, 2010; Zarrindast et al., 2010), suggesting that the hippocampus contributes to several aspects of alcohol dependence and can be implicated in the phenomena linked to alcohol use disorders (AUD). For example, alcohol dependence is linked to decreased hippocampus volume (Sullivan et al., 1995; Beresford et al., 2006), altered hippocampal morphology (Bengochea and Gonzalo, 1990; Durazzo et al., 2011), and deficits in hippocampus-dependent learning and memory (Brandt et al., 1983; Glenn and Parsons, 1991; Sullivan et al., 2000a, 2000b, 2002). Preclinical studies show that chronic in vivo exposure to ethanol, and withdrawal and abstinence from ethanol enhances the expression and function of hippocampal GluN receptors (Trevisan et al., 1994; Smothers et al., 1997; Marszalek-Grabska et al., 2021). Notably, reduced ethanol seeking behaviors in animal models and craving in human subjects is observed with memantine, a non-competitive GluN antagonist (Krishnan-Sarin et al., 2015; Vengeliene et al., 2015). Coincidentally, reduced hippocampal GluN expression is observed with memantine treatment in hippocampal neurons under the influence of ethanol, suggesting that memantine may produce its effects by altering ethanol-induced hippocampal GluN expression (Maler et al., 2005). However, this suggested relationship needs to be validated. In addition to ethanol's effects on GluNs, there is data to support ethanol's bidirectional effects on GluA receptors in the hippocampus. For example, ethanol exposure has an inhibitory effect on GluA receptor expression and function in hippocampal neuronal cultures, and hippocampal CA1 and CA3 regions ex vivo (Martin et al., 1995; Weiner et al., 1999; Costa et al., 2000; Crowder et al., 2002; Carta et al., 2003), and the inhibitory effect is reversed to unregulation of GluA receptors and function during withdrawal (Carta et al., 2002). More interesting is the fact that GluA receptors seem to play a role in ethanol seeking-behaviors and not ethanol drinking, however, the role of hippocampal GluAs in these behavioral outcomes is yet to be investigated (Sanchis-Segura et al., 2006).

In addition to the studies that have investigated the role of ionotrophic GluRs (GluNs and GluAs) in ethanol taking and seeking behaviors, there are reports on ethanols effect on metabotrophic GluRs (mGluRs) and the role of these receptors in ethanol taking and seeking behaviors. For example, chronic ethanol exposure, in vivo, alters transcription of mGluRs in a sub-region and receptor subtype manner, with decreases in mGluR3 and mGluR5 expression in the DG and CA3, and decreases mGluR7 in the CA1 and CA3 (Simonyi et al., 2004). More notable is that, stimulation of mGluR2 systemically reduced cue-induced reinstatement of alcohol seeking behavior, an effect that was associated with increased *c*-fos gene expression in the hippocampus (Zhao et al., 2006). However, the specific role of hippocampal mGluRs in ethanol drinking and seeking behaviors is still unknown. Lastly, chronic ethanol experience-induced increase in the extracellular glutamate levels in the hippocampus could be attributed to increases in glutamate release or diminished clearance. The attribution to diminished clearance is supported by studies that have revealed decreased expression of glutamate transporters in the hippocampus (Aal-Aaboda et al., 2015; Alshehri et al., 2017). Given the correlational relationship between reduced glutamate transporters and chonic ethanol-induced glutamate release, it is tempting to speculate that altered function of glutamate transporters in the hippocampus by ethanol could facilitate context driven ethanol seeking behaviors.

In the context of the above hypothesis, few studies have attempted to investigate the role of hippocampus in context driven reinstatement of ethanol seeking behaviors. Correlative studies demonstrate that reinstatement of ethanol seeking driven by ethanol context is accompanied by increases in transcription and protein expression of markers of neuronal activation in the dorsal hippocampus (Topple et al., 1998; Dayas et al., 2007; Marinelli et al., 2007; Felipe et al., 2021). Systemic treatment with an opioid antagonist reduced ethanol seeking triggered by ethanol context, and correspondingly reduced ethanol reinstatement-induced neuronal activity in the hippocampus (Dayas et al., 2007). However, site specific antagonism of opioid receptors in the dorsal hippocampus did not reduce ethanol seeking behaviors, suggesting a more complex role of brain opioid receptors in ethanol-seeking behaviors (Marinelli et al., 2010). More notable is that pharmacological inactivation of the dorsal hippocampus prevents reinstatement of ethanol seeking triggered by ethanol context, indicating a direct role of the hippocampus in ethanol context memories and motivation to seek ethanol (Felipe et al., 2021). Taken together, while the role of the hippocampus in ethanol seeking is confirmed, the specific role of the distinct circuits within the hippocampus, and between the hippocampus and other regions involved in ethanol seeking is yet to be determined.

Alcohol and hippocampus-dependent behaviors

Preclinical studies show that high doses, but not low doses of ethanol impair memory and cognition. For example, acute high-dose ethanol administration ($1-2\ \mathrm{mg\ kg^{-1}}$) impairs hippocampus-dependent learning and memory in the Morris Water Maze (Matthews et al.,

1995; Markwiese et al., 1998; Shimizu et al., 1998; Berry and Matthews, 2004), the radial arm maze (Matthews et al., 1995; White et al., 1997), the sandbox maze (Rajendran and Spear, 2004), and contextual fear conditioning (Melia et al., 1996; Gulick and Gould, 2007). Preclinical studies also show that prolonged ethanol consumption results in deficits in hippocampus-dependent cognitive function, which were shown to be irreversible after prolonged abstinence (Bond and Di Giusto, 1976; Beatty et al., 1984; Cippitelli et al., 2010; Ehrlich and Humpel, 2012). In contrast, low dose ethanol administration (0.25–5 mg kg^{-1}) does not produce any deficits in hippocampus-dependent learning and memory (Rajendran and Spear, 2004; Gulick and Gould, 2007). These results coincide with findings from human studies, where light to moderate alcohol intake does not produce profound deficits in cognitive function, and higher alcohol intake correlated with worsened cognitive performance dependent on the hippocampus (Hassing, 2018; Zhang et al., 2020; Yan et al., 2021). In support of this relationship, in humans, AUD is associated with significant health problems, particularly cognitive impairments, with over 50% of individuals suffering from moderate to severe AUD reporting memory and cognitive dysfunction (Ingle and Weingartner, 1995; Vetreno et al., 2011; Stavro et al., 2013). For example, chronic alcohol consumption leads to impairments in learning and memory, attention and executive function, and abstraction (Klisz and Parsons, 1977; Bates et al., 2002; Vetreno et al., 2011). More notable is that these deficits persisted into abstinence, and therefore whether complete recovery from cognitive dysfunction with prolonged abstinence is possible in individuals with moderate to severe AUD is unknown (Fein et al., 1990; Stavro et al., 2013).

In addition to the cognitive deficits, some individuals with severe AUD suffer a condition known as Wernicke–Korsakoff syndrome (WKS). WKS in an indirect effect of chronic alcohol consumption, and is directly related to the thiamine deficiency produced by chronic alcohol consumption. WKS patients exhibit extensive damage to the hippocampus, observed as reduced hippocampal volume, reduced hippocampal activity and more importantly reduced thalamo-hippocampal connectivity (Sullivan and Marsh, 2003; Caulo et al., 2005; Sullivan and Pfefferbaum, 2009; Segobin et al., 2019), suggesting that these alterations in hippocampal structure, morphology and circuitry, may produce hippocampus-dependent learning and memory deficits that could contribute to the negative affect state in AUD patients suffering from WKS (Jones et al., 1975; Brand et al., 2005).

In conclusion, based on preclinical and clinical studies, it is evident that deficits in hippocampal learning and memory functions depends on the dose of ethanol administered or amount of alcohol consumed. The altered hippocampal function could lead to strong ethanol/alcohol–context associations, which may assist with alcohol-seeking behavior and AUD.

Conclusions

This chapter has briefly reviewed synaptic plasticity in the hippocampus and its importance for learning and memory, the effects of addictive drugs on various forms of hippocampal plasticity, and the role of hippocampal function in drug reward. Here, we focused on cocaine and alcohol as exemplars of these phenomena, but it is likely that many of the processes and mechanisms discussed above extend to other drugs of abuse as well. In sum, drug addiction can be conceptualized as a learning and memory disorder, and ample evidence supports a role for hippocampus-dependent learning and memory, as well as hippocampal plasticity, in the development and maintenance of drug addiction.

Acknowledgments

Funds from the Department of Veterans Affairs (BX003304) and National Institute on Alcoholism and Alcohol Abuse (AA020098) provided salary support. A part of the chapter has been recently published as a review article by the author.

References

Aal-Aaboda, M., Alhaddad, H., Osowik, F., Nauli, S.M., Sari, Y., 2015. Effects of (R)-(-)-5-methyl-1-nicotinoyl-2-pyrazoline on glutamate transporter 1 and cysteine/glutamate exchanger as well as ethanol drinking behavior in male, alcohol-preferring rats. J. Neurosci. Res. 93, 930–937.

Abraham, W.C., Bear, M.F., 1996. Metaplasticity: the plasticity of synaptic plasticity. Trends Neurosci. 19, 126–130.

Abrous, D.N., Adriani, W., Montaron, M.F., Aurousseau, C., Rougon, G., Le Moal, M., Piazza, P.V., 2002. Nicotine self-administration impairs hippocampal plasticity. J. Neurosci. 22, 3656–3662.

Adlaf, E.W., Vaden, R.J., Niver, A.J., Manuel, A.F., Onyilo, V.C., Araujo, M.T., Dieni, C.V., Vo, H.T., King, G.D., Wadiche, J.I., Overstreet-Wadiche, L., 2017. Adult-born neurons modify excitatory synaptic transmission to existing neurons. Elife 6.

Aguayo, L.G., 1990. Ethanol potentiates the GABAA-activated Cl-current in mouse hippocampal and cortical neurons. Eur. J. Pharmacol. 187, 127–130.

Akers, K.G., Martinez-Canabal, A., Restivo, L., Yiu, A.P., De Cristofaro, A., Hsiang, H.L., Wheeler, A.L., Guskjolen, A., Niibori, Y., Shoji, H., Ohira, K., Richards, B.A., Miyakawa, T., Josselyn, S.A., Frankland, P.W., 2014. Hippocampal neurogenesis regulates forgetting during adulthood and infancy. Science 344, 598–602.

Allan, A.M., Harris, R.A., 1986. Gamma-aminobutyric acid and alcohol actions: neurochemical studies of long sleep and short sleep mice. Life Sci. 39, 2005–2015.

Allen, E., 1912. The cessation of the mitosis in the central nervous system of the albino rat. J. Comp. Neurol. 22, 547–568.

Alshehri, F.S., Althobaiti, Y.S., Sari, Y., 2017. Effects of administered ethanol and methamphetamine on glial glutamate transporters in rat striatum and Hippocampus. J. Mol. Neurosci. 61, 343–350.

Altman, J., 1963. Autoradiographic investigation of cell proliferation in the brains of rats and cats. Anat. Rec. 145, 573–591.

Altman, J., Das, G.D., 1965. Autoradiographic and histological evidence of postnatal hippocampal neurogenesis in rats. J. Comp. Neurol. 124, 319–335.

Altman, J., Das, G.D., 1967. Postnatal neurogenesis in the Guinea-pig. Nature 214, 1098–1101.

Altman, J., Everitt, B.J., Glautier, S., Markou, A., Nutt, D., Oretti, R., Phillips, G.D., Robbins, T.W., 1996. The biological, social and clinical bases of drug addiction: commentary and debate. Psychopharmacology (Berl) 125, 285–345.

Amaral, D.G., Scharfman, H.E., Lavenex, P., 2007. The dentate gyrus: fundamental neuroanatomical organization (dentate gyrus for dummies). Prog. Brain Res. 163, 3–22.

Amaral, D.G., Witter, M.P., 1989. The three-dimensional organization of the hippocampal formation: a review of anatomical data. Neuroscience 31, 571–591.

Anacker, C., Hen, R., 2017. Adult hippocampal neurogenesis and cognitive flexibility—linking memory and mood. Nat. Rev. Neurosci. 18, 335–346.

Andersen, P., 1975. [Isolated brain slices. A new preparation for theoretical and clinical research]. Tidsskrift for den Norske laegeforening : tidsskrift for praktisk Medicin, Ny Raekke 95, 349–351.

Andersen, P., Bruland, H., Kaada, B.R., 1961. Activation of the dentate area by septal stimulation. Acta Physiol. Scand. 51, 17–28.

Andersen, P., Holmqvist, B., Voorhoeve, P.E., 1966. Excitatory synapses on hippocampal apical dendrites activated by entorhinal stimulation. Acta Physiol. Scand. 66, 461–472.

Ardila, A., Rosselli, M., Strumwasser, S., 1991. Neuropsychological deficits in chronic cocaine abusers. Int. J. Neurosci. 57, 73–79.

Atkins, C.M., Selcher, J.C., Petraitis, J.J., Trzaskos, J.M., Sweatt, J.D., 1998. The MAPK cascade is required for mammalian associative learning. Nat. Neurosci. 1, 602–609.

Avchalumov, Y., Oliver, R.J., Trenet, W., Heyer Osorno, R.E., Sibley, B.D., Purohit, D.C., Contet, C., Roberto, M., Woodward, J.J., Mandyam, C.D., 2021. Chronic ethanol exposure differentially alters neuronal function in the medial prefrontal cortex and dentate gyrus. Neuropharmacology 185, 108438.

Baione, V., Belvisi, D., Cortese, A., Cetta, I., Tartaglia, M., Millefiorini, E., Berardelli, A., Conte, A., 2019. Cortical M1 plasticity and metaplasticity in patients with multiple sclerosis. Mult. Scler. Relat. Disord. 38, 101494.

Baram, T.Z., Hirsch, E., Snead 3rd, O.C., Schultz, L., 1992. Corticotropin-releasing hormone-induced seizures in infant rats originate in the amygdala. Ann. Neurol. 31, 488–494.

Barbieri, M., Ossato, A., Canazza, I., Trapella, C., Borelli, A.C., Beggiato, S., Rimondo, C., Serpelloni, G., Ferraro, L., Marti, M., 2016. Synthetic cannabinoid JWH-018 and its halogenated derivatives JWH-018-Cl and JWH-018-Br impair Novel Object Recognition in mice: behavioral, electrophysiological and neurochemical evidence. Neuropharmacology 109, 254–269.

Bardo, M.T., 1998. Neuropharmacological mechanisms of drug reward: beyond dopamine in the nucleus accumbens. Crit. Rev. Neurobiol. 12, 37–67.

Barr, J.L., Renner, K.J., Forster, G.L., 2010. Withdrawal from chronic amphetamine produces persistent anxiety-like behavior but temporally-limited reductions in monoamines and neurogenesis in the adult rat dentate gyrus. Neuropharmacology 59, 395–405.

Barria, A., Muller, D., Derkach, V., Griffith, L.C., Soderling, T.R., 1997. Regulatory phosphorylation of AMPA-type glutamate receptors by CaM-KII during long-term potentiation. Science 276, 2042–2045.

Basavarajappa, B.S., Ninan, I., Arancio, O., 2008. Acute ethanol suppresses glutamatergic neurotransmission through endocannabinoids in hippocampal neurons. J. Neurochem. 107, 1001–1013.

Bates, M.E., Bowden, S.C., Barry, D., 2002. Neurocognitive impairment associated with alcohol use disorders: implications for treatment. Exp. Clin. Psychopharmacol. 10, 193–212.

Beatty, W.W., Bengtson, K.R., Lunn, R.J., Staton, R.D., Brumback, R.A., 1984. Comparative effects of long-term ethanol consumption and forebrain lesions on maze learning and active avoidance behavior in rats. Alcohol 1, 465–470.

Bengochea, O., Gonzalo, L.M., 1990. Effect of chronic alcoholism on the human hippocampus. Histol. Histopathol. 5, 349–357.

Benoy, A., Dasgupta, A., Sajikumar, S., 2018. Hippocampal area CA2: an emerging modulatory gateway in the hippocampal circuit. Exp. Brain Res. 236, 919–931.

Beresford, T.P., Arciniegas, D.B., Alfers, J., Clapp, L., Martin, B., Du, Y., Liu, D., Shen, D., Davatzikos, C., 2006. Hippocampus volume loss due to chronic heavy drinking. Alcohol Clin. Exp. Res. 30, 1866–1870.

Berry, R.B., Matthews, D.B., 2004. Acute ethanol administration selectively impairs spatial memory in C57BL/6J mice. Alcohol 32, 9–18.

Beveridge, T.J., Smith, H.R., Daunais, J.B., Nader, M.A., Porrino, L.J., 2006. Chronic cocaine self-administration is associated with altered functional activity in the temporal lobes of non human primates. Eur. J. Neurosci. 23, 3109–3118.

Bison, S., Crews, F., 2003. Alcohol withdrawal increases neuropeptide Y immunoreactivity in rat brain. Alcohol Clin. Exp. Res. 27, 1173–1183.

Bliss, T.V., Collingridge, G.L., 1993. A synaptic model of memory: long-term potentiation in the hippocampus. Nature 361, 31–39.

Bliss, T.V., Gardner-Medwin, A.R., 1973. Long-lasting potentiation of synaptic transmission in the dentate area of the unanaesthetized rabbit following stimulation of the perforant path. J. Physiol. 232, 357–374.

Bliss, T.V., Lomo, T., 1973. Long-lasting potentiation of synaptic transmission in the dentate area of the anaesthetized rabbit following stimulation of the perforant path. J. Physiol. 232, 331–356.

Blitzer, R.D., Connor, J.H., Brown, G.P., Wong, T., Shenolikar, S., Iyengar, R., Landau, E.M., 1998. Gating of CaMKII by cAMP-regulated protein phosphatase activity during LTP. Science 280, 1940–1942.

Blitzer, R.D., Gil, O., Landau, E.M., 1990. Long-term potentiation in rat hippocampus is inhibited by low concentrations of ethanol. Brain Res. 537, 203–208.

Bolla, K.I., Rothman, R., Cadet, J.L., 1999. Dose-related neurobehavioral effects of chronic cocaine use. J. Neuropsychiatry Clin. Neurosci. 11, 361–369.

Bond, N.W., Di Giusto, E.L., 1976. Impairment of Hebb-Williams maze performance following prolonged alcohol consumption in rats. Pharmacol. Biochem. Behav. 5, 85–86.

Brand, M., Fujiwara, E., Borsutzky, S., Kalbe, E., Kessler, J., Markowitsch, H.J., 2005. Decision-making deficits of korsakoff patients in a new gambling task with explicit rules: associations with executive functions. Neuropsychology 19, 267–277.

Brandalise, F., Gerber, U., 2014. Mossy fiber-evoked subthreshold responses induce timing-dependent plasticity at hippocampal CA3 recurrent synapses. Proc. Natl. Acad. Sci. U. S. A. 111, 4303–4308.

Brandt, J., Butters, N., Ryan, C., Bayog, R., 1983. Cognitive loss and recovery in long-term alcohol abusers. Arch. Gen. Psychiatr. 40, 435–442.

Brown, T.E., Lee, B.R., Ryu, V., Herzog, T., Czaja, K., Dong, Y., 2010. Reducing hippocampal cell proliferation in the adult rat does not prevent the acquisition of cocaine-induced conditioned place preference. Neurosci. Lett. 481, 41–46.

Brun, V.H., Leutgeb, S., Wu, H.Q., Schwarcz, R., Witter, M.P., Moser, E.I., Moser, M.B., 2008. Impaired spatial representation in CA1 after lesion of direct input from entorhinal cortex. Neuron 57, 290–302.

Budygin, E.A., Oleson, E.B., Mathews, T.A., Lack, A.K., Diaz, M.R., McCool, B.A., Jones, S.R., 2007. Effects of chronic alcohol exposure on dopamine uptake in rat nucleus accumbens and caudate putamen. Psychopharmacology (Berl) 193, 495–501.

Burgess, N., Maguire, E.A., O'Keefe, J., 2002. The human hippocampus and spatial and episodic memory. Neuron 35, 625–641.

Cadete-Leite, A., Tavares, M.A., Pacheco, M.M., Volk, B., Paula-Barbosa, M.M., 1989. Hippocampal mossy fiber-CA3 synapses after chronic alcohol consumption and withdrawal. Alcohol 6, 303–310.

Cameron, H.A., McKay, R., 1998. Stem cells and neurogenesis in the adult brain. Curr. Opin. Neurobiol. 8, 677–680.

Canales, J.J., 2013. Deficient plasticity in the hippocampus and the spiral of addiction: focus on adult neurogenesis. Curr. Topics Behav. Neurosci. 15, 293–312.

Carta, M., Ariwodola, O.J., Weiner, J.L., Valenzuela, C.F., 2003. Alcohol potently inhibits the kainate receptor-dependent excitatory drive of hippocampal interneurons. Proc. Natl. Acad. Sci. U. S. A. 100, 6813–6818.

Carta, M., Olivera, D.S., Dettmer, T.S., Valenzuela, C.F., 2002. Ethanol withdrawal upregulates kainate receptors in cultured rat hippocampal neurons. Neurosci. Lett. 327, 128–132.

Castilla-Ortega, E., Blanco, E., Serrano, A., Ladrón de Guevara-Miranda, D., Pedraz, M., Estivill-Torrús, G., Pavón, F.J., Rodríguez de Fonseca, F., Santín, L.J., 2016a. Pharmacological reduction of adult hippocampal neurogenesis modifies functional brain circuits in mice exposed to a cocaine conditioned place preference paradigm. Addiction Biol. 21, 575–588.

Castilla-Ortega, E., Ladron de Guevara-Miranda, D., Serrano, A., Pavon, F.J., Suarez, J., Rodriguez de Fonseca, F., Santin, L.J., 2017. The impact of cocaine on adult hippocampal neurogenesis: potential neurobiological mechanisms and contributions to maladaptive cognition in cocaine addiction disorder. Biochem. Pharmacol. 141, 100–117.

Castilla-Ortega, E., Santin, L.J., 2020. Adult hippocampal neurogenesis as a target for cocaine addiction: a review of recent developments. Curr. Opin. Pharmacol. 50, 109–116. https://doi.org/10.1016/j.coph.2019.10.002. 31708413.

Castilla-Ortega, E., Serrano, A., Blanco, E., Araos, P., Suárez, J., Pavón, F.J., Rodríguez de Fonseca, F., Santín, L.J., 2016b. A place for the hippocampus in the cocaine addiction circuit: potential roles for adult hippocampal neurogenesis. Neurosci. Biobehav. Rev. 66, 15–32.

Castillo, P.E., Schoch, S., Schmitz, F., Sudhof, T.C., Malenka, R.C., 2002. RIM1alpha is required for presynaptic long-term potentiation. Nature 415, 327–330.

Catlow, B.J., Badanich, K.A., Sponaugle, A.E., Rowe, A.R., Song, S., Rafalovich, I., Sava, V., Kirstein, C.L., Sanchez-Ramos, J., 2010. Effects of MDMA ("ecstasy") during adolescence on place conditioning and hippocampal neurogenesis. Eur. J. Pharmacol. 628, 96–103.

Caulo, M., Van Hecke, J., Toma, L., Ferretti, A., Tartaro, A., Colosimo, C., Romani, G.L., Uncini, A., 2005. Functional MRI study of diencephalic amnesia in Wernicke-Korsakoff syndrome. Brain 128, 1584–1594.

Cervo, L., Mukherjee, S., Bertaglia, A., Samanin, R., 1997. Protein kinases A and C are involved in the mechanisms underlying consolidation of cocaine place conditioning. Brain Res. 775, 30–36.

Chandler, L.J., Sutton, G., 2005. Acute ethanol inhibits extracellular signal-regulated kinase, protein kinase B, and adenosine 3′:5′-cyclic monophosphate response element binding protein activity in an age- and brain region-specific manner. Alcohol Clin. Exp. Res. 29, 672–682.

Chevaleyre, V., Castillo, P.E., 2002. Assessing the role of Ih channels in synaptic transmission and mossy fiber LTP. Proc. Natl. Acad. Sci. U. S. A. 99, 9538–9543.

Chevaleyre, V., Siegelbaum, S.A., 2010. Strong CA2 pyramidal neuron synapses define a powerful disynaptic cortico-hippocampal loop. Neuron 66, 560–572.

Childress, A.R., Mozley, P.D., McElgin, W., Fitzgerald, J., Reivich, M., O'Brien, C.P., 1999. Limbic activation during cue-induced cocaine craving. Am. J. Psychiatr. 156, 11–18.

Cippitelli, A., Zook, M., Bell, L., Damadzic, R., Eskay, R.L., Schwandt, M., Heilig, M., 2010. Reversibility of object recognition but not spatial memory impairment following binge-like alcohol exposure in rats. Neurobiol. Learn. Mem. 94, 538–546.

Citri, A., Malenka, R.C., 2008. Synaptic plasticity: multiple forms, functions, and mechanisms. Neuropsychopharmacology 33, 18–41.

Claus, D., Kim, J.S., Kornhuber, M.E., Ahn, Y.S., 1982. [Effect of ethanol on the neurotransmitters glutamate and GABA]. Arch. Psychiatr. Nervenkr. 232, 183–189.

Collingridge, G.L., Kehl, S.J., McLennan, H., 1983. Excitatory amino acids in synaptic transmission in the Schaffer collateral-commissural pathway of the rat hippocampus. J. Physiol. 334, 33–46.

Collingridge, G.L., Peineau, S., Howland, J.G., Wang, Y.T., 2010. Long-term depression in the CNS. Nat. Rev. Neurosci. 11, 459–473.

Contet, C., Kim, A., Le, D., Iyengar, S.K., Kotzebue, R.W., Yuan, C.J., Kieffer, B.L., Mandyam, C.D., 2014. mu-Opioid receptors mediate the effects of chronic ethanol binge drinking on the hippocampal neurogenic niche. Addiction Biol. 19 (5), 770–780. https://doi.org/10.1111/adb.12040. 23461397.

Contractor, A., Swanson, G., Heinemann, S.F., 2001. Kainate receptors are involved in short- and long-term plasticity at mossy fiber synapses in the hippocampus. Neuron 29, 209–216.

Costa, E.T., Soto, E.E., Cardoso, R.A., Olivera, D.S., Valenzuela, C.F., 2000. Acute effects of ethanol on kainate receptors in cultured hippocampal neurons. Alcohol Clin. Exp. Res. 24, 220–225.

Crestani, A.P., Krueger, J.N., Barragan, E.V., Nakazawa, Y., Nemes, S.E., Quillfeldt, J.A., Gray, J.A., Wiltgen, B.J., 2019. Metaplasticity contributes to memory formation in the hippocampus. Neuropsychopharmacology 44, 408–414.

Crews, F.T., Nixon, K., 2003. Alcohol, neural stem cells, and adult neurogenesis. Alcohol Res. Health 27, 197–204.

Crews, F.T., Nixon, K., 2009. Mechanisms of neurodegeneration and regeneration in alcoholism. Alcohol Alcohol 44, 115–127.

Crews, F.T., Nixon, K., Wilkie, M.E., 2004. Exercise reverses ethanol inhibition of neural stem cell proliferation. Alcohol 33, 63–71.

Criado, J.R., Liu, T., Ehlers, C.L., Mathe, A.A., 2011. Prolonged chronic ethanol exposure alters neuropeptide Y and corticotropin-releasing factor levels in the brain of adult Wistar rats. Pharmacol. Biochem. Behav. 99, 104–111.

Crowder, T.L., Ariwodola, O.J., Weiner, J.L., 2002. Ethanol antagonizes kainate receptor-mediated inhibition of evoked GABA(A) inhibitory postsynaptic currents in the rat hippocampal CA1 region. J. Pharmacol. Exp. Therapeut. 303, 937–944.

Cull-Candy, S., Brickley, S., Farrant, M., 2001. NMDA receptor subunits: diversity, development and disease. Curr. Opin. Neurobiol. 11, 327–335.

Dan, Y., Poo, M.M., 2006. Spike timing-dependent plasticity: from synapse to perception. Physiol. Rev. 86, 1033–1048.

Danielson, N.B., Kaifosh, P., Zaremba, J.D., Lovett-Barron, M., Tsai, J., Denny, C.A., Balough, E.M., Goldberg, A.R., Drew, L.J., Hen, R., Losonczy, A., Kheirbek, M.A., 2016. Distinct contribution of adult-born hippocampal granule cells to context encoding. Neuron 90, 101–112.

Davidson, M., Shanley, B., Wilce, P., 1995. Increased NMDA-induced excitability during ethanol withdrawal: a behavioural and histological study. Brain Res. 674, 91–96.

Davidson, M.D., Wilce, P., Shanley, B.C., 1993. Increased sensitivity of the hippocampus in ethanol-dependent rats to toxic effect of N-methyl-D-aspartic acid in vivo. Brain Res. 606, 5–9.

Dayas, C.V., Liu, X., Simms, J.A., Weiss, F., 2007. Distinct patterns of neural activation associated with ethanol seeking: effects of naltrexone. Biol. Psychiatr. 61, 979–989.

Debanne, D., Gahwiler, B.H., Thompson, S.M., 1994. Asynchronous pre- and postsynaptic activity induces associative long-term depression in area CA1 of the rat hippocampus in vitro. Proc. Natl. Acad. Sci. U. S. A. 91, 1148–1152.

del Olmo, N., Miguéns, M., Higuera-Matas, A., Torres, I., García-Lecumberri, C., Solís, J.M., Ambrosio, E., 2006. Enhancement of hippocampal long-term potentiation induced by cocaine self-administration is maintained during the extinction of this behavior. Brain Res. 1116, 120–126.

Deneau, G., Yanagita, T., Seevers, M.H., 1969. Self-administration of psychoactive substances by the monkey. Psychopharmacologia 16, 30–48.

Deng, W., Saxe, M.D., Gallina, I.S., Gage, F.H., 2009. Adult-born hippocampal dentate granule cells undergoing maturation modulate learning and memory in the brain. J. Neurosci. 29, 13532–13542.

Deroche-Gamonet, V., Revest, J.M., Fiancette, J.F., Balado, E., Koehl, M., Grosjean, N., Abrous, D.N., Piazza, P.V., 2019. Depleting adult dentate gyrus neurogenesis increases cocaine-seeking behavior. Mol. Psychiatr. 24, 312–320.

Derrick, B.E., York, A.D., Martinez Jr., J.L., 2000. Increased granule cell neurogenesis in the adult dentate gyrus following mossy fiber stimulation sufficient to induce long-term potentiation. Brain Res. 857, 300–307.

Deschaux, O., Vendruscolo, L.F., Schlosburg, J.E., Diaz-Aguilar, L., Yuan, C.J., Sobieraj, J.C., George, O., Koob, G.F., Mandyam, C.D., 2014. Hippocampal neurogenesis protects against cocaine-primed relapse. Addiction Biol. 19 (4), 562–574. https://doi.org/10.1111/adb.12019. 23278919.

Dhaliwal, J., Lagace, D.C., 2011. Visualization and genetic manipulation of adult neurogenesis using transgenic mice. Eur. J. Neurosci. 33, 1025–1036.

Dhanabalan, G., Le Maître, T.W., Bogdanovic, N., Alkass, K., Druid, H., 2018. Hippocampal granule cell loss in human chronic alcohol abusers. Neurobiol. Dis. 120, 63–75.

Dolleman-Van der Weel, M.J., Witter, M.P., 2000. Nucleus reuniens thalami innervates gamma aminobutyric acid positive cells in hippocampal field CA1 of the rat. Neurosci. Lett. 278, 145–148.

Dranovsky, A., Hen, R., 2006. Hippocampal neurogenesis: regulation by stress and antidepressants. Biol. Psychiatr. 59, 1136–1143.

Duncan, K., Ketz, N., Inati, S.J., Davachi, L., 2012. Evidence for area CA1 as a match/mismatch detector: a high-resolution fMRI study of the human hippocampus. Hippocampus 22, 389–398.

Dupret, D., Revest, J.M., Koehl, M., Ichas, F., De Giorgi, F., Costet, P., Abrous, D.N., Piazza, P.V., 2008. Spatial relational memory requires hippocampal adult neurogenesis. PLoS One 3, e1959.

Durand, D., Carlen, P.L., 1984. Impairment of long-term potentiation in rat hippocampus following chronic ethanol treatment. Brain Res. 308, 325–332.

Durazzo, T.C., Tosun, D., Buckley, S., Gazdzinski, S., Mon, A., Fryer, S.L., Meyerhoff, D.J., 2011. Cortical thickness, surface area, and volume of the brain reward system in alcohol dependence: relationships to relapse and extended abstinence. Alcohol Clin. Exp. Res. 35, 1187–1200.

Ehrlich, D., Humpel, C., 2012. Chronic vascular risk factors (cholesterol, homocysteine, ethanol) impair spatial memory, decline cholinergic neurons and induce blood-brain barrier leakage in rats in vivo. J. Neurol. Sci. 322, 92–95.

Eisch, A.J., Barrot, M., Schad, C.A., Self, D.W., Nestler, E.J., 2000. Opiates inhibit neurogenesis in the adult rat hippocampus. Proc. Natl. Acad. Sci. U.S.A. 97, 7579–7584.

Eisch, A.J., Harburg, G.C., 2006. Opiates, psychostimulants, and adult hippocampal neurogenesis: insights for addiction and stem cell biology. Hippocampus 16, 271–286.

Eisch, A.J., Mandyam, C.D., 2004. Beyond BrdU: basic and clinical implications for analysis of endogenous cell cycle proteins. In: Progress in Stem Cell Research. Nova Science Publishers Inc.

Elgersma, Y., Silva, A.J., 1999. Molecular mechanisms of synaptic plasticity and memory. Curr. Opin. Neurobiol. 9, 209–213.

Enikolopov, G., Overstreet-Wadiche, L., Ge, S., 2015. Viral and transgenic reporters and genetic analysis of adult neurogenesis. Cold Spring Harbor Perspect. Biol. 7, a018804.

Epp, J.R., Silva Mera, R., Kohler, S., Josselyn, S.A., Frankland, P.W., 2016. Neurogenesis-mediated forgetting minimizes proactive interference. Nat. Commun. 7, 10838.

Ernst, A., Alkass, K., Bernard, S., Salehpour, M., Perl, S., Tisdale, J., Possnert, G., Druid, H., Frisen, J., 2014. Neurogenesis in the striatum of the adult human brain. Cell 156, 1072–1083.

España, R.A., Oleson, E.B., Locke, J.L., Brookshire, B.R., Roberts, D.C., Jones, S.R., 2010. The hypocretin-orexin system regulates cocaine self-administration via actions on the mesolimbic dopamine system. Eur. J. Neurosci. 31, 336–348.

Fein, G., Bachman, L., Fisher, S., Davenport, L., 1990. Cognitive impairments in abstinent alcoholics. West. J. Med. 152, 531–537.

Feldman, D.E., 2012. The spike-timing dependence of plasticity. Neuron 75, 556–571.

Felipe, J.M., Palombo, P., Bianchi, P.C., Zaniboni, C.R., Anésio, A., Yokoyama, T.S., Engi, S.A., Carneiro-de-Oliveira, P.E., Planeta, C.D.S., Leão, R.M., Cruz, F.C., 2021. Dorsal hippocampus plays a causal role in context-induced reinstatement of alcohol-seeking in rats. Behav. Brain Res. 398, 112978.

Fijał, K., Nowak, E., Leśkiewicz, M., Budziszewska, B., Filip, M., 2015. Working memory deficits and alterations of ERK and CREB phosphorylation following withdrawal from cocaine self-administration. Pharmacol. Rep. 67, 881–889.

Fino, E., Deniau, J.M., Venance, L., 2009. Brief subthreshold events can act as Hebbian signals for long-term plasticity. PLoS One 4, e6557.

Fox, C.J., Russell, K.I., Wang, Y.T., Christie, B.R., 2006. Contribution of NR2A and NR2B NMDA subunits to bidirectional synaptic plasticity in the hippocampus in vivo. Hippocampus 16, 907–915.

Frankland, P.W., Josselyn, S.A., 2016. Hippocampal neurogenesis and memory clearance. Neuropsychopharmacology 41, 382–383.

Frasca, A., Aalbers, M., Frigerio, F., Fiordaliso, F., Salio, M., Gobbi, M., Cagnotto, A., Gardoni, F., Battaglia, G.S., Hoogland, G., Di Luca, M., Vezzani, A., 2011. Misplaced NMDA receptors in epileptogenesis contribute to excitotoxicity. Neurobiol. Dis. 43, 507–515.

Friedman, D.P., Aggleton, J.P., Saunders, R.C., 2002. Comparison of hippocampal, amygdala, and perirhinal projections to the nucleus accumbens: combined anterograde and retrograde tracing study in the Macaque brain. J. Comp. Neurol. 450, 345–365.

Fuchs, R.A., Eaddy, J.L., Su, Z.I., Bell, G.H., 2007. Interactions of the basolateral amygdala with the dorsal hippocampus and dorsomedial prefrontal cortex regulate drug context-induced reinstatement of cocaine-seeking in rats. Eur. J. Neurosci. 26, 487–498.

Fuchs, R.A., Evans, K.A., Ledford, C.C., Parker, M.P., Case, J.M., Mehta, R.H., See, R.E., 2005. The role of the dorsomedial prefrontal cortex, basolateral amygdala, and dorsal hippocampus in contextual reinstatement of cocaine seeking in rats. Neuropsychopharmacology 30, 296–309.

Fujii, S., Yamazaki, Y., Sugihara, T., Wakabayashi, I., 2008. Acute and chronic ethanol exposure differentially affect induction of hippocampal LTP. Brain Res. 1211, 13–21.

Galinato, M.H., Lockner, J.W., Fannon-Pavlich, M.J., Sobieraj, J.C., Staples, M.C., Somkuwar, S.S., Ghofranian, A., Chaing, S., Navarro, A.I., Joea, A., Luikart, B.W., Janda, K.D., Heyser, C., Koob, G.F., Mandyam, C.D., 2018a. A synthetic small-molecule Isoxazole-9 protects against methamphetamine relapse. Mol. Psychiatr. 23 (3), 629–638. https://doi.org/10.1038/mp.2017.46. 28348387.

Galinato, M.H., Takashima, Y., Fannon, M.J., Quach, L.W., Morales Silva, R.J., Mysore, K.K., Terranova, M.J., Dutta, R.R., Ostrom, R.W., Somkuwar, S.S., Mandyam, C.D., 2018b. Neurogenesis during abstinence is necessary for context-driven methamphetamine-related memory. J. Neurosci. 38, 2029–2042.

Garavan, H., Kaufman, J.N., Hester, R., 2008. Acute effects of cocaine on the neurobiology of cognitive control. Philos. Trans. R. Soc. Lond. B Biol. Sci. 363, 3267–3276.

Garcia-Fuster, M.J., Flagel, S.B., Mahmood, S.T., Mayo, L.M., Thompson, R.C., Watson, S.J., Akil, H., 2011. Decreased proliferation of adult hippocampal stem cells during cocaine withdrawal: possible role of the cell fate regulator FADD. Neuropsychopharmacology 36, 2303–2317.

Garcia-Fuster, M.J., Perez, J.A., Clinton, S.M., Watson, S.J., Akil, H., 2010. Impact of cocaine on adult hippocampal neurogenesis in an animal model of differential propensity to drug abuse. Eur. J. Neurosci. 31, 79–89

Garthe, A., Behr, J., Kempermann, G., 2009. Adult-generated hippocampal neurons allow the flexible use of spatially precise learning strategies. PLoS One 4, e5464.

Ge, S., Goh, E.L., Sailor, K.A., Kitabatake, Y., Ming, G.L., Song, H., 2006. GABA regulates synaptic integration of newly generated neurons in the adult brain. Nature 439, 589–593.

Ge, S., Yang, C.H., Hsu, K.S., Ming, G.L., Song, H., 2007. A critical period for enhanced synaptic plasticity in newly generated neurons of the adult brain. Neuron 54, 559–566.

Gebhardt, C., Mosienko, V., Alenina, N., Albrecht, D., 2019. Priming of LTP in amygdala and hippocampus by prior paired pulse facilitation paradigm in mice lacking brain serotonin. Hippocampus 29, 610–618.

Gehlert, D.R., Cippitelli, A., Thorsell, A., Le, A.D., Hipskind, P.A., Hamdouchi, C., Lu, J., Hembre, E.J., Cramer, J., Song, M., McKinzie, D., Morin, M., Ciccocioppo, R., Heilig, M., 2007. 3-(4-Chloro-2-morpholin-4-yl-thiazol-5-yl)-8-(1-ethylpropyl)-2,6-dimethyl-imidazo [1,2-b]pyridazine: a novel brain-penetrant, orally available corticotropin-releasing factor receptor 1 antagonist with efficacy in animal models of alcoholism. J. Neurosci. 27, 2718–2726.

George, O., Mandyam, C.D., Wee, S., Koob, G.F., 2008. Extended access to cocaine self-administration produces long-lasting prefrontal cortex-dependent working memory impairments. Neuropsychopharmacology 33, 2474–2482.

George, O., Sanders, C., Freiling, J., Grigoryan, E., Vu, S., Allen, C.D., Crawford, E., Mandyam, C.D., Koob, G.F., 2012. Recruitment of medial prefrontal cortex neurons during alcohol withdrawal predicts cognitive impairment and excessive alcohol drinking. Proc. Natl. Acad. Sci. U. S. A. 109, 18156–18161.

Gheusi, G., Lepousez, G., Lledo, P.M., 2013. Adult-born neurons in the olfactory bulb: integration and functional consequences. Curr. Topics Behav. Neurosci. 15, 49–72.

Gibson, D.A., Harris, B.R., Prendergast, M.A., Hart, S.R., Blanchard 2nd, J.A., Holley, R.C., Pedigo, N.W., Littleton, J.M., 2003. Polyamines contribute to ethanol withdrawal-induced neurotoxicity in rat hippocampal slice cultures through interactions with the NMDA receptor. Alcohol Clin. Exp. Res. 27, 1099–1106.

Gilpin, N.W., Smith, A.D., Cole, M., Weiss, F., Koob, G.F., Richardson, H.N., 2009. Operant behavior and alcohol levels in blood and brain of alcohol-dependent rats. Alcohol Clin. Exp. Res. 33, 2113–2123.

Glenn, S.W., Parsons, O.A., 1991. Impaired efficiency in female alcoholics' neuropsychological performance. J. Clin. Exp. Neuropsychol. 13, 895–908.

Gobin, C., Schwendt, M., 2017. The effects of extended-access cocaine self-administration on working memory performance, reversal learning and incubation of cocaine-seeking in adult male rats. J. Addiction Prev. 5.

Gold, A.E., Kesner, R.P., 2005. The role of the CA3 subregion of the dorsal hippocampus in spatial pattern completion in the rat. Hippocampus 15, 808–814.

Goncalves, J.T., Schafer, S.T., Gage, F.H., 2016. Adult neurogenesis in the Hippocampus: from stem cells to behavior. Cell 167, 897–914.

Goodman, J., Packard, M.G., 2016. Memory systems and the addicted brain. Front. Psychiatr. 7, 24.

Gould, E., Reeves, A.J., Graziano, M.S., Gross, C.G., 1999. Neurogenesis in the neocortex of adult primates. Science 286, 548–552.

Grant, S., London, E.D., Newlin, D.B., Villemagne, V.L., Liu, X., Contoreggi, C., Phillips, R.L., Kimes, A.S., Margolin, A., 1996. Activation of memory circuits during cue-elicited cocaine craving. Proc. Natl. Acad. Sci. U. S. A. 93, 12040–12045.

Gray, R., Johnston, D., 1985. Rectification of single GABA-gated chloride channels in adult hippocampal neurons. J. Neurophysiol. 54, 134–142.

Griffin 3rd, W.C., Lopez, M.F., Becker, H.C., 2009. Intensity and duration of chronic ethanol exposure is critical for subsequent escalation of voluntary ethanol drinking in mice. Alcohol Clin. Exp. Res. 33, 1893–1900.

Gu, H., Salmeron, B.J., Ross, T.J., Geng, X., Zhan, W., Stein, E.A., Yang, Y., 2010. Mesocorticolimbic circuits are impaired in chronic cocaine users as demonstrated by resting-state functional connectivity. Neuroimage 53, 593–601.

Guan, X., Zhang, R., Xu, Y., Li, S., 2009. Cocaine withdrawal enhances long-term potentiation in rat hippocampus via changing the activity of corticotropin-releasing factor receptor subtype 2. Neuroscience 161, 665–670.

Gulick, D., Gould, T.J., 2007. Acute ethanol has biphasic effects on short- and long-term memory in both foreground and background contextual fear conditioning in C57BL/6 mice. Alcohol Clin. Exp. Res. 31, 1528–1537.

Gutierrez, R., Heinemann, U., 1999. Synaptic reorganization in explanted cultures of rat hippocampus. Brain Res. 815, 304–316.

Han, J., Li, Y., Wang, D., Wei, C., Yang, X., Sui, N., 2010. Effect of 5-aza-2-deoxycytidine microinjecting into hippocampus and prelimbic cortex on acquisition and retrieval of cocaine-induced place preference in C57BL/6 mice. Eur. J. Pharmacol. 642, 93–98.

Hansson, A.C., Nixon, K., Rimondini, R., Damadzic, R., Sommer, W.H., Eskay, R., Crews, F.T., Heilig, M., 2010. Long-term suppression of forebrain neurogenesis and loss of neuronal progenitor cells following prolonged alcohol dependence in rats. Int. J. Neuropsychopharmacol. 13, 583–593.

Harris, E.W., Cotman, C.W., 1986. Long-term potentiation of Guinea pig mossy fiber responses is not blocked by N-methyl D-aspartate antagonists. Neurosci. Lett. 70, 132–137.

Harris, E.W., Ganong, A.H., Cotman, C.W., 1984. Long-term potentiation in the hippocampus involves activation of N-methyl-D-aspartate receptors. Brain Res. 323, 132–137.

Hassing, L.B., 2018. Light alcohol consumption does not protect cognitive function: a longitudinal prospective study. Front. Aging Neurosci. 10, 81.

He, J., Nixon, K., Shetty, A.K., Crews, F.T., 2005. Chronic alcohol exposure reduces hippocampal neurogenesis and dendritic growth of newborn neurons. Eur. J. Neurosci. 21, 2711–2720.

Hebb, D.O., 1949. The Organization of Behavior; a Neuropsychological Theory. Wiley, New York.

Hegemann, R.U., Abraham, W.C., 2019. Electrophysiological investigation of metabotropic glutamate receptor-dependent metaplasticity in the Hippocampus. Methods Mol. Biol. 1941, 79–91.

Hernandez-Rabaza, V., Hontecillas-Prieto, L., Velazquez-Sanchez, C., Ferragud, A., Perez-Villaba, A., Arcusa, A., Barcia, J.A., Trejo, J.L., Canales, J.J., 2008. The hippocampal dentate gyrus is essential for generating contextual memories of fear and drug-induced reward. Neurobiol. Learn. Mem. 90, 553–559.

Hill, A.S., Sahay, A., Hen, R., 2015. Increasing adult hippocampal neurogenesis is sufficient to reduce anxiety and depression-like behaviors. Neuropsychopharmacology 40, 2368–2378.

Hitchcock, L.N., Lattal, K.M., 2018. Involvement of the dorsal hippocampus in expression and extinction of cocaine-induced conditioned place preference. Hippocampus 28, 226–238.

Hoffman, A.F., Oz, M., Yang, R., Lichtman, A.H., Lupica, C.R., 2007. Opposing actions of chronic Delta9-tetrahydrocannabinol and cannabinoid antagonists on hippocampal long-term potentiation. Learn. Mem. 14, 63–74.

Hoffman, P.L., 2003. NMDA receptors in alcoholism. Int. Rev. Neurobiol. 56, 35–82.

Hoffman, P.L., Rabe, C.S., Moses, F., Tabakoff, B., 1989. N-methyl-D-aspartate receptors and ethanol: inhibition of calcium flux and cyclic GMP production. J. Neurochem. 52, 1937–1940.

Hrabetova, S., Sacktor, T.C., 2001. Transient translocation of conventional protein kinase C isoforms and persistent downregulation of atypical protein kinase Mzeta in long-term depression. Brain Res. Mol. Brain Res. 95, 146–152.

Hrabetova, S., Serrano, P., Blace, N., Tse, H.W., Skifter, D.A., Jane, D.E., Monaghan, D.T., Sacktor, T.C., 2000. Distinct NMDA receptor subpopulations contribute to long-term potentiation and long-term depression induction. J. Neurosci. 20, Rc81.

Huang, Y.Y., Levine, A., Kandel, D.B., Yin, D., Colnaghi, L., Drisaldi, B., Kandel, E.R., 2014. D1/D5 receptors and histone deacetylation mediate the gateway effect of LTP in hippocampal dentate gyrus. Learn. Mem. 21, 153–160.

Hunt, D.L., Puente, N., Grandes, P., Castillo, P.E., 2013. Bidirectional NMDA receptor plasticity controls CA3 output and heterosynaptic metaplasticity. Nat. Neurosci. 16, 1049–1059.

Hyman, S.E., Malenka, R.C., Nestler, E.J., 2006. Neural mechanisms of addiction: the role of reward-related learning and memory. Annu. Rev. Neurosci. 29, 565–598.

Ieraci, A., Herrera, D.G., 2007. Single alcohol exposure in early life damages hippocampal stem/progenitor cells and reduces adult neurogenesis. Neurobiol. Dis. 26, 597–605.

Ihunwo, A.O., Tembo, L.H., Dzamalala, C., 2016. The dynamics of adult neurogenesis in human hippocampus. Neural Regen. Res. 11, 1869–1883.

Ingle, K.G., Weingartner, H.J., 1995. Cognitive deficits in alcoholism: approaches to theoretical modeling. Alcohol Health Res. World 19, 155–158.

Ito, Y., Tabata, K., Makimura, M., Fukuda, H., 2001. Acute and chronic intracerebroventricular morphine infusions affect long-term potentiation differently in the lateral perforant path. Pharmacol. Biochem. Behav. 70, 353–358.

Itzhak, Y., Liddie, S., Anderson, K.L., 2013. Sodium butyrate-induced histone acetylation strengthens the expression of cocaine-associated contextual memory. Neurobiol. Learn. Mem. 102, 34–42.

Izumi, Y., Nagashima, K., Murayama, K., Zorumski, C.F., 2005. Acute effects of ethanol on hippocampal long-term potentiation and long-term depression are mediated by different mechanisms. Neuroscience 136, 509–517.

Jedlicka, P., Vnencak, M., Krueger, D.D., Jungenitz, T., Brose, N., Schwarzacher, S.W., 2015. Neuroligin-1 regulates excitatory synaptic transmission, LTP and EPSP-spike coupling in the dentate gyrus in vivo. Brain Struct. Funct. 220, 47–58.

Jones, B.P., Moskowitz, H.R., Butters, N., Glosser, G., 1975. Psychophysical scaling of olfactory, visual, and auditory stimuli by alcoholic Korsakoff patients. Neuropsychologia 13, 387–393.

Jones, E.G., 1994. The neuron doctrine 1891. J. Hist. Neurosci. 3, 3–20.

Kameyama, K., Lee, H.K., Bear, M.F., Huganir, R.L., 1998. Involvement of a postsynaptic protein kinase: A substrate in the expression of homosynaptic long-term depression. Neuron 21, 1163–1175.

Kandel, E.R., Tauc, L., 1965. Mechanism of heterosynaptic facilitation in the giant cell of the abdominal ganglion of Aplysia depilans. J. Physiol. 181, 28–47.

Kauer, J.A., Malenka, R.C., Nicoll, R.A., 1988. NMDA application potentiates synaptic transmission in the hippocampus. Nature 334, 250–252.

Keller, E., Cummins, J.T., von Hungen, K., 1983. Regional effects of ethanol on glutamate levels, uptake and release in slice and synaptosome preparations from rat brain. Subst. Alcohol Actions Misuse 4, 383–392.

Kelley, A.E., 2004. Memory and addiction: shared neural circuitry and molecular mechanisms. Neuron 44, 161–179.

Kelley, B.J., Yeager, K.R., Pepper, T.H., Beversdorf, D.Q., 2005. Cognitive impairment in acute cocaine withdrawal. Cognit. Behav. Neurol. 18, 108–112.

Kempermann, G., Gage, F.H., Aigner, L., Song, H., Curtis, M.A., Thuret, S., Kuhn, H.G., Jessberger, S., Frankland, P.W., Cameron, H.A., Gould, E., Hen, R., Abrous, D.N., Toni, N., Schinder, A.F., Zhao, X., Lucassen, P.J., Frisén, J., 2018. Human adult neurogenesis: evidence and remaining questions. Cell Stem Cell 23, 25–30.

Kempermann, G., Song, H., Gage, F.H., 2015. Neurogenesis in the adult Hippocampus. Cold Spring Harbor Perspect. Biol. 7, a018812.

Kerr, K.M., Agster, K.L., Furtak, S.C., Burwell, R.D., 2007. Functional neuroanatomy of the parahippocampal region: the lateral and medial entorhinal areas. Hippocampus 17, 697–708.

Kerstetter, K.A., Ballis, M.A., Duffin-Lutgen, S., Carr, A.E., Behrens, A.M., Kippin, T.E., 2012. Sex differences in selecting between food and cocaine reinforcement are mediated by estrogen. Neuropsychopharmacology 37, 2605–2614.

Kheirbek, M.A., Tannenholz, L., Hen, R., 2012. NR2B-dependent plasticity of adult-born granule cells is necessary for context discrimination. J. Neurosci. 32, 8696–8702.

Kilts, C.D., Schweitzer, J.B., Quinn, C.K., Gross, R.E., Faber, T.L., Muhammad, F., Ely, T.D., Hoffman, J.M., Drexler, K.P., 2001. Neural activity related to drug craving in cocaine addiction. Arch. Gen. Psychiatr. 58, 334–341.

Kirkwood, A., Bear, M.F., 1994. Homosynaptic long-term depression in the visual cortex. J. Neurosci. 14, 3404–3412.

Kiss, J., Csáki, A., Bokor, H., Shanabrough, M., Leranth, C., 2000. The supramammillo-hippocampal and supramammillo-septal glutamatergic/aspartatergic projections in the rat: a combined [3H]D-aspartate autoradiographic and immunohistochemical study. Neuroscience 97, 657–669.

Kitamura, T., Saitoh, Y., Takashima, N., Murayama, A., Niibori, Y., Ageta, H., Sekiguchi, M., Sugiyama, H., Inokuchi, K., 2009. Adult neurogenesis modulates the hippocampus-dependent period of associative fear memory. Cell 139, 814–827.

Klausberger, T., Somogyi, P., 2008. Neuronal diversity and temporal dynamics: the unity of hippocampal circuit operations. Science 321, 53–57.

Klisz, D.K., Parsons, O.A., 1977. Hypothesis testing in younger and older alcoholics. J. Stud. Alcohol 38, 1718–1729.

Köhler, C., 1985. Intrinsic projections of the retrohippocampal region in the rat brain. I. The subicular complex. J. Comp. Neurol. 236, 504–522.

Kohr, G., Jensen, V., Koester, H.J., Mihaljevic, A.L., Utvik, J.K., Kvello, A., Ottersen, O.P., Seeburg, P.H., Sprengel, R., Hvalby, O., 2003. Intracellular domains of NMDA receptor subtypes are determinants for long-term potentiation induction. J. Neurosci. 23, 10791–10799.

Koob, G.F., Sanna, P.P., Bloom, F.E., 1998. Neuroscience of addiction. Neuron 21, 467–476.

Koob, G.F., Volkow, N.D., 2010. Neurocircuitry of addiction. Neuropsychopharmacology 35, 217–238.

Koob, G.F., Volkow, N.D., 2016. Neurobiology of addiction: a neurocircuitry analysis. Lancet Psychiatr. 3, 760–773.

Kramer, J., Dick, D.M., King, A., Ray, L.A., Sher, K.J., Vena, A., Vendruscolo, L.F., Acion, L., 2020. Mechanisms of alcohol addiction: bridging human and animal studies. Alcohol Alcohol 55, 603–607.

Krishnan-Sarin, S., O'Malley, S.S., Franco, N., Cavallo, D.A., Morean, M., Shi, J., Pittman, B., Krystal, J.H., 2015. N-methyl-D-aspartate receptor antagonism has differential effects on alcohol craving and drinking in heavy drinkers. Alcohol Clin. Exp. Res. 39, 300–307.

Krueger, D.D., Tuffy, L.P., Papadopoulos, T., Brose, N., 2012. The role of neurexins and neuroligins in the formation, maturation, and function of vertebrate synapses. Curr. Opin. Neurobiol. 22, 412–422.

Kyzar, E.J., Floreani, C., Teppen, T.L., Pandey, S.C., 2016. Adolescent alcohol exposure: burden of epigenetic reprogramming, synaptic remodeling, and adult psychopathology. Front. Neurosci. 10, 222.

Lacar, B., Linker, S.B., Jaeger, B.N., Krishnaswami, S., Barron, J., Kelder, M., Parylak, S., Paquola, A., Venepally, P., Novotny, M., O'Connor, C., Fitzpatrick, C., Erwin, J., Hsu, J.Y., Husband, D., McConnell, M.J., Lasken, R., Gage, F.H., 2016. Nuclear RNA-seq of single neurons reveals molecular signatures of activation. Nat. Commun. 7, 11022.

Lasseter, H.C., Xie, X., Ramirez, D.R., Fuchs, R.A., 2010. Sub-region specific contribution of the ventral hippocampus to drug context-induced reinstatement of cocaine-seeking behavior in rats. Neuroscience 171, 830–839.

Le Maître, T.W., Dhanabalan, G., Bogdanovic, N., Alkass, K., Druid, H., 2018. Effects of alcohol abuse on proliferating cells, stem/progenitor cells, and immature neurons in the adult human Hippocampus. Neuropsychopharmacology 43, 690–699.

Lee, H.K., Kameyama, K., Huganir, R.L., Bear, M.F., 1998. NMDA induces long-term synaptic depression and dephosphorylation of the GluR1 subunit of AMPA receptors in hippocampus. Neuron 21, 1151–1162.

Lenoir, M., Serre, F., Cantin, L., Ahmed, S.H., 2007. Intense sweetness surpasses cocaine reward. PLoS One 2, e698.

Lepousez, G., Nissant, A., Lledo, P.M., 2015. Adult neurogenesis and the future of the rejuvenating brain circuits. Neuron 86, 387–401.

Lepousez, G., Valley, M.T., Lledo, P.M., 2013. The impact of adult neurogenesis on olfactory bulb circuits and computations. Annu. Rev. Physiol. 75, 339–363.

Letzkus, J.J., Kampa, B.M., Stuart, G.J., 2006. Learning rules for spike timing-dependent plasticity depend on dendritic synapse location. J. Neurosci. 26, 10420–10429.

Lisman, J., 1989. A mechanism for the Hebb and the anti-Hebb processes underlying learning and memory. Proc. Natl. Acad. Sci. U. S. A. 86, 9574–9578.

Lisman, J.E., Grace, A.A., 2005. The hippocampal-VTA loop: controlling the entry of information into long-term memory. Neuron 46, 703–713.

Liu, L., Wong, T.P., Pozza, M.F., Lingenhoehl, K., Wang, Y., Sheng, M., Auberson, Y.P., Wang, Y.T., 2004. Role of NMDA receptor subtypes in governing the direction of hippocampal synaptic plasticity. Science 304, 1021–1024.

Liu, X., Weiss, F., 2002. Additive effect of stress and drug cues on reinstatement of ethanol seeking: exacerbation by history of dependence and role of concurrent activation of corticotropin-releasing factor and opioid mechanisms. J. Neurosci. 22, 7856–7861.

Liu, X., Weiss, F., 2003. Stimulus conditioned to foot-shock stress reinstates alcohol-seeking behavior in an animal model of relapse. Psychopharmacology (Berl) 168, 184–191.

Lomo, T., 2003. The discovery of long-term potentiation. Philos. Trans. R. Soc. Lond. B Biol. Sci. 358, 617–620.

London, E.D., Cascella, N.G., Wong, D.F., Phillips, R.L., Dannals, R.F., Links, J.M., Herning, R., Grayson, R., Jaffe, J.H., Wagner Jr., H.N., 1990. Cocaine-induced reduction of glucose utilization in human brain. A study using positron emission tomography and [fluorine 18]-fluorodeoxyglucose. Arch. Gen. Psychiatr. 47, 567–574.

Lopez, M.F., Becker, H.C., 2005. Effect of pattern and number of chronic ethanol exposures on subsequent voluntary ethanol intake in C57BL/6J mice. Psychopharmacology (Berl) 181, 688–696.

Loughlin, S.E., Foote, S.L., Grzanna, R., 1986. Efferent projections of nucleus locus coeruleus: morphologic subpopulations have different efferent targets. Neuroscience 18, 307–319.

Lovinger, D.M., White, G., Weight, F.F., 1989. Ethanol inhibits NMDA-activated ion current in hippocampal neurons. Science 243, 1721–1724.

Lukoyanov, N.V., Madeira, M.D., Paula-Barbosa, M.M., 1999. Behavioral and neuroanatomical consequences of chronic ethanol intake and withdrawal. Physiol. Behav. 66, 337–346.

Luo, A.H., Tahsili-Fahadan, P., Wise, R.A., Lupica, C.R., Aston-Jones, G., 2011. Linking context with reward: a functional circuit from hippocampal CA3 to ventral tegmental area. Science 333, 353–357.

Lutzu, S., Castillo, P.E., 2021. Modulation of NMDA receptors by G-protein-coupled receptors: role in synaptic transmission, plasticity and beyond. Neuroscience 456, 27–42. https://doi.org/10.1016/j.neuroscience.2020.02.019. 32105741.

Lynch, G., Larson, J., Kelso, S., Barrionuevo, G., Schottler, F., 1983. Intracellular injections of EGTA block induction of hippocampal long-term potentiation. Nature 305, 719–721.

Lynch, G.S., Dunwiddie, T., Gribkoff, V., 1977. Heterosynaptic depression: a postsynaptic correlate of long-term potentiation. Nature 266, 737–739.

Lynch, M.A., 2004. Long-term potentiation and memory. Physiol. Rev. 84, 87–136.

Ma, L., Steinberg, J.L., Cunningham, K.A., Bjork, J.M., Lane, S.D., Schmitz, J.M., Burroughs, T., Narayana, P.A., Kosten, T.R., Bechara, A., Moeller, F.G., 2018. Altered anterior cingulate cortex to hippocampus effective connectivity in response to drug cues in men with cocaine use disorder. Psychiatry Res. Neuroimaging. 271, 59–66.

Macey, D.J., Schulteis, G., Heinrichs, S.C., Koob, G.F., 1996. Time-dependent quantifiable withdrawal from ethanol in the rat: effect of method of dependence induction. Alcohol 13, 163–170.

Maglóczky, Z., Acsády, L., Freund, T.F., 1994. Principal cells are the postsynaptic targets of supramammillary afferents in the hippocampus of the rat. Hippocampus 4, 322–334.

Mahar, I., Bambico, F.R., Mechawar, N., Nobrega, J.N., 2014. Stress, serotonin, and hippocampal neurogenesis in relation to depression and antidepressant effects. Neurosci. Biobehav. Rev. 38, 173–192.

Majchrowicz, E., 1975. Induction of physical dependence upon ethanol and the associated behavioral changes in rats. Psychopharmacologia 43, 245–254.

Malenka, R.C., Bear, M.F., 2004. LTP and LTD: an embarrassment of riches. Neuron 44, 5–21.

Malenka, R.C., Kauer, J.A., Zucker, R.S., Nicoll, R.A., 1988. Postsynaptic calcium is sufficient for potentiation of hippocampal synaptic transmission. Science 242, 81–84.

Malenka, R.C., Nicoll, R.A., 1999. Long-term potentiation—a decade of progress? Science 285, 1870–1874.

Maler, J.M., Esselmann, H., Wiltfang, J., Kunz, N., Lewczuk, P., Reulbach, U., Bleich, S., Rüther, E., Kornhuber, J., 2005. Memantine inhibits ethanol-induced NMDA receptor up-regulation in rat hippocampal neurons. Brain Res. 1052, 156–162.

Malinow, R., Schulman, H., Tsien, R.W., 1989. Inhibition of postsynaptic PKC or CaMKII blocks induction but not expression of LTP. Science 245, 862–866.

Mandyam, C.D., Koob, G.F., 2012. The addicted brain craves new neurons: putative role for adult-born progenitors in promoting recovery. Trends Neurosci. 35, 250–260.

Mandyam, C.D., Wee, S., Crawford, E.F., Eisch, A.J., Richardson, H.N., Koob, G.F., 2008. Varied access to intravenous methamphetamine self-administration differentially alters adult hippocampal neurogenesis. Biol. Psychiatr. 64, 958–965.

Marinelli, P.W., Funk, D., Juzytsch, W., Lê, A.D., 2010. Opioid receptors in the basolateral amygdala but not dorsal hippocampus mediate context-induced alcohol seeking. Behav. Brain Res. 211, 58–63.

Marinelli, P.W., Funk, D., Juzytsch, W., Li, Z., Lê, A.D., 2007. Effects of opioid receptor blockade on the renewal of alcohol seeking induced by context: relationship to c-fos mRNA expression. Eur. J. Neurosci. 26, 2815–2823.

Markram, H., Gerstner, W., Sjostrom, P.J., 2011. A history of spike-timing-dependent plasticity. Front. Synaptic Neurosci. 3, 4.

Markram, H., Gerstner, W., Sjostrom, P.J., 2012. Spike-timing-dependent plasticity: a comprehensive overview. Front. Synaptic Neurosci. 4, 2.

Markwiese, B.J., Acheson, S.K., Levin, E.D., Wilson, W.A., Swartzwelder, H.S., 1998. Differential effects of ethanol on memory in adolescent and adult rats. Alcohol Clin. Exp. Res. 22, 416–421.

Marszalek-Grabska, M., Smaga, I., Surowka, P., Grochecki, P., Slowik, T., Filip, M., Kotlinska, J.H., 2021. Memantine prevents the WIN 55,212-2 evoked cross-priming of ethanol-induced conditioned place preference (CPP). Int. J. Mol. Sci. 22.

Martens, U., Wree, A., 2001. Distribution of [3H]MK-801, [3H]AMPA and [3H]Kainate binding sites in rat hippocampal long-term slice cultures isolated from external afferents. Anat. Embryol. 203, 491–500.

Martin, D., Tayyeb, M.I., Swartzwelder, H.S., 1995. Ethanol inhibition of AMPA and kainate receptor-mediated depolarizations of hippocampal area CA1. Alcohol Clin. Exp. Res. 19, 1312–1316.

Martinez Jr., J.L., Derrick, B.E., 1996. Long-term potentiation and learning. Annu. Rev. Psychol. 47, 173–203.

Massa, F., Koehl, M., Wiesner, T., Grosjean, N., Revest, J.M., Piazza, P.V., Abrous, D.N., Oliet, S.H., 2011. Conditional reduction of adult neurogenesis impairs bidirectional hippocampal synaptic plasticity. Proc. Natl. Acad. Sci. U. S. A. 108, 6644–6649.

Matsuzaki, M., Honkura, N., Ellis-Davies, G.C., Kasai, H., 2004. Structural basis of long-term potentiation in single dendritic spines. Nature 429, 761–766.

Matthews, D.B., Simson, P.E., Best, P.J., 1995. Acute ethanol impairs spatial memory but not stimulus/response memory in the rat. Alcohol Clin. Exp. Res. 19, 902–909.

McGlinchey, E.M., Aston-Jones, G., 2018. Dorsal Hippocampus drives context-induced cocaine seeking via inputs to lateral septum. Neuropsychopharmacology 43, 987–1000.

McMullen, P.A., Saint-Cyr, J.A., Carlen, P.L., 1984. Morphological alterations in rat CA1 hippocampal pyramidal cell dendrites resulting from chronic ethanol consumption and withdrawal. J. Comp. Neurol. 225, 111–118.

McNamara, C.G., Tejero-Cantero, Á., Trouche, S., Campo-Urriza, N., Dupret, D., 2014. Dopaminergic neurons promote hippocampal reactivation and spatial memory persistence. Nat. Neurosci. 17, 1658–1660.

McNaughton, B.L., Barnes, C.A., Gerrard, J.L., Gothard, K., Jung, M.W., Knierim, J.J., Kudrimoti, H., Qin, Y., Skaggs, W.E., Suster, M., Weaver, K.L., 1996. Deciphering the hippocampal polyglot: the hippocampus as a path integration system. J. Exp. Biol. 199, 173–185.

Melia, K.R., Ryabinin, A.E., Corodimas, K.P., Wilson, M.C., Ledoux, J.E., 1996. Hippocampal-dependent learning and experience-dependent activation of the hippocampus are preferentially disrupted by ethanol. Neuroscience 74, 313–322.

Mellor, J., Nicoll, R.A., 2001. Hippocampal mossy fiber LTP is independent of postsynaptic calcium. Nat. Neurosci. 4, 125–126.

Mellor, J., Nicoll, R.A., Schmitz, D., 2002. Mediation of hippocampal mossy fiber long-term potentiation by presynaptic Ih channels. Science 295, 143–147.

Mendez, I.A., Montgomery, K.S., LaSarge, C.L., Simon, N.W., Bizon, J.L., Setlow, B., 2008. Long-term effects of prior cocaine exposure on Morris water maze performance. Neurobiol. Learn. Mem. 89, 185–191.

Meyers, R.A., Zavala, A.R., Neisewander, J.L., 2003. Dorsal, but not ventral, hippocampal lesions disrupt cocaine place conditioning. Neuroreport 14, 2127–2131.

Meyers, R.A., Zavala, A.R., Speer, C.M., Neisewander, J.L., 2006. Dorsal hippocampus inhibition disrupts acquisition and expression, but not consolidation, of cocaine conditioned place preference. Behav. Neurosci. 120, 401–412.

Miki, T., Kuma, H., Yokoyama, T., Sumitani, K., Matsumoto, Y., Kusaka, T., Warita, K., Wang, Z.Y., Hosomi, N., Imagawa, T., K, S.B., Itoh, S., Nakamura, Y., Takeuchi, Y., 2008. Early postnatal ethanol exposure induces fluctuation in the expression of BDNF mRNA in the developing rat hippocampus. Acta Neurobiol. Exp. 68, 484–493.

Min, M.Y., Asztely, F., Kokaia, M., Kullmann, D.M., 1998. Long-term potentiation and dual-component quantal signaling in the dentate gyrus. Proc. Natl. Acad. Sci. U. S. A. 95, 4702–4707.

Ming, G.L., Song, H., 2011. Adult neurogenesis in the mammalian brain: significant answers and significant questions. Neuron 70, 687–702.

Mittenberg, W., Motta, S., 1993. Effects of chronic cocaine abuse on memory and learning. Arch. Clin. Neuropsychol. 8, 477–483.

Moore, D.B., Madorsky, I., Paiva, M., Barrow Heaton, M., 2004. Ethanol exposure alters neurotrophin receptor expression in the rat central nervous system: effects of neonatal exposure. J. Neurobiol. 60, 114–126.

Moreno-Jiménez, E.P., Terreros-Roncal, J., Flor-García, M., Rábano, A., Llorens-Martín, M., 2021. Evidences for adult hippocampal neurogenesis in humans. J. Neurosci. 41, 2541–2553.

Morishita, W., Lu, W., Smith, G.B., Nicoll, R.A., Bear, M.F., Malenka, R.C., 2007. Activation of NR2B-containing NMDA receptors is not required for NMDA receptor-dependent long-term depression. Neuropharmacology 52, 71–76.

Mulholland, P.J., Harris, B.R., Wilkins, L.H., Self, R.L., Blanchard, J.A., Holley, R.C., Littleton, J.M., Prendergast, M.A., 2003. Opposing effects of ethanol and nicotine on hippocampal calbindin-D28k expression. Alcohol 31, 1–10.

Mulkey, R.M., Malenka, R.C., 1992. Mechanisms underlying induction of homosynaptic long-term depression in area CA1 of the hippocampus. Neuron 9, 967–975.

Müller, C., Remy, S., 2018. Septo-hippocampal interaction. Cell Tissue Res. 373, 565–575.

Nagerl, U.V., Eberhorn, N., Cambridge, S.B., Bonhoeffer, T., 2004. Bidirectional activity-dependent morphological plasticity in hippocampal neurons. Neuron 44, 759–767.

Nakashiba, T., Young, J.Z., McHugh, T.J., Buhl, D.L., Tonegawa, S., 2008. Transgenic inhibition of synaptic transmission reveals role of CA3 output in hippocampal learning. Science 319, 1260–1264.

Nakazawa, T., Komai, S., Tezuka, T., Hisatsune, C., Umemori, H., Semba, K., Mishina, M., Manabe, T., Yamamoto, T., 2001. Characterization of Fyn-mediated tyrosine phosphorylation sites on GluR epsilon 2 (NR2B) subunit of the N-methyl-D-aspartate receptor. J. Biol. Chem. 276, 693–699.

Nakazawa, T., Komai, S., Watabe, A.M., Kiyama, Y., Fukaya, M., Arima-Yoshida, F., Horai, R., Sudo, K., Ebine, K., Delawary, M., Goto, J., Umemori, H., Tezuka, T., Iwakura, Y., Watanabe, M., Yamamoto, T., Manabe, T., 2006. NR2B tyrosine phosphorylation modulates fear learning as well as amygdaloid synaptic plasticity. EMBO J. 25, 2867–2877.

Nawarawong, N.N., Nickell, C.G., Hopkins, D.M., Pauly, J.R., Nixon, K., 2021. Functional activation of newborn neurons following alcohol-induced reactive neurogenesis. Brain Sci. 11.

Nelson, T.E., Ur, C.L., Gruol, D.L., 2005. Chronic intermittent ethanol exposure enhances NMDA-receptor-mediated synaptic responses and NMDA receptor expression in hippocampal CA1 region. Brain Res. 1048, 69–79.

Nicoll, R.A., Malenka, R.C., 1995. Contrasting properties of two forms of long-term potentiation in the hippocampus. Nature 377, 115–118.

Niibori, Y., Yu, T.S., Epp, J.R., Akers, K.G., Josselyn, S.A., Frankland, P.W., 2012. Suppression of adult neurogenesis impairs population coding of similar contexts in hippocampal CA3 region. Nat. Commun. 3, 1253.

Nixon, K., 2006. Alcohol and adult neurogenesis: roles in neurodegeneration and recovery in chronic alcoholism. Hippocampus 16, 287–295.

Nixon, K., Crews, F.T., 2002. Binge ethanol exposure decreases neurogenesis in adult rat hippocampus. J. Neurochem. 83, 1087–1093.

Nixon, K., Crews, F.T., 2004. Temporally specific burst in cell proliferation increases hippocampal neurogenesis in protracted abstinence from alcohol. J. Neurosci. 24, 9714–9722.

Nixon, K., Kim, D.H., Potts, E.N., He, J., Crews, F.T., 2008. Distinct cell proliferation events during abstinence after alcohol dependence: microglia proliferation precedes neurogenesis. Neurobiol. Dis. 31, 218–229.

Noonan, M.A., Bulin, S.E., Fuller, D.C., Eisch, A.J., 2010. Reduction of adult hippocampal neurogenesis confers vulnerability in an animal model of cocaine addiction. J. Neurosci. 30, 304–315.

Noonan, M.A., Choi, K.H., Self, D.W., Eisch, A.J., 2008. Withdrawal from cocaine self-administration normalizes deficits in proliferation and enhances maturity of adult-generated hippocampal neurons. J. Neurosci. 28, 2516–2526.

North, A., Swant, J., Salvatore, M.F., Gamble-George, J., Prins, P., Butler, B., Mittal, M.K., Heltsley, R., Clark, J.T., Khoshbouei, H., 2013. Chronic methamphetamine exposure produces a delayed, long-lasting memory deficit. Synapse 67, 245–257.

O'Dell, L.E., Roberts, A.J., Smith, R.T., Koob, G.F., 2004. Enhanced alcohol self-administration after intermittent versus continuous alcohol vapor exposure. Alcohol Clin. Exp. Res. 28, 1676–1682.

O'Keefe, J., Dostrovsky, J., 1971. The hippocampus as a spatial map. Preliminary evidence from unit activity in the freely-moving rat. Brain Res. 34, 171–175.

Opendak, M., Offit, L., Monari, P., Schoenfeld, T.J., Sonti, A.N., Cameron, H.A., Gould, E., 2016. Lasting adaptations in social behavior produced by social disruption and inhibition of adult neurogenesis. J. Neurosci. 36, 7027–7038.

Pang, K.K.L., Sharma, M., Krishna, K.K., Behnisch, T., Sajikumar, S., 2019. Long-term population spike-timing-dependent plasticity promotes synaptic tagging but not cross-tagging in rat hippocampal area CA1. Proc. Natl. Acad. Sci. U. S. A. 116, 5737–5746.

Papadopoulos, T., Korte, M., Eulenburg, V., Kubota, H., Retiounskaia, M., Harvey, R.J., Harvey, K., O'Sullivan, G.A., Laube, B., Hulsmann, S., Geiger, J.R., Betz, H., 2007. Impaired GABAergic transmission and altered hippocampal synaptic plasticity in collybistin-deficient mice. EMBO J. 26, 3888–3899.

Papadopoulos, T., Soykan, T., 2011. The role of collybistin in gephyrin clustering at inhibitory synapses: facts and open questions. Front. Cell. Neurosci. 5, 11.

Pelkey, K.A., Chittajallu, R., Craig, M.T., Tricoire, L., Wester, J.C., McBain, C.J., 2017. Hippocampal GABAergic inhibitory interneurons. Physiol. Rev. 97, 1619–1747.

Penasco, S., Rico-Barrio, I., Puente, N., Gomez-Urquijo, S.M., Fontaine, C.J., Egana-Huguet, J., Achicallende, S., Ramos, A., Reguero, L., Elezgarai, I., Nahirney, P.C., Christie, B.R., Grandes, P., 2019. Endocannabinoid long-term depression revealed at medial perforant path excitatory synapses in the dentate gyrus. Neuropharmacology 153, 32–40.

Perez, M.F., Gabach, L.A., Almiron, R.S., Carlini, V.P., De Barioglio, S.R., Ramirez, O.A., 2010. Different chronic cocaine administration protocols induce changes on dentate gyrus plasticity and hippocampal dependent behavior. Synapse 64, 742–753.

Perry, A.N., Westenbroek, C., Becker, J.B., 2013. The development of a preference for cocaine over food identifies individual rats with addiction-like behaviors. PLoS One 8, e79465.

Phillips, R.G., LeDoux, J.E., 1992. Differential contribution of amygdala and hippocampus to cued and contextual fear conditioning. Behav. Neurosci. 106, 274–285.

Pian, J.P., Criado, J.R., Milner, R., Ehlers, C.L., 2010. N-methyl-D-aspartate receptor subunit expression in adult and adolescent brain following chronic ethanol exposure. Neuroscience 170, 645–654.

Pierce, R.C., Kalivas, P.W., 1997. A circuitry model of the expression of behavioral sensitization to amphetamine-like psychostimulants. Brain Res. Brain Res. Rev. 25, 192–216.

Piskorowski, R.A., Chevaleyre, V., 2012. Synaptic integration by different dendritic compartments of hippocampal CA1 and CA2 pyramidal neurons. Cell. Mol. Life Sci. 69, 75–88.

Pitkänen, A., Pikkarainen, M., Nurminen, N., Ylinen, A., 2000. Reciprocal connections between the amygdala and the hippocampal formation, perirhinal cortex, and postrhinal cortex in rat. A review. Ann. N. Y. Acad. Sci. 911, 369–391.

Powrozek, T.A., Sari, Y., Singh, R.P., Zhou, F.C., 2004. Neurotransmitters and substances of abuse: effects on adult neurogenesis. Curr. Neurovascular Res. 1, 251–260.

Prendergast, M.A., Harris, B.R., Mullholland, P.J., Blanchard 2nd, J.A., Gibson, D.A., Holley, R.C., Littleton, J.M., 2004. Hippocampal CA1 region neurodegeneration produced by ethanol withdrawal requires activation of intrinsic polysynaptic hippocampal pathways and function of N-methyl-D-aspartate receptors. Neuroscience 124, 869–877.

Prior, P.L., Galduroz, J.C., 2011. Glutamatergic hyperfunctioning during alcohol withdrawal syndrome: therapeutic perspective with zinc and magnesium. Med. Hypotheses 77, 368–370.

Pu, L., Bao, G.B., Xu, N.J., Ma, L., Pei, G., 2002. Hippocampal long-term potentiation is reduced by chronic opiate treatment and can be restored by re-exposure to opiates. J. Neurosci. 22, 1914–1921.

Qi, S., Tan, S.M., Wang, R., Higginbotham, J.A., Ritchie, J.L., Ibarra, C.K., Arguello, A.A., Christian, R.J., Fuchs, R.A., 2022. Optogenetic inhibition of the dorsal hippocampus CA3 region during early-stage cocaine-memory reconsolidation disrupts subsequent context-induced cocaine seeking in rats. Neuropsychopharmacology 47, 1473–1483.

Rajendran, P., Spear, L.P., 2004. The effects of ethanol on spatial and nonspatial memory in adolescent and adult rats studied using an appetitive paradigm. Ann. N. Y. Acad. Sci. 1021, 441–444.

Ramirez, D.R., Bell, G.H., Lasseter, H.C., Xie, X., Traina, S.A., Fuchs, R.A., 2009. Dorsal hippocampal regulation of memory reconsolidation processes that facilitate drug context-induced cocaine-seeking behavior in rats. Eur. J. Neurosci. 30, 901–912.

Ramon y Cajal, S., 1928. Degeneration and Regeneration of the Nervous System. Hafner, New York.

Recinto, P., Samant, A.R., Chavez, G., Kim, A., Yuan, C.J., Soleiman, M., Grant, Y., Edwards, S., Wee, S., Koob, G.F., George, O., Mandyam, C.D., 2012. Levels of neural progenitors in the hippocampus predict memory impairment and relapse to drug seeking as a function of excessive methamphetamine self-administration. Neuropsychopharmacology 37, 1275–1287.

Reynolds, J.N., Prasad, A., MacDonald, J.F., 1992. Ethanol modulation of GABA receptor-activated Cl-currents in neurons of the chick, rat and mouse central nervous system. Eur. J. Pharmacol. 224, 173–181.

Rice, A.C., Bullock, M.R., Shelton, K.L., 2004. Chronic ethanol consumption transiently reduces adult neural progenitor cell proliferation. Brain Res. 1011, 94–98.

Richardson, H.N., Chan, S.H., Crawford, E.F., Lee, Y.K., Funk, C.K., Koob, G.F., Mandyam, C.D., 2009. Permanent impairment of birth and survival of cortical and hippocampal proliferating cells following excessive drinking during alcohol dependence. Neurobiol. Dis. 36, 1–10.

Richardson, N.R., Roberts, D.C., 1996. Progressive ratio schedules in drug self-administration studies in rats: a method to evaluate reinforcing efficacy. J. Neurosci. Methods 66, 1–11.

Riedel, G., Davies, S.N., 2005. Cannabinoid function in learning, memory and plasticity. Handb. Exp. Pharmacol. 445–477.

Roberto, M., Nelson, T.E., Ur, C.L., Brunelli, M., Sanna, P.P., Gruol, D.L., 2003. The transient depression of hippocampal CA1 LTP induced by chronic intermittent ethanol exposure is associated with an inhibition of the MAP kinase pathway. Eur. J. Neurosci. 17, 1646–1654.

Roberto, M., Nelson, T.E., Ur, C.L., Gruol, D.L., 2002. Long-term potentiation in the rat hippocampus is reversibly depressed by chronic intermittent ethanol exposure. J. Neurophysiol. 87, 2385–2397.

Robinson, T.E., Berridge, K.C., 2000. The psychology and neurobiology of addiction: an incentive-sensitization view. Addiction 95 (Suppl. 2), S91–S117.

Rogers, J.L., See, R.E., 2007. Selective inactivation of the ventral hippocampus attenuates cue-induced and cocaine-primed reinstatement of drug-seeking in rats. Neurobiol. Learn. Mem. 87, 688–692.

Rolls, E.T., 2015. Diluted connectivity in pattern association networks facilitates the recall of information from the hippocampus to the neocortex. Prog. Brain Res. 219, 21–43.

Salmanzadeh, F., Fathollahi, Y., Semnanian, S., Shafizadeh, M., 2003. Dependence on morphine impairs the induction of long-term potentiation in the CA1 region of rat hippocampal slices. Brain Res. 965, 108–113.

Sanchis-Segura, C., Borchardt, T., Vengeliene, V., Zghoul, T., Bachteler, D., Gass, P., Sprengel, R., Spanagel, R., 2006. Involvement of the AMPA receptor GluR-C subunit in alcohol-seeking behavior and relapse. J. Neurosci. 26, 1231–1238.

Sanna, E., Serra, M., Cossu, A., Colombo, G., Follesa, P., Cuccheddu, T., Concas, A., Biggio, G., 1993. Chronic ethanol intoxication induces differential effects on GABAA and NMDA receptor function in the rat brain. Alcohol Clin. Exp. Res. 17, 115–123.

Sanna, P.P., Simpson, C., Lutjens, R., Koob, G., 2002. ERK regulation in chronic ethanol exposure and withdrawal. Brain Res. 948, 186–191.

Santucci, A.C., 2008. Adolescent cocaine residually impairs working memory and enhances fear memory in rats. Exp. Clin. Psychopharmacol 16, 77–85.

Santucci, A.C., Capodilupo, S., Bernstein, J., Gomez-Ramirez, M., Milefsky, R., Mitchell, H., 2004. Cocaine in adolescent rats produces residual memory impairments that are reversible with time. Neurotoxicol. Teratol. 26, 651–661.

Saxe, M.D., Battaglia, F., Wang, J.W., Malleret, G., David, D.J., Monckton, J.E., Garcia, A.D., Sofroniew, M.V., Kandel, E.R., Santarelli, L., Hen, R., Drew, M.R., 2006. Ablation of hippocampal neurogenesis impairs contextual fear conditioning and synaptic plasticity in the dentate gyrus. Proc. Natl. Acad. Sci. U. S. A. 103, 17501–17506.

Schluter, O.M., Schnell, E., Verhage, M., Tzonopoulos, T., Nicoll, R.A., Janz, R., Malenka, R.C., Geppert, M., Sudhof, T.C., 1999. Rabphilin knock-out mice reveal that rabphilin is not required for rab3 function in regulating neurotransmitter release. J. Neurosci. 19, 5834–5846.

Schummers, J., Browning, M.D., 2001. Evidence for a role for GABA(A) and NMDA receptors in ethanol inhibition of long-term potentiation. Brain Res Mol Brain Res 94, 9–14.

Scoville, W.B., Milner, B., 1957. Loss of recent memory after bilateral hippocampal lesions. J. Neurol. Neurosurg. Psychiatr. 20, 11–21.

Segobin, S., Laniepce, A., Ritz, L., Lannuzel, C., Boudehent, C., Cabé, N., Urso, L., Vabret, F., Eustache, F., Beaunieux, H., Pitel, A.L., 2019. Dissociating thalamic alterations in alcohol use disorder defines specificity of Korsakoff's syndrome. Brain 142, 1458–1470.

Sheela Rani, C.S., Ticku, M.K., 2006. Comparison of chronic ethanol and chronic intermittent ethanol treatments on the expression of GABA(A) and NMDA receptor subunits. Alcohol 38, 89–97.

Sheng, M., Pak, D.T., 2000. Ligand-gated ion channel interactions with cytoskeletal and signaling proteins. Annu. Rev. Physiol. 62, 755–778.

Shimizu, K., Matsubara, K., Uezono, T., Kimura, K., Shiono, H., 1998. Reduced dorsal hippocampal glutamate release significantly correlates with the spatial memory deficits produced by benzodiazepines and ethanol. Neuroscience 83, 701–706.

Shin, J., Berg, D.A., Zhu, Y., Shin, J.Y., Song, J., Bonaguidi, M.A., Enikolopov, G., Nauen, D.W., Christian, K.M., Ming, G.L., Song, H., 2015. Single-cell RNA-seq with waterfall reveals molecular cascades underlying adult neurogenesis. Cell Stem Cell 17, 360–372.

Shipman, S.L., Nicoll, R.A., 2012. A subtype-specific function for the extracellular domain of neuroligin 1 in hippocampal LTP. Neuron 76, 309–316.

Simonyi, A., Christian, M.R., Sun, A.Y., Sun, G.Y., 2004. Chronic ethanol-induced subtype- and subregion-specific decrease in the mRNA expression of metabotropic glutamate receptors in rat hippocampus. Alcohol Clin. Exp. Res. 28, 1419–1423.

Skrede, K.K., Westgaard, R.H., 1971. The transverse hippocampal slice: a well-defined cortical structure maintained in vitro. Brain Res. 35, 589–593.

Smith, D.A., Browning, M., Dunwiddie, T.V., 1993. Cocaine inhibits hippocampal long-term potentiation. Brain Res. 608, 259–265.

Smith, M.A., Weiss, S.R., Berry, R.L., Zhang, L.X., Clark, M., Massenburg, G., Post, R.M., 1997. Amygdala-kindled seizures increase the expression of corticotropin-releasing factor (CRF) and CRF-binding protein in GABAergic interneurons of the dentate hilus. Brain Res. 745, 248–256.

Smothers, C.T., Mrotek, J.J., Lovinger, D.M., 1997. Chronic ethanol exposure leads to a selective enhancement of N-methyl-D-aspartate receptor function in cultured hippocampal neurons. J. Pharmacol. Exp. Therapeut. 283, 1214–1222.

Snell, L.D., Nunley, K.R., Lickteig, R.L., Browning, M.D., Tabakoff, B., Hoffman, P.L., 1996. Regional and subunit specific changes in NMDA receptor mRNA and immunoreactivity in mouse brain following chronic ethanol ingestion. Brain Res. Mol. Brain Res. 40, 71–78.

Snyder, J.S., Grigereit, L., Russo, A., Seib, D.R., Brewer, M., Pickel, J., Cameron, H.A., 2016. A transgenic rat for specifically inhibiting adult neurogenesis. eNeuro 3.

Snyder, J.S., Hong, N.S., McDonald, R.J., Wojtowicz, J.M., 2005. A role for adult neurogenesis in spatial long-term memory. Neuroscience 130, 843–852.

Snyder, J.S., Kee, N., Wojtowicz, J.M., 2001. Effects of adult neurogenesis on synaptic plasticity in the rat dentate gyrus. J. Neurophysiol. 85, 2423–2431.

Soltesz, I., Jones, R.S., 1995. The direct perforant path input to CA1: excitatory or inhibitory? Hippocampus 5, 101–103.

Somkuwar, S.S., Fannon, M.J., Staples, M.C., Zamora-Martinez, E.R., Navarro, A.I., Kim, A., Quigley, J.A., Edwards, S., Mandyam, C.D., 2016. Alcohol dependence-induced regulation of the proliferation and survival of adult brain progenitors is associated with altered BDNF-TrkB signaling. Brain Struct. Funct. 221, 4319–4335.

Spronk, D.B., van Wel, J.H., Ramaekers, J.G., Verkes, R.J., 2013. Characterizing the cognitive effects of cocaine: a comprehensive review. Neurosci. Biobehav. Rev. 37, 1838–1859.

Spyraki, C., Fibiger, H.C., Phillips, A.G., 1982. Cocaine-induced place preference conditioning: lack of effects of neuroleptics and 6-hydroxydopamine lesions. Brain Res. 253, 195–203.

Squire, L.R., Stark, C.E., Clark, R.E., 2004. The medial temporal lobe. Annu. Rev. Neurosci. 27, 279–306.

Squire, L.R., Wixted, J.T., 2011. The cognitive neuroscience of human memory since H.M. Annu. Rev. Neurosci. 34, 259–288.

Staples, M.C., Kim, A., Mandyam, C.D., 2015. Dendritic remodeling of hippocampal neurons is associated with altered NMDA receptor expression in alcohol dependent rats. Mol. Cell. Neurosci. 65, 153–162.

Stavro, K., Pelletier, J., Potvin, S., 2013. Widespread and sustained cognitive deficits in alcoholism: a meta-analysis. Addiction Biol. 18, 203–213.

Stramiello, M., Wagner, J.J., 2010. Cocaine enhancement of long-term potentiation in the CA1 region of rat hippocampus: lamina-specific mechanisms of action. Synapse 64, 644–648.

Stuart, G.J., Sakmann, B., 1994. Active propagation of somatic action potentials into neocortical pyramidal cell dendrites. Nature 367, 69–72.

Sudai, E., Croitoru, O., Shaldubina, A., Abraham, L., Gispan, I., Flaumenhaft, Y., Roth-Deri, I., Kinor, N., Aharoni, S., Ben-Tzion, M., Yadid, G., 2011. High cocaine dosage decreases neurogenesis in the hippocampus and impairs working memory. Addiction Biol. 16, 251–260.

Sudhof, T.C., Czernik, A.J., Kao, H.T., Takei, K., Johnston, P.A., Horiuchi, A., Kanazir, S.D., Wagner, M.A., Perin, M.S., De Camilli, P., et al., 1989. Synapsins: mosaics of shared and individual domains in a family of synaptic vesicle phosphoproteins. Science 245, 1474–1480.

Suh, J., Rivest, A.J., Nakashiba, T., Tominaga, T., Tonegawa, S., 2011. Entorhinal cortex layer III input to the hippocampus is crucial for temporal association memory. Science 334, 1415–1420.

Sullivan, E.V., Fama, R., Rosenbloom, M.J., Pfefferbaum, A., 2002. A profile of neuropsychological deficits in alcoholic women. Neuropsychology 16, 74–83.

Sullivan, E.V., Marsh, L., 2003. Hippocampal volume deficits in alcoholic Korsakoff's syndrome. Neurology 61, 1716–1719.

Sullivan, E.V., Marsh, L., Mathalon, D.H., Lim, K.O., Pfefferbaum, A., 1995. Anterior hippocampal volume deficits in nonamnesic, aging chronic alcoholics. Alcohol Clin. Exp. Res. 19, 110–122.

Sullivan, E.V., Pfefferbaum, A., 2009. Neuroimaging of the wernicke-korsakoff syndrome. Alcohol Alcohol 44, 155–165.

Sullivan, E.V., Rosenbloom, M.J., Lim, K.O., Pfefferbaum, A., 2000a. Longitudinal changes in cognition, gait, and balance in abstinent and relapsed alcoholic men: relationships to changes in brain structure. Neuropsychology 14, 178–188.

Sullivan, E.V., Rosenbloom, M.J., Pfefferbaum, A., 2000b. Pattern of motor and cognitive deficits in detoxified alcoholic men. Alcohol Clin. Exp. Res. 24, 611–621.

Swanson, L.W., Mogenson, G.J., Simerly, R.B., Wu, M., 1987. Anatomical and electrophysiological evidence for a projection from the medial preoptic area to the 'mesencephalic and subthalamic locomotor regions' in the rat. Brain Res. 405, 108–122.

Swanson, L.W., Wyss, J.M., Cowan, W.M., 1978. An autoradiographic study of the organization of intrahippocampal association pathways in the rat. J. Comp. Neurol. 181, 681–715.

Sweatt, J.D., 2004. Mitogen-activated protein kinases in synaptic plasticity and memory. Curr. Opin. Neurobiol. 14, 311–317.

Taffe, M.A., Kotzebue, R.W., Crean, R.D., Crawford, E.F., Edwards, S., Mandyam, C.D., 2010. Long-lasting reduction in hippocampal neurogenesis by alcohol consumption in adolescent nonhuman primates. Proc. Natl. Acad. Sci. U. S. A. 107, 11104–11109.

Tashiro, A., Sandler, V.M., Toni, N., Zhao, C., Gage, F.H., 2006. NMDA-receptor-mediated, cell-specific integration of new neurons in adult dentate gyrus. Nature 442, 929–933.

Thomas, M.J., Kalivas, P.W., Shaham, Y., 2008. Neuroplasticity in the mesolimbic dopamine system and cocaine addiction. Br. J. Pharmacol. 154, 327–342.

Thompson, A.M., Gosnell, B.A., Wagner, J.J., 2002. Enhancement of long-term potentiation in the rat hippocampus following cocaine exposure. Neuropharmacology 42, 1039–1042.

Thompson, A.M., Swant, J., Gosnell, B.A., Wagner, J.J., 2004. Modulation of long-term potentiation in the rat hippocampus following cocaine self-administration. Neuroscience 127, 177–185.

Thompson, A.M., Swant, J., Wagner, J.J., 2005. Cocaine-induced modulation of long-term potentiation in the CA1 region of rat hippocampus. Neuropharmacology 49, 185–194.

Topple, A.N., Hunt, G.E., McGregor, I.S., 1998. Possible neural substrates of beer-craving in rats. Neurosci. Lett. 252, 99–102.

Tremwel, M.F., Hunter, B.E., 1994. Effects of chronic ethanol ingestion on long-term potentiation remain even after a prolonged recovery from ethanol exposure. Synapse 17, 141–148.

Trevisan, L., Fitzgerald, L.W., Brose, N., Gasic, G.P., Heinemann, S.F., Duman, R.S., Nestler, E.J., 1994. Chronic ingestion of ethanol up-regulates NMDAR1 receptor subunit immunoreactivity in rat hippocampus. J. Neurochem. 62, 1635–1638.

Trommer, B.L., Liu, Y.B., Pasternak, J.F., 1996. Long-term depression at the medial perforant path-granule cell synapse in developing rat dentate gyrus. Brain Res Dev Brain Res 96, 97–108.

Tropea, T.F., Kosofsky, B.E., Rajadhyaksha, A.M., 2008. Enhanced CREB and DARPP-32 phosphorylation in the nucleus accumbens and CREB, ERK, and GluR1 phosphorylation in the dorsal hippocampus is associated with cocaine-conditioned place preference behavior. J. Neurochem. 106, 1780–1790.

Turrigiano, G., 2012. Homeostatic synaptic plasticity: local and global mechanisms for stabilizing neuronal function. Cold Spring Harbor Perspect. Biol. 4, a005736.

Turrigiano, G.G., Leslie, K.R., Desai, N.S., Rutherford, L.C., Nelson, S.B., 1998. Activity-dependent scaling of quantal amplitude in neocortical neurons. Nature 391, 892–896.

Turrigiano, G.G., Nelson, S.B., 2004. Homeostatic plasticity in the developing nervous system. Nat. Rev. Neurosci. 5, 97–107.

Valdez, G.R., Roberts, A.J., Chan, K., Davis, H., Brennan, M., Zorrilla, E.P., Koob, G.F., 2002. Increased ethanol self-administration and anxiety-like behavior during acute ethanol withdrawal and protracted abstinence: regulation by corticotropin-releasing factor. Alcohol Clin. Exp. Res. 26, 1494–1501.

Valzachi, M.C., Teodorov, E., Marcourakis, T., Bailey, A., Camarini, R., 2013. Enhancement of behavioral sensitization, anxiety-like behavior, and hippocampal and frontal cortical CREB levels following cocaine abstinence in mice exposed to cocaine during adolescence. PLoS One 8, e78317.

van Dam, E.J., Ruiter, B., Kamal, A., Ramakers, G.M., Gispen, W.H., de Graan, P.N., 2002. N-methyl-D-aspartate-induced long-term depression is associated with a decrease in postsynaptic protein kinase C substrate phosphorylation in rat hippocampal slices. Neurosci. Lett. 320, 129–132.

van Groen, T., Kadish, I., Wyss, J.M., 2002. Species differences in the projections from the entorhinal cortex to the hippocampus. Brain Res. Bull. 57, 553–556.

van Groen, T., Wyss, J.M., 1990. Extrinsic projections from area CA1 of the rat hippocampus: olfactory, cortical, subcortical, and bilateral hippocampal formation projections. J. Comp. Neurol. 302, 515–528.

van Strien, N.M., Cappaert, N.L., Witter, M.P., 2009. The anatomy of memory: an interactive overview of the parahippocampal-hippocampal network. Nat. Rev. Neurosci. 10, 272–282.

Vendruscolo, L.F., Estey, D., Goodell, V., Macshane, L.G., Logrip, M.L., Schlosburg, J.E., McGinn, M.A., Zamora-Martinez, E.R., Belanoff, J.K., Hunt, H.J., Sanna, P.P., George, O., Koob, G.F., Edwards, S., Mason, B.J., 2015.

Glucocorticoid receptor antagonism decreases alcohol seeking in alcohol-dependent individuals. J. Clin. Invest. 125, 3193–3197.

Vendruscolo, L.F., Roberts, A.J., 2014. Operant alcohol self-administration in dependent rats: focus on the vapor model. Alcohol 48, 277–286.

Vengeliene, V., Olevska, A., Spanagel, R., 2015. Long-lasting effect of NMDA receptor antagonist memantine on ethanol-cue association and relapse. J. Neurochem. 135, 1080–1085.

Vertes, R.P., Fortin, W.J., Crane, A.M., 1999. Projections of the median raphe nucleus in the rat. J. Comp. Neurol. 407, 555–582.

Vetreno, R.P., Hall, J.M., Savage, L.M., 2011. Alcohol-related amnesia and dementia: animal models have revealed the contributions of different etiological factors on neuropathology, neurochemical dysfunction and cognitive impairment. Neurobiol. Learn. Mem. 96, 596–608.

Vianna, M.R., Alonso, M., Viola, H., Quevedo, J., de Paris, F., Furman, M., de Stein, M.L., Medina, J.H., Izquierdo, I., 2000. Role of hippocampal signaling pathways in long-term memory formation of a nonassociative learning task in the rat. Learn. Mem. 7, 333–340.

Vidal-Infer, A., Arenas, M.C., Daza-Losada, M., Aguilar, M.A., Miñarro, J., Rodríguez-Arias, M., 2012. High novelty-seeking predicts greater sensitivity to the conditioned rewarding effects of cocaine. Pharmacol. Biochem. Behav. 102, 124–132.

Volkow, N.D., Morales, M., 2015. The brain on drugs: from reward to addiction. Cell 162, 712–725.

Volkow, N.D., Wang, G.J., Tomasi, D., Baler, R.D., 2013. Unbalanced neuronal circuits in addiction. Curr. Opin. Neurobiol. 23, 639–648.

Vorel, S.R., Liu, X., Hayes, R.J., Spector, J.A., Gardner, E.L., 2001. Relapse to cocaine-seeking after hippocampal theta burst stimulation. Science 292, 1175–1178.

Wang, S., Scott, B.W., Wojtowicz, J.M., 2000. Heterogenous properties of dentate granule neurons in the adult rat. J. Neurobiol. 42, 248–257.

Wang, Y., Cui, H., Wang, W., Zhao, B., Lai, J., 2012. The region-specific activation of Ca2+/calmodulin dependent protein kinase II and extracellular signal-regulated kinases in hippocampus following chronic alcohol exposure. Brain Res. Bull. 89, 191–196.

Wayner, M.J., Chitwood, R., Armstrong, D.L., Phelix, C., 1997. Ethanol affects hypothalamic neurons projecting to the hippocampus and inhibits dentate granule cell LTP. Alcohol 14, 1–7.

Weiner, J.L., Dunwiddie, T.V., Valenzuela, C.F., 1999. Ethanol inhibition of synaptically evoked kainate responses in rat hippocampal CA3 pyramidal neurons. Mol. Pharmacol. 56, 85–90.

Weisskopf, M.G., Castillo, P.E., Zalutsky, R.A., Nicoll, R.A., 1994. Mediation of hippocampal mossy fiber long-term potentiation by cyclic AMP. Science 265, 1878–1882.

Wells, A.M., Lasseter, H.C., Xie, X., Cowhey, K.E., Reittinger, A.M., Fuchs, R.A., 2011. Interaction between the basolateral amygdala and dorsal hippocampus is critical for cocaine memory reconsolidation and subsequent drug context-induced cocaine-seeking behavior in rats. Learn. Mem. 18, 693–702.

Werner, C.T., Mitra, S., Auerbach, B.D., Wang, Z.J., Martin, J.A., Stewart, A.F., Gobira, P.H., Iida, M., An, C., Cobb, M.M., Caccamise, A., Salvi, R.J., Neve, R.L., Gancarz, A.M., Dietz, D.M., 2020. Neuroadaptations in the dorsal hippocampus underlie cocaine seeking during prolonged abstinence. Proc. Natl. Acad. Sci. U. S. A. 117, 26460–26469.

Wexler, B.E., Gottschalk, C.H., Fulbright, R.K., Prohovnik, I., Lacadie, C.M., Rounsaville, B.J., Gore, J.C., 2001. Functional magnetic resonance imaging of cocaine craving. Am. J. Psychiatr. 158, 86–95.

White, A.M., Simson, P.E., Best, P.J., 1997. Comparison between the effects of ethanol and diazepam on spatial working memory in the rat. Psychopharmacology (Berl) 133, 256–261.

White, N.M., 1996. Addictive drugs as reinforcers: multiple partial actions on memory systems. Addiction 91, 921–949 discussion 951-965.

Wigstrom, H., Gustafsson, B., Huang, Y.Y., 1986. Mode of action of excitatory amino acid receptor antagonists on hippocampal long-lasting potentiation. Neuroscience 17, 1105–1115.

Wilce, P.A., Le, F., Matsumoto, I., Shanley, B.C., 1993. Ethanol inhibits NMDA-receptor mediated regulation of immediate early gene expression. Alcohol Alcohol Suppl. (2), 359–363.

Wilkins Jr., L.H., Prendergast, M.A., Blanchard, J., Holley, R.C., Chambers, E.R., Littleton, J.M., 2006. Potential value of changes in cell markers in organotypic hippocampal cultures associated with chronic EtOH exposure and withdrawal: comparison with NMDA-induced changes. Alcohol Clin. Exp. Res. 30, 1768–1780.

Wirkner, K., Poelchen, W., Koles, L., Muhlberg, K., Scheibler, P., Allgaier, C., Illes, P., 1999. Ethanol-induced inhibition of NMDA receptor channels. Neurochem. Int. 35, 153–162.

Witter, M.P., 1993. Organization of the entorhinal-hippocampal system: a review of current anatomical data. Hippocampus 3, 33–44. Spec No.

Witter, M.P., Van Hoesen, G.W., Amaral, D.G., 1989. Topographical organization of the entorhinal projection to the dentate gyrus of the monkey. J. Neurosci. 9, 216–228.

Wood, S.C., Fay, J., Sage, J.R., Anagnostaras, S.G., 2007. Cocaine and Pavlovian fear conditioning: dose-effect analysis. Behav. Brain Res. 176, 244–250.

Wooden, J.I., Thompson, K.R., Guerin, S.P., Nawarawong, N.N., Nixon, K., 2021. Consequences of adolescent alcohol use on adult hippocampal neurogenesis and hippocampal integrity. Int. Rev. Neurobiol. 160, 281–304.

Wright, J.W., Kramar, E.A., Myers, E.D., Davis, C.J., Harding, J.W., 2003. Ethanol-induced suppression of LTP can be attenuated with an angiotensin IV analog. Regul. Pept. 113, 49–56.

Wu, P.H., Mihic, S.J., Liu, J.F., Le, A.D., Kalant, H., 1993. Blockade of chronic tolerance to ethanol by the NMDA antagonist, (+)-MK-801. Eur. J. Pharmacol. 231, 157–164.

Wyss, J.M., Van Groen, T., 1992. Connections between the retrosplenial cortex and the hippocampal formation in the rat: a review. Hippocampus 2, 1–11.

Xie, X., Ramirez, D.R., Lasseter, H.C., Fuchs, R.A., 2010. Effects of mGluR1 antagonism in the dorsal hippocampus on drug context-induced reinstatement of cocaine-seeking behavior in rats. Psychopharmacology (Berl) 208, 1–11.

Xu, W., Sudhof, T.C., 2013. A neural circuit for memory specificity and generalization. Science 339, 1290–1295.

Yamazaki, Y., Jia, Y., Niu, R., Sumikawa, K., 2006. Nicotine exposure in vivo induces long-lasting enhancement of NMDA receptor-mediated currents in the hippocampus. Eur. J. Neurosci. 23, 1819–1828.

Yan, Z., Yingjie, Z., Na, A., Qi, Q., Wei, L., Wenzheng, W., Lin, S., Shifu, X., 2021. The effects of light-to-moderate alcohol consumption on the cognitive function of community nondemented male elderly: a cohort study. Behav. Neurol. 2021, 5681913.

Yang, K., Lei, G., Xie, Y.F., MacDonald, J.F., Jackson, M.F., 2014. Differential regulation of NMDAR and NMDAR-mediated metaplasticity by anandamide and 2-AG in the hippocampus. Hippocampus 24, 1601–1614.

Yasuda, H., Barth, A.L., Stellwagen, D., Malenka, R.C., 2003. A developmental switch in the signaling cascades for LTP induction. Nat. Neurosci. 6, 15–16.

Yun, S., Reynolds, R.P., Masiulis, I., Eisch, A.J., 2016. Re-evaluating the link between neuropsychiatric disorders and dysregulated adult neurogenesis. Nat. Med. 22, 1239–1247.

Zahr, N.M., Mayer, D., Vinco, S., Orduna, J., Luong, R., Sullivan, E.V., Pfefferbaum, A., 2009. In vivo evidence for alcohol-induced neurochemical changes in rat brain without protracted withdrawal, pronounced thiamine deficiency, or severe liver damage. Neuropsychopharmacology 34, 1427–1442.

Zarrindast, M.R., Meshkani, J., Rezayof, A., Beigzadeh, R., Rostami, P., 2010. Nicotinic acetylcholine receptors of the dorsal hippocampus and the basolateral amygdala are involved in ethanol-induced conditioned place preference. Neuroscience 168, 505–513.

Zhang, R., Shen, L., Miles, T., Shen, Y., Cordero, J., Qi, Y., Liang, L., Li, C., 2020. Association of low to moderate alcohol drinking with cognitive functions from middle to older age among US adults. JAMA Netw. Open 3, e207922.

Zhao, C., Deng, W., Gage, F.H., 2008. Mechanisms and functional implications of adult neurogenesis. Cell 132, 645–660.

Zhao, Y., Dayas, C.V., Aujla, H., Baptista, M.A., Martin-Fardon, R., Weiss, F., 2006. Activation of group II metabotropic glutamate receptors attenuates both stress and cue-induced ethanol-seeking and modulates c-fos expression in the hippocampus and amygdala. J. Neurosci. 26, 9967–9974.

Zhou, Q., Homma, K.J., Poo, M.M., 2004. Shrinkage of dendritic spines associated with long-term depression of hippocampal synapses. Neuron 44, 749–757.

Zucker, R.S., Regehr, W.G., 2002. Short-term synaptic plasticity. Annu. Rev. Physiol. 64, 355–405.

CHAPTER

8

Amygdala circuits

Lieselot L.G. Carrette[a], *Elizabeth A. Sneddon*[b] *and Olivier George*[a]

[a]Department of Psychiatry, University of California San Diego, La Jolla, CA, United States; [b]Department of Psychology and Center for Neuroscience and Behavior, Miami University, Oxford, OH, United States

Introduction

The amygdala consists of several nuclei with distinct connectional and functional characteristics in humans and animals. The basolateral complex, also known as the basolateral amygdala (BLA) (Amunts et al., 2005), the cortical nucleus, the medial nucleus, the central nucleus (CeA), and the intercalated cell clusters are among these nuclei. The BLA and the CeA represent two of the main input and output regions of the amygdala, respectively, and the role of their circuitry in addiction will be the focus of this chapter.

The BLA consists of both γ-aminobutyric acidergic (GABA) interneurons and glutamatergic (Glut) neurons (Liu et al., 2021) that process emotional and motivational stimuli. The BLA receives salient auditory sensory information through the lateral nucleus from the auditory thalamus, and primary auditory cortex (AC) from both aversive and rewarding stimuli, and the BLA is reciprocally connected to the hippocampus (HPC) (Aggleton, 2000; Fanselow and LeDoux, 1999; Ghashghaei and Barbas, 2002; Janak and Tye, 2015; John et al., 2013; Lüthi and Lüscher, 2014; Morrison and Salzman, 2010). The BLA also receives input from several brain regions involved in addiction-related behaviors, including the prefrontal cortex (PFC), insular cortex (IC), locus coeruleus (LC), nucleus basalis of Meynert (NBM), and ventral tegmental area (VTA) (Fig. 8.1). Emotion-related information from these regions is processed by the BLA and thus plays a critical role in aversive and reward learning (Killcross et al., 1997; Hatfield et al., 1996), instrumental conditioning (Balleine et al., 2003; Blundell et al., 2001; Ostlund and Balleine, 2008), decision-making, and motivated behavior (Wassum and Izquierdo, 2015). The classic view of the amygdala proposed that the BLA sends dense glutamatergic projections

Neurocircuitry of Addiction
https://doi.org/10.1016/B978-0-12-823453-2.00003-5

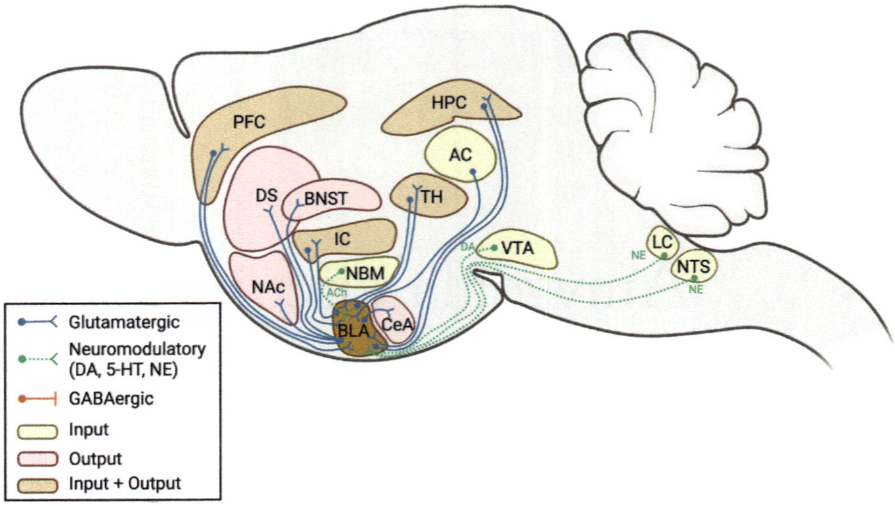

FIGURE 8.1 **Projections from the basolateral amygdala (BLA).** Input (*yellow*), output (*red*), and combined input and output (*orange*) regions. *AC*, auditory cortex; *BLA*, basolateral amygdala; *BNST*, bed nucleus of the stria terminalis; *DS*, dorsal striatum; *HPC*, hippocampus; *IC*, insular cortex; *LC*, locus coeruleus; *NAc*, nucleus accumbens; *NBM*, nucleus basalis of Meynert; *NTS*, nucleus tractus solitarius; *PFC*, prefrontal cortex; *TH*, thalamus; *VTA*, ventral tegmental area. Dopamine (DA), serotonin (5-HT), and norepinephrine (NE) neurons are indicated as neuromodulatory.

to CeA, which then processes the information to control several downstream regions involved in the physiological and behavioral response to threats, emotions, and motivational cues and contexts. More recent findings support that parallel processing in the BLA and CeA mediate different aspects of emotional processing (Balleine et al., 2003; Phillips et al., 2003). The BLA not only projects to the CeA but also to other regions, including the nucleus accumbens (NAc), dorsomedial striatum (DMS), PFC, HPC, bed nucleus of the stria terminalis (BNST), IC, and TH.

Converging evidence demonstrates a crucial role of the BLA in addiction-like behavior. Lesion studies show that the BLA is necessary for cocaine- (Whitelaw et al., 1996; McLaughlin and See, 2003; Meil and See, 1997) and heroin-seeking behavior (Fuchs and See, 2002). In addition, pharmacological studies show that the BLA is involved in acquisition and extinction of methamphetamine-conditioned place preference (Goodman et al., 2019), memory consolidation of cue-cocaine pairing (Gabriele and See, 2010) and, also, reconsolidation of heroin withdrawal memories (Yuan et al., 2020). These studies support a role for the BLA in addictive-like behaviors and provide a strong rationale for investigating how specific projections to and from the BLA differentially contribute to these behaviors.

The CeA consists of a highly interconnected network of heterogeneous GABAergic neurons with various subpopulations that co-express different peptides (Gilpin, 2012; Roberts et al., 1982; van den Burg and Stoop, 2019). The primary input of the CeA is the BLA, but other brain regions that are associated with addiction-related behaviors also project to the

CeA, including the parabrachial nuclei (PBN), paraventricular nucleus of the TH (PVT), hypothalamus (HPT), raphe nuclei (RN), VTA, substantia nigra (SN), IC, LC, periaqueductal gray (PAG), and nucleus of the tractus solitarius (NTS). The CeA plays an important role in the emotional processing of salient stimuli coming from the BLA, particularly in orchestrating appropriate physiological and behavioral responses in the context of food and drug consumption (Cai et al., 2014; Hardaway et al., 2019), appetitive behaviors (Kim et al., 2017), positive and negative encoding (Beyeler et al., 2016), fear (Namburi et al., 2015), anxiety (Zhou et al., 2021), and pain (Finnegan et al., 2006; Neugebauer et al., 2003; Zhou et al., 2021) through modulation of activity in the PVN, PVT, HPT, RN, VTA/SN, LC, PAG, NTS, and BNST as downstream regions it projects to (Fig. 8.2).

Converging evidence demonstrates a key role for the CeA in addiction-like behavior, particularly in the emergence of somatic and motivational withdrawal symptoms after chronic drug use/exposure, and also, in mediating excessive drug self-administration after a period of abstinence (Koob et al., 2014). For instance, the CeA mediates escalation of alcohol drinking and withdrawal in alcohol-dependent rats (de Guglielmo et al., 2019). Activation of the CeA is critical for drug-seeking behavior and drug-taking, particularly during withdrawal and after protracted abstinence from opioids (Li et al., 2008; Ma et al., 2008), nicotine (Funk et al., 2016), methamphetamine (Li et al., 2014), and cocaine (Lu et al., 2005, 2007; Xi et al., 2013; Erb et al., 2001; McFarland et al., 2004). CeA lesions impair aversive and appetitive conditioning (Campeau and Davis, 1995; Gallagher et al., 1990). Optogenetic activation of the CeA, while not rewarding on its own, intensifies appetitive motivation for sucrose and cocaine (Tom et al., 2019; Warlow et al., 2020). Moreover, while CeA stimulation typically

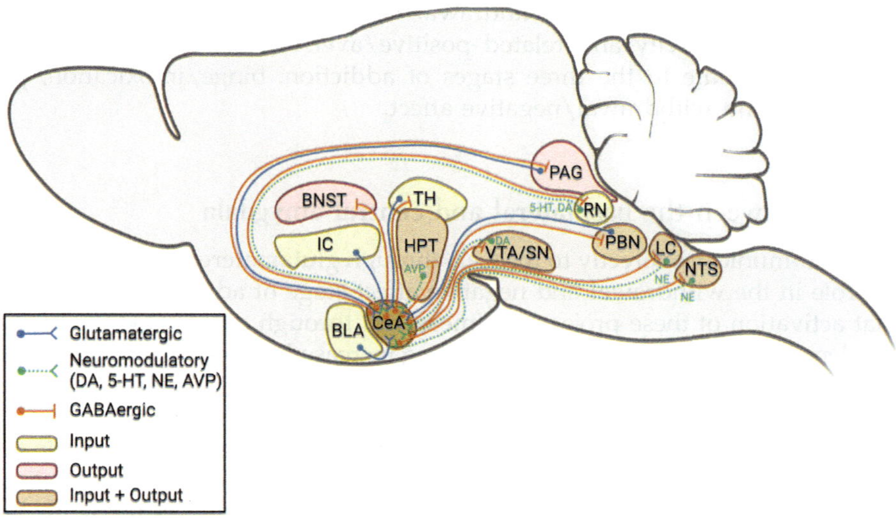

FIGURE 8.2 **Projections from the central nucleus of the amygdala (CeA).** Input (*yellow*), output (*red*) and combined input and output (*orange*) regions. *BLA*, basolateral amygdala; *BNST*, bed nucleus of the stria terminalis; *HPT*, hypothalamus; *IC*, insular cortex; *LC*, locus coeruleus; *NTS*, nucleus tractus solitarius; *PAG*, periaqueductal gray; *PBN*, parabrachial nuclei; *RN*, raphe nuclei; *TH*, thalamus; *VTA*, ventral tegmental area. Dopamine (DA), serotonin (5-HT) and norepinephrine (NE) neurons are indicated as neuromodulatory.

potentiates negatively-valenced defensive freezing and avoidance with an electric shock, it can also result in maladaptive attraction to adverse shock stimuli (Warlow et al., 2020), showing that the CeA attributes incentive salience and reinforces behavioral strategies to stimuli, even if they are aversive. Because the CeA receives emotionally aversive and rewarding information via afferents and promotes avoidant or reinforcing behavioral responses through its efferents projections, it is not surprising that the CeA has been a major focus of addiction research.

The overall goal of this chapter is to discuss amygdalar circuits that are involved in addiction-like behaviors. To this end, we provide a short introduction of the different projection regions and early studies that provide correlational evidence for the role of specific circuits in these behaviors based on data from anatomy, anterograde/retrograde tracing, fiber photometry, electrophysiology, pharmacology, and lesion studies. Then, we focus on recent studies that use circuit specific chemo-and optogenetic manipulations to demonstrate a causal role for specific BLA and CeA input and output projections in addiction-related behaviors (Figs. 8.1 and 8.2 and Table 8.1). These circuits include pathways connecting the BLA/CeA to brain regions involved in stress/withdrawal (LC, BNST, HPT, HPT), impulsivity (VTA, SNC, BNST), pain (PAG, PBN), decision making (PFC, IC), memory (HPC, LC, PVT), cue and context learning/reward and aversion (NAc, PBN, PVT, VTA/SNC, NTS), emotional processing (IC, LC, PVT), malaise (IC, PBN), anxiety (LC, BNST), arousal (RN), and frustration (PVT). We focus our interest on addiction-like behaviors with significant translational relevance to substance use disorders, including operant self-administration studies, intracranial self-stimulation (ICSS) tests, conditioned place preference (CPP), conditioned place aversion (CPA), real-time place preference (RTPP), and real-time place avoidance (RTPA), abstinence, extinction and reinstatement studies, free-feeding or drinking studies (including two-bottle choice), studies related to withdrawal, nociception, aversion, anxiety and negative emotional states, impulsivity and related positive/aversive learning. Lastly, we establish which circuits contribute to the three stages of addiction, binge/intoxication, preoccupation/anticipation, and withdrawal/negative affect.

Local circuit between the basolateral and central amygdala

The BLA communicates directly to the CeA through glutamatergic projections that play an important role in the withdrawal and negative affect stage of addiction. Retrograde tracing shows that activation of these projections (measured through *c*-Fos colocalization) increases negative valence and affective behavior, including increased anxiety-like behavior in the open field test in male mice (C57, 25–35 g) (McCall et al., 2017). Neuronal activity of the BLA-CeA projection neurons (measured through a method of optogenetic-mediated phototagging) also increases following exposure to a predictive cue to the aversive tastant quinine in an operant task in male mice (C57) (Beyeler et al., 2016). Moreover, synaptic strength of this projection (measured through electrophysiology and retrobead tracing) increases following a fear conditioning task in male mice (C57, 6–12 weeks), while it decreases following the delivery of a sucrose reward (Namburi et al., 2015). Selective photoinhibition of the BLA^{Glut} projections to the CeA in male mice (C57, 6–12 weeks) suppresses the freezing response in a fear conditioning task, while their photostimulation causes real-time place aversion (Namburi et al., 2015).

TABLE 8.1 Summary of the confirmed causal contribution of amygdalar circuitry in behaviors relevant to the three stages of addiction. *Arrows* (↙ and ↗) indicate respective decrease and increase of the behavior by stimulation of the circuit.

Stage of addiction	Behavior	BLA circuits	CeA circuits
Binge/ intoxication	Intrinsic reward	↗ BLA^{Glut} → NAc (Stuber et al., 2011) ↙ BLA^{Glut} → NAc shell (Lafferty et al., 2020) ↗ $BLA^{Ppp1r1b}$ → CeA (Kim et al., 2017)	↗ CeA^{Htr2a} → PBN (Douglass et al., 2017) ↗ CeA^{Pnoc} → PBN, BNST, NTS (Hardaway et al., 2019) ↗ CeA^{NTS} → PBN (Torruella-Suárez et al., 2020) ↗ CeA^{Sst} → SN (Steinberg et al., 2020)
Binge/ intoxication	Drug intake	Alcohol: ↙ BLA^{Glut} → NAc shell (Millan et al., 2017) ↗ $mPFC^{NPY,Glut}$ → BLA (Robinson et al., 2019) Cocaine: ↗ BLA^{Glut} → NAc $shell^{FSIs}$ (Yu et al., 2017)	Alcohol: ↗ CeA^{NT} → PBN (Torruella-Suárez et al., 2020) ↗ aIC^{Glut} → CeA (Haaranen, Schäfer, et al., 2020)
Withdrawal/ negative affect	Intrinsic aversion/ avoidance	↗ BLA^{GABA} → CeA (Namburi et al., 2015) ↗ BLA^{Rspo2} → CeA (Kim et al., 2017) ↗ LC^{NE} → BLA (McCall et al., 2017) ↗ BLA^{Glut} → PL (Song et al., 2019)	↗ CeA^{GABA} → LH^{Hcrt1} (Weera et al., 2021) ↗ CeA^{CRF} → LC (McCall et al., 2015) ↗ pIC^{Glut} → CeA (Gehrlach et al., 2019; Schiff et al., 2018) ↗ PBN^{CGRP} → CeA (Han et al., 2015)
Withdrawal/ negative affect	Drug withdrawal	N/A	Alcohol: ↗ CeA^{CRF} → BNST (de Guglielmo et al., 2019) ↘ CeA^{GABA} → PAG (Avegno et al., 2018)
Preoccupation/ anticipation	Conditioned response to cues	↗ NBM^{ACh} → BLA (Crouse et al., 2020)	↗ $aPVT^{Glut}$ → CeA (Do-Monte et al., 2017)
Preoccupation/ anticipation	Drug-seeking behavior	Alcohol: ↙ BLA^{Glut} → NAc shell (Millan et al., 2017) ↙ BLA^{AMPARs} → NAc shell (Lee et al., 2013) Cocaine: ↗ BLA^{Glut} → NAc core (Puaud et al., 2021)	N/A
Preoccupation/ anticipation	Impulsivity	N/A	↘ $CeA^{D2R,GABA}$ → $BNST^{GABA}$ (Kim et al., 2018)

(Continued)

TABLE 8.1 Summary of the confirmed causal contribution of amygdalar circuitry in behaviors relevant to the three stages of addiction. *Arrows* (↙ and ↗) indicate respective decrease and increase of the behavior by stimulation of the circuit.—cont'd

Stage of addiction	Behavior	BLA circuits	CeA circuits
Preoccupation/ anticipation	Reinstatement	Cocaine: ↗ BLA^{Glut} → NAc core (Stefanik and Kalivas, 2013) ↗ $lOFC^{Glut}$ → BLA (Arguello et al., 2017) ↗ VTA^{DA} → BLA (Mahler et al., 2019)	Methamphetamine: ↗ aIC^{Glut} → CeA (Venniro et al., 2017)
Preoccupation/ anticipation	Memory	↗ BLA^{Glut} → aIC (Gil-Lievana et al., 2020)[nd] Opioid: ↗ BLA^{Glut} → ACC (Shao et al., 2021)	Morphine: ↗ PVT^{Glut} (LC) → CeA (Wang et al., 2021) ↗ PVT^{Glut} → CeA (Keyes et al., 2020)
Preoccupation/ anticipation	Incentive salience	N/A	↗ CeA^{Sst} → SN (Steinberg et al., 2020) Morphine: ↗ RN^{DA} → CeA (Lin et al., 2020)

Collectively, these studies show that projections from the BLA to the CeA are involved in negative valence encoding and aversive learning, two critical processes in the development of negative reinforcement in addiction.

Another key function of the BLA to CeA projection is its role in the modulation of pain (Neugebauer et al., 2003; Zhou et al., 2021; Ren et al., 2010). Optogenetic activation of the excitatory BLA^{Glut} to CeA projections increases pain thresholds in male mice (CaMKII-Cre, 8–10 weeks) and alleviates pain-induced anxiety-like behavior in the open field and elevated plus maze (Zhou et al., 2021). Optogenetic inhibition produces the opposite effect (Zhou et al., 2021). Since the BLA is rich in mu-opioid receptors (MORs), its projections to the CeA are important for mediating the analgesic effects of opioids. MOR activation in the BLA primarily attenuates inhibitory presynaptic GABAergic inputs on BLA to CeA projection neurons, thus, disinhibits the projection in male rats (80–120 g) (as shown with electrophysiology and retrograde tracing) resulting in a reduction of pain effects as described above (Finnegan et al., 2006).

Therefore, projections from the BLA^{Glut} to CeA are involved in negative affect, as they increase avoidance behaviors (Namburi et al., 2015), aversion (Beyeler et al., 2016), and reduce pain responses (Neugebauer et al., 2000; Zhou et al., 2021), which are all key aspects of the withdrawal/negative affect stage of addiction (Table 8.1; Fig. 8.3). But the CeA does not only mediate aversive behavior. There are two spatially segregated, genetically distinct populations of BLA to CeA projection neurons: *R*-spondin 2 (Rspo2) expressing BLA neurons elicit defensive behaviors and inhibit appetitive behaviors in male mice (Rspo2-Cre backcrossed on C57, 6–12 weeks), but protein phosphatase 1 regulatory subunit 1B (Ppp1r1b)

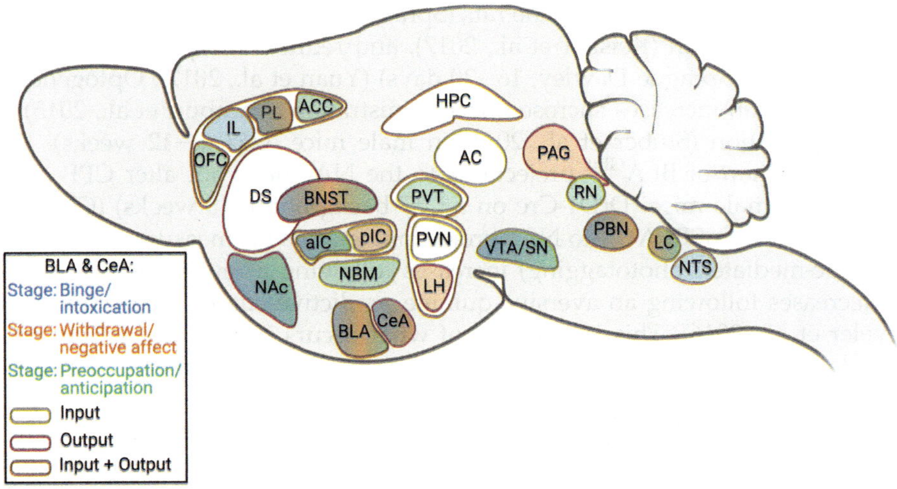

FIGURE 8.3 **Causal contribution of amygdalar circuitry in behaviors relevant to the three stages of addiction.** Binge/intoxication (*blue*), withdrawal/negative affect (*orange*), and preoccupation/anticipation (*green*). Regions that fit under more than one stage of addiction colored with a combination of the colors of the stages. Region outlines characterized by input (*yellow* border), output (*red* border), and combined input and output (*orange* border) regions for the BLA and CeA. *AC*, auditory cortex; *ACC*, anterior cingulate cortex; *BLA*, basolateral amygdala; *BNST*, bed nucleus of the stria terminalis; *CeA*, central nucleus of the amygdala; *DS*, dorsal striatum; *HPC*, hippocampus; *HPT*, hypothalamus; *IC*, insular cortex; *LC*, locus coeruleus; *lOFC*, lateral orbitofrontal cortex; *mPFC*, medial prefrontal cortex; *NAc*, nucleus accumbens; *NBM*, nucleus basalis of Meynert; *NTS*, nucleus tractus solitarius; *PAG*, periaqueductal gray; *PBN*, parabrachial nuclei; *PL*, prelimbic cortex; *RN*, raphe nuclei; *TH*, thalamus; *VTA*, ventral tegmental area.

expressing BLA neurons stimulate appetitive behaviors and inhibit defensive behaviors in male mice (Cartpt-Cre backcrossed on C57, 6–12 weeks) (Kim et al., 2017). This finding suggests that the BLA to CeA circuit may contribute to other aspects of addiction, for example, drug taking and intoxication.

Basolateral amygdala circuitry

Projections from BLA to NAc in addiction

The NAc is involved in reward, aversion, and motivation (Salgado and Kaplitt, 2015). The NAc itself can be subdivided in the central core and surrounding shell (Salgado and Kaplitt, 2015). In humans and animals, the NAc is involved in various psychiatric disorders including but, not limited to, depression-like behavior, obsessive compulsive-like behavior, anxiety-like behavior, and addiction-related behaviors (Salgado and Kaplitt, 2015). Early studies show that lesioning of the NAc and the BLA blocks the acquisition of cocaine-seeking behavior (Whitelaw et al., 1996). As the NAc is involved in reward and motivation, multiple studies have investigated the role of BLA projections to NAc in reward intake and seeking. Both the BLA and the NAc are activated (as measured by *c*-Fos) during cocaine reinstatement in male rats (Sprague Dawley, 275–325 g) (McGlinchey et al., 2016). Ablation of BLA^{Glut} neurons that project to the NAc as a whole, blocks extinction of alcohol-seeking behavior and attenuates alcohol reinstatement in male rats (Sprague Dawley, 225–275 g) following chronic alcohol self-administration (Keistler et al., 2017), and reduces morphine-induced locomotor activity in male rats (Sprague Dawley, 16–20 days) (Yuan et al., 2017). Optogenetic stimulation of this projection increases sucrose self-administration (Namburi et al., 2015) and intracranial self-stimulation (Stuber et al., 2011) in male mice (C57, 6–12 weeks). In contrast, optogenetic inhibition of BLA^{Glut} projections to the NAc does not alter CPP of cocaine in adult male and female mice (DrD1-Cre on a C57 background, 10 weeks) (Christoffel et al., 2021). The excitability of BLA^{Glut} to NAc projection neurons (as measured through a method of optogenetic-mediated phototagging) increases following a rewarding sucrose predictive cue and decreases following an aversive quinine predictive cue in an operant conditioning task (Beyeler et al., 2016). This is opposite of what occurs in BLA projections to the CeA, and these data suggest that BLA^{Glut} projections to the NAc are inherently rewarding and are involved in reward-taking and -seeking behaviors, which are important aspects of the binge/intoxication and preoccupation/anticipation stages of addiction.

Distinct projections from the BLA to the NAc core and shell may mediate different aspects of addictive behavior. For instance, chemogenetic inhibition of the BLA^{Glut} to NAc core projection prevents the acquisition of cue-induced cocaine seeking under a second order ratio schedule of reinforcement in male rats (Sprague Dawley) (Puaud et al., 2021), and optogenetic inhibition of this projection also suppresses cue-induced reinstatement of cocaine in male rats (Sprague Dawley, 250–300 g) (Stefanik and Kalivas, 2013). Thus, increased drug seeking through BLA projections to the NAc core is an important aspect of the preoccupation/anticipation stage of addiction. However, the BLA^{Glut} to NAc shell projection also plays a role in habitual consummatory behaviors, which are integral for the binge/intoxication stage and preoccupation/anticipation stages of addiction. For example, optogenetic activation of the BLA^{Glut} to NAc shell projection reduces both alcohol and sucrose intake in a cued operant task and in a homecage paradigm in male rats (Long Evans) (Millan et al., 2017) and prevents incubation of cocaine craving (i.e., increased cocaine seeking following abstinence) in male rats (Sprague Dawley, 28–30 days) (Lee et al., 2013). Optogenetic inhibition of BLA^{Glut} projections to the rostral NAc shell increases food intake in an operant task in male mice (C57, 8 weeks, 25–30 g) (Reed et al., 2018). BLA^{Glut} neurons innervate NAc shell medium spiny neurons (MSNs), and GABA fast-spiking interneurons (FSIs). Optogenetic stimulation of BLA^{Glut} projections to NAc $shell^{FSIs}$ accelerates the acquisition of cocaine self-administration in male and female mice (C57, 7–12 weeks, ~ 25 g) (Yu et al., 2017). Accordingly, optogenetic inhibition of this projection increases habitual, or inflexible, unproductive responding for sucrose in a seeking paradigm in male and female mice (DrD1-Cre back-crossed on C57, 12 weeks, 25–30 g) (Lafferty et al., 2020). Reduced responding through BLA projections to the NAc shell is important for adaptive motivated behavior and correct habitual responding regulating both the binge/intoxication and preoccupation/anticipation stages of the addiction cycle.

Collectively, these findings show that activation of BLA^{Glut} projections to the NAc core facilitates encoding of drug-paired cues and the expression of drug seeking behavior (Puaud et al., 2021; Stefanik and Kalivas, 2013), while activation of BLA^{Glut} projections to NAc shell suppresses habitual behavior (Lafferty et al., 2020), drug intake (Millan et al., 2017), and drug-seeking behavior (Millan et al., 2017; Yu et al., 2017), which are key aspects of both the binge/intoxication stage and the preoccupation/anticipation stage of addiction (Table 8.1; Fig. 8.3).

Projections from BLA to DMS in addiction

The dorsal striatum (DS) plays a role in decision-making, motivation, and emotional processing and consists of MSNs, cholinergic interneurons, and GABAergic interneurons (Yager et al., 2015). It is split into the DMS and dorsolateral striatum (DLS) subregions (Kim et al., 2013), which are innervated by the BLA (Kita and Kitai, 1990). The DMS promotes goal-directed behaviors while the DLS promotes habit-like behavior (Kim et al., 2013; Koob and Volkow, 2010). Chronic intermittent alcohol exposure in male rats (Long Evans 3–6 months) increases glutamate release in the DMS (measured using optogenetics and electrophysiology) and strengthens BLA synaptic inputs onto DMS neurons (Ma et al., 2017). Accordingly, muscimol inactivation of the DMS reduces alcohol-seeking behavior after 2 weeks of self-administration in male rats (Long Evans, 300 g) (Corbit et al., 2012) and Daun02 inactivation of DMS neuronal ensembles attenuates methamphetamine-seeking behavior in male rats (Sprague Dawley, 175–350 g) (Caprioli et al., 2017). We are not aware of data showing a casual role for the BLA^{Glut}-to-DMS circuit in mediating addiction-related behaviors, the data summarized above suggest that BLA^{Glut}-to-DMS circuit activity, which increases following drug exposure, may promote drug seeking and taking.

As drug intake becomes more habitual, there is a shift from DMS to DLS activation. Muscimol inactivation of the DMS after 8 weeks of alcohol self-administration (in contrast to the 2-week time point described above) does not affect alcohol-seeking behavior, but DLS inactivation at this time point reduces alcohol-seeking behavior in male rats (Long Evans, 300 g) (Corbit et al., 2012). Chronic drug exposure thus increases activity in the BLA^{Glut}-to-DLS circuit, which drives habitual behavior, another key aspect of the binge/intoxication phase. More research is needed to determine the causal role of BLA^{Glut} circuit projections to the DMS and DLS in mediating specific aspects of addiction-like behavior.

Reciprocal circuits between BLA and PFC in addiction

The PFC is involved in cognition, impulsivity, and risk-taking (Miller, 2000). It is part of the isocortex in the forebrain and divided into the anterior cingulate cortex (ACC) (Guercio et al., 2020), prelimbic cortex (PL) (Peters et al., 2008), infralimbic cortex (IL) (Logrip and Zorrilla, 2014), and orbitofrontal cortex (OFC) (Lasseter et al., 2014). The ACC and dorsal PL are sometimes grouped together as the dorsomedial PFC, and the ventral PL and IL are grouped together as the ventromedial PFC. All PFC subdivisions have bidirectional connections with the BLA as shown by viral tracing (Ottersen, 1982) and electron microscopy (Bacon et al., 1996). Lesions of the mPFC and ACC facilitate acquisition of cocaine self-administration in male rats (Listar hooded, 250–320 g) (Weissenborn et al., 1997). However, pharmacological inactivation of the PL decreases responding for a cocaine-paired stimulus during extinction and reinstatement in a model of cocaine-seeking behavior in male rats (Sprague Dawley, 300–325 g) (McLaughlin and See, 2003), and simultaneous pharmacological inhibition of the OFC and BLA using baclofen and muscimol suppresses drug context-induced cocaine-seeking behavior in male rats (Sprague Dawley, 250–300 g) (Lasseter et al., 2011). Similarly, photoinhibition of lateral OFC^{Glut} projections to BLA reduces cue-induced reinstatement of cocaine-seeking behavior in male rats (Sprague Dawley, 250–275 g) (Arguello et al., 2017). Thus, these results indicate that OFC^{Glut} projections to BLA may promote drug-seeking behavior during relapse. In addition, inhibition of the PL-BLA pathway through activation of NPY1 receptor or chemogenetic inhibition of the PL-BLA pathway reduces binge-like alcohol drinking in male and female mice (NPY1R-Cre+ backcrossed on C57, 10 weeks) (Robinson et al., 2019). These results demonstrate that while the PFC inhibits acquisition of drug taking, PFC projections to the BLA promote drug seeking when animals are exposed to drug-associated cues. While inactivation of reciprocal BLA^{Glut} projections to the OFC does not alter cue-induced reinstatement of cocaine-seeking behavior, optogenetic inhibition of BLA^{Glut} projections to PL or BLA^{Glut} projections to ACC blocks conditioned place aversion to opioid withdrawal in male mice (C57, 8–12) (Song et al., 2019; Shao et al., 2021). These results suggest that the BLA^{Glut} projections to the PL and OFC facilitate aversion and are involved in the withdrawal/negative affect stage of addiction. Together, these results demonstrate an important role of reciprocal mPFC-BLA circuits in all stages of addiction (Table 8.1; Fig. 8.3).

Reciprocal circuits between BLA and HPC in addiction

The HPC is an isocortical structure that plays an important role in learning and memory (O'Reilly and Rudy, 2001). Tracing studies have established that the BLA sends efferent projections to the HPC (Pitkänen et al., 2000; McCall et al., 2017) and receives afferent inputs from the HPC (Ottersen, 1982), all of which are glutamatergic. Immunohistochemical and pharmacological approaches show that the BLA, ventral HPC (vHPC) (Kutlu et al., 2018) and dorsal HPC (dHPC) (Zarrindast et al., 2010) contribute to addiction-like behaviors. For example, pharmacological inactivation of the dHPC blocks the acquisition and expression of cocaine CPP in male rats (Sprague Dawley, 275–300 g) (Meyers et al., 2003) and inactivation of the vHPC using baclofen and muscimol decreases cocaine-seeking behavior in an operant task in male rats (Sprague Dawley, 250–300) (Lasseter et al., 2010), suggesting a key role for this circuit in the preoccupation/anticipation stage of addiction.

Learning facilitated by the HPC is important for conditioned responses. For example, lesions of the dHPC disrupt fear conditioning to an auditory cue in male rats (Long Evans, ~90 days) (Quinn et al., 2008) and, pharmacological inactivation of the BLA weakens Pavlovian fear conditioning in male mice (C57, 4–6 months, 27–32 g) (Calandreau et al., 2005). BLA^{Glut} projections to vHPC are activated (as indicated by *c*-Fos expression) by both positive and negative valence cues in operant conditioning tasks in male mice (C57) (Beyeler et al., 2016). Moreover, this circuit plays a role in anxiety-like behavior since photoinhibition of BLA^{Glut} projections to vHPC reduces, while stimulation promotes, anxiety-like behavior in an elevated plus-maze task with male mice (C57, 5–6 weeks) (Felix-Ortiz et al., 2013).

These studies show that the BLA^{Glut} projections to the HPC play a role in cue and context conditioning, which is a critical process in the preoccupation and anticipation stage of addiction. Moreover, it facilitates anxiety-like behavior, which is often comorbid with addiction-related behaviors. More research is needed to determine the causal roles of BLA^{Glut} projections to HPC and reciprocal HPC-to-BLA projections in specific addiction-related behaviors.

Projections from BLA to BNST in addiction

The BNST, located in the basal forebrain and part of the extended amygdala, consists of interneurons and glutamatergic and GABAergic projection neurons (Ju et al., 1989; Ju and Swanson, 1989). It plays an important role in stress and anxiety-like behaviors particularly in response to threat as well as feeding behavior, goal-directed behaviors, and behavioral inhibition in response to unfamiliar situations (Stamatakis et al., 2014). Specifically for drug studies, immunohistochemistry shows an increase in Fos expression in both the BNST and BLA following chronic morphine exposure in male rats (Sprague Dawley, 200–250 g) that is associated with increased morphine place preference (Harris and Aston-Jones, 2003). This abstinence-induce increases in Fos expression in the BNST and BLA was replicated after chronic oxycodone exposure in male and female rats (Sprague Dawley, 350–400 g and 280–350 g, respectively) (Simpson et al., 2020). Moreover, optogenetic activation BLA^{Glut} projections to BNST increases anxiety-like behavior in the elevated plus-maze in male mice (C57) (Crowley et al., 2016). These studies suggest that BLA projections to the BNST may be important for mediating addiction-related behaviors and in the facilitation of anxiety-like behavior, which is often comorbid with addiction.

Reciprocal circuits between BLA and IC in addiction

The IC, the part of the isocortex that surrounds the rhinal fissure, is involved in diverse functions that include salience detection, interoception, and processing of emotion and pain (Uddin et al., 2017). In relation to addiction-related behaviors, the IC processes interoceptive effects of drug and natural rewards and their integration with attention, executive function, and emotions (Droutman et al., 2015). Lesioning or pharmacological inactivation of the IC disrupts craving for amphetamine, cocaine-seeking behavior, and nicotine self-administration in various animal models of addiction (Contreras et al., 2007; Cosme et al., 2015; Pushparaj et al., 2015). The anterior insula (aIC) promotes reward- and drug-seeking behavior, whereas the posterior insula (pIC) is associated with avoidance behavior and aversive states (Gehrlach et al., 2019; Schiff et al., 2018). Pharmacological inactivation of the aIC decreases cue and context-induced reinstatement of cocaine-seeking behavior in male rats (Sprague Dawley, 250–275 g) (Cosme et al., 2015; Arguello et al., 2017) and nicotine-seeking behavior in male rats (Long Evans, 300–325 g) (Pushparaj et al., 2015), Reciprocal glutamatergic projections exist between the BLA and the IC (Gil-Lievana et al., 2020; Kayyal et al., 2019; McGinnis et al., 2020). Following withdrawal from chronic alcohol vapor exposure, the activity of aIC^{Glut} projections to BLA is increased (as measured by electrophysiology) in male rats (Sprague Dawley, 10 weeks, 300 g) (McGinnis et al., 2020).

While chemogenetic activation of the BLA and IC separately each reduce alcohol intake in an intermittent access model, activation of IC^{Glut} projections to BLA does not alter alcohol intake in male rats (Alko Alcohol, 10 weeks) (Haaranen, Schäfer, et al., 2020). Optogenetic inhibition of BLA^{Glut} projections to the aIC results in accelerated extinction and impaired reinstatement in a RTPP paradigm using male and female mice (TH-Cre backcrossed on C57, 3–4 months, 23–35 g) (Gil-Lievana et al., 2020). These results demonstrate that BLA^{Glut} projections to the IC have a role in the maintenance of rewarding contextual memory, extinction, and reinstatement. Overall, these results suggest that reciprocal projections between BLA and IC have roles in mediating addiction-related behaviors, although the specific roles of IC projections to BLA and BLA projections to pIC in mediating addictive-related behaviors are yet to be determined.

Reciprocal circuits between BLA and TH in addiction

The TH is located in the forebrain, above the brainstem, and between the midbrain and cortex. It consists of clusters of thalamic nuclei: the anterior nuclei, lateral nuclei, medial nuclei (MTN), intralaminar nuclei, paraventricular nuclei (PVT), and the reticular nucleus

(TRN) (Torrico and Munakomi, 2021). These glutamatergic nuclei participate in the integration of sensory information and underlie motivational states to guide behavioral responses for reward (Van der Werf et al., 2002). Studies using viral tracing and immunohistochemistry established the presence of TH^{Glut} to BLA projections (McDonald, 1998; van Vulpen and Verwer, 1989) and projections from the BLA to TRN (Zikopoulos and Barbas, 2012).

As part of their role in motivational states, regulating hunger and food intake, chemogenetic inhibition of PVT^{Glut}-to-BLA projection neurons increases free feeding in a homecage, while excitation of this circuit decreases food cue responses in a food discrimination task using male mice (C57, 10–16 weeks) (Livneh et al., 2017). On the other hand, photostimulation of BLA projections to the TRN increases activity in the auditory cortex following an auditory cue in male and female mice (CamKIIa-Cre backcrossed on C57, 7–15 weeks, 17–27 g) (Aizenberg et al., 2019). These results indicate that the BLA-TRN circuit may integrate valence information to selectively amplify sound processing in the auditory cortex. Overall, these results suggest that the projections to and from the BLA and TH are involved in regulating motivation and salience to cue responding, but more work is needed to identify the precise roles of sub-circuits in mediating specific addiction-related behaviors.

Projections from VTA to BLA in addiction

The VTA consists of dopaminergic, glutamatergic, and GABAergic neurons located in the midbrain that form the origin of the mesocorticolimbic DA system (Beier et al., 2015). The VTA is widely implicated in the brain reward circuit and plays an important role in reward processing, motivational salience, associative learning, and positively-valenced emotions (Bouarab et al., 2019). Viral tracing and fast-scan cyclic voltammetry identified VTA^{DA}-to-BLA projections (Albanese and Minciacchi, 1983). As the VTA is strongly implicated in positive reinforcement, VTA^{DA} projections to the BLA may be essential for mediating addiction-related behaviors. Chemogenetic activation of VTA^{DA} projections to BLA increases cocaine cue-induced reinstatement and food intake in an operant task in male rats (hemizygous TH-Cre, 250–400 g) (Mahler et al., 2019). This result shows that VTA^{DA} projections to the BLA promotes cocaine cue-induced reinstatement (Mahler et al., 2019), but more work is needed to elucidate the potential role of this circuit in drug intake and other aspects of addiction-like behavior.

Projections from LC to BLA in addiction

The LC, a small nucleus in the pons of the brainstem, is the principal site for brain synthesis of norepinephrine (NE), an important regulator of emotions and learned behavior (Breton-Provencher et al., 2021). The LC is involved in physiological responses to stress (Valentino and Van Bockstaele, 2008), arousal (Carter et al., 2010), behavioral flexibility (Snyder et al., 2012), and pain processing (Hickey et al., 2014). The LC^{NE} system is a major component of the centrally mediated fight-or-flight response, activated by numerous environmental stressors, including social and predator stress (Valentino and Van Bockstaele, 2008). As the LC^{NE} is involved in many aversive states, it is possible that the LC^{NE} to BLA projection is essential for the withdrawal/negative affect stage of addiction.

Photostimulation of LC^{NE} projection neurons to the BLA increases NE release in the BLA, which is anxiogenic in the elevated zero maze test and promotes aversion in a CPA task in male mice (C57, 25–35 g) (McCall et al., 2017). Moreover, retrograde tracer imaging shows that LC^{NE} projection neurons preferentially synapse on BLA neurons that project to the HPC and CeA and promote anxiety-like behavior (McCall et al., 2017). These results suggest that activity of LC^{NE} projections to the BLA are important for avoidance and aversion (McCall et al., 2017), and activation of this circuit promotes anxiety-like behavior, which is often co-morbid with addiction.

Projections from the NBM to BLA in addiction

The NBM is a basal forebrain structure that sends acetylcholine (ACh) projections to the BLA (Woolf, 1991). The NBM is involved in the maintenance of attentional and arousal processes as well as learning and memory (Koulousakis et al., 2019). Optogenetic and electrophysiological approaches confirm the presence of a NBM^{ACh}-to-BLA circuit in mice (ChAT-Cre and ChAT tau-eGFP) (Jiang et al., 2016). Photostimulation of this projection improves responding for a cued food reward in male and female mice (ChAT-IRES-Cre backcrossed on C57, 5–7 months), indicating that the NBM^{ACh} to BLA projection enhances cue-reward learning in an operant task (Crouse et al., 2020). This study did not find the projection to be inherently rewarding, as photostimulation does not cause RTPP, but another study did report CPP associated with stimulation of the NBM^{ACh}-to-BLA circuit in male mice (Chat-Cre, adult) (Aitta-aho et al., 2018). In addition, optical stimulation of NBM^{ACh} projections to BLA during fear conditioning results in a strengthening of fear memories in mice (ChAT-Cre) (Jiang et al., 2016). Thus, the NBM^{ACh}-to-BLA circuit has a role in the preoccupation/anticipation stage through its involvement in cue conditioning and memory formation (Table 8.1; Fig. 8.3).

Central amygdala circuits

Reciprocal circuits between CeA and PBN in addiction

The PBN is a group of pontine nuclei that contains a large population of diverse glutamatergic neurons involved in processing visceral, nociceptive, and thermoreceptive inputs (e.g., taste, pain, threat, and malaise) from the spinal cord and NTS and is involved in directing central autonomic control (e.g., blood sugar control, energy balance, sodium intake, thermoregulation, respiration, and fluid satiation) to the HPT, TH, and amygdala (Chiang et al., 2019). The CeA receives nociceptive information through the spino-parabrachio-amygdaloid pain pathway, and activation of this pathway in a rat arthritis model (through knee joint injections) enhances CeA excitability through increased mGluR1 expression (Neugebauer et al., 2003). Inflammatory pain in male mice (C57, 8–10 weeks old), increases activity of CeA-projecting PBN neurons (measured using electrophysiology) that results in acute anxiety-like behavior in the elevated plus-maze and open field tasks (Zhou et al., 2021). Thus, reciprocal projections between CeA and PBN may have a key role in the withdrawal/negative affect stages of addiction.

During aversive learning procedures that incorporate painful stimuli, affective and motivational aspects of the pain experience are transmitted to the CeA through calcitonin gene-related peptide (CGRP)-expressing PBN neurons, which regulate vasodilation and affective pain transmission, to generate memories for future avoidance of painful situations (Han et al., 2015). Footshock in mice ($Calca^{Cre}$ backcrossed on C57) activates PBN^{CGRP} neurons (as measured through Fos expression), and their inactivation with toxins blocks pain signals and attenuates learning (Han et al., 2015). Direct infusion of CGRP into the CeA of these mice induces freezing behavior (Han et al., 2015). Finally, optogenetic activation of CGRP neurons in the PBN or CeA is sufficient for aversive learning (Han et al., 2015). These projections thus encode averse signals and regulate aversive memories and responses. PBN^{CGRP} neurons also are activated in male mice ($Calca^{Cre}$ backcrossed on C57, 7–9 weeks), following conditions that reduce food intake, as measured through Fos expression (Carter et al., 2013). Chemogenetic stimulation of PBN^{CGRP} projection neurons to the CeA in these mice reduces food intake (Carter et al., 2013) and induces conditioned taste aversion (Carter et al., 2015), while their inhibition reduces malaise-induced appetite suppression and starvation (Carter et al., 2013). Tracer studies show that some PBN afferents important for feeding behavior specifically synapse onto CeA neurons expressing protein kinase C-δ (PKC-δ). $CeA^{PKC-\delta}$ neurons of male mice are activated (as measured by *c*-Fos expression) in conditions of satiety, nausea and low palatability, and inhibit feeding in mice when optogenetically activated, without inducing anxiety-like behavior (Cai et al., 2014). $CeA^{PKC-\delta}$ neurons themselves project back to the PBN, but optogenetic activation of $CeA^{PKC-\delta}$ projections to PBN does not decrease feeding (Cai et al., 2014). These studies suggest that the PBN-to-CeA circuit is involved in aversive behaviors and may be critical for mediating drug withdrawal effects on affect and behavior.

Other afferent projections from the PBN synapse onto CeA neurons that express serotonin receptor 5-HT 2a (Htr2a). CeA^{Htr2a} neurons are activated (measured *in vivo* using calcium signaling) during feeding in female mice (Htr2a-Cre backcrossed to C57, 1–4 month), and optogenetic activation of these neurons is positively reinforcing for male mice (Htr2a-Cre backcrossed to C57, 1–4 month) (Douglass et al., 2017). Optogenetic stimulation of reciprocal CeA^{Htr2a} projections to PBN increases food intake and is intrinsically rewarding in mice, measured using RTPP and ICSS (Douglass et al., 2017). CeA neurons expressing the neuropeptide prepronociceptin (Pnoc) are also activated (as measured by *c*-Fos immunohistochemistry) by palatable food consumption in male mice (Pnoc-IRES-Cre × Ai9, 8–24 weeks) and promote palatable food consumption as their ablation or chemogenetic inhibition reduces palatable food intake (Hardaway et al., 2019). CeA^{Pnoc} neurons project to the PBN, BNST, and NTS. Optogenetic activation of these projections promote RTPP and ICSS, but contrary to CeA^{Htr2a} neurons, this stimulation does not affect feeding behavior. No overlap has been observed between CeA^{Htr2a} and CeA^{Pnoc} projection neurons to the PBN (Hardaway et al., 2019). Together, these studies provide strong evidence that activation of CeA projections to the PBN is rewarding.

CeA neurons expressing the neuropeptide neurotensin (NT), which is critical in reward and anxiety signaling, are activated (Fos measurement by fluorescent *in situ* hybridization) during alcohol consumption in male mice (C57, 10 weeks) (Torruella-Suárez et al., 2020). Optogenetic stimulation of CeA^{NT} projections to the PBN in male mice (NTS-IRES-Cre) results in RTPP, ICSS, and increases consumption of alcohol and palatable fluids such as sucrose and saccharin solutions without altering consumption of neutral or aversive fluids (Torruella-Suárez et al., 2020).

Taken together, these studies implicate a broad role for reciprocal CeA-PBN circuits in addiction. While PBN^{CGRP} projection neurons to the CeA promote aversive effects (Han et al., 2015) relevant for drug withdrawal, CeA projections (Htr2a, Pnoc, NT) to PBN are inherently rewarding (Douglass et al., 2017; Hardaway et al., 2019; Torruella-Suárez et al., 2020), and CeA^{NT} promote alcohol consumption (Torruella-Suárez et al., 2020) (Table 8.1; Fig. 8.3).

Reciprocal circuits between CeA and PVT in addiction

The PVT is a thalamic cluster of glutamatergic nuclei that participates in the integration of sensory information and underlies motivational states to guide behavioral responses for reward (Van der Werf et al., 2002). Neurons in the PVT are activated (as measured by *c*-Fos immunohistochemistry) by context and cues associated with reward (Matzeu et al., 2017) and aversion (Do-Monte et al., 2015). It is activated by various stressors and emotionally related contexts, with chemogenetic activation of PVT^{Glut} projections to CeA causing depression-like behaviors and stress susceptibility in a model of unpredictable stress in male mice (C57, 7–9 weeks) (Zhao et al., 2021). PVT projections to the CeA also have a role in fear-related behavior, such that inactivation of PVT^{Glut} projections to CeA prevent retrieval of fear memories in male rats (Sprague Dawley, 300–360 g) (Do-Monte et al., 2015) and male and female mice (Som-Cre backcrossed on C57, 6–9 weeks) (Penzo et al., 2015). Reciprocal projections from CeA to PVT have been linked to feeding cessation under threat (Petrovich et al., 2021). Therefore, the PVT-CeA circuit processes information related to cues, stress and aversive memory, and may have a role in addiction-related behavior.

Chemogenetic inhibition of the PVT^{Glut}-CeA pathway attenuates retrieval of memories related to morphine withdrawal in a CPA test in male mice (C57, 8–12 weeks) (Wang et al., 2021) and the formation of memories related to morphine intoxication in a CPP test in male mice (C57, 5–12 weeks) (Keyes et al., 2020). The PVT also mediates expectations and the emotional response to reward omission, which is another important process in addiction. When a cued reward, such as sucrose, is not delivered when it is expected, the anterior PVT is activated (measured using *in vivo* electrode recording) and sucrose-seeking and anxiety-like behavior increases in male rats (Sprague Dawley, 320–420 g) (Do-Monte et al., 2017). Photoinhibition of PVT^{Glut} projections to the CeA reduces sucrose-seeking behavior (Do-Monte et al., 2017). These results indicate that activation of PVT^{Glut} projections to the CeA enhances context-induced memories and drug-seeking.

Together, these studies demonstrate that activation of the PVT^{Glut} projections to the CeA contributes to the preoccupation/anticipation stage in the addiction cycle through formation and retrieval of reinforcing and aversive morphine memory (Keyes et al., 2020; Wang et al., 2021) or reward-seeking behavior under negative outcomes (Do-Monte et al., 2017) (Table 8.1; Fig. 8.3). The role of the reciprocal CeA^{GABA} projection to the PVT in relation to addiction-like behaviors is unclear.

Reciprocal circuits between CeA and HPT in addiction

The hypothalamus (HPT), located below the thalamus, is part of the limbic system and consists of a number of small nuclei (Flament-Durand, 1980). It regulates certain metabolic and autonomic processes, including body temperature, hunger, thirst, fatigue, sleep, and circadian rhythm regulation (Flament-Durand, 1980; Pop et al., 2018). It also links the nervous system to the endocrine system via the pituitary gland and secretes NT, corticotropin-releasing factor (CRF), oxytocin, and/or arginine-vasopressin (AVP) through parvocellular or magnocellular neurosecretory neurons (Flament-Durand, 1980).

The hypothalamic-pituitary-adrenal (HPA) axis is activated during acute drug intoxication and during withdrawal from chronic administration of all major drugs with abuse potential (Koob and Volkow, 2010). The paraventricular nucleus of the hypothalamus (PVN) consists of magnocellular, parvocellular, and long-projecting neurons (Qin et al., 2018). It is one of the most important autonomic control centers in the brain, with essential roles in controlling stress, metabolism, growth, reproduction, immunity, and other more traditional autonomic functions (Qin et al., 2018). The PVN is activated (as measured through *c*-Fos expression) by naloxone-precipitated morphine withdrawal in male rats (Sprague-Dawley, 220–240) (Laorden et al., 2002). The PVN locally releases CRF in response to stress to initiate the stress response in male and female mice (Crfr1-gfp) (Jiang et al., 2018). Early-life and acute adult stress increase AVP secretion and the density of HPT^{AVP} projections to the CeA^{GABA} projections in male rats (Wistar, 280 g) (Hernández et al., 2016). These studies suggest that PVN projections to the CeA may promote behaviors related to the withdrawal/negative affect stage.

The lateral hypothalamus (LH) plays an important role in modulating motivated behavior. Optogenetic activation of LH^{GABA} cells produces RTPP (Jennings et al., 2015), whereas activation of both LH^{Glut} and hypocretin-expressing (Hcrt1) LH cells produces RTPA in male mice (Vgat-IRES-Cre, Vglut-IRES-Cre, and Hcrt-Cre, respectively, 8–16 weeks) (de Jong et al., 2019; Jennings et al., 2013; Giardino et al., 2018). In male rats (Wistar, adult), predator odor stress activates (as measured through *c*-Fos activation) CeA^{GABA} projections to the LH in animals that exhibit persistent avoidance of the odor-paired context, and these high-avoidance animals drink higher quantities of alcohol for weeks after stress exposure (Edwards et al., 2013; Weera et al., 2021). Chemogenetic inhibition of this CeA^{GABA} to LH projection attenuates avoidance and stimulation of the projection in naive animals produces CPA (Weera et al., 2021). Overall, the reciprocal HPT-CeA circuit is essential for modulating stress coping, which makes this circuit a priomising target for modulation of drug withdrawal and negative affect (Table 8.1; Fig. 8.3).

Reciprocal circuits between CeA and RN in addiction

The RN are found in the brainstem (Kirby et al., 2011). They are the primary location for 5-HT production and release, which plays an important role in addiction vulnerability (Kirby et al., 2011). RN^{5-HT} neuron firing is inhibited by acute cocaine administration (Cunningham and Lakoski, 1988) and withdrawal from chronic morphine (Jolas et al., 2000). The RN is also a source of DA neurons (Ochi and Shimizu, 1978) that are involved in arousal, social interaction, fear response, and play a role in encoding incentive salience (Lin et al., 2021). The RN is reciprocally connected with the CeA (Lin et al., 2020; Vertes, 1991). Activity (measured by calcium imaging) of RN^{5-HT} projection neurons to the CeA increases following footshock in male mice (C57, 8–12 weeks) and chemogenetic activation of these neurons decreases locomotion in an open field and increases anxiety-like behavior on the elevated plus-maze (Ren et al., 2018).

Dopaminergic CeA cells are activated (calcium signals measured with fiber photometry) in responses to cues that predict sucrose reward or footshock in male and female mice (DAT-Cre, 8–12 weeks) (Lin et al., 2020). Loss of DA by Crispr-Cas9 knockdown of tyrosine hydroxylase in the RN of male mice (C57, 8–12 weeks) reduces high-fat food- or morphine-induced CPP, fear conditioning-induced freezing, and morphine withdrawal-induced place CPA (Lin et al., 2020), indicating that RN^{DA} projections to the CeA are involved in encoding incentive salience, which may have implications for addiction-related behaviors. As yet, the potential role of CeA projections to RN in addiction-related behaviors has not been explored.

Reciprocal circuits between CeA and VTA/SN in addiction

As mentioned previously, the VTA has dopaminergic, glutamatergic and GABAergic cells (Beier et al., 2015) and is well known for its involvement in motivation and reward (Koob and Volkow, 2010). The VTA is associated with the initial, positive, rewarding effects of alcohol, opioids, and nicotine (Koob and Volkow, 2010; Morikawa and Morrisett, 2010). The substantia nigra (SN) is another dopaminergic center located in the ventral midbrain, part of the basal ganglia, and has fewer glutamatergic DA neurons than the VTA (Mingote et al., 2015), but it too plays an important role in reward and movement (Berridge and Robinson, 1998). VTA^{DA} neurons are involved in mediating the hedonic effects of drugs, and they respond to both rewarding and aversive stimuli, as well as cues that predict those stimuli (Bromberg-Martin et al., 2010). Stimuli activate distinct neurons in the SN to drive salience and inhibit distinct neurons in the VTA to drive aversive learning (Matsumoto and Hikosaka, 2009). Retrograde tracing shows that the VTA and SN both have reciprocal connections with the CeA (Loughlin and Fallon, 1983). Blocking DA receptors in the CeA attenuates the effect of self-administered cocaine (Caine et al., 1995), DA levels (measured with microdialysis) in the CeA increase during cocaine withdrawal and reinstatement (Tran-Nguyen et al., 1998), and dopamine 2 receptor antagonism in the CeA increases food consumption (Anderberg et al., 2014).

In a study of fear generalization, inhibition of VTA^{DA} projections to the CeA enhances discrimination and fear learning in male and female mice (DAT-Cre, 3–7 months), but stimulation of DA terminals in the CeA does not increase preference in a RTPP test (Jo et al., 2018). This suggests that DA from VTA projections in the CeA is not inherently reinforcing. Alcohol dependence activates VTA^{DA} projections to the CeA during withdrawal (measured with *c*-Fos and slice electrophysiology) in male rats (Long Evans, 300 g), and these neurons may contribute to alcohol withdrawal-related behavior and negative affect (Avegno et al., 2021). Leptin receptor (LepR)-expressing VTA neurons primarily innervate and synapse onto CeA neurons expressing cocaine and amphetamine-regulated transcript (CART), a neuropeptide that produces behaviors psychostimulant-like effects in mice (LepRb-EGFPf or iZ/WAP transgenic mouse lines) (Leshan et al., 2010). Leptin decreases DA efflux in the CeA, leading to reduced CART expression (Leshan et al., 2010), which may normalize alcohol withdrawal effects, as CART itself in the CeA has been suggested to mediate the early signs of anxiety-like behavior induced by alcohol withdrawal in a social interaction test in male rats (Sprague-Dawley, 230–250 g) (Dandekar et al., 2008). Finally, there are also $VTA^{GABA,\ non-DA}$ projections to the CeA that have a role in defensive behavior in male mice (C57, 6–8 weeks) (Zhou et al., 2019). Reciprocal CeA^{CRF} projections to the VTA are anxiolytic, with effects that are mediated by CRF1 receptors (CRFR1) in the VTA. Depletion of CRF in the CeA reduces prefrontal cortex DA release, increases anxiety-like behavior in the light/dark box and elevated plus-maze, and facilitates fear conditioning in male mice (CRH flox × Camk2a-CreERT2, 10–14 weeks) (Dedic et al., 2018). These findings suggest that the CeA-to-VTA circuit may play a role in the withdrawal/negative affect stage of drug addiction.

Lesion studies show that SN^{DA} projections to the CeA are involved in surprise-induced enhancement of attention in an associative learning task in male rats (Long-Evans, 350–400 g) (Lee et al., 2006), which underscores their role in mediating incentive salience. Reciprocal CeA-to-SN projection neurons expressing somatostatin (Sst) are activated (measured by calcium imaging) by both appetitive and aversive stimuli in male mice (C57, >8 weeks), but their activity declines with successive presentations, indicating their role in incentive salience (Steinberg et al., 2020). Moreover, optogenetic stimulation of CeA-to-SN neurons does not produce CPP or CPA, but mice self-stimulate and show RTPP for optogenetic activation of this circuit, indicating that it is inherently rewarding (Steinberg et al., 2020). These findings show a clear role for reciprocal CeA-SN projections in reward and incentive salience that may have relevance for drug use and drug craving.

Circuitry from IC to CeA in addiction

The IC processes interoceptive effects of drug and natural rewards, with aIC projections promoting reward- and drug-seeking behavior and pIC projections promoting avoidance behavior and aversive states (see BLA section above). The pIC is also known as the visceral or interoceptive insula and is a major cortical convergence site for sensory signals (pain hypersensitivity, drug craving, and visceral malaise) (Gogolla et al., 2014). The CeA is one of the major outputs of the IC (Ponserre et al., 2020). Projections from the IC to $CeA^{PKC-\delta}$ and CeA^{Htr2a} neurons provide feeding-related signals in male mice (Cai et al., 2014; Douglass et al., 2017). Given its role in reward, aversion, and drug-seeking behaviors, IC circuit activity may be important for all stages of the addiction cycle.

Reinstatement after voluntary abstinence with a mutually exclusive choice between food and methamphetamine selectively activates aIC^{Glut} projections to CeA (measured by *c*-Fos) in male rats (Sprague-Dawley, 300–350 g) and chemogenetic inhibition of this circuit decreases methamphetamine-seeking behavior (Venniro et al., 2017). Chemogenetic activation of aIC^{Glut} projections to CeA also increases alcohol reward in male rats (Alko Alcohol, 10 weeks) (Haaranen, Schäfer, et al., 2020). While optogenetic activation of the aIC and CeA each individually suppress alcohol consumption in a limited access model of binge drinking, selective chemogenetic activation of aIC^{Glut} to CeA projections increases alcohol drinking (Haaranen, Schäfer, et al., 2020). This discrepancy could be explained by selective activation of the excitatory projection, as aIC stimulation also activates the pIC (Haaranen, Scuppa, et al., 2020), which through its projection to the CeA causes aversive states in male rats (Alko Alcohol, 10 weeks) and could thus impose an opposite effect on the behavioral outcome. Nevertheless, selective activation of aIC^{Glut} projections to CeA promotes alcohol intake and seeking, and may have similar effects for other drugs.

Optogenetic stimulation of pIC^{Glut} projections to CeA elicits defensive reactions with robust RTPA and increases in respiratory rate, immobility, and anxiety-like behaviors in male mice (C57, 2–6 months) (Gehrlach et al., 2019; Schiff et al., 2018). Conversely, selective inhibition of pIC^{Glut} projections to CeA prevents predator-odor-mediated avoidance of a food source without affecting food consumption itself (Gehrlach et al., 2019), as well as appropriate responses to rewarding and aversive conditioned stimuli (Schiff et al., 2018). Finally, optogenetic activation of the IC^{Glut}-to-CeA circuit suppresses licking behavior in thirsty male mice and induces avoidance behavior (Schiff et al., 2018). Collectively these results show that the IC-to-CeA circuit promotes reward (aIC) and aversion (pIC), and is important in the learning and expression of anticipatory behaviors in response to associated cues.

Reciprocal circuits between CeA and LC in addiction

The LC is the principal site for brain synthesis of NE, an important regulator of emotions and arousal (see BLA section), and the target of many drugs (Valentino and Volkow, 2019). The CeA is highly innervated by NE afferents from the LC (Asan, 1998). Some LC projections likely converge (in a synergistic way) on CeA neurons that receive PVT inputs that, as discussed above, drive morphine withdrawal memory retrieval (Wang et al., 2021). To our knowledge, no circuit-based study has manipulated LC^{NE}-to-CeA circuit activity, but tracing studies have visualized the circuitry and muscimol inhibition of the LC inhibits morphine withdrawal memory retrieval in a CPA test with male mice (C57, 8–12 weeks) (Wang et al., 2021), suggesting a potential role for the LC^{NE}-CeA circuit in drug withdrawal and craving.

The CeA also sends projections to the LC (Pomrenze et al., 2015; Reyes et al., 2008). Chemo- and optogenetic activation of CeA-to-LC projections promotes CRF release in the LC, activates CRFR1 receptors in that brain region, and promotes anxiety-like behavior and aversive behavior in a CPA test, open field, light–dark box, elevated zero maze, and RTPA test in male mice (C57, 9–10 weeks) (McCall et al., 2015; Paretkar and Dimitrov, 2018). Opioids typically reduce amygdalar CRF in the LC, but reduced sensitivity to opioids due to tolerance can result in stress-induced activation of the arousal system (Reyes et al., 2008; Valentino and Volkow, 2019). Chemogenetic activation of CeA^{CRF}-to-LC projections in male mice (C57, 9–10 weeks) also improves working memory performance in the Y-maze and novel object recognition memory tests (Paretkar and Dimitrov, 2018). The latter highlights the importance of activating specific projections rather than a whole population of neurons, as general CeA^{CRF} activation causes anxiety-like behavior that negatively impacts working memory performance. Therefore, CeA^{CRF} projections to LC likely have a role in drug withdrawal.

Circuitry from CeA to BNST in addiction

The BNST is important for mediating behavioral responses under stress, fear, and anxiety (see BLA section). Early lesion and activation studies suggested that the BNST is involved in a sustained state of avoidance, apprehension, and risk-assessment similar to anxiety, while the CeA is involved in acute fear (Walker et al., 2003). However, the CeA is now clearly recognized as an essential mediator of anxiety-like behavior through activation of the BNST (Herman et al., 2013; Pomrenze et al., 2015, 2019). Pharmacological studies show that the CeA^{CRF} projections to BNST mediate footshock-induced reinstatement of cocaine-, morphine-, and heroin-seeking behavior in male rats (Long Evans, 350–450 g or Sprague-Dawley, 225–250 g) (Erb et al., 2001; McFarland et al., 2004). When superfused with alcohol, CeA^{CRF} projections to BNST exhibit increases in firing rate (measured using a combination of electrophysiology and retrograde tracing) in male mice (Crhr1-gfp, 2–6 months) (Herman et al., 2013). Moreover, Daun02 inhibition of CeA^{CRF} projections to BNST reduces dependence-induced somatic signs of withdrawal and alcohol drinking in male rats (Crh-Cre, 200–225 g) (de Guglielmo et al., 2019). Thus, the CeA-to-BNST circuit has critical roles in drug taking, drug seeking, and drug withdrawal.

As mentioned above, $CeA^{PKC-\delta}$ and CeA^{Pnoc} neurons that project to the PBN also project to the BNST. Optogenetic stimulation of CeA^{Pnoc} projections to BNST are inherently rewarding, similar to PBN and NTS projections in male mice (Pnoc-IRES-Cre × Ai9, 8–24 weeks) (Hardaway et al., 2019). This is surprising considering the prominent role CeA-to-BNST projections play in anxiety-like behavior, and suggests a possible role for this circuit in the binge/intoxication stage of addiction. CeA^{D2R} neurons are largely non-overlapping with $CeA^{PKC-\delta}$ and CeA^{CRF} neurons and innervate both the BNST and VTA. Photoactivation of $CeA^{D2R,GABA}$ projections to the BNST decreases impulsivity in male mice ($Drd2^{-/-}$, 7–8 weeks) (Kim et al., 2018), which may have importance for addiction-related outcomes. The results described in this section highlight the importance of studying neuron-specific pathways and demonstrate key roles of CeA-BNST circuits in all stages of addiction (Table 8.1; Fig. 8.3).

Reciprocal circuits between CeA and PAG in addiction

The PAG is a midbrain region consisting of GABAergic interneurons and glutamatergic projection neurons that play a critical role in the control of pain (Taylor et al., 2019). Pain signals and stress activate enkephalin neurons, which indirectly inhibit ascending pain signals from the spinal cord (Behbehani, 1995) and produce analgesia (George et al., 2019). In addition, the PAG promotes defensive responses and learned avoidance behavior in response to threats and stress. Antero- and retrograde tracing shows reciprocal projections between the PAG and CeA (Rizvi et al., 1991) which consist of a homogeneous population of projections from the lateral CeA directed to the ventrolateral PAG and intrinsically heterogeneous projections from the medial CeA directed to the rostral, dorsolateral/lateral and ventrolateral PAG (Li and Sheets, 2018). Inflammatory pain (paw injection of complete Freud's adjuvant) decreases excitability of regular spiking projection neurons from the medial CeA^{GABA} to rostral PAG, which regulate defensive behaviors in male and female mice (C57, 4–10 weeks), whereas fast-spiking CeA projections to the dorsolateral/lateral PAG that evoke escape behaviors in response to pain are not affected (Li and Sheets, 2018). Electrical stimulation of the CeA or PAG has an analgesic effects on the nociceptive tail-flick response of male rats (Wistar, 140–160 g), that is contingent on mu-opioid receptor (MOR) activity in the PAG (Oliveira and Prado, 2001). Therefore, reciprocal projections between the CeA and PAG may be important for drug withdrawal and negative affect.

Optogenetic silencing of CeA^{GABA} projections to vlPAG induces thermal hyperalgesia in naive male rats (Wistar, 300 g) (Avegno et al., 2018). The activity of this projection is reduced (as measured with electrophysiological recordings) during withdrawal in alcohol-dependent rats. Increases in nociception observed during inhibition of CeA^{GABA}-vlPAG projection neurons is likely mediated by increased activity of vlPAG inhibitory interneurons and lower activity of $vlPAG^{MOR}$ projection neurons (Avegno et al., 2018). Accordingly, optogenetic activation of the CeA^{GABA}-to-vlPAG projection reduces hyperalgesia during withdrawal in alcohol-dependent rats, while optogenetic silencing mimics alcohol withdrawal-induced hyperalgesia in naive rats (Avegno et al., 2018). As mentioned (in the BNST section), alcohol withdrawal also increases CCL2 expression in CeA-to-PAG and CeA-to-BNST projections, which reduces anxiety-like behavior in the social interaction task of male rats (Wistar,

180–200 g) (Harper et al., 2020). These results suggest that the CeA^{GABA}-to-PAG circuit may represent a top-down control that can be used as a "brake" on negative emotional states.

CeA projections to PAG mediate pain and analgesia, and are highly relevant for the hyperalgesia effects of opioid and alcohol withdrawal through PAG^{MOR} activity, but more work is needed to confirm a potential role for PAG projections to CeA in addiction-related outcomes.

Reciprocal circuits between CeA and NTS in addiction

The NTS is a series of sensory nuclei (clusters of nerve cell bodies) embedded in the brainstem medulla (Jean et al., 1991). The solitary tract, a white bundle of nerve fibers, innervates the NTS (Jean et al., 1991). The function of the NTS is to contribute to autonomic regulation (Jean et al., 1991). Electrophysiology recordings show that alcohol enhances NTS^{NE} signaling (Aimino et al., 2018) and nicotine activates catecholamine expressing NTS neurons (Page et al., 2019). Stimulation of the CeA^{Pnoc} projections to NTS has a rewarding effect in male mice (Pnoc-IRES-Cre × Ai9, 8–24 weeks) similar to CeA^{Pnoc} projections to the PBN and BNST (Hardaway et al., 2019). The few studies on the NTS indicate that this brain region may play a role in the binge/intoxication stage of addiction, but a potential role for reciprocal NTS projections to CeA is less clear.

Conclusions

Early studies suggested that the role of the BLA may be limited to the control of behavior by reward-related and withdrawal-related cues, while the CeA may be limited to the control of the behavioral and physiological response to withdrawal. However, there is now converging evidence that this view was too simplistic, and that the role of the BLA and CeA in drug addiction highly depends on the specific sub-circuits controlling or under the control of the BLA and CeA. The field has only recently started to explore the role of these sub-circuits using pathway-specific and cell-specific tools. Nevertheless, several amygdalar circuits have been identified as critical for positive reinforcement during the binge/intoxication stage (Fig. 8.3, Table 8.1), including the BLA-NAc, BLA-CeA, mPFC-BLA, CeA-PBN, CeA-SN, and aIC–CeA pathways. Indeed, stimulation of these pathways usually promote reward-seeking behavior, place preference, self-stimulation and consummatory behaviors, probably by increasing the relevance of cues for drug intake and/or by increasing drug reward.

On the other hand, several pathways appear to be critical for the withdrawal/negative affect stage including the BLA-CeA, BLA-PL, LC-BLA, CeA-BNST, CeA-LH, pIC-CeA, PBN-CeA and CeA-PAG pathways (Fig. 8.3, Table 8.1). Indeed, stimulation of these pathways promotes withdrawal-like behavior, anxiety-like behavior, depression-like behavior, RTPA (intrinsic aversion), and hyperalgesia, all of which are aversive and may drive drug taking and seeking through negative reinforcement mechanisms.

Finally, several pathways appear critical for the preoccupation/anticipation stage including the BLA-NAc, BLA-ACC, BLA-aIC, VTA-BLA, lOFC-BLA, NBM-BLA, CeA-BNST, PVT-CeA, CeA-SN and RN-CeA pathways, Fig. 8.3, Table 8.1). Stimulation of these pathways increases cue- and context-induced responding and attention to drug cues, impulsivity, reward-related memories, incubation of craving, and drug-seeking behavior (i.e., relapse-like behavior).

Advanced techniques such as chemogenetics and optogenetics to investigate the role of the BLA and CeA circuitry in addiction-related behaviors in rodent models have added great insights into which mechanisms may promote different aspects of the addiction cycle. Although these studies have added greatly to the addiction field, most of the studies discussed in this chapter only used male subjects. There is a lack of data on BLA and CeA circuitry in addiction-related behaviors using these techniques in females and, therefore, our understanding of whether these circuits drive addiction-related behavior similarly or differently in males and females is yet to be determined. This is a major issue as we know that there are important sex differences in drug effects and substance use disorders (McHugh et al., 2018), and that some of these brain regions show neuroanatomical and functional sex differences (Hamann, 2005).

Overall, this chapter shows that BLA and CeA circuits are involved in all stages of drug addiction. In addition, specific clusters of nuclei, subregions, and sub-circuits that project to or from the BLA and CeA are essential for the emergence of specific addiction-related phenotypes. Dissecting the function of amygdala sub-circuits is a critical step in understanding the role of each sub-circuit in drug addiction, and this process is greatly facilitated by recent advancements in circuit-based and imaging technologies.

Funding sources

This work was supported by the National Institutes of Health (R01AA022977, R01AA0236081, U01DA044451, U01DA043799, R01AA026081, P60AA006420, TRDRP T32IR5384, and TRDRP 27IR-0047A to OG and F99NS118727 to EAS) and the Preclinical Alcohol Research Consortium at the University of California, San Diego.

References

Aggleton, J.P., 2000. The Amygdala: A Functional Analysis. http://orca.cf.ac.uk/id/eprint/34922.

Aimino, M.A., Coker, C.R., Silberman, Y., 2018. Acute ethanol modulation of neurocircuit function in the nucleus of the tractus solitarius. Brain Res. Bull. 138, 5–11.

Aitta-aho, T., Hay, Y.A., Phillips, B.U., Bussey, T.J., Paulsen, O., Apergis-Schoute, J., 2018. Basal forebrain and brainstem cholinergic neurons differentially impact amygdala circuits and learning-related behavior. Curr. Biol. 28 (16), P2557–P2569.

Aizenberg, M., Rolón-Martínez, S., Pham, T., Rao, W., Haas, J.S., Geffen, M.N., 2019. Projection from the amygdala to the thalamic reticular nucleus amplifies cortical sound responses. Cell Rep. 28 (3), 605–615.e4.

Albanese, A., Minciacchi, D., 1983. Organization of the ascending projections from the ventral tegmental area: a multiple fluorescent retrograde tracer study in the rat. J. Comp. Neurol. 216 (4), 406–420.

Amunts, K., Kedo, O., Kindler, M., Pieperhoff, P., Mohlberg, H., Shah, N.J., Habel, U., Schneider, F., Zilles, K., 2005. Cytoarchitectonic mapping of the human amygdala, hippocampal region and entorhinal cortex: intersubject variability and probability maps. Anat. Embryol. 210 (5–6), 343–352.

Anderberg, R.H., Anefors, C., Bergquist, F., Nissbrandt, H., Skibicka, K.P., 2014. Dopamine signaling in the amygdala, increased by food ingestion and GLP-1, regulates feeding behavior. Physiol. Behav. 136, 135–144.

Arguello, A.A., Richardson, B.D., Hall, J.L., Wang, R., Hodges, M.A., Mitchell, M.P., Stuber, G.D., Rossi, D.J., Fuchs, R.A., 2017. Role of a lateral orbital frontal cortex-basolateral amygdala circuit in cue-induced cocaine-seeking behavior. Neuropsychopharmacology: Official Publication of the American College of Neuropsychopharmacology 42 (3), 727–735.

Asan, E., 1998. The Catecholaminergic Innervation of the Rat Amygdala. Springer.

Avegno, E.M., Kasten, C.R., Snyder 3rd, W.B., Kelley, L.K., Lobell, T.D., Templeton, T.J., Constans, M., Wills, T.A., Middleton, J.W., Gilpin, N.W., 2021. Alcohol dependence activates ventral tegmental area projections to central amygdala in male mice and rats. Addiction Biol. 26 (4), e12990.

Avegno, E.M., Lobell, T.D., Itoga, C.A., Baynes, B.B., Whitaker, A.M., Weera, M.M., Edwards, S., Middleton, J.W., Gilpin, N.W., 2018. Central amygdala circuits mediate hyperalgesia in alcohol-dependent rats. J. Neurosci.: The Official Journal of the Society for Neuroscience 38 (36), 7761–7773.

Bacon, S.J., Headlam, A.J., Gabbott, P.L., Smith, A.D., 1996. Amygdala input to medial prefrontal cortex (mPFC) in the rat: a light and electron microscope study. Brain Res. 720 (1–2), 211–219.

Balleine, B.W., Killcross, A.S., Dickinson, A., 2003. The effect of lesions of the basolateral amygdala on instrumental conditioning. J. Neurosci.: The Official Journal of the Society for Neuroscience 23 (2), 666–675.

Behbehani, M.M., 1995. Functional characteristics of the midbrain periaqueductal gray. Prog. Neurobiol. 46 (6), 575–605.

Beier, K.T., Steinberg, E.E., DeLoach, K.E., Xie, S., Miyamichi, K., Schwarz, L., Gao, X.J., Kremer, E.J., Malenka, R.C., Luo, L., 2015. Circuit architecture of VTA dopamine neurons revealed by systematic input-output mapping. Cell 162 (3), 622–634.

Berridge, K.C., Robinson, T.E., 1998. What is the role of dopamine in reward: hedonic impact, reward learning, or incentive salience? Brain Research. Brain Research Reviews 28 (3), 309–369.

Beyeler, A., Namburi, P., Glober, G.F., Simonnet, C., Calhoon, G.G., Conyers, G.F., Luck, R., Wildes, C.P., Tye, K.M., 2016. Divergent routing of positive and negative information from the amygdala during memory retrieval. Neuron 90 (2), 348–361.

Blundell, P., Hall, G., Killcross, S., 2001. Lesions of the basolateral amygdala disrupt selective aspects of reinforcer representation in rats. J. Neurosci.: The Official Journal of the Society for Neuroscience 21 (22), 9018–9026.

Bouarab, C., Thompson, B., Polter, A.M., 2019. VTA GABA neurons at the interface of stress and reward. Front. Neural Circ. 13, 78.

Breton-Provencher, V., Drummond, G.T., Sur, M., 2021. Locus coeruleus norepinephrine in learned behavior: anatomical modularity and spatiotemporal integration in targets. Front. Neural Circ. 15, 638007.

Bromberg-Martin, E.S., Matsumoto, M., Hikosaka, O., 2010. Dopamine in motivational control: rewarding, aversive, and alerting. Neuron 68 (5), 815–834.

Cai, H., Haubensak, W., Anthony, T.E., Anderson, D.J., 2014. Central amygdala PKC-δ+ neurons mediate the influence of multiple anorexigenic signals. Nat. Neurosci. 17 (9), 1240–1248.

Caine, S.B., Heinrichs, S.C., Coffin, V.L., Koob, G.F., 1995. Effects of the dopamine D-1 antagonist SCH 23390 microinjected into the accumbens, amygdala or striatum on cocaine self-administration in the rat. Brain Res. 692 (1–2), 47–56.

Calandreau, L., Desmedt, A., Decorte, L., Jaffard, R., 2005. A different recruitment of the lateral and basolateral amygdala promotes contextual or elemental conditioned association in Pavlovian fear conditioning. Learn. Mem. 12 (4), 383–388.

Campeau, S., Davis, M., 1995. Involvement of the central nucleus and basolateral complex of the amygdala in fear conditioning measured with fear-potentiated startle in rats trained concurrently with auditory and visual conditioned stimuli. J. Neurosci.: The Official Journal of the Society for Neuroscience 15 (3), 2301–2311.

Caprioli, D., Venniro, M., Zhang, M., Bossert, J.M., Warren, B.L., Hope, B.T., Shaham, Y., 2017. Role of dorsomedial striatum neuronal ensembles in incubation of methamphetamine craving after voluntary abstinence. J. Neurosci.: The Official Journal of the Society for Neuroscience 37 (4), 1014–1027.

Carter, M.E., Han, S., Palmiter, R.D., 2015. Parabrachial calcitonin gene-related peptide neurons mediate conditioned taste aversion. J. Neurosci.: The Official Journal of the Society for Neuroscience 35 (11), 4582–4586.

Carter, M.E., Soden, M.E., Zweifel, L.S., Palmiter, R.D., 2013. Genetic identification of a neural circuit that suppresses appetite. Nature 503 (7474), 111–114.

Carter, M.E., Yizhar, O., Chikahisa, S., Nguyen, H., Adamantidis, A., Nishino, S., Deisseroth, K., de Lecea, L., 2010. Tuning arousal with optogenetic modulation of locus coeruleus neurons. Nat. Neurosci. 13 (12), 1526–1533.

Chiang, M.C., Bowen, A., Schier, L.A., Tupone, D., Uddin, O., Heinricher, M.M., 2019. Parabrachial complex: a hub for pain and aversion. J. Neurosci.: The Official Journal of the Society for Neuroscience 39 (42), 8225–8230.

Christoffel, D.J., Walsh, J.J., Hoerbelt, P., Heifets, B.D., Llorach, P., Lopez, R.C., Ramakrishnan, C., Deisseroth, K., Malenka, R.C., 2021. Selective filtering of excitatory inputs to nucleus accumbens by dopamine and serotonin. Proc. Natl. Acad. Sci. U. S. A. 118 (24). https://doi.org/10.1073/pnas.2106648118.

Contreras, M., Ceric, F., Torrealba, F., 2007. Inactivation of the interoceptive insula disrupts drug craving and malaise induced by lithium. Science 318 (5850), 655–658.

Corbit, L.H., Nie, H., Janak, P.H., 2012. Habitual alcohol seeking: time course and the contribution of subregions of the dorsal striatum. Biol. Psychiatr. 72 (5), 389–395.

Cosme, C.V., Gutman, A.L., LaLumiere, R.T., 2015. The dorsal agranular insular cortex regulates the cued reinstatement of cocaine-seeking, but not food-seeking, behavior in rats. Neuropsychopharmacology: Official Publication of the American College of Neuropsychopharmacology 40 (10), 2425–2433.

Crouse, R.B., Kim, K., Batchelor, H.M., Girardi, E.M., Kamaletdinova, R., Chan, J., Rajebhosale, P., Pittenger, S.T., Role, L.W., Talmage, D.A., Jing, M., Li, Y., Gao, X.-B., Mineur, Y.S., Picciotto, M.R., 2020. Acetylcholine is released in the basolateral amygdala in response to predictors of reward and enhances the learning of cue-reward contingency. Elife 9. https://doi.org/10.7554/eLife.57335.

Crowley, N.A., Bloodgood, D.W., Hardaway, J.A., Kendra, A.M., McCall, J.G., Al-Hasani, R., McCall, N.M., Yu, W., Schools, Z.L., Krashes, M.J., Lowell, B.B., Whistler, J.L., Bruchas, M.R., Kash, T.L., 2016. Dynorphin controls the gain of an amygdalar anxiety circuit. Cell Rep. 14 (12), 2774–2783.

Cunningham, K.A., Lakoski, J.M., 1988. Electrophysiological effects of cocaine and procaine on dorsal raphe serotonin neurons. Eur. J. Pharmacol. 148 (3), 457–462.

Dandekar, M.P., Singru, P.S., Kokare, D.M., Lechan, R.M., Thim, L., Clausen, J.T., Subhedar, N.K., 2008. Importance of cocaine- and amphetamine-regulated transcript peptide in the central nucleus of amygdala in anxiogenic responses induced by ethanol withdrawal. Neuropsychopharmacology: Official Publication of the American College of Neuropsychopharmacology 33 (5), 1127–1136.

Dedic, N., Kühne, C., Jakovcevski, M., Hartmann, J., Genewsky, A.J., Gomes, K.S., Anderzhanova, E., Pöhlmann, M.L., Chang, S., Kolarz, A., Vogl, A.M., Dine, J., Metzger, M.W., Schmid, B., Almada, R.C., Ressler, K.J., Wotjak, C.T., Grinevich, V., Chen, A., Deussing, J.M., 2018. Chronic CRH depletion from GABAergic, long-range projection neurons in the extended amygdala reduces dopamine release and increases anxiety. Nat. Neurosci. 21 (6), 803–807.

de Guglielmo, G., Kallupi, M., Pomrenze, M.B., Crawford, E., Simpson, S., Schweitzer, P., Koob, G.F., Messing, R.O., George, O., 2019. Inactivation of a CRF-dependent amygdalofugal pathway reverses addiction-like behaviors in alcohol-dependent rats. Nat. Commun. 10 (1), 1238.

De Jong, J.W., Atiyeh Afjei, S., Pollak Dorocic, I., Peck, J.R., Liu, C., Kim, C.K., Tian, L., Deisseroth, K., Lammel, S., 2019. A neural circuit mechanism for encoding aversive stimuli in the mesolimbic dopamine system. Neuron 101, 133–151.

Do-Monte, F.H., Minier-Toribio, A., Quiñones-Laracuente, K., Medina-Colón, E.M., Quirk, G.J., 2017. Thalamic regulation of sucrose seeking during unexpected reward omission. Neuron 94 (2), 388–400.e4.

Do-Monte, F.H., Quiñones-Laracuente, K., Quirk, G.J., 2015. A temporal shift in the circuits mediating retrieval of fear memory. Nature 519 (7544), 460–463.

Douglass, A.M., Kucukdereli, H., Ponserre, M., Markovic, M., Gründemann, J., Strobel, C., Alcala Morales, P.L., Conzelmann, K.-K., Lüthi, A., Klein, R., 2017. Central amygdala circuits modulate food consumption through a positive-valence mechanism. Nat. Neurosci. 20 (10), 1384–1394.

Droutman, V., Read, S.J., Bechara, A., 2015. Revisiting the role of the insula in addiction. Trends Cognit. Sci. 19 (7), 414–420.

Edwards, S., Baynes, B.B., Carmichael, C.Y., Zamora-Martinez, E.R., Barrus, M., Koob, G.F., Gilpin, N.W., 2013. Traumatic stress reactivity promotes excessive alcohol drinking and alters the balance of prefrontal cortex-amygdala activity. Transl. Psychiatry 3, e296.

Erb, S., Salmaso, N., Rodaros, D., Stewart, J., 2001. A role for the CRF-containing pathway from central nucleus of the amygdala to bed nucleus of the stria terminalis in the stress-induced reinstatement of cocaine seeking in rats. Psychopharmacology 158 (4), 360–365.

Fanselow, M.S., LeDoux, J.E., 1999. Why we think plasticity underlying Pavlovian fear conditioning occurs in the basolateral amygdala. Neuron 23 (2), 229–232.

Felix-Ortiz, A.C., Beyeler, A., Seo, C., Leppla, C.A., Wildes, C.P., Tye, K.M., 2013. BLA to vHPC inputs modulate anxiety-related behaviors. Neuron 79 (4), 658–664.

Finnegan, T.F., Chen, S.-R., Pan, H.-L., 2006. Mu opioid receptor activation inhibits GABAergic inputs to basolateral amygdala neurons through Kv1.1/1.2 channels. J. Neurophysiol. 95 (4), 2032–2041.

Flament-Durand, J., 1980. The hypothalamus: anatomy and functions. Acta Psychiatr. Belg. 80 (4), 364–375.

Fuchs, R.A., See, R.E., 2002. Basolateral amygdala inactivation abolishes conditioned stimulus- and heroin-induced reinstatement of extinguished heroin-seeking behavior in rats. Psychopharmacology 160 (4), 425–433.

Funk, D., Coen, K., Tamadon, S., Hope, B.T., Shaham, Y., Lê, A.D., 2016. Role of central amygdala neuronal ensembles in incubation of nicotine craving. J. Neurosci.: The Official Journal of the Society for Neuroscience 36 (33), 8612–8623.

Gabriele, A., See, R.E., 2010. Reversible inactivation of the basolateral amygdala, but not the dorsolateral caudate putamen, attenuates consolidation of cocaine-cue associative learning in a reinstatement model of drug-seeking. Eur. J. Neurosci. 32 (6), 1024–1029.

Gallagher, M., Graham, P.W., Holland, P.C., 1990. The amygdala central nucleus and appetitive Pavlovian conditioning: lesions impair one class of conditioned behavior. J. Neurosci.: The Official Journal of the Society for Neuroscience 10 (6), 1906–1911.

Gehrlach, D.A., Dolensek, N., Klein, A.S., Roy Chowdhury, R., Matthys, A., Junghänel, M., Gaitanos, T.N., Podgornik, A., Black, T.D., Reddy Vaka, N., Conzelmann, K.-K., Gogolla, N., 2019. Aversive state processing in the posterior insular cortex. Nat. Neurosci. 22 (9), 1424–1437.

George, D.T., Ameli, R., Koob, G.F., 2019. Periaqueductal gray sheds light on dark areas of psychopathology. Trends Neurosci. 42 (5), 349–360.

Ghashghaei, H.T., Barbas, H., 2002. Pathways for emotion: interactions of prefrontal and anterior temporal pathways in the amygdala of the rhesus monkey. Neuroscience 115 (4), 1261–1279.

Giardino, W.J., Eban-Rothschild, A., Christoffel, D.J., Li, S.-B., Malenka, R.C., de Lecea, L., 2018. Parallel circuits from the bed nuclei of stria terminalis to the lateral hypothalamus drive opposing emotional states. Nat. Neurosci. 21 (8), 1084–1095.

Gil-Lievana, E., Balderas, I., Moreno-Castilla, P., Luis-Islas, J., McDevitt, R.A., Tecuapetla, F., Gutierrez, R., Bonci, A., Bermúdez-Rattoni, F., 2020. Glutamatergic basolateral amygdala to anterior insular cortex circuitry maintains rewarding contextual memory. Communications Biology 3 (1), 139.

Gilpin, N.W., 2012. Corticotropin-releasing factor (CRF) and neuropeptide Y (NPY): effects on inhibitory transmission in central amygdala, and anxiety- & alcohol-related behaviors. Alcohol 46 (4), 329–337.

Gogolla, N., Takesian, A.E., Feng, G., Fagiolini, M., Hensch, T.K., 2014. Sensory integration in mouse insular cortex reflects GABA circuit maturation. Neuron 83 (4), 894–905.

Goodman, J., Hsu, E., Packard, M.G., 2019. NMDA receptors in the basolateral amygdala mediate acquisition and extinction of an amphetamine conditioned place preference. Behav. Neurosci. 133 (4), 428–436.

Guercio, L.A., Wimmer, M.E., Schmidt, H.D., Swinford-Jackson, S.E., Pierce, R.C., Vassoler, F.M., 2020. Deep brain stimulation of the infralimbic cortex attenuates cocaine priming-induced reinstatement of drug seeking. Brain Res. 1746, 147011.

Haaranen, M., Schäfer, A., Järvi, V., Hyytiä, P., 2020. Chemogenetic stimulation and silencing of the insula, amygdala, nucleus accumbens, and their connections differentially modulate alcohol drinking in rats. Front. Behav. Neurosci. 14, 580849.

Haaranen, M., Scuppa, G., Tambalo, S., Järvi, V., Bertozzi, S.M., Armirotti, A., Sommer, W.H., Bifone, A., Hyytiä, P., 2020. Anterior insula stimulation suppresses appetitive behavior while inducing forebrain activation in alcohol-preferring rats. Transl. Psychiatry 10 (1), 1–11.

Hamann, S., 2005. Sex differences in the responses of the human amygdala. Neuroscientist: A Review Journal Bringing Neurobiology, Neurology and Psychiatry 11 (4), 288–293.

Han, S., Soleiman, M.T., Soden, M.E., Zweifel, L.S., Palmiter, R.D., 2015. Elucidating an affective pain circuit that creates a threat memory. Cell 162 (2), 363–374.

Hardaway, J.A., Halladay, L.R., Mazzone, C.M., Pati, D., Bloodgood, D.W., Kim, M., Jensen, J., DiBerto, J.F., Boyt, K.M., Shiddapur, A., Erfani, A., Hon, O.J., Neira, S., Stanhope, C.M., Sugam, J.A., Saddoris, M.P., Tipton, G., McElligott, Z., Jhou, T.C., Kash, T.L., 2019. Central amygdala prepronociceptin-expressing neurons mediate palatable food consumption and reward. Neuron 102 (5), 1037–1052.e7.

Harper, K.M., Knapp, D.J., Todd, C.A., Balan, I., Aurelian, L., Criswell, H.E., Breese, G.R., 2020. Phenotyping CCL2 containing central amygdala neurons controlling alcohol withdrawal-induced anxiety. Front. Cell. Neurosci. 14, 580583.

Harris, G.C., Aston-Jones, G., 2003. Enhanced morphine preference following prolonged abstinence: association with increased Fos expression in the extended amygdala. Neuropsychopharmacology: Official Publication of the American College of Neuropsychopharmacology 28 (2), 292–299.

Hatfield, T., Han, J.S., Conley, M., Gallagher, M., Holland, P., 1996. Neurotoxic lesions of basolateral, but not central, amygdala interfere with Pavlovian second-order conditioning and reinforcer devaluation effects. J. Neurosci.: The Official Journal of the Society for Neuroscience 16 (16), 5256–5265.

Herman, M.A., Contet, C., Justice, N.J., Vale, W., Roberto, M., 2013. Novel subunit-specific tonic GABA currents and differential effects of ethanol in the central amygdala of CRF receptor-1 reporter mice. J. Neurosci.: The Official Journal of the Society for Neuroscience 33 (8), 3284–3298.

Hernández, V.S., Hernández, O.R., Perez de la Mora, M., Gómora, M.J., Fuxe, K., Eiden, L.E., Zhang, L., 2016. Hypothalamic vasopressinergic projections innervate central amygdala GABAergic neurons: implications for anxiety and stress coping. Front. Neural Circ. 10, 92.

Hickey, L., Li, Y., Fyson, S.J., Watson, T.C., Perrins, R., Hewinson, J., Teschemacher, A.G., Furue, H., Lumb, B.M., Pickering, A.E., 2014. Optoactivation of locus ceruleus neurons evokes bidirectional changes in thermal nociception in rats. J. Neurosci.: The Official Journal of the Society for Neuroscience 34 (12), 4148–4160.

Janak, P.H., Tye, K.M., 2015. From circuits to behaviour in the amygdala. Nature 517 (7534), 284–292.

Jean, A., 1991. The nucleus tractus solitarius: neuroanatomic, neurochemical and functional aspects. Arch. Int. Physiol. Biochim. Biophys. 99 (5), A3–A52.

Jennings, J.H., Rizzi, G., Stamatakis, A.M., Ung, R.L., Stuber, G.D., 2013. The inhibitory circuit architecture of the lateral hypothalamus orchestrates feeding. Science 341 (6153), 1517–1521.

Jennings, J.H., Ung, R.L., Resendez, S.L., Stamatakis, A.M., Taylor, J.G., Huang, J., Veleta, K., Kantak, P.A., Aita, M., Shilling-Scrivo, K., Ramakrishnan, C., Deisseroth, K., Otte, S., Stuber, G.D., 2015. Visualizing hypothalamic network dynamics for appetitive and consummatory behaviors. Cell 160 (3), 516–527.

Jiang, L., Kundu, S., Lederman, J.D., López-Hernández, G.Y., Ballinger, E.C., Wang, S., Talmage, D.A., Role, L.W., 2016. Cholinergic signaling controls conditioned fear behaviors and enhances plasticity of cortical-amygdala circuits. Neuron 90 (5), 1057–1070.

Jiang, Z., Rajamanickam, S., Justice, N.J., 2018. Local corticotropin-releasing factor signaling in the hypothalamic paraventricular nucleus. J. Neurosci.: The Official Journal of the Society for Neuroscience 38 (8), 1874–1890.

John, Y.J., Bullock, D., Zikopoulos, B., Barbas, H., 2013. Anatomy and computational modeling of networks underlying cognitive-emotional interaction. Front. Hum. Neurosci. 7, 101.

Jolas, T., Nestler, E.J., Aghajanian, G.K., 2000. Chronic morphine increases GABA tone on serotonergic neurons of the dorsal raphe nucleus: association with an up-regulation of the cyclic AMP pathway. Neuroscience 95 (2), 433–443.

Jo, Y.S., Heymann, G., Zweifel, L.S., 2018. Dopamine neurons reflect the uncertainty in fear generalization. Neuron 100 (4), 916–925.e3.

Ju, G., Swanson, L.W., 1989. Studies on the cellular architecture of the bed nuclei of the stria terminalis in the rat: I. Cytoarchitecture. J. Comp. Neurol. 280 (4), 587–602.

Ju, G., Swanson, L.W., Simerly, R.B., 1989. Studies on the cellular architecture of the bed nuclei of the stria terminalis in the rat: II. Chemoarchitecture. J. Comp. Neurol. 280 (4), 603–621.

Kayyal, H., Yiannakas, A., Kolatt Chandran, S., Khamaisy, M., Sharma, V., Rosenblum, K., 2019. Activity of insula to basolateral amygdala projecting neurons is necessary and sufficient for taste valence representation. J. Neurosci.: The Official Journal of the Society for Neuroscience 39 (47), 9369–9382.

Keistler, C.R., Hammarlund, E., Barker, J.M., Bond, C.W., DiLeone, R.J., Pittenger, C., Taylor, J.R., 2017. Regulation of alcohol extinction and cue-induced reinstatement by specific projections among medial prefrontal cortex, nucleus accumbens, and basolateral amygdala. J. Neurosci.: The Official Journal of the Society for Neuroscience 37 (17), 4462–4471.

Keyes, P.C., Adams, E.L., Chen, Z., Bi, L., Nachtrab, G., Wang, V.J., Tessier-Lavigne, M., Zhu, Y., Chen, X., 2020. Orchestrating opiate-associated memories in thalamic circuits. Neuron 107 (6), 1113–1123.e4.

Killcross, S., Robbins, T.W., Everitt, B.J., 1997. Different types of fear-conditioned behaviour mediated by separate nuclei within amygdala. Nature 388 (6640), 377–380.

Kim, B., Yoon, S., Nakajima, R., Lee, H.J., Lim, H.J., Lee, Y.-K., Choi, J.-S., Yoon, B.-J., Augustine, G.J., Baik, J.-H., 2018. Dopamine D2 receptor-mediated circuit from the central amygdala to the bed nucleus of the stria terminalis regulates impulsive behavior. Proc. Natl. Acad. Sci. U. S. A. 115 (45), E10730–E10739.

Kim, H., Lee, D., Jung, M.W., 2013. Signals for previous goal choice persist in the dorsomedial, but not dorsolateral striatum of rats. J. Neurosci.: The Official Journal of the Society for Neuroscience 33 (1), 52–63.

Kim, J., Zhang, X., Muralidhar, S., LeBlanc, S.A., Tonegawa, S., 2017. Basolateral to central amygdala neural circuits for appetitive behaviors. Neuron 93 (6), 1464–1479.e5.

Kirby, L.G., Zeeb, F.D., Winstanley, C.A., 2011. Contributions of serotonin in addiction vulnerability. Neuropharmacology 61 (3), 421–432.

Kita, H., Kitai, S.T., 1990. Amygdaloid projections to the frontal cortex and the striatum in the rat. J. Comp. Neurol. 298 (1), 40–49.

Koob, G.F., Buck, C.L., Cohen, A., Edwards, S., Park, P.E., Schlosburg, J.E., Schmeichel, B., Vendruscolo, L.F., Wade, C.L., Whitfield Jr., T.W., George, O., 2014. Addiction as a stress surfeit disorder. Neuropharmacology 76 Pt B, 370–382.

Koob, G.F., Volkow, N.D., 2010. Neurocircuitry of addiction. Neuropsychopharmacology: Official Publication of the American College of Neuropsychopharmacology 35 (1), 217–238.

Koulousakis, P., Andrade, P., Visser-Vandewalle, V., Sesia, T., 2019. The nucleus basalis of Meynert and its role in deep brain stimulation for cognitive disorders: a historical perspective. J. Alzheim. Dis.: JAD 69 (4), 905–919.

Kutlu, M.G., Connor, D.A., Tumolo, J.M., Cann, C., Garrett, B., Gould, T.J., 2018. Nicotine modulates contextual fear extinction through changes in ventral hippocampal GABAergic function. Neuropharmacology 141, 192–200.

Lafferty, C.K., Yang, A.K., Mendoza, J.A., Britt, J.P., 2020. Nucleus accumbens cell type- and input-specific suppression of unproductive reward seeking. Cell Rep. 30 (11), 3729–3742.e3.

Laorden, M.L., Núñez, C., Almela, P., Milanés, M.V., 2002. Morphine withdrawal-induced c-fos expression in the hypothalamic paraventricular nucleus is dependent on the activation of catecholaminergic neurones. J. Neurochem. 83 (1), 132–140.

Lasseter, H.C., Wells, A.M., Xie, X., Fuchs, R.A., 2011. Interaction of the basolateral amygdala and orbitofrontal cortex is critical for drug context-induced reinstatement of cocaine-seeking behavior in rats. Neuropsychopharmacology: Official Publication of the American College of Neuropsychopharmacology 36 (3), 711–720.

Lasseter, H.C., Xie, X., Arguello, A.A., Wells, A.M., Hodges, M.A., Fuchs, R.A., 2014. Contribution of a mesocorticolimbic subcircuit to drug context-induced reinstatement of cocaine-seeking behavior in rats. Neuropsychopharmacology: Official Publication of the American College of Neuropsychopharmacology 39 (3), 660–669.

Lasseter, H.C., Xie, X., Ramirez, D.R., Fuchs, R.A., 2010. Sub-region specific contribution of the ventral hippocampus to drug context-induced reinstatement of cocaine-seeking behavior in rats. Neuroscience 171, 830–839.

Lee, B.R., Ma, Y.-Y., Huang, Y.H., Wang, X., Otaka, M., Ishikawa, M., Neumann, P.A., Graziane, N.M., Brown, T.E., Suska, A., Guo, C., Lobo, M.K., Sesack, S.R., Wolf, M.E., Nestler, E.J., Shaham, Y., Schlüter, O.M., Dong, Y., 2013. Maturation of silent synapses in amygdala-accumbens projection contributes to incubation of cocaine craving. Nat. Neurosci. 16 (11), 1644–1651.

Lee, H.J., Youn, J.M., O, M.J., Gallagher, M., Holland, P.C., 2006. Role of substantia nigra-amygdala connections in surprise-induced enhancement of attention. J. Neurosci.: The Official Journal of the Society for Neuroscience 26 (22), 6077–6081.

Leshan, R.L., Opland, D.M., Louis, G.W., Leinninger, G.M., Patterson, C.M., Rhodes, C.J., Münzberg, H., Myers Jr., M.G., 2010. Ventral tegmental area leptin receptor neurons specifically project to and regulate cocaine- and amphetamine-regulated transcript neurons of the extended central amygdala. J. Neurosci.: The Official Journal of the Society for Neuroscience 30 (16), 5713–5723.

Li, J.-N., Sheets, P.L., 2018. The central amygdala to periaqueductal gray pathway comprises intrinsically distinct neurons differentially affected in a model of inflammatory pain. J. Physiol. 596 (24), 6289–6305.

Lin, R., Liang, J., Luo, M., 2021. The raphe dopamine system: roles in salience encoding, memory expression, and addiction. Trends Neurosci. 44 (5), 366–377.

Lin, R., Liang, J., Wang, R., Yan, T., Zhou, Y., Liu, Y., Feng, Q., Sun, F., Li, Y., Li, A., Gong, H., Luo, M., 2020. The raphe dopamine system controls the expression of incentive memory. Neuron 106 (3), 498–514.e8.

Liu, J., Hu, T., Zhang, M.-Q., Xu, C.-Y., Yuan, M.-Y., Li, R.-X., 2021. Differential efferent projections of GABAergic neurons in the basolateral and central nucleus of amygdala in mice. Neurosci. Lett. 745, 135621.

Livneh, Y., Ramesh, R.N., Burgess, C.R., Levandowski, K.M., Madara, J.C., Fenselau, H., Goldey, G.J., Diaz, V.E., Jikomes, N., Resch, J.M., Lowell, B.B., Andermann, M.L., 2017. Homeostatic circuits selectively gate food cue responses in insular cortex. Nature 546 (7660), 611–616.

Li, X., Zeric, T., Kambhampati, S., Bossert, J.M., Shaham, Y., 2014. The central amygdala nucleus is critical for incubation of methamphetamine craving. Neuropsychopharmacology: Official Publication of the American College of Neuropsychopharmacology 40 (5), 1297–1306.

Li, Y.-Q., Li, F.-Q., Wang, X.-Y., Wu, P., Zhao, M., Xu, C.-M., Shaham, Y., Lu, L., 2008. Central amygdala extracellular signal-regulated kinase signaling pathway is critical to incubation of opiate craving. J. Neurosci.: The Official Journal of the Society for Neuroscience 28 (49), 13248–13257.

Logrip, M.L., Zorrilla, E.P., 2014. Differential changes in amygdala and frontal cortex Pde10a expression during acute and protracted withdrawal. Front. Integr. Neurosci. 8, 30.

Loughlin, S.E., Fallon, J.H., 1983. Dopaminergic and non-dopaminergic projections to amygdala from substantia nigra and ventral tegmental area. Brain Res. 262 (2), 334–338.

Lu, L., Hope, B.T., Dempsey, J., Liu, S.Y., Bossert, J.M., Shaham, Y., 2005. Central amygdala ERK signaling pathway is critical to incubation of cocaine craving. Nat. Neurosci. 8 (2), 212–219.

Lu, L., Uejima, J.L., Gray, S.M., Bossert, J.M., Shaham, Y., 2007. Systemic and central amygdala injections of the mGluR(2/3) agonist LY379268 attenuate the expression of incubation of cocaine craving. Biol. Psychiatr. 61 (5), 591–598.

Lüthi, A., Lüscher, C., 2014. Pathological circuit function underlying addiction and anxiety disorders. Nat. Neurosci. 17 (12), 1635–1643.

Ma, D.Y., Xu, M.Y., Yang, H.C., Yang, L.Z., 2008. Effect of inhibition of the central nucleus of the amygdala and drug experience on the regions underlying footshock-induced reinstatement of morphine seeking. J. Int. Med. Res. 36 (5), 992–1000.

Mahler, S.V., Brodnik, Z.D., Cox, B.M., Buchta, W.C., Bentzley, B.S., Quintanilla, J., Cope, Z.A., Lin, E.C., Riedy, M.D., Scofield, M.D., Messinger, J., Ruiz, C.M., Riegel, A.C., España, R.A., Aston-Jones, G., 2019. Chemogenetic manipulations of ventral tegmental area dopamine neurons reveal multifaceted roles in cocaine abuse. J. Neurosci.: The Official Journal of the Society for Neuroscience 39 (3), 503–518.

Ma, T., Barbee, B., Wang, X., Wang, J., 2017. Alcohol induces input-specific aberrant synaptic plasticity in the rat dorsomedial striatum. Neuropharmacology 123, 46–54.

Matsumoto, M., Hikosaka, O., 2009. Two types of dopamine neuron distinctly convey positive and negative motivational signals. Nature 459 (7248), 837–841.

Matzeu, A., Cauvi, G., Kerr, T.M., Weiss, F., Martin-Fardon, R., 2017. The paraventricular nucleus of the thalamus is differentially recruited by stimuli conditioned to the availability of cocaine versus palatable food. Addiction Biol. 22 (1), 70–77.

McCall, J.G., Al-Hasani, R., Siuda, E.R., Hong, D.Y., Norris, A.J., Ford, C.P., Bruchas, M.R., 2015. CRH engagement of the locus coeruleus noradrenergic system mediates stress-induced anxiety. Neuron 87 (3), 605–620.

McCall, J.G., Siuda, E.R., Bhatti, D.L., Lawson, L.A., McElligott, Z.A., Stuber, G.D., Bruchas, M.R., 2017. Locus coeruleus to basolateral amygdala noradrenergic projections promote anxiety-like behavior. Elife 6, e18247.

McDonald, A.J., 1998. Cortical pathways to the mammalian amygdala. Prog. Neurobiol. 55 (3), 257–332.

McFarland, K., Davidge, S.B., Lapish, C.C., Kalivas, P.W., 2004. Limbic and motor circuitry underlying footshock-induced reinstatement of cocaine-seeking behavior. J. Neurosci.: The Official Journal of the Society for Neuroscience 24 (7), 1551–1560.

McGinnis, M.M., Parrish, B.C., McCool, B.A., 2020. Withdrawal from chronic ethanol exposure increases postsynaptic glutamate function of insular cortex projections to the rat basolateral amygdala. Neuropharmacology 172, 108129.

McGlinchey, E.M., James, M.H., Mahler, S.V., Pantazis, C., Aston-Jones, G., 2016. Prelimbic to accumbens core pathway is recruited in a dopamine-dependent manner to drive cued reinstatement of cocaine seeking. J. Neurosci.: The Official Journal of the Society for Neuroscience 36 (33), 8700–8711.

McHugh, R.K., Votaw, V.R., Sugarman, D.E., Greenfield, S.F., 2018. Sex and gender differences in substance use disorders. Clin. Psychol. Rev. 66, 12–23.

McLaughlin, J., See, R.E., 2003. Selective inactivation of the dorsomedial prefrontal cortex and the basolateral amygdala attenuates conditioned-cued reinstatement of extinguished cocaine-seeking behavior in rats. Psychopharmacology 168 (1–2), 57–65.

Meil, W.M., See, R.E., 1997. Lesions of the basolateral amygdala abolish the ability of drug associated cues to reinstate responding during withdrawal from self-administered cocaine. Behav. Brain Res. 87 (2), 139–148.

Meyers, R.A., Zavala, A.R., Neisewander, J.L., 2003. Dorsal, but not ventral, hippocampal lesions disrupt cocaine place conditioning. Neuroreport 14 (16), 2127–2131.

Millan, E.Z., Kim, H.A., Janak, P.H., 2017. Optogenetic activation of amygdala projections to nucleus accumbens can arrest conditioned and unconditioned alcohol consummatory behavior. Neuroscience 360, 106–117.

Miller, E.K., 2000. The prefontral cortex and cognitive control. Nat. Rev. Neurosci. 1 (1), 59–65.

Mingote, S., Chuhma, N., Kusnoor, S.V., Field, B., Deutch, A.Y., Rayport, S., 2015. Functional connectome analysis of dopamine neuron glutamatergic connections in forebrain regions. J. Neurosci.: The Official Journal of the Society for Neuroscience 35 (49), 16259–16271.

Morikawa, H., Morrisett, R.A., 2010. Ethanol action on dopaminergic neurons in the ventral tegmental area: interaction with intrinsic ion channels and neurotransmitter inputs. Int. Rev. Neurobiol. 91, 235–288.

Morrison, S.E., Salzman, C.D., 2010. Re-valuing the amygdala. Curr. Opin. Neurobiol. 20 (2), 221–230.

Namburi, P., Beyeler, A., Yorozu, S., Calhoon, G.G., Halbert, S.A., Wichmann, R., Holden, S.S., Mertens, K.L., Anahtar, M., Felix-Ortiz, A.C., Wickersham, I.R., Gray, J.M., Tye, K.M., 2015. A circuit mechanism for differentiating positive and negative associations. Nature 520 (7549), 675–678.

Neugebauer, V., Li, W., Bird, G.C., Bhave, G., Gereau 4th, R.W., 2003. Synaptic plasticity in the amygdala in a model of arthritic pain: differential roles of metabotropic glutamate receptors 1 and 5. J. Neurosci.: The Official Journal of the Society for Neuroscience 23 (1), 52–63.

Neugebauer, V., Zinebi, F., Russell, R., Gallagher, J.P., Shinnick-Gallagher, P., 2000. Cocaine and kindling alter the sensitivity of group II and III metabotropic glutamate receptors in the central amygdala. J. Neurophysiol. 84 (2), 759–770.

Ochi, J., Shimizu, K., 1978. Occurrence of dopamine-containing neurons in the midbrain raphe nuclei of the rat. Neurosci. Lett. 8 (4), 317–320.

Oliveira, M.A., Prado, W.A., 2001. Role of PAG in the antinociception evoked from the medial or central amygdala in rats. Brain Res. Bull. 54, 55–63.

O'Reilly, R.C., Rudy, J.W., 2001. Conjunctive representations in learning and memory: principles of cortical and hippocampal function. Psychol. Rev. 108 (2), 311–345.

Ostlund, S.B., Balleine, B.W., 2008. Differential involvement of the basolateral amygdala and mediodorsal thalamus in instrumental action selection. J. Neurosci.: The Official Journal of the Society for Neuroscience 28 (17), 4398–4405.

Ottersen, O.P., 1982. Connections of the amygdala of the rat. IV: corticoamygdaloid and intraamygdaloid connections as studied with axonal transport of horseradish peroxidase. J. Comp. Neurol. 205 (1), 30–48.

Page, S.J., Zhu, M., Appleyard, S.M., 2019. Effects of acute and chronic nicotine on catecholamine neurons of the nucleus of the solitary tract. Am. J. Physiol. Regul. Integr. Comp. Physiol. 316 (1), R38–R49.

Paretkar, T., Dimitrov, E., 2018. The central amygdala corticotropin-releasing hormone (CRH) neurons modulation of anxiety-like behavior and hippocampus-dependent memory in mice. Neuroscience 390, 187–197.

Penzo, M.A., Robert, V., Tucciarone, J., De Bundel, D., Wang, M., Van Aelst, L., Darvas, M., Parada, L.F., Palmiter, R.D., He, M., Huang, Z.J., Li, B., 2015. The paraventricular thalamus controls a central amygdala fear circuit. Nature 519 (7544), 455–459.

Peters, J., LaLumiere, R.T., Kalivas, P.W., 2008. Infralimbic prefrontal cortex is responsible for inhibiting cocaine seeking in extinguished rats. J. Neurosci.: The Official Journal of the Society for Neuroscience 28 (23), 6046–6053.

Petrovich, G.D., 2021. The function of paraventricular thalamic circuitry in adaptive control of feeding behavior. Front. Behav. Neurosci. 2021, 671096. https://doi.org/10.3389/fnbeh.2021.671096, 27 April 2021.

Phillips, A.G., Ahn, S., Howland, J.G., 2003. Amygdalar control of the mesocorticolimbic dopamine system: parallel pathways to motivated behavior. Neurosci. Biobehav. Rev. 27 (6), 543–554.

Pitkänen, A., Pikkarainen, M., Nurminen, N., Ylinen, A., 2000. Reciprocal connections between the amygdala and the hippocampal formation, perirhinal cortex, and postrhinal cortex in rat. A review. Ann. N. Y. Acad. Sci. 911, 369–391.

Pomrenze, M.B., Millan, E.Z., Hopf, F.W., Keiflin, R., Maiya, R., Blasio, A., Dadgar, J., Kharazia, V., De Guglielmo, G., Crawford, E., Janak, P.H., George, O., Rice, K.C., Messing, R.O., 2015. A transgenic rat for investigating the anatomy and function of corticotrophin releasing factor circuits. Front. Neurosci. 9, 487.

Pomrenze, M.B., Tovar-Diaz, J., Blasio, A., Maiya, R., Giovanetti, S.M., Lei, K., Morikawa, H., Hopf, F.W., Messing, R.O., 2019. A corticotropin releasing factor network in the extended amygdala for anxiety. J. Neurosci.: The Official Journal of the Society for Neuroscience 39 (6), 1030–1043.

Ponserre, M., Peters, C., Fermani, F., Conzelmann, K., Klein, R., 2020. The insula cortex contacts distinct output streams of the central amygdala. J. Neurosci. 40 (46), 8870–8882.

Pop, M.G., Crivii, C., Opincariu, I., 2018. Anatomy and function of the hypothalamus. In: Hypothalamus in Health and Diseases. IntechOpen.

Puaud, M., Higuera-Matas, A., Brunault, P., Everitt, B.J., Belin, D., 2021. The basolateral amygdala to nucleus accumbens core circuit mediates the conditioned reinforcing effects of cocaine-paired cues on cocaine seeking. Biol. Psychiatr. 89 (4), 356–365.

Pushparaj, A., Kim, A.S., Musiol, M., Trigo, J.M., Le Foll, B., 2015. Involvement of the rostral agranular insular cortex in nicotine self-administration in rats. Behav. Brain Res. 290, 77–83.

Qin, C., Li, J., Tang, K., 2018. The paraventricular nucleus of the hypothalamus: development, function, and human diseases. Endocrinology 159 (9), 3458–3472.

Quinn, J.J., Wied, H.M., Ma, Q.D., Tinsley, M.R., Fanselow, M.S., 2008. Dorsal hippocampus involvement in delay fear conditioning depends upon the strength of the tone-footshock association. Hippocampus 18 (7), 640–654.

Reed, S.J., Lafferty, C.K., Mendoza, J.A., Yang, A.K., Davidson, T.J., Grosenick, L., Deisseroth, K., Britt, J.P., 2018. Co-ordinated reductions in excitatory input to the nucleus accumbens underlie food consumption. Neuron 99 (6), 1260–1273.e4.

Ren, J., Friedmann, D., Xiong, J., Liu, C.D., Ferguson, B.R., Weerakkody, T., DeLoach, K.E., Ran, C., Pun, A., Sun, Y., Weissbourd, B., Neve, R.L., Huguenard, J., Horowitz, M.A., Luo, L., 2018. Anatomically defined and functionally distinct dorsal raphe serotonin sub-systems. Cell 175 (2), 472–487.e20.

Ren, W., Neugebauer, V., 2010. Pain-related increase of excitatory transmission and decrease of inhibitory transmission in the central nucleus of the amygdala are mediated by mGluR1. Mol. Pain 6, 93.

Reyes, B.A.S., Drolet, G., Van Bockstaele, E.J., 2008. Dynorphin and stress-related peptides in rat locus coeruleus: contribution of amygdalar efferents. J. Comp. Neurol. 508 (4), 663–675.

Reyes, B.A.S., Valentino, R.J., Van Bockstaele, E.J., 2008. Stress-induced intracellular trafficking of corticotropin-releasing factor receptors in rat locus coeruleus neurons. Endocrinology 149 (1), 122–130.

Rizvi, T.A., Ennis, M., Behbehani, M.M., Shipley, M.T., 1991. Connections between the central nucleus of the amygdala and the midbrain periaqueductal gray: topography and reciprocity. J. Comp. Neurol. 303 (1), 121–131.

Roberts, G.W., Woodhams, P.L., Polak, J.M., Crow, T.J., 1982. Distribution of neuropeptides in the limbic system of the rat: the amygdaloid complex. Neuroscience 7 (1), 99–131.

Robinson, S.L., Marrero, I.M., Perez-Heydrich, C.A., Sepulveda-Orengo, M.T., Reissner, K.J., Thiele, T.E., 2019. Medial prefrontal cortex neuropeptide Y modulates binge-like ethanol consumption in C57BL/6J mice. Neuropsychopharmacology: Official Publication of the American College of Neuropsychopharmacology 44 (6), 1132–1140.

Salgado, S., Kaplitt, M.G., 2015. The nucleus accumbens: a comprehensive review. Stereotact. Funct. Neurosurg. 93 (2), 75–93.

Schiff, H.C., Bouhuis, A.L., Yu, K., Penzo, M.A., Li, H., He, M., Li, B., 2018. An insula-central amygdala circuit for guiding tastant-reinforced choice behavior. J. Neurosci.: The Official Journal of the Society for Neuroscience 38 (6), 1418–1429.

Shao, D., Cao, Z., Fu, Y., Yang, H., Gao, P., Zheng, P., Lai, B., 2021. Projection from the basolateral amygdala to the anterior cingulate cortex facilitates the consolidation of long-term withdrawal memory. Addiction Biol. e13048.

Simpson, S., Kimbrough, A., Boomhower, B., McLellan, R., Hughes, M., Shankar, K., de Guglielmo, G., George, O., 2020. Depletion of the microbiome alters the recruitment of neuronal ensembles of oxycodone intoxication and withdrawal. eNeuro 7 (3). https://doi.org/10.1523/ENEURO.0312-19.2020.

Snyder, K., Wang, W.-W., Han, R., McFadden, K., Valentino, R.J., 2012. Corticotropin-releasing factor in the norepinephrine nucleus, locus coeruleus, facilitates behavioral flexibility. Neuropsychopharmacology: Official Publication of the American College of Neuropsychopharmacology 37 (2), 520–530.

Song, J., Shao, D., Guo, X., Zhao, Y., Cui, D., Ma, Q., Sheng, H., Ma, L., Lai, B., Chen, M., Zheng, P., 2019. Crucial role of feedback signals from prelimbic cortex to basolateral amygdala in the retrieval of morphine withdrawal memory. Sci. Adv. 5 (2), eaat3210.

Stamatakis, A.M., Sparta, D.R., Jennings, J.H., McElligott, Z.A., Decot, H., Stuber, G.D., 2014. Amygdala and bed nucleus of the stria terminalis circuitry: implications for addiction-related behaviors. Neuropharmacology 76 Pt B, 320–328.

Stefanik, M.T., Kalivas, P.W., 2013. Optogenetic dissection of basolateral amygdala projections during cue-induced reinstatement of cocaine seeking. Front. Behav. Neurosci. 7, 213.

Steinberg, E.E., Gore, F., Heifets, B.D., Taylor, M.D., Norville, Z.C., Beier, K.T., Földy, C., Lerner, T.N., Luo, L., Deisseroth, K., Malenka, R.C., 2020. Amygdala-midbrain connections modulate appetitive and aversive learning. Neuron 106 (6), 1026–1043.e9.

Stuber, G.D., Sparta, D.R., Stamatakis, A.M., Van Leeuwen, W.A., Hardjoprajitno, J.E., Cho, S., Tye, K.M., Kempadoo, K.A., Zhang, F., Deisseroth, K., Bonci, A., 2011. Excitatory transmission from the amygdala to nucleus accumbens facilitates reward seeking. Nature 475 (7356), 377–382.

Taylor, N.E., Pei, J., Zhang, J., Vlasov, K., Y, Davis, T., Taylor, E., Weng, F., Van Dort, C.,J., Solt, K., Brown, E.N., 2019. The role of glutamatergic and dopaminergic neurons in the periaqueductal gray/dorsal raphe: separating analgesia and anxiety. eNeuro 6 (1). ENEURO.0018-18.2019.

Tom, R.L., Ahuja, A., Maniates, H., Freeland, C.M., Robinson, M.J.F., 2019. Optogenetic activation of the central amygdala generates addiction-like preference for reward. Eur. J. Neurosci. 50 (3), 2086–2100.

Torrico, T.J., Munakomi, S., 2021. Neuroanatomy, thalamus. In: StatPearls. StatPearls Publishing.

Torruella-Suárez, M.L., Vandenberg, J.R., Cogan, E.S., Tipton, G.J., Teklezghi, A., Dange, K., Patel, G.K., McHenry, J.A., Hardaway, J.A., Kantak, P.A., Crowley, N.A., DiBerto, J.F., Faccidomo, S.P., Hodge, C.W., Stuber, G.D., McElligott, Z.A., 2020. Manipulations of central amygdala neurotensin neurons alter the consumption of ethanol and sweet fluids in mice. J. Neurosci.: The Official Journal of the Society for Neuroscience 40 (3), 632–647.

Tran-Nguyen, L.T., Fuchs, R.A., Coffey, G.P., Baker, D.A., O'Dell, L.E., Neisewander, J.L., 1998. Time-dependent changes in cocaine-seeking behavior and extracellular dopamine levels in the amygdala during cocaine withdrawal. Neuropsychopharmacology: Official Publication of the American College of Neuropsychopharmacology 19 (1), 48–59.

Uddin, L.Q., Nomi, J.S., Hébert-Seropian, B., Ghaziri, J., Boucher, O., 2017. Structure and function of the human insula. J. Clin. Neurophysiol.: Official Publication of the American Electroencephalographic Society 34 (4), 300–306.

Valentino, R.J., Van Bockstaele, E., 2008. Convergent regulation of locus coeruleus activity as an adaptive response to stress. Eur. J. Pharmacol. 583 (2–3), 194–203.

Valentino, R.J., Volkow, N.D., 2019. Drugs, sleep, and the addicted brain. Neuropsychopharmacology: Official Publication of the American College of Neuropsychopharmacology 45 (1), 3–5.

van den Burg, E.H., Stoop, R., 2019. Neuropeptide signalling in the central nucleus of the amygdala. Cell Tissue Res. 375 (1), 93–101.

Van der Werf, Y.D., Witter, M.P., Groenewegen, H.J., 2002. The intralaminar and midline nuclei of the thalamus. Anatomical and functional evidence for participation in processes of arousal and awareness. Brain Research. Brain Research Reviews 39 (2–3), 107–140.

van Vulpen, E.H., Verwer, R.W., 1989. Organization of projections from the mediodorsal nucleus of the thalamus to the basolateral complex of the amygdala in the rat. Brain Res. 500 (1–2), 389–394.

Venniro, M., Caprioli, D., Zhang, M., Whitaker, L.R., Zhang, S., Warren, B.L., Cifani, C., Marchant, N.J., Yizhar, O., Bossert, J.M., Chiamulera, C., Morales, M., Shaham, Y., 2017. The anterior insular Cortex→Central amygdala glutamatergic pathway is critical to relapse after contingency management. Neuron 96 (2), 414–427.e8.

Vertes, R.P., 1991. A PHA-L analysis of ascending projections of the dorsal raphe nucleus in the rat. J. Comp. Neurol. 313 (4), 643–668.

Walker, D.L., Toufexis, D.J., Davis, M., 2003. Role of the bed nucleus of the stria terminalis versus the amygdala in fear, stress, and anxiety. Eur. J. Pharmacol. 463 (1–3), 199–216.

Wang, Y., Pan, Y., Cai, Z., Lei, C., Guo, X., Cui, D., Yuan, Y., Lai, B., Zheng, P., 2021. Inputs from paraventricular nucleus of thalamus and locus coeruleus contribute to the activation of central nucleus of amygdala during context-induced retrieval of morphine withdrawal memory. Exp. Neurol. 338, 113600.

Warlow, S.M., Naffziger, E.E., Berridge, K.C., 2020. The central amygdala recruits mesocorticolimbic circuitry for pursuit of reward or pain. Nat. Commun. 11 (1), 1–15.

Wassum, K.M., Izquierdo, A., 2015. The basolateral amygdala in reward learning and addiction. Neurosci. Biobehav. Rev. 57, 271–283.

Weera, M.M., Shackett, R.S., Kramer, H.M., Middleton, J.W., Gilpin, N.W., 2021. Central amygdala projections to lateral hypothalamus mediate avoidance behavior in rats. J. Neurosci.: The Official Journal of the Society for Neuroscience 41 (1), 61–72.

Weissenborn, R., Robbins, T.W., Everitt, B.J., 1997. Effects of medial prefrontal or anterior cingulate cortex lesions on responding for cocaine under fixed-ratio and second-order schedules of reinforcement in rats. Psychopharmacology 134 (3), 242–257.

Whitelaw, R.B., Markou, A., Robbins, T.W., Everitt, B.J., 1996. Excitotoxic lesions of the basolateral amygdala impair the acquisition of cocaine-seeking behaviour under a second-order schedule of reinforcement. Psychopharmacology 127 (3), 213–224.

Woolf, N.J., 1991. Cholinergic systems in mammalian brain and spinal cord. Prog. Neurobiol. 37 (6), 475–524.

Xi, Z.-X., Li, X., Li, J., Peng, X.-Q., Song, R., Gaál, J., Gardner, E.L., 2013. Blockade of dopamine D3 receptors in the nucleus accumbens and central amygdala inhibits incubation of cocaine craving in rats. Addiction Biol. 18 (4), 665–677.

Yager, L.M., Garcia, A.F., Wunsch, A.M., Ferguson, S.M., 2015. The ins and outs of the striatum: role in drug addiction. Neuroscience 301, 529–541.

Yuan, K., Cao, L., Xue, Y.-X., Luo, Y.-X., Liu, X.-X., Kong, F.-N., Tabarak, S., Liao, F., Meng, S.-Q., Han, Y., Wu, P., Bao, Y.-P., Zhang, W., Lu, L., Shi, J., 2020. Basolateral amygdala is required for reconsolidation updating of heroin-associated memory after prolonged withdrawal. Addiction Biol. 25 (4), e12793.

Yuan, K., Sheng, H., Song, J., Yang, L., Cui, D., Ma, Q., Zhang, W., Lai, B., Chen, M., Zheng, P., 2017. Morphine treatment enhances glutamatergic input onto neurons of the nucleus accumbens via both disinhibitory and stimulating effect. Addiction Biol. 22 (6), 1756–1767.

Yu, J., Yan, Y., Li, K.-L., Wang, Y., Huang, Y.H., Urban, N.N., Nestler, E.J., Schlüter, O.M., Dong, Y., 2017. Nucleus accumbens feedforward inhibition circuit promotes cocaine self-administration. Proc. Natl. Acad. Sci. U. S. A. 114 (41), E8750–E8759.

Zarrindast, M.R., Meshkani, J., Rezayof, A., Beigzadeh, R., Rostami, P., 2010. Nicotinic acetylcholine receptors of the dorsal hippocampus and the basolateral amygdala are involved in ethanol-induced conditioned place preference. Neuroscience 168, 505–513.

Zhao, D., Liu, C., Cui, M., Liu, J., Meng, F., Lian, H., Wang, D., Hu, F., Liu, D., Li, C., 2021. The paraventricular thalamus input to central amygdala controls depression-related behaviors. Exp. Neurol. 342, 113744.

Zhou, W., Li, Y., Meng, X., Liu, A., Mao, Y., Zhu, X., Meng, Q., Jin, Y., Zhang, Z., Tao, W., 2021. Switching of delta opioid receptor subtypes in central amygdala microcircuits is associated with anxiety states in pain. J. Biol. Chem. 296, 100277.

Zhou, Z., Liu, X., Chen, S., Zhang, Z., Liu, Y., Montardy, Q., Tang, Y., Wei, P., Liu, N., Li, L., Song, R., Lai, J., He, X., Chen, C., Bi, G., Feng, G., Xu, F., Wang, L., 2019. A VTA GABAergic neural circuit mediates visually evoked innate defensive responses. Neuron 103 (3), 473–488.e6.

Zikopoulos, B., Barbas, H., 2012. Pathways for emotions and attention converge on the thalamic reticular nucleus in primates. J. Neurosci.: The Official Journal of the Society for Neuroscience 32 (15), 5338–5350.

CHAPTER

9

Bed Nucleus of Stria Terminalis (BNST) circuits

Samuel W. Centanni, Jordan A. Brown, Kellie M. Williford, Elizabeth A. Flook, Joseph R. Luchsinger and Danny G. Winder

Vanderbilt Center for Addiction Research, Vanderbilt University School of Medicine, Nashville, TN, United States

Introduction

The bed nucleus of the stria terminalis (BNST) is a limbic forebrain structure nestled below the lateral ventricles, surrounding the anterior commissure, and its neighboring regions, the striatum, thalamus, and hypothalamus. The BNST is an integral component of the extended amygdala, a network of brain areas that span the anterior/posterior gradient of the brain starting anterior in the nucleus accumbens, continuing through the transition areas, and into the BNST and the central nucleus of the amygdala. The BNST has functional outputs relevant for reward and stress, and it is interconnected with brain areas involved in generating and regulating mood and overall emotional state. Various brain circuits are regulated by BNST outputs, and complex intrinsic microcircuits regulate the overall activity state of the BNST and modulate outputs to other brain areas. The BNST integrates cortical and subcortical inputs to determine affective state and whether a stimulus/situation will produce fear, anxiety, depression, irritability, or reward motivation/goal-directed behavior. On the cellular level, this highly heterogeneous brain area contains a diverse population of cell types and inputs, thus allowing for nuanced regulation of emotional state and behavioral responses.

The BNST is involved in all phases of addiction, including the binge/intoxication stage, preoccupation stage, and withdrawal/negative affect stage (Koob and Schulkin, 2018; Koob and Volkow, 2010), but especially the last of these. Withdrawal is defined by negative emotional states that drive drug use via negative reinforcement mechanisms (i.e., avoidance of withdrawal symptoms). Negative affect is a major contributor to relapse in abstinent

Neurocircuitry of Addiction
https://doi.org/10.1016/B978-0-12-823453-2.00011-4

individuals with a substance use disorder (SUD). In this chapter, we will provide an overview of the BNST from an intrinsic and extrinsic circuit perspective, focusing on anatomy, physiology, pharmacology, and BNST afferents/efferents. The focus will then shift to the BNST in addiction and the role it plays in regulating the negative emotional states associated with addiction. At this time, studies of the human BNST are in their infancy, but researchers are beginning to utilize improved imaging techniques to gain insight into human BNST processes important for addiction and other affective disorders. For this reason, much of this chapter focuses on preclinical rodent studies. The chapter concludes with a discussion of the few human BNST studies in addiction, and how improvements in technology at the preclinical and clinical research level could yield novel insights into how BNST circuits may be targeted for diagnosing and treating SUDs.

BNST subregions and cell types

The BNST can be divided into several subregions and is composed of numerous cell types that are classified by expression of neurotransmitters, neuropeptides, ion channels, and other proteins. There have been considerable efforts to categorize BNST cell-type heterogeneity, and the emergence of new tools has recently enabled functional characterization of these cell groups, enhancing our understanding of the role of the BNST in various affective, social, and reward-related behaviors.

Anatomical subregions of the BNST

The rodent BNST is typically divided into 12–18 anatomical subregions (Alheid et al., 1998; Dong and Swanson, 2004a; Ju et al., 1989; Moga et al., 1989), the projections and functions of which have been thoroughly reviewed (Ch'ng et al., 2018; Flanigan and Kash, 2020; Lebow and Chen, 2016) and are summarized here. Standard nomenclature divides the BNST into anterior (aBNST) and posterior (pBNST) divisions, defined in relation to a bundle of fibers associated with the stria terminalis. The pBNST contains three subnuclei: the principal nucleus (BNSTpr), interfascicular nucleus (BNSTif), and transverse nucleus (BNSTtr). The aBNST can be further divided into dorsal (dBNST) and ventral divisions (vBNST), defined in relation to the anterior commissure, and collectively contains nine commonly accepted subnuclei. The dBNST contains the oval nucleus (BNSTov), juxtacapsular nucleus (BNSTjx), and anterolateral nucleus (BNSTal) (these three are collectively referred to as the dorsolateral BNST (dlBNST)), and anteromedial nucleus (BNSTam). The vBNST contains the fusiform nucleus (BNSTfu), the magnocellular nucleus (BNSTmg), the rhomboid nucleus (BNSTrh), the dorsomedial nucleus (BNSTdm), and the ventral nucleus (BNSTv). BNST subregion heterogeneity is critical in achieving its integrative function in "valence surveillance" (the integration of environmental contextual assessment with internal affective and motivational state) (Lebow and Chen, 2016), with different subregions mediating distinct, and sometimes competing, effects on behavior. For example, the BNST is a major modulator of the Hypothalamic-Pituitary-Adrenal (HPA) axis, which is responsible for mediating the neuroendocrine stress response. The aBNST, and in particular, the BNSTdm, drives activation of the

HPA axis, while the pBNST inhibits HPA axis activity (Choi et al., 2007, 2008a; Radley et al., 2009). This is likely driven in part by inhibitory intra-BNST connectivity, with the BNSTpr providing input to the BNSTam, BNSTmg, and BNSTdm. The small size of many BNST subnuclei and technical limitations has made precise functional characterization challenging, but existing work in this area is briefly summarized below.

Anterior BNST

In addition to driving activation of the HPA axis, the aBNST is involved in social vigilance, mediating responses to social threats, and stress-induced impairments in reward and prosocial behaviors (Dumais et al., 2016; Duque-Wilckens et al., 2018; Duque-Wilckens et al., 2020; Forray and Gysling, 2004; Jasnow et al., 2004; Klampfl et al., 2016). Within the aBNST, the BNSTov integrates information about mood and negative valence, and generally promotes anxiety-like behavior (Kim et al., 2013). The BNSTal is involved in the integration of mating behaviors, bonding, and neuroendocrine state with mood, pain processing, exteroceptive sensory information, threats, and digestive homeostasis. The BNSTam integrates drinking and fluid homeostasis information with HPA axis activation and fight-or-flight responses through connectivity with brainstem nuclei (Bienkowski and Rinaman, 2013; Bruijnzeel et al., 1999; Dong and Swanson, 2004b, 2006a, 2006b; Ide et al., 2013; Klampfl et al., 2016; Krettek and Price, 1978; Lange et al., 2017; Park et al., 2012; Romero and Butler, 2007).

The vBNST contains the highest concentration of noradrenergic (norepinephrine, noradrenaline, NE) fibers in the brain (Kilts and Anderson, 1986; Phelix et al., 1992). It plays a key role in arousal and mediates cardiovascular response integration through connectivity with the nucleus of the solitary tract (NTS) and central amygdala (CeA) (Dunn and Williams, 1995; Forray et al., 2000; Roder and Ciriello, 1993). Noradrenaline is released in the vBNST tonically and also in response to immobilization stress, footshock, fox odor exposure, forced swim stress, and unreceived anticipated reward (Briand et al., 2010; Cecchi et al., 2002; Fendt et al., 2005; Forray and Gysling, 2004; Palij and Stamford, 1992; Park et al., 2013). The vBNST is involved in regulation of social behaviors. For example, the vBNST decreases pro-social behaviors after exposure to alcohol, and may regulate aggressive and sexual behaviors through connectivity to the ventromedial hypothalamus (VMH) (Dong and Swanson, 2004a, 2006a; Duque-Wilckens et al., 2020; Kim et al., 2015; Marcinkiewcz et al., 2015). In some cases, the vBNST opposes dBNST effects, for example, by providing direct inhibitory input to the paraventricular nucleus of the hypothalamus (PVN) to inhibit HPA axis activity in the face of inescapable stressors, while simultaneously promoting active coping strategies through inhibition of the ventrolateral periaqueductal grey (vlPAG) (Radley and Johnson, 2018). Finally, the vBNST drives feeding and reward behavior, which will be discussed in more detail later in this chapter. Most sub-nuclei in the vBNST have not been well characterized individually, with the exception of the BNSTmg and BNSTdm, which are both involved in neuroendocrine and autonomic control of fluid and nutrient homeostasis and are largely responsible for aBNST-induced activation of the HPA axis. The BNSTdm also modulates approach and avoidance behavior via the PVN, integrating social information with reward or stress responses and adjusting mood accordingly (Dong and Swanson, 2006a, 2006b; McFadden et al., 2012; Ventura-Silva et al., 2012).

Posterior BNST

The pBNST is the most sexually dimorphic region of the extended amygdala across species and modulates many sex-specific social behaviors including mating and reproduction, parental care, and social defense and aggression behaviors (Campi et al., 2013; Goodson and Kabelik, 2009; Laflamme et al., 1998; Ventura-Silva et al., 2012). The BNSTif and BNSTtr likely play an important role in mediating many of these behaviors through their possible role in social recognition (Dong and Swanson, 2004b; Petrulis and Johnston, 1999). The BNSTpr is the most heavily studied of the posterior nuclei. It plays a role in stress responses and aggression and, as mentioned above, is critical in the integrative function of the BNST as a whole through its intra-BNST projections to subregions like the BNSTmg and BNSTdm (Dong and Swanson, 2004a; Nelson and Trainor, 2007; Ventura-Silva et al., 2012). The pBNST may combine social information with reward cues via interconnectivity with the ventral tegmental area (VTA), a midbrain region important for reward and motivated behavior (see Chapter 1 of this book). Posterior BNST-VTA circuits may be important for the assignment of valence to social interactions and, through the principal nucleus, bi-directional regulation of the motivation to engage in social behavior and/or HPA axis activity (Choi et al., 2007, 2008b; Herman and Larson, 2001; Lebow et al., 2012).

Anatomy of the human BNST

The human BNST is a sub-cortical brain region roughly the size of a sunflower seed that lies in the center of the brain on either side of the fornix. In contrast to the 12–18 subregions typically described in the rodent BNST, the human BNST is divided into 4 subregions: lateral, medial, ventral, and central, based on a post-mortem study of immunohistochemical markers and anatomy (Walter et al., 1991). The lateral, medial and central subdivisions are largely situated above the anterior commissure and are differentiated immunohistochemically. Both the lateral and medial subdivisions are characterized by high density of substance P fibers and neuropeptide Y immunoreactivity but are differentiated by the presence (lateral) or absence (medial) of neuropeptide Y immunolabelled neurons. The central subdivision is largely characterized by somatostatin fiber immunoreactivity, and the ventral subdivision is situated below the anterior commissure. Rodent studies often describe functional differences between BNST subregions; in humans, however, the BNST is examined as a whole region owing to its small size and deep location combined with limitations in neuroimaging resolution. For these reasons, the following sections describe BNST cell type heterogeneity, pharmacology and electrophysiology based primarily on rodent literature.

BNST cell type heterogeneity

Integrative function of the BNST is facilitated by extensive cell type heterogeneity. BNST neurons can be categorized in a variety of ways, including which neurotransmitter is released, expression of specific proteins/neuropeptides, and activity profiles assessed using electrophysiological techniques.

Neurotransmitters and neuromodulators: The vast majority of neurons in the BNST (~90%) release GABA, form symmetric synapses, and express vGAT (vesicular GABA transporter). Approximately 10% of BNST neurons release glutamate, form asymmetric synapses, and express vGlut2 (vesicular glutamate transporter 2). There is also a very small proportion of neurons that expresses vGlut3, but these neurons also express GAD67 for GABA production, typically release GABA, and form symmetric synapses, suggesting they are primarily inhibitory (Kudo et al., 2012; Moffitt et al., 2018; Rodriguez-Romaguera et al., 2020; Welch et al., 2019). GABAergic and glutamatergic neurons in the BNST play distinct roles in stress, anxiety, and reward seeking that have been especially well studied in the vBNST (Companion and Thiele, 2018; Jennings et al., 2013b). The BNST is also a hub for monoamine signaling, and different distributions of cells expressing monoamine receptors are expressed throughout the region. For example, cells expressing the D2 dopamine receptor (D2R) are fairly evenly distributed throughout the dBNST and vBNST, with slightly higher expression in the dlBNST. In contrast, D1 dopamine receptor (D1R)-expressing cells are sparse, with expression in a small number of cells primarily restricted to the dBNST, but with a striking lack of presence in the rat BNSTov (Krawczyk et al., 2011a; Lu et al., 2021; Yoon and Baik, 2015). Adrenergic versus non-adrenergic cells expressing alpha2 adrenergic receptor (alpha2-AR) (autoreceptor vs. heteroreceptor populations, respectively) have differential effects on BNST activity and differential involvement in stress-induced reinstatement of drug seeking (including opiates and cocaine), analgesia, sedation, and cognitive function in an input-specific manner (Flavin et al., 2014; Harris et al., 2018; Perez et al., 2020). Cell populations defined by expression of distinct serotonin (5-HT) receptor subtypes can also have opposing effects on the expression of fear- and anxiety-like behaviors (Hessel et al., 2020; Marcinkiewcz et al., 2019). See below for more information regarding the effects of GABAergic, glutamatergic, and monoaminergic transmission on BNST signaling and function.

Neuropeptides/Proteins: BNST cells can be defined by expression of neuropeptides and/or the receptors for those neuropeptides. These include cell bodies expressing corticotropin-releasing factor (CRF), somatostatin (SOM), neuropeptide Y (NPY), neurotensin (NT), arginine vasopressin (AVP), nociceptin (NOC), substance P (SP), galanin (GAL), cholecystokinin (CCK), enkephalin (ENK), dynorphin (DYN), and oxytocin (OT), as well as cells expressing the receptors for those peptides plus pituitary adenylate cyclase-activating peptide (PACAP) and orexin (OX) (Ju and Swanson, 1989; Lesur et al., 1989; Walter et al., 1991). While not a neuropeptide, protein kinase C delta (PKCd) is a common marker of an anatomically and functionally distinct cell population in the BNST and CeA (Fetterly et al., 2019; Haubensak et al., 2010; Ye and Veinante, 2019). It is important to note that, while there is often overlap, the cell population expressing the receptor for a neuropeptide is not equivalent to the population expressing the peptide itself. For example, there exist complex bi-directional interactions between CRF and OT systems in the regulation of maternal social behaviors wherein OT neurons express CRF-receptor 2 (CRFR2) and CRF neurons express OTR in the BNST (Dabrowska et al., 2011; Klampfl and Bosch, 2019; Martinon and Dabrowska, 2018). There are also varying degrees of overlap between neuropeptides; for example, a large percentage of NOC neurons co-express either SOM, CCK, or PKCd, but have little-to-no overlap with ENK, CRF, or NT cells (Rodriguez-Romaguera et al., 2020). SOM overlaps heavily with SP cells, but has almost no colocalization with PKCd (Shimada et al., 1989; Ye and Veinante,

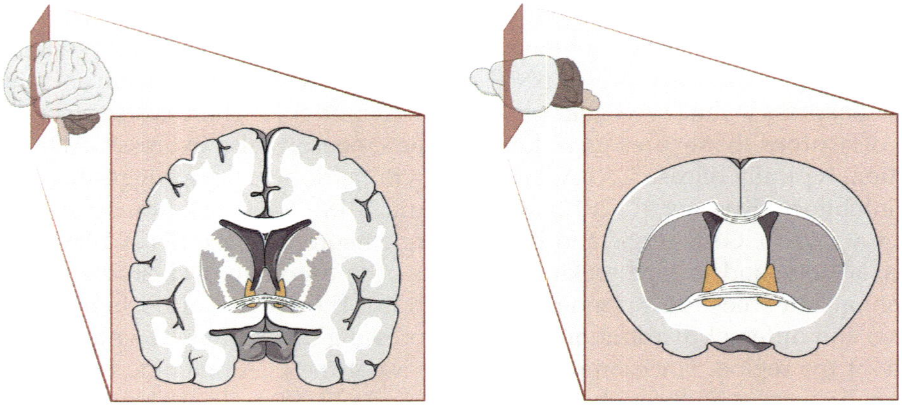

FIGURE 9.1 Illustration of human and mouse brains cut in coronal view at the location of the red plane. Human brain is on the left and mouse brain is on the right. Bed nucleus of the stria terminalis in each brain is highlighted in yellow. *Adapted from Servier Medical Art.*

2019). Furthermore, CRF-expressing and PKCd-expressing cells generally exhibit a low degree of overlap, but stress may alter co-expression of CRF and PKCd in BNST cells (Fetterly et al., 2019). The expression profiles and function of many of these cell types have been extensively characterized, while others are just beginning to be investigated (for reviews, see (Ch'ng et al., 2018; Flanigan and Kash, 2020; Kash et al., 2015; Lebow and Chen, 2016)). See Fig. 9.2 for an illustrated summary of what is known about peptide expression in BNST cells across sub-regions. Recent advances in single-cell profiling have also resulted in new categorization schemes for BNST cells based on their genetic profiles, with one group identifying 11 distinct subpopulations and another finding 41 separate cell types (Rodriguez-Romaguera et al., 2020; Welch et al., 2019). Future work may reveal even more nuance in the identification and function of BNST subpopulations.

Electrophysiological: It is a common method for neurons to be classified (e.g., in cortex, striatum, and amygdala) based on electrophysiological profiles (Kreitzer, 2009; Markram et al., 2004; Pape and Pare, 2010; Sah et al., 2003; Seung and Sümbül, 2014; van Aerde and Feldmeyer, 2015). Knowledge of the physiological properties of cell types can provide insight into their functional roles, and characterization of synaptic responses enables identification of cells *in vivo* to understand activity in awake and behaving animals. While many studies have classified BNST cells according to electrophysiological profiles, this work has suffered from the presence of considerable differences across species, and difficulty in identifying the functional/behavioral relevance of each cell type (Daniel et al., 2017; Silberman et al., 2013). In general, four BNST cell types have been described: Type I, Type II, and Type III, and "other" (neurons not fitting into any of these classifications (Daniel et al., 2017; Silberman et al., 2013). Type I neurons are typically characterized by their regular firing rate (and as such, have also been termed Regular Spiking Cells) but show spike frequency adaptation after prolonged depolarization (Rodríguez-Sierra et al., 2013). Additionally, they show prominent

Cell Type in BNST	Behavioral Correlate
AVP	↑↓ Sickness ↑ Social ↑ Reproduction
CRF	↑ Anxiety ↑ Relapse
CCK	↑ Positive Valence
DYN	↑ Dysphoria
ENK	↓ Anxiety ↑ Fear
NOC	↓ Anxiety ↑ Feeding
NPY	↓ Anxiety ↓ Pain ↓ EtOH Binge ↑ Feeding
NT	↑ Reward ↑ Reinforcement
OXT	↑ Maternal behavior ↑ Agression
PKCd	↓ Feeding
SOM	↓ Anxiety ↑ Fear

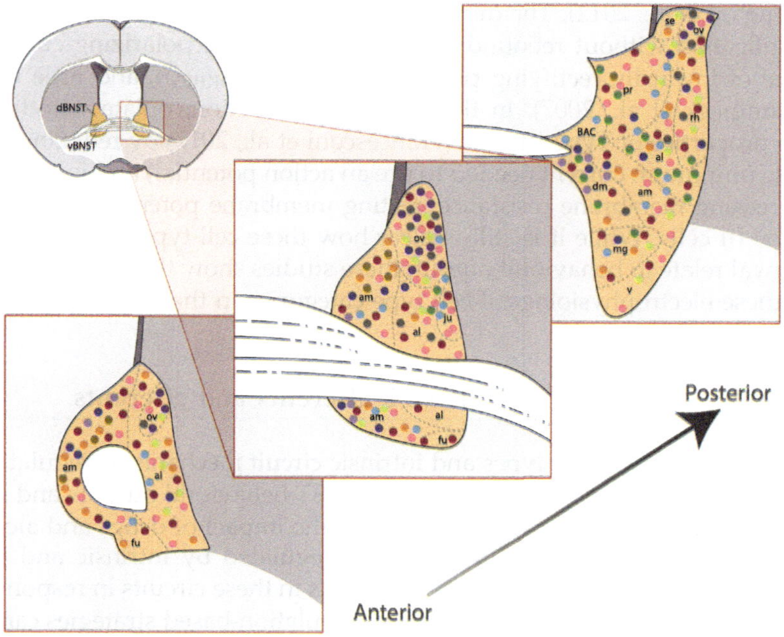

FIGURE 9.2 Diagram of cell-type distribution in the BNST. Three planes of the BNST are shown. Planes progress from anterior to posterior when moving from left to right. *Cell types included:* AVP, *arginine vasopressin;* CCK, *cholecystokinin;* CRF, *corticotropin releasing factor;* DYN, *dynorphin;* ENK, *enkephalin;* NOC, *nociception;* NPY, *neuropeptide Y;* NT, *neurotensin;* OXT, *oxytocin;* PKCd, *protein kinase C delta;* SOM, *somatostatin. References contributing to this figure in footnote*[1].

depolarization sag following a hyperpolarizing step, meaning they depolarize to a slightly less-hyperpolarized level after initial hyperpolarization. Type I cells also do not show burst firing after injection of depolarizing current, and they do not show Low-Threshold Spiking (LTS), meaning they require significant stimulation to fire an action potential (Gauss and Seifert, 2000; Hammack et al., 2007; Monteggia et al., 2000; Szücs et al., 2010). Type II neurons are characterized by more pronounced depolarization sag in response to hyperpolarization, which is followed by rebound spiking upon termination of the injection of hyperpolarizing current, and generally show prevalent LTS (Hammack et al., 2007). The majority of Type II neurons also display burst firing, leading to the alternate name of Low-Threshold Bursting (LTB) cells, meaning less current is needed to evoke an action potential (Rodríguez-Sierra et al., 2013). However, the presence of bursting is highly variable within Type II neurons, with some displaying rapid consecutive spikes at membrane potentials more depolarized than −70 mV, and others exclusively responding with single spikes (Daniel et al., 2017; Rodríguez-Sierra et al., 2013). While most still include these neurons in the Type II classification, one group separated these cells into their own division termed Type O, which resemble Type II but show regular, oscillatory firing after hyperpolarization and single spikes after depolarization (Rodríguez-Sierra et al., 2013; Szücs et al., 2010). In one example of the intersection between neuropeptide signaling and electrophysiological profiles, NPY reduces aversion associated with pain and stress by decreasing the excitability of Type II cells specifically

(Rangani et al., 2012). The defining feature of Type III neurons is the presence of fast inward rectification without rebound firing following hyperpolarizing current (indicating the presence of inwardly rectifying potassium channels ($I_{K(IR)}$)), and little to no depolarization sag (Hammack et al., 2007). In the context of addiction, opiate withdrawal[11] specifically alters the properties of Type III cells (Francesconi et al., 2017) by reducing the normally high rheobase (minimum current needed to fire an action potential) and inward rectification, while also increasing membrane resistance, resting membrane potential, and excitability specifically in Type III cells. While it is still unclear how these cell-type specific alterations in opiate withdrawal relate to behavioral output, these studies show that there may be functional relevance to these electrophysiological cell type categories in the context of addiction.

BNST afferents and efferents

The diversity of cell types and intrinsic circuit mechanisms regulating activity in the BNST highlight the complexity and range of BNST behavioral outputs and how it can impact overall affective state. In order to understand the impact of drugs and alcohol on BNST circuitry, we must first establish the basal states regulated by intrinsic and extrinsic BNST circuits. From there, we can determine dysfunctions in these circuits in response to drugs and alcohol. *In vivo* and *ex vivo* pharmacological manipulation-based strategies can then be used to modulate or mitigate BNST circuit effects on behavior. Although pharmacological interventional approaches have gleaned significant insights into the mechanisms underlying BNST circuity, this approach has produced mixed results in terms of treatments. The following overview of BNST microcircuitry, BNST pharmacology, BNST afferents and efferents, and their effects on behavior will provide context for the pharmacological studies conducted in addiction models discussed in greater detail later in the chapter. Fig. 9.3 shows a graphical representation of the inputs and outputs into the BNST.

Glutamate/GABA

The BNST is largely composed of GABAergic neurons interspersed with glutamatergic neurons (Cassell et al., 1999; Poulin et al., 2009). Two major fiber tracts connect the BNST to downstream brain regions, and these are the stria terminalis/dorsal bundle and the ansa peduncularis/ventral bundle, or the amygdalofugal pathway (Dong et al., 2001).

Glutamate pharmacology

Numerous pharmacological studies have focused on ionotropic and metabotropic glutamate signaling, given the dense expression of both types of receptors in the BNST, and the high number of excitatory glutamatergic inputs to the BNST (Vranjkovic et al., 2017). Pharmacologically activating metabotropic glutamate receptors (mGluRs) decreases glutamatergic transmission in the BNST, as evidenced by decreased frequency of spontaneous excitatory postsynaptic currents (sEPSC), decreased sEPSC amplitude, decreased field EPSCs (entire BNST excitatory signaling), and increased long-term synaptic depression (LTD) (Gosnell et al., 2011; Grueter et al., 2006, 2008; Grueter and Winder, 2005; McElligott and Winder, 2008). mGluRs are categorized into three classes (type I, II, III) and numerous compounds have been developed to target individual subtypes or classes. Pharmacologically

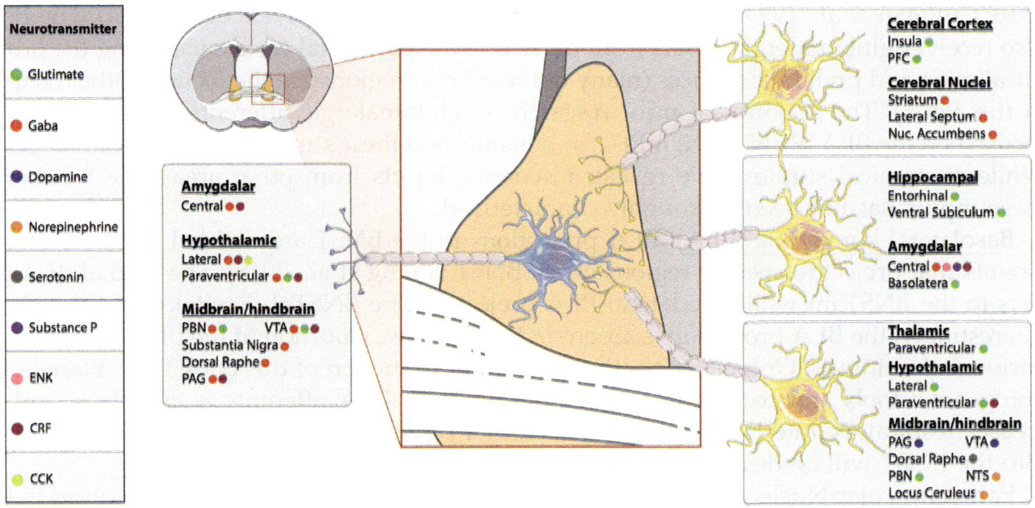

FIGURE 9.3 Diagram of key inputs and outputs from the BNST. Yellow neurons represent regions projecting to the BNST (BNST afferents) with specific regions identified in boxes on the right. Blue neuron represents regions receiving projections from the BNST (BNST efferents). Associated neurotransmitters are demarcated by colored dots next to each regional input. *Adapted from Servier Medical Art.*

manipulating mGluR signaling represents an exciting area of research for modulating activity in the BNST. Similarly, ionotropic AMPA (AMPAR) and NMDA (NMDAR) receptors in the BNST play a key role in the overall activity state of the BNST. Blocking local glutamatergic neurotransmission in the BNST by targeting ionotropic glutamate receptors with antagonists reduces anxiety-like behavior (Kim et al., 2013), and ionotropic glutamate receptor antagonists applied directly to the BNST slice *ex vivo* blocks long-term potentiation (LTP) (Glangetas et al., 2015). Furthermore, subunit-specific pharmacology has greatly improved in recent years, facilitating a wave of research dedicated to examining the impact of individual glutamate receptor subunits on BNST activity. For example, the GluN2 subunit of the NMDAR has several isoforms that dictate its synaptic localization and pharmacological profile. GluN2B-containing NMDARs can be present outside of the synapse, and deletion of this subunit eliminates LTP in the BNST and prevents ethanol from modulating BNST activity, highlighting a role for this subunit in mediating the effects of alcohol in the BNST (Wills et al., 2012). In addition, GluN2D-containing NMDARs exhibit prolonged deactivation kinetics and increased glutamate sensitivity as compared to other GluN2-containing NMDARs. Genetically deleting this subunit in the BNST increases depressive-like behavior in animals and increases glutamatergic drive onto stress-sensitive CRF-positive cells in the BNST (Salimando et al., 2020). As the pharmacological tools to study glutamate improve, targeted approaches to modulating glutamatergic activity in the BNST could alter addiction-related behaviors.

Glutamatergic afferents

The BNST receives glutamatergic input from various brain regions including the basolateral amygdala (BLA), entorhinal cortex (EC), lateral hypothalamus (LH), olfactory bulb, parabrachial nucleus (PBN), insular cortex (insula), the ventral subiculum of the hippocampus (HPC) and the paraventricular thalamus (PVT) (Canteras and Swanson, 1992; Ch'ng et al.,

2018; Cullinan et al., 1993; Dong et al., 2001; McDonald, 1998; Myers et al., 2014). The BNST also receives glutamatergic inputs from regions of the prefrontal cortex, including the orbital, infralimbic and prelimbic cortices (many of these brain regions are the focus of other chapters in this book). The majority of prior research on glutamatergic afferents in the BNST have focused on the BLA, PVN, PBN, mPFC, and insula, and these studies will be described below. While anatomical studies have revealed synaptic inputs from other areas, the function of these inputs has not been thoroughly characterized.

Basolateral Amygdala (BLA): BLA projections to the BNST are divided into two parallel circuits that project to specific regions of the BNST (Ch'ng et al., 2018). The medial BLA projects to the BNSTam while the lateral BLA projects to the BNSTal (Krettek and Price, 1978). Interestingly, the BLA projection is absent in the BNSTov, a portion of the BNST that receives various other inputs. Optogenetic activation (see introduction of this book for explanation of optogenetic tools and techniques) of BNST-projecting BLA afferents is anxiolytic and decreases respiratory rate (Kim et al., 2013) Further optogenetic characterization of this input into the BNST will be described in later sections.

Paraventricular Nucleus (PVN): The PVN, a nucleus in the hypothalamus involved in hormonal regulation, sends a glutamatergic onto the BNSTal that contribute to regulating the stress-response hormone corticotrophin releasing factor (CRF, CRH) (Berk and Finkelstein, 1982; Myers et al., 2014). Additionally, the PVN sends an excitatory orexin/dynorphin co-expressing projection to the BNST (Peyron et al., 1998).

Parabrachial Nucleus (PBN): The PBN provides a glutamatergic input onto cells in the BNST. This synapse has been associated with increased arousal and food-seeking/consummatory behavior in a stressed state (Carter et al., 2013; Palmiter, 2018). Optogenetic stimulation of PBN synapses in the BNST reveals two BNST cell populations that are either activated or inhibited by PBN stimulation. Activation of PBN inputs to BNST increases phasic calcium activity and anxiety-like behavior (Jaramillo et al., 2020). Moreover, PBN projections specifically onto BNST CRF cells are sensitive to noradrenaline, as washing on noradrenaline decreases evoked glutamatergic activity (Fetterly et al., 2019), outlining a strong role for this specific input in regulating reward and arousal.

Medial prefrontal cortex (mPFC): The BNST receives glutamatergic input from the mPFC, a brain region involved in cognitive control and decision making. This input is endocannabinoid (eCB) sensitive (Massi et al., 2008; Radley et al., 2009). One study showed that mPFC inputs from the prelimbic area of the mPFC synapse onto cells in the BNSTov that themselves project onto PVN neurons (Radley et al., 2009). Another study demonstrated that projections from the infralimbic subregion of the mPFC synapse onto VTA-projecting BNST neurons (Massi et al., 2008), potentially outlining a role for the BNST in relaying cortical information to downstream regions to regulate the reward behavior.

Insular cortex (insula): The BNST receives glutamatergic input from the insula, a brain area involved in interoception. These inputs are modulated by eCB signaling (Centanni et al., 2019b; Reichard et al., 2017), but not noradrenergic signaling (Fetterly et al., 2019). Increased activity in CRF-positive cells in the BNST following optogenetic insular input activation was diminished with application of a cannabinoid 1 receptor (CB1R) agonist (Centanni et al., 2019b). Moreover, neuronal activity in the insula-BNST circuit (measured by *in vivo* activity sensors for calcium, glutamate, and GABA) is positively correlated with active escape behavior during restraint stress (Luchsinger et al., 2021), suggesting a distinct role for this circuit in regulating behavioral response during a stressor.

GABA pharmacology

GABAergic cells in the BNST vastly outnumber glutamate cells and form microcircuits that create a balance with glutamatergic signaling to control overall BNST activity. There are two main classes of GABA receptors (GABARs) in the brain: ionotropic $GABA_AR$ and metabotropic $GABA_BR$. $GABA_ARs$ form tetramers containing multiple combinations of alpha, beta, gamma, and/or delta subunits. These different combinations dictate synaptic localization, GABA affinity, and affinity for subunit-specific pharmacological compounds. $GABA_BRs$ are typically localized presynaptically in many parts of the brain and serve as autoreceptors to inhibit neurotransmitter release. The diversity of GABARs in the brain highlights these receptors as particularly intriguing for pharmacologically altering inhibitory/excitatory balance. Bidirectionally modulating GABAergic activity in the BNST alters affective state, with $GABA_AR$ antagonists and agonists producing and preventing anxiety-like behavior in rodents, respectively (Egli and Winder, 2003; Fendt et al., 2003). To date, a major treatment option for anxiety disorders is the benzodiazepine class of drugs; these $GABA_AR$ agonists increase GABAergic transmission in the BNST and elsewhere in the brain. Given its role in affective state, the BNST likely plays a major role in the overall impact of benzodiazepines in reducing anxiety, and further studies exploring specific GABAR pharmacology in the BNST will be essential for developing new treatments for addiction and affective disorders.

GABAergic afferents

The primary GABAergic input into the BNST originates in the central amygdala (CeA) (Vranjkovic et al., 2017). The CeA to BNST circuit expresses various neuropeptides including ENK, SP, and/or NT (Ch'ng et al., 2018). Less predominant GABAergic inputs to the BNST originate from the striatum, lateral septum, and nucleus accumbens (NAcc) shell (Cullinan et al., 1993; Dong et al., 2001; Hurley et al., 1991; McDonald, 1998; Myers et al., 2014; Takagishi and Chiba, 1991; Vertes, 2004).

Neuromodulators

Neuropeptide pharmacology

The BNST is intricately involved in the extrahypothalamic stress response system. For this reason, one of the most comprehensively studied neuropeptides in the BNST is CRF, which is often referred to as the "stress response hormone." CRF receptors (CRFRs) are densely expressed in the BNST, and CRF levels in the BNST (and elsewhere in the brain) increase in response to stress. Pharmacologically activating CRFRs or increasing the peptide itself in the BNST increases anxiety-like behavior, supports conditioned place aversion, and produces inhibitory avoidance in rodents (Liang et al., 2001; Sahuque et al., 2006), and inversely, stressors and anxiety-promoting behaviors increase CRF mRNA expression in the BNST (Funk et al., 2006), illustrating a tight relationship between stress, anxiety, and CRF. NPY is another densely expressed neuropeptide in the BNST that is expressed in cells that are distinct from CRF-positive cells and has an anti-anxiety profile that opposes CRF effects on affective state (Heilig et al., 1994). NPY expression in the BNST is decreased during anxiety- and depressive-like behaviors (Desai et al., 2014), and evidence supports the notion that NPY exerts its anti-anxiety actions through inhibition of GABAergic transmission via presynaptic NPY receptors (NPYRs).

The neuropeptide dynorphin, a member of the opioid family, is expressed in moderate levels in the BNST, and emerging research suggests that dynorphin in the BNST plays a key role in the dysphoria associated with withdrawal from drugs and alcohol (Koob and Le Moal, 2008). It exerts these actions through the kappa opioid receptor (KOR), and KOR agonists support conditioned aversion and decreased social interactions (Robles et al., 2014). In the BNST, negative affective behaviors increase prodynorphin, a precursor to dynorphin, mRNA expression, and KORs inhibit both GABAergic signaling (Li et al., 2012) and glutamatergic neurotransmission (Crowley et al., 2016), highlighting the modulatory influence of dynorphin/KOR signaling on excitatory/inhibitory balance in the BNST. Moreover, KOR agonist actions in the BNST are in part through inhibition of glutamatergic inputs from the BLA, but not the PFC (Crowley et al., 2016). Dynorphin signaling through the KOR may be a promising target for understanding BNST circuitry and treating addiction.

Neuropeptide afferents

Neurons in the BNST receive and send neuropeptide-expressing projections from and to several brain regions. Neuropeptide signaling is prominent and interconnected in the BNST with cells often expressing multiple peptides. CRF-positive neurons from the CeA and PVN, and CRF-positive interneurons, synapse onto cell bodies in the BNST and regulate cell excitability (Vranjkovic et al., 2017). CRF signaling has been linked to excitation and inhibition in the BNST via actions on distinct presynaptic or postsynaptic receptors (Kash and Winder, 2006; Silberman et al., 2013). Inhibitory drive onto CRF-positive neurons in the BNST is enhanced through NPY activation (Pleil et al., 2015a), further showing the interconnectedness of neuropeptide signaling in the BNST.

As mentioned above, numerous other neuropeptides are expressed in the BNST (Fig. 9.1). While each of these neuropeptides modulates BNST activity, to date very few studies have examined their roles in addiction. To stay within the scope of this chapter, the focus will remain on BNST neuropeptides implicated in addiction (for extensive review on all BNST neuropeptides (see Kash et al., 2015). As better pharmacological targets emerge, research may uncover new BNST-centric targets for treating addiction.

Monoamines

The BNST receives several midbrain afferents containing a wide variety of monoamine neuromodulators. Intrinsic BNST circuitry relies heavily on monoaminergic neurotransmission, thus pharmacologically targeting these neuromodulators in the BNST can drastically impact BNST activity.

Dopamine pharmacology

Dopamine is considered an integral neuromodulator involved in reward, and nearly every drug of abuse has been linked to its actions on dopamine neurotransmission. Dopamine increases spontaneous glutamatergic signaling, primarily acting through D1Rs (Kash et al., 2008b), and decreases GABAergic signaling in the BNST, primarily acting through the D2Rs (Krawczyk et al., 2014) . Further, dopamine results in depolarization of CRF-positive cells in the BNST (Silberman et al., 2013). Dopamine enhances glutamatergic transmission in the BNST in an activity- and CRFR1-dependent manner (Kash et al., 2008b). In addition, dopamine produces depolarization in CRF-positive cells in the BNST (Silberman et al., 2013). These studies suggest that dopamine-CRF interactions may be important for mediating the role of the BNST in addiction.

Dopaminergic afferents

The BNST receives dopaminergic input from the VTA and PAG (Freedman and Cassell, 1994; Meloni, 2006). The VTA and PAG are heavily implicated in reward and arousal, highlighting the involvement of the BNST in reward-mediated circuitry. Additionally, a D2R-expressing inhibitory input projects from the CeA onto GABAergic and non-GABAergic neurons in the BNST (Kim et al., 2018). Dopaminergic innervation is diffuse across the dlBNST with dense localization of fibers in the BNSTov, and the BNSTjx (Freedman and Cassell, 1994; Krawczyk et al., 2011a; Meloni, 2006; Phelix et al., 1992). D1Rs and D2Rs are expressed throughout the anterior BNST, with only D2Rs localized to the BNSTov (Krawczyk et al., 2011a). Drugs of abuse such as cocaine, alcohol, morphine, and nicotine increase extracellular dopamine release in the BNST in a dose-dependent manner (Carboni et al., 2000), decreasing inhibitory and excitatory transmission in the BNSTov through activation of presynaptic D2R or alpha2-AR, respectively (Krawczyk et al., 2011a). Projections from the VTA and PAG synapse primarily onto CRF-positive neurons in the dBNST (Meloni, 2006).

Noradrenaline pharmacology

Dopamine can be converted to another monoamine, noradrenaline (NE, norepinephrine) by the enzyme dopamine beta-hydroxylase. Noradrenergic transmission in the BNST influence both excitatory and inhibitory transmission. Adrenergic receptors (ARs) are classified as either alpha(1−2) or beta(1−3). Agonists for alpha2a- and alpha1-ARs decrease glutamatergic transmission in both the dBNST and vBNST, whereas a beta-AR agonist decreases glutamatergic transmission in the dBNST but not vBNST. Application of noradrenaline increases spontaneous inhibitory transmission in VTA-projecting neurons in the BNST. This effect is dependent on alpha1-ARs (Dumont and Williams, 2004). Noradrenaline also decreases glutamate signaling in the vBNST and in some, and a subset of cells in the dBNST (Egli et al., 2005; McElligott and Winder, 2008). Interestingly, noradrenergic signaling through alpha1-and alpha2-ARs decreases excitatory (Dumont and Williams, 2004; Egli et al., 2005; Fetterly et al., 2019; McElligott and Winder, 2008; Shields et al., 2009) and inhibitory drive onto BNST cells (Shields et al., 2009). Specifically, alpha2-AR inhibition of glutamatergic synaptic transmission in the BNST occurs through alpha2a-AR activation. Conversely, signaling through beta-AR enhances both excitatory (Egli et al., 2005; Nobis et al., 2011) and inhibitory (Dumont and Williams, 2004) drive onto neurons in the BNST. Guanfacine, an alpha2a-AR partial agonist, can have excitatory and inhibitory effects in the dBNST, depending on cell type and dose (Egli et al., 2005). Conversely, signaling through beta-AR enhances both excitatory (Egli et al., 2005; Nobis et al., 2011) and inhibitory (Dumont and Williams, 2004) drive onto neurons in the BNST. Noradrenergic signaling increases CRF and glutamate signaling in the BNST (Nobis et al., 2011; Shields et al., 2009; Silberman et al., 2013). Isoproterenol, a beta-AR agonist, results in increased excitability of BNST neurons through increased spontaneous

(Nobis et al., 2011) and evoked excitatory synaptic events (Egli et al., 2005). Isoproterenol increases spontaneous glutamatergic transmission in the BNST through activation of beta1-AR in a CRFR-dependent manner (Nobis et al., 2011). This and several other studies have shown a role for noradrenergic signaling in the BNST and in the effects of drugs of abuse. Collectively, noradrenaline signaling in the BNST is complex and subregion and cell-type specific, yet highly influential on BNST circuitry.

Noradrenergic afferents

The BNST receives one of the densest noradrenergic projections originating from the nucleus tractus solitarius (NTS) of the ventral noradrenergic bundle (Banihashemi and Rinaman, 2006; Egli et al., 2005; Flavin et al., 2014; Forray and Gysling, 2004; Ricardo and Tongju Koh, 1978; Shields et al., 2009). Additionally, the BNST receives a sparse noradrenergic input from the locus coeruleus. The vBNST is densely innervated by alpha1-AR- and alpha2-AR-expressing noradrenergic cells, which can influence both excitatory and inhibitory transmission. Stimulation of the ventral noradrenergic bundle results in noradrenaline release in the BNST as measured by *in vivo* fast-scan cyclic voltammetry (Park et al., 2009). Noradrenergic and non-noradrenergic inputs to the BNST are altered by several pharmacological agents that target adrenergic receptors (Flavin et al., 2014; Harris et al., 2018; Perez et al., 2020). In addition, axons from the PBN form peri-somatic connections with BNST neurons and these synapses are regulated by noradrenergic signaling. Guanfacine inhibits glutamatergic input from the PBN onto CRF-positive neurons in the BNST (Fetterly et al., 2019; Flavin et al., 2014). Both noradrenaline and guanfacine reduce glutamatergic transmission from the PBN onto CRF-positive neurons in the BNST (Fetterly et al., 2019). Conversely, guanfacine has no effect on glutamatergic transmission from the BLA or insula, suggesting input-dependent effects of noradrenergic modulation (Fetterly et al., 2019; Flavin et al., 2014).

Serotonin pharmacology

Serotonin receptors (5HTRs) are also expressed in the BNST, and the influence of 5HT signaling on BNST activity is well established. 5HT signaling and pharmacology have been extensively studied for their anti-depressant actions. Selective serotonin reuptake inhibitors (SSRIs) are one of the most widely prescribed classes of medications for depression and given the role of the BNST in affective state, the effects of SSRIs are mediated at least in part through actions on BNST circuitry. Depression is highly comorbid with substance and alcohol use disorders, driving numerous lines of research focused on 5HT pharmacology and addiction. However, the actions of 5HT specifically on BNST circuitry have not been fully elucidated. Similar to other monoamines, 5HT can modulate both inhibitory and excitatory neurotransmission in the BNST, depending on the specific composition of 5HTR subunits. Postsynaptic responses of serotonin in the BNST vary, ranging from purely hyperpolarizing, depolarizing, a combination of the two or no postsynaptic response, with hyperpolarization being the most common response (Guo et al., 2009; Levita et al., 2004). The two most prominent 5HTRs in the BNST are the excitatory G_s-coupled $5HT_7$ and inhibitory G_i-coupled $5HT_{1A}$ G-protein-coupled receptor (GPCR) (Guo et al., 2009). As expected, this has revealed complex effects of serotonin on the BNST. Pharmacologically activating $5HT_{1A}$Rs in BNST generates an anxiolytic phenotype while activating $5HT_2$Rs produces an anxiogenic phenotype (Levita et al., 2004). Subunit specific circuitry has been explored in the BNST as well. Activation of

$5HT_{2C}$Rs led to decreased anxiety by blunting BNST output to the VTA and lateral hypothalamus (Marcinkiewcz et al., 2016). With expanding pharmacological compounds targeting specific 5HTR subunits, examining the direct actions of these compounds on BNST activity will provide unique insight into the role of the BNST in regulating mood and emotional state through 5HT signaling.

Serotonergic afferents

The caudal regions of the dorsal raphe nucleus have reciprocal 5HT connections with the dBNST (Block and Hoffman, 1987; Commons et al., 2003; Lowry et al., 2008). It is hypothesized that CRF release during stress activates serotonergic neurons in the dorsal raphe through CRFR2 activation (Hammack et al., 2002). It is hypothesized that BNST projections to the dorsal raphe influences 5HT signaling in that region via effects on CRF signaling. 5HT acts on presynaptic receptors to alter glutamatergic transmission in the BNST and serotonergic input to the BNST is linked with anxiety (Guo and Rainnie, 2010). It is also hypothesized that 5HT modulates release of neuropeptides, such as CRF, through activation of presynaptic 5HTRs, but the precise mechanism underlying this effect is not fully characterized. The BNST-dorsal raphe reciprocal circuits are hypothesized to function as a negative feedback loop in response to stress or anxiety-provoking stimuli (Hammack et al., 2007).

Endogenous cannabinoids

Endogenous cannabinoids (endocannabinoids, eCBs) and their primary receptor in the CNS, CB1R, and the lesser characterized CB2R, are ubiquitously expressed throughout the brain (Devane et al., 1992; Howlett, 2002; Sugiura et al., 1995) and modulate both glutamatergic and GABAergic signaling (Kreitzer and Regehr, 2001; Ohno-Shosaku et al., 2001). eCBs exhibit unique retrograde neurotransmission as they are synthesized on demand postsynaptically in response to GABA or glutamate release, and are then trafficked to the presynaptic bouton, where they bind to presynaptic CB1Rs that inhibit neurotransmitter release through a G_i-coupled GPCR signaling pathway (Castillo et al., 2012; Piomelli, 2003). CB1Rs in the BNST are expressed on both GABA and glutamate neurons and can therefore act to reduce inhibitory and/or excitatory signaling in the BNST, making this system an intriguing target for controlling neurotransmitter release from intrinsic BNST circuitry and extrinsic BNST inputs (Bedse et al., 2019). CB1R agonists applied to BNST slices inhibit both excitatory and inhibitory postsynaptic potentials, and this suppression is prevented by a CB1R antagonist (Puente et al., 2010). Compounds targeting the enzymes regulating the two endogenous CB1R ligands, 2-archidonylglycerol (2AG) and anandamide (AEA) have garnered significant attention as pharmacological targets. Drugs that inhibit the AEA-degrading enzyme FAAH and the 2AG-degrading enzyme MAGL are currently being tested in clinical trials for neurological disorders (Huggins et al., 2012; Kerbrat et al., 2016; van Esbroeck et al., 2017) and have thus far proven to be relatively safe with few side effects, creating the possibility for testing these compounds for treating addiction and negative affective disorders. In addition, pharmacological compounds targeting enzymes involved in eCB synthesis have been tested in a number of preclinical models of negative affect (Bluett et al., 2014, 2017; Centanni et al., 2019b; Holleran et al., 2016). Specifically, in the BNST, pharmacologically increasing 2-AG levels via inhibition of a 2-AG degrading enzyme in an acute BNST slice preparation decreases the frequency of spontaneous excitatory post synaptic potentials (Centanni et al., 2019b).

Endocannabinoid modulation of BNST afferents

Endocannabinoids act through their endogenous receptors, CB1R or CB2R, to influence the activity of GABAergic and non-GABAergic cells in the BNST. Specifically, eCB regulation of BNST inputs from the mPFC, insula, CeA, BLA, and ventral subiculum have been investigated in rodent models. Glutamatergic inputs from the infralimbic cortex (IL, a subregion of the mPFC) and ventral subiculum onto the BNST directly affect the excitatory BNST projections to the VTA through an eCB-sensitive pathway (Caillé et al., 2009; Georges and Aston-Jones, 2002; Jalabert et al., 2009; Massi et al., 2008). Furthermore, infusion of CB1R agonist into the BNST blunts the excitatory drive of IL onto downstream VTA DA neurons (Massi et al., 2008). This study provides the framework of an IL–> BNST–> VTA circuit originating from the IL onto DA neurons in the VTA that requires CB1R activity in the BNST. Similarly, infusion of a CB1R antagonist into the BNST prevented stimulation-induced LTP in the mPFC of stressed mice (Glangetas et al., 2013). *Ex vivo* extracellular field recordings revealed that CB1R agonism inhibits evoked excitation and inhibition in the BNST, and these effects were reversed by CB1R antagonism (Puente et al., 2010). CB1R agonism decreases excitatory responses in CRF-positive cells in the BNST following optical stimulation of the insular terminals (Centanni et al., 2019b). Presynaptic CB1R activation inhibits inputs from the CeA and BLA onto BNST neurons (Lange et al., 2017). Conversely, inputs from the MeA are not affected by CB1R activation (Lange et al., 2017). While a majority of endocannabinoid work has focused on CB1Rs, recent studies also show a role for CB2R activation in the BNST in negative affective behaviors (Gomes-de-Souza et al., 2021): this study found that CB1Rs and CB2Rs are located in the anterior and posterior portions of the BNST.

BNST efferents

Circuit mapping approaches have revealed that the BNST projects to several brain regions such as the PBN, LH, medial preoptic area, substantia nigra, dorsal raphe, NTS, PVN, PAG, CeA, and the VTA (Ch'ng et al., 2018; Jennings et al., 2013b; Kim et al., 2013; Mahler and Aston-Jones, 2012). The connections between the BNST and the CeA, PVN, PAG and VTA are reciprocal and have been well-studied (Dong and Swanson, 2004a; Georges and Aston-Jones, 2002; Jalabert et al., 2009; Kim et al., 2013; Kudo et al., 2012; Silberman et al., 2013). Glutamatergic and GABAergic neurons in the BNST synapse onto dopaminergic and non-dopaminergic neurons in the VTA influencing multiple pathways (Dong and Swanson, 2006a, 2006b; Geisler and Zahm, 2005; Kudo et al., 2012). The majority of BNST efferents to the VTA are GABAergic and are associated with anxiolytic-like behavioral effects, however a small portion of glutamatergic efferents from the BNST to VTA have been associated with anxiogenic-like and aversive effects (Jennings et al., 2013b). Glutamatergic BNST projections to the VTA are activated by stress, and GABAergic vBNST projections to the VTA are inhibited by stress (Companion and Thiele, 2018). Activation of glutamatergic inputs from the BNST to VTA produce conditioned place aversion, reduce reward-seeking behavior, and increase anxiety-like behavior in mice (Jennings et al., 2013b). Conversely, activation of GABAergic vBNST efferents to the VTA increase reward-seeking behavior, produce conditioned place preference, and reduce anxiety-like behavior (Jennings et al., 2013b). It is through these pathways that the BNST modulates activity of dopamine neurons in the VTA (Georges and Aston-Jones, 2002; Jalabert et al., 2009). BNST efferents synapse onto dopamine and GABA cells in the VTA (Georges and Aston-Jones, 2002). Application of noradrenaline in the BNST increases spontaneous inhibitory transmission in VTA-projecting BNST neurons, and this effect is dependent on alpha1-ARs (Dumont and Williams, 2004). Future studies will need to parse the individual effects of each on stress- and addiction-related outcomes.

The BNST sends dense projections to the PAG in the midbrain; specifically these are CRF-containing projections originating in the BNSTov (Dong and Swanson, 2004a). Activation of the BNST-PAG pathway results in CRF release from BNST terminals onto dopaminergic neurons in the PAG, depolarizing them and resulting in downstream DA release from PAG terminals in the BNST. Dopamine activates D1R on CRF-positive neurons in the BNST resulting in release of CRF and downstream modulation of glutamatergic synaptic transmission in the BNST via actions at CRFR1 (Bowers et al., 2003; Kash et al., 2008b; Silberman et al., 2013).

The BNST acts as a relay between the IL and VTA dopamine neurons (Massi et al., 2008). The IL provides phasic glutamatergic control of BNST neurons through AMPAR, NMDAR and $GABA_AR$ activity (Massi et al., 2008). Similarly, the BNST relays information between the prelimbic area of the mPFC (PL) and the PVN (Radley et al., 2009). As described in a previous section, the BNST receives glutamatergic input from regions of the prefrontal cortex, including the orbital, infralimbic and prelimbic cortices. The PL modulates activity of the HPA axis through PVN neurons and this pathway is involved in acute emotional responses (Radley et al., 2009). However, there is only a weak projection from the PL to the PVN that seems unlikely to mediate this response to stress. Therefore, it was hypothesized the PL acts through a relay brain region to exert its effects on the PVN, and the BNST has been investigated as the potential relay between the PL and PVN. Specifically, projections from BNST to PVN and from PL to BNST were confirmed using anterograde and retrograde tracing techniques (Radley et al., 2009). Predominantly GABAergic projections from the vBNST synapse onto CRF-positive neurons in the PVN, although some sparse projections are glutamatergic and CRF-expressing (Ch'ng et al., 2018). This pathway allows the BNST to drive HPA axis activation and modulate the production of stress hormones such as CRF. Ablation of GABAergic neurons in the BNST results in an enhanced stress response in the PVN, evidenced by stress-induced increases in nuclear expression of cfos protein, and CRF mRNA (Radley et al., 2009). This suggests the GABAergic projection from the BNST to the PVN is necessary for the stress response initiated by the mPFC. This response is similar to enhanced stress-induced activation of PVN neurons that is observed following mPFC ablation (Radley et al., 2009). Furthermore, exposure to stress results in a switch from LTD to LTP in the BNST following mPFC stimulation (Glangetas et al., 2013). This effect is due to CB1R actions on glutamatergic terminals in the BNST and is absent in CB1R knockout animals (Glangetas et al., 2013). These results, in addition to evidence showing that CB1R activation on mPFC glutamatergic terminals in the BNST control neuronal response to cortical stimulation, suggest a CB1R-sensitive di-synaptic circuit from the mPFC to the PVN through the BNST that is necessary for generating stress responses.

The lateral hypothalamus receives two non-overlapping projections from the BNST that express either CRF or cholecystokinin (CCK) (Giardino et al., 2018). These pathways respond differently to various emotional states. For example, CRF-positive cells respond more to predator odor, while CCK-positive cells respond more to odor of the opposite sex. Both CRF and CCK cells in the BNST receive intra-BNST projections, with CRF-positive cells receiving projections from the BNSTal and CCK-positive cells receiving inputs from the BNSTam and the medial pBNST. Both CRF-positive and CCK-positive neurons in the BNST receive inputs from the MeA and the medial preoptic area.

Effects of acute and chronic drug exposure on the BNST

BNST efferents, afferents, and cell type-specific microcircuits have all been heavily associated with drugs of abuse (Briand et al., 2010; Dumont et al., 2005; Grueter et al., 2006; Kash et al., 2008a; Pleil et al., 2015a; Reisiger et al., 2014; Sartor and Aston-Jones, 2012; Silberman et al., 2013). In addition to playing a critical role in the withdrawal/negative affect component of substance use disorders (discussed in detail below), the BNST is also a site of numerous acute effects of drugs of abuse, many of which may prime the region for its role in mediating drug relapse/reinstatement. For instance, morphine, nicotine, cocaine, and alcohol increase extracellular dopamine in the BNST in a dose-dependent manner (Carboni et al., 2000). Recent work found that drugs of abuse including morphine, nicotine, cocaine, alcohol, and amphetamine also increase noradrenaline transmission in the BNST, with all except morphine increasing noradrenaline in a dose-dependent manner (Jadzic et al., 2021). Cocaine, morphine, nicotine, or THC administration result in increased ERK phosphorylation in the dlBNST through a dopamine D1R-dependent mechanism (Valjent et al., 2004). In addition to these commonalities, drugs of abuse also have distinct mechanisms of action within the BNST, which are summarized below.

Alcohol

Alcohol directly modulates BNST neurotransmission, as bath application of alcohol onto an acute slice containing the BNST results in decreased amplitude of NMDAR-dependent currents and long-term potentiation (Kash et al., 2009; Weitlauf et al., 2004; Wills et al., 2012). A large portion of research on the role of the BNST in addiction has focused on alcohol use disorder. The BNST has been linked to the both alcohol consumption and alcohol withdrawal-induced anxiety and depression. Commonly used methods to evaluate the underlying mechanisms of alcohol use disorder is to use a binge-drinking and/or intoxication model using continuous or limited access to alcohol, systemic administration, or contingent access (Holleran and Winder, 2016). Acute exposure to alcohol increases cfos expression in the BNST suggesting that the BNST directly responds to alcohol via increased neuronal activation (Saalfield and Spear, 2019; Sharko et al., 2016). A single acute exposure to alcohol decreased expression of DNA methyltransferase (DNMT), an enzyme linked to epigenetic regulation of gene expression, in the BNST that was increased following a second systemic alcohol injection (Sakharkar et al., 2014). Stress and alcohol modulate phosphorylated

CREB (pCREB) expression in the BNST and this effect can be blocked by NMDAR antagonism (Blundell and Adamec, 2007). A moderate-dose alcohol exposure that produces conditioned place aversion (CPA) is blunted by previous stress exposure and results in a reduction in pCREB expression in the BNST (Schreiber et al., 2019). Alcohol increases noradrenaline release (Jadzic et al., 2021) and dopamine release in the BNST as measured by *in vivo* voltammetry (Carboni et al., 2000). Alcohol-induced conditioned place preference (CPP) results in increased intrinsic excitability of neurons in the vBNST (Pati et al., 2019). This effect was not seen following alcohol-induced CPA or alcohol exposure in home cage, suggesting specific effects on the rewarding properties of alcohol in the BNST.

Neuromodulators such as CRF and NPY have also been linked to alcohol use. Persistent alcohol drinking in stressed mice compared to non-stressed mice is correlated with increased CRF mRNA levels in the BNST (Albrechet-Souza et al., 2017). Administration of a CRFR2 antagonist dose-dependently increases alcohol consumption, regardless of exposure to stress while a CRFR1 antagonist directly infused into the BNST reduces alcohol intake in unstressed mice (Albrechet-Souza et al., 2017). Activation of NPY1R results in enhanced inhibitory neurotransmission onto CRF neurons in the BNST, an effect that has been associated with decreased alcohol drinking (Pleil et al., 2015a). Alpha-melanocyte stimulating hormone (alpha-MSH), a key component of the melanocortin system, is reduced in rats exposed to chronic alcohol (Navarro et al., 2008). Alpha-MSH has been associated with regulation of dopamine release in the VTA to NAcc pathway, a circuit heavily involved in drugs of abuse, further implicating the BNST to VTA circuit in alcohol consumption (Centanni et al., 2019a).

Non-contingent methods, such as chronic intermittent ethanol (CIE), that allow for precise measurements of exposure and result in high blood alcohol levels are often used to study alcohol use disorder in animal models (Holleran and Winder, 2016). This method produces alcohol dependence in animals and can be used to measure effects on alcohol drinking. Alterations in synaptic plasticity of glutamatergic inputs to the BNST have been associated with response-contingent and non-response-contingent alcohol exposure effects. Specifically, exposure to acute and chronic non-response-contingent alcohol administration resulted in alterations in expression and function of the NMDAR subunit GluN2B (Kash et al., 2008c, 2009; Wills et al., 2012). Additionally, CIE produces an increase in expression of GluN2B in the BNST (Kash et al., 2009). CIE results in increased basal activity of CRF-positive neurons in the BNST in a manner similar to stress exposure (Snyder et al., 2019), and this effect requires noradrenergic signaling through beta-ARs. CIE enhances basal activity in VTA-projecting neurons in the BNST via a CRFR1-dependent mechanism, and moreover, binge-like alcohol drinking is reduced following inhibition of BNST CRF projections onto the VTA (Rinker et al., 2017). *Ex vivo* application of alcohol attenuates the beginning phase of high frequency LTP in the dBNST through depression of NMDAR function that requires GABAergic inhibition (Weitlauf, 2004). This effect on NMDAR synaptic transmission is dependent on GluN2B expressing NMDARs (Kash et al., 2008c, 2009; Wills et al., 2012). Interestingly, CIE increases the expression of GluN2B expressing NMDARs in the BNST and increases excitatory postsynaptic currents and enhances LTP induction through a GluN2B-dependent mechanism (Kash et al., 2008c, 2009; Wills et al., 2012). Alcohol produces a greater effect on NMDAR-evoked excitatory and GABAergic inhibitory postsynaptic currents in BNST neurons in adolescent mice relative to adults (Wills et al., 2013), highlighting unique effects of alcohol on BNST circuitry during adolescence. Chronic alcohol drinking can also impact downstream signaling molecules in the BNST. Chronic alcohol drinking increases protein levels of Homer, an mGluR5-scaffolding protein, and activated extracellular signal-related kinase (ERK) in the BNST, suggesting mGluR5 phosphorylation as a potential adaptive response to alcohol consumption (Campbell et al., 2019). To further this observation, transgenic animals with a point mutation in mGluR5 preventing phosphorylation by ERK exhibited increased alcohol-drinking (Campbell et al., 2019). These transgenic animals were determined to be insensitive to alcohol aversion and this effect is mimicked by ERK inhibition in the BNST.

Alcohol results in increased activation of GABAergic and non-GABAergic neurons in the BNSTal (Crankshaw et al., 2003; Leriche et al., 2008). Disruption of GABAergic signaling (Hyytiä and Koob, 1995) or dopaminergic signaling (Eiler et al., 2003) results in decreased alcohol-seeking behaviors. Inhibition of GABA signaling in the BNST decreases alcohol self-administration in rats (Hyytiä and Koob, 1995). This supports the proposed role of reciprocal VTA-BNST circuits in mediating the rewarding effects of alcohol. Binge alcohol intake is decreased following silencing of GABAergic BNST neurons that project to the VTA. Similarly, self-administration of alcohol is decreased following injection of a dopamine D1R antagonist into the BNST in a dose-dependent manner (Eiler et al., 2003).

Opioids

Mice that have undergone morphine CPP have increased levels of pCREB, a marker of neuronal activity, in the BNST (García-Carmona et al., 2013), and acute heroin exposure increases cfos expression in the BNST (Singh et al., 2005). After morphine CPP, there is an increase in pCREB co-expression in CRF-positive neurons in the BNST. Acute opioid withdrawal results in increased GABAergic synaptic activity in the BNST potentially through a noradrenergic-sensitive pathway. This effect potentially modulates downstream inhibitory projections onto VTA neurons (Dumont and Williams, 2004). Pharmacologically targeting the BNST opioid system has been shown to impact opioid-seeking behavior. Injection of an opiate receptor antagonist, methylnaloxonium, into the BNST dose-dependently decreases heroin-seeking behavior in heroin-dependent rats (Walker et al., 2000), while having no effect on heroin-seeking behavior in non-heroin-dependent animals. Heroin and morphine also impact BNST neuropeptide systems other than opioids, as both drugs increase NPY levels in the BNST, which may play a role in the acute anxiolytic effects of these drugs (D'Este et al., 2006; Desai et al., 2013). During acute withdrawal, injection of a CRFR1 antagonist into the BNST decreases fentanyl-associated cue-conditioned reinforcement (Gyawali et al., 2020).

Cocaine

The effects of cocaine on BNST activity are the most extensively studied of stimulant drugs. In addition to increasing DA and NE release in the BNST, more complex effects of cocaine on monoamine signaling in BNST have been reported (Carboni et al., 2000; Jadzic et al., 2021; Melchior et al., 2021). Early work sought to understand the effects of cocaine on BNST noradrenaline reuptake but produced conflicting results, with findings of increases, decreases, or no change in noradrenaline transporter (NET) availability after chronic cocaine self-administration, though it is possible that species differences and/or duration of cocaine exposure may contribute to the discrepancies (Belej et al., 1996; Macey et al., 2004). Chronic cocaine can also alter dopamine and noradrenaline receptor signaling and expression. For example, long access (6 h) to cocaine significantly reduced the number of BNST neurons expressing alpha1-AR compared to short-access (1 h) and drug-naïve rats, and this may mediate increased motivation to obtain cocaine and escalation of cocaine self-administration in rats with long access to cocaine (Wee et al., 2008). The beta1-AR agonist isoproterenol increases spontaneous glutamatergic transmission in the BNST through activation of beta1-AR via a CRFR1-dependent mechanism, and this effect occurs through activation of dopamine-insensitive glutamatergic synapses and is occluded by repeated *in vivo* exposure to cocaine (Nobis et al., 2011). Chronic cocaine self-administration alters dopamine modulation of GABAergic signaling in the BNSTov. Specifically, there is sparse expression of D1R in the BNST at baseline, and bath application of dopamine causes a D2R -dependent decrease in $GABA_A$R-mediated inhibitory transmission, but after 15 days of cocaine self-administration, bath application of dopamine causes a D1R-mediated increase in $GABA_A$R-mediated IPSCs, and this effect was not seen in rats passively given cocaine or after the acquisition phase of self-administration (Krawczyk et al., 2011b).

Cocaine self-administration leads to dopamine-induced reduction of NMDAR-mediated currents in the BNSTov of rats (Krawczyk et al., 2014), which is one of many cocaine-mediated alterations in BNST excitability and plasticity (Harris and Winder, 2018). Chronic cocaine self-administration leads to increases in excitatory transmission in several BNST subregions. This can be seen by self-administration-induced increases in the AMPAR/NMDAR ratio (a measure of postsynaptic strength) in the BNSTov. The mechanism underlying this increase in postsynaptic strength occurs via increases in AMPAR-mediated EPSCs in the lateral vBNST through a GluN2B-dependent mechanism in VTA-projecting neurons in the dlBNST but not the BNSTam (Debacker et al., 2015; Dumont et al., 2005). However, in the BNSTjx, long-access cocaine administration blocks high frequency stimulation-induced LTP of excitatory transmission (Francesconi et al., 2009).

Cocaine can also impact LTD of excitatory signaling. Activation of group I mGluRs with DHPG ((RS)-3,5-dihydroxyphenylglycin) in the dBNST induces ERK1-dependent LTD (DHPG-LTD) (Grueter et al., 2006). Systemic injection or self-administration of cocaine produces a transient, mGluR5-dependent inhibition of DHPG-LTD, the length of which is likely dependent on duration of cocaine exposure. A single dose of cocaine inhibits DHPG-LTD for less than 4 h, while 10 days of exposure produces robust inhibition of DHPG-LTD present for at least 24 h, but less than 10 days, after the last injection (Grueter et al., 2008). Cocaine also impairs NMDAR-dependent LTD in the dlBNST (Debacker et al., 2015). Interestingly, a single systemic injection of cocaine or *ex vivo* brain slice cocaine incubation in mice each lead to an NMDAR-dependent short-term potentiation of DA-enhanced glutamatergic transmission in the dlBNST (Kash et al., 2008b). These data may suggest differences in acute verses chronic cocaine effects on NMDAR-mediated signaling in the BNST.

The NMDAR-dependent short-term potentiation described above by Kash and colleagues also requires downstream activation of D1R, D2R, and CRFR1 (Kash et al., 2008b). This and other studies have implicated cocaine in neuropeptide and hormone-based signaling pathways (Corominas et al., 2010). For example, chronic gestational cocaine treatment leads to reduced OT receptor binding and may play a role in cocaine-driven increases in maternal aggression (Jarrett et al., 2006). Also, chronic cocaine injections result in increased $FKBP_5$

(FK_{506}-binding protein $_{51}$) mRNA levels in the BNST, which is a co-chaperone of the glucocorticoid receptor complex and reduces GR sensitivity to corticosteroids (Connelly and Unterwald, 2019; Wochnik et al., 2005).

Several other behavioral and physiological effects of cocaine are also mediated by effects of the drug in the BNST. For example, cocaine causes cardiovascular changes such as increased bradycardiac and tachycardiac responses of the baroreflex, but synaptic inactivation in the BNST with $CoCl_2$ reverses these baroreflex changes (Cruz et al., 2013; Glangetas et al., 2015; Nader et al., 2012). Cocaine administration also results in increased locomotor activity, and the locomotor effect of subthreshold cocaine doses can be potentiated by inducing LTP in the BNST via a ventral subiculum–> BNTS–> VTA circuit (Cruz et al., 2013; Glangetas et al., 2015; Nader et al., 2012). Additionally, loss of environmental enrichment increases vulnerability to cocaine addiction in part through increases in CRF mRNA expression in the BNST (Cruz et al., 2013; Glangetas et al., 2015; Nader et al., 2012). Finally, cocaine also has positive (rewarding) and negative (anxiogenic) properties, that are mediated at least in part by drug effects in the BNST, and one way to measure these opposing properties is via a runway model of cocaine self-administration. In this task, animals are trained to run a straight alley from a start box to a goal box for intravenous cocaine administration, and both the latency to initiate approach (to assess the positive component) and the number of retreats away from the goal box prior to entering (to assess the negative component) are measured (characterized and reviewed in (Ettenberg, 2009; Ettenberg and Geist, 1991)). Using this task, inactivation of the BNST with lidocaine 15 min prior to each runway trial over 14 days decreased approach times and suppressed retreat behavior (away from the goal box) (Wenzel et al., 2011). This effect may be mediated by $5HT_{1B}$ autoreceptor signaling in the BNST and not CRF signaling, as both pretreatment (10 min before each trial) and posttreatment (5 min after) with the $5HT_{1B}$ agonist CP 94,253 reduces retreat behavior, but CRF receptor antagonism has no effect (Ettenberg et al., 2015; Klein et al., 2017).

Amphetamines

Much work has been done in recent years to characterize the effects of amphetamines on BNST activation during different phases of the addiction cycle. A series of studies by the Zuloaga group showed that chronic methamphetamine exposure leads to desensitization of the BNST to subsequent exposure to methamphetamine or stress; more specifically, mice exposed to 10 consecutive days of methamphetamine, with or without a subsequent withdrawal period, show reductions in cfos expression in the BNST upon exposure to a challenge dose of methamphetamine or exposure to forced swim stress, compared to mice receiving saline prior to drug or stress exposure (Jacobskind et al., 2018, 2019; Zuloaga et al., 2016). However, this adaptation may be dependent on dose and/or the presence of a withdrawal period, as García-Carmona and colleagues found an increase in the number of cfos-positive neurons in the BNSTov immediately following 10 days of 2 mg kg^{-1} methamphetamine, compared to 5 mg kg^{-1} used by the Zuloaga group (García-Carmona et al., 2018). They also found that following chronic methamphetamine and seven days of withdrawal, with no challenge dose of drug, there was no change in overall cfos expression in BNSTov neurons but found an increase in the number of cfos-positive CRF cells specifically, as well as an increase in the number of CRF cells, suggesting that chronic amphetamine exposure may have cell type-specific effects, shifting BNST activation patterns to favor CRF-positive over CRF-negative cells. Finally, a single dose of amphetamine increases cfos expression in the BNSTov in the home cage but not a novel environment, and this neuronal activation occurs in ENK-positive but not CRF-positive cells (Colussi-Mas et al., 2005; Day et al., 2001). Together, these findings highlight the need for more subregion and cell-type specific experiments to improve our understanding of amphetamine effects in the BNST.

Nicotine

Acute nicotine injections dose-dependently increase cfos expression in the BNST; more specifically, nicotine preferentially increases the number of CRF-positive cells that express cfos at higher doses (0.135 mg kg^{-1}), but a low nicotine dose (0.045 mg kg^{-1}) preferentially increases the number of CRF-negative cfos-expressing cells (Matta et al., 1997). Much higher concentrations of nicotine injection (1 mg kg^{-1}) also decrease levels of NPY in the BNST (Kotagale et al., 2014). However, more recent studies have reported that passive, acute injections of nicotine does not result in these BNST adaptations in adults (Shram et al., 2007). Most work in adults has focused on measuring BNST adaptations following chronic, active self-administration and/or nicotine exposure in conjunction with other drugs of abuse. Caillé and colleagues found that excitatory inputs from the infralimbic cortex into the BNST have heightened responsiveness after nicotine self-administration, but not after passive nicotine infusion (Caillé et al., 2009). Follow-up studies found that chronic nicotine self-administration may "prime" IL→BNST circuits, enabling the subsequent expression of LTP in response to 10 Hz stimulation in a CB1R-dependent manner. This induction of evoked spike potentiation in the BNST was maintained during passive forced abstinence, but abolished following active extinction training, suggesting this IL-BNST circuit plasticity is sensitive to learning (Reisiger et al., 2014). Chronic nicotine self-administration also alters stress responsivity of the BNST, resulting in fewer stress-induced cfos-positive vBNST neurons that project to the PVN, and thus resulting in disinhibition of the HPA axis and enhanced neuroendocrine stress response. A few studies have also examined interactions between nicotine and other drugs and found that co-administration of nicotine with alcohol or THC enhances cfos expression in the BNST above that of either drug alone (Leão et al., 2015; Valjent et al., 2009).

The prevalence of nicotine use in younger populations has precipitated efforts to understand nicotine effects on the developing adolescent brain. Repeated exposure to nicotine in adolescent rats (beginning at postnatal day 32 (P32)) induces significant increases in BNST dendritic branching/elaboration and increased total length of dendrites (Smith et al., 2015). These changes may persist into adulthood, and because increased dendritic surface area is closely related to greater synapse numbers and increases the likelihood and speed of action potential generation, nicotine-induced dendritic elaboration in adolescence may be a mechanism mediating increased anxiety-like behavior seen later in life (Smith et al., 2015). Earlier in life, acute injection of nicotine in rat pups increased the number of cfos-positive cells in the dlBNST at P7 and P10, but not P5, and increased Arc-positive cells (another marker of neuronal activity) at P10 but not before, despite this early developmental period (P4-14) being one marked by stress hypo-responsiveness in rodents (Levine, 2005; Sapolsky and Meaney, 1986; Schmitt et al., 2008; Vazquez et al., 2006).

Cannabinoids

Cannabinoids have been studied for their strong anxiolytic properties (and anxiogenic properties in certain individuals and/or at higher doses), suggesting BNST circuitry may play a central role in its effects. Cannabinoids inhibit glutamatergic transmission from the IL to the BNST through activation of presynaptic CB1Rs (Massi et al., 2008). Delta (9)-tetrahydrocannabinol (THC) is the major psychoactive component of marijuana and acts as an agonist at CB1Rs. Chronic exposure to THC can have interesting effects on subsequent drug exposure. Chronic THC before heroin injection results in a suppression of heroin-induced increase in locomotion (Singh et al., 2005), and the BNST may play a role in this effect, as chronic THC attenuates heroin-induced increases in cfos expression in the BNST. This effect of THC exposure on heroin response was also seen following perinatal exposure to THC and adolescent exposure to heroin (Singh et al., 2006).

Another cannabinoid, cannabidiol (CBD) has gained popularity recently for its ability to treat certain forms of epilepsy and is an intriguing compound for several affective disorders for its perceived lack of psychoactive properties and low abuse potential. The role of CBD in emotional regulation and its effects on BNST circuitry have not been fully elucidated, however research suggests an interaction with 5HT, as CBD injected directly into the BNST decreases anxiety-like behavior and contextual fear conditioning mediated through $5HT_{1A}$Rs (Gomes et al., 2011, 2012). Moreover, systemic injection of CBD activates $5HT_{1A}$Rs to decrease cardiovascular responses to acute restraint stress (Gomes et al., 2013). Microinjection of CBD into the BNST can also attenuate contextual fear behavior (Gomes et al., 2012), and this effect is blocked by pre-treatment with a $5HT_{1A}$R antagonist. While much work remains to be done to understand the direct actions of CBD on the BNST and the brain as a whole, these initial studies provide intriguing rationale for further exploring its role in negative affective disorders.

Long term effects of drugs of abuse on the BNST

Initial drug use is often driven by stress relieving and rewarding properties. However chronic drug use changes the response to drugs, causing a homeostatic shift from that of taking a drug for its rewarding, positive effects (positive reinforcement) to taking a drug to maintain this newly established baseline, and in turn decreasing the rewarding properties. This shift in response can lead to increased drug intake in an attempt to recapture the rewarding effects, which promotes the "vicious cycle" of addiction, wherein behavior shifts to avoiding the negative symptoms of withdrawal (negative reinforcement). Withdrawal and abstinence are synonymous with intense negative emotional state, which is predominantly driven by the BNST and other areas associated with the extended amygdala. Regardless of whether an individual is diagnosed with an alcohol or substance use disorder, chronic drug exposure can induce changes in BNST activity that persist long after an individual has stopped taking the drug.

Early withdrawal

Upon cessation of drug taking following chronic high-dose exposure, individuals can experience a wide range of acute or early withdrawal symptoms. Drug withdrawal severity depends on a number of factors including type of drug, duration and amount of drug use, physical and mental health, sex, etc. Withdrawal can manifest as both physical symptoms (e.g., sickness, seizures, sweating) and affective symptoms (e.g., depression, anxiety, irritability, dysphoria). Withdrawal phenotypes are mediated by changes in brain homeostasis caused by chronic exposure to drugs or alcohol, and these symptoms subside as a new drug-free homeostasis is established. While physical withdrawal symptoms typically dissipate after days or weeks, changes in mood and affective state can persist for months or even years into abstinence (see below). Preclinical models of withdrawal generally consist of forced or voluntary chronic exposure to drugs or alcohol, followed by forced or voluntary cessation of drug exposure or availability.

The BNST plays a major role in regulating affective state and is therefore a prime candidate for regulating the negative affect symptoms associated with acute withdrawal. As highlighted above, nearly all drugs of abuse impact BNST circuitry; therefore much research has been dedicated to studying the role of the BNST in drug and alcohol withdrawal. Alcohol use disorder (AUD) produces robust physical and affective withdrawal symptoms in patients. At the level of the BNST, acute withdrawal can produce physiological changes that collectively promote a negative affective state. Preclinical rodent models of alcohol withdrawal have outlined increases in neuronal excitability and activation (Kash et al., 2009; Marcinkiewcz et al., 2015), spontaneous glutamate release onto BNST neurons (Pleil et al., 2015a; Silberman et al., 2013), and LTP (Wills et al., 2012), all of which are consistent with a hyperactive BNST state. Interestingly, spontaneous inhibitory neurotransmission is also increased in the BNST following chronic alcohol exposure (Pleil et al., 2016), suggesting increased GABA release from GABAergic efferents such as the central amygdala. BNST hyperactivity after chronic alcohol exposure is heavily regulated by neuromodulatory systems. Manipulations of CRF (Silberman et al., 2013), $5HT_{2c}$ (Marcinkiewcz et al., 2015), GluN2B (Kash et al., 2009; Wills et al., 2012), and KOR (Erikson et al., 2018) each bi-directionally impact alcohol withdrawal-induced changes in BNST activity. Several genes in the BNST are upregulated during alcohol withdrawal including genes related to the endocannabinoid, opioid, dopamine, and serotonin systems (Contet et al., 2011). This highlights the broad activity changes in the BNST that occur during early alcohol withdrawal.

Opiate withdrawal also induces pronounced changes in the BNST including increased expression of cfos (Aston-Jones et al., 1999). Noradrenergic inputs onto BNST neurons are activated specifically during opiate withdrawal and abolish withdrawal-induced place aversion (Aston-Jones et al., 1999; Delfs et al., 2000). Microinjection of a beta-AR antagonist into the BNST attenuated opiate withdrawal symptoms including decreased somatic symptoms such as teeth chattering and eye twitching, and withdrawal-induced place aversion.

Lesioning the alpha1-AR and alpha2-AR noradrenergic projections to the BNST also abolished opiate withdrawal-induced place aversion (Aston-Jones et al., 1999; Delfs et al., 2000).

The VTA-BNST circuitry has been implicated in both opiate and alcohol withdrawal. Increases in GABAergic signaling in VTA-projecting BNST neurons during morphine withdrawal is attributed to increased activation of alpha1-and beta2-AR in the VTA (Dumont and Williams, 2004), suggesting that BNST projections to the VTA may contribute to opiate withdrawal-induced anhedonia and negative affect by inhibiting dopaminergic signaling in the VTA. Moreover, CRF enhances presynaptic glutamatergic transmission onto VTA-projecting BNST neurons (Silberman et al., 2013), and this effect is blocked following chronic intermittent alcohol exposure and withdrawal. Interestingly, BNST CRF neurons that do not project to the VTA or LH exhibit increased excitability in alcohol withdrawal, and non-CRF cells that project to the VTA and LH show a similar alcohol withdrawal-induced increase in excitability, suggesting dysfunctional GABAergic microcircuitry in the BNST (Pati et al., 2020). Taken together CRF microcircuitry in the BNST is impacted by alcohol withdrawal and influence the activity of BNST projections to the LH, VTA and other brain regions.

The involvement of the BNST in stimulant withdrawal has also been explored. Following chronic nicotine exposure, overexpression of CRF in the BNST diminishes withdrawal-induced anxiety-like symptoms in rodents (Qi et al., 2016). This study also showed that prolonged overexpression of BNST CRF prevents the increase in dysphoria-like state associated with nicotine withdrawal. This was shown to act possibly through a CRFR2-mediated pathway, which can have opposite effects on downstream circuitry than its counterpart CRFR1s.

While numerous sex differences in the BNST have been established, how these differences impact withdrawal has yet to be fully explored. The neurohormone arginine vasopressin (AVP) is expressed at a higher density in the BNST of males than females (Rood et al., 2013). Interestingly, in withdrawal following chronic amphetamine exposure, female rats, but not male rats, show increased numbers of AVP-expressing cells, with a higher number of cells during oestrus versus diestrus (Ahumada et al., 2017). Thus, the BNST may play an important role in sexually dimorphic responses to stimulant withdrawal.

Protracted abstinence

Protracted abstinence is an indefinite period of time following the initial immediate withdrawal symptoms and is often synonymous with varying intensity of affective symptoms such as anxiety, depression, dysphoria, irritability, etc. Preclinical models for addiction typically use one of two abstinence protocols: (1) forced abstinence or simply removing the drug and/or its context, or (2) voluntary abstinence by either pairing the drug with an adverse consequence or a more rewarding alternative such as social interaction. The abstinence period has been hypothesized to be characterized in part by incubation of drug craving that potentiates over time and continues even after the initial withdrawal symptoms subside (Pickens et al., 2011). The neurocircuitry driving negative affective symptoms during alcohol or drug abstinence is not completely clear, however, the BNST appears to play a role in these processes and effects.

One study by Francesconi et al. observed similar impairments in long-term potentiation of intrinsic excitability in the BNST during protracted abstinence after self-administration of alcohol, cocaine, and heroin. Protracted withdrawal from all three drugs prevented a high frequency stimulation-induced shift towards hyperpolarization of the action potential threshold, suggesting disruption in long-term potentiation in the BNST in withdrawal. Moreover, these changes were blocked by systemic administration of a CRFR1 antagonist in the alcohol model (Francesconi et al., 2009), suggesting a role for this system in regulating withdrawal-induced changes in BNST synaptic plasticity. Protracted abstinence from alcohol leads to decreased short-term plasticity (Vranjkovic et al., 2018), increased spontaneous glutamate release onto BNST neurons (Centanni et al., 2019b), and increased intrinsic firing threshold (Francesconi et al., 2009). As discussed above, alcohol decreases glutamatergic neurotransmission when bath applied acutely to BNST slices (Kash et al., 2009; Weitlauf et al., 2004; Wills et al., 2012), suggesting that alcohol withdrawal and abstinence engender a rebound of spontaneous glutamatergic neurotransmission that may relate to increases in negative affect. BNST slice electrophysiology experiments suggest that alcohol abstinence-induced increase in BNST glutamatergic signaling can be reversed by IP injection of the NMDAR antagonist ketamine or by bath application of the endocannabinoid-degradation inhibitor JZL-184 (Centanni et al., 2019b; Vranjkovic et al., 2018). Time of administration was important in both studies. Ketamine prevented abstinence-induced plasticity when administered at the start of abstinence, whereas JZL-184 prevented deficits when administered later in the protracted abstinence period (Centanni et al., 2019b; Vranjkovic et al., 2018). Increased glutamatergic drive onto the BNST suggests larger circuitry may be involved in mediating alterations in BNST output activity during alcohol abstinence. For example, the insula drives increased BNST neuronal activity during abstinence, evidenced by increased cfos expression and spontaneous glutamatergic drive onto BNST neurons (Centanni et al., 2019b), providing evidence for a discrete circuit involved in alcohol abstinence-induced negative affect. However, given the numerous glutamatergic inputs discussed above, a number of other inputs may also contribute to this hyperactivity.

BNST circuitry is also engaged during protracted abstinence from chronic morphine exposure. Rats treated chronically with morphine exhibit enhanced morphine preference five weeks into abstinence, and the magnitude of morphine preference is positively correlated with the magnitude of cfos-positive cells in the BNST (Harris and Aston-Jones, 2003). As discussed above, noradrenaline may play a part in this effect, as alpha2-AR containing noradrenergic neurons in the NTS, the major noradrenaline input to the BNST, are activated during protracted morphine abstinence by exposure to a previously morphine-paired environment (Harris and Aston-Jones, 2003, 2007).

In addition to depressants, the effects of protracted abstinence from stimulants on BNST signaling has also been examined. Seven days into withdrawal from chronic methamphetamine treatment, rats exhibit increases in cfos expression in CRF-positive cells in the BNST, as well as an increase in the number of CRF cells in the BNST (García-Carmona et al., 2018), suggesting cell-type-specific effects of chronic methamphetamine, and perhaps preferentially activating CRF-positive over CRF-negative cells in the BNST. Protracted abstinence has proven to be a difficult phase of the addiction cycle to target experimentally, and while evidence supports a major role for the BNST in this phase, much more work is needed to fully understand the larger circuits driving long-term changes in affective state that can trigger relapse.

Moreover, the driving factors underlying individual variability in the ability to cope with stress throughout abstinence should be a major focus of research moving forward.

Relapse

Patients often cite stress and negative affective symptoms such as anxiety and depression as the leading driver of craving and relapse, and the severity of symptoms is highly correlated with relapse susceptibility (Fox et al., 2017; Grant et al., 2016). Preventing relapse through prophylactic treatment strategies or diagnosing individual vulnerability to relapse is a major goal in addiction research. It is difficult to predict if, or when, any individual will relapse, but many cases can be linked to emerging or sustained negative emotional states. Stress-induced relapse often manifests in one of two ways, both of which implicate BNST circuitry. One involves an acute exteroceptive stressor such as losing a job or the death of a loved one, while the other involves interoceptive stress, such as the omnipresent anxiety, depression, and/or dysphoria that accompanies the constant pressure to avoid drugs and maintain abstinence. Addiction is often equated with a maladaptive stress response system, or the inability to appropriately cope with stress, therefore stress during abstinence can very often trigger relapse.

Preclinical models have been developed to test stress-induced relapse-like behavior in rodents. One commonly used model is the conditioned place preference (CPP) in which preference for the drug-paired side in a drug-free state is measured as drug-seeking behavior. Another model involves operant conditioning procedures, in which animals learn to press a lever in order to receive a drug. After the reinforced responding is extinguished (by allowing animals to perform the response in the absence of reinforcer deliveries), rodents are subjected to an exteroceptive stressor (e.g., mild foot shock) that increases non-reinforced (i.e., no drug) operant responding for several drugs including heroin, cocaine, alcohol, nicotine, and methamphetamine; this phenomenon is referred to as stress-induced reinstatement of drug-seeking behavior (Mantsch et al., 2016).

The BNST has been implicated in reinstatement behavior (Erb et al., 2001b; Erb and Stewart, 1999), in part due to its involvement in the extrahypothalamic stress response system (HPA axis) and the dense expression of CRF and other neuromodulators of BNST activity. Pharmacological inactivation of the BNST, via GABAR agonist microinfusion, blocks footshock stress-induced reinstatement of cocaine-seeking behavior (McFarland et al., 2004; Shaham et al., 2000). Further, lesioning the noradrenergic bundle, which sends dense projections to the BNST, was sufficient to block footshock-induced reinstatement of heroin-seeking behavior (Shaham et al., 2000). Interestingly, chemogenetically activating G_i-coupled signaling in BNST neurons, which has an overall excitatory effect in the BNST (see next section), is sufficient to induce cocaine reinstatement without a stressor (Perez et al., 2020). As outlined above, efferents from the BNST synapse onto dopamine and GABA cells in the VTA, and this circuit has been linked to stress and is necessary for cue-induced cocaine-seeking behavior (Mahler et al., 2012), including cocaine CPP (Sartor and Aston-Jones, 2012), highlighting the intricate relationship between VTA reward circuitry and BNST affective circuitry.

Noradrenaline is involved in mediating stress-induced reinstatement of drug seeking behavior. Blocking beta1-and beta2-AR in the BNST via local infusion decreases stress-induced reinstatement of cocaine seeking, while activation of beta-AR signaling causes reinstatement of cocaine CPP (Vranjkovic et al., 2012). Activating alpha2-AR induces reinstatement of cocaine CPP (Wang et al., 2001) and reinstates nicotine-seeking behavior (Yamada and Bruijnzeel, 2011). Noradrenaline signaling also interacts with CRF signaling in the BNST. In drug reinstatement models, cocaine-seeking behavior induced by a beta2-AR agonist is blocked by injection of a CRFR1 antagonist (Bornstein et al., 1998), outlining a unique relationship between these two signaling modalities in the BNST. It was later shown that beta-AR signaling in the BNST modulates CRF signaling onto downstream VTA neurons and is critical for stress-induced cocaine seeking behavior (McReynolds et al., 2014b). Inhibition of alpha-AR signaling blocks stress-induced reinstatement of heroin-seeking behavior (Erb, 2000). Stress and chronic alcohol exposure act similarly upon beta-ARs to increase neuronal excitability of CRF-positive neurons in the BNST (Snyder et al., 2019). Signaling through alpha2a heteroreceptors (receptors located on non-noradrenergic neurons) are necessary for stress-induced reinstatement of cocaine-seeking behavior (Perez et al., 2020). This study went on to show that a low dose of guanfacine, an alpha2a-AR agonist that does not recruit cfos activity in BNST neurons, was shown to block stress-induced reinstatement of cocaine CPP. These studies and others (Brown et al., 2011; McReynolds et al., 2014a, 2014b) provide evidence of a BNST circuit involving neuropeptide and monoamine signaling that underlies stress-induced reinstatement of drug-seeking behavior.

The BNST CRF system is also directly involved in reinstatement of drug-seeking behavior, as CRF mRNA is elevated in the BNST after stress-induced reinstatement of heroin-seeking behavior (Shalev et al., 2001). Local injection of a CRFR1 antagonist into the BNST decreases foot shock-induced reinstatement of cocaine and morphine seeking, while intra-BNST infusion of CRF itself increases reinstatement of cocaine-seeking behavior (Vranjkovic et al., 2014; Wang et al., 2006). Interconnectivity with the CeA plays a role as well, as pharmacologically inactivating the CeA (via GABAR agonist microinfusion) in one hemisphere and CRF activity in the contralateral BNST decreases stress-induced reinstatement of cocaine seeking (Sakanaka et al., 1986). Further, an ipsilateral connection from the CeA onto neurons expressing CRF in the dlBNST is critical for expression of stress-induced reinstatement of cocaine-seeking behavior (Salmaso et al., 2001). This CeA projection to the BNST has also been implicated in negative affect observed during morphine withdrawal (Nakagawa et al., 2005).

Dynorphin and KOR in the BNST have also garnered attention for their role in stress-induced reinstatement of drug seeking. Activation of KOR with a systemic agonist induces a strong stress response that is sufficient to drive reinstatement of alcohol seeking behavior, and the number of cfos-positive cells in the BNST after KOR agonist injection was positively correlated with lever pressing (Le et al., 2018). Furthermore, blocking KOR with site-specific delivery of an antagonist into the BNST prevented the systemic agonist-induced reinstatement of alcohol-seeking behavior (Le et al., 2018), implicating a role for the BNST in KOR stress-facilitation of reinstatement behavior.

The orexin system is another intriguing candidate for modulating BNST signaling in addiction because of its role in arousal and reward processing. Orexin receptors are expressed in the BNST, and the BNST sends projections to orexin neurons in the LH. Pharmacological inactivation of the BNST blocks cocaine CPP, and increases cfos expression in LH orexin neurons, outlining a potential circuit in which GABAergic BNST projections disinhibit LH orexin cells to induce relapse-like behavior (Mahler and Aston-Jones, 2012). Further, cue-induced reinstatement of alcohol-seeking behavior is blocked by intra-BNST infusion of an orexin receptor antagonist (Ubaldi et al., 2016). Additionally, the neuropeptide pituitary adenylate cyclase-activating polypeptide (PACAP) has been implicated in drug relapse-like behavior. For example, PACAP transcript levels are increased after 10 days of cocaine self-administration, and elevated BNST PACAP levels drive reinstatement of cocaine-seeking behavior (Miles et al., 2018). In all, neuropeptides and the neurocircuitry they regulate offer highly promising targets in the BNST for modulation of relapse-like behaviors.

Chemogenetic and optogenetic circuit manipulation in the BNST

The development of chemogenetic and optogenetic tools has enabled researchers to better understand the role of the BNST in the context of addiction in a cell-type and circuit-specific manner. Optogenetics relies on the expression of light-activated ion channels or pumps in neurons to drive temporally precise activation or inhibition of their activity (Fenno et al., 2011; Repina et al., 2017) (See Salling Chapter in this book). Many optogenetic studies in the BNST have helped to clarify the often opposing effects of BNST subpopulations and afferents on behavior. For example, channelrhodopsin (ChR2)-mediated activation of BNST afferents in the VTA is appetitive (mice show a real-time place preference for stimulation) with no effect on anxiety-like behavior (Kim et al., 2013). Dissecting this circuit further, however, revealed that ChR2 activation specifically in GABAergic vBNST neurons projecting to the VTA is appetitive and decreases anxiety-like behavior, while photostimulation of VTA-projecting glutamatergic vBNST neurons is aversive and anxiogenic (Jennings et al., 2013b). Optogenetic excitation of global BNST afferents in the LH is anxiolytic but has no effect on real-time place preference (Kim et al., 2013). However, specific stimulation of GABAergic BNST afferents in the LH produces robust place preference and also drives avid food consumption, especially of highly palatable foods (Jennings et al., 2013a). Interestingly, ChR2 activation of BNST CRF-positive or CCK-positive cells induces an aversive or appetitive state, respectively, as does activation of their terminals projecting specifically to the LH, but the activity of these cells has no effect on food intake (Giardino et al., 2018), suggesting a different cell subpopulation may mediate this output of the BNST→LH circuit.

A better understanding of the BNST and its intricate circuitry has been possible through the use of chemogenetic strategies, namely designer receptors exclusively activated by designer drugs (DREADDs). DREADDs are muscarinic acetylcholine receptors that have been modified to drive G_i-, G_q-, or G_s-coupled GPCR signaling pathways upon administration of the 'designer drug' clozapine-N-oxide (CNO), which is an otherwise inert compound (Roth, 2016) (see Salling chapter in this book). One benefit of this approach is that it can be used to mimic endogenous signaling pathways of various receptors expressed in BNST neurons (Grueter et al., 2006; Harris et al., 2018; McElligott et al., 2010; Perez et al., 2020; Pina et al., 2020). Indeed, work from Mazzone and colleagues showed that G_q-, but not G_s- or G_i-, DREADD activation in BNST GABAergic neurons promotes anxiety-like behavior, and that this could be recapitulated through stimulation of the G_q-coupled $5HT_{2C}R$ in the BNST (Mazzone et al., 2018). Although G_i-DREADDs are typically considered to have inhibitory actions, and G_q- and G_s-to have excitatory ones, chemogenetic studies in the BNST have urged caution regarding these assumptions. For example, both optogenetic activation and G_q-DREADD activation of BNST CRF-positive cells is aversive, demonstrating canonical G_q-driven cellular activation, and Gi-DREADD expression decreases resting membrane potential and spiking activity, fitting with canonical inhibitory G_i signaling actions (Giardino et al., 2018). However, work from the Winder lab has reliably shown that G_i-DREADD activation can also have excitatory effects in BNST neurons, increasing BNST activity and anxiety-like behavior (Harris et al., 2018; Perez et al., 2020). This work highlights the need for careful interpretation of "activation" and "inhibition" using G_q- and G_i-coupled DREADDs in this region, as GPCR signaling pathways can be quite complex.

Although there have been numerous chemogenetic and optogenetic studies investigating the role of the BNST and specific cell types within it on outputs such as anxiety-like behavior, fear, feeding, pain processing, and aggression (Bayless et al., 2019; Bruzsik et al., 2021; Emmons et al., 2021; Giardino et al., 2018; Gungor et al., 2015; Jaramillo et al., 2020; Jennings et al., 2013a, 2013b; Kim et al., 2013; Rodriguez-Romaguera et al., 2020; Xiao et al., 2020), to date there have been no optogenetic manipulations, and relatively few chemogenetic manipulations, of the BNST in the context of addiction. Of the studies that exist, several have specifically examined chemogenetic inhibition of VTA-projecting BNST neurons on alcohol consumption and preference. Studies by Pina and colleagues found that G_i-DREADD expression in the BNST, and specifically in VTA-projecting BNST neurons, blocked alcohol CPP when CNO was administered 30 min before testing (Pina and Cunningham, 2017; Pina et al., 2015). They also found that G_i-DREADD activation in the BNST blunts the increase in cfos typically seen following alcohol cue exposure. Other studies demonstrated that activation of G_i-DREADDs in VTA-projecting dlBNST CRF cells reduces binge-like alcohol consumption in a standard drinking-in-the-dark (DID) model in mice (Companion and Thiele, 2018; Rinker et al., 2017). Driving G_i-DREADD signaling in BNST CRF-positive neurons also suppresses binge-like alcohol consumption in mice (Pleil et al., 2015b). Conversely, driving G_s-DREADD signaling in these neurons does not affect alcohol consumption but blocks NPY Y1R-mediated suppression of binge-like alcohol drinking (Pleil et al., 2015b). G_i-DREADD activation in BNST-projecting mPFC neurons does not impact alcohol consumption but does rescue alcohol-induced suppression of marble-burying behavior (Hwa et al., 2020). This G_i-DREADD activation also increases predator odor avoidance in both non-alcohol- and alcohol-exposed mice, blocking alcohol-induced increases in predator odor investigation in the latter group (Hwa et al., 2020). One study from the Winder lab investigated the effects of G_q-DREADD activation in the BNST in relation to the negative affective component of prolonged alcohol abstinence. They reported that G_q-DREADD activation in dBNST neurons receiving input from the insula mimics increases in anxiety-like behavior and BNST cfos expression normally seen during forced abstinence from chronic alcohol drinking (Centanni et al., 2019b). In another study from the Winder group, G_i-DREADD expression in the dBNST was sufficient to drive reinstatement of cocaine conditioned place preference, mimicking the effects of the G_i-coupled alpha2-AR heteroreceptor on stress-induced reinstatement (Perez et al., 2020). Together, these studies highlight that BNST chemogenetic and optogenetic manipulation research is still in its infancy, but current work reinforces the importance of the BNST in mediating drug intake, withdrawal, and reinstatement.

Translational work in the human BNST

Despite substantial rodent research highlighting the role of the BNST in psychopathology, BNST research in humans is still an emerging field. The first neuroimaging investigation of the BNST was published in 2014 (Avery et al., 2014) and detailed the structural and functional connectivity of the BNST (see Figs. 9.1–9.3 in Avery et al., 2014) with 108 other brain regions. As the BNST had not been examined using neuroimaging in humans before, this study used ultra-high resolution (7T) magnetic resonance imaging (MRI) to manually define the location of the BNST. Results from this study showed structural connectivity between the BNST and regions of the basal ganglia (NAcc, pallidum, caudate, putamen), the limbic system (subcallosal cortex, amygdala, hippocampus), the thalamus, and the temporal pole. The functional connectivity, which was measured at rest and is referred to as resting state functional connectivity, showed BNST connectivity with the basal ganglia (caudate, NAcc, putamen, pallidum), limbic region (hippocampus), the thalamus, and the paracingulate cortex. In a more exploratory approach, Avery et al. (2014) also demonstrated functional connectivity between the BNST and parts of the subcallosal cortex, parahippocampal gyrus, anterior insula, anterior cingulate cortex, medial frontal gyrus, superior frontal gyrus, inferior frontal gyrus, middle frontal gyrus, posterior cingulate cortex, calcarine fissure, precuneus, and precentral gyrus. These first *in vivo* human BNST results laid a foundation for future BNST imaging studies in humans and provided important evidence for translational validity of converging BNST findings in rodents and humans.

After the first human BNST publication in 2014, the number of BNST studies in humans has been steadily increasing. Early studies provided critical replication of the findings from

BOX 9.1

Images from DTI and fMRI human studies of stress and addiction related neurocircuitry.

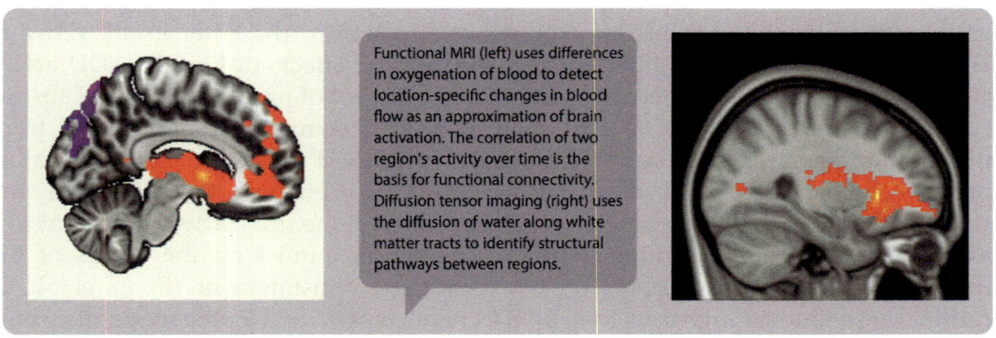

Avery et al. (2014) and expanded to include connectivity with more brain regions. Using high-field MRI, Torrisi and colleagues replicated previous findings and also showed BNST functional connectivity with the hypothalamus, periaqueductal gray, parieto-occipital sulcus, habenula, and posterior insula (Torrisi et al., 2018). One recent structural connectivity study also demonstrated BNST connectivity with the anterior insula (Flook et al., 2020). In addition to information about which regions have structural connectivity with the BNST, the main white matter paths from the BNST have also been described. In 2015, a structural connectivity study identified three major white matter pathways from the BNST: the anterior bundle, the posterior bundle, and the ventral bundle (Krüger et al., 2015). The posterior bundle follows the stria terminalis to the amygdala and has also been identified in rodent models. The ventral bundle follows the ansa peduncularis from the BNST to the amygdala and hypothalamus and has been shown in rodent studies as well. Finally, the anterior bundle connects the BNST to the orbitofrontal cortex via the caudate and NAcc, a pathway that yet to be identified in rodents. This study also identified numerous projections between the BNST and brainstem, but the heterogeneity of the connection between individuals prevented the identification of a specific pathway. The summation of these human studies reflects patterns of BNST connectivity that largely replicate rodent research, showing that the human BNST has connectivity with regions associated with critical processes including emotion, motivation, and decision making.

Since these early studies, an important evolution of human BNST research has been to investigate BNST function and connectivity in pathology. Rodent studies have demonstrated a role for the BNST in behaviors related to psychopathology that human studies have only recently begun to investigate. Of these, anxiety has been the most extensively studied (for early examples see (Alvarez et al., 2011; Somerville et al., 2010). Congruent with the rodent literature describing the role of the BNST in anxiety-like behaviors, human studies have shown alterations in BNST connectivity during anxiety-inducing tasks and in patients who have an anxiety disorder. For example, during a threatening condition (anticipation of a shock), healthy participants show decreased BNST functional connectivity with the NAcc, mPFC, precuneus, and ventromedial PFC (vmPFC) compared to a nonthreatening condition (Torrisi et al., 2018). Furthermore, participants with either a general anxiety disorder or social anxiety disorder demonstrate decreased BNST functional connectivity with the orbitofrontal cortex and dorsolateral PFC at rest compared to non-anxious participants (Torrisi et al., 2019). This decrease in functional connectivity has also been shown in a threatening task for participants with social anxiety. Higher social anxiety scores were associated with decreased functional connectivity between the BNST and amygdala during presentation of a cue that signified the subsequent presentation of either a neutral or a threatening image (Clauss et al., 2019). During the presentation of the unpredictable neutral or threatening images, higher social anxiety was associated with increased BNST functional connectivity with the vmPFC and posterior cingulate cortex (Clauss et al., 2019). In addition to studies of anxiety, the BNST has also been linked to disorders that are highly comorbid with addiction, such as post-traumatic stress disorder (PTSD) (Miles and Maren, 2019), depression (Fitzgerald et al., 2018), and obsessive compulsive disorder (Islam et al., 2015). These studies in humans provide critical translational evidence for differences in BNST connectivity associated with anxiety and encourage future studies translating rodent findings to humans.

Strong rodent evidence supports a role for the BNST in driving negative affect behaviors during abstinence; in humans, however, very few studies of BNST circuitry exist. One study found increased BNST-amygdala functional connectivity during fearful face viewing in abstinent patients with a history of multiple relapses of alcohol use disorder (O'Daly et al., 2012), possibly suggesting an increased response to threat during abstinence. A more recent study of BNST structural connectivity examined regions known to have BNST connectivity and showed increased BNST-hypothalamus connectivity and decreased BNST-vmPFC connectivity in abstinent women with a history of alcohol use disorder compared to female controls; there were no differences seen in men (Flook et al., 2021). Given the roles of the hypothalamus in the brain's major stress pathway, increased BNST-hypothalamus structural connectivity in abstinent women could help explain why women experience greater anxiety symptoms during abstinence than men (Conway et al., 2006). Understanding this difference could also help to explain why women are more likely to relapse in response to stress or anxiety (Becker and Koob, 2016). These first studies of BNST connectivity differences in abstinence provide translational support for the role of the BNST in anxiety during abstinence, but more studies are needed to better understand the factors that contribute to differences in connectivity.

Future of BNST circuitry and addiction

Numerous seminal studies highlighted throughout this chapter collectively paint an elaborate portrait of the BNST's expansive role in addiction. Emerging literature is now building on these foundational studies to incorporate the complex circuitry mediating changes in the BNST brought on by drug exposure. The advancement of exciting new tools for studying circuitry began with the development of optogenetic and chemogenetic viruses that allow for isolating and manipulating specific cell types and circuits, including many studies that have directly examined BNST circuitry using these strategies (described above). Not only have the basic chemogenetic and optogenetic tools significantly evolved, but these tools have facilitated a wave of novel instruments for manipulating circuits *in vivo* and *ex vivo*. In conjunction with circuit manipulation tools, the evolution of genetically engineered indicators designed to detect calcium, neurotransmitters, voltage, pH, etc., now allows for monitoring of endogenous circuit activity, providing researchers with a way of identifying dysfunctional circuits in disease states such as addiction. Moreover, highly specific viral promoters provide targeted expression to multiple different cell types in the same area (e.g., INTRSECT (Fenno et al., 2014)), as well as multiple areas within a cell (e.g., axon, nucleus, mitochondria). Utilizing these strategies will be critical for understanding microcircuitry in complex, heterogeneous brain structures like the BNST. Transsynaptic, retrograde, and anterograde viral trafficking provide ways to specifically isolate input and output neurons in the BNST, thus nuanced changes in BNST neuronal circuits in different phases of the addiction cycle can now be detected with much greater precision than in the past. Combining these strategies with the established genetic mouse models and emerging genetic tools such as CRISPR allow for precise cell-type manipulation, which is critical in such heterogeneous brain areas as the BNST. Lastly, identifying the larger circuits beyond the direct inputs and outputs of the BNST is now possible with the use of rabies tracing in combination with retrograde and anterograde viruses (e.g., TRIO (Schwarz et al., 2015)). Coupling these viral technologies with improved neuronal imaging techniques with higher resolution microscopy and whole brain imaging of lipid-cleared brains using light sheet microcopy has significantly narrowed the gap between human imaging and preclinical imaging studies. Mapping BNST circuitry and determining how it relates to affective behavior is an essential step towards developing new ways to treat and diagnose affective disorders and negative affective symptoms that drive all phases of addiction.

The evolution of new tools to probe BNST circuits in preclinical models will complement the continued advances in clinical models as well. Methodological advancements of the last decade have revolutionized neuroimaging and enabled the *in vivo* observation of small neural structures in humans, including the BNST. One main advancement has been the availability of high-resolution MRI, notably the widespread use of 3T MRI machines and the increasing use of 7T machines. Here, 3T and 7T refer to the strength of the magnetic field produced in unit Tesla. Stronger magnetic fields can be used to acquire higher resolution, which is important for distinguishing the boundaries of a small structure like the BNST. In addition to increases in magnetic field strength, acquisition has also been substantially improved by the advent of multi-band or multi-shot planar imaging, which allows for rapid collection of data and improves image quality (Moeller et al., 2010). As the technology and these techniques continue to improve, *in vivo* investigation of the BNST in humans will become more prevalent and substantially increase the scope of the existing literature. Future advances could even facilitate the investigation of BNST subregions, allowing for more direct comparisons to rodent research.

References

Ahumada, C., Bahamondes, C., Cerda, C.A., Silva, R.A., Cruz, G., Moya, P.R., Sotomayor-Zárate, R., Renard, G.M., 2017. Amphetamine treatment affects the extra-hypothalamic vasopressinergic system in a sex- and nucleus-dependent manner. J. Neuroendocrinol. 29, 1–8.

Albrechet-Souza, L., Viola, T.W., Grassi-Oliveira, R., Miczek, K.A., de Almeida, R.M.M., 2017. Corticotropin releasing factor in the bed nucleus of the stria terminalis in socially defeated and non-stressed mice with a history of chronic alcohol intake. Front. Pharmacol. 8, 762.

Alheid, G.F.F., Beltramino, C.A.A., de Olmos, J.S.S., Forbes, M.S.S., Swanson, D.J.J., Heimer, L., 1998. The neuronal organization of the supracapsular part of the stria terminalis in the rat: the dorsal component of the extended amygdala. Neuroscience 84, 967–996.

Alvarez, R.P., Chen, G., Bodurka, J., Kaplan, R., Grillon, C., 2011. Phasic and sustained fear in humans elicits distinct patterns of brain activity. Neuroimage 55, 389–400.

Aston-Jones, G., Delfs, J.M., Druhan, J., Zhu, Y., 1999. The bed nucleus of the stria terminalis. A target site for noradrenergic actions in opiate withdrawal. Ann. N. Y. Acad. Sci. 877, 486–498.

Avery, S.N., Clauss, J.A., Winder, D.G., Woodward, N., Heckers, S., Blackford, J.U., 2014. BNST neurocircuitry in humans. Neuroimage 91, 311–323.

Bamshad, M., Cooper, T.T., Karom, M., Elliott Albers, H., 1996. Glutamate and vasopressin interact to control scent marking in Syrian hamsters (Mesocricetus auratus). Brain Res. 731, 213–216.

Banihashemi, L., Rinaman, L., 2006. Noradrenergic inputs to the bed nucleus of the stria terminalis and paraventricular nucleus of the hypothalamus underlie hypothalamic-pituitary-adrenal axis but not hypophagic or conditioned avoidance responses to systemic yohimbine. J. Neurosci. 26, 11442–11453.

Bayless, D.W., Yang, T., Mason, M.M., Susanto, A.A.T., Lobdell, A., Shah, N.M., 2019. Limbic neurons shape sex recognition and social behavior in sexually naive males. Cell 176, 1190, 1205.e1120.

Becker, J.B., Koob, G.F., 2016. Sex differences in animal models: focus on addiction. Pharmacol. Rev. 68, 242–263.

Bedse, G., Centanni, S.W., Winder, D.G., Patel, S., 2019. Endocannabinoid signaling in the central amygdala and bed nucleus of the stria terminalis: implications for the pathophysiology and treatment of alcohol use disorder. Alcohol Clin. Exp. Res. 43, 2014–2027.

Belej, T., Manji, D., Sioutis, S., Barros, H.M.T., Nobrega, J.N., 1996. Changes in serotonin and norepinephrine uptake sites after chronic cocaine: pre- vs. post-withdrawal effects. Brain Res. 736, 287–296.

Berk, M.L., Finkelstein, J.A., 1982. Efferent connections of the lateral hypothalamic area of the rat: an autoradiographic investigation. Brain Res. Bull. 8, 511–526.

Bienkowski, M.S., Rinaman, L., 2013. Common and distinct neural inputs to the medial central nucleus of the amygdala and anterior ventrolateral bed nucleus of stria terminalis in rats. Brain Struct. Funct. 218, 187–208.

Block, C.H., Hoffman, G.E., 1987. Neuropeptide and monoamine components of the parabrachial pontine complex. Peptides 8, 267–283.

Bluett, R.J., Baldi, R., Haymer, A., Gaulden, A.D., Hartley, N.D., Parrish, W.P., Baechle, J., Marcus, D.J., Mardam-Bey, R., Shonesy, B.C., et al., 2017. Endocannabinoid signalling modulates susceptibility to traumatic stress exposure. Nat. Commun. 8, 14782.

Bluett, R.J., Gamble-George, J.C., Hermanson, D.J., Hartley, N.D., Marnett, L.J., Patel, S., 2014. Central anandamide deficiency predicts stress-induced anxiety: behavioral reversal through endocannabinoid augmentation. Transl. Psychiatry 4, e408.

Blundell, J., Adamec, R., 2007. The NMDA receptor antagonist CPP blocks the effects of predator stress on pCREB in brain regions involved in fearful and anxious behavior. Brain Res. 1136, 59–76.

Bornstein, S.R., Webster, E.L., Torpy, D.J., Richman, S.J., Mitsiades, N., Igel, M., Lewis, D.B., Rice, K.C., Joost, H.G., Tsokos, M., et al., 1998. Chronic effects of a nonpeptide corticotropin-releasing hormone type I receptor antagonist on pituitary-adrenal function, body weight, and metabolic regulation. Endocrinology 139, 1546–1555.

Bosch, O.J., Pförtsch, J., Beiderbeck, D.I., Landgraf, R., Neumann, I.D., 2010. Maternal behaviour is associated with vasopressin release in the medial preoptic area and bed nucleus of the stria terminalis in the rat. J. Neuroendocrinol. 22, 420–429.

Bowers, L.K., Swisher, C.B., Behbehani, M.M., 2003. Membrane and synaptic effects of corticotropin-releasing factor on periaqueductal gray neurons of the rat. Brain Res. 981, 52–57.

Briand, L.A., Vassoler, F.M., Pierce, R.C., Valentino, R.J., Blendy, J.A., 2010. Ventral tegmental afferents in stress-induced reinstatement: the role of cAMP response element-binding protein. J. Neurosci. 30, 16149–16159.

Brown, Z.J., Nobrega, J.N., Erb, S., 2011. Central injections of noradrenaline induce reinstatement of cocaine seeking and increase c-fos mRNA expression in the extended amygdala. Behav. Brain Res. 217, 472–476.

Bruijnzeel, A.W., Stam, R., Compaan, J.C., Croiset, G., Akkermans, L.M.A., Olivier, B., Wiegant, V.M., 1999. Long-term sensitization of Fos-responsivity in the rat central nervous system after a single stressful experience. Brain Res. 819, 15–22.

Bruzsik, B., Biro, L., Zelena, D., Sipos, E., Szebik, H., Sarosdi, K.R., Horvath, O., Farkas, I., Csillag, V., Finszter, C.K., et al., 2021. Somatostatin neurons of the bed nucleus of stria terminalis enhance associative fear memory consolidation in mice. J. Neurosci. 41, 1982–1995. JN-RM-1944-1920.

Caillé, S., Guillem, K., Cador, M., Manzoni, O., Georges, F., 2009. Voluntary nicotine consumption triggers in vivo potentiation of cortical excitatory drives to midbrain dopaminergic neurons. J. Neurosci. 29, 10410–10415.

Calcagnoli, F., de Boer, S.F., Beiderbeck, D.I., Althaus, M., Koolhaas, J.M., Neumann, I.D., 2014. Local oxytocin expression and oxytocin receptor binding in the male rat brain is associated with aggressiveness. Behav. Brain Res. 261, 315–322.

Campbell, R.R., Domingo, R.D., Williams, A.R., Wroten, M.G., McGregor, H.A., Waltermire, R.S., Greentree, D.I., Goulding, S.P., Thompson, A.B., Lee, K.M., et al., 2019. Increased alcohol-drinking induced by manipulations of mGlu5 phosphorylation within the bed nucleus of the stria terminalis. J. Neurosci. 39, 2745–2761.

Campi, K.L., Jameson, C.E., Trainor, B.C., 2013. Sexual dimorphism in the brain of the monogamous California mouse (peromyscus californicus). Brain Behav. Evol. 81, 236–249.

Canteras, N.S., Swanson, L.W., 1992. Projections of the ventral subiculum to the amygdala, septum, and hypothalamus: a PHAL anterograde tract-tracing study in the rat. J. Comp. Neurol. 324, 180–194.

Carboni, E., Silvagni, A., Rolando, M.T., Di Chiara, G., 2000. Stimulation of in vivo dopamine transmission in the bed nucleus of stria terminalis by reinforcing drugs. J. Neurosci. Off. J. Soc. Neurosci. 20. RC102-RC102.

Carter, M.E., Soden, M.E., Zweifel, L.S., Palmiter, R.D., 2013. Genetic identification of a neural circuit that suppresses appetite. Nature 503, 111–114.

Cassell, M.D., Freedman, L.J., Shi, C., 1999. The intrinsic organization of the central extended amygdala. Ann. N. Y. Acad. Sci. 877, 217–241.

Castillo, P.E., Younts, T.J., Chavez, A.E., Hashimotodani, Y., 2012. Endocannabinoid signaling and synaptic function. Neuron 76, 70–81.

Cecchi, M., Khoshbouei, H., Javors, M., Morilak, D.A., 2002. Modulatory effects of norepinephrine in the lateral bed nucleus of the stria terminalis on behavioral and neuroendocrine responses to acute stress. Neuroscience 112, 13–21.

Centanni, S.W., Bedse, G., Patel, S., Winder, D.G., 2019a. Driving the downward spiral: alcohol-induced dysregulation of extended amygdala circuits and negative affect. Alcohol Clin. Exp. Res. 43, 2000–2013.

Centanni, S.W., Morris, B.D., Luchsinger, J.R., Bedse, G., Fetterly, T.L., Patel, S., Winder, D.G., 2019b. Endocannabinoid control of the insular-bed nucleus of the stria terminalis circuit regulates negative affective behavior associated with alcohol abstinence. Neuropsychopharmacology 44, 526–537.

Ch'ng, S., Fu, J., Brown, R.M., McDougall, S.J., Lawrence, A.J., 2018. The intersection of stress and reward: BNST modulation of aversive and appetitive states. Prog. Neuro-Psychopharmacol. Biol. Psychiatry 87, 108–125.

Choi, D.-s., Wei, W., Deitchman, J.K., Kharazia, V.N., Lesscher, H.M.B., McMahon, T., Wang, D., Qi, Z.-h., Sieghart, W., Zhang, C., et al., 2008a. Protein kinase C delta regulates ethanol intoxication and enhancement of GABA-stimulated tonic current. J. Neurosci. 28, 11890–11899.

Choi, D.C., Furay, A.R., Evanson, N.K., Ostrander, M.M., Ulrich-Lai, Y.M., Herman, J.P., 2007. Bed nucleus of the stria terminalis subregions differentially regulate hypothalamic-pituitary-adrenal axis activity: implications for the integration of limbic inputs. J. Neurosci. 27, 2025–2034.

Choi, D.C., Furay, A.R., Evanson, N.K., Ulrich-Lai, Y.M., Nguyen, M.M.N., Ostrander, M.M., Herman, J.P., 2008b. The role of the posterior medial bed nucleus of the stria terminalis in modulating hypothalamic-pituitary-adrenocortical axis responsiveness to acute and chronic stress. Psychoneuroendocrinology 33, 659–669.

Chronwall, B.M., DiMaggio, D.A., Massari, V.J., Pickel, V.M., Ruggiero, D.A., O'Donohue, T.L., 1985. The anatomy of neuropeptide-y-containing neurons in rat brain. Neuroscience 15, 1159–1181.

Chung, S., Kim, H.J., Kim, H.J., Choi, S.H., Cho, J.H., Cho, Y.H., Kim, D.-H., Shin, K.H., 2014. Desipramine and citalopram attenuate pretest swim-induced increases in prodynorphin immunoreactivity in the dorsal bed nucleus of the stria terminalis and the lateral division of the central nucleus of the amygdala in the forced swimming test. Neuropeptides 48, 273–280.

Ciccocioppo, R., Fedeli, A., Economidou, D., Policani, F., Weiss, F., Massi, M., 2003. The bed nucleus is a neuroanatomical substrate for the anorectic effect of corticotropin-releasing factor and for its reversal by nociceptin/orphanin FQ. J. Neurosci. 23, 9445.

Clauss, J.A., Avery, S.N., Benningfield, M.M., Blackford, J.U., 2019. Social anxiety is associated with BNST response to unpredictability. Depress. Anxiety 36, 666–675.

Colussi-Mas, J., Panayi, F., Ne Scarna, H., Renaud, B., Bérod, A., Lambás-Señ, L., 2005. Blockade of b-adrenergic receptors prevents amphetamine-induced behavioural sensitization in rats: a putative role of the bed nucleus of the stria terminalis. Int. J. Neuropsychopharmacol. 8, 569–581.

Commons, K.G., Connolley, K.R., Valentino, R.J., 2003. A neurochemically distinct dorsal raphe-limbic circuit with a potential role in affective disorders. Neuropsychopharmacology 28, 206–215.

Companion, M.A., Thiele, T.E., 2018. Assessment of ventral tegmental area-projecting GABAergic neurons from the bed nucleus of the stria terminalis in modulating binge-like ethanol intake. Eur. J. Neurosci. 48, 3335–3343.

Connelly, K.L., Unterwald, E.M., 2019. Chronic cocaine administration upregulates FKBP5 in the extended amygdala of male and female rats. Drug Alcohol Depend. 199, 101–105.

Consiglio, A.R., Borsoi, A., Pereira, G.A.M., Lucion, A.B., 2005. Effects of oxytocin microinjected into the central amygdaloid nucleus and bed nucleus of stria terminalis on maternal aggressive behavior in rats. Physiol. Behav. 85, 354–362.

Contet, C., Gardon, O., Filliol, D., Becker, J.A., Koob, G.F., Kieffer, B.L., 2011. Identification of genes regulated in the mouse extended amygdala by excessive ethanol drinking associated with dependence. Addiction Biol. 16, 615–619.

Conway, K.P., Compton, W., Stinson, F.S., Grant, B.F., 2006. Lifetime comorbidity of DSM-IV mood and anxiety disorders and specific drug use disorders. J. Clin. Psychiatr. 67, 247–258.

Corominas, M., Roncero, C., Casas, M., 2010. Corticotropin Releasing Factor and Neuroplasticity in Cocaine Addiction. Elsevier Inc., pp. 1–9

Crankshaw, D.L., Briggs, J.E., Olszewski, P.K., Shi, Q., Grace, M.K., Billington, C.J., Levine, A.S., 2003. Effects of intracerebroventricular ethanol on ingestive behavior and induction of c-Fos immunoreactivity in selected brain regions. Physiol. Behav. 79, 113–120.

Crowley, N.A., Bloodgood, D.W., Hardaway, J.A., Kendra, A.M., McCall, J.G., Al-Hasani, R., McCall, N.M., Yu, W., Schools, Z.L., Krashes, M.J., et al., 2016. Dynorphin controls the gain of an amygdalar anxiety circuit. Cell Rep. 14, 2774–2783.

Cruz, F.C., Alves, F.H.F., Leão, R.M., Planeta, C.S., Crestani, C.C., 2013. Role of the bed nucleus of the stria terminalis in cardiovascular changes following chronic treatment with cocaine and testosterone: a role beyond drug seeking in addiction? Neuroscience 253, 29–39.

Cullinan, W.E., Herman, J.P., Watson, S.J., 1993. Ventral subicular interaction with the hypothalamic paraventricular nucleus: evidence for a relay in the bed nucleus of the stria terminalis. J. Comp. Neurol. 332, 1–20.

Cummings, S., Elde, R., Ells, J., Lindall, A., 1983. Corticotropin-releasing factor immunoreactivity is widely distributed within the central nervous system of the rat: an immunohistochemical study. J. Neurosci. 3, 1355–1368.

D'Este, L., Casini, A., Pontieri, F.E., Renda, T.G., 2006. Changes in neuropeptide FF and NPY immunohistochemical patterns in rat brain under heroin treatment. Brain Res. 1083, 151–158.

Dabrowska, J., Hazra, R., Ahern, T.H., Guo, J.-D., McDonald, A.J., Mascagni, F., Muller, J.F., Young, L.J., Rainnie, D.G., 2011. Neuroanatomical evidence for reciprocal regulation of the corticotrophin-releasing factor and oxytocin systems in the hypothalamus and the bed nucleus of the stria terminalis of the rat: implications for balancing stress and affect. Psychoneuroendocrinology 36, 1312–1326.

Daniel, S.E., Guo, J., Rainnie, D.G., 2017. A comparative analysis of the physiological properties of neurons in the anterolateral bed nucleus of the stria terminalis in the *Mus musculus, Rattus norvegicus* , and *Macaca mulatta.* J. Comp. Neurol. 525, 2235–2248.

Dawe, K.L., Wakerley, J.B., Fulford, A.J., 2010. Nociceptin/orphanin FQ and the regulation of neuronal excitability in the rat bed nucleus of the stria terminalis: interaction with glucocorticoids. Stress 13, 516–527.

Day, H.E.W., Badiani, A., Uslaner, J.M., Oates, M.M., Vittoz, N.M., Robinson, T.E., Watson, S.J., Akil, H., 2001. Environmental novelty differentially affects c-fos mRNA expression induced by amphetamine or cocaine in subregions of the bed nucleus of the stria terminalis and amygdala. J. Neurosci. 21, 732–740.

Day, H.E.W., Curran, E.J., Watson Jr., S.J., Akil, H., 1999. Distinct neurochemical populations in the rat central nucleus of the amygdala and bed nucleus of the stria terminalis: evidence for their selective activation by interleukin-1β. J. Comp. Neurol. 413, 113–128.

De Bundel, D., Zussy, C., Espallergues, J., Gerfen, C.R., Girault, J.A., Valjent, E., 2016. Dopamine D2 receptors gate generalization of conditioned threat responses through mTORC1 signaling in the extended amygdala. Mol. Psychiatr. 21, 1545–1553.

Debacker, J., Hawken, E.R., Normandeau, C.P., Jones, A.A., Di Prospero, C., Mechefske, E., Gardner Gregory, J., Hayton, S.J., Dumont, É.C., 2015. GluN2B-containing NMDA receptors blockade rescues bidirectional synaptic plasticity in the bed nucleus of the stria terminalis of cocaine self-administering rats. Neuropsychopharmacology 40, 394–405.

Delfs, J.M., Zhu, Y., Druhan, J.P., Aston-Jones, G., 2000. Noradrenaline in the ventral forebrain is critical for opiate withdrawal-induced aversion. Nature 403, 430–434.

Desai, S.J., Borkar, C.D., Nakhate, K.T., Subhedar, N.K., Kokare, D.M., 2014. Neuropeptide Y attenuates anxiety- and depression-like effects of cholecystokinin-4 in mice. Neuroscience 277, 818–830.

Desai, S.J., Upadhya, M.A., Subhedar, N.K., Kokare, D.M., 2013. NPY mediates reward activity of morphine, via NPY Y1 receptors, in the nucleus accumbens shell. Behav. Brain Res. 247, 79–91.

Devane, W.A., Breuer, A., Sheskin, T., Jarbe, T.U., Eisen, M.S., Mechoulam, R., 1992. A novel probe for the cannabinoid receptor. J. Med. Chem. 35, 2065–2069.

Dong, H.-W., Petrovich, G.D., Watts, A.G., Swanson, L.W., 2001. Basic organization of projections from the oval and fusiform nuclei of the bed nuclei of the stria terminalis in adult rat brain. J. Comp. Neurol. 436, 430–455.

Dong, H.-W., Swanson, L.W., 2004a. Organization of axonal projections from the anterolateral area of the bed nuclei of the stria terminalis. J. Comp. Neurol. 468, 277–298.

Dong, H.-W., Swanson, L.W., 2004b. Projections from bed nuclei of the stria terminalis, posterior division: implications for cerebral hemisphere regulation of defensive and reproductive behaviors. J. Comp. Neurol. 471, 396–433.

Dong, H.-W., Swanson, L.W., 2006a. Projections from bed nuclei of the stria terminalis, magnocellular nucleus: implications for cerebral hemisphere regulation of micturition, defecation, and penile erection. J. Comp. Neurol. 494, 108–141.

Dong, H.W., Swanson, L.W., 2006b. Projections from bed nuclei of the stria terminalis, dorsomedial nucleus: implications for cerebral hemisphere integration of neuroendocrine, autonomic, and drinking responses. J. Comp. Neurol. 494, 75–107.

Dumais, K.M., Alonso, A.G., Immormino, M.A., Bredewold, R., Veenema, A.H., 2016. Involvement of the oxytocin system in the bed nucleus of the stria terminalis in the sex-specific regulation of social recognition. Psychoneuroendocrinology 64, 79–88.

Dumont, E.C., Mark, G.P., Mader, S., Williams, J.T., 2005. Self-administration enhances excitatory synaptic transmission in the bed nucleus of the stria terminalis. Nat. Neurosci. 8, 413–414.

Dumont, E.C., Williams, J.T., 2004. Noradrenaline triggers GABAA inhibition of bed nucleus of the stria terminalis neurons projecting to the ventral tegmental area. J. Neurosci. 24, 8198–8204.

Dunn, J.D., Williams, T.J., 1995. Cardiovascular responses to electrical stimulation of the bed nucleus of the stria terminalis. J. Comp. Neurol. 352, 227–234.

Duque-Wilckens, N., Steinman, M.Q., Busnelli, M., Chini, B., Yokoyama, S., Pham, M., Laredo, S.A., Hao, R., Perkeybile, A.M., Minie, V.A., et al., 2018. Oxytocin receptors in the anteromedial bed nucleus of the stria terminalis promote stress-induced social avoidance in female California mice. Biol. Psychiatr. 83, 203–213.

Duque-Wilckens, N., Steinman, M.Q., Laredo, S.A., Hao, R., Perkeybile, A.M., Bales, K.L., Trainor, B.C., 2016. Inhibition of vasopressin V1a receptors in the medioventral bed nucleus of the stria terminalis has sex- and context-specific anxiogenic effects. Neuropharmacology 110, 59–68.

Duque-Wilckens, N., Torres, L.Y., Yokoyama, S., Minie, V.A., Tran, A.M., Petkova, S.P., Hao, R., Ramos-Maciel, S., Rios, R.A., Jackson, K., et al., 2020. Extrahypothalamic oxytocin neurons drive stress-induced social vigilance and avoidance. Proc. Natl. Acad. Sci. U. S. A 117, 26406–26413.

Egli, R.E., Kash, T.L., Choo, K., Savchenko, V., Matthews, R.T., Blakely, R.D., Winder, D.G., 2005. Norepinephrine modulates glutamatergic transmission in the bed nucleus of the stria terminalis. Neuropsychopharmacology 30, 657–668.

Egli, R.E., Winder, D.G., 2003. Dorsal and ventral distribution of excitable and synaptic properties of neurons of the bed nucleus of the stria terminalis. J. Neurophysiol. 90, 405–414.

Eiler, W.J.A., Seyoum, R., Foster, K.L., Mailey, C., June, H.L., 2003. D1 Dopamine Receptor Regulates Alcohol-Motivated Behaviors in the Bed Nucleus of the Stria Terminalis in Alcohol-Preferring (P) Rats, vol 48. Synapse, New York, N.Y., pp. 45–56

Emmons, R., Sadok, T., Rovero, N.G., Belnap, M.A., Henderson, H.J.M., Quan, A.J., Del Toro, N.J., Halladay, L.R., 2021. Chemogenetic manipulation of the bed nucleus of the stria terminalis counteracts social behavioral deficits induced by early life stress in C57BL/6J mice. J. Neurosci. Res. 99, 90–109.

Erb, S., 2000. Alpha-2 adrenergic receptor agonists block stress-induced reinstatement of cocaine seeking. Neuropsychopharmacology 23, 138–150.

Erb, S., Shaham, Y., Stewart, J., 2001. Stress-induced relapse to drug seeking in the rat: role of the bed nucleus of the stria terminalis and amygdala. Stress (Amsterdam, Netherlands) 4, 289–303.

Erb, S., Stewart, J., 1999. A role for the bed nucleus of the stria terminalis, but not the amygdala, in the effects of corticotropin-releasing factor on stress-induced reinstatement of cocaine seeking. J. Neurosci. 19, RC35.

Erikson, C.M., Wei, G., Walker, B.M., 2018. Maladaptive behavioral regulation in alcohol dependence: role of kappa-opioid receptors in the bed nucleus of the stria terminalis. Neuropharmacology 140, 162–173.

Ettenberg, A. Opponent Process Properties of Self-Administered Cocaine. (Elsevier Ltd), pp. 721-728.

Ettenberg, A., 2009. The Runway Model of Drug Self-Administration. Elsevier, pp. 271–277.

Ettenberg, A., Cotten, S.W., Brito, M.A., Klein, A.K., Ohana, T.A., Margolin, B., Wei, A., Wenzel, J.M., 2015. CRF antagonism within the ventral tegmental area but not the extended amygdala attenuates the anxiogenic effects of cocaine in rats. Pharmacol. Biochem. Behav. 138, 148–155.

Ettenberg, A., Geist, T.D., 1991. Animal model for investigating the anxiogenic effects of self-administered cocaine. Psychopharmacology 103, 455–461.

Fendt, M., Endres, T., Apfelbach, R., 2003. Temporary inactivation of the bed nucleus of the stria terminalis but not of the amygdala blocks freezing induced by trimethylthiazoline, a component of fox feces. J. Neurosci. 23, 23–28.

Fendt, M., Siegl, S., Steiniger-Brach, B., 2005. Noradrenaline transmission within the ventral bed nucleus of the stria terminalis is critical for fear behavior induced by trimethylthiazoline, a component of fox odor. J. Neurosci. 25, 5998–6004.

Fenno, L., Yizhar, O., Deisseroth, K., 2011. The development and application of optogenetics. Annu. Rev. Neurosci. 34, 389–412.

Fenno, L.E., Mattis, J., Ramakrishnan, C., Hyun, M., Lee, S.Y., He, M., Tucciarone, J., Selimbeyoglu, A., Berndt, A., Grosenick, L., et al., 2014. INTRSECT: single-component targeting of cells using multiple-feature Boolean logic. Nat. Methods 11, 763–772.

Fetterly, T.L., Basu, A., Nabit, B.P., Awad, E., Williford, K.M., Centanni, S.W., Matthews, R.T., Silberman, Y., Winder, D.G., 2019. alpha2A-adrenergic receptor activation decreases parabrachial nucleus excitatory drive onto BNST CRF neurons and reduces their activity in vivo. J. Neurosci. 39, 472–484.

Fink, G., Sumner, B.E.H., Rosie, R., Grace, O., Quinn, J.P., 1996. Estrogen control of central neurotransmission: effect on mood, mental state, and memory. Cell. Mol. Neurobiol. 16, 325–344.

Fitzgerald, P.B., Segrave, R., Richardson, K.E., Knox, L.A., Herring, S., Daskalakis, Z.J., Bittar, R.G., 2018. A pilot study of bed nucleus of the stria terminalis deep brain stimulation in treatment-resistant depression. Brain Stimul. 11, 921–928.

Flanigan, M.E., Kash, T.L., 2020. Coordination of social behaviors by the bed nucleus of the stria terminalis. Eur. J. Neurosci. 55, 2404–2420 ejn.14991-ejn.14991.

Flavin, S.A., Matthews, R.T., Wang, Q., Muly, E.C., Winder, D.G., 2014. 2A-adrenergic receptors filter parabrachial inputs to the bed nucleus of the stria terminalis. J. Neurosci. 34, 9319–9331.

Flook, E.A., Feola, B., Avery, S.N., Winder, D.G., Woodward, N.D., Heckers, S., Blackford, J.U., 2020. BNST-insula structural connectivity in humans. Neuroimage 210.

Flook, E.A., Feola, B., Benningfield, M.M., Silveri, M.M., Winder, D.G., Blackford, J.U., 2021. Alterations in connectivity of the bed nucleus of the stria terminalis during early abstinence in individuals with alcohol use disorder. Alcohol Clin. Exp. Res. 45, 1028–1038.

Forray, M.I., Gysling, K., 2004. Role of noradrenergic projections to the bed nucleus of the stria terminalis in the regulation of the hypothalamic–pituitary–adrenal axis. Brain Res. Rev. 47 (1-3), 145–160. https://doi.org/10.1016/j.brainresrev.2004.07.011 15572169.

Forray, M.I., Gysling, K., Andrés, M.E., Bustos, G., Araneda, S., 2000. Medullary noradrenergic neurons projecting to the bed nucleus of the stria terminalis express mRNA for the NMDA-NR1 receptor. Brain Res. Bull. 52, 163–169.

Fox, H.C., Milivojevic, V., Angarita, G.A., Stowe, R., Sinha, R., 2017. Peripheral immune system suppression in early abstinent alcohol-dependent individuals: links to stress and cue-related craving. J. Psychopharmacol. 31, 883–892.

Francesconi, W., Berton, F., Repunte-Canonigo, V., Hagihara, K., Thurbon, D., Lekic, D., Specio, S.E., Greenwell, T.N., Chen, S.A., Rice, K.C., et al., 2009. Protracted withdrawal from alcohol and drugs of abuse impairs long-term potentiation of intrinsic excitability in the juxtacapsular bed nucleus of the stria terminalis. J. Neurosci. 29, 5389–5401.

Francesconi, W., Szücs, A., Berton, F., Koob, G.F., Vendruscolo, L.F., Sanna, P.P., 2017. Opiate dependence induces cell type-specific plasticity of intrinsic membrane properties in the rat juxtacapsular bed nucleus of stria terminalis (jcBNST). Psychopharmacology 234, 3485–3498.

Freedman, L.J., Cassell, M.D., 1994. Distribution of dopaminergic fibers in the central division of the extended amygdala of the rat. Brain Res. 633, 243–252.

Funk, D., Li, Z., Lê, A.D., 2006. Effects of environmental and pharmacological stressors on c-fos and corticotropin-releasing factor mRNA in rat brain: relationship to the reinstatement of alcohol seeking. Neuroscience 138, 235–243.

García-Carmona, J.-A., Milanés, M.-V., Laorden, M.-L., 2013. Brain stress system response after morphine-conditioned place preference. Int. J. Neuropsychopharmacol. 16, 1999–2011.

García-Carmona, J.A., Georgiou, P., Zanos, P., Bailey, A., Laorden, M.L., 2018. Methamphetamine withdrawal induces activation of CRF neurons in the brain stress system in parallel with an increased activity of cardiac sympathetic pathways. N. Schmied. Arch. Pharmacol. 391, 423–434.

Gauss, R., Seifert, R., 2000. Pacemaker oscillations in heart and brain: a key role for hyperpolarization-activated cation channels. Chronobiol. Int. 17, 453–469.

Geisler, S., Zahm, D.S., 2005. Afferents of the ventral tegmental area in the rat-anatomical substratum for integrative functions. J. Comp. Neurol. 490, 270–294.

Georges, F., Aston-Jones, G., 2002. Activation of ventral tegmental area cells by the bed nucleus of the stria terminalis: a novel excitatory amino acid input to midbrain dopamine neurons. J. Neurosci. 22, 5173–5187.

Giardino, W.J., Eban-Rothschild, A., Christoffel, D.J., Li, S.-B., Malenka, R.C., de Lecea, L., 2018. Parallel circuits from the bed nuclei of stria terminalis to the lateral hypothalamus drive opposing emotional states. Nat. Neurosci. 21, 1084–1095.

Glangetas, C., Fois, G.R.R., Jalabert, M., Lecca, S., Valentinova, K., Meye, F.J.J., Diana, M., Faure, P., Mameli, M., Caille, S., et al., 2015. Ventral subiculum stimulation promotes persistent hyperactivity of dopamine neurons and facilitates behavioral effects of cocaine. Cell Rep. 13, 2287–2296.

Glangetas, C., Girard, D., Groc, L., Marsicano, G., Chaouloff, F., Georges, F., 2013. Stress switches cannabinoid type-1 (CB1) receptor-dependent plasticity from LTD to LTP in the bed nucleus of the stria terminalis. J. Neurosci. 33, 19657–19663.

Gomes, F.V., Alves, F.H.F., Guimarães, F.S., Correa, F.M.A., Resstel, L.B.M., Crestani, C.C., 2013. Cannabidiol administration into the bed nucleus of the stria terminalis alters cardiovascular responses induced by acute restraint stress through 5-HT1A receptor. Eur. Neuropsychopharmacol. 23, 1096–1104.

Gomes, F.V., Reis, D.G., Alves, F.H.F., Corrêa, F.M.A., Guimarães, F.S., Resstel, L.B.M., 2012. Cannabidiol injected into the bed nucleus of the stria terminalis reduces the expression of contextual fear conditioning via 5-HT $_{1A}$ receptors. J. Psychopharmacol. 26, 104–113.

Gomes, F.V., Resstel, L.B.M., Guimarães, F.S., 2011. The anxiolytic-like effects of cannabidiol injected into the bed nucleus of the stria terminalis are mediated by 5-HT1A receptors. Psychopharmacology 213, 465–473.

Gomes-de-Souza, L., Bianchi, P.C., Costa-Ferreira, W., Tomeo, R.A., Cruz, F.C., Crestani, C.C., 2021. CB1 and CB2 receptors in the bed nucleus of the stria terminalis differently modulate anxiety-like behaviors in rats. Prog. Neuro Psychopharmacol. Biol. Psychiatr. 110, 110284.

Goodson, J.L., Kabelik, D., 2009. Dynamic Limbic Networks and Social Diversity in Vertebrates: From Neural Context to Neuromodulatory Patterning. Academic Press, pp. 429–441.

Gosnell, H.B., Silberman, Y., Grueter, B.A., Duvoisin, R.M., Raber, J., Winder, D.G., 2011. mGluR8 modulates excitatory transmission in the bed nucleus of the stria terminalis in a stress-dependent manner. Neuropsychopharmacology 36, 1599–1607.

Grant, B.F., Saha, T.D., Ruan, W.J., Goldstein, R.B., Chou, S.P., Jung, J., Zhang, H., Smith, S.M., Pickering, R.P., Huang, B., et al., 2016. Epidemiology of DSM-5 drug use disorder: results from the national epidemiologic survey on alcohol and related conditions-III. JAMA Psychiatr. 73, 39–47.

Gray, T.S., Magnuson, D.J., 1987. Neuropeptide neuronal efferents from the bed nucleus of the stria terminalis and central amygdaloid nucleus to the dorsal vagal complex in the rat. J. Comp. Neurol. 262, 365–374.

Gray, T.S., Magnuson, D.J., 1992. Peptide immunoreactive neurons in the amygdala and the bed nucleus of the stria terminalis project to the midbrain central gray in the rat. Peptides 13, 451–460.

Grueter, B.A., Gosnell, H.B., Olsen, C.M., Schramm-Sapyta, N.L., Nekrasova, T., Landreth, G.E., Winder, D.G., 2006. Extracellular-signal regulated kinase 1-dependent metabotropic glutamate receptor 5-induced long-term depression in the bed nucleus of the stria terminalis is disrupted by cocaine administration. J. Neurosci. 26, 3210–3219.

Grueter, B.A., McElligott, Z.A., Robison, A.J., Mathews, G.C., Winder, D.G., 2008. In vivo metabotropic glutamate receptor 5 (mGluR5) antagonism prevents cocaine-induced disruption of postsynaptically maintained mGluR5-dependent long-term depression. J. Neurosci. 28, 9261–9270.

Grueter, B.A., Winder, D.G., 2005. Group II and III metabotropic glutamate receptors suppress excitatory synaptic transmission in the dorsolateral bed nucleus of the stria terminalis. Neuropsychopharmacology 30, 1302–1311.

Gungor, N.Z., Yamamoto, R., Paré, D., Pare, D., Paré, D., 2015. Optogenetic study of the projections from the bed nucleus of the stria terminalis to the central amygdala. J. Neurophysiol. 114, 2903–2911.

Guo, J.D., Hammack, S.E., Hazra, R., Levita, L., Rainnie, D.G., 2009. Bi-directional modulation of bed nucleus of stria terminalis neurons by 5-HT: molecular expression and functional properties of excitatory 5-HT receptor subtypes. Neuroscience 164, 1776–1793.

Guo, J.D., Rainnie, D.G., 2010. Presynaptic 5-HT(1B) receptor-mediated serotonergic inhibition of glutamate transmission in the bed nucleus of the stria terminalis. Neuroscience 165, 1390–1401.

Gyawali, U., Martin, D.A., Sulima, A., Rice, K.C., Calu, D.J., 2020. Role of BNST CRFR1 receptors in incubation of fentanyl seeking. Front. Behav. Neurosci. 14, 153.

Hammack, S.E., Mania, I., Rainnie, D.G., 2007. Differential expression of intrinsic membrane currents in defined cell types of the anterolateral bed nucleus of the stria terminalis. J. Neurophysiol. 98, 638–656.

Hammack, S.E., Richey, K.J., Schmid, M.J., LoPresti, M.L., Watkins, L.R., Maier, S.F., 2002. The role of corticotropin-releasing hormone in the dorsal raphe nucleus in mediating the behavioral consequences of uncontrollable stress. J. Neurosci. 22, 1020–1026.

Harris, G.C., Aston-Jones, G., 2003. Enhanced morphine preference following prolonged abstinence: association with increased Fos expression in the extended amygdala. Neuropsychopharmacology 28, 292–299.

Harris, G.C., Aston-Jones, G., 2007. Activation in extended amygdala corresponds to altered hedonic processing during protracted morphine withdrawal. Behav. Brain Res. 176, 251–258.

Harris, N.A., Isaac, A.T., Günther, A., Merkel, K., Melchior, J., Xu, M., Eguakun, E., Perez, R., Nabit, B.P., Flavin, S., et al., 2018. Dorsal BNST alpha2A-adrenergic receptors produce HCN-dependent excitatory actions that initiate anxiogenic behaviors. J. Neurosci. 38, 8922–8942.

Harris, N.A., Winder, D.G., 2018. Synaptic plasticity in the bed nucleus of the stria terminalis: underlying mechanisms and potential ramifications for reinstatement of drug- and alcohol-seeking behaviors. ACS Chem. Neurosci. 9, 2173–2187.

Haubensak, W., Kunwar, P.S., Cai, H., Ciocchi, S., Wall, N.R., Ponnusamy, R., Biag, J., Dong, H.-W.W., Deisseroth, K., Callaway, E.M., et al., 2010. Genetic dissection of an amygdala microcircuit that gates conditioned fear. Nature 468, 270–276.

Hawley, D.F., Bardi, M., Everette, A.M., Higgins, T.J., Tu, K.M., Kinsley, C.H., Lambert, K.G., 2010. Neurobiological constituents of active, passive, and variable coping strategies in rats: integration of regional brain neuropeptide Y levels and cardiovascular responses. Stress 13, 172–183.

Heilig, M., Koob, G.F., Ekman, R., Britton, K.T., 1994. Corticotropin-releasing factor and neuropeptide Y: role in emotional integration. Trends Neurosci. 17, 80–85.

Herman, J.P., Larson, B.R., 2001. Differential regulation of forebrain glutamic acid decarboxylase mRNA expression by aging and stress. Brain Res. 912, 60–66.

Hessel, M., Pape, H.C., Seidenbecher, T., 2020. Stimulation of 5-HT receptors in anterodorsal BNST guides fear to predictable and unpredictable threat. Eur. Neuropsychopharmacol. 39, 56–69.

Holleran, K.M., Wilson, H.H., Fetterly, T.L., Bluett, R.J., Centanni, S.W., Gilfarb, R.A., Rocco, L.E.R., Patel, S., Winder, D.G., 2016. Ketamine and MAG lipase inhibitor-dependent reversal of evolving depressive-like behavior during forced abstinence from alcohol drinking. Neuropsychopharmacology Off. Publ. Am. Coll. Neuropsychopharmacol. 41, 2062–2071.

Holleran, K.M., Winder, D.G., 2016. Preclinical voluntary drinking models for alcohol abstinence-induced affective disturbances in mice. Gene Brain Behav. 16, 8–14.

Howlett, A.C., 2002. The cannabinoid receptors. Prostag. Other Lipid Mediat. 68–69, 619–631.

Huggins, J.P., Smart, T.S., Langman, S., Taylor, L., Young, T., 2012. An efficient randomised, placebo-controlled clinical trial with the irreversible fatty acid amide hydrolase-1 inhibitor PF-04457845, which modulates endocannabinoids but fails to induce effective analgesia in patients with pain due to osteoarthritis of the knee. Pain 153, 1837–1846.

Hurley, K.M., Herbert, H., Moga, M.M., Saper, C.B., 1991. Efferent projections of the infralimbic cortex of the rat. J. Comp. Neurol. 308, 249–276.

Hwa, L.S., Neira, S., Flanigan, M.E., Stanhope, C.M., Pina, M.M., Pati, D., Hon, O.J., Yu, W., Kokush, E., Calloway, R., et al., 2020. Alcohol drinking alters stress response to predator odor via BNST kappa opioid receptor signaling in male mice. Elife 9, 1–53.

Hyytiä, P., Koob, G.F., 1995. GABAA receptor antagonism in the extended amygdala decreases ethanol self-administration in rats. Eur. J. Pharmacol. 283, 151–159.

Ide, S., Hara, T., Ohno, A., Tamano, R., Koseki, K., Naka, T., Maruyama, C., Kaneda, K., Yoshioka, M., Minami, M., 2013. Opposing roles of corticotropin-releasing factor and neuropeptide Y within the dorsolateral bed nucleus of the stria terminalis in the negative affective component of pain in rats. J. Neurosci. 33, 5881–5894.

Islam, L., Franzini, A., Messina, G., Scarone, S., Gambini, O., 2015. Deep brain stimulation of the nucleus accumbens and bed nucleus of stria terminalis for obsessive-compulsive disorder: a case series. World Neurosurg. 83, 657–663.

Jacobskind, J.S., Rosinger, Z.J., Brooks, M.L., Zuloaga, D.G., 2019. Stress-induced neural activation is altered during early withdrawal from chronic methamphetamine. Behav. Brain Res. 366, 67–76.

Jacobskind, J.S., Rosinger, Z.J., Gonzalez, T., Zuloaga, K.L., Zuloaga, D.G., 2018. Chronic methamphetamine exposure attenuates neural activation in hypothalamic–pituitary–adrenal axis-associated brain regions in a sex-specific manner. Neuroscience 380, 132–145.

Jadzic, D., Bassareo, V., Carta, A.R., Carboni, E., 2021. Nicotine, cocaine, amphetamine, morphine, and ethanol increase norepinephrine output in the bed nucleus of stria terminalis of freely moving rats. Addiction Biol. 26, e12864.

Jalabert, M., Aston-Jones, G., Herzog, E., Manzoni, O., Georges, F., 2009. Role of the bed nucleus of the stria terminalis in the control of ventral tegmental area dopamine neurons. Prog. Neuro Psychopharmacol. Biol. Psychiatr. 33, 1336–1346.

Jaramillo, A.A., Williford, K.M., Marshall, C., Winder, D.G., Centanni, S.W., 2020. BNST transient activity associates with approach behavior in a stressful environment and is modulated by the parabrachial nucleus. Neurobiol. Stress 13, 100247.

Jarrett, T.M., McMurray, M.S., Walker, C.H., Johns, J.M., 2006. Cocaine treatment alters oxytocin receptor binding but not mRNA production in postpartum rat dams. Neuropeptides 40, 161–167.

Jasnow, A.M., Davis, M., Huhman, K.L., 2004. Involvement of central amygdalar and bed nucleus of the stria terminalis corticotropin-releasing factor in behavioral responses to social defeat. Behav. Neurosci. 118, 1052–1061.

Jennings, J.H., Rizzi, G., Stamatakis, A.M., Ung, R.L., Stuber, G.D., 2013a. The inhibitory circuit architecture of the lateral hypothalamus orchestrates feeding. Science 341, 1517–1521.

Jennings, J.H., Sparta, D.R., Stamatakis, A.M., Ung, R.L., Pleil, K.E., Kash, T.L., Stuber, G.D., 2013b. Distinct extended amygdala circuits for divergent motivational states. Nature 496, 224–228.

Ju, G., Swanson, L.W., 1989. Studies on the cellular architecture of the bed nuclei of the stria terminalis in the rat: I. cytoarchitecture. J. Comp. Neurol. 280, 587–602.

Ju, G., Swanson, L.W., Simerly, R.B., 1989. Studies on the cellular architecture of the bed nuclei of the stria terminalis in the rat: II. Chemoarchitecture. J. Comparative Neurol. 280, 603–621.

Kash, T.L., Baucum 2nd, A.J., Conrad, K.L., Colbran, R.J., Winder, D.G., 2009. Alcohol exposure alters NMDAR function in the bed nucleus of the stria terminalis. Neuropsychopharmacology 34, 2420–2429.

Kash, T.L., Matthews, R.T., Winder, D.G., 2008a. Alcohol inhibits NR2B-containing NMDA receptors in the ventral bed nucleus of the stria terminalis. Neuropsychopharmacology 33, 1379–1390.

Kash, T.L., Nobis, W.P., Matthews, R.T., Winder, D.G., 2008b. Dopamine enhances fast excitatory synaptic transmission in the extended amygdala by a CRF-R1-dependent process. J. Neurosci. 28, 13856–13865.

Kash, T.L., Nobis, W.P., Matthews, R.T., Winder, D.G., 2008c. The extended amygdala by a CRF-R1-dependent process, 28, 13856–13865.

Kash, T.L., Pleil, K.E., Marcinkiewcz, C.A., Lowery-Gionta, E.G., Crowley, N., Mazzone, C., Sugam, J., Hardaway, J.A., McElligott, Z.A., 2015. Neuropeptide regulation of signaling and behavior in the BNST. Mol. Cell. 38, 1–13.

Kash, T.L., Winder, D.G., 2006. Neuropeptide Y and corticotropin-releasing factor bi-directionally modulate inhibitory synaptic transmission in the bed nucleus of the stria terminalis. Neuropharmacology 51, 1013–1022.

Kerbrat, A., Ferre, J.C., Fillatre, P., Ronziere, T., Vannier, S., Carsin-Nicol, B., Lavoue, S., Verin, M., Gauvrit, J.Y., Le Tulzo, Y., et al., 2016. Acute neurologic disorder from an inhibitor of fatty acid amide hydrolase. N. Engl. J. Med. 375, 1717–1725.

Khoshbouei, H., Cecchi, M., Morilak, D.A., 2002. Modulatory effects of galanin in the lateral bed nucleus of the stria terminalis on behavioral and neuroendocrine responses to acute stress. Neuropsychopharmacology 27, 25–34.

Kilts, C.D., Anderson, C.M., 1986. The simultaneous quantification of dopamine, norepinephrine and epinephrine in micropunched rat brain nuclei by on-line trace enrichment HPLC with electrochemical detection: distribution of catecholamines in the limbic system. Neurochem. Int. 9, 437–445.

Kim, B., Yoon, S., Nakajima, R., Lee, H.J., Lim, H.J., Lee, Y.-K., Choi, J.-S., Yoon, B.-J., Augustine, G.J., Baik, J.-H., 2018. Dopamine D2 receptor-mediated circuit from the central amygdala to the bed nucleus of the stria terminalis regulates impulsive behavior. Proc. Natl. Acad. Sci. U S A 115, E10730–E10739.

Kim, S.Y., Adhikari, A., Lee, S.Y., Marshel, J.H., Kim, C.K., Mallory, C.S., Lo, M., Pak, S., Mattis, J., Lim, B.K., et al., 2013. Diverging neural pathways assemble a behavioural state from separable features in anxiety. Nature 496, 219–223.

Kim, Y., Venkataraju, K.U., Pradhan, K., Mende, C., Taranda, J., Turaga, S.C., Arganda-Carreras, I., Ng, L., Hawrylycz, M.J., Rockland, K.S., et al., 2015. Mapping social behavior-induced brain activation at cellular resolution in the mouse. Cell Rep. 10, 292–305.

Klampfl, S.M., Bosch, O.J., 2019. When mothers neglect their offspring: an activated CRF system in the BNST is detrimental for maternal behavior. Arch. Wom. Ment. Health 22, 409–415.

Klampfl, S.M., Brunton, P.J., Bayerl, D.S., Bosch, O.J., 2016. CRF-R1 activation in the anterior-dorsal BNST induces maternal neglect in lactating rats via an HPA axis-independent central mechanism. Psychoneuroendocrinology 64, 89–98.

Klein, A.K., Brito, M.A., Akhavan, S., Flanagan, D.R., Le, N., Ohana, T., Patil, A.S., Purvis, E.M., Provenzano, C., Wei, A., et al., 2017. Attenuation of the anxiogenic effects of cocaine by 5-HT1B autoreceptor stimulation in the bed nucleus of the stria terminalis of rats. Psychopharmacology 234, 485–495.

Koob, G.F., Le Moal, M., 2008. Addiction and the brain antireward system. Annu. Rev. Psychol. 59, 29–53.

Koob, G.F., Schulkin, J., 2018. Addiction and stress: an allostatic view. Neurosci. Biobehav. Rev. 106, 245–262.

Koob, G.F., Volkow, N.D., 2010. Neurocircuitry of addiction. Neuropsychopharmacology 35, 217–238.

Kotagale, N.R., Walke, S., Shelkar, G.P., Kokare, D.M., Umekar, M.J., Taksande, B.G., 2014. Agmatine attenuates nicotine induced conditioned place preference in mice through modulation of neuropeptide Y system. Behav. Brain Res. 262, 118–124.

Krawczyk, M., deBacker, J., Mason, X., Jones, A.A., Dumont, E.C., 2014. Dopamine decreases NMDA currents in the oval bed nucleus of the stria terminalis of cocaine self-administering rats. Prog. Neuro-Psychopharmacol. Biol. Psychiatry 51, 83–88.

Krawczyk, M., Georges, F., Sharma, R., Mason, X., Berthet, A., Bézard, E., Dumont, É.C., 2011a. Double-dissociation of the catecholaminergic modulation of synaptic transmission in the oval bed nucleus of the stria terminalis. J. Neurophysiol. 105, 145–153.

Krawczyk, M., Sharma, R., Mason, X., de Backer, J., Jones, A.A., Dumont, É.C., 2011b. A switch in the neuromodulatory effects of dopamine in the oval bed nucleus of the stria terminalis associated with cocaine self-administration in rats. J. Neurosci. 31, 8928–8935.

Kreitzer, A.C., 2009. Physiology and pharmacology of striatal neurons. Annu. Rev. Neurosci. 32, 127–147.

Kreitzer, A.C., Regehr, W.G., 2001. Retrograde inhibition of presynaptic calcium influx by endogenous cannabinoids at excitatory synapses onto Purkinje cells. Neuron 29, 717–727.

Krettek, J.E., Price, J.L., 1978. Amygdaloid projections to subcortical structures within the basal forebrain and brainstem in the rat and cat. J. Comp. Neurol. 178, 225–253.

Krüger, O., Shiozawa, T., Kreifelts, B., Scheffler, K., Ethofer, T., 2015. Three distinct fiber pathways of the bed nucleus of the stria terminalis to the amygdala and prefrontal cortex. Cortex J. Devoted study Nervous System Behav. 66, 60–68.

Kudo, T., Uchigashima, M., Miyazaki, T., Konno, K., Yamasaki, M., Yanagawa, Y., Minami, M., Watanabe, M., 2012. Three types of neurochemical projection from the bed nucleus of the stria terminalis to the ventral tegmental area in adult mice. J. Neurosci. 32, 18035–18046.

Laflamme, N., Nappi, R.E., Drolet, G., Labrie, C., Rivest, S., 1998. Expression and neuropeptidergic characterization of estrogen receptors (ERα and ERβ) throughout the rat brain: anatomical evidence of distinct roles of each subtype. J. Neurobiol. 36, 357–378.

Land, B.B., Bruchas, M.R., Lemos, J.C., Xu, M., Melief, E.J., Chavkin, C., 2008. The dysphoric component of stress is encoded by activation of the dynorphin κ-opioid system. J. Neurosci. 28, 407.

Lange, M.D., Daldrup, T., Remmers, F., Szkudlarek, H.J., Lesting, J., Guggenhuber, S., Ruehle, S., Jüngling, K., Seidenbecher, T., Lutz, B., et al., 2017. Cannabinoid CB1 receptors in distinct circuits of the extended amygdala determine fear responsiveness to unpredictable threat. Mol. Psychiatr. 22, 1422–1430.

Le, A.D., Funk, D., Coen, K., Tamadon, S., Shaham, Y., 2018. Role of kappa-opioid receptors in the bed nucleus of stria terminalis in reinstatement of alcohol seeking. Neuropsychopharmacology 43, 838–850.

Leão, R.M., Cruz, F.C., Vendruscolo, L.F., de Guglielmo, G., Logrip, M.L., Planeta, C.S., Hope, B.T., Koob, G.F., George, O., 2015. Chronic nicotine activates stress/reward-related brain regions and facilitates the transition to compulsive alcohol drinking. J. Neurosci. 35, 6241–6253.

Lebow, M., Neufeld-Cohen, A., Kuperman, Y., Tsoory, M., Gil, S., Chen, A., 2012. Susceptibility to PTSD-like behavior is mediated by corticotropin-releasing factor receptor type 2 levels in the bed nucleus of the stria terminalis. J. Neurosci. 32, 6906–6916.

Lebow, M.A., Chen, A., 2016. Overshadowed by the amygdala: the bed nucleus of the stria terminalis emerges as key to psychiatric disorders. Mol. Psychiatr. 21, 450–463.

Lee, Y., Fitz, S., Johnson, P.L., Shekhar, A., 2008. Repeated stimulation of CRF receptors in the BNST of rats selectively induces social but not panic-like anxiety. Neuropsychopharmacology 33, 2586–2594.

Leriche, M., Méndez, M., Zimmer, L., Bérod, A., 2008. Acute ethanol induces Fos in GABAergic and non-GABAergic forebrain neurons: a double-labeling study in the medial prefrontal cortex and extended amygdala. Neuroscience 153, 259–267.

Lesur, A., Gaspar, P., Alvarez, C., Berger, B., 1989. Chemoanatomic compartments in the human bed nucleus of the stria terminalis. Neuroscience 32, 181–194.

Levine, S., 2005. Developmental determinants of sensitivity and resistance to stress. Psychoneuroendocrinology 30, 939–946.

Levita, L., Hammack, S.E., Mania, I., Li, X.Y., Davis, M., Rainnie, D.G., 2004. 5-hydroxytryptamine1A-like receptor activation in the bed nucleus of the stria terminalis: electrophysiological and behavioral studies. Neuroscience 128, 583–596.

Li, C., Pleil, K.E., Stamatakis, A.M., Busan, S., Vong, L., Lowell, B.B., Stuber, G.D., Kash, T.L., 2012. Presynaptic inhibition of gamma-aminobutyric acid release in the bed nucleus of the stria terminalis by kappa opioid receptor signaling. Biol. Psychiatr. 71, 725–732.

Liang, K.C., Chen, H.C., Chen, D.Y., 2001. Posttraining infusion of norepinephrine and corticotropin releasing factor into the bed nucleus of the stria terminalis enhanced retention in an inhibitory avoidance task. Chin. J. Physiol. 44, 33–43.

Lowry, C.A., Hale, M.W., Evans, A.K., Heerkens, J., Staub, D.R., Gasser, P.J., Shekhar, A., 2008. Serotonergic systems, anxiety, and affective disorder. Ann. N. Y. Acad. Sci. 1148, 86–94.

Lu, J., Cheng, Y., Xie, X., Woodson, K., Bonifacio, J., Disney, E., Barbee, B., Wang, X., Zaidi, M., Wang, J., 2021. Whole-brain mapping of direct inputs to dopamine D1 and D2 receptor-expressing medium spiny neurons in the posterior dorsomedial striatum. eNeuro 8, 1–15.

Luchsinger, J.R., Fetterly, T.L., Williford, K.M., Salimando, G.J., Doyle, M.A., Maldonado, J., Simerly, R.B., Winder, D.G., Centanni, S.W., 2021. Delineation of an insula-BNST circuit engaged by struggling behavior that regulates avoidance in mice. Nat. Commun. 12, 3561.

Macey, D.J., Rice, W.N., Freedland, C.S., Whitlow, C.T., Porrino, L.J., 2004. Patterns of functional activity associated with cocaine self-administration in the rat change over time. Psychopharmacology 172, 384–392.

Mahler, S.V., Aston-Jones, G.S., 2012. Fos activation of selective afferents to ventral tegmental area during cue-induced reinstatement of cocaine seeking in rats. J. Neurosci. 32, 13309–13325.

Mahler, S.V., Smith, R.J., Moorman, D.E., Sartor, G.C., Aston-Jones, G., 2012. Multiple roles for orexin/hypocretin in addiction. Prog. Brain Res. 198, 79–121.

Mantsch, J.R., Baker, D.A., Funk, D., Lê, A.D., Shaham, Y., 2016. Stress-induced reinstatement of drug seeking: 20 years of progress. Neuropsychopharmacology 41, 335–356.

Marcinkiewcz, C.A., Bierlein-De La Rosa, G., Dorrier, C.E., McKnight, M., Diberto, J.F., Pati, D., Gianessi, C.A., Hon, O.J., Tipton, G., McElligott, Z.A., et al., 2019. Sex-dependent modulation of anxiety and fear by 5-HT1A receptors in the bed nucleus of the stria terminalis. ACS Chem. Neurosci. 10, 3154–3166.

Marcinkiewcz, C.A., Dorrier, C.E., Lopez, A.J., Kash, T.L., 2015. Ethanol induced adaptations in 5-HT2c receptor signaling in the bed nucleus of the stria terminalis: implications for anxiety during ethanol withdrawal. Neuropharmacology 89, 157–167.

Marcinkiewcz, C.A., Mazzone, C.M., D'Agostino, G., Halladay, L.R., Hardaway, J.A., DiBerto, J.F., Navarro, M., Burnham, N., Cristiano, C., Dorrier, C.E., et al., 2016. Serotonin engages an anxiety and fear-promoting circuit in the extended amygdala. Nature 537, 97–101.

Markram, H., Toledo-Rodriguez, M., Wang, Y., Gupta, A., Silberberg, G., Wu, C., 2004. Interneurons of the neocortical inhibitory system. Nat. Rev. Neurosci. 5, 793–807.

Martinon, D., Dabrowska, J., 2018. Corticotropin-releasing factor receptors modulate oxytocin release in the dorsolateral bed nucleus of the stria terminalis (BNST) in male rats. Front. Neurosci. 12, 183-183.

Martinon, D., Lis, P., Roman, A.N., Tornesi, P., Applebey, S.V., Buechner, G., Olivera, V., Dabrowska, J., 2019. Oxytocin receptors in the dorsolateral bed nucleus of the stria terminalis (BNST) bias fear learning toward temporally predictable cued fear. Transl. Psychiatry 9, 140.

Massi, L., Elezgarai, I., Puente, N., Reguero, L., Grandes, P., Manzoni, O.J., Georges, F., 2008. Cannabinoid receptors in the bed nucleus of the stria terminalis control cortical excitation of midbrain dopamine cells in vivo. J. Neurosci. 28, 10496–10508.

Matta, S.G., Valentine, J.D., Sharp, B.M., 1997. Nicotinic activation of CRH neurons in extrahypothalamic regions of the rat brain. Endocrine 7, 245–253.

Mazzone, C.M., Pati, D., Michaelides, M., DiBerto, J., Fox, J.H., Tipton, G., Anderson, C., Duffy, K., McKlveen, J.M., Hardaway, J.A., et al., 2018. Acute engagement of Gq-mediated signaling in the bed nucleus of the stria terminalis induces anxiety-like behavior. Mol. Psychiatr. 23, 143–153.

McDonald, A.J., 1998. Cortical pathways to the mammalian amygdala. Prog. Neurobiol. 55, 257–332.

McElligott, Z.A., Klug, J.R., Nobis, W.P., Patel, S., Grueter, B.A., Kash, T.L., 2010. Distinct Forms of G Q -receptor-dependent Plasticity of Excitatory Transmission in the BNST Are Differentially Affected by Stress. Proc. Natl. Acad. Sci. 107, 2271–2276.

McElligott, Z.A., Winder, D.G., 2008. Alpha1-adrenergic receptor-induced heterosynaptic long-term depression in the bed nucleus of the stria terminalis is disrupted in mouse models of affective disorders. Neuropsychopharmacology 33, 2313–2323.

McFadden, K., Griffin, T.A., Levy, V., Wolfe, J.H., Valentino, R.J., 2012. Overexpression of corticotropin-releasing factor in Barrington's nucleus neurons by adeno-associated viral transduction: effects on bladder function and behavior. Eur. J. Neurosci. 36, 3356–3364.

McFarland, K., Davidge, S.B., Lapish, C.C., Kalivas, P.W., 2004. Limbic and motor circuitry underlying footshock-induced reinstatement of cocaine-seeking behavior. J. Neurosci. 24, 1551–1560.

McReynolds, J.R., Peña, D.F., Blacktop, J.M., Mantsch, J.R., 2014a. Neurobiological mechanisms underlying relapse to cocaine use: contributions of CRF and noradrenergic systems and regulation by glucocorticoids. Stress 17, 22–38.

McReynolds, J.R., Vranjkovic, O., Thao, M., Baker, D.A., Makky, K., Lim, Y., Mantsch, J.R., 2014b. Beta-2 adrenergic receptors mediate stress-evoked reinstatement of cocaine-induced conditioned place preference and increases in CRF mRNA in the bed nucleus of the stria terminalis in mice. Psychopharmacology 231, 3953–3963.

Meddle, S.L., Bishop, V.R., Gkoumassi, E., van Leeuwen, F.W., Douglas, A.J., 2007. Dynamic changes in oxytocin receptor expression and activation at parturition in the rat brain. Endocrinology 148, 5095–5104.

Melchior, J.R., Perez, R.E., Salimando, G.J., Luchsinger, J.R., Basu, A, Winder, D.G., 2021. Cocaine Augments Dopa mine-Mediated Inhibition of Neuronal Activity in the Dorsal Bed Nucleus of the Stria Terminalis. J. Neurosci. 41 (27), 5876–5893. https://doi.org/10.1523/JNEUROSCI.0284-21.2021 34035141.

Meloni, E.G., 2006. Behavioral and anatomical interactions between dopamine and corticotropin-releasing factor in the rat. J. Neurosci. 26, 3855–3863.

Miles, O.W., Maren, S., 2019. Role of the bed nucleus of the stria terminalis in PTSD: insights from preclinical models. Front. Behav. Neurosci. 13, 68-68.

Miles, O.W., Thrailkill, E.A., Linden, A.K., May, V., Bouton, M.E., Hammack, S.E., 2018. Pituitary adenylate cyclase-activating peptide in the bed nucleus of the stria terminalis mediates stress-induced reinstatement of cocaine seeking in rats. Neuropsychopharmacology 43, 978–986.

Moaddab, M., Dabrowska, J., 2017. Oxytocin receptor neurotransmission in the dorsolateral bed nucleus of the stria terminalis facilitates the acquisition of cued fear in the fear-potentiated startle paradigm in rats. Neuropharmacology 121, 130–139.

Moeller, S., Yacoub, E., Olman, C.A., Auerbach, E., Strupp, J., Harel, N., Uğurbil, K., 2010. Multiband multislice GE-EPI at 7 tesla, with 16-fold acceleration using partial parallel imaging with application to high spatial and temporal whole-brain fMRI. Magn. Reson. Med. 63, 1144–1153.

Moffitt, J.R., Bambah-Mukku, D., Eichhorn, S.W., Vaughn, E., Shekhar, K., Perez, J.D., Rubinstein, N.D., Hao, J., Regev, A., Dulac, C., et al., 2018. Molecular, spatial, and functional single-cell profiling of the hypothalamic preoptic region. Science 362, eaau5324.

Moga, M.M., Saper, C.B., Gray, T.S., 1989. Bed nucleus of the stria terminalis: cytoarchitecture, immunohistochemistry, and projection to the parabrachial nucleus in the rat. J. Comp. Neurol. 283, 315–332.

Monteggia, L.M., Eisch, A.J., Tang, M.D., Kaczmarek, L.K., Nestler, E.J., 2000. Cloning and localization of the hyperpolarization-activated cyclic nucleotide-gated channel family in rat brain. Mol. Brain Res. 81, 129–139.

Morilak, D.A., Cecchi, M., Khoshbouei, H., 2003. Interactions of norepinephrine and galanin in the central amygdala and lateral bed nucleus of the stria terminalis modulate the behavioral response to acute stress. Life Sci. 73, 715–726.

Myers, B., Mark Dolgas, C., Kasckow, J., Cullinan, W.E., Herman, J.P., 2014. Central stress-integrative circuits: forebrain glutamatergic and GABAergic projections to the dorsomedial hypothalamus, medial preoptic area, and bed nucleus of the stria terminalis. Brain Struct. Funct. 219, 1287–1303.

Nader, J., Claudia, C., Rawas, R.E., Favot, L., Jaber, M., Thiriet, N., Solinas, M., 2012. Loss of environmental enrichment increases vulnerability to cocaine addiction. Neuropsychopharmacology 37, 1579–1587.

Naik, R.R., de Jong, T.R., 2017. Transient and persistent behavioral and molecular changes in primiparous female Wistar rats. Eur. J. Neurosci. 45, 797–804.

Nakagawa, T., Yamamoto, R., Fujio, M., Suzuki, Y., Minami, M., Satoh, M., Kaneko, S., 2005. Involvement of the bed nucleus of the stria terminalis activated by the central nucleus of the amygdala in the negative affective component of morphine withdrawal in rats. Neuroscience 134, 9–19.

Navarro, M., Cubero, I., Knapp, D.J., Breese, G.R., Thiele, T.E., 2008. Decreased immunoreactivity of the melanocortin neuropeptide alpha-melanocyte-stimulating hormone (alpha-MSH) after chronic ethanol exposure in Sprague-Dawley rats. Alcohol Clin. Exp. Res. 32, 266–276.

Neal, C.R., Swann, J.M., Newman, S.W., 1989. The colocalization of substance P and prodynorphin immunoreactivity in neurons of the medial preoptic area, bed nucleus of the stria terminalis and medial nucleus of the amygdala of the Syrian hamster. Brain Res. 496, 1–13.

Neal Jr., C.R., Mansour, A., Reinscheid, R., Nothacker, H.-P., Civelli, O., Watson Jr., S.J., 1999. Localization of orphanin FQ (nociceptin) peptide and messenger RNA in the central nervous system of the rat. J. Comp. Neurol. 406, 503–547.

Nelson, R.J., Trainor, B.C., 2007. Neural Mechanisms of Aggression. Nature Publishing Group, pp. 536–546.

Nobis, W.P., Kash, T.L., Silberman, Y., Winder, D.G., 2011. β-Adrenergic receptors enhance excitatory transmission in the bed nucleus of the stria terminalis through a corticotrophin-releasing factor receptor–dependent and cocaine-regulated mechanism. Biol. Psychiatr. 69, 1083–1090.

Normandeau, C.P., Torruella Suárez, M.L., Sarret, P., McElligott, Z.A., Dumont, E.C., 2018a. Neurotensin and dynorphin Bi-Directionally modulate CeA inhibition of oval BNST neurons in male mice. Neuropharmacology 143, 113–121.

Normandeau, C.P., Ventura-Silva, A.P., Hawken, E.R., Angelis, S., Sjaarda, C., Liu, X., Pêgo, J.M., Dumont, É.C., 2018b. A key role for neurotensin in chronic-stress-induced anxiety-like behavior in rats. Neuropsychopharmacology 43, 285–293.

O'Daly, O.G., Trick, L., Scaife, J., Marshall, J., Ball, D., Phillips, M.L., Williams, S.S., Stephens, D.N., Duka, T., 2012. Withdrawal-associated increases and decreases in functional neural connectivity associated with altered emotional regulation in alcoholism. Neuropsychopharmacology 37, 2267–2276.

Ohno-Shosaku, T., Maejima, T., Kano, M., 2001. Endogenous cannabinoids mediate retrograde signals from depolarized postsynaptic neurons to presynaptic terminals. Neuron 29, 729–738.

Otero-Garcia, M., Martin-Sanchez, A., Fortes-Marco, L., Martínez-Ricós, J., Agustin-Pavón, C., Lanuza, E., Martínez-García, F., 2014. Extending the socio-sexual brain: arginine-vasopressin immunoreactive circuits in the telencephalon of mice. Brain Struct. Funct. 219, 1055–1081.

Palij, P., Stamford, J.A., 1992. Real-time monitoring of endogenous noradrenaline release in rat brain slices using fast cyclic voltammetry: 1. Characterisation of evoked noradrenaline efflux and uptake from nerve terminals in the bed nucleus of stria terminalis, pars ventralis. Brain Res. 587, 137–146.

Palmiter, R.D., 2018. The parabrachial nucleus: CGRP neurons function as a general alarm. Trends Neurosci. 41, 280–293.

Pape, H.-C., Pare, D., 2010. Plastic synaptic networks of the amygdala for the acquisition, expression, and extinction of conditioned fear. Physiol. Rev. 90, 419–463.

Park, J., Bucher, E.S., Fontillas, K., Owesson-White, C., Ariansen, J.L., Carelli, R.M., Wightman, R.M., 2013. Opposing catecholamine changes in the bed nucleus of the stria terminalis during intracranial self-stimulation and its extinction. Biol. Psychiatr. 74, 69–76.

Park, J., Kile, B.M., Mark Wightman, R., 2009. *In vivo* voltammetric monitoring of norepinephrine release in the rat ventral bed nucleus of the stria terminalis and anteroventral thalamic nucleus. Eur. J. Neurosci. 30, 2121–2133.

Park, J., Wheeler, R.A., Fontillas, K., Keithley, R.B., Carelli, R.M., Wightman, R.M., 2012. Catecholamines in the bed nucleus of the stria terminalis reciprocally respond to reward and aversion. Biol. Psychiatr. 71, 327–334.

Pati, D., Pina, M.M., Kash, T.L., 2019. Ethanol-induced conditioned place preference and aversion differentially alter plasticity in the bed nucleus of stria terminalis. Neuropsychopharmacology 44 (11), 1843–1854. https://doi.org/10.1038/s41386-019-0349-0 30795004.

Pati, D., Marcinkiewcz, C.A., DiBerto, J.F., Cogan, E.S., McElligott, Z.A., Kash, T.L., 2020. Chronic intermittent ethanol exposure dysregulates a GABAergic microcircuit in the bed nucleus of the stria terminalis. Neuropharmacology 168, 107759.

Perez, R.E., Basu, A., Nabit, B.P., Harris, N.A., Folkes, O.M., Patel, S., Gilsbach, R., Hein, L., Winder, D.G., 2020. α2A-adrenergic heteroreceptors are required for stress-induced reinstatement of cocaine conditioned place preference. Neuropsychopharmacology 45, 1473–1481.

Petrulis, A., Johnston, R.E., 1999. Lesions centered on the medial amygdala impair scent-marking and sex- odor recognition but spare discrimination of individual odors in female golden hamsters. Behav. Neurosci. 113, 345–357.

Peyron, C., Tighe, D.K., van den Pol, A.N., de Lecea, L., Heller, H.C., Sutcliffe, J.G., Kilduff, T.S., 1998. Neurons containing hypocretin (orexin) project to multiple neuronal systems. J. Neurosci. 18, 9996–10015.

Phelix, C.F., Liposits, Z., Paull, W.K., 1992. Monoamine innervation of bed nucleus of stria terminalis: an electron microscopic investigation. Brain Res. Bull. 28, 949–965.

Pickens, C.L., Airavaara, M., Theberge, F., Fanous, S., Hope, B.T., Shaham, Y., 2011. Neurobiology of the incubation of drug craving. Trends Neurosci. 34, 411–420.

Pina, M.M., Cunningham, C.L., 2017. Ethanol-seeking behavior is expressed directly through an extended amygdala to midbrain neural circuit. Neurobiol. Learn. Mem. 137, 83–91.

Pina, M.M., Pati, D., Hwa, L.S., Wu, S.Y., Mahoney, A.A., Omenyi, C.G., Navarro, M., Kash, T.L., 2020. The kappa opioid receptor modulates GABA neuron excitability and synaptic transmission in midbrainprojections from the insular cortex. Neuropharmacology 165, 107831.

Pina, M.M., Young, E.A., Ryabinin, A.E., Cunningham, C.L., 2015. The bed nucleus of the stria terminalis regulates ethanol-seeking behavior in mice. Neuropharmacology 99, 627–638.

Piomelli, D., 2003. The molecular logic of endocannabinoid signalling. Nat. Rev. Neurosci. 4, 873–884.

Pleil, K.E., Helms, C.M., Sobus, J.R., Daunais, J.B., Grant, K.A., Kash, T.L., 2016. Effects of chronic alcohol consumption on neuronal function in the non-human primate BNST. Addiction Biol. 21, 1151–1167.

Pleil, K.E., Lopez, A., McCall, N., Jijon, A.M., Bravo, J.P., Kash, T.L., 2012. Chronic stress alters neuropeptide Y signaling in the bed nucleus of the stria terminalis in DBA/2J but not C57BL/6J mice. Neuropharmacology 62, 1777–1786.

Pleil, K.E., Lowery-Gionta, E.G., Crowley, N.A., Li, C., Marcinkiewcz, C.A., Rose, J.H., McCall, N.M., Maldonado-Devincci, A.M., Morrow, A.L., Jones, S.R., et al., 2015a. Effects of chronic ethanol exposure on neuronal function in the prefrontal cortex and extended amygdala. Neuropharmacology 99, 735–749.

Pleil, K.E., Rinker, J.A., Lowery-Gionta, E.G., Mazzone, C.M., McCall, N.M., Kendra, A.M., Olson, D.P., Lowell, B.B., Grant, K.A., Thiele, T.E., et al., 2015b. NPY signaling inhibits extended amygdala CRF neurons to suppress binge alcohol drinking. Nat. Neurosci. 18, 545–552.

Poulin, J.-F., Chevalier, B., Laforest, S., Drolet, G., 2006. Enkephalinergic afferents of the centromedial amygdala in the rat. J. Comp. Neurol. 496, 859–876.

Poulin, J.F., Arbour, D., Laforest, S., Drolet, G., 2009. Neuroanatomical characterization of endogenous opioids in the bed nucleus of the stria terminalis. Prog. Neuro-Psychopharmacol. Biol. Psychiatry 33, 1356–1365.

Puente, N., Elezgarai, I., Lafourcade, M., Reguero, L., Marsicano, G., Georges, F., Manzoni, O.J., Grandes, P., 2010. Localization and function of the cannabinoid CB1 receptor in the anterolateral bed nucleus of the stria terminalis. PLoS One 5, e8869.

Qi, X., Guzhva, L., Yang, Z., Febo, M., Shan, Z., Wang, K.K.W., Bruijnzeel, A.W., Elsevier, B.B.V., 2016. Overexpression of CRF in the BNST diminishes dysphoria but not anxiety-like behavior in nicotine withdrawing rats. Eur. Neuropsychopharmacol. 26, 1378–1389.

Radley, J.J., Gosselink, K.L., Sawchenko, P.E., 2009. A discrete GABAergic relay mediates medial prefrontal cortical inhibition of the neuroendocrine stress response. J. Neurosci. 29, 7330–7340.

Radley, J.J., Johnson, S.B., 2018. Anteroventral Bed Nuclei of the Stria Terminalis Neurocircuitry: Towards an Integration of HPA axis Modulation with Coping Behaviors - Curt Richter Award Paper 2017, pp. 239–249.

Rangani, R.J., Upadhya, M.A., Nakhate, K.T., Kokare, D.M., Subhedar, N.K., 2012. Nicotine evoked improvement in learning and memory is mediated through NPY Y1 receptors in rat model of Alzheimer's disease. Peptides 33, 317–328.

Reichard, R.A., Subramanian, S., Desta, M.T., Sura, T., Becker, M.L., Ghobadi, C.W., Parsley, K.P., Zahm, D.S., 2017. Abundant collateralization of temporal lobe projections to the accumbens, bed nucleus of stria terminalis, central amygdala and lateral septum. Brain Struct. Funct. 222, 1971–1988.

Reisiger, A.R., Kaufling, J., Manzoni, O., Cador, M., Georges, F., Caille, S., 2014. Nicotine self-administration induces CB1-dependent LTP in the bed nucleus of the stria terminalis. J. Neurosci. 34, 4285–4292.

Repina, N.A., Rosenbloom, A., Mukherjee, A., Schaffer, D.V., Kane, R.S., 2017. At light speed: advances in optogenetic systems for regulating cell signaling and behavior. Ann. Rev. Chem. Biomol. Eng. 8, 13–39.

Ricardo, J.A., Tongju Koh, E., 1978. Anatomical evidence of direct projections from the nucleus of the solitary tract to the hypothalamus, amygdala, and other forebrain structures in the rat. Brain Res. 153, 1–26.

Rigney, N., Whylings, J., Mieda, M., de Vries, G.J., Petrulis, A., 2019. Sexually dimorphic vasopressin cells modulate social investigation and communication in sex-specific ways. Eneuro 6. ENEURO.0415-0418.2019.

Rinker, J.A., Marshall, S.A., Mazzone, C.M., Lowery-Gionta, E.G., Gulati, V., Pleil, K.E., Kash, T.L., Navarro, M., Thiele, T.E., 2017. Extended amygdala to ventral tegmental area corticotropin-releasing factor circuit controls binge ethanol intake. Biol. Psychiatr. 81, 930–940.

Robles, C.F., McMackin, M.Z., Campi, K.L., Doig, I.E., Takahashi, E.Y., Pride, M.C., Trainor, B.C., 2014. Effects of kappa opioid receptors on conditioned place aversion and social interaction in males and females. Behav. Brain Res. 262, 84–93.

Roder, S., Ciriello, J., 1993. Contribution of bed nucleus of the stria terminalis to the cardiovascular responses elicited by stimulation of the amygdala. J. Auton. Nerv. Syst. 45, 61–75.

Rodi, D., Zucchini, S., Simonato, M., Cifani, C., Massi, M., Polidori, C., 2008. Functional antagonism between nociceptin/orphanin FQ (N/OFQ) and corticotropin-releasing factor (CRF) in the rat brain: evidence for involvement of the bed nucleus of the stria terminalis. Psychopharmacology 196, 523–531.

Rodriguez-Romaguera, J., Ung, R.L., Nomura, H., Otis, J.M., Basiri, M.L., Namboodiri, V.M.K., Zhu, X., Elliott Robinson, J., McHenry, J.A., Kosyk, O., et al., 2020. Prepronociceptin Expressing Neurons in the Extended Amygdala Encode and Promote Rapid Arousal Responses to Motivationally Salient Stimuli. bioRxiv), p. 2020, 2001.2021.914341-912020.914301.914321.914341.

Rodríguez-Sierra, O.E., Turesson, H.K., Pare, D., 2013. Contrasting distribution of physiological cell types in different regions of the bed nucleus of the stria terminalis. J. Neurophysiol. 110, 2037–2049.

Romero, L.M., Butler, L.K., 2007. Endocrinology of stress. Int. J. Comp. Psychol. 20, 89–95.

Rood, B.D., De Vries, G.J., 2011. Vasopressin innervation of the mouse (Mus musculus) brain and spinal cord. J. Comp. Neurol. 519, 2434–2474.

Rood, B.D., Stott, R.T., You, S., Smith, C.J., Woodbury, M.E., De Vries, G.J., 2013. Site of origin of and sex differences in the vasopressin innervation of the mouse (Mus musculus) brain. J. Comp. Neurol. 521, 2321–2358.

Roth, B.L., 2016. DREADDs for neuroscientists. Neuron 89, 683–694.

Saalfield, J., Spear, L., 2019. Fos activation patterns related to acute ethanol and conditioned taste aversion in adolescent and adult rats. Alcohol 78, 57–68.

Sah, P., Faber, E.S.L., Lopez De Armentia, M., Power, J., 2003. The amygdaloid complex: anatomy and physiology. Physiol. Rev. 83, 803–834.

Sahuque, L.L., Kullberg, E.F., McGeehan, A.J., Kinder, J.R., Hicks, M.P., Blanton, M.G., Janak, P.H., Olive, M.F., 2006. Anxiogenic and aversive effects of corticotropin-releasing factor (CRF) in the bed nucleus of the stria terminalis in the rat: role of CRF receptor subtypes. Psychopharmacology (Berl) 186, 122–132.

Sakanaka, M., Shibasaki, T., Lederis, K., 1986. Distribution and efferent projections of corticotropin-releasing factor-like immunoreactivity in the rat amygdaloid complex. Brain Res. 382, 213–238.

Sakharkar, A.J., Zhang, H., Tang, L., Baxstrom, K., Shi, G., Moonat, S., Pandey, S.C., 2014. Effects of histone deacetylase inhibitors on amygdaloid histone acetylation and neuropeptide Y expression: a role in anxiety-like and alcohol-drinking behaviours. Int. J. Neuropsychopharmacol. 17, 1207–1220.

Salimando, G.J., Hyun, M., Boyt, K.M., Winder, D.G., 2020. BNST GluN2D-containing NMDA receptors influence anxiety- and depressive-like behaviors and ModulateCell-specific excitatory/inhibitory synaptic balance. J. Neurosci. 40, 3949–3968.

Salmaso, N., Rodaros, D., Stewart, J., Erb, S., 2001. A role for the CRF-containing pathway from central nucleus of the amygdala to bed nucleus of the stria terminalis in the stress-induced reinstatement of cocaine seeking in rats. Psychopharmacology 158, 360–365.

Sapolsky, R.M., Meaney, M.J., 1986. Maturation of the Adrenocortical Stress Response: Neuroendocrine Control Mechanisms and the Stress Hyporesponsive Period. Elsevier, pp. 65–76.

Sartor, G.C., Aston-Jones, G., 2012. Regulation of the ventral tegmental area by the bed nucleus of the stria terminalis is required for expression of cocaine preference. Eur. J. Neurosci. 36, 3549–3558.

Schmitt, H.F., Huang, L.Z., Son, J.H., Pinzon-Guzman, C., Slaton, G.S., Winzer-Serhan, U.H., 2008. Acute nicotine activates c-fos and activity-regulated cytoskeletal associated protein mRNA expression in limbic brain areas involved in the central stress-response in rat pups during a period of hypo-responsiveness to stress. Neuroscience 157, 349–359.

Schreiber, A.L., McGinn, M.A., Edwards, S., Gilpin, N.W., 2019. Predator odor stress blunts alcohol conditioned aversion. Neuropharmacology 144, 82–90.

Schroeder, L.E., Furdock, R., Quiles, C.R., Kurt, G., Perez-Bonilla, P., Garcia, A., Colon-Ortiz, C., Brown, J., Bugescu, R., Leinninger, G.M., 2019. Mapping the populations of neurotensin neurons in the male mouse brain. Neuropeptides 76, 101930.

Schwarz, L.A., Miyamichi, K., Gao, X.J., Beier, K.T., Weissbourd, B., DeLoach, K.E., Ren, J., Ibanes, S., Malenka, R.C., Kremer, E.J., et al., 2015. Viral-genetic tracing of the input-output organization of a central noradrenaline circuit. Nature 524, 88–92.

Seung, H.S., Sümbül, U., 2014. Neuronal cell types and connectivity: lessons from the retina. Neuron 83, 1262–1272.

Shaham, Y., Highfield, D., Delfs, J., Leung, S., Stewart, J., 2000. Clonidine blocks stress-induced reinstatement of heroin seeking in rats: an effect independent of locus coeruleus noradrenergic neurons. Eur. J. Neurosci. 12, 292–302.

Shalev, U., Morales, M., Hope, B., Yap, J., Shaham, Y., 2001. Time-dependent changes in extinction behavior and stress-induced reinstatement of drug seeking following withdrawal from heroin in rats. Psychopharmacology (Berl) 156, 98–107.

Sharko, A.C., Kaigler, K.F., Fadel, J.R., Wilson, M.A., 2016. Ethanol-induced anxiolysis and neuronal activation in the amygdala and bed nucleus of the stria terminalis. Alcohol 50, 19–25.

Shields, A.D., Wang, Q., Winder, D.G., 2009. α2A-adrenergic receptors heterosynaptically regulate glutamatergic transmission in the bed nucleus of the stria terminalis. Neuroscience 163, 339–351.

Shimada, S., Inagaki, S., Kubota, Y., Ogawa, N., Shibasaki, T., Takagi, H., 1989. Coexistence of peptides (corticotropin releasing factor/neurotensin and substance P/somatostatin) in the bed nucleus of the stria terminalis and central amygdaloid nucleus of the rat. Neuroscience 30, 377–383.

Shram, M.J., Funk, D., Li, Z., Lê, A.D., 2007. Acute nicotine enhances c-fos mRNA expression differentially in reward-related substrates of adolescent and adult rat brain. Neurosci. Lett. 418, 286–291.

Silberman, Y., Matthews, R.T., Winder, D.G., 2013. A corticotropin releasing factor pathway for ethanol regulation of the ventral tegmental area in the bed nucleus of the stria terminalis. J. Neurosci. 33, 950–960.

Singh, M.E., McGregor, I.S., Mallet, P.E., 2005. Repeated exposure to Δ9-tetrahydrocannabinol alters heroin-induced locomotor sensitisation and Fos-immunoreactivity. Neuropharmacology 49, 1189–1200.

Singh, M.E., McGregor, I.S., Mallet, P.E., 2006. Perinatal exposure to Δ9-tetrahydrocannabinol alters heroin-induced place conditioning and fos-immunoreactivity. Neuropsychopharmacology 31, 58–69.

Smith, K.C., Ehlinger, D.G., Smith, R.F., 2015. Adolescent nicotine alters dendritic morphology in the bed nucleus of the stria terminalis. Neurosci. Lett. 590, 111–115.

Snyder, A.E., Salimando, G.J., Winder, D.G., Silberman, Y., 2019. Chronic intermittent ethanol and acute stress similarly modulate BNST CRF neuron activity via noradrenergic signaling. Alcohol Clin. Exp. Res. 43, 1695–1701.

Somerville, L.H., Whalen, P.J., Kelley, W.M., 2010. Human bed nucleus of the stria terminalis indexes hypervigilant threat monitoring. Biol. Psychiatr. 68, 416–424.

Steinman, M.Q., Duque-Wilckens, N., Greenberg, G.D., Hao, R., Campi, K.L., Laredo, S.A., Laman-Maharg, A., Manning, C.E., Doig, I.E., Lopez, E.M., et al., 2016. Sex-specific effects of stress on oxytocin neurons correspond with responses to intranasal oxytocin. Biol. Psychiatr. 80, 406–414.

Steinman, M.Q., Laredo, S.A., Lopez, E.M., Manning, C.E., Hao, R.C., Doig, I.E., Campi, K.L., Flowers, A.E., Knight, J.K., Trainor, B.C., 2015. Hypothalamic vasopressin systems are more sensitive to the long term effects of social defeat in males versus females. Psychoneuroendocrinology 51, 122–134.

Sugiura, T., Kondo, S., Sukagawa, A., Nakane, S., Shinoda, A., Itoh, K., Yamashita, A., Waku, K., 1995. 2-Arachidonoylglycerol: a possible endogenous cannabinoid receptor ligand in brain. Biochem. Biophys. Res. Commun. 215, 89–97.

Szücs, A., Berton, F., Nowotny, T., Sanna, P., Francesconi, W., 2010. Consistency and diversity of spike dynamics in the neurons of bed nucleus of stria terminalis of the rat: a dynamic clamp study. PLoS One 5 e11920-e11920.

Takagishi, M., Chiba, T., 1991. Efferent projections of the infralimbic (area 25) region of the medial prefrontal cortex in the rat: an anterograde tracer PHA-L study. Brain Res. 566, 26–39.

Torrisi, S., Alvarez, G.M., Gorka, A.X., Fuchs, B., Geraci, M., Grillon, C., Ernst, M., 2019. Resting-state connectivity of the bed nucleus of the stria terminalis and the central nucleus of the amygdala in clinical anxiety. J. Psychiatr. Neurosci. JPN 44, 1–11.

Torrisi, S., Gorka, A.X., Gonzalez-Castillo, J., O'Connell, K., Balderston, N., Grillon, C., Ernst, M., 2018. Extended amygdala connectivity changes during sustained shock anticipation. Transl. Psychiatry 8, 33-33.

Ubaldi, M., Giordano, A., Severi, I., Li, H., Kallupi, M., de Guglielmo, G., Ruggeri, B., Stopponi, S., Ciccocioppo, R., Cannella, N., 2016. Activation of hypocretin-1/orexin-A neurons projecting to the bed nucleus of the stria terminalis and paraventricular nucleus is critical for reinstatement of alcohol seeking by neuropeptide S. Biol. Psychiatr. 79, 452–462.

Uchida, K., Otsuka, H., Morishita, M., Tsukahara, S., Sato, T., Sakimura, K., Itoi, K., 2019. Female-biased sexual dimorphism of corticotropin-releasing factor neurons in the bed nucleus of the stria terminalis. Biol. Sex Differ. 10, 6.

Valjent, E., Mitchell, J.M., Besson, M.-J.J., Caboche, J., Maldonado, R., 2009. Behavioural and biochemical evidence for interactions between Δ9-tetrahydrocannabinol and nicotine. Br. J. Pharmacol. 135, 564–578.

Valjent, E., Pagès, C., Hervé, D., Girault, J.-A.A., Caboche, J., Pages, C., Herve, D., Girault, J.-A.A., Caboche, J., 2004. Addictive and non-addictive drugs induce distinct and specific patterns of ERK activation in mouse brain. Eur. J. Neurosci. 19, 1826–1836.

van Aerde, K.I., Feldmeyer, D., 2015. Morphological and physiological characterization of pyramidal neuron subtypes in rat medial prefrontal cortex. Cerebr. Cortex 25, 788–805.

van Esbroeck, A.C.M., Janssen, A.P.A., Cognetta 3rd, A.B., Ogasawara, D., Shpak, G., van der Kroeg, M., Kantae, V., Baggelaar, M.P., de Vrij, F.M.S., Deng, H., et al., 2017. Activity-based protein profiling reveals off-target proteins of the FAAH inhibitor BIA 10-2474. Science 356, 1084–1087.

van Leeuwen, F., Caffé, R., 1983. Vasopressin-immunoreactive cell bodies in the bed nucleus of the stria terminalis of the rat. Cell Tissue Res. 228, 525–534.

Vazquez, D.M., Bailey, C., Dent, G.W., Okimoto, D.K., Steffek, A., López, J.F., Levine, S., 2006. Brain corticotropin-releasing hormone (CRH) circuits in the developing rat: effect of maternal deprivation. Brain Res. 1121, 83–94.

Veenema, A.H., Beiderbeck, D.I., Lukas, M., Neumann, I.D., 2010. Distinct correlations of vasopressin release within the lateral septum and the bed nucleus of the stria terminalis with the display of intermale aggression. Horm. Behav. 58, 273–281.

Veinante, P., Stoeckel, M.-E., Lasbennes, F., Freund-Mercier, M.-J., 2003. c-Fos and peptide immunoreactivities in the central extended amygdala of morphine-dependent rats after naloxone-precipitated withdrawal. Eur. J. Neurosci. 18, 1295–1305.

Ventura-Silva, A.P., Pêgo, J.M., Sousa, J.C., Marques, A.R., Rodrigues, A.J., Marques, F., Cerqueira, J.J., Almeida, O.F.X., Sousa, N., 2012. Stress shifts the response of the bed nucleus of the stria terminalis to an anxiogenic mode. Eur. J. Neurosci. 36, 3396–3406.

Vertes, R.P., 2004. Differential Projections of the Infralimbic and Prelimbic Cortex in the Rat, vol 51. Synapse, New York, N.Y., pp. 32–58

Vranjkovic, O., Gasser, P.J., Gerndt, C.H., Baker, D.A., Mantsch, J.R., 2014. Stress-induced cocaine seeking requires a beta-2 adrenergic receptor-regulated pathway from the ventral bed nucleus of the stria terminalis that regulates CRF actions in the ventral tegmental area. J. Neurosci. 34, 12504–12514.

Vranjkovic, O., Hang, S., Baker, D.A., Mantsch, J.R., 2012. β-Adrenergic receptor mediation of stress-induced reinstatement of extinguished cocaine-induced conditioned place preference in mice: roles for β_1 and β_2 adrenergic receptors. J. Pharmacol. Exp. Therapeut. 342, 541–551.

Vranjkovic, O., Pina, M., Kash, T.L., Winder, D.G., 2017. The bed nucleus of the stria terminalis in drug-associated behavior and affect: a circuit-based perspective. Neuropharmacology 122, 100–106.

Vranjkovic, O., Winkler, G., Winder, D.G., 2018. Ketamine administration during a critical period after forced ethanol abstinence inhibits the development of time-dependent affective disturbances. Neuropsychopharmacology 43, 1915–1923.

Walker, J.R., Ahmed, S.H., Gracy, K.N., Koob, G.F., 2000. Microinjections of an opiate receptor antagonist into the bed nucleus of the stria terminalis suppress heroin self-administration in dependent rats. Brain Res. 854, 85–92.

Walter, A., Mai, J.K., Lanta, L., Gorcs, T., 1991. Differential distribution of immunohistochemical markers in the bed nucleus of the stria terminalis in the human brain. J. Chem. Neuroanat. 4, 281–298.

Wang, J., Fang, Q., Liu, Z., Lu, L., 2006. Region-specific effects of brain corticotropin-releasing factor receptor type 1 blockade on footshock-stress- or drug-priming-induced reinstatement of morphine conditioned place preference in rats. Psychopharmacology (Berl) 185, 19–28.

Wang, L., Goebel-Stengel, M., Stengel, A., Wu, S.V., Ohning, G., Taché, Y., 2011. Comparison of CRF-immunoreactive neurons distribution in mouse and rat brains and selective induction of Fos in rat hypothalamic CRF neurons by abdominal surgery. Brain Res. 1415, 34–46.

Wang, X., Cen, X., Lu, L., 2001. Noradrenaline in the bed nucleus of the stria terminalis is critical for stress-induced reactivation of morphine-conditioned place preference in rats. Eur. J. Pharmacol. 432, 153–161.

Wang, Y., Kim, J., Schmit, M.B., Cho, T.S., Fang, C., Cai, H., 2019. A bed nucleus of stria terminalis microcircuit regulating inflammation-associated modulation of feeding. Nat. Commun. 10, 2769.

Wee, S., Mandyam, C.D., Lekic, D.M., Koob, G.F., 2008. α1-Noradrenergic system role in increased motivation for cocaine intake in rats with prolonged access. Eur. Neuropsychopharmacol. 18, 303–311.

Weitlauf, C., Egli, R.E., Grueter, B.A., Winder, D.G., 2004. High-frequency stimulation induces ethanol-sensitive long-term potentiation at glutamatergic synapses in the dorsolateral bed nucleus of the stria terminalis. J. Neurosci. 24, 5741–5747.

Welch, J.D., Kozareva, V., Ferreira, A., Vanderburg, C., Martin, C., Macosko, E.Z., 2019. Single-cell multi-omic integration compares and contrasts features of brain cell identity. Cell 177, 1873–1887.e1817.

Wenzel, J.M., Waldroup, S.A., Haber, Z.M., Su, Z.I., Ben-Shahar, O., Ettenberg, A., 2011. Effects of lidocaine-induced inactivation of the bed nucleus of the stria terminalis, the central or the basolateral nucleus of the amygdala on the opponent-process actions of self-administered cocaine in rats. Psychopharmacology 217, 221–230.

Whylings, J., Rigney, N., Peters, N.V., de Vries, G.J., Petrulis, A., 2020. Sexually dimorphic role of BNST vasopressin cells in sickness and social behavior in male and female mice. Brain Behav. Immun. 83, 68–77.

Wills, T.A., Kash, T.L., Winder, D.G., 2013. Developmental changes in the acute ethanol sensitivity of glutamatergic and GABAergic transmission in the BNST. Alcohol 47, 531–537.

Wills, T.A., Klug, J.R., Silberman, Y., Baucum, A.J., Weitlauf, C., Colbran, R.J., Delpire, E., Winder, D.G., 2012. GluN2B subunit deletion reveals key role in acute and chronic ethanol sensitivity of glutamate synapses in bed nucleus of the stria terminalis. Proc. Natl. Acad. Sci. U. S. A. 109, E278–E287.

Wochnik, G.M., Ruegg, J., Abel, G.A., Schmidt, U., Holsboer, F., Rein, T., 2005. FK506-binding proteins 51 and 52 differentially regulate dynein interaction and nuclear translocation of the glucocorticoid receptor in mammalian cells. J. Biol. Chem. 280, 4609–4616.

Xiao, Q., Zhou, X., Wei, P., Xie, L., Han, Y., Wang, J., Cai, A., Xu, F., Tu, J., Wang, L., 2021. A new GABAergic so matostatin projection from the BNST onto accumbal parvalbumin neurons controls anxiety. Mol. Psychiatr. 26 (9), 4719–4741. https://doi.org/10.1038/s41380-020-0816-3 32555286.

Yamada, H., Bruijnzeel, A.W., 2011. Stimulation of alpha2-adrenergic receptors in the central nucleus of the amygdala attenuates stress-induced reinstatement of nicotine seeking in rats. Neuropharmacology 60, 303–311.

Ye, J., Veinante, P., 2019. Cell-type specific parallel circuits in the bed nucleus of the stria terminalis and the central nucleus of the amygdala of the mouse. bioRxiv 224, 1067–1095.

Yohn, C.N., Leithead, A.B., Becker, E.A., 2017. Increased vasopressin expression in the BNST accompanies paternally induced territoriality in male and female California mouse offspring. Horm. Behav. 93, 9–17.

Yoon, Y.R., Baik, J.H., 2015. Melanocortin 4 receptor and dopamine D2 receptor expression in brain areas involved in food intake. Endocrinol. Metab. 30, 576–583.

Zuloaga, D.G., Johnson, L.A., Weber, S., Raber, J., 2016. Immediate and lasting effects of chronic daily methamphetamine exposure on activation of cells in hypothalamic-pituitary-adrenal axis-associated brain regions. Psychopharmacology 233, 381–392.

CHAPTER

10

Noradrenergic circuits

Zoé A. McElligott[a, b, c], *Madigan L. Bedard*[c], *Sara Y. Conley*[d], *Isabel M. Bravo*[a], *Elizabeth S. Cogan*[a] *and Anthony M. Downs*[a]

[a]Bowles Center for Alcohol Studies, University of North Carolina at Chapel Hill, Chapel Hill, NC, United States; [b]Department of Psychiatry, University of North Carolina at Chapel Hill, Chapel Hill, NC, United States; [c]Department of Pharmacology, University of North Carolina at Chapel Hill, Chapel Hill, NC, United States; [d]Neuroscience Curriculum, University of North Carolina at Chapel Hill, Chapel Hill, NC, United States

Norepinephrine (NE) is a neurotransmitter/neuromodulator found both within the central nervous system (CNS) and the peripheral nervous system (PNS). NE, also referred to as noradrenaline (especially in the United Kingdom), is a biogenic amine, and more specifically a catecholamine due to the catechol group contained within the molecule (see Fig. 10.1). Evidence strongly suggests that NE signaling in the brain has profound effects on behavior. Too much or too little NE signaling results in perturbation of behaviors, and this "U-shaped" dose–response relationship has been well studied with respect to the noradrenergic system especially in relationship to arousal and memory (Baldi and Bucherelli, 2005).

Over the past several decades, addiction researchers have been guided by two theories of addiction. First, the Incentive-Salience Hypothesis (Berridge and Robinson, 2016) which postulates that substance use disorders are driven by "excessive wanting" of a substance driven by environmental and interoceptive cues, without corresponding enhancement of how much the substance is "liked." Second, the Allostasis Hypothesis (Fronk et al., 2020; Koob, 2003), which posits that repeated cycles of intoxication and withdrawal lead to the shifting of "allostatic set points" in effect (i.e., emotion), thereby leading to a situation in which individuals switch from using substances for their positive reinforcing properties (i.e., "feeling good"), to using substances for their negative reinforcement properties (i.e., to avoid or escape "feeling bad"). Because NE cell bodies send processes throughout the brain to multiple anatomical

Neurocircuitry of Addiction
https://doi.org/10.1016/B978-0-12-823453-2.00007-2

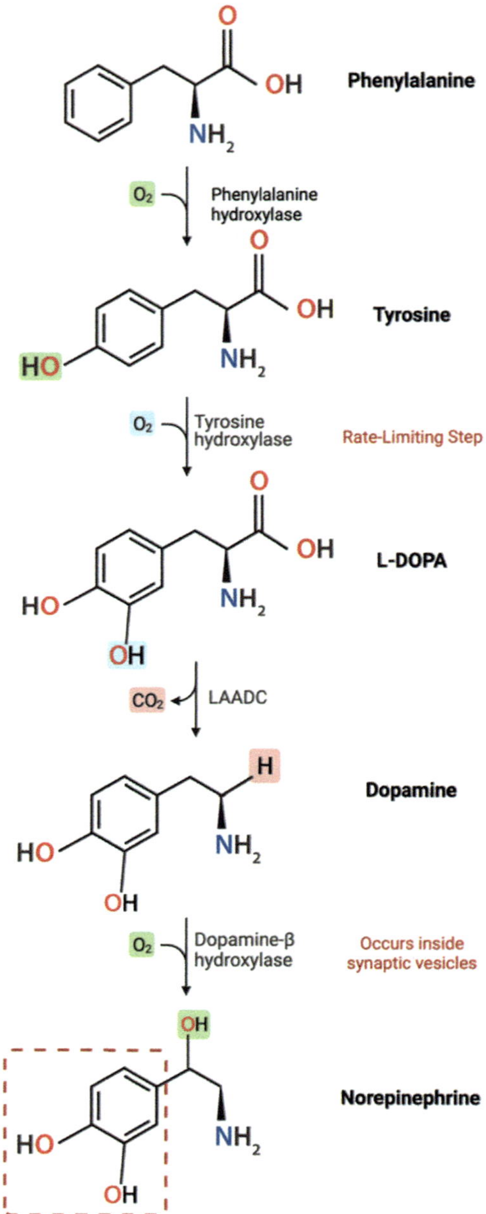

FIGURE 10.1 Norepinephrine chemical structure. Catabolism of norepinephrine from phenylamine. Changes between steps are highlighted. Catechol group in product is *dashed box* (dopamine, norepinephrine, and epinephrine are catecholamines).

targets, and because research has highlighted the critical involvement of NE in the regulation of emotional memory and stress (Tully and Bolshakov, 2010), there is a place for NE in both of the addiction theories mentioned above. Thus, understanding changes in the noradrenergic system by reinforcing substances and how NE signaling impacts the consumption of drugs is important for our understanding of addiction neurobiology.

It is important to note that the vast majority of the experiments discussed in this chapter were performed in rodent models, however, we will note when other species have been used. Additionally, it should be noted that most experiments have only been conducted in male subjects. We indicate below where female subjects were studied and we emphasize and underscore that the need for female research subjects is essential in both preclinical and clinical research (where the need expands to include men, women, and non-binary research subjects), especially in systems like the noradrenergic system which has been noted for sex differences.

Norepinephrine synthesis, storage, receptors, transporters, and metabolism

Reinforcing substances can impact neurotransmitter production, storage, signaling, and metabolism, thereby altering behavior. For example, some drugs, like cocaine, are best known for impeding neurotransmitter re-uptake from the synapse, while others work as direct agonists or antagonists of receptors or ion channels. Drugs like heroin are agonists at the μ-opioid receptor, and caffeine is a potent antagonist of the A_{2A} adenosine receptor. In addition to impeding re-uptake, cocaine also blocks sodium channels, highlighting that drugs may target multiple receptors, channels and/or proteins in the brain, and consequently have multiple effects. Indeed, alcohol/ethanol has so many molecular and cellular targets that it is hard to generate a list, though modulation of $GABA_A$ and NMDA receptors would be high on said list. This diversity of drug targets underscores the complexity of pharmacology. Moreover, drug effects on neurons may be direct, indirect, or both. In this introductory section we describe the basics of the noradrenergic/NE (these will be used interchangeably) system such that our readers have context for subsequent sections where we describe the experimentally derived role of this system in substance use and substance use disorders (SUDs).

The synthesis and packaging of NE begins with the essential amino acid phenylalanine, which is converted within the cytoplasm to the amino acid tyrosine by the enzyme phenylalanine hydroxylase. Tyrosine is then modified by the enzyme tyrosine hydroxylase (TH) to l-3,4-dihydroxyphenylalanine (also known as levodopa or L-dopa). TH is the rate limiting enzyme in the synthesis of both dopamine and NE, and the rate at which it converts tyrosine to L-dopa can be altered by phosphorylation. TH can be phosphorylated on several different serine (Ser) residues: Ser8, Ser19, Ser31, and Ser40 (Dunkley et al., 2004). Ser8 and Ser19 phosphorylation alone do not directly regulate the activity of TH, however Ser31 phosphorylation, and to a greater extent Ser40 phosphorylation enhance enzymatic activity. Finally, Ser19 phosphorylation can promote Ser40 phosphorylation exhibiting a property known as hierarchical phosphorylation. Differences in the phosphorylation state of TH can be regulated by stress, anti-depressants, and reinforcing substances (Nestler et al., 1990; Ong et al., 2011a,b). Following the formation of L-dopa, the enzyme l-amino acid-decarboxylase (LAADC) removes the carboxyl group on L-dopa converting it to dopamine. Dopamine is then packed into synaptic vesicles by the vesicular monoamine transporter (vMAT). In the CNS, the vMAT2 isoform packages dopamine into synaptic vesicles, whereas vMAT1 packages dopamine in peripheral endocrine cells like the adrenal chromaffin cells (Erickson et al., 1996). It is worth noting that vMATs also package other biogenic amines like serotonin and histamine. Once inside the synaptic vesicle, dopamine is converted to NE via addition of a hydroxyl group to the β-carbon by the aptly named enzyme dopamine β-hydroxylase (DBH). Expression of DBH in a cell defines the neuron as a noradrenergic neuron. Interestingly there is some evidence that noradrenergic neurons may also be able to release dopamine (Kempadoo et al., 2016; Takeuchi et al., 2016).

Once NE is packaged in synaptic vesicles, it is available for release into the extracellular space where it may engage adrenergic receptors. Adrenergic receptors are named so because they are also typically stimulated by epinephrine (adrenaline). Epinephrine is one biosynthetic step subsequent to the synthesis of NE and is not produced in purely noradrenergic cells. All adrenergic receptors are 7-transmembrane g-protein coupled receptors (GPCRs), and they are grouped into three families: the α_1, the α_2, and the β families. Each family consists of three distinct receptor subtypes produced from unique gene products (see Table 10.1). Canonically the α_1-adrenergic receptors are coupled to G_q g-proteins (activating the phospholipase C signaling cascade often resulting in an increase in intracellular calcium levels), the α_2-adrenergic receptors are coupled to the $G_{i/o}$ g-proteins (inhibiting adenylate cyclase and

TABLE 10.1 Cellular effects of the three families of noradrenergic receptors: α1, α2, and β. Each receptor family has three subtypes, each encoded by a unique gene. Norepinephrine has varying affinities across the families and subtypes

<table>
<tr><th></th><th></th><th>Family Subtypes</th><th>Encoding Gene</th><th>NE K_i Human (nM)</th></tr>
<tr><td rowspan="3">α_1</td><td rowspan="3">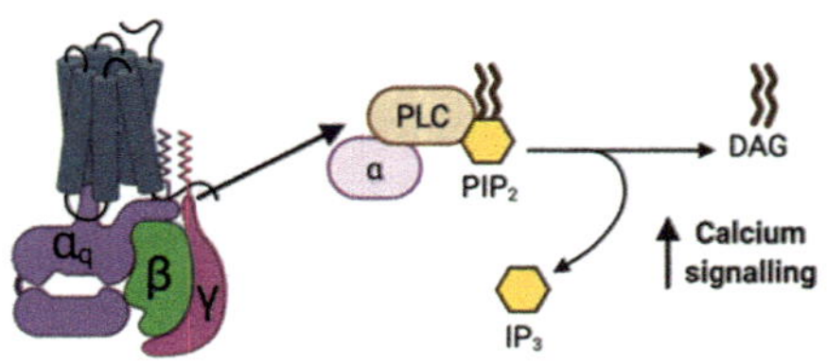
</td><td>A</td><td>ADRA1A</td><td>8,709</td></tr>
<tr><td>B</td><td>ADRA1B</td><td>7,585</td></tr>
<tr><td>D</td><td>ADRA1D</td><td>>10,000</td></tr>
<tr><td rowspan="3">α_2</td><td rowspan="3">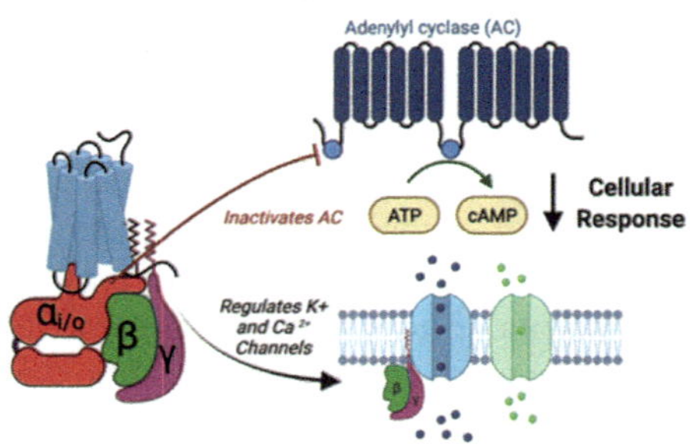
</td><td>A</td><td>ADRA2A</td><td>1196</td></tr>
<tr><td>B</td><td>ADRA2B</td><td>1,542</td></tr>
<tr><td>C</td><td>ADRA2C</td><td>968</td></tr>
<tr><td rowspan="3">β</td><td rowspan="3">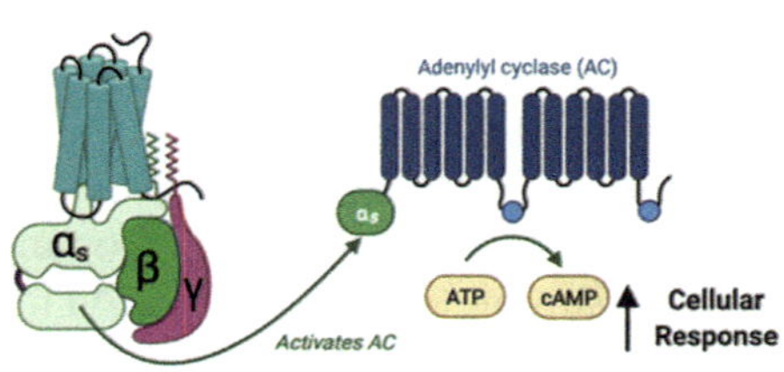
</td><td>1</td><td>ADRB1</td><td>3570</td></tr>
<tr><td>2</td><td>ADRB2</td><td>>10,000</td></tr>
<tr><td>3</td><td>ADRB3</td><td>4,300</td></tr>
</table>

reducing cAMP, activating potassium channels, and inhibiting calcium channels), and the β-adrenergic receptors are coupled to G_s g-proteins (stimulating adenylate cyclase and the production of cAMP and subsequent activation of PKA signaling pathways). However, there are examples of non-canonical g-protein signaling, especially at the β-adrenergic receptors (Galaz-Montoya et al., 2017). NE has the highest affinity for α_2-adrenergic receptors, followed by α_1-and β-adrenergic receptors. All three receptor subtypes can be expressed post-synaptically on a number of neurons, and there are examples of expression on astrocytes as well. The α_2-adrenergic receptors are also expressed pre-synaptically as auto-receptors that regulate NE release by engaging mechanisms to reduce NE release when activated (e.g. negatively regulating presynaptic calcium channels). Thus, they serve as sensors for negative feedback. There is evidence that α_2-adrenergic receptors are also expressed on pre-synaptic terminals of glutamate and GABA neurons, and regulate the release of those neuro-transmitters via interactions with ion channels, and inhibition of adenylyl cyclase (Giovannitti et al., 2015; Harris et al., 2018; Shields et al., 2009).

In addition to autoreceptors limiting the release of NE, several other mechanisms control NE levels in the synapse. Noradrenergic neurons express the norepinephrine transporter (NET) which clears NE from the synapse using the electrical-chemical gradient of sodium ions (symport of NE and Na^+). In addition, NE is cleared by the dopamine transporter (DAT), the serotonin transporter (SERT), and several non-selective organic cation transporters (OCTs). Once back inside the cell, NE can be degraded into dihydroxymandelic acid by the mitochondrial bound enzyme monoamine oxidase (MAO). Additionally, extracellular NE can be broken down into normetanephrine by the enzyme catechol-0-methyltransferase (COMT). In both instances, the byproducts are then metabolized further into the end-stage metabolite vanillylmandelic acid (VMA, Fig. 10.2). It is thought that most of the NE taken up into tissues is metabolized, but there is some evidence for NE recycling which may be altered in disease states (Kies et al., 2004).

Anatomy/development of norepinephrine circuits

The cell bodies of CNS NE neurons are located in the hindbrain, specifically the pons and the medulla oblongata, however the axons traverse and innervate almost the entire CNS to varying degrees. These cell groups are numbered A1-A7, and are referred to by these numbers or the nucleus where they reside, which are often interchangeable. The vast majority of NE neurons are in the pontine nucleus called the locus coeruleus (LC/A6). Latin for "blue spot," the LC is naturally pigmented blue by melanin in primates, however other typical laboratory vertebrates (e.g. mice and rats) lack this pigmentation. The projection targets of the A6/LC are vast, including many forebrain areas via the dorsal noradrenergic bundle (DNAB). Often textbooks and review articles state that the A6/LC/DNAB is the only source of NE to the forebrain, but in fact noradrenergic neurons in the rostral ventrolateral medulla (RVLM) and the nucleus of the tractus solitarius (NTS) (the A1 and A2 cell groups respectively), supply substantial NE to various forebrain nuclei via the ventral noradrenergic bundle (VNAB).

Scientists have investigated which noradrenergic neuronal populations innervate various brain regions by retrograde and anterograde tracing techniques using chemical tracers or viruses, or using intersectional strategies to label genetically distinct neurons (Saleeba et al., 2019). These studies have suggested that the cells of the A2/NTS and A1/RVLM project to the ventral forebrain including the bed nucleus of the stria terminalis (BNST), a component

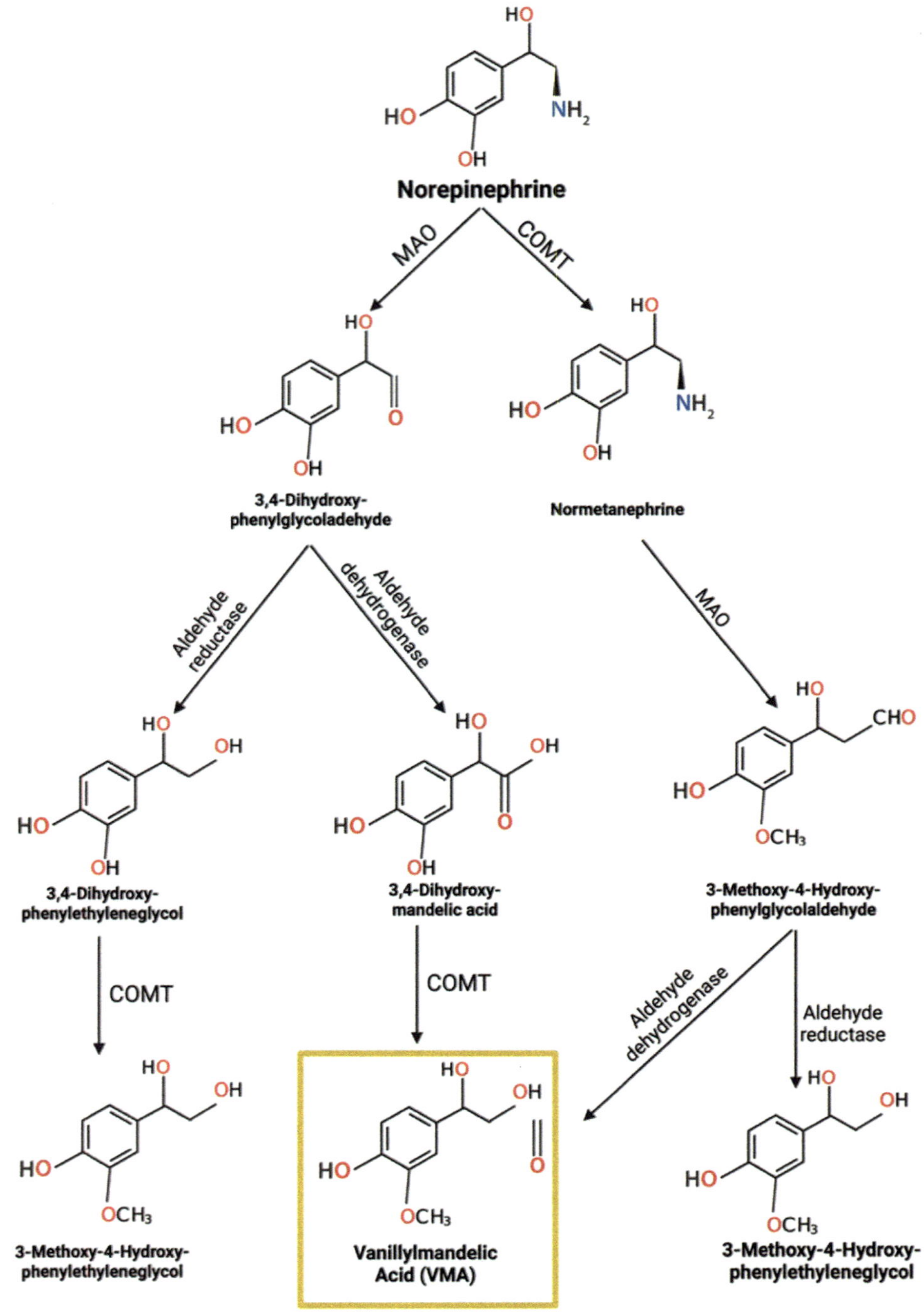

FIGURE 10.2 Metabolism of norepinephrine into vanillylmandelic acid (*yellow box*) via two different routes. Other metabolites 3,4-dihydroxyphenyethyleneglycol and 3-methoxy-4-hydroxyphenylethyleneglycol are other metabolites that are often associated with NE turnover.

of the extended amygdala that has been identified as an important nexus for various behaviors related to substance use disorders. Additionally, the VNAB also innervates the paraventricular nucleus of the hypothalamus (PVN), which is critical for the corporeal stress response (see the HPA axis chapter in this book, additional discussion below). Interestingly, using an antibody that targets DBH conjugated to a saporin toxin, Banihashemi and Rinaman demonstrated that BNST-projecting NE neurons collateralize and also send projections to the PVN (Banihashemi and Rinaman, 2006). This suggests that if one of these collateralizing neurons is activated, it may release NE in both of these brain regions at relatively the same time, affecting post-synaptic neurons, and incoming afferents in both regions simultaneously.

The developmental origins of the various NE neurons are somewhat anatomically distinct. Using an intersectional strategy with multiple transgenic lines, the Jensen Lab has elegantly investigated the developmental fate of noradrenergic neurons (Robertson et al., 2013). Neurons in the A6/LC almost exclusively originate in the first developmental rhombomere (Aroca et al., 2006) and thus derive from an embryonic lineage that express the engrailed one gene. In contrast, many (but not all) of the other noradrenergic neurons, including the A2/NTS and A1/RVLM are from the rhombomere four developmental lineage, which express the homeobox B1 gene. With intersectional transgenic lines, the Jensen Lab was able to fluorescently label noradrenergic neurons of different developmental origins and track their projection target regions. As prior anatomical studies had shown, developmental inputs from the A2/NTS and A1/RVLM were strongest in the BNST, PVN, and in the posterior aspect of the basolateral amygdala (BLA). Both the BLA and BNST had less, yet significant input from the A6/LC. Intriguingly, they also found that there was substantial NE innervation in the insular cortex from the homeobox B1 lineage, which was not previously known, as all cortical NE innervation was thought to be from the LC. Another benefit of this work was that it showed details of the varicosities (the swellings associated with transmitter release sites) from these distinct NE neuron populations. The projections from rhombomere 4 (originating mainly in the A2/NTS and A1/RVLM regions) had thick axonal projections with large varicosities, while projections from rhombomere 1 (mainly A6/LC) were much finer in structure. It has yet to be determined if this striking anatomical distinction results in functional differences between NE release from each of these projections.

Other studies have demonstrated that noradrenergic innervation of discrete brain regions is complex. Injection of an antibody against DBH, conjugated to a saporin toxin which when internalized into the cell kills NE neurons, into the BNST of rats depleted DBH-positive fibers in both the BNST and the medial paraventricular nucleus of the hypothalamus (mPVN). As mentioned above, these data also suggest that BNST-projecting NE neurons send axon collaterals to the mPVN (Banihashemi and Rinaman, 2006). In contrast to this evidence for NE neuron collateralization in the medullary NE neurons, the pontine A6/LC NE neurons appear to have distinct modules, with separate functional neuronal ensembles projecting to the prefrontal cortex and the subcortical BLA (Uematsu et al., 2017). Indeed, studies have examined how A6/LC neurons differ morphologically, based on distinct molecular markers (neuropeptides and receptors) and in terms of their projection targets, but it is not known how these distinctions may multiplex to affect function, nor how reinforcing substances may influence these different populations (Schwarz and Luo, 2015). Finally, using the rabies virus based "tracing the relationship between input and output" or TRIO method, Schwarz et al. Found that A6/LC neurons that send projections to distinct circuits (the olfactory bulb, auditory cortex, hippocampus, cerebellum and medulla) within the brain receive inputs from similar nuclei (Schwarz et al., 2015). It is important to note, however, that rabies based synaptic labeling does not necessarily mean functional fast synaptic transmission (ie. glutamatergic and/or GABAergic synaptic transmission) in the way that neuroscientists often presume when they contemplate circuits. As an example we, and others, have not found GABAergic inhibition of the LC by CeA terminals expressing channelrhodopsin in the hindbrain (McCall et al., 2015; Torruella-Suárez et al., 2020), however these same terminals appear to release neuropeptides (corticotropin releasing factor—CRF, sometimes referred to as corticotropin releasing hormone or CRH, McCall et al., 2015) in the A6/LC suggesting that there is "functional connectivity" between these nuclei. Taken together, these studies underscore how much there remains to learn about basic noradrenergic circuitries, and how substance use may differentially alter discrete NE circuits. (For a basic overview of the inputs and outputs to the A6/LC and A1/RVLM and A2/NTS, see Fig. 10.3).

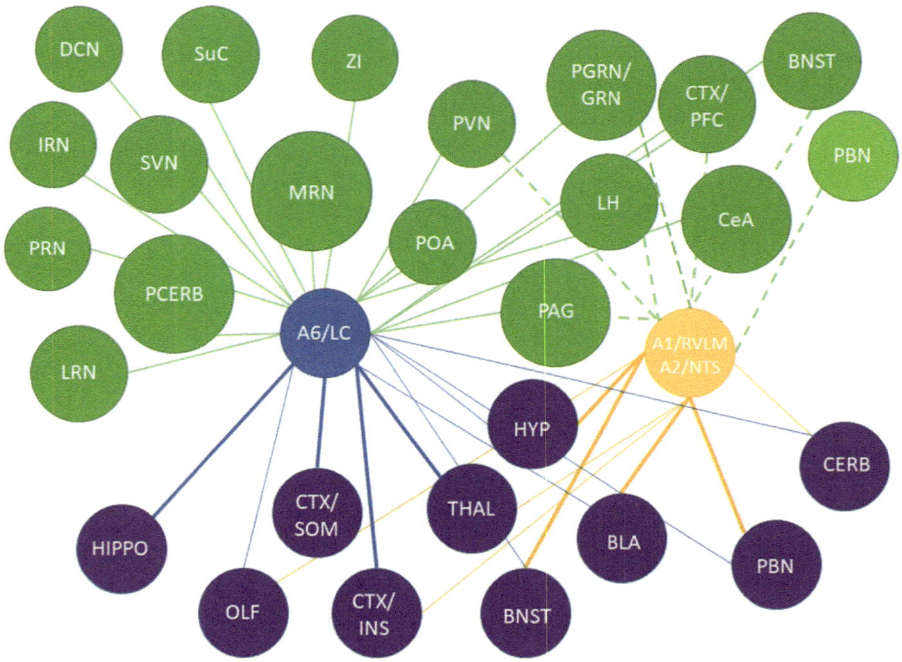

FIGURE 10.3 Diagram of major inputs (afferents) and outputs (efferents) of the A6/LC (*blue*) and A1/RVLM and A2/NTS (*yellow*). *Green circles* represent input nuclei and are sized corresponding to the strength of the input to the A6/LC. *Solid green lines* are targets that have been confirmed with pseudorabies tracing, where *dashed green lines* are targets that have been confirmed with classic retro- and anterograde tracing. *Purple circles* represent output nuclei targeted byf the noradrenergic neurons as labeled in an intersectional DBH x developmental rhombomere (A6/LC x rhombomere1—*blue*; A1/RVLM and A2/NTS x rhombomere4—*yellow*) fashion. *Thicker lines* represent stronger input than *thinner lines* to a given *purple nucleus*. It is worth noting that some of these connections appear to be reciprocal between the noradrenergic nuclei and the brain region of interest, however, we do not currently know the extent of the way these circuits influence each other. Abbreviations: *BLA*, basolateral amygdala; *BNST*, bed nucleus of the stria terminalis; *CeA*, central nucleus of the amygdala; *CERB*, cerebellum; *CTX/INS*, insular cortex; *CTX/PFC*, prefrontal cortex; *CTX/SOM*, somtosensory cortex; *DCN*, deep cerebellar nuclei; *HIPPO*, hippocampus; *HYP*, hypothalamus; *INR*, intermediate reticular nucleus; *LC*, locus coeruleus; *LH*, lateral hypothalamus; *LRN*, lateral reticular nucleus; *MRN*, midbrain reticular nucleus; *PAG*, periaquaductal gray; *PBN*, parabrachial nucleus; *PCERB*, Purkinje cells of the cerebellum; *PGRN/GRN*, perigigantocellular/gigantocellular nucleus; *POA*, preoptic area; *PRN*, pontine reticular neucleus; *PVN*, paraventricular nucleus of the hypothalamus; *SuC*, superior colliculous; *SVN*, spinal vestibular nucleus; *THAL*, thalamus; *ZI*, zona incerta. *This figure compiles data from the following sources.*

Norepinephrine involvement in stress, arousal, and locomotion

As a neuromodulator that innervates the vast majority of the brain, NE is positioned to regulate many physiological processes. In particular, noradrenergic systems play prominent roles in regulating arousal responses, stress responses, and locomotor behaviors. As all of these physiological phenomena influence, and are influenced by, the response to drugs, it is important to consider the role of NE in these processes.

Activation of LC neurons regulates arousal, sleep behavior and wakefulness. Using a combination of chemogenetic techniques, and pharmacology, the Weinshenker group demonstrated that activating G_q-GPCR signaling in the LC, results in the release of NE in the ventral periaqueductal gray (vPAG), where NE binds to α_1-adrenergic receptors on astrocytes leading to the activation of vPAG dopamine neurons and waking behavior (Porter-Stransky et al., 2019). LC neurons are almost always tonically active, but their activity changes across the sleep–wake cycle, where neuronal firing decreases during slow-wave sleep, and their firing ceases only during rapid-eye-movement, or REM sleep. Modulation of LC neuron activity that maintains firing and prevents REM sleep periods leads to disruptions of memory consolidation and alters related behavior (Swift et al., 2018).

Noradrenergic signaling regulates the neuroendocrine stress response. This is in large part due to the direct and indirect influence of NE on HPA axis activity (Herman et al., 2016). Briefly, stimulation of the parvocellular PVN neurons by NE causes synthesis and release of CRF. This CRF release stimulates adrenocorticotropic hormone (ACTH) production by the anterior pituitary, which then travels through the bloodstream to act on the adrenal cortex to induce production of mineralo- and glucocorticoids such as cortisol (or corticosterone in rodents). Cortisol subsequently enables the stress response via mobilization of energy stores and suppression of non-essential systems such as the immune, digestive, and reproductive systems. Additionally, cortisol acts in the brain to decrease CRF and ACTH synthesis, thereby acting as its own negative regulator (Herman et al., 2003). Peripherally, NE is a key component in the sympathetic nervous system (SNS), which mediates the fight-or-flight response. When presented with a stressful stimulus, preganglionic neurons in the interomediolateral gray matter of the spinal cord release acetylcholine (ACh), which then either activates postganglionic NE neurons directly, or stimulates epinephrine and norepinephrine production and release into the bloodstream by the adrenal medulla (Goldstein, 1987). This noradrenergic signaling reaches many organs of the body and serves to dilate the pupils, and increase heartrate and respiration, among other responses (Karemaker, 2017). Preganglionic sympathetic neurons receive direct inputs from brain areas such as the PVN and insular cortex, as well as the noradrenergic A2/NTS and A1/RVLM areas (Fisher et al., 2009). As one might expect, these neurons are also indirectly influenced by other fear- and stress-related brain regions, such as the amygdala and BNST (Buijs and Van Eden, 2000; Crestani et al., 2013; Lebow and Chen, 2016). Thus, peripheral NE signaling via the SNS, in concert with central NE signaling upon the HPA axis, prime the body to respond to urgent threats. In the short term, elevated HPA axis and SNS activity can be highly advantageous, allowing an organism to escape an imminently dangerous situation. However, sustained activation of these systems has been shown to contribute to a variety of deleterious effects including inflammation, chronic pain, depression, and anxiety (Faravelli et al., 2012; Hannibal and Bishop, 2014; Pariante and Lightman, 2008; Silverman and Sternberg, 2012).

Noradrenergic systems also influence ambulatory behavior, which makes it challenging, and somewhat confounding, to study noradrenergic systems in rodent models because most of the behavioral assays depend on locomotor actions. Acute and chronic blockade of NET with selective inhibitors decreases locomotion in the open field (Mitchell et al., 2006). Similarly, NET knockout mice exhibit lower locomotor behavior at baseline (Mitchell et al., 2006), but enhanced locomotor response to psychostimulants (Xu et al., 2000). Recent data, however, has shed some light on how DBH knockout mice respond to novelty and how this may influence their locomotor behavior. As with NET knockout mice, DBH knockout mice exhibit reduced locomotion in a novel environment, although they do not exhibit a neophobic response in the novelty-suppressed feeding task (Lustberg et al., 2020).

Neurochemical techniques used for measuring brain NE cell and circuit activity

As mentioned in earlier chapters, multiple methods are used to investigate how substances of abuse engage the noradrenergic system, and the role that the noradrenergic system plays in the manifestation of behaviors associated with substance use. Here, we will not repeat explanations of circuit monitoring and manipulation covered in Chapter 1, but we will briefly review neurochemical techniques that will be referred to in the following section of this chapter.

Neurotransmitter detection: There are a variety of techniques that can be used to directly or indirectly measure NE in the brain. Some of these techniques determine the exact amount of analyte that is available to measure, while others give a relative value of how much analyte is released relative to what exists in the background (typically called "background subtracted" techniques). The difference between what is measured in a given technique is important to understand when designing experiments and interpreting data.

Turn-over assays sample pieces of brain tissue and then use chemical detection (usually high-performance liquid chromatography coupled with either electrochemical or fluorescent detection) to measure levels of a neurotransmitter and its metabolites. The ratio of metabolite to transmitter is used to index the turn-over rate. If there is enhanced metabolite to transmitter levels, it is presumed that there is enhanced neurotransmitter release.

In vivo microdialysis describes a procedure in which a probe with a semi-permeable membrane is implanted into a brain region and the dialysis fluid is sampled periodically (usually in 20–30 min intervals but can be done more frequently). The fluid samples are then run through high-performance liquid chromatography coupled to electrochemical or fluorescent detection as above. This allows for comparison of neurotransmitter levels in samples collected at baseline, and then following a stimulus (e.g. a drug, or cue).

In vivo/ex vivo amperometry is an electrochemical technique in which a carbon fiber microelectrode is continuously held at a certain potential (usually +0.7 V) to detect neurotransmitter. This is usually used with exogenous neurotransmitter application to measure transmitter uptake through transporters like NET.

In vivo/ex vivo fast-scan cyclic voltammetry is an electrochemical technique in which a carbon fiber microelectrode is held at a given potential (usually −0.4 V) and rapidly ramped (usually at a rate of 400 V s) to a positive potential (usually +1.3 V), at a sub-second sampling frequency (usually 10 Hz). This allows for the oxidation and reduction of released compounds and the detection of these compounds based on location of the probe, the response to various pharmacological treatment, and calibration of the carbon fiber microelectrode. The major confound with fast-scan cyclic voltammetry is that biogenic monoamines usually oxidize and reduce at almost the same exact potential, and it is nearly impossible to distinguish between the analytes. In order to accurately conclude one is detecting the desired analyte, specific circumstances must be considered. For example, one must record in a brain region where one is confident that the analyte is the principal neurotransmitter released, and/or use pharmacological validation of the recording with uptake inhibitors and/or autoreceptor agonists or antagonists. Additionally, using optogenetic strategies to release the biogenic amine is another way that we can be confident that we are detecting a particular biogenic amine (e.g., NE).

In vivo/ex vivo biosensors are a method that uses viral or transgenic techniques to deliver proteins that encode a receptor moiety that leads to a change in fluorescence intensity when activated and can be detected with either microscopy or an optical fiber detection system (fiber photometry). For example, the $GRAB_{NE}$ sensor has been successfully used to detect NE release in vivo (Feng et al., 2019).

Manipulating/probing NE circuits

There have not been many, studies in which specific NE circuits or afferents to specific NE nuclei have been manipulated in the context of reinforcing drugs. There have, however, been some experiments conducted by our lab and others in which NE circuits have been investigated for their effects on behavior and cellular physiology, which we will highlight here.

The Jensen lab has used an intersectional approach to express Gq-coupled Designer Receptors Exclusively Activated by Designer Drugs (DREADDs, a chemogenetic technique) in either A6/LC neurons or in majority A1/RVLM and A2/NTS (those that express the Hoxb1 gene) neurons in mice. Chemogenetic stimulation of A6/LC neurons drove avoidance ("anxiety-like") behaviors, but also decreased locomotor behaivors (Sciolino et al., 2016). In contrast, when activating the Hoxb1-NE expressing neurons, there was a decrease in avoidance behavior and "depressive-like" behaviors (Chen et al., 2019). There also appear to be some funcitonal distinction between different types of NE neurons. Our lab performs whole cell electrophysiology in NE neurons and we have observed different firing patters in the LC and A2/NTS (for examples Fig. 10.4). These physiological differences may have functional and behaivoral consequences.

While the A6/LC was originally thought to be a rather heterogenous structure, recent studies have begun to functionally untangle various "modules" within the A6/LC based on its target projections (Fig. 10.5). The Waterhouse lab retrogradely labeled neurons projecting to the orbital frontal cortex, the medial PFC, the anterior cingulate cortex, and the M1 motor cortex, and assayed these neurons for mRNA expression of catecholaminergic markers,

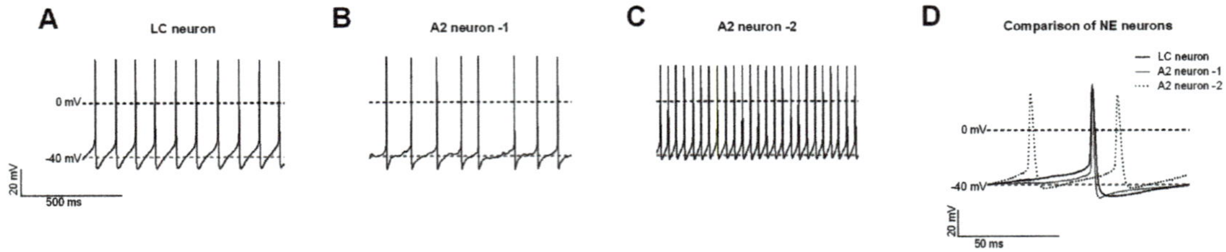

FIGURE 10.4 Representations of NE neuron ex vivo physiology in A6/LC and A2/NTS neurons. (A) Spontaneous firing of an A6/LC neuron (B) An A2/NTS neuron and (C) a separate A2/NTS neuron. Time scale is 1 s for A–C to show different firing patterns. (D) A representative spike from each of the recordings in A–C on a 100 ms time scale to show differences in shape of the action potentials (*Gray dashed line* at −40 mV and *black dashed line* at 0 mV in all recordings)

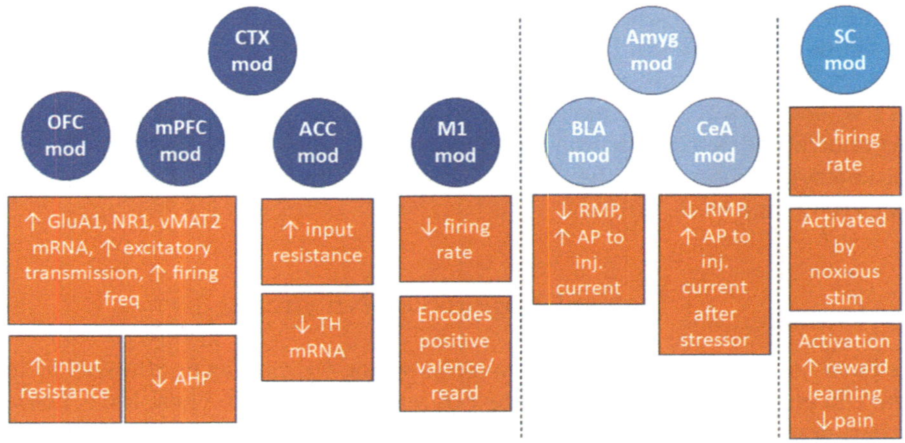

FIGURE 10.5 Distinct modules of the A6/LC. Anatomical, physiological, and behavioral studies have demonstrated that the A6/LC is not a homogenous structure, but rather distinct circuits defined by A6/LC outputs with individual characteristics. This figure summarizes some of what is known about the distinct properties of these modules. Abbreviations: *ACC*, anterior cingulate cortex; *AHP*, after hyperpolarization potential; *Amyg*, amygdala; *AP*, action potential; brain regions; *BLA*, basolateral amygdala; *CeA*, central nucleus of the amygdala; *CTX*, cortex; *electrophysiology RMP*, resting membrane potential; *M1*, M1 motor cortex; *mPFC*, medial prefrontal cortex; *mRNAs, GluA1*, AMPA glutamate receptor subunit 1; *NR1*, NMDA receptor subunit 1; *OFC*, orbital frontal cortex; *SC*, spinal column; *TH*, tyrosine hydroxylase; *vMAT2*, vesicular monoamine transporter 2.

various receptor and channel subunits, cellular physiology, and anatomical overlap (Chandler et al., 2014). The projection neurons to the M1 motor cortex did not anatomically or functionally overlap with the other projections. Overall, the A6/LC projections to the medial PFC and the orbital frontal cortex had characteristics both electrophysiologically and by mRNA expression that would suggest a propensity for greater release of NE in these target structures.

Probing the function of the LC in pain behavior in male Wistar rats, the Pickering Lab has found that there may be differences along the dorsal–ventral axis of the LC with regard to the modulation of pain behavior. Optogenetic stimulation of the A6/LC had opposite outcome in thermal nociception depending on if the dorsal portion or the ventral portion of the A6/LC was transduced by channelrhodopsin. Stimulation of the ventral A6/LC promoted anti-nociception, whereas stimulation of the dorsal A6/LC increased pain sensitivity (Hickey et al., 2014). Further studies (Li et al., 2016) using a retrograde labeling method demonstrated that a ventral portion of the LC formed a largely distinct module that projected to the spinal cord (differentiating it from a PFC projecting module). These neurons also exhibited differences in physiology as compared to other LC neurons, and had lower spontaneous firing frequencies in vivo, but were excited by aversive stimuli. Further work, targeting these same projection populations demonstrated that activating the spinal cord projecting module could also induce conditioned place preference, underscoring a role for this module/projection in reward learning behavior. The PFC projecting module, however, promoted "anxiety-like" behavior (Hirschberg et al., 2017).

In addition to differences between A6/LC neurons projecting to the spinal cord versus PFC, and as referenced above, A6/LC neurons exhibit at least some distinct projections to the amygdala and PFC. Using retrograde labeling (retrobeads) in mice, we found that there are distinct physiological differences between A6/LC neurons projecting to each of these target regions. Our previously unpublished data demonstrate that BLA projecting neurons have a significantly lower "resting membrane potential" (in quotes because this is the average membrane potential as A6/LC neurons do not "rest") compared to PFC projecting neurons, and there is a trend for the BLA projecting neurons to also have lower ex vivo spontaneous firing rate. In contrast, when cells are clamped at a membrane potential of −70 mV (where spontaneous firing ceases) and then current steps are injected, we find that BLA-projecting neurons fired more action potentials over the depolarization period with increasing current injection reative to the PFC-projecting neurons (Fig. 10.6). Similar to our data, the Chandler lab investigated LC projections to the PFC versus the CeA in late adolescent male Sprague-Dawley rats (Borodovitsyna et al., 2020), and found that there were baseline electrophysiological differences in mPFC versus CeA projecting A6/LC neurons. Furthermore, these

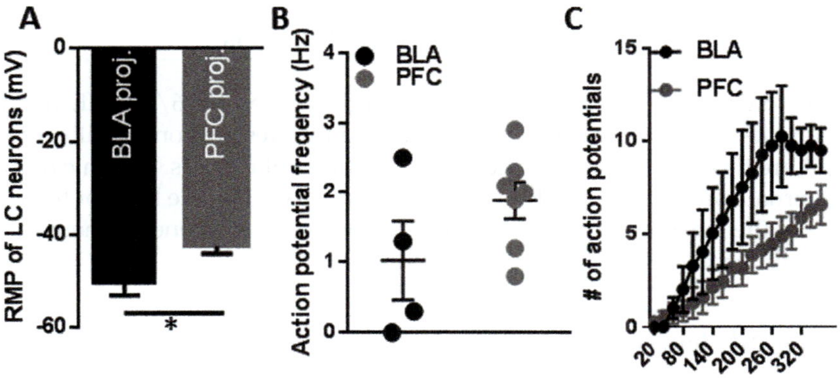

FIGURE 10.6 (A) Resting membrane potential (RMP) differences between BLA and PFC projecting A6/LC neurons. (B) Trend for a difference in Action Potential (AP) frequency between basolateral amygdala (BLA) and prefrontal cortex (PFC) projecting LC neurons. (C) Significant interaction ($P < .0001$) between # of action potentials and injected current BLA and PFC projecting A6/LC neurons.

differences were exacerbated by an acute stressor (restraint and predator odor combination). Somewhat in contrast to the data from the Pickering lab, using a chemogenetic strategy they found that the mPFC projecting A6/LC module promoted exploratory behavior, while the CeA projecting module promoted "anxiety-like" behavior. These differences could be due to the age of the animals, differences in strain, and the influence of distinct stressors versus noxious stimuli.

In a series of elegant studies, the Sur lab has begun to investigate the modulation and encoding of A6/LC NE neurons. They have found that local circuit inhibitory (GABA) control over LC neurons can alter arousal states, and that these arousal states can differ depending on (Breton-Provencher and Sur, 2019) if the neurons project only to peri-coerulear GABA neurons versus the A6/LC itself. A very recent study by the same group used a go-no-go assay to demonstrate that the phasic firing of the A6/LC correlates to goal directed behavior (Breton-Provencher et al., 2022), where activity is enhanced prior to the behavior and subsequent to reinforcement. A6/LC neurons exhibit phasic activity for both positive and negative reinforcement, however firing frequency is higher during negative reinforcement. Further, their study provides evidence that neuronal activity of A6/LC neurons during unexpected reward helps to shape future behavioral outcomes/learning. Finally, this study suggested that cell firing encoding the positive valence response was limited to a subset of neurons, while the negative valence response was broad across all neurons in the A6/LC. Examining this further in a circuit like fashion, silencing A6/LC inputs to motor cortex reduced accuracy for a positive valence response when stimuli was of low intensity, while silencing dorsal medial or motor cortex did not affect negative valence outcomes. This study demonstrates the complexity of neuronal encoding of motivational states by the A6/LC and future work will undoubtedly investigate the role of exposure and withdrawal to reinforcing drugs on these complicated behaviors and physiology.

Indeed, it will be intruiging to investigate how these distinct projecting A6/LC modules are modulated by reinforcing drugs, drug dependence, and how they contribute to the learned behaviors surrounding drug use.

Norepinephrine and opioids

Opioid receptors are expressed on noradrenergic neurons. A6/LC NE neurons express both μ-OR and κ-OR, both of which can be engaged by prescription and illicit opioids. Classically, μ-OR are thought to mediate the euphoric effects of opioids. Chronic opioid exposure results in internalization of the μ-OR in A6/LC NE neurons in male but not female rats, highlighting one of the ways that both the opioid system and noradrenergic neurons themselves show sexual dimorphisms (Enman et al., 2019).

Manipulating NE levels

DBH knockout mice (Thomas et al., 1995) have been utilized in many different experimental paradigms to investigate the role of NE in behavior. Importantly, DBH knockout mice are embryonically lethal, due to cardiovascular failures, unless there is synthesis of

NE via other sources. To circumvent lethality, a compound called dihydroxyphenylserine (DOPS) can be administered to produce NE through conversion by LAADC. Using DOPS, animals are viable, and can be used to investigate the role of NE in substance use. Olson and colleagues (Olson et al., 2006) found that NE was required for the establishment of morphine-induced CPP, such that DBH knockout mice failed to show CPP for multiple doses of morphine, while their wild-type litter mates exhibited robust dose-dependent CPP. Moreover, restoration of NE using DOPS rescued the loss of morphine CPP in DBH knockout mice. Using viral technologies to replace DBH in specific noradrenergic cell groups, they found that restoring DBH to the A2/NTS cell groups rescued morphine-induced CPP in DBH knockout mice, whereas restoration to the A6/LC did not rescue morphine-induced CPP in those mice. These results suggest a critical role for NE, especially that originating in the A1 and A2 medullary cell groups, in reward learning behaviors.

Norepineprhine has also been implicated in mediating negative valence associations with opioid withdrawal (Delfs et al., 2000). Indeed, lesions of the forebrain ventral noradrenergic projections (VNAB) from the A1/A2 cell groups attenuates opioid withdrawal-induced CPA, while not disrupting general aversive learning. Conversely, lesions of LC projections (DNAB) do not attenuate opioid withdrawal-induced CPA, again strongly suggesting that VNAB projections are critical for negative valence behaviors associated with opioid withdrawal. Surprisingly, lesions of neither the DNAB nor the VNAB independently changed somatic behaviors associated with opioid withdrawal, and somatic withdrawal signs correlate with NE release in the bed nucleus of the stria terminalis (Delfs et al., 2000; Fox et al., 2017).

It is not surprising perhaps that noradrenergic signaling, even within the same brain region, may promote both positive and negative experiences with opioid use. As referenced above, catecholamines operate on a U-shaped curve and therefore concentrations of synaptic NE may preferentially activate some receptors (like the high affinity α_2-ARs) while leaving others relatively unstimulated (the lower affinity β-ARs for example). Additionally, NE can modulate plasticity events based on the duration of receptor agonist exposure (McElligott and Winder, 2008). Thus, how NE is signaling within a given brain region and across brain regions may have multidimensional effects on how an animal responds to drugs.

Manipulating post-synaptic receptors

As with the VNAB lesions discussed above, blocking β-ARs in the bed nucleus of the stria terminalis similarly attenuates the expression of opioid withdrawal-induced CPA. In contrast to what is observed with VNAB and LC lesions, however, β-AR blockade in the BNST does attenuate the expression of somatic withdrawal behaviors (Delfs et al., 2000).

Studies have also examined how the noradrenergic system may play a role in stress-induced reinstatement of opioid-seeking behavior. Shaham and colleagues found that stimulating α2-ARs systemically, or via injection into the ventricles, attenuated stress-induced reinstatement of heroin-seeking behavior, however direct injection into the LC/A6 did not attenuate stress-induced reinstatement (Shaham et al., 2000b). As injection of α2-AR agonists directly into the LC/A6 leads to reductions in LC/A6 neuronal firing rate, but fails to attenuate stress-induced reinstatement of heroin-seeking behavior, this suggests that LC/A6 neurons do not mediate this behavior. Similarly, stress (intermittent foot shock) enhances morphine CPP, an effect which was attenuated by injection of α2-AR agonist into the bed nucleus of the stria terminalis (Wang et al., 2001), which, as noted above, mainly receives inputs from the medullary A1/A2 adrenergic cell groups.

α1b-ARs play a role both in both the sensitivity to and the reinforcing properties of opioids (Drouin et al., 2002). Global knock out of the α1b-AR attenuates enhancement of locomotor behavior after a single injection of morphine, as well as behavioral sensitization after repeated morphine injections. Additionally, these mice exhibit reductions in the oral consumption of morphine and do not develop a CPP for morphine at a dose of 5 mg kg^{-1}, implicating the α1b-AR in the rewarding and reinforcing effects of opioids. Furthermore, if wild-type animals are pretreated with an injection of an α1-AR antagonist, there is no distinction in locomotor activation between α1b-AR knockout and wild-type animals. This suggests that α1b-AR mediate locomotor effects of injected opioids in animals.

Other neurotransmitter systems modulate noradrenergic systems, and this is especially true for interactions of the hypothalamic orexin/hypocretin and amygdalar CRF systems with LC/A6 NE neurons. For example, pharmacological activation of the LC/A6 via stimulation of orexin receptors promotes opioid withdrawal-like behaviors in both morphine-dependent morphine-naïve rats (Ghaemi-Jandabi et al., 2017). In congruence with these data, blockade of orexin-1 receptors (HCRTR1) prevents opioid withdrawal behaviors, and this is dependent on $GABA_A$ receptor signaling in the LC (Davoudi et al., 2016). Indeed, within-slice precipitated morphine withdrawal (when naloxone is added to the slice to dislodge morphine from opioid receptors) reduces GABAergic signaling onto LC neurons, and this effect is greater with the addition of orexin A (Davoudi et al., 2019).

Similarly, CRF signaling modulates LC function (McCall et al., 2015; Valentino et al., 2013; Van Bockstaele and Valentino, 2013). Chronic morphine sensitizes the LC to the effects of CRF signaling and stress, as demonstrated by an increase in firing rate of LC neurons in response to focal CRF application (Xu et al., 2004). Recent data shows that chronic morphine exposure recruits CRF receptor type 1 (CRFR1) to the plasma membrane in male and female rats (Enman et al., 2019). Furthermore, blockade of CRFR1 prevents morphine-induced CPP, morphine withdrawal behaviors, and morphine-induced reduction of NE turnover in multiple brain regions including the nucleus accumbens and cerebral cortex (Funada et al., 2001; Lasheras et al., 2015).

Regulation of NE physiology and release by opioid system

As described above, the noradrenergic system can modulate physiological and behavioral response to opioids. However, NE and the opioid system share a bidirectional relationship, wherein changes in NE neuron physiology and activity are mediated by endogenous opioid signaling and exogenous opioid exposure.

LC neuron physiology has long been studied in the context of opioid withdrawal (Rasmussen, 1991). Opioid withdrawal precipitated by naloxone, a rapidly activating opioid receptor antagonist, increases the firing rate of LC neurons in vivo for hours following naloxone administration (Rasmussen et al., 1990). Furthermore, there is strong evidence that activation of glutamatergic receptors plays a significant role in mediating this increase in firing rate as intraventricular administration of kynurenic acid, an excitatory amino acid antagonist, attenuates withdrawal-induced increases in LC neuron firing rate (Rasmussen et al., 1991; Tung et al., 1990). Supporting this notion, there is evidence for an increase in excitatory synaptic plasticity, as demonstrated by an increase in spontaneous excitatory postsynaptic currents, on LC neurons following morphine withdrawal (Torrecilla et al., 2008), although it is not clear which circuits are affected. Systemic modulation of glutamatergic autoreceptors that regulate the release of glutamate also tunes the firing rate of LC neurons during opioid withdrawal (Rasmussen et al., 2004; Vandergriff and Rasmussen, 1999).

Changes in intracellular signaling pathways have also been implicated in cellular plasticity in LC neurons following opioid withdrawal. Morphine withdrawal increases the activity of adenylate cyclase and cyclic AMP-dependent protein kinase, but interestingly rats with increased propensity to self-administer opioids, and expressing more extensive opioid withdrawal, have higher basal activity of LC neurons and increased responding to a cell permeable activator of cyclic AMP-dependent kinase (Guitart et al., 1993). Downregulation of cyclic AMP response element binding protein (CREB), a transcription factor important in synaptic plasticity, in the LC attenuates both LC neuronal firing and the expression of opioid withdrawal behaviors (Han et al., 2006). Collectively, these experiments demonstrate that the activity level of LC neurons and the plasticity of excitatory synaptic inputs onto these neurons strongly influence opioid withdrawal behaviors. These data are intriguing when taken in the context of reports that lesioning the LC does not influence opioid withdrawal behaviors. This could suggest that functional lesions of the LC may result in neuronal adaptations that allow for the expression of opioid withdrawal behaviors, and underscores the critical contribution of opioid-NE sytem crosstalk in these outcomes.

Using radioligand tracing of NE in slices of rat and guinea pig cortex, Werling and colleagues demonstrated that pharmacologic activation of μ, κ, and δ opioid receptors inhibits NE release to varying degrees. This effect was rescued by naloxone administration, although naloxone itself produced slight inhibition of NE release (Werling et al., 1987). Inhibitory modulation of NE release by the opioid system helps to fine-tune the stress response. Curtis et al. showed that antagonism of CRF receptors preventes increases in tonic firing rate of LC NE neurons induced by a predator odor stress exposure. Interestingly, this effect is mediated by opioids, such that pretreatment with naloxone blocks the CRF antagonist effect, demonstrating cross-talk between CRF and opioid systems in the LC (Curtis et al., 2012). Further, Quirarte and colleagues found that administration of the endogenous opioid receptor agonist β-endorphin blocks stress-induced NE release in the amygdala (dialysis probe was placed between the CeA and BLA) when administered before, immediately following, and 30 min after foot shock, whereas naloxone potentiated NE release in the same region. This evidence points to the role of endogenous opioids in the regulation of memory storage through modulation of NE release in the amygdala, and suggests a possible mechanism whereby exogenous opioids may act to pathologically alter NE neurotransmission (Quirarte et al., 1998).

Because of the established role for NE in opioid reward and opioid withdrawal-mediated aversion, and due to the dense expression of opioid receptors on NE neurons, researchers have been curious if opioid exposure and withdrawal modulates plasticity in noradrenergic circuits. As mentioned above, there is evidence that chronic opioid exposure (morphine pellet implantation) increases glutamatergic synaptic transmission onto LC NE neurons as compared to mice impanted with placebo pellets, suggesting enhancement of synaptic plasticity (Torrecilla et al., 2008). Due to the importance of noradrenergic projections to the BNST in mediating various opioid-related behaviors (see above), we (McElligott and colleagues) were interested in probing if noradrenergic projections to the BNST are themselves modified by opioid withdrawal (McElligott et al., 2013). Using fast-scan cyclic voltammetry, we demonstrated that in Sprague-Dawley rats (an inbred-outbred strain), morphine withdrawal augments activity in noradrenergic synapses, by reducing the efficacy of the α2-AR autoreceptor for NE, and reducing the efficiency of NET to clear NE from the synapse. Interestingly, we found that morphine withdrawal does not potentiate noradrenergic synapses of a different strain of rat, the Lewis rat. This was significant for two reasons: (1) Lewis rats are a genetic model of stress disorders and show elevated self-administration of opioids (George and Goldberg, 1989; Picetti et al., 2012); and, (2) at baseline, naïve Lewis rats had reduced α2-AR autoreceptor and NET function as compared to naïve Sprague-Dawley rats, akin to the reduction observed in morphine-dependent Sprague-Dawley rats. Using Sprauge-Dawley rats, the Akil lab investigated the potential role of the noradrenergic system in the BNST in individual differences in responsivity to opioid withdrawal (Cecchi et al., 2007). They demonstrated that Sprague-Dawley rats that exhibit high responsivity to novel environments exhibit more profound somatic signs of opioid withdrawal and exhibit higher levels of β1-ARs at baseline. Selective blockade of β1-ARs in the BNST reduces both the elevated opioid withdrawal symptoms and opioid withdrawal-induced CPA observed in high novelty-responding rats. These experiments show that individual and genetic differences in noradrenergic signaling in the BNST may account for differences in opioid withdrawal outcomes and associated learned behaviors.

Norepinephrine and alcohol

From a clinical perspective, there is strong rationale to investigate a role for noradrenergic systems in alcohol use disorder (AUD). Different studies have reported divergent results related to DBH activity level and the association with alcohol-related behaviors. Examining college students, La Grange et al. found that there was a positive correlation between DBH activity (as measured with the conversion of tyramine to octopamine) and alcohol consumption in female college students, but not males (La Grange et al., 1995), suggesting potential sex differences in the interaction of NE dynamics and alcohol behaviors. DBH activity is reduced, however, in plasma of abstinent people with AUD diagnosises (Köhnke et al., 2002), and the presence of the DBH*444A polymorphism, which reduces DBH activity, is significantly elevated in patients with AUD (Köhnke et al., 2006) while the DBH*1021C→T allele which accounts for the 35% to 52% of the genetic variation in multiple ethnic groups (Zabetian et al., 2001) does not (Köhnke et al., 2002). In a clinical study, blockade of α2-ARs, which potentiates central NE release (Herr et al., 2012), led to alterations in alcohol metabolism (reduction in blood-alcohol content over time), decreases in the stimulating properties of alcohol, and enhancement of the sedative properties of alcohol (McDougle et al., 1995), demonstrating that noradrenergic signaling can alter multiple effects of alcohol, both peripherally and centrally (Haass-Koffler et al., 2018).

Multiple alcohol exposure paradigms engage noradrenergic circuitry. Intraperitoneal injection of ethanol enhances the co-expression of cFos protein (a proxy for neuronal activity) and

TH in both LC and A2/NTS of male Long-Evans rats (Thiele et al., 2000). Further, binge-like ethanol consumption (>80 mg dL^{-1}) significantly increases cFos/TH co-expression in the LC and A2/NTS of male C57BL6/J mice, whereas sub-binge ethanol consumption does not (Burnham and Thiele, 2017). Moreover, acute alcohol exposure increases NE release, presumably from both the DNAB (measured in the medial prefrontal cortex) and the VNAB (measured in the basal forebrain), but one week of alcohol self-administration attenuates NE release (relative to baseline) in the medial prefrontal cortex of male Long-Evans rats (Jaime et al., 2020). In another experiment, however, acute alcohol exposure increased NE levels in the nucleus accumbens only in animals that had previously experienced social isolation stress (Karkhanis et al., 2014). Discrepancies between these studies may have to do with the route of alcohol administration (i.v. vs. i.p.) and/or the different brain regions examined, which may receive different degrees of NE innervation.

Manipulating NE levels

NE signaling plays a strong role in several alcohol-related behaviors. To study how NE signaling regulates alcohol-related behaviors, the Palmiter lab used DBH knockout mice that lack norepinephrine and compared them to their haplo-sufficient controls (animals that carry one copy of the DBH gene) (Weinshenker et al., 2000). Weinshenker and colleagues found that DBH knockout mice demonstrated enhanced ethanol-induced hypothermia, which slowed ethanol metabolism at room temperature. This temperature-dependent effect, however, could not account for the enhanced effect of alcohol sedation observed in the DBH knockout mice, which was rescued by restoring central NE levels. Furthermore, when mice were allowed to freely consume alcohol or water in a two bottle choice assay, DBH knockout animals consumed less alcohol and exhibited reduced preference for the alcohol bottle, while their consumption of sucrose and quinine solutions remained unchanged. These data strongly support the notion that NE, especially centrally acting NE, plays a broad role in mediating the behavioral effects of alcohol, including the voluntary consumption and preference for alcohol. In contrast to these studies, acute blockade of NET with systemic desipramine, also enhances the sedative properties of ethanol, and this effect is potentiated or attenuated by activating or inhibiting the α2-AR respectively, and is occluded by prior stress experience (Boyce-Rustay et al., 2008). The discrepancy in these studies could be partially attributed to the concept that catecholamines are thought to regulate behavior in a "U" type fashion (as described earlier in the chapter), where too much or too little signaling may lead to aberrant behavioral output.

Interestingly, a recent study using electrochemical detection methods (FSCV) demonstrated that NE release in the central nucleus of the amygdala (CeA) is not modulated by acute alcohol application to the CeA, but ex vivo NE release is reduced by CRF (Hedges et al., 2020), which is interesting because NE induces CRF release throughout the extended amygdala, including in the CeA (McElligott et al., 2010; Nobis et al., 2011).

Manipulating post-synaptic receptors

Because of the relationship between alcohol dependence and stress, researchers have investigated how altering adrenergic signaling can modulate alcohol-seeking behavior and alcohol consumption in alcohol-dependent rats. Walker and colleagues demonstrated that blockade of α1-ARs reduced alcohol self-administration in alcohol-dependent animals

(Walker et al., 2008). Similarly in a different drinking paradigm, the intermittent access model, α1-AR blockade reduces alcohol consumption and preference, and reduces anxiety-like behavior following ethanol drinking in rats (Skelly and Weiner, 2014). Similar reductions in anxiety-like behavior (this time measuring marble burying, considered a defensive behavior) are observed following α1-AR blockade in mice that have undergone alcohol exposure in the chronic intermittent ethanol and forced swim-stress model (den Hartog et al., 2020). In a genetic model of excessive alcohol consumption, the alcohol preferring P rat, α1-AR blockade reduces voluntary alcohol consumption (Rasmussen et al., 2009), and combination α1-AR blockade with opioid receptor blockade (naltrexone) further suppresses alcohol consumption behaviors, again suggesting significant cross-talk between endogenous opioid and adrenergic systems (Rasmussen et al., 2015). Additionally, there is clinical evidence that blockade of α1-ARs reduces alcohol consumption in humans with comorbid AUD and post-traumatic stress disorder (Simpson et al., 2015, 2018).

Beta adrenoceptors have also been investigated preclinically for potential therapeutic value in AUD. Gilpin and Koob showed that blocking central, but not peripheral β-ARs reduced alcohol self-administration at all doses tested in alcohol-dependent male Wistar rats (Gilpin and Koob, 2010). There is evidence that alcohol acts locally through β-AR receptor-mediated mechanisms to potentiate GABAergic signaling in the basolateral amygdala, a structure associated with learning both appetitive and aversive cues (Silberman et al., 2012). These data strongly suggest that α1-and β-AR blockers may have potential as pharmacotherapeutics for treating AUD in humans. Interestingly, the highest doses of both α1-and β-AR antagonists reduced consumption in rats not dependent on alcohol, further suggesting a role for the noradrenergic system in baseline alcohol reinforcement.

Norepinephrine and psychostimulants

Akin to the dopamine and serotonin transporters, NET is a substrate for psychostimulants. Psychostimulants, like cocaine and methylphenidate, physically block NET activity while amphetamines can cause reverse transport of catecholamines via NET. Additionally, cathinone substances that are in some cases more potent reinforcers than "traditional" psychostimulants, also have efficacy at blocking activity of all three of the aforementioned biogenic monoamine transporters (Gannon et al., 2018). In contrast to cocaine, which blocks DAT, NET, and SERT with similar efficacy, the cathinone substances more efficaciously block DAT activity.

Manipulating NE levels

As with opioids and alcohol, DBH knockout mice have been examined in the context of psychostimulants (Schank et al., 2006; Weinshenker et al., 2002). Intriguingly, DBH knockout mice are super-sensitive to the locomotor stimulating effects and stereotypy-inducing effects of amphetamines and cocaine. Paradoxically, DBH knockout mice exhibit reduced dopamine release in the nucleus accumbens, dorsal striatum, and prefrontal cortex in response to amphetamine administration, as compared to littermate controls. These studies also showed alterations in dopamine receptor binding (suggesting differential expression) in striatum may account for these effects. Thus, there are compensatory mechanisms that account for the lack of NE tone in DBH knockout mice, which may be developmental in nature.

When NE is specifically depleted from the medial prefrontal cortex (using a pharmacological method), male C57BL/6JIco mice do not exhibit amphetamine-induced CPP, but they do exhibit enhancement of amphetamine locomotor effects (Ventura et al., 2003). Furthermore, this study demonstrated that medial prefrontal cortical NE is critical for mediating elevations of dopamine levels in the nucleus accumbens after amphetamine administration. These data further suggest a tight link between noradrenergic and dopaminergic systems in regulating the behavioral response to psychostimulants.

Chronic NE depletion, as is the case with DBH knockout mice, may be different from acute manipulation of NE levels or signaling. Data suggest that NE signaling is unlikely to play a role in some aspects of cocaine reinforcement. Upon depletion of NE by the use of selective DBH inhibitors, rats maintain normal rates of cocaine self-administration (Schroeder et al., 2010). Inhibition of DBH, however, reduces the breakpoint for cocaine reinforcement in experiments where a progressive ratio schedule of reinforcement is used, and it prevents both stress-induced (footshock and yohimbine administration) and cocaine-primed reinstatement of cocaine-seeking behavior (Schroeder et al., 2013). Intriguingly, and similar to the DBH knockout mice discussed above, NET knockout mice showed enhanced locomotor behavior when challenged with either cocaine or amphetamine, which may be attributable to modulation of midbrain dopamine neuron function (Xu et al., 2000).

Manipulating post-synaptic receptors

There is strong evidence that α1-ARs, especially in the prefrontal cortex, play a role in mediating the psychomotor effects of psychostimulants (Blanc et al., 1994). As was described above with opioids, mice lacking α1b receptors (global α1b knock out mice) show reduced locomotor hyperactivity and behavioral sensitization responses to both amphetamine and cocaine, as well as reduced oral consumption of cocaine (Drouin et al., 2002). Similarly, as with opioids, pretreatment with a selective α1-AR agonist prevents α1b-AR knockout effects on the locomotor response to cocaine or amphetamine in mice, again suggesting that α1b-AR, which is highly expressed in the prefrontal cortex, is responsible mediating α1-AR effects on locomotor stimulating effects of psychostimulants. Further, α1b-AR knockout mice, when administered amphetamine, do not exhibit increased dopamine release in the nucleus accumbens (Auclair et al., 2002), akin to experiments where NE is depleted in the medial prefrontal cortex (see above).

Similar to what was described above for stress-induced reinstatement of opioid-seeking behavior, stressful experiences also reinstate cocaine-seeking behavior in animals, and a role for the noradrenergic system has been investigated in this behavior. Stimulating α2-ARs, known to decrease NE release, attenuated stress-induced reinstatement of cocaine-seeking behavior in rats, but does not alter cocaine-priming induced reinstatement of cocaine seeking in rats (Erb et al., 2000). As temporary inactivation of both the BNST and the CeA blocks stress-induced cocaine reinstatement behaviors (Shaham et al., 2000a), researchers were keen to identify if noradrenergic signaling within the extended amygdala plays a role in mediating these behaviors. To directly test this, researchers microinfused specific adrenergic drugs into extended amygdala sub-regions. Direct injection of β-AR antagonists into the BNST attenuated stress-induced reinstatement of cocaine seeking, while β-AR blockade in the CeA completely prevented stress-induced reinstatement of cocaine seeking (Leri et al., 2002). Interestingly, these manipulations did not alter reinstatement of cocaine seeking induced by a priming dose of cocaine, suggesting that noradrenergic signaling in the extended amygdala is critical for stress-induced, but not drug priming-induced relapse-like behaviors in rodents.

As demonstrated above, there appears to be a role for NE in priming-induced reinstatement of cocaine seeking, but it does not seem to be modulated by manipulation of adrenergic receptors in the extended amygdala. Stimulation of CNS α1-ARs, however, restores priming-induced reinstatement of cocaine seeking, and blockade of α1-ARs specifically in the mPFC, but not the VTA or NAc, prevents priming-induced reinstatement of cocaine seeking (Schmidt et al., 2017). In clinical studies from Rajita Sinha's lab, α2-AR stimulation reduces cue-induced craving, arousal and anxiety in persons abstinent from cocaine use (Fox et al., 2012). Additionally, individuals that received α2-AR agonist exhibit enhanced activity in the prefrontal cortex as compared to the placebo group. These data demonstrate that targeting adrenergic receptors may be a means for increasing prefrontal cortical function which may inhibit cocaine relapse.

Like with alcohol, there is evidence that the endogenous opioid system influences psychostimulant-related behaviors via the noradrenergic system. Activation of the κ-OR system is associated with stress and dysphoric behavior (Crowley and Kash, 2015). Systemic injection of a κ-OR agonist drives reinstatement of a cocaine-induced CPP, and this effect is attenuated by prior injection of a κ-OR blocker into the A6/LC. Similarly, mice lacking the κ-OR do not show κ-OR-mediated reinstatement of cocaine CPP, but viral restoration of κ-OR in the LC rescues this reinstatement behavior (Al-Hasani et al., 2013).

Norepinephrine and other substances of abuse

Nicotine

Norepinephrine release (as measured by turnover assays) in the periphery—including the heart and brown adipose tissue—is enhanced by nicotine (Yoshida et al., 1994). In rats, both acute and chronic subcutaneous injection of nicotine increases both NE transmitter and metabolite levels in cortical and striatal regions, but not the ventral tegmental area (VTA) (Liang et al., 2008; Singer et al., 2004), and these increases may be attenuated by an analog of the neuropeptide neurotensin (Liang et al., 2008). Direct infusion of low-dose nicotine into multiple brain regions increases NE release, but decreases NE release in other areas (e.g., VTA) (Shearman et al., 2005). Cigarettes, and the non-nicotine components therein, also inhibit the function of monoamine oxidase, which, in combination with nicotine, increases extracellular concentrations of NE (Lewis et al., 2007). Thus, nicotine may increase NE release via multiple mechanisms. Agonists for nicotinic acetylcholine receptors produce NE release in hippocampal slices and in the prefrontal cortex (Barik and Wonnacott, 2006; Rao et al., 2003). Furthermore, intravenous nicotine, but not focal application of nicotine on the brain slice, increases the firing rate of LC neurons (Svensson and Engberg, 1980), suggesting an indirect action of nicotine on these cells. NE also plays a role in regulating cues associated with nicotine, as well as nicotine withdrawal and consumption behaviors. NET transporter blockers alleviate nicotine withdrawal effects and reduce self-administration in rat models (Paterson et al., 2008). Furthermore, α_2-AR activation reduces nicotine craving in response to both stress and cued imagery in humans (Fox et al., 2012).

Cannabinoids

There is striking evidence that endocannabinoid (eCB) systems engage noradrenergic circuitry (Carvalho and Van Bockstaele, 2012). The exogenous cannabinoid Δ9-tetrahydrocannabinol (THC), the active component of marijuana, activates reward circuitry and induces dopamine release in the NAc of male Sprague-Dawley CAMM rats, but systemic stimulation of α_2-ARs (intraperitoneal clonidine) completely blocks this effect (Jentsch et al., 1998). In addition, THC administration increases NE turnover ratios in the prefrontal cortex (Jentsch et al., 1997), and a synthetic CB1 agonist dose-dependently increases NE release in the prefrontal cortex as measured by microdialysis (Oropeza et al., 2005). Early autoradiography and in situ hybridization studies demonstrated cannabinoid receptor 1 (CB1) binding in both the LC/A6 and NTS/A2 (Herkenham et al., 1991; Mailleux and Vanderhaeghen, 1992), but it is important to remember that these techniques are not cell type-specific. Immunohistochemical and electron microscopy have determined that CB1 receptors are located both somatodendritically and on axon terminals of LC neurons that were co-stained with antibodies for tyrosine hydroxylase (Scavone et al., 2010). Furthermore, CB1 agonists increase cFos labeling in tyrosine hydroxylase (TH)-positive LC neurons, suggesting that these cells are indeed activated by cannabinoids (Patel and Hillard, 2003).

The activity of NE neurons may be modulated by descending inputs from excitatory and inhibitory afferents. This concept is particularly important when taken into context with electrophysiological studies. Intravenous administration of synthetic cannabinoid agonists elevate the firing rate of LC neurons in vivo, an effect that is blocked by cannabinoid receptor antagonism. Direct infusion into the LC, intracerebroventricular injections, and application of cannabinoid receptor agonists to LC slices, however, fail to change the spontaneous firing rate of LC neurons (Mendiguren and Pineda, 2006) suggesting that cannabinoid receptor-induced enhancement of LC firing rates is due to complex circuit actions (but see Muntoni et al., 2006). Also, application of THC to NTS/A2 brain slices elevates the spontaneous firing rate of putative NE neurons (Himmi et al., 1996, 1998).

There is also evidence for differential distribution of CB1 receptors on subsets of NE terminals. Immunohistochemical data suggest that CB1 receptors are more densely expressed on LC/A6 terminals in the prefrontal cortex than NTS/A2 terminals in the nucleus accumbens (Carvalho et al., 2010). These differences in distribution of CB1 receptors may inform how NE levels are modulated in these brain regions during cannabis use, but it is important to remember that there are many CB receptors in these brain regions on other terminals that may influence NE release via circuit effects.

Noradrenergic circuitry also influences endocannabinoid system function. For example, activation of postsynaptic α_2-ARs in the hypothalamus leads to endocannabinioid synthesis and subsequent eCB-mediated inhibition of glutamate release (Kuzmiski et al., 2009).

Additionally, there is some evidence for complex interactions between β-ARs and CB1 receptors using bioluminescence resonance engery transfer (BRET) and cell signaling to show physical interactions between these receptor classes (Hudson et al., 2010).

Norepinephrine, natural rewards/psychosocial reward

Feeding behavior

The relationship between brain NE systems and feeding behavior is well established and is tightly linked with the noradrenergic system's influence over sleep behavior. NE release has a diurnal rhythm, and within the PVN, peak NE release (measured by microdialysis) occurs 1 h prior to the onset of the dark (i.e., active) phase, and is accompanied by a marked increase in feeding during the first hour of the dark phase in rodents (Morien et al., 1995). Injection of NE directly into the hypothalamus/PVN produces marked increases in consummatory behaviors (eating and drinking) (Grossman, 1960; Leibowitz, 1978). Interestingly the increase in feeding behaviors appears to be mediated by stimulation of α_2-ARs and has demonstratable interactions with circulating glucose and corticosterone levels (Jhanwar-Uniyal et al., 1988; Leibowitz, 1988; Roland et al., 1986). Furthermore, radioligand binding studies have demonstrated that α_2-AR expression in the PVN is also diurnal and that the times of highest expression levels match the times when peak feeding responses occur (Jhanwar-Uniyal et al., 1986). This is also interesting because (as mentioned above) stimulation of hypothalamic α_2-ARs promotes the release of endocannabinoids that also enhance food consumption (Koch et al., 2015).

Rats that have been trained to associate the presentation of a lever with a food reward (a type of Pavlovian conditioning) can engage with the conditioned stimulus in different ways. It is thought that animals that show enhanced engagement with the lever have enhanced motivational and emotional association with the cue that predicts the availability of the food and are termed "sign-trackers" (Robinson and Flagel, 2009) and animals that exhibit this type of behavior are thought to attribute the cue with enhanced value or "incentive salience" which has implications for substance use disorders (Flagel et al., 2009). Systemic blockade of β-ARs reduces "sign-tracking" behaviors in rats and decreases neuronal activity in brain regions associated with "motivated behaviors" including multiple striatal and amygdalar brain regions (Cogan et al., 2019).

Exercise

Access to a wheel for running (24 h) or limited treadmill running increases NE levels in the pons/medula and spinal cord, and increases NE metabolites in the hippocampus and prefrontal cortex as compared to a sedentary control group, suggesting that exercise upregulates NE availability and signaling in multiple brain structures (Dunn et al., 1996). Furthermore, in a microdialysis experiment, treadmill running elevated the release of NE in the prefrontal cortex compared to baseline levels (Pagliari and Peyrin, 1995). Chronic exercise increases NE levels in the LC and protects against stress-induced (footshock) NE depletion, and exercise reduces anxiety-like behaviors and enhances the production of galanin in the LC/A6 of rats (Sciolino et al., 2012). Specific deletion of galanin from NE neurons shifts coping strategies in various aversive assays to enhance active coping mechanisms (i.e., enhanced digging/burying behavior) in rats (Tillage et al., 2020). Finally, in humans, plasma NE levels rise during increases in strenuous exercise, and increase to a greater extent in persons who undergo endurance training prior to the sample collection (Greiwe et al., 1999).

Gambling behavior

Studies in clinical populations have implicated the noradrenergic system in gambling behavior and monetary reward (Zakeri and Potenza, 2012). In a human neuroimaging study using positron emission tomography (PET) with a ligand that binds to NET, researchers found that persons with decreased NET expression in their thalamus exhibited higher aversive responses to monetary loss (Takahashi et al., 2013). Additionally, persons diagnosed as pathological gamblers exhibit higher levels of NE metabolite in the cerebrospinal fluid (CSF), suggesting higher NE turnover in the CNS, in addition to higher quantities of NE in the urine, as compared to healthy controls (Roy et al., 1988). The authors of that study suggested that increased noradrenergic tone in persons diagnosed with pathological gambling disorder may promote enhanced sensation-seeking behaviors in those individuals. Another study reported that behavioral measures of extroverted personality traits are positively correlated with CNS NE metabolite levels in CSF, plasma, and urine, further suggesting a possible link between traits associated with gambling behavior and the noradrenergic system (Roy et al., 1989). Plasma NE levels also increase in response to winning in a gambling-like game and show sustained elevation for up to 30 min after a winning streak (Shinohara et al., 1999). While plasma NE increases in both pathological gamblers and controls during gambling, plasma NE levels are significantly higher during gambling in those that qualify as "problem gamblers" (Meyer et al., 2004). While it is difficult to parse plasma NE from central noradrenergic effects in these studies, the association of healthy recreational gambling with significantly elevated arousal responses strongly suggests that central noradrenergic signaling may contribute to the effects reported above (Miller and Gordh, 2021).

Social behavior

NE is implicated in the development of social bonds between dams and pups (Thomas and Palmiter, 1997). One of the earliest studies with the DBH knockout mouse demonstrated that the surge in NE that immediately precedes parturition is critical for the establishment for the development of social bonds between the dam and her pups. Due to this deficit, the dams reduce their caretaking behaviors (e.g. gathering of the pups in the nest), and these behavioral deficits result in large decreases in survival rates in pups (as low as a 20% survival rate). If DBH knockout pups are cross fostered with wild-type dams, or if wild-type pups who have already nursed on their wild-type dam are cross fostered with DBH knockout dams, survival rates normalized. Additionally, virgin DBH knockout females exhibit deficits in pup retrieval assays. Recent studies by the Shea laboratory (Dvorkin and Shea, 2022) have demonstrated a tight temporal coupling between the phasic activity of LC neurons (measured as a change in calcium dynamics with fiber photometry and with in vivo electrophysiology) and pup retrieval, suggesting that the LC may promote goal-directed behavior in this task. Additionally, Dvorkin and Shea found that tonic LC activity is altered during other maternal behaviors such as pup grooming and nest building. Other evidence has shown that in particular β-AR activation promotes the consolidation of maternal behaviors (Moffat et al., 1993). Thus it appears that differential LC activity shapes multiple pup/dam social behaviors. As has been commented on earlier, release of different quantities of NE due to either phasic bursts or changes in tonic firing may engage different adrenergic receptors (due to their different affinities for NE) and different circuits due to their receptor expression densities. Similarly, there is substantial evidence that NE plays an important role in memory formation following mating behavior. NE levels increase in the accessory olfactory bulb in female mice for at least 4 h following a mating episode (Brennan et al., 1995). Furthermore, blockade of α-ARs in the same brain region prevents the learned association with a male mating partner (Kaba and Keverne, 1988). Additional studies in these domains will certainly be highly informative as to the role that NE plays in socially motivated behaviors, and how these may be shaped by drugs.

Conclusions

The studies discussed in this chapter highlight the important role that the noradrenergic system plays with regard to misused drugs as well as natural and naturalistic rewards. Overlaid on these topics is the significant influence that NE has over learning mechanisms (especially "emotional learning") and the role of NE in stress behaviors. The noradrenergic system is robustly affected by drugs, and noradrenergic signaling influences both appetitive and aversive aspects of drug use and misuse. Pharmacological targeting of the noradrenergic system and NE receptors have strong therapeutic potential for the treatment of substance use disorders. Finally, studies that focus on the role of specific NE circuits on functional outcomes related to addiction are in the early stages, but they are ongoing and have the potential to significantly change the direction of the field in coming years.

References

Al-Hasani, R., McCall, J.G., Foshage, A.M., Bruchas, M.R., 2013. Locus coeruleus kappa-opioid receptors modulate reinstatement of cocaine place preference through a noradrenergic mechanism. Off. Publ. Am. Coll. Neuropsychopharmacol. 38, 2484–2497. https://doi.org/10.1038/npp.2013.151.

Aroca, P., Lorente-Cánovas, B., Mateos, F.R., Puelles, L., 2006. Locus coeruleus neurons originate in alar rhombomere 1 and migrate into the basal plate: studies in chick and mouse embryos. J. Comp. Neurol. 496, 802–818. https://doi.org/10.1002/cne.20957.

Auclair, A., Cotecchia, S., Glowinski, J., Tassin, J.-P., 2002. D-amphetamine fails to increase extracellular dopamine levels in mice lacking alpha 1b-adrenergic receptors: relationship between functional and nonfunctional dopamine release. Off. J. Soc. Neurosci. 22, 9150–9154.

Baldi, E., Bucherelli, C., 2005. The inverted "u-shaped" dose-effect relationships in learning and memory: modulation of arousal and consolidation. Nonlinearity. Biol. Toxicol. Med. 3, 9–21. https://doi.org/10.2201/nonlin.003.01.002.

Banihashemi, L., Rinaman, L., 2006. Noradrenergic inputs to the bed nucleus of the stria terminalis and paraventricular nucleus of the hypothalamus underlie hypothalamic-pituitary-adrenal axis but not hypophagic or conditioned avoidance responses to systemic yohimbine. Off. J. Soc. Neurosci. 26, 11442–11453. https://doi.org/10.1523/JNEUROSCI.3561-06.2006.

Barik, J., Wonnacott, S., 2006. Indirect modulation by alpha7 nicotinic acetylcholine receptors of noradrenaline release in rat hippocampal slices: interaction with glutamate and GABA systems and effect of nicotine withdrawal. Mol. Pharmacol. 69, 618–628. https://doi.org/10.1124/mol.105.018184.

Berridge, K.C., Robinson, T.E., 2016. Liking, wanting, and the incentive-sensitization theory of addiction. Am. Psychol. 71, 670–679. https://doi.org/10.1037/amp0000059.

Blanc, G., Trovero, F., Vezina, P., Hervé, D., Godeheu, A.M., Glowinski, J., Tassin, J.P., 1994. Blockade of prefronto-cortical alpha 1-adrenergic receptors prevents locomotor hyperactivity induced by subcortical D-amphetamine injection. Eur. J. Neurosci. 6, 293–298. https://doi.org/10.1111/j.1460-9568.1994.tb00272.x.

Borodovitsyna, O., Duffy, B.C., Pickering, A.E., Chandler, D.J., 2020. Anatomically and functionally distinct locus coeruleus efferents mediate opposing effects on anxiety-like behavior. Neurobiol. Stress. 13, 100284. https://doi.org/10.1016/j.ynstr.2020.100284.

Boyce-Rustay, J.M., Palachick, B., Hefner, K., Chen, Y.-C., Karlsson, R.-M., Millstein, R.A., Harvey-White, J., Holmes, A., 2008. Desipramine potentiation of the acute depressant effects of ethanol: modulation by alpha2-adrenoreceptors and stress. Neuropharmacology 55, 803–811. https://doi.org/10.1016/j.neuropharm.2008.06.032.

Brennan, P.A., Kendrick, K.M., Keverne, E.B., 1995. Neurotransmitter release in the accessory olfactory bulb during and after the formation of an olfactory memory in mice. Neuroscience 69, 1075–1086. https://doi.org/10.1016/0306-4522(95)00309-7.

Breton-Provencher, V., Drummond, G.T., Feng, J., Li, Y., Sur, M., 2022. Spatiotemporal dynamics of noradrenaline during learned behaviour. Nature. https://doi.org/10.1038/s41586-022-04782-2.

Breton-Provencher, V., Sur, M., 2019. Active control of arousal by a locus coeruleus GABAergic circuit. Nat. Neurosci. 22, 218–228. https://doi.org/10.1038/s41593-018-0305-z.

Buijs, R.M., Van Eden, C.G., 2000. The integration of stress by the hypothalamus, amygdala and prefrontal cortex: balance between the autonomic nervous system and the neuroendocrine system. Prog. Brain Res. 126, 117–132. https://doi.org/10.1016/S0079-6123(00)26011-1.

Burnham, N.W., Thiele, T.E., 2017. Voluntary binge-like ethanol consumption site-specifically increases c-fos immunoexpression in male C57BL6/J mice. Neuroscience 367, 159–168. https://doi.org/10.1016/j.neuroscience.2017.10.027.

Carvalho, A.F., Mackie, K., Van Bockstaele, E.J., 2010. Cannabinoid modulation of limbic forebrain noradrenergic circuitry. Eur. J. Neurosci. 31, 286–301. https://doi.org/10.1111/j.1460-9568.2009.07054.x.

Carvalho, A.F., Van Bockstaele, E.J., 2012. Cannabinoid modulation of noradrenergic circuits: implications for psychiatric disorders. Prog. Neuro-Psychopharmacol. Biol. Psychiatry 38, 59–67. https://doi.org/10.1016/j.pnpbp.2012.01.008.

Cecchi, M., Capriles, N., Watson, S.J., Akil, H., 2007. Beta1 adrenergic receptors in the bed nucleus of stria terminalis mediate differential responses to opiate withdrawal. Off. Publ. Am. Coll. Neuropsychopharmacol. 32, 589–599. https://doi.org/10.1038/sj.npp.1301140.

Chandler, D.J., Gao, W.-J., Waterhouse, B.D., 2014. Heterogeneous organization of the locus coeruleus projections to prefrontal and motor cortices. Proc. Natl. Acad. Sci. U.S.A. 111, 6816–6821. https://doi.org/10.1073/pnas.1320827111.

Chen, Y.-W., Das, M., Oyarzabal, E.A., Cheng, Q., Plummer, N.W., Smith, K.G., Jones, G.K., Malawsky, D., Yakel, J.L., Shih, Y.-Y.I., Jensen, P., 2019. Genetic identification of a population of noradrenergic neurons implicated in attenuation of stress-related responses. Mol. Psychiatr. 24, 710–725. https://doi.org/10.1038/s41380-018-0245-8.

Cogan, E.S., Shapses, M.A., Robinson, T.E., Tronson, N.C., 2019. Disrupting reconsolidation: memory erasure or blunting of emotional/motivational value? Off. Publ. Am. Coll. Neuropsychopharmacol. 44, 399–407. https://doi.org/10.1038/s41386-018-0082-0.

Crestani, C.C., Alves, F.H., Gomes, F.V., Resstel, L.B., Correa, F.M., Herman, J.P., 2013. Mechanisms in the bed nucleus of the stria terminalis involved in control of autonomic and neuroendocrine functions: a review. Curr. Neuropharmacol. 11, 141–159. https://doi.org/10.2174/1570159X11311020002.

Crowley, N.A., Kash, T.L., 2015. Kappa opioid receptor signaling in the brain: circuitry and implications for treatment. Prog. Neuro-Psychopharmacol. Biol. Psychiatry. 62, 51–60. https://doi.org/10.1016/j.pnpbp.2015.01.001.

Curtis, A.L., Leiser, S.C., Snyder, K., Valentino, R.J., 2012. Predator stress engages corticotropin-releasing factor and opioid systems to alter the operating mode of locus coeruleus norepinephrine neurons. Neuropharmacology 62, 1737–1745. https://doi.org/10.1016/j.neuropharm.2011.11.020.

Davoudi, M., Azizi, H., Mirnajafi-Zadeh, J., Semnanian, S., 2019. Decrease of inhibitory synaptic currents of locus coeruleus neurons via orexin type 1 receptors in the context of naloxone-induced morphine withdrawal. J. Physiol. Sci. JPS 69, 281–293. https://doi.org/10.1007/s12576-018-0645-1.

Davoudi, M., Azizi, H., Mirnajafi-Zadeh, J., Semnanian, S., 2016. The blockade of GABAA receptors attenuates the inhibitory effect of orexin type 1 receptors antagonist on morphine withdrawal syndrome in rats. Neurosci. Lett. 617, 201–206. https://doi.org/10.1016/j.neulet.2016.02.022.

Delfs, J.M., Zhu, Y., Druhan, J.P., Aston-Jones, G., 2000. Noradrenaline in the ventral forebrain is critical for opiate withdrawal-induced aversion. Nature 403, 430–434. https://doi.org/10.1038/35000212.

den Hartog, C.R., Blandino, K.L., Nash, M.L., Sjogren, E.R., Grampetro, M.A., Moorman, D.E., Vazey, E.M., 2020. Noradrenergic tone mediates marble burying behavior after chronic stress and ethanol. Psychopharmacology (Berl.) 237, 3021–3031. https://doi.org/10.1007/s00213-020-05589-7.

Drouin, C., Darracq, L., Trovero, F., Blanc, G., Glowinski, J., Cotecchia, S., Tassin, J.-P., 2002. Alpha1b-adrenergic receptors control locomotor and rewarding effects of psychostimulants and opiates. Off. J. Soc. Neurosci. 22, 2873–2884. https://doi.org/10.1523/JNEUROSCI.22-07-02873.200.

Dunkley, P.R., Bobrovskaya, L., Graham, M.E., von Nagy-Felsobuki, E.I., Dickson, P.W., 2004. Tyrosine hydroxylase phosphorylation: regulation and consequences. J. Neurochem. 91, 1025–1043. https://doi.org/10.1111/j.1471-4159.2004.02797.x.

Dunn, A.L., Reigle, T.G., Youngstedt, S.D., Armstrong, R.B., Dishman, R.K., 1996. Brain norepinephrine and metabolites after treadmill training and wheel running in rats. Med. Sci. Sports Exerc. 28, 204–209. https://doi.org/10.1097/00005768-199602000-00008.

Dvorkin, R., Shea, S.D., 2022. Precise and pervasive phasic bursting in locus coeruleus during maternal behavior in mice. J. Neurosci. Off. J. Soc. Neurosci. 42, 2986–2999. https://doi.org/10.1523/JNEUROSCI.0938-21.2022.

Enman, N.M., Reyes, B.A.S., Shi, Y., Valentino, R.J., Van Bockstaele, E.J., 2019. Sex differences in morphine-induced trafficking of mu-opioid and corticotropin-releasing factor receptors in locus coeruleus neurons. Brain Res. 1706, 75–85. https://doi.org/10.1016/j.brainres.2018.11.001.

Erb, S., Hitchcott, P.K., Rajabi, H., Mueller, D., Shaham, Y., Stewart, J., 2000. Alpha-2 adrenergic receptor agonists block stress-induced reinstatement of cocaine seeking. Off. Publ. Am. Coll. Neuropsychopharmacol. 23, 138–150. https://doi.org/10.1016/S0893-133X(99)00158-X.

Erickson, J.D., Schafer, M.K., Bonner, T.I., Eiden, L.E., Weihe, E., 1996. Distinct pharmacological properties and distribution in neurons and endocrine cells of two isoforms of the human vesicular monoamine transporter. Proc. Natl. Acad. Sci. U.S.A. 93, 5166–5171. https://doi.org/10.1073/pnas.93.10.5166.

Faravelli, C., Lo Sauro, C., Lelli, L., Pietrini, F., Lazzeretti, L., Godini, L., Benni, L., Fioravanti, G., Talamba, G.A., Castellini, G., Ricca, V., 2012. The role of life events and HPA axis in anxiety disorders: a review. Curr. Pharmaceut. Des. 18, 5663–5674. https://doi.org/10.2174/138161212803530907.

Feng, J., Zhang, C., Lischinsky, J.E., Jing, M., Zhou, J., Wang, H., Zhang, Y., Dong, A., Wu, Z., Wu, H., Chen, W., Zhang, P., Zou, J., Hires, S.A., Zhu, J.J., Cui, G., Lin, D., Du, J., Li, Y., 2019. A genetically encoded fluorescent sensor for rapid and specific in vivo detection of norepinephrine. Neuron 102. https://doi.org/10.1016/j.neuron.2019.02.037, 745-761.e8.

Fisher, J.P., Young, C.N., Fadel, P.J., 2009. Central sympathetic overactivity: maladies and mechanisms. Auton. Neurosci. Basic Clin. 148, 5–15. https://doi.org/10.1016/j.autneu.2009.02.003.

Flagel, S.B., Akil, H., Robinson, T.E., 2009. Individual differences in the attribution of incentive salience to reward-related cues: implications for addiction. Neuropharmacology 56 (Suppl. 1), 139–148. https://doi.org/10.1016/j.neuropharm.2008.06.027.

Fox, H.C., Seo, D., Tuit, K., Hansen, J., Kimmerling, A., Morgan, P.T., Sinha, R., 2012. Guanfacine effects on stress, drug craving and prefrontal activation in cocaine dependent individuals: preliminary findings. J. Psychopharmacol. Oxf. Engl. 26, 958–972. https://doi.org/10.1177/0269881111430746.

Fox, M.E., Rodeberg, N.T., Wightman, R.M., 2017. Reciprocal catecholamine changes during opiate exposure and withdrawal. Off. Publ. Am. Coll. Neuropsychopharmacol. 42, 671–681. https://doi.org/10.1038/npp.2016.135.

Fronk, G.E., Sant'Ana, S.J., Kaye, J.T., Curtin, J.J., 2020. Stress allostasis in substance use disorders: promise, progress, and emerging priorities in clinical research. Annu. Rev. Clin. Psychol. 16, 401–430. https://doi.org/10.1146/annurev-clinpsy-102419-125016.

Funada, M., Hara, C., Wada, K., 2001. Involvement of corticotropin-releasing factor receptor subtype 1 in morphine withdrawal regulation of the brain noradrenergic system. Eur. J. Pharmacol. 430, 277–281. https://doi.org/10.1016/s0014-2999(01)01402-9.

Galaz-Montoya, M., Wright, S.J., Rodriguez, G.J., Lichtarge, O., Wensel, T.G., 2017. β2-Adrenergic receptor activation mobilizes intracellular calcium via a non-canonical cAMP-independent signaling pathway. J. Biol. Chem. 292, 9967–9974. https://doi.org/10.1074/jbc.M117.787119.

Gannon, B.M., Baumann, M.H., Walther, D., Jimenez-Morigosa, C., Sulima, A., Rice, K.C., Collins, G.T., 2018. The abuse-related effects of pyrrolidine-containing cathinones are related to their potency and selectivity to inhibit the dopamine transporter. Off. Publ. Am. Coll. Neuropsychopharmacol. 43, 2399–2407. https://doi.org/10.1038/s41386-018-0209-3.

George, F.R., Goldberg, S.R., 1989. Genetic approaches to the analysis of addiction processes. Trends Pharmacol. Sci. 10, 78–83. https://doi.org/10.1016/0165-6147(89)90083-7.

Ghaemi-Jandabi, M., Azizi, H., Ahmadi-Soleimani, S.M., Semnanian, S., 2017. Intracoerulear microinjection of orexin-A induces morphine withdrawal-like signs in rats. Brain Res. Bull. 130, 107–111. https://doi.org/10.1016/j.brainresbull.2017.01.010.

Gilpin, N.W., Koob, G.F., 2010. Effects of β-adrenoceptor antagonists on alcohol drinking by alcohol-dependent rats. Psychopharmacology (Berl.) 212, 431–439. https://doi.org/10.1007/s00213-010-1967-8.

Giovannitti, J.A., Thoms, S.M., Crawford, J.J., 2015. Alpha-2 adrenergic receptor agonists: a review of current clinical applications. Anesth. Prog. 62, 31–39. https://doi.org/10.2344/0003-3006-62.1.31.

Goldstein, D.S., 1987. Stress-induced activation of the sympathetic nervous system. Baillieres Clin. Endocrinol. Metab. 1, 253–278. https://doi.org/10.1016/s0950-351x(87)80063-0.

Greiwe, J.S., Hickner, R.C., Shah, S.D., Cryer, P.E., Holloszy, J.O., 1999. Norepinephrine response to exercise at the same relative intensity before and after endurance exercise training. J. Appl. Physiol. Bethesda Md. 86, 531–535. https://doi.org/10.1152/jappl.1999.86.2.531.

Grossman, S.P., 1960. Eating or drinking elicited by direct adrenergic or cholinergic stimulation of hypothalamus. Science 132, 301–302. https://doi.org/10.1126/science.132.3422.301.

Guitart, X., Kogan, J.H., Berhow, M., Terwilliger, R.Z., Aghajanian, G.K., Nestler, E.J., 1993. Lewis and Fischer rat strains display differences in biochemical, electrophysiological and behavioral parameters: studies in the nucleus accumbens and locus coeruleus of drug naive and morphine-treated animals. Brain. Res. 611, 7–17. https://doi.org/10.1016/0006-8993(93)91770-s.

Haass-Koffler, C.L., Swift, R.M., Leggio, L., 2018. Noradrenergic targets for the treatment of alcohol use disorder. Psychopharmacology (Berl.) 235, 1625–1634. https://doi.org/10.1007/s00213-018-4843-6.

Han, M.-H., Bolaños, C.A., Green, T.A., Olson, V.G., Neve, R.L., Liu, R.-J., Aghajanian, G.K., Nestler, E.J., 2006. Role of cAMP response element-binding protein in the rat locus ceruleus: regulation of neuronal activity and opiate withdrawal behaviors. Off. J. Soc. Neurosci. 26, 4624–4629. https://doi.org/10.1523/JNEUROSCI.4701-05.2006.

Hannibal, K.E., Bishop, M.D., 2014. Chronic stress, cortisol dysfunction, and pain: a psychoneuroendocrine rationale for stress management in pain rehabilitation. Phys. Ther. 94, 1816–1825. https://doi.org/10.2522/ptj.20130597.

Harris, N.A., Isaac, A.T., Günther, A., Merkel, K., Melchior, J., Xu, M., Eguakun, E., Perez, R., Nabit, B.P., Flavin, S., Gilsbach, R., Shonesy, B., Hein, L., Abel, T., Baumann, A., Matthews, R., Centanni, S.W., Winder, D.G., 2018. Dorsal BNST α2a-adrenergic receptors produce HCN-dependent excitatory actions that initiate anxiogenic behaviors. Off. J. Soc. Neurosci. 38, 8922–8942. https://doi.org/10.1523/JNEUROSCI.0963-18.2018.

Hedges, D.M., Yorgason, J.T., Brundage, J.N., Wadsworth, H.A., Williams, B., Steffensen, S.C., Roberto, M., 2020. Corticotropin releasing factor, but not alcohol, modulates norepinephrine release in the rat central nucleus of the amygdala. Neuropharmacology 179, 108293. https://doi.org/10.1016/j.neuropharm.2020.108293.

Herkenham, M., Lynn, A.B., Johnson, M.R., Melvin, L.S., de Costa, B.R., Rice, K.C., 1991. Characterization and localization of cannabinoid receptors in rat brain: a quantitative in vitro autoradiographic study. Off. J. Soc. Neurosci. 11, 563–583.

Herman, J.P., Figueiredo, H., Mueller, N.K., Ulrich-Lai, Y., Ostrander, M.M., Choi, D.C., Cullinan, W.E., 2003. Central mechanisms of stress integration: hierarchical circuitry controlling hypothalamo-pituitary-adrenocortical responsiveness. Front. Neuroendocrinol. 24, 151–180. https://doi.org/10.1016/j.yfrne.2003.07.001.

Herman, J.P., McKlveen, J.M., Ghosal, S., Kopp, B., Wulsin, A., Makinson, R., Scheimann, J., Myers, B., 2016. Regulation of the hypothalamic-pituitary-adrenocortical stress response. Compr. Physiol. 6, 603–621. https://doi.org/10.1002/cphy.c150015.

Herr, N.R., Park, J., McElligott, Z.A., Belle, A.M., Carelli, R.M., Wightman, R.M., 2012. In vivo voltammetry monitoring of electrically evoked extracellular norepinephrine in subregions of the bed nucleus of the stria terminalis. J. Neurophysiol. 107, 1731–1737. https://doi.org/10.1152/jn.00620.2011.

Hickey, L., Li, Y., Fyson, S.J., Watson, T.C., Perrins, R., Hewinson, J., Teschemacher, A.G., Furue, H., Lumb, B.M., Pickering, A.E., 2014. Optoactivation of locus ceruleus neurons evokes bidirectional changes in thermal nociception in rats. Off. J. Soc. Neurosci. 34, 4148–4160. https://doi.org/10.1523/JNEUROSCI.4835-13.2014.

Himmi, T., Dallaporta, M., Perrin, J., Orsini, J.C., 1996. Neuronal responses to delta 9-tetrahydrocannabinol in the solitary tract nucleus. Eur. J. Pharmacol. 312, 273–279. https://doi.org/10.1016/0014-2999(96)00490-6.

Himmi, T., Perrin, J., El Ouazzani, T., Orsini, J.C., 1998. Neuronal responses to cannabinoid receptor ligands in the solitary tract nucleus. Eur. J. Pharmacol. 359, 49–54. https://doi.org/10.1016/s0014-2999(98)00630-x.

Hirschberg, S., Li, Y., Randall, A., Kremer, E.J., Pickering, A.E., 2017. Functional dichotomy in spinal- vs prefrontal-projecting locus coeruleus modules splits descending noradrenergic analgesia from ascending aversion and anxiety in rats. Elife 6, e29808. https://doi.org/10.7554/eLife.29808.

Hudson, B.D., Hébert, T.E., Kelly, M.E.M., 2010. Physical and functional interaction between CB1 cannabinoid receptors and beta2-adrenoceptors. Br. J. Pharmacol. 160, 627–642. https://doi.org/10.1111/j.1476-5381.2010.00681.x.

Jaime, S., Vena, A.A., Gonzales, R.A., 2020. Intravenous ethanol administration and operant self-administration alter extracellular norepinephrine concentration in the mesocorticolimbic systems of male long evans rats. Alcohol Clin. Exp. Res. 44, 1529–1539. https://doi.org/10.1111/acer.14397.

Jentsch, J.D., Andrusiak, E., Tran, A., Bowers, M.B., Roth, R.H., 1997. Delta 9-tetrahydrocannabinol increases prefrontal cortical catecholaminergic utilization and impairs spatial working memory in the rat: blockade of dopaminergic effects with HA966. Off. Publ. Am. Coll. Neuropsychopharmacol. 16, 426–432. https://doi.org/10.1016/S0893-133X(97)00018-3.

Jentsch, J.D., Wise, A., Katz, Z., Roth, R.H., 1998. Alpha-noradrenergic receptor modulation of the phencyclidine- and delta9-tetrahydrocannabinol-induced increases in dopamine utilization in rat prefrontal cortex. Synap. N. Y. N 28, 21–26. https://doi.org/10.1002/(SICI)1098-2396(199801)28:1<21::AID-SYN3>3.0.CO;2-E.

Jhanwar-Uniyal, M., Papamichael, M.J., Leibowitz, S.F., 1988. Glucose-dependent changes in alpha 2-noradrenergic receptors in hypothalamic nuclei. Physiol. Behav. 44, 611–617. https://doi.org/10.1016/0031-9384(88)90326-5.

Jhanwar-Uniyal, M., Roland, C.R., Leibowitz, S.F., 1986. Diurnal rhythm of alpha 2-noradrenergic receptors in the paraventricular nucleus and other brain areas: relation to circulating corticosterone and feeding behavior. Life Sci. 38, 473–482. https://doi.org/10.1016/0024-3205(86)90073-1.

Kaba, H., Keverne, E.B., 1988. The effect of microinfusions of drugs into the accessory olfactory bulb on the olfactory block to pregnancy. Neuroscience 25, 1007–1011. https://doi.org/10.1016/0306-4522(88)90053-x.

Karemaker, J.M., 2017. An introduction into autonomic nervous function. Physiol. Meas. 38, R89–R118. https://doi.org/10.1088/1361-6579/aa6782.

Karkhanis, A.N., Locke, J.L., McCool, B.A., Weiner, J.L., Jones, S.R., 2014. Social isolation rearing increases nucleus accumbens dopamine and norepinephrine responses to acute ethanol in adulthood. Alcohol Clin. Exp. Res. 38, 2770–2779. https://doi.org/10.1111/acer.12555.

Kempadoo, K.A., Mosharov, E.V., Choi, S.J., Sulzer, D., Kandel, E.R., 2016. Dopamine release from the locus coeruleus to the dorsal hippocampus promotes spatial learning and memory. Proc. Natl. Acad. Sci. U.S.A. 113, 14835–14840. https://doi.org/10.1073/pnas.1616515114.

Kies, P., Wichter, T., Schäfers, M., Paul, M., Schäfers, K.P., Eckardt, L., Stegger, L., Schulze-Bahr, E., Rimoldi, O., Breithardt, G., Schober, O., Camici, P.G., 2004. Abnormal myocardial presynaptic norepinephrine recycling in patients with Brugada syndrome. Circulation 110, 3017–3022. https://doi.org/10.1161/01.CIR.0000146920.35020.44.

Koch, M., Varela, L., Kim, J.G., Kim, J.D., Hernández-Nuño, F., Simonds, S.E., Castorena, C.M., Vianna, C.R., Elmquist, J.K., Morozov, Y.M., Rakic, P., Bechmann, I., Cowley, M.A., Szigeti-Buck, K., Dietrich, M.O., Gao, X.-B., Diano, S., Horvath, T.L., 2015. Hypothalamic POMC neurons promote cannabinoid-induced feeding. Nature 519, 45–50. https://doi.org/10.1038/nature14260.

Köhnke, M.D., Kolb, W., Köhnke, A.M., Lutz, U., Schick, S., Batra, A., 2006. DBH*444G/A polymorphism of the dopamine-beta-hydroxylase gene is associated with alcoholism but not with severe alcohol withdrawal symptoms. J. Neural. Transm. 113, 869–876. https://doi.org/10.1007/s00702-005-0365-6. Vienna Austria 1996.

Köhnke, M.D., Zabetian, C.P., Anderson, G.M., Kolb, W., Gaertner, I., Buchkremer, G., Vonthein, R., Schick, S., Lutz, U., Köhnke, A.M., Cubells, J.F., 2002. A genotype-controlled analysis of plasma dopamine beta-hydroxylase in healthy and alcoholic subjects: evidence for alcohol-related differences in noradrenergic function. Biol. Psychiatr. 52, 1151–1158. https://doi.org/10.1016/s0006-3223(02)01427-0.

Koob, G.F., 2003. Alcoholism: allostasis and beyond. Alcohol Clin. Exp. Res. 27, 232–243. https://doi.org/10.1097/01.ALC.0000057122.36127.C2.

Kuzmiski, J.B., Pittman, Q.J., Bains, J.S., 2009. Metaplasticity of hypothalamic synapses following in vivo challenge. Neuron 62, 839–849. https://doi.org/10.1016/j.neuron.2009.05.027.

La Grange, L., Jones, T.D., Erb, L., Reyes, E., 1995. Alcohol consumption: biochemical and personality correlates in a college student population. Addict. Behav. 20, 93–103. https://doi.org/10.1016/0306-4603(94)00049-5.

Lasheras, M.C., Laorden, M.L., Milanés, M.V., Núñez, C., 2015. Corticotropin-releasing factor 1 receptor mediates the activity of the reward system evoked by morphine-induced conditioned place preference. Neuropharmacology 95, 168–180. https://doi.org/10.1016/j.neuropharm.2014.12.021.

Lebow, M.A., Chen, A., 2016. Overshadowed by the amygdala: the bed nucleus of the stria terminalis emerges as key to psychiatric disorders. Mol. Psychiatr. 21, 450–463. https://doi.org/10.1038/mp.2016.1.

Leibowitz, S.F., 1988. Hypothalamic paraventricular nucleus: interaction between alpha 2-noradrenergic system and circulating hormones and nutrients in relation to energy balance. Neurosci. Biobehav. Rev. 12, 101–109. https://doi.org/10.1016/s0149-7634(88)80002-2.

Leibowitz, S.F., 1978. Paraventricular nucleus: a primary site mediating adrenergic stimulation of feeding and drinking. Pharmacol. Biochem. Behav. 8, 163–175. https://doi.org/10.1016/0091-3057(78)90333-7.

Leri, F., Flores, J., Rodaros, D., Stewart, J., 2002. Blockade of stress-induced but not cocaine-induced reinstatement by infusion of noradrenergic antagonists into the bed nucleus of the stria terminalis or the central nucleus of the amygdala. J. Neurosci. Off. J. Soc. Neurosci. 22, 5713–5718. https://doi.org/10.1523/JNEUROSCI.22-13-05713.2002.

Lewis, A., Miller, J.H., Lea, R.A., 2007. Monoamine oxidase and tobacco dependence. Neurotoxicology 28, 182–195. https://doi.org/10.1016/j.neuro.2006.05.019.

Li, Y., Hickey, L., Perrins, R., Werlen, E., Patel, A.A., Hirschberg, S., Jones, M.W., Salinas, S., Kremer, E.J., Pickering, A.E., 2016. Retrograde optogenetic characterization of the pontospinal module of the locus coeruleus with a canine adenoviral vector. Brain Res. 1641, 274–290. https://doi.org/10.1016/j.brainres.2016.02.023.

Liang, Y., Boules, M., Shaw, A.M., Williams, K., Fredrickson, P., Richelson, E., 2008. Effect of a novel neurotensin analog, NT69L, on nicotine-induced alterations in monoamine levels in rat brain. Brain Res. 1231, 6–15. https://doi.org/10.1016/j.brainres.2008.07.037.

Lustberg, D., Tillage, R.P., Bai, Y., Pruitt, M., Liles, L.C., Weinshenker, D., 2020. Noradrenergic circuits in the forebrain control affective responses to novelty. Psychopharmacology (Berl.) 237, 3337–3355. https://doi.org/10.1007/s00213-020-05615-8.

Mailleux, P., Vanderhaeghen, J.J., 1992. Distribution of neuronal cannabinoid receptor in the adult rat brain: a comparative receptor binding radioautography and in situ hybridization histochemistry. Neuroscience 48, 655–668. https://doi.org/10.1016/0306-4522(92)90409-u.

McCall, J.G., Al-Hasani, R., Siuda, E.R., Hong, D.Y., Norris, A.J., Ford, C.P., Bruchas, M.R., 2015. CRH engagement of the locus coeruleus noradrenergic system mediates stress-induced anxiety. Neuron 87, 605–620. https://doi.org/10.1016/j.neuron.2015.07.002.

McDougle, C.J., Krystal, J.H., Price, L.H., Heninger, G.R., Charney, D.S., 1995. Noradrenergic response to acute ethanol administration in healthy subjects: comparison with intravenous yohimbine. Psychopharmacology (Berl.) 118, 127–135. https://doi.org/10.1007/BF02245830.

McElligott, Z.A., Fox, M.E., Walsh, P.L., Urban, D.J., Ferrel, M.S., Roth, B.L., Wightman, R.M., 2013. Noradrenergic synaptic function in the bed nucleus of the stria terminalis varies in animal models of anxiety and addiction. Neuropsychopharmacol. Off. Publ. Am. Coll. 38, 1665–1673. https://doi.org/10.1038/npp.2013.63.

McElligott, Z.A., Klug, J.R., Nobis, W.P., Patel, S., Grueter, B.A., Kash, T.L., Winder, D.G., 2010. Distinct forms of Gq-receptor-dependent plasticity of excitatory transmission in the BNST are differentially affected by stress. Proc. Natl. Acad. Sci. U.S.A. 107, 2271–2276. https://doi.org/10.1073/pnas.0905568107.

McElligott, Z.A., Winder, D.G., 2008. Alpha1-adrenergic receptor-induced heterosynaptic long-term depression in the bed nucleus of the stria terminalis is disrupted in mouse models of affective disorders. Neuropsychopharmacol. Off. Publ. Am. Coll. 33, 2313–2323. https://doi.org/10.1038/sj.npp.1301635.

Mendiguren, A., Pineda, J., 2006. Systemic effect of cannabinoids on the spontaneous firing rate of locus coeruleus neurons in rats. Eur. J. Pharmacol. 534, 83–88. https://doi.org/10.1016/j.ejphar.2006.01.002.

Meyer, G., Schwertfeger, J., Exton, M.S., Janssen, O.E., Knapp, W., Stadler, M.A., Schedlowski, M., Krüger, T.H.C., 2004. Neuroendocrine response to casino gambling in problem gamblers. Psychoneuroendocrinology 29, 1272–1280. https://doi.org/10.1016/j.psyneuen.2004.03.005.

Miller, L., Gordh, A.S., 2021. High recreational gamblers show increased stimulatory effects of an acute laboratory gambling challenge. J. Gambl. Stud. 37, 299–318. https://doi.org/10.1007/s10899-020-09952-3.

Mitchell, H.A., Ahern, T.H., Liles, L.C., Javors, M.A., Weinshenker, D., 2006. The effects of norepinephrine transporter inactivation on locomotor activity in mice. Biol. Psychiatr. 60, 1046–1052. https://doi.org/10.1016/j.biopsych.2006.03.057.

Moffat, S.D., Suh, E.J., Fleming, A.S., 1993. Noradrenergic involvement in the consolidation of maternal experience in postpartum rats. Physiol. Behav. 53, 805–811. https://doi.org/10.1016/0031-9384(93)90192-i.

Morien, A., Wellman, P.J., Fojt, J., 1995. Diurnal rhythms of paraventricular hypothalamic norepinephrine and food intake in rats. Pharmacol. Biochem. Behav. 52, 169–174. https://doi.org/10.1016/0091-3057(95)00084-a.

Muntoni, A.L., Pillolla, G., Melis, M., Perra, S., Gessa, G.L., Pistis, M., 2006. Cannabinoids modulate spontaneous neuronal activity and evoked inhibition of locus coeruleus noradrenergic neurons. Eur. J. Neurosci. 23, 2385–2394. https://doi.org/10.1111/j.1460-9568.2006.04759.x.

Nestler, E.J., McMahon, A., Sabban, E.L., Tallman, J.F., Duman, R.S., 1990. Chronic antidepressant administration decreases the expression of tyrosine hydroxylase in the rat locus coeruleus. Proc. Natl. Acad. Sci. U.S.A. 87, 7522–7526. https://doi.org/10.1073/pnas.87.19.7522.

Nobis, W.P., Kash, T.L., Silberman, Y., Winder, D.G., 2011. β-Adrenergic receptors enhance excitatory transmission in the bed nucleus of the stria terminalis through a corticotrophin-releasing factor receptor-dependent and cocaine-regulated mechanism. Biol. Psychiatr. 69, 1083–1090. https://doi.org/10.1016/j.biopsych.2010.12.030.

Olson, V.G., Heusner, C.L., Bland, R.J., During, M.J., Weinshenker, D., Palmiter, R.D., 2006. Role of noradrenergic signaling by the nucleus tractus solitarius in mediating opiate reward. Science 311, 1017–1020. https://doi.org/10.1126/science.1119311.

Ong, L.K., Bobrovskaya, L., Walker, F.R., Day, T.A., Dickson, P.W., Dunkley, P.R., 2011a. The effect of social defeat on tyrosine hydroxylase phosphorylation in the rat brain and adrenal gland. Neurochem. Res. 36, 27–33. https://doi.org/10.1007/s11064-010-0255-7.

Ong, L.K., Guan, L., Stutz, B., Dickson, P.W., Dunkley, P.R., Bobrovskaya, L., 2011b. The effects of footshock and immobilization stress on tyrosine hydroxylase phosphorylation in the rat locus coeruleus and adrenal gland. Neuroscience 192, 20–27. https://doi.org/10.1016/j.neuroscience.2011.06.087.

Oropeza, V.C., Page, M.E., Van Bockstaele, E.J., 2005. Systemic administration of WIN 55,212-2 increases norepinephrine release in the rat frontal cortex. Brain Res. 1046, 45–54. https://doi.org/10.1016/j.brainres.2005.03.036.

Pagliari, R., Peyrin, L., 1995. Norepinephrine release in the rat frontal cortex under treadmill exercise: a study with microdialysis. J. Appl. Physiol. Bethesda. Md. 78, 2121–2130. https://doi.org/10.1152/jappl.1995.78.6.2121.

Pariante, C.M., Lightman, S.L., 2008. The HPA axis in major depression: classical theories and new developments. Trends. Neurosci. 31, 464–468. https://doi.org/10.1016/j.tins.2008.06.006.

Patel, S., Hillard, C.J., 2003. Cannabinoid-induced Fos expression within A10 dopaminergic neurons. Brain. Res. 963, 15–25. https://doi.org/10.1016/s0006-8993(02)03797-6.

Paterson, N.E., Semenova, S., Markou, A., 2008. The effects of chronic versus acute desipramine on nicotine withdrawal and nicotine self-administration in the rat. Psychopharmacology (Berl.) 198, 351–362. https://doi.org/10.1007/s00213-008-1144-5.

Picetti, R., Caccavo, J.A., Ho, A., Kreek, M.J., 2012. Dose escalation and dose preference in extended-access heroin self-administration in Lewis and Fischer rats. Psychopharmacology (Berl.) 220, 163–172. https://doi.org/10.1007/s00213-011-2464-4.

Porter-Stransky, K.A., Centanni, S.W., Karne, S.L., Odil, L.M., Fekir, S., Wong, J.C., Jerome, C., Mitchell, H.A., Escayg, A., Pedersen, N.P., Winder, D.G., Mitrano, D.A., Weinshenker, D., 2019. Noradrenergic transmission at alpha1-adrenergic receptors in the ventral periaqueductal gray modulates arousal. Biol. Psychiatr. 85, 237–247. https://doi.org/10.1016/j.biopsych.2018.07.027.

Quirarte, G.L., Galvez, R., Roozendaal, B., McGaugh, J.L., 1998. Norepinephrine release in the amygdala in response to footshock and opioid peptidergic drugs. Brain. Res. 808, 134–140. https://doi.org/10.1016/s0006-8993(98)00795-1.

Rao, T.S., Correa, L.D., Adams, P., Santori, E.M., Sacaan, A.I., 2003. Pharmacological characterization of dopamine, norepinephrine and serotonin release in the rat prefrontal cortex by neuronal nicotinic acetylcholine receptor agonists. Brain. Res. 990, 203–208. https://doi.org/10.1016/s0006-8993(03)03532-7.

Rasmussen, D.D., Alexander, L.L., Raskind, M.A., Froehlich, J.C., 2009. The alpha1-adrenergic receptor antagonist, prazosin, reduces alcohol drinking in alcohol-preferring (P) rats. Alcohol Clin. Exp. Res. 33, 264–272. https://doi.org/10.1111/j.1530-0277.2008.00829.x.

Rasmussen, D.D., Kincaid, C.L., Froehlich, J.C., 2015. Prazosin + naltrexone decreases alcohol drinking more effectively than does either drug alone in P rats with a protracted history of extensive voluntary alcohol drinking, dependence, and multiple withdrawals. Alcohol Clin. Exp. Res. 39, 1832–1841. https://doi.org/10.1111/acer.12828.

Rasmussen, K., 1991. Afferent effects on locus coeruleus in opiate withdrawal. Prog. Brain Res. 88, 207–216. https://doi.org/10.1016/s0079-6123(08)63810-8.

Rasmussen, K., Beitner-Johnson, D.B., Krystal, J.H., Aghajanian, G.K., Nestler, E.J., 1990. Opiate withdrawal and the rat locus coeruleus: behavioral, electrophysiological, and biochemical correlates. Off. J. Soc. Neurosci. 10, 2308–2317.

Rasmussen, K., Hsu, M.-A., Vandergriff, J., 2004. The selective mGlu2/3 receptor antagonist LY341495 exacerbates behavioral signs of morphine withdrawal and morphine-withdrawal-induced activation of locus coeruleus neurons. Neuropharmacology 46, 620–628. https://doi.org/10.1016/j.neuropharm.2003.11.013.

Rasmussen, K., Krystal, J.H., Aghajanian, G.K., 1991. Excitatory amino acids and morphine withdrawal: differential effects of central and peripheral kynurenic acid administration. Psychopharmacology (Berl.) 105, 508–512. https://doi.org/10.1007/BF02244371.

Robertson, S.D., Plummer, N.W., de Marchena, J., Jensen, P., 2013. Developmental origins of central norepinephrine neuron diversity. Nat. Neurosci. 16, 1016–1023. https://doi.org/10.1038/nn.3458.

Robinson, T.E., Flagel, S.B., 2009. Dissociating the predictive and incentive motivational properties of reward-related cues through the study of individual differences. Biol. Psychiatr. 65, 869–873. https://doi.org/10.1016/j.biopsych.2008.09.006.

Roland, C.R., Bhakthavatsalam, P., Leibowitz, S.F., 1986. Interaction between corticosterone and alpha-2-noradrenergic system of the paraventricular nucleus in relation to feeding behavior. Neuroendocrinology 42, 296–305. https://doi.org/10.1159/000124455.

Roy, A., Adinoff, B., Roehrich, L., Lamparski, D., Custer, R., Lorenz, V., Barbaccia, M., Guidotti, A., Costa, E., Linnoila, M., 1988. Pathological gambling. A psychobiological study. Arch. Gen. Psychiatr. 45, 369–373. https://doi.org/10.1001/archpsyc.1988.01800280085011.

Roy, A., De Jong, J., Linnoila, M., 1989. Extraversion in pathological gamblers. Correlates with indexes of noradrenergic function. Arch. Gen. Psychiatr. 46, 679–681. https://doi.org/10.1001/archpsyc.1989.01810080009001.

Saleeba, C., Dempsey, B., Le, S., Goodchild, A., McMullan, S., 2019. A student's guide to neural circuit tracing. Front. Neurosci. 13, 897. https://doi.org/10.3389/fnins.2019.00897.

Scavone, J.L., Mackie, K., Van Bockstaele, E.J., 2010. Characterization of cannabinoid-1 receptors in the locus coeruleus: relationship with mu-opioid receptors. Brain Res. 1312, 18–31. https://doi.org/10.1016/j.brainres.2009.11.023.

Schank, J.R., Ventura, R., Puglisi-Allegra, S., Alcaro, A., Cole, C.D., Liles, L.C., Seeman, P., Weinshenker, D., 2006. Dopamine beta-hydroxylase knockout mice have alterations in dopamine signaling and are hypersensitive to cocaine. Neuropsychopharmacol. Off. Publ. Am. Coll. 31, 2221–2230. https://doi.org/10.1038/sj.npp.1301000.

Schmidt, K.T., Schroeder, J.P., Foster, S.L., Squires, K., Smith, B.M., Pitts, E.G., Epstein, M.P., Weinshenker, D., 2017. Norepinephrine regulates cocaine-primed reinstatement via α1-adrenergic receptors in the medial prefrontal cortex. Neuropharmacology 119, 134–140. https://doi.org/10.1016/j.neuropharm.2017.04.005.

Schroeder, J.P., Cooper, D.A., Schank, J.R., Lyle, M.A., Gaval-Cruz, M., Ogbonmwan, Y.E., Pozdeyev, N., Freeman, K.G., Iuvone, P.M., Edwards, G.L., Holmes, P.V., Weinshenker, D., 2010. Disulfiram attenuates drug-primed reinstatement of cocaine seeking via inhibition of dopamine β-hydroxylase. Neuropsychopharmacol. Off. Publ. Am. Coll. 35, 2440–2449. https://doi.org/10.1038/npp.2010.127.

Schroeder, J.P., Epps, S.A., Grice, T.W., Weinshenker, D., 2013. The selective dopamine β-hydroxylase inhibitor nepicastat attenuates multiple aspects of cocaine-seeking behavior. Neuropsychopharmacol. Off. Publ. Am. Coll. 38, 1032–1038. https://doi.org/10.1038/npp.2012.267.

Schwarz, L.A., Luo, L., 2015. Organization of the locus coeruleus-norepinephrine system. Curr. Biol. CB 25, R1051–R1056. https://doi.org/10.1016/j.cub.2015.09.039.

Schwarz, L.A., Miyamichi, K., Gao, X.J., Beier, K.T., Weissbourd, B., DeLoach, K.E., Ren, J., Ibanes, S., Malenka, R.C., Kremer, E.J., Luo, L., 2015. Viral-genetic tracing of the input-output organization of a central noradrenaline circuit. Nature 524, 88–92. https://doi.org/10.1038/nature14600.

Sciolino, N.R., Dishman, R.K., Holmes, P.V., 2012. Voluntary exercise offers anxiolytic potential and amplifies galanin gene expression in the locus coeruleus of the rat. Behav. Brain Res. 233, 191–200. https://doi.org/10.1016/j.bbr.2012.05.001.

Sciolino, N.R., Plummer, N.W., Chen, Y.-W., Alexander, G.M., Robertson, S.D., Dudek, S.M., McElligott, Z.A., Jensen, P., 2016. Recombinase-dependent mouse lines for chemogenetic activation of genetically defined cell types. Cell Rep. 15, 2563–2573. https://doi.org/10.1016/j.celrep.2016.05.034.

Shaham, Y., Erb, S., Stewart, J., 2000a. Stress-induced relapse to heroin and cocaine seeking in rats: a review. Brain Res. Rev. 33, 13–33. https://doi.org/10.1016/s0165-0173(00)00024-2.

Shaham, Y., Highfield, D., Delfs, J., Leung, S., Stewart, J., 2000b. Clonidine blocks stress-induced reinstatement of heroin seeking in rats: an effect independent of locus coeruleus noradrenergic neurons. Eur. J. Neurosci. 12, 292–302. https://doi.org/10.1046/j.1460-9568.2000.00899.x.

Shearman, E., Rossi, S., Sershen, H., Hashim, A., Lajtha, A., 2005. Locally administered low nicotine-induced neurotransmitter changes in areas of cognitive function. Neurochem. Res. 30, 1055–1066. https://doi.org/10.1007/s11064-005-7132-9.

Shields, A.D., Wang, Q., Winder, D.G., 2009. alpha2A-adrenergic receptors heterosynaptically regulate glutamatergic transmission in the bed nucleus of the stria terminalis. Neuroscience 163, 339–351. https://doi.org/10.1016/j.neuroscience.2009.06.022.

Shinohara, K., Yanagisawa, A., Kagota, Y., Gomi, A., Nemoto, K., Moriya, E., Furusawa, E., Furuya, K., Terasawa, K., 1999. Physiological changes in Pachinko players; beta-endorphin, catecholamines, immune system substances and heart rate. Appl. Hum. Sci. J. Physiol. Anthropol. 18, 37–42. https://doi.org/10.2114/jpa.18.37.

Silberman, Y., Ariwodola, O.J., Weiner, J.L., 2012. β1-adrenoceptor activation is required for ethanol enhancement of lateral paracapsular GABAergic synapses in the rat basolateral amygdala. J. Pharmacol. Exp. Therapeut. 343, 451–459. https://doi.org/10.1124/jpet.112.196022.

Silverman, M.N., Sternberg, E.M., 2012. Glucocorticoid regulation of inflammation and its functional correlates: from HPA axis to glucocorticoid receptor dysfunction. Ann. N. Y. Acad. Sci. 1261, 55–63. https://doi.org/10.1111/j.1749-6632.2012.06633.x.

Simpson, T.L., Malte, C.A., Dietel, B., Tell, D., Pocock, I., Lyons, R., Varon, D., Raskind, M., Saxon, A.J., 2015. A pilot trial of prazosin, an alpha-1 adrenergic antagonist, for comorbid alcohol dependence and posttraumatic stress disorder. Alcohol Clin. Exp. Res. 39, 808–817. https://doi.org/10.1111/acer.12703.

Simpson, T.L., Saxon, A.J., Stappenbeck, C., Malte, C.A., Lyons, R., Tell, D., Millard, S.P., Raskind, M., 2018. Double-blind randomized clinical trial of prazosin for alcohol use disorder. Am. J. Psychiatr. 175, 1216–1224. https://doi.org/10.1176/appi.ajp.2018.17080913.

Singer, S., Rossi, S., Verzosa, S., Hashim, A., Lonow, R., Cooper, T., Sershen, H., Lajtha, A., 2004. Nicotine-induced changes in neurotransmitter levels in brain areas associated with cognitive function. Neurochem. Res. 29, 1779–1792. https://doi.org/10.1023/b:nere.0000035814.45494.15.

Skelly, M.J., Weiner, J.L., 2014. Chronic treatment with prazosin or duloxetine lessens concurrent anxiety-like behavior and alcohol intake: evidence of disrupted noradrenergic signaling in anxiety-related alcohol use. Brain Behav. 4, 468–483. https://doi.org/10.1002/brb3.230.

Svensson, T.H., Engberg, G., 1980. Effect of nicotine on single cell activity in the noradrenergic nucleus locus coeruleus. Acta Physiol. Scand. Suppl. 479, 31–34.

Swift, K.M., Gross, B.A., Frazer, M.A., Bauer, D.S., Clark, K.J.D., Vazey, E.M., Aston-Jones, G., Li, Y., Pickering, A.E., Sara, S.J., Poe, G.R., 2018. Abnormal locus coeruleus sleep activity alters sleep signatures of memory consolidation and impairs place cell stability and spatial memory. Curr. Biol. CB 28. https://doi.org/10.1016/j.cub.2018.09.054, 3599-3609.e4.

Takahashi, H., Fujie, S., Camerer, C., Arakawa, R., Takano, H., Kodaka, F., Matsui, H., Ideno, T., Okubo, S., Takemura, K., Yamada, M., Eguchi, Y., Murai, T., Okubo, Y., Kato, M., Ito, H., Suhara, T., 2013. Norepinephrine in the brain is associated with aversion to financial loss. Mol. Psychiatr. 18, 3–4. https://doi.org/10.1038/mp.2012.7.

Takeuchi, T., Duszkiewicz, A.J., Sonneborn, A., Spooner, P.A., Yamasaki, M., Watanabe, M., Smith, C.C., Fernández, G., Deisseroth, K., Greene, R.W., Morris, R.G.M., 2016. Locus coeruleus and dopaminergic consolidation of everyday memory. Nature 537, 357–362. https://doi.org/10.1038/nature19325.

Thiele, T.E., Cubero, I., van Dijk, G., Mediavilla, C., Bernstein, I.L., 2000. Ethanol-induced c-fos expression in catecholamine- and neuropeptide Y-producing neurons in rat brainstem. Alcohol Clin. Exp. Res. 24, 802–809.

Thomas, S.A., Matsumoto, A.M., Palmiter, R.D., 1995. Noradrenaline is essential for mouse fetal development. Nature 374, 643–646. https://doi.org/10.1038/374643a0.

Thomas, S.A., Palmiter, R.D., 1997. Impaired maternal behavior in mice lacking norepinephrine and epinephrine. Cell 91, 583–592. https://doi.org/10.1016/s0092-8674(00)80446-8.

Tillage, R.P., Sciolino, N.R., Plummer, N.W., Lustberg, D., Liles, L.C., Hsiang, M., Powell, J.M., Smith, K.G., Jensen, P., Weinshenker, D., 2020. Elimination of galanin synthesis in noradrenergic neurons reduces galanin in select brain areas and promotes active coping behaviors. Brain Struct. Funct. 225, 785–803. https://doi.org/10.1007/s00429-020-02035-4.

Torrecilla, M., Quillinan, N., Williams, J.T., Wickman, K., 2008. Pre- and postsynaptic regulation of locus coeruleus neurons after chronic morphine treatment: a study of GIRK-knockout mice. Eur. J. Neurosci. 28, 618–624. https://doi.org/10.1111/j.1460-9568.2008.06348.x.

Torruella-Suárez, M.L., Vandenberg, J.R., Cogan, E.S., Tipton, G.J., Teklezghi, A., Dange, K., Patel, G.K., McHenry, J.A., Hardaway, J.A., Kantak, P.A., Crowley, N.A., DiBerto, J.F., Faccidomo, S.P., Hodge, C.W., Stuber, G.D., McElligott, Z.A., 2020. Manipulations of central amygdala neurotensin neurons alter the consumption of ethanol and sweet fluids in mice. J. Neuro Oncol. 40, 632–647. https://doi.org/10.1523/JNEUROSCI.1466-19.2019.

Tully, K., Bolshakov, V.Y., 2010. Emotional enhancement of memory: how norepinephrine enables synaptic plasticity. Mol. Brain 3, 15. https://doi.org/10.1186/1756-6606-3-15.

Tung, C.S., Grenhoff, J., Svensson, T.H., 1990. Morphine withdrawal responses of rat locus coeruleus neurons are blocked by an excitatory amino-acid antagonist. Acta Physiol. Scand. 138, 581–582. https://doi.org/10.1111/j.1748-1716.1990.tb08888.x.

Uematsu, A., Tan, B.Z., Ycu, E.A., Cuevas, J.S., Koivumaa, J., Junyent, F., Kremer, E.J., Witten, I.B., Deisseroth, K., Johansen, J.P., 2017. Modular organization of the brainstem noradrenaline system coordinates opposing learning states. Nat. Neurosci. 20, 1602–1611. https://doi.org/10.1038/nn.4642.

Valentino, R.J., Van Bockstaele, E., Bangasser, D., 2013. Sex-specific cell signaling: the corticotropin-releasing factor receptor model. Trends Pharmacol. Sci. 34, 437–444. https://doi.org/10.1016/j.tips.2013.06.004.

Van Bockstaele, E.J., Valentino, R.J., 2013. Neuropeptide regulation of the locus coeruleus and opiate-induced plasticity of stress responses. Adv. Pharmacol. San Diego Calif 68, 405–420. https://doi.org/10.1016/B978-0-12-411512-5.00019-1.

Vandergriff, J., Rasmussen, K., 1999. The selective mGlu2/3 receptor agonist LY354740 attenuates morphine-withdrawal-induced activation of locus coeruleus neurons and behavioral signs of morphine withdrawal. Neuropharmacology 38, 217–222. https://doi.org/10.1016/s0028-3908(98)00196-8.

Ventura, R., Cabib, S., Alcaro, A., Orsini, C., Puglisi-Allegra, S., 2003. Norepinephrine in the prefrontal cortex is critical for amphetamine-induced reward and mesoaccumbens dopamine release. J. Neuro Oncol. 23, 1879–1885.

Walker, B.M., Rasmussen, D.D., Raskind, M.A., Koob, G.F., 2008. alpha1-noradrenergic receptor antagonism blocks dependence-induced increases in responding for ethanol. Alcohol Fayettev. N 42, 91–97. https://doi.org/10.1016/j.alcohol.2007.12.002.

Wang, X., Cen, X., Lu, L., 2001. Noradrenaline in the bed nucleus of the stria terminalis is critical for stress-induced reactivation of morphine-conditioned place preference in rats. Eur. J. Pharmacol. 432, 153–161. https://doi.org/10.1016/s0014-2999(01)01487-x.

Weinshenker, D., Miller, N.S., Blizinsky, K., Laughlin, M.L., Palmiter, R.D., 2002. Mice with chronic norepinephrine deficiency resemble amphetamine-sensitized animals. Proc. Natl. Acad. Sci. U.S.A. 99, 13873–13877. https://doi.org/10.1073/pnas.212519999.

Weinshenker, D., Rust, N.C., Miller, N.S., Palmiter, R.D., 2000. Ethanol-associated behaviors of mice lacking norepinephrine. J. Neuro Oncol. 20, 3157–3164.

Werling, L.L., Brown, S.R., Cox, B.M., 1987. Opioid receptor regulation of the release of norepinephrine in brain. Neuropharmacology 26, 987–996. https://doi.org/10.1016/0028-3908(87)90077-3.

Xu, F., Gainetdinov, R.R., Wetsel, W.C., Jones, S.R., Bohn, L.M., Miller, G.W., Wang, Y.M., Caron, M.G., 2000. Mice lacking the norepinephrine transporter are supersensitive to psychostimulants. Nat. Neurosci. 3, 465–471. https://doi.org/10.1038/74839.

Xu, G.-P., Van Bockstaele, E., Reyes, B., Bethea, T., Valentino, R.J., 2004. Chronic morphine sensitizes the brain norepinephrine system to corticotropin-releasing factor and stress. J. Neuro Oncol. 24, 8193–8197. https://doi.org/10.1523/JNEUROSCI.1657-04.2004.

Yoshida, T., Sakane, N., Umekawa, T., Kondo, M., 1994. Effect of nicotine on sympathetic nervous system activity of mice subjected to immobilization stress. Physiol. Behav. 55, 53–57. https://doi.org/10.1016/0031-9384(94)90009-4.

Zabetian, C.P., Anderson, G.M., Buxbaum, S.G., Elston, R.C., Ichinose, H., Nagatsu, T., Kim, K.S., Kim, C.H., Malison, R.T., Gelernter, J., Cubells, J.F., 2001. A quantitative-trait analysis of human plasma-dopamine beta-hydroxylase activity: evidence for a major functional polymorphism at the DBH locus. Am. J. Hum. Genet. 68, 515–522. https://doi.org/10.1086/318198.

Zakeri, K., Potenza, M.N., 2012. The neuropsychopharmacology of pathological gambling. Curr. Psychiatr. Rev. 8. https://doi.org/10.2174/157340012798994911.

CHAPTER

11

Cholinergic modulation of circuits

Nii A. Addy[a,b,c,d,e], Christie D. Fowler[f] and Robert J. Wickham[g]

[a]Department of Psychiatry, Yale School of Medicine, New Haven, CT, United States; [b]Yale Tobacco Center of Regulatory Science, Yale School of Medicine, New Haven, CT, United States; [c]Department of Cellular and Molecular Physiology, Yale School of Medicine, New Haven, CT, United States; [d]Interdepartmental Neuroscience Program, Yale University, New Haven, CT, United States; [e]Wu Tsai Institute, Yale University, New Haven, CT, United States; [f]Department of Neurobiology and Behavior, University of California, Irvine, Irvine, CA, United States; [g]Department of Psychology, Lafayette College, Easton, PA, United States

In this chapter, we introduce the neuromodulatory actions of acetylcholine and the effects of drug exposure on acetylcholine processes in brain pathways and circuits. We start with the discovery of acetylcholine, and then describe the anatomy and localization of acetylcholine neurons and their projections in the brain, the actions of acetylcholine at their receptors in various brain pathways and circuits, and how the neuromodulatory actions of acetylcholine mediate drug effects in the brain and drug-associated and addiction-related behaviors.

Drug use is common among the general population. Of those over the age of 12 in the US, 65.5% report using alcohol, 26% using tobacco cigarettes, and 16.7% using illicit substances for the prior year. However, only a subset of these individuals, 5.3% for alcohol and 3% for illicit substances (Samhsa, 2019), develop a substance use disorder with its defined detrimental physical, physiological, psychological, and social consequences. In individuals who continue to use substances, despite these adverse consequences, and for those who try to quit, there are several characteristic behaviors associated with prolonged drug use. As an example, for someone seeking to quit smoking cigarettes, there are several factors that make it very difficult for these individuals to "kick the habit." The individual seeking to quit may be accustomed to smoking every time they go to the bar. Thus, they may find it very difficult to resist the urge to smoke any time they are at the bar. This difficulty and inability to quit could result from the intense cigarette cravings that they feel when they're at the bar with friends, while at other times they may start smoking at the bar, out of habit. For other individuals attempting to quit smoking, they may have previously developed a

Neurocircuitry of Addiction
https://doi.org/10.1016/B978-0-12-823453-2.00004-7

routine of taking smoking breaks at work, and this may be a routine they had developed over a number of years. In an attempt to quit smoking, they may decide to skip their smoking breaks, but may notice that it's extremely difficult to concentrate at certain times of the day. In this circumstance, they may start smoking again to regain their focus, making it that much more difficult to quit.

In instances where individuals are struggling with the excessive use of an illicit substance (like cocaine, amphetamine, or heroin), they sometime choose or are recommended to relocate to a treatment facility for a period of time. This approach can be particularly helpful in instances where the substance use is compromising the safety of the individual or their loved ones. At specialized treatment and recovery facilities, individuals may have some success in decreasing their substance use and achieving periods of abstinence. The major challenges typically occur when these individuals leave the recovery facility. Oftentimes, they will describe the intense drug cravings they experience once they return to familiar environments. Unfortunately, these intense cravings can lead to unintended drug relapse, and sometimes binge drug use. For others who manage to remain abstinent for a period of time, the increased susceptibility to relapse may occur during stressful periods, for instance before an exam or intense evaluation at work, after losing a job or a loved one, or after another type of stressful life event. In still other scenarios, particularly with opioids, individuals may continue using drugs in order to get relief from the intense physical and psychological withdrawal symptoms associated with drug abstinence.

In each of these scenarios, drug-related behaviors are mediated, at some level, by the neurobiological actions of acetylcholine across multiple brain circuits. In this chapter, we'll first recount the discovery of acetylcholine, introduce what is known and unknown about acetylcholine actions at cholinergic receptors throughout the brain, consider the role of brain loci, circuits and pathways, and then discuss how these acetylcholine mechanisms mediate motivated behavior and other behaviors associated with substance use and substance use disorders.

The discovery of acetylcholine

Acetylcholine, the first neurotransmitter discovered, was experimentally identified as a cell-to-cell messenger in 1921 in a classic experiment by Otto Loewi. In this experiment, he isolated two, still-beating frog hearts each in their own liquid-filled chamber. The major difference between these two hearts was that one of these hearts had an intact vagus nerve, which upon stimulation, caused the heart to beat more slowly. He then took the liquid of the vagus-containing heart and added it to the heart with the vagus nerve removed. In doing so, he found that the second heart also started to beat more slowly. He hypothesized that something, which he termed "vagusstoff", was released from the vagus nerve of the first heart, and could be transferred to the second heart, causing heart activity to slow. Acetylcholine had actually been previously discovered and isolated in 1913 by Henry Noble and Arthur Ewins (Ewins, 1914). But acetylcholine had not been observed in the body until 1929 by Dale and Dudley (1929). As a result, it wasn't immediately clear that the "vagusstoff" identified by Loewi was acetylcholine (although Loewi and others knew that "vagusstoff" was a choline ester). Even after acetylcholine was discovered, there was ongoing debate as to whether it was important for neuronal communication, and whether its actions were mediated by chemical or electrical communication. This was part of a general debate in the field about the processes underlying neuronal communication. Eventually, with additional experimental evidence collected by Dale and others, acetylcholine was characterized as a chemical messenger, or neurotransmitter (reviewed in Tansey, 2006).

From nodes to circuits

The framework of understanding the role of specific brain regions (loci) in biological functions and behaviors, emerged from years of groundbreaking research studies that revealed the important functions and roles of many different brain regions. As an example, the discovery and identification of the visual cortex emerged from observations by Bartolomeo Panizza in 1855. Panizza observed and noted that stroke patients became blind after damage to a specific area of the brain, an area that was later labeled as the visual cortex (Panizza, 1855). Prior to Panizza's work and others, one of the prevailing frameworks was that different brain regions collectively and equally mediated functions in the brain (reviewed in Zago et al., 2000). Early understanding of the role of the hippocampus in memory were largely due to findings from patient HM, who lost the ability to gain new memories, after surgical temporal lobe removal, that was performed to minimize his seizure episodes (reviewed in Squire, 2009). Our understanding of brain processes underlying reward-related behavior also benefited greatly from brain region targeted studies-based on classical, initial brain stimulation experiments performed in rats by Olds and Milner in 1954 (Olds and Milner, 1954). In describing the impact of these early brain stimulation studies, Wise and Bozrath stated "Animals will work for stimulation of some parts of their own brains: this suggests that the brain has specialized circuitry for mediation of reward" (Wise and Bozarth, 1981). Indeed, these intracranial self-stimulation (ICSS) studies, in which an animal spins a wheel or presses a lever to receive electrical stimulation in specific brain regions, set a foundation for subsequent experiments, which provided new insights into brain-region specific mechanisms underlying drug use, drug-related behavior and substance use disorders. As will be discussed throughout this chapter, with the advent of additional tools for recording activity across multiple brain regions, and tools to manipulate circuits and pathways, the field has gained a deeper appreciation and understanding for the role of circuit activity in drug-related behavior and substance use disorders.

Acetylcholine anatomy and circuitry

Acetylcholine neurons are mainly identified by the presence of choline acetyltransferase (ChAT), the enzyme involved in the synthesis of the neurotransmitter. In the chemical synthesis pathway, acetylcholine is produced when the ChAT enzyme transforms choline and acetyl coenzyme A into acetylcholine, with the byproduct of coenzyme A. The axon terminals of acetylcholine neurons can be further identified by the presence of the vesicular acetylcholine transporter, which functions to load acetylcholine molecules into vesicles for synaptic release from the axon terminal. Acetylcholine neurons in the brain were originally identified as being localized in two main clusters of brain loci, known as complexes (Fig. 11.1). The first is the basal forebrain complex, which includes the medial septum, the ventral diagonal band, the horizontal diagonal band, and the nucleus basalis (reviewed in Newman et al., 2012; Perez-Lloret and Barrantes, 2016). These four brain loci were originally termed Ch 1 through Ch 4 by Musulam, as a reference to cholinergic cell group 1 through

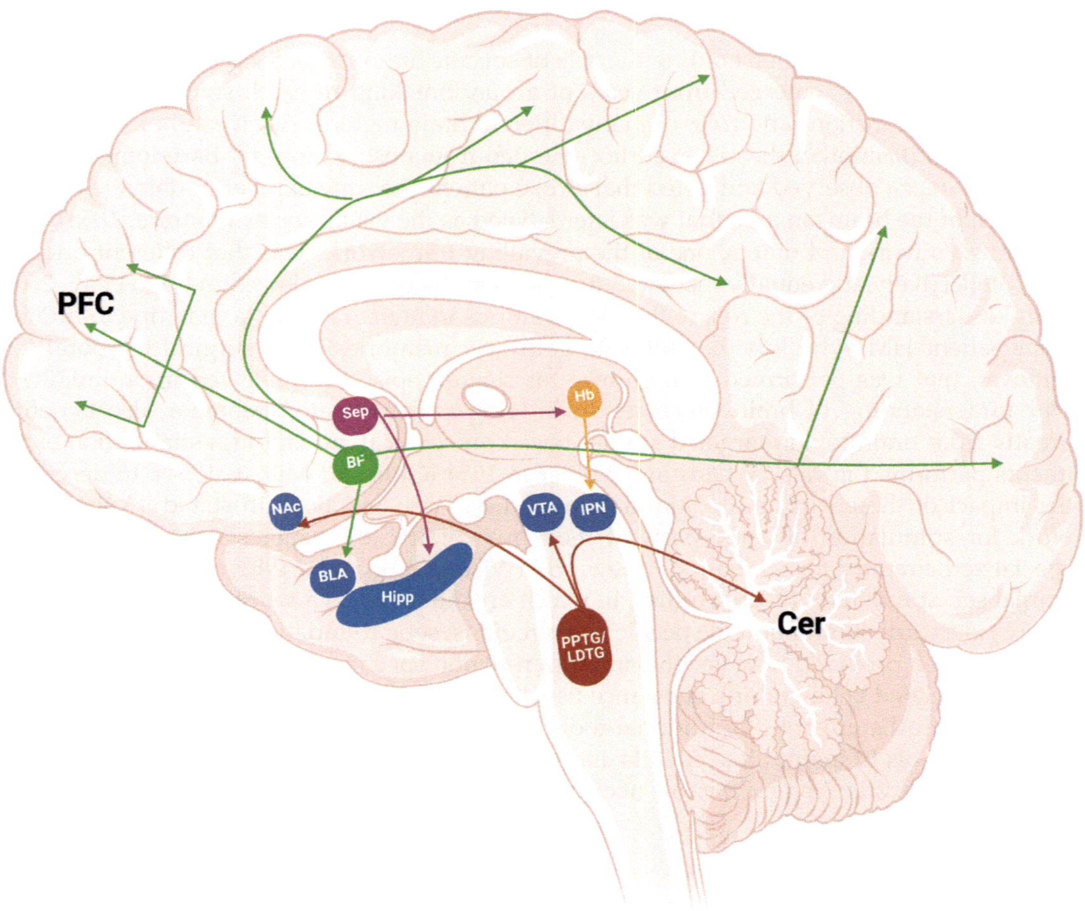

FIGURE 11.1 Overview of cholinergic circuits in the brain. Cholinergic innervation is widespread throughout the brain. There are four major sources of acetylcholine in the brain that are highly relevant for addiction circuits. *Red*: The pedunculopontine tegmentum (PPTg) and laterodorsal tegmentum (LDTg) innervate the ventral tegmental area (VTA) as well as the nucleus accumbens (NAc), with some innervation to the cerebellum (Cer). *Green*: The basal forebrain (BF), specially the nucleus basalis, innervates large portions of the cortex and amygdala. *Purple*: The septum (Sep) innervates the hippocampus (Hipp) and the habenula (Hb). *Orange*: Cholinergic neurons within the habenula innervate the interpeduncular nucleus (IPNs). It should be noted that there are local cholinergic neurons within the nucleus accumbens and the hippocampus as well.

cholinergic cell group 4 (Mesulam et al., 1983). The second cluster containing cholinergic neurons is the brainstem complex. This complex includes the laterodorsal tegmentum (LDTg) and the pedunculopontine tegmentum (PPTg), referred to as Ch 5 and Ch 6 (Mesulam et al., 1983). These two complexes, which house the cell bodies of acetylcholine neurons in the aforementioned nuclei, project and send their axons throughout the brain (Fig. 11.1). The basal forebrain complex projects to several forebrain areas, including the frontal cortex, hippocampus, amygdala, olfactory area/bulb, and visual cortex. The brainstem complex projects to midbrain and other relay structures, including the substantia nigra (SN) and ventral tegmental area (VTA), thalamus, basal ganglia/striatum, as well as the cerebellum and pons, among others. Further investigations have identified cholinergic neurons in other discrete regions, including interneurons within the VTA and a dense cholinergic pathway from the habenula (Hb) to the interpeduncular nucleus (IPN) (Groenewegen et al., 1986; Lammel et al., 2012; Hsu et al., 2013)

Consistent with the actions of serotonin and norepinephrine, acetylcholine modulates several brain regions and circuits throughout the brain, and it is thus known as a neuromodulator. In the context of substance use disorders, one of the key areas of research focus has been acetylcholine regulation of the dopamine system. This is due to the known roles of dopamine in reward processing, reward consummatory behavior, and reward-seeking behavior (reviewed in (Ikemoto, 2007). But we note that acetylcholine also regulates other neurotransmitter and neuromodulatory systems, both directly and indirectly. In later sections of this chapter, we'll consider how acetylcholine concentration changes in brain regions and pathways, leading to changes in neuronal activity to initiate and modulate neuronal function, biochemical processes, circuit function, and ultimately behavioral processes. Similar to many of the neurotransmitter systems discussed in this textbook thus far, acetylcholine released from neurons acts by binding to acetylcholine receptors (AChRs), both within and outside of the synapse (McGehee and Role, 1995; Fowler et al., 2020). AChRs are expressed on neurons throughout the brain, on pre-synaptic axon terminals, on the soma (cell body), and on post-synaptic dendrites (McGehee and Role, 1995; Kenny and Markou, 2004; Fowler et al., 2020). Cholinergic receptors are also present on other cell types in the brain, particularly glial cells, including astrocytes and immune cells reviewed in (Van Der Zee et al., 1993; Gamage et al., 2020).

Similar to acetylcholine being the first identified neurotransmitter, acetylcholine receptors were also the first identified neurotransmitter receptors. The idea of a "receptive substance" was first proposed by John Newport Langley in 1905, when it was hypothesized that a "receptive substance" in the muscle of a fowl must be receiving a signal from nicotine to transduce that signal into a muscle contraction, in his experiment [Langley (1907) reviewed in Changeux (2012, 2020)]. With the availability of toxins that targeted the acetylcholine system, and with the use of improved purification techniques to isolate brain proteins, two types of acetylcholine receptors were eventually identified and isolated. One class of acetylcholine receptors were identified as nicotinic acetylcholine receptors (nAChRs) which, as the name implies, are activated by nicotine (reviewed in Albuquerque et al., 2009). These fast-acting ionotropic receptors are permeable to the cations, sodium and calcium. The influx of these cations through nAChRs can depolarize neurons, leading to downstream changes including neurotransmitter release, activation of nearby channels that are sensitive to voltage changes, and activation of intracellular processes that are also sensitive to voltage changes or are directly activated by calcium. Structurally, nAChRs are made up of 5 subunits, and the receptors exist either as homomeric (made up of 5 identical α subunits) or heteromeric receptors (made up of either 2 α and 3 β, or 3 α and 2 β subunits). The known nAChR subunits include α2 through α10 and β2, β3, and β4 (Parikh and Sarter 2008; Picciotto et al., 2008). Subtypes of nicotinic receptors also have different properties, depending on the subunit composition of the receptors. Some of these subtype-specific properties include differences in activation kinetics, localization on different neuronal cell types in the brain, different permeability to specific cations, as well as different desensitization rates (McGehee and Role, 1995; Picciotto, 1998).

The other class of acetylcholine receptors are the muscarinic receptors (mAChRs), which are activated by the mushroom toxin, muscarine. These are slow-acting receptors that are associated with, or "coupled to," intracellular G-proteins, and are thus termed G protein-coupled receptors, or GPCRs (reviewed in Digby et al., 2010). Activation of these GPCRs leads to a host of downstream intracellular processes. There are 2 types of G-proteins coupled to AChRs, termed Gq and Gi/Go, and they lead to either excitatory (Gq) or inhibitory (Gi/Go) actions within the neuron. Muscarinic receptors exist in five known subtypes, M1 through M5 (Eglen, 2005). M1, M3, and M5 mAChRs are Gq-coupled receptors that exert that actions on phospholipase C (PLC) and its downstream processes (reviewed in Digby et al., 2010). M2 and M4 mAChRs are Gi/o-coupled receptors, which inhibit the action of adenylyl cyclase and its downstream processes (reviewed in Digby et al., 2010).

Both nicotinic and muscarinic AChRs are located widely throughout the brain. As noted earlier, they exist on neurons and on non-neuronal cells, including classes of immune cells in the brain where they play important roles in many critical processes influencing brain circuit activity, function, and ultimately behavior. For the purposes of this chapter, we'll primarily focus on AChR actions in neurons. As noted earlier, neuronal AChRs are located on the soma (cell body) as well as on pre-synaptic terminals and on post-synaptic dendrites. Depending on the localization (pre-synaptic or post-synaptic) and the cell type (for instance, dopamine, glutamate, acetylcholine or other neuronal cell types), and the subtype of nAChR or mAChR, acetylcholine actions at AChRs can have vastly different effects on neuronal communication and excitability.

To better understand the actions of AChRs in the brain, let's first consider the localization and consequences associated with pre-synaptic and post-synaptic AChRs. We'll start with pre-synaptic nicotinic receptors, which are permeable to sodium and calcium (as mentioned earlier). These nAChRs can thus change the pre-synaptic membrane potential and depolarize the membrane. The entry of calcium through pre-synaptic nAChRs, in particular, can directly induce calcium-dependent neurotransmitter release (Soliakov et al., 1995; Sacaan et al., 1996). This calcium mediated neurotransmitter release can occur either as a direct result of depolarization (to facilitate vesicular release of neurotransmitters), or through the recruitment of other voltage gated calcium channels that depolarize the pre-synaptic membrane to facilitate neurotransmitter release. It is important to note that this promotion of neurotransmitter release, by pre-synaptic nAChRs, can have differential effects on the activity of specific brain regions, depending on the cell types where nAChRs are located. For instance, pre-synaptic nAChRs on glutamate versus GABA cells could have opposing effects on overall excitation or inhibition, respectively, of a brain pathway.

Many pre-synaptic muscarinic receptor mechanisms have been extensively studied outside of the brain, especially at the neuromuscular junction. Within the brain, pre-synaptic mAChRs mechanisms have been investigated in the hippocampus, primarily within the context of synaptic plasticity with implications in memory function. In the rat hippocampus, pre-synaptic M2 and M4 mAChRs (coupled to Gi/Go) have been shown to inhibit pre-synaptic terminals (via PLC), thereby inhibiting glutamate release [Qian and Saggau (1997) also reviewed in Fernandez de Sevilla et al. (2021)]. In contrast, M1 receptors on pre-synaptic terminals, for instance on glutamatergic cells in the prefrontal cortex, can facilitate neurotransmitter release (Oda et al., 2018). Pre-synaptic mAChR mechanisms have also been studied in other brain regions and pathways. For instance, pre-synaptic M4 mAChRs on cholinergic terminals in VTA can act as autoreceptors. Early evidence from brain slices in adult male mice suggested that when these pre-synaptic M4 mAChRs are activated, they likely provide feedback to limit the neuronal activity, and thus limit the release of acetylcholine, from these neurons (Tzavara et al., 2004). Additionally, M3 (Gq coupled) receptors on cell bodies (for instance on GABA cells/interneurons) can enhance cell firing, increase GABA release, and thus facilitate inhibition in regions like the VTA (Yeomans, 2012).

For post-synaptic AChRs, the initial mechanisms of action are very similar to pre-synaptic AChRs. Indeed, post-synaptic nAChRs are also permeable to sodium and calcium and can directly depolarize neurons and/or activate voltage gated channels that can further depolarize the postsynaptic neuron. Furthermore, nAChRs activation or inhibition, is sufficient to alter neuronal firing. Within the VTA, activation of AChRs, with carbachol, is sufficient to induce dopamine neuron burst firing (Zhang et al., 2005). Evidence from electrophysiology studies in male mice strongly suggests that β2* nAChRs (* denotes the presence of β2 subunits) play a critical role in regulating dopamine neuronal firing in the VTA (Mameli-Engvall et al., 2006). For post-synaptic mAChRs, actions at these receptors engage the same G protein coupled mechanisms described for pre-synaptic mAChRs. The only difference for post-synaptic mAChRs is that their activation influences post-synaptic processes, with downstream biochemical processes that are activated by G protein targets, leading to engagement of intracellular cascades associated with plasticity and neuroadaptations. For instance, the post-synaptic effects of activating AChRs on dopamine neurons within the VTA are particularly important in the context of drug reward, reward-related learning and neuronal plasticity associated with drug exposure that facilitates dependence and relapse (as will be discussed later in this section). A specific example from the VTA, which is highly relevant to the behaviors discussed in this chapter, are the M5 mAChRs on post-synaptic dopamine neurons, which are suggested to be key mAChR regulators of dopamine firing activity in the VTA, thereby facilitating dopamine release in target regions (Basile et al., 2002; Forster et al., 2002). Of course, any drug-related changes in acetylcholine levels in the VTA (or other brain regions) can lead to activation of pre-synaptic and post-synaptic AChRs to influence overall activity of the VTA, leading to downstream changes in signaling in circuits throughout the brain. We should also note that acetylcholine is released into the synaptic cleft, which may then move out of the cleft via volume transmission to target non-synaptic AChRs (Yamasaki et al., 2010). However, in this extracellular space, acetylcholine is eventually degraded by the enzyme acetylcholinesterase, thereby producing the metabolites of choline and acetic acid. Thus, several factors, including acetylcholine concentration, the affinity and localization of specific nAChRs and mAChRs, the number of active AChRs present, and the rate of clearance by acetylcholinesterase, can all influence how the neuromodulatory effects of acetylcholine occur in brain pathways and circuits.

Given the rich arborization of cholinergic axons and projections, and the diverse actions and cellular localizations of nAChRs and mAChRs throughout the brain, acetylcholine can modulate the actions of several neurotransmitters and cell types. As briefly described earlier, acetylcholine regulation of dopamine circuits, for instance, plays a critical role in drug-related behaviors. This cholinergic regulation of dopamine activity is mediated by both actions of brainstem cholinergic nuclei and their projections, as well actions of the basal forebrain nuclei and its projections (Lodge and Grace, 2006; Maskos, 2008).

Acetylcholine mediated behaviors

As a brief overview, we note the large number of processes which ACh is known to mediate. These include reward processing, as well as consummatory behavior and seeking behaviors for both natural rewards and substances of abuse. The most prominent example of cholinergic receptor action in drug reward are the reinforcing effects of nicotine, which are initially mediated by nAChRs in the VTA (Corrigall et al., 1994). Notably, many behaviors and processes associated with long term nicotine use and addiction are mediated by nAChR receptor mechanisms in several downstream target regions of the VTA (reviewed in Picciotto et al., 2008), including several regions of the mesolimbic circuit such as the nucleus accumbens (NAc), hippocampus, and prefrontal cortex (Corrigall et al., 1994; Levin 2002, 2013). But this is not only the case for nicotine, as acetylcholine mechanisms mediate relapse-related behavior for heroin, cocaine and alcohol (Lof et al., 2007; Zhou et al., 2007; You et al., 2008). Acetylcholine signaling also plays a critical role in attentional processes. Initial, strong evidence for basal forebrain projections playing an important role in attentional processes came from brain lesion studies. In this early work, investigators showed that inhibition, ablation, or disruption of these pathways disrupted attentional performance in various preclinical animal models (reviewed in (Parikh and Bangasser, 2020). Subsequent studies, using electrochemical techniques to measure neurotransmitter levels, in dialysate samples, from specific areas in the cortex, also revealed changes in total acetylcholine concentrations during attentional tasks, showing changes in overall acetylcholine levels, over long periods of time, during attentional tasks that were correlated with the attentional demands of the task (Himmelheber et al., 1997; Passetti et al., 2000; Arnold et al., 2002). Examination of real time, rapid (or phasic) acetylcholine changes in prefrontal cortex also revealed that increases in rapidly changing acetylcholine levels are critical for attentional tasks associated with cue detection, which is a critical process in repeated use of some drugs (Parikh et al., 2007; Parikh and Sarter, 2008).

Acetylcholine is also implicated in several other behaviors associated with reward and attention. In particular, acetylcholine plays a key role in learning and memory, with several studies delineating roles of hippocampal nAChRs in memory processes (Levin, 2002). Indeed, the role of acetylcholine disruptions and perturbations play a well-known role in neurodegenerative diseases, such as Alzheimer's Disease and other disorders associated with memory deficits (Lombardo and Maskos, 2015). Acetylcholine has also been implicated in regulating motivation, hedonia, anhedonia and anxiety (Hoebel et al., 2007; Nunes et al., 2013), as well as behaviors that are critical for survival, including sleep, food intake and food-related learning (Rada et al., 2000; Sharf et al., 2006; Sharf and Ranaldi, 2006; Mineur et al., 2011; Luppi and Fort, 2019).

Throughout the rest of this chapter, we will introduce and discuss the critical roles of acetylcholine in specific brain pathways and circuits. We will then discuss how acetylcholine modulates brain activity in specific circuits to influence behavioral outcomes and processes. We will also consider the interaction between substance use and acetylcholine—namely the effects of drugs of abuse on acetylcholine processes in the brain and how acetylcholine mediates the effects of these substances through actions within brain circuits. Finally, we will consider acetylcholine actions that mediate the behavioral effects of drug use and misuse, including drug-seeking, dependence and withdrawal-related behaviors.

Reward-related signaling: mesopontine tegmentum to VTA circuit

While the role of the VTA in drug-related behaviors has been discussed in previous chapters, one of the key regulators of VTA neuronal activity centers around its cholinergic inputs. The VTA is a heterogenous group of neurons, comprised of dopamine, GABAergic, glutamatergic, and even glutamate and dopamine co-releasing neurons (Zell et al., 2020). Moving forward, we will primarily focus on dopamine (DA) neurons given their canonical role in drug-related behaviors. VTA neurons have two major modes of firing: burst firing (high frequency phasic firing) and tonic firing (low, pacemaker-like firing) (Grace and Bunney 1984a,b). Burst firing typically produces robust and rapid elevations of dopamine in the NAc that are associated with the euphoric effects of many drugs of abuse and play a major role in reward-related learning, such as encoding both the hedonic value of reward as well as reward-predictive cues (Schultz and Romo, 1990; Day et al., 2007). The regulation of VTA DA neuron activity is quite complex, largely due to the diversity of inputs into the VTA that control its activity (Fig. 11.1). Two major drivers of VTA DA neuron bursting are cholinergic and glutamatergic inputs. Glutamatergic inputs activate NMDA receptors on VTA DA neurons, thereby transitioning the neurons from tonic to bursting (Zweifel et al., 2009). Meanwhile, cholinergic input acting on somatodendritic β2* nAChRs, as well as M5 receptors, serve as a "gate" to allow VTA dopamine neurons to burst following NMDA receptor activation (Yeomans et al., 2001; Mameli-Engvall et al., 2006; Yeomans, 2012). Thus, both cholinergic and glutamatergic inputs modulate VTA DA neuronal activity and responses to reward-related stimuli.

The major source of acetylcholine to the VTA arises from a pair of brain regions in the aforementioned brainstem complex, or mesopontine tegmentum, that are comprized of not only cholinergic neurons, but also GABAergic and glutamatergic neurons. These two brain regions are the LDTg and the PPTg (Maskos, 2008). Charles Blaha and colleagues sought to assess whether cholinergic input from these areas differentially influenced dopamine release from VTA and SN cells (Blaha and Winn, 1993; Blaha et al., 1996). There are two key things to remember about this circuitry before going further. First, these researchers were heavily leaning on work that showed that the LDTg preferentially innervates the VTA, and the PPTg preferentially innervates the SN (Cornwall et al., 1990). Second, they were also relying on work that showed that the VTA primarily projects to the NAc, and the SN primarily projects to the caudate-putamen (CP), or dorsal striatum (Ungerstedt, 1971; Ikemoto, 2007). Thus, they proposed two separate circuits: (1) LDTg to VTA to NAc, and (2) PPTg to SN to CP. The experimental approach in male adult mice was to inject the acetylcholinesterase inhibitor neostigmine (which blocks acetylcholinesterase from degrading acetylcholine, thereby raising acetylcholine levels) into the VTA or SN, and then compare dopamine release in the NAc (Circuit 1) or the CP (Circuit 2) using chronoamperometry. In control sham-lesioned animals, they found: (1) increasing acetylcholine levels in the VTA increased dopamine release in the NAc and (2) increasing acetylcholine levels in the SN increased dopamine release in the CP. Next, they examined the lesioned animals. They found that pairing a LDTg lesion with increased acetylcholine in the VTA resulted in decreased dopamine release in the NAc. Similarly, pairing a PPTg lesion with increased acetylcholine in the SN resulted in decreased dopamine release in the CP. These data support the hypothesis for both proposed circuits: acetylcholine from the LDTg activates the VTA and in turn causes dopamine release in the NAc, whereas acetylcholine from the PPTg activates the SN and in turn causes dopamine release in the CP.

However, when one takes a closer look at these circuits and realizes that the projections are not as discretely defined, the question arises: What about that small fraction of PPTg neurons that project to the VTA? Indeed, more recent studies have shown that PPTg neurons are very important for controlling dopamine neuron bursting within the VTA (Lokwan et al., 1999; Floresco et al., 2003; Grace et al., 2007), indicating that the PPTg can also regulate dopamine release in the NAc. Therefore, the current hypothesis is that LDTg neurons can activate the small fraction of PPTg neurons that project to the VTA, suggesting two additional circuits (Circuit 3) LDT to PPTg to VTA to NAc and (Circuit 4) LDTg to VTA to NAc (Grace et al., 2007). The precise debate about differential functions between the PPTg and LDTg are beyond the scope of this chapter so we will consider these as relatively interchangeable. Thus, in subsequent sections, we will specify when the PPTg or LDTg were isolated for investigation. However, the reader should be aware that functional distinctions in these various regions and circuits are still being unraveled.

Role of VTA acetylcholine in drug reward

The functional role of cholinergic, glutamatergic, and GABAergic inputs to the VTA are not well established, but numerous studies report an important role for the LDTg/PPTg in reward-related learning (Pan and Hyland, 2005; Steidl and Veverka, 2015; Steidl et al., 2017), and it is likely that all three inputs play a role. One of the major drivers of acetylcholine release in the VTA arises from consummatory rewarding behaviors, such as eating and drinking (Rada et al., 2000) and sensory processing (Reese et al., 1995; Pan and Hyland, 2005). Interestingly, male rats have been shown to self-administer both carbachol, a nonselective cholinergic receptor agonist, and physostigmine, another acetylcholinesterase inhibitor like neostigmine, directly into the VTA (Ikemoto and Wise, 2002), suggesting that acetylcholine underlies reinforcement processing. The idea that cholinergic input into the VTA is important for reward and reinforcement fits with an optogenetic study that selectively targeted LDTg axonal inputs to the VTA. In this study in mice (Steidl et al., 2017), a virus encoding the excitatory channelrhodopsin was injected into either cholinergic or glutamatergic neurons, and the terminals in the VTA were optically stimulated during a conditioned place preference test. Either cholinergic or glutamatergic terminals were stimulated while the animal was in one of the conditioned place preference chambers. Then, after a training period, animals were given the choice to explore either the optically stimulated-paired chamber (light-paired chamber) or chamber not paired with light (control chamber). A robust conditioned place preference was exhibited with selective optical activation of cholinergic LDTg axon terminals in the VTA (Steidl et al., 2017). In contrast, selective activation of glutamatergic LDTg axon terminals in the VTA reduced the total amount of time spent in the light-paired chamber, suggesting conditioned aversion. Together, these results indicate potentially opposing roles for cholinergic and glutamatergic LDTg inputs. Interestingly, optical stimulation of glutamatergic terminals also caused the mice to enter the light-paired chamber more frequently, despite spending less time in that chamber overall. The caveat here is that it is possible that glutamatergic input to the VTA from the LDTg might trigger an approach to rewarding stimuli (the light-paired chamber), as stimulating those inputs when the mouse enters the light-paired chamber increased entries into that chamber. Based on this evidence, cholinergic inputs to VTA from LDTg appear to drive reward-related learning processes, whereas glutamatergic inputs appear to drive aversion and/or approach behaviors to rewarding stimuli.

Another way to assess the contributions of acetylcholine from the LDTg/PPTg is via administration of cholinergic agonists and antagonists directly into the VTA. This approach is relatively simple and examines all cholinergic inputs into the VTA at the same time (e.g., from both the LDTg and PPTg). Cholinergic activation of VTA nAChRs play a major role in controlling the activity of dopamine neurons. We mentioned before that β2* nAChRs are critical for allowing VTA dopamine neurons to switch from tonic to burst firing. Prior and subsequent studies have highlighted a functional role for β2* nAChRs within the VTA. Both α4β2* and α6β2* nAChRs are critical for driving the rewarding effects of nicotine and play important roles in VTA burst firing, whereas α6β2* nAChRs appear to be more important in driving phasic dopamine release in the NAc (Corrigall et al., 1994; Liu et al., 2012; Wickham et al., 2013). Moreover, the M5 mAChR receptor also plays a major role in driving phasic DA release, suggesting that both nAChRs and mAChRs are important for controlling VTA neuron activity (Forster et al., 2002). Below, we will explore how VTA nAChRs and mAChRs receptors may play roles in reward-related behaviors.

VTA mAChRs in drug reward

Muscarinic AChRs localized on VTA neuron dendrites play a major role in driving eating/consummatory behaviors and associated learning (e.g., operant conditioning for food reward), while nAChRs appear to play little to no role (Sharf et al., 2006; Sharf and Ranaldi, 2006). Since the M5 receptor is the main subtype expressed by VTA dopamine neurons, M5 mAChRs are thought to be the primary receptor regulating food consumption and food reward-related learning, although other mAChRs may also contribute to signaling in this region (Yeomans, 2012). The idea that VTA M5 receptor function is important for consumption of other substances of abuse was further explored using knockout mice lacking the M5 receptor. M5 knockout mice show reduced cocaine and morphine reinforcement, suggesting that M5 activation in the VTA may function as a general "reward" signal, especially since it modulates dopamine release from VTA terminals in the NAc (Basile et al., 2002; Forster et al., 2002; Fink-Jensen et al., 2003; Forster and Blaha, 2003). These findings are in line with previously discussed optogenetic studies showing a role for cholinergic input from the LDTg in reward-related learning.

VTA nAChRs in drug reward

The function of nAChRs in nicotine reward is relatively well studied and quite complex. Almost 35 years ago, Bill Corrigall and colleagues showed that infusion of DHβE, a β2* nAChR specific antagonist, into the VTA of male Long-Evans rats reduced nicotine self-administration (Corrigall et al., 1994). Pioneering work by Marina Picciotto showed that mice lacking the β2 subunit fail to self-administer nicotine, implying that nAChRs with β2 receptors are important for nicotine-taking behaviors (Picciotto et al., 1998). Subsequent work by Stéphanie Pons and colleagues took advantage of knockout mouse and viral vector strategies to show that mice lacking α4, α6, or β2 nAchR subunits do not experience the rewarding effects of nicotine. Using lentiviral approaches, restoring VTA expression of α4, α6, or β2 in the respective knockout mice produced robust nicotine self-administration, demonstrating that α4α6β2* nAChRs may be the major player in driving nicotine reinforcement in the VTA.

One feature of nAChRs that complicates our understanding of their function is that nAChRs desensitize rapidly to nicotine. At concentrations of nicotine that are comparable to those experienced by humans smokers, α7 receptors are the slowest to desensitize while the β2* nAChRs are the fastest (note: the converse is true at supraphysiologically high, but behaviorally irrelevant, levels of nicotine) (Wooltorton et al., 2003). There is a bit of a paradox here: nicotine stays in the blood for hours in a human smoker, but β2*nAChRs desensitize on the order of seconds to minutes. This does NOT match the experience of a human smoker, who will experience euphoria and positive mood for much longer than it takes for β2* nAChRs to desensitize. So why does a smoker still have a "buzz" if the purported *required* nAChR is stuck in a desensitized state? In this case, the differences between both (a) the rate of desensitization between α7 and β2*nAChRs and (b) the location of the specific nAChR expression contributes to these effects (Fig. 11.2), which we will explore in greater detail below.

Cholinergic receptors are located both pre- and post-synaptically within the VTA. For example, β2* nAChRs are located on VTA DA cell bodies as well as the GABA terminals innervating those cell bodies, whereas α7 receptors are located primarily on glutamatergic terminals (potentially arising from the PPTg/LDTg, prefrontal cortex, or other brain areas) (Jones and Wonnacott, 2004). When a smoker first takes a puff of a cigarette, nicotine enters the brain and activates β2* and α7 nAChRs. Before desensitization begins: (1) nicotine activates α7 nAChRs on glutamate terminals, increasing glutamate release onto VTA DA neurons and causing burst-firing; (2) nicotine activates β2* nAChRs on VTA DA neurons causing burst-firing; and (3) nicotine activates β2* nAChRs on GABA terminals, leading inhibition of the VTA DA neurons (Picciotto et al., 2008). The first two excitatory events outweigh the third inhibitory event, and thus, VTA DA neurons burst and produce dopamine release in the NAc, likely providing the "buzz" from smoking. However, over a matter of seconds, the β2* nAChRs

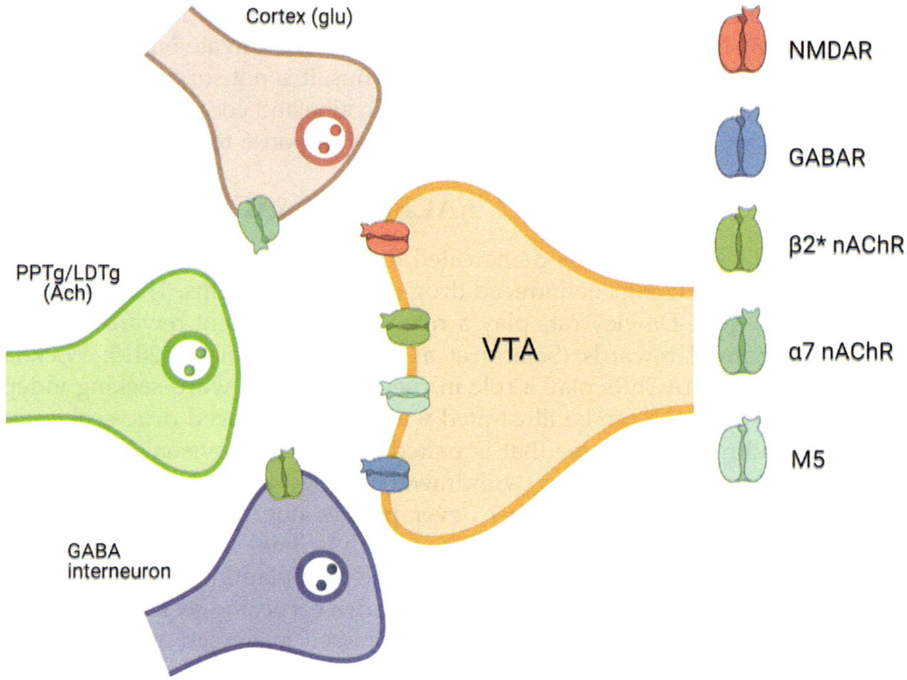

FIGURE 11.2 Cholinergic regulation of the VTA. Glutamatergic, GABAergic, and cholinergic inputs are well positioned to regulate VTA activity. Acetylcholine in particular can influence VTA activity both directly by stimulating postsynaptic β2* nAChRs or M5 receptors, or indirectly by eliciting glutamate release via α7 nAChRs. Nicotine can directly stimulate both β2*nAChRs on VTA neurons and α7 nAChRs on glutamate terminals which lead to increased burst-firing and phasic DA release. After nicotine has been in the brain for some time (~seconds to a minutes), β2*nAChRs desensitize and are rendered effectively nonfunctional. However, nicotine can still act on presynaptic glutamate terminals via the slowly desensitizing α7 nAChR, eliciting glutamate release and causing VTA neuron bursting. This mechanism helps account for the fact that smokers experience euphoria for several minutes after smoking a cigarette despite β2* nAChRs being in a desensitized state.

desensitize, rendering most of them nonfunctional, thereby leaving only event 1 from above intact, since α7 nAChRs desensitize on a much slower time scale at these nicotine concentrations (Giniatullin et al., 2005). In other words—differences in desensitization rates of these two receptors shift the VTA nicotine response toward a more glutamatergic dominated process, which may be the predominant mechanism that produces nicotine reward. A second consequence of this desensitization is related to the salience of smoking-related cues and their role in nicotine craving. Mice lacking β2 nAChR subunits have higher baseline levels of conditioned reinforcement, a behavioral assay that measures the reinforcing value of environmental cues (Brunzell et al., 2006). Thus, it is possible that desensitization of β2* nAChRs enhance the saliency of nicotine product related cues. Along these lines, PPTg inputs to the VTA likely play a role in driving some of the enhanced saliency of smoking cues given their ability to release both acetylcholine and glutamate. Environmental cues increase PPTg firing rate and increases the release of both glutamate and acetylcholine in the VTA (Pan and Hyland, 2005). In the case when the β2* nAChRs, but not the α7 nAChRs, are desensitized, cholinergic release activates α7-containing nAChRs on glutamate terminals, thereby enhancing NMDAR activation on VTA DA neurons (Picciotto et al., 2008). Moreover, PPTg neurons likely directly activate NMDARs via glutamate release from terminals in the VTA (Yau et al., 2016). Thus, it is not surprising that alterations of PPTg activity influences self-administration of both nicotine and cocaine in rats (Corrigall et al., 2002), as they are well positioned to influence the VTA response to environmental cues.

Functional differences between VTA nAChR and mAChR

Work done by Nii Addy's lab has demarcated the functional differences between nAChRs and mAChRs in the VTA using cue-induced drug-seeking paradigms. They showed that VTA nAChRs in male Sprague-Dawley rats play a role in cue-dependent reward-seeking for drug rewards, but not natural rewards (Solecki et al., 2013; Addy et al., 2015; Wickham et al., 2015). In contrast, VTA mAChRs play a role in cue-dependent reward-seeking independently of reward type. These results can be illustrated with the cue-induced drug-seeking paradigm, in which rats self-administer cocaine that is paired with an audiovisual cue for 10 days and then undergo a period of abstinence (withdrawal) for several days. When rats are placed back into the self-administration chamber, lever presses only produce the audiovisual cue while cocaine is omitted. Intra-VTA infusions of mecamylamine—a nonselective nAChR antagonist (meaning it blocks all nAChR subtypes) —and scopolamine—a nonselective mAChR antagonist—decreases the ability of these cues to drive cocaine-seeking behavior (Solecki et al., 2013). Interestingly, an experiment that addressed a similar question using sucrose self-administration in male Sprague-Dawley rats found that blockade of VTA mAChRs, but not nAChRs, decreased cue-induced sucrose-seeking (Addy et al., 2015). These experiments suggest that VTA nAChRs may selectively play a role in cue-induced drug-seeking, while VTA mAChRs may play a role in more general cue-induced reward-seeking. Other recent work by the Addy lab has shown overlapping roles of cholinergic receptor subtypes in mediating withdrawal effects from drugs of abuse. For example, in male rats that have undergone cocaine self-administration, intra-VTA infusions of mecamylamine or scopolamine reduced anxiety-like behavior during cocaine withdrawal (Nunes et al., 2019). Intra-VTA infusions of mecamylamine and scopolamine also reduced anxiety-like behavior in cocaine-naïve rats. Notably, cocaine-abstinent rats were more sensitive to the anxiety-reducing (anxiolytic) effects on mecamylamine or scopolamine, suggesting that function of both nAChRs and mAChRs in the VTA is highly dependent on drug use history.

Cholinergic circuits in the NAc

While inputs from the LDTg/PPTg to the VTA have been extensively studied, the function of LDTg/PPTg projections directly to the NAc has only recently been explored. The LDTg broadly innervates the striatum, with the greatest innervation in the NAc core and medial striatum (Dautan et al., 2014). This innervation consists of glutamatergic, GABAergic, and cholinergic terminals, with cholinergic inputs playing the most important role in driving reward-related behavior. In work spearheaded by Bárbara Coimbra in Ana João Rodrigues's lab, it was shown that optical simulation of LDTg terminals in the NAc increased the motivation of Wistar Han rats to obtain food reward, whereas optical inhibition of the same terminals reduced the motivation of rats to obtain food reward (Coimbra et al., 2019). These effects were produced by stimulation of cholinergic terminals, but not glutamatergic and GABAergic terminals, which highlights the importance of LDTg acetylcholine release into the NAc input in this behavior. These data mirror that of the optical stimulation of LDTg cholinergic axons into the VTA, suggesting a broader role of acetylcholine for influencing VTA-NAc circuits in reward-related learning. As mentioned above, the PPTg, and also likely the LDTg, influences both nicotine and cocaine self-administration in the VTA, but it is largely unknown how cholinergic input to the NAc affects drug-related behaviors.

Not all cholinergic inputs into the NAc originate from the LDTg/PPTg. There is a small population of cholinergic interneurons in the NAc that play an important role in fine-tuning the dopamine output of the VTA, which we will explore next. In the previous section, we centered our focus on the ACh receptors on VTA DA cell bodies and on the terminals of inputs to these neurons. In the following section, we will primarily focus on the role of cholinergic interneurons in modulating DA neurotransmission at the axon terminal in the NAc.

Tonically active cholinergic interneurons in the NAc

A key feature of cholinergic interneurons in the NAc is a "pause" in the firing rate that occurs during exposure to an environmental stimulus, which occurs with a similar latency to the burst firing observed in VTA neurons (Schultz and Romo, 1990; Aosaki et al., 1994). As such, these NAc cholinergic interneurons are termed tonically active neurons (TANs) and VTA dopamine neurons are called DANs. One possible explanation for the TAN pause is that dopamine released from the DANs activates dopamine D2 receptors on TANs, thereby inhibiting their activity. However, the connection here is bidirectional. TANs also innervate the dopamine neuron terminals. Thus, environmental cues increase VTA dopamine neuron activity, increase dopamine release onto TANs in the NAc, thereby inhibiting TANs and reducing cholinergic release back onto the dopamine neuron terminals in NAc (Fig. 11.3). The next section addresses the consequence of this bidirectional communication.

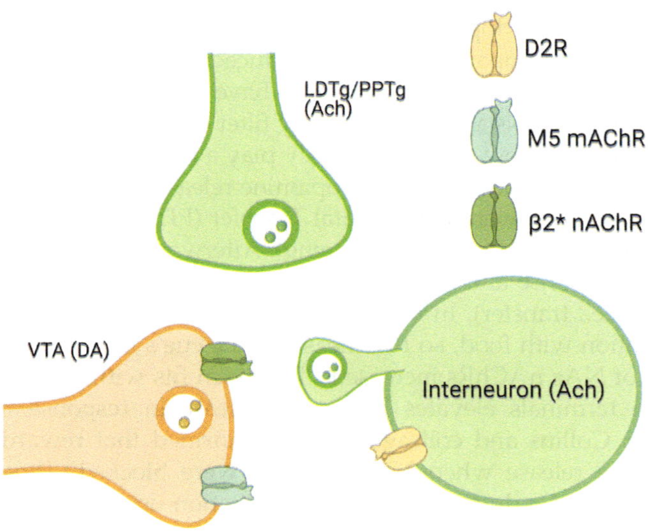

FIGURE 11.3 Cholinergic regulation of the NAc. Both cholinergic input from the LDTg/PPTg and local cholinergic interneurons can influence DA release by stimulating presynaptic M5 or β2*nAChRs. Upon DA release from the VTA, D2 receptor activation suppresses cholinergic interneuron activity, which in turn reduces presynaptic β2*nAChR activation. Reduction in β2*nAChR activation relieves the VTA terminal from short-term depression, allowing greater phasic DA release at high frequencies of firing.

In work led by Stephanie Cragg and Margaret Rice in the dorsal striatum of guinea pig brain slices, and work by Hui Zhang and David Sulzer in the nucleus accumbens of mouse brain slices, it was demonstrated that the effects of reduced cholinergic input to the dopamine neuron terminals actually *decreases* dopamine release when dopamine neurons fire at *low* frequencies, but i*ncreases* dopamine release when dopamine neurons fire at high frequencies or burst-fire (Rice and Cragg, 2004; Zhang and Sulzer, 2004). In mouse brain slices, Cragg and Rice stimulated the medial forebrain bundle (the axons connecting VTA dopamine neurons to the NAc) and used fast-scan cyclic voltammetry to measure phasic (<1 s) dopamine release. Interestingly, they found that when they used stimulation which mimicked the activity of bursting neurons (multiple stimulations, high firing rate), the amount of phasic dopamine release was not that much different than what was produced by a single stimulation, which mimics tonic dopamine neuron firing. In other words, dopamine neuron phasic release in the striatum is not very sensitive to the frequency of firing. This is thought to occur due to a process called short-term depression, in which neurons exhaust their neurotransmitter stores and subsequent action potentials generate diminished neurotransmitter release. However, when the experimenters bath applied mecamylamine (the nAChR antagonist) onto the brain slice, the relationship between phasic dopamine release and dopamine neuron firing rate became more linear: lower frequencies produced low levels of dopamine, whereas high frequencies produced high levels of dopamine. Thus, it is thought that reductions of nAChR activation on dopamine terminals can produce higher levels of dopamine when these neurons fire at high frequencies. Similarly, DHβE, a β2*nAChR selective antagonist, or nicotine which rapidly desensitizes β2*nAChRs, produced identical results.

In summary, when VTA dopamine neurons fire the first action potential of a burst, they release dopamine onto TANs, which results in inhibition of TANs (i.e., the "pause" mentioned above). The net effect of this action is a reduction of cholinergic release, thereby limiting β2*nAChR activation on dopamine axon terminals. This feedback suppresses the release of dopamine from the first action potential within the burst and prevents short-term depression, facilitating the release of dopamine in response to subsequent action potentials. Thus, cholinergic TANs may serve as a frequency filter, allowing biologically important stimuli that produce burst-firing to produce high levels of dopamine. Moreover, this frequency filter exaggerates the gap between the amounts of dopamine release produced by high and low-frequency firing, allowing stimuli that drive high-frequency firing to have greater saliency.

What is the functional consequence of the TANs and this frequency filter on behavior? Work lead by Anne Collins and Kate Wassum's lab show that TANs likely play a role in motivation in reward-learning, mainly through cholinergic modulation of dopamine release (Collins et al., 2016). Using a behavioral approach called Pavlovian Instrumental Transfer (PIT), they trained male rats to associate a cue with food reward (Pavlovian conditioning). Afterward, they trained the same rats to learn an instrumental response and assessed the influence of the previously learned cue on instrumental behavior (i.e., transfer). In other words, the cue has some motivating properties because of its association with food, so PIT measures the cue's motivational valence on other behaviors. Blockade of NAc nAChRs increased PIT, which fits with the idea that blocking nAChRs on dopamine terminals elevates dopamine release in response to reward-predictive environmental cues. Collins and colleagues then confirmed that reward-predictive cues evoked more dopamine release when NAc nAChRs were blocked. These data suggest that pausing of TAN firing and reductions of nAChR activation on presynaptic

DA terminals play a key role in amplifying the saliency of environmental cues. Therefore, it is no wonder that one of the major drivers of craving in those who use tobacco or e-cigarette products are the environmental cues that are associated with smoking. The saliency of nicotine product cues is probably exaggerated due to the constant desensitization of β2*nAChRs on dopamine terminals and consequentially elevated dopamine release in response to those cues. Interestingly, PIT was reduced and phasic dopamine release decreased when blocking mAChRs in the NAc. While not the only possible explanation, it is known that activation of M5 mAChRs on dopamine terminals enhances phasic dopamine release, so it would not be surprising that blocking M5 mAChRs results in reduced PIT and phasic dopamine release (Shin et al., 2015). However, whether or not the M5 mAChR activation effects are tied to the firing rate of the dopamine neurons, like nAChRs are, is unknown.

Comparison of cholinergic input to the VTA and NAc

You may have noted a similarity between the role of nAChRs located within the VTA and on VTA terminals in downstream brain regions. In both cases, desensitization of β2* nAChRs leads to enhanced phasic dopamine neurotransmission. Thus, smoking-associated cues that are present predominantly when β2* nAChRs are in a desensitized state gain enhanced saliency and ability to produce craving in smokers. Identifying these mechanisms is important in understanding potential pharmacotherapeutic treatments. For example, varenicline, a partial α4β2* nAChR agonist, in theory could slow down the desensitization of β2* nAChRs by effectively preventing nicotine from binding them. Varenicline, a partial agonist of the α4β2* nAChRs and full agonist of α7 nAChRS, does help curb nicotine craving in part by reducing the saliency of environmental cues (Garcia-Rivas et al., 2019). Indeed, Vernon Garcia-Rivas's work in Véronique Deroche-Gamonet's lab illustrated this using a clever behavioral paradigm. In this paradigm, male Sprague-Dawley rats were trained to self-administer intravenous nicotine which coincided with presentation of a light cue. However, one group of rats were trained in near total darkness whereas another group were trained with ambient levels of light. Animals trained in the darkness viewed the cue light as more salient compared to animals trained in the ambient light, since the cue light appeared brighter. After self-administration training, the light treatment for each group was reversed, and it was found that animals originally trained in the dark exhibited decreases in self-administration, whereas animals trained with ambient light exhibited increases in self-administration after the switch. Thus—this paradigm is a way to assess the saliency of the light cue. When the cue's saliency increases, so does self-administration of nicotine and vice-versa. When animals that were originally trained in ambient light had the light removed *and* were given a systemic injection of varenicline, no increase in self-administration occurred. While varenicline itself did decrease the rewarding value of nicotine alone, it effectively blunted the increased levels of self-administration produced by increasing the saliency of the light (i.e., by removing the ambient light). Again, these data point to a role for β2* nAChR desensitization in driving the effects of smoking-related cues on nicotine consumption. The current theory for varenicline's mechanism of action is that it prevents nicotine from desensitizing the β2* nAChRs, likely both at the level of VTA cell bodies and VTA terminals, which will reduce the saliency of smoking-related cues in addition to reducing the rewarding properties of nicotine.

Role of acetylcholine in the basolateral amygdala

In addition to its effects on reward function in the mesolimbic dopamine system (i.e., VTA to NAc), acetylcholine also plays a key role in mediating many anxiety-related behaviors. For instance, injection of physostigmine (acetylcholinesterase inhibitor) causes anxiogenic-like and pro-depressive-like behaviors in mice (Mineur et al., 2018). More specifically, the basolateral amygdala (BLA) plays an important role in mediating anxiety-like responses and expresses many AChRs. The pathogenesis of excess anxiety centers around hyperexcitability of the BLA, and withdrawal from substances of abuse, depends to some degree on BLA activity (Belujon et al., 2016). The major source of cholinergic input to the BLA arises from the nucleus basalis (NB) of the basal forebrain. Optogenetic stimulation of the NB increases the activity of BLA neurons, and this activation is dependent on both nAChRs and mAChRs (Jiang et al., 2016), with β2* nAChR and α7 nAChRs playing prominent roles. While the behavioral role of mAChRs are less understood, there is evidence to suggest that nAChRs play a role in mediating some of the anxiogenic effects of withdrawal or brain trauma-induced anxiety. In a rat model of mild brain injury, the resulting increases in anxiety-like behaviors were associated with decreased GABAergic inputs with increased expression of α7 receptors in BLA neurons (Klein and Yakel, 2006). Interestingly, a clinical trial of an α7 negative allosteric modulator reduced BLA responses to fearful stimuli in individuals with generalized anxiety disorder (Almeida-Suhett et al., 2014). These data suggest that cholinergic inputs into the BLA modulate anxiety and may depend on nAChR signaling. During abstinence, smokers that also have post-traumatic stress disorder experience more severe anxiety symptoms precipitated by withdrawal (Vujanovic et al., 2010), suggesting a potential interaction between cholinergic signaling and trauma on anxiety.

The BLA is also an important site of stimulus-reward learning, similar to the VTA-to-NAc circuit. Recent work by Richard Crouse in Marina Picciotto's lab showed that acetylcholine is released in the BLA in response to rewarding stimuli and their predictors, much like VTA dopamine release that occurs in response to rewards and reward-predictive cues (Schultz and Romo, 1990; Crouse et al. 2020). Optical stimulation of the NB-to-BLA circuit even enhanced reward-related learning, suggesting that cholinergic function within the BLA may help generate stimulus-reward associations. This finding is backed up by prior behavioral work showing a role for BLA acetylcholine in stimulus-reward learning. For example, cocaine-induced long-term potentiation in the mouse amygdala is more robust after nAChR activation (Huang et al., 2013). Similarly, nAChR blockade in the BLA prevents the development of conditioned place preference for ethanol, which hints that activation of these receptors stymie the association between the rewarding properties of ethanol and contextual stimuli (Zarrindast et al., 2010). Additionally, mAChR activation is also likely important for forming associations between drugs and environmental cues. Pharmacological blockade of mAChRs in the BLA prevents the association between cocaine and an environmental stimulus (See et al., 2003). Given that the BLA is highly important in relapse of drug-taking behavior (Whitelaw et al., 1996; Fuchs et al., 2002; Ito et al., 2006), it is tempting to suggest that cholinergic modulation in the BLA may contribute to drug relapse; however, there is not yet data to support this hypothesis.

Role of acetylcholine in the prefrontal cortex

The prefrontal cortex (PFC) plays a role in various processes, including attention, memory, response inhibition, and decision making, among others (Miller and Cohen, 2001). Acetylcholine, more broadly, is thought to play an important role in attentional processes within the PFC, and thereby may influence how drug-related stimuli are processed or attended to. Like in the BLA, the main supplier of cholinergic input to the prefrontal cortex is the NB. Selective cholinergic lesions of the NB reduce visual attention in a five-choice serial reaction time task (McGaughy et al., 2002), while acetylcholine release is elevated in the PFC during completion of the task. Current evidence suggests that cholinergic signaling through β2* nAChRs are responsible for the attentional functions of acetylcholine (Guillem et al., 2011). Smokers, especially those that started during adolescence, tend to have aberrant attentional function (Jacobsen et al., 2005). Other studies have implicated PFC acetylcholine signaling in the encoding of relevant environmental cues, which may be important for driving the effects of cues on drug taking and reward learning. These data suggest that cholinergic input to the PFC from the NB is responsible for attentional and environmental cue processes, which are typically hypofunctional after prolonged drug use (Jacobsen et al., 2005).

The precise role of PFC acetylcholine in drug addiction is relatively less understood compared to acetylcholine's role in other addiction-related brain areas. We know that acetylcholine levels are elevated during consumption of some drugs of abuse, particularly stimulants like cocaine and amphetamines (Ichikawa et al., 2002), which can lead to the development of psychomotor sensitization to stimulants (Sarter et al., 2006; Sarter et al., 2012). Blockade of medial PFC mAChRs reduces cocaine self-administration, suggesting a potential role for acetylcholine in driving drug reinforcement (Ikemoto and Goeders 2000). However, the role of acetylcholine function in the PFC in drug addiction warrants further investigation.

Aversion-related signaling: habenula to interpeduncular circuit

The habenula (Hb) was first identified by Serres in 1824 and then characterized in anatomic detail in 1911 by Ramon y Cajal (1911). This relatively small structure is located bilaterally on the midline, adjacent to the dorsal third ventricle, and provides a functional connection between the limbic forebrain and midbrain. Although this structure is relatively conserved across species, asymmetrical development of the right and left habenula is found in fish, reptiles and amphibians. The thin skull of these animals allows for light to enter and activate the photoreactive cells of the pineal gland, thereby contributing to the development of habenula bilateral asymmetry in size and signaling mechanisms (Concha and Wilson, 2001). In contrast, mammals with thicker skulls do not appear to have pineal photoreactive cells, leading to largely symmetrical habenula structures between hemispheres. The habenula receives input from the stria medullaris, which contains axons from the septum, nucleus of the diagonal band, basal ganglia, lateral hypothalamus, lateral preoptic area, and NB. The habenula is divided into the medial (MHb) and lateral (LHb) regions based on differences in cellular morphology, signaling mechanisms, afferent/efferent projections, and function.

Medial habenulo-interpeduncular (MHb-IPN) circuit

The dorsal and ventral regions of the MHb exhibit distinct patterns of gene expression that are likely related to the different functions of these sub-regions. The dorsal MHb contains several proteins and peptides implicated in pain regulation, including neurokinin1, substance P, μ opioid receptor, G-protein coupled receptor 139 (GPR139), and tachykinin receptor 1 (Contestabile et al., 1987; Aizawa et al., 2012; Wagner et al., 2014). Activation of μ opioid receptors induces inhibitory G-protein and ERK1/2 signaling in habenular neurons, leading to downstream activation of the kinase RSK2. Interestingly, selective knockdown of RSK2 in the MHb of male mice prevents the μ opioid receptor agonist, morphine, from alleviating pain (Darcq et al., 2012), which thereby defines a molecular mechanism of pain processing in the MHb. Interestingly, activation of GPR139 in these same cells appears to counteract the inhibitory effect of μ opioid receptors on neuronal activity in the MHb of male and female mice (Stoveken et al., 2020), providing evidence for dynamic intracellular balance of pain regulation.

A prominent feature of the MHb is the dense expression of cholinergic signaling factors, which include choline acetyltransferase, acetylcholine, acetylcholinesterase and the vesicular acetylcholine transporter, as well as the α3, α4, α5, β2 and β4 nAChR subunits (Contestabile et al., 1987; Grady et al., 2009; Aizawa et al., 2012). Nicotinic AChRs are mainly localized in cholinergic and glutamatergic co-expressing neurons, but α6 and α4 nAChR subunits have also been identified in non-cholinergic neurons (Shih et al., 2014). The majority of neurons fire tonic spontaneous action potentials at baseline levels, suggesting sustained neurotransmitter release at the axonal terminals (McCormick and Prince, 1987; Ren et al., 2011; Gorlich et al., 2013). In cholinergic neurons, hyperpolarization-activated cyclic nucleotide-gated (HCN) pacemaker channels maintain a spontaneous tonic firing rate of 2-10 Hz in MHb neurons of mice (Gorlich et al., 2013). Further, nicotine enhances intrinsic neuronal excitability via actions on α5β2* or α3β4* nAChRs, and the neuropeptide neurokinin has also been shown to mediate MHb neuronal excitability in mice (Gorlich et al., 2013; Dao et al., 2014). The MHb neurons send well-characterized projections to the interpeduncular nucleus, a pathway termed the fasciculus retroflexus. Of note, the fasciculus retroflexus appears to be among the first fiber tracts that form in the developing human fetus (Cho et al., 2014), which terminates in the midline-localized structure of the IPN. The lateral IPN receives substance P and glutamatergic fibers from the dorsal MHb, whereas the central and intermediate regions receive cholinergic and glutamatergic fibers from the ventral MHb (Contestabile et al., 1987; Kawaja et al., 1988; Ren et al., 2011). Moreover, the axonal fibers extending into the central region display a striking pattern of innervation as they begin at the base of the IPN, then zigzag upward through the structure while forming *en passant* synaptic connections (Kawaja et al., 1988). It is thought that this organization allows for the integration of information from both the left and right MHbs (Lenn et al., 1983). Pre-synaptic nAChRs on these habenular axons modulate the release of glutamate and acetylcholine (Grady et al., 2009). The IPN neurons send broad ascending and descending projections to various brain regions. The most prominent of these projections are the tegmental nuclei, medial septum/nucleus of the diagonal band, hippocampus, raphe and periaqueductal gray (Shibata and Suzuki, 1984; Groenewegen et al., 1986; Montone et al., 1988; Klemm, 2004). Further, IPN signaling leads to subsequent downstream effects on the reward-related mesolimbic pathway via cholinergic signaling. Specifically, IPN GABAergic neurons expressing α4β2α5* and α3β4α5* nAChRs terminate in the cholinergic DTg, which then release acetylcholine into the VTA as described above (Groenewegen et al., 1986; Lammel et al., 2012; Hsu et al., 2013). The DTg and raphe neurons also send reciprocal projections back to the IPN (Groenewegen et al., 1986), and the nucleus of the tractus solitarius relays peripheral body signals into the IPN (Tuesta et al., 2017). Therefore, given the multiple feed-forward and feed-back mechanisms of the IPN, it has been characterized as a central hub for circuit integration.

MHb-IPN nicotine-mediated behaviors

Functionally, the MHb-IPN pathway regulates nicotine intake by mediating the aversive properties of the drug. For instance, α5* nAChRs and the MHb-IPN pathway neurons have both been implicated in regulating nicotine consumption at high doses of the drug in mice and rats (Fowler et al., 2011), as well as symptoms associated with nicotine withdrawal in male mice (Salas et al., 2009; Zhao-Shea et al., 2013). With chronic nicotine use, brain regions regulating the aversive response to nicotine may also become less responsive, thus promoting further drug intake leading to dependence. Men and women with allelic gene variation in the α5-α3-β4 nAChR subunit gene cluster, *CHRNA5-CHRNA3-CHRNB4*, exhibit increased vulnerability to nicotine addiction, as evidenced by a higher likelihood of becoming dependent on nicotine and increased number of cigarettes consumed per day (Bierut et al., 2008; Saccone et al., 2009). Investigations into the function of the α5, α3 and β4 nAChR subunits that are expressed in the MHb-IPN circuit have revealed the underlying mechanisms mediating this vulnerability. Adult male and female mice lacking the α5 nAChR gene do not differ in intravenous nicotine self-administration at moderate rewarding doses, but do exhibit an increased level of responding at higher doses of nicotine, compared to wildtype controls (Fowler et al., 2011). These findings suggest that α5* nAChRs do not regulate the reinforcing properties of the drug, but rather mediate the aversive response to high doses. Indeed, rewarding doses of nicotine similarly reduce ICSS brain reward thresholds (indicative of increased brain reward function) in adult α5 knockout and wildtype male mice (Fowler et al., 2013). However, as the unit dose of nicotine increases, wildtype mice exhibit an attenuation of nicotine's lowering effects on brain reward thresholds, with increased aversive signaling more prominent as the dose escalates. In contrast, α5 knockout mice still exhibit nicotine-induced reductions of reward-related threshold values at these higher nicotine doses. Moreover, a high dose of nicotine maintains its rewarding value in adult α5 knockout, but not wildtype, male mice, as assessed in a conditioned place preference procedure (Jackson et al., 2010). Together, these studies indicate that α5* nAChRs control aversion signaling. In addition to the α5 nAChR subunit, the α3 and β4 nAChR subunits have also been implicated in mediating the aversive effects of nicotine. Transgenic overexpression of the β4 nAChR subunit leads to an enhanced aversive response to nicotine, as evidenced by decreased oral consumption of a nicotine solution in adult male mice (Frahm et al., 2011). The above nAChR-mediated effects have been localized to the MHb-IPN pathway. Re-expression of α5 nAChR subunits in the MHb-IPN pathway of adult male α5 knockout mice results in a "rescued" behavioral phenotype, as nicotine intake becomes normalized to wildtype levels (Fowler et al., 2011), and viral-mediated α3 nAChR gene knockdown in the MHb or IPN results in increased nicotine intake at higher doses with intravenous self-administration in adult male rats (Elayouby et al., 2020). Nicotine intake can be further modulated by alternate mechanisms that act on the MHb-IPN synaptic region. For instance, a subtype of projection neurons in the IPN also release nitric oxide from the cell body within the IPN, which serves to retrogradely inhibit signals from MHb axon terminals (Ables et al., 2017), and the peptide GLP-1 also acts on the MHb-IPN synaptic region to decrease nicotine intake (Tuesta et al., 2017), as demonstrated in adult male and female mice and adult male rats. Taken together, these findings indicate a dynamic signaling process occurring at MHb axonal terminals in the IPN, which regulates the addictive properties of nicotine and inserts a "stop signal" on nicotine intake that is mediated by alterations in the intensity of aversive effects of higher doses of nicotine.

Cessation of nicotine use results in an aversive withdrawal syndrome, which can persist from weeks to months in men and women (Shiffman and Jarvik, 1976). When someone experiences the aversive physical and affective symptoms of withdrawal, this can promote re-consumption of the drug to alleviate negative symptoms (Piasecki et al., 2000). Cholinergic signaling has been shown to play an essential role in these processes. Men and women with allelic genetic variation in the α4 nAChR subunit gene, *CHRNA4*, report intense withdrawal symptoms when quitting smoking (Lazary et al., 2014), and allelic variation in the α3 nAChR subunit, *CHRNA3*, is associated with increased withdrawal symptoms and drug craving (Sarginson et al., 2011). In rodent studies, chronic nicotine administration is most often achieved with subcutaneously implanted minipumps or via administration in the drinking water. Following chronic nicotine exposure in adult male mice, β4* nAChR binding sites are significantly increased in the MHb (Meyers et al., 2015), and β4 and β3 subunit mRNA are increased in the IPN (Zhao-Shea et al., 2013), suggesting an increased ability of the cell to respond with higher receptor numbers. However, the baseline level of MHb neuronal activity does not appear to change during chronic nicotine administration (Gorlich et al., 2013; Shih et al., 2014), but during nicotine withdrawal, nicotine-induced activity is dramatically decreased following short-term nicotine administration (3 and 14 days in adult male and female mice) (Shih et al., 2014) but increased after longer periods of administration (28 days in mice, sex unspecified) (Gorlich et al., 2013). Induction of the withdrawal state may be achieved by removal of the nicotine source for a more gradual spontaneous withdrawal, similar to someone quitting smoking. Alternatively, a nAChR antagonist, such as mecamylamine, is commonly administered to rodents to immediately block the direct actions of nicotine on nAChRs and thereby precipitate withdrawal. Quantitative assessment of the somatic signs of withdrawal includes characterizing the behaviors of shaking, scratching, head nods, chewing, and increased grooming, whereas the affective signs of withdrawal may include assessments of anxiety-related behaviors, conditioned place aversion, or elevated brain reward ICSS thresholds. Although the general nicotinic receptor antagonist, mecamylamine, is commonly used to precipitate withdrawal, other antagonists selective for α3β4*, α4β2* or α7* nAChRs are also highly effective (Damaj et al., 2003). This evidence highlights the potential receptor subtypes that likely mediate the withdrawal state. Interestingly, administration of an antagonist selective for the α6* nAChR exerts an opposing effect with a reduction in the expression of a withdrawal-induced conditioned place aversion in adult male mice (Jackson et al., 2009). Indeed, cholinergic signaling mechanisms in the MHb-IPN pathway neurons critically regulate the withdrawal state via nicotinic receptor signaling, which has been demonstrated in knockout mouse models. Specifically, adult male and female mice lacking the α2, α5, or β4 nAChR subunit exhibit few nicotine somatic withdrawal symptoms (Salas et al., 2004, 2009). Interestingly, the somatic withdrawal-mediating effects of the α2 nAChR subunit, which is expressed in the IPN, appears to be dependent on the context. In a familiar environment, adult α2 knockout male and female mice exhibit fewer somatic signs of withdrawal (Salas et al., 2009), but in an unfamiliar environment, adult α2 knockout male and female mice exhibit an increase in the number of somatic and affective signs of withdrawal, as assessed by a cued fear conditioning paradigm (Lotfipour et al., 2013). Increased anxiety-related behaviors are also exhibited during nicotine withdrawal, but these are lessened in adult male mice lacking the β2 nAChR subunit (Jackson et al., 2008). Of further interest, while the β2* nAChR may mediate affective anxiety-related components, it does not appear to modulate somatic behaviors during withdrawal in adult male and female mice (Salas et al., 2004; Jackson et al., 2008). Consistent with the role of the MHb in withdrawal, adult male and female mice lacking the μ opioid receptor also demonstrate an attenuation of somatic signs during withdrawal (Berrendero et al., 2002). While data from gene knockout models provide compelling findings, it is important to recognize that these strategies remove the receptor subunit from the entire brain and body throughout development. Thus, direct MHb-IPN manipulations are necessary to more clearly link this brain structure with the effects of nicotine withdrawal. Injection of the nAChR antagonist mecamylamine directly into the MHb or IPN is sufficient to elicit an increase in withdrawal symptoms in nicotine-exposed adult male and female mice (Salas et al., 2009), and disruption of HCN pacemaker activity in cholinergic MHb neurons can also induce somatic and anxiety-related withdrawal symptoms in mice (Gorlich et al., 2013). Further, administration of the substance P receptor neurokinin 1 antagonist or neurokinin B receptor antagonist directly into the MHb increases the somatic signs of nicotine withdrawal in adult male and female mice (Dao et al., 2014). Therefore, these data together support the notion that the MHb-IPN circuitry is an essential regulator of aversion experienced during nicotine withdrawal, and that this occurs via multiple signaling mechanisms.

Signaling of neurons in the MHb also appears to be important for other psychological states. For instance, substance P, mu opioid receptors, and phosphodiesterase 2A have all been implicated in stress and pain-related behavioral responses. Selective destruction of the MHb GPR151-expressing cells results in impulsive and compulsive behavior, hyperactivity, environmental maladaptation, and learning deficits, as examined in male and female adult mice (Kobayashi et al., 2013). Moreover, fear-related processing appears to involve a circuit from the medial amygdala to the bed nucleus of the anterior commissure and subsequently to substance P-expressing neurons of the dorsal MHb (Yamaguchi et al., 2013). The anxiety-related effects of nicotine also appears to involve a circuit originating in the hippocampus and projecting to the triangular septal nucleus and then to cholinergic neurons of the ventral MHb, which subsequently terminate in the central IPN (Yamaguchi et al., 2013). Therefore, given that α4*, β3* and β4* nAChRs are expressed in the ventral MHb cholinergic neurons, it is not surprising that these subunits have also been implicated in anxiety-related behaviors in male and female mice (Ross et al., 2000; Salas et al., 2003; Booker et al., 2007). Since nicotine dependence exhibits high comorbidity with other maladaptive psychiatric states (Hughes et al., 1986; Heffner et al., 2013), these findings support the notion that common neurobiological mechanisms may underlie drug dependence and affective disorders.

Lateral habenula (LHb)

The LHb processes negative reward-, aversion- and depression-associated signals. LHb neurons are mainly glutamatergic, but there are also sparse GABAergic local interneurons. Cholinergic signaling is mediated by AChRs located on cells within this region, although more research is needed to fully characterize LHb cholinergic function. Furthermore, some MHb fibers project into the LHb but the neurotransmitter content of these neurons are unknown. A reciprocal LHb-MHb connection has not been found, although a small number of projections from the LHb to the IPN have been documented (Kim and Chang, 2005), thus further integration may occur in the IPN. The majority of LHb glutamatergic axons extend along the fasciculus retroflexus, but they exhibit diversity in their innervation to a variety of structures, including the raphe, central gray, substantia nigra pars compacta, reticular formation and rostral medial tegmental area. LHb glutamatergic axons neurons display a heterogeneous pattern of activity that includes tonic, burst oscillation or silent profiles at rest (Kim and Chang, 2005). In male rhesus monkeys, activation of the LHb with electrical stimulation results in excitation of RMTg neurons and subsequent inhibition of the vast majority of dopamine neurons in the VTA (Hong et al., 2011). In adult male rats, this pathway has been shown to mediate a conditioned avoidance response to cocaine infusions, decrease intravenous cocaine self-administration and reduce cocaine-seeking behavior during reinstatement (Friedman et al., 2010; Jhou et al., 2013). Further, the LHb receives feedback from GABAergic and glutamatergic projections of the VTA (Root et al., 2014). As noted above, limited cholinergic signaling has been documented in the LHb with only the presence of mAChRs, including the M2 (Wagner et al., 2014). Injection of a mAChR antagonist into the LHb has been shown to increase impulsive cocaine-seeking behaviors in a cocaine-associated environment in adult male rats (Zapata et al., 2017). The LHb is also important for depression and, given the high comorbidity of drug use disorders with depression, it is perhaps not surprising that similar brain regions may underlie drug dependence and affective disorders. In an initial study, humans with severe major depressive disorder were administered deep brain stimulation into the LHb, which profoundly alleviated the depressive state (Sartorius et al., 2010). These remarkable findings led to further investigations to discern the mechanisms of LHb signaling, and this research field recently merged with a renewed interest for the therapeutic potential of ketamine, a well-known tranquilizer used in veterinary medicine and street drug with high abuse potential (also known as 'Special K'). Specifically, intravenous infusion of ketamine can rapidly alleviate symptoms of depression in patients unresponsive to other pharmacotherapies (Phillips et al., 2019). Ketamine suppresses burst firing of the LHb via actions on the glutamatergic NMDA receptor (Yang et al., 2018), and the anti-muscarinic drug scopolamine has also been shown to alleviate depressive symptoms (Witkin et al., 2020), suggesting that further investigations may be warranted into the potential role of LHb cholinergic signaling in mediating (and perhaps treating) depression in humans.

Septal circuits

Located on the midline in the forebrain, the septum is an evolutionarily conserved part of the limbic system, although septal size and shape have a dramatically different appearance across species (Andy and Stephan, 1968). In rodents, the septum has been mainly divided into the lateral, medial and triangular regions, and are often grouped together with the nucleus of the diagonal band and bed nucleus of the stria terminalis. In humans, the septum appears to be characteristically different, consisting of two main subdivisions: the septum pellucidum and septum verum (Andy and Stephan, 1968). However, it is thought that these divisions contain the same neuronal groupings as that found in lower mammals, except with a much smaller triangular septum (Andy and Stephan, 1968).

Septo-hippocampal circuit

A large number of cholinergic neurons are found in the medial septum and nucleus of the diagonal band that project to the hippocampus, which accounts for the majority of acetylcholine released in the hippocampus (Tsanov, 2018). Cholinergic signaling in the hippocampus has generally been linked to exploratory behavior, learning and memory function, and sensory processing. Of note, many of these neurons co-express other signaling molecules, such as glutamate and neuropeptides, indicating that pre-synaptic nAChRs likely mediate multiple neurotransmitter systems through actions on mediating release into the synapse. One of the co-released neuropeptides, galanin, has been linked to nicotine dependence. For instance, allelic variation in the galanin receptor gene is associated with decreased likelihood to develop nicotine dependence in men and women, a finding that is supported by behavioral genetic knockout studies in adult male mice (Jackson et al., 2011). However, galanin is expressed in other reward-related brain regions as well, so the septo-hippocampal pathway may not be the circuit underlying these effects. A feedback mechanism for cholinergic tone is generated by reciprocal projections from the hippocampus back to the lateral septum, which then projects to the medial septum (Tsanov, 2018). Together, these feedforward and feedback circuits are thought to underlie correlational theta rhythms of 5-12 Hz between the two brain structures, which has been proposed to be important for learning and memory function. Cholinergic activation of mAChRs in the hippocampus have also been associated with the theta rhythms characteristic of REM sleep (Yamada and Ueda, 2019). Indeed, sleep disturbances are commonly found across the drug use trajectory for many substances of abuse. This has led to the theory that an altered sleep architecture may underlie various aspects of drug use and dependence, such as those found with alcohol (Koob and Colrain, 2020). In addition, the hippocampus has been implicated in cognitive deficits that occur when someone attempts to quit tobacco or nicotine vape use. Withdrawal from nicotine is characterized by deficits in hippocampal-dependent learning tasks, which can persist for a few days (Zeid et al., 2018). Such cognitive deficits may propagate relapse to drug use, since administration of nicotine alleviates these cognitive deficits through nicotine's actions on the hippocampal nAChRs. It is further important to note that when nicotine exposure occurs during early developmental stages, such as with maternal smoking during pregnancy or vaping during adolescence, longer-term effects are induced on hippocampal synaptic plasticity and signaling, which can then propagate more prolonged deficits in learning and memory function, as well as other maladaptive behavioral patterns (Zeid et al., 2018).

Septo-habenula circuit

The MHb receives multiple inputs from septal nuclei. For instance, the triangular nucleus sends cholinergic and glutamatergic input to the MHb, while GABAergic input originates from the medial septum and nucleus of the diagonal band (Contestabile and Fonnum, 1983; Qin and Luo, 2009). Given the role of the MHb in mediating the aversive effects of nicotine and nicotine withdrawal, as described above, septal input likely provides upstream modulation of withdrawal effects, although this postulation requires further investigation. Of note, the IPN sends projections back to the medial septum/nucleus of the diagonal band, thereby generating another level of feedback within this extended circuit.

Cerebellum

The cerebellum, Latin for "little brain", is localized caudal to the main cerebral cortex, near the brainstem. The intricate layers of crossing fibers within this structure have been well-defined for their involvement in mediating various aspects of movement, including coordination, precision and timing. Cholinergic fibers innervating the cerebellum mainly originate from the medulla, reticular formation and sensory nuclei. A wide variety of nAChRs, including those expressing the $\alpha3$, $\alpha4$, $\beta2$ and $\beta4$ subunits, are localized in the Purkinje, granule and deep cerebellar regions, and depending on their specific location, cerebellar nAChRs can mediate the release of glutamate, GABA or norepinephrine from axon terminals (Turner and Kellar, 2005; Turner et al., 2011). During development, cholinergic signaling controls the proliferation and survival of cerebellar granule cells, and thus, tobacco and e-cigarette nicotine use during pregnancy can result in altered cellular connectivity and function in the developing brain (Dwyer et al., 2009). Recent investigations have also begun to link cerebellar circuits with aspects of drug use. In adult human PET and fMRI imaging studies, many brain regions are differentially activated during drug relapse, including the cerebellum. For instance, increased cerebellar activation occurs when someone is exposed to cues associated with prior drug taking (e.g., drug paraphernalia or smells), and such cerebellar activation during drug craving has been demonstrated in individuals for nicotine, cocaine and alcohol (Jasinska et al., 2014). In one interesting study led by Nora Volkow, researchers brought cocaine users into the laboratory environment. When these men and women were told that they were going to receive cocaine and then were administered a cocaine infusion, glucose metabolism increased in the cerebellum and thalamus. This effect was not due to the cocaine infusion itself, since infusion of cocaine, after being told to expect a placebo infusion, did not result in such an effect on cerebellar activity (Volkow et al., 2003). Thus, the cerebellum appears to be important for cue-associated predictions of drug availability in individuals with prior drug use.

Conclusions

In this chapter, we began with the discovery of acetylcholine and the subsequent discovery of acetylcholine receptors. We then discussed rodent studies where researchers delineated and identified cholinergic pathways and circuits in the brain. With this context, we next reviewed the role of cholinergic projections in the brain that mediate behaviors such as approach behavior, reward, aversion, and avoidance behaviors. We also highlighted specific midbrain circuits where acetylcholine modulates the activity of dopamine, glutamate, GABA and other neurotransmitters to regulate drug reward and withdrawal behaviors, as well as cue-mediated behavior for natural rewards and for drugs that are used and misused by humans. We also considered the role of acetylcholine in the habenula, IPN, and hippocampal pathways and how acetylcholine actions in those circuits mediate learning, memory and aversion related behavior.

Throughout this chapter, readers may notice that vast majority of cited preclinical acetylcholine studies were performed in male rats and mice. This historical use of male animals is particularly evident in many of the early, and even ongoing, electrophysiological, molecular, and behavioral investigations of acetylcholine actions in the brain. As has been appropriately addressed elsewhere (Becker and Koob, 2016; Zakiniaeiz et al., 2016), this sole reliance on male animals is problematic for neuroscience research for several reasons. As it pertains to this chapter, a focus on male rodents limits our broader understanding of acetylcholine mechanisms across males and females, and prevents any possibility of identifying potentially highly relevant sex-differences. Sex differences can exist across a range of levels, from anatomical to molecular to behavior. Of relevance, estrogen has been shown to act as a positive allosteric modulator of $\alpha4\beta2^*$ nAChRs and appears to interact with cholinergic signaling in the hippocampus (Paradiso et al., 2001; Rudick et al., 2003; Towart et al., 2003), findings which have implications for both the male and female brain. Furthermore, an understanding of these mechanisms across females and males has important implications on both our understanding on the basic neurobiology and our understanding of the potential clinical implications of preclinical findings. In more recent work, particularly examinations of $\alpha5$ nAChR mechanisms and investigations of habenula and IPN pathways, there has been more appropriate inclusion of male and female animals. However, it is critically important that this approach be applied more recently across all levels of preclinical analysis, as is now mandated for National Institutes of Health (NIH) funded research.

References

Ables, J.L., Gorlich, A., Antolin-Fontes, B., Wang, C., Lipford, S.M., Riad, M.H., Ren, J., Hu, F., Luo, M., Kenny, P.J., Heintz, N., Ibanez-Tallon, I., 2017. Retrograde inhibition by a specific subset of interpeduncular alpha5 nicotinic neurons regulates nicotine preference. Proc. Natl. Acad. Sci. U. S. A. 114 (49), 13012–13017.

Addy, N.A., Nunes, E.J., Wickham, R.J., 2015. Muscarinic, but not nicotinic, acetylcholine receptor blockade in the ventral tegmental area attenuates cue-induced sucrose-seeking. Behav. Brain. Res. 291, 372–376.

Aizawa, H., Kobayashi, M., Tanaka, S., Fukai, T., Okamoto, H., 2012. Molecular characterization of the subnuclei in rat habenula. J. Comp. Neurol. 520 (18), 4051–4066.

Albuquerque, E.X., Pereira, E.F., Alkondon, M., Rogers, S.W., 2009. Mammalian nicotinic acetylcholine receptors: from structure to function. Physiol. Rev. 89 (1), 73–120.

Almeida-Suhett, C.P., Prager, E.M., Pidoplichko, V., Figueiredo, T.H., Marini, A.M., Li, Z., Eiden, L.E., Braga, M.F., 2014. Reduced GABAergic inhibition in the basolateral amygdala and the development of anxiety-like behaviors after mild traumatic brain injury. PLoS One 9 (7), e102627.

Andy, O.J., Stephan, H., 1968. The septum in the human brain. J. Comp. Neurol. 133 (3), 383–410.

Aosaki, T., Tsubokawa, H., Ishida, A., Watanabe, K., Graybiel, A.M., Kimura, M., 1994. Responses of tonically active neurons in the primate's striatum undergo systematic changes during behavioral sensorimotor conditioning. J. Neurosci. 14 (6), 3969–3984.

Arnold, H.M., Burk, J.A., Hodgson, E.M., Sarter, M., Bruno, J.P., 2002. Differential cortical acetylcholine release in rats performing a sustained attention task versus behavioral control tasks that do not explicitly tax attention. Neuroscience 114 (2), 451–460.

Basile, A.S., Fedorova, I., Zapata, A., Liu, X., Shippenberg, T., Duttaroy, A., Yamada, M., Wess, J., 2002. Deletion of the M5 muscarinic acetylcholine receptor attenuates morphine reinforcement and withdrawal but not morphine analgesia. Proc. Natl. Acad. Sci. U. S. A. 99 (17), 11452–11457.

Becker, J.B., Koob, G.F., 2016. Sex differences in animal models: focus on addiction. Pharmacol. Rev. 68 (2), 242–263.

Belujon, P., Jakobowski, N.L., Dollish, H.K., Grace, A.A., 2016. Withdrawal from acute amphetamine induces an amygdala-driven attenuation of dopamine neuron activity: reversal by ketamine. Neuropsychopharmacology 41 (2), 619–627.

Berrendero, F., Kieffer, B.L., Maldonado, R., 2002. Attenuation of nicotine-induced antinociception, rewarding effects, and dependence in mu-opioid receptor knock-out mice. J. Neurosci. 22 (24), 10935–10940.

Bierut, L.J., Stitzel, J.A., Wang, J.C., Hinrichs, A.L., Grucza, R.A., Xuei, X., Saccone, N.L., Saccone, S.F., Bertelsen, S., Fox, L., Horton, W.J., Breslau, N., Budde, J., Cloninger, C.R., Dick, D.M., Foroud, T., Hatsukami, D., Hesselbrock, V., Johnson, E.O., Kramer, J., Kuperman, S., Madden, P.A., Mayo, K., Nurnberger Jr., J., Pomerleau, O., Porjesz, B., Reyes, O., Schuckit, M., Swan, G., Tischfield, J.A., Edenberg, H.J., Rice, J.P., Goate, A.M., 2008. Variants in nicotinic receptors and risk for nicotine dependence. Am. J. Psychiatr. 165 (9), 1163–1171.

Blaha, C.D., Allen, L.F., Das, S., Inglis, W.L., Latimer, M.P., Vincent, S.R., Winn, P., 1996. Modulation of dopamine efflux in the nucleus accumbens after cholinergic stimulation of the ventral tegmental area in intact, pedunculopontine tegmental nucleus-lesioned, and laterodorsal tegmental nucleus-lesioned rats. J. Neurosci. 16 (2), 714–722.

Blaha, C.D., Winn, P., 1993. Modulation of dopamine efflux in the striatum following cholinergic stimulation of the substantia nigra in intact and pedunculopontine tegmental nucleus-lesioned rats. J. Neurosci. 13 (3), 1035–1044.

Booker, T.K., Butt, C.M., Wehner, J.M., Heinemann, S.F., Collins, A.C., 2007. Decreased anxiety-like behavior in beta3 nicotinic receptor subunit knockout mice. Pharmacol. Biochem. Behav. 87 (1), 146–157.

Brunzell, D.H., Chang, J.R., Schneider, B., Olausson, P., Taylor, J.R., Picciotto, M.R., 2006. beta2-Subunit-containing nicotinic acetylcholine receptors are involved in nicotine-induced increases in conditioned reinforcement but not progressive ratio responding for food in C57BL/6 mice. Psychopharmacology (Berl) 184 (3–4), 328–338.

Changeux, J.P., 2012. The nicotinic acetylcholine receptor: the founding father of the pentameric ligand-gated ion channel superfamily. J. Biol. Chem. 287 (48), 40207–40215.

Changeux, J.P., 2020. Discovery of the first neurotransmitter receptor: the acetylcholine nicotinic receptor. Biomolecules 10 (4).

Cho, K.H., Mori, S., Jang, H.S., Kim, J.H., Abe, H., Rodriguez-Vazquez, J.F., Murakami, G., 2014. The habenulo-interpeduncular and mammillothalamic tracts: early developed fiber tracts in the human fetal diencephalon. Childs. Nerv. Syst. 30 (9), 1477–1484.

Coimbra, B., Soares-Cunha, C., Vasconcelos, N.A.P., Domingues, A.V., Borges, S., Sousa, N., Rodrigues, A.J., 2019. Role of laterodorsal tegmentum projections to nucleus accumbens in reward-related behaviors. Nat. Commun. 10 (1), 4138.

Collins, A.L., Aitken, T.J., Greenfield, V.Y., Ostlund, S.B., Wassum, K.M., 2016. Nucleus accumbens acetylcholine receptors modulate dopamine and motivation. Neuropsychopharmacology 41 (12), 2830–2838.

Concha, M.L., Wilson, S.W., 2001. Asymmetry in the epithalamus of vertebrates. J. Anat. 199 (Pt 1–2), 63–84.

Contestabile, A., Fonnum, F., 1983. Cholinergic and GABAergic forebrain projections to the habenula and nucleus interpeduncularis: surgical and kainic acid lesions. Brain. Res. 275 (2), 287–297.

Contestabile, A., Villani, L., Fasolo, A., Franzoni, M.F., Gribaudo, L., Oktedalen, O., Fonnum, F., 1987. Topography of cholinergic and substance P pathways in the habenulo-interpeduncular system of the rat. An immunocytochemical and microchemical approach. Neuroscience 21 (1), 253–270.

Cornwall, J., Cooper, J.D., Phillipson, O.T., 1990. Afferent and efferent connections of the laterodorsal tegmental nucleus in the rat. Brain. Res. Bull. 25 (2), 271–284.

Corrigall, W.A., Coen, K.M., Adamson, K.L., 1994. Self-administered nicotine activates the mesolimbic dopamine system through the ventral tegmental area. Brain. Res. 653 (1–2), 278–284.

Corrigall, W.A., Coen, K.M., Zhang, J., Adamson, L., 2002. Pharmacological manipulations of the pedunculopontine tegmental nucleus in the rat reduce self-administration of both nicotine and cocaine. Psychopharmacology (Berl) 160 (2), 198–205.

Crouse, R.B., Kim, K., Batchelor, H.M., Girardi, E.M., Kamaletdinova, R., Chan, J., Rajebhosale, P., Pittenger, S.T., Role, L.W., Talmage, D.A., Jing, M., Li, Y., Gao, X.B., Mineur, Y.S., Picciotto, M.R., 2020. Acetylcholine is released in the basolateral amygdala in response to predictors of reward and enhances the learning of cue-reward contingency. Elife 9.

Dale, H.H., Dudley, H.W., 1929. The presence of histamine and acetylcholine in the spleen of the ox and the horse. J. Physiol. 68 (2), 97–123.

Damaj, M.I., Kao, W., Martin, B.R., 2003. Characterization of spontaneous and precipitated nicotine withdrawal in the mouse. J. Pharmacol. Exp. Therapeut. 307 (2), 526–534.

Dao, D.Q., Perez, E.E., Teng, Y., Dani, J.A., De Biasi, M., 2014. Nicotine enhances excitability of medial habenular neurons via facilitation of neurokinin signaling. J. Neurosci. 34 (12), 4273–4284.

Darcq, E., Befort, K., Koebel, P., Pannetier, S., Mahoney, M.K., Gaveriaux-Ruff, C., Hanauer, A., Kieffer, B.L., 2012. RSK2 signaling in medial habenula contributes to acute morphine analgesia. Neuropsychopharmacology 37 (5), 1288–1296.

Dautan, D., Huerta-Ocampo, I., Witten, I.B., Deisseroth, K., Bolam, J.P., Gerdjikov, T., Mena-Segovia, J., 2014. A major external source of cholinergic innervation of the striatum and nucleus accumbens originates in the brainstem. J. Neurosci. 34 (13), 4509–4518.

Day, J.J., Roitman, M.F., Wightman, R.M., Carelli, R.M., 2007. Associative learning mediates dynamic shifts in dopamine signaling in the nucleus accumbens. Nat. Neurosci. 10 (8), 1020–1028.

Digby, G.J., Shirey, J.K., Conn, P.J., 2010. Allosteric activators of muscarinic receptors as novel approaches for treatment of CNS disorders. Mol. Biosyst. 6 (8), 1345–1354.

Dwyer, J.B., McQuown, S.C., Leslie, F.M., 2009. The dynamic effects of nicotine on the developing brain. Pharmacol. Ther. 122 (2), 125–139.

Eglen, R.M., 2005. Muscarinic receptor subtype pharmacology and physiology. Prog. Med. Chem. 43, 105–136.

Elayouby, K.S., Ishikawa, M., Dukes, A.J., Smith, A.C.W., Lu, Q., Fowler, C.D., Kenny, P.J., 2021. alpha3* Nicotinic acetylcholine receptors in the habenula-interpeduncular nucleus circuit regulate nicotine intake. J. Neurosci. 41 (8), 1779–1787.

Ewins, A.J., 1914. Acetylcholine, a new active principle of ergot. Biochem. J. 8 (1), 44–49.

Fernandez de Sevilla, D., Nunez, A., Buno, W., 2021. Muscarinic receptors, from synaptic plasticity to its role in network activity. Neuroscience 456, 60–70.

Fink-Jensen, A., Fedorova, I., Wortwein, G., Woldbye, D.P., Rasmussen, T., Thomsen, M., Bolwig, T.G., Knitowski, K.M., McKinzie, D.L., Yamada, M., Wess, J., Basile, A., 2003. Role for M5 muscarinic acetylcholine receptors in cocaine addiction. J. Neurosci. Res. 74 (1), 91–96.

Floresco, S.B., West, A.R., Ash, B., Moore, H., Grace, A.A., 2003. Afferent modulation of dopamine neuron firing differentially regulates tonic and phasic dopamine transmission. Nat. Neurosci. 6 (9), 968–973.

Forster, G.L., Blaha, C.D., 2003. Pedunculopontine tegmental stimulation evokes striatal dopamine efflux by activation of acetylcholine and glutamate receptors in the midbrain and pons of the rat. Eur. J. Neurosci. 17 (4), 751–762.

Forster, G.L., Yeomans, J.S., Takeuchi, J., Blaha, C.D., 2002. M5 muscarinic receptors are required for prolonged accumbal dopamine release after electrical stimulation of the pons in mice. J. Neurosci. 22 (1), RC190.

Fowler, C.D., Lu, Q., Johnson, P.M., Marks, M.J., Kenny, P.J., 2011. Habenular alpha5 nicotinic receptor subunit signalling controls nicotine intake. Nature 471 (7340), 597–601.

Fowler, C.D., Tuesta, L., Kenny, P.J., 2013. Role of alpha5* nicotinic acetylcholine receptors in the effects of acute and chronic nicotine treatment on brain reward function in mice. Psychopharmacology (Berl) 229, 503–513.

Fowler, C.D., Turner, J.R., Imad Damaj, M., 2020. Molecular mechanisms associated with nicotine pharmacology and dependence. Handb. Exp. Pharmacol. 258, 373–393.

Frahm, S., Slimak, M.A., Ferrarese, L., Santos-Torres, J., Antolin-Fontes, B., Auer, S., Filkin, S., Pons, S., Fontaine, J.F., Tsetlin, V., Maskos, U., Ibanez-Tallon, I., 2011. Aversion to nicotine is regulated by the balanced activity of beta4 and alpha5 nicotinic receptor subunits in the medial habenula. Neuron 70 (3), 522–535.

Friedman, A., Lax, E., Dikshtein, Y., Abraham, L., Flaumenhaft, Y., Sudai, E., Ben-Tzion, M., Ami-Ad, L., Yaka, R., Yadid, G., 2010. Electrical stimulation of the lateral habenula produces enduring inhibitory effect on cocaine seeking behavior. Neuropharmacology 59 (6), 452–459.

Fuchs, R.A., Weber, S.M., Rice, H.J., Neisewander, J.L., 2002. Effects of excitotoxic lesions of the basolateral amygdala on cocaine-seeking behavior and cocaine conditioned place preference in rats. Brain. Res. 929 (1), 15–25.

Gamage, R., Wagnon, I., Rossetti, I., Childs, R., Niedermayer, G., Chesworth, R., Gyengesi, E., 2020. Cholinergic modulation of glial function during aging and chronic neuroinflammation. Front. Cell. Neurosci. 14, 577912.

Garcia-Rivas, V., Fiancette, J.F., Cannella, N., Carbo-Gas, M., Renault, P., Tostain, J., Deroche-Gamonet, V., 2019. Varenicline targets the reinforcing-enhancing effect of nicotine on its associated salient cue during nicotine self-administration in the rat. Front. Behav. Neurosci. 13, 159.

Giniatullin, R., Nistri, A., Yakel, J.L., 2005. Desensitization of nicotinic ACh receptors: shaping cholinergic signaling. Trends. Neurosci. 28 (7), 371–378.

Gorlich, A., Antolin-Fontes, B., Ables, J.L., Frahm, S., Slimak, M.A., Dougherty, J.D., Ibanez-Tallon, I., 2013. Reexposure to nicotine during withdrawal increases the pacemaking activity of cholinergic habenular neurons. Proc. Natl. Acad. Sci. U. S. A. 110 (42), 17077–17082.

Grace, A.A., Bunney, B.S., 1984. The control of firing pattern in nigral dopamine neurons: burst firing. J. Neurosci. 4 (11), 2877–2890.

Grace, A.A., Bunney, B.S., 1984. The control of firing pattern in nigral dopamine neurons: single spike firing. J. Neurosci. 4 (11), 2866–2876.

Grace, A.A., Floresco, S.B., Goto, Y., Lodge, D.J., 2007. Regulation of firing of dopaminergic neurons and control of goal-directed behaviors. Trends. Neurosci. 30 (5), 220–227.

Grady, S.R., Moretti, M., Zoli, M., Marks, M.J., Zanardi, A., Pucci, L., Clementi, F., Gotti, C., 2009. Rodent habenulo-interpeduncular pathway expresses a large variety of uncommon nAChR subtypes, but only the alpha3beta4* and alpha3beta3beta4* subtypes mediate acetylcholine release. J. Neurosci. 29 (7), 2272–2282.

Groenewegen, H.J., Ahlenius, S., Haber, S.N., Kowall, N.W., Nauta, W.J., 1986. Cytoarchitecture, fiber connections, and some histochemical aspects of the interpeduncular nucleus in the rat. J. Comp. Neurol. 249 (1), 65–102.

Guillem, K., Bloem, B., Poorthuis, R.B., Loos, M., Smit, A.B., Maskos, U., Spijker, S., Mansvelder, H.D., 2011. Nicotinic acetylcholine receptor beta2 subunits in the medial prefrontal cortex control attention. Science 333 (6044), 888–891.

Heffner, J.L., Anthenelli, R.M., Adler, C.M., Strakowski, S.M., Beavers, J., DelBello, M.P., 2013. Prevalence and correlates of heavy smoking and nicotine dependence in adolescents with bipolar and cannabis use disorders. Psychiatr. Res. 210 (3), 857–862.

Himmelheber, A.M., Sarter, M., Bruno, J.P., 1997. Operant performance and cortical acetylcholine release: role of response rate, reward density, and non-contingent stimuli. Brain Res Cogn Brain Res 6 (1), 23–36.

Hoebel, B.G., Avena, N.M., Rada, P., 2007. Accumbens dopamine-acetylcholine balance in approach and avoidance. Curr. Opin. Pharmacol. 7 (6), 617–627.

Hong, S., Jhou, T.C., Smith, M., Saleem, K.S., Hikosaka, O., 2011. Negative reward signals from the lateral habenula to dopamine neurons are mediated by rostromedial tegmental nucleus in primates. J. Neurosci. 31 (32), 11457–11471.

Hsu, Y.W., Tempest, L., Quina, L.A., Wei, A.D., Zeng, H., Turner, E.E., 2013. Medial habenula output circuit mediated by alpha5 nicotinic receptor-expressing GABAergic neurons in the interpeduncular nucleus. J. Neurosci. 33 (46), 18022–18035.

Huang, Y.Y., Kandel, D.B., Kandel, E.R., Levine, A., 2013. Nicotine primes the effect of cocaine on the induction of LTP in the amygdala. Neuropharmacology 74, 126–134.

Hughes, J.R., Hatsukami, D.K., Mitchell, J.E., Dahlgren, L.A., 1986. Prevalence of smoking among psychiatric outpatients. Am. J. Psychiatr. 143 (8), 993–997.

Ichikawa, J., Chung, Y.C., Li, Z., Dai, J., Meltzer, H.Y., 2002. Cholinergic modulation of basal and amphetamine-induced dopamine release in rat medial prefrontal cortex and nucleus accumbens. Brain. Res. 958 (1), 176–184.

Ikemoto, S., 2007. Dopamine reward circuitry: two projection systems from the ventral midbrain to the nucleus accumbens-olfactory tubercle complex. Brain. Res. Rev. 56 (1), 27–78.

Ikemoto, S., Goeders, N.E., 2000. Intra-medial prefrontal cortex injections of scopolamine increase instrumental responses for cocaine: an intravenous self-administration study in rats. Brain. Res. Bull. 51 (2), 151–158.

Ikemoto, S., Wise, R.A., 2002. Rewarding effects of the cholinergic agents carbachol and neostigmine in the posterior ventral tegmental area. J. Neurosci. 22 (22), 9895–9904.

Ito, R., Robbins, T.W., McNaughton, B.L., Everitt, B.J., 2006. Selective excitotoxic lesions of the hippocampus and basolateral amygdala have dissociable effects on appetitive cue and place conditioning based on path integration in a novel Y-maze procedure. Eur. J. Neurosci. 23 (11), 3071–3080.

Jackson, K.J., Chen, X., Miles, M.F., Harenza, J., Damaj, M.I., 2011. The neuropeptide galanin and variants in the GalR1 gene are associated with nicotine dependence. Neuropsychopharmacology 36 (11), 2339–2348.

Jackson, K.J., Marks, M.J., Vann, R.E., Chen, X., Gamage, T.F., Warner, J.A., Damaj, M.I., 2010. Role of alpha5 nicotinic acetylcholine receptors in pharmacological and behavioral effects of nicotine in mice. J. Pharmacol. Exp. Therapeut. 334 (1), 137–146.

Jackson, K.J., Martin, B.R., Changeux, J.P., Damaj, M.I., 2008. Differential role of nicotinic acetylcholine receptor subunits in physical and affective nicotine withdrawal signs. J. Pharmacol. Exp. Therapeut. 325 (1), 302–312.

Jackson, K.J., McIntosh, J.M., Brunzell, D.H., Sanjakdar, S.S., Damaj, M.I., 2009. The role of alpha6-containing nicotinic acetylcholine receptors in nicotine reward and withdrawal. J. Pharmacol. Exp. Therapeut. 331 (2), 547–554.

Jacobsen, L.K., Krystal, J.H., Mencl, W.E., Westerveld, M., Frost, S.J., Pugh, K.R., 2005. Effects of smoking and smoking abstinence on cognition in adolescent tobacco smokers. Biol. Psychiatr. 57 (1), 56–66.

Jasinska, A.J., Stein, E.A., Kaiser, J., Naumer, M.J., Yalachkov, Y., 2014. Factors modulating neural reactivity to drug cues in addiction: a survey of human neuroimaging studies. Neurosci. Biobehav. Rev. 38, 1–16.

Jhou, T.C., Good, C.H., Rowley, C.S., Xu, S.P., Wang, H., Burnham, N.W., Hoffman, A.F., Lupica, C.R., Ikemoto, S., 2013. Cocaine drives aversive conditioning via delayed activation of dopamine-responsive habenular and midbrain pathways. J. Neurosci. 33 (17), 7501–7512.

Jiang, L., Kundu, S., Lederman, J.D., Lopez-Hernandez, G.Y., Ballinger, E.C., Wang, S., Talmage, D.A., Role, L.W., 2016. Cholinergic signaling controls conditioned fear behaviors and enhances plasticity of cortical-amygdala circuits. Neuron 90 (5), 1057–1070.

Jones, I.W., Wonnacott, S., 2004. Precise localization of alpha7 nicotinic acetylcholine receptors on glutamatergic axon terminals in the rat ventral tegmental area. J. Neurosci. 24 (50), 11244–11252.

Kawaja, M.D., Flumerfelt, B.A., Hrycyshyn, A.W., 1988. Topographical and ultrastructural investigation of the habenulo-interpeduncular pathway in the rat: a wheat germ agglutinin-horseradish peroxidase anterograde study. J. Comp. Neurol. 275 (1), 117–127.

Kenny, P.J., Markou, A., 2004. The ups and downs of addiction: role of metabotropic glutamate receptors. Trends. Pharmacol. Sci. 25 (5), 265–272.

Kim, U., Chang, S.Y., 2005. Dendritic morphology, local circuitry, and intrinsic electrophysiology of neurons in the rat medial and lateral habenular nuclei of the epithalamus. J. Comp. Neurol. 483 (2), 236–250.

Klein, R.C., Yakel, J.L., 2006. Functional somato-dendritic alpha7-containing nicotinic acetylcholine receptors in the rat basolateral amygdala complex. J. Physiol. 576 (Pt 3), 865–872.

Klemm, W.R., 2004. Habenular and interpeduncularis nuclei: shared components in multiple-function networks. Med. Sci. Monit. 10 (11), RA261–273.

Kobayashi, Y., Sano, Y., Vannoni, E., Goto, H., Suzuki, H., Oba, A., Kawasaki, H., Kanba, S., Lipp, H.P., Murphy, N.P., Wolfer, D.P., Itohara, S., 2013. Genetic dissection of medial habenula-interpeduncular nucleus pathway function in mice. Front. Behav. Neurosci. 7, 17.

Koob, G.F., Colrain, I.M., 2020. Alcohol use disorder and sleep disturbances: a feed-forward allostatic framework. Neuropsychopharmacology 45 (1), 141–165.

Lammel, S., Lim, B.K., Ran, C., Huang, K.W., Betley, M.J., Tye, K.M., Deisseroth, K., Malenka, R.C., 2012. Input-specific control of reward and aversion in the ventral tegmental area. Nature 491 (7423), 212–217.

Langley, J.N., 1907. On the contraction of muscle, chiefly in relation to the presence of "receptive" substances: Part I. J. Physiol. 36 (4–5), 347–384.

Lazary, J., Dome, P., Csala, I., Kovacs, G., Faludi, G., Kaunisto, M., Dome, B., 2014. Massive withdrawal symptoms and affective vulnerability are associated with variants of the CHRNA4 gene in a subgroup of smokers. PLoS One 9 (1), e87141.

Lenn, N.J., Wong, V., Hamill, G.S., 1983. Left-right pairing at the crest synapses of rat interpeduncular nucleus. Neuroscience 9 (2), 383–389.

Levin, E.D., 2002. Nicotinic receptor subtypes and cognitive function. J. Neurobiol. 53 (4), 633–640.

Levin, E.D., 2013. Complex relationships of nicotinic receptor actions and cognitive functions. Biochem. Pharmacol. 86 (8), 1145–1152.

Liu, L., Zhao-Shea, R., McIntosh, J.M., Gardner, P.D., Tapper, A.R., 2012. Nicotine persistently activates ventral tegmental area dopaminergic neurons via nicotinic acetylcholine receptors containing alpha4 and alpha6 subunits. Mol. Pharmacol. 81 (4), 541–548.

Lodge, D.J., Grace, A.A., 2006. The laterodorsal tegmentum is essential for burst firing of ventral tegmental area dopamine neurons. Proc. Natl. Acad. Sci. U. S. A. 103 (13), 5167–5172.

Lof, E., Olausson, P., deBejczy, A., Stomberg, R., McIntosh, J.M., Taylor, J.R., Soderpalm, B., 2007. Nicotinic acetylcholine receptors in the ventral tegmental area mediate the dopamine activating and reinforcing properties of ethanol cues. Psychopharmacology (Berl) 195 (3), 333–343.

Lokwan, S.J., Overton, P.G., Berry, M.S., Clark, D., 1999. Stimulation of the pedunculopontine tegmental nucleus in the rat produces burst firing in A9 dopaminergic neurons. Neuroscience 92 (1), 245–254.

Lombardo, S., Maskos, U., 2015. Role of the nicotinic acetylcholine receptor in Alzheimer's disease pathology and treatment. Neuropharmacology 96 (Pt B), 255–262.

Lotfipour, S., Byun, J.S., Leach, P., Fowler, C.D., Murphy, N.P., Kenny, P.J., Gould, T.J., Boulter, J., 2013. Targeted deletion of the mouse alpha2 nicotinic acetylcholine receptor subunit gene (Chrna2) potentiates nicotine-modulated behaviors. J. Neurosci. 33 (18), 7728–7741.

Luppi, P.H., Fort, P., 2019. Sleep-wake physiology. Handb. Clin. Neurol. 160, 359–370.

Mameli-Engvall, M., Evrard, A., Pons, S., Maskos, U., Svensson, T.H., Changeux, J.P., Faure, P., 2006. Hierarchical control of dopamine neuron-firing patterns by nicotinic receptors. Neuron 50 (6), 911–921.

Maskos, U., 2008. The cholinergic mesopontine tegmentum is a relatively neglected nicotinic master modulator of the dopaminergic system: relevance to drugs of abuse and pathology. Br. J. Pharmacol. 153 (Suppl. 1), S438–S445.

McCormick, D.A., Prince, D.A., 1987. Acetylcholine causes rapid nicotinic excitation in the medial habenular nucleus of Guinea pig, in vitro. J. Neurosci. 7 (3), 742–752.

McGaughy, J., Dalley, J.W., Morrison, C.H., Everitt, B.J., Robbins, T.W., 2002. Selective behavioral and neurochemical effects of cholinergic lesions produced by intrabasalis infusions of 192 IgG-saporin on attentional performance in a five-choice serial reaction time task. J. Neurosci. 22 (5), 1905–1913.

McGehee, D.S., Role, L.W., 1995. Physiological diversity of nicotinic acetylcholine receptors expressed by vertebrate neurons. Annu. Rev. Physiol. 57, 521–546.

Mesulam, M.M., Mufson, E.J., Levey, A.I., Wainer, B.H., 1983. Cholinergic innervation of cortex by the basal forebrain: cytochemistry and cortical connections of the septal area, diagonal band nuclei, nucleus basalis (substantia innominata), and hypothalamus in the rhesus monkey. J. Comp. Neurol. 214 (2), 170–197.

Meyers, E.E., Loetz, E.C., Marks, M.J., 2015. Differential expression of the beta4 neuronal nicotinic receptor subunit affects tolerance development and nicotinic binding sites following chronic nicotine treatment. Pharmacol. Biochem. Behav. 130, 1–8.

Miller, E.K., Cohen, J.D., 2001. An integrative theory of prefrontal cortex function. Annu. Rev. Neurosci. 24, 167–202.

Mineur, Y.S., Abizaid, A., Rao, Y., Salas, R., DiLeone, R.J., Gundisch, D., Diano, S., De Biasi, M., Horvath, T.L., Gao, X.B., Picciotto, M.R., 2011. Nicotine decreases food intake through activation of POMC neurons. Science 332 (6035), 1330–1332.

Mineur, Y.S., Cahuzac, E.L., Mose, T.N., Bentham, M.P., Plantenga, M.E., Thompson, D.C., Picciotto, M.R., 2018. Interaction between noradrenergic and cholinergic signaling in amygdala regulates anxiety- and depression-related behaviors in mice. Neuropsychopharmacology 43 (10), 2118–2125.

Montone, K.T., Fass, B., Hamill, G.S., 1988. Serotonergic and non-serotonergic projections from the rat interpeduncular nucleus to the septum, hippocampal formation and raphe: a combined immunocytochemical and fluorescent retrograde labelling study of neurons in the apical subnucleus. Brain Res. Bull. 20 (2), 233–240.

Newman, E.L., Gupta, K., Climer, J.R., Monaghan, C.K., Hasselmo, M.E., 2012. Cholinergic modulation of cognitive processing: insights drawn from computational models. Front. Behav. Neurosci. 6, 24.

Nunes, E.J., Bitner, L., Hughley, S.M., Small, K.M., Walton, S.N., Rupprecht, L.E., Addy, N.A., 2019. Cholinergic receptor blockade in the VTA attenuates cue-induced cocaine-seeking and reverses the anxiogenic effects of forced abstinence. Neuroscience 413, 252–263.

Nunes, E.J., Randall, P.A., Podurgiel, S., Correa, M., Salamone, J.D., 2013. Nucleus accumbens neurotransmission and effort-related choice behavior in food motivation: effects of drugs acting on dopamine, adenosine, and muscarinic acetylcholine receptors. Neurosci. Biobehav. Rev. 37 (9 Pt A), 2015–2025.

Oda, S., Tsuneoka, Y., Yoshida, S., Adachi-Akahane, S., Ito, M., Kuroda, M., Funato, H., 2018. Immunolocalization of muscarinic M1 receptor in the rat medial prefrontal cortex. J. Comp. Neurol. 526 (8), 1329–1350.

Olds, J., Milner, P., 1954. Positive reinforcement produced by electrical stimulation of septal area and other regions of rat brain. J. Comp. Physiol. Psychol. 47 (6), 419–427.

Pan, W.X., Hyland, B.I., 2005. Pedunculopontine tegmental nucleus controls conditioned responses of midbrain dopamine neurons in behaving rats. J. Neurosci. 25 (19), 4725–4732.

Panizza, B., 1855. Osservazioni sul neuroticottica. Gior IR Ist Lomb Sci Lett Art 7, 237–252.

Paradiso, K., Zhang, J., Steinbach, J.H., 2001. The C terminus of the human nicotinic alpha4beta2 receptor forms a binding site required for potentiation by an estrogenic steroid. J. Neurosci. 21 (17), 6561–6568.

Parikh, V., Bangasser, D.A., 2020. Cholinergic signaling dynamics and cognitive control of attention. Curr Top Behav Neurosci 45, 71–87.

Parikh, V., Kozak, R., Martinez, V., Sarter, M., 2007. Prefrontal acetylcholine release controls cue detection on multiple timescales. Neuron 56 (1), 141–154.

Parikh, V., Sarter, M., 2008. Cholinergic mediation of attention: contributions of phasic and tonic increases in prefrontal cholinergic activity. Ann. N. Y. Acad. Sci. 1129, 225–235.

Passetti, F., Dalley, J.W., O'Connell, M.T., Everitt, B.J., Robbins, T.W., 2000. Increased acetylcholine release in the rat medial prefrontal cortex during performance of a visual attentional task. Eur. J. Neurosci. 12 (8), 3051–3058.

Perez-Lloret, S., Barrantes, F.J., 2016. Deficits in cholinergic neurotransmission and their clinical correlates in Parkinson's disease. NPJ. Parkinsons. Dis. 2, 16001.

Phillips, J.L., Norris, S., Talbot, J., Birmingham, M., Hatchard, T., Ortiz, A., Owoeye, O., Batten, L.A., Blier, P., 2019. Single, repeated, and maintenance ketamine infusions for treatment-resistant depression: a randomized controlled trial. Am. J. Psychiatr. 176 (5), 401–409.

Piasecki, T.M., Niaura, R., Shadel, W.G., Abrams, D., Goldstein, M., Fiore, M.C., Baker, T.B., 2000. Smoking withdrawal dynamics in unaided quitters. J. Abnorm. Psychol. 109 (1), 74–86.

Picciotto, M.R., 1998. Common aspects of the action of nicotine and other drugs of abuse. Drug. Alcohol. Depend. 51 (1–2), 165–172.

Picciotto, M.R., Addy, N.A., Mineur, Y.S., Brunzell, D.H., 2008. It is not "either/or": activation and desensitization of nicotinic acetylcholine receptors both contribute to behaviors related to nicotine addiction and mood. Prog. Neurobiol. 84 (4), 329–342.

Picciotto, M.R., Zoli, M., Rimondini, R., Lena, C., Marubio, L.M., Pich, E.M., Fuxe, K., Changeux, J.P., 1998. Acetylcholine receptors containing the beta2 subunit are involved in the reinforcing properties of nicotine. Nature 391 (6663), 173–177.

Qian, J., Saggau, P., 1997. Presynaptic inhibition of synaptic transmission in the rat hippocampus by activation of muscarinic receptors: involvement of presynaptic calcium influx. Br. J. Pharmacol. 122 (3), 511–519.

Qin, C., Luo, M., 2009. Neurochemical phenotypes of the afferent and efferent projections of the mouse medial habenula. Neuroscience 161 (3), 827–837.

Rada, P.V., Mark, G.P., Yeomans, J.J., Hoebel, B.G., 2000. Acetylcholine release in ventral tegmental area by hypothalamic self-stimulation, eating, and drinking. Pharmacol. Biochem. Behav. 65 (3), 375–379.

Ramon y Cajal, S., 1911. Histologie du système nerveux de l'homme & des vertébrés, II. Maloine, Paris, France.

Reese, N.B., Garcia-Rill, E., Skinner, R.D., 1995. Auditory input to the pedunculopontine nucleus: II. Unit responses. Brain. Res. Bull. 37 (3), 265–273.

Ren, J., Qin, C., Hu, F., Tan, J., Qiu, L., Zhao, S., Feng, G., Luo, M., 2011. Habenula "cholinergic" neurons co-release glutamate and acetylcholine and activate postsynaptic neurons via distinct transmission modes. Neuron 69 (3), 445–452.

Rice, M.E., Cragg, S.J., 2004. Nicotine amplifies reward-related dopamine signals in striatum. Nat. Neurosci. 7 (6), 583–584.

Root, D.H., Mejias-Aponte, C.A., Zhang, S., Wang, H.L., Hoffman, A.F., Lupica, C.R., Morales, M., 2014. Single rodent mesohabenular axons release glutamate and GABA. Nat. Neurosci. 17 (11), 1543–1551.

Ross, S.A., Wong, J.Y., Clifford, J.J., Kinsella, A., Massalas, J.S., Horne, M.K., Scheffer, I.E., Kola, I., Waddington, J.L., Berkovic, S.F., Drago, J., 2000. Phenotypic characterization of an alpha 4 neuronal nicotinic acetylcholine receptor subunit knock-out mouse. J. Neurosci. 20 (17), 6431–6441.

Rudick, C.N., Gibbs, R.B., Woolley, C.S., 2003. A role for the basal forebrain cholinergic system in estrogen-induced disinhibition of hippocampal pyramidal cells. J. Neurosci. 23 (11), 4479–4490.

Sacaan, A.I., Menzaghi, F., Dunlop, J.L., Correa, L.D., Whelan, K.T., Lloyd, G.K., 1996. Epibatidine: a nicotinic acetylcholine receptor agonist releases monoaminergic neurotransmitters: in vitro and in vivo evidence in rats. J. Pharmacol. Exp. Therapeut. 276 (2), 509–515.

Saccone, N.L., Wang, J.C., Breslau, N., Johnson, E.O., Hatsukami, D., Saccone, S.F., Grucza, R.A., Sun, L., Duan, W., Budde, J., Culverhouse, R.C., Fox, L., Hinrichs, A.L., Steinbach, J.H., Wu, M., Rice, J.P., Goate, A.M., Bierut, L.J.,

2009. The CHRNA5-CHRNA3-CHRNB4 nicotinic receptor subunit gene cluster affects risk for nicotine dependence in African-Americans and in European-Americans. Cancer. Res. 69 (17), 6848–6856.

Salas, R., Pieri, F., De Biasi, M., 2004. Decreased signs of nicotine withdrawal in mice null for the beta4 nicotinic acetylcholine receptor subunit. J. Neurosci. 24 (45), 10035–10039.

Salas, R., Pieri, F., Fung, B., Dani, J.A., De Biasi, M., 2003. Altered anxiety-related responses in mutant mice lacking the beta4 subunit of the nicotinic receptor. J. Neurosci. 23 (15), 6255–6263.

Salas, R., Sturm, R., Boulter, J., De Biasi, M., 2009. Nicotinic receptors in the habenulo-interpeduncular system are necessary for nicotine withdrawal in mice. J. Neurosci. 29 (10), 3014–3018.

Samhsa, 2019. 2019 National Survey of Drug Use and Health (NSDUH), 106. College of Health Sciences, Rockville, MD, p. 128 (5).

Sarginson, J.E., Killen, J.D., Lazzeroni, L.C., Fortmann, S.P., Ryan, H.S., Schatzberg, A.F., Murphy Jr., G.M., 2011. Markers in the 15q24 nicotinic receptor subunit gene cluster (CHRNA5-A3-B4) predict severity of nicotine addiction and response to smoking cessation therapy. Am. J. Med. Genet. B. Neuropsychiatr. Genet. 156B (3), 275–284.

Sarter, M., Bruno, J.P., Parikh, V., Martinez, V., Kozak, R., Richards, J.B., 2006. Forebrain dopaminergic-cholinergic interactions, attentional effort, psychostimulant addiction and schizophrenia. EXS 98, 65–86.

Sarter, M., Lustig, C., Taylor, S.F., 2012. Cholinergic contributions to the cognitive symptoms of schizophrenia and the viability of cholinergic treatments. Neuropharmacology 62 (3), 1544–1553.

Sartorius, A., Kiening, K.L., Kirsch, P., von Gall, C.C., Haberkorn, U., Unterberg, A.W., Henn, F.A., Meyer-Lindenberg, A., 2010. Remission of major depression under deep brain stimulation of the lateral habenula in a therapy-refractory patient. Biol. Psychiatr. 67 (2), e9–e11.

Schultz, W., Romo, R., 1990. Dopamine neurons of the monkey midbrain: contingencies of responses to stimuli eliciting immediate behavioral reactions. J. Neurophysiol. 63 (3), 607–624.

See, R.E., McLaughlin, J., Fuchs, R.A., 2003. Muscarinic receptor antagonism in the basolateral amygdala blocks acquisition of cocaine-stimulus association in a model of relapse to cocaine-seeking behavior in rats. Neuroscience 117 (2), 477–483.

Sharf, R., McKelvey, J., Ranaldi, R., 2006. Blockade of muscarinic acetylcholine receptors in the ventral tegmental area prevents acquisition of food-rewarded operant responding in rats. Psychopharmacology (Berl) 186 (1), 113–121.

Sharf, R., Ranaldi, R., 2006. Blockade of muscarinic acetylcholine receptors in the ventral tegmental area disrupts food-related learning in rats. Psychopharmacology (Berl) 184 (1), 87–94.

Shibata, H., Suzuki, T., 1984. Efferent projections of the interpeduncular complex in the rat, with special reference to its subnuclei: a retrograde horseradish peroxidase study. Brain. Res. 296 (2), 345–349.

Shiffman, S.M., Jarvik, M.E., 1976. Smoking withdrawal symptoms in two weeks of abstinence. Psychopharmacology (Berl) 50 (1), 35–39.

Shih, P.Y., Engle, S.E., Oh, G., Deshpande, P., Puskar, N.L., Lester, H.A., Drenan, R.M., 2014. Differential expression and function of nicotinic acetylcholine receptors in subdivisions of medial habenula. J. Neurosci. 34 (29), 9789–9802.

Shin, J.H., Adrover, M.F., Wess, J., Alvarez, V.A., 2015. Muscarinic regulation of dopamine and glutamate transmission in the nucleus accumbens. Proc. Natl. Acad. Sci. U. S. A. 112 (26), 8124–8129.

Solecki, W., Wickham, R.J., Behrens, S., Wang, J., Zwerling, B., Mason, G.F., Addy, N.A., 2013. Differential role of ventral tegmental area acetylcholine and N-methyl-d-aspartate receptors in cocaine-seeking. Neuropharmacology 75C, 9–18.

Soliakov, L., Gallagher, T., Wonnacott, S., 1995. Anatoxin-a-evoked [3H]dopamine release from rat striatal synaptosomes. Neuropharmacology 34 (11), 1535–1541.

Squire, L.R., 2009. The legacy of patient H.M. for neuroscience. Neuron 61 (1), 6–9.

Steidl, S., Veverka, K., 2015. Optogenetic excitation of LDTg axons in the VTA reinforces operant responding in rats. Brain. Res. 1614, 86–93.

Steidl, S., Wang, H., Ordonez, M., Zhang, S., Morales, M., 2017. Optogenetic excitation in the ventral tegmental area of glutamatergic or cholinergic inputs from the laterodorsal tegmental area drives reward. Eur. J. Neurosci. 45 (4), 559–571.

Stoveken, H.M., Zucca, S., Masuho, I., Grill, B., Martemyanov, K.A., 2020. The orphan receptor GPR139 signals via Gq/11 to oppose opioid effects. J. Biol. Chem. 295 (31), 10822–10830.

Tansey, E.M., 2006. Henry Dale and the discovery of acetylcholine. C R Biol 329 (5–6), 419–425.

Towart, L.A., Alves, S.E., Znamensky, V., Hayashi, S., McEwen, B.S., Milner, T.A., 2003. Subcellular relationships between cholinergic terminals and estrogen receptor-alpha in the dorsal hippocampus. J. Comp. Neurol. 463 (4), 390–401.

Tsanov, M., 2018. Differential and complementary roles of medial and lateral septum in the orchestration of limbic oscillations and signal integration. Eur. J. Neurosci. 48 (8), 2783–2794.

Tuesta, L.M., Chen, Z., Duncan, A., Fowler, C.D., Ishikawa, M., Lee, B.R., Liu, X.A., Lu, Q., Cameron, M., Hayes, M.R., Kamenecka, T.M., Pletcher, M., Kenny, P.J., 2017. GLP-1 acts on habenular avoidance circuits to control nicotine intake. Nat. Neurosci. 20 (5), 708–716.

Turner, J.R., Kellar, K.J., 2005. Nicotinic cholinergic receptors in the rat cerebellum: multiple heteromeric subtypes. J. Neurosci. 25 (40), 9258–9265.

Turner, J.R., Ortinski, P.I., Sherrard, R.M., Kellar, K.J., 2011. Cerebellar nicotinic cholinergic receptors are intrinsic to the cerebellum: implications for diverse functional roles. Cerebellum 10 (4), 748–757.

Tzavara, E.T., Bymaster, F.P., Davis, R.J., Wade, M.R., Perry, K.W., Wess, J., McKinzie, D.L., Felder, C., Nomikos, G.G., 2004. M4 muscarinic receptors regulate the dynamics of cholinergic and dopaminergic neurotransmission: relevance to the pathophysiology and treatment of related CNS pathologies. Faseb. J. 18 (12), 1410–1412.

Ungerstedt, U., 1971. Stereotaxic mapping of the monoamine pathways in the rat brain. Acta. Physiol. Scand. Suppl. 367, 1–48.

Van Der Zee, E.A., De Jong, G.I., Strosberg, A.D., Luiten, P.G., 1993. Muscarinic acetylcholine receptor-expression in astrocytes in the cortex of young and aged rats. Glia 8 (1), 42–50.

Volkow, N.D., Wang, G.J., Ma, Y., Fowler, J.S., Zhu, W., Maynard, L., Telang, F., Vaska, P., Ding, Y.S., Wong, C., Swanson, J.M., 2003. Expectation enhances the regional brain metabolic and the reinforcing effects of stimulants in cocaine abusers. J. Neurosci. 23 (36), 11461–11468.

Vujanovic, A.A., Marshall-Berenz, E.C., Beckham, J.C., Bernstein, A., Zvolensky, M.J., 2010. Posttraumatic stress symptoms and cigarette deprivation in the prediction of anxious responding among trauma-exposed smokers: a laboratory test. Nicotine. Tob. Res. 12 (11), 1080–1088.

Wagner, F., French, L., Veh, R.W., 2014. Transcriptomic-anatomic analysis of the mouse habenula uncovers a high molecular heterogeneity among neurons in the lateral complex, while gene expression in the medial complex largely obeys subnuclear boundaries. Brain. Struct. Funct. (in press).

Whitelaw, R.B., Markou, A., Robbins, T.W., Everitt, B.J., 1996. Excitotoxic lesions of the basolateral amygdala impair the acquisition of cocaine-seeking behaviour under a second-order schedule of reinforcement. Psychopharmacology (Berl) 127 (3), 213–224.

Wickham, R., Solecki, W., Rathbun, L., McIntosh, J.M., Addy, N.A., 2013. Ventral tegmental area alpha6beta2 nicotinic acetylcholine receptors modulate phasic dopamine release in the nucleus accumbens core. Psychopharmacology (Berl) 229 (1), 73–82.

Wickham, R.J., Solecki, W.B., Nunes, E.J., Addy, N.A., 2015. Distinct effects of ventral tegmental area NMDA and acetylcholine receptor blockade on conditioned reinforcement produced by food-associated cues. Neuroscience 301, 384–394.

Wise, R.A., Bozarth, M.A., 1981. Brain substrates for reinforcement and drug self-administration. Prog. Neuro Psychopharmacol. 5 (5–6), 467–474.

Witkin, J.M., Smith, J.L., Golani, L.K., Brooks, E.A., Martin, A.E., 2020. Involvement of muscarinic receptor mechanisms in antidepressant drug action. Adv. Pharmacol. 89, 311–356.

Wooltorton, J.R., Pidoplichko, V.I., Broide, R.S., Dani, J.A., 2003. Differential desensitization and distribution of nicotinic acetylcholine receptor subtypes in midbrain dopamine areas. J. Neurosci. 23 (8), 3176–3185.

Yamada, R.G., Ueda, H.R., 2019. Molecular mechanisms of REM sleep. Front. Neurosci. 13, 1402.

Yamaguchi, T., Danjo, T., Pastan, I., Hikida, T., Nakanishi, S., 2013. Distinct roles of segregated transmission of the septo-habenular pathway in anxiety and fear. Neuron (in press).

Yamasaki, M., Matsui, M., Watanabe, M., 2010. Preferential localization of muscarinic M1 receptor on dendritic shaft and spine of cortical pyramidal cells and its anatomical evidence for volume transmission. J. Neurosci. 30 (12), 4408–4418.

Yang, Y., Cui, Y., Sang, K., Dong, Y., Ni, Z., Ma, S., Hu, H., 2018. Ketamine blocks bursting in the lateral habenula to rapidly relieve depression. Nature 554 (7692), 317–322.

Yau, H.J., Wang, D.V., Tsou, J.H., Chuang, Y.F., Chen, B.T., Deisseroth, K., Ikemoto, S., Bonci, A., 2016. Pontomesencephalic tegmental afferents to VTA non-dopamine neurons are necessary for appetitive pavlovian learning. Cell. Rep. 16 (10), 2699–2710.

Yeomans, J., Forster, G., Blaha, C., 2001. M5 muscarinic receptors are needed for slow activation of dopamine neurons and for rewarding brain stimulation. Life. Sci. 68 (22–23), 2449–2456.

Yeomans, J.S., 2012. Muscarinic receptors in brain stem and mesopontine cholinergic arousal functions. Handb. Exp. Pharmacol. 208, 243–259.

You, Z.B., Wang, B., Zitzman, D., Wise, R.A., 2008. Acetylcholine release in the mesocorticolimbic dopamine system during cocaine seeking: conditioned and unconditioned contributions to reward and motivation. J. Neurosci. 28 (36), 9021–9029.

Zago, S., Nurra, M., Scarlato, G., Silani, V., 2000. Bartolomeo Panizza and the discovery of the brain's visual center. Arch. Neurol. 57 (11), 1642–1648.

Zakiniaeiz, Y., Cosgrove, K.P., Potenza, M.N., Mazure, C.M., 2016. Balance of the sexes: addressing sex differences in preclinical research. Yale J. Biol. Med. 89 (2), 255–259.

Zapata, A., Hwang, E.K., Lupica, C.R., 2017. Lateral habenula involvement in impulsive cocaine seeking. Neuropsychopharmacology 42 (5), 1103–1112.

Zarrindast, M.R., Meshkani, J., Rezayof, A., Beigzadeh, R., Rostami, P., 2010. Nicotinic acetylcholine receptors of the dorsal hippocampus and the basolateral amygdala are involved in ethanol-induced conditioned place preference. Neuroscience 168 (2), 505–513.

Zeid, D., Kutlu, M.G., Gould, T.J., 2018. Differential effects of nicotine exposure on the Hippocampus across lifespan. Curr. Neuropharmacol. 16 (4), 388–402.

Zell, V., Steinkellner, T., Hollon, N.G., Warlow, S.M., Souter, E., Faget, L., Hunker, A.C., Jin, X., Zweifel, L.S., Hnasko, T.S., 2020. VTA glutamate neuron activity drives positive reinforcement absent dopamine Co-release. Neuron 107 (5), 864–873 e864.

Zhang, H., Sulzer, D., 2004. Frequency-dependent modulation of dopamine release by nicotine. Nat. Neurosci. 7 (6), 581–582.

Zhang, L., Liu, Y., Chen, X., 2005. Carbachol induces burst firing of dopamine cells in the ventral tegmental area by promoting calcium entry through L-type channels in the rat. J. Physiol. 568 (Pt 2), 469–481.

Zhao-Shea, R., Liu, L., Pang, X., Gardner, P.D., Tapper, A.R., 2013. Activation of GABAergic neurons in the interpeduncular nucleus triggers physical nicotine withdrawal symptoms. Curr. Biol. 23 (23), 2327–2335.

Zhou, W., Liu, H., Zhang, F., Tang, S., Zhu, H., Lai, M., Kalivas, P.W., 2007. Role of acetylcholine transmission in nucleus accumbens and ventral tegmental area in heroin-seeking induced by conditioned cues. Neuroscience 144 (4), 1209–1218.

Zweifel, L.S., Parker, J.G., Lobb, C.J., Rainwater, A., Wall, V.Z., Fadok, J.P., Darvas, M., Kim, M.J., Mizumori, S.J., Paladini, C.A., Phillips, P.E., Palmiter, R.D., 2009. Disruption of NMDAR-dependent burst firing by dopamine neurons provides selective assessment of phasic dopamine-dependent behavior. Proc. Natl. Acad. Sci. U. S. A. 106 (18), 7281–7288.

CHAPTER

12

Gut-brain axis

Kelly M. Abshire[a] *and Lorenzo Leggio*[a, b, c, d, e]

[a]Clinical Psychoneuroendocrinology and Neuropsychopharmacology Section, Translational Addiction Medicine Branch, National Institute on Drug Abuse and National Institute on Alcohol Abuse and Alcoholism, National Institutes of Health, Baltimore, MD, United States; [b]Medication Development Program, National Institute on Drug Abuse Intramural Research Program, National Institutes of Health, Baltimore, MD, United States; [c]Center for Alcohol and Addiction Studies, Department of Behavioral and Social Sciences, School of Public Health, Brown University, Providence, RI, United States; [d]Division of Addiction Medicine, Department of Medicine, School of Medicine, Johns Hopkins University, Baltimore, MD, United States; [e]Department of Neuroscience, Georgetown University Medical Center, Washington, DC, United States

Introduction

Traditionally, addiction research and efforts toward the development of new therapeutics have targeted areas of the brain associated with reward processing and negative reinforcement. However, addictive substances also have consequences across many physiological systems. In fact, research has recently uncovered many ways in which mechanisms outside of the nervous system influence neurocircuitries and thus result in behavioral changes. An example of these more recent approaches is the work on the potential role of the gut-brain axis. Recent studies have been able to directly tie addictive behaviors to gastro-intestinal tract-based peptides, such as ghrelin and GLP-1, as well as certain changes in the gut microbiome. By further elucidating the roles these systems play in the development and maintenance of addiction and drug-seeking behaviors, perhaps we can better define these previously uncharacterized physiological connections and explore new targets and modalities for therapy.

Neurocircuitry of Addiction
https://doi.org/10.1016/B978-0-12-823453-2.00013-8

The gut-brain axis

Akin to most diseases, addiction is a complex medical disorder that impacts our physiology in to varying degrees in multiple locations. While the brain is the obvious place to begin investigating the mechanisms underlying alcohol and substance use disorders, considering the influence of other biological systems may produce a more comprehensive understanding of how drugs can impact our body and behavior. Put simply, the gut-brain axis refers to the bidirectional mechanisms in which our brain and our gut communicate with each other.

There is growing evidence that both the 'ascending' signals from peripheral organs to the brain, as well as the 'descending' signals from the brain to the periphery contribute to neuropsychiatric disorders, including addiction. One such example is the gut-brain axis, which has been extensively investigated for its role in obesity and food-related behaviors, but less so for its role in addiction. Of note, there is converging evidence that alcohol-, drug- and food-seeking behaviors share common neurobiological mechanisms. Neural pathways, including neuroendocrine modulators that regulate appetite, influence the use of alcohol and other addictive drugs. Clinically, there is high comorbidity between eating disorders, obesity, and AUD, and food and alcohol consumption are inter-related. Medications that reduce drinking also reduce food intake (e.g., naltrexone and topiramate). While complex, studying the gut-brain axis and other body–brain pathways is an opportunity to identify novel treatment targets for addiction.

Bidirectional communication between gut and brain involve mesolimbic brain regions associated with reward processing, such as the ventral tegmental area and nucleus accumbens, as well as the hypothalamus. Interestingly, many of these regions contain receptors for gut-derived peptides, like ghrelin and GLP-1, which act as hormones with both peripheral and central effects. An admittedly less explored but increasingly pertinent aspect of the gut-brain axis is the microbiome. While research is still in its infancy, there is increasing evidence that the microbes in our gastrointestinal tract can modify pathways essential for neurotransmitter production and gene transcription in the central nervous system.

This chapter will provide an overview of the emerging literature on the role of gut-brain communications in addiction, with a specific focus on ghrelin, GLP-1, and gut microbiome.

Gastrointestinal neuroendocrine pathways

Ghrelin

Ghrelin is a 28-amino acid orexigenic peptide produced and released primarily from endocrine cells in the stomach (Kojima et al., 1999). Preproghrelin is the 117 amino acid precursor polypeptide encoded by the *GHRL* gene on Chromosome 3, which is then post-translationally cleaved to form des-acyl ghrelin (Gualillo et al., 2006). Next, the Ghrelin-*O*-Acyl-Transferase (GOAT) enzyme acetylates the peptide to form the active acyl-ghrelin (hereto referred to as ghrelin) (Yang et al., 2008). To assert physiological effects, ghrelin binds to and activates the growth hormone secretagogue receptor 1a (GHS-R1a), also known as the ghrelin receptor. Expressed throughout peripheral (e.g., gut, pancreas, thyroid, adipose tissue) and central (e.g., hypothalamus, ventral tegmental area, amygdala, hippocampus, Edinger-Westphal nucleus) tissues, this G-protein-coupled receptor has widespread physiological impacts (Gahete et al., 2014; Gnanapavan et al., 2002; Guan et al., 1997; Howard et al., 1996) (Fig. 12.1).

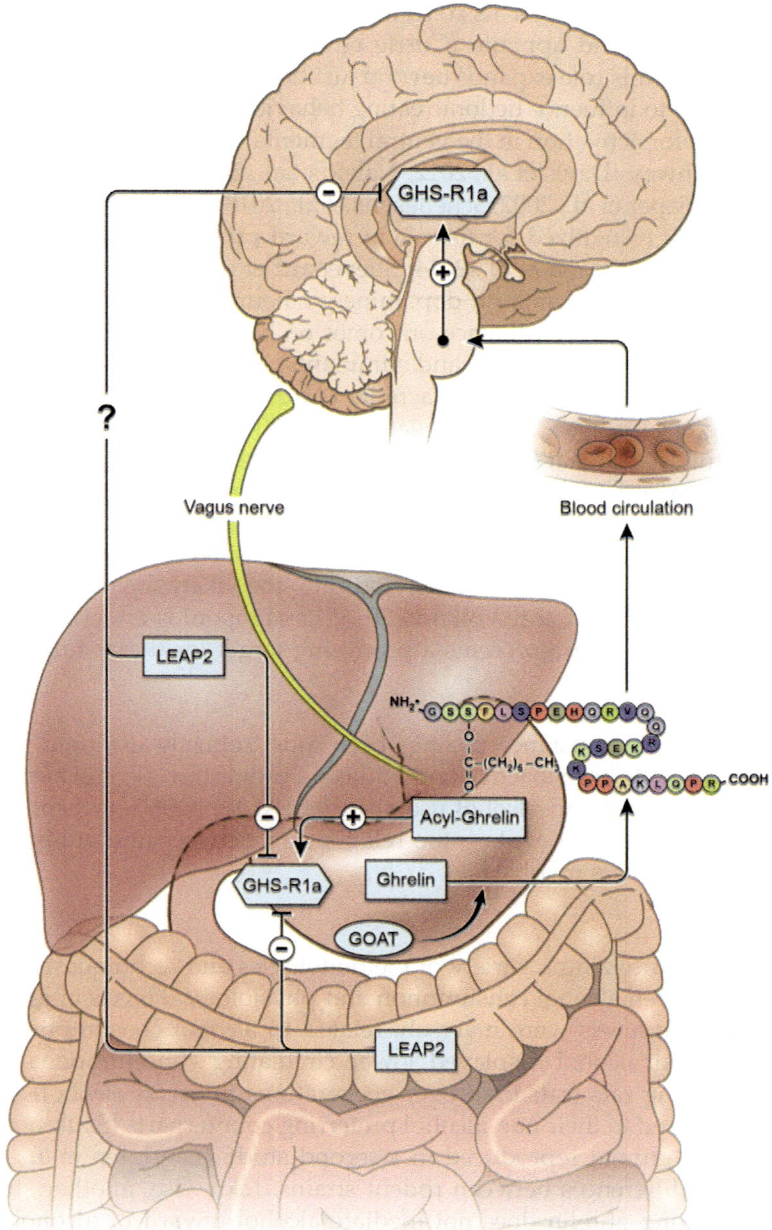

FIGURE 12.1 A simplified schematic outline of the ghrelin system. Abbreviations: *GHS-R1a*, growth hormone secretagogue receptor 1a; *GOAT*, ghrelin-O-acyltransferase; *LEAP2*, liver-expressed antimicrobial peptide 2. *Reprinted from Farokhnia, M., Faulkner, M.L., Piacentino, D., Lee, M.R., Leggio, L., 2019. Ghrelin: from a gut hormone to a potential therapeutic target for alcohol use disorder. Physiol. Behav. 204, 49–57. Copyright (2019), with permission from Elsevier.*

Ghrelin is most well-known for its roles in modulating energy metabolism and, notably, stimulating food intake and appetite (Currie et al., 2005; Schéle et al., 2016; Wren et al., 2000, 2001). However, this role expands beyond just homeostatic feeding functions, as ghrelin has also been shown to influence hedonic eating behaviors (i.e., eating for pleasure/reward), likely through receptor activation in the ventral tegmental area, nucleus accumbens, and mesolimbic reward pathway (Davis et al., 2012; Naleid et al., 2005; Olszewski et al., 2008; Perelló and Zigman, 2012; Saper et al., 2002; Schellekens et al., 2013; Wei et al., 2015). Further, ghrelin has been increasingly recognized for its role in reward processing by acting throughout the central nervous system (Mason et al., 2014; Stievenard et al., 2017). For example, the activation of GHS-R1a receptors located on dopaminergic neurons in the VTA (i.e., at the seat of mesolimbic reward pathways) influence outcomes on behavioral measures related to multiple addictive drugs (including alcohol and stimulants), such as conditioned place preference (CPP; a proxy of reward) and locomotor activity (Abizaid et al., 2006; Guan et al., 1997; Jerlhag, 2008; Jerlhag et al., 2006a, 2007; Schuette et al., 2013). In addition, ghrelin acts on the hypothalamic-pituitary-adrenal (HPA) axis, suggesting its potential relevance as a modulator of stress-related behaviors (Bali and Singh Jaggi, 2016; Currie et al., 2012; Labarthe et al., 2014; Meyer et al., 2014; Schellekens et al., 2013; Spencer et al., 2012, 2015). As it applies to addiction, ghrelin activity in neural circuits important for positive reinforcement (drug reward) and negative reinforcement (stress relief) indicate the likely involvement of ghrelin in drug-seeking behavior (Koob and Volkow, 2016; Panagopoulos and Ralevski, 2014). Thus, modulating ghrelin signaling represents a promising target for therapeutic intervention.

Ghrelin and alcohol

The role of ghrelin in substance use has been most robustly explored in the context of alcohol. In addition to its psychoactive and addictive properties, alcohol also contains caloric content. Therefore, alcohol and alcohol use disorder (AUD) have represented an intriguing, yet complex, starting place to explore the relationship between the gut-brain axis and the neuroendocrine biomarkers involved.

Preclinical studies

Preclinical studies, utilizing a variety of methodologies and techniques, have investigated the relationship between alcohol consumption and physiological levels of ghrelin. One study found plasma ghrelin levels were inversely related to alcohol consumption—i.e., rats that chronically consumed alcohol displayed lower circulating concentrations of ghrelin, and high-alcohol preferring rats (rats bred over geenerations to prefer alcohol) displayed lower ghrelin levels compared to their non-alcohol preferring counterparts (Szulc et al., 2013). However, these results were not reproduced in a second study (Landgren et al., 2012), possibly due to phenotypic differences between rodent strains. Like-wise, another study found that endogenous circulating ghrelin does not mediate alcohol reward or alcohol intake in male NMRI mice (Jerlhag et al., 2014). Conversely, systemic administration of exogenous ghrelin increases alcohol intake in male Sprague-Dawley rats (Cepko et al., 2014), but those results have not been consistently replicated across species, and specifically in male C57BL/6J mice (Lyons et al., 2008), possibly because of species and strain differences.

When examining the roles of ghrelin in alcohol-related behaviors, both central and peripheral levels and actions of the peptide must be considered. Primarily considered a peripheral peptide, ghrelin does cross the blood–brain-barrier (BBB) to exert central actions, although this topic remains controversial and studies suggest potential species-specific differences in the ability and directionality of ghrelin in crossing the BBB—human acyl-ghrelin crosses the BBB bidirectionally, and mouse ghrelin crosses the BBB either from the periphery to the brain (desacyl-ghrelin) or from the brain to the periphery (acyl-ghrelin) (Banks et al., 2002). Though controversial, there is also evidence that ghrelin may be produced centrally, mainly in the hypothalamus (Cabral et al., 2017; Ferrini et al., 2009). Moreover, central administration of exogenous ghrelin into the VTA and laterodorsal tegmental area (LDTg) increases home cage alcohol consumption in male C57B1/6 and GHS-R1A knock-out mice as well as male Sprague-Dawley rats (Cepko et al., 2014; Jerlhag et al., 2009; Jerlhag et al., 2011), though the same was not observed when ghrelin was administered into the paraventricular nucleus (PVNs), lateral hypothalamus (LHs), or nucleus accumbens (NAcs) of rats (Schneider et al., 2007). Preclinical genetic studies also offer insight: ghrelin peptide (*Ghrl*) knockout mice do not display the same levels of alcohol-induced dopamine release in the NAc, nor do they display the same level of alcohol-induced locomotor stimulation compared relative to wild-type controls (Jerlhag et al., 2011). In addition to lower alcohol-induced hyperlocomotion, *Ghrl* knockout animals also display lower alcohol consumption and attenuations in alcohol-conditioned place preference relative to wild-type control mice (Bahi et al., 2013).

Interestingly, GHS-R1a receptor expression is increased in the prefrontal cortex, nucleus accumbens, hippocampus, amygdala, and VTA following prolonged alcohol exposure in high-alcohol-preferring versus low-alcohol-preferring rats (Landgren et al., 2011b). Outside of the "classical reward pathways," ghrelin also targets the amygdala, modulating alcohol-related GABAergic and serotonergic transmission (Cruz et al., 2013; Hansson et al., 2014; Yoshimoto et al., 2017). Moreover, ghrelin acting on hippocampal GHS-R1a influences memory formation (Diano et al., 2006), and both acute and chronic alcohol administration increase ghrelin and dopamine release in the LH (Yoshimoto et al., 2017). Altogether, these findings suggest that central ghrelin signaling has wide-ranging impacts on neural circuitry tat are important for mediating alcohol effects on the brain and for the control of alcohol-related behaviors.

To develop innovative therapeutics for AUD, some researchers are targeting the link between alcohol and central ghrelin signaling through pharmacological and genetic manipulation of GHS-R1a function. Studies using various animal models (mice, rats, and prairie voles) have shown that GHS-R1a antagonism leads to reduced alcohol consumption (Bahi et al., 2013; Gomez et al., 2015; Gomez and Ryabinin, 2014; Kaur and Ryabinin, 2010; Landgren et al., 2012; Stevenson et al., 2015). Similarly, both ghrelin receptor (GHRS) knockout mice and rats self-administer and consume less alcohol than wild-type controls (Jerlhag et al., 2009; Zallar et al., 2019). In addition to alcohol intake, GHS-R1a antagonism in mice, rats, and prairie voles also attenuates alcohol-induced mesolimbic dopamine activity, as evidenced by reductions in locomotor stimulation, conditioned place preference, and dopamine release in the nucleus accumbens after alcohol administration (Bahi et al., 2013; Jerlhag et al., 2009; Kaur and Ryabinin, 2010; Landgren et al., 2012; Stevenson et al., 2016; Suchankova et al., 2015a). Combined, these findings suggests that GHS-R1a plays an important role in modulating the rewarding effects of alcohol. Of note, the effects of GHS-R1a antagonists seem to be more pronounced in the context of chronic alcohol exposure (Suchankova et al., 2013b). These findings imply that sensitivity of the ghrelin system may change with prolonged alcohol exposure, and thus, that treatment with GHS-R1a antagonists may have higher efficacy in chronic, heavy drinking individuals.

Human studies

Akin to preclinical studies, research on the ghrelin system, as it relates to alcohol consumption in humans, is complex, but shows therapeutic promise. In both healthy volunteers and social drinkers, plasma ghrelin levels are lower following acute oral alcohol consumption (Calissendorff et al., 2005, 2006; Ralevski et al., 2017a; Zimmermann et al., 2007). One mechanistic theory for this decrease involves alcohol directly inhibiting ghrelin secretion in the stomach. However, when social drinkers are given intravenous alcohol, plasma levels of fasting-induced ghrelin are attenuated compared to saline-treated controls (Leggio et al., 2013), indicating that alcohol may influence ghrelin signaling systemically, in addition to locally in the stomach. A recent set of translational experiments suggests that, overall, the caloric content of alcohol may play a role in its effects on ghrelin levels, but it is unlikely to be the sole explanation of how alcohol leads to acute reductions in peripheral endogenous ghrelin levels (Deschaine et al., 2021).

In individuals with AUD, active drinkers have lower circulating ghrelin levels and lower ghrelin production compared to healthy controls and abstinent AUD patients (Addolorato et al., 2006; Badaoui et al., 2008), although one study did report the opposite effect (Kraus et al., 2005). Many studies have reported that AUD patients in withdrawal and/or who abstain from alcohol have increased levels of circulating ghrelin (Kim et al., 2005; Kraus et al., 2005; Leggio et al., 2012; Wurst et al., 2007). In one study, patients who began to drink again, while receiving treatment, had higher baseline levels of ghrelin than patients who abstained, which suggests ghrelin could be a biomarker predictive of subsequent relapse (Leggio et al., 2012). Moreover, higher circulating ghrelin levels are positively associated with alcohol craving, as measured by a variety of questionnaires (Addolorato et al., 2006; Akkisi Kumsar and Dilbaz, 2015; Anne Koopmann et al., 2012; Leggio et al., 2012; Wurst et al., 2007). A study of social drinkers reported a direct relationship between fasting ghrelin levels and personality measures indicative of higher reward sensitivity and impulsivity (Ralevski et al., 2017b).

Like-wise, when exogenous ghrelin is administered to individuals with AUD in a bar-lab cue-reactivity experimental setting, participants that receive ghrelin, compared to placebo controls, report higher levels of alcohol craving, but no differences in craving for juice (Leggio et al., 2014). A similar study also found that, after intravenous ghrelin administration, individuals with AUD exhibited increases in self-administration of alcohol using a progressive ratio schedule, shorter time to initiate self-administration of alcohol, and increased activation in the amygdala in the presence of alcohol cues (Farokhnia et al., 2018). In terms of subjective response to alcohol, participants in this study also reported higher ratings of 'feel(ing) high' under the ghrelin condition. Furthermore, there was a significant interaction between ghrelin, but not placebo, and breath alcohol concentration (BrAC) for Biphasic Alcohol Effects Scale (BAES) stimulation, Drug Effects Questionnaire (DEQ) 'like the effects', 'feel high', and 'feel intoxicated'. These findings suggest a role for ghrelin in increasing motivation to self-administer alcohol that may be mediated by effects on the subjective effects of alcohol. Interestingly, food craving as measured by the General Food Craving Questionnaire (G-FQ-S) scores, but not alcohol craving as measured by the Alcohol Urge Questionnare (AUQ), also increased in the IV ghrelin condition, though this is likely due to participants having access to alcohol but not food during the experiment (Farokhnia et al., 2018). This study also found that, during a brain neuroimaging experiment, systemic ghrelin administration leads to increased amygdala activation in the presence of alcohol cues. Other neuroimaging studies have also identified positive correlations between circulating ghrelin concentrations and mesolimbic (i.e., ventral striatum [VS]) reactivity to alcohol cues and alcohol craving (Koopmann et al., 2019). A mediation analysis for this same study found that the VS response to alcohol cue-reactivity fully mediated the relationship between blood acyl ghrelin levels and cue-induced alcohol craving. Another neuroimaging study found a similar association between acylated-ghrelin and alcohol cue-induced activation of the bilateral insula (Bach et al., 2019). Taken together, these findings indicate that ghrelin signaling likely contributes to the alcohol-related pathophysiology, specifically as it pertains to reward sensitivity and self-control.

Many of the above studies conclude that targeting ghrelin signaling, either through reducing systemic levels of the activated peptide or antagonizing its actions at the GHS-R1a receptor, represents a promising direction for the development of novel therapeutic interventions for reducing alcohol craving. Indeed, GHS-R1a antagonism is a target in current studies for novel pharmacotherapies to treat AUD, but the results are still preliminary. The first clinical study of a ghrelin receptor inverse agonist in humans showed promising results with a reduction in cue-induced alcohol craving, but further testing is needed to verify whether this is an efficacious treatment option for AUD (Lee et al., 2020). Importantly, this trial showed that the GHS-R1α inverse agonist, PF-5190457, possessed an acceptable concentration-time profile for daily oral use and was safe when administered concomitantly with alcohol. In a heavy drinking sample, PF-5190457 administered alone or with alcohol did not have any significant adverse effects, including sedation, which has been observed in non-AUD samples (Lee et al., 2020). Therefore, PF-5190457 and other potential compounds targeting the ghrelin system represent a course of pharmacological treatment that is safe and well tolerated.

Genetic analyses related to the ghrelin system are interesting but limited. One study found the rs2232165 SNP of GHSR to be associated with heavy alcohol drinking, and other studies have reported significant associations between GHSR polymorphisms and risk/severity of AUD (Landgren et al., 2008, 2011a; Suchankova et al., 2016). One case–control study offered preliminary findings suggesting an association between a Leu72Met missense polymorphism in the pre-pro-ghrelin gene and AUD diagnosis, alcohol consumption and subjective responses to alcohol consumption (Suchankova et al., 2017). Especially considering the high constitutive activity of GHS-R1a (Mear et al., 2013), and prior work showing a lack of association between the ghrelin peptide gene (*GHRL*) haplotypes and AUD diagnosis and severity (Landgren et al., 2008, 2010, 2011a; Suchankova et al., 2016), targeting GHS-R1a, via receptor blockade or through other components of the ghrelin system, represents a potentially promising therapeutic direction for treating AUD.

Ghrelin and cannabinoids

Much like ghrelin, cannabinoids are well known for their orexigenic effects on feeding behavior and metabolism (Cota et al., 2003). Though very few experiments have been conducted to examine the crosstalk between these systems, there is some evidence to indicate a connection between ghrelin and cannabinoid signaling.

Preclinical studies

Only two studies have been published, at the time of this writing, directly examining the relationship between cannabis and ghrelin. Mazidi et al. (2014) found that rats that were administered *C. sativa* had significantly elevated blood ghrelin levels 30 and 60 min post-ingestion compared to controls. More recently, it was reported that Δ9-tetrahydrocannabinol (THC)-induced CPP is dose-dependently attenuated by systemic administration of a GHSR-1A antagonist, JMV2959, administration in rats. In addition, when administered 20 min prior to THC, JMV2959 dose-dependently attenuates THC-induced changes in behavioral stimulation, such as locomotion duration, distance traveled, and average speed. Utilizing Win55, 212-2, a synthetic aminoalkylindole cannabinoid, Charalambous and collegues also showed that JMV2959-treated rats intravenously self-administer less of the synthetic cannabinoid, while ghrelin pretreatment increased Win55, 212-2 self-administration (Charalambous et al., 2021). These experiments suggest GHSR-1A may play an important role in mediating the rewarding and stimulating effects of cannabinoids. However, Win55, 212-2 has some important distinctions from THC, including a higher affinity for the cannabinoid receptor CB1, lower lipophilicity and higher rate of excretion, and it seems to precipitate more noticeable spontaneous withdrawal symptoms in rats (Sharma et al., 2012; Aceto et al., 2001). These caveats should be kept in mind when comparing results from studies that use this drug to studies that focus on THC or cannabis.

Additionally, many groups have used cannabinoid CB1 receptor antagonists and agonists to explore the relationship between ghrelin and endocannabinoid (eCB) signaling. Systemic administration of two CB1 receptor antagonists, rimonabant and oleoylethanolamide (OEA), reduce plasma ghrelin levels and food intake in fasted rats (Cani et al., 2004). When infused directly into the PVN, rimonabant reverses ghrelin-induced hyperphagia (Tucci et al., 2004). A recent study identified an interesting relationship between CB1 signaling, ghrelin, and alcohol consumption. In that study, the peripherally active CB1 receptor inverse agonist, JD5037, reduced alcohol consumption in mice, but this effect was not observed in animals deficient in the CB1 receptor, ghrelin peptide, or GHS-R1a (Godlewski et al., 2019). Further, JD5037 treatment inhibited the formation of biologically active acyl-ghrelin without affecting plasma levels of des-acyl-ghrelin, its inactive form. Through a series of experiments involving neonatal capsaicin treatment for the selective blockade of vagal afferent signaling, intact vagal afferent activity was shown to be necessary for CB1 receptor or GHS-R1a signaling to reduce alcohol drinking. Therefore, CB1 receptor signaling in ghrelin-producing cells plays a critical role modulating both the formation of active ghrelin and its signaling in gastric vagal afferents, resulting in a reduction of alcohol drinking (Godlewski et al., 2019). These studies indicate a complex physiological interaction between ghrelin and endocannabinoid signaling systems.

The leading mechanistic theory for interaction between ghrelin and endocannabinoid systems involves mediation by hypothalamic AMP-activated protein kinase (AMPK), an enzyme considered to be a key regulator of energy homeostasis, which acts both centrally and peripherally (Kola et al., 2006; Xue and Kahn, 2006). Both cannabinoids (specifically Δ9-tetrahydrocannabinol [THC]) and ghrelin stimulate AMPK activity in the hypothalamus and heart, and inhibit activity in the liver and adipose tissue (Kola et al., 2005). Another study reported that animals lacking CB1 function, through either genetic knockout or pharmacological blockade, displayed blunted ghrelin-induced AMPK activity in the hypothalamus (Kola et al., 2008). In this same study, ghrelin did not induce orexigenic effects in CB1-knockout mice. As AMPK is a key player in appetite regulation (Minokoshi et al., 2004), Kola and colleagues surmised that the effects of ghrelin on appetite and AMPK signaling in the hypothalamus are dependent upon the presence and function of CB1. In a similar study, the enhanced AMPK activity seen with ghrelin or CB1 agonist administration was attenuated in mice lacking GHS-R1a (Lim et al., 2013). Therefore, it appears that both ghrelin and cannabinoid signaling pathways must be intact for ghrelin or cannabinoids to act on AMPK and exert orexigenic effects.

Another area of interest involving cannabinoid and ghrelin intractions being investigated is the dopaminergic reward pathway. In mice, peripheral administration of rimonabant attenuates ghrelin-induced locomotor stimulation and NAc dopamine release, but not ghrelin-induced food intake. This same study found intra-VTA administration of rimonabant also attenuates ghrelin-induced locomotor stimulation without affecting food intake (Kalafateli et al., 2018). While the systemic findings are contradictory to prior reports that the orexigenic effects of ghrelin depend on CB1 receptor presence and function, the site-specific study suggests that VTA CB1 receptors are required for ghrelin to activate the mesolimbic dopamine pathway. Given the recently proposed theory of ghrelin and cannabinoid receptors in the VTA underlying non-homeostatic (i.e., hedonic) feeding (Edwards and Abizaid, 2016), more research is needed in this field to determine how crosstalk between ghrelin and cannabinoids may influence addiction-related behavior.

Human studies

Though human studies are currently limited, we may expect more in the future due to (1) the increasingly established overlap between cannabis-induced physiological actions and the metabolic neuroendocrine system, and (2) the changing state of cannabis legality in the US opening the field of cannabinoid research. At this point, only two clinical studies linking cannabis use to ghrelin have been conducted. The first involved HIV-positive adult men who smoked medical cannabis or placebo for HIV-associated neuropathic pain. In this study, blood ghrelin levels were dose-dependently positively correlated with THC levels (Riggs et al., 2012). In a more recent study, appetitive and metabolic hormones were measured over a timecourse of THC administration through a variety of modalities (oral, smoked, and vaporized). Farokhnia and colleagues found a significant main effect of THC on circulating ghrelin levels, with post-hoc analysis indicating total ghrelin levels during the oral cannabis session were higher than the smoked or vaporized sessions (Farokhnia et al., 2020). However, it is important to note that while significant effects were found for total ghrelin, defined as acyl (active) + des-acyl (inactive) ghrelin, no effect was found for just acyl-ghrelin. Though there appears to be a clear link between ghrelin and cannabinoid signaling, more studies are required to elucidate the intricacies of this relationship.

Ghrelin and nicotine

Nicotine is affects appetite regulation and energy homeostasis (Jo et al., 2002; Zoli and Picciotto, 2012). Like-wise, several experiments involving nicotine and ghrelin have been conducted in the interest of investigating their overlapping role in reward sensitivity and food- and nicotine-seeking behaviors.

Preclinical studies

Very few studies, to our knowledge, have investigated the direct association between nicotine intake and circulating ghrelin levels. In one such study, it was reported that rats exposed to cigarette smoke for 4 weeks had significantly higher blood acyl-ghrelin levels compared to controls. However, the cigarette smoke-exposed animals also displayed lower body weight and the authors speculate the difference in circulating ghrelin levels could be secondary to this difference in energy balance between groups (Tomoda et al., 2012). Another group exposed rats to cigarette smoke for 8 weeks and reported no differences in serum ghrelin levels, although this discrepancy could be due to the study measuring total ghrelin instead of acyl-ghrelin, and/or the time difference since last nicotine exposure, among other potential reasons (Ypsilantis et al., 2012). In a study comparing oral, smoked, and intraperitoneal nicotine administration in rats, all nicotine-treated groups had higher ghrelin levels than controls (Ali et al., 2015). Despite relatively few studies connecting nicotine and ghrelin, there is ample evidence to suggest that ghrelin and nicotinic signaling systems have interaction effects on mesolimbic reward pathway activity and addiction-related behaviors.

Nicotinic acetylcholine receptors (nAChRs) are located throughout the central reward pathway, specifically the VTA, and modulate dopaminergic neuronal activity (Charpantier et al., 1998; Jerlhag et al., 2006b; Klink et al., 2001; Larsson et al., 2002; Léna and Changeux, 1997). A series of experiments used selective nAchR antagonists to show that ghrelin-induced locomotor stimulation and increases in dopamine concentration in the NAc are mediated by VTA nAChRs in rats (Jerlhag et al., 2008). Conversely, treatment with a ghrelin receptor antagonist attenuates nicotine-induced hyperlocomotion, conditioned place preference, and NAc dopamine release (Jerlhag and Engel, 2011; Wellman et al., 2011). Paired with a study showing that ghrelin stimulates nicotine-induced dopamine release in the rat striatum (Palotai et al., 2013), it is evident that ghrelin modulates nicotine-induced reward signaling. Thus, manipulating ghrelin signaling represents a potential target for treatment of nicotine dependence.

Human studies

Human data relating circulating ghrelin levels to smoking status has produced mixed results. These discrepancies are likely due, at least partially, to differences in methodology, as well as data and sample collection techniques and timepoints. Two studies reported that smoking status is associated with ghrelin levels, with current smokers displaying the highest concentrations of blood ghrelin (Fagerberg et al., 2003; Langenberg et al., 2005). However, other studies have shown no association between baseline ghrelin levels and smoking status (Kokkinos et al., 2007; Mutschler et al., 2012; Pöykkö et al., 2006). Only one study we are aware of differentiated between total and acyl-ghrelin, and they found acyl-ghrelin levels to be higher in smokers, but no group differences in total ghrelin levels (Koopmann et al., 2015). In an abstinent smoking sample, a reduction in plasma ghrelin levels was found after 2 months of abstinence (Lee et al., 2006). Another study reported that higher ghrelin levels increased risk of relapse, and those who relapsed showed a reduction in ghrelin levels 48 h after smoking cessation (al'Absi et al., 2014; Lemieux and al'Absi, 2018). No studies have shown a correlation between circulating ghrelin levels and nicotine craving or withdrawal (al'Absi et al., 2014; Mutschler et al., 2012).

Experiments exploring the acute effect of nicotine on ghrelin levels have also produced mixed results. One group found nonsmokers, but not smokers, exhibit a significant decline in ghrelin levels after smoking 2 cigarettes (Kokkinos et al., 2007). In a different study, smokers and nonsmokers alike displayed an increase in ghrelin levels shortly after smoking 1 cigarette (Bouros et al., 2006). Protocols using gum as the modality of nicotine delivery found no change in circulating ghrelin levels in nonsmokers after nicotine delivery (Kroemer et al., 2015; Pilhatsch et al., 2014). Lastly, a genetic analysis identified a variation of the *GHSR* gene that appears to be positively correlated with severity of cigarette smoking (Suchankova et al., 2016).

Given the varied outcome of the above studies, it may be helpful for the field to implement standardized approaches to better elucidate the relationship between nicotine and ghrelin signaling. In the only study to measure acyl-ghrelin, there were significant positive associations between acyl-ghrelin levels, smoking status, number of cigarettes consumed per day, and Fagerstom Test for Nicotine Dependence (FTND), while none of these associations were present for total ghrelin levels (Koopmann et al., 2015). Therefore, distinguishing between acyl-, desacyl-, and total-ghrelin represents a more informative approach for future experiments.

Ghrelin and opioids

Preclinical studies

Current literature on the relationship between ghrelin and opioid addiction is limited to just a few preclinical studies. Nevertheless, there are data to suggest a role for central ghrelin signaling in opioid reinforcement. In a series of studies by Sustkova-Fiserova and colleagues, a ghrelin receptor antagonist, JMV2959, was used to explore the interplay of ghrelin and opioids in influencing mesolimbic reward circuit activity. In the first of these experiments, it was shown that pretreatment with systemic JMV2959 in male Wistar rats dose-dependently reduced both morphine-induced dopamine release in the NAc and morphine-induced stereotyped behavior (i.e., reduced sniffing and gnawing and abolished licking) (Sustkova-Fiserova et al., 2014). A decrease in morphine-induced condition placed preference, dopaminergic sensitization, and behavioral sensitization, as well as a modulation of dopamine metabolism within the NAc, were all observed after systemic JMV2959 administration in rats (Jerabek et al., 2017). These findings were followed up by two studies showing that JMV2959 reverses morphine and fentanyl-induced increases in levels of the eCB anandamide, and exaggerated opioid-induced decreases in levels of the eCB 2-arachidonoylglycerol (2-AG) in the nucleus accumbens shell (NACSh) (Sustkova-Fiserova et al., 2017; Sustkova-Fiserova et al., 2016). In another study, ghrelin receptor antagonist-induced attenuation of opioid-related behavioral effects was replicated, and reduced fentanyl-evoked accumbens GABA efflux was observed in rats (Sustkova-Fiserova et al., 2017). In more recent experiments, male Wistar rats underwent a place conditioning procedure with fentanyl for 8 days and received systemic JMV2959 (or saline control), either as a single dose or repeatedly, over the 8 conditioning days. In this study, JMV2959 significantly and dose-dependently attenuated fentanyl-induced conditioned place preference (CPP) (Sustkova-Fiserova et al., 2020). Pretreatment with JMV2959 also reduced fentanyl self-administration and fentanyl seeking/relapse-like behavior. Finally, JMV2959 attenuated fentanyl-induced dopamine influx in the NAc, and increased dopamine metabolism by monoamines, as evident by increased accumbal 3,4-dihydroxyphenylacetic acid (DOPAC) (Sustkova-Fiserova et al., 2020).

Other groups have reported similar effects: for example, systemic JMV2959 pretreatment attenuates morphine-induced locomotor stimulation, CPP, and extracellular levels of dopamine in the NAc of mice (Engel et al., 2015). Another study reported that intracerebroventricular ghrelin infusion enhances motivation to self-administer heroin in rats, as measured by increases in progressive ratio breakpoints. However, ghrelin receptor blockade did not attenuate heroin self-administration or food deprivation-induced reinstatement of extinguished heroin-seeking behavior (Maric et al., 2012). Collectively, these preclinical experiments highlight the potential role of ghrelin signaling in opioid effects and its potential as a target for the development of novel treatment strategies to combat opioid addiction.

Ghrelin and stimulants

Much preclinical and clinical research has been conducted to explore physiological interactions between the ghrelin system and stimulant drugs, including cocaine, amphetamine, and methamphetamine.

Preclinical studies

While most studies investigating the relationship between psychostimulants and ghrelin have examined cocaine, there are also some experiments that used other psuchostimulant drugs. For example, studies have found an increase in serum ghrelin levels after injecting 3,4-methylenedioxymethamphetamine (MDMA) and methamphetamine in rats fed *ab libitum* (Crowley et al., 2005; Kobeissy et al., 2008). However, there is no question that cocaine studies form the bulk of this literature, and this will be our focus below.

An early finding showed a positive correlation between peripheral baseline levels of total ghrelin and active lever presses during reinstatement of extinguished cocaine responding after exposure to cocaine-associated conditioned stimuli (i.e., cues) in rats (Tessari et al., 2007). This finding suggests that ghrelin may modulate cue-triggered reinstatement of cocaine-seeking behavior. Subsequent experiments reported increases in cocaine-induced hyperlocomotion after systemic and central (injected into the NAc) ghrelin administration in rats (Jang et al., 2013; Wellman et al., 2005, 2008), indicating that ghrelin plays a role in locomotor sensitization in cocaine use. Similarly, ghrelin administered systemically or centrally into the VTA or NAc potentiates cocaine-induced CPP (Davis et al., 2007; Dunn et al., 2019; Schuette et al., 2013). Interestingly, mice treated with an acyl-ghrelin vaccine did not exhibit changes in cocaine-induced CPP relative to control animals, while a ghrelin receptor antagonist, JMV2959, attenuated this effect, suggesting that the rewarding effects of cocaine do not require peripherally synthesized acyl-ghrelin (Wenthur et al., 2019).

Other studies have utilized GHS-R1a antagonism or knockout to explore the role of ghrelin in psychostimulant-related drug-seeking behavior and reward sensitivity. When peripherally administered, JMV2959 attenuates both cocaine- and amphetamine-induced locomotor activity, accumbal dopamine release, and CPP (Jerlhag et al., 2010). When ghrelin is administered directly into the VTA, pretreatment with JMV2959 blocks the ghrelin-induced potentiation of cocaine-induced CPP (Dunn et al., 2019). Similarly, sub-chronic pretreatment of JMV2959 attenuates amphetamine-induced locomotor stimulation (Suchankova et al., 2015a). Another group also confirmed this relationship by showing that rats pretreated with JMV2959, as well as rats genetically modified to knockout the ghrelin receptor, display attenuated locomotor sensitization compared to control animals when administered cocaine (Clifford et al., 2012). Another study reported that *Ghrl* knockout mice show reduced cocaine-induced locomotor stimulation and sensitization, as well as changes to mesolimbic dopamine processing (Abizaid et al., 2011). It souhld also be noted that several studies using genetic manipulation have reported no differences in cocaine-induced hyperlocomotion in *Ghrl* or *Ghrs* knockout animals (Clifford et al., 2011, 2012).

Human studies

To our knowledge, only one study has examined the direct relationship between stimulants and ghrelin. In this experiment, 8 experienced cocaine users received intravenous cocaine, and no differences in total or acyl-ghrelin where observed after the cocaine administration, compared to baseline levels (Bouhlal et al., 2017). Two genetic studies did not find any connection between *GHRL* polymorphisms and stimulant use, although one study conducted in Swedish amphetamine users and matched controls did identify a *GHRL* SNP rs4684677, which was associated with Addiction Severity Index (ASI) composite score for drug use (Suchankova et al., 2013a; Yoon et al., 2005). Suchankova and colleagues did identify a *GHSR* SNP that was more common in the amphetamine-dependent sample compared to controls (Suchankova et al., 2013a). Akin to genetic findings ascertained from studies investigating other drugs of abuse, it seems that genetic variation in the ghrelin receptor gene (*GHSR*) is more robustly tied to drug use that of the ghrelin peptide gene (*GHLR*).

GLP-1

Glucagon-like peptide-1 (GLP-1) is a 30 amino-acid peptide hormone mainly produced and secreted peripherally from the L-cells of the intestines, and centrally from the hindbrain, in response to nutrient intake (Alvarez et al., 1996; Brubaker and Anini, 2003; Holst, 2007; Novak et al., 1987). GLP-1 is considered to be an incretin given its abilities to stimulate insulin release and reduce glucagon secretion (Holst, 2007; Kreymann et al., 1987; Matsuyama et al., 1988). This observation has led to GLP-1 analogues being approved for the treatment of obesity and type II diabetes (Gentilella et al., 2019; Srivastava and Apovian, 2018). Also defined as an anorexigenic peptide, GLP-1 is most known for its role in feeding behavior, gastric emptying, and energy regulation (Hayes et al., 2008; Näslund et al., 2005; Turton et al., 1996).

Both peripheral and central GLP-1 receptors (GLP-1R) are important for the peptide's regulatory functions on feeding and metabolism. Activation of GLP-1R in the hypothalamus and hindbrain are sufficient for mediating food intake and gastric emptying (Hayes et al., 2008, 2009; Shughrue et al., 1996). Furthermore, GLP-1R is distributed throughout the central nervous system (Merchenthaler et al., 1999). Of particular importance to the addiction field are receptors located in the mesolimbic reward pathway. In particular, GLP-1R activation and antagonism in neurons projecting from the nucleus of the solitary tract to the VTA and NAc modify food intake, particularly of highly palatable food (Alhadeff et al., 2012), which suggests that GLP-1 actions in the mesolimbic system are not only physiologically relevant for energy regulation, but potentially also modulate reward signaling in neuropsychiatric disorders, including in addictive behaviors (Fig. 12.2).

GLP-1 and alcohol

The concept of targeting GLP-1 receptors as a form of pharmacotherapy for alcohol use disorder is still fairly novel, with the first study indicating its potential efficacy being published in 2012. However, GLP-1 research has rapidly expanded since then and represents a promising avenue for innovative therapeutic options for AUD.

Preclinical studies

The first study to investigate the relationship between GLP-1 signaling and AUD used systemic administration of a GLP-1 receptor agonist, Exendin-4 (Ex4), to test its effects on various measures of alcohol-induced reward, alcohol consumption, and alcohol-seeking behavior in male mice and rats (Egecioglu et al., 2013c). These experiments showed that systemically administered Ex4 reduced alcohol-induced locomotor activity and attenuated alcohol-induced accumbal dopamine release compared to vehicle treatment, and a single dose of Ex4 attenuated alcohol CPP, while repeated treatment with Ex4 block the ability for alcohol to produce CPP in mice (Egecioglu et al., 2013c). Using an operant alcohol progressive ratio test, the same study showed that Ex4-treated rats exhibited fewer responses for alcohol, and a lower alcohol breakpoint, exemplifying a reduction in alcohol-seeking behavior and/or motivation to work for alcohol (Egecioglu et al., 2013c). Collectively, these results suggest that Ex4 attenuates alcohol reward and suppresses alcohol-induced activation of the mesolimbic reward pathway. These findings were extended by experiments that showed that direct stimulation of VTA GLP-1 receptors, either by Ex4 or the GLP-1 peptide itself, reduced alcohol intake in mice and rats (Bornebusch et al., 2019; Shirazi et al., 2013).

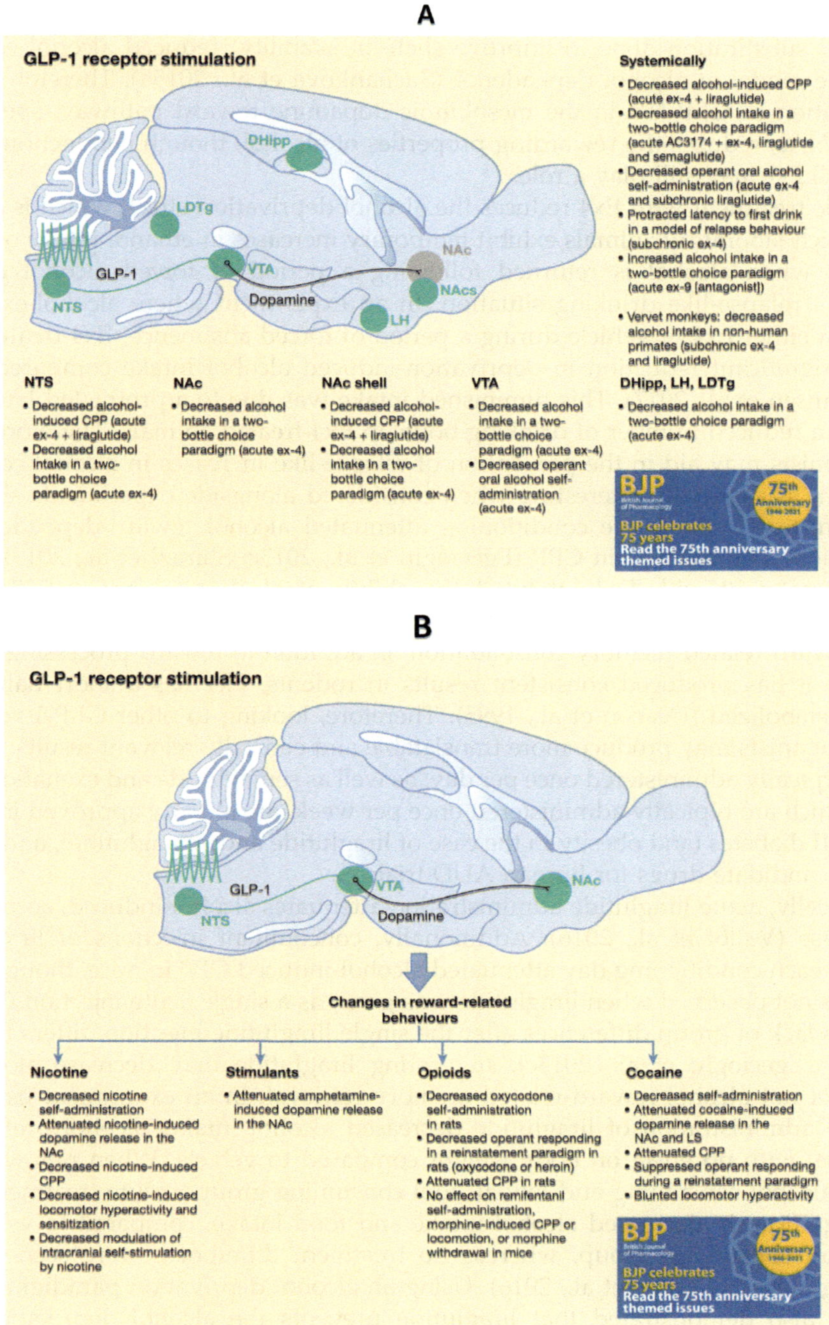

FIGURE 12.2 (A) Effects of glucagon-like peptide 1 (GLP-1) receptor stimulation on alcohol reward-related behaviors in preclinical models. (B) Effects of GLP-1 receptor stimulation in various substance reward-related behaviors in preclinical models. Abbreviations: *CPP*, conditioned place preference; *DHipp*, dorsal hippocampus; *ex-4*, exenatide; *ex-9*, exendin 9–39; *LDTgs*, laterodorsal tegmental nucleus; *LH*, lateral hypothalamus; *LS*, lateral septum; *NAc*, nucleus accumbens; *NAcs*, nucleus accumbens shell; *NTSs*, nucleus tractus solitarius; *VTA*, ventral tegmental area. *Reprinted from Kruse Klausen, M., Thomsen, M., Wortwein, G., Fink-Jensen, A., 2022. The role of glucagon-like peptide 1 (GLP-1) in addictive disorders. Br. J. Pharmacol. 179, 625–641. Copyright (2022), with permission from Wiley.*

Other studies report that AC3174 ([Leu14]exendin-4; an exenatide analog with a single amino-acid substitution done to improve shelf-life stability) reduced alcohol consumption in a mouse model of alcohol dependence (Suchankova et al., 2015a). Therefore, it is likely that activation of GLP-1Rs in the mesolimbic dopamine reward pathway, specifically the VTA and NAc, reduces the rewarding properties of alcohol, though endogenously released systemic GLP-1 may still play a role.

Systemic treatment with Ex4 reduces the alcohol deprivation effect, which is a phenomenon in which laboratory animals exhibit temporary increases in ethanol intake over baseline conditions when alcohol is returned following a period of forced alcohol deprivation, modeling a relapse-like drinking situation. In an experiment where alcohol-exposed mice were given either Ex4 or vehicle during a period of forced abstinence, Ex4-treated mice displayed a significant reduction in deprivation-induced alcohol intake compared to control mice (Thomsen et al., 2017). This diminished intake was due to a protracted latency to first drink and a reduced number of drinking bouts in Ex4-treated animals. Therefore, GLP-1 receptor agonists may aid in the prevention of relapse-like increases in alcohol consumption. This finding is especially interesting when considered alongside experiments showing that Ex4 administered after place conditioning attenuated alcohol reward-dependent memory consolidation, as measured in CPP (Egecioglu et al., 2013c; Shirazi et al., 2013). Moreover, repeated treatment with Ex4 inhibited the ability of alcohol to induce CPP (Egecioglu et al., 2013c). Taken together, these findings suggest GLP-1 analogues can influence alcohol-reward related memory consolidation, in addition to reward processing.

Though it has produced consistent results in rodents, Ex4 has a short half-life and is quickly metabolized (Deacon et al., 1995). Therefore, looking to other GLP-1 receptor analogues or agonists may produce more translatable and clinically relevant results. Liraglutide, which is typically administered once per day, as well as semaglutide and exenatide extended-release, which are typically administered once per week, are already approved in humans to treat type II diabetes (and obesity in the case of liraglutide and semaglutide), and may represent ideal candidate drugs for human AUD trials.

Preclinically, acute liraglutide administration attenuates alcohol-induced, accumbal dopamine release (Vallöf et al., 2016). Additionally, concomitant injections of liraglutide and alcohol on each conditioning day attenuated alcohol-induced CPP in mice, though this attenuation was not observed when liraglutide was given as a single acute injection (Vallöf et al., 2016). This lack of group differences after the single liraglutide injection differs from studies using Ex4 (Egecioglu et al., 2013c), suggesting liraglutide may decrease alcohol-related reward, but not alcohol reward-related memory retrieval. In an experiment using outbred rats, acute administration of liraglutide decreased alcohol intake, alcohol preference, and food intake, with no effect on body weight compared to vehicle. When rats were divided into high-alcohol consuming and low-alcohol consuming groups, acute treatment with liraglutide significantly decreased alcohol intake and food intake, compared to vehicle, in the high-alcohol consuming group, whereas no treatment differences were seen in the low-consuming animals (Vallöf et al., 2016). Using an alcohol deprivation paradigm, Vallöf and colleagues also demonstrated that liraglutide prevents the alcohol deprivation effect in rats, providing evidence that liraglutide could hinder relapse-like drinking. Furthermore, repeated treatment with liraglutide reduced alcohol intake in outbred rats, and decreased operant self-administration of alcohol in selectively bred Sardinian alcohol-preferring (sP) rats

(Vallöf et al., 2016). Similarly, in alcohol-preferring African vervet monkeys, liraglutide reduced alcohol consumption over a duration of 2 weeks after repeat treatments and without significant impact on water intake or apparent drug-related side-effects (Thomsen et al., 2019). Lastly, liraglutide modulates the subjective response to alcohol withdrawal. In a set of experiments using an elevated plus maze test, liraglutide prevented alcohol withdrawal-induced anxiety in rats (Sharma et al., 2015).

Although these studies provide robust evidence that GLP-1 receptor agonists modulate alcohol-induced reward processing, the precise physiological mechanisms and neurocircuits involved are still largely unknown. In addition to their central locations, GLP-1 receptors are widely expressed throughout the periphery, including the hepatic portal system, vagal afferents, and pancreatic B-cells (Kanoski et al., 2011; Orskov et al., 1988). In the above studies on alcohol, GLP-1 analogues were administered almost exclusively in the periphery. However, in experiments using mice, both Ex4 and liraglutide seem to be able to cross the BBB (Hunter and Hölscher, 2012; Kastin and Akerstrom, 2003), and an increasing amount of evidence suggests that centrally located GLP-1R are the primary regulators of GLP-1 effects on drug reinforcement. To this point, genetic ablation of central GLP-1R signaling abolished the ability of Ex4 administration to reduce alcohol intake, while hedonic feeding was only partially blocked (Sirohi et al., 2016). This latter observation suggests that central GLP-1 signaling is required to regulate alcohol reward, but both central and peripheral GLP-1 signaling are involved in feeding behavior. Furthermore, Marty et al. (2020) looked specifically at targeting of G-protein receptor 119 (GPR119), which is primarily located in pancreatic cells and in the gastro-intestinal tract, where its activation promotes the downstream release of endogenous GLP-1 (Chu et al., 2007; Fredriksson et al., 2003; Hansen et al., 2011; Lan et al., 2012; Overton et al., 2006; Soga et al., 2005). This study found that administration of two different GPR119 agonists did not impact alcohol consumption (Marty et al., 2020). Like-wise, pharmacological inhibition of dipeptidyl peptidase-4 (DPP-4), the enzyme responsible for degrading GLP-1 (Deacon et al., 1995), also failed to significantly modify alcohol intake in the same study. However, when this same cohort of animals was injected with liraglutide or semaglutide, alcohol intake was significantly suppressed, although only semaglutide reduced ethanol preference (Marty et al., 2020). These experiments suggest that endogenous circulating GLP-1 may not be adequate to activate central GLP-1Rs, and their associated neurocircuitries, to impact alcohol-related signaling.

There is accumulating evidence surrounding the importance of GLP-1R signaling in the nucleus of the solitary tract (NTS) in feeding behavior and reward processing. In fact, activation of GLP-1Rs in the NTS blocked alcohol-induced locomotor stimulation, accumbal dopamine release, and CPP (Vallöf et al., 2019). Moreover, in mice pretreated with a GLP-1R antagonist directly in the NTS and then dosed with systemic Ex4, the GLP-1 did not inhibit alcohol-induced locomotor stimulation compared to vehicle (Vallöf et al., 2019). Lastly, genetic knockdown of GLP-1R in the NTS attenuates the anorectic and weight-reducing effects of acute and chronic administration of liraglutide (Fortin et al., 2020). NTS GABAergic neurons, in particular, may play a key role in GLP-1R reward signaling, as selectively silencing these neurons attenuates the food intake and body weight-reducing effects of liraglutide (Fortin et al., 2020). In summary, there is clear evidence that GLP-1-signaling modulates alcohol reward and other related behaviors, as well as the circuits that underlie those behaviors. GLP-1R agonists represent a promising and innovative therapeutic tool for the treatment of AUD, but more work is needed to elucidate the precise mechanisms underlying the observed neuronal and behavioral outcomes.

Human studies

As of this writing, clinical trials for GLP-1 analog usage to treat AUD may be underway, but no results are currently published. However, it is known that genetic variation in GLP-1R is associated with AUD diagnosis in humans (Suchankova et al., 2015b). Moreover, these findings were replicated when splitting the cohort by race, and through comparison to an additional independent sample (Suchankova et al., 2015b). Suchankova and colleagues completed an additional analysis where they functionally validated these findings in a smaller sample of social drinkers. Here, they discovered the *GLP1R* 168*Ser* allele of the rs6923761 SNP was associated with increased BrAC and subjects reaching a binge level of 80 mg% of BrAC while self-administering alcohol. This allele was also significantly correlated with higher BOLD signaling in the globus pallidus when receiving rewarding feedback during an fMRI session (Suchankova et al., 2015b). *In vitro* studies of the 168*Ser* allele have associated it with lower GLP-1R cell surface expression, which also led to lower efficacy of agonist response (Koole et al., 2011). Therefore, it seems likely genetic variations in GLP-1R affect receptor expression and signaling, leading to phenotypic differences which may influence the development and severity of alcohol use disorder.

GLP-1 and cannabinoids

Preclinical studies

The interplay between GLP-1 and endocannabinoid signaling is not well understood. Also, to our knowledge, there are no preclinical studies investigating the direct relationship between GLP-1 and cannabis use (i.e., exogenous cannabinoids).

Although the direct effect of cannabis on GLP-1 has not been investigated in preclinical studies, experiments involving pharmacological and genetic manipulation of CB1 receptors do provide some information regarding the relationship between GLP-1 and eCB signaling. GLP-1 and eCBs regulate feeding behavior and energy metabolism. There is little evidence to suggest crosstalk of these systems in central reward pathways, but GLP-1 and eCBs may interact peripherally in the regulation of insulin secretion, and this interaction may indirectly influence some of the appetitive effects of cannabis use. For example, CB1 receptor knockout mice display higher postprandial GLP-1 levels following a glucose challenge compared to wildtype control animals (González-Mariscal et al., 2016). In addition, CB1 knockout mice have lower plasma insulin levels, and when subcutaneously infused with GLP-1, CB1 knockout mice show significantly lower blood glucose levels and greater early phase insulin secretion. Gonzalez-Mariscal and colleagues conducted a series of experiments in mouse insulinoma cells and reported that eCBs down-regulated GLP-1R-mediated cAMP accumulation and insulin secretion (González-Mariscal et al., 2016). However, cellular interactions do not necessarily translate to behavioral changes, and some studies have reported that GLP-1 does not mediate CB1 receptor effects on food intake, feeding behavior, or body weight (Bojanowska and Radziszewska, 2011; Cani et al., 2004).

Human studies

A few clinical studies have inquired into the relationship between cannabis and GLP-1, though results are still somewhat inconclusive. One study examined different modalities of cannabis intake on metabolic hormones and reported that GLP-1 levels in the blood were lower after cannabis exposure (Farokhnia et al., 2020). Similarly, a separate study reported that subjects who were administered THC displayed an attenuated GLP-1 response to food intake compared to the placebo group, but no group differences were present during the fasting state (Weltens et al., 2019). Moreover, these results were replicated in an experiment using a CB receptor agonist where, again, post-drug fasting GLP-1 levels were comparable across groups, but subjects in the CBR agonist group displayed suppressed levels of GLP-1 following an oral glucose tolerance test (Chia et al., 2017). These findings suggest that GLP-1 may attenuate the hyperphagic effects of cannabinoids in the context of food intake. However, authors of the above studies speculate the relationship between cannabinoids and GLP-1 is likely not direct, with insulin or glucose-dependent insulinotropic polypeptide (GIP) potentially acting as the primary target of cannabinoids, which then modulates changes in circulating GLP-1. Overall, more research into the relationship between cannabis and GLP-1, and related metabolic pathways, is needed.

GLP-1 and nicotine

Given the known effects of GLP-1R and nicotine receptors on mesolimbic reward circuit function, investigating the interaction between these compounds may provide understanding of the suitability of GLP-1R targeting drugs for the treatment of nicotine addiction. There is evidence to suggest that GLP-1 may influence nicotine-related motivated behaviors and reward processing. First, a single pre-treatment dose of systemic Ex4 in mice significantly reduces nicotine-induced locomotor activity, accumbal dopamine release, and CPP (Egecioglu et al., 2013a). In addition, systemic Ex4 blocks nicotine-induced locomotor sensitization (Egecioglu et al., 2013a). These findings indicate that GLP-1 receptors regulate nicotine-induced activation of the mesolimbic dopamine system. Furthermore, systemic treatment with Ex4 or sitagliptin, an inhibitor of the GLP-1 degrading enzyme dipeptidyl peptidase-4 (DPP4), reduced nicotine self-administration but did not change responses to food rewards (Tuesta et al., 2017). The same study showed that *Glp1r* knockout mice consume more nicotine, but not food, than their wildtype littermates across a range of nicotine doses, resulting in an upward shift in the dose–response curve. Moreover, nicotine administration reduced response to food reinforcers similarly across genotype groups, suggesting that GLP-1 is likely not involved in the anorectic effects of nicotine (Tuesta et al., 2017). Taken together, these results indicate that GLP-1 transmission selectively regulates the motivational properties of nicotine.

Tuesta and colleagues also examined the role of specific neurocircuits in GLP-1 regulation of nicotine-related behaviors. Through the use of DREADDs, the authors chemogenetically activated GLP-1 neurons in the NTS, as opposed the NTS as a whole, and found a marked decrease in nicotine intake in these mice compared to control groups; thus revealing nicotine likely preferentially activates GLP-1 neurons in the NTS (Tuesta et al., 2017). The authors surmise that NTS terminals release GLP-1, which then stimulates habenular inputs to enhance activation of the interpeduncular nucleus (IPNs). Infusion of Ex4 into the IPN reduces nicotine intake in rats, while infusion of a GLP-1 receptor antagonist into the IPN increases nicotine intake in rats without affecting food intake (Tuesta et al., 2017). Finally, *Glp1r* knockout mice showed diminished nicotine-induced IPN activity (Tuesta et al., 2017). Overall, these studies propose a potential circuit mechanism through which GLP-1 activates medial habenular-IPN circuitry to dampen the rewarding effects of nicotine.

Human studies

At the time of this writing, there is only one published pilot trial investigating the relationship between nicotine addiction and GLP-1 but more may be in various stages of development. A group of prediabetic and/or overweight smokers were given subcutaneous once-weekly extended-release exenatide or placebo, in addition to nicotine replacement therapy (patch) and smoking cessation counseling. Following 6 weeks of treatment, abstinent indivuduals treated with exenatide displayed significantly increased rates of abstinence, less craving, and dampened withdrawal symptoms relative to the placebo group (Yammine et al., 2021). Additionally, exenatide reduced post-cessation weight more than placebo, which is an important consideration because many smokers gain weight after quitting, precipitating or worsening obesity and type 2 diabetes among this population (Yammine et al., 2021; Bush et al., 2016). Therefore, this is an area that warrants additional investigation given the substantial preclinical and emerging clinical evidence supporting the potential of GLP-1-regulating pharmacotherapies as treatments for nicotine addiction.

GLP-1 and opioids

Preclinical studies

Currently, there are only a few preclinical studies investigating the interaction between opioid/opiate drugs and GLP-1. In the first of these studies, administration of linagliptin, a selective DPP4 inhibitor, blocked the expression, acquisition, and reinstatement of morphine-induced CPP (Łupina et al., 2020). These findings suggest that inhibition GLP-1 degradation attenuates morphine-seeking behavior and morphine reward processing. Similarly, rats pretreated with Ex4, either systemically or directly in the nucleus accumbens shell, self-administer less oxycodone than vehicle-treated controls (Zhang et al., 2020). In addition, both systemic and intra-accumbens shell infusion of Ex4 results in dose-dependent attenuation of oxycodone-seeking behavior during reinstatement tests (Zhang et al., 2020). Another study found that liraglutide-treated rats self-administered less heroin, did not escalate heroin self-administration over trials, and displayed increased latency to self-administer heroin, compared to a vehicle-treated group (Douton et al., 2022). These studies offer promising, though preliminary, evidence that a physiological increase of GLP-1 may reduce opioid drug-seeking behavior and opioid drug reinforcement without producing adverse feeding effects or affecting opioid drug-induced analgesia. However, these findings have not been consistently replicated. In fact, one study reported that systemic treatment with Ex4 had no effect on morphine-induced CPP, withdrawal, or locomotor stimulation in mice (Bornebusch et al., 2019). Moreover, neither Ex4 treatment nor genetic knockout of GLP-1 receptors affected self-administration of remifentanil, a short-acting synthetic opioid (Bornebusch et al., 2019). It is difficult to speculate why such varying results are observed between studies, but exploring the mechanisms underlying GLP-1 and opioid signaling would be the ideal starting point to better inform researchers on how and where to administer potentially therapeutic compounds for the efficient treatment of opioid/opiate use disorders. Therefore, more work is needed to fully elucidate the direct interplay between GLP-1 and opioid signaling and the cellular/circuit mechanisms involved. At this time, no clinical studies on opioid use and GLP-1 have been published.

GLP-1 and stimulants

Psychostimulants primarily exert their reinforcing effects by binding to dopamine transporters to increase the level of synaptic and extra-synaptic dopamine levels in the nucleus accumbens (Kalivas, 2007). Targeting GLP-1R receptors in these classical reward pathways represents a potential therapeutic target for reducing cocaine and amphetamine misuse and addiction in humans.

Preclinical studies

In rats, acute cocaine self-administration doubles endogenous GLP-1 levels peripherally (You et al., 2019). However, following 14 days of cocaine self-administration training, the rats underwent extinction testing. On day 1 of extinction, saline administration caused circulating GLP-1 to increase to levels observed with cocaine intake, but this effect was extinguished within 2 weeks (You et al., 2019). Systemic pretreatment with Ex4 attenuates amphetamine as well as cocaine-induced hyperlocomotion, accumbal dopamine release, and CPP in mice (Egecioglu et al., 2013b). These results, demonstrating the efficacy of Ex4 modulation of cocaine and amphetamine reward processing, are consistent with the results of other studies using similar paradigms (Graham et al., 2013; Sørensen et al., 2015). One group found that Ex4 decreases amphetamine-induced locomotor activity in rats without inducing anxiety-like behavior (Erreger et al., 2012). A similar reduction in amphetamine-stimulated hyperlocomotion in mice was also observed with administration of a DPP4 inhibitor (Lautar et al., 2005). Therefore, the GLP-1R appears to play a key role in regulating psychostimulant reward processing and reinforcement.

Though GLP-1 receptors are located both centrally and peripherally, and the above experiments all involved systemically administered GLP-1R regulators, it is central GLP-1 signaling that is thought to mediate the rewarding effects and addictive properties of psychostimulants. This notion is supported by work showing that systemically administered Ex4 is unable to attenuate amphetamine-induced CPP in mice with genetic ablation of central GLP-1 signaling (Sirohi et al., 2016). A similar study reported that animals with genetic ablation of GLP-1R exhibit augmentations in cocaine-induced locomotor activity and CPP, but these responses are restored to control levels when GLP-1R function is selectively restored in GABAergic neurons located in the dorsal lateral septum (LS) (Harasta et al., 2015). In fact, systemic and local administration of Ex4 reduce cocaine-induced increases in extracellular dopamine levels in the LS (Reddy et al., 2016). The same study further characterized the role of GLP-1R in dopamine homeostasis by treating brain slices containing the LS with GLP-1, which increases surface levels of dopamine transporters (DATs) and dopamine reuptake. These findings imply that GLP-1 signaling regulates cocaine effects on DAT-dependent cellular processes in the LS. To investigate whether GLP-1R signaling regulates DAT function through a retrograde signal, levels of 2-AG, an endogenous cannabinoid retrograde messenger with a known role in reward, and arachidonic acid (AA), a biproduct of 2-AG degradation known to impair DAT-mediated dopamine reuptake (Chen et al., 2003; L'hirondel et al., 1995; Zhang and Reith, 1996), were measured in the LS following systemic Ex4 injection. Following systemic Ex4 administration, there was a significant reduction of 2-AG and AA levels in the LS, implying a reduction of endocannabinoid metabolism. Furthermore, AA itself appeared to reduce dopamine transporter function (Reddy et al., 2016). Therefore, GLP-1 signaling in the LS may modulate DAT function, and this may be important for the rewarding effects of cocaine.

Regions of the mesolimbic pathway other than the LS have also been theorized to have pivotal actions in GLP-1 and cocaine reward processing. For example, Ex4 administered systemically and directly into the NAc dose-dependently attenuate cocaine-seeking behavior in rats (Hernandez et al., 2019). Furthermore, immunohistochemical analysis revealed peripherally injected fluoro-Ex4 colocalizes with glial fibrillary acidic protein (GFAP)-positive astrocytes and neuronal nuclear protein (NeuN)-positive neurons in the NAc core and shell, observed via confocal microscopy. Using *in vivo* electrophysiology, Ex4 also increased the frequency of action potentials in the NAc of cocaine-experienced rats (Hernandez et al., 2019). Moreover, intravenous cocaine infusion evokes phasic dopamine release in the NAc shell and core (Fortin and Roitman, 2017), which is thought to contribute to the reward-based learning, motivation, and reinforcement that facilitate drug use (Covey et al., 2014). This cocaine-induced increase in accumbal dopamine signaling in the NAc core, but not NAc shell, is attenuated by central administration of Ex4, but the magnitude of cocaine-stimulated dopamine reuptake is not affected by central GLP-1R agonism (Fortin and Roitman, 2017). These findings suggest that GLP-1R activation attenuates the rewarding effects of cocaine by suppressing the excitability of dopamine neurons, although this could be site-specific and warrants additional experimentation.

In rats, intra-VTA administration of Ex4 reduces cocaine, but not sucrose, self-administration as indicated by a reduction in lever presses and breakpoint in a progressive ratio paradigm (Schmidt et al., 2016). Furthermore, cocaine activates GLP-1 neurons in the NTS (Schmidt et al., 2016) that project monosynaptically to the VTA (Alhadeff et al., 2012). A possible compensatory mechanism for this relationship involves corticosterone-related pathways and mechanisms. Indeed, plasma corticosterone is elevated by cocaine intake, and exogenous corticosterone administration to rats leads to activation of GLP-1 producing neurons in the NTS (Schmidt et al., 2016). Administration of exogenous corticosterone into the fourth ventricle reduces cocaine self-administration, and this effect is blocked when animals are pretreated with a GLP-1 receptor antagonist, EX9-39, directly in the VTA. Moreover, when GLP-1 receptors in the VTA are selectively knocked down, animals displayed a significant increase in breakpoint and total cocaine infusions (Schmidt et al., 2016). Furthermore, systemic and direct infusion of Ex4 into the VTA dose-dependently reduces cocaine-seeking behavior (Hernandez et al., 2018). Peripherally administered Ex4 binds to dopamine neurons in the VTA, and blocking intra-VTA GLP-1R with an antagonist abolishes the ability of peripherally administered Ex4 to attenuate cocaine-seeking behavior (Hernandez et al., 2018). Therefore, endogenous GLP-1 signaling in the VTA is necessary to selectively regulate drug-motivated behavior.

Human studies

To date, only one clinical study has been published on the relationship between stimulants and GLP-1. Following intravenous cocaine administration, there was a significant reduction in serum GLP-1 levels (Bouhlal et al., 2017). Given the preclinical literature documenting how GLP-1 analogues decrease cocaine consumption, the authors speculate that cocaine-induced reductions of circulating GLP1- levels may promote cocaine use and further decreases GLP-1 concentration to initiate a positive feedback loop. Interestingly, GLP-1 levels are also associated with subjective factors of cocaine use, specifically feeling high and feeling anxious (Bouhlal et al., 2017). This observation indicates a role for GLP-1 in emotional regulation associated with cocaine use. However, it is important to note that this human experimental study compared GLP-1 levels and other metabolic hormones before and after intravenous administration of cocaine, without a placebo-matched comparison group. More studies are needed to explore the crosstalk between stimulant use and GLP-1 signaling, including exploring the potential efficacy of a GLP-1 receptor agonist for the treatment of stimulant addiction.

Microbiome

The gastro-intestinal tract is the densely populated home to the gut microbiota: a wide-variety of bacteria, yeasts, fungi, and viruses, numbering at approximately 10^{14} total cells. The colon hosts the highest microbial population with a density of $10^{11}-10^{12}$ cells per gram of bowel content, while the duodenum is at the lower end with $10^{2}-10^{4}$ cells per gram (Derrien and van Hylckama Vlieg, 2015; Faith et al., 2010; O'Hara and Shanahan, 2006). Altogether, the microbiome genome is ~150 fold larger than the human genome (Qin et al., 2010). Every individual has a unique flora composed of 100-1000 different species of microbes, with bacteria being the most common (Qin et al., 2010; Zoetendal et al., 1998). Collectively, the gut microbiome plays an important role in regulating host physiology and maintaining gut and immune homeostasis. Though evidence suggests the gut microbiome can be remarkably stable over the lifetime, variables such as diet, medications, and stress all affect the gut microbiome (Aziz et al., 2013; Faith et al., 2013; Kelly et al., 2015; Sandhu et al., 2017; Singh et al., 2017; Turnbaugh et al., 2009; Wu et al., 2017; Xu et al., 2017).

Under normal conditions, the relationship between an individual and their microbiome is symbiotic: microbes in the gut protect their host from foreign organisms and provide immune regulatory functions, often by breaking down larger molecules to provide beneficial metabolites (DeGruttola et al., 2016). Dysbiosis refers to a disturbance in gut microbiome homeostasis and can entail a loss of beneficial organisms, overgrowth of pathogenic organisms, or a loss of overall microbial diversity (DeGruttola et al., 2016; Myers and Hawrelak, 2004). Alterations in the diversity, quantity, and location of microbes has been tied to many diseases such as diabetes, obesity, cancer, and inflammatory bowel disease (Pflughoeft and Versalovic, 2012; Shreiner et al., 2015), as well as neuropsychiatric disorders including multiple sclerosis, Parkinson's Disease, Alzheimer's, depression, anxiety, and anorexia (Foster and McVey Neufeld, 2013; Seitz et al., 2019; Tremlett et al., 2017).

As evident through the above reviews linking the gut microbiome to various metabolic and psychiatric disease states, there is clearly a connection between the gut and the brain, but exact regulatory mechanisms remain largely unknown. Dysbiosis-induced changes in metabolite production, intestinal permeability, immune regulation, and neuronal signaling are all theorized to play a role in behavioral changes and disease pathology (Fig. 12.3). Given

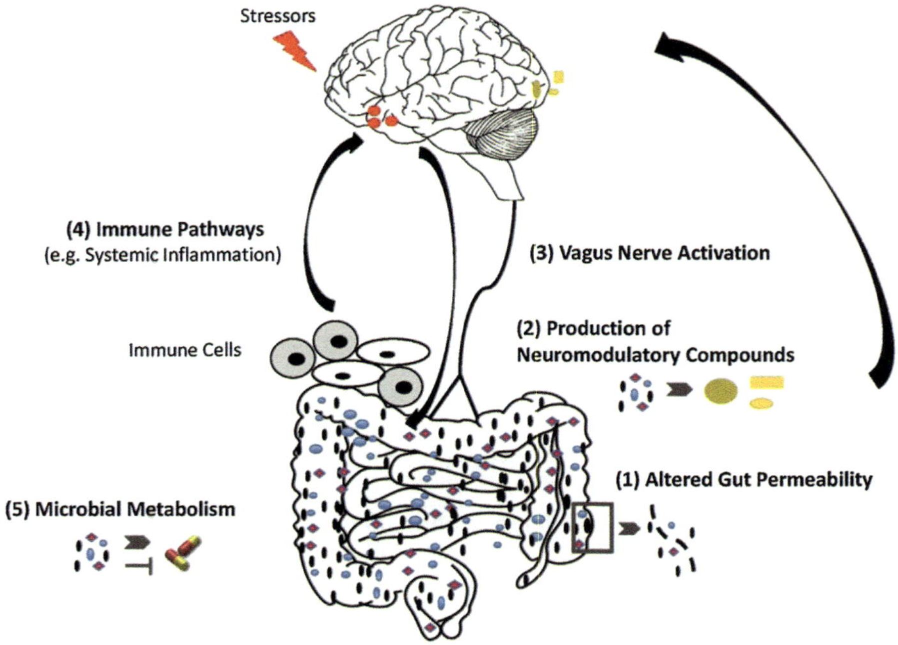

FIGURE 12.3 There is a growing body of work indicating interactions between the host, the brain, and the gut microbiome, facilitated by the following. (1) Increased gut permeability enables either microbes or microbial metabolites to enter the bloodstream. (2) Gut microbes produce neuromodulatory metabolites (e.g., short chain fatty acids), as well as induce the production of host-derived vitamins (B12), neurotransmitters (e.g., serotonin), and hormones (e.g., peptide YY) that may impact neurological and host health. (3) Bidirectional interactions may occur directly via innervation of the vagus nerve, providing a direct line of communication between the enteric and central nervous system. (4) In addition, gut–brain interactions can occur through immune-mediated inflammatory pathways, such as (A) microbial-driven systemic inflammation linked to the progression of neurodegenerative diseases, and (B) stressors that can alter the gut via inflammatory pathways. (5) Finally, gut microbes can metabolize xenobiotics, impacting brain function. *Reprinted from Tremlett, H., Bauer, K.C., Appel-Cresswell, S., Finlay, B.B., Waubant, E., 2017. The gut microbiome in human neurological disease: a review. Ann. Neurol. 81, 369–382. Copyright (2017), with permission from Wiley.*

the influence many psychoactive drugs have on feeding behavior and metabolism, it is no surprise there is a growing literature associating changes in the gut microbiome to chronic substance misuse (Meckel and Kiraly, 2019). Perhaps by elucidating the precise mechanisms involved and further defining the bidirectional crosstalk between the gut and brain, new therapeutic targets can be identified for the treatment of substance use disorders and their sequalae.

Drug-induced changes in diversity and taxonomic structure of the microbiome and in metabolism (resulting metabolites)

One of the key tenants of a healthy microbiome is microbial diversity. When healthy diversity is disturbed, including through the usage of psychoactive drugs, dysbiosis occurs and thus begins a chain reaction. One of the most direct examples of dysbiosis-related change involves metabolites released from the gut to the rest of the body. Foremost among these are short-chain fatty acids, bile acids, and tryptophan metabolites.

Short-chain fatty acids

Short-chain fatty acids (SCFAs) are metabolites produced by bacteria through anaerobic fermentation of dietary fibers and proteins (Roy et al., 2006), and are essential for the maintenance of intestinal homeostasis. SCFAs activate G protein-coupled receptors both locally in the GI tract and systemically in a variety of cell types, including epithelial cells, neurons, hepatocytes, adipocytes, and enteroendocrine cells (Stilling et al., 2016). In addition, SCFAs are the primary energy source of colonocytes. From the GI tract, SCFAs are also transported to the liver via the hepatic portal vein, and from there into systemic circulation (Koh et al., 2016). Locally, SCFAs serve a protective role in preserving intestinal barrier function and attenuating inflammatory markers (Cresci et al., 2017; Elamin et al., 2013; Ratajczak et al., 2019). Systemically, SCFAs are known for their inhibitory effect on histone deacetylases (HDACs), and this modulation of gene expression may contribute to their widespread immunomodulatory and anti-inflammatory effects (Johnstone, 2002; Koh et al., 2016). Centrally, SCFAs are able to cross the BBB and influence neurophysiology and behavior (Oldendorf, 1973). For example, social stress reduces the frequency of pathways involved in fatty acid biosynthesis and metabolism (Bharwani et al., 2016), and administering SCFAs attenuates depressive-like and anxious-like behaviors induced by psychosocial stress in mice (Sun et al., 2016; van de Wouw et al., 2018). Other neuronal functions, such as microglial homeostasis and hypothalamic appetite regulation, are also modulated by SCFAs (Erny et al., 2015; Frost et al., 2014).

Bile acids

Bile acids are the metabolic product of cholesterol catabolism, which occurs primarily in the liver and secondarily in the microbiota of the intestines. In brief, the liver breaks down cholesterol to form cholic acid and chenodeoxycholic acid, which are then transported into the gall bladder before being secreted into the duodenum postprandially to be converted into deoxycholic and lithocholic acids, respectively, or a derivative thereof (Fiorucci et al., 2021). Bile acids can influence the microbial composition of the colon (Parséus et al., 2017; Wahlström et al., 2016). However, this relationship is bidirectional, and so microbiome composition and resultant metabolites also influence the synthesis of bile acids in the liver, uptake in the ileum, and modification in the colon (Sayin et al., 2013; Wahlström et al., 2016). Importantly, certain bile acids also exert regulatory functions on inflammation, immune markers, mucosal barriers, and cell renewal (Sun and Chang, 2014).

Tryptophan metabolites

Tryptophan is an essential amino acid that must be obtained through dietary proteins (Le Floc'h et al., 2011). Once tryptophan is absorbed in the gut, it can enter circulation, and, in its free form, can cross the BBB to participate in serotonin synthesis in the central nervous system (Ruddick et al., 2006). Within the gastrointestinal tract, tryptophan is metabolized via three pathways, all of which are regulated by the microbiota (Agus et al., 2018). The bioavailability of tryptophan and its metabolites is dependent upon the balance of these pathways, which also impacts downstream changes in inflammation, immune response, and neurotransmission (Waclawiková and El Aidy, 2018).

Two of the pathways ingested tryptophan may traverse are that of serotonin synthesis (1%–3%) or metabolism to aryl hydrocarbon receptor (AhR) ligands (4%–6%) (Gao et al., 2018). In the gut, Trp hydroxylase 1 enzyme, located in the enterochromaffin cells, produces 5-HT. While this 5-HT does not cross the BBB, it does have wide ranging effects on gastric motility, vasodilation, secretion, and nutrient absorption (Agus et al., 2018; Mawe and Hoffman, 2013). In the case of AhR ligands, intestinal microorganisms directly transform tryptophan into several metabolites, including tryptamine and indole, and its derivatives. AhR signaling is a critical aspect of intestinal homeostasis, and AhR ligands play a crucial role in maintenance of epithelial barrier integrity, host immunity, and reducing inflammation (Agus et al., 2018; Dodd et al., 2017; Galligan, 2018; Lamas et al., 2018).

However, greater than 90% of tryptophan is metabolized by the kynurenine pathway (Badawy, 2017; Stone and Darlington, 2002). Located in the gut, indoleamine-2,3-dioxygenase (IDO) is the first and rate limiting enzyme of this pathway, which converts tryptophan into kynurenine that is then used to produce the downstream metabolites kynurenic acid, anthranilic acid, and quinolinic acid (Badawy, 2017; Yeung et al., 2015). Of note, the two main metabolites, kynurenic acid and quinolinic acid are considered to be, respectively, neuroprotective and neurotoxic (O'Mahony et al., 2015; Vécsei et al., 2013). Induction of IDO via proinflammatory cytokines shifts the metabolism of tryptophan toward the kynurenine pathway and away from serotonin synthesis (Yeung et al., 2015). This inflammation-induced reduction in serotonin production, and resultant production of neurotoxic metabolites, may promote depression-like behavior through multiple mechanisms. First, increased IDO activation leads to lower levels of tryptophan available for central conversion to 5-HT as it is instead being converted to kynurenine. Additionally, the resultant metabolite, quinolinic acid, is a potent NMDA receptor agonist and its overproduction may lead to overstimulation of NMDA receptors, resulting in apoptosis, hippocampal atrophy, and oxidative stress (Wichers and Maes, 2004).

Microbial diversity

Multiple studies have reported that alcohol and substance use in humans and animals promote shifts in microbial abundance and composition in the gut (for reviews see Qin et al. (2021) and Temko et al. (2017)). While intestinal dysbiosis has been linked to many substance use disorders, establishing causal relationships is complicated due to the bidirectional nature of the gut-brain axis and the unique balance and diversity of species found across individuals (Salavrakos et al., 2021). Although diet, stress, and other environmental factors mold each person's microenvironment individually, overarchingly, the most abundant phyla are *Firmicutes* and *Bacteroidetes*, followed by *Proteobacteria* and *Actinobacteria*, and to a lesser extent *Verrucomicrobia* and *Fusobacteria* (Sun and Chang, 2014). Dysbiosis-induced changes in the structural and functional profile of the microbiome are likely major contributors to the pathophysiology of many immune, metabolic, cancerous, and immune disorders. Moreover, dysbiosis has been linked to widespread dysfunction, ranging from cardiac phenotypes to behavioral expressions (Salavrakos et al., 2021; Sun and Chang, 2014). Therefore, elucidating the precise microbial changes that define maladaptive microbiotic responses to drugs of abuse is paramount to understanding the bi-directional relationship between the gut microbiome and substance use disorders.

Alcohol

Alcohol is understandably one of the most studied drugs in relation to the gut microbiome, considering its simultaneous caloric and psychoactive properties and typical oral route of administration. Indeed, clinical studies report that AUD is associated with an increase in endotoxin production and a decrease in autochthonous bacterial taxa (Bajaj, 2019). For example, group differences have been identified between patients who overconsume alcohol and controls, where the alcohol overconsumption group had higher relative abundance of *Proteobacteria* and the genera *Sutterella* (*Proteobacteria*), *Clostridium*, and *Holdemania* (both *Firmicutes*), and a lower relative abundance of *Faecilbacterium* (Bjørkhaug et al., 2019). *Proteobacteria* contain endotoxins, specifically lipopolysaccharide (LPS), that are gram-negative, are unstable over time, and have been proposed as a biomarker for dysbiosis (Shin et al., 2015). Other studies report changes in *Clostribium* and *Holdemania* levels in association with alcohol consumption, withdrawal, and intestinal permeability, but their exact role in GI-related disease remains unclear (Leclercq et al., 2014; Mutlu et al., 2012). Conversely, *Faecilbacterium* species are known to produce SCFAs and are considered markers of gut health (Cao et al., 2014; Fujimoto et al., 2013; Machiels et al., 2014). Other studies confirmed these links between AUD and dysbiosis with increased *Proteobacteria* abundance and lower *Bacteroidaceae* abundance in individuals diagnosed with AUD (Chen et al., 2011; Mutlu et al., 2012).

Furthermore, the type of alcohol consumed, amount of alcohol consumed, and comorbidity of liver cirrhosis and hepatic disease may also be reflected in the composition of the microbiome and account for some interindividual differences. In one randomized, crossover, controlled intervention trial, bacterial composition varied significantly after just 20 days of drinking red wine, de-alcoholized red wine, or gin. The results of this study showed that red wine increased the abundance of *Proteobacteria*, *Fusobacteria*, *Firmicutes*, and *Bacteroidetes*, while also decreasing *Clostridium* (Queipo-Ortuño et al., 2012). In addition, red wine and de-alcoholized red wine were associated with increased abundance of *Bifidobacterium*, which is thought to be beneficial for gut health (Gibson et al., 1995). On the other hand, gin intake led to an increase in *Bacteroides* and *Clostridium* (Queipo-Ortuño et al., 2012). Red wine contains dietary polyphenols, which are associated with increased commensal bacteria and improved gut health, specifically through the reduction of *Clostridium*, which has been linked to gastrointestinal disease, though it should be noted that alcohol on its own is likely detrimental (Engen et al., 2015; Guarner and Malagelada, 2003). In addition, studies have found differences between individuals with alcohol-related cirrhosis, AUD without cirrhosis, and healthy controls. In a shotgun metagenomics analysis performed in a Russian cohort, participants with alcohol-related cirrhosis displayed increased dysbiosis compared to individuals with AUD without cirrhosis and healthy individuals. Furthermore, patients with cirrhosis displayed divergent markers of dysbiosis, compared to the non-cirrhotic AUD group, as evident through distinct bacterial taxa associated with each condition. Along with an increase in the severity of dysbiosis, cirrhotic patients displayed a substantial decrease in commensal *Bacteroidales* and an increase in taxa such as *Lactobacillus* and *Streptococcus*, which are normally associated with the oral cavity (Dubinkina et al., 2017). Intra- and inter-study comparisons with cohorts self-identifying as other racial identities yielded similar results to the Russian sample (Dubinkina et al., 2017; Qin et al., 2014). These changes are likely related to the liver and gut microbiome feedback loop, where one is able to modulate the other, namely through the hepatic portal vein and bile secretion, thus dysfunction in one organ has consequences in the other (Betrapally et al., 2017; Cesaro et al., 2011; Schnabl and Brenner, 2014; Tripathi et al., 2018).

The above changes in microbial homeostasis inherently shift the metabolite profile. Notably, stools from individuals with AUD displayed lower levels of SCFAs, decreased amounts of fatty alcohols with antioxidant properties, lower concentrations of the phytochemicals camphene, known to attenuate hepatic steatosis, and caryophyllene, a CB2 receptor agonist, and finally, elevated levels of the oxidative stress biomarker, tetradecane (Couch et al., 2015). Further, currently drinking patients with cirrhosis have a more potentially toxic bile acid profile compared to abstinent cirrhotic patients and healthy controls (Bajaj et al., 2017). Altogether, evidence suggests that short- and long-term alcohol misuse induces changes in microbial diversity, shifting the metabolite profile, and leading to a proinflammatory and endotoxic environment.However, whether changes in gut microbiome (either preceding the development of AUD or representing a consequence of AUD) are causally related to AUD remains to be determined.

Cannabinoids

Studies investigating the relationship between exogenous cannabinoids and the gut microbiome are sparse. In the first (Cluny et al., 2015), prevented weight gain in diet-induced obesity (DIO) mice in addition to increasing the *Firmicutes:Bacteroidetes* ratio, which is also restored with weight loss (Ley et al., 2006). *Akkermansia muciniphila* abundance was also increased in DIO mice chronically treated with THC, which is notable given that this bacteria is associated with fat storage and adipose tissue metabolism related to weight loss (Everard et al., 2013).

In a second study, *A. muciniphila* was significantly elevated in a murine model for multiple sclerosis (MSs), which was attenuated by concurrent THC and cannabidiol (CBD) exposure, though levels were still elevated above that of naive controls (Al-Ghezi et al., 2019). This reduction is important given that LPS biosynthesis, a key function of gram-negative bacteria such as *A. muciniphila*, has broad physiological impacts ranging from induction of a proinflammatory environment to demyelination of neurons and disruption of the BBB (Escribano et al., 2017; Felts et al., 2005). Brain lysates from MS animals showed significantly elevated levels of LPS, but these concentrations were attenuated in animals treated with THC and CBD. Cannabinoid-treated MS mice also displayed global increases in SCFA production and an anti-inflammatory shift in the circulating cytokine profile, implying that treatment with THC and CBD induced systemic improvements in inflammation and production of therapeutically beneficial metabolites. The various treatment groups also exhibited significant alterations to the abundance of various taxa, including MS-associated increases in *Verrucomicrobia* and *Proteobacteria* that were normalized by THC and CBD treatment. Changes in *Bacteroidetes*, *Firmicutes*, and *Tenericutes* were also seen in response to cannabinoid exposure (Al-Ghezi et al., 2019). Un-like other drugs of abuse, cannabinoids appear to have mixed to semi-protective properties, and may even have therapeutic potential for dysbiosis-related disease, although many more studies are needed to confirm whether or not this is true and to investigate the full scope of cannabinoid effects in the gut.

Nicotine

To our knowledge, very few clinical studies have investigated the impact of nicotine use on the gut microbiome, although the field has experienced a recent growth spurt yielding many promising outcomes. One analysis in a cohort of adults from Bangladesh reported that four taxa (class *Erysipelotrichi*, order *Erysipelotrichale*, family *Erysipelotrichaceae*, and genus *Catenbacterium*) showed a positive dose–response association between relative abundance and number of packs of cigarettes smoked per day (Nolan-Kenney et al., 2019). Interestingly, the aforementioned taxa are also associated with high-fat diets and inflammation (Dinh et al., 2015; Greiner and Bäckhed, 2011; Kaakoush, 2015). In patients with Crohn's Disease, smokers have lower levels of gut microbial gene richness, genus diversity, and species diversity, as well as lower proportions of the genera *Collinsella*, *Enterorhabdus*, and *Gordonibacter*, compared to their non-smoking counterparts (Opstelten et al., 2016). Individuals with and without Crohn's Disease who smoke also display higher *Bacteriodes-Prevotella* than non-smokers in both categories (Benjamin et al., 2011). These results are in line with findings from another study which examined changes in the gut microbiome in smokers over the course of smoking cessation. Here, α-diversity of the intestinal microbiota was markedly improved following 4 and 8 weeks of smoking cessation, and there was an increase of sequences from *Firmicutes* and *Actinobacteria* and decrease from *Proteobacteria* and *Bacteroidetes* (Biedermann et al., 2013, 2014). Current smokers, and to a lower but still significant extent, former smokers, display higher rates of *Clostridium difficile* infection (Rogers et al., 2012). Even in infants, exposure to nicotine via "thirdhand smoking" was associated with lower α-diversity, lower abundance of *Bifidobacterium*, and higher abundance of *Enterococcus* (Northrup et al., 2021).

Preclinical studies have also demonstrated a tangible link between nicotine exposure and the intestinal microbiome. First, in rats, exposure to cigarette smoke for 4 weeks was associated with a reduction in the concentration several organic acids, decreased abundance of *Bifidobacterium*, and elevated pH levels (Tomoda et al., 2011). Another study done in mice reported that 8 weeks of cigarette exposure yielded increased abundance of *Clostridium* species, and decreased abundance of *Firmicutes*, *Enterobacteriaceae*, and segmented filamentous bacteria (Wang et al., 2012). Chronic (24 weeks) exposure to cigarette smoke increased the activity of *Lachnospiraceae* species, a butyrate producer associated with colonic inflammation, and profoundly altered gut microbiota-related mucin composition and cytokine/chemokine production in mice (Allais et al., 2016). However, many preclinical studies suggest that nicotine-induced changes to the intestinal flora likely have many substantial modulators, such as diet and sex (Chi et al., 2017; Wang et al., 2019; Yang et al., 2021). As such, elucidating the precise mechanisms whereby tobacco-based nicotine products modify, in conjunction with other physiological and environmental factors, will be of great importance when investigating the role nicotine plays in human microbiome health and disease.

Though many of the above studies show deleterious impacts of cigarette smoking on the intestinal microbiome, the importance of consummatory modality, e.g., nicotine from a tobacco cigarette versus E-cigarette, is less understood. To our knowledge, only one clinical study has compared tobacco smokers, E-cigarette smokers, and control subjects; tobacco smokers displayed elevated *Prevotella*, lower *Bacteroides*, and lower Shannon diversity, a measure of α-diversity, compared to both other groups, but E-cigarette smokers did not differ from non-smoking controls (Stewart et al., 2018). However, another study using an *in vivo* murine model and *ex vivo* murine and human cells concluded that the propylene glycol and vegetable glycerol e-liquid (i.e, the vehicle), not nicotine, induced widespread and dramatic changes to the genetic composition of the gut microbiome. Moreover, nicotine appeared to play an anti-inflammatory role in this study (Sharma et al., 2021). Therefore, further experiments are needed to distinguish the harmful effects of nicotine from the effects of other tobacco and e-cigarette-related carcinogens on the gut microbiome.

Opioids

Like alcohol, there is an immediately evident connection between opioid use and gut health given the ability of opioids to disrupt gastrointestinal function, a phenomenon also known as opioid-induced constipation. This reduction of intestinal motility stems from opioid-induced inhibition of coordinated myoenteric activity, which can reduce transit time and lead to bacterial overgrowth (Balzan et al., 2007). While there is a considerable preclinical literature connecting opioid use to dysbiosis, clinical studies tend to either investigate short-term opioid use in the context of post-operative pain relief, and those that have investigated chronic opioid misuse/addiction, there are often confounding variables and comorbidities clouding interpretation of the results.

For example, one study compared the gut flora of a sample of people with SUDs against that of healthy controls (Xu et al., 2017). The sample with SUDs included individuals who used heroin, heroin + ephedrine, and heroin + methamphetamine, while participants all also regularly smoked and consumed alcohol. The results of this study indicated that SUDs may influence the functional diversity of the putative metagenome, yielding evidence that pathways involving translation, DNA replication and repair, and cell growth and death were upregulated in people with SUDs, while cellular processing and signaling, as well as metabolism, were diminished. The authors also found that genus *Thauera*, *Paracoccus*, and *Prevotella* may be tied to SUDs. Despite these findings, group differences cannot be directly attributed to opioid use and, instead, may be due to alcohol and cigarette consumption, or lifestyle differences between the SUDs and control groups (Xu et al., 2017). Other clinical analyses include findings in patients with liver cirrhosis, where individuals undergoing opioid therapy displayed significantly greater dysbiosis compared to the non-opioid group. This included an opioid-related reduction in relative abundance of autochthonous families, specifically *Ruminococcaceae* and *Clostridiales XIV*, reduced relative abundance of *Bacteroidaceae*, and increased endotoxemia (Acharya et al., 2017). Another study reported associations between opioid use and microbial differences, most notably in relative abundance of *Bifidobacterium*, in African American men with type 2 diabetes (Barengolts et al., 2018). In a cohort of hospitalized patients, opioid use was associated with an increase in α-diversity, possibly due to increased microbial growth in the gut as a result of delayed gastrointestinal transit time (Vincent et al., 2016). Lastly, a metagenomic analysis showed that opioid use was associated with beta-diversity in a Dutch population-based cohort of 1135 individuals (Zhernakova et al., 2016).

Preclinical studies further exemplify the dysbiotic effects of morphine on the gastrointestinal system. In a non-human primate model, 84 days of tridaily intramuscular morphine injections (gradually increased from 2 mg/kg the first week to 4 mg/kg from week 3 on) induced dysbiosis and altered microbiome composition as measured through beta-diversity. Morphine-treated animals also displayed significant alterations in fecal metabolites, including significant increases in several secondary bile acids, while concurrently, there were decreases in primary bile acids, such as cholate and glycocholate (Sindberg et al., 2019). In morphine-treated mice, there was a significant expansion of gram-positive Firmicutes and a reduction in the abundance of the phyla Bacteroidetes, thus reducing the Bacteroidestes/Firmicutes ratio in these animals. Within the Firmicutes phylum, morphine-exposed animals showed elevated abundance of *Enterococcaceae*, *Staphylococcaceae*, *Bacillaceae*, *Streptococcaceae*, and *Erysipelotrichaceae* families (Banerjee et al., 2016). In addition, reductions in the abundance of *Lactobacillus* and *Clostridium* were found in morphine-exposed animals. Concurrently, morphine-experienced mice displayed elevated levels of cholesterol in the liver and lower levels of unconjugated ursodeoxycholate, a secondary bile acid, suggesting that disruption in the bacterial communities has deleterious downstream effects on hepatic circulation and cholesterol catabolism. Interestingly, this study also found that fecal transplants from morphine-exposed mice induced bacteria translocation to the liver in morphine-naïve mice, also sparking an immune-response evident by an elevation in IL-6 concentrations (Banerjee et al., 2016).

Other studies have reported that mice with an implanted morphine pellet display reduced relative abundance and, specifically, reduced levels of Bacteroidetes (*Bacteriodales*) and Firmicutes (*Clostridiales* and *Lactobacillales*), and enhanced amounts of Proteobacteria (*Enterobacteriales*) in an order analysis of fecal samples (Kang et al., 2017). Following one day of morphine exposure, compared to placebo, mice displayed a significant shift in the gut microbiome and metabolon, with *Enterococcus faecalis* representing a potential biomarker for morphine-induced dysbiosis considering its robust increase. Overall, morphine-induced microbial dysbiosis was associated with an increase of potentially pathogenic communities, a decrease in microbial communities associated with cellular stress tolerance, as well as a reduction of bile acids and gut biotransformation of morphine-3-glucuronide/morphine. Moreover, morphine-induced analgesic tolerance was accelerated by concurrent *E. faecalis* infection (Wang et al., 2018). Furthermore, chronic morphine exposure leads to sepsis in mice due to increased bacterial translocation, increased virulence of pathogens, immune dysregulation, and disrupted gut barrier function (Babrowski et al., 2012; Banerjee et al., 2013; Hilburger et al., 1997).

Akin to the above findings by Wang et al. (2018), there is growing evidence that the gut microbiome modulates other physiological effects of morphine. For example, one study showed that animals with depleted microbiomes following administration of a broad-spectrum antibiotic cocktail also displayed decreased antinociceptive tolerance, as measured by tail-immersion and acetic acid stretch assays, following chronic morphine (Kang et al., 2017). Vancomycin, which when orally administered has 0% bioavailability and is not absorbed from the intestine, similarly prevented morphine antinociceptive tolerance. Combined, these findings suggest the gut microbiome, particularly vancomycin-sensitive Gram-positive bacteria, affects the development of morphine tolerance. However, in that study, brain morphine concentrations did not differ between antibiotic- and saline-treated groups, nor did naloxone-precipitated induced withdrawal. Therefore, antibiotics likely did not affect the distribution of morphine (Kang et al., 2017).

However, another study produced different results, specifically that antibiotic-treated animals displayed antinociceptive tolerance to continuous and intermittent morphine administration (Lee et al., 2018). These seemingly discrepant results may be due to variation in the antibiotic cocktail, as well as differences in the morphine administration route in the two studies. This latter study also reported that morphine treatment did significantly effect beta-diversity, though there were differences between routes of administration; intermittent intraperitoneal morphine administration yielded greater relative abundance of *Ruminococcus* and decreased *Lactibacillus*, while implanted sub-dermal morphine pellets (i.e, chronic slow release) led to increased relative abundance of the genera Clostridium and family

Rikenellaceae (Lee et al., 2018). Therefore, there seems to be differential outcomes between continuous and intermittent morphine exposure patterns (or perhaps between routes of administration), as only intermittent morphine administration was associated with increased gut permeability, as well as altered microglial morphology and hyperalgesia. Since intermittent morphine administration is associated with repeated periods of withdrawal and its resultant immunomodulatory consequences, withdrawal associated with opioid use may explain some of the observed differences and represents an important factor when considering the translational power of these preclinical studies (Eisenstein et al., 2006).

Psychostimulants

Though psychostimulant impact on the gut microbiota is not as well studied as some other classes of drugs, recent work offers some insight into a complex but interesting relationship. To our knowledge, there is only one clinical study examining the role of cocaine use on the gut microbiome. In a sample of patients with and without HIV, cocaine use was associated with higher relative abundance of *Bacteroidetes* (Volpe et al., 2014). When comparing all conditions of HIV status and cocaine use, there was a significant difference in abundance of *Proteobacteria* between groups, with HIV-positive cocaine users displaying the highest concentration (Volpe et al., 2014).

In preclinical studies, cocaine induces disruption of gut homeostasis, particularly through alterations of butyrate-producing bacteria, in mice treated with intraperitoneal cocaine daily for 7 days (Chivero et al., 2019). Specifically, cocaine-exposed mice displayed increased relative abundance of genera *Barnesiella*, and unclassified members of *Porphyromonadaceae, Bacteriodales* and *Proteobacteria*, as well as decreased adundance of *Mucispirillum, Butyricicoccus, Pseudoflavonifractor,* and unclassified *Rumino* (Chivero et al., 2019). In that study, cocaine also increased total and phosphorylated NF-κB in the GI tract, further suggesting its role in modulating gut homeostasis. In addition, cocaine decreased *trans*-epithelial electrical resistance in epithelial cells, suggesting reduced barrier integrity. *In vivo*, FITC Dextran (4 kDa) was utilized to measure intestinal permeability, and, indeed, cocaine-exposed animals had higher blood FITC Dextran levels, implying cocaine administration exacerbated intestinal permeability (Chivero et al., 2019).

Kiraly and colleagues have also demonstrated an important link between the gut microbiome and cocaine-related phenotypes. Depletion of the gut microbiota via administration of a cocktail of antibiotics, which did not alter cocaine metabolism or corticosterone, yielded an increased sensitivity to the behavioral effects of intraperitoneal cocaine, as seen in CPP and locomotor sensitization tasks (Kiraly et al., 2016). Though both antibiotic-treated and control mice displayed robust CPP at a high dose (10 mg/kg) of cocaine, only antibiotic-treated animals displayed robust CPP at a lower dose (5 mg/kg). Similarly, locomotor activity was significantly elevated in both treatment and control groups following a 10 mg/kg dose of cocaine, but only the antibiotic-treated cohort displayed elevated levels following a 5 mg/kg dose. Additionally, in the absence of cocaine, antibiotic treatment showed no effect on CPP or locomotor activity. Interestingly, the above CPP findings at the 5 mg/kg dose were reversed when antibiotic-treated mice were given SCFA supplementation, suggesting bacterial fermentation products may mediate cocaine-related behaviors (Kiraly et al., 2016). It should be noted that Lee et al. (2018) observed decreased cocaine CPP formation at a 10 mg/kg dose following antibiotic administration. However, differences in antibiotic cocktail makeup and duration of use should be considered. Another interesting avenue Kiraly and colleagues explored was the relationship between antibiotic treatment, cocaine, and the transcriptional profile of the NAc. For example, levels of Bdnf were increased by antibiotic treatment, and levels of the Bdnf receptor—tyrosine receptor kinase B (Ntrk2), were decreased in antibiotic- and cocaine-treated mice (Kiraly et al., 2016). This suggests that antibiotic depletion of the gut microbiome may alter Bdnf-Trkb signaling in the NAc and cause consequential behavioral changes, which has been reported in previous literature (Graham et al., 2007, 2009). Additionally, transcript levels of the Drd1 dopamine receptor and Glu2 AMPA receptor in the NAc increased in animals receiving both antibiotics and cocaine (Kiraly et al., 2016). Considering that Drd1 is an important mediator of cocaine reward and (mis)use, and Glu2 has been linked to increased behavioral responses to lower doses of cocaine, these findings suggest the gut microbiome may influence the neurocircuitry of cocaine misuse (Wolf 2010; Boudreau and Wolf, 2005: Kelz et al., 1999).

As cocaine is often smoked (Scorza et al., 2019), investigated the effect of volatilized cocaine with two common adulterants, caffeine and phenacetin, on the gut microbiota in rats. Following 14 days of chronic exposure, there was a decrease in phylogenetic bacterial diversity and significant alteration in community composition in cocaine and phenacetin-treated rats compared to control animals. Furthermore, Scorza and colleagues found that genes involved in butyrate synthesis pathways were upregulated in the feces of cocaine-treated rats. The authors also observed reduced aromatic amino acid decarboxylase, indicating a cocaine-induced alteration in bacterial populations that metabolize tryptophan and other related neuroactive compounds (Scorza et al., 2019).

Methamphetamine also alters gut microbiota composition. In an experiment comparing the gut microbiota of animals tested for methamphetamine-induced CPP to controls, two different studies found that animals treated with methamphetamine had higher fecal microbial diversity (Bornebusch et al., 2019; Ning et al., 2017). Specifically, *Proteobacteria, Ruminococcaceae, Bacillus, Cetobacterium, Fusobacteria,* and *Aeromonas* phylotypes were all elevated in the methamphetamine exposed animals, while *Phascolarctobacterium*, belonging to the family *Acidaminococcaceae,* was more abundant in the control group. In conjunction with these findings, propionate was also lower in methamphetamine-exposed rats (Ning et al., 2017). Taken together, the above studies indicate promising preliminary data linking stimulant use and its behavioral effects to the gut microbiome, with a particular emphasis on the role of SCFAs. However, additional studies are needed to further elucidate these relationships.

Conclusions

Although the literature reviewed in this chapter is not meant to be comprehensive, we have provided examples (ghrelin and GLP-1) from gastrointestinal neuroendocrine systems that support a critical role of gut-brain endocrine mechanisms in the development and maintenance of alcohol and substance use disorders. In some cases, the literature is very preliminary, while in other cases, the gain in knowledge has led to translational efforts toward developing potential new treatments for patients living with addiction. The literature on the gut microbiome and addiction is also very intriguing, yet most of the work is correlational in nature, especially that conducted in humans, therefore additional work is needed to shed light on the potential causal role of the gut microbiome in addiction-related behaviors.

Funding and disclosure

The authors are supported by the National Institutes of Health, Intramural Research Programs of the National Institute on Drug Abuse and the National Institute on Alcohol Abuse and Alcoholism. The content of this article is solely the responsibility of the authors and does not necessarily represent the official views of the National Institutes of Health. The authors report no conflict of interest.

References

Abizaid, A., Liu, Z.-W., Andrews, Z.B., Shanabrough, M., Borok, E., Elsworth, J.D., Tschöp, M.H., 2006. Ghrelin modulates the activity and synaptic input organization of midbrain dopamine neurons while promoting appetite. J. Clin. Invest. 116 (12), 3229–3239.

Abizaid, A., Mineur, Y.S., Roth, R.H., Elsworth, J.D., Sleeman, M.W., Picciotto, M.R., Horvath, T.L., 2011. Reduced locomotor responses to cocaine in ghrelin-deficient mice. Neuroscience 192, 500–506. https://doi.org/10.1016/j.neuroscience.2011.06.001.

Aceto, M.D., Scates, S.M., Martin, B.B., 2001. Spontaneous and precipitated withdrawal with a synthetic cannabinoid, WIN 55212-2. Eur. J. Pharmacol. 416 (1–2), 75–81. https://doi.org/10.1016/s0014-2999(01)00873-1.

Acharya, C., Betrapally, N.S., Gillevet, P.M., Sterling, R.K., Akbarali, H., White, M.B., Bajaj, J.S., 2017. Chronic opioid use is associated with altered gut microbiota and predicts readmissions in patients with cirrhosis. Aliment Pharmacol. Ther. 45 (2), 319–331. https://doi.org/10.1111/apt.13858.

Addolorato, G., Capristo, E., Leggio, L., Ferrulli, A., Abenavoli, L., Malandrino, N., Gasbarrini, G., 2006. Relationship between ghrelin levels, alcohol craving, and nutritional status in current alcoholic patients. Alcohol. Clin. Exp. Res. 30 (11), 1933–1937. https://doi.org/10.1111/j.1530-0277.2006.00238.x.

Agus, A., Planchais, J., Sokol, H., 2018. Gut microbiota regulation of tryptophan metabolism in health and disease. Cell Host Microbe 23 (6), 716–724. https://doi.org/10.1016/j.chom.2018.05.003.

Akkisi Kumsar, N., Dilbaz, N., 2015. Relationship between craving and ghrelin, adiponectin, and resistin levels in patients with alcoholism. Alcohol. Clin. Exp. Res. 39 (4), 702–709. https://doi.org/10.1111/acer.12689.

Al-Ghezi, Z.Z., Busbee, P.B., Alghetaa, H., Nagarkatti, P.S., Nagarkatti, M., 2019. Combination of cannabinoids, delta-9-tetrahydrocannabinol (THC) and cannabidiol (CBD), mitigates experimental autoimmune encephalomyelitis (EAE) by altering the gut microbiome. Brain Behav. Immun. 82, 25–35. https://doi.org/10.1016/j.bbi.2019.07.028.

al'Absi, M., Lemieux, A., Nakajima, M., 2014. Peptide YY and ghrelin predict craving and risk for relapse in abstinent smokers. Psychoneuroendocrinology 49, 253–259. https://doi.org/10.1016/j.psyneuen.2014.07.018.

Alhadeff, A.L., Rupprecht, L.E., Hayes, M.R., 2012. GLP-1 neurons in the nucleus of the solitary tract project directly to the ventral tegmental area and nucleus accumbens to control for food intake. Endocrinology 153 (2), 647–658. https://doi.org/10.1210/en.2011-1443.

Ali, S.S., Hamed, E.A., Ayuob, N.N., Shaker Ali, A., Suliman, M.I., 2015. Effects of different routes of nicotine administration on gastric morphology and hormonal secretion in rats. Exp. Physiol. 100 (8), 881–895. https://doi.org/10.1113/EP085015.

Allais, L., Kerckhof, F.-M., Verschuere, S., Bracke, K.R., De Smet, R., Laukens, D., Van de Wiele, T., 2016. Chronic cigarette smoke exposure induces microbial and inflammatory shifts and mucin changes in the murine gut. Environ. Microbiol. 18 (5), 1352–1363. https://doi.org/10.1111/1462-2920.12934.

Alvarez, E., Roncero, I., Chowen, J.A., Thorens, B., Blázquez, E., 1996. Expression of the glucagon-like peptide-1 receptor gene in rat brain. J. Neurochem. 66 (3), 920–927.

Aziz, Q., Doré, J., Emmanuel, A., Guarner, F., Quigley, E., 2013. Gut microbiota and gastrointestinal health: current concepts and future directions. Neuro Gastroenterol. Motil. 25 (1), 4–15.

Babrowski, T., Holbrook, C., Moss, J., Gottlieb, L., Valuckaite, V., Zaborin, A., Alverdy, J.C., 2012. *Pseudomonas aeruginosa* virulence expression is directly activated by morphine and is capable of causing lethal gut-derived sepsis in mice during chronic morphine administration. Ann. Surg. 255 (2), 386–393. https://doi.org/10.1097/SLA.0b013e3182331870.

Bach, P., Bumb, J.M., Schuster, R., Vollstädt-Klein, S., Reinhard, I., Rietschel, M., Koopmann, A., 2019. Effects of leptin and ghrelin on neural cue-reactivity in alcohol addiction: two streams merge to one river? Psychoneuroendocrinology 100, 1–9. https://doi.org/10.1016/j.psyneuen.2018.09.026.

Badaoui, A., De Saeger, C., Duchemin, J., Gihousse, D., De Timary, P., Stärkel, P., 2008. Alcohol dependence is associated with reduced plasma and fundic ghrelin levels. Eur. J. Clin. Invest. 38 (6), 397–403. https://doi.org/10.1111/j.1365-2362.2008.01947.x.

Badawy, A.A.B., 2017. Tryptophan availability for kynurenine pathway metabolism across the life span: control mechanisms and focus on aging, exercise, diet and nutritional supplements. Neuropharmacology 112, 248–263. https://doi.org/10.1016/j.neuropharm.2015.11.015.

Bahi, A., Tolle, V., Fehrentz, J.-A., Brunel, L., Martinez, J., Tomasetto, C.-L., Karam, S.M., 2013. Ghrelin knockout mice show decreased voluntary alcohol consumption and reduced ethanol-induced conditioned place preference. Peptides 43, 48–55. https://doi.org/10.1016/j.peptides.2013.02.008.

Bajaj, J.S., 2019. Alcohol, liver disease and the gut microbiota. Nat. Rev. Gastroenterol. Hepatol. 16 (4), 235–246. https://doi.org/10.1038/s41575-018-0099-1.

Bajaj, J.S., Kakiyama, G., Zhao, D., Takei, H., Fagan, A., Hylemon, P., Gillevet, P.M., 2017. Continued alcohol misuse in human cirrhosis is associated with an impaired gut-liver Axis. Alcohol. Clin. Exp. Res. 41 (11), 1857–1865. https://doi.org/10.1111/acer.13498.

Bali, A., Singh Jaggi, A., 2016. An integrative review on role and mechanisms of ghrelin in stress, anxiety and depression. Curr. Drug Targets 17 (5), 495–507.

Balzan, S., de Almeida Quadros, C., de Cleva, R., Zilberstein, B., Cecconello, I., 2007. Bacterial translocation: overview of mechanisms and clinical impact. J. Gastroenterol. Hepatol. 22 (4), 464–471. https://doi.org/10.1111/j.1440-1746.2007.04933.x.

Banerjee, S., Meng, J., Das, S., Krishnan, A., Haworth, J., Charboneau, R., Roy, S., 2013. Morphine induced exacerbation of sepsis is mediated by tempering endotoxin tolerance through modulation of miR-146a. Sci. Rep. 3 (1), 1977. https://doi.org/10.1038/srep01977.

Banerjee, S., Sindberg, G., Wang, F., Meng, J., Sharma, U., Zhang, L., Roy, S., 2016. Opioid-induced gut microbial disruption and bile dysregulation leads to gut barrier compromise and sustained systemic inflammation. Mucosal Immunol. 9 (6), 1418–1428. https://doi.org/10.1038/mi.2016.9.

Banks, W.A., Tschöp, M., Robinson, S.M., Heiman, M.L., 2002. Extent and direction of ghrelin transport across the blood–brain barrier is determined by its unique primary structure. J. Pharmacol. Exp. Therapeut. 302 (2), 822–827. https://doi.org/10.1124/jpet.102.034827.

Barengolts, E., Green, S.J., Eisenberg, Y., Akbar, A., Reddivari, B., Layden, B.T., Chlipala, G., 2018. Gut microbiota varies by opioid use, circulating leptin and oxytocin in African American men with diabetes and high burden of chronic disease. PLoS One 13 (3), e0194171. https://doi.org/10.1371/journal.pone.0194171.

Benjamin, J.L., Hedin, C.R.H., Koutsoumpas, A., Ng, S.C., McCarthy, N.E., Prescott, N.J., Whelan, K., 2011. Smokers with active Crohn's disease have a clinically relevant dysbiosis of the gastrointestinal microbiota. Inflamm. Bowel Dis. 18 (6), 1092–1100. https://doi.org/10.1002/ibd.21864.

Betrapally, N.S., Gillevet, P.M., Bajaj, J.S., 2017. Gut microbiome and liver disease. Transl. Res. 179, 49–59. https://doi.org/10.1016/j.trsl.2016.07.005.

Bharwani, A., Mian, M.F., Foster, J.A., Surette, M.G., Bienenstock, J., Forsythe, P., 2016. Structural & functional consequences of chronic psychosocial stress on the microbiome & host. Psychoneuroendocrinology 63, 217–227. https://doi.org/10.1016/j.psyneuen.2015.10.001.

Biedermann, L., Brülisauer, K., Zeitz, J., Frei, P., Scharl, M., Vavricka, S.R., Schuppler, M., 2014. Smoking cessation alters intestinal microbiota: insights from quantitative investigations on human fecal samples using FISH. Inflamm. Bowel Dis. 20 (9), 1496–1501. https://doi.org/10.1097/mib.0000000000000129.

Biedermann, L., Zeitz, J., Mwinyi, J., Sutter-Minder, E., Rehman, A., Ott, S.J., Rogler, G., 2013. Smoking cessation induces profound changes in the composition of the intestinal microbiota in humans. PLoS One 8 (3), e59260. https://doi.org/10.1371/journal.pone.0059260.

Bjørkhaug, S.T., Aanes, H., Neupane, S.P., Bramness, J.G., Malvik, S., Henriksen, C., Valeur, J., 2019. Characterization of gut microbiota composition and functions in patients with chronic alcohol overconsumption. Gut Microb. 10 (6), 663–675. https://doi.org/10.1080/19490976.2019.1580097.

Bojanowska, E., Radziszewska, E., 2011. Combined stimulation of glucagon-like peptide-1 receptor and inhibition of cannabinoid CB1 receptor act synergistically to reduce food intake and body weight in the rat. J. Physiol. Pharmacol. 62 (4), 395–402.

Bornebusch, A.B., Fink-Jensen, A., Wörtwein, G., Seeley, R.J., Thomsen, M., 2019. Glucagon-like peptide-1 receptor agonist treatment does not reduce abuse-related effects of opioid drugs. eNeuro 6 (2). https://doi.org/10.1523/eneuro.0443-18.2019.

Boudreau, A.C., Wolf, M.E., 2005. Behavioral sensitization to cocaine is associated with increased AMPA receptor surface expression in the nucleus accumbens. J. Neurosci. : 25 (40), 9144–9151. https://doi.org/10.1523/JNEUROSCI.2252-05.2005.

Bouhlal, S., Ellefsen, K.N., Sheskier, M.B., Singley, E., Pirard, S., Gorelick, D.A., Leggio, L., 2017. Acute effects of intravenous cocaine administration on serum concentrations of ghrelin, amylin, glucagon-like peptide-1, insulin, leptin and peptide YY and relationships with cardiorespiratory and subjective responses. Drug Alcohol Depend. 180, 68–75. https://doi.org/10.1016/j.drugalcdep.2017.07.033.

Bouros, D., Tzouvelekis, A., Anevlavis, S., Doris, M., Tryfon, S., Froudarakis, M., Kukuvitis, A., 2006. Smoking acutely increases plasma ghrelin concentrations. Clin. Chem. 52 (4), 777–778. https://doi.org/10.1373/clinchem.2005.065243.

Brubaker, P.L., Anini, Y., 2003. Direct and indirect mechanisms regulating secretion of glucagon-like peptide-1 and glucagon-like peptide-2. Can. J. Physiol. Pharmacol. 81 (11), 1005–1012.

Bush, T., Lovejoy, J.C., Deprey, M., Carpenter, K.M., 2016. The effect of tobacco cessation on weight gain, obesity, and diabetes risk. Obesity (Silver Spring, Md.) 24 (9), 1834–1841. https://doi.org/10.1002/oby.21582.

Cabral, A., López Soto, E.J., Epelbaum, J., Perelló, M., 2017. Is ghrelin synthesized in the central nervous system? Int. J. Mol. Sci. 18 (3), 638. Retrieved from. https://www.mdpi.com/1422-0067/18/3/638.

Calissendorff, J., Danielsson, O., Brismar, K., Röjdmark, S., 2006. Alcohol ingestion does not affect serum levels of peptide YY but decreases both total and octanoylated ghrelin levels in healthy subjects. Metabolism 55 (12), 1625–1629.

Calissendorff, J., Danielsson, O., Brismar, K., Röjdmark, S., 2005. Inhibitory effect of alcohol on ghrelin secretion in normal man. Eur. J. Endocrinol. 152 (5), 743–747.

Cani, P.D., Montoya, M.L., Neyrinck, A.M., Delzenne, N.M., Lambert, D.M., 2004. Potential modulation of plasma ghrelin and glucagon-like peptide-1 by anorexigenic cannabinoid compounds, SR141716A (rimonabant) and oleoylethanolamide. Br. J. Nutr. 92 (5), 757–761. https://doi.org/10.1079/bjn20041256.

Cao, Y., Shen, J., Ran, Z.H., 2014. Association between Faecalibacterium prausnitzii reduction and inflammatory bowel disease: a meta-analysis and systematic review of the literature. Gastroenterol Res Pract 2014, 872725. https://doi.org/10.1155/2014/872725.

Cepko, L.C.S., Selva, J.A., Merfeld, E.B., Fimmel, A.I., Goldberg, S.A., Currie, P.J., 2014. Ghrelin alters the stimulatory effect of cocaine on ethanol intake following mesolimbic or systemic administration. Neuropharmacology 85, 224–231. https://doi.org/10.1016/j.neuropharm.2014.05.030.

Cesaro, C., Tiso, A., Del Prete, A., Cariello, R., Tuccillo, C., Cotticelli, G., Loguercio, C., 2011. Gut microbiota and probiotics in chronic liver diseases. Dig. Liver Dis. 43 (6), 431–438. https://doi.org/10.1016/j.dld.2010.10.015.

Charalambous, C., Havlickova, T., Lapka, M., Puskina, N., Šlamberová, R., Kuchar, M., Sustkova-Fiserova, M., 2021. Cannabinoid-induced conditioned place preference, intravenous self-administration, and behavioral stimulation influenced by ghrelin receptor antagonism in rats. Int. J. Mol. Sci. 22 (5), 2397. https://doi.org/10.3390/ijms22052397.

Charpantier, E., Barnéoud, P., Moser, P., Besnard, F., Sgard, F., 1998. Nicotinic acetylcholine subunit mRNA expression in dopaminergic neurons of the rat substantia nigra and ventral tegmental area. Neuroreport 9 (13), 3097–3101. Retrieved from. https://journals.lww.com/neuroreport/Fulltext/1998/09140/Nicotinic_acetylcholine_subunit_mRNA_expression_in.33.aspx.

Chen, N., Appell, M., Berfield, J.L., Reith, M.E., 2003. Inhibition by arachidonic acid and other fatty acids of dopamine uptake at the human dopamine transporter. Eur. J. Pharmacol. 478 (2–3), 89–95.

Chen, Y., Yang, F., Lu, H., Wang, B., Chen, Y., Lei, D., Li, L., 2011. Characterization of fecal microbial communities in patients with liver cirrhosis. Hepatology 54 (2), 562–572. https://doi.org/10.1002/hep.24423.

Chi, L., Mahbub, R., Gao, B., Bian, X., Tu, P., Ru, H., Lu, K., 2017. Nicotine alters the gut microbiome and metabolites of gut–brain interactions in a sex-specific manner. Chem. Res. Toxicol. 30 (12), 2110–2119. https://doi.org/10.1021/acs.chemrestox.7b00162.

Chia, C.W., Carlson, O.D., Liu, D.D., González-Mariscal, I., Santa-Cruz Calvo, S., Egan, J.M., 2017. Incretin secretion in humans is under the influence of cannabinoid receptors. Am. J. Physiol. Endocrinol. Metab. 313 (3), E359–E366. https://doi.org/10.1152/ajpendo.00080.2017.

Chivero, E.T., Ahmad, R., Thangaraj, A., Periyasamy, P., Kumar, B., Kroeger, E., Buch, S., 2019. Cocaine induces inflammatory gut milieu by compromising the mucosal barrier integrity and altering the gut microbiota colonization. Sci. Rep. 9 (1), 12187. https://doi.org/10.1038/s41598-019-48428-2.

Chu, Z.L., Jones, R.M., He, H., Carroll, C., Gutierrez, V., Lucman, A., Leonard, J., 2007. A role for beta-cell-expressed G protein-coupled receptor 119 in glycemic control by enhancing glucose-dependent insulin release. Endocrinology 148 (6), 2601–2609. https://doi.org/10.1210/en.2006-1608.

Clifford, P.S., Rodriguez, J., Schul, D., Hughes, S., Kniffin, T., Hart, N., Wellman, P.J., 2012. Attenuation of cocaine-induced locomotor sensitization in rats sustaining genetic or pharmacologic antagonism of ghrelin receptors. Addiction Biol. 17 (6), 956–963. https://doi.org/10.1111/j.1369-1600.2011.00339.x.

Clifford, S., Zeckler, R.A., Buckman, S., Thompson, J., Hart, N., Wellman, P.J., Smith, R.G., 2011. Impact of food restriction and cocaine on locomotion in ghrelin- and ghrelin-receptor knockout mice. Addiction Biol. 16 (3), 386–392. https://doi.org/10.1111/j.1369-1600.2010.00253.x.

Cluny, N.L., Keenan, C.M., Reimer, R.A., Le Foll, B., Sharkey, K.A., 2015. Prevention of diet-induced obesity effects on body weight and gut microbiota in mice treated chronically with Δ9-tetrahydrocannabinol. PLoS One 10 (12), e0144270. https://doi.org/10.1371/journal.pone.0144270.

Cota, D., Marsicano, G., Lutz, B., Vicennati, V., Stalla, G., Pasquali, R., Pagotto, U., 2003. Endogenous cannabinoid system as a modulator of food intake. Int. J. Obes. 27 (3), 289–301.

Couch, R.D., Dailey, A., Zaidi, F., Navarro, K., Forsyth, C.B., Mutlu, E., Keshavarzian, A., 2015. Alcohol induced alterations to the human fecal VOC metabolome. PLoS One 10 (3), e0119362. https://doi.org/10.1371/journal.pone.0119362.

Covey, D.P., Roitman, M.F., Garris, P.A., 2014. Illicit dopamine transients: reconciling actions of abused drugs. Trends Neurosci. 37 (4), 200–210. https://doi.org/10.1016/j.tins.2014.02.002.

Cresci, G.A., Glueck, B., McMullen, M.R., Xin, W., Allende, D., Nagy, L.E., 2017. Prophylactic tributyrin treatment mitigates chronic-binge ethanol-induced intestinal barrier and liver injury. J. Gastroenterol. Hepatol. 32 (9), 1587–1597. https://doi.org/10.1111/jgh.13731.

Crowley, W.R., Ramoz, G., Keefe, K.A., Torto, R., Kalra, S.P., Hanson, G.R., 2005. Differential effects of methamphetamine on expression of neuropeptide Y mRNA in hypothalamus and on serum leptin and ghrelin concentrations in ad libitum-fed and schedule-fed rats. Neuroscience 132 (1), 167–173. https://doi.org/10.1016/j.neuroscience.2004.11.037.

Cruz, M.T., Herman, M.A., Cote, D.M., Ryabinin, A.E., Roberto, M., 2013. Ghrelin increases GABAergic transmission and interacts with ethanol actions in the rat central nucleus of the amygdala. Neuropsychopharmacology 38 (2), 364–375.

Currie, P.J., Khelemsky, R., Rigsbee, E.M., Dono, L.M., Coiro, C.D., Chapman, C.D., Hinchcliff, K., 2012. Ghrelin is an orexigenic peptide and elicits anxiety-like behaviors following administration into discrete regions of the hypothalamus. Behav. Brain Res. 226 (1), 96–105.

Currie, P.J., Mirza, A., Fuld, R., Park, D., Vasselli, J.R., 2005. Ghrelin is an orexigenic and metabolic signaling peptide in the arcuate and paraventricular nuclei. Am. J. Physiol. Regul. Integr. Comp. Physiol. 289 (2), R353–R358.

Davis, J., Perello, M., Choi, D., Magrisso, I., Kirchner, H., Pfluger, P., Benoit, S., 2012. GOAT induced ghrelin acylation regulates hedonic feeding. Horm. Behav. 62 (5), 598–604.

Davis, K.W., Wellman, P.J., Clifford, P.S., 2007. Augmented cocaine conditioned place preference in rats pretreated with systemic ghrelin. Regul. Pept. 140 (3), 148–152. https://doi.org/10.1016/j.regpep.2006.12.003.

Deacon, C.F., Johnsen, A.H., Holst, J.J., 1995. Degradation of glucagon-like peptide-1 by human plasma in vitro yields an N-terminally truncated peptide that is a major endogenous metabolite in vivo. J. Clin. Endocrinol. Metab. 80 (3), 952–957. https://doi.org/10.1210/jcem.80.3.7883856.

DeGruttola, A.K., Low, D., Mizoguchi, A., Mizoguchi, E., 2016. Current understanding of dysbiosis in disease in human and animal models. Inflamm. Bowel Dis. 22 (5), 1137–1150. https://doi.org/10.1097/mib.0000000000000750.

Derrien, M., van Hylckama Vlieg, J.E.T., 2015. Fate, activity, and impact of ingested bacteria within the human gut microbiota. Trends Microbiol. 23 (6), 354–366. https://doi.org/10.1016/j.tim.2015.03.002.

Deschaine, S.L., Farokhnia, M., Gregory-Flores, A., Zallar, L.J., You, Z.B., Sun, H., Leggio, L., 2021. A closer look at alcohol-induced changes in the ghrelin system: novel insights from preclinical and clinical data. Addiction Biol. e13033. https://doi.org/10.1111/adb.13033.

Diano, S., Farr, S.A., Benoit, S.C., McNay, E.C., da Silva, I., Horvath, B., Banks, W.A., 2006. Ghrelin controls hippocampal spine synapse density and memory performance. Nat. Neurosci. 9 (3), 381–388.

Dinh, D.M., Volpe, G.E., Duffalo, C., Bhalchandra, S., Tai, A.K., Kane, A.V., Ward, H.D., 2015. Intestinal microbiota, microbial translocation, and systemic inflammation in chronic HIV infection. J. Infect. Dis. 211 (1), 19–27.

Dodd, D., Spitzer, M.H., Van Treuren, W., Merrill, B.D., Hryckowian, A.J., Higginbottom, S.K., Sonnenburg, J.L., 2017. A gut bacterial pathway metabolizes aromatic amino acids into nine circulating metabolites. Nature 551 (7682), 648–652. https://doi.org/10.1038/nature24661.

Douton, J.E., Horvath, N., Mills-Huffnagle, S., Nyland, J.E., Hajnal, A., Grigson, P.S., 2022. Glucagon-like peptide-1 receptor agonist, liraglutide, reduces heroin self-administration and drug-induced reinstatement of heroin-seeking behaviour in rats. Addiction Biol. 27 (2), e13117. https://doi.org/10.1111/adb.13117.

Dubinkina, V.B., Tyakht, A.V., Odintsova, V.Y., Yarygin, K.S., Kovarsky, B.A., Pavlenko, A.V., Govorun, V.M., 2017. Links of gut microbiota composition with alcohol dependence syndrome and alcoholic liver disease. Microbiome 5 (1), 141. https://doi.org/10.1186/s40168-017-0359-2.

Dunn, D.P., Bastacky, J.M.R., Gray, C.C., Abtahi, S., Currie, P.J., 2019. Role of mesolimbic ghrelin in the acquisition of cocaine reward. Neurosci. Lett. 709, 134367. https://doi.org/10.1016/j.neulet.2019.134367.

Edwards, A., Abizaid, A., 2016. Driving the need to feed: insight into the collaborative interaction between ghrelin and endocannabinoid systems in modulating brain reward systems. Neurosci. Biobehav. Rev. 66, 33–53. https://doi.org/10.1016/j.neubiorev.2016.03.032.

Egecioglu, E., Engel, J.A., Jerlhag, E., 2013a. The glucagon-like peptide 1 analogue Exendin-4 attenuates the nicotine-induced locomotor stimulation, accumbal dopamine release, conditioned place preference as well as the expression of locomotor sensitization in mice. PLoS One 8 (10), e77284.

Egecioglu, E., Engel, J.A., Jerlhag, E., 2013b. The glucagon-like peptide 1 analogue, exendin-4, attenuates the rewarding properties of psychostimulant drugs in mice. PLoS One 8 (7), e69010.

Egecioglu, E., Steensland, P., Fredriksson, I., Feltmann, K., Engel, J.A., Jerlhag, E., 2013c. The glucagon-like peptide 1 analogue Exendin-4 attenuates alcohol mediated behaviors in rodents. Psychoneuroendocrinology 38 (8), 1259–1270. https://doi.org/10.1016/j.psyneuen.2012.11.009.

Eisenstein, T.K., Rahim, R.T., Feng, P., Thingalaya, N.K., Meissler, J.J., 2006. Effects of opioid tolerance and withdrawal on the immune system. J. Neuroimmune Pharmacol. 1 (3), 237–249. https://doi.org/10.1007/s11481-006-9019-1.

Elamin, E.E., Masclee, A.A., Dekker, J., Pieters, H.-J., Jonkers, D.M., 2013. Short-chain fatty acids activate AMP-activated protein kinase and ameliorate ethanol-induced intestinal barrier dysfunction in Caco-2 cell monolayers. J. Nutr. 143 (12), 1872–1881. https://doi.org/10.3945/jn.113.179549.

Engel, J.A., Nylander, I., Jerlhag, E., 2015. A ghrelin receptor (GHS-R1A) antagonist attenuates the rewarding properties of morphine and increases opioid peptide levels in reward areas in mice. Eur. Neuropsychopharmacol 25 (12), 2364–2371. https://doi.org/10.1016/j.euroneuro.2015.10.004.

Engen, P.A., Green, S.J., Voigt, R.M., Forsyth, C.B., Keshavarzian, A., 2015. The gastrointestinal microbiome: alcohol effects on the composition of intestinal microbiota. Alcohol Res. Curr. Rev. 37 (2), 223–236. Retrieved from. https://pubmed.ncbi.nlm.nih.gov/26695747. https://www.ncbi.nlm.nih.gov/pmc/articles/PMC4590619/.

Erny, D., Hrabě de Angelis, A.L., Jaitin, D., Wieghofer, P., Staszewski, O., David, E., Prinz, M., 2015. Host microbiota constantly control maturation and function of microglia in the CNS. Nat. Neurosci. 18 (7), 965–977. https://doi.org/10.1038/nn.4030.

Erreger, K., Davis, A.R., Poe, A.M., Greig, N.H., Stanwood, G.D., Galli, A., 2012. Exendin-4 decreases amphetamine-induced locomotor activity. Physiol. Behav. 106 (4), 574–578. https://doi.org/10.1016/j.physbeh.2012.03.014.

Escribano, B.M., Medina-Fernández, F.J., Aguilar-Luque, M., Agüera, E., Feijoo, M., Garcia-Maceira, F.I., Luque, E., 2017. Lipopolysaccharide binding protein and oxidative stress in a multiple sclerosis model. Neurotherapeutics 14 (1), 199–211.

Everard, A., Belzer, C., Geurts, L., Ouwerkerk, J.P., Druart, C., Bindels, L.B., Cani, P.D., 2013. Cross-talk between *Akkermansia muciniphila* and intestinal epithelium controls diet-induced obesity. Proc. Natl. Acad. Sci. U. S. A. 110 (22), 9066–9071. https://doi.org/10.1073/pnas.1219451110.

Fagerberg, B., Hultén, L.M., Hulthe, J., 2003. Plasma ghrelin, body fat, insulin resistance, and smoking in clinically healthy men: the atherosclerosis and insulin resistance study. Metabolism 52 (11), 1460–1463. https://doi.org/10.1016/S0026-0495(03)00274-9.

Faith, J.J., Guruge, J.L., Charbonneau, M., Subramanian, S., Seedorf, H., Goodman, A.L., Leibel, R.L., 2013. The long-term stability of the human gut microbiota. Science 341 (6141).

Faith, J.J., Rey, F.E., O'donnell, D., Karlsson, M., McNulty, N.P., Kallstrom, G., Gordon, J.I., 2010. Creating and characterizing communities of human gut microbes in gnotobiotic mice. ISME J. 4 (9), 1094–1098.

Farokhnia, M., Grodin, E., Lee, M., Oot, E., Blackburn, A., Stangl, B., Ramchandani, V., 2018. Exogenous ghrelin administration increases alcohol self-administration and modulates brain functional activity in heavy-drinking alcohol-dependent individuals. Mol. Psychiatry 23 (10), 2029–2038.

Farokhnia, M., McDiarmid, G.R., Newmeyer, M.N., Munjal, V., Abulseoud, O.A., Huestis, M.A., Leggio, L., 2020. Effects of oral, smoked, and vaporized cannabis on endocrine pathways related to appetite and metabolism: a randomized, double-blind, placebo-controlled, human laboratory study. Transl. Psychiatry 10 (1). https://doi.org/10.1038/s41398-020-0756-3, 71-71.

Felts, P.A., Woolston, A.-M., Fernando, H.B., Asquith, S., Gregson, N.A., Mizzi, O.J., Smith, K.J., 2005. Inflammation and primary demyelination induced by the intraspinal injection of lipopolysaccharide. Brain 128 (7), 1649–1666. https://doi.org/10.1093/brain/awh516.

Ferrini, F., Salio, C., Lossi, L., Merighi, A., 2009. Ghrelin in central neurons. Curr. Neuropharmacol. 7 (1), 37–49.

Fiorucci, S., Distrutti, E., Carino, A., Zampella, A., Biagioli, M., 2021. Bile acids and their receptors in metabolic disorders. Prog. Lipid Res. 82, 101094. https://doi.org/10.1016/j.plipres.2021.101094.

Fortin, S.M., Lipsky, R.K., Lhamo, R., Chen, J., Kim, E., Borner, T., Hayes, M.R., 2020. GABA neurons in the nucleus tractus solitarius express GLP-1 receptors and mediate anorectic effects of liraglutide in rats. Sci. Transl. Med. 12 (533). https://doi.org/10.1126/scitranslmed.aay8071.

Fortin, S.M., Roitman, M.F., 2017. Central GLP-1 receptor activation modulates cocaine-evoked phasic dopamine signaling in the nucleus accumbens core. Physiol. Behav. 176, 17–25. https://doi.org/10.1016/j.physbeh.2017.03.019.

Foster, J.A., McVey Neufeld, K.-A., 2013. Gut–brain axis: how the microbiome influences anxiety and depression. Trends Neurosci. 36 (5), 305–312. https://doi.org/10.1016/j.tins.2013.01.005.

Fredriksson, R., Höglund, P.J., Gloriam, D.E.I., Lagerström, M.C., Schiöth, H.B., 2003. Seven evolutionarily conserved human rhodopsin G protein-coupled receptors lacking close relatives. FEBS Lett. 554 (3), 381–388. https://doi.org/10.1016/S0014-5793(03)01196-7.

Frost, G., Sleeth, M.L., Sahuri-Arisoylu, M., Lizarbe, B., Cerdan, S., Brody, L., Bell, J.D., 2014. The short-chain fatty acid acetate reduces appetite via a central homeostatic mechanism. Nat. Commun. 5 (1), 3611. https://doi.org/10.1038/ncomms4611.

Fujimoto, T., Imaeda, H., Takahashi, K., Kasumi, E., Bamba, S., Fujiyama, Y., Andoh, A., 2013. Decreased abundance of Faecalibacterium prausnitzii in the gut microbiota of Crohn's disease. J. Gastroenterol. Hepatol. 28 (4), 613–619. https://doi.org/10.1111/jgh.12073.

Gahete, M.D., Rincon-Fernandez, D., Villa-Osaba, A., Hormaechea-Agulla, D., Ibanez-Costa, A., Martinez-Fuentes, A.J., Luque, R.M., 2014. Ghrelin gene products, receptors, and GOAT enzyme: biological and pathophysiological insight. J. Endocrinol. 220 (1), R1–**R**24.

Galligan, J.J., 2018. Beneficial actions of microbiota-derived tryptophan metabolites. Neuro Gastroenterol. Motil. 30 (2), e13283. https://doi.org/10.1111/nmo.13283.

Gao, J., Xu, K., Liu, H., Liu, G., Bai, M., Peng, C., Yin, Y., 2018. Impact of the gut microbiota on intestinal immunity mediated by tryptophan metabolism. Front. Cell. Infect. Microbiol. 8. https://doi.org/10.3389/fcimb.2018.00013, 13-13.

Gentilella, R., Pechtner, V., Corcos, A., Consoli, A., 2019. Glucagon-like peptide-1 receptor agonists in type 2 diabetes treatment: are they all the same? Diabetes/metabolism research and reviews 35 (1), e3070.

Gibson, G.R., Beatty, E.R., Wang, X., Cummings, J.H., 1995. Selective stimulation of bifidobacteria in the human colon by oligofructose and inulin. Gastroenterology 108 (4), 975–982. https://doi.org/10.1016/0016-5085(95)90192-2.

Gnanapavan, S., Kola, B., Bustin, S.A., Morris, D.G., McGee, P., Fairclough, P., Korbonits, M.r., 2002. The tissue distribution of the mRNA of ghrelin and subtypes of its receptor, GHS-R, in humans. J. Clin. Endocrinol. Metab. 87 (6), 2988–2991.

Godlewski, G., Cinar, R., Coffey, N.J., Liu, J., Jourdan, T., Mukhopadhyay, B., Kunos, G., 2019. Targeting peripheral CB(1) receptors reduces ethanol intake via a gut-brain axis. Cell Metab. 29 (6), 1320–1333. https://doi.org/10.1016/j.cmet.2019.04.012 e1328.

Gomez, J.L., Cunningham, C.L., Finn, D.A., Young, E.A., Helpenstell, L.K., Schuette, L.M., Ryabinin, A.E., 2015. Differential effects of ghrelin antagonists on alcohol drinking and reinforcement in mouse and rat models of alcohol dependence. Neuropharmacology 97, 182–193. https://doi.org/10.1016/j.neuropharm.2015.05.026.

Gomez, J.L., Ryabinin, A.E., 2014. The effects of ghrelin antagonists [D-Lys3]-GHRP-6 or JMV2959 on ethanol, water, and food intake in C57BL/6J mice. Alcohol. Clin. Exp. Res. 38 (9), 2436–2444. https://doi.org/10.1111/acer.12499.

González-Mariscal, I., Krzysik-Walker, S.M., Kim, W., Rouse, M., Egan, J.M., 2016. Blockade of cannabinoid 1 receptor improves GLP-1R mediated insulin secretion in mice. Mol. Cell. Endocrinol. 423, 1–10. https://doi.org/10.1016/j.mce.2015.12.015.

Graham, D.L., Edwards, S., Bachtell, R.K., DiLeone, R.J., Rios, M., Self, D.W., 2007. Dynamic BDNF activity in nucleus accumbens with cocaine use increases self-administration and relapse. Nat. Neurosci. 10 (8), 1029–1037. https://doi.org/10.1038/nn1929.

Graham, D.L., Erreger, K., Galli, A., Stanwood, G.D., 2013. GLP-1 analog attenuates cocaine reward. Mol. Psychiatry 18 (9), 961–962.

Graham, D.L., Krishnan, V., Larson, E.B., Graham, A., Edwards, S., Bachtell, R.K., Simmons, D., Gent, L.M., Berton, O., Bolanos, C.A., DiLeone, R.J., Parada, L.F., Nestler, E.J., Self, D.W., 2009. Tropomyosin-related kinase B in the mesolimbic dopamine system: region-specific effects on cocaine reward. Biol. Psychiatry 65 (8), 696–701. https://doi.org/10.1016/j.biopsych.2008.09.032.

Greiner, T., Bäckhed, F., 2011. Effects of the gut microbiota on obesity and glucose homeostasis. TEM (Trends Endocrinol. Metab.) 22 (4), 117–123.

Gualillo, O., Lago, F., Casanueva, F.F., Dieguez, C., 2006. One ancestor, several peptides: post-translational modifications of preproghrelin generate several peptides with antithetical effects. Mol. Cell. Endocrinol. 256 (1–2), 1–8.

Guan, X.-M., Yu, H., Palyha, O.C., McKee, K.K., Feighner, S.D., Sirinathsinghji, D.J., Howard, A.D., 1997. Distribution of mRNA encoding the growth hormone secretagogue receptor in brain and peripheral tissues. Mol. Brain Res. 48 (1), 23–29.

Guarner, F., Malagelada, J.R., 2003. Gut flora in health and disease. Lancet 361 (9356), 512–519. https://doi.org/10.1016/s0140-6736(03)12489-0.

Hansen, K.B., Rosenkilde, M.M., Knop, F.K., Wellner, N., Diep, T.A., Rehfeld, J.F., Hansen, H.S., 2011. 2-Oleoyl glycerol is a GPR119 agonist and signals GLP-1 release in humans. J. Clin. Endocrinol. Metab. 96 (9), E1409–E1417. https://doi.org/10.1210/jc.2011-0647.

Hansson, C., Alvarez-Crespo, M., Taube, M., Skibicka, K.P., Schmidt, L., Karlsson-Lindahl, L., Dickson, S.L., 2014. Influence of ghrelin on the central serotonergic signaling system in mice. Neuropharmacology 79, 498–505.

Harasta, A.E., Power, J.M., Von Jonquieres, G., Karl, T., Drucker, D.J., Housley, G.D., Klugmann, M., 2015. Septal glucagon-like peptide 1 receptor expression determines suppression of cocaine-induced behavior. Neuropsychopharmacology 40 (8), 1969–1978.

Hayes, M.R., Bradley, L., Grill, H.J., 2009. Endogenous hindbrain glucagon-like peptide-1 receptor activation contributes to the control of food intake by mediating gastric satiation signaling. Endocrinology 150 (6), 2654–2659. https://doi.org/10.1210/en.2008-1479.

Hayes, M.R., Skibicka, K.P., Grill, H.J., 2008. Caudal brainstem processing is sufficient for behavioral, sympathetic, and parasympathetic responses driven by peripheral and hindbrain glucagon-like-peptide-1 receptor stimulation. Endocrinology 149 (8), 4059–4068. https://doi.org/10.1210/en.2007-1743.

Hernandez, N.S., Ige, K.Y., Mietlicki-Baase, E.G., Molina-Castro, G.C., Turner, C.A., Hayes, M.R., Schmidt, H.D., 2018. Glucagon-like peptide-1 receptor activation in the ventral tegmental area attenuates cocaine seeking in rats. Neuropsychopharmacology 43 (10), 2000–2008. https://doi.org/10.1038/s41386-018-0010-3.

Hernandez, N.S., O'Donovan, B., Ortinski, P.I., Schmidt, H.D., 2019. Activation of glucagon-like peptide-1 receptors in the nucleus accumbens attenuates cocaine seeking in rats. Addiction Biol. 24 (2), 170–181. https://doi.org/10.1111/adb.12583.

Hilburger, M.E., Adler, M.W., Truant, A.L., Meissler Jr., J.J., Satishchandran, V., Rogers, T.J., Eisenstein, T.K., 1997. Morphine induces sepsis in mice. J. Infect. Dis. 176 (1), 183–188. https://doi.org/10.1086/514021.

Holst, J.J., 2007. The physiology of glucagon-like peptide 1. Physiol. Rev. 87 (4), 1409–1439. https://doi.org/10.1152/physrev.00034.2006.

Howard, A.D., Feighner, S.D., Cully, D.F., Arena, J.P., Liberator, P.A., Rosenblum, C.I., Anderson, J., 1996. A receptor in pituitary and hypothalamus that functions in growth hormone release. Science 273 (5277), 974–977.

Hunter, K., Hölscher, C., 2012. Drugs developed to treat diabetes, liraglutide and lixisenatide, cross the blood brain barrier and enhance neurogenesis. BMC Neurosci. 13 (1), 33. https://doi.org/10.1186/1471-2202-13-33.

Jang, J.K., Kim, W.Y., Cho, B.R., Lee, J.W., Kim, J.-H., 2013. Microinjection of ghrelin in the nucleus accumbens core enhances locomotor activity induced by cocaine. Behav. Brain Res. 248, 7–11. https://doi.org/10.1016/j.bbr.2013.03.049.

Jerabek, P., Havlickova, T., Puskina, N., Charalambous, C., Lapka, M., Kacer, P., Sustkova-Fiserova, M., 2017. Ghrelin receptor antagonism of morphine-induced conditioned place preference and behavioral and accumbens dopaminergic sensitization in rats. Neurochem. Int. 110, 101–113. https://doi.org/10.1016/j.neuint.2017.09.013.

Jerlhag, E., 2008. Preclinical study: systemic administration of ghrelin induces conditioned place preference and stimulates accumbal dopamine. Addiction Biol. 13 (3-4), 358–363.

Jerlhag, E., Egecioglu, E., Dickson, S., Svensson, L., Engel, J., 2006a. Central administration of the orexigenic peptide ghrelin stimulates parameters associated with reward. Alcohol. Clin. Exp. Res. 30 (9), 842.

Jerlhag, E., Egecioglu, E., Dickson, S.L., Douhan, A., Svensson, L., Engel, J.A., 2007. Preclinical study: ghrelin administration into tegmental areas stimulates locomotor activity and increases extracellular concentration of dopamine in the nucleus accumbens. Addiction Biol. 12 (1), 6–16.

Jerlhag, E., Egecioglu, E., Dickson, S.L., Engel, J.A., 2010. Ghrelin receptor antagonism attenuates cocaine-and amphetamine-induced locomotor stimulation, accumbal dopamine release, and conditioned place preference. Psychopharmacology 211 (4), 415–422.

Jerlhag, E., Egecioglu, E., Dickson, S.L., Svensson, L., Engel, J.A., 2008. Alpha-conotoxin MII-sensitive nicotinic acetylcholine receptors are involved in mediating the ghrelin-induced locomotor stimulation and dopamine overflow in nucleus accumbens. Eur. Neuropsychopharmacol. 18 (7), 508–518. https://doi.org/10.1016/j.euroneuro.2008.02.006.

Jerlhag, E., Egecioglu, E., Landgren, S., Salomé, N., Heilig, M., Moechars, D., Engel, J.A., 2009. Requirement of central ghrelin signaling for alcohol reward. Proc. Natl. Acad. Sci. U. S. A. 106 (27), 11318–11323. https://doi.org/10.1073/pnas.0812809106.

Jerlhag, E., Engel, J.A., 2011. Ghrelin receptor antagonism attenuates nicotine-induced locomotor stimulation, accumbal dopamine release and conditioned place preference in mice. Drug Alcohol Depend. 117 (2), 126–131. https://doi.org/10.1016/j.drugalcdep.2011.01.010.

Jerlhag, E., Grøtli, M., Luthman, K., Svensson, L., Engel, J.A., 2006b. Role of the subunit composition of central nicotinic acetylcholine receptors for the stimulatory and dopamine-enhancing effects of ethanol. Alcohol Alcohol. 41 (5), 486–493. https://doi.org/10.1093/alcalc/agl049.

Jerlhag, E., Ivanoff, L., Vater, A., Engel, J.A., 2014. Peripherally circulating ghrelin does not mediate alcohol-induced reward and alcohol intake in rodents. Alcohol. Clin. Exp. Res. 38 (4), 959–968. https://doi.org/10.1111/acer.12337.

Jerlhag, E., Landgren, S., Egecioglu, E., Dickson, S.L., Engel, J.A., 2011. The alcohol-induced locomotor stimulation and accumbal dopamine release is suppressed in ghrelin knockout mice. Alcohol 45 (4), 341–347. https://doi.org/10.1016/j.alcohol.2010.10.002.

Jo, Y.H., Talmage, D.A., Role, L.W., 2002. Nicotinic receptor-mediated effects on appetite and food intake. J. Neurobiol. 53 (4), 618–632.

Johnstone, R.W., 2002. Histone-deacetylase inhibitors: novel drugs for the treatment of cancer. Nat. Rev. Drug Discov. 1 (4), 287–299. https://doi.org/10.1038/nrd772.

Kaakoush, N.O., 2015. Insights into the role of Erysipelotrichaceae in the human host. Front. Cell. Infect. Microbiol. 5, 84.

Kalafateli, A.L., Vallöf, D., Jörnulf, J.W., Heilig, M., Jerlhag, E., 2018. A cannabinoid receptor antagonist attenuates ghrelin-induced activation of the mesolimbic dopamine system in mice. Physiol. Behav. 184, 211–219. https://doi.org/10.1016/j.physbeh.2017.12.005.

Kalivas, P.W., 2007. Cocaine and amphetamine-like psychostimulants: neurocircuitry and glutamate neuroplasticity. Dialogues Clin. Neurosci. 9 (4), 389–397. https://doi.org/10.31887/DCNS.2007.9.4/pkalivas.

Kang, M., Mischel, R.A., Bhave, S., Komla, E., Cho, A., Huang, C., Akbarali, H.I., 2017. The effect of gut microbiome on tolerance to morphine mediated antinociception in mice. Sci. Rep. 7 (1), 42658. https://doi.org/10.1038/srep42658.

Kanoski, S.E., Fortin, S.M., Arnold, M., Grill, H.J., Hayes, M.R., 2011. Peripheral and central GLP-1 receptor populations mediate the anorectic effects of peripherally administered GLP-1 receptor agonists, liraglutide and exendin-4. Endocrinology 152 (8), 3103–3112. https://doi.org/10.1210/en.2011-0174.

Kastin, A., Akerstrom, V., 2003. Entry of exendin-4 into brain is rapid but may be limited at high doses. Int. J. Obes. 27 (3), 313–318.

Kaur, S., Ryabinin, A.E., 2010. Ghrelin receptor antagonism decreases alcohol consumption and activation of perioculomotor urocortin-containing neurons. Alcohol. Clin. Exp. Res. 34 (9), 1525–1534. https://doi.org/10.1111/j.1530-0277.2010.01237.x.

Kelly, J., Kennedy, P., Cryan, J., Dinan, T., Clarke, G., Hyland, N., 2015. Breaking down the barriers: the gut microbiome, intestinal permeability and stress-related psychiatric disorders. Front. Cell. Neurosci. 9 (392). https://doi.org/10.3389/fncel.2015.00392.

Kelz, M.B., Chen, J., Carlezon Jr., W.A., Whisler, K., Gilden, L., Beckmann, A.M., Steffen, C., Zhang, Y.J., Marotti, L., Self, D.W., Tkatch, T., Baranauskas, G., Surmeier, D.J., Neve, R.L., Duman, R.S., Picciotto, M.R., Nestler, E.J., 1999. Expression of the transcription factor deltaFosB in the brain controls sensitivity to cocaine. Nature 401 (6750), 272–276. https://doi.org/10.1038/45790.

Kim, D.-J., Yoon, S.-J., Choi, B., Kim, T.-S., Woo, Y.S., Kim, W., Kim, Y.-K., 2005. Increased fasting plasma ghrelin levels during alcohol abstinence. Alcohol Alcohol. 40 (1), 76–79.

Kiraly, D.D., Walker, D.M., Calipari, E.S., Labonte, B., Issler, O., Pena, C.J., Nestler, E.J., 2016. Alterations of the host microbiome affect behavioral responses to cocaine. Sci. Rep. 6, 35455. https://doi.org/10.1038/srep35455.

Klink, R., de Kerchove d'Exaerde, A., Zoli, M., Changeux, J.-P., 2001. Molecular and physiological diversity of nicotinic acetylcholine receptors in the midbrain dopaminergic nuclei. J. Neurosci. 21 (5), 1452–1463.

Kobeissy, F.H., Jeung, J.A., Warren, M.W., Geier, J.E., Gold, M.S., 2008. Preclinical study: changes in leptin, ghrelin, growth hormone and neuropeptide-Y after an acute model of MDMA and methamphetamine exposure in rats. Addiction Biol. 13 (1), 15–25. https://doi.org/10.1111/j.1369-1600.2007.00083.x.

Koh, A., De Vadder, F., Kovatcheva-Datchary, P., Bäckhed, F., 2016. From dietary fiber to host physiology: short-chain fatty acids as key bacterial metabolites. Cell 165 (6), 1332–1345. https://doi.org/10.1016/j.cell.2016.05.041.

Kojima, M., Hosoda, H., Date, Y., Nakazato, M., Matsuo, H., Kangawa, K., 1999. Ghrelin is a growth-hormone-releasing acylated peptide from stomach. Nature 402 (6762), 656–660.

Kokkinos, A., Tentolouris, N., Kyriakaki, E., Argyrakopoulou, G., Doupis, J., Psallas, M., Katsilambros, N., 2007. Differentiation in the short- and long-term effects of smoking on plasma total ghrelin concentrations between male nonsmokers and habitual smokers. Metabolism 56 (4), 523–527. https://doi.org/10.1016/j.metabol.2006.11.012.

Kola, B., Boscaro, M., Rutter, G.A., Grossman, A.B., Korbonits, M., 2006. Expanding role of AMPK in endocrinology. TEM (Trends Endocrinol. Metab.) 17 (5), 205–215. https://doi.org/10.1016/j.tem.2006.05.006.

Kola, B., Farkas, I., Christ-Crain, M., Wittmann, G., Lolli, F., Amin, F., Korbonits, M., 2008. The orexigenic effect of ghrelin is mediated through central activation of the endogenous cannabinoid system. PLoS One 3 (3), e1797. https://doi.org/10.1371/journal.pone.0001797.

Kola, B., Hubina, E., Tucci, S.A., Kirkham, T.C., Garcia, E.A., Mitchell, S.E., Korbonits, M., 2005. Cannabinoids and ghrelin have both central and peripheral metabolic and cardiac effects via AMP-activated protein kinase. J. Biol. Chem. 280 (26), 25196–25201. https://doi.org/10.1074/jbc.C500175200.

Koob, G.F., Volkow, N.D., 2016. Neurobiology of addiction: a neurocircuitry analysis. Lancet Psychiatry 3 (8), 760–773.

Koole, C., Wootten, D., Simms, J., Valant, C., Miller, L.J., Christopoulos, A., Sexton, P.M., 2011. Polymorphism and ligand dependent changes in human glucagon-like peptide-1 receptor (GLP-1R) function: allosteric rescue of loss of function mutation. Mol. Pharmacol. 80 (3), 486. https://doi.org/10.1124/mol.111.072884.

Koopmann, A., Bach, P., Schuster, R., Bumb, J.M., Vollstädt-Klein, S., Reinhard, I., Kiefer, F., 2019. Ghrelin modulates mesolimbic reactivity to alcohol cues in alcohol-addicted subjects: a functional imaging study. Addiction Biol. 24 (5), 1066–1076. https://doi.org/10.1111/adb.12651.

Koopmann, A., Bez, J., Lemenager, T., Hermann, D., Dinter, C., Reinhard, I., Kiefer, F., 2015. Effects of cigarette smoking on plasma concentration of the appetite-regulating peptide ghrelin. Ann. Nutr. Metab. 66 (2–3), 155–161. https://doi.org/10.1159/000381834.

Koopmann, A., von der Goltz, C., Grosshans, M., Dinter, C., Vitale, M., Wiedemann, K., Kiefer, F., 2012. The association of the appetitive peptide acetylated ghrelin with alcohol craving in early abstinent alcohol dependent individuals. Psychoneuroendocrinology 37 (7), 980–986. https://doi.org/10.1016/j.psyneuen.2011.11.005.

Kraus, T., Schanze, A., Gröschl, M., Bayerlein, K., Hillemacher, T., Reulbach, U., Bleich, S., 2005. Ghrelin levels are increased in alcoholism. Alcohol. Clin. Exp. Res. 29 (12), 2154–2157.

Kreymann, B., Ghatei, M.A., Williams, G., Bloom, S.R., 1987. Glucagon-like peptide-1 7-36: a physiological incretin in man. Lancet 330 (8571), 1300–1304. https://doi.org/10.1016/S0140-6736(87)91194-9.

Kroemer, N.B., Wuttig, F., Bidlingmaier, M., Zimmermann, U.S., Smolka, M.N., 2015. Nicotine enhances modulation of food-cue reactivity by leptin and ghrelin in the ventromedial prefrontal cortex. Addiction Biol. 20 (4), 832–844. https://doi.org/10.1111/adb.12167.

L'hirondel, M., Cheramy, A., Godeheu, G., Glowinski, J., 1995. Effects of arachidonic acid on dopamine synthesis, spontaneous release, and uptake in striatal synaptosomes from the rat. J. Neurochem. 64 (3), 1406–1409.

Labarthe, A., Fiquet, O., Hassouna, R., Zizzari, P., Lanfumey, L., Ramoz, N., Tolle, V., 2014. Ghrelin-derived peptides: a link between appetite/reward, GH axis, and psychiatric disorders? Front. Endocrinol. 5, 163.

Lamas, B., Natividad, J.M., Sokol, H., 2018. Aryl hydrocarbon receptor and intestinal immunity. Mucosal Immunol. 11 (4), 1024–1038. https://doi.org/10.1038/s41385-018-0019-2.

Lan, H., Lin, H.V., Wang, C.F., Wright, M.J., Xu, S., Kang, L., Kowalski, T.J., 2012. Agonists at GPR119 mediate secretion of GLP-1 from mouse enteroendocrine cells through glucose-independent pathways. Br. J. Pharmacol. 165 (8), 2799–2807. https://doi.org/10.1111/j.1476-5381.2011.01754.x.

Landgren, S., Berglund, K., Jerlhag, E., Fahlke, C., Balldin, J., Berggren, U., Engel, J.A., 2011a. Reward-related genes and personality traits in alcohol-dependent individuals: a pilot case control study. Neuropsychobiology 64 (1), 38–46. https://doi.org/10.1159/000324992.

Landgren, S., Engel, J.A., Hyytiä, P., Zetterberg, H., Blennow, K., Jerlhag, E., 2011b. Expression of the gene encoding the ghrelin receptor in rats selected for differential alcohol preference. Behav. Brain Res. 221 (1), 182–188.

Landgren, S., Jerlhag, E., Hallman, J., Oreland, L., Lissner, L., Strandhagen, E., Engel, J.A., 2010. Genetic variation of the ghrelin signaling system in females with severe alcohol dependence. Alcohol. Clin. Exp. Res. 34 (9), 1519–1524. https://doi.org/10.1111/j.1530-0277.2010.01236.x.

Landgren, S., Jerlhag, E., Zetterberg, H., Gonzalez-Quintela, A., Campos, J., Olofsson, U., Engel, J.A., 2008. Association of pro-ghrelin and GHS-R1A gene polymorphisms and haplotypes with heavy alcohol use and body mass. Alcohol. Clin. Exp. Res. 32 (12), 2054–2061. https://doi.org/10.1111/j.1530-0277.2008.00793.x.

Landgren, S., Simms, J.A., Hyytiä, P., Engel, J.A., Bartlett, S.E., Jerlhag, E., 2012. Ghrelin receptor (GHS-R1A) antagonism suppresses both operant alcohol self-administration and high alcohol consumption in rats. Addiction Biol. 17 (1), 86–94. https://doi.org/10.1111/j.1369-1600.2010.00280.x.

Langenberg, C., Bergstrom, J., Laughlin, G.A., Barrett-Connor, E., 2005. Ghrelin and the metabolic syndrome in older adults. J. Clin. Endocrinol. Metab. 90 (12), 6448–6453. https://doi.org/10.1210/jc.2005-1358.

Larsson, A., Svensson, L., Söderpalm, B., Engel, J.A., 2002. Role of different nicotinic acetylcholine receptors in mediating behavioral and neurochemical effects of ethanol in mice. Alcohol 28 (3), 157–167. https://doi.org/10.1016/s0741-8329(02)00244-6.

Lautar, S.L., Rojas, C., Slusher, B.S., Wozniak, K.M., Wu, Y., Thomas, A.G., Belyakov, S., 2005. DPP IV inhibitor blocks mescaline-induced scratching and amphetamine-induced hyperactivity in mice. Brain Res. 1048 (1), 177–184. https://doi.org/10.1016/j.brainres.2005.04.069.

Le Floc'h, N., Otten, W., Merlot, E., 2011. Tryptophan metabolism, from nutrition to potential therapeutic applications. Amino Acids 41 (5), 1195–1205.

Leclercq, S., Matamoros, S., Cani, P.D., Neyrinck, A.M., Jamar, F., Stärkel, P., Delzenne, N.M., 2014. Intestinal permeability, gut-bacterial dysbiosis, and behavioral markers of alcohol-dependence severity. Proc. Natl. Acad. Sci. U. S. A. 111 (42), E4485–E4493. https://doi.org/10.1073/pnas.1415174111.

Lee, H., Joe, K.-H., Kim, W., Park, J., Lee, D.-H., Sung, K.-W., Kim, D.-J., 2006. Increased leptin and decreased ghrelin level after smoking cessation. Neurosci. Lett. 409 (1), 47–51. https://doi.org/10.1016/j.neulet.2006.09.013.

Lee, K., Vuong, H.E., Nusbaum, D.J., Hsiao, E.Y., Evans, C.J., Taylor, A., 2018. The gut microbiota mediates reward and sensory responses associated with regimen-selective morphine dependence. Neuropsychopharmacology 43 (13), 2606–2614. https://doi.org/10.1038/s41386-018-0211-9.

Lee, M.R., Tapocik, J.D., Ghareeb, M., Schwandt, M.L., Dias, A.A., Le, A.N., Leggio, L., 2020. The novel ghrelin receptor inverse agonist PF-5190457 administered with alcohol: preclinical safety experiments and a phase 1b human laboratory study. Mol. Psychiatry 25 (2), 461–475. https://doi.org/10.1038/s41380-018-0064-y.

Leggio, L., Ferrulli, A., Cardone, S., Nesci, A., Miceli, A., Malandrino, N., Addolorato, G., 2012. Ghrelin system in alcohol-dependent subjects: role of plasma ghrelin levels in alcohol drinking and craving. Addiction Biol. 17 (2), 452–464. https://doi.org/10.1111/j.1369-1600.2010.00308.x.

Leggio, L., Schwandt, M.L., Oot, E.N., Dias, A.A., Ramchandani, V.A., 2013. Fasting-induced increase in plasma ghrelin is blunted by intravenous alcohol administration: a within-subject placebo-controlled study. Psychoneuroendocrinology 38 (12), 3085–3091. https://doi.org/10.1016/j.psyneuen.2013.09.005.

Leggio, L., Zywiak, W.H., Fricchione, S.R., Edwards, S.M., de la Monte, S.M., Swift, R.M., Kenna, G.A., 2014. Intravenous ghrelin administration increases alcohol craving in alcohol-dependent heavy drinkers: a preliminary investigation. Biological psychiatry 76 (9), 734–741. https://doi.org/10.1016/j.biopsych.2014.03.019.

Lemieux, A.M., al'Absi, M., 2018. Changes in circulating peptide YY and ghrelin are associated with early smoking relapse. Biol. Psychol. 131, 43–48. https://doi.org/10.1016/j.biopsycho.2017.03.007.

Léna, C., Changeux, J.-P., 1997. Pathological mutations of nicotinic receptors and nicotine-based therapies for brain disorders. Curr. Opin. Neurobiol. 7 (5), 674–682. https://doi.org/10.1016/S0959-4388(97)80088-8.

Ley, R.E., Turnbaugh, P.J., Klein, S., Gordon, J.I., 2006. Microbial ecology: human gut microbes associated with obesity. Nature 444 (7122), 1022–1023. https://doi.org/10.1038/4441022a.

Lim, C.T., Kola, B., Feltrin, D., Perez-Tilve, D., Tschöp, M.H., Grossman, A.B., Korbonits, M., 2013. Ghrelin and cannabinoids require the ghrelin receptor to affect cellular energy metabolism. Mol. Cell. Endocrinol. 365 (2), 303–308. https://doi.org/10.1016/j.mce.2012.11.007.

Łupina, M., Talarek, S., Kotlińska, J., Gibuła-Tarłowska, E., Listos, P., Listos, J., 2020. The role of linagliptin, a selective dipeptidyl peptidase-4 inhibitor, in the morphine rewarding effects in rats. Neurochem. Int. 133, 104616. https://doi.org/10.1016/j.neuint.2019.104616.

Lyons, A.M., Lowery, E.G., Sparta, D.R., Thiele, T.E., 2008. Effects of food availability and administration of orexigenic and anorectic agents on elevated ethanol drinking associated with drinking in the dark procedures. Alcohol. Clin. Exp. Res. 32 (11), 1962–1968. https://doi.org/10.1111/j.1530-0277.2008.00784.x.

Machiels, K., Joossens, M., Sabino, J., De Preter, V., Arijs, I., Eeckhaut, V., Vermeire, S., 2014. A decrease of the butyrate-producing species Roseburia hominis and Faecalibacterium prausnitzii defines dysbiosis in patients with ulcerative colitis. Gut 63 (8), 1275–1283. https://doi.org/10.1136/gutjnl-2013-304833.

Maric, T., Sedki, F., Ronfard, B., Chafetz, D., Shalev, U., 2012. A limited role for ghrelin in heroin self-administration and food deprivation-induced reinstatement of heroin seeking in rats. Addiction Biol. 17 (3), 613–622. https://doi.org/10.1111/j.1369-1600.2011.00396.x.

Marty, V.N., Farokhnia, M., Munier, J.J., Mulpuri, Y., Leggio, L., Spigelman, I., 2020. Long-acting glucagon-like peptide-1 receptor agonists suppress voluntary alcohol intake in male Wistar rats. Front. Neurosci. 14. https://doi.org/10.3389/fnins.2020.599646, 599646–599646.

Mason, B., Wang, Q., Zigman, J., 2014. The central nervous system sites mediating the orexigenic actions of ghrelin. Annu. Rev. Physiol. 76, 519–533.

Matsuyama, T., Komatsu, R., Namba, M., Watanabe, N., Itoh, H., Tarui, S., 1988. Glucagon-like peptide-1 (7–36 amide): a potent glucagonostatic and insulinotropic hormone. Diabetes Res. Clin. Pract. 5 (4), 281–284. https://doi.org/10.1016/S0168-8227(88)80063-9.

Mawe, G.M., Hoffman, J.M., 2013. Serotonin signalling in the gut—functions, dysfunctions and therapeutic targets. Nat. Rev. Gastroenterol. Hepatol. 10 (8), 473–486. https://doi.org/10.1038/nrgastro.2013.105.

Mazidi, M., Taraghdari, S.B., Rezaee, P., Kamgar, M., Jomezadeh, M.R., Hasani, O.A., Nematy, M., 2014. The effect of hydroalcoholic extract of Cannabis Sativa on appetite hormone in rat. J. Compl. Integr. Med. 11 (4), 253–257. https://doi.org/10.1515/jcim-2014-0006.

Mear, Y., Enjalbert, A., Thirion, S., 2013. GHS-R1a constitutive activity and its physiological relevance. Front. Neurosci. 7 (87). https://doi.org/10.3389/fnins.2013.00087.

Meckel, K.R., Kiraly, D.D., 2019. A potential role for the gut microbiome in substance use disorders. Psychopharmacology 236 (5), 1513–1530. https://doi.org/10.1007/s00213-019-05232-0.

Merchenthaler, I., Lane, M., Shughrue, P., 1999. Distribution of pre-pro-glucagon and glucagon-like peptide-1 receptor messenger RNAs in the rat central nervous system. J. Comp. Neurol. 403 (2), 261–280. https://doi.org/10.1002/(SICI)1096-9861(19990111)403:2<261::AID-CNE8>3.0.CO;2-5.

Meyer, R.M., Burgos-Robles, A., Liu, E., Correia, S.S., Goosens, K.A., 2014. A ghrelin–growth hormone axis drives stress-induced vulnerability to enhanced fear. Mol. Psychiatry 19 (12), 1284–1294.

Minokoshi, Y., Alquier, T., Furukawa, N., Kim, Y.-B., Lee, A., Xue, B., Birnbaum, M.J., 2004. AMP-kinase regulates food intake by responding to hormonal and nutrient signals in the hypothalamus. Nature 428 (6982), 569–574.

Mutlu, E.A., Gillevet, P.M., Rangwala, H., Sikaroodi, M., Naqvi, A., Engen, P.A., Keshavarzian, A., 2012. Colonic microbiome is altered in alcoholism. Am. J. Physiol. Gastrointest. Liver Physiol. 302 (9), G966–G978. https://doi.org/10.1152/ajpgi.00380.2011.

Mutschler, J., Graf, N., Spanaus, K.S., Rössler, W., Hergan, K., Binkert, C.A., Gutzeit, A., 2012. Circulating ghrelin levels are not associated with craving and withdrawal symptoms in acute nicotine withdrawal. Psychiatr. Danub. 24 (2), 229–230.

Myers, S.P., Hawrelak, J., 2004. The causes of intestinal dysbiosis: a review. Altern. Med. Rev. 9 (2), 180–197.

Naleid, A.M., Grace, M.K., Cummings, D.E., Levine, A.S., 2005. Ghrelin induces feeding in the mesolimbic reward pathway between the ventral tegmental area and the nucleus accumbens. Peptides 26 (11), 2274–2279.

Näslund, E., Schmidt, P.T., Hellström, P.M., 2005. Gut peptide hormones: importance for food intake. Scand. J. Gastroenterol. 40 (3), 250–258.

Ning, T., Gong, X., Xie, L., Ma, B., 2017. Gut microbiota analysis in rats with methamphetamine-induced conditioned place preference. Front. Microbiol. 8, 1620. https://doi.org/10.3389/fmicb.2017.01620.

Nolan-Kenney, R., Wu, F., Hu, J., Yang, L., Kelly, D., Li, H., Chen, Y., 2019. The association between smoking and gut microbiome in Bangladesh. Nicotine Tob. Res. 22 (8), 1339–1346. https://doi.org/10.1093/ntr/ntz220.

Northrup, T.F., Stotts, A.L., Suchting, R., Matt, G.E., Quintana, P.J.E., Khan, A.M., Stewart, C.J., 2021. Thirdhand smoke associations with the gut microbiomes of infants admitted to a neonatal intensive care unit: an observational study. Environ. Res. 197, 111180. https://doi.org/10.1016/j.envres.2021.111180.

Novak, U., Wilks, A., Buell, G., McEwen, S., 1987. Identical mRNA for preproglucagon in pancreas and gut. Eur. J. Biochem. 164 (3), 553–558.

O'Hara, A.M., Shanahan, F., 2006. The gut flora as a forgotten organ. EMBO Rep. 7 (7), 688–693. https://doi.org/10.1038/sj.embor.7400731.

O'Mahony, S.M., Clarke, G., Borre, Y.E., Dinan, T.G., Cryan, J.F., 2015. Serotonin, tryptophan metabolism and the brain-gut-microbiome axis. Behav. Brain Res. 277, 32–48. https://doi.org/10.1016/j.bbr.2014.07.027.

Oldendorf, W.H., 1973. Carrier-mediated blood–brain barrier transport of short-chain monocarboxylic organic acids. Am. J. Physiol. Leg. Content 224 (6), 1450–1453.

Olszewski, P.K., Schiöth, H.B., Levine, A.S., 2008. Ghrelin in the CNS: from hunger to a rewarding and memorable meal? Brain Res. Rev. 58 (1), 160–170.

Opstelten, J.L., Plassais, J., van Mil, S.W.C., Achouri, E., Pichaud, M., Siersema, P.D., Cervino, A.C.L., 2016. Gut microbial diversity is reduced in smokers with Crohn's disease. Inflamm. Bowel Dis. 22 (9), 2070–2077. https://doi.org/10.1097/MIB.0000000000000875.

Orskov, C., Holst, J.J., Nielsen, O.V., 1988. Effect of truncated glucagon-like peptide-1 [proglucagon-(78-107) amide] on endocrine secretion from pig pancreas, antrum, and nonantral stomach. Endocrinology 123 (4), 2009–2013. https://doi.org/10.1210/endo-123-4-2009.

Overton, H.A., Babbs, A.J., Doel, S.M., Fyfe, M.C.T., Gardner, L.S., Griffin, G., Reynet, C., 2006. Deorphanization of a G protein-coupled receptor for oleoylethanolamide and its use in the discovery of small-molecule hypophagic agents. Cell Metab. 3 (3), 167–175. https://doi.org/10.1016/j.cmet.2006.02.004.

Palotai, M., Bagosi, Z., Jászberényi, M., Csabafi, K., Dochnal, R., Manczinger, M., Szabó, G., 2013. Ghrelin amplifies the nicotine-induced dopamine release in the rat striatum. Neurochem. Int. 63 (4), 239–243. https://doi.org/10.1016/j.neuint.2013.06.014.

Panagopoulos, V.N., Ralevski, E., 2014. The role of ghrelin in addiction: a review. Psychopharmacology 231 (14), 2725–2740.

Parséus, A., Sommer, N., Sommer, F., Caesar, R., Molinaro, A., Ståhlman, M., Bäckhed, F., 2017. Microbiota-induced obesity requires farnesoid X receptor. Gut 66 (3), 429–437. https://doi.org/10.1136/gutjnl-2015-310283.

Perelló, M., Zigman, J.M., 2012. The role of ghrelin in reward-based eating. Biol. Psychiatry 72 (5), 347–353.

Pflughoeft, K.J., Versalovic, J., 2012. Human microbiome in health and disease. Annu. Rev. Pathol. 7 (1), 99–122. https://doi.org/10.1146/annurev-pathol-011811-132421.

Pilhatsch, M., Scheuing, H., Kroemer, N., Kobiella, A., Bidlingmaier, M., Farger, G., Zimmermann, U.S., 2014. Nicotine administration in healthy non-smokers reduces appetite but does not alter plasma ghrelin. Hum. Psychopharmacol. Clin. Exp. 29 (4), 384–387. https://doi.org/10.1002/hup.2405.

Pöykkö, S.M., Kellokoski, E., Ukkola, O., Kauma, H., Päivänsalo, M., Kesäniemi, Y.A., Hörkkö, S., 2006. Plasma ghrelin concentrations are positively associated with carotid artery atherosclerosis in males. J. Intern. Med. 260 (1), 43–52. https://doi.org/10.1111/j.1365-2796.2006.01661.x.

Qin, C., Hu, J., Wan, Y., Cai, M., Wang, Z., Peng, Z., Yang, W., 2021. Narrative review on potential role of gut microbiota in certain substance addiction. Prog. Neuro Psychopharmacol. Biol. Psychiatry 106, 110093. https://doi.org/10.1016/j.pnpbp.2020.110093.

Qin, J., Li, R., Raes, J., Arumugam, M., Burgdorf, K.S., Manichanh, C., Yamada, T., 2010. A human gut microbial gene catalogue established by metagenomic sequencing. Nature 464 (7285), 59–65.

Qin, N., Yang, F., Li, A., Prifti, E., Chen, Y., Shao, L., Li, L., 2014. Alterations of the human gut microbiome in liver cirrhosis. Nature 513 (7516), 59–64. https://doi.org/10.1038/nature13568.

Queipo-Ortuño, M.I., Boto-Ordóñez, M., Murri, M., Gomez-Zumaquero, J.M., Clemente-Postigo, M., Estruch, R., Tinahones, F.J., 2012. Influence of red wine polyphenols and ethanol on the gut microbiota ecology and biochemical biomarkers. Am. J. Clin. Nutr. 95 (6), 1323–1334. https://doi.org/10.3945/ajcn.111.027847.

Ralevski, E., Horvath, T.L., Shanabrough, M., Hayden, R., Newcomb, J., Petrakis, I., 2017a. Ghrelin is supressed by intravenous alcohol and is related to stimulant and sedative effects of alcohol. Alcohol Alcohol. 52 (4), 431–438.

Ralevski, E., Shanabrough, M., Newcomb, J., Gandelman, E., Hayden, R., Horvath, T.L., Petrakis, I., 2017b. Ghrelin is related to personality differences in reward sensitivity and impulsivity. Alcohol Alcohol. 53 (1), 52–56. https://doi.org/10.1093/alcalc/agx082.

Ratajczak, W., Rył, A., Mizerski, A., Walczakiewicz, K., Sipak, O., Laszczyńska, M., 2019. Immunomodulatory potential of gut microbiome-derived short-chain fatty acids (SCFAs). Acta Biochim. Pol. 66 (1), 1–12.

Reddy, I., Pino, J., Weikop, P., Osses, N., Sørensen, G., Bering, T., Wortwein, G., 2016. Glucagon-like peptide 1 receptor activation regulates cocaine actions and dopamine homeostasis in the lateral septum by decreasing arachidonic acid levels. Transl. Psychiatry 6 (5) e809-e809.

Riggs, P.K., Vaida, F., Rossi, S.S., Sorkin, L.S., Gouaux, B., Grant, I., Ellis, R.J., 2012. A pilot study of the effects of cannabis on appetite hormones in HIV-infected adult men. Brain Res. 1431, 46–52. https://doi.org/10.1016/j.brainres.2011.11.001.

Rogers, M.A., Greene, M.T., Saint, S., Chenoweth, C.E., Malani, P.N., Trivedi, I., Aronoff, D.M., 2012. Higher rates of *Clostridium difficile* infection among smokers. PLoS One 7 (7), e42091. https://doi.org/10.1371/journal.pone.0042091.

Roy, C.C., Kien, C.L., Bouthillier, L., Levy, E., 2006. Short-chain fatty acids: ready for prime time? Nutr. Clin. Pract. 21 (4), 351–366. https://doi.org/10.1177/0115426506021004351.

Ruddick, J.P., Evans, A.K., Nutt, D.J., Lightman, S.L., Rook, G.A., Lowry, C.A., 2006. Tryptophan metabolism in the central nervous system: medical implications. Expert Rev. Mol. Med. 8 (20), 1.

Salavrakos, M., Leclercq, S., De Timary, P., Dom, G., 2021. Microbiome and substances of abuse. Prog. Neuro Psychopharmacol. Biol. Psychiatry 105, 110113. https://doi.org/10.1016/j.pnpbp.2020.110113.

Sandhu, K.V., Sherwin, E., Schellekens, H., Stanton, C., Dinan, T.G., Cryan, J.F., 2017. Feeding the microbiota-gut-brain axis: diet, microbiome, and neuropsychiatry. Transl. Res. 179, 223–244.

Saper, C.B., Chou, T.C., Elmquist, J.K., 2002. The need to feed: homeostatic and hedonic control of eating. Neuron 36 (2), 199–211.

Sayin, S.I., Wahlström, A., Felin, J., Jäntti, S., Marschall, H.-U., Bamberg, K., Bäckhed, F., 2013. Gut microbiota regulates bile acid metabolism by reducing the levels of tauro-beta-muricholic acid, a naturally occurring FXR antagonist. Cell Metab. 17 (2), 225–235. https://doi.org/10.1016/j.cmet.2013.01.003.

Schéle, E., Bake, T., Rabasa, C., Dickson, S.L., 2016. Centrally administered ghrelin acutely influences food choice in rodents. PLoS One 11 (2), e0149456.

Schellekens, H., Dinan, T.G., Cryan, J.F., 2013. Taking two to tango: a role for ghrelin receptor heterodimerization in stress and reward. Front. Neurosci. 7, 148.

Schmidt, H.D., Mietlicki-Baase, E.G., Ige, K.Y., Maurer, J.J., Reiner, D.J., Zimmer, D.J., Olivos, D.R., 2016. Glucagon-like peptide-1 receptor activation in the ventral tegmental area decreases the reinforcing efficacy of cocaine. Neuropsychopharmacology 41 (7), 1917–1928.

Schnabl, B., Brenner, D.A., 2014. Interactions between the intestinal microbiome and liver diseases. Gastroenterology 146 (6), 1513–1524. https://doi.org/10.1053/j.gastro.2014.01.020.

Schneider, E.R., Rada, P., Darby, R.D., Leibowitz, S.F., Hoebel, B.G., 2007. Orexigenic peptides and alcohol intake: differential effects of orexin, galanin, and ghrelin. Alcohol. Clin. Exp. Res. 31 (11), 1858–1865. https://doi.org/10.1111/j.1530-0277.2007.00510.x.

Schuette, L.M., Gray, C.C., Currie, P.J., 2013. Microinjection of ghrelin into the ventral tegmental area potentiates cocaine-induced conditioned place preference. J. Behav. Brain Sci. 3 (8), 276.

Scorza, C., Piccini, C., Martínez Busi, M., Abin Carriquiry, J.A., Zunino, P., 2019. Alterations in the gut microbiota of rats chronically exposed to volatilized cocaine and its active adulterants caffeine and phenacetin. Neurotox. Res. 35 (1), 111–121. https://doi.org/10.1007/s12640-018-9936-9.

Seitz, J., Trinh, S., Herpertz-Dahlmann, B., 2019. The microbiome and eating disorders. Psychiatr. Clin. 42 (1), 93–103.

Sharma, A., Lee, J., Fonseca, A.G., Moshensky, A., Kothari, T., Sayed, I.M., Das, S., 2021. E-cigarettes compromise the gut barrier and trigger inflammation. iScience 24 (2). https://doi.org/10.1016/j.isci.2021.102035, 102035–102035.

Sharma, A.N., Pise, A., Sharma, J.N., Shukla, P., 2015. Glucagon-like peptide-1 (GLP-1) receptor agonist prevents development of tolerance to anti-anxiety effect of ethanol and withdrawal-induced anxiety in rats. Metab. Brain Dis. 30 (3), 719–730.

Sharma, P., Murthy, P., Bharath, M.M., 2012. Chemistry, metabolism, and toxicology of cannabis: clinical implications. Iran. J. Psychiatry 7 (4), 149–156.

Shin, N.R., Whon, T.W., Bae, J.W., 2015. Proteobacteria: microbial signature of dysbiosis in gut microbiota. Trends Biotechnol. 33 (9), 496–503. https://doi.org/10.1016/j.tibtech.2015.06.011.

Shirazi, R.H., Dickson, S.L., Skibicka, K.P., 2013. Gut peptide GLP-1 and its analogue, Exendin-4, decrease alcohol intake and reward. PLoS One 8 (4), e61965.

Shreiner, A.B., Kao, J.Y., Young, V.B., 2015. The gut microbiome in health and in disease. Curr. Opin. Gastroenterol. 31 (1), 69–75. https://doi.org/10.1097/MOG.0000000000000139.

Shughrue, P.J., Lane, M.V., Merchenthaler, I., 1996. Glucagon-like peptide-1 receptor (GLP1-R) mRNA in the rat hypothalamus. Endocrinology 137 (11), 5159–5162. https://doi.org/10.1210/en.137.11.5159.

Sindberg, G.M., Callen, S.E., Banerjee, S., Meng, J., Hale, V.L., Hegde, R., Buch, S., 2019. Morphine potentiates dysbiotic microbial and metabolic shifts in acute SIV infection. J. Neuroimmune Pharmacol. 14 (2), 200–214. https://doi.org/10.1007/s11481-018-9805-6.

Singh, R.K., Chang, H.-W., Yan, D., Lee, K.M., Ucmak, D., Wong, K., Zhu, T.H., 2017. Influence of diet on the gut microbiome and implications for human health. J. Transl. Med. 15 (1), 1–17.

Sirohi, S., Schurdak, J.D., Seeley, R.J., Benoit, S.C., Davis, J.F., 2016. Central & peripheral glucagon-like peptide-1 receptor signaling differentially regulate addictive behaviors. Physiol. Behav. 161, 140–144. https://doi.org/10.1016/j.physbeh.2016.04.013.

Soga, T., Ohishi, T., Matsui, T., Saito, T., Matsumoto, M., Takasaki, J., Furuichi, K., 2005. Lysophosphatidylcholine enhances glucose-dependent insulin secretion via an orphan G-protein-coupled receptor. Biochem. Biophys. Res. Commun. 326 (4), 744–751. https://doi.org/10.1016/j.bbrc.2004.11.120.

Sørensen, G., Reddy, I.A., Weikop, P., Graham, D.L., Stanwood, G.D., Wortwein, G., Fink-Jensen, A., 2015. The glucagon-like peptide 1 (GLP-1) receptor agonist exendin-4 reduces cocaine self-administration in mice. Physiol. Behav. 149, 262–268. https://doi.org/10.1016/j.physbeh.2015.06.013.

Spencer, S.J., Emmerzaal, T.L., Kozicz, T., Andrews, Z.B., 2015. Ghrelin's role in the hypothalamic-pituitary-adrenal axis stress response: implications for mood disorders. Biol. Psychiatry 78 (1), 19–27.

Spencer, S.J., Xu, L., Clarke, M.A., Lemus, M., Reichenbach, A., Geenen, B., Andrews, Z.B., 2012. Ghrelin regulates the hypothalamic-pituitary-adrenal axis and restricts anxiety after acute stress. Biol Psychiatry 72 (6), 457–465.

Srivastava, G., Apovian, C., 2018. Future pharmacotherapy for obesity: new anti-obesity drugs on the horizon. Curr. Obes. Rep. 7 (2), 147–161.

Stevenson, J.R., Buirkle, J.M., Buckley, L.E., Young, K.A., Albertini, K.M., Bohidar, A.E., 2015. GHS-R1A antagonism reduces alcohol but not sucrose preference in prairie voles. Physiol. Behav. 147, 23–29. https://doi.org/10.1016/j.physbeh.2015.04.001.

Stevenson, J.R., Francomacaro, L.M., Bohidar, A.E., Young, K.A., Pesarchick, B.F., Buirkle, J.M., O'Bryan, C.M., 2016. Ghrelin receptor (GHS-R1A) antagonism alters preference for ethanol and sucrose in a concentration-dependent manner in prairie voles. Physiol. Behav. 155, 231–236. https://doi.org/10.1016/j.physbeh.2015.12.017.

Stewart, C.J., Auchtung, T.A., Ajami, N.J., Velasquez, K., Smith, D.P., De La Garza, R., Petrosino, J.F., 2018. Effects of tobacco smoke and electronic cigarette vapor exposure on the oral and gut microbiota in humans: a pilot study. PeerJ 6, e4693. https://doi.org/10.7717/peerj.4693.

Stievenard, A., Méquinion, M., Andrews, Z.B., Destée, A., Chartier-Harlin, M.-C., Viltart, O., Vanbesien-Mailliot, C.C., 2017. Is there a role for ghrelin in central dopaminergic systems? Focus on nigrostriatal and mesocorticolimbic pathways. Neurosci. Biobehav. Rev. 73, 255–275.

Stilling, R.M., van de Wouw, M., Clarke, G., Stanton, C., Dinan, T.G., Cryan, J.F., 2016. The neuropharmacology of butyrate: the bread and butter of the microbiota-gut-brain axis? Neurochem. Int. 99, 110–132. https://doi.org/10.1016/j.neuint.2016.06.011.

Stone, T.W., Darlington, L.G., 2002. Endogenous kynurenines as targets for drug discovery and development. Nat. Rev. Drug Discov. 1 (8), 609–620. https://doi.org/10.1038/nrd870.

Suchankova, P., Engel, J.A., Jerlhag, E., 2015a. Sub-chronic ghrelin receptor blockade attenuates alcohol- and amphetamine-induced locomotor stimulation in mice. Alcohol Alcohol. 51 (2), 121–127. https://doi.org/10.1093/alcalc/agv100.

Suchankova, P., Jerlhag, E., Jayaram-Lindström, N., Nilsson, S., Toren, K., Rosengren, A., Franck, J., 2013a. Genetic variation of the ghrelin signalling system in individuals with amphetamine dependence. PLoS One 8 (4), e61242.

Suchankova, P., Nilsson, S., von der Pahlen, B., Santtila, P., Sandnabba, K., Johansson, A., Jerlhag, E., 2016. Genetic variation of the growth hormone secretagogue receptor gene is associated with alcohol use disorders identification test scores and smoking. Addiction Biol. 21 (2), 481–488. https://doi.org/10.1111/adb.12277.

Suchankova, P., Steensland, P., Fredriksson, I., Engel, J.A., Jerlhag, E., 2013b. Ghrelin receptor (GHS-R1A) antagonism suppresses both alcohol consumption and the alcohol deprivation effect in rats following long-term voluntary alcohol consumption. PLoS One 8 (8), e71284. https://doi.org/10.1371/journal.pone.0071284.

Suchankova, P., Yan, J., Schwandt, M.L., Stangl, B.L., Caparelli, E.C., Momenan, R., Leggio, L., 2015b. The glucagon-like peptide-1 receptor as a potential treatment target in alcohol use disorder: evidence from human genetic association studies and a mouse model of alcohol dependence. Transl. Psychiatry 5 (6). https://doi.org/10.1038/tp.2015.68 e583–e583.

Suchankova, P., Yan, J., Schwandt, M.L., Stangl, B.L., Jerlhag, E., Engel, J.A., Leggio, L., 2017. The Leu72Met polymorphism of the prepro-ghrelin gene is associated with alcohol consumption and subjective responses to alcohol: preliminary findings. Alcohol Alcohol. 52 (4), 425–430. https://doi.org/10.1093/alcalc/agx021.

Sun, J., Chang, E.B., 2014. Exploring gut microbes in human health and disease: pushing the envelope. Genes Dis. 1 (2), 132–139. https://doi.org/10.1016/j.gendis.2014.08.001.

Sun, J., Wang, F., Hong, G., Pang, M., Xu, H., Li, H., Liu, J., 2016. Antidepressant-like effects of sodium butyrate and its possible mechanisms of action in mice exposed to chronic unpredictable mild stress. Neurosci. Lett. 618, 159–166. https://doi.org/10.1016/j.neulet.2016.03.003.

Sustkova-Fiserova, M., Charalambous, C., Havlickova, T., Lapka, M., Jerabek, P., Puskina, N., Syslova, K., 2017. Alterations in rat accumbens endocannabinoid and GABA content during fentanyl treatment: the role of ghrelin. Int. J. Mol. Sci. 18 (11), 2486. Retrieved from. https://www.mdpi.com/1422-0067/18/11/2486.

Sustkova-Fiserova, M., Jerabek, P., Havlickova, T., Kacer, P., Krsiak, M., 2014. Ghrelin receptor antagonism of morphine-induced accumbens dopamine release and behavioral stimulation in rats. Psychopharmacology 231 (14), 2899–2908.

Sustkova-Fiserova, M., Jerabek, P., Havlickova, T., Syslova, K., Kacer, P., 2016. Ghrelin and endocannabinoids participation in morphine-induced effects in the rat nucleus accumbens. Psychopharmacology 233 (3), 469–484.

Sustkova-Fiserova, M., Puskina, N., Havlickova, T., Lapka, M., Syslova, K., Pohorala, V., Charalambous, C., 2020. Ghrelin receptor antagonism of fentanyl-induced conditioned place preference, intravenous self-administration, and dopamine release in the nucleus accumbens in rats. Addiction Biol. 25 (6), e12845. https://doi.org/10.1111/adb.12845.

Szulc, M., Mikolajczak, P.L., Geppert, B., Wachowiak, R., Dyr, W., Bobkiewicz-Kozlowska, T., 2013. Ethanol affects acylated and total ghrelin levels in peripheral blood of alcohol-dependent rats. Addiction Biol. 18 (4), 689–701. https://doi.org/10.1111/adb.12025.

Temko, J.E., Bouhlal, S., Farokhnia, M., Lee, M.R., Cryan, J.F., Leggio, L., 2017. The microbiota, the gut and the brain in eating and alcohol use disorders: a 'Ménage à Trois'? Alcohol Alcohol. 52 (4), 403–413. https://doi.org/10.1093/alcalc/agx024.

Tessari, M., Catalano, A., Pellitteri, M., Di Francesco, C., Marini, F., Gerrard, P.A., Melotto, S., 2007. Preclinical study: correlation between serum ghrelin levels and cocaine-seeking behaviour triggered by cocaine-associated conditioned stimuli in rats. Addiction Biol. 12 (1), 22–29. https://doi.org/10.1111/j.1369-1600.2007.00052.x.

Thomsen, M., Dencker, D., Wörtwein, G., Weikop, P., Egecioglu, E., Jerlhag, E., Molander, A., 2017. The glucagon-like peptide 1 receptor agonist Exendin-4 decreases relapse-like drinking in socially housed mice. Pharmacol. Biochem. Behav. 160, 14–20. https://doi.org/10.1016/j.pbb.2017.07.014.

Thomsen, M., Holst, J.J., Molander, A., Linnet, K., Ptito, M., Fink-Jensen, A., 2019. Effects of glucagon-like peptide 1 analogs on alcohol intake in alcohol-preferring vervet monkeys. Psychopharmacology 236 (2), 603–611.

Tomoda, K., Kubo, K., Asahara, T., Andoh, A., Nomoto, K., Nishii, Y., Kimura, H., 2011. Cigarette smoke decreases organic acids levels and population of bifidobacterium in the caecum of rats. J. Toxicol. Sci. 36 (3), 261–266. https://doi.org/10.2131/jts.36.261.

Tomoda, K., Kubo, K., Nishii, Y., Yamamoto, Y., Yoshikawa, M., Kimura, H., 2012. Changes of ghrelin and leptin levels in plasma by cigarette smoke in rats. J. Toxicol. Sci. 37 (1), 131–138.

Tremlett, H., Bauer, K.C., Appel-Cresswell, S., Finlay, B.B., Waubant, E., 2017. The gut microbiome in human neurological disease: a review. Ann. Neurol. 81 (3), 369–382. https://doi.org/10.1002/ana.24901.

Tripathi, A., Debelius, J., Brenner, D.A., Karin, M., Loomba, R., Schnabl, B., Knight, R., 2018. The gut–liver axis and the intersection with the microbiome. Nat. Rev. Gastroenterol. Hepatol. 15 (7), 397–411. https://doi.org/10.1038/s41575-018-0011-z.

Tucci, S.A., Rogers, E.K., Korbonits, M., Kirkham, T.C., 2004. The cannabinoid CB1 receptor antagonist SR141716 blocks the orexigenic effects of intrahypothalamic ghrelin. Br. J. Pharmacol. 143 (5), 520–523. https://doi.org/10.1038/sj.bjp.0705968.

Tuesta, L.M., Chen, Z., Duncan, A., Fowler, C.D., Ishikawa, M., Lee, B.R., Kenny, P.J., 2017. GLP-1 acts on habenular avoidance circuits to control nicotine intake. Nat. Neurosci. 20 (5), 708–716. https://doi.org/10.1038/nn.4540.

Turnbaugh, P.J., Ridaura, V.K., Faith, J.J., Rey, F.E., Knight, R., Gordon, J.I., 2009. The effect of diet on the human gut microbiome: a metagenomic analysis in humanized gnotobiotic mice. Sci. Transl. Med. 1 (6), 6ra14–16ra14.

Turton, M., O'shea, D., Gunn, I., Beak, S., Edwards, C., Meeran, K., Lambert, P., 1996. A role for glucagon-like peptide-1 in the central regulation of feeding. Nature 379 (6560), 69–72.

Vallöf, D., Maccioni, P., Colombo, G., Mandrapa, M., Jörnulf, J.W., Egecioglu, E., Jerlhag, E., 2016. The glucagon-like peptide 1 receptor agonist liraglutide attenuates the reinforcing properties of alcohol in rodents. Addiction Biol. 21 (2), 422–437. https://doi.org/10.1111/adb.12295.

Vallöf, D., Vestlund, J., Jerlhag, E., 2019. Glucagon-like peptide-1 receptors within the nucleus of the solitary tract regulate alcohol-mediated behaviors in rodents. Neuropharmacology 149, 124–132. https://doi.org/10.1016/j.neuropharm.2019.02.020.

van de Wouw, M., Boehme, M., Lyte, J.M., Wiley, N., Strain, C., O'Sullivan, O., Cryan, J.F., 2018. Short-chain fatty acids: microbial metabolites that alleviate stress-induced brain–gut axis alterations. J. Physiol. 596 (20), 4923–4944. https://doi.org/10.1113/JP276431.

Vécsei, L., Szalárdy, L., Fülöp, F., Toldi, J., 2013. Kynurenines in the CNS: recent advances and new questions. Nat. Rev. Drug Discov. 12 (1), 64–82. https://doi.org/10.1038/nrd3793.

Vincent, C., Miller, M.A., Edens, T.J., Mehrotra, S., Dewar, K., Manges, A.R., 2016. Bloom and bust: intestinal microbiota dynamics in response to hospital exposures and *Clostridium difficile* colonization or infection. Microbiome 4, 12. https://doi.org/10.1186/s40168-016-0156-3.

Volpe, G.E., Ward, H., Mwamburi, M., Dinh, D., Bhalchandra, S., Wanke, C., Kane, A.V., 2014. Associations of cocaine use and HIV infection with the intestinal microbiota, microbial translocation, and inflammation. J. Stud. Alcohol Drugs 75 (2), 347–357. https://doi.org/10.15288/jsad.2014.75.347.

Waclawiková, B., El Aidy, S., 2018. Role of microbiota and tryptophan metabolites in the remote effect of intestinal inflammation on brain and depression. Pharmaceuticals 11 (3), 63. Retrieved from. https://www.mdpi.com/1424-8247/11/3/63.

Wahlström, A., Sayin, S.I., Marschall, H.-U., Bäckhed, F., 2016. Intestinal crosstalk between bile acids and microbiota and its impact on host metabolism. Cell Metab. 24 (1), 41–50. https://doi.org/10.1016/j.cmet.2016.05.005.

Wang, F., Meng, J., Zhang, L., Johnson, T., Chen, C., Roy, S., 2018. Morphine induces changes in the gut microbiome and metabolome in a morphine dependence model. Sci. Rep. 8 (1), 3596. https://doi.org/10.1038/s41598-018-21915-8.

Wang, H., Zhao, J.-X., Hu, N., Ren, J., Du, M., Zhu, M.-J., 2012. Side-stream smoking reduces intestinal inflammation and increases expression of tight junction proteins. World J. Gastroenterol. 18 (18), 2180–2187. https://doi.org/10.3748/wjg.v18.i18.2180.

Wang, R., Li, S., Jin, L., Zhang, W., Liu, N., Wang, H., Wu, C., 2019. Four-week administration of nicotinemoderately impacts blood metabolic profile and gut microbiota in a diet-dependent manner. Biomed. Pharmacother. 115, 108945. https://doi.org/10.1016/j.biopha.2019.108945.

Wei, X., Sun, B., Chen, K., Lv, B., Luo, X., Yan, J., 2015. Ghrelin signaling in the ventral tegmental area mediates both reward-based feeding and fasting-induced hyperphagia on high-fat diet. Neuroscience 300, 53–62.

Wellman, P.J., Clifford, P.S., Rodriguez, J., Hughes, S., Eitan, S., Brunel, L., Martinez, J., 2011. Pharmacologic antagonism of ghrelin receptors attenuates development of nicotine induced locomotor sensitization in rats. Regul. Pept. 172 (1), 77–80. https://doi.org/10.1016/j.regpep.2011.08.014.

Wellman, P.J., Davis, K.W., Nation, J.R., 2005. Augmentation of cocaine hyperactivity in rats by systemic ghrelin. Regul. Pept. 125 (1), 151–154. https://doi.org/10.1016/j.regpep.2004.08.013.

Wellman, P.J., Hollas, C.N., Elliott, A.E., 2008. Systemic ghrelin sensitizes cocaine-induced hyperlocomotion in rats. Regul. Pept. 146 (1), 33–37. https://doi.org/10.1016/j.regpep.2007.07.007.

Weltens, N., Depoortere, I., Tack, J., Van Oudenhove, L., 2019. Effect of acute Δ9-tetrahydrocannabinol administration on subjective and metabolic hormone responses to food stimuli and food intake in healthy humans: a randomized, placebo-controlled study. Am. J. Clin. Nutr. 109 (4), 1051–1063. https://doi.org/10.1093/ajcn/nqz007.

Wenthur, C.J., Gautam, R., Zhou, B., Vendruscolo, L.F., Leggio, L., Janda, K.D., 2019. Ghrelin receptor influence on cocaine reward is not directly dependent on peripheral acyl-ghrelin. Sci. Rep. 9 (1). https://doi.org/10.1038/s41598-019-38549-z, 1841–1841.

Wichers, M.C., Maes, M., 2004. The role of indoleamine 2,3-dioxygenase (Ido) in the pathophysiology of interferon-alpha-induced depression. J. Psychiatry Neurosci. 29 (1), 11–17. Retrieved from. https://pubmed.ncbi.nlm.nih.gov/14719046.

Wolf, M.E., 2010. Regulation of AMPA receptor trafficking in the nucleus accumbens by dopamine and cocaine. Neurotox. Res. 18 (3–4), 393–409. https://doi.org/10.1007/s12640-010-9176-0.

Wren, A., Seal, L., Cohen, M., Brynes, A., Frost, G., Murphy, K., Bloom, S., 2001. Ghrelin enhances appetite and increases food intake in humans. J. Clin. Endocrinol. Metab. 86 (12), 5992.

Wren, A., Small, C., Ward, H., Murphy, K., Dakin, C., Taheri, S., Ghatei, M., 2000. The novel hypothalamic peptide ghrelin stimulates food intake and growth hormone secretion. Endocrinology 141 (11), 4325–4328.

Wu, H., Esteve, E., Tremaroli, V., Khan, M.T., Caesar, R., Mannerås-Holm, L., Planas-Fèlix, M., 2017. Metformin alters the gut microbiome of individuals with treatment-naive type 2 diabetes, contributing to the therapeutic effects of the drug. Nat. Med. 23 (7), 850.

Wurst, F.M., Graf, I., Ehrenthal, H.D., Klein, S., Backhaus, J., Blank, S., Junghanns, K., 2007. Gender differences for ghrelin levels in alcohol-dependent patients and differences between alcoholics and healthy controls. Alcohol. Clin. Exp. Res. 31 (12), 2006–2011.

Xu, Y., Xie, Z., Wang, H., Shen, Z., Guo, Y., Gao, Y., Wang, K., 2017. Bacterial diversity of intestinal microbiota in patients with substance use disorders revealed by 16S rRNA gene deep sequencing. Sci. Rep. 7 (1), 1–9.

Xue, B., Kahn, B.B., 2006. AMPK integrates nutrient and hormonal signals to regulate food intake and energy balance through effects in the hypothalamus and peripheral tissues. J. Physiol. 574 (1), 73–83. https://doi.org/10.1113/jphysiol.2006.113217.

Yammine, L., Green, C.E., Kosten, T.R., de Dios, C., Suchting, R., Lane, S.D., Verrico, C.D., Schmitz, J.M., 2021. Exenatide adjunct to nicotine patch facilitates smoking cessation and may reduce post-cessation weight gain: a pilot randomized controlled trial. Nicotine Tob. Res. 23 (10), 1682–1690. https://doi.org/10.1093/ntr/ntab066.

Yang, J., Brown, M.S., Liang, G., Grishin, N.V., Goldstein, J.L., 2008. Identification of the acyltransferase that octanoylates ghrelin, an appetite-stimulating peptide hormone. Cell 132 (3), 387–396.

Yang, Y., Yang, C., Lei, Z., Rong, H., Yu, S., Wu, H., Guo, J., 2021. Cigarette smoking exposure breaks the homeostasis of cholesterol and bile acid metabolism and induces gut microbiota dysbiosis in mice with different diets. Toxicology 450, 152678. https://doi.org/10.1016/j.tox.2021.152678.

Yeung, A.W., Terentis, A.C., King, N.J., Thomas, S.R., 2015. Role of indoleamine 2,3-dioxygenase in health and disease. Clin. Sci. (Lond.) 129 (7), 601–672. https://doi.org/10.1042/cs20140392.

Yoon, S.-J., Pae, C.-U., Lee, H., Choi, B., Kim, T.-S., Lyoo, I.K., Kim, D.-J., 2005. Ghrelin precursor gene polymorphism and methamphetamine dependence in the Korean population. Neurosci. Res. 53 (4), 391–395. https://doi.org/10.1016/j.neures.2005.08.013.

Yoshimoto, K., Nagao, M., Watanabe, Y., Yamaguchi, T., Ueda, S., Kitamura, Y., Hattori, H., 2017. Enhanced alcohol-drinking behavior associated with active ghrelinergic and serotoninergic neurons in the lateral hypothalamus and amygdala. Pharmacol. Biochem. Behav. 153, 1–11.

You, Z.B., Wang, B., Gardner, E.L., Wise, R.A., 2019. Cocaine and cocaine expectancy increase growth hormone, ghrelin, GLP-1, IGF-1, adiponectin, and corticosterone while decreasing leptin, insulin, GIP, and prolactin. Pharmacol. Biochem. Behav. 176, 53–56. https://doi.org/10.1016/j.pbb.2018.11.001.

Ypsilantis, P., Politou, M., Anagnostopoulos, C., Tsigalou, C., Kambouromiti, G., Kortsaris, A., Simopoulos, C., 2012. Effects of cigarette smoke exposure and its cessation on body weight, food intake and circulating leptin, and ghrelin levels in the rat. Nicotine Tob. Res. 15 (1), 206–212. https://doi.org/10.1093/ntr/nts113.

Zallar, L.J., Beurmann, S., Tunstall, B.J., Fraser, C.M., Koob, G.F., Vendruscolo, L.F., Leggio, L., 2019. Ghrelin receptor deletion reduces binge-like alcohol drinking in rats. J. Neuroendocrinol. 31 (7), e12663. https://doi.org/10.1111/jne.12663.

Zhang, L., Reith, M.E., 1996. Regulation of the functional activity of the human dopamine transporter by the arachidonic acid pathway. Eur. J. Pharmacol. 315 (3), 345–354.

Zhang, Y., Kahng, M.W., Elkind, J.A., Weir, V.R., Hernandez, N.S., Stein, L.M., Schmidt, H.D., 2020. Activation of GLP-1 receptors attenuates oxycodone taking and seeking without compromising the antinociceptive effects of oxycodone in rats. Neuropsychopharmacology 45 (3), 451–461. https://doi.org/10.1038/s41386-019-0531-4.

Zhernakova, A., Kurilshikov, A., Bonder, M.J., Tigchelaar, E.F., Schirmer, M., Vatanen, T., Fu, J., 2016. Population-based metagenomics analysis reveals markers for gut microbiome composition and diversity. Science 352 (6285), 565–569. https://doi.org/10.1126/science.aad3369.

Zimmermann, U.S., Buchmann, A., Steffin, B., Dieterle, C., Uhr, M., 2007. Clinical study: alcohol administration acutely inhibits ghrelin secretion in an experiment involving psychosocial stress. Addiction Biol. 12 (1), 17–21. https://doi.org/10.1111/j.1369-1600.2006.00026.x.

Zoetendal, E.G., Akkermans, A.D., De Vos, W.M., 1998. Temperature gradient gel electrophoresis analysis of 16S rRNA from human fecal samples reveals stable and host-specific communities of active bacteria. Appl. Environ. Microbiol. 64 (10), 3854–3859. https://doi.org/10.1128/AEM.64.10.3854-3859.1998.

Zoli, M., Picciotto, M.R., 2012. Nicotinic regulation of energy homeostasis. Nicotine Tob. Res. 14 (11), 1270–1290. https://doi.org/10.1093/ntr/nts159.

CHAPTER

13

Circadian circuits

Mackenzie C. Gamble[a, b] *and Ryan W. Logan*[b, c]

[a]Molecular and Translational Medicine, Graduate Medical Sciences, Department of Medicine, Boston University School of Medicine, Boston, MA, United States; [b]Department of Pharmacology and Experimental Therapeutics, Boston University School of Medicine, Boston, MA, United States; [c]Center for Systems Neuroscience, Boston University, Boston, MA, United States

Introduction

Substance use disorders (SUDs) are associated with disruptions to sleep and circadian rhythms. There is a bidirectional relationship between sleep, rhythms, and addiction, whereby repeated use of substances leads to sleep and circadian rhythm disruptions, while chronic disruptions in sleep and rhythms contribute to substance use risk and dependence vulnerability. Repeated substance use and withdrawal can also lead to persistent, long-lasting effects on circadian rhythms that promote craving and relapse. In addition, prolonged circadian misalignment (*e.g.*, social "jet-lag" and shift work) or evening preference (*i.e.*, night owls) are risk factors for substance use and dependence. Substance use is also highly comorbid with other psychiatric disorders that are linked to sleep and circadian rhythm disruptions, including depression and bipolar disorder. For some suffering with mood disorders, substance use may be an attempt to ameliorate mood instability and sleep issues, further compounding mood and substance use-related health problems. Depression susceptibility also varies by season and peaks along with substance use during winter months, suggesting possible circadian involvement in seasonality of substance use and mood liability. Circadian rhythms also regulate diurnal variations in the sensitivity and responsivity to nearly every substance. For example, the hedonic value of alcohol, cocaine, and morphine peaks and troughs at different times of day, indicating circadian modulation of reward responses to substances. Thus, both the response to substances and the vulnerability to substance dependence are influenced by circadian rhythms.

Neurocircuitry of Addiction
https://doi.org/10.1016/B978-0-12-823453-2.00009-6

The role of circadian rhythms in the regulation of brain processes and behaviors associated with substance use and dependence is only beginning to be understood. The hierarchical organization of the system, from genes to organ systems, enables the circadian system to directly regulate or indirectly modulate across biological scales, including molecular, cellular, and neural circuit pathways that are involved in the transition to substance dependence. Additionally, the consequences of substance use on circadian rhythms may persist during abstinence and contribute to relapse. Approaches to mitigate the impact of substance-related alterations on sleep and circadian rhythms may be an effective strategy for reducing cravings and relapse propensity. Continued in-depth investigation into the biological roles of sleep and circadian rhythms in motivation, reward, and substance use and dependence will be useful for developing therapeutics aimed at treating substance use disorders. Here, we describe the anatomical organization of the circadian system and discuss the role of circadian rhythms in the regulation of neural circuits involved in reward, motivation, and addiction. In addition, we highlight the impact of sleep and circadian disruptions on craving, relapse, and dependence across drug classes.

Circadian rhythms

Circadian rhythms are ~24-h oscillations in nearly every biological and physiological process in the brain and body. The circadian system enables an organism to adapt to changes in the environment to ultimately optimize function and to promote survival. In mammals, the circadian system is hierarchically organized, like a symphonic orchestra, whereby the "conductor" housed within the anterior hypothalamus of the brain called the suprachiasmatic nucleus (SCNs), coordinates and synchronizes the "orchestra" of oscillators in the rest of the body (Fig. 13.1) (Reppert and Weaver, 2002; Yoo et al., 2004). Temporal coordination of central and peripheral oscillators across the body, along with alignment of these oscillators to the environment, are key to overall health (Logan and McClung, 2019). Alterations and disruptions to, or misalignment of, the circadian system has negative health consequences that contribute to the emergence, development, and progression of neurological and psychiatric diseases.

Functional and anatomical organization of the circadian system

The SCN receives distinct types of input, both photic (*i.e.*, light) and non-photic (*e.g.*, arousal, metabolic, sleep), that controls circadian timing and entrainment (Fig. 13.2). Non-photic inputs also modulate the effects of photic inputs to the SCN that help entrain to the environmental light–dark cycles. Environmental light is received by the retina in the eye then relayed via glutamatergic retinal ganglion cells through the retinohypothalamic tract and peptidergic projections from the intergeniculate leaflet (IGL) to the SCN (Hattar et al., 2002, 2006). Non-photic inputs, such as arousal, sleep-wake state, and locomotor activity, are mainly transmitted to the SCN via serotonergic neurons of the medial raphe nucleus, GABAergic neurons of the IGL, and dopaminergic midbrain neurons (Grippo et al., 2017; Rosenwasser, 2009; Rosenwasser and Turek, 2015). Both photic and non-photic information

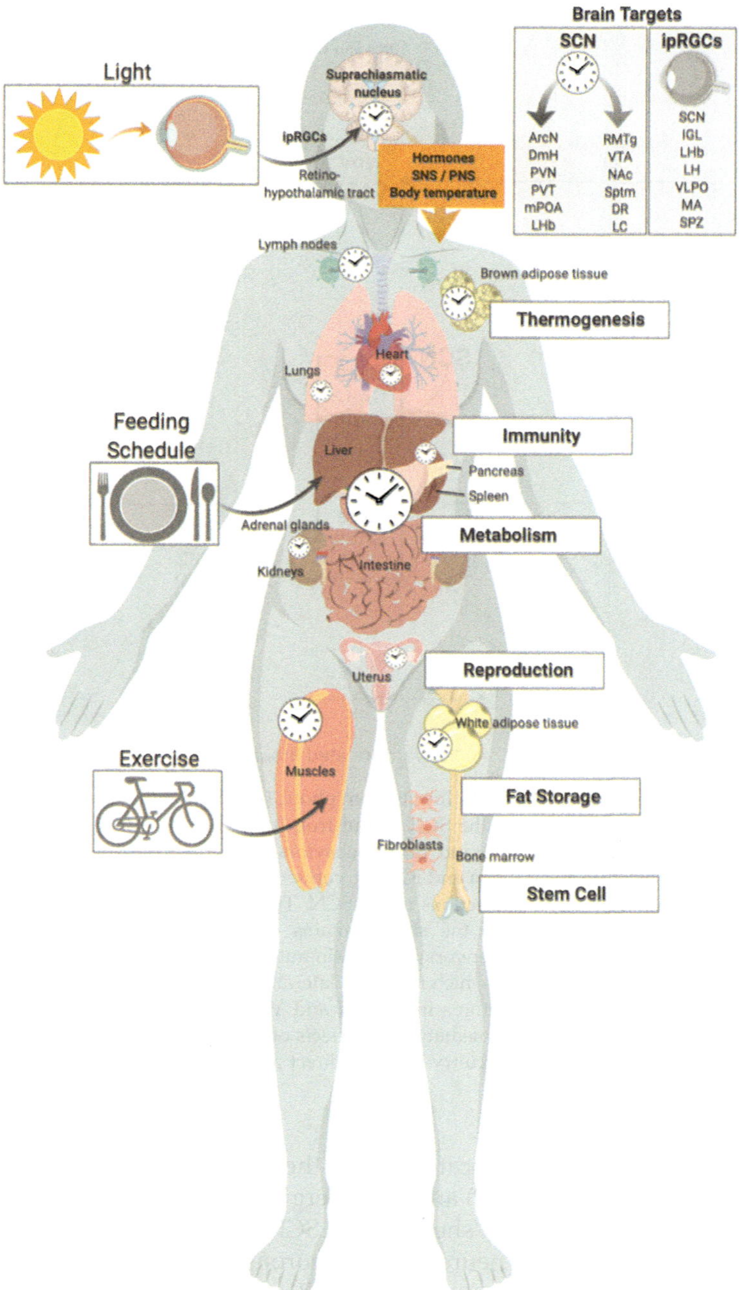

FIGURE 13.1 **The circadian rhythm system.** The circadian timing system is hierarchically organized, whereby photic information (*i.e.*, light) is received via the retina and relayed through the retinohypothalamic tract (RHT) to the suprachiasmatic nucleus (SCNs) to coordinate the timing of rhythms in the brain and body. The SCN communicates timing information to other regions in the brain and to peripheral tissues through direct and indirect innervation, and hormonal control. These pathways maintain coordination among tissues and synchronization to the external environment. Extra-SCN brain regions and peripheral tissues contain functional molecular clocks to maintain tissue and cell-type homeostasis and metabolic programming. Feeding schedules and exercise can also entrain central and peripheral clocks. Circadian rhythms are key regulators of thermogenesis, immune function, metabolism, reproduction, and stem cell development. *ArcN*, arcuate nucleus; *DmH*, dorsomedial hypothalamus; *DR*, dorsal raphe; *IGL*, intergeniculate leaflet; *LC*, locus coeruleus; *LH*, lateral hypothalamus; *LHb*, lateral habenula; *MA*, medial amygdala; *mPOA*, medial preoptic area; *NAc*, nucleus accumbens; *PVNs*, paraventricular nucleus of the hypothalamus; *PVTs*, paraventricular nucleus of the thalamus; *RMTgs*, rostromedial tegmental nucleus; *Sptm*, septum; *SPZ*, subparaventricular zone; *VLPOs*, ventrolateral preoptic nucleus; *VTA*, ventral tegmental area.

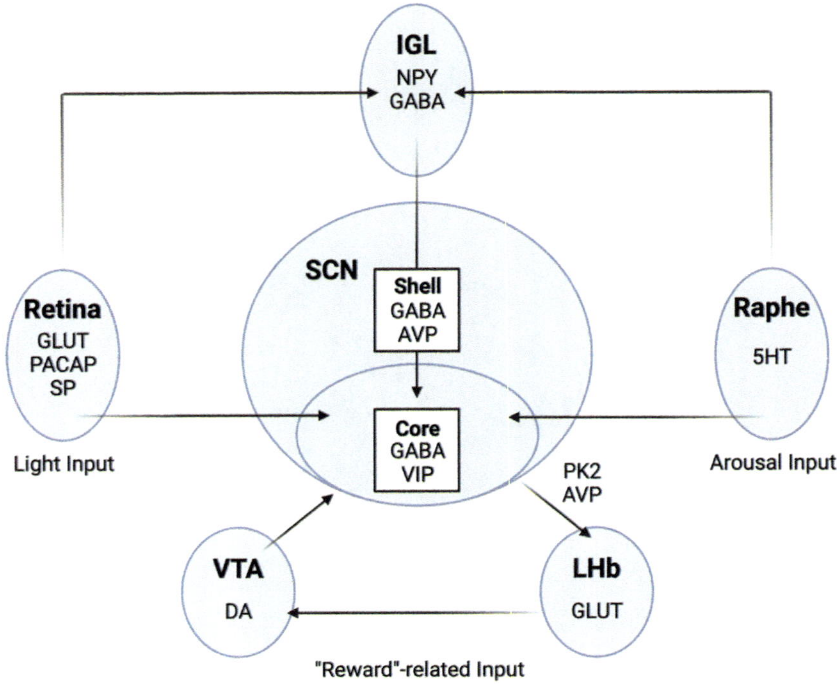

FIGURE 13.2 **Neural circuitry of the SCN.** Inputs from photic (*i.e.*, light) and non-photic (*e.g.*, food, locomotion, arousal, substances) afferents converge on the SCN. Input from the retina to the SCN is primarily glutamatergic (GLUT), while inputs that mediate arousal and other behaviors, are primarily from the raphe nuclei (RN) and serotonergic (5HT). Projections from the retina and RN also converge in the intergeniculate leaflet (IGL), which sends neuropeptide Y (NPY) and GABAergic projections to the SCN. The core of the SCN contains groups of vasoactive intestinal peptide (VIP) neurons, whereas the shell contains primarily arginine vasopressin (AVP) neurons, responsible for "coupling" the oscillatory networks to sustain autonomous rhythms in the SCN. Outputs from the core include prokineticin 2 (PK2) and AVP, which reach the lateral habenula (LHb). The LHb directly modulates the 5HT and dopamine neurotransmission rhythms in the RN and VTA, respectively. The VTA and RN send direct inputs to the SCN and may be involved in mediating the effects of substances on circadian rhythms and the role of circadian disturbances on reward neural circuitry through direct and indirect modulation of reward-related neural circuitry.

is relayed to the "core" of the SCN located within the ventrolateral portion, comprised mostly of vasoactive intestinal peptide (VIP) and GABAergic neurons (Rosenwasser, 2009). VIP and GABAergic neurons project to the "shell" of the SCN, the dorsomedial portion, which consists mostly of vasopressin (VP) neurons. VIP neurons in the core mainly synchronize the SCN to environmental light–dark cycles, while VP neurons in the shell are responsible for sending the timing information to rest of the brain and body. Together the core and shell are capable of self-sustaining rhythms of cell firing via coupling of network activity between core and shell (Mieda et al., 2015; Tso et al., 2017). In addition, individual SCN neurons are capable of independently generating rhythms of molecular and physiological activity (Flourakis et al., 2015). Astrocytes and microglia in the SCN and other brain regions are also essential to both rhythm generation and maintenance (Barca-Mayo et al., 2017; Brancaccio et al., 2013, 2017; Tso et al., 2017).

Through the regulation of hormones and the autonomic nervous system, the SCN coordinates and maintains rhythms in the rest of the brain and throughout the body. In the brain, the SCN directly projects to nearby hypothalamic and thalamic areas, including the medial preoptic area (mPOA), dorsomedial hypothalamus (DmHs), paraventricular nucleus (PVNs), paraventricular thalamus (PVTs), and lateral habenula (LHb). The SCN also indirectly projects to other areas of the brain through multi-synaptic connections, including the ventral tegmental area (VTA) (Cheng et al., 2005; Luo and Aston-Jones, 2009) through the mPOA and the nucleus accumbens (NAcs) through the PVT (Alamilla and Aguilar-Roblero, 2010). Thus, the SCN sends direct or indirect projections to several brain regions that are involved in reward and motivation (Figs. 13.2 and 13.3). Lesions of the SCN alter depressive-like behaviors in rodent models (Tataroglu et al., 2004; Tuma et al., 2005), possibly via SCN modulation of the VTA, LHb, and mPOA (Li et al., 2009). In contrast, SCN lesions fail to have any discernible effects on reward and motivated behaviors (Albrecht, 2011). However, SCN function is impacted by substance use. For example, the pattern and rate of neuronal firing in the SCN is affected by methamphetamine, cannabinoids, nicotine, and cocaine (Brager et al., 2010, 2011c; McElroy et al., 2009; Prosser and Glass, 2009; Prosser et al., 2008; Ruby et al., 2009a, b). Alcohol also affects the SCN by altering the timing (*e.g.*, phase and period) of circadian-dependent locomotor activity (Ruby et al., 2009a; Seggio et al., 2007, 2009). Therefore, addictive drugs may alter the temporal function of the SCN that in turn impacts other brain regions and tissues across the body that are directly or indirectly regulated by SCN-dependent relay of timing information.

Circadian rhythms in brain and periphery: role of the molecular clock

Almost every cell in the body expresses the molecular machinery required for rhythmic function. In cells, circadian rhythms are regulated across every level of gene and protein regulation including transcription and translation, as well as post-transcriptional (or translational) and epigenetic pathways (Bass and Takahashi, 2010, 2013; Fontenot et al., 2017; Nobuya Koike et al., 2012; Koike et al., 2012; Partch et al., 2014; Takahashi, 2017a, b). Through a series of interlocking, autoregulatory transcriptional and translational positive and negative feedback loops, specific molecular and cellular processes follow near 24-h oscillations (Fig. 13.4) . The positive loop is driven primarily by the dimerization of the transcription factors Circadian Locomotor Output Cycles Kaput (CLOCK) and Brain and Muscle ARNT-Like 1 (BMAL1) that are recruited to enhancer elements in gene promoters called E-boxes.

CLOCK/BMAL1 protein complexes promote the transcription of hundreds to thousands of transcripts. The transcription factor neuronal PAS domain-containing protein 2 (NPAS2) can also dimerize with BMAL1 to regulate circadian-dependent transcription. NPAS2 is

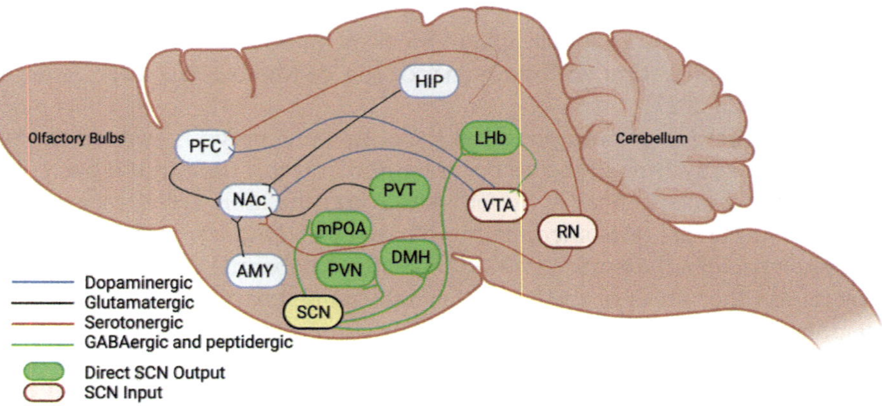

FIGURE 13.3 Links between neural circuitry of reward and circadian rhythms. The circadian timing system regulates reward-related neural circuitry at the cellular level through the expression and function of molecular clock machinery and at the circuit level through direct or indirect connections from the SCN. The SCN projects to other hypothalamic areas which then send projections throughout the brain. Other direct projections include the medial preoptic area (mPOA) and lateral habenula (LHb). Direct SCN outputs receive monosynaptic afferents and/or diffusible signals. The ventral tegmental area (VTA) and raphe nuclei (RN) send direct inputs to the SCN and may underlie the relationships between circadian rhythms and substance use and dependence. *AMY*, amygdala; *DmH*, dorsomedial hypothalamus; *HIP*, hippocampus; *NAc*, nucleus accumbens; *PFC*, prefrontal cortex; *PVN*, paraventricular nucleus; *PVT*, paraventricular thalamus.

preferentially expressed in the mammalian forebrain (*e.g.*, striatum) and peripheral tissues such as the liver (DePoy et al., 2021; Dioum et al., 2002; Franken et al., 2006; Garcia et al., 2000; Ozburn et al., 2015, 2017; Parekh et al., 2019; Reick et al., 2001; Rutter et al., 2001; Zhou et al., 1997). Several of the transcripts controlled by CLOCK/BMAL1-dependent transcription encode for the canonical circadian genes, *Period (Per1,2)* and *Cryptochromes (Cry1,2)*. Once translated in the nucleus, PER and CRY proteins build within the cytoplasm and form heterodimers that eventually translocate to the nucleus, interacting directly with CLOCK/BMAL1 complexes to inhibit their own transcription (Fig. 13.4). Several kinases control the timing of PER/CRY nuclear translocation and their degradation. Other transcripts regulated by CLOCK/BMAL1 encode for the nuclear orphan receptors, REV-ERB alpha and beta, and receptor-related orphan receptors (ROR alpha and beta), also feedback to modulate the transcriptional activity of CLOCK/BMAL1. For example, REV-ERB-alpha and ROR-alpha repress and activate transcription of *Bmal1*, respectively, via promoter response elements. CLOCK/BMAL1 complexes also control the expression of nicotinamide phosphoribosyltransferase (NAMPT), which is the rate-limiting enzyme of nicotinamide adenine dinucleotide (NAD+) biosynthesis from nicotinamide (NAM). NAM is modified by NAMPT to produce nicotinamide mononucleotide, which in turn is converted to NAD+ by several adenyltransferases (Fig. 13.4). Thus, NAMPT oscillations control circadian fluctuations in NAD+ levels, which in turn modulate Sirtuin 1 (SIRT1) activity and signaling. High levels of NAD+ promote SIRT1 activation. SIRT1 interacts directly with CLOCK/BMAL1 to deacetylate BMAL1 and inhibit CLOCK-dependent transcription. The rhythms of transcripts across

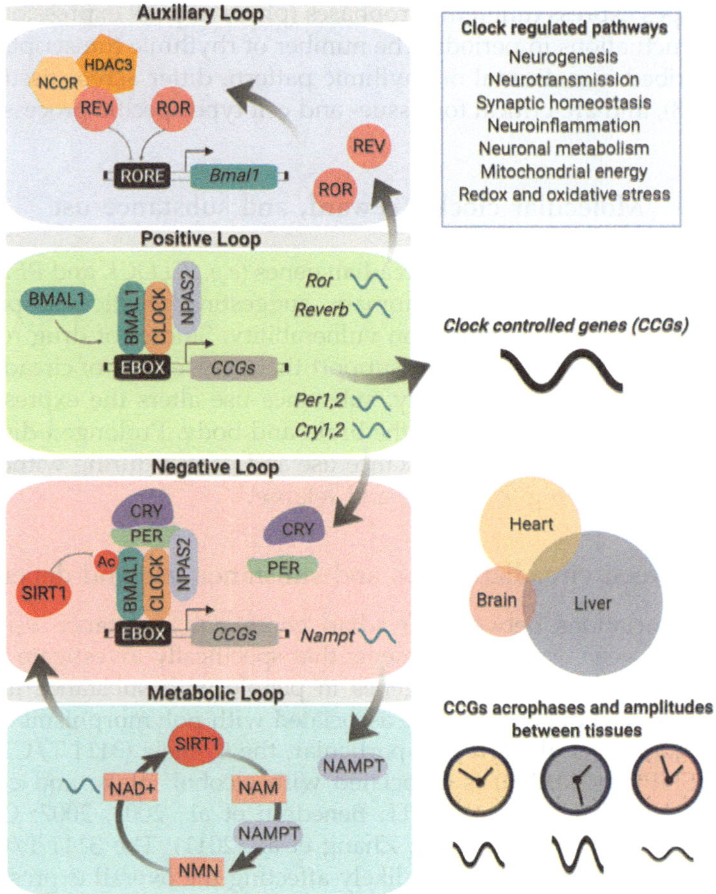

FIGURE 13.4 **The molecular clock.** A series of transcriptional and translational feedback loops that oscillate with a near-24-h cycle comprise the molecular clock in mammals. The positive loop is driven by the heterodimerization of either circadian locomotor output cycles protein kaput (CLOCK) or neuronal PAS domain-containing protein 2 (NPAS2) with brain and muscle ARNT-like 1 (BMAL1). These heterodimers bind to enhancer boxes (E-boxes) in gene promoters to regulate the transcription of clock-controlled genes (CCGs), including those encoding period (PER) proteins and cryptochrome (CRY) proteins. PER and CRY proteins accumulate in the cytoplasm during the circadian cycle, eventually dimerizing and shuttling to the nucleus to inhibit their own transcription, thus closing the negative-feedback loop. The auxiliary loop includes the nuclear retinoic acid receptor-related orphan receptors (RORα and RORβ) and REV-ERBs (REV-ERBα and REV-ERBβ), which are also transcriptionally regulated by CLOCK/BMAL1 heterodimers. REV-ERBα (REV in the figure) and RORα repress and activate the transcription of *Bmal1*, respectively, by inhibiting and activating the ROR or REV-ERB response elements (RREs). CLOCK/BMAL1 complexes also control the expression of nicotinamide phosphoribosyltransferase (NAMPT), which is the rate-limiting enzyme of NAD^+ biosynthesis from nicotinamide (NAM). NAM is modified by NAMPT to produce nicotinamide mononucleotide (NMN), which is then converted to NAD^+. NAMPT oscillations control circadian fluctuations in NAD^+ levels, which in turn modulate Sirtuin 1 (SIRT1) activity. High levels of NAD^+ promote SIRT1 activation. SIRT1 interacts directly with CLOCK/BMAL1 to deacetylate BMAL1 and inhibit CLOCK-driven transcription. Between tissues and cell types, CCGs and other molecular and cellular rhythms may be expressed with different circadian parameters, including phase, amplitude, and period.

tissues and cell types express different acrophases (phase of peak expression by time of day), amplitudes and fluctuations in periods. The number of rhythmic transcripts and which transcripts are transcribed in a diurnal or rhythmic pattern, differ across tissues and cell types (Ruben et al., 2018), and are critical for tissue- and cell type-specific processes and functions.

Molecular clocks, reward, and substance use

Mutations and variants in canonical circadian genes (*e.g.*, *CLOCK* and *PER2*) are associated with substance use and dependence in humans, suggesting genetic disruption of molecular clock components contributes to addiction vulnerability. Studies of drug reward-related behaviors in mutant and knockout animals support the involvement of circadian genes in substance use and dependence. Additionally, substance use alters the expression of circadian genes that lead to disrupted rhythms in the brain and body. Prolonged disruptions in sleep and rhythms occur during repeated substance use and persist during withdrawal and abstinence, potentially contributing to craving and relapse.

Associations between circadian genes and substance use and dependence

Most of the associations between circadian genes and substance use in humans are revealed by targeted gene arrays experiments that specifically investigate the occurrence of polymorphisms in canonical circadian genes in people with substance use disorders. For example, alcohol use and dependence are associated with polymorphisms in *CLOCK* (Kovanen et al., 2010; Sjoholm et al., 2010). In particular, the C allele (3111 T/C single nucleotide polymorphism (SNP), rs1801260) is associated with alcohol intake and consumption, and psychiatric disorders (Barclay et al., 2011; Benedetti et al., 2003, 2007; Chen et al., 2013; McCarthy et al., 2012; Soria et al., 2010; Zhang et al., 2011). The 3111 T/C SNP is located within the 3′ untranslated region (UTR), likely affecting the overall expression and stability of *CLOCK* leading to altered molecular clock function (Ozburn et al., 2016). A dominant-negative CLOCK protein in male and female mice (BALB/c background) leads to increased alcohol drinking (Renee Ozburn et al., 2013) and increased cocaine self-administration (McClung et al., 2005; Ozburn et al., 2012).

Other studies find associations between polymorphisms in PERs and use of alcohol along with other substances. For example, a PER2 SNP (rs56013859) predicts drinking amount and frequency in people who are alcohol dependent (Kovanen et al., 2010; Spanagel et al., 2005a, b). Variants in PER1 and PER2 are related to compulsive drinking in adolescents and heavy drinking in adults (Dong et al., 2011). Further, variants in PER1 and PER2 are also associated with stress-induced drinking (Blomeyer et al., 2013) and disrupted sleep (Comasco et al., 2010). Cocaine dependence is associated with a polymorphic repeat region in PER2 (Shumay et al., 2012). In mice, *Per1* and *Per2* mutations alter behavioral responses to alcohol, cocaine, methamphetamine, and morphine. For example, *Per1* and *Per2* mutant male mice (Brager:

B6·129S7-Per2tm1Brd/J, Gamsby: C57BL/6J, Perreau-Lenz: 129SvEvBrd/C57BL/6-Tyrc-Brd, Zghoul: 129SvEvBrd/C57/BL6-Tyrc-Brd) voluntarily consume more alcohol (Brager et al., 2011a; Dong et al., 2011; Gamsby et al., 2013; Perreau-Lenz et al., 2009; Zghoul et al., 2007). Flies with deletion of *Per* (or *Timeless*; PER binding partner) abolishes alcohol tolerance and metabolism (Liao et al., 2016; Pohl et al., 2013). In response to cocaine, *Per2* male mutant mice have increased locomotor sensitization, while *Per1* mutant male mice (mixed C57BL/6Tyrc-Brd and 129S7 background) do not exhibit sensitization (Abarca et al., 2002), like *Per* mutant flies (Andretic et al., 1999). *Per1* mutant male mice on C57BL/6J background also show reduced cocaine-induced conditioned place preference (Abarca et al., 2002), further supporting the differential roles of *Per1* and *Per2* in promoting or attenuating cocaine reward, respectively. *Per2* also modulates behavioral responses to opioids, as *Per2* mutant male mice (C57BL/6J background) display reduced morphine tolerance and withdrawal (Perreau-Lenz et al., 2010).

Other circadian genes including *Cry* and several kinases that phosphorylate PER and CRY proteins to modulate the pace of the molecular clock, casein-kinase 1 epsilon (*CK1ε*) and delta (*CK1δ*) (Eide et al., 2005; Meng et al., 2008), are involved in alcohol dependence and relapse of male Wistar rats (Perreau-Lenz et al., 2012). Collectively, studies in humans and animals provide connections between circadian genes and substance use, dependence, and withdrawal. Chronotherapies are effective for other disorders like depression, yet remain largely unexplored in the treatment of SUDs. This represents a gap in the field and additional investigations into the potential role of circadian genes in substance use are needed, particularly to assess whether targeting the molecular clock may be a viable therapeutic strategy for curbing substance use and the effects of withdrawal. For example,when male Wistar rats are subjected to a long-term drinking paradigm punctuated by repeated deprivation periods designed to model relapse-like alcohol consumption, pharmacological inhibition of CK1ε/δ, a post-translational regulator of clock genes, reduces relapse to alcohol drinking, but only when administered at specific times of day or circadian phases. This suggests pharmacologically stabilizing high-amplitude rhythms is therapeutically effective at reducing alcohol craving and relapse (Perreau-Lenz et al., 2012). Simiarly, it has also been shown to attenuate fentanyl seeking in a reinstatement model using Sprague-Dawley rats (Wager et al., 2014), however, whether this effect is specific to targeting of the molecular clock needs to be determined.

Substance use alters circadian genes in the brain

Substance use alters molecular, physiological, and behavioral rhythms. People with alcohol dependence exhibit reduced expression of circadian genes in peripheral blood mononuclear cells (PBMCs), persisting for at least one week into withdrawal (Huang et al., 2010). Using fibroblasts derived from skin biopsies collected from patients, the periodicity of fibroblast molecular rhythms is inversely correlated with severity of alcohol dependence and withdrawal (McCarthy et al., 2013). While only a few studies have examined the relationship between substance use, dependence, and circadian gene expression rhythms, animal studies provide insights into (1) the potential consequences of substances on molecular rhythms and (2) the role of substance-induced molecular rhythm disruptions in reward, craving, and relapse, as discussed below.

Alcohol alters the expression of circadian genes in nearly every tissue from rodent models surveyed to date. The extent of alcohol-induced alterations in circadian gene expression are contingent on frequency, dose, duration and route of administration of alcohol. For example, consumption of an alcohol-containing liquid diet over a period of weeks shifts the expression of *Per* rhythms in the arcuate nucleus of the hypothalamus and in the SCN toward the transition from lights on to lights off of male Sprague-Dawley rats (Chen et al., 2004), with minimal effects on other circadian genes in the SCN in male C57BL/6J (Filiano et al., 2013). Voluntary alcohol drinking for longer durations (*e.g.*, 6–12 months), reduces the expression of arginine vasopressin (AVP), VIP, and somatostatin (SST) in the SCN of male Wistar rats (Madeira et al., 1997). These cell types are critical for communication between cells within the SCN to maintain temporal coordination (Aton et al., 2005; Yan et al., 2007). Indeed, changes in AVP, VIP, and SST signaling persist into alcohol withdrawal in male C57BL/6J mice and Long Evans rats, suggesting this signaling pathway may mediate alcohol effects on circadian period and phase (Logan et al., 2012; Rosenwasser et al., 2005; Seggio et al., 2009).

Cocaine alters the expression of circadian genes across brain regions. In the hippocampus, following chronic cocaine administration (daily injection of cocaine for 14 days) increases the amplitude of *Per1* and *Per2* rhythms and reduces the amplitude of *Bmal1* and *Cry1* rhythms of C3H/HeJ male mice (Uz et al., 2005). Chronic administration of cocaine (daily injection for 21 days) also leads to blunted rhythmic expression of *Per1, Per2, Per3, Cry*, and *Bmal1* in hippocampus and several reward-related brain regions (Wang et al., 2019). This includes *Per1* expression in the NAc core and NAc shell, *Per2* expression in the NAc core, *Per3* expression in the NAc shell and VTA, *Cry* expression in the NAc core, NAc shell, and VTA, and *Bmal1* expression in the NAc shell and VTA. Cocaine administered daily via injection for seven days also alters the rhythms of *Per1* and *Per3* in the NAc of male C57BL/6J mice (Falcon et al., 2013) and *Per1* and *Clock* in the caudate putamen of male Sprague-Dawley rats following seven days of cocaine intravenous self-administration (Lynch et al., 2008), along with other genes in the striatum (Brami-Cherrier et al., 2020). Notably, 14 days of repeated cocaine administration enhances binding of the circadian transcription factor NPAS2 to the promoters of *Per1* and *Per3* in the striatum (NAc and CPu) in male C57BL/6J mice (Falcon et al., 2013), suggesting a mechanism by which cocaine alters circadian gene expression through activation of NPAS2-dependent circadian transcription in the striatum. Abolishment of *striatal Per1* rhythm by pinealectomy, also attenuates diurnal rhythms of locomotor sensitization to cocaine in C3H/HeJ mice (Uz et al., 2003), suggesting PER rhythms are involved in neural and behavioral plasticity induced by repeated cocaine exposure.

Substances such as methamphetamine and opioids alter circadian gene expression rhythms in the striatum and other brain regions. For example, chronic administration of methamphetamine (daily injections for six days) reverses diurnal peak expression of *Per1* and *Per2* in the striatum and alters the diurnal rhythm of expression of *Bmal1* and *Rev-erbα* in male Wistar rats and male mice, yet no effects on these genes were found in the SCN (Iijima et al., 2002; Nikaido et al., 2001; Webb et al., 2009; Wongchitrat et al., 2013). Additionally, methamphetamine repeatedly administered at the same circadian phase across weeks and months lengthens the period of locomotor activity rhythms and surprisingly restores behavioral rhythms in otherwise arrhythmic rodent models (Mohawk et al., 2009; Salaberry et al., 2017). Un-like other psychostimulants, including cocaine, methamphetamine seems to entrain molecular, physiological, and behavioral rhythms, presumably via a distributed network of oscillators in the brain that may be independent of the SCN (Tataroglu et al., 2006). Indeed, recent evidence shows that methamphetamine exposure reinstates dorsal striatal multi-unit neural activity rhythms after SCN lesion in male C57 B/6J mice (Miyazaki et al., 2021), although the mechanism underlying this effect remains unclear. Repeated opioid administration and opioid withdrawal enhance the amplitude of *Per* gene rhythms in the forebrain and frontal cortex of male Wistar rats (Ammon et al., 2003; Hood et al., 2010). Inhibiting PER1 in frontal cortex and striatum prevents morphine-induced conditioned place preference and morphine-induced activation of secondary messenger signaling cascades involving cAMP response element-binding protein (CREB) signaling in male BALB/c mice (Li et al., 2008). Thus, *Per1* may act as an immediate early gene activated in response to opioids that in turn leads to induction of CREB-dependent transcription of target genes known to be involved in cellular and synaptic plasticity (Barrot et al., 2002; Berger et al., 2011; Carlezon et al., 1998, 2005; Dong et al., 2006; Green et al., 2006; Guitart et al., 1992; Han et al., 2006; Lane-Ladd et al., 1997; Larson et al., 2011; Olson et al., 2005; Self et al., 1998; Wallace et al., 2009; Widnell et al., 1996).

Alterations of circadian gene expression by drugs of abuse are likely due to signaling pathways involved in modulating the activity and synaptic function of various neural cell types, including but not limited to glutamatergic and dopaminergic neurotransmission, and cellular metabolism. Glutamatergic signaling via N-Methyl-D-aspartic acid (NMDA) activation induces the expression of *Per1* and *Per2* via changes in calcium transients and CREB-mediated transcription in male 129/SvEvBrd, BALB/c, and C57BL/6J mice (Albrecht et al., 1997; Shigeyoshi et al., 1997). Strengthening of excitatory synapses in the striatum and other brain regions after chronic administration of cocaine or opioids may therefore impact the expression and function of circadian genes (Parekh et al., 2018a, b, 2019). Ketamine, a high affinity NMDA receptor antagonist and dissociative anesthetic, may reduce the amplitude of circadian gene expression by directly altering the recruitment of CLOCK/BMAL1 dimers to promoters at certain times of day (Bellet et al., 2011). Extensive crosstalk between dopamine signaling and molecular clocks has been established in the striatum: for example, activation of the dopamine receptor type 1 (D1R) induces the expression of *Per1, Npas2, Clock,* and *Bmal1*, while activation of dopamine type 2 (D2R) and type 3 (D3R) receptors reduces the expression of *Clock* and *Per1* (Imbesi et al., 2009). In male C3H/HeJ mice, the locomotor response to D2/D3 receptor agonists is circadian-dependent, implicating a role for molecular clocks in the regulation of this behavior (Akhisaroglu et al., 2005).

Interactions between opioid receptor signaling pathways and the molecular clock modulate reward and sensitization behaviors. Morphine enhances the rhythmic amplitude of *Per1* and *Per2* in several brain regions, including striatum, forebrain, and frontal cortex of rodents (Ammon et al., 2003; Ammon-Treiber and Hollt, 2005). Presumably through action in the striatum, PER1 potentiates morphine-induced conditioned place preference and locomotor sensitization through epigenetic regulation of extracellular signal-regulated kinase and CREB (Perreau-Lenz et al., 2017). Similarly, PER2 may potentiate the analgesic and withdrawal effects of morphine (Perreau-Lenz et al., 2010). Further dissection of the mechanisms underlying the relationships between opioids and molecular rhythms are needed to better understand the role of circadian genes in the diurnal modulation of opioid reward and dependence. Alterations in the expression and function of circadian genes, particularly those encoding the circadian transcription factors, including CLOCK and NPAS2, may have effects 'downstream' of the molecular clock, for example on synaptic and neural circuit functions that regulate substance reward, craving, and relapse.

Connections between molecular clocks, energetics, and neural circuits involved in reward

The brain consumes more oxygen and glucose than any other organ, relying mostly on energy substrates from the vasculature to fuel neural activity. Adenosine triphosphate (ATP) is the primary carrier of energy, secreted via calcium-dependent exocytosis from astrocytes and generated within neurons via glycolysis, lactate production, mitochondrial oxidative phosphorylation, and the tricarboxylic acid (TCA) cycle (Mukherjee et al., 2010; Parekh et al., 2018a; Roybal et al., 2007). In the brain, ATP synthesis pathways are regulated by circadian-dependent environmental (*e.g.,* feeding rhythms) and biological rhythms (*e.g.,* molecular clocks) (King et al., 1997a, b; Sidor et al., 2015; Spencer et al., 2012). For example, the molecular clock directly controls the transcription of several key metabolic factors including N. AD+ and other rate-limiting enzymes of energy substrate production (Marcheva et al., 2013; Peek et al., 2015; Ramsey et al., 2009), which may, in turn, regulate rhythms of extracellular ATP (de Goede et al., 2018; Marpegan et al., 2011; Shumay et al., 2012; Womac et al., 2009; Yamazaki et al., 1994). Diurnal variations have been demonstrated in ATP release, calcium homeostasis, and extracellular glutamate feedback to molecular clocks (Blomeyer et al., 2013). ATP can be co-released with neurotransmitters including dopamine, GABA, and glutamate, and may be involved in the circadian regulation of neurotransmission (Freyberg and Logan, 2018). Extracellular ATP binds and activates purine receptors on presynaptic and postsynaptic neurons and nearby astrocytes. For instance, ATP activation of presynaptic ionotropic P2X receptors enhances glutamatergic neurotransmission by increasing spontaneous glutamate release, whereas binding to the metabotropic P2YRs inhibits further release (Freyberg and Logan, 2018). P2X receptors also modulate dopaminergic, glutamatergic, and GABAergic neurotransmission in mesolimbic neural circuitry (Freyberg and Logan, 2018). Activation of P2X4 receptors by ATP increases midbrain dopamine neuron firing and extracellular dopamine levels in the striatum. Through actions at presynaptic and postsynaptic sites, P2X and P2Y receptors are involved in alcohol drinking and amphetamine sensitization. P2X4R deletion or reduced expression increases alcohol intake and preference while blocking P2Y1R precludes amphetamine locomotor sensitization in male C57BL/6J mice and various rat strains (Freyberg and Logan, 2018). Given the functional relationships between ATP, purinergic receptors, and molecular clocks, these findings implicate purine receptors as mediators of the impact of substances on cellular and synaptic plasticity, molecular rhythms, and energetics.

ATP is used to synthesize another purine, adenosine (Lindberg et al., 2015). Adenosine is a major neuromodulator of arousal, sleep-wake states, and circadian rhythms (Benington and Heller, 1995; Porkka-Heiskanen et al., 1997, 2000; Ruby et al., 2014; Saper et al., 2005; Strecker et al., 2000). Notably, adenosine is implicated in substance reward and dependence. Adenosine activates several receptor subtypes (A1, A2A, A2B, and A3) that are largely located on presynaptic terminals. A2A receptors are highly expressed in the striatum and hippocampus and A2A receptor expression is upregulated by chronic cocaine administration, including following intravenous self-administration, injection, and binge models, in male Fisher, Wistar, and

Sprague-Dawley rats (Bailey et al., 2005; Frankowska et al., 2013; Marcellino et al., 2007; Yang et al., 2011). However, A2A receptors in the striatum and hippocampus differentially impact cocaine behaviors. Deletion of A2A receptors in the striatum enhances cocaine sensitization, whereas A2A receptor deletion in the hippocampus attenuates cocaine sensitization (Shen et al., 2008; Soria et al., 2006). A2A receptors form heteromeric receptors with D2Rs on GABAergic striatal neurons (Marinovic et al., 2002; Pinna et al., 1997; Wydra et al., 2015), and when activated, reduces dopamine binding affinity at D2Rs, thereby enhancing GABA release and reducing cocaine-seeking behavior in male Wistar rats (Borroto-Escuela et al., 2016; Pintsuk et al., 2016). Thus, adenosine acts at A2A receptors to modulate dopaminergic and glutamatergic neurotransmission in neural circuits that regulate substance reward. Whether circadian rhythms, sleep-wake cycles or diurnal variations in arousal are directly involved in these processes remains an area worthy of future investigation, particularly relevant for understanding the associations between sleep, circadian disruptions and addiction.

Circadian variations in other energy substrates of the brain may control neural circuit function related to reward. Lactate is another major source of brain energetics. Astrocytes utilize extracellular glutamate to activate glycolysis, converting glycogen to pyruvate then lactate. Lactate is then transported to neurons, entering the TCA cycle to produce ATP, collectively fueling neuronal metabolism and energetics to meet and sustain activity-dependent demands (Yellen, 2018). Variations in extracellular lactate depend on sleep-wake cycles (Kalinchuk et al., 2003; Rempe and Wisor, 2014), suggesting circadian rhythms in neuronal activity and synaptic transmission drive or are driven by time-of-day dependent changes in glycolysis and lactate in the brain. Evidence for the latter is provided by data indicating that molecular clocks control transcription of the enzyme that catalyzes lactate production and that lactate transporters are diurnally expressed in the brain (Dioum et al., 2002; Kaasik and Lee, 2004). Preventing lactate transport in the brain reduces cocaine reward and cocaine-seeking behavior in male Sprague Dawley rats (Boury-Jamot et al., 2016; Zhang et al., 2016). NAD+ is also involved in neurotransmission and substance reward, and is an essential metabolic and redox factor and is important for brain energetics (Canto et al., 2015; Requardt et al., 2010, 2012).

Accumulating NAD+ enhances the deacetylase activity of SIRT1 and SIRT1 regulates the transcription of tyrosine hydroxylase (TH) via interactions with CLOCK in the midbrain, and thereby modulates dopaminergic neurotransmission in the striatum (Logan et al., 2019). SIRT1 may also control the postsynaptic response of GABAergic striatal neurons to cocaine and other substances (Ferguson et al., 2013, 2015, 2018), suggesting coupling between molecular clocks, energetics and associated metabolic factors, and neurotransmission important for mediating drug reward.

Circadian modulation of neural circuitry involved in substance reward

Almost every cell in the brain and body expresses the machinery required to generate and sustain molecular rhythms. Molecular clocks are important for directly or indirectly controlling cellular functions, including various aspects of brain energetics and neurotransmission, that aid in the communication of cells and circuits within and between brain regions. In addition, the "conductor" of circadian rhythms in the brain and body, the SCN, receives inputs from brain regions involved in arousal, reward, and motivation, and sends direct and indirect projections to brain regions that are involved in reward processing. Through these connections, the SCN may modulate reward and motivated behaviors.

The conductor of circadian rhythms: role of the suprachiasmatic nucleus (SCN) in the synchronization and coordination of circadian rhythms

The SCN is the primary circadian pacemaker, comprised of ~20,000 densely packed neurons in the anterior hypothalamus, above the optic chiasm. The SCN synchronizes rhythms to the environment, mainly by receiving photic input (*e.g.*, light) through the eyes via glutamatergic projections from intrinsically photosensitive retinal ganglion cells (ipRGCs) (Hattar et al., 2002, 2003, 2006). Neurons in the SCN core receive synaptic inputs from glutamatergic and peptidergic projections from the retina, GABAergic and peptidergic projections from the thalamic IGL, and serotonergic projections from dorsal and medial raphe nuclei. Inputs to the SCN from the IGL and raphe convey behavioral state signals to the pacemaker, including arousal, activity, and sleep-wake information (Rosenwasser, 2009). The SCN core projects to VP GABAergic neurons in the shell. Both core and shell SCN neurons project to other areas of the brain, that relay timing information to the rest of the body via humoral, paracrine, and autonomic nervous system outputs (Rosenwasser, 2009). The SCN conveys circadian signals to the rest of the body to orchestrate and coordinate clocks in peripheral tissues, organs, and cells. Other signals, such as food and exercise, can also entrain brain and peripheral clocks.

SCN neural circuit efferents

Circadian regulation of substance use and dependence involves connections between the SCN and other brain regions involved in reward and motivation. The SCN sends direct projections to the mPOA, dorsomedial hypothalamus (DmHs), and the LHb. Several of these regions then project to areas that are critical for reward processing. For instance, orexinergic neurons in the DmH encode information related to arousal, energy, and reward, and innervate to the VTA (Aston-Jones et al., 2001, 2009; Balcita-Pedicino and Sesack, 2007; de Lecea, 2012). The VTA is the major source for dopamine in the brain and controls various reward-related behaviors, in part, through projections to the ventral and dorsal striatum. Located within the ventral striatum, the NAc is a major integrator of emotional and sensorimotor information to guide goal-directed and motivated behaviors (Aleyasin et al., 2018; Anderson et al., 2017; Arango-Lievano et al., 2014; Atkins et al., 1999; Beitner-Johnson and Nestler, 1991, 1993; Berger et al., 2011; Brown et al., 2011; Cahill et al., 2016, 2017; Calipari et al., 2016, 2019; Damez-Werno et al., 2012; Dong et al., 2006; Dumitriu et al., 2012; Ferguson et al., 2013; Graziane et al., 2016; Liu et al., 2010; Mary Kay Lobo et al., 2013; Lobo et al., 2013; Ma et al., 2016; Terwilliger et al., 1991). The VTA also projects to the prefrontal cortex (PFC), involved in decision-making, cognition, and impulsivity, and altered dopamine signaling in the PFC is associated with substance dependence (Goldstein and Volkow, 2011). Major serotonergic areas of the brain include the dorsal and medial raphe nuclei which receive indirect inputs from the SCN (Deurveilher and Semba, 2005). Serotonin neurons and receptors in the raphe are involved in the regulation of drug reward, including cocaine-seeking behavior and craving, presumably through interactions with dopaminergic and GABAergic signaling in the NAc (You et al., 2016). Another region that projects to the

NAc is the PVT, which has reciprocal connections with the SCN (Alamilla and Aguilar-Roblero, 2010). The PVT is also involved in drug reward and drug-seeking behaviors (Colavito et al., 2013; Matzeu et al., 2014; Neumann et al., 2016).

Each of the SCN target regions described above has functional molecular clocks and exhibit diurnal and circadian rhythms in neuronal activity and firing (Logan et al., 2014). For example, neurons in the VTA display robust firing and gene expression rhythms *in vivo*, which are lost in *ex vivo* slices of VTA (Abe et al., 2002; Logan et al., 2015). Given the inputs from the SCN to the VTA, loss of molecular and cellular rhythms when the VTA is removed from intact neural circuits suggests the SCN may regulate circadian rhythms in the VTA (Luo and Aston-Jones, 2009). In support of this, ablation of the SCN by lesion significantly alters the expression rhythms of dopamine transporter and TH in the NAc, presumably from terminals of VTA dopaminergic neurons that receive indirect inputs from the SCN (Sleipness et al., 2007). Some brain areas, for example the LHb and mPOA, express high levels of prokineticin 2 (PK2) receptors that are targeted by PK2 peptide released from SCN terminals in those regions, then send their own projections to the VTA (Cheng et al., 2005; Li et al., 2009). Thus, PK2 release from the SCN and action at the receptors in areas that directly project to the VTA could be a major modulator of dopamine neurotransmission from VTA to NAc, and other striatal and cortical areas. Much work is necessary to further anatomically and functionally define SCN outputs, especially in relation to behavior, including reward and motivation.

SCN neural circuit afferents

The SCN receives multiple inputs from other areas of the brain. For example, input from ipRGCs through the retinohypothalamic tract (RHT) entrains the circadian pacemaker to environmental light–dark cycles (Rosenwasser, 2009). RHT terminals release glutamate, pituitary adenyl cyclase activating peptide and substance-P in response to photic stimulation (*i.e.*, light). iPRGCs also project to the peri-habenular and thalamic regions, including the IGL (Hattar et al., 2002, 2003, 2006; LeGates et al., 2014), which is mostly comprised of neuropeptide Y (NPY) and GABA neurons that project to the SCN to mediate the effects of arousal, locomotor activity, and benzodiazepines on circadian timing. Another major afferent to the SCN originates from the median raphe nucleus, providing a major serotonergic input to the circadian timing system to mediate effects of light and arousal on the SCN (Rosenwasser, 2009). Other inputs to the circadian system include cholinergic projections from the forebrain, noradrenergic projections from the brainstem, and histaminergic projections from the posterior hypothalamus (Rosenwasser, 2009). The SCN also receives dopaminergic inputs from reward-related brain regions, including the VTA of the midbrain (see next section) (Grippo and Guler, 2019; Grippo et al., 2017; Korshunov et al., 2017).

Midbrain dopaminergic inputs to the SCN

Dopaminergic signaling is involved in reward-seeking behaviors, and circadian rhythms and wakefulness (Isaac and Berridge, 2003; Luo et al., 2018; Qu et al., 2010). Substances that alter dopamine neurotransmission, such as methamphetamine, have been shown to alter circadian entrainment (Mohawk et al., 2009; Tataroglu et al., 2006). Investigations into the role of dopamine neurotransmission in circadian rhythms has revealed food-entrainable and methamphetamine-sensitive circadian oscillators (Blum et al., 2014; Pendergast and Yamazaki, 2018; Tataroglu et al., 2006), both of which seem to be independent of the SCN. However, selective activation of dopamine receptor subtype 1 (D1R)-containing neurons in the SCN leads to phase shifts of behavioral rhythms when the circadian system is most sensitive to light (Jones et al., 2015). Indeed, selective genetic ablation of *Drd1* in the SCN slows behavioral entrainment to light following a phase shift of the light–dark cycle, rescued by restoration of DRD1 expression in the SCN (Grippo et al., 2017). D1R-dependent signaling in SCN neurons is modulated by direct projections from dopamine neurons in the VTA (Grippo et al., 2017). Through these VTA to SCN dopaminergic pathways, seeking or consumption of food (Grippo et al., 2020) and drugs may alter SCN activity, leading to disturbances in the circadian system, and thereby affecting reward-seeking behaviors through a feed-forward loop. However, the direct roles of D1R-dependent signaling in the SCN in circadian rhythms and substance reward and dependence has yet to be established. It's plausible that chronic administration of substances leads to long-lasting plasticity in the SCN and associated circadian disturbances that contribute to craving and relapse behaviors (Brager et al., 2010; Brager et al., 2011c, 2013; Hammer et al., 2010; Lindsay et al., 2014; McElroy et al., 2009; Prosser and Glass, 2009; Prosser et al., 2008; Ruby et al., 2009a). However, the direct involvement of the SCN in midbrain dopamine circuit modulation of drug-related and reward-related behaviors requires further investigation.

Raphe serotonergic inputs to the SCN

The SCN receives direct and indirect inputs from the raphe nuclei. Rhythmic release of serotonin modulates SCN activity (Morin, 1999; Rosenwasser, 2009). Raphe nuclei also project to the lateral habenula, another brain region that receives afferents from the SCN and is involved in regulating circadian rhythms (Bano-Otalora and Piggins, 2017; Mendoza, 2017) and reward-seeking behaviors (Velasquez et al., 2014; Zapata et al., 2017). Serotonergic afferents to the SCN from the raphe mediate effects of arousal, wakefulness, and locomotor activity on the SCN and circadian system. Intriguingly, the raphe nuclei are involved in substance reward, seeking, and dependence behaviors: for example, median and dorsal raphe serotonergic neurons modulate compulsive cocaine self-administration and stress-induced relapse behaviors (Li and Kirby, 2016; Verheij et al., 2018). To date, there is limited evidence directly linking the raphe nuclei to SCN functions and circadian rhythms in the context of substance use and dependence. Most investigations have focused on projections from the raphe nuclei to known areas of reward modulation, including the lateral habenula and VTA (Nakamura, 2013). Given the role of the raphe in arousal, wakefulness, and other circadian-related behaviors, there is a strong possibility that raphe-to-SCN circuitry is involved in sleep and circadian disturbances associated with substance use, dependence, and withdrawal.

Environmental circadian perturbations and substance use

Changes in photoperiod, light–dark schedules, and light at night

The demand of modern society requires repeated adaptations to changes in environmental and social schedules. Repeated, chronic perturbations or disturbances to sleep and circadian rhythms because of social, work, and other demands negatively impact health. For example, chronic shift work, where an individual works overnight or alternating schedules between days and nights, has been identified as a public health hazard (Costa, 2010; Jehan et al., 2017). Higher rates of substance use and dependence have been reported in chronic shift workers (Trinkoff and Storr, 1998). Other environmental factors that have negative health consequences via circadian impacts include disrupted sleep schedules, prolonged and frequent light during the night, and irregular feeding schedules. It is likely that the combination of sleep disturbances and circadian disruptions contribute to the negative health consequences including the increased vulnerability to substance use and dependence.

Studies in animals have provided insights into the impact of circadian disruptions on drug reward and drug-related behaviors. Experimental manipulation of repeatedly shifting the light–dark cycle or adjusting the photoperiod (*i.e.*, number of hours of light and dark within a 24-h period) has been shown to decrease and increase reward-related behaviors in animals, depending on the species, experimental approach, substance, sex, and reward behaviors. For example, repeated shifts of light–dark cycles reduces voluntary alcohol drinking in Fisher and Lewis rats in both males and females (Rosenwasser et al., 2010), and increases alcohol intake in male Sprague-Dawley rats (Gauvin et al., 1997). Repeated phase shifting increases methamphetamine consumption in male Sprague-Dawley rats (Doyle et al., 2015). In a selectively bred line of rats that consumes comparatively high levels of alcohol, called high alcohol drinking male and female rats, repeated phase shifting leads to lower alcohol drinking in males and higher alcohol drinking in females (Clark et al., 2007), suggesting sex-specific effects of circadian perturbations on alcohol drinking in rats. In contrast, changes in photoperiod and repeated phase shifting has no measurable effect on alcohol drinking in male C57BL/6J and C3H/HeJ mice (Rosenwasser and Fixaris, 2013). However, mice under constant conditions, such as constant light or constant dark (24-hours of continuous light or dark), exhibit reduced alcohol consumption relative to mice on normal light–dark cycles (Rosenwasser and Fixaris, 2013).

Sleep alterations or manipulations also affect drug reward and drug-seeking behaviors. For instance, acute sleep deprivation increases both sucrose- and cocaine-seeking behaviors in male Sprague-Dawley rats and mice (Chen et al., 2015; Liu et al., 2016). Shorter photoperiods (*e.g.*, winter-like) reduce cocaine craving and relapse-like behaviors in male Sprague-Dawley rats, while longer photoperiods (*e.g.*, summer-like) have minimal impact on these behaviors. Interestingly, reduced cocaine craving and relapse behaviors persist after rats are returned to a standard light–dark cycle, suggesting that environmental perturbations of the circadian system lead to persistent changes in circadian and reward neural circuits (LeGates et al., 2012; Sorg et al., 2011).

Neural plasticity in reward-related neural circuits after circadian perturbations may be driven by the circadian oscillations of various hormones and peptides in the brain, including glucocorticoids (Liston et al., 2013). Glucocorticoid signaling in the brain regulates the entrainment and phase of circadian rhythms to perturbed light–dark cycles (Gibson et al., 2010; Kiessling et al., 2010). Changes in light–dark cycles may also lead to a phenomenon, called "neurotransmitter switching", whereby cells in the brain "switch" from primarily producing a main neurotransmitter to synthesis and release of another neurotransmitter: for example, the number of neurons primarily synthesizing and releasing dopamine in the hypothalamus (lateral preoptic, paraventricular nucleus, periventricular nucleus) are significantly higher during shorter photoperiods in rats, while longer photoperiods effectively induce these same neurons to produce and release somatostatin (Dulcis et al., 2013). These hypothalamic neurons that switch from dopamine to somatostatin production and release send projections to corticotropin releasing hormone (CRH) producing neurons in the PVN (Dulcis et al., 2013), suggesting a neural circuit by which changes in photoperiods, or the amount of light during the day, modulates the release of CRH and, by extension, the stress response. The impact of environmental perturbations on stress responses and their interactions with substance reward and dependence may occur via direct hypothalamic outputs to CRH neurons in the PVN.

Circadian "misalignment" and substance use vulnerability: a focus on adolescents

Among rodents, non-human primates, and humans, circadian rhythms begin to change during the transition from childhood to adolescence, mostly around puberty (Logan et al., 2018). During adolescence, the timing of sleep begins to shift later in the day accompanied by a delay in circadian rhythms (Randler, 2008; Roenneberg et al., 2004), coinciding with an 'evening' preference, or chronotype, and slower accumulation of homeostatic sleep drive (Carskadon, 2011). Adolescents are more likely to have less sleep, greater daytime sleepiness, and more sleep disturbances (Carskadon, 2011). Delayed sleep timing along with early school start times may contribute to sleep loss (Crowley et al., 2014; Touitou, 2013). Other factors that impact sleep include social pressure from peers and decreased parental restrictions and monitoring (Logan et al., 2018). In addition, more exposure to light at night further exacerbates sleep and circadian disturbances, particularly misalignment of circadian rhythms (Logan et al., 2018). Circadian misalignment during adolescence occurs when the biologically driven tendency for later sleep-wake timing conflicts with earlier sleep-wake schedules demanded by environmental pressures. Prolonged circadian misalignment likely has negative health consequences and may contribute to vulnerability for developing mood and substance use disorders.

Circadian misalignment is associated with increased substance use during adolescence (McKnight-Eily et al., 2011; Paiva et al., 2016; Sivertsen et al., 2015). Adolescence is a critical developmental period of increased risky behaviors and susceptibility for substance use in general (Chen and Kandel, 1995), and sleep and circadian disturbances may contribute to this vulnerability. For example, greater weekday—weekend differences in sleep timing contribute to circadian misalignment and are called "social jet lag", which has been associated with increased alcohol use and mood lability in adolescents (Hasler et al., 2017). Notably, pronounced circadian misalignment during adolescence predicted higher alcohol dependence scale scores (Skinner and Allen, 1982) two years later (Hasler et al., 2017), suggesting a relationship between sleep, circadian rhythms, and risk for chronic substance use. Several studies in adolescents have demonstrated that circadian misalignment impacts neural circuitry important for controlling mood and reward (Adan et al., 2010; Caci et al., 2004; Drennan et al., 1991; Hasler et al., 2010, 2012b; Merikanto et al., 2015; Miller et al., 2015; Tonetti et al., 2010). During a monetary reward task, adolescents who had a larger weekday—weekend differences in sleep timing had significantly reduced prefrontal cortical activity during both reward anticipation and delivery (Hasler et al., 2012a). Later sleep timing is also associated with enhanced ventral striatal activity during a monetary reward task

(Forbes et al., 2012; Holm et al., 2009). Sleep deprivation likely contributes to changes in prefrontal and striatal activity in response to reward in adolescents (Franzen et al., 2016; Germain et al., 2016). Together, these findings suggest that circadian misalignment and sleep loss impacts cortical and striatal circuitry in response to rewards. Future studies should parse the relative contribution of sleep and circadian rhythms to neural circuit function and their potential roles in other behaviors known to contribute to substance use vulnerability during adolescence, including risk-taking behaviors and impulsivity.

Chronotype impacts reward neural circuit functions

Chrono-type is a complex trait with genetic, biological, and environmental factors contributing to whether an individual has more of a preference for early or late parts of the day, often referred to as "morning" or "evening" preferences, respectively (Horne and Ostberg, 1976). A morning chronotype is related to a preference for activities during the earlier part of the day, with peak productivity in the morning. An evening chronotype is related to a preference for activities later in the day or evening, with peak productivity in the evening or night hours. Importantly, variants of circadian genes have been linked to chronotype in humans. For example, variants in *PER* genes have been associated with morning chronotype (Johansson et al., 2003), whereas variants in *CLOCK* have been associated with evening chronotype (Kennaway, 2010). A few of these circadian gene variants are also associated with psychiatric disorders including substance use disorders (Kennaway, 2010; Logan et al., 2014), suggesting genetic drivers underlying the relationships between chronotype and substance use.

Chrono-type also predicts the responses of several brain regions to rewards (Forbes et al., 2009). For example, glucose metabolism, a measure of brain activity during neuroimaging tasks, is increased in the afternoon and evening compared to the morning in the ventral striatum and PFC of adolescents and young adults (Buysse et al., 2004; Germain and Kupfer, 2008; Hasler et al., 2012b). In addition, an evening chronotype is correlated with attenuated neural responses to reward tasks, particularly during the day compared to the evening in adolescents (Hasler et al., 2012a). However, young adults (~20 years old) with an evening chronotype exhibit a reduced PFC response to reward anticipation and increased ventral striatum response to reward delivery, compared to individuals with a primarily morning chronotype. Notably, the reduced PFC response and enhanced ventral striatum response predicted higher alcohol use and greater risk for alcohol dependence (Hasler et al., 2017). Furthermore, an evening chronotype has important implications for mood disorders including depression and comorbidity with substance use (Giannotti et al., 2002), suggesting chronotype may be associated with vulnerability to comorbid psychiatric disorders. Collectively, these findings demonstrate robust relationships between chronotype and neural circuit reward function, as well as their contributions to the substance use vulnerability.

Loss of rhythms and loss of control

In humans and animal models, self-administration of rewarding substances closely follows diurnal and circadian variation. In nocturnal rodents, voluntary self-administration of alcohol and cocaine occurs mainly during the dark phase of the light–dark cycle (Aalto and Kiianmaa, 1986; Agabio et al., 1996; Boyle et al., 1997; Dole et al., 1985; Lynch and Taylor, 2004; Pasley et al., 1987; Roberts et al., 2002; Trujillo et al., 2011). Cocaine self-administration also follows a free-running rhythm under constant darkness conditions, suggesting that cocaine-seeking and intake behaviors are modulated by SCN-dependent mechanisms (Bass et al., 2010). In humans, alcohol consumption peaks during the early evening hours, likely due to social and work schedules. However, in people who are dependent on alcohol, cravings for the drug intensify during the early morning hours and ultimately contribute to increases in alcohol consumption during early to mid-morning hours (Danel et al., 2003). Opioid use and overdoses also follow a diurnal pattern, with peaks in the early evening and nadirs in the early morning (Eacret et al., 2020). Therefore, the circadian system may "gate" or modulate the timing of reward-seeking and motivated behaviors critical for regulating substance use. The transition from use to dependence is marked by a loss of the diurnal pattern or circadian rhythm of substance use and seeking. A loss of control of substance use is foundational to substance dependence and is predominantly characterized by intense cravings and binges. Extended, intermittent access to alcohol, for example, leads to increases in alcohol intake, primarily owed to marked increases in alcohol drinking during the light phase when nocturnal rodents typically consume less (Perreau-Lenz et al., 2012). Similarly, extended access to nicotine results in increased intake of nicotine during the light phase and reduced intake during the dark phase in rodents (O'Dell et al., 2007). The loss of control, or diurnal modulation of substance seeking that occurs over months in rodents, has important therapeutic implications, as pharmacological targeting of the molecular clock has been shown to effectively reduce substance intake by restoring the diurnal pattern of intake (Vengeliene et al., 2013). The timing of administration of the intervention, whether pharmacological or behavioral, could be beneficial in the treatment of substance use disorders.

Conclusions

Our understanding of how SCN afferent and efferent circuits modulate addiction-related outcomes is severely limited and requires more attention. The majority of studies to date have provide a foundation for characterizing the impact of drugs of abuse on circadian rhythms and molecular clocks in the brain and other tissues. The recent advent of new technologies will facilitate investigation of the role of circadian rhythms in addiction-related behaviors. More specifically, the field is increasingly able to examine the role of temporality of cellular, circuit and molecular processes important for controlling drug reward, drug taking and drug seeking. While the SCN forms direct or indirect connections with many brain regions involved in drug-related behaviors, the direct role of the SCN as a key node in the circuit, whether related to sleep, wake, arousal, or other circadian rhythms, is limited. Presumably, alterations in circadian rhythms that impact the SCN could lead to altered function of downstream brain regions that receive SCN inputs.

Another area that requires greater attention are sex differences and sex-specific mechanisms that may contribute to the role of circadian rhythms in substance use disorders and drug-related behaviors. For example, among chronic shift-workers, alcohol consumption is lower in women than men (Dorrian and Skinner, 2012; Dorrian et al., 2017). Further, there is much we do not know about the interaction of sex and circadian rhythms in regulating alcohol consumption in mice and rats. Changing light–dark schedules to model shiftwork in C57BL/6J mice results in increased alcohol consumption in females compared to males (Rizk et al., 2022). Interestingly, genetic ablation of the molecular clock specifically in the striatum leads to increased alcohol consumption in male relative to female C57BL/6J mice (de Zavalia et al., 2021). Sex-specific effects on genetic alterations on the molecular clock have also been observed for cocaine-seeking behaviors, by which NPAS2-deficiency selectively increases cocaine self-administration and reinstatement in female mice (DePoy et al., 2021). These few studies provide a basis and rationale for exploring interactions between sex, circadian rhythms, and drug reward, seeking and taking.

Growing skepticism as to whether sleep and circadian rhythms are primary contributors to substance use and dependence has been due, in part, to the overall limited evidence that directly links sleep and circadian-dependent mechanisms to various aspects of addictive behavior. The onus lies on researchers and clinicians in the field to clearly define the impact of sleep and circadian disruptions on substance use, dependence, craving and relapse, and to also investigate the potential of targeting sleep and circadian mechanisms in the treatment of substance use disorders. A smattering of preclinical findings strongly suggests that disruption of circadian rhythms, either via environmental changes or genetic ablations of circadian genes, provide a foundation for investigating relationships between circadian rhythms and addiction.

References

Aalto, J., Kiianmaa, K., 1986. REM-sleep deprivation-induced increase in ethanol intake: role of brain monoaminergic neurons. Alcohol 3 (6), 377–381. https://www.ncbi.nlm.nih.gov/pubmed/3814349.

Abarca, C., Albrecht, U., Spanagel, R., 2002. Cocaine sensitization and reward are under the influence of circadian genes and rhythm. Proc. Natl. Acad. Sci. U.S.A. 99 (13), 9026–9030. https://doi.org/10.1073/pnas.142039099.

Abe, M., Herzog, E.D., Yamazaki, S., Straume, M., Tei, H., Sakaki, Y., Menaker, M., Block, G.D., 2002. Circadian rhythms in isolated brain regions. J. Neurosci. 22 (1), 350–356. https://www.ncbi.nlm.nih.gov/pubmed/11756518.

Adan, A., Natale, V., Caci, H., Prat, G., 2010. Relationship between circadian typology and functional and dysfunctional impulsivity. Chronobiol. Int. 27 (3), 606–619. https://doi.org/10.3109/07420521003663827, 10.3109/07420521003663827.

Agabio, R., Cortis, G., Fadda, F., Gessa, G.L., Lobina, C., Reali, R., Colombo, G., 1996. Circadian drinking pattern of Sardinian alcohol-preferring rats. Alcohol Alcohol 31 (4), 385–388. https://doi.org/10.1093/oxfordjournals.alcalc.a008166.

Akhisaroglu, M., Kurtuncu, M., Manev, H., Uz, T., 2005. Diurnal rhythms in quinpirole-induced locomotor behaviors and striatal D2/D3 receptor levels inmice. Pharmacol. Biochem. Behav. 80 (3), 371–377. https://doi.org/10.1016/j.pbb.2004.11.016.

Alamilla, J., Aguilar-Roblero, R., 2010. Glutamate and GABA neurotransmission from the paraventricular thalamus to the suprachiasmatic nuclei in the rat. J. Biol. Rhythm. 25 (1), 28–36. https://doi.org/10.1177/0748730409357771, 10.1177/0748730409357771.

Albrecht, U., 2011. The circadian clock, reward, and memory. Front. Mol. Neurosci. 4, 41. https://doi.org/10.3389/fnmol.2011.00041.

Albrecht, U., Sun, Z.S., Eichele, G., Lee, C.C., 1997. A differential response of two putative mammalian circadian regulators, mper1 and mper2, to light. Cell 91 (7), 1055–1064. https://doi.org/10.1016/s0092-8674(00)80495-x.

Aleyasin, H., Flanigan, M.E., Golden, S.A., Takahashi, A., Menard, C., Pfau, M.L., Multer, J., Pina, J., McCabe, K.A., Bhatti, N., Hodes, G.E., Heshmati, M., Neve, R.L., Nestler, E.J., Heller, E.A., Russo, S.J., 2018. Cell-type-specific role of DeltaFosB in nucleus accumbens in modulating intermale aggression. J. Neurosci. 38 (26), 5913–5924. https://doi.org/10.1523/JNEUROSCI.0296-18.2018, 10.1523/JNEUROSCI.0296-18.2018. Epub 2018 Jun 11.

Ammon, S., Mayer, P., Riechert, U., Tischmeyer, H., Hollt, V., 2003. Microarray analysis of genes expressed in the frontal cortex of rats chronically treated with morphine and after naloxone precipitated withdrawal. Brain Res. Mol. Brain Res. 112 (1–2), 113–125. https://www.ncbi.nlm.nih.gov/pubmed/12670709.

Ammon-Treiber, S., Hollt, V., 2005. Morphine-induced changes of gene expression in the brain. Addiction Biol. 10 (1), 81–89. https://doi.org/10.1080/13556210412331308994, 10.1080/13556210412331308994.

Anderson, E.M., Wissman, A.M., Chemplanikal, J., Buzin, N., Guzman, D., Larson, E.B., Neve, R.L., Nestler, E.J., Cowan, C.W., Self, D.W., 2017. BDNF-TrkB controls cocaine-induced dendritic spines in rodent nucleus accumbens dissociated from increases in addictive behaviors. Proc. Natl. Acad. Sci. U.S.A. 114 (35), 9469–9474. https://doi.org/10.1073/pnas.1702441114, 10.1073/pnas.1702441114. Epub 2017 Aug 14.

Andretic, R., Chaney, S., Hirsh, J., 1999. Requirement of circadian genes for cocaine sensitization in Drosophila. Science 285 (5430), 1066–1068. https://www.ncbi.nlm.nih.gov/pubmed/10446052.

Arango-Lievano, M., Schwarz, J.T., Vernov, M., Wilkinson, M.B., Bradbury, K., Feliz, A., Marongiu, R., Gelfand, Y., Warner-Schmidt, J., Nestler, E.J., Greengard, P., Russo, S.J., Kaplitt, M.G., 2014. Cell-type specific expression of p11 controls cocaine reward. Biol. Psychiatr. 76 (10), 794–801. https://doi.org/10.1016/j.biopsych.2014.02.012. https://pubmed.ncbi.nlm.nih.gov/30682435/. https://doi.org/S0006-3223(14)00107-3 [pii].

Aston-Jones, G., Chen, S., Zhu, Y., Oshinsky, M.L., 2001. A neural circuit for circadian regulation of arousal. Nat. Neurosci. 4 (7), 732–738. https://doi.org/10.1038/89522.

Aston-Jones, G., Smith, R.J., Moorman, D.E., Richardson, K.A., 2009. Role of lateral hypothalamic orexin neurons in reward processing and addiction. Neuropharmacology 56 (Suppl. 1), 112–121. https://doi.org/10.1016/j.neuropharm.2008.06.060.

Atkins, J.B., Chlan-Fourney, J., Nye, H.E., Hiroi, N., Carlezon Jr., W.A., Nestler, E.J., 1999. Region-specific induction of deltaFosB by repeated administration of typical versus atypical antipsychotic drugs. Synapse 33 (2), 118–128. https://doi.org/10.1002/(SICI)1098-2396(199908)33:2<118::AID-SYN2>3.0.CO;2-L.

Aton, S.J., Colwell, C.S., Harmar, A.J., Waschek, J., Herzog, E.D., 2005. Vasoactive intestinal polypeptide mediates circadian rhythmicity and synchrony in mammalian clock neurons. Nat. Neurosci. 8 (4), 476–483. https://doi.org/10.1038/nn1419.

Bailey, A., Gianotti, R., Ho, A., Kreek, M.J., 2005. Persistent upregulation of mu-opioid, but not adenosine, receptors in brains of long-term withdrawn escalating dose "binge" cocaine-treated rats. Synapse 57 (3), 160–166. https://doi.org/10.1002/syn.20168.

Balcita-Pedicino, J.J., Sesack, S.R., 2007. Orexin axons in the rat ventral tegmental area synapse infrequently onto dopamine and gamma-aminobutyric acid neurons. J. Comp. Neurol. 503 (5), 668–684. https://doi.org/10.1002/cne.21420.

Bano-Otalora, B., Piggins, H.D., 2017. Contributions of the lateral habenula to circadian timekeeping. Pharmacol. Biochem. Behav. 162, 46–54. https://doi.org/10.1016/j.pbb.2017.06.007.

Barca-Mayo, O., Pons-Espinal, M., Follert, P., Armirotti, A., Berdondini, L., De Pietri Tonelli, D., 2017. Astrocyte deletion of Bmal1 alters daily locomotor activity and cognitive functions via GABA signalling. Nat. Commun. 8, 14336. https://doi.org/10.1038/ncomms14336.

Barclay, N.L., Eley, T.C., Mill, J., Wong, C.C., Zavos, H.M., Archer, S.N., Gregory, A.M., 2011. Sleep quality and diurnal preference in a sample of young adults: associations with 5HTTLPR, PER3, and CLOCK 3111. Am. J. Med. Genet. B Neuropsychiatr. Genet. 156B (6), 681–690. https://doi.org/10.1002/ajmg.b.31210, 10.1002/ajmg.b.31210. Epub 2011 Jun 28.

Barrot, M., Olivier, J.D., Perrotti, L.I., DiLeone, R.J., Berton, O., Eisch, A.J., Impey, S., Storm, D.R., Neve, R.L., Yin, J.C., Zachariou, V., Nestler, E.J., 2002. CREB activity in the nucleus accumbens shell controls gating of behavioral responses to emotional stimuli. Proc. Natl. Acad. Sci. U.S.A. 99 (17), 11435–11440. https://doi.org/10.1073/pnas.172091899.

Bass, J., Takahashi, J.S., 2010. Circadian integration of metabolism and energetics. Science 330 (6009), 1349–1354. https://doi.org/10.1126/science.1195027.

Bass, C.E., Jansen, H.T., Roberts, D.C., 2010. Free-running rhythms of cocaine self-administration in rats held under constant lighting conditions. Chronobiol. Int. 27 (3), 535–548. https://doi.org/10.3109/07420521003664221.

Beitner-Johnson, D., Nestler, E.J., 1991. Morphine and cocaine exert common chronic actions on tyrosine hydroxylase in dopaminergic brain reward regions. J. Neurochem. 57 (1), 344–347. https://www.ncbi.nlm.nih.gov/pubmed/1675665.

Beitner-Johnson, D., Nestler, E.J., 1993. Chronic morphine impairs axoplasmic transport in the rat mesolimbic dopamine system. Neuroreport 5 (1), 57–60. https://www.ncbi.nlm.nih.gov/pubmed/7506589.

Bellet, M.M., Vawter, M.P., Bunney, B.G., Bunney, W.E., Sassone-Corsi, P., 2011. Ketamine influences CLOCK:-BMAL1 function leading to altered circadian gene expression. PLoS One 6 (8), e23982. https://doi.org/10.1371/journal.pone.0023982, 10.1371/journal.pone.0023982. Epub 2011 Aug 24.

Benedetti, F., Serretti, A., Colombo, C., Barbini, B., Lorenzi, C., Campori, E., Smeraldi, E., 2003. Influence of CLOCK gene polymorphism on circadian mood fluctuation and illness recurrence in bipolar depression. Am. J. Med. Genet. B Neuropsychiatr. Genet. 123B (1), 23–26. https://doi.org/10.1002/ajmg.b.20038.

Benedetti, F., Dallaspezia, S., Fulgosi, M.C., Lorenzi, C., Serretti, A., Barbini, B., Colombo, C., Smeraldi, E., 2007. Actimetric evidence that CLOCK 3111 T/C SNP influences sleep and activity patterns in patients affected by bipolar depression. Am. J. Med. Genet. B Neuropsychiatr. Genet. 144B (5), 631–635. https://doi.org/10.1002/ajmg.b.30475.

Benington, J.H., Heller, H.C., 1995. Restoration of brain energy metabolism as the function of sleep. Prog. Neurobiol. 45 (4), 347–360. https://doi.org/10.1016/0301-0082(94)00057-o.

Berger, A.K., Green, T., Siegel, S.J., Nestler, E.J., Hammer Jr., R.P., 2011. cAMP response element binding protein phosphorylation in nucleus accumbens underlies sustained recovery of sensorimotor gating following repeated D-like receptor agonist treatment in rats. Biol. Psychiatr. 69 (3), 288–294. https://doi.org/10.1016/j.biopsych.2010.08.032.

Blomeyer, D., Buchmann, A.F., Lascorz, J., Zimmermann, U.S., Esser, G., Desrivieres, S., Schmidt, M.H., Banaschewski, T., Schumann, G., Laucht, M., 2013. Association of PER2 genotype and stressful life events with alcohol drinking in young adults. PLoS One 8 (3), e59136. https://doi.org/10.1371/journal.pone.0059136, 10.1371/journal.pone.0059136. Epub 2013 Mar 22.

Blum, I.D., Zhu, L., Moquin, L., Kokoeva, M.V., Gratton, A., Giros, B., Storch, K.F., 2014. A highly tunable dopaminergic oscillator generates ultradian rhythms of behavioral arousal. Elife 3. https://doi.org/10.7554/eLife.05105.

Borroto-Escuela, D.O., Wydra, K., Pintsuk, J., Narvaez, M., Corrales, F., Zaniewska, M., Agnati, L.F., Franco, R., Tanganelli, S., Ferraro, L., Filip, M., Fuxe, K., 2016. Understanding the functional plasticity in neural networks of the basal Ganglia in cocaine use disorder: a role for allosteric receptor-receptor interactions in A2A-D2 heteroreceptor complexes. Neural Plast. 2016, 4827268. https://doi.org/10.1155/2016/4827268.

Boury-Jamot, B., Carrard, A., Martin, J.L., Halfon, O., Magistretti, P.J., Boutrel, B., 2016. Disrupting astrocyte-neuron lactate transfer persistently reduces conditioned responses to cocaine. Mol. Psychiatr. 21 (8), 1070–1076. https://doi.org/10.1038/mp.2015.157.

Boyle, A.E., Smith, B.R., Amit, Z., 1997. A descriptive analysis of the structure and temporal pattern of voluntary ethanol intake within an acquisition paradigm. J. Stud. Alcohol 58 (4), 382–391. https://doi.org/10.15288/jsa.1997.58.382.

Brager, A.J., Ruby, C.L., Prosser, R.A., Glass, J.D., 2010. Chronic ethanol disrupts circadian photic entrainment and daily locomotor activity in the mouse. Alcohol Clin. Exp. Res. 34 (7), 1266–1273. https://doi.org/10.1111/j.1530-0277.2010.01204.x, 10.1111/j.1530-0277.2010.01204.x. Epub 2010 May 7.

Brager, A., Prosser, R.A., Glass, J.D., 2011a. Acamprosate-responsive brain sites for suppression of ethanol intake and preference. Am. J. Physiol. Regul. Integr. Comp. Physiol. 301 (4), R1032–R1043. https://doi.org/10.1152/ajpregu.00179.2011, 10.1152/ajpregu.00179.2011. Epub 2011 Jun 22.

Brager, A.J., Ruby, C.L., Prosser, R.A., Glass, J.D., 2011c. Acute ethanol disrupts photic and serotonergic circadian clock phase-resetting in the mouse. Alcohol Clin. Exp. Res. 35 (8), 1467–1474. https://doi.org/10.1111/j.1530-0277.2011.01483.x, 10.1111/j.1530-0277.2011.01483.x. Epub 2011 Apr 4.

Brager, A.J., Stowie, A.C., Prosser, R.A., Glass, J.D., 2013. The mPer2 clock gene modulates cocaine actions in the mouse circadian system. Behav. Brain Res. 243, 255–260. https://doi.org/10.1016/j.bbr.2013.01.014, 10.1016/j.bbr.2013.01.014. Epub 2013 Jan 17.

Brami-Cherrier, K., Lewis, R.G., Cervantes, M., Liu, Y., Tognini, P., Baldi, P., Sassone-Corsi, P., Borrelli, E., 2020. Cocaine-mediated circadian reprogramming in the striatum through dopamine D2R and PPARgamma activation. Nat. Commun. 11 (1), 4448. https://doi.org/10.1038/s41467-020-18200-6.

Brancaccio, M., Maywood, E.S., Chesham, J.E., Loudon, A.S., Hastings, M.H., 2013. A Gq-Ca2+ axis controls circuit-level encoding of circadian time in the suprachiasmatic nucleus. Neuron 78 (4), 714–728. https://doi.org/10.1016/j.neuron.2013.03.011, 10.1016/j.neuron.2013.03.011. Epub 2013 Apr 25.

Brancaccio, M., Patton, A.P., Chesham, J.E., Maywood, E.S., Hastings, M.H., 2017. Astrocytes control circadian time-keeping in the suprachiasmatic nucleus via glutamatergic signaling. Neuron 93 (6), 1420–1435 e1425. https://doi.org/10.1016/j.neuron.2017.02.030, 10.1016/j.neuron.2017.02.030. Epub 2017 Mar 9.

Brown, T.E., Lee, B.R., Mu, P., Ferguson, D., Dietz, D., Ohnishi, Y.N., Lin, Y., Suska, A., Ishikawa, M., Huang, Y.H., Shen, H., Kalivas, P.W., Sorg, B.A., Zukin, R.S., Nestler, E.J., Dong, Y., Schluter, O.M., 2011. A silent synapse-based mechanism for cocaine-induced locomotor sensitization. J. Neurosci. 31 (22), 8163–8174. https://doi.org/10.1523/JNEUROSCI.0016-11.2011, 10.1523/JNEUROSCI.0016-11.2011.

Buhr, E.D., Takahashi, J.S., 2013. Molecular components of the Mammalian circadian clock. Handb. Exp. Pharmacol. (217), 3–27. https://doi.org/10.1007/978-3-642-25950-0_1, 10.1007/978-3-642-25950-0_1.

Buysse, D.J., Nofzinger, E.A., Germain, A., Meltzer, C.C., Wood, A., Ombao, H., Kupfer, D.J., Moore, R.Y., 2004. Regional brain glucose metabolism during morning and evening wakefulness in humans: preliminary findings. Sleep 27 (7), 1245–1254. https://www.ncbi.nlm.nih.gov/pubmed/15586778.

Caci, H., Robert, P., Boyer, P., 2004. Novelty seekers and impulsive subjects are low in morningness. Eur. Psychiatr. 19 (2), 79–84. https://doi.org/10.1016/j.eurpsy.2003.09.007.

Cahill, M.E., Bagot, R.C., Gancarz, A.M., Walker, D.M., Sun, H., Wang, Z.-J., Heller, E.A., Feng, J., Kennedy, P.J., Koo, J.W., Cates, H.M., Neve, R.L., Shen, L., Dietz, D.M., Nestler, E.J., 2016. Bidirectional synaptic structural plasticity after chronic cocaine administration occurs through Rap1 small GTPase signaling. Neuron 89 (3), 566–582. https://doi.org/10.1016/j.neuron.2016.01.031.

Cahill, M.E., Walker, D.M., Gancarz, A.M., Wang, Z.J., Lardner, C.K., Bagot, R.C., Neve, R.L., Dietz, D.M., Nestler, E.J., 2017. The dendritic spine morphogenic effects of repeated cocaine use occur through the regulation of serum response factor signaling. Mol. Psychiatr. 23 (6), 1474–1486. https://doi.org/10.1038/mp.2017.116, 10.1038/mp.2017.116. https://www.ncbi.nlm.nih.gov/pmc/articles/PMC5709273/#!po=70.9302.

Calipari, E.S., Bagot, R.C., Purushothaman, I., Davidson, T.J., Yorgason, J.T., Pena, C.J., Walker, D.M., Pirpinias, S.T., Guise, K.G., Ramakrishnan, C., Deisseroth, K., Nestler, E.J., 2016. In vivo imaging identifies temporal signature of D1 and D2 medium spiny neurons in cocaine reward. Proc. Natl. Acad. Sci. U.S.A. 113 (10), 2726–2731. https://doi.org/10.1073/pnas.1521238113, 10.1073/pnas.1521238113. Epub 2016 Feb 1.

Calipari, E.S., Godino, A., Salery, M., Damez-Werno, D.M., Cahill, M.E., Werner, C.T., Gancarz, A.M., Peck, E.G., Jlayer, Z., Rabkin, J., Landry, J.A., Smith, A.C.W., Defilippi, P., Kenny, P.J., Hurd, Y.L., Neve, R.L., Dietz, D.M., Nestler, E.J., 2019. Synaptic microtubule-associated protein EB3 and SRC phosphorylation mediate structural and behavioral adaptations during withdrawal from cocaine self-administration. J. Neurosci. 39 (29), 5634–5646. https://doi.org/10.1523/JNEUROSCI.0024-19.2019.

Canto, C., Menzies, K.J., Auwerx, J., 2015. NAD(+) metabolism and the control of energy homeostasis: a balancing act between mitochondria and the nucleus. Cell Metabol. 22 (1), 31–53. https://doi.org/10.1016/j.cmet.2015.05.023.

Carlezon Jr., W.A., Thome, J., Olson, V.G., Lane-Ladd, S.B., Brodkin, E.S., Hiroi, N., Duman, R.S., Neve, R.L., Nestler, E.J., 1998. Regulation of cocaine reward by CREB. Science 282 (5397), 2272–2275. https://www.ncbi.nlm.nih.gov/pubmed/9856954.

Carlezon Jr., W.A., Duman, R.S., Nestler, E.J., 2005. The many faces of CREB. Trends Neurosci. 28 (8), 436–445 https://doi.org/S0166-2236(05)00158-X (pii).

Carskadon, M.A., 2011. Sleep in adolescents: the perfect storm. Pediatr. Clin. 58 (3), 637–647. https://doi.org/10.1016/j.pcl.2011.03.003, 10.1016/j.pcl.2011.03.003.

Chen, K., Kandel, D.B., 1995. The natural history of drug use from adolescence to the mid-thirties in a general population sample. Am. J. Publ. Health 85 (1), 41–47. https://www.ncbi.nlm.nih.gov/pubmed/7832260.

Chen, C.P., Kuhn, P., Advis, J.P., Sarkar, D.K., 2004. Chronic ethanol consumption impairs the circadian rhythm of pro-opiomelanocortin and period genes mRNA expression in the hypothalamus of the male rat. J. Neurochem. 88 (6), 1547–1554 https://doi.org/2300 (pii).

Chen, Q., Huang, C.Q., Hu, X.Y., Li, S.B., Zhang, X.M., 2013. Functional CLOCK gene rs1554483 G/C polymorphism is associated with susceptibility to Alzheimer's disease in the Chinese population. J. Int. Med. Res. 41 (2), 340–346. https://doi.org/10.1177/0300060513476430.

Chen, B., Wang, Y., Liu, X., Liu, Z., Dong, Y., Huang, Y.H., 2015. Sleep regulates incubation of cocaine craving. J. Neurosci. 35 (39), 13300–13310. https://doi.org/10.1523/JNEUROSCI.1065-15.2015.

Cheng, M.Y., Bittman, E.L., Hattar, S., Zhou, Q.Y., 2005. Regulation of prokineticin 2 expression by light and the circadian clock. BMC Neurosci. 6, 17. https://doi.org/10.1186/1471-2202-6-17.

Clark, J.W., Fixaris, M.C., Belanger, G.V., Rosenwasser, A.M., 2007. Repeated light-dark phase shifts modulate voluntary ethanol intake in male and female high alcohol-drinking (HAD1) rats. Alcohol Clin. Exp. Res. 31 (10), 1699–1706. https://doi.org/10.1111/j.1530-0277.2007.00476.x.

Colavito, V., Fabene, P.F., Grassi-Zucconi, G., Pifferi, F., Lamberty, Y., Bentivoglio, M., Bertini, G., 2013. Experimental sleep deprivation as a tool to test memory deficits in rodents. Front. Syst. Neurosci. 7, 106. https://doi.org/10.3389/fnsys.2013.00106.

Comasco, E., Nordquist, N., Gokturk, C., Aslund, C., Hallman, J., Oreland, L., Nilsson, K.W., 2010. The clock gene PER2 and sleep problems: association with alcohol consumption among Swedish adolescents. Ups. J. Med. Sci. 115 (1), 41–48. https://doi.org/10.3109/03009731003597127.

Costa, G., 2010. Shift work and health: current problems and preventive actions. Saf Health Work 1 (2), 112–123. https://doi.org/10.5491/SHAW.2010.1.2.112.

Crowley, S.J., Van Reen, E., LeBourgeois, M.K., Acebo, C., Tarokh, L., Seifer, R., Barker, D.H., Carskadon, M.A., 2014. A longitudinal assessment of sleep timing, circadian phase, and phase angle of entrainment across human adolescence. PLoS One 9 (11), e112199. https://doi.org/10.1371/journal.pone.0112199 eCollection 2014.

Damez-Werno, D., LaPlant, Q., Sun, H., Scobie, K.N., Dietz, D.M., Walker, I.M., Koo, J.W., Vialou, V.F., Mouzon, E., Russo, S.J., Nestler, E.J., 2012. Drug experience epigenetically primes Fosb gene inducibility in rat nucleus accumbens. J. Neurosci. 32 (30), 10267–10272. https://doi.org/10.1523/JNEUROSCI.1290-12.2012.

Danel, T., Jeanson, R., Touitou, Y., 2003. Temporal pattern in consumption of the first drink of the day in alcohol-dependent persons. Chronobiol. Int. 20 (6), 1093–1102. https://doi.org/10.1081/cbi-120025533.

de Goede, P., Wefers, J., Brombacher, E.C., Schrauwen, P., Kalsbeek, A., 2018. Circadian rhythms in mitochondrial respiration. J. Mol. Endocrinol. 60 (3), R115–R130. https://doi.org/10.1530/JME-17-0196. Epub 2018 Jan 29.

de Lecea, L., 2012. Hypocretins and the neurobiology of sleep-wake mechanisms. Prog. Brain Res. 198, 15–24. https://doi.org/10.1016/B978-0-444-59489-1.00003-3.

de Zavalia, N., Schoettner, K., Goldsmith, J.A., Solis, P., Ferraro, S., Parent, G., Amir, S., 2021. *Bmal1* in the striatum influences alcohol intake in a sexually dimorphic manner. Commun Biol 4, 1227. https://doi.org/10.1038/s42003-021-02715-9.

DePoy, L.M., Becker-Krail, D.D., Zong, W., Petersen, K., Shah, N.M., Brandon, J.H., Miguelino, A.M., Tseng, G.C., Logan, R.W., McClung, C.A., 2021. Circadian-dependent and sex-dependent increases in intravenous cocaine self-administration in Npas2 mutant mice. J. Neurosci. 41 (5), 1046–1058. https://doi.org/10.1523/jneurosci.1830-20.2020.

Deurveilher, S., Semba, K., 2005. Indirect projections from the suprachiasmatic nucleus to major arousal-promoting cell groups in rat: implications for the circadian control of behavioural state. Neuroscience 130 (1), 165–183. https://doi.org/10.1016/j.neuroscience.2004.08.030.

Dioum, E.M., Rutter, J., Tuckerman, J.R., Gonzalez, G., Gilles-Gonzalez, M.A., McKnight, S.L., 2002. NPAS2: a gas-responsive transcription factor. Science 298 (5602), 2385–2387. https://doi.org/10.1126/science.1078456. Epub 2002 Nov 20.

Dole, V.P., Ho, A., Gentry, R.T., 1985. Toward an analogue of alcoholism in mice: criteria for recognition of pharmacologically motivated drinking. Proc. Natl. Acad. Sci. U. S. A. 82 (10), 3469–3471. https://doi.org/10.1073/pnas.82.10.3469.

Dong, Y., Green, T., Saal, D., Marie, H., Neve, R., Nestler, E.J., Malenka, R.C., 2006. CREB modulates excitability of nucleus accumbens neurons. Nat. Neurosci. 9 (4), 475–477. https://doi.org/10.1038/nn1661.

Dong, L., Bilbao, A., Laucht, M., Henriksson, R., Yakovleva, T., Ridinger, M., Desrivieres, S., Clarke, T.K., Lourdusamy, A., Smolka, M.N., Cichon, S., Blomeyer, D., Treutlein, J., Perreau-Lenz, S., Witt, S.,

Leonardi-Essmann, F., Wodarz, N., Zill, P., Soyka, M., Albrecht, U., Rietschel, M., Lathrop, M., Bakalkin, G., Spanagel, R., Schumann, G., 2011. Effects of the circadian rhythm gene period 1 (per1) on psychosocial stress-induced alcohol drinking. Am. J. Psychiatr. 168 (10), 1090–1098. https://doi.org/10.1176/appi.ajp.2011.10111579. Epub 2011 Aug 9.

Dorrian, J., Skinner, N., 2012. Alcohol consumption patterns of shiftworkers compared with dayworkers. Chronobiol. Int. 29 (5), 610–618. https://doi.org/10.3109/07420528.2012.675848.

Dorrian, J., Heath, G., Sargent, C., Banks, S., Coates, A., 2017. Alcohol use in shiftworkers. Accid. Anal. Prev. 99 (Pt B), 395–400. https://doi.org/10.1016/j.aap.2015.11.011.

Doyle, S.E., Feng, H., Garber, G., Menaker, M., Lynch, W.J., 2015. Effects of circadian disruption on methamphetamine consumption in methamphetamine-exposed rats. Psychopharmacology 232 (12), 2169–2179. https://doi.org/10.1007/s00213-014-3845-2. Epub 2014 Dec 30.

Drennan, M.D., Klauber, M.R., Kripke, D.F., Goyette, L.M., 1991. The effects of depression and age on the Horne-Ostberg morningness-eveningness score. J. Affect. Disord. 23 (2), 93–98. https://www.ncbi.nlm.nih.gov/pubmed/1753041.

Dulcis, D., Jamshidi, P., Leutgeb, S., Spitzer, N.C., 2013. Neurotransmitter switching in the adult brain regulates behavior. Science 340 (6131), 449–453. https://doi.org/10.1126/science.1234152.

Dumitriu, D., Laplant, Q., Grossman, Y.S., Dias, C., Janssen, W.G., Russo, S.J., Morrison, J.H., Nestler, E.J., 2012. Subregional, dendritic compartment, and spine subtype specificity in cocaine regulation of dendritic spines in the nucleus accumbens. J. Neurosci. 32 (20), 6957–6966. https://doi.org/10.1523/JNEUROSCI.5718-11.2012.

Eacret, D., Veasey, S.C., Blendy, J.A., 2020. Bidirectional relationship between opioids and disrupted sleep: putative mechanisms. Mol. Pharmacol. 98 (4), 445–453. https://doi.org/10.1124/mol.119.119107.

Eide, E.J., Kang, H., Crapo, S., Gallego, M., Virshup, D.M., 2005. Casein kinase I in the mammalian circadian clock. Methods Enzymol. 393, 408–418. https://doi.org/10.1016/S0076-6879(05)93019-X.

Falcon, E., Ozburn, A., Mukherjee, S., Roybal, K., McClung, C.A., 2013. Differential regulation of the period genes in striatal regions following cocaine exposure. PLoS One 8 (6), e66438. https://doi.org/10.1371/journal.-pone.0066438. Print 2013.

Ferguson, D., Koo, J.W., Feng, J., Heller, E., Rabkin, J., Heshmati, M., Renthal, W., Neve, R., Liu, X., Shao, N., Sartorelli, V., Shen, L., Nestler, E.J., 2013. Essential role of SIRT1 signaling in the nucleus accumbens in cocaine and morphine action. J. Neurosci. 33 (41), 16088–16098. https://doi.org/10.1523/JNEUROSCI.1284-13.2013.

Ferguson, D., Shao, N., Heller, E., Feng, J., Neve, R., Kim, H.D., Call, T., Magazu, S., Shen, L., Nestler, E.J., 2015. SIRT1-FOXO3a regulate cocaine actions in the nucleus accumbens. J. Neurosci. 35 (7), 3100–3111. https://doi.org/10.1523/JNEUROSCI.4012-14.2015.

Ferguson, L.B., Ozburn, A.R., Ponomarev, I., Metten, P., Reilly, M., Crabbe, J.C., Harris, R.A., Mayfield, R.D., 2018. Genome-wide expression profiles drive discovery of novel compounds that reduce binge drinking in mice. Neuropsychopharmacology 43 (6), 1257–1266. https://doi.org/10.1038/npp.2017.301. Epub 2017 Dec 18.

Filiano, A.N., Millender-Swain, T., Johnson Jr., R., Young, M.E., Gamble, K.L., Bailey, S.M., 2013. Chronic ethanol consumption disrupts the core molecular clock and diurnal rhythms of metabolic genes in the liver without affecting the suprachiasmatic nucleus. PLoS One 8 (8), e71684. https://doi.org/10.1371/journal.pone.0071684 eCollection 2013.

Flourakis, M., Kula-Eversole, E., Hutchison, A.L., Han, T.H., Aranda, K., Moose, D.L., White, K.P., Dinner, A.R., Lear, B.C., Ren, D., Diekman, C.O., Raman, I.M., Allada, R., 2015. A conserved bicycle model for circadian clock control of membrane excitability. Cell 162 (4), 836–848. https://doi.org/10.1016/j.cell.2015.07.036.

Fontenot, M.R., Berto, S., Liu, Y., Werthmann, G., Douglas, C., Usui, N., Gleason, K., Tamminga, C.A., Takahashi, J.S., Konopka, G., 2017. Novel transcriptional networks regulated by CLOCK in human neurons. Genes Dev. 31 (21), 2121–2135. https://doi.org/10.1101/gad.305813.117. Epub 2017 Dec 1.

Forbes, E.E., Hariri, A.R., Martin, S.L., Silk, J.S., Moyles, D.L., Fisher, P.M., Brown, S.M., Ryan, N.D., Birmaher, B., Axelson, D.A., Dahl, R.E., 2009. Altered striatal activation predicting real-world positive affect in adolescent major depressive disorder. Am. J. Psychiatr. 166 (1), 64–73. https://doi.org/10.1176/appi.ajp.2008.07081336.

Forbes, E.E., Dahl, R.E., Almeida, J.R., Ferrell, R.E., Nimgaonkar, V.L., Mansour, H., Sciarrillo, S.R., Holm, S.M., Rodriguez, E.E., Phillips, M.L., 2012. PER2 rs2304672 polymorphism moderates circadian-relevant reward circuitry activity in adolescents. Biol. Psychiatr. 71 (5), 451–457. https://doi.org/10.1016/j.biopsych.2011.10.012. Epub 2011 Dec 2.

Franken, P., Dudley, C.A., Estill, S.J., Barakat, M., Thomason, R., O'Hara, B.F., McKnight, S.L., 2006. NPAS2 as a transcriptional regulator of non-rapid eye movement sleep: genotype and sex interactions. Proc. Natl. Acad. Sci. U.S.A. 103 (18), 7118–7123. https://doi.org/10.1073/pnas.0602006103. Epub 2006 Apr 24.

Frankowska, M., Marcellino, D., Adamczyk, P., Filip, M., Fuxe, K., 2013. Effects of cocaine self-administration and extinction on D2-like and A2A receptor recognition and D2-like/Gi protein coupling in rat striatum. Addiction Biol. 18 (3), 455–466. https://doi.org/10.1111/j.1369-1600.2012.00452.x.

Franzen, P.L., Buysse, D.J., Forbes, E.E., Jones, N.P., Ohlsen, T.J., Germain, A., 2016. Sleep restriction lowers striatal responses to the receipt of monetary reward in adolescents. Sleep 39S, A93.

Freyberg, Z., Logan, R.W., 2018. The intertwined roles of circadian rhythms and neuronal metabolism fueling drug reward and addiction. Curr. Opin. Physiol. 5, 80–89. https://doi.org/10.1016/j.cophys.2018.08.004.

Gamsby, J.J., Templeton, E.L., Bonvini, L.A., Wang, W., Loros, J.J., Dunlap, J.C., Green, A.I., Gulick, D., 2013. The circadian Per1 and Per2 genes influence alcohol intake, reinforcement, and blood alcohol levels. Behav. Brain Res. 249, 15–21. https://doi.org/10.1016/j.bbr.2013.04.016. Epub 2013 Apr 20.

Garcia, J.A., Zhang, D., Estill, S.J., Michnoff, C., Rutter, J., Reick, M., Scott, K., Diaz-Arrastia, R., McKnight, S.L., 2000. Impaired cued and contextual memory in NPAS2-deficient mice. Science 288 (5474), 2226–2230. https://www.ncbi.nlm.nih.gov/pubmed/10864874.

Gauvin, D.V., Baird, T.J., Vanecek, S.A., Briscoe, R.J., Vallett, M., Holloway, F.A., 1997. Effects of time-of-day and photoperiod phase shifts on voluntary ethanol consumption in rats. Alcohol Clin. Exp. Res. 21 (5), 817–825. https://www.ncbi.nlm.nih.gov/pubmed/9267531.

Germain, A., Kupfer, D.J., 2008. Circadian rhythm disturbances in depression. Hum. Psychopharmacol. 23 (7), 571–585. https://doi.org/10.1002/hup.964.

Germain, A., McNamee, R., Khan, H., McMakin, D.L., Franzen, P., Forbes, E.E., 2016. Sleep restriction amplifies neural response to reward cues compared to normal sleep and sleep deprivation. Sleep 39S, A94.

Giannotti, F., Cortesi, F., Sebastiani, T., Ottaviano, S., 2002. Circadian preference, sleep and daytime behaviour in adolescence. J. Sleep Res. 11 (3), 191–199. https://www.ncbi.nlm.nih.gov/pubmed/12220314.

Gibson, E.M., Wang, C., Tjho, S., Khattar, N., Kriegsfeld, L.J., 2010. Experimental "jet lag" inhibits adult neurogenesis and produces long-term cognitive deficits in female hamsters. PLoS One 5 (12), e15267. https://doi.org/10.1371/journal.pone.0015267.

Goldstein, R.Z., Volkow, N.D., 2011. Dysfunction of the prefrontal cortex in addiction: neuroimaging findings and clinical implications. Nat. Rev. Neurosci. 12 (11), 652–669. https://doi.org/10.1038/nrn3119.

Graziane, N.M., Sun, S., Wright, W.J., Jang, D., Liu, Z., Huang, Y.H., Nestler, E.J., Wang, Y.T., Schluter, O.M., Dong, Y., 2016. Opposing mechanisms mediate morphine- and cocaine-induced generation of silent synapses. Nat. Neurosci. 19 (7), 915–925. https://doi.org/10.1038/nn.4313. Epub 2016 May 30.

Green, T.A., Alibhai, I.N., Hommel, J.D., DiLeone, R.J., Kumar, A., Theobald, D.E., Neve, R.L., Nestler, E.J., 2006. Induction of inducible cAMP early repressor expression in nucleus accumbens by stress or amphetamine increases behavioral responses to emotional stimuli. J. Neurosci. 26 (32), 8235–8242. https://doi.org/10.1523/JNEUROSCI.0880-06.2006.

Grippo, R.M., Guler, A.D., 2019. Dopamine signaling in circadian photoentrainment: consequences of desynchrony. Yale J. Biol. Med. 92 (2), 271–281. https://www.ncbi.nlm.nih.gov/pubmed/31249488.

Grippo, R.M., Purohit, A.M., Zhang, Q., Zweifel, L.S., Guler, A.D., 2017. Direct midbrain dopamine input to the suprachiasmatic nucleus accelerates circadian entrainment. Curr. Biol. 27 (16), 2465–2475 e2463. https://doi.org/10.1016/j.cub.2017.06.084. Epub 2017 Aug 3.

Grippo, R.M., Tang, Q., Zhang, Q., Chadwick, S.R., Gao, Y., Altherr, E.B., Sipe, L., Purohit, A.M., Purohit, N.M., Sunkara, M.D., Cios, K.J., Sidikpramana, M., Spano, A.J., Campbell, J.N., Steele, A.D., Hirsh, J., Deppmann, C.D., Wu, M., Scott, M.M., Guler, A.D., 2020. Dopamine signaling in the suprachiasmatic nucleus enables weight Gain associated with hedonic feeding. Curr. Biol. 30 (7), 1352–1355. https://doi.org/10.1016/j.cub.2020.03.034.

Guitart, X., Thompson, M.A., Mirante, C.K., Greenberg, M.E., Nestler, E.J., 1992. Regulation of cyclic AMP response element-binding protein (CREB) phosphorylation by acute and chronic morphine in the rat locus coeruleus. J. Neurochem. 58 (3), 1168–1171. https://www.ncbi.nlm.nih.gov/pubmed/1531356.

Hammer, S.B., Ruby, C.L., Brager, A.J., Prosser, R.A., Glass, J.D., 2010. Environmental modulation of alcohol intake in hamsters: effects of wheel running and constant light exposure. Alcohol Clin. Exp. Res. 34 (9), 1651–1658. https://doi.org/10.1111/j.1530-0277.2010.01251.x. Epub 2010 Jun 21.

Han, M.H., Bolanos, C.A., Green, T.A., Olson, V.G., Neve, R.L., Liu, R.J., Aghajanian, G.K., Nestler, E.J., 2006. Role of cAMP response element-binding protein in the rat locus ceruleus: regulation of neuronal activity and opiate withdrawal behaviors. J. Neurosci. 26 (17), 4624–4629. https://doi.org/10.1523/JNEUROSCI.4701-05.2006.

Hasler, B.P., Allen, J.J., Sbarra, D.A., Bootzin, R.R., Bernert, R.A., 2010. Morningness-eveningness and depression: preliminary evidence for the role of the behavioral activation system and positive affect. Psychiatr. Res. 176 (2–3), 166–173. https://doi.org/10.1016/j.psychres.2009.06.006. Epub 2010 Feb 4.

Hasler, B.P., Dahl, R.E., Holm, S.M., Jakubcak, J.L., Ryan, N.D., Silk, J.S., Phillips, M.L., Forbes, E.E., 2012a. Weekend-weekday advances in sleep timing are associated with altered reward-related brain function in healthy adolescents. Biol. Psychol. 91 (3), 334–341. https://doi.org/10.1016/j.biopsycho.2012.08.008. Epub 2012 Aug 30.

Hasler, B.P., Germain, A., Nofzinger, E.A., Kupfer, D.J., Krafty, R.T., Rothenberger, S.D., James, J.A., Bi, W., Buysse, D.J., 2012b. Chronotype and diurnal patterns of positive affect and affective neural circuitry in primary insomnia. J. Sleep Res. 21 (5), 515–526. https://doi.org/10.1111/j.1365-2869.2012.01002.x. Epub 2012 Feb 27.

Hasler, B.P., Casement, M.D., Sitnick, S.L., Shaw, D.S., Forbes, E.E., 2017. Eveningness among late adolescent males predicts neural reactivity to reward and alcohol dependence 2 years later. Behav. Brain Res. 327, 112–120. https://doi.org/10.1016/j.bbr.2017.02.024. Epub 2017 Feb 28.

Hattar, S., Liao, H.W., Takao, M., Berson, D.M., Yau, K.W., 2002. Melanopsin-containing retinal ganglion cells: architecture, projections, and intrinsic photosensitivity. Science 295 (5557), 1065–1070. https://doi.org/10.1126/science.1069609.

Hattar, S., Lucas, R.J., Mrosovsky, N., Thompson, S., Douglas, R.H., Hankins, M.W., Lem, J., Biel, M., Hofmann, F., Foster, R.G., Yau, K.W., 2003. Melanopsin and rod-cone photoreceptive systems account for all major accessory visual functions in mice. Nature 424 (6944), 76–81. https://doi.org/10.1038/nature01761. Epub 2003 Jun 15.

Hattar, S., Kumar, M., Park, A., Tong, P., Tung, J., Yau, K.W., Berson, D.M., 2006. Central projections of melanopsin-expressing retinal ganglion cells in the mouse. J. Comp. Neurol. 497 (3), 326–349. https://doi.org/10.1002/cne.20970.

Holm, S.M., Forbes, E.E., Ryan, N.D., Phillips, M.L., Tarr, J.A., Dahl, R.E., 2009. Reward-related brain function and sleep in pre/early pubertal and mid/late pubertal adolescents. J. Adolesc. Health 45 (4), 326–334. https://doi.org/10.1016/j.jadohealth.2009.04.001. Epub 2009 May 31.

Hood, S., Cassidy, P., Cossette, M.-P., Weigl, Y., Verwey, M., Robinson, B., Stewart, J., Amir, S., 2010. Endogenous dopamine regulates the rhythm of expression of the clock protein PER2 in the rat dorsal striatum via daily activation of D2 dopamine receptors. J. Neurosci. 30 (42), 14046–14058. https://doi.org/10.1523/JNEUROSCI.2128-10.2010.

Horne, J.A., Ostberg, O., 1976. A self-assessment questionnaire to determine morningness-eveningness in human circadian rhythms. Int. J. Chronobiol. 4 (2), 97–110. https://www.ncbi.nlm.nih.gov/pubmed/1027738.

Huang, M.C., Ho, C.W., Chen, C.H., Liu, S.C., Chen, C.C., Leu, S.J., 2010. Reduced expression of circadian clock genes in male alcoholic patients. Alcohol Clin. Exp. Res. 34 (11), 1899–1904. https://doi.org/10.1111/j.1530-0277.2010.01278.x. Epub 2010 Aug 24.

Iijima, M., Nikaido, T., Akiyama, M., Moriya, T., Shibata, S., 2002. Methamphetamine-induced, suprachiasmatic nucleus-independent circadian rhythms of activity and mPer gene expression in the striatum of the mouse. Eur. J. Neurosci. 16 (5), 921–929 https://doi.org/2140 (pii).

Imbesi, M., Yildiz, S., Dirim Arslan, A., Sharma, R., Manev, H., Uz, T., 2009. Dopamine receptor-mediated regulation of neuronal "clock" gene expression. Neuroscience 158 (2), 537–544. https://doi.org/10.1016/j.neuroscience.2008.10.044.

Isaac, S.O., Berridge, C.W., 2003. Wake-promoting actions of dopamine D1 and D2 receptor stimulation. J. Pharmacol. Exp. Therapeut. 307 (1), 386–394. https://doi.org/10.1124/jpet.103.053918.

Jehan, S., Zizi, F., Pandi-Perumal, S.R., Myers, A.K., Auguste, E., Jean-Louis, G., McFarlane, S.I., 2017. Shift work and sleep: medical implications and management. Sleep Med. Disord. 1 (2). https://www.ncbi.nlm.nih.gov/pubmed/29517053.

Johansson, C., Willeit, M., Smedh, C., Ekholm, J., Paunio, T., Kieseppa, T., Lichtermann, D., Praschak-Rieder, N., Neumeister, A., Nilsson, L.G., Kasper, S., Peltonen, L., Adolfsson, R., Schalling, M., Partonen, T., 2003. Circadian clock-related polymorphisms in seasonal affective disorder and their relevance to diurnal preference. Neuropsychopharmacology 28 (4), 734–739. https://doi.org/10.1038/sj.npp.1300121.

Jones, J.R., Tackenberg, M.C., McMahon, D.G., 2015. Manipulating circadian clock neuron firing rate resets molecular circadian rhythms and behavior. Nat. Neurosci. 18 (3), 373–375. https://doi.org/10.1038/nn.3937. Epub 2015 Feb 2.

Kaasik, K., Lee, C.C., 2004. Reciprocal regulation of haem biosynthesis and the circadian clock in mammals. Nature 430 (6998), 467–471. https://doi.org/10.1038/nature02724.

Kalinchuk, A.V., Urrila, A.S., Alanko, L., Heiskanen, S., Wigren, H.K., Suomela, M., Stenberg, D., Porkka-Heiskanen, T., 2003. Local energy depletion in the basal forebrain increases sleep. Eur. J. Neurosci. 17 (4), 863–869. https://doi.org/10.1046/j.1460-9568.2003.02532.x.

Kennaway, D.J., 2010. Clock genes at the heart of depression. J. Psychopharmacol. 24 (2 Suppl. l), 5–14. https://doi.org/10.1177/1359786810372980.

Kiessling, S., Eichele, G., Oster, H., 2010. Adrenal glucocorticoids have a key role in circadian resynchronization in a mouse model of jet lag. J. Clin. Invest. 120 (7), 2600–2609. https://doi.org/10.1172/JCI41192.

King, D.P., Vitaterna, M.H., Chang, A.M., Dove, W.F., Pinto, L.H., Turek, F.W., Takahashi, J.S., 1997a. The mouse Clock mutation behaves as an antimorph and maps within the W19H deletion, distal of Kit. Genetics 146 (3), 1049–1060. https://www.ncbi.nlm.nih.gov/pubmed/9215907.

King, D.P., Zhao, Y., Sangoram, A.M., Wilsbacher, L.D., Tanaka, M., Antoch, M.P., Steeves, T.D., Vitaterna, M.H., Kornhauser, J.M., Lowrey, P.L., Turek, F.W., Takahashi, J.S., 1997b. Positional cloning of the mouse circadian clock gene. Cell 89 (4), 641–653. https://www.ncbi.nlm.nih.gov/pubmed/9160755.

Koike, N., Yoo, S.H., Huang, H.C., Kumar, V., Lee, C., Kim, T.K., Takahashi, J.S., 2012. Transcriptional architecture and chromatin landscape of the core circadian clock in mammals. Science 338 (6105), 349–354. https://doi.org/10.1126/science.1226339. Epub 2012 Aug 30.

Korshunov, K.S., Blakemore, L.J., Trombley, P.Q., 2017. Dopamine: a modulator of circadian rhythms in the central nervous system. Front. Cell. Neurosci. 11, 91. https://doi.org/10.3389/fncel.2017.00091.

Kovanen, L., Saarikoski, S.T., Haukka, J., Pirkola, S., Aromaa, A., Lonnqvist, J., Partonen, T., 2010. Circadian clock gene polymorphisms in alcohol use disorders and alcohol consumption. Alcohol Alcohol 45 (4), 303–311. https://doi.org/10.1093/alcalc/agq035. Epub 2010 Jun 16.

Lane-Ladd, S.B., Pineda, J., Boundy, V.A., Pfeuffer, T., Krupinski, J., Aghajanian, G.K., Nestler, E.J., 1997. CREB (cAMP response element-binding protein) in the locus coeruleus: biochemical, physiological, and behavioral evidence for a role in opiate dependence. J. Neurosci. 17 (20), 7890–7901. https://www.ncbi.nlm.nih.gov/pubmed/9315909.

Larson, E.B., Graham, D.L., Arzaga, R.R., Buzin, N., Webb, J., Green, T.A., Bass, C.E., Neve, R.L., Terwilliger, E.F., Nestler, E.J., Self, D.W., 2011. Overexpression of CREB in the nucleus accumbens shell increases cocaine reinforcement in self-administering rats. J. Neurosci. 31 (45), 16447–16457. https://doi.org/10.1523/JNEUROSCI.3070-11.2011.

LeGates, T.A., Altimus, C.M., Wang, H., Lee, H.K., Yang, S., Zhao, H., Kirkwood, A., Weber, E.T., Hattar, S., 2012. Aberrant light directly impairs mood and learning through melanopsin-expressing neurons. Nature 491 (7425), 594–598. https://doi.org/10.1038/nature11673. Epub 2012 Nov 14.

LeGates, T.A., Fernandez, D.C., Hattar, S., 2014. Light as a central modulator of circadian rhythms, sleep and affect. Nat. Rev. Neurosci. 15 (7), 443–454. https://doi.org/10.1038/nrn3743. Epub 2014 Jun 11.

Li, C., Kirby, L.G., 2016. Effects of cocaine history on postsynaptic GABA receptors on dorsal raphe serotonin neurons in a stress-induced relapse model in rats. Eur. Neuropsychopharmacol 26 (1), 45–54. https://doi.org/10.1016/j.euroneuro.2015.11.009.

Li, S.X., Wang, Z.R., Li, J., Peng, Z.G., Zhou, W., Zhou, M., Lu, L., 2008. Inhibition of Period1 gene attenuates the morphine-induced ERK-CREB activation in frontal cortex, hippocampus, and striatum in mice. Am. J. Drug Alcohol Abuse 34 (6), 673–682. https://doi.org/10.1080/00952990802308197.

Li, J.D., Hu, W.P., Zhou, Q.Y., 2009. Disruption of the circadian output molecule prokineticin 2 results in anxiolytic and antidepressant-like effects in mice. Neuropsychopharmacology 34 (2), 367–373. https://doi.org/10.1038/npp.2008.61.

Liao, J., Seggio, J.A., Ahmad, S.T., 2016. Mutations in the circadian gene period alter behavioral and biochemical responses to ethanol in Drosophila. Behav. Brain Res. 302, 213–219. https://doi.org/10.1016/j.bbr.2016.01.041. Epub 2016 Jan 20.

Lindberg, D., Shan, D., Ayers-Ringler, J., Oliveros, A., Benitez, J., Prieto, M., McCullumsmith, R., Choi, D.S., 2015. Purinergic signaling and energy homeostasis in psychiatric disorders. Curr. Mol. Med. 15 (3), 275–295. https://www.ncbi.nlm.nih.gov/pubmed/25950756.

Lindsay, J.H., Glass, J.D., Amicarelli, M., Prosser, R.A., 2014. The mammalian circadian clock in the suprachiasmatic nucleus exhibits rapid tolerance to ethanol in vivo and in vitro. Alcohol Clin. Exp. Res. 38 (3), 760–769. https://doi.org/10.1111/acer.12303. Epub 2014 Feb 11.

Liston, C., Cichon, J.M., Jeanneteau, F., Jia, Z., Chao, M.V., Gan, W.B., 2013. Circadian glucocorticoid oscillations promote learning-dependent synapse formation and maintenance. Nat. Neurosci. 16 (6), 698–705. https://doi.org/10.1038/nn.3387. Epub 2013 Apr 28.

Liu, Y., Aragona, B.J., Young, K.A., Dietz, D.M., Kabbaj, M., Mazei-Robison, M., Nestler, E.J., Wang, Z., 2010. Nucleus accumbens dopamine mediates amphetamine-induced impairment of social bonding in a monogamous rodent species. Proc. Natl. Acad. Sci. U.S.A. 107 (3), 1217–1222. https://doi.org/10.1073/pnas.0911998107.

Liu, Z., Wang, Y., Cai, L., Li, Y., Chen, B., Dong, Y., Huang, Y.H., 2016. Prefrontal cortex to accumbens projections in sleep regulation of reward. J. Neurosci. 36 (30), 7897–7910. https://doi.org/10.1523/JNEUROSCI.0347-16.2016.

Lobo, M.K., Zaman, S., Damez-Werno, D.M., Koo, J.W., Bagot, R.C., DiNieri, J.A., Nugent, A., Finkel, E., Chaudhury, D., Chandra, R., Riberio, E., Rabkin, J., Mouzon, E., Cachope, R., Cheer, J.F., Han, M.-H., Dietz, D.M., Self, D.W., Hurd, Y.L., Vialou, V., Nestler, E.J., 2013. ΔFosB induction in striatal medium spiny neuron subtypes in response to chronic pharmacological, emotional, and optogenetic stimuli. J. Neurosci. 33 (47), 18381–18395. https://doi.org/10.1523/JNEUROSCI.1875-13.2013.

Logan, R.W., McClung, C.A., 2019. Rhythms of life: circadian disruption and brain disorders across the lifespan. Nat. Rev. Neurosci. 20 (1), 49–65. https://doi.org/10.1038/s41583-018-0088-y.

Logan, R.W., McCulley 3rd, W.D., Seggio, J.A., Rosenwasser, A.M., 2012. Effects of withdrawal from chronic intermittent ethanol vapor on the level and circadian periodicity of running-wheel activity in C57BL/6J and C3H/HeJ mice. Alcohol Clin. Exp. Res. 36 (3), 467–476. https://doi.org/10.1111/j.1530-0277.2011.01634.x.

Logan, R.W., Williams 3rd, W.P., McClung, C.A., 2014. Circadian rhythms and addiction: mechanistic insights and future directions. Behav. Neurosci. 128 (3), 387–412. https://doi.org/10.1037/a0036268.

Logan, R.W., Edgar, N., Gillman, A.G., Hoffman, D., Zhu, X., McClung, C.A., 2015. Chronic stress induces brain region-specific alterations of molecular rhythms that correlate with depression-like behavior in mice. Biol. Psychiatr. 78 (4), 249–258. https://doi.org/10.1016/j.biopsych.2015.01.011.

Logan, R.W., Hasler, B.P., Forbes, E.E., Franzen, P.L., Torregrossa, M.M., Huang, Y.H., Buysse, D.J., Clark, D.B., McClung, C.A., 2018. Impact of sleep and circadian rhythms on addiction vulnerability in adolescents. Biol. Psychiatr. 83 (12), 987–996. https://doi.org/10.1016/j.biopsych.2017.11.035.

Logan, R.W., Parekh, P.K., Kaplan, G.N., Becker-Krail, D.D., Williams 3rd, W.P., Yamaguchi, S., Yoshino, J., Shelton, M.A., Zhu, X., Zhang, H., Waplinger, S., Fitzgerald, E., Oliver-Smith, J., Sundarvelu, P., Enwright 3rd, J.F., Huang, Y.H., McClung, C.A., 2019. NAD+ cellular redox and SIRT1 regulate the diurnal rhythms of tyrosine hydroxylase and conditioned cocaine reward. Mol. Psychiatr. 24 (11), 1668–1684. https://doi.org/10.1038/s41380-018-0061-1.

Luo, A.H., Aston-Jones, G., 2009. Circuit projection from suprachiasmatic nucleus to ventral tegmental area: a novel circadian output pathway. Eur. J. Neurosci. 29 (4), 748–760. https://doi.org/10.1111/j.1460-9568.2008.06606.x. Epub 2008 Feb 5.

Luo, Y.J., Li, Y.D., Wang, L., Yang, S.R., Yuan, X.S., Wang, J., Cherasse, Y., Lazarus, M., Chen, J.F., Qu, W.M., Huang, Z.L., 2018. Nucleus accumbens controls wakefulness by a subpopulation of neurons expressing dopamine D1 receptors. Nat. Commun. 9 (1), 1576. https://doi.org/10.1038/s41467-018-03889-3.

Lynch, W.J., Taylor, J.R., 2004. Sex differences in the behavioral effects of 24-h/day access to cocaine under a discrete trial procedure. Neuropsychopharmacology 29 (5), 943–951. https://doi.org/10.1038/sj.npp.1300389.

Lynch, W.J., Girgenti, M.J., Breslin, F.J., Newton, S.S., Taylor, J.R., 2008. Gene profiling the response to repeated cocaine self-administration in dorsal striatum: a focus on circadian genes. Brain Res. 1213, 166–177. https://doi.org/10.1016/j.brainres.2008.02.106.

Ma, Y.Y., Wang, X., Huang, Y., Marie, H., Nestler, E.J., Schluter, O.M., Dong, Y., 2016. Re-silencing of silent synapses unmasks anti-relapse effects of environmental enrichment. Proc. Natl. Acad. Sci. U.S.A. 113 (18), 5089–5094. https://doi.org/10.1073/pnas.1524739113. Epub 2016 Apr 18.

Madeira, M.D., Andrade, J.P., Lieberman, A.R., Sousa, N., Almeida, O.F., Paula-Barbosa, M.M., 1997. Chronic alcohol consumption and withdrawal do not induce cell death in the suprachiasmatic nucleus, but lead to irreversible depression of peptide immunoreactivity and mRNA levels. J. Neurosci. 17 (4), 1302–1319. https://www.ncbi.nlm.nih.gov/pubmed/9006974.

Marcellino, D., Roberts, D.C., Navarro, G., Filip, M., Agnati, L., Lluis, C., Franco, R., Fuxe, K., 2007. Increase in A2A receptors in the nucleus accumbens after extended cocaine self-administration and its disappearance after cocaine withdrawal. Brain Res. 1143, 208–220. https://doi.org/10.1016/j.brainres.2007.01.079.

Marcheva, B., Ramsey, K.M., Peek, C.B., Affinati, A., Maury, E., Bass, J., 2013. Circadian clocks and metabolism. Handb. Exp. Pharmacol. (217), 127–155. https://doi.org/10.1007/978-3-642-25950-0_6.

Marinovic, A.C., Zheng, B., Mitch, W.E., Price, S.R., 2002. Ubiquitin (UbC) expression in muscle cells is increased by glucocorticoids through a mechanism involving Sp1 and MEK1. J. Biol. Chem. 277 (19), 16673–16681. https://doi.org/10.1074/jbc.M200501200.

Marpegan, L., Swanstrom, A.E., Chung, K., Simon, T., Haydon, P.G., Khan, S.K., Liu, A.C., Herzog, E.D., Beaule, C., 2011. Circadian regulation of ATP release in astrocytes. J. Neurosci. 31 (23), 8342–8350. https://doi.org/10.1523/JNEUROSCI.6537-10.2011.

Matzeu, A., Zamora-Martinez, E.R., Martin-Fardon, R., 2014. The paraventricular nucleus of the thalamus is recruited by both natural rewards and drugs of abuse: recent evidence of a pivotal role for orexin/hypocretin signaling in this thalamic nucleus in drug-seeking behavior. Front. Behav. Neurosci. 8, 117. https://doi.org/10.3389/fnbeh.2014.00117 eCollection 2014.

McCarthy, M.J., Nievergelt, C.M., Kelsoe, J.R., Welsh, D.K., 2012. A survey of genomic studies supports association of circadian clock genes with bipolar disorder spectrum illnesses and lithium response. PLoS One 7 (2), e32091. https://doi.org/10.1371/journal.pone.0032091.

McCarthy, M.J., Fernandes, M., Kranzler, H.R., Covault, J.M., Welsh, D.K., 2013. Circadian clock period inversely correlates with illness severity in cells from patients with alcohol use disorders. Alcohol Clin. Exp. Res. 37 (8), 1304–1310. https://doi.org/10.1111/acer.12106. Epub 2013 Mar 29.

McClung, C.A., Sidiropoulou, K., Vitaterna, M., Takahashi, J.S., White, F.J., Cooper, D.C., Nestler, E.J., 2005. Regulation of dopaminergic transmission and cocaine reward by the Clock gene. Proc. Natl. Acad. Sci. U.S.A. 102 (26), 9377–9381. https://doi.org/10.1073/pnas.0503584102.

McElroy, B., Zakaria, A., Glass, J.D., Prosser, R.A., 2009. Ethanol modulates mammalian circadian clock phase resetting through extrasynaptic GABA receptor activation. Neuroscience 164 (2), 842–848. https://doi.org/10.1016/j.neuroscience.2009.08.020. Epub 2009 Aug 18.

McKnight-Eily, L.R., Eaton, D.K., Lowry, R., Croft, J.B., Presley-Cantrell, L., Perry, G.S., 2011. Relationships between hours of sleep and health-risk behaviors in US adolescent students. Prev. Med. 53 (4–5), 271–273. https://doi.org/10.1016/j.ypmed.2011.06.020. Epub 2011 Aug 5.

Mendoza, J., 2017. Circadian neurons in the lateral habenula: clocking motivated behaviors. Pharmacol. Biochem. Behav. 162, 55–61. https://doi.org/10.1016/j.pbb.2017.06.013.

Meng, Q.J., Logunova, L., Maywood, E.S., Gallego, M., Lebiecki, J., Brown, T.M., Sladek, M., Semikhodskii, A.S., Glossop, N.R., Piggins, H.D., Chesham, J.E., Bechtold, D.A., Yoo, S.H., Takahashi, J.S., Virshup, D.M., Boot-Handford, R.P., Hastings, M.H., Loudon, A.S., 2008. Setting clock speed in mammals: the CK1 epsilon tau mutation in mice accelerates circadian pacemakers by selectively destabilizing PERIOD proteins. Neuron 58 (1), 78–88. https://doi.org/10.1016/j.neuron.2008.01.019.

Merikanto, I., Kronholm, E., Peltonen, M., Laatikainen, T., Vartiainen, E., Partonen, T., 2015. Circadian preference links to depression in general adult population. J. Affect. Disord. 188, 143–148. https://doi.org/10.1016/j.jad.2015.08.061. Epub 2015 Sep. 1.

Mieda, M., Ono, D., Hasegawa, E., Okamoto, H., Honma, K., Honma, S., Sakurai, T., 2015. Cellular clocks in AVP neurons of the SCN are critical for interneuronal coupling regulating circadian behavior rhythm. Neuron 85 (5), 1103–1116. https://doi.org/10.1016/j.neuron.2015.02.005.

Miller, M.A., Rothenberger, S.D., Hasler, B.P., Donofry, S.D., Wong, P.M., Manuck, S.B., Kamarck, T.W., Roecklein, K.A., 2015. Chronotype predicts positive affect rhythms measured by ecological momentary assessment. Chronobiol. Int. 32 (3), 376–384. https://doi.org/10.3109/07420528.2014.983602. Epub 2014 Nov 20.

Miyazaki, S., Tahara, Y., Colwell, C.S., Block, G.D., Nakamura, W., Nakamura, T.J., 2021. Chronic methamphetamine uncovers a circadian rhythm in multiple-unit neural activity in the dorsal striatum which is independent of the suprachiasmatic nucleus. Neurobiol. Sleep Circadian Rhythms 11, 100070. https://doi.org/10.1016/j.nbscr.2021.100070.

Mohawk, J.A., Baer, M.L., Menaker, M., 2009. The methamphetamine-sensitive circadian oscillator does not employ canonical clock genes. Proc. Natl. Acad. Sci. U.S.A. 106 (9), 3519–3524. https://doi.org/10.1073/pnas.0813366106. Epub 2009 Feb 9.

Morin, L.P., 1999. Serotonin and the regulation of mammalian circadian rhythmicity. Ann. Med. 31 (1), 12–33. https://www.ncbi.nlm.nih.gov/pubmed/10219711.

Mukherjee, S., Coque, L., Cao, J.L., Kumar, J., Chakravarty, S., Asaithamby, A., Graham, A., Gordon, E., Enwright 3rd, J.F., DiLeone, R.J., Birnbaum, S.G., Cooper, D.C., McClung, C.A., 2010. Knockdown of Clock in the ventral tegmental area through RNA interference results in a mixed state of mania and depression-like behavior. Biol. Psychiatr. 68 (6), 503–511. https://doi.org/10.1016/j.biopsych.2010.04.031. Epub 2010 Jun 29.

Nakamura, K., 2013. The role of the dorsal raphe nucleus in reward-seeking behavior. Front. Integr. Neurosci. 7, 60. https://doi.org/10.3389/fnint.2013.00060.

Neumann, P.A., Wang, Y., Yan, Y., Wang, Y., Ishikawa, M., Cui, R., Huang, Y.H., Sesack, S.R., Schluter, O.M., Dong, Y., 2016. Cocaine-induced synaptic alterations in thalamus to nucleus accumbens projection. Neuropsychopharmacology 41 (9), 2399–2410. https://doi.org/10.1038/npp.2016.52. Epub 2016 Apr 14.

Nikaido, T., Akiyama, M., Moriya, T., Shibata, S., 2001. Sensitized increase of period gene expression in the mouse caudate/putamen caused by repeated injection of methamphetamine. Mol. Pharmacol. 59 (4), 894–900. http://www.ncbi.nlm.nih.gov/entrez/query.fcgi?cmd=Retrieve&db=PubMed&dopt=Citation&list_uids=11259635.

O'Dell, L.E., Chen, S.A., Smith, R.T., Specio, S.E., Balster, R.L., Paterson, N.E., Markou, A., Zorrilla, E.P., Koob, G.F., 2007. Extended access to nicotine self-administration leads to dependence: circadian measures, withdrawal measures, and extinction behavior in rats. J. Pharmacol. Exp. Therapeut. 320 (1), 180–193 https://doi.org/jpet.106.105270 (pii).

Olson, V.G., Zabetian, C.P., Bolanos, C.A., Edwards, S., Barrot, M., Eisch, A.J., Hughes, T., Self, D.W., Neve, R.L., Nestler, E.J., 2005. Regulation of drug reward by cAMP response element-binding protein: evidence for two functionally distinct subregions of the ventral tegmental area. J. Neurosci. 25 (23), 5553–5562. https://doi.org/10.1523/JNEUROSCI.0345-05.2005.

Ozburn, A.R., Larson, E.B., Self, D.W., McClung, C.A., 2012. Cocaine self-administration behaviors in ClockDelta19 mice. Psychopharmacology 223 (2), 169–177. https://doi.org/10.1007/s00213-012-2704-2. Epub 2012 Apr 26.

Ozburn, A.R., Falcon, E., Twaddle, A., Nugent, A.L., Gillman, A.G., Spencer, S.M., Arey, R.N., Mukherjee, S., Lyons-Weiler, J., Self, D.W., McClung, C.A., 2015. Direct regulation of diurnal Drd3 expression and cocaine reward by NPAS2. Biol. Psychiatr. 77 (5), 425–433. https://doi.org/10.1016/j.biopsych.2014.07.030. Epub 2014 Aug 13.

Ozburn, A.R., Purohit, K., Parekh, P.K., Kaplan, G.N., Falcon, E., Mukherjee, S., Cates, H.M., McClung, C.A., 2016. Functional implications of the CLOCK 3111T/C single-nucleotide polymorphism. Front. Psychiatr. 7, 67. https://doi.org/10.3389/fpsyt.2016.00067 eCollection 2016.

Ozburn, A.R., Kern, J., Parekh, P.K., Logan, R.W., Liu, Z., Falcon, E., Becker-Krail, D., Purohit, K., Edgar, N.M., Huang, Y., McClung, C.A., 2017. NPAS2 regulation of anxiety-like behavior and GABAA receptors. Front. Mol. Neurosci. 10, 360. https://doi.org/10.3389/fnmol.2017.00360.

Paiva, T., Gaspar, T., Matos, M.G., 2016. Mutual relations between sleep deprivation, sleep stealers and risk behaviours in adolescents. Sleep Sci. 9 (1), 7–13. https://doi.org/10.1016/j.slsci.2016.02.176. Epub 2016 Feb 23.

Parekh, P.K., Becker-Krail, D., Sundaravelu, P., Ishigaki, S., Okado, H., Sobue, G., Huang, Y., McClung, C.A., 2018a. Altered GluA1 (Gria1) function and accumbal synaptic plasticity in the ClockDelta19 model of bipolar mania. Biol. Psychiatr. 84 (11), 817–826. https://doi.org/10.1016/j.biopsych.2017.06.022. Epub 2017 Jun 27.

Parekh, P.K., Sidor, M.M., Gillman, A., Becker-Krail, D., Bettelini, L., Arban, R., Alvaro, G.S., Zambello, E., Mutinelli, C., Huang, Y., Large, C.H., McClung, C.A., 2018b. Antimanic efficacy of a novel Kv3 potassium channel modulator. Neuropsychopharmacology 43 (2), 435–444. https://doi.org/10.1038/npp.2017.155. Epub 2017 Aug 31.

Parekh, P.K., Logan, R.W., Ketchesin, K.D., Becker-Krail, D., Shelton, M.A., Hildebrand, M.A., Barko, K., Huang, Y.H., McClung, C.A., 2019. Cell-type-specific regulation of nucleus accumbens synaptic plasticity and cocaine reward sensitivity by the circadian protein, NPAS2. J. Neurosci. 39 (24), 4657–4667. https://doi.org/10.1523/JNEUROSCI.2233-18.2019.

Partch, C.L., Green, C.B., Takahashi, J.S., 2014. Molecular architecture of the mammalian circadian clock. Trends Cell Biol. 24 (2), 90–99. https://doi.org/10.1016/j.tcb.2013.07.002. Epub 2013 Aug 1.

Pasley, J.N., Powell, E.W., Halberg, F., 1987. Strain differences in circadian drinking behaviors of ethanol and water in rats. Prog. Clin. Biol. Res. 227B, 467–471. https://www.ncbi.nlm.nih.gov/pubmed/3628356.

Peek, C.B., Ramsey, K.M., Levine, D.C., Marcheva, B., Perelis, M., Bass, J., 2015. Circadian regulation of cellular physiology. Methods Enzymol. 552, 165–184. https://doi.org/10.1016/bs.mie.2014.10.006. Epub 2015 Jan 5.

Pendergast, J.S., Yamazaki, S., 2018. The mysterious food-entrainable oscillator: insights from mutant and engineered mouse models. J. Biol. Rhythm. 33 (5), 458–474. https://doi.org/10.1177/0748730418789043.

Perreau-Lenz, S., Zghoul, T., de Fonseca, F.R., Spanagel, R., Bilbao, A., 2009. Circadian regulation of central ethanol sensitivity by the mPer2 gene. Addiction Biol. 14 (3), 253–259. https://doi.org/10.1111/j.1369-1600.2009.00165.x.

Perreau-Lenz, S., Sanchis-Segura, C., Leonardi-Essmann, F., Schneider, M., Spanagel, R., 2010. Development of morphine-induced tolerance and withdrawal: involvement of the clock gene mPer2. Eur. Neuropsychopharmacol 20 (7), 509–517. https://doi.org/10.1016/j.euroneuro.2010.03.006.

Perreau-Lenz, S., Vengeliene, V., Noori, H.R., Merlo-Pich, E.V., Corsi, M.A., Corti, C., Spanagel, R., 2012. Inhibition of the casein-kinase-1-epsilon/delta prevents relapse-like alcohol drinking. Neuropsychopharmacology 37 (9), 2121–2131. https://doi.org/10.1038/npp.2012.62. Epub 2012 May 2.

Perreau-Lenz, S., Hoelters, L.-S., Leixner, S., Sanchis-Segura, C., Hansson, A., Bilbao, A., Spanagel, R., 2017. mPer1 promotes morphine-induced locomotor sensitization and conditioned place preference via histone deacetylase activity. Psychopharmacology 234 (11), 1713–1724. https://doi.org/10.1007/s00213-017-4574-0.

Pinna, A., Wardas, J., Cristalli, G., Morelli, M., 1997. Adenosine A2A receptor agonists increase Fos-like immunoreactivity in mesolimbic areas. Brain Res. 759 (1), 41–49. https://doi.org/10.1016/s0006-8993(97)00214-x.

Pintsuk, J., Borroto-Escuela, D.O., Pomierny, B., Wydra, K., Zaniewska, M., Filip, M., Fuxe, K., 2016. Cocaine self-administration differentially affects allosteric A2A-D2 receptor-receptor interactions in the striatum. Relevance for cocaine use disorder. Pharmacol. Biochem. Behav. 144, 85–91. https://doi.org/10.1016/j.pbb.2016.03.004.

Pohl, J.B., Ghezzi, A., Lew, L.K., Robles, R.B., Cormack, L., Atkinson, N.S., 2013. Circadian genes differentially affect tolerance to ethanol in Drosophila. Alcohol Clin. Exp. Res. 37 (11), 1862–1871. https://doi.org/10.1111/acer.12173. Epub 2013 Jun 28.

Porkka-Heiskanen, T., Strecker, R.E., Thakkar, M., Bjorkum, A.A., Greene, R.W., McCarley, R.W., 1997. Adenosine: a mediator of the sleep-inducing effects of prolonged wakefulness. Science 276 (5316), 1265–1268. https://doi.org/10.1126/science.276.5316.1265.

Porkka-Heiskanen, T., Strecker, R.E., McCarley, R.W., 2000. Brain site-specificity of extracellular adenosine concentration changes during sleep deprivation and spontaneous sleep: an in vivo microdialysis study. Neuroscience 99 (3), 507–517. https://doi.org/10.1016/s0306-4522(00)00220-7.

Prosser, R.A., Glass, J.D., 2009. The mammalian circadian clock exhibits acute tolerance to ethanol. Alcohol Clin. Exp. Res. 33 (12), 2088–2093. https://doi.org/10.1111/j.1530-0277.2009.01048.x. Epub 2009 Sep. 9.

Prosser, R.A., Mangrum, C.A., Glass, J.D., 2008. Acute ethanol modulates glutamatergic and serotonergic phase shifts of the mouse circadian clock in vitro. Neuroscience 152 (3), 837–848. https://doi.org/10.1016/j.neuroscience.2007.12.049. Epub 2008 Jan 29.

Qu, W.M., Xu, X.H., Yan, M.M., Wang, Y.Q., Urade, Y., Huang, Z.L., 2010. Essential role of dopamine D2 receptor in the maintenance of wakefulness, but not in homeostatic regulation of sleep, in mice. J. Neurosci. 30 (12), 4382–4389. https://doi.org/10.1523/JNEUROSCI.4936-09.2010.

Ramsey, K.M., Yoshino, J., Brace, C.S., Abrassart, D., Kobayashi, Y., Marcheva, B., Hong, H.K., Chong, J.L., Buhr, E.D., Lee, C., Takahashi, J.S., Imai, S., Bass, J., 2009. Circadian clock feedback cycle through NAMPT-mediated NAD+ biosynthesis. Science 324 (5927), 651–654. https://doi.org/10.1126/science.1171641. Epub 2009 Mar 19.

Randler, C., 2008. Morningness-eveningness comparison in adolescents from different countries around the world. Chronobiol. Int. 25 (6), 1017–1028. https://doi.org/10.1080/07420520802551519.

Reick, M., Garcia, J.A., Dudley, C., McKnight, S.L., 2001. NPAS2: an analog of clock operative in the mammalian forebrain. Science 293 (5529), 506–509. https://doi.org/10.1126/science.1060699.

Rempe, M.J., Wisor, J.P., 2014. Cerebral lactate dynamics across sleep/wake cycles. Front. Comput. Neurosci. 8, 174. https://doi.org/10.3389/fncom.2014.00174.

Renee Ozburn, A., Falcon, E., Mukherjee, S., Gillman, A., Arey, R., Spencer, S., McClung, C.A., 2013. The role of clock in ethanol-related behaviors. Neuropsychopharmacology 38 (12), 2393–2400. https://doi.org/10.1038/npp.2013.138. https://www.ncbi.nlm.nih.gov/pmc/articles/PMC3799058/#__ffn_sectitle.

Reppert, S.M., Weaver, D.R., 2002. Coordination of circadian timing in mammals. Nature 418 (6901), 935–941. https://doi.org/10.1038/nature00965.

Requardt, R.P., Wilhelm, F., Rillich, J., Winkler, U., Hirrlinger, J., 2010. The biphasic NAD(P)H fluorescence response of astrocytes to dopamine reflects the metabolic actions of oxidative phosphorylation and glycolysis. J. Neurochem. 115 (2), 483–492. https://doi.org/10.1111/j.1471-4159.2010.06940.x.

Requardt, R.P., Hirrlinger, P.G., Wilhelm, F., Winkler, U., Besser, S., Hirrlinger, J., 2012. Ca(2)(+) signals of astrocytes are modulated by the NAD(+)/NADH redox state. J. Neurochem. 120 (6), 1014–1025. https://doi.org/10.1111/j.1471-4159.2012.07645.x.

Rizk, A.A., Jenkins, B.W., Al-Sabagh, Y., Hamidullah, S., Reitz, C.J., Rasouli, M., Martino, T.A., Khokhar, J.Y., 2022. The impact of sex, circadian disruption, and the Clock$^{\Delta19/\Delta19}$ genotype on alcohol drinking in mice. Genes 13 (4), 701. https://doi.org/10.3390/genes13040701.

Roberts, D.C., Brebner, K., Vincler, M., Lynch, W.J., 2002. Patterns of cocaine self-administration in rats produced by various access conditions under a discrete trials procedure. Drug Alcohol Depend. 67 (3), 291–299. https://www.ncbi.nlm.nih.gov/pubmed/12127200.

Roenneberg, T., Kuehnle, T., Pramstaller, P.P., Ricken, J., Havel, M., Guth, A., Merrow, M., 2004. A marker for the end of adolescence. Curr. Biol. 14 (24), R1038–R1039. https://doi.org/10.1016/j.cub.2004.11.039.

Rosenwasser, A.M., 2009. Functional neuroanatomy of sleep and circadian rhythms. Brain Res. Rev. 61 (2), 281–306. https://doi.org/10.1016/j.brainresrev.2009.08.001.

Rosenwasser, A.M., Fixaris, M.C., 2013. Chronobiology of alcohol: studies in C57BL/6J and DBA/2J inbred mice. Physiol. Behav. 110–111, 140–147. https://doi.org/10.1016/j.physbeh.2013.01.001. Epub 2013 Jan 10.

Rosenwasser, A.M., Turek, F.W., 2015. Neurobiology of circadian rhythm regulation. Sleep Med. Clin. 10 (4), 403–412. https://doi.org/10.1016/j.jsmc.2015.08.003. Epub 2015 Sep. 11.

Rosenwasser, A.M., Logan, R.W., Fecteau, M.E., 2005. Chronic ethanol intake alters circadian period-responses to brief light pulses in rats. Chronobiol. Int. 22 (2), 227–236. https://doi.org/10.1081/cbi-200053496.

Rosenwasser, A.M., Clark, J.W., Fixaris, M.C., Belanger, G.V., Foster, J.A., 2010. Effects of repeated light-dark phase shifts on voluntary ethanol and water intake in male and female Fischer and Lewis rats. Alcohol 44 (3), 229–237. https://doi.org/10.1016/j.alcohol.2010.03.002. Epub 2010 May 20.

Roybal, K., Theobold, D., Graham, A., DiNieri, J.A., Russo, S.J., Krishnan, V., Chakravarty, S., Peevey, J., Oehrlein, N., Birnbaum, S., Vitaterna, M.H., Orsulak, P., Takahashi, J.S., Nestler, E.J., Carlezon Jr., W.A., McClung, C.A., 2007. Mania-like behavior induced by disruption of CLOCK. Proc. Natl. Acad. Sci. U.S.A. 104 (15), 6406–6411 https://doi.org/0609625104 (pii).

Ruben, M.D., Wu, G., Smith, D.F., Schmidt, R.E., Francey, L.J., Lee, Y.Y., Anafi, R.C., Hogenesch, J.B., 2018. A database of tissue-specific rhythmically expressed human genes has potential applications in circadian medicine. Sci. Transl. Med. 10 (458). https://doi.org/10.1126/scitranslmed.aat8806.

Ruby, C.L., Brager, A.J., DePaul, M.A., Prosser, R.A., Glass, J.D., 2009a. Chronic ethanol attenuates circadian photic phase resetting and alters nocturnal activity patterns in the hamster. Am. J. Physiol. Regul. Integr. Comp. Physiol. 297 (3), R729–R737. https://doi.org/10.1152/ajpregu.00268.2009. Epub 2009 Jun 24.

Ruby, C.L., Prosser, R.A., DePaul, M.A., Roberts, R.J., Glass, J.D., 2009b. Acute ethanol impairs photic and nonphotic circadian phase resetting in the Syrian hamster. Am. J. Physiol. Regul. Integr. Comp. Physiol. 296 (2), R411–R418. https://doi.org/10.1152/ajpregu.90782.2008. Epub 2008 Dec 10.

Ruby, C.L., O'Connor, K.M., Ayers-Ringler, J., Choi, D.S., 2014. Adenosine and glutamate in neuroglial interaction: implications for circadian disorders and alcoholism. Adv Neurobiol 11, 103–119. https://doi.org/10.1007/978-3-319-08894-5_6.

Rutter, J., Reick, M., Wu, L.C., McKnight, S.L., 2001. Regulation of clock and NPAS2 DNA binding by the redox state of NAD cofactors. Science 293 (5529), 510–514. https://doi.org/10.1126/science.1060698.

Salaberry, N.L., Mateo, M., Mendoza, J., 2017. The clock gene rev-erbalpha regulates methamphetamine actions on circadian timekeeping in the mouse brain. Mol. Neurobiol. 54 (7), 5327–5334. https://doi.org/10.1007/s12035-016-0076-z. Epub 2016 Sep. 1.

Saper, C.B., Scammell, T.E., Lu, J., 2005. Hypothalamic regulation of sleep and circadian rhythms. Nature 437 (7063), 1257–1263. https://doi.org/10.1038/nature04284.

Seggio, J.A., Logan, R.W., Rosenwasser, A.M., 2007. Chronic ethanol intake modulates photic and non-photic circadian phase responses in the Syrian hamster. Pharmacol. Biochem. Behav. 87 (3), 297–305. https://doi.org/10.1016/j.pbb.2007.05.001.

Seggio, J.A., Fixaris, M.C., Reed, J.D., Logan, R.W., Rosenwasser, A.M., 2009. Chronic ethanol intake alters circadian phase shifting and free-running period in mice. J. Biol. Rhythm. 24 (4), 304–312. https://doi.org/10.1177/0748730409338449.

Self, D.W., Genova, L.M., Hope, B.T., Barnhart, W.J., Spencer, J.J., Nestler, E.J., 1998. Involvement of cAMP-dependent protein kinase in the nucleus accumbens in cocaine self-administration and relapse of cocaine-seeking behavior. J. Neurosci. 18 (5), 1848–1859. https://www.ncbi.nlm.nih.gov/pubmed/9465009.

Shen, H.Y., Coelho, J.E., Ohtsuka, N., Canas, P.M., Day, Y.J., Huang, Q.Y., Rebola, N., Yu, L., Boison, D., Cunha, R.A., Linden, J., Tsien, J.Z., Chen, J.F., 2008. A critical role of the adenosine A2A receptor in extrastriatal neurons in modulating psychomotor activity as revealed by opposite phenotypes of striatum and forebrain A2A receptor knock-outs. J. Neurosci. 28 (12), 2970–2975. https://doi.org/10.1523/JNEUROSCI.5255-07.2008.

Shigeyoshi, Y., Taguchi, K., Yamamoto, S., Takekida, S., Yan, L., Tei, H., Moriya, T., Shibata, S., Loros, J.J., Dunlap, J.C., Okamura, H., 1997. Light-induced resetting of a mammalian circadian clock is associated with rapid induction of the mPer1 transcript. Cell 91 (7), 1043–1053. https://doi.org/10.1016/s0092-8674(00)80494-8.

Shumay, E., Fowler, J.S., Wang, G.J., Logan, J., Alia-Klein, N., Goldstein, R.Z., Maloney, T., Wong, C., Volkow, N.D., 2012. Repeat variation in the human PER2 gene as a new genetic marker associated with cocaine addiction and brain dopamine D2 receptor availability. Transl. Psychiatry 2, e86. https://doi.org/10.1038/tp.2012.11.

Sidor, M.M., Spencer, S.M., Dzirasa, K., Parekh, P.K., Tye, K.M., Warden, M.R., Arey, R.N., Enwright 3rd, J.F., Jacobsen, J.P., Kumar, S., Remillard, E.M., Caron, M.G., Deisseroth, K., McClung, C.A., 2015. Daytime spikes in dopaminergic activity drive rapid mood-cycling in mice. Mol. Psychiatr. 5. https://doi.org/10.1038/mp.2014.167.

Sivertsen, B., Skogen, J.C., Jakobsen, R., Hysing, M., 2015. Sleep and use of alcohol and drug in adolescence. A large population-based study of Norwegian adolescents aged 16 to 19 years. Drug Alcohol Depend. 149, 180–186. https://doi.org/10.1016/j.drugalcdep.2015.01.045. Epub 2015 Feb 11.

Sjoholm, L.K., Kovanen, L., Saarikoski, S.T., Schalling, M., Lavebratt, C., Partonen, T., 2010. CLOCK is suggested to associate with comorbid alcohol use and depressive disorders. J. Circadian Rhythms 8, 1. https://doi.org/10.1186/1740-3391-8-1.

Skinner, H.A., Allen, B.A., 1982. Alcohol dependence syndrome: measurement and validation. J. Abnorm. Psychol. 91 (3), 199–209. https://doi.org/10.1037//0021-843x.91.3.199.

Sleipness, E.P., Sorg, B.A., Jansen, H.T., 2007. Diurnal differences in dopamine transporter and tyrosine hydroxylase levels in rat brain: dependence on the suprachiasmatic nucleus. Brain Res. 1129 (1), 34–42. https://doi.org/10.1016/j.brainres.2006.10.063.

Sorg, B.A., Stark, G., Sergeeva, A., Jansen, H.T., 2011. Photoperiodic suppression of drug reinstatement. Neuroscience 176, 284–295. https://doi.org/10.1016/j.neuroscience.2010.12.022. Epub 2010 Dec 24.

Soria, G., Castane, A., Ledent, C., Parmentier, M., Maldonado, R., Valverde, O., 2006. The lack of A2A adenosine receptors diminishes the reinforcing efficacy of cocaine. Neuropsychopharmacology 31 (5), 978–987. https://doi.org/10.1038/sj.npp.1300876.

Soria, V., Martinez-Amoros, E., Escaramis, G., Valero, J., Perez-Egea, R., Garcia, C., Gutierrez-Zotes, A., Puigdemont, D., Bayes, M., Crespo, J.M., Martorell, L., Vilella, E., Labad, A., Vallejo, J., Perez, V., Menchon, J.M., Estivill, X., Gratacos, M., Urretavizcaya, M., 2010. Differential association of circadian genes with mood disorders: CRY1 and NPAS2 are associated with unipolar major depression and CLOCK and VIP with bipolar disorder. Neuropsychopharmacology 35 (6), 1279–1289. https://doi.org/10.1038/npp.2009.230. Epub 2010 Jan 13.

Spanagel, R., Pendyala, G., Abarca, C., Zghoul, T., Sanchis-Segura, C., Magnone, M.C., Lascorz, J., Depner, M., Holzberg, D., Soyka, M., Schreiber, S., Matsuda, F., Lathrop, M., Schumann, G., Albrecht, U., 2005a. The clock gene Per2 influences the glutamatergic system and modulates alcohol consumption. Nat. Med. 11 (1), 35–42 https://doi.org/nm1163 (pii).

Spanagel, R., Rosenwasser, A.M., Schumann, G., Sarkar, D.K., 2005b. Alcohol consumption and the body's biological clock. Alcohol Clin. Exp. Res. 29 (8), 1550–1557. https://www.ncbi.nlm.nih.gov/pubmed/16156052.

Spencer, S., Torres-Altoro, M.I., Falcon, E., Arey, R., Marvin, M., Goldberg, M., Bibb, J.A., McClung, C.A., 2012. A mutation in CLOCK leads to altered dopamine receptor function. J. Neurochem. 123 (1), 124–134. https://doi.org/10.1111/j.1471-4159.2012.07857.x. Epub 2012 Jul 27.

Strecker, R.E., Morairty, S., Thakkar, M.M., Porkka-Heiskanen, T., Basheer, R., Dauphin, L.J., Rainnie, D.G., Portas, C.M., Greene, R.W., McCarley, R.W., 2000. Adenosinergic modulation of basal forebrain and preoptic/anterior hypothalamic neuronal activity in the control of behavioral state. Behav. Brain Res. 115 (2), 183–204. https://doi.org/10.1016/s0166-4328(00)00258-8.

Takahashi, J.S., 2017a. Enriching the circadian proteome. Cell Metabol. 25 (1), 1–2. https://doi.org/10.1016/j.cmet.2016.12.014.

Takahashi, J.S., 2017b. Transcriptional architecture of the mammalian circadian clock. Nat. Rev. Genet. 18 (3), 164–179. https://doi.org/10.1038/nrg.2016.150. Epub 2016 Dec 19.

Tataroglu, O., Aksoy, A., Yilmaz, A., Canbeyli, R., 2004. Effect of lesioning the suprachiasmatic nuclei on behavioral despair in rats. Brain Res. 1001 (1–2), 118–124. https://doi.org/10.1016/j.brainres.2003.11.063.

Tataroglu, O., Davidson, A.J., Benvenuto, L.J., Menaker, M., 2006. The methamphetamine-sensitive circadian oscillator (MASCO) in mice. J. Biol. Rhythm. 21 (3), 185–194. https://doi.org/10.1177/0748730406287529.

Terwilliger, R.Z., Beitner-Johnson, D., Sevarino, K.A., Crain, S.M., Nestler, E.J., 1991. A general role for adaptations in G-proteins and the cyclic AMP system in mediating the chronic actions of morphine and cocaine on neuronal function. Brain Res. 548 (1–2), 100–110. https://www.ncbi.nlm.nih.gov/pubmed/1651140.

Tonetti, L., Adan, A., Caci, H., De Pascalis, V., Fabbri, M., Natale, V., 2010. Morningness-eveningness preference and sensation seeking. Eur. Psychiatr. 25 (2), 111–115. https://doi.org/10.1016/j.eurpsy.2009.09.007. Epub 2009 Nov 18.

Touitou, Y., 2013. Adolescent sleep misalignment: a chronic jet lag and a matter of public health. J. Physiol. Paris 107 (4), 323–326. https://doi.org/10.1016/j.jphysparis.2013.03.008. Epub 2013 Mar 29.

Trinkoff, A.M., Storr, C.L., 1998. Work schedule characteristics and substance use in nurses. Am. J. Ind. Med. 34 (3), 266–271. https://doi.org/10.1002/(sici)1097-0274(199809)34:3<266::aid-ajim9>3.0.co;2-t.

Trujillo, J.L., Do, D.T., Grahame, N.J., Roberts, A.J., Gorman, M.R., 2011. Ethanol consumption in mice: relationships with circadian period and entrainment. Alcohol 45 (2), 147–159. https://doi.org/10.1016/j.alcohol.2010.08.016. Epub 2010 Sep. 29.

Tso, C.F., Simon, T., Greenlaw, A.C., Puri, T., Mieda, M., Herzog, E.D., 2017. Astrocytes regulate daily rhythms in the suprachiasmatic nucleus and behavior. Curr. Biol. 27 (7), 1055–1061. https://doi.org/10.1016/j.cub.2017.02.037. Epub 2017 Mar 23.

Tuma, J., Strubbe, J.H., Mocaer, E., Koolhaas, J.M., 2005. Anxiolytic-like action of the antidepressant agomelatine (S 20098) after a social defeat requires the integrity of the SCN. Eur. Neuropsychopharmacol 15 (5), 545–555 https://doi.org/S0924-977X(05)00040-4 (pii).

Uz, T., Akhisaroglu, M., Ahmed, R., Manev, H., 2003. The pineal gland is critical for circadian *Period1* expression in the striatum and for circadian cocaine sensitization in mice. Neuropsychopharmacology 28, 2117–2123. https://doi.org/10.1038/sj.npp.1300254.

Uz, T., Ahmed, R., Akhisaroglu, M., Kurtuncu, M., Imbesi, M., Arslan Dirim, A., Manev, H., 2005. Effect of fluoxetine and cocaine on the expression of clock genes in the mouse hippocampus and striatum. Neuroscience 134 (4), 1309–1316. https://doi.org/10.1016/j.neuroscience.2005.05.003.

Velasquez, K.M., Molfese, D.L., Salas, R., 2014. The role of the habenula in drug addiction. Front. Hum. Neurosci. 8, 174. https://doi.org/10.3389/fnhum.2014.00174.

Vengeliene, V., Noori, H.R., Spanagel, R., 2013. The use of a novel drinkometer system for assessing pharmacological treatment effects on ethanol consumption in rats. Alcohol Clin. Exp. Res. 37 (Suppl. 1), E322–E328. https://doi.org/10.1111/j.1530-0277.2012.01874.x.

Verheij, M.M.M., Contet, C., Karel, P., Latour, J., van der Doelen, R.H.A., Geenen, B., van Hulten, J.A., Meyer, F., Kozicz, T., George, O., Koob, G.F., Homberg, J.R., 2018. Median and dorsal raphe serotonergic neurons control moderate versus compulsive cocaine intake. Biol. Psychiatr. 83 (12), 1024–1035. https://doi.org/10.1016/j.biopsych.2017.10.031.

Wager, T.T., Chandrasekaran, R.Y., Bradley, J., Rubitski, D., Berke, H., Mente, S., Butler, T., Doran, A., Chang, C., Fisher, K., Knafels, J., Liu, S., Ohren, J., Marconi, M., DeMarco, G., Sneed, B., Walton, K., Horton, D., Rosado, A., Mead, A., 2014. Casein kinase 1δ/ε inhibitor PF-5006739 attenuates opioid drug-seeking behavior. ACS Chem. Neurosci. 5 (12), 1253–1265.

Wallace, D.L., Han, M.H., Graham, D.L., Green, T.A., Vialou, V., Iniguez, S.D., Cao, J.L., Kirk, A., Chakravarty, S., Kumar, A., Krishnan, V., Neve, R.L., Cooper, D.C., Bolanos, C.A., Barrot, M., McClung, C.A., Nestler, E.J., 2009. CREB regulation of nucleus accumbens excitability mediates social isolation-induced behavioral deficits. Nat. Neurosci. 12 (2), 200–209. https://doi.org/10.1038/nn.2257. Epub 2009 Jan 18.

Wang, D.-Q., Wang, X.-L., Wang, C.-Y., Wang, Y., Li, S.-X., Liu, K.-Z., 2019. Effects of chronic cocaine exposure on the circadian rhythmic expression of the clock genes in reward-related brain areas in rats. Behav. Brain Res. 363, 61–69. https://doi.org/10.1016/j.bbr.2019.01.035. Epub 2019 Jan 22.

Webb, I.C., Baltazar, R.M., Lehman, M.N., Coolen, L.M., 2009. Bidirectional interactions between the circadian and reward systems: is restricted food access a unique zeitgeber? Eur. J. Neurosci. 30 (9), 1739–1748. https://doi.org/10.1111/j.1460-9568.2009.06966.x. Epub 2009 Oct 28.

Widnell, K.L., Self, D.W., Lane, S.B., Russell, D.S., Vaidya, V.A., Miserendino, M.J., Rubin, C.S., Duman, R.S., Nestler, E.J., 1996. Regulation of CREB expression: in vivo evidence for a functional role in morphine action in the nucleus accumbens. J. Pharmacol. Exp. Therapeut. 276 (1), 306–315. https://www.ncbi.nlm.nih.gov/pubmed/8558448.

Womac, A.D., Burkeen, J.F., Neuendorff, N., Earnest, D.J., Zoran, M.J., 2009. Circadian rhythms of extracellular ATP accumulation in suprachiasmatic nucleus cells and cultured astrocytes. Eur. J. Neurosci. 30 (5), 869–876. https://doi.org/10.1111/j.1460-9568.2009.06874.x. Epub 2009 Aug 27.

Wongchitrat, P., Mukda, S., Phansuwan-Pujito, P., Govitrapong, P., 2013. Effect of amphetamine on the clock gene expression in rat striatum. Neurosci. Lett. 542, 126–130. https://doi.org/10.1016/j.neulet.2013.03.009. Epub 2013 Mar 18.

Wydra, K., Suder, A., Borroto-Escuela, D.O., Filip, M., Fuxe, K., 2015. On the role of A(2)A and D(2) receptors in control of cocaine and food-seeking behaviors in rats. Psychopharmacology (Berl) 232 (10), 1767–1778. https://doi.org/10.1007/s00213-014-3818-5.

Yamazaki, S., Ishida, Y., Inouye, S., 1994. Circadian rhythms of adenosine triphosphate contents in the suprachiasmatic nucleus, anterior hypothalamic area and caudate putamen of the rat—negative correlation with electrical activity. Brain Res. 664 (1–2), 237–240. https://www.ncbi.nlm.nih.gov/pubmed/7895035.

Yan, L., Karatsoreos, I., Lesauter, J., Welsh, D.K., Kay, S., Foley, D., Silver, R., 2007. Exploring spatiotemporal organization of SCN circuits. Cold Spring Harbor Symp. Quant. Biol. 72, 527–541. https://doi.org/10.1101/sqb.2007.72.037.

Yang, S.L., Han, J.Y., Kim, Y.B., Nam, S.Y., Song, S., Hong, J.T., Oh, K.W., 2011. Increased non-rapid eye movement sleep by cocaine withdrawal: possible involvement of A2A receptors. Arch Pharm. Res. (Seoul) 34 (2), 281–287. https://doi.org/10.1007/s12272-011-0214-0.

Yellen, G., 2018. Fueling thought: management of glycolysis and oxidative phosphorylation in neuronal metabolism. J. Cell Biol. 217 (7), 2235–2246. https://doi.org/10.1083/jcb.201803152.

Yoo, S.H., Yamazaki, S., Lowrey, P.L., Shimomura, K., Ko, C.H., Buhr, E.D., Siepka, S.M., Hong, H.K., Oh, W.J., Yoo, O.J., Menaker, M., Takahashi, J.S., 2004. PERIOD2::LUCIFERASE real-time reporting of circadian dynamics reveals persistent circadian oscillations in mouse peripheral tissues. Proc. Natl. Acad. Sci. U.S.A. 101 (15), 5339–5346. https://doi.org/10.1073/pnas.0308709101. Epub 2004 Feb 12.

You, I.J., Wright, S.R., Garcia-Garcia, A.L., Tapper, A.R., Gardner, P.D., Koob, G.F., David Leonardo, E., Bohn, L.M., Wee, S., 2016. 5-HT1A autoreceptors in the dorsal raphe nucleus convey vulnerability to compulsive cocaine seeking. Neuropsychopharmacology 41 (5), 1210–1222. https://doi.org/10.1038/npp.2015.268.

Zapata, A., Hwang, E.K., Lupica, C.R., 2017. Lateral habenula involvement in impulsive cocaine seeking. Neuropsychopharmacology 42 (5), 1103–1112. https://doi.org/10.1038/npp.2016.286.

Zghoul, T., Abarca, C., Sanchis-Segura, C., Albrecht, U., Schumann, G., Spanagel, R., 2007. Ethanol self-administration and reinstatement of ethanol-seeking behavior in Per1(Brdm1) mutant mice. Psychopharmacology 190 (1), 13–19. https://doi.org/10.1007/s00213-006-0592-z.

Zhang, J., Liao, G., Liu, C., Sun, L., Liu, Y., Wang, Y., Jiang, Z., Wang, Z., 2011. The association of CLOCK gene T3111C polymorphism and hPER3 gene 54-nucleotide repeat polymorphism with Chinese Han people schizophrenics. Mol. Biol. Rep. 38 (1), 349–354. https://doi.org/10.1007/s11033-010-0114-2. Epub 2010 Apr 3.

Zhang, Y., Xue, Y., Meng, S., Luo, Y., Liang, J., Li, J., Ai, S., Sun, C., Shen, H., Zhu, W., Wu, P., Lu, L., Shi, J., 2016. Inhibition of lactate transport erases drug memory and prevents drug relapse. Biol. Psychiatr. 79 (11), 928–939. https://doi.org/10.1016/j.biopsych.2015.07.007.

Zhou, Y.D., Barnard, M., Tian, H., Li, X., Ring, H.Z., Francke, U., Shelton, J., Richardson, J., Russell, D.W., McKnight, S.L., 1997. Molecular characterization of two mammalian bHLH-PAS domain proteins selectively expressed in the central nervous system. Proc. Natl. Acad. Sci. U.S.A. 94 (2), 713–718. http://www.ncbi.nlm.nih.gov/entrez/query.fcgi?cmd=Retrieve&db=PubMed&dopt=Citation&list_uids=9012850.

Index

'*Note:* Page numbers followed by "f" indicate figures, "t" indicate tables and "b" indicate boxes.'

W

9780128234532